ENGLISH PLACE-NAME SOCIETY. VOLUME LXXVIII
FOR 2000–2001

GENERAL EDITOR

VICTOR WATTS

THE PLACE-NAMES OF
LEICESTERSHIRE

PART II

THE SURVEY OF ENGLISH PLACE-NAMES
UNDERTAKEN WITH THE APPROVAL AND SUPPORT OF
THE BRITISH ACADEMY

THE PLACE-NAMES OF

LEICESTERSHIRE

BY

BARRIE COX

PART TWO

FRAMLAND HUNDRED

NOTTINGHAM
ENGLISH PLACE-NAME SOCIETY
2002

Published by the English Place-Name Society,
School of English Studies, University of Nottingham,
Nottingham NG7 2RD.

Registered Charity No. 257891

ISBN 0 904889 63 7

Typeset by Paul Cavill & Printed in Great Britain
by Woolnough Bookbinding, Irthlingborough, Northants.

CONTENTS

vii

PREFACE

The magnificent collection of medieval deeds, cartularies and compotus rolls in the Duke of Rutland's muniments rooms, library and galleries in Belvoir Castle is central to this survey of the place-names of the Framland Hundred of Leicestershire. To the late Duke of Rutland I owe a great debt of gratitude for his unfailing kindness and patience during the years in which I was extracting place-name materials from his superb treasure-house of historical record.

To the former staff of the Leicestershire Record Office, New Walk, Leicester, I offer my best thanks for their untiring assistance, as I do to those members of the present staff of the Record Office for Leicestershire, Leicester and Rutland at Wigston Magna.

The Lincolnshire Archives Office, Lincoln, houses the great bulk of the surviving Glebe Terriers of the early Leicestershire parishes. Its staff has provided me with splendid help in locating and presenting these manuscripts and such other records as I have requested there.

My gratitude is due also to Dr Anne Tarver who has drawn the detailed parish map for the Hundred. As always, her work is exemplary.

Finally, my best thanks are due Mrs Janet Rudkin, Dr Bonnie Millar-Heggie and especially to Dr Paul Cavill of the English Place-Name Society for their meticulous application in preparing for publication the camera-ready copy of what I hope will prove to be a user-friendly volume.

Barrie Cox

INTRODUCTION
TO THE PLACE-NAMES
OF FRAMLAND HUNDRED

Framland Hundred comprises the north-eastern corner of Leicestershire. The uplands of the Wolds are central to it and dominant. To their north, the Hundred takes in a tranche of the Vale of Belvoir. To their south, the upper Wreake Valley is part of the Hundred's territory, together with a strip of land running south-east across the northern edge of High Leicestershire. A detached portion of the Hundred is situated high on this upland at Withcote.

The townships of the Vale of Belvoir lie on flat claylands which are drained by streams flowing north to the river Trent. Those on the Wolds for the most part exploit light soils produced by Marlstone, Northampton Sands Ironstone and Lincolnshire Limestone. Here and there is a capping of Boulder Clay. The gravel terraces and heavier soils of the upper Wreake Valley to the south are very fertile and especially rich in meadowland.

The Iron Age Corieltauvi are the earliest people to have influenced the later toponomy of the Hundred, with their great hill-fort at Burrough on the Hill affecting many minor names and field-names in the environs of that township. Prehistoric trackways are Sewstern Lane, which now forms the county boundary with Lincolnshire for some ten miles and the ancient routeway which enters the Hundred in Clawson, Hose and Harby parish in the Vale of Belvoir, climbs the escarpment of the Wolds near Brock Hill and runs due south to cross the river Wreake at the ford at Melton Mowbray and onwards past the hill fort on Burrough Hill. It was to become a military road, the *Ferdgate* of the Anglo-Saxons (with Old English *ferd* 'an army, a troop'). To these trackways may perhaps be added the route which the Romans later exploited across the line of the Wolds.

The principal remains of the Roman period are sited on the Wolds. A small town (a *vicus*) lay at Goadby Marwood. Ironworking and quarrying for building stone were especially important. Iron slag from the smelting of ironstone is known from Goadby Marwood, Eaton, Sproxton and Knipton. Routes particularly used as made roads during the Roman occupation were the important line across the Wolds (Margary 58a) from

Ermine Street to the Fosse Way, the above-mentioned Sewstern Lane and the lesser known King Street Lane running from the *vicus* at Goadby Marwood to that at Thistleton across the border in Rutland. Beside this road was sited the Roman villa at Wymondham.

The earliest known remains of the Anglo-Saxons in the Hundred are the pagan inhumation cemetery at Melton Mowbray, that at Sysonby, and the mixed inhumation/cremation cemetery at Saxby (sometimes referred to as the Stapleford Park site), all on the gravel terraces of the upper Wreake Valley. In addition, inhumations have been found at Knipton which occupies a small valley opening into the Vale of Belvoir. On the Wolds themselves lie the identifiably early Anglo-Saxon settlement sites (with names in *hām*) at Waltham on the Wolds and Wycomb and probably the lost *Whenham* in Ab Kettleby parish and *Hygham* in Scalford parish. Wycomb is an example of the very early compound appellative *wīc-hām* which is believed to identify an Anglo-Saxon settlement in very close relationship with a Romano-British *vicus* (in this case, the small town at Goadby Marwood), while Waltham on the Wolds, *Whenham* and *Hygham* all lie in close proximity to Margary 58a, the Roman road across the Wolds. To these early settlements may be added Wymondham (with its Roman villa) which lies on the Roman King Street Lane running between the *vici* at Goadby Marwood and Thistleton.

The earliest evidence for the Scandinavian settlement in the Hundred is constituted by those townships whose names are compounded with a Scandinavian personal name as first element and Old English *tūn* 'a village, an estate'. These are considered to be original Anglo-Saxon settlements appropriated by and renamed with reference to the men of the Viking army which disbanded in 877. In the Vale of Belvoir such villages are Barkestone and Long Clawson, while on the Wolds themselves is Croxton Kerrial. In the upper Wreake Valley are Sproxton and Coston. However, this part of the Hundred is especially noted for its settlement names in *bȳ* 'a farmstead, a village'. These sites may mark a later dividing-up of original larger Anglo-Saxon estates. On small tributary streams flowing south into the rivers Eye and Wreake are Saltby, Stonesby, Saxby, Freeby, Wyfordby, Brentingby and Sysonby, while higher into the Wolds are Goadby Marwood, Ab Kettleby and Wartnaby. South of the principal watercourse and on streams flowing northwards to join it are Great Dalby, Little Dalby and Eye Kettleby. At the chief river crossing lies Melton Mowbray, its Old English name having a Scandinavianized first element. The river-name Wreake is Scandinavian, having replaced the name of the English river Eye in the latter's lower reaches. The great impact of the Scandinavian settlement is also to be seen clearly in the vocabulary of the local medieval field-names.

The name of the Framland Wapentake (later Hundred) is also of Scandinavian origin. Its moot-site was located at the present-day Great Framlands on the long, high, south-pointing ridge some two miles from the Roman road Margary 58a across the Wolds and beside the prehistoric trackway that led south from the Vale of Belvoir to ford the river Wreake at Melton Mowbray. Framland (probably 'Fræna's grove') must have been an isolated clump of trees which served as a landmark for travellers to their moot in an area which Domesday Book shows to have been very largely cleared of woodland by 1086. The trackway is that which the Anglo-Saxons styled the *Ferdgate*. It was later used as a saltway (as were Sewstern Lane and Margary 58a).

The impact of the Norman Conquest on the major names of the Hundred is limited to its two medieval castle sites, that at Belvoir and that at Sauvey in Withcote parish. The name of Belvoir Castle, founded by Robert de Todenei in the eleventh century, is Old French. That of Sauvey Castle, founded by King John in 1211, appears to be English, but with a deal of phonetic alteration by its Norman keepers.

The Normans, however, were also instrumental in founding the religious houses of Croxton Abbey, Belvoir Priory and the great leper Hospital of St Lazarus at Burton Lazars. As the Wolds were prime sheep-rearing lands, Croxton Abbey developed granges at Branston, Nether Broughton, Croxton Kerrial and probably those known at Bescaby, Coston, Hose and Saltby. But other great houses beyond the boundaries of the Hundred also had granges here. Garendon Abbey owned granges at Goadby Marwood, Ringlethorpe and Sysonby. Vaudey Abbey in Lincolnshire possessed those at Burton Lazars and Sewstern, while Kirby Bellars Priory held the grange at Buckminster. That at Eaton was the property either of Croxton Abbey or of Leicester Abbey, while Tutbury Priory in Staffordshire held the grange at Wymondham.

Such Norman foundations later developed associated hunting parks. That at Croxton Kerrial is earliest mentioned in the 1290 inspeximus of a charter of 1189. The park at Burton Lazars had come into being by 1300, while the Old Park at Belvoir is first recorded in 1343. Its New Park was established by 1525. To these should be added a park at Cold Overton, initial mention of which is in 1218. Cold Overton, although a detached member township of the Framland Hundred, is presently in the civil parish of Knossington and Cold Overton: it will be treated with the place-names of Gartree Hundred.

NOTES ON ARRANGEMENT

1.   The Framland Hundred name is discussed first, followed by the names of regions. After these, the place-names are treated within the civil parishes. Within each civil parish, the townships are dealt with in alphabetical order. For each township, the township name is followed by names of primary historical or etymological interest, also arranged in alphabetical order. At the end of these sections, all the remaining names related to the township appearing on the 1956–67 O.S. 6" maps, on the 1951–66 O.S. 2½" maps and on the 1967–8 O.S. 1" maps (and any names recorded only locally) are listed with such early forms and etymological comment as can be provided. These names, however, are sometimes of obvious origin or are ones about whose history it is unwise to speculate. The forms of all names in the above sections are presented in the order: spelling, date, source. The final section for each township lists field-names, divided into modern (i.e. post-1750) and earlier. The pre-1750 field-names are printed in italic.

2.   Place-names believed to be no longer current are marked '(lost)', e.g. 'BURROWCHURCH (lost)'. This does not necessarily mean that the site to which the name was once applied is unknown. We are dealing primarily with names and it is the names which are lost. Such names are printed in italic in the index. Place-names marked '(local)' are believed to be current locally.

3.   In explaining the various toponyms, summary reference is always made, by printing the elements in bold type, to the analysis of elements at the end of this volume and to the more extended treatment of these in *English Place-Name Elements* (EPNS 25 and 26), in the *Addenda and Corrigenda* to these volumes in JEPNS 1 and in *The Vocabulary of English Place-Names* (CENS), in progress; e.g. '*Sletyng* 1316 (*v.* **sléttr, eng**)',

4.   Manuscript sources of the early spellings of the names are indicated by printing the abbreviations for the sources in italic. The abbreviations for published sources are printed in roman type.

5.   Where two dates are given for a spelling, e.g. '1189 (1332)' or '1258 (e.15)', the first date is the date at which the document purports to have been composed, the second the date of the copy that has come down to us. Sources whose dates cannot be fixed to a particular year are dated by century, e.g. '12', '13', '14' etc. (often more specifically 'e.13', 'm.13', 'l.13' etc., early, mid and late thirteenth century respectively); by regnal date, e.g. 'Edw 1', 'Hy 2', 'John' etc.; or by a range of years, e.g. '1282 x 91', such a date meaning that the form belongs to a particular year within those limits but cannot be more precisely fixed.

6.   The sign '(p)' after a source indicates that the particular spelling given appears in that source as a person's surname, not primarily as a reference to a place; thus '*Bokminstre* 1298 Fine (p)' refers to one *Simon de Bokminstre*, bearing *Bokminstre* as his surname.

7.   When a letter or letters (sometimes words or phrases) in an early place-name form are enclosed in parentheses, it means that spellings with and without the enclosed letter(s) occur; e.g. '*Botel(s)ford*' means that the forms *Botelford* and *Botelsford* are found. When only one part of a place-name spelling is given as a variant, preceded or followed by a hyphen or '~', it means that the particular spelling only differs in respect of the cited part from the preceding or following spelling, e.g. '*Redmild ~, Redmyld Beke*'.

8.   When an entry reads, e.g. 'ACRELANDS LANE, 1846 White', the name appears in its modern spelling in the source quoted.

9.   Cross references to other names are sometimes given with *supra* or *infra*, the former referring to a name already dealt with, the latter to a name dealt with later in the text.

10.   When a place-name is compared with an example from another county, that county is indicated; e.g. 'cf. Braunston, Ru 74' which refers to Braunston in Rutland and to a specific page in the EPNS survey *The Place-Names of Rutland*.

11.   In order to save space in presenting early spellings of a name, *et passim* and *et freq* are sometimes used to indicate that the preceding form occurs from time to time or frequently from the date of the last quoted source to that of the following one.

12.   Putative forms of place-name elements which appear asterisked in the analysis of elements at the end of this volume are not asterisked in the text, although the discussion will often make it clear which are on independent record and which are inferred.

ABBREVIATIONS AND BIBLIOGRAPHY

Abbreviations printed in roman type refer to printed sources and those in italic to manuscript sources.

a.	*ante*.
AAS	Reports and Papers of the Associated Architectural Societies.
Abbr	*Placitorum Abbrevatio* (RC), 1811.
abl.sg.	ablative singular.
AC	Ancient Charters (PRS 10), 1883.
acc.pl.	accusative plural.
acc.sg.	accusative singular.
AD	*Catalogue of Ancient Deeds* (PRO), in progress.
adj.	adjective, adjectival.
adv.	adverb.
AFr	Anglo-French.
AN	Anglo-Norman.
Anderson	O. S. Anderson, *The English Hundred-Names*, Lund 1934.
Angl	Anglian dialect of Old English.
Anglo-Scand	Anglo-Scandinavian.
ASC	*The Anglo-Saxon Chronicle*, ed. B. Thorpe (RS), 1861.
Ass	Assize Rolls in various publications.
Ave	Avenue (in street-names).
Banco	*Index of Placita de Banco 1327–8* (PRO Lists and Indexes 32), 1909; De Banco Rolls in Farnham.
BCS	*Cartularium Saxonicum*, ed. W. de G. Birch, 3 vols., 1885–93.
Bd	Bedfordshire.
BdHu	*The Place-Names of Bedfordshire and Huntingdonshire* (EPNS 3), 1926.
BelCartA	Small Cartulary of Belvoir Priory (Add MS 98), Duke of Rutland's Muniments Room, Belvoir Castle, Leics.
BelCartB	Large Cartulary of Belvoir Priory (Add MS 105), Duke of Rutland's Muniments Room, Belvoir Castle, Leics.
Berkeley	*Catalogue of the Charters at Berkeley Castle*, ed. I. H. Jeayes, 1892.
BHosp	Barrow Hospital Trustees MSS, The Record Office for Leicestershire, Leicester and Rutland, Wigston Magna.

Bk	Buckinghamshire; *The Place-Names of Buckinghamshire* (EPNS 2), 1925.
BL	British Library.
Blore	T. Blore, *History and Antiquities of the County of Rutland*, 1811.
BM	*Index to the Charters and Rolls in the Department of Manuscripts, British Museum*, 1900–12.
BodlCh	*Calendar of Charters and Rolls preserved in the Bodleian Library*, ed. W. H. Turner and H. O. Coxe, 1878.
Boniface	W. Levison, *Vitae Sancti Bonifatii Archiepiscopi Moguntini*, 1905.
BPR	*The Register of Edward the Black Prince* (PRO), 4 vols., 1930–3.
Brase	*Calendar of the Muniments of Brasenose College, Oxford* (NRA).
Brase	Unpublished plans in Brasenose College Library, Oxford.
Braye	Braye MSS, The Record Office for Leicestershire, Leicester and Rutland, Wigston Magna.
BrCart	The Breedon Cartulary (Latin MS 222), Rylands Library, Manchester.
Brk	Berkshire; *The Place-Names of Berkshire* (EPNS 49–51), 1973–6.
Burton	W. Burton, *The Description of Leicestershire*, 1622.
c.	*circa.*
Ca	Cambridgeshire; *The Place-Names of Cambridgeshire and the Isle of Ely* (EPNS 19), 1943.
Camd	Publications of the Camden Society.
Camden	W. Camden, *Britannia*, ed. R. Gough, 3 vols., 1789.
CartAnt	*The Cartae Antiquae Rolls* 1–20 (PRS NS 17, 33), 1939, 1960.
CCR	Croxton Kerrial Court Rolls, Duke of Rutland's Muniments Room, Belvoir Castle, Leics.
CENS	Publications of the Centre for English Name Studies, University of Nottingham, Nottingham.
cent.	century.
cf.	compare.
Ch	*Calendar of Charter Rolls* (PRO), 6 vols., 1903–27.
Ch	Cheshire; *The Place-Names of Cheshire* (EPNS 44–7), 1970–2, (EPNS 48, 54), 1981, (EPNS 74), 1997.
ChancR	Chancellor's Rolls (as footnotes to *Pipe Rolls* (PRS), in progress).
ChancW	*Calendar of Chancery Warrants* (PRO), in progress.
Chap	*Chapter Acts, Lincoln Cathedral* (LRS 12, 13, 15).

Charyte	Charyte's Novum Rentale of Leicester Abbey, incorporating Geryn's Rental (Bodleian Laud Misc 625), Bodleian Library, Oxford.
ChPr	*Chronicon Petroburgense* (Camd 47), 1849.
Clay	Clayton MSS, The Record Office for Leicestershire, Leicester and Rutland, Wigston Magna.
ClR	*Rotuli Litterarum Clausarum* (RC), 1833–44.
Cl(s)	Close(s) (in field-names).
Comp	Compotus Rolls, Duke of Rutland's Muniments Room, Belvoir Castle, Leics.; The Record Office for Leicestershire, Leicester and Rutland, Wigston Magna; in Middleton MSS, Nottingham University Archives, Nottingham.
comp.	comparative.
comp. adj.	comparative adjective.
Conant	Conant MSS, The Record Office for Leicestershire, Leicester and Rutland, Wigston Magna.
ContGerm	Continental Germanic.
CoPleas	Common Pleas in various publications.
Coram	Coram Rege Rolls in various publications.
CRCart	Roll Cartulary of Croxton Abbey (II.29.iii), Duke of Rutland's Muniments Room, Belvoir Castle, Leics.
Cresc	Crescent (in street-names).
Crox	The Large Cartulary of Croxton Abbey (Add. MS 70), Duke of Rutland's Muniments Room, Belvoir Castle, Leics.
CroxR	Croxton Abbey Register (Add. MS 71), Duke of Rutland's Muniments Room, Belvoir Castle, Leics.
Ct	Court Rolls in the Ferrers MSS, the Hazlerigg MSS, the Rothley Temple Deeds and the Winstanley MSS, The Record Office for Leicestershire, Leicester and Rutland, Wigston Magna; in the Middleton MSS, Nottingham University Archives, Nottingham; in PRO.
Cu	Cumberland; *The Place-Names of Cumberland* (EPNS 20–2), 1950–2.
Cur	*Curia Regis Rolls* (PRO), in progress.
Curtis	J. Curtis, *A Topographical History of the County of Leicester*, 1831.
d.	died.
Dane	F. M. Stenton, *Documents illustrative of the Social and Economic History of the Danelaw*, 1920.
dat.sg.	dative singular.
DB	Domesday Book; *Domesday Book: Leicestershire*, ed. P. Morgan, 1979.

Db	Derbyshire; *The Place-Names of Derbyshire* (EPNS 27–9), 1959.
Deed	Miscellaneous deeds in The Record Office for Leicestershire, Leicester and Rutland, Wigston Magna; in Lincolnshire Archives Office, Lincoln; in private collections.
def.art.	definite article.
DEPN	E. Ekwall, *The Concise Oxford Dictionary of English Place-Names*, 4th edn, 1960.
Derby	*Descriptive Catalogue of Derbyshire Charters*, ed. I. H. Jeayes, 1906.
dial.	dialect(al).
Dixie	Dixie or Market Bosworth Grammar School MSS, The Record Office for Leicestershire, Leicester and Rutland, Wigston Magna.
DKR	*Reports of the Deputy Keeper of the Public Records* (PRO).
DS	*Danmarks Stednavne*, Copenhagen 1922 ff.
Dugd	W. Dugdale, *Monasticon Anglicanum*, 6 vols. in 8, 1817–30.
Dun	Duncombe and Jeffreys Estate Deeds, The Record Office for Leicestershire, Leicester and Rutland, Wigston Magna.
e.	early.
ECP	*Early Chancery Proceedings* (PRO Lists and Indexes 1–10).
ed.	edited by.
EDD	J. Wright, *The English Dialect Dictionary*, 6 vols., 1898–1905.
edn	edition.
Edw 1, Edw 2	Regnal date, t. Edward I, t. Edward II etc.
el.	place-name element.
ELiW	*Early Lincoln Wills*, ed. A. Gibbons, 1888.
EMBI	*Early Maps of the British Isles*, ed. G. R. Crone, 1961.
eModE	early Modern English.
EnclA	Enclosure Awards in various publications.
EnclA	Unpublished Enclosure Awards, The Record Office for Leicestershire, Leicester and Rutland, Wigston Magna.
EpCB	*An Episcopal Court Book for the Diocese of Lincoln 1514–20* (LRS 61), 1967.
EPNS	Publications of the English Place-Name Society.
esp.	especially.
Ess	Essex; *The Place-Names of Essex* (EPNS 12), 1935.
et freq	*et frequenter* (and frequently (thereafter)).
et passim	and occasionally (thereafter).
ExchAO	Exchequer Augmentation Office Miscellaneous Books in Farnham.
FA	*Feudal Aids* (PRO), 6 vols., 1899–1920.

Fane	Fane MSS, The Record Office for Leicestershire, Leicester and Rutland, Wigston Magna.
Farnham	G. F. Farnham, *Leicestershire Medieval Village Notes*, 6 vols., 1929–33.
FB	Stathern Field Book, The Record Office for Leicestershire, Leicester and Rutland, Wigston Magna.
FConc	*Final Concords of the County of Lincoln* (LRS 17), 1920.
Fd	Field (in field-names).
Fees	*The Book of Fees* (PRO), 3 vols., 1921–31.
Feilitzen	O. von Feilitzen, *The Pre-Conquest Personal Names of Domesday Book*, Uppsala 1937.
fem.	feminine.
FF	Feet of Fines in various publications.
Fm	Farm.
Field	J. Field, *A History of English Field-Names*, 1993.
Finch	Finch MSS, The Record Office for Leicestershire, Leicester and Rutland, Wigston Magna.
Fine	*Calendar of Fine Rolls* (PRO), in progress.
FineR	*Excerpta e rotulis finium* (RC), 2 vols., 1835–6.
f.n(s).	field-name(s).
For	*Select Pleas of the Forest* (Seld 13), 1901.
Forssner	T. Forssner, *Continental Germanic Personal Names in England*, Uppsala 1916.
Förstemann	B. Förstemann, *Altdeutsches Namenbuch: Personennamen*, 2nd edn, Bonn 1900.
Fr	French.
France	*Calendar of Documents preserved in France* (RS), 1899.
freq	frequently.
GarCart	Cartulary of Garendon Abbey (BL Lansdown 415), British Library, London.
GarCh	Garendon Abbey Charters, The Record Office for Leicestershire, Leicester and Rutland, Wigston Magna.
gen.pl.	genitive plural.
gen.sg.	genitive singular.
Gilb	*Gilbertine Charters* (LRS 18), 1922.
GildR	Merchant Gild Rolls in RFL and RBL.
Gl	Gloucestershire; *The Place-Names of Gloucestershire* (EPNS 38–41), 1964–5.
Gox	The Goxhill Leiger, Peterborough Dean and Chapter MS 23.
GR	*John of Gaunt's Register 1379–1383* (Camd 3rd Series 56–7), 1911, 1937.
Gret	Gretton MSS, The Record Office for Leicestershire, Leicester and Rutland, Wigston Magna.

Gt.	Great.
Ha	Hampshire.
Hastings	*The Manuscripts of the late Reginald Rawdon Hastings of the Manor House, Ashby de la Zouch*, vol. 1 (HMC), 1928.
Hazlerigg	Hazlerigg MSS, The Record Office for Leicestershire, Leicester and Rutland, Wigston Magna.
HB	*The Registers of Bishop Henry Burghersh 1320–42* (LRS 87), 1999.
HDW	Hunt, Dickins and Willat Deeds, The Record Office for Leicestershire, Leicester and Rutland, Wigston Magna.
HMC	Historical Manuscripts Commission.
HMCVar	Historical Manuscripts Commission Reports on Manuscripts in Various Collections, 1901–23.
Ho.	House.
Hosp	*The Hospitallers in England* (Camd 65), 1855.
HP	Hall Papers in RBL.
Hrt	Hertfordshire; *The Place-Names of Hertfordshire*, (EPNS 15), 1938.
Hy 1, Hy 2	Regnal date, t. Henry I, t. Henry II etc.
ib, *ib*	*ibidem.*
Inqaqd	*Inquisitiones ad quod Damnum* (RC), 1803.
Ipm	*Calendar of Inquisitions post mortem* (PRO), in progress.
IpmR	*Inquisitiones post mortem* (RC), 4 vols., 1802–28.
ISLR	F. A. Greenhill, *The Incised Slabs of Leicestershire and Rutland*, 1958.
JEPNS	Journal of the English Place-Name Society.
John	Regnal date, t. John.
KB	Cartulary of Kirby Bellars Priory, Rockingham Castle Library, Rockingham, Northants.
Kelly	*Kelly's Directory of the Counties of Leicester and Rutland*, 1925.
L	Lincolnshire; *The Place-Names of Lincolnshire* (EPNS 58, 64–6, 71, 73, 77), 1985–2001, in progress.
l.	late.
La	Lancashire.
LAS	Transactions of the Leicestershire Archaeological Society, later Leicestershire Archaeological and Historical Society.
Lat	Latin.
Laz	Cartulary of Burton Lazars (BL Cotton Nero C XII), British Library, London.
LCDeeds	Leicester Corporation Deeds, The Record Office for Leicestershire, Leicester and Rutland, Wigston Magna.
Lease	Unpublished leases in local and private collections.

Lei   Leicestershire; *The Place-Names of Leicestershire* (EPNS 75), 1998, in progress.
LeicSurv   *The Leicestershire Survey*, ed. C. F. Slade, 1956.
LeicW   *Leicester Wills*, ed. H. Hartopp, 2 vols., 1902–20.
Leland   *The Itinerary of John Leland*, ed. L. Toulmin-Smith, 5 vols., 1906–10.
LEpis   *Lincoln Episcopal Records* (LRS 2), 1912.
LGerm   Low German.
Lib   *Calendar of Liberate Rolls* (PRO), in progress.
LibCl   Liber Cleri in *The State of the Church*, vol.1 (LRS 23), 1926.
Lind   E. H. Lind, *Norsk-Isländska Personbinamn från Medeltiden*, Uppsala 1920–1.
Lindkvist   H. Lindkvist, *Middle English Place-Names of Scandinavian Origin*, Uppsala 1912.
LML   *Leicestershire Marriage Licences 1570–1729*, ed. H. Hartopp, 1910.
LN   *Liber Niger Scaccarii*, 1774.
LP   *Letters and Papers Foreign and Domestic, Henry VIII* (PRO), 1864–1933.
LPeace   *Some Sessions of the Peace in Lincolnshire 1360–75* (LRS 30), 1937.
LRS   Publications of the Lincolnshire Record Society.
Lt.   Little.
LTD   Liber de terris Dominicalibus of Leicester Abbey (BL Cotton Galba B III), British Library, London.
Lundgren-Brate   M. F. Lundgren and E. Brate, *Personnamn från Medeltiden*, Stockholm, 1892–3.
LWills   *Lincoln Wills* (LRS 5, 10, 24), 1914–30.
m.   mid.
MagBrit   D. Lysons and S. Lysons, *Magna Britannia being a Concise Topographical Account of the several Counties of Great Britain*, 1816.
Map   Various printed maps.
Map   Unpublished maps in local and private collections.
Margary   I. D. Margary, *Roman Roads in Britain*, vol. 1, 1955.
masc.   masculine.
Mdw   Meadow (in field-names).
ME   Middle English.
MemR   *Memoranda Rolls* (PRS NS 11, 21, 31).
MHW   The Matriculus of Hugh de Wells in *Rotuli Hugonis de Welles* (LRS 3), 1912.
MiD   Middleton MSS, University of Nottingham Archives, Nottingham.

MinAccts	*Ministers' Accounts: List of the Lands of Dissolved Religious Houses* (PRO Lists and Indexes, Supplementary Series III, vols. 1–4).
MinAccts	Unpublished Ministers' Accounts, The Record Office for Leicestershire, Leicester and Rutland, Wigston Magna.
Misc	*Calendar of Inquisitions Miscellaneous* (PRO), in progress.
MiscAccts	Miscellaneous accounts in local and private collections.
MktHPR	Market Harborough Parish Records, The Record Office for Leicestershire, Leicester and Rutland, Wigston Magna.
MLat	Medieval Latin.
ModE	Modern English.
ModEdial.	Modern English dialect(al).
MS(S)	Manuscript(s).
Mx	Middlesex; *The Place-Names of Middlesex* (EPNS 18), 1942.
n.d.	not dated.
neut.	neuter.
Nichols	J. Nichols, *The History and Antiquities of the County of Leicester*, 4 vols. in 8, 1795–1811.
nom.pl.	nominative plural.
NordKult	*Nordisk Kultur*, vol. 7, Stockholm 1947.
Norw	Norwegian.
NQ	*Notes and Queries.*
NRA	National Register of Archives.
NS	New series in a run of publications.
Nt	Nottinghamshire; *The Place-Names of Nottinghamshire* (EPNS 17), 1940.
Nth	Northamptonshire; *The Place-Names of Northamptonshire* (EPNS 10), 1933.
num.	numeral.
O	First edition O.S. 1" maps.
OblR	*Rotuli de Oblatis* (RC), 1835.
obl.sg.	oblique singular.
OBret	Old Breton.
ODan	Old Danish.
OE	Old English.
OED	*A New English Dictionary*, ed. J. A. H. Murray *et al.*, 1884–1928; re-issued with a supplement in 1933 as *The Oxford English Dictionary.*
OEScand	Old East Scandinavian.
OFr	Old French.
OFris	Old Frisian.
OGer	Old German.
OIcel	Old Icelandic.

ON	Old Norse.
ONFr	Old Northern French.
O.S.	The Ordnance Survey.
OSax	Old Saxon.
OScand	Old Scandinavian.
OSut	*The Rolls and Registers of Bishop Oliver Sutton* (LRS 39, 43, 48, 52, 60), 1948–65.
OSwed	Old Swedish.
Ox	Oxfordshire; *The Place-Names of Oxfordshire* (EPNS 23–4), 1953–4.
P	*Pipe Rolls* (PRS), in progress.
(p)	place-name used as a personal name.
Pap	*Calendar of Entries in the Papal Registers* (PRO), in progress.
pa.part.	past participle.
Pat	*Calendar of Patent Rolls* (PRO), in progress.
Pat	Patent Rolls in the Public Record Office.
PatR	*Rotuli Litterarum Patentium* (RC), 1835.
Peake	Peake MSS (Neville of Holt), The Record Office for Leicestershire, Leicester and Rutland, Wigston Magna.
perh.	perhaps.
pers.n(s).	personal name(s).
P.H.	Public House.
Plan	Unpublished plans in The Record Office for Leicestershire, Leicester and Rutland, Wigston Magna.
p.n.	place-name.
PN-ing	E. Ekwall, *English Place-Names in -ing*, 2nd edn, Lund 1962.
PNL	M. Gelling, *Place-Names in the Landscape*, 1984.
Pochin	Pochin MSS, The Record Office for Leicestershire, Leicester and Rutland, Wigston Magna.
Polyolbion	M. Drayton, *Polyolbion*, ed. J. W. Hebel, 1961.
poss.	possible, possibly.
ppl.adj.	participial adjective.
PR	Parish Registers in various publications.
PraesR	*Praestitia Roll* (PRS 75, NS 37), 1964.
PRep	*The Register of Bishop Philip Repingdon* (LRS 57–8), 1963.
prep.	preposition.
pres.part.	present participle.
presum.	presumably.
PRO	Records preserved in or published by the Public Record Office.
prob.	probable, probably.
PRS	Publications of the Pipe Roll Society.
q.v.	*quod vide.*
R.	River.

RB	Romano-British.
RBE	*Red Book of the Exchequer* (RS 99), 1896.
RBL	*Records of the Borough of Leicester*, vols. 1–3, ed. M. Bateson 1899–1905; vol. 4, ed. H. Stocks 1923; vols. 5–6, ed. G. A. Chinnery 1965–7.
RC	Publications of the Record Commission.
Rd	Road (in street-names).
Reaney	P. H. Reaney, *A Dictionary of English Surnames*, revised by R. M. Wilson, 3rd edn with appendix by D. Hey, 1995.
Redin	M. Redin, *Uncompounded Personal Names in Old English*, Uppsala 1915.
Reeve	Documents in the Reeve Collection, Lincolnshire Archives Office, Lincoln.
Reg	*Regesta Regum Anglo-Normannorum*, 1913–1968.
RegAnt	*Registrum Antiquissimum of the Cathedral Church of Lincoln* (LRS 27–9, 51), 1931–58.
Rental	Various published rentals.
Rental	Various unpublished rentals in local and private collections.
RFL	*Register of the Freemen of Leicester*, ed. H. Hartopp, 2 vols., 1927–33.
RGrav	*Rotuli Ricardi Gravesend Episcopi Lincolniensis* (LRS 20), 1925.
RGros	*Rotuli Roberti Grosseteste Episcopi Lincolniensis* (LRS 11), 1914.
RH	*Rotuli Hundredorum* (RC), 1812–8.
RHug	*Rotuli Hugonis de Welles Episcopi Lincolniensis* (LRS 3,6), 1912–3.
Ric 1, Ric 2	Regnal dates, t. Richard I, t. Richard II etc.
RS	Rolls Series.
RTAL	*Rotulus Taxationis Archidiaconatus Leicestrie* (LRS 3), 1912.
RTemple	Rothley Temple Deeds, The Record Office for Leicestershire, Leicester and Rutland, Wigston Magna.
Ru	Rutland; *The Place-Names of Rutland* (EPNS 67–9), 1994.
Rut	Duke of Rutland's MSS, Muniments Room, Belvoir Castle, Leics.
RydCart	*The Rydware Cartulary* (Salt 16), 1895.
S	P. H. Sawyer, *Anglo-Saxon Charters*, 1968.
Sa	Shropshire; *The Place-Names of Shropshire* (EPNS 62–3, 70, 76) 1990–2001, in progress.
Sale	Particulars of sales in local and private collections.
Salt	Publications of the William Salt Society.
Saxton	C. Saxton, *Atlas of England and Wales*, 1576.
sb.	substantive.

Scand   Scandinavian.

Seld   Publications of the Selden Society.

Sf   Suffolk.

Sloane   Sloane MSS, The British Library, London.

s.n.   *sub nomine.*

SNav   *Stamford Navigation: Report of Robert Whitworth, Engineer,* 1786.

SNPh   *Studia Neophilologica.*

So   Somerset.

Speed   J. Speed, *The Theatre of the Empire of Great Britain,* 1610.

SPNLY   G. Fellows Jensen, *Scandinavian Personal Names in Lincolnshire and Yorkshire,* Copenhagen 1968.

SR   Subsidy Rolls in various publications.

Sr   Surrey; *The Place-Names of Surrey* (EPNS 11), 1934.

SSNEM   G. Fellows Jensen, *Scandinavian Settlement Names in the East Midlands,* Copenhagen 1978.

St   Staffordshire.

St   Street (in street-names).

Stephen   Regnal date, t. Stephen.

Stix   Cartulary of Stixwould Priory (BL MS Add. 46701), British Library, London.

sup.   superlative.

surn(s).   surname(s).

Surv   Surveys in local and private collections.

s.v.   *sub voce.*

Sx   Sussex; *The Place-Names of Sussex* (EPNS 6–7), 1929–30.

t.   *tempore.*

TA   Tithe Awards, The Record Office for Leicestershire, Leicester and Rutland, Wigston Magna.

Tax   *Taxatio Ecclesiastica* (RC), 1802.

Templar   *Records of the Templars in England in the Twelfth Century,* ed. B. A. Lees, 1935.

Terrier   Terriers in local and private collections.

Thoresby   Thoresby House MSS, Nottinghamshire Record Office, Nottingham.

TRE   *tempore Regis Edwardi,* the DB term for 'on the day that King Edward the Confessor was alive and dead'.

TutP   *Cartulary of Tutbury Priory* (HMC vol. JP2), 1962.

v.   *vide.*

Val   *The Valuation of Norwich,* ed. W. E. Lunt, 1926.

vb.   verb.

vbl.sb.   verbal substantive.

VCHL   *Victoria County History of Leicestershire,* in progress.

VE	*Valor Ecclesiasticus* (RC), 1810–34.
VEPN	*The Vocabulary of English Place-Names* (CENS), in progress.
Visit	*Visitations of Religious Houses in the Diocese of Lincoln* (LRS 14, 21, 33, 35, 37), 1918–47.
We	Westmorland; *The Place-Names of Westmorland* (EPNS 42–3), 1967.
White	*History, Gazetteer and Directory of Leicestershire and Rutland*, ed. W. White, 1846, 1863, 1877.
Will	Unpublished wills in local and private collections.
Will	Wills in various publications.
wk.obl.	weak oblique.
Wm 1, Wm 2	Regnal date, t. William I, t. William II.
Wo	Worcestershire; *The Place-Names of Worcestershire* (EPNS 4), 1927.
WoCart	John de Wodeford's Cartulary (BL Claudius A XIII), British Library, London.
Wright	J. Wright, *The History and Antiquities of the County of Rutland*, 1684.
WSax	West Saxon dialect of Old English.
Wyg	Wyggeston Hospital MSS, The Record Office for Leicestershire, Leicester and Rutland, Wigston Magna.
YE	Yorkshire East Riding; *The Place-Names of the East Riding of Yorkshire and York* (EPNS 14), 1937.
YN	Yorkshire North Riding; *The Place-Names of the North Riding of Yorkshire* (EPNS 5), 1928.
YW	Yorkshire West Riding; *The Place-Names of the West Riding of Yorkshire* (EPNS 30–7), 1961–3.
*	a postulated form.
1"	O.S. 1" maps, editions of 1967–8.
2½"	O.S. 2½" maps, editions of 1951–66.
6"	O.S. 6" maps, editions of 1956–67.
(x2), (x3)	Two instances of a particular name; three instances etc.

FRAMLAND HUNDRED

Framland Hundred

Franelund 1086 DB, c.1130 LeicSurv, 1167, 1168 P *et freq* to 1193 ib, *Franelun* 1086 DB, c.1130 LeicSurv, *Franlund* 1086 DB, 13 (1404) *Laz*
Franeslund 1166 P
Frenelund 1175 ChancR, 1176, 1177 P, *Frenelun* 1195, 1197 ib
Freneslund' 1175, 1191 P
Framelund' c.1130 LeicSurv, 1184 P, 1241 (e.15) *BelCartB et passim* to c.1291 Tax (freq), e.14 *BelCartA*, 1307 Fine, *Frameland(e)* 1248 Abbr, 1267 Cur *et passim* to 1428 FA, *Framelond(e)* 1209 × 35 RHug, 1241 (e.14) *BelCartA et passim* to 1314 *GarCart et freq* to 1402, 1428 FA, *Framelound'* 1284 Ass, c.1291 Tax, Edw 1 (e.15) *BelCartB*
Frameslund 1247 Fees
Fremelund 1180 P, *Fremeland* 1326 Fine
Framlund' 13 (1404) *Laz*, *Framlond(e)* 1381, 1382 Cl *et passim* to 1448, 1449 *Rut*, 1480 *MiD*, 1509 LP, *Framland(e)* c.1291 Tax, 13 *GarCart*, e.14 *BelCartA et passim* to 1457 *Ct*, 1480 *MiD et freq*

The division is styled
wapentac, -tak, -taco, -tacum, -tagio 1086 DB (freq) *et freq* to 1227 Fees, 1284 Abbr
hundred, -i, -um c.1130 LeicSurv, 1231 Cl, 1247 Fees *et freq*

v. **vápnatak, hundred**.

The first el. of Framland is a Scand pers.n., either *Fræna* or an unrecorded **Fráni* or **Fræni* (*v.* Anderson 46). *Fræna* appears in ASC(E) as the name of a Danish jarl killed at the Battle of Ashdown in 871. Another leader called *Fræna* is recorded for 993 in ASC(E). The second el. is Scand **lundr** 'a grove, a small wood'. The name was given to a clump of trees which must have formed a distinctive landmark on higher ground in an area not particularly well wooded. The grove acted as the marker for the moot-site of the men of the wapentake. This small wood appears to have been still present as late as 1276 RH when *bosco de Framelund* is recorded. It lay close to what is now the covert called Scalford Gorse. By 1400 Ipm, *Framelande* is described as an enclosure (cf. *Framlande hedge* 1550 *Pochin*, *v.* **hecg**). The name survives in Great Framlands (*q.v.*) which is located two miles north of Melton Mowbray. The moot-site is at the head of a high, southward-shooting ridge, two miles south of the Roman road Margary 58a across the Wolds, joining the Fosse Way with Ermine Street, and beside an ancient trackway also used in the Roman period. This track entered the county in the Vale of Belvoir, climbed Brock Hill in Clawson, Hose and Harby parish and ran southwards to cross R. Wreake at Melton Mowbray. It is referred to as *le Ferdgate* 13 AD ('the military road', *v.* **ferd**, **gata**) and was later used as a saltway.

Names of Regions

VALE OF BELVOIR
  (*de*) *Valle Beauver* 1250 Cl
  le Vaal 1339 *Pat*, *la Vale* 1375 Cl
  the Vale of Beauer 1449 *WoCart, the Valle of Bever* 1516 *Wyg, the Vale of Bever* c.1545 Leland, 1613 Polyolbion
  le Vale de Beluere 1511 *Wyg, le Vale of Bever* 1520 *ib*

The following forms are affixed to township names:
  ~ *in vall* 1332 SR, ~ *in Valle* 1416 Nichols
  ~ *in le Vale* 1338 Hosp, 1449 *WoCart*, 1451 *Wyg et passim* to 1530 *ib*, 1553 Pat
  ~ *in the Vayle* 1510 *Wyg*, ~ *in the Vale* 1556 *Rut*, 1564 Fine *et passim* to 1618 LML, 1666 LeicW
  ~ *in le Wall'* 1517, 1519 *Wyg*, ~ *in the Wayll'* 1552 AAS

  v. **val**.

THE WOLDS
Early forms for these uplands are affixed to township names and the following are from such names in Framland Hundred:
  ~ *super Wald'* c.1130 LeicSurv, 1316 *RTemple*, ~ *super Waldas* 1325 *MiD*
  ~ *de Wauz* 1209 Derby
  ~ *super le Wold*(*e*) 1316 FA, 1408 Inqaqd *et passim* to 1499 *RTemple*, 1539 *Deed*, ~ *super Woldas* Edw 2 *MiD*, ~ *super Wolde* 1529 *RTemple*, ~ *super le Woldes* 1604 SR
  ~ *de le Woldys* 1505 *RTemple*, ~ *on the Woldys* 1552 *Rut*, ~ *on the Wolds* 1607 LML
  ~ *super le Oldes* 1553 Pat, ~ *vpon Olds* 1610 Speed, ~ *on the Ould* 1613 Polyolbion, ~ *on the Olds* 1688, 1707 LML

  v. **wald**; here used to denote a high tract of open land rather than forest land.

Belvoir

1. BELVOIR

Belveder 1130 P, *Belvedeire* 1146 Reg, *Beluedeir* e.13 (e.15) *BelCartB*, 1269 (e.14) *BelCartA*, *Belvether* Hy 1 (1331) Ch, *Belveher* 1198 (1301) ib
Bello videre 1145 BM, Hy 2 *Rut*, 1431 Pat, *Bellouidere* e.13 (e.14) *BelCartA*, e.13 (e.15), Hy 3 (e.15) *BelCartB*
Belveeir 1152 BM, *Belueeir* 1167, 1168, 1169 P *et passim* to 1241 (e.14) *BelCartA*, *Belueeyr* 1.12 (e.14) *ib*, *Bealveeir* 1168 P, *Bealueeir* 1172, 1183 ib
Belveir 1168 ChancR, 1236 Fees, *Belueir* 1.12 *Rut*, 1191 P *et passim* to e.13, John *Rut*, *Bealveir* 1172 P, *Beelueir* 1.12 *Rut*, *Belweir* 1.Hy 2 BM, *Beluair* 1.12 *Rut*, *Balveir* Hy 2 BM
Belveer 1155 × 58 (1333) Ch, 1216 PatR, *Belueer* Hy 1 (e.15) *BelCartB*, c.1150 BM, Stephen *Rut et passim* to e.13 *ib*, John (e.15) *BelCartB*, *Beelueer* Hy 2 *Rut*
Beluar' c.1130 LeicSurv, *Beluer* 1155 × 68 *Rut*, 1196 ChancR, e.13 *Rut et passim* to Hy 3, 1317 *ib et freq* to 1408, 1542 *ib*, *Belver* 1236 Fees, 1242 Ipm *et passim* to 1312 ib *et freq* to 1441 Cl, 1449 Pat *et passim* to 1540 *Rut*, 1549 Pat, *Belvere* 1306 Banco, 1307 IpmR, 1324 Ipm
Baluero m.13 (e.15) *BelCartB*, Hy 3 *Rut*
Beluero c.1130 LeicSurv, Hy 2 *Rut et passim* to 1263, 1268, Hy 3 *ib* (freq) *et freq* to 1408, 1411 *ib et passim* to 1517 *Wyg*, 1534 *Rut*, *Belueru'* 1288, 1305, 1307 *ib*, *Beluerum* 1305, 1323, 1380, 1444, 1451 *ib*, *Belvero* 1230 RHug, 1249 RGros *et passim* to 1261, 1263 Cl *et freq* to 1334, 1349 ib *et passim* to 1452 Pap, 1486 Pat, *Belvor* 1601 *Terrier*
Belvour 1497 *Rut*, *Belvoier* 1541 *ib*, *Belvoyer* 1544 *ib*, *Belvoyr* 1555 *ib*, *Belvoire* 1605, c.1612 *Terrier*
Bealuer 13 (e.15) *BelCartB*, *Bealvour* 1462 Pat, *Bealvoir* 1464, 1467, 1475 ib

4

Bellover 1462, 1464, 1467, 1475 Pat, *Bello vero* 1482 *Rut*, *Bellever* c.1545 Leland, *Bellevoire* c.1545 ib

Bauveer 1150 × 60 BM, *Bauveir* 1236 Fees, *Bauver* 1287 Ipm

Beauueer 1215 PraesR, 1537 *Rut*, *Beauveer* 1216 ClR, 1216 PatR, 1294 Ipm, *Beauveir* 1262 AD, 1408 Pat, 1441 Cl

Beauuer John *Rut*, e.13 (e.14) *BelCartA*, e.Hy 3 *Rut et passim* to 1331 *ib et freq* to 1420, 1437 *Comp et passim* to 1489 *Wyg*, *Beauuere* 1286 (e.15) *BelCartB*, *Beauver* 1224 Cur, 1234 Cl *et passim* to 1311 Ipm *et freq* to 1413, 1416 *Comp et passim* to 1477 Cl, *Beauvere* 1321 Pat, *Beawver* 1364 Misc

Beauuoir(e) 1224 (e.15) *BelCartB*, 1427 *Comp*, 1443 *MiD*, *Beauvoir(e)* 1301 ChancW, 1302, 1431 Pat *et passim* to 1475 ib, *Beauvoier* 1445, 1473 *Comp*, *Beauuoiere* 1486 *ib*, *Beauvour* 1462 Pat

Beuveir 1217 BM, 1236 Fees, *Beuveyr* 1236 ib, 1285 Fine, 1285 Ipm, *Beuvayr* 1285 ib

Beuuer John, 1252, 1261 *Rut et freq* to 1312, 1431 *ib*, *Beuver* 1212, 1236 Fees *et freq* to 1363 Ipm, 1424 *Wyg*, *Beuvoir* 1172 RBE

Beuer 1388, 1408 *Rut et passim* to 1579 EMBI, *Beuere* 1395 *Rut*, 1404 *Wyg*, *Bever* 1400 *Rut*, 1412 FA *et passim* to 1549 Pat, 1610 Speed, *Bevor* 1508 Ipm, *Bevyr* 1373, 1495 ib, *Bevour* 1462, 1464 Pat *et passim* to 1495 Ipm, *Beyuer* 1524 *Wyg*, *Beyver* 1531 *ib*, 1549 Pat, *Beywer* 1542 *Rut*

Beauer 1252, 1460 *Rut*, 1482, 1489 *Wyg*, *Beaver* 1495 *Rut*, 1507 Ipm, 1545 MemR, 1604 LML, *Beavoire* 1388 Ipm, *Beavoure* 1498 ib, *Beavoyr* 1552 Nichols

'Beautiful view', *v.* **bel**[2], **beau**, **vedeir**. An OFr place-name, in origin identical with the ModE sb. *belvedere* 'a summer-house erected on an eminence for the purpose of viewing the surrounding scene'. Belvoir Castle crowns an eastern headland of the Wolds, with commanding views to the north and east across the Vale of Belvoir. It was founded in the late 11th cent. by Robert de Todenei, standard bearer of William the Conqueror. It is noteworthy that while the older *bel* occurs in the earliest spellings of the name, *beu/beau* is also present in forms from the middle of the 12th cent. onwards.

BELVOIR CASTLE
> *castrum de Belvedeire* 1146 Reg, *castro de Beauveer* 1216 PatR
> *de Castello* Hy 1 (1333) Ch (p), *castello de Beluario* 1189 CartAnt,
>   ~ *de Belvero* 1287 *Pat*, ~ *de Beauver(e)* 1321, 1354 *ib, castelli de*
>   *Beauver* 1361 *ib*, ~ *de Beavoire* 1388 *ib, castellum de Bello*
>   *Videre* 1431 *ib*
> *Bevercastell* 1439 *Pat, Belwer Castell* 1539 *Rut, Bellever Castelle*
>   c.1545 Leland, *Beuer cast.* 1576 Saxton, 1579 EMBI, *Beaver*
>   *Castle* 1618 LML, *Belvoir Castle* 1863, 1877 White

v. **castel(l)**. Note also MLat *castrum* and MLat *castellum*, both 'a castle'.

Recorded parts of the castle are:
> *le Courtehous Yerde* 1531 *Comp* (*v.* **court-hous, geard**); *le*
>   *Gatehouse* 1542 *Rut* (*v.* **gate-hous**); *Hallegarth'* 1425 *Comp, le*
>   *Hallȝerd* 1423 *Wyg, le halleyerd* 1424 *ib, le hall yerd* 1424 *ib* (*v.*
>   **hall, garðr, geard**); *the Kechen close* 1542 *Rut* (*v.* **kicchen,**
>   **clos(e)**); *le Mote* 1356 Nichols (*v.* **mote**); *le Ward* 1292 OSut, *le*
>   *Castleward* 1555 *Rut* (*v.* **warde**).

ST MARY'S PRIORY (lost)
> *prioratus de Belvero* 1220 MHW
> *priorie Sancte Marie Belver* 1449 *Pat, priorie de Bevour* 1462, 1464,
>   1467, 1475 *ib, priorie vel celle de Belver* 1549 *ib*

The priory, which was sited below the castle on the north side, was a Benedictine house founded c.1076 by Robert de Todenei who established the castle. Note MLat *prioratus* and MLat *prioria*, both meaning 'a priory', and MLat *cella* 'a daughter-house'.

BLACKBERRY HILL
> *montis de Blakeburugh* 12 (e.15) *BelCartB*, ~ *de Blakeberg(e)* 1252
>   *Rut*, ~ *de Blakeberge* 1257 Nichols
> *Blakeberough* 12 (e.15), m.13 (e.15) *BelCartB, Blakeberew* John
>   (e.15) *ib*, *Blakebergwe* 1252 Ipm, *Blakeberugh* 1343 ib,
>   *Blakebergh* 1393 Nichols, 1395 Cl, *Blakebargh'* 1423, 1427
>   *Comp, Blakeborugh'* 1428 *Rut, Blakeberu(e)* 1449 *WoCart*
> *Blackberghe* 1414 Nichols, *Blackeborough* 1531 *Comp, Blackborow*
>   1601 *Terrier, Blackburrow* 1605 *ib*

Blackborow hill 1601 *Terrier, Blackburrow hill* 1611 × 13 *ib,*
  Blackborrowe hill 1625 *ib*
Blackberry Hill 1795 Map, 1803 *EnclA,* 1815 Map, 1846, 1877
  White

'The dark, densely overgrown hill', *v.* **blæc, berg**. Note MLat *mons*
(*montis* gen.sg.) 'a hill'.

SALTBECK
  Saltbec 1154 × 59 *Rut, Saltebec* John *ib,* 1252 (e.14) *BelCartA,* Edw
    1 *Rut,* Edw 1 (e.15) *BelCartB, Saltbec'* 1253 *Rut*
  Saltbek' 1292 (e.15) *BelCartB,* 1417, 1423 *Comp,* 1424 *Wyg,* 1425,
    1426, 1427 *Comp, Saltebek'* 1292 (e.15) *BelCartB,* 1531 *Comp,*
    Saltbeck 1374 (e.15) *BelCartB,* 1424 *Wyg, Saltbeke* 1413 *Comp,*
    Salt beck 1824 O
  Saltbecks 1806 Map, *Bushy Salt becks* c.1729 Nichols

'The salty stream', *v.* **salt**^{2}, **bekkr**. Saltbeck is now the name of a
copse on the lower slope of the Wolds escarpment in the extreme north
of the parish (hence *Bushy ~* c.1729, *v.* **busshi**). *Redmyld Saltbek'* 1424
Wyg is recorded in adjoining Redmile parish, but identification of the
course of the particular stream is not obvious today, possibly because of
alterations caused by modern drainage. It is noteworthy that the defunct
Belvoir Spa 1824 O (*v.* **spa**) lay only a half mile south-west of Saltbeck
copse. Chalybeate springs hereabouts may have been the source of the
stream. Salt domes are known in the Lower Lias formations which
underlie the Wolds and ironstone is still worked at Saltby (*q.v.*) some
five miles to the south-east. The stream evidently contained iron salts or
other minerals in solution enough to establish its name early in the
medieval period.

THE AVENUE, *v.* **avenue**. BRIERY COTTAGE, BRIERY WOOD, *v.* **brērig**.
CALCROFT'S CLOSE, *Calcrofts Close* 1795 *EnclA,* 1806 Map, *Calcrofts*
1824 O. *William Calcroft* 1630 LML was resident in neighbouring
Bottesford, *Robert Calcroft* 1641 ib in the same village. *John Calcroft*
1707 ib, 1736 *Terrier* is recorded in adjoining Redmile, while *William
Calcroft* 1877 White was a farmer and grazier of nearby Muston.
CARLISLE WOOD, named from the father of the fifth Duchess of Rutland,
the Earl of Carlisle. THE DEVON is *The Deven Field* 1789 Nichols, 1791
EnclA, The Deven 1840 *TA,* named from R. Devon which flows along

its boundary. DUCHESS GARDEN is sited beside the Mausoleum, built 1826–8; the Mausoleum's altar is a monument to the fifth Duchess of Rutland who died in 1825. The garden was named in her honour. FIR HOLT, *the Fir Holt* 1803 *EnclA*, *v.* **firr(e)**, **holt**. KENNELS WOOD, 1925 Kelly, cf. *Kennels* 1806 Map, *Dog Kennel* 1824 O, *v.* **kenel**; the kennels of the Belvoir Foxhounds. THE MAUSOLEUM, *v.* **mausoleum**. MIDDLESDALE, *Middesdale* 1449 *WoCart*, *Middledale* 1601, 1605, 1612, 1704 *Terrier*, *Middlesdale* 1605, 1612 *ib*, *Midlesdale*, *Midle dale* 1625 *ib*, *Long*, *Short Middle Dale* 1803 *EnclA*, *v.* **dalr**; **middes** appears to be later confused with **middel**, cf. *Middles dale* in Pickwell f.ns. (b) and *Medlisdale* in Leesthorpe f.ns. (b). OLD PARK WOOD, 1795 *EnclA*, *the Park Wood* 1803 *ib*, *Holdpark* 1343 Ipm, *le Park* 1356 (1449) *WoCart*, *Beverpark* 1386 Ipm, *Beauver park* 1394 ib, *the Parke* 1601, 1605, 1612, 1625 *Terrier*, *Old Park* 1795 *EnclA*, 1806 Map, *v.* **ald**, **park**. THE PEACOCK is *Peacock Inn* 1846, 1863, 1877 White, *Peacock Hotel* 1925 Kelly; a peacock is part of the coat of arms of the Manners family, the Dukes of Rutland. SIR JOHN'S WOOD was named from the Rev. Sir John Thoroton, incumbent of Bottesford and friend and domestic chaplain to the fifth Duke of Rutland. He died in 1820. He was knighted by George IV when Prince Regent and supervised the remodelling of Belvoir into the shape of a medieval castle (work completed c.1830) after the death of the architect James Wyatt in 1813. WESTMINSTER is now the name of a large fishpond, first recorded as *Westminster pondes* 1611 *Rut*, *v.* **ponde**. The present pond lies just to the east of the site of St Mary's Priory and the ponds may formerly have been its stews. The origin of the name is obscure since it seems unlikely that by 1611 Westminster was a transferred name (but cf. Windsor Hill (forms from 1601) to the south of the castle). Perhaps the priory church was seen as the 'west minster' in relation to the 'east minster', the lost St James's Church in Old Church Wood, Woolsthorpe, about one mile away across the valley of R. Devon. WEST WONG, 1795 *EnclA*, *le Weste Wong'* 1424 *Wyg*, *le Westwong* 1424 *ib*, *v.* **west**, **vestr**, **vangr**.

FIELD-NAMES

In (a), forms dated 1803 are *EnclA*. Forms throughout dated Hy 2, John, 13, 1305, 1314, 1354, 1384, 1400, 1413, 1417, 1425, 1426, 1427, 1437, 1477, 1478, 1511, 1525, 1531, 1540, 1542 and 1555 are *Rut*; John (e.15), 1200 × 50 (e.15), 1275 (e.15) and 1329 (e.15) are *BelCartB*; 1424 and 1532 are *Wyg*.

(a) the Paddock 1803 (*v.* **paddock**); Priory Holt Wood 1803 (*v.* **holt** and St Mary's Priory *supra*).

(b) *Castelgate* 1314 (*v.* **castel(l)**, **gata**; the principal road to the castle); *Castell Row* 1531 (*v.* **castel(l)**, **vrá**); *Chaveneis leasis* c.1545 Leland (with the surn. *Chaveney*, presum. an early form of *Cheyney*, *v.* **lǣs**); *Cobbescroftes* 1413 (an OE pers.n. **Cobba* is postulated by Insley in JEPNS **10** 42 from *Cobbecroft* 13 (Ess 637), but note also OE **cobb(e)** 'a roundish mass, a lump' which may have been used topographically; *cob* used as the name for a stocky horse is not recorded before the early 19th cent. (*v.* OED *s.v.* cob, sb.[1], 4), but cf. *crofto Palefridi* and *Gyldyngcroft'*, *infra*, which also may refer to horses, *v.* **croft**); *Cow Crofte* 1531 (*v.* **cū**, **croft**); *Easthorpmore* 1413 (*v.* **mōr**[1]; moorland lying between Belvoir and Easthorpe in Bottesford parish); *Forewonge* 1437 (*v.* **fore**, **vangr**); *Granthamesgathe* John (*v.* **gata**; the road to Grantham to the east); *Graueleyplace* 1424 (*v.* **place**; with the generic *place*, a surn. would normally be expected (*v.* Reaney *s.n.* Graveley), but better here is **graveli**); *Grete Close* 1531, *the great close* 1540 (*v.* **grēat**, **clos(e)**); *Gyldyngcroft'* 1425, *Geldyngcroft* 1426 (*v.* **croft**), *Geldinge Close* 1531, *the Geldyng close* 1540 (*v.* **clos(e)**) (all with ME **geldyng** 'a castrated horse', from ON *geldingr*; in Belvoir f.ns., *croft* appears to be replaced by *close*, cf. *Leicroft* and *Longecroft'*, *infra*); *Harlondes* 1314 ('boundary selions', *v.* **hār**[2], **land**); *Hornecrofte close* 1531 (*v.* **horn**, **croft**, **clos(e)**); *landa* 1417, 1426, *le laund* 1427 (*v.* **launde**); *Langmore* 1413 (*v.* **lang**[1], **mōr**[1]); *langewong'* 1413 (*v.* **lang**[1], **vangr**); *Leicroft* 1394 Ipm, 1413, *Leycroft* 1386, 1394 Ipm, 1441 Cl (*v.* **croft**), *le leyclose* 1531, *the Ley close* 1540 (*v.* **clos(e)**; perh. with ME **laie** 'a pool' rather than **lēah** 'a clearing in woodland'); *Longecroft'* 1275 (e.15), *Longcroft* 1305 (*v.* **croft**), *Longeclose* 1531 (*v.* **clos(e)**) (*v.* **lang**[1]); *Neathouse meadow* 1656 Nichols (*v.* **neethowse**); *Neuweye* John (*v.* **nīwe**, **weg**); *New Parke* 1525, *le Newparke* 1531, *the newe parke at Belver* 1540 (*v.* **nīwe**, **park**, cf. Old Park (Wood) *supra*); *Northwel'* John (e.15), (*le) Northwell'* 1200 × 50 (e.15) (*v.* **norð**, **wella**); *Ogberdeswell'*, *Oggeberdeswelle* John, John (e.15) (*v.* **wella**; with the OGer pers.n. *Ogebert* (Förstemann 1178)); *crofto Palefridi* 1284 Nichols (perh. 'the palfrey croft', with MLat *palefridus* 'a palfrey, a saddle-horse' and MLat *croftum* 'a croft', but the croft suggests that rather than *palefridus*, we may have a Latinization of the surn. *Palfrey* (by metonomy for *Palfreyman*) from OFr *palefrei* 'a palfrey, a saddle-horse', *v.* Reaney *s.n.*); *Pecok croft* 1275 (e.15), *Pekokcroft'* 1305 (perh. 'the peacock croft', *v.* **pecok**, **croft**; the bird was served as a delicacy at aristocratic tables in the Middle Ages, but because this was a croft, the surn. *Peacock* may be preferable as the specific, *v.* Reaney *s.n.* and cf. *crofto Palefridi*, *supra*; but also cf. *Cowe Crofte*, *supra*); *le Peterstone Lane* 1555 (*v.* **lane**; presum. with an early use of **peterstone** 'a fragment of fossil encrinite', *v.* EDD *s.v.*; such fossils are to be found in the fields between Belvoir and Muston); *Prattesplace* 1400 (*v.* **place**; with the surn. *Pratt*); *Redelandes* 1314 (*v.* **rēad**, **land**); *Redmildeheng'* 1275 (e.15) (*v.* **eng**), *Redmildegate* 1314 (*v.* **gata**) (Redmile parish adjoins to the west); *Saltbekwong* 1437 (*v.* **vangr** and Saltbeck *supra*); *Southcroftes* 1531 (*v.* **sūð**, **croft**); *Southynges* 1413 (*v.* **sūð**, **eng**); *Sowthbrygge* 1413 (*v.* **sūð**, **brycg**); *Sowthell'* 13 (*v.* **sūð**, **wella**, cf. *Northwel'*, *supra*); *Spittelhousclose* 1531 (*v.* **spitel-hous**, **clos(e)**; presum. the close lay next to the infirmary of St Mary's Priory); *Staynewong'* 1413 (*v.* **steinn**, **vangr**); *Tawstonthinge* 1531, *v.* **thing** and Toston Hill in Easthorpe); *le Warenne*

1352 Ipm, *Beavoyr Waren* 1552 Nichols; earlier *warranam* 1292 OSut (MLat *waranna* 'a game preserve') (*v.* **wareine**; the vernacular instance of *warren* predates the earliest citation in OED by 25 years); *le Wellesty* 1384 (*v.* **wella**; with **stīg** or **stig**); *Westgate* Hy 2, 1354, 1426, *le Westgate* 1329 (e.15) (*v.* **west, vestr, gata**); *le West lane* 1477, 1478, *Westelane* 1511, *West lane* 1532 (*v.* **west, lane**; presum. the same road as *Westgate*); *Ynglandeswange* 1531 (*v.* **vangr**; with the surn. *England*; Reaney *s.n.* notes that 'there is no authority for . . . *ing-land* "meadow-land"').

2. HARSTON

Herstan 1086 DB, *Herston* 1428 FA, 1498 Cl
Harestan c.1130 LeicSurv, 1156 (1318) Ch, 1180 ChancR (p), 1191 P *et freq* to e.13 *Rut*, 1223 RHug *et passim* to 1276 RH, Edw 1 *CroxR*, *Harestane* 1212 RBE (p), *Harastan* c.1270 (1449) *WoCart* (p), 1290 Ch, *Harestun* c.1155 *Rut*, *Harestuna* 12 (e.15) *BelCartB*, *Hareston'* 1180 P (p), 1197 ib *et passim* to 1369 *Rut*, 1396, 1407 *BelCartB*, 1535 VE
Harstan 1195 P, 1205 Fine, e.13 *Rut* (p) *et passim* to 1321 *ib* (p), 1322 *ib* (p), 1347 *ib* (p), *Harstane* e.14 *BelCartA*, *Harstuna* Hy 1 (1333) Ch, Hy 2 (e.15) *BelCartB*, *Harstona* Hy 3 *Rut*, 1472 Derby, 1577 LEpis, *Harston* 1253 × 58 RHug, Edw 1 *Rut* (p), 1316 FA *et passim* to 1360 (1449) *WoCart*, 1369 *Rut et freq*

'The boundary-stone', *v.* **hār**[2], **stān**, cf. Hoarstone, Wo 250. OE *hār* 'grey, lichen-covered' is frequently used with words denoting objects forming boundary marks, or lying on boundaries, so that it has long been thought that *hār* came to mean 'boundary'. In this Leics. example, the use of the definite declension for the adj. (i.e. *hāra*) is perhaps significant since this usage usually indicated that the item modified was the one expected in that context; thus the combination *hār* plus *stān* was something more than simply the addition of adj. to noun as 'grey stone', but rather 'boundary-stone'. The eastern boundary of the township is the division between Leics. and Lincs.

BLACK HOLT, *v.* **blæc, holt**. HARSTON WOOD, 1824 O, *The Wood* 1840 *TA*. THE RECTORY, *(The) Rectory* 1840 *TA*, 1877 White, *The Old Rectory* 1925 Kelly; it is *the Parsonage House* 1605[1], 1605[2], 1612 *Terrier et passim* to 1707 (18) *ib*, *v.* **personage**. ST MICHAEL AND ALL ANGELS' CHURCH, *ecclesie de Harestan* 1220 MHW, *The Church* 1707, 1707 (18) *Terrier*, *Church (St Michael)* 1846, 1863 White, *St Michael* *and All Angels* 1877 ib. Note also *the Churchyard* 1605[1], 1707, 1707 (18) *Terrier, the Church Yarde* 1605[2], 1625 *ib, the churchyarde* 1612 *ib, Church Yard* 1840 *TA, v.* **chirche-ȝeard**.

FIELD-NAMES

Undated forms in (a) are 1840 *TA*, while those dated 1791 are *EnclA*. Forms throughout dated 1601, 1605[1], 1605[2], 1612, 1625, 1674, 1693, 1703, 1707 and 1707 (18) are *Terrier*.

(a) The Four Acre, The Five ~, The Six ~, The Eight ~, The Ten Acre, Bottom, Top Ten Acre, The Thirteen ~, The Nineteen Acre (*v.* **æcer**); Barn Cl (x2); Beck Fd 1791 (*the Becke* 1605[1], 1605[2], *the Becks* 1707, 1707 (18), *the Beck furlonge* 1601, 1605[1], 1612, 1625, *Becke furlonge* 1605[2], *the Beck furlong* 1707, 1707 (18), *v.* **bekkr**); The Bottom Cl (*v.* **bottom**); Croxton Bridle Rd (*v.* **brigdels**; Croxton Kerrial parish adjoins to the south); Croxton Rd 1791 (*Croxton gate* 1605[1], 1612, *v.* **gata**); First, Second Croxton Lane; Croxton Fd; The Cutwells (*Cattwell* 1601, 1605[1], 1612, 1707, *Catwell* 1605[2], 1625, 1707 (18), 'spring or stream frequented by wild-cats', *v.* **cat(t), wella**); The Dale (*v.* **dalr**); Denton Rd 1791 (Denton parish in Lincs. adjoins to the east); Denton Wells (*Denton Welles* 1601, ~ *Wells* 1605[1], 1605[2], 1612, 1625, 1707, 1707 (18), *v.* **wella**); Harston Devon 1803 *EnclA*, The Deven (*The Devyn* 1601), the Deven Cl 1791, Far ~ ~, Deven Cl (closes beside R. Devon); Doctor's Cl; Far ~ ~, Middle ~ ~, Drift Cl, Drift Hill Side (*v.* **sīde**) (*v.* **drift**); Dropwell Hill 1791 (*the hill aboue dropwell* 1612, *Dropwell* 1601, 1605[2], 1612, 1625, 1707, 1707 (18), *Droppwell* 1605[1], *v.* **dropi, wella, aboven**); Far Pasture; First Pasture; West ~ ~, Flatten Cl (poss. 'flat meadow', *v.* **flatr, eng**); Gorse Cl (*v.* **gorst**); Grantham Gate (1605[1], 1605[2], 1612, 1625, *v.* **gata**; the road to Grantham in Lincs., presum. Denton Rd *supra*); Green Hill (*Greenehill* 1601, 1605[1], 1605[2], 1612, 1625, *v.* **grēne[1], hyll**); Gulson's Pasture (with the surn. *Gulson*); Far Hill Top, First Hill Top, Top Hill Side (*v.* **sīde**); The Hollow (cf. *the Hollow guttur* 1605[1], 1605[2], 1612, 1625, 1707, ~ ~ *gutter* 1707 (18), *v.* **holh, goter**); Home Cl (x3) (*v.* **home**); Far ~ ~ ~, Horse Pool Hill (*horsepoolehill* 1601, *Horsepoole hill* 1605[2], 1625, *horspool hill* 1612, *Horsepool hill* 1707, *Horse-pool-hill* 1707 (18), *v.* **hors, pōl, hyll**); The Ings 1840, the Ings Cl 1791 (*the Inge* 1605[1], 1605[2], 1612, *the Ings* 1707, 1707 (18), *v.* **eng**); Kirk Hill 1840, Kirkhill Cl 1791 (*Kyrke hill* 1601, *Kyrkhill* 1601, 1605[1], 1612, *Kirkehill* 1605[2], *Kirkhill* 1625, *Under Kyrkhill* 1605[2], 1612, 1625, *Under Kirkhill* 1707, 1707 (18), *Church hill* 1605[1], 1605[2], 1612, 1625, *Church-hill* 1707, 1707 (18), *v.* **kirkja, cirice, hyll**; both Scand and English forms of the name of this hill in the great West Fd exist side by side in the same terriers); Knipton Rd 1791 (*v.* Knipton *infra*); Long Cl; (the) Long Fd 1791; Long Dale Fd 1791, Longdale Rd 1840 (*long dales* 1601, 1612, *longe dalls* 1605[2], *long dalls* 1605[1], 1625, *the Long Dales* 1707, 1707 (18), *v.* **lang[1], deill**); Far ~, South ~, Longlands (*v.* **lang[1], land**); Long Pasture; Meadow Cl (*the Meddow* 1605[2], *the medow* 1707, *the Meadow* 1707 (18), *v.* **mǣd** (**mǣdwe** obl.sg.)); Middle Hill; Far Moor, Far ~ ~, Long Moor (cf. *Short Moores* 1601, 1605[1], 1612, 1625,

Shorte Moores 1605², *v.* **mōr**¹); Nix's Cl (with the surn. *Nix*); Nordale Cl 1840, (the) Nordale Fd 1791 (*v.* **norð, dalr**); Pasture Cl (cf. *the Common Pasture* 1601, *v.* **commun, pasture**); Porter's bottom ~, Porter's middle Cl (with the surn. *Porter*); Pudding Bag (referring either to sticky soil or to a rounded enclosure, *v.* Field 41); Far ~ ~, Rough Ground (*v.* **rūh**¹, **grund**); Second Pasture; Sewstern and Newark Rd 1791 (is *Salt'lane* 1426 *Rut* (*v.* **saltere, lane**); it is *the Streete* 1601, 1605¹, 1605², 1612, 1625, *the Kinges streete* 1605², 1625, *the Kings Streete* 1612, *the Street* 1707, 1707 (18) (*v.* **strǣt**); with reference to James I; an early trackway adopted as a Roman road and later a saltway, nowadays called Sewstern Lane); the Stone Pitt 1791, Stone pit, ~ ~ Cl 1840, Stone Pit(t) Rd 1791 (cf. *(the) Stonnpytt hill* 1601, *Stonnpitt hill* 1605¹, 1605², 1625, *Stonpitt hill* 1605², 1612, 1625, *Stonepitt Hill* 1707, 1707 (18), *v.* **stān-pytt**); Top ~ ~, Thorney Mere (*Thornye Meere* 1601, *Thorney Meer(e)* 1605², 1625, *thornie meere* 1612, *Thorny meer* 1707, 1707 (18), *Thurnye Meere* 1605¹, *v.* **þornig, þyrniht, (ge)mǣre**); the Thurn 1791 (cf. *thirndich, thirnedig* Hy 3 *Crox, v.* **þyrne, dīc, dík**); Town end Cl (*v.* **tūn, ende**); Water Mdw (poss. a meadow with an irrigation system, *v.* Field 90–1); West Fd (*The West(e) Feild(e)* 1601, 1605¹, 1605², 1612, *The West Field* 1707, *v.* **west, feld**; one of the great fields of the village); Willow Holt (*v.* **wilig, holt**); Bottom ~ ~, Wood Cl, Hallam's Wood Cl (with the surn. *Hallam*); Woolsthorpe Bridle Rd (*v.* **brigdels**; Woolsthorpe parish adjoins to the north); Far, Near Woolsthorpe hills (*Wolsthorp hill* 1601, *Wolstrop(p) hill* 1605¹, 1605², 1612, 1625, *Woostrope hill* (sic) 1707, 1707 (18)); Woolsthorpe Rd 1791.

(b) *Bassett home* 1601, ~ *holme* 1605¹, 1605², 1612, 1625, *Basset holm(e)* 1707, 1707 (18) (*v.* **holmr**; with the surn. *Basset(t)*, from OFr *basset* 'of low stature'); *the Cleyes* 1601, 1605¹, 1605², 1612, 1625, *the Cleys* 1707, 1707 (18), *the Clays* 1707, 1707 (18), *the Upper end(e) of the Cleyes* 1605², 1612, *the Longe Cleyes* 1610, 1605¹, 1605², 1612, 1625, *the Long Cleys* 1707, 1707 (18), *the Short(e) Cleyes* 1601, 1605¹, 1605², 1612, 1625, *the Short Cleys* 1707, 1707 (18), *the Cley furlong(e)* 1605¹, 1605², 1707, 1707 (18), *the Clay furlong* 1612 (*v.* **clæg**); *the Clyffe* 1601, 1605¹, 1612, *the Cliffe* 1605², 1625, 1707 (18), *the Cliff* 1707, *the Further syde of the Clyffe* 1612, *Under the Clyffe* 1601, *under the Cliffe* 1612, 1625, 1707 (*v.* **clif**); *Thomas Crosse his lande* 1605¹, 1612; *Croxton Meere* 1601, *(the) Croxton Mere* 1707, 1707 (18) (*v.* **(ge)mǣre**; Croxton Kerrial parish adjoins to the south); *Depslade* 1625 (*v.* **dēop, slæd**); *the Devin hill* 1601, 1605¹, 1605², 1612, 1625, *the Deven hill* 1707, *the Devon hill* 1707 (18) (*v.* The Devon in Belvoir *supra*); *the Dike* 1605², 1625, 1707 (18), *the Dyke* 1605¹, 1612, 1707 (*v.* **dík**; in the great West Fd); *Dunesho* 1205 Fine, 1205 FF ('Dunn's spur of land', *v.* **hōh**; the pers.n. *Dunn* is OE, cf. *Dun(n)esby* in adjoining Branston f.ns. (b)); *the Earle of Rutland his grounde* 1605¹ (*v.* **grund**; referring to the fifth Earl of Rutland whose seat was Belvoir Castle); *the Easte Feilde* 1601, 1605¹, 1605², 1612, 1625, *the East Feild* 1703, 1707, ~ ~ *Field* 1707 (18) (*v.* **ēast, feld**; one of the great fields of the village); *Frethegestwong'* Hy 3 *Crox* (*v.* **vangr**; with the OScand pers.n. *Friðgestr* which appears in late OE sources as *Friðgest* and, as in the Liber Vitae of Thorney Abbey, as *Freðegyst, Freþegist* (*v.* Feilitzen 254–5, SPNLY 86)); *Grantham Gate furlonge* 1601, 1605¹, 1605², 1612, 1625, ~ ~ *Furlong* 1707, 1707 (18) (*v.* Grantham Gate in f.ns. (a) *supra*); *Gravill furlong* 1625 (*v.* **gravel**); *Gravill pittes* 1625 (*v.* **gravel, pytt**); *the Guttur* 1601 (in the great West Fd and prob. to be identified with *the Hollow guttur, v.* The Hollow in f.ns. (a) *supra*); *the heades* 1612, *the Hades* 1707 (18) (*v.* hēafod); *the Hill* 1601, 1605[1] *et passim* to 1707 (18) (*v.* hyll); *the Homestall* 1605[1], 1605[2], 1612, 1703, 1707, 1707 (18), *the Homestead* 1674, 1693 (*v.* hām-stall, hām-stede; the home buildings of *the Parsonage House* and Rectory *supra*); (*the*) *Iredale Furlong* 1707, 1707 (18) (perh. 'the Irishman's portion of land', referring to a Viking who had been in Ireland before coming to England, *v.* Íri, deill); *Mr Jacksons Grounde* 1601, *Jarvas* ~ ~ ~, *Jarvis Jackson his ground* 1605[1], 1605[2], *Gervace Jackson his ground* 1612, *Mr Jackson his land* 1612 (*v.* grund); *Knipton Bridge* 1601, 1605[1], 1605[2] *et passim* to 1707 (18) (*v.* brycg and Knipton *infra*); *Knipton Furlonge* 1601, 1605[2], 1625, ~ *Furlong* 1612, 1707, 1707 (18) (selions adjoining the boundary with Knipton); *Lincolne Gate* 1601, 1605[1], 1605[2], 1612, *Lincoln Gate* 1707, 1707 (18) (*v.* gata; presum. here a name for the ancient trackway, later Roman road, now known as Sewstern Lane which forms the county boundary to the east of Harston and runs to the Fosse Way at Newark and thence to Lincoln); *the Long(e) furlong(e)* 1605[1], 1605[2], 1612, 1625 (*v.* lang[1]); *the Long Headland* 1601 (*v.* lang[1], hēafod-land); *longe headlea* 1605[1] (*v.* headley; this appears to be an alternative style for the previous f.n., presum. referring to a grass-covered headland); *the Common Meere* 1601, *the Meere* 1605[1], 1605[2], *the Mere* 1707 (*v.* commun, (ge)mǣre; the northern boundary of the great North Fd); *the Meere Lees* 1601, (*the*) *Meere leyes* 1605[1], *the Mare Leyes* 1605[1], 1605[2], 1612, 1625, (*the*) *Mare Leys* 1707, 1707 (18), *Mare Lea Balk* 1707, *Mare Ley Baulk* 1707 (18) (*v.* balca) (*v.* (ge)mǣre, leys; meadows on the eastern boundary of the township); *the Myddle Furlonge* 1601, 1612, *the Mydle Furlong* 1601, 1612, *the Mid(d)le Furlonge* 1605[1], 1605[2], 1612, 1625, *the Middle Furlong* 1707, 1707 (18) (*v.* middel; in the great South Fd); *Millgate* 1605[1] (*v.* myln, gata); *Milne hookes* 1612, *Millhooks* 1605[2], 1612, 1707 (18) (*v.* myln, hōc); *Northalls* 1605[1], 1605[2], 1612, 1625, 1707, *North-Halls* 1707 (18) (*v.* norð, halh); *the North Feild(e)* 1601, 1605[1], 1605[2], 1612, 1625, 1707, ~ ~ *Field* 1707 (18) (*v.* norð, feld; one of the great fields of the township); *Nuegate* 1601, *Newgate* 1605[1], 1605[2], 1612, *Newgates* 1707, 1707 (18) (*v.* nīwe, gata and cf. *Neuweye* in Belvoir f.ns. (b)); *Owsell welles* 1601, *oowsin wells* 1605[1], *No(w)sin Wells* 1605[2], *Oosin wells* 1612, 1707, *Owsin Wells* 1707, 1707 (18) (*v.* ōsle, wella, cf. Izle Beck in Long Clawson f.ns. (a)); *the Parsonage ground* 1605[1] (*v.* personage, grund); *the Rofe* 1707, 1707 (18) (*v.* rūh[2]); *the Round Knowl* 1707, 1707 (18) (*v.* round, cnoll); *Schyremere* 1426 *Rut* (*v.* scīr[1], (ge)mǣre; the county boundary formed in part by Sewstern Lane to the east of the village); *the South Feild(e)* 1601, 1605[1], 1605[2], 1612, 1625, 1703, 1707, ~ ~ *Field* 1707 (18) (*v.* sūð, feld; one of the great fields of the township); *Toftes* 1205 Fine, 1205 FF (*v.* toft); *the Towne furlong(e)* 1601, 1605[1], 1605[2], 1612 *et passim* to 1707 (18) (*v.* tūn; the furlong next to the village in the great East Fd); *the Towne Street(e)* 1605[1], 1605[2], 1612, 1707, *the Town Street* 1707 (18) (*v.* tūn, strǣt; the main street of the village); *the Upper Furlong(e)* 1601, 1605[1], 1605[2] *et passim* to 1707 (18) (in the great North Fd); *Mr Welby's ground* 1707 (18) (*v.* grund; the surn. *Welby* was that of a family originating in the settlement of this name nine miles to the south-west); *Whyt(t)moore heades* 1601, 1605[1], *Whitmore heades* 1612, *Whitemoore heads* 1605[2], 1625, *Whitmore heads* 1707, 1707 (18) (because of the name's longevity, perh. 'headlands abutting on *Whitmore* (i.e. dry moorland)', *v.* hwīt, mōr[1], hēafod, although *Whitmore* could be a surn. here, *v.* Reaney *s.n.*); *Wolstropp pittes*

1601, 1625, ~ *pyttes* 1605[1], ~ *pitts* 1612, *Wolstrop pitts* 1605[2], *Woolstrop(e) pitts* 1707, 1707 (18) ('the pits next to Woolsthorpe', *v.* **pytt**; presum. stone-pits, Woolsthorpe parish in Lincs. adjoining to the north); *the Wrooes* 1601, *the Rowes* 1605[1], 1605[2], 1612, 1625, *the Rows* 1707, 1707 (18) (*v.* **vrá**); *Wrogate* 1625 (*v.* **vrá, gata**).

3. KNIPTON

> *Gniptone* 1086 DB, *Gnipton'* c.1130 LeicSurv, 12 (e.15) *BelCartB*, 1206 Abbr *et passim* to 1366, 1369 *Rut*, *Gniptona* l.12 *ib* (p), 1228 *ib* (p), *Gniptun'* a.1166 (e.15) *BelCartB*, l.12 *GarCart*, l.12 *BHosp* (p), *Gniptune* c.1235 (1407) *Laz* (p), *Gniptuna* Hy 1 (1333) Ch, Hy 2 (e.15) *BelCartB* (p), *Gnypton'* e.13 (e.14) *BelCartA* (p), c.1207 (e.15) *BelCartB*, 1238 RGros *et passim* to 1252 *Rut*, 1252 Misc *et freq* to 1449 *WoCart*, 1451 *Rut et passim* to 1489 *Wyg*, 1500, 1511 *Rut*, (~ *iuxta Beauuer* 1316 (1449) *WoCart*)
> *Gnippeton'* 12 (e.15) *BelCartB*, c.1250 (e.15) *ib*, *Gnipeton'* e.Hy 3 *Rut* (p), 1225 Cur (p)
> *Cnipetone* 1086 DB, 1235 × 53 Dugd
> *Knipton'* 1208, 1229 Pat (p), l.Hy 3 *Rut* (p), *Knipton* 1487 Cl, 1576 Saxton, 1606 LML *et freq*, *Kniptona* 1156 (1318) Ch, Hy 2 Dugd, *Kniptun* 1236 Fees, *Knypton'* 1243 Cur, 1277 Cl *et passim* to 1449 *WoCart*, 1454 *Rut et freq* to 1530 *ib*, 1553 Pat *et passim* to 1576 LibCl, 1577 LEpis, *Knypeton* 1539 *Deed*

'The farmstead, village below the steep hillside', *v.* **gnípa, tūn,** cf. Knipe, We 2 191 and Gnipe Howe, YN 122. Knipton lies in a narrow valley with hills rising steeply on each side. Pagan Anglo-Saxon burials here suggest that an earlier OE name for the site was supplanted after the Scand settlements.

ALL SAINTS' CHURCH, *Church (All Saints)* 1846, 1877 White; recorded earlier as *ecclesie de Gnipton* 1220 MHW, *ecclesia(m) de Gnipton* 1238, 1240 RGros, *ecclesiam de Gnypton* 1238 ib, *ecclesie de Gnupton* 1281 *Pat*, ~ *de Gnapton* 1340 *ib*, ~ *de Knypton* 1456 *ib*. Note also *the Churchyarde* 1601, 1605 *Terrier*, *the Churcheyarde* 1625 *ib*, *the Church Yard* 1803 *EnclA*, 1821 *Terrier*, *v.* **chirche-ȝeard**. THE CARRIER, a water channel related to Knipton Reservoir. GRANBY WOOD, named from the Marquis of Granby, the title of the eldest son of the Duke of Rutland, whose seat is Belvoir Castle. THE HIGH LEYS, 1803 *EnclA*, *the High Leas(e)* 1601, 1605, 1704 *Terrier*, *the High Lees* 1612 *ib*, *the highe leas* 1625 *ib*, *v*. **hēah**[1], **leys**. KING'S WOOD. KNIPTON COTTAGE, 1863 White, *v*. **cotage**. KNIPTON HO., *Knipton House* 1863 White. KNIPTON LODGE, 1824 O, 1863 White, *The Lodge* 1925 Kelly, *v*. **loge**. KNIPTON PASTURE is *the Common pasture* 1601, 1605, 1612, 1625 *Terrier*, *Knipton Common Pasture* 1803 *EnclA*, *v*. **commun**, **pasture**. KNIPTON RESERVOIR, 1806 Map, 1824 O, *Reservoir* 1846, 1877 White; built to supply water for the Nottingham and Grantham Canal (*The Grantham Canal* 1822 *Terrier*). THE RECTORY, 1821 *Terrier*, 1877 White, 1925 Kelly, *the Rectory House* 1803 *EnclA*; it is *the Parsonage house* 1601, 1605, 1625, 1704 *Terrier*, *the personage house* 1612 *ib*, *v*. **personage**. RESERVOIR WOOD, *v*. Knipton Reservoir *supra*. RUTLAND ARMS (P.H.) (lost), *Rutland Arms* 1846, 1863 White; referring to the Dukes of Rutland of Belvoir Castle. WINDSOR HILL, *Winsore hill* 1601 *Terrier*, *Wynser hill* 1605 *ib*, *Winser hill* 1612 *ib*. At this date, the transferred name of royal Windsor seems unlikely (but cf. Westminster in Belvoir *supra*); the generic may be OE **ōra** 'a bank, an edge', but earlier forms are needed to identify the specific.

FIELD-NAMES

Undated forms in (a) are 1803 *EnclA*. Forms throughout dated 1449 are *WoCart*, while those of 1601, 1605, 1612, 1625 and 1704 are *Terrier*.

(a) the Cherry Yard (a small enclosure with cherry-trees, *v*. **cheri(e)**, **geard**, cf. the Nut Yard *infra*); the Church Nook (*v*. **nōk**); Copton Fd (*coppethorne* 1428 *Rut*, *copethorn* 1449, *Copthorne feilde* 1601, 1625, *Coppethorne Feilde* 1605, *Copling feild* 1704 (*v*. **feld**), *copethornegate* 1449 (*v*. **gata**); 'the pollarded thorn-tree', *v*. **copped**, **þorn**, naming one of the great fields of the village); Debdale Fd (*deep(e)dale* 1601, 1605, 1612, 1625, *dibdale* 1704, *v*. **dēop**, **dalr**); (the) East Cl; Frog Hall Hollow (poss. an ironical name for a spot where frogs abounded, but *Hall* may be a reflex of OE *halh* 'a water-meadow, dry ground in marsh, *v*. **frogga**, **halh**, **holh**, cf. Frog Hall, Ru 207); Gorsey Close Wood (*v*. **gorstig**); the Great Cl; the Holme (*the holmes* 1601, 1612, 1625, *the holms* 1605, *v*. **holmr**); the Jug (presum. descriptive of shape and/or wetness); Knipton Mill; Larkcliff Fd (*Larkecliff(e)* 1601, *Larkeclyf(f)e* 1605, *Larkliffe*, *Larklyffe* 1625, *Larke Cliffe* 1601, 1625, 1704, 'steep hillside frequented by larks', *v*. **lāwerce**, **clif**); Little Cl (x2); March Cl, March Fd (*le Marsshe* 1428 *Rut*, *March(e) Feilde* 1601, 1605, *Marshe Feilde* 1625, *March Feild* 1704, 'the field beside the marsh', *v*. **mersc**, **feld**; one of the great fields of the township); Mill Cl (*the Mille cloase* 1601, *the Mill Closse* 1605, *the myll close* 1625, *v*. **myln**, **clos(e)**)); the Mill Hill; the Mill Holme (*Milne Holme* 1435 Nichols, *Mylne*

Holme 1436 Cl, *the Mill holme* 1601, 1625, *the Millholm* 1605, *v.* **myln, holmr** and *the Watermill* in f.ns. (b)); the New Cls (*the New cloase* 1601, *the New*(*e*) *Closse* 1605, 1612, *the new*(*e*) *cloase* 1625, *v.* **nīwe, clos(e)**); the Nithingworth (*Nydingworth* 1601, 1704, *Nythingworth* 1605, *Nithingworth* 1612, *Nydingeworthe* 1625; the first el. is OE **nīðing** 'a niggard, a wretch, a sluggard, a coward' còmpounded with OE **worð** 'an enclosure, a small enclosure containing a dwelling'; *nīðing* used as a sb. or even as a by-name seems unlikely; its use as an adj. is unrecorded, but such a construction indicating a poor site, one from which produce was hard to come by, would make reasonable sense); Old House Cl; the Nut Yard (a small enclosure with nut-bearing trees, *v.* **hnutu, geard,** cf. the Cherry Yard *supra*); the Park Leys (*Park Lease* 1601, 1704, (*the*) *Parke Leas* 1605, 1612, *Park Leas* 1625, *v.* **park, leys**; relating either to the Old Park or to the *New Parke*, both in Belvoir); Tenter Cl (*v.* **tentour**); Wheat Hill Fd (*Wheathill Feilde* 1601, 1605, 1625, *Weathil feild* 1704 (*v.* **feld**; one of the great fields of the village), *Wheathill* 1601, 1605, *Under Wheathill* 1601, 1605, 1625, *Wheathill breach*(*e*) 1601, 1605, ~ *breche* 1625 (*v.* **brēc**), *Wheathill Waye* 1601, 1605, 1625 (*v.* **weg**), 'the hill where wheat is grown', *v.* **hwǣte, hyll**).

(b) *Aldemulne* 1252 Misc, 1257 Nichols, *Holdmylne* 1252 *Rut*, 1252 Misc (*v.* **ald, myln**); *Annis*(*e*)*balkes* 1601, *Annesbalkes* 1625 (*v.* **balca**; with the surn. *Annis*, from OFr *Anés* the vernacular form of *Agnes, v.* Reaney *s.n.*); *Arden his house* 1601, 1605, 1612, *Ardens house* 1625 (with the surn. *Arden*); *Richard Armson his peece* 1601, 1605, 1612, ~ *Armesone* ~ ~ 1625 (*v.* **pece**; with the surn. *Armson, v.* Reaney *s.n.*); *arnoldis ake* (sic) 1449 (either with the OGer pers.n. *Arnold* or with the surn. *Arnold, v.* Reaney *s.n.*; the second el. is prob. **æcer** 'a plot of land', being a mistranscription of its later spelling *aker* into the cartulary); *Barstongat* 1441 *Rut, Barston gate* 1601, *Barkston gate* 1605, *Barkestone gate* 1625 (*v.* **gata**; Barkestone lies to the north-west); *Robert Bertram his cloase* 1601, *Robert Bartram his Closse* 1605, ~ ~ *his Cloase* 1625 (*v.* **clos(e)**), *Robert Bertram his Wonge, Bartrame his Wonge* 1601, *Bartram his Wonge* 1605, 1612, 1625, *Robert Bartrams wonge* 1625 (*v.* **vangr**) (with the surn. *Bartram, v.* Reaney *s.n.*); *Beane lease* 1601, 1605 (*v.* **leys**; presum. with the surn. *Bean, v.* Reaney *s.n.*); *Belvor gate* 1601, *Belvoire gate* 1605, 1612, *Belvoier gate* 1625 (*v.* **gata**; the road to Belvoir Castle); *Blakke Borowe close* 1525 *Rut, Blakeborowe Close* 1531 *Comp, Blakborowe close* 1540 *Rut, Blackborow cloase* 1601, *Blak*(*e*)*burrow Closse* 1605, 1612, *Blackborrowe close* 1625 (*v.* **clos(e)**), *Blackborow lane* 1601, *Blakburrow lane* 1612, *Blackborrowe lane* 1625 (*v.* **lane**); *Blakeberou* ~, *Blakeborou wellis* 1449 (*v.* **wella**), *Under Blackburrow* 1605 (*v.* Blackberry Hill in Belvoir); *blakethyng* 1441 *Rut* (*v.* **thing**; with the surn. *Black* or *Blake*); *Bostone hoale* 1601, 1605, *Boston hoale* 1625 (*v.* **hol**[1]; prob. with the surn. *Boston*, cf. Boston Lane in Hose); *bradelond* 1449 (*v.* **brād, land**); *brakendole* 1449 (*v.* **brakni, dāl**); *Branston ditch* 1601, ~ *Dyche* 1605, ~ *dytch* 1612, *Branstone dytche* 1625 (*v.* **dīc**), *Branston gate* 1601, 1605, 1612, 1625 (*v.* **gata**), *Branston hedge* 1601, 1605, 1612, *Branstone* ~, *Braunston hedge* 1625 (*v.* **hecg**) (Branston lies immediately to the south-west; both ditch and hedge were boundary markers); *le brantepyttys* 1297 *Rut, le branpittes* 1444 *ib* ('the steep-sided pits', *v.* **brant, pytt**); *le breche* 1297 *Rut, the Breach* 1601, 1605, 1612, *the bre*(*a*)*che* 1625 (*v.* **brēc**); *the brinke* 1601, *the Brinkes* 1605, 1612, *the Brinckes* 1625 (*v.* **brink**); *Brodesyke* 1462 *Rut, Broadsyke*

1605, *broad(e)sike* 1610, *Broadsyck(e)* 1612, *Broad(e)sick(e)* 1625, *broadsike waye* 1601, *Broadsyke Waye* 1605, *Broadsicke waye* 1625 (*v.* **weg**) ('the broad piece of meadow along the stream', *v.* **brād, sík**); *bryggefurlonge* 1200 × 50 (1449) *WoCart* (*v.* **brycg, furlang**); *the bull swayth* 1601, *the Bull Swath(e)* 1605, 1612, 1625 ('the strip of grassland used for grazing the bull', *v.* **bula, swathe**); *le cattisterne* 1297 *Rut* (*v.* **þyrne**; most prob. 'thorn-scrub frequented by wild-cats' (with **cat(t)**), but note *Joh' le Cat* 1336 GildR of Leicester, so that alternatively 'le Cat's thorns' is poss.; *þyrne* > *terne* is a common development in Framland Hundred, cf. Sewstern); *chapill pitts* 1601, *Chappell pittes* 1605, 1612, 1625 (*v.* **chapel(e), pytt**); *neethire* ~, *clayfurlonge* 1410 *Rut*, *clay forlong* 1601, *Claye furlonge* 1605, 1625 (*v.* **neoðera, clǣg, furlang**); *le Coldhyl* 1444 *Rut*, *could(e)hill* 1601, *Coldhill* 1605, 1612, 1625 (*v.* **cald, hyll**); *colle lease* 1704 (*v.* **leys**; the first el. is either the surn. *Colle* (*v.* Reaney *s.n.*) or ON **kollr** 'a hill' from which it derives); *the Common at the Mill* 1601, ~ ~ *at the Myll* 1605 (*v.* **commun, myln**); *le Cowmes* 1428 *Rut*, *under the comes* 1601, *Under the Coomes* 1605, 1612, 1625 (*v.* **cumb**); *Croxtondikes, Croxtondykes* c.1270 (1449) *WoCart*, *Crouxtondykes* 1449 (*v.* **dík**), *Croxton hedge* 1601, 1605, 1625 (*v.* **hecg**) (Croxton Kerrial parish adjoins to the south; both hedge and ditch were boundary markers, cf. *Branston ditch*, ~ *hedge, supra*); *the upper ende of the dale* 1601 (*v.* **dalr**); *the Dales* 1605 (with **dalr** or **deill**); *the dytches* 1605, 1625 (*v.* **díc**); *Edlin his shrobbs* 1601, *Edlyns Shrubbs* 1605, ~ *Shrubs* 1625 (*v.* **scrobb, scrubb**; with the surn. *Edlin, v.* Reaney *s.n.*); *(le) Estfurlonge* c.1270 (1449) *WoCart*, 1449 (*v.* **ēast, furlang**); *Filbow(e) well* 1601, 1625 (*v.* **boga, wella**; the first el. could be OE *fille* 'thyme' or some such plant (cf. OE *cerfille* 'chervil') with *boga* in the sense 'a curving hillside', but earlier forms are needed); *Fulwellehill'* 1410 *Rut*, *fullwellehille* 1417 *ib* (*v.* **fūl, wella, hyll**); *galowtres* 1449 (referring to the local gallows, *v.* **galg-trēow** and *gallohill* in adjoining Croxton Kerrial f.ns. (b))); *gorefurlonge* 1449 (*v.* **gāra, furlang**); *Grandham gate* 1605, 1625 (*v.* **gata**; the road to Grantham to the east in Lincs.); *la Grene* c.1270 (1449) *WoCart* (p) (*v.* **grēne²**); *le Grenecrofte* 1428 *Rut*, *Greencrofte* 1601, 1625, *Greencraft* 1605, *Greenecraft* 1704 (*v.* **grēne¹, croft**); *le grenegate* 1449 (*v.* **grēne¹, gata**); *the gutter* 1601, 1625, *the Guttur* 1605 (in the Park Leys *supra*), *the Gutter in Litledale* 1601, *the Guttur in Lyttledale* 1605, 1612, *the Gutter against Thomas Worsdale his Cloase* 1601, ~ ~ ~ ~ *Worsdall* ~ ~ 1605, *the Gutter against Thomas Worsdales Cloase* (*v.* **clos(e)**) (*v.* **goter**); *atte Hall* 1387 Pat (p), 1398 Banco (p) (*v.* **atte**), *le Stonhalle* 1428 *Rut* (*v.* **stān**), *Knypton Hall* 1521 *ib* (*v.* **hall**; the stone-built manor house of the village), *the haull grounde* 1605, *the hall grounde* 1625 (*v.* **grund**), *the haull land* 1605, *the hall lande* 1625 (*v.* **land**), *the hall peece* 1605, 1612 (*v.* **pece**); *harenab* 1449, *hareneb* 1601, *harenebb* 1605, 1612, *the hare nebbe* 1625 (the first el. is more prob. **hār²** 'grey, lichen-covered' than *hara* 'a hare', with ON **nabbi** 'a projecting peak, a knoll' replaced by OE **nebb** 'a beak, a beak-shaped thing' in later spellings); *Harston brigge* 1449 (*v.* **brycg**), *harstonhyl* 1441 *Rut* (*v.* **hyll**) (*v.* Harston *supra*); *harwythyng* 1441 *Rut* (a tenement, *v.* **thing**; with the surn. *Harvey*, from OFr *Hervé* 'battle worthy'); *Hawthornstye* 1428 (*v.* **hagu-þorn, stīg**); *herring hole* 1601, *horringe hoale* 1605, *herringe hole* 1625 (*v.* **hol¹**; prob. with the surn. *Herring*; how much weight can be given to the 1605 form is uncertain, but if significant, then OE **horing* 'a filthy place' (from *horu* 'filth, dirt' plus the p.n.-forming suffix *-ing²*) may be thought of; but cf. *Bostone hoale* above, where the first el. is similarly a surn., this from the p.n. Boston in Lincs.); *heynehowys* 1297 *Rut, heinehous* 1449 ('the house in a lofty position', *v.* **hēah**[1] (**hēan** wk.obl.), **hūs**); *the High(e) Thorne* 1601, 1605, 1625 (*v.* **hēah**[1], **þorn**); *the high way(e)* 1601, 1605, ~ ~ *waie* 1625 (*v.* **hēah-weg**); *the north ende of the hill* 1601, *the hill toppe* 1601, 1625, *the Topp(e) of the hill* 1605, 1612, 1625 (*v.* **topp**), *Under the hill* 1601, 1625 (all furlong names); *the Homestall* 1605, 1625 (*v.* **hām-stall**; the home buildings of *the Parsonage house*, *v.* The Rectory *supra*); *Roger House hedland* 1601, ~ ~ *headland* 1605, *Rodger House headlande* 1625 (*v.* **hēafod-land**), *Roger House land(e)* 1601, 1605, 1612 (*v.* **land**) (*Roger House* is cited 1625 *Terrier*); *le horcharde wonge* 1417 *Rut* (*v.* **orceard, vangr**); *Horsepooles* 1601, 1605, 1625 (*v.* **hors, pōl**[1] and cf. Horse Pool Hill in Harston f.ns. (a)); *hyldbaldwell'* c.1270 (1449) *WoCart* (*v.* **wella**; with the OE pers.n. *Hildebald*); *the Inge* 1601, 1605, 1612, 1625, 1704 (*v.* **eng**); *langelond* 1200 × 50 (1449) *WoCart, langlond'* 1449 *ib, longland* 1462 *Rut, Longlands* 1601, *longlandes* 1605, 1625 (*v.* **lang**[1],**land**); *Longdole* 1601, 1612, *longdale* 1625 (*v.* **lang**[1], **dāl**); *Long(e)dike* 1601, *longedyke* 1605, *Long dyke* 1605, 1612, 1625 (*v.* **lang**[1], **dík**); *long dytche* 1625 (*v.* **lang**[1], **dīc**; a different feature from the preceding f.n.); *longefurlonge* 1449 (*v.* **lang**[1], **furlang**); *Long sike* 1601, *long syke* 1605, 1612, *longe sicke* 1625 (*v.* **lang**[1], **sík**); *Long Swaythes* 1601, *the long(e) swathes* 1605, 1612, 1625 (*v.* **lang**[1], **swathe**); *Lyttledale* 1297 *Rut*, 1605, 1625, *Litledale* 1601, 1625, *Littledale Feild(e)* 1601, 1605, *Litledale feild(e)* 1601, 1625, 1704, *Lyttledale Feild(e)* 1605, 1612, 1704 (*v.* **lȳtel, lítill, dalr**; eventually 'the little valley' gave its name to one of the great fields of the village); *lyttle wonge* 1605 (*v.* **lȳtel, lítill, vangr**); *Mayden gate* 1601, 1625, *Maiden gate* 1605, 1612, *Maydengatewelle* 1428 *Rut* (*v.* **wella**) ('the road where the girls congregate', *v.* **mægden, gata**); *le meeres* 1410 *Rut, lez meres* 1428 *ib, meres* 1449 (*v.* **(ge)mǣre**); *midilfurlong'* Hy 3 *Crox*, 1449, *the middle forlonge* 1601, *the Mid(d)le furlonge* 1605, 1612, 1625 (*v.* **middel, furlang**); *(the) Mill hurste* 1601, 1612, 1625, *the Myll hurst* 1605 (*v.* **myln, hyrst** and Knipton Mill in f.ns. (a)); *le More* 1428 (*v.* **mōr**[1]); *myculclyf* 1410 *Rut, miculclife gate* 1417 *ib, Mikulclyfgate* 1462 *ib* (*v.* **gata**) ('the great slope', *v.* **micel, mikill, clif**); *Neate damm(e)s* 1601, 1605, *Neat dams* 1612, 1625 (*v.* **nēat, damme**; artificially made pond(s) for watering cattle); *Neat Sike* 1601, *Neat(e) Syke* 1605, 1612, *Neatsicke* 1625 (*v.* **nēat, sík**); *Norman Bridge* 1601, 1605, 1612, 1625 (*v.* **brycg**; as only late forms are recorded, it is uncertain whether the first el. is an original OE **Norðman** 'a Northman, a Norwegian', or because of the post-Conquest siting of Belvoir Castle, is ME **Norman** (from OFr *Normand* 'a Norman of Normandy'), or even, if a bridge at a boundary, a 'no man's bridge', is **nān-mann**; note also *normangate* in both Bottesford and Redmile parishes); *northebrige* 1449 (*v.* **norð, brycg**); *the Parsonage Balke* 1601, 1605, 1625, *the Personage Balke* 1612 (*v.* **balca**), *the Parsonage Barne* 1605, 1625 (*v.* **bern**), *the Parsonage Cloase* 1601, 1625, ~ ~ *Closse* 1605, *the Personage Closse* 1612 (*v.* **clos(e)**), *the parsonage meddow* 1601, ~ ~ *medowe* 1625 (*v.* **mǣd (mǣdwe** obl.sg.)), *the Parsonage Orchyarde* 1601, ~ ~ *Orchard(e)* 1605, 1625 (*v.* **orceard**), *the parsonage pingle* 1601 (*v.* **pingel**) (*v.* **personage**); *the Parsons Balke* 1605, 1625, *the Persons Balke* 1612 (*v.* **persone, balca**); *the Part(e)able dole* 1601, 1605, 1612, 1625 (*v.* **partable, dāl**); *Peesdal* 1441 *Rut, Pesdal* 1441 *ib*, 1449, *pesedale* 1449, *peasedale* 1601, 1625, *Peasdall* 1605 (*v.* **pise, deill**); *Pesowe* 1428 *Rut, Pissaw(e)*

1601, 1625, 1704, *Pyssaw* 1605 (*v.* **pise, haugr**); *Powell* 1601, 1605, 1612, 1625 (*v.* **wella**; the first el. may be a reduced form of OE **pohha** 'a bag, a pouch' used as a by-name, or used of a bag-shaped topographical feature); *Watson Proudloue his cloase* 1601, 1605, ~ ~ *his Closse* 1612, *Watson Prowdlove his cloase* 1625 (*v.* **clos(e)**); *Nethurresduldal'* 1441 *Rut*, *Nethur Restuldale* 1462 *ib* (*v.* **neoðera, wræs(t)el**; with either **dalr** or **deill**); *the Rundle* 1601, 1605, 1625 (*v.* **rynel**); *Sadelbridges* 1601, *Saddle Brigges* 1605, 1625, *Saddle Briggs* 1612 (*v.* **brycg, bryggja**; the first el. is perh. ME **schadel** 'a parting of the ways; a cross-way' (*v.* OED *s.v.* gateshodel) rather than **sadol** 'a saddle', referring to a saddle-shaped dip in a hill formation or to bridges crossing two arms of a stream, giving them a saddle-shaped appearance); *le Salowe* 1428 *Rut*, *at the Sallow tree* 1601, 1605, 1612, 1625 (*v.* **salh**); *the Seven Lease* 1601, *(the) Seaven Lease* 1605, 1625 (*v.* **seofon, leys**; when compounded with a numeral, *leys* represents grassland units of tenure corresponding to *lands* similarly used of arable); *Sheepcoat(e) Lease* 1601, *Sheep(e)cote Lease* 1605, 1625, *Sheepcoat Leas* 1612 (*v.* **scēp-cot, leys**); *Simson his Wonge* 1601, *Thomas Symson his Wonge* 1605, 1612, 1625, *Symsons wonge* 1625 (*v.* **vangr**); *the Sondpytt* 1625 (*v.* **sand-pytt**); *spincwelle* 1449, *Spinkwel* 1601, 1605, 1612, 1625, *spincwellehill'* 1449 (*v.* **hyll**), *Spynkewelledale* 1410 *Rut* (*v.* **dalr**) (*v.* **wella**; with ME **spink** 'a finch' which was especially used of the chaffinch); *the Springe heade in Powell* 1601, 1605, 1612 (*v.* **spring**[1], **hēafod** and *Powell*, *supra*); *Stedfordsty* 1428 *Rut* (*v.* **stede, ford, stīg**; in this context, *stede* must refer to something concrete, such as the site of a building); *the Stigh* 1601, 1605, 1612, *the Stygh* 1612, *the Stighe* 1625 (*v.* **stig**); *stokbrig* 1449 ('the log bridge', *v.* **stocc, brycg, bryggja**); *the stone, the Stonne* 1605, 1625 (*v.* **stān**; presum. some kind of (boundary?) marker); *stonfurlonge* c.1270 (1449) *WoCart*, *le stonfurlong'* 1297 *Rut* (*v.* **stān, furlang**); *the stone middow* 1601, *the Stonn Meddow* 1605, 1612 (*v.* **stān, stoned, mæd** (**mædwe** obl.sg.); some meadows in Leics. named 'the stone meadow' are also styled 'the stoned meadow' or are recorded as having been cleared of stones; or reference may be to '*a* stoned meadow' without specifying that the field in question carried the description as a permanent f.n., i.e. '*the* stoned meadow'; whether a 'stone meadow' always implied 'a meadow cleared of stones (to facilitate mowing?)' is uncertain, *v.* the *Stoned Medowe* in Branston f.ns. (b)); *the stonepitt* 1601, *the Stonnpytt* 1605, *the stone pitts* 1601, *the stonne pittes* 1605, *the Stonpitts* 1612, *the Stonepittes* 1625 (*v.* **stān-pytt**); *the Sweeting(e) tree* 1601, 1605, 1625 ('the sweet-apple tree', *v.* **sweeting**); *Tebbot lane* 1447, 1505 *Rut* ('Tebbot's lane', *v.* **lane**; the surn. is from the OFr pers.n. *Theobald/Tibaut*, *v.* Reaney *s.n.* Theobald and cf. *terra Henrici de Thebeltoft* in Wymondham f.ns. (b)); *thirspittes, turpyttes* 1449 ('the giant's or demon's pits', *v.* **þyrs, pytt**); *thornfurlong* 1449 (*v.* **þorn, furlang**); *Thorpes* 1449, *the Thorpes* 1601, 1625, *the Thorppes* 1605, 1612 (*v.* **þorp**); *Thorpdale* 1410 *Rut* (*v.* **þorp, dalr**); *Threthorndale* 1428 *Rut* (*v.* **þrēo, þorn**; the final el. is prob. **deill**); *Trygebarne* 1454 *Rut* (*v.* **bern**; with the surn. *Trigg*, from ON *tryggr* 'true, faithful, trustworthy', also used as a pers.n., *v.* Reaney *s.n.* and cf. *Ade Trigge* 1348 (c.1430) *KB* of Sewstern); *Wade* 1205 Fine, 1205 FF (*v.* **(ge)wæd**); *wadecliue* Hy 3 *Crox*, *Watcliffe* 1601, 1605, 1625, 1704, *Watclyffe* 1605, 1612 (*v.* **(ge)wæd, clif**); *the Warrande walle* 1601, *the Warrant(e) Wall* 1605, *the Warren Wall(e)* 1612, 1625 (*v.* **wareine, wall**); *waudyng* 1449 (perh. 'the meadow at the ford', *v.* **(ge)wæd, eng** (with AFr *au* for *a*, i.e. *waud-* < *wad-*); **wald** with *u* for *l* due to AN influence is tempting as first el., but is otherwise absent from names in this immediate area); *the Watermill* 1601, 1605, *the water myll* 1625 (*v.* **water-mylne**); *Westcliffe* 1601, 1625, *Westclyfe* 1605, *West(e)clyffe* 1605, 1612 (*v.* **west, clif**); *the West(e) Feilde* 1601, 1605, 1612, *the West Feild* 1704 (*v.* **west, feld**; one of the great fields of the township); *Whinydole* 1601, *Whynnydole* 1605, 1625, *Whinnidole* 1612 (*v.* **whinny, dāl**); *white cross* 1449 (*v.* **hwīt, cros**; prob. a standing cross made of limestone); *wlruncroft* 1449 ('Wulfrūn's small enclosed field', *v.* **croft**; the OE pers.n. *Wulfrūn* is fem.); *Wolsthorppesacre* 1428 *Rut* ('the plot of arable land adjoining Woolsthorpe', *v.* **æcer**; Woolsthorpe in Lincs. adjoins to the north); *Thomas Worsdale his cloase* 1601, *~ Worsdall ~ ~* 1605, *Thomas Worsdales Cloase* 1625 (*v.* **clos(e)**); *Thomas Worsdale his turneyarde* 1601, *Thomas Worsdall his Turneyard* 1605 (the compound **turnyard** is otherwise unrecorded; it appears to denote an enclosure with a rotary apparatus of some kind, such as a horse-gin, a horse-mill, a windlass; cf. 'an Engine called a Turne, or the Turne Engine . . . by which great Weights are lifted up' 1688, *v.* OED *s.v.* turn sb. 7); *Thomas Worsdale his Wonge* 1601, 1612, 1625, *~ Worsdall ~ ~* 1605 (*v.* **vangr**); *Willyam Worsdale his hedlande* 1601, *Willm. Worsdales headland* 1625 (*v.* **hēafod-land**); *Wulverstang* 1444 *Rut* ('Wulfhere's spit of land', *v.* **tang, tangi**; the pers.n. *Wulfhere* is OE).

Bottesford

1. BOTTESFORD

Botlesford c.1130 LeicSurv, Hy 1 (1333) Ch, 1176 P *et passim* to 1203 Ass, John *Rut, Botlesforde* e.13, e.Hy 3 *Rut*, 1224 RHug, 1230 *Rut et freq* to Edw 1 *ib* (freq), 1335 Cl *et passim* to 1427 *Comp*, 1489 Cl, *Bottlesford'* Hy 3 *Rut, Bottlesforth'* 1339 *ib*, *Botlisford'* e.Hy 3 *ib* (freq), e.13 *Wyg*, 1240 *Rut et freq* to 1317, 1318 *ib et passim* to 1333 Ch, *Bottlisford'* Hy 3, 1310 *Rut*, *Botlisforda* c.1240, 1247 *ib, Botlisfort* e.Hy 3 *ib, Botlisforth'* 1332 *ib*

Botelesford(e) Hy 2 (e.15) *BelCartB*, l.12 (e.14) *BelCartA*, 1224 RHug *et passim* to 1329 *Rut*, 1339 Pat *et freq* to 1449, 1451 *Rut et passim* to 1489 Ipm, 1493 *Wyg, Botelesforth'* 1317 *Rut*, *Botellesford'* 1281, 1287 *ib et passim* to 1465 *Wyg*, 1466 *Rut*, *Bottellesford(e)* 1350, 1384 *Wyg*, 1395 *Rut et passim* to 1487 *ib*, 1490 *Wyg, Bottellesford' in le Vale* 1492 *ib, Bottelesford'* Edw 1 *Rut*, 1488 *Wyg*, 1533, 1544 *Rut, Botelisford'* m.13 (e.15), Hy 3 (e.15) *BelCartB et passim* to 1308, 1332 *Rut et freq* to 1349 *Wyg*, 1351 *Rut, Bottellisford'* 1395 *ib, Botilesford'* 1325 *Wyg*, *Bottillesford(e)* 1237 *Rut*, 1324 *Wyg*, 1337 *Rut*, 1338 *Wyg*, *Botillesford'* 1281, 1325, 1349 *Rut*, 1482 *Wyg, Botilesforth'* Hy 3 *Crox, Botilisford'* Hy 3, Edw 1, 1332 *Rut, Botylisford'* 1289 *ib*, *Botillisford'* 1307, 1341 *ib, Bottilisford* 1427 *Terrier, Bottylisford* 1427 *ib, Bottillisford'* 1331 *ib, Bottillisforthe* Hy 3 *Rut*, *Botullesford'* 1342 *Wyg, Botullesforth'* 1333 *Rut*

Botelsford(e) 1224 RHug, 1274 Ass (p) *et passim* to 1462 *Wyg*, *Botellsford* 1413 *Comp, Bottelsforde* 1544 *Rut, Botilsford'* Hy 3 (e.15) *BelCartB, Bottilsford'* 1312 *Wyg*, 1331 *Rut*, 1427 *Terrier*, *Bottylsford* 1427 *ib, Botillsford'* 1482 *Wyg*

Botleford 1236 Fees, *Botelford* 1258 (e.15) *BelCartB*, 1381 *Rut*, 1482 *Wyg*, 1544 *Rut, Bottelleford* 1525 *Comp, Bottelford(e)* 1544 *Rut, Bottilford'* e.Hy 3, 1236, 1247 *ib, Botilford* 1259 (Edw 1) *CroxR, Botillforde* 1482 *Wyg, Botilleford'* 1482 *ib*

Botesford 1086 DB, 1339 Pat, 1368 *Rut et passim* to 1429 *ib,* 1508 Ipm, *Botesforth* 1486 Pat, *Botysford(e)* 1388 *Rut,* 1546 AAS, *Botisford* 1516 *Wyg, Bottesford(e)* 1400 *Rut,* 1404 *Wyg et passim* to 1415, 1423 *Comp et freq, Bottesford other wise cald Bottlesford* 1516 *Wyg, Bottesford alias Botlisford* 1516 *ib, Bottesford al' dict' Botlesford* 1518 *ib, Bottesford otherwyse cald Botlesford* 1518 *ib, Bottesforth(e)* 1535 VE, 1541 *Rut et passim* to 1593 *ib, Bottisford(e)* 1427 *Comp,* 1516 *Wyg et passim* to 1531 *ib, Bottysford'* 1388, 1513 *Rut et passim* to 1553 Pat, *Bottysforth(e)* 1535 VE, 1546 AAS, *Bot(t)isforthe* 1539 *Rut,* 1581 LEpis
Bottsforthe 1611 *Rut*
Bothesford 1155 × 68 *Rut, Bodlesford* 1236 Fees

'The ford at the dwelling' (literally 'the ford of the dwelling'), *v.* **botl, ford**. The two final forms listed above indicate the influence of OE **boðl**, an alternative form of *botl. Bottellesford' in le Vale* 1492 *Wyg* relates the settlement to the Vale of Belvoir (*v.* **val**). Bottesford stands on R. Devon, hence the ford.

BECKINGTHORPE
Beclinctorp Edw 1 *Rut, Beclingthorp* Edw 1 *ib*
Belingthorp (sic) Edw 1 *Rut*
Beckingthorpe 1599 *Rut,* 1618 LeicW, *Beckingthorp* 1610 ib

This is a difficult name. Formally, *Beck(l)ing-* could represent an OE **Be(o)ccelingas* 'Be(o)ccel's people' (*v.* **-ingas** and cf. Beckling, Sf) or OE **Bece-ling* 'the place at the stream' (*v.* **-ing²**, **-ling**), with Scandinavianization of the palatal *c* and reference to R. Devon (perh. cf. Beckering (L) which is *Bechelinge* 1086 DB). However, the addition of *þorp* to such early names would be unusual. The most satisfactory explanation is that Beckingthorpe means 'Berkling's farmstead', with the ON pers.n. *Berklingr, v.* Lind 20. Loss of *r* may be assigned to the weak pronunciation of the consonant in AN (*v.* Feilitzen 84) and attraction to *bekkr* 'a stream' since the settlement is beside R. Devon, while loss of *l* can be ascribed to AFr influence, especially because of the proximity of the French stronghold of Belvoir Castle. The peculiarly northern Scandinavian nature of the pers.n. may arise from the settlement's lying adjacent to Normanton *infra, v.* **þorp**.

HARDWICK (lost)

> *Herdewic* e.Hy 3 *Rut, Herdwic* e.13 *ib*, Hy 3 (e.15) *BelCartB,*
> *Herdewyk'* 1252 (e.14) *BelCartA*, 1425 *Comp, Herdwyke* 1253
> *Rut, Herdwyk* 1292 (e.15) *BelCartB*, 1374 (e.15) *ib*, 1437 *Comp*
> *Hardewic* 13 (e.15) *BelCartB, Hardewyk* 1374 (e.15) *ib, Hardewik*
> 1531 *Comp*

'The herd farm', *v.* **heorde-wīc**.

WESTTHORPE (lost)

> *Westorp'* 1249, 1305 *Wyg, Westhorp'* 1287, 1450 *ib*, 1458 *Rut*, 1482
> *Wyg, Westhorpp'* 1486 *Rut, Westthorp'* 1516 *Wyg, Westthorpe*
> 1523 LeicW
> *Vestropp'* 1488 *Wyg* bis

'The western farmstead', *v.* **west, vestr, þorp**. Easthorpe has survived, *v. infra*.

WINTERBECK

> *Wynterbeck* 1325 *Wyg, Wynterbek'* 1352 *Rut*, 1404 *Wyg, Wynterbeke*
> 1427 *Terrier, Wynturbek* 1463 *Wyg, winterbeck(e)* 1605 *Terrier,*
> *wynterbeck* 1625 *ib, Winterbeck* 1736 *ib*, 1850 *TA*
> *Winterbeck drain* 1771 *Plan*, 1772 *EnclA*

'The stream which flows chiefly in winter', *v.* **winter, vinter, bekkr, drain**.

ACACIA HO. ACRELANDS LANE, 1846 White, *Acrelandes* 1567 *Terrier, acre landes* 1625 *ib, Acrelands* 1736 *ib*, 1772 *EnclA*, cf. *Acrelands Meadow* 1772 *ib, Acrelands Pasture* 1771 *Plan*, 1772 *EnclA*, *v.* **æcer, land**. ALBERT ST, named from Albert, Prince Consort of Victoria, *v.* Queen St *infra*. ARNOLD LODGE. BACK ST, 1863, 1877 White, *v.* **back**. BARKESTONE LANE, the road to Barkestone which lies to the south-west. BEACON HILL, the site of a former signalling beacon, *v.* **(ge)bēacon**. BECKINGTHORPE FM, cf. *Beckingthorpe house* 1877 White, *v.* Beckingthorpe *supra*. BLACK BULL (P.H.) (lost), *Black Bull* 1846, 1863, 1877 White. BOTTESFORD NURSERY, *v.* **nursery**. BOTTESFORD SCHOOL (lost), *Bottesford School* 1736 *Terrier*. BOTTESFORD VINERIES, *v.* **vinery**. BOTTESFORD WHARF, 1824 O, *v* **hwearf**; on the now disused Nottingham and Grantham Canal. CHAPEL ST, 1863, 1877 White; named from the Primitive Methodist Chapel. THE CHESTNUTS. CHURCH FM, *Church farm* 1925 Kelly, *v.* St Mary's Church *infra*. CHURCH ST, 1846, 1863, 1877 White; as for Church Fm. CRAVEN HO., *Craven house* 1877 White. DEBDALES, *Dibdale* 1679 *Terrier*, *Debdale* 1736 *ib*, cf. *Debdale fellde* 1567 *ib*, *de(e)pdale feild* 1605 *ib*, *Debbdale feild* 1626 *Rut*, *Debdale Field* 1771 *Plan*, 1772 *EnclA* (*v.* **feld**; one of the great fields of the village), *depdale hole* 1605 *Terrier* (*v.* **hol**[1]), 'the deep valley', *v.* **dēop, dalr**. DEVON FM, *Devon farm* 1925 Kelly, DEVON LANE, both named from R. Devon which runs through the village. EADY FM, *þe ette*, *þe etty* 1427 *Terrier*, *þe est syd etty* 1427 *ib* (*v.* **ēast, sīde**), *þe west syde ette*, *þe west syd þe etty* 1427 *ib* (*v.* **west, sīde**), *Etyforlong'* Edw 1 *Rut* (*v.* **furlang**), *etytong'* 1427 *Terrier* (*v.* **tang, tangi**), *the Eaty ground* 1736 *ib* (*v.* **grund**), *Eatie Pasture* 1772 *EnclA*, *v.* **ete**. EARL OF RUTLAND'S HOSPITAL, 1846, 1863, 1877 White; earlier it is *the Hospital* 1709 *Terrier*, *The Mens Hospital of Bottesford*, *the Hospital or Alms House in Bottesford called the Mens Hospital* 1730 *EnclA* (*v.* **almes-hous**); founded c.1590 by the fourth Countess; Roger, fifth Earl of Rutland, endowed it in 1612 with land in Muston, cf. Hospital Fm in that township, *v.* **hospital**. THE ELMS. FLEMING'S ALMSHOUSES, *Fleming's Hospital* 1846, 1863 White; founded in 1620 by the Rev. Samuel Fleming, rector, for four poor widows, cf. *the Women's Hospital* 1736 *Terrier*, *v.* **hospital**. FLEMING'S BRIDGE, built at the south entrance to the churchyard by the Rev. Samuel Fleming. GRANBY (P.H.) (lost), *Granby* 1846, 1863 White, *Granby Inn* 1877 *ib*; named from the Marquis of Granby, heir of the Duke of Rutland. The most renowned marquis was John Manners, Marquis of Granby from 1721 to 1770, who became a national hero as leader of the victorious cavalry charge at Warburg in 1760. Many taverns throughout England were named in his honour. THE GREEN, *a la grene* Edw 1 *Rut* (p), *le Grene* l.13, 1333 *Wyg*, *The Green* 1863, 1877 White, 1925 Kelly, *v.* **grēne**[2]. GREENFIELD, 1925 Kelly. THE GRIMMER, cf. *Grimmer Furlong* 1736 *Terrier*, *v.* **grīma** 'a boundary marker', cf. *Grimebroc*, Ch **3** 158. This stream forms for part of its course the parish boundary with Redmile. HIGH ST, 1846, 1863, 1877 White. HILL FM is *Canal farm* 1925 Kelly, named from the Nottingham and Grantham Canal. THE LODGE. MARKET ST, 1877 White. MIDDLESTILE BRIDGE, 1824 O, *v.* **middel, stīg**; names with *stīg* 'a path' are freq. attracted to *stigel* 'a stile' in Framland Hundred. MILL LANE, 1877 White, cf. *Water Mill* 1846, 1864 *ib*, *v.* **water-mylne**. THE NOOK, *v.* **nōk**. NOOK LANE 1877 White, *v.* The Nook *supra*. NOTTINGHAM RD, 1877 White; the road to Nottingham. PARTICULAR

BAPTIST CHAPEL. PINFOLD LANE, v. **pynd-fald**. PROVIDENCE COTTAGE (local). QUEEN ST, 1846, 1863, 1877 White; named in honour of Queen Victoria, cf. Albert St *supra*. RECTORY COVERT, v. **cover(t)**, RECTORY FM, *Rectory F.* 1824 O, *Rectory farm* 1925 Kelly; *The Rectory* is recorded 1877 White, 1925 Kelly. Its predecessor is *the parsonage* 1605 *Terrier, The Parsonage House* 1736 *ib*, v. **personage**. RED LION (P.H.), *Red Lion* 1846, 1863, 1877 White, 1925 Kelly. RUTLAND ARMS (P.H.), *Rutland Arms* 1846, 1863, 1877 White, 1925 Kelly; named with reference to the Dukes of Rutland of nearby Belvoir Castle. ST MARY'S CHURCH, *Church (St Mary)* 1846, 1877 White; it is earlier recorded as *eccelesie de Botlesford* a.1219 RHug, 1351, 1352 *Pat*, ~ *de Botillisford* 1220 MHW, ~ *de Botelesford* 1339, 1373, 1400 *Pat*, ~ *de Bottesford* 1462, 1464, 1467, 1475 *ib, eccelesie parochialis de Bottellesford* 1470 *ib*. SCRIMSHAW'S WINDMILL, 1863 White, cf. *Thomas Scrimshaw* (baker) and *Ann Scrimshaw* resident in neighbouring Muston in 1846 ib, and *Thomas Scrimshaw* (farmer), resident in Bottesford in 1863 ib. VINE COTTAGE, 1877 White, v. **cotage**. WINTERBECK BRIDGE, *Wynterbecke bryge* 1567 *Terrier*, v. **brycg** and Winterbeck *supra*.

FIELD-NAMES

Forms in (a) dated 1771 are *Plan*, 1772 are *EnclA*, 1806 are *Lease* and 1825 are *Terrier*. Forms throughout dated Hy 2 are Nichols; those dated e.13, e.Hy 3, 1236[1], 1236[2], 1253, Hy 3, 1275, 1281, 1285, 1287, 1292, 1295, 13, 1304, Edw 1, Edw 1[1], Edw 1[2], 1314, 1325, 1326, Edw 2, 1333[1], 1337[1], 1347[1], 1351, 1366, 1392, 1426, 1447, 1449, 1542 and 1626 are *Rut*; 1247 are Ass; 1252 (e.14) and e.14 are *BelCartA*; 1254 are Cur; Hy 3 (e.15), 1292 (e.15), 1293 (e.15), 13 (e.15) and 1374 are *BelCartB*; c.1290, p.1290, 1296, 1297, 1298, 1299, 1.13, 1333[2], 1337[2], 1338, 1340, 1341, 1342[1], 1342[2], 1347[2], 1350, 1398, 1404, 1409, 1413[2], 1423, 1424[1], 1424[2], 1427[3], 1433, 1451 and 1463 are *Wyg*; 1381 are SR; 1413[1], 1425, 1437, 1438, 1442, 1443 and 1531 are *Comp*; 1427[1], 1427[2], 1567, 1579, 1605, 1625, 1679, 1.17 and 1736 are *Terrier*; 1539 are Fine; 1545 are *Deed*.

(a) Bellands 1772, ~ Pasture 1771, 1772 (*belland* 1427[1], *bellands, bellandys* 1427[2], *Bellondes* 1567, *Belandes* 1625, *Bellands* 1736, *northbellands, north bellandys* 1427[2] (v. **norð**), v. **land**; at least eight instances of *bellands* are known in Framland Hundred, and because the f.n. appears to be common, it may well be that **bēan** 'bean' rather than **belle** 'a bell-shaped hill' is its first el., with the development

ME *ben(e)landes* > *bellandes* through assimilation, cf. the more usual *ban(e)landes* > *ballandes* > *bal(l)ance* (*v.* Nth 266); in Framland Hundred, OE *bēan* normally gives ME *ben(e)*, while elsewhere in Leics., ME *ban(e)* is its usual reflex; however, *belle* cannot be discounted, *v. le Benlandes* in f.ns. (b) *infra*); Bottesford Mill 1824 O (a windmill); Caddow Bank 1772 (*v.* **banke**); *Cadowbanks drain* 1772 (*v.* **drain**) (*v.* **cad(d)aw, cad(d)owe** and *Cawdaw hill* in Branston f.ns. (b)); Dale Cl 1772, 1825 (*v.* **dalr**); Glebe Wongs 1771, 1772 (*v.* **glebe, vangr**); Hall Cl 1771 (cf. *atte Halle* 1381 (p), *hallwongedyke* 1427[1], 1427[2], *halwong(e)dyke* 1427[1], *the Hall Wong* 1736, *v.* **atte, hall, vangr, dík**); Hill Fd 1771, 1772 (*le Hill* 1253, *þe hyll* 1427[1], *the Hill* 1625, 1736, *ye hyll felde* 1567, *The Hill feild(e)* 1625, ~ ~ *Field* 1736, *Bottesford Hill Field* 1736, *v.* **hyll, feld**; one of the great fields of the village); Hough Hedge 1772 (*v.* **hecg**; prob. with the surn. *Hough*, but OE **hōh** 'a headland' is poss. as the first el.); Huntershorn 1824 O (*v.* **huntere, horn**; perh. descriptive of the shape of a headland); The Meadows 1772 (cf. *medowdyk(e)* 1427[2], *the medow dyche* 1567, *Meadow Dike* 1736 (*v.* **mǣd (mǣdwe** obl.sg.), **dík, dīc**), *the Meadow Side* 1736 (*v.* **sīde**)); Middle Fd 1771, 1772 (*midle feild* 1605, *middle feild* 1625, 1626, *the Midle Field* 1736, *v.* **middel, feld**; one of the great fields of the village); Lammas Cl 1772 (*v.* **lammas**; a close used for grazing after August 1st); Morelands Pasture 1772 (*v.* **mōr**[1], **land**); New Pasture 1771, 1772; Redmile Beck 1772 (*Reddmyld* ~, *Reddymyld* ~, *Redmild* ~, *Redmyld Beke* 1427[2], *Redmell becke* 1567, *v.* **bekkr**; Redmile parish adjoins to the south); Rundle 1772 (*v.* **rynel**); Sands Pasture 1772 (*le Sandes* l.13, Edw 1, 1351, 1404, *þe Sandys* 1427[2], *ye Sandes* 1567, *the sandes* 1625, *estsandes* 1295, 1404, *le estsandis* 1337[1] (*v.* **ēast**), *le Westsandes* c.1290, *Westsandes* 1404, 1427[1], *West Sands, Westsandys* 1427[2] (*v.* **west**), 'the sandy soil', *v.* **sand**); Sheep Pasture 1771, 1772; Sixteen Acre Cl 1806; Tenter Cl 1772 (*v.* **tentour**); Thatch Mdw 1771 (cf. *Thacholm* Hy 2, e.13, *Thakholm* e.14 (*v.* **holmr**), *le Thak'* 1281, *le Thack'* Edw 1[1], Edw 1[2], 1304, *þe Take, þe thak* 1427[2], *le Thakk'* 1463, *thack* 1567, *takedeyl* 1252 (e.14), *Thachedeyl* 1253, *thackedayle* 1292 (e.15), *Thakdeil* 1326, *Thacdeyles* Edw 2, *Thakdayll'* 1347[1], *thakdayle* 1374 (e.15) (*v.* **deill**), *houertakdeyle* 1252 (e.14), *Ouerthachedeyl* 1253, *ouirthackedeyle* 1292 (e.15), *ouerthakdayle* 1374 (e.15) (*v.* **uferra**), *v.* **þæc, þak**; the Scand form dominates); Twelve Acre Cl 1806 (*Twelueacres* 1292, *Twelfacres* 1298, *le twelueakeris* Edw 1, *le Twelueacris* Edw 2, *Twelfacris* 1337[1], *Twelffacres* 1404, *les twelfe acres* 1409, *v.* **twelf, æcer**).

(b) *akerdick'* 1295 (*v.* **æcer-dīc, dík**); *Alredwro* 1337[1], *halredwro, halyred wro* 1427[2] (*v.* **vrá**; with the ME reflex of the OE pers.n. *Ælfrēd*); *arkelgraue* 1295 (with the ME reflex of the Scand pers.n. *Arnketill*; the second el. is OE **grāf** 'a grove, a copse'); *Barlyakir, Barlyakre* Edw 1, *barliacre* e.14, *Barley Acres* 1567, *barly acres* 1625 (*v.* **bærlic, æcer**); *Basiltoftes* 1413 (*v.* **toft**; either with the OFr pers.n. *Basile* (English form *Basil*) or with its ME surn. reflex *Basil*); *the Bastardes* 1625, *the Bastards* 1736 (OFr **bastard** when applied to land was derogatory and was used of fields of abnormal shape or of low yield); *the bastard leys* 1567 (*v.* **leys**; poss. an earlier form of, or related to, the preceding f.n. feature, but Field 96 notes that Bastard Leys as a f.n. type could refer to selions of the old great fields not completely swarded over in the improved management of pasture from the 16th cent. onwards); *beenill* 1427[1], *benhyll* 1427[2], *beane hill* 1625, *Bean Hill* 1736, *Benhillforlong'* Edw 1 (*v.* **furlang**), *benehilgate* 1295, *Benhilgate* Edw 1, *benylgatt* 1427[1] (*v.* **gata**), *benilmedow* 1427[2] (*v.* **mǣd** (**mǣdwe** obl.sg.) ('the hill where beans are grown', *v.* **bēan, hyll**); *le Benlandes* 1.13, 1404 (*v.* **bēan, land** and Bellands in f.ns. (a) *supra*); *Beltons* 1736 (the surn. *Belton* in the possessive case; the family prob. originated in Belton (Lincs.), eight miles to the east rather than in Belton (Rutland), 20 miles to the south); *Bidilhawedland* Edw 1 ('the beadle's headland', *v.* **bydel, hēafod-land**); *Bingham gate furlong* 1605, 1625 (*v.* **gata**; land beside the road to Bingham which lies six miles to the west in Notts.); *blacpyt forlonge* 1567 (*v.* **blæc, pytt, furlang**); *bondemanisbrode* 1337[1], *bondmansbrod* 1427[2] (*v.* **bondeman, brǣdu**); *boosam wonge* 1625 (*v.* **bōs** (**bōsum** dat.pl.), **vangr**); *Bordland'* 1438 (*v.* **bord-land**); *borland forlonge* 1567 (this may belong with the preceding f.n.; if not, then with OE **bōr**[1] 'a hill, an eminence', *v.* **land, furlang**); *Bottesford browke* 1542 (*v.* **brōc**; presum. an alternative name for R. Devon); *Bottesfordheye* 1254 (*v.* **(ge)hæg**; *Bottesford Medowys* 1567, *Bottesforde Meadowes* 1579, *Bottesford Meadow(s)* 1.17, 1736, *Bottesforde farre medowe* 1625 (cf. *the far medowe syde* 1625, *v.* **feor, sīde**), *Bottesforde high meadow* 1625 (*the Hygh Medowe* 1567, *v.* **hēah**[1]) (*v.* **mǣd** (**mǣdwe** obl.sg.)); *bradebeck'* 1295, *bradbeke, brodebeke* 1427[2], *the broadbeck* 1736, *Bradebekeforlong* Edw 1, *brodbecke forlong* 1567 (*v.* **furlang**), *brodbeke gatt* 1427[2] (*v.* **gata**), *brodbecke hyll forlong* 1567 (*v.* **hyll**) (*v.* **brād, bekkr**); *le Breches* Edw 1, *Breches* 1427[1] (*v.* **brēc**); *Brendelandes, le Brendelandis* 1236, *le Brenlandis* 1297, *Brenlandes, Brandland'* 1404, *northbrendeland'* 1337[1] (*v.* **norð**) ('land(s) cleared by burning', *v.* **brende**[2], **land**); *le Brodegate* 1337[1], *brodegatte* 1427[2] (*v.* **brād, gata**); *byrnelandys, byrnlands* 1427[2] ('land(s) cleared by burning', *v.* **bryne, land**); *John Calcrofts Bushes* 1736 (*v.* **busc**), *John Calcrofts Headland* 1736 (*v.* **hēafod-land**) (note also *Rycherd Calcroft* 1567 and *William Calcrofte* 1625, both of Bottesford, and cf. Calcroft's Cl in adjoining Belvoir parish); *Caldwell, ~ forlonge* 1567 (*v.* **furlang**), *Caldewellesic* e.13, e.Hy 3, Hy 3, Hy 3 (e.15), *Caldewallesike, Kald(e)wallesike* Edw 1, *Caudewellesyke, Caudewellsike, -syke, Caudewelsyke* 1427[2] (*v.* **sīk**), *Caldewelsike furlong* Edw 1, *caudewellsyke forlong* 1427[1] (*v.* **furlang**) ('the cold spring or stream', *v.* **cald, wella**); *Calverhillwong'* 1374 (e.15) (*v.* **calf** (**calfra** gen.pl.), **hyll, vangr** and Calving Hills in Normanton f.ns. (a)); *le castelgate* 1295, *Kastelgate* p.1290, *le Castellgate* 1304, *le castilgate* 1337[1], *castellgat, le castellgatt* 1427[2], *þe Castell gatte, le Castulgatt, Castyllgatt* 1427[1], *Castelgate* 1463, *Castell gate* 1567, *Castellgate forlonge* 1567 (*v.* **furlang**), *castell gatt hyll* 1427[1] (*v.* **hyll**) ('the road to the castle', *v.* **castel(l), gata**; the road to Belvoir Castle continued through Easthorpe (*q.v.* for later forms)); *Catewade* 1567, *Catwadlond* 1253, 1374 (e.15), *cattwadlond* 1293 (e.15) (*v.* **land**) ('the ford frequented by wild-cats', *v.* **cat(t), (ge)wæd**); *þe checer* 1427[2], *þe checur* 1427[1], *the Checker* 1567, *the Chekers* 1.17 (*v.* **cheker**); *Clayholm* 1427[2], 1625, *Clayholmfurlong* 1297, 1.13, 1404, *Cleholme forlong* 1567 (*v.* **furlang**) (*v.* **clæg, holmr**); *the Clefeld* 1567 (*v.* **clæg, feld**; one of the great fields of the village); *Cleforlonge* 1567 (*v.* **clæg, furlang**); *le Cliff* 1252 (e.14), 1253, 1374 (e.15), *le Clif* 1253, 1374 (e.15), *le clyf, Clyff'* 1292 (e.15), *le clife* 1374 (e.15), *the Cliffe* 1625, *cliffe furlong* 1625, *shortclyf* 1427[1], *short clife* 1625, *Short Cliff* 1736, *Short clyf forlong(e)* 1567 (*v.* **sc(e)ort, furlang**) ('the steep slope', *v.* **clif**; *the Coal pit way* 1736, *the Cole pit gate, the Coalpit gate* 1736 (*v.* **gata**) (*v.* **col-pytt**; the pit was a place where charcoal was made); *Cokes furres forlonge* 1567 (*v.* **furlang**), *Cooke furrowes* 1625 (*v.* **furh**; the first el. is prob. the ME occupational surn. *Cook, v.* Reaney *s.n.*); *Cokeswrogate* 1451 (*v.* **vrá, gata**; the first el. is either the surn. *Cook* or **cocc**[2] 'a woodcock'); *coksty* e.14, *Cokstye* 1427[2], *Cokstylles* 1567 ('the path where woodcock are numerous', *v.* **cocc**[2], **stīg**; the latest form shows attraction to *stigel* 'a stile'); *Collesdeyle* e.hy 3, *Coledeyle* 1252 (e.14), 1253, 1292 (e.15), *coldeyl* e.14, *Colddayle* 1374 (e.15), *coldayle* 1427[2], *Coldellebuts* 1427[2] (*v.* **butte**) (*v.* **deill**; the first el. is a Scand pers.n., either ON *Kollr*, an original by-name meaning 'the bald-headed one', or ON *Kolr* (ODan *Kol*)); *Cooslades* 1736 (*v.* **cū, slæd**); *Coleuillemiclewong* 1253, *coluilmiclewong'* 1292 (e.15), *Coluylmikylwong* 1374 (e.15), *Coluilewonge* e.14 (*v.* **micel, mikill, vangr**), *colleuelwylows* 1427[2] (*v.* **wilig**) (all with the family name *de Colville*, cf. *Henricus de Colevile* e.14 of Bottesford); *the Common gate* 1736 (*v.* **commun, gata**); *Coupeland* 1253, 1374 (e.15), *coupland* 1292 (e.15) (*v.* **kaupa-land**); *Cowedoles* 1625 (*v.* **cū, dāl**); *Cowslophyll'* 1427[2], *Cowslop hyll* 1567, *Cowslipp hill* l.17, *Cowslip hill* 1736 (*v.* **cū-sloppe, hyll**); *Great Crabbesforowes, Near Crabbesforowes* 1625 (*v.* **furh**; either with the surn. *Crabb* (*v.* Reaney *s.n.*) or, less likely, with **crabbe**); *le Croft Close* 1253 (*v.* **croft, clos(e)**); *crosfurlong'* 1427[2], *Crossefurlong* 1449 (*v.* **cross, furlang**); *crouthorn* 1337[1] ('the thorn patch frequented by crows', *v.* **crāwe, þorn**); *contra Crucem* 1427[1] ('next to the cross', with MLat *contra* 'against, next to' and MLat *crux* (*crucem* acc.sg.) 'a cross'); *crucem Agathe* Edw 2 (with MLat *crux* 'a cross' and the OFr fem. pers.n. *Agatha*); *Crunbull'* 1427[2] (*v.* **crymel**); *dedwong'* 1427[2] (*v.* **dēad, vangr**; a field associated with the discovery of an early burial site or of a recently dead body); *Diuenewong'* 1253, *dyunwong'* 1292 (e.15), *Dyuenwong'* 1374 (e.15) ('the in-field beside R. Devon', *v.* **vangr**); *the dockes* 1567 (*v.* **docce**); *the Ducks Nest* 1736 (*v.* **dūce, nest**; beside R. Devon); *the Duke of Rutlands Headland* 1736 (*v.* **hēafod-land**); *Duuepittis* 1236[1], 1236[2] *duwfpytts, duwfpyttis* 1427[2], *dowve pytts* 1567 (*v.* **dūfe, pytt**; the meaning of the compound is uncertain, but poss. it refers to ground pocked by digging for minerals and reminiscent of the holes of a dovecote, cf. Dove Holes, Db 64 and 399, and Pigeon Holes in Long Clawson f.ns. (a)); *Emmeslande* 1442, 1443 (*v.* **land**; either with the fem. pers.n. *Emm*, the English form of Norman *Emma* (OGer *Emma, Imma*), or with its ME surn. reflex *Emm(s)*, *v.* Reaney *s.n.*); *the Eighty-Three Leys* 1736 (*v.* **leys**; when compounded with a numeral, *leys* represents grassland units of tenure corresponding to *lands* similarly used of arable); *felbrygreins, felebryggreins* 1427[1] (*v.* **fjǫl, brycg, bryggja**; the final el. is either ON **rein** 'a boundary strip' or less likely ON **grein** 'a fork of a stream'); *the foremedowes* 1567 (*v.* **fore, mæd** (**mædwe** obl.sg.)); *forera Hamsterlays* 1427[1] (with MLat *forera* 'a headland', cf. *John Hampsterley* 1413 of Bottesford); *foreram cantarie Sancti Petri* 1427[1] (with MLat *forera* 'a headland' and MLat *cantaria* 'a chantry'; presum. the chantry was part of St Mary's Church, since no separate chantry chapel is recorded in the township); *John Forrests headland* 1736 (*v.* **hēafod-land**), *John Forrests headley* 1736 (*v.* **headley**; it is uncertain whether *headley*, which recurs in later Leics. f.ns., is always an alternative for *headland* or can refer to another agrarian feature such as a swarded-over selion used for grazing or the end unit of an individual's holding of grouped units of pasture as in the *Eighty-three Leys, supra*; but cf. *longe headlea* 1605 *Terrier* in Harston f.ns. (b) *supra*, which appears to replace *the Long Headland* 1601 *ib*); *Gasgell medow* 1427[1] (*v.* **mæd** (**mædwe** obl.sg.); the northern surn. *Gaskell* (*v.* Reaney *s.n.* and Cu 133 *s.n.* Gatesgill) seems unlikely here at this early date; poss. is Scand **gás** 'a goose' compounded with Scand **skáli** 'a shed'); *the gate howsse* 1605 (*v.* **gate-hous**); *Geuelok(e)* e.14 (*v.* **gafeluc**); *godegate* e.14 (*v.* **gōd²**, **goðr**, **gata**); *Godwinbarns* 1342¹, 1342², *Gudwynbarns* 1404 (presum. with **bern** 'a barn' in the pl. rather than with Scand *barn* 'a child' in the possessive case indicating 'the child of Gōdwin's property', *v.* VEPN *s.v.* **barn**), *Godwynhedland* 1341, *Godwinhedland'* 1342¹, 1342², *Gudwynhedland'* 1404 (*v.* **hēafod-land**) (both with the OE pers.n. *Gōdwine* or, less likely, its ME surn. reflex *Goodwin*, *v.* Reaney *s.n.*); *Gorebrod(e)* Edw 1, *gorbrod'* 1337¹, 1427², *gorbrode* 1567, *lyttylgorebrod'* e.14 (*v.* **lȳtel**, **lítill**), *mikelgorebrod'* e.14 (*v.* **micel**, **mikill**), *nedergorbrod* 1427² (*v.* **neoðera**), *ouergorbrod* 1427² (*v.* **uferra**) (*v.* **gorebrode**); *the gorse forlong* 1567 (*v.* **gorst**, **furlang**); *the Granary Close* 1736 (*v.* **granary**); *Great Bush Furlong* 1736 (*v.* **busc**); *le Grene in Westhorp'* 1287 (*v.* **grēne²** and Westthorpe *supra*); *Ryc' Grenham hedland* 1567 (*v.* **hēafod-land**; Richard Grenham is otherwise unrecorded); *le Grenlane* 1350, 1398, *le Grenelane* 1409 (*v.* **grēne¹**, **lane**); *grene lays*, *greneleys* 1427², *(the) Grenleys* 1567, *greene leies*, *Greene Leyes* 1625, *Green Leys* 1736, *nedergreneleys* 1427² (*v.* **neoðera**), *ouergrenelays* 1427¹, 1427² (*v.* **uferra**), *schort grenelays* 1427² (*v.* **sc(e)ort**) (*v.* **grēne¹**, **lǣs**); *the grippes* 1625 (*v.* **gryppe**); *Hamsterley land* 1423, *Hamsterleyland'* 1424¹, 1424² (*v.* **land**), *hamsterlays* 1427² bis, *Hampsterleys* 1463 (in the possessive case), *Hamsterley place* 1433 (*v.* **place**) (cf. *John Hampsterley* 1413 of Bottesford); *hamstrell*, *hamstryll* 1567 (either OE **hām-stall** 'the (enclosure of a) homestead' and later 'the farm-yard' (supposing an instrusive *r*, cf. *the hamstell* in neighbouring Easthorpe f.ns. (b)), or 'the hill where corn-weevils abound', *v.* **hamstra**, **hyll**); *harddeyles*, *herdeyls* 1427² (*v.* **heard**, **deill**; describing land hard to till); *Hard(e)hilles* Edw 1, l.13, e.14, *Hardhillis* 1281, 1351, *Hardhyll'* 1404 (*v.* **heard**, **hyll**; again alluding to land hard to till); *Hardewik Leys* 1531 (*v.* **lǣs** and Hardwick *supra*); *longharelonds* 1427², *long harelandes forlong* 1567 (*v.* **lang¹**, **furlang**), *schortharelondeys* 1427², *short harelandes forlonge* 1567 (*v.* **sc(e)ort**, **furlang**) (prob. alluding to furlongs on a boundary, *v.* **hār²**, **land**); *Harewellesike* Edw 1¹, Edw 1², *harewellsyke*, *harwelsyke* 1427² (*v.* **hār²**, **wella**, **sík**, cf. *Harewell* in Croxton Kerrial f.ns. (b) and Hardwell Cl (*harewell*) in Holwell f.ns. (a)); *Harewong'* 1253 (*v.* **vangr**; with **hār²** or **hara**); *hassokes* 1427², *le Hassokkes* 1463 (*v.* **hassuc**); *heltun ruschus* 1427¹ ('the rush-bed towards Elton', *v.* **risc**; Elton in Notts. adjoins to the west); *the hemp landes* 1625 (*v.* **hænep**, **land**, **hempland**); *Herdwykwonge* 1437 (*v.* **vangr** and Hardwick *supra*); *herle acres* 1427¹ (*v.* **æcer**; the first el. is the ME reflex of OE **eorl** 'a nobleman', later 'an earl', but it may be used as a surn. here, *v.* Reaney *s.n.* Earl; there is no particular connection with the Earls of Rutland, the first of that title created in 1526); *hingoldysmer'*, *hynggodsmer'* 1427² ('Ingold's boundary', *v.* **(ge)mǣre**; the pers.n. *Ingold* is Anglo-Scand (from ON *Ingjaldr*)); *le Holewong'* Edw 1¹, Edw 1², *hol(l)wong'* 1427², *hollow wonge forlonge* 1567 (*v.* **furlang**) ('the in-field in the hollow', *v.* **hol²**, **holh**, **vangr**); *Holmeshyll'* 1438 (*v.* **holmr**, **hyll**); *del Hoo* 1247 Ass (p) (*v.* **hōh**); *husemilne* 1252 (e.14), *Husmilne* 1253, *housemilne* 1374 (e.15) ('the mill with the house attached', *v.* **hūs**, **myln**); *the hyll forlonge* 1567 (*v.* **hyll**, **furlang**); *þe hylgatt* 1427¹, *hyllgatt* 1427² (*v.* **hyll**, **gata**); *Jonismere* Edw 1¹, Edw 1² ('John's boundary', *v.* **(ge)mǣre**; the OFr pers.n, *Johan* (from Hebrew *Johanen*), usually latinized to *Johannes* in early MSS, gave the ME pers.n. and surn. *John*); *the*

king(e)s highway 1605, 1625 (referring to the Nottingham to Grantham road and to
James I, *v.* **hēah-weg**); *le kirkehous* 1433 (*v.* **kirkja, hūs**); *laferikhilles* e.14 (*v.*
lāwerce, lāferce, hyll); *lauutona* l.13, *Lawton* 1404 (either 'the farm on the hill' or
'the farm by the mound', *v.* **hlāw, tūn**, cf. Lawton, Ch **2** 320); *ledbeterforows* 1427[2]
(*v.* **furh**; with the ME occupational surn. *Ledbetere* 'a worker in lead', *v.* Reaney *s.n.*
Leadbeater); *linecroft* 1252 (e.14), *lynecroft* 1292 (e.15), *lincroft* 1295, *lyncroft* e.14,
1374 (e.15) (*v.* **līn, croft**); *linestigate* 1295, *lynsey gatt* 1427[2] (*v. Lynstygate* in
Normanton f.ns. (b) *infra*); *le Longclif* 1296, *Longcliffe* 1347[2], *Longcliff'* 1404, (*le*)
Longclyff' 1404, *Longclyf* 1427[1] bis, *longclyff* 1427[2] bis, *Longeclyffe, longclyfe* 1567,
long clife 1605, 1625, *long cliffe* 1625, *Long Cliff* 1736 (*v.* **lang[1], clif**); *longedeyle*
1252 (e.14), *Long(e)deyl* 1253, *long deyle* 1292 (e.15), *longedaylle* 1374 (e.15) (*v.*
lang[1], langr, deill); *Long doles* 1567, 1736 (*v.* **lang[1], dāl**); *long furlong'* 1427 bis,
longe forlonge 1567, *the longe furlonge* 1625 (*v.* **lang[1], furlang**); *the long hadland*
1625, *the Long Headland* 1625, 1736 (*v.* **hēafod-land**); *Lucaslande* 1443 (*v.* **land**;
with the ME surn. *Lucas*); *Lusiaker* e.Hy 3, 13 (e.15) (*v.* **æcer**), *Lusihalfaker* (*v.* **half-**
aker) (with the ME surn. *Lucy*); *Mannisheuid* 1281, *Mannesheued'* 1299, *Manneshed*
1404 bis, *Manshedde* 1427[1], *manshede* 1427[2], *Maneshed* 1567 (two interpretations
appear poss.: (i) literally 'the man's head', *v.* **mann, hēafod**, cf. Manshead
(Hundred), BdHu 112, for which it has been suggested that the allusion is to the
impaling of a man's head on a stake; (ii) 'the headland belonging to the community',
v. **(ge)mænnes, hēafod**; since the reference appears not to be to a traditional, ritual
meeting-place, the second interpretation is perh. to be preferred, although OE *ǣ*
usually gave ME *e*, cf. *mennessefurlong'* in Muston f.ns. (b) *infra*; the OE pers.n.
Mann in the possessive case would be unlikely compounded with *hēafod* as
'headland'); *þe Mere* 1427[2], *þe meres* 1427[1] (*v.* **(ge)mǣre**); *middelfurlong'* 1252
(e.14), *Middilforlong* 1253, *le middelforlong'* 1374 (e.15), *mydulfurlong'* 1427[2], *the*
Midle Furlong 1736, *nethermiddulforlong'* 1252 (e.14), *le Nethermiddilforlong* 1253
(*v.* **neoðera**) (*v.* **middel, furlang**; the middle furlong of the great Middle Fd);
middilfurlong super le withclays 1292 (e.15) (*v.* **middel, furlang** and *le Witeclais*,
infra); *midfurlong'* 1337[1] (*v.* **midd, furlang**); *mickelmerehil* 1295, *Mikulmerhil'*
1342[1], *Mikulmerhille* 1342[2], *mukelmerehil'* 1392, *Myculmarhill'* 1404,
mykyllmerehyll 1427[3] (*v.* **micel, mikill, (ge)mǣre, hyll**; as second el., **mere[1]** 'a pool'
would appear to make happier sense, but modern topography does not obviously
signal this, unless the location is to be identified with *the west poole* in Easthorpe
f.ns. (b)); *milnecroft* 1252 (e.14), 1253, e.14, 1374 (e.15), *le milnecroft* 1292 (e.15)
(*v.* **myln, croft**); *milnestyes* 1427[2] bis, *Nether myllstylles forlong, Over myllstylles*
forlonge 1567 (*v.* **neoðera, uferra, furlang**) (*v.* **myln**; with **stīg** or **stig**, the 1567
forms having been attracted to *stigel* 'a stile'); *musendoles* 1567 ('the shares of land
towards Muston', *v.* **dāl**; Muston *infra* lies to the south-east); *Mustonbek* 1463 (*v.*
bekkr; this is an alternative name for R. Devon which flows from Muston through
Bottesford); *Mustundale* Hy 3, 13 (*v.* **dalr**; a hollow towards Muston); *myclemore*
dole 1567, *Micklemore dool* 1736 (these forms may belong with *mickelmere(hil)*,
supra; if not, then *v.* **micel, mikill, mōr[1], dāl**); *mykulplott* 1427[1] (*v.* **micel, mikill**,
plot); *þe mylnse* (sic) 1427[1], *betwynne ye myllnes* 1567 (*v.* **myln, betwēonan**); *the*
neither holte 1625 (*v.* **neoðera, holt**); *the netes pasture* 1567 (*v.* **nēat, pasture**);
Normangatt 1427[1] (prob. 'the road of the Northmen or Norwegians', *v.* **Norðman,**

gata and *Normangate*, its continuation in adjacent Redmile; but cf. *Norman Bridge* in Knipton f.ns. (b)); *Offerton Hedge* 1736 (presum. the hedge to property of a family called *Offerton* since there is no evidence for a lost farmstead or settlement of this name); *orstungatt* 1427¹, *orson gate* 1567 (*v.* **gata**), *orson way* 1567 (*v.* **weg**), *orston foote gate* 1625 (*v.* **fote-gate**), *Orson foot way* 1736 (*v.* **fote-waye**) (the road and the footpath to Orston which lies to the north-west in Notts.; note the typical loss of *t* in the group -*ston* which occurred in local p.ns. from the 16th cent. onwards); *osbutterlands, osbutterlond* 1427¹, *osbutterlond(y)s* 1427² (*v.* **austr, butere, land**); *ouerberu* 1337¹, *Longouerberehye* p.1290, *Longouerbergh'* 1404, *longouerborow* 1427² bis, *longhorbrow* 1427², *long orboro* 1567, *Long arborrowes* 1625 (*v.* **lang¹**), *oldouerborow, howldhouerborow* 1427², *Old orboro* 1567 (*v.* **ald**), *Orbora, Over garbrough* (sic) 1736 (because of the inconsistency of forms, it is difficult to decide whether the generic of this f.n. is *berg* 'a hill' or *burh* 'a fortified place'; if the latter, then a meaning 'the upper fortified place' may be adduced (*v.* **uferra, burh (byrig** dat.sg.)), perh. referring to an early fortified site on the hill north-east of the village, cf. *Byristede* in Normanton f.ns. (b) *infra* and Overbury, Wo 153; if the generic is *berg*, then a simple furlong name is indicated, i.e. '(the furlong) across the hill' (*v.* **ofer³, berg**); it is poss. that 17th and 18th cent. forms have been influenced by *eorð-burh* 'fortification with ramparts of earth'); *ouercotestys* 1427¹ (*v.* **ofer³, cot, stig**); *houerpools* 1427¹, *Overpoles forlong* 1567 (*v.* **ofer³, pōl¹, furlang**); *Paskedenholm* 1304, Edw 1, *Paskedenhoml* (sic) Edw 1 (*v.* **holmr**), *Paskedn ~, Phaskeden lane* Edw 1 (*v.* **lane**) (cf. *Alan Phaskeden* Edw 1 of Bottesford); *ye person hedlande* 1567, *the parsons headland* 1736 (*v.* **persone, hēafod-land**); *Prestegate* 1413², 1463, *prestgatt(e)* 1427², *preestgate* 1463, *Priestgate* 1736, *Prestgate forlonge* 1567, *Preist(e)gate furlonge* 1625 (*v.* **furlang**), *prest gatt syde* 1427² (*v.* **sīde**) ('the priest's path or road', *v.* **prēost, gata**); *the prestes hadland* 1625 (*v.* **prēost, hēafod-land**); *þe prest welows* 1427² (*v.* **prēost, wilig**); *le Pyngull'* 1350, 1398, 1409 (*v.* **pingel**); *le redhert* 1337¹ bis, *redȝerth* 1427² bis, *Redeyerth* 1463, *Rederth ~, Redeyerth forlonge* 1567, *the redd earth furlonge* 1625 (*v.* **furlang**) ('the red soil', *v.* **rēad, eorðe**; prob. to the south-west towards Redmile (*q.v.*)); *the Red ground* 1736 (*v.* **grund**); *Redmile Footway* 1736 (*v.* **fote-waye**; the footpath to Redmile); *Redemyldgate* 1298, *Redmyldgate* 1404 ('the road to Redmile', *v.* **gata**); *Redwong* 1253, e.14, 1374 (e.15), *redewong'* 1292 (e.15) bis (*v.* **rēad, vangr**; red soil is again indicated); *Sandhill'* 1337², 1340, 1427², *sand heyll* 1427², *Sandyll'* 1427² bis, *Sandhyll forlonge* 1567 (*v.* **furlang**), *Sandhilhedland* 1404, *Sandhilheuedland'* 1409 (*v.* **hēafod-land**) (*v.* **sand, hyll**; a hill with sandy soil); *the Sand pittes* 1625 (*v.* **sand-pytt**); *Sandwong'* 1252 (e.14), 1253 (e.15), 1374 (e.15), *sandwonge* e.14 (*v.* **sand, sandr, vangr**); *scamdeyll, skamdeyl* e.14, *Skamdayl* Edw 1, *Scamdayl* Edw 2 (*v.* **skammr, deill**); *Scheperd well* 1427¹ (*v.* **scēp-hirde, wella**); *sedygatt* 1427¹ (*v.* **gata**; ostensibly 'the road where seed or grain abounds', but this as a concept seems unlikely and the earliest citation in OED for *seedy* 'abounding in seed' is for 1574; poss. as the first el. is OE (**ge)set** 'a fold, a place for animals', but more forms are needed); *Setcopp'* 1404, *sedcop* 1427², *sydcop* 1625, *Side Cop* 1736, *sydecop forlonge* 1567 (*v.* **furlang**), *sydcop hill* 1625 (*v.* **set-copp**); *sikewong'* 1252 (e.14), 1253, 1292 (e.15), *sykewong* 1374 (e.15) (*v.* **sīk, vangr**); *smaleeng* e.14, *smal(h)yng'* 1427² (*v.* **smæl, smal(r), eng**); *smal furlong'* 1427¹ (*v.* **smæl, furlang**); *le Smithisdeil*

Hy 3, *Smithesdeyl, smithedeyl* e.14, *Smithisdeil* 1314, *Smithesdeil* 1333[1], *smythysdale* 1337[1], *Smithesdeyll* 1366, *smeth deyle, smyth dayle* 1427[2], *neder smyth deyls* 1427[2] (*v.* **neoðera**), *Smyth doles* 1567, *Smithdoles* 1625, 1736 (*v.* **smið, smiðr, deill**; in the later forms, *deill* has been replaced by **dāl**); *þe Soke* 1427[2] bis ('the drain', *v.* **soc**); *sowthholme* 1427[2] (*v.* **sūð, holmr**); *stenwytt well'* 1427[2] (*v.* **steinn, vað, wella**; too distant from Stenwith beyond the county boundary in Lincs. to be related to it other than in etymology); *the stint furlong* 1625 (*v.* **stynt**); *Stocbechil* Edw 1, *stokbechille* 1337[1], *stokbekhyll'* 1427[2] (*v.* **stocc, stokkr, bekkr, hyll**); *Stochil* 1295 (*v.* **stocc, hyll**); *Stodgate* 13, 13 (e.15) (*v.* **stōd, gata**); *Stongate* e.Hy 3, 1426 (*v.* **stān, gata**); *Stowegate* 1275, 1275 (e.15) (*v.* **stōw, gata**); *Stowegren, stowgrene forlonge* 1567 (*v.* **stōw, grene**[2], **furlang**); *in tyll' Sty* 1404 ('(the furlong running) up to the path', *v.* **untyll, stīg**); *þe stytong'* 1427[2] (*v.* **stīg, tang, tangi**); *Stywolde* 1545 (*v.* **wald**; with **stīg** or **stig**); *sukewonge* e.14 (*v.* **soc, vangr**; cf. *þe Soke, supra*); *Swartketilwong'* 1253, *swarketelwong'* 1374 (e.15) (*v.* **vangr**; with the Scand pers.n. *Svartketill*); *swerdeacre* e.14 (prob. 'the sword-shaped piece of land', *v.* **sword, æcer**, although the ME occupational surn. *Swerd* used of a sword-maker is poss. as the first el.); *swynemore forlonge* 1567, *Swinemore furlonge* 1625 ('the furlong next to the waste ground used for pasturing pigs', *v.* **swīn, mōr, furlang**); *swithmore* 1337[1], *Swythmore* 1413[2], *le Swythmore* 1451, *swythmor' furlong'* 1427[2] (*v.* **furlang**) ('the waste ground cleared by burning', *v.* **sviða, mōr**[1], **mór**); *Taustongate* 1427[2], *Tawstongate* 1463 (*v.* **gata** and Toston Hill); *Templewong'* 1253, 1292 (e.15), 1374 (e.15) ('the in-field belonging to the Knights Templars', *v.* **temple, vangr**); *thirnelsick'* 1295, *thyrnelsike* 1337[1] bis, *thirnelsyke* 1427[2] (*v.* **þyrne, hyll, sík**); *Thornham hadland* 1427[1] (*v.* **hēafod-land**; poss. with the surn. *Thornham*, otherwise *v.* **þorn, hamm**); *Thorwong'* 1424[1], 1424[2] (*v.* **vangr**; with the Anglo-Scand pers.n. *Þór*); *Toftis* 1252 (e.14), 1253, 1292 (e.15), *Thoftis* e.14, *Toftes* 1374 (e.15) (*v.* **toft**); *the Town Side* 1736 (*v.* **tūn, sīde**); *Typolde doles* 1567 (*v.* **dāl**; prob. with the ME surn. *Tebold*, from the OFr pers.n. *Theobald, Teobaud, v.* Reaney *s.n.* Theobald); *Tyrspitwong'* 1253, *thirsputwong* 1292 (e.15), *thirspitwong'* 1374 (e.15), *Thrspitteswong* 1449 (*v.* **þyrs, pytt, vangr**; poss. identical with *thorsepytwong'* in Muston f.ns. (b)); *under þe hege* 1427[1] (*v.* **under, hecg**; a furlong name); *viam Regiam* 1427[1] ('the king's highway', with reference to the Nottingham to Grantham road and to Henry VI); *Wadehil* 1236, *Wadhil* 1337[1] (*v.* **hyll** and cf. *Rog' Wade* 1236 of Bottesford); *Walkerhou* 1325, *Walkerhowe* 1326, 1427[2], *Walkerhow* 1427[1], *Walcrow forlonge* 1567 (*v.* **furlang**), *Walker Hoe* 1625, *Walker How* 1736 (*v.* **walcere**; with either OE **hōh** 'a headland' or more likely ON **haugr** 'a hill'); *Wardcroft* 1337[1] (*v.* **croft**; with the surn. *Ward*); *þe waren thorns* 1427[2] (*v.* **wareine, þorn**); *waterstals* 1427[1], *Waterstalles forlonge* 1567 (*v.* **furlang**) (*v.* **wæter, stall**); *le Wenge* 1253, *le weng'* 1337[1], *del Wenge in le Witeclais* 1252 (e.14), *le Wyng' in le withclays* 1292 (e.15), *le wong' in le Whitclays* 1377 (e.15) (*v.* **vengi** and *le Witeclais, infra*, and cf. Wing, Ru 228; OScand **vengi** is a derivative of ON **vangr** which replaces it in the 1377 (e.15) form); *westbryg* 1427[2] (*v.* **west, vestr, brycg, bryggja**); *West hyll* 1427[1] (*v.* **west, hyll**); *Weyleys* 1427[1], *weeyleys* 1427[2] (*v.* **weg, lǣs**); *weywyllis* 1427[2] (*v.* **weg, wilig**); *Winterbecfurlong* e.13, *Wynterbecke forlonge* 1567, *winterbeck furlonge* 1625 (*v.* **furlang** and Winterbeck *supra*); *le Witeclais* 1252 (e.14), *le Wytecleys* 1253 bis, *Witeclays* Hy 3, *Witecleyes* 1285, *le withclays*

1292 (e.15), *le whiteclays* 1374 (e.15), *Whiteclayes* 1424[1], *Whytecleys* 1424[2], *Medilewhytcleys* 1424[2], *Middelwhiteclayes* 1424[1] (*v.* **meðal, middel**) ('the white clay selions', *v.* **hwīt, clǣg**); *le wrongland'* 1337[1], *Wronglandes* 1341, 1404, *Wrongland'* 1342[1], 1342[2], *Wronglandis* 1409, *wronglands* 1427[1], 1427[2], *Wronglandys* 1427[2], *Schortwronglandes* 1341, 1404, *Scortwrongland'* 1342[2] (*v.* **sc(e)ort**), *Long Ranglands* 1736, *Wronglandes forlonge* 1567 (*v.* **furlang**), *wranglandes* ~, *wrongelandes hill* 1625 ('the crooked or twisted selions', *v.* **wrang, vrangr, land**); *Withinbusc* Hy 3, *Wythambusk, Wythombusk* e.14, *Wythinnbusk', le Wythunbuske* 1347[1], *Wytham boske* 1567 (*v.* **wīðign, buskr**); *withins,* ~ *buttes* 1625 (*v.* **wīðign, butte**); *þe wroo* 1427[2], *þe wrow* 1427[1], *wro,* ~ *furlong* 1625 (*v.* **vrá**); *Wylnehall* 1539 (*v.* **wiligen, halh**); *wymbisshwong* 1447 (*v.* **vangr**, cf. *Walter de Wynebisch* 1325 of Bottesford); *Wyngfurlong'* 1427[1], 1427[2], *wynfurlong'* 1427[2] (*v.* **vengi, furlang**, cf. *le Wenge, supra*).

2. EASTHORPE

Estthorp c.1240 *Rut, Estthorpe* 1467 Pat, 1531 *Wyg*
Estorp 1276 RH, *Esthorp'* Edw 1 *Rut*, 1320 LAS (p), 1449, 1458 *Rut et freq* to 1519, 1521 *Wyg, Esthorpe* 1372 Nichols, 1475 Pat, 1524 *Wyg*, 1534, 1539 Fine, *Esthorpp'* 1486 *Rut*
Estrop' 1482 *Wyg, Estropp'* 1487 *Rut*, 1488 *Wyg, Estrope* 1544 *Rut*
Eastroppe 1579 Fine, *Eastropp* 1626 LML
Eastthorpe 1584 Ipm, *Easthorpe* 1609 LML *et freq*

'The eastern outlying farmstead', *v.* **ēast, þorp**, cf. Westthorpe *supra*.

TOSTON HILL
    Toxtonhyl 1304 *Rut, Toxtonul* 1314 *ib, Toxtonehil* Edw 2 *ib*
    Tustonhyll 1427 *Terrier*
    Tawsten hyll 1567 *Terrier, Tawesting hill* 1625 *ib*
    Toston Hill 1736 *Terrier*, 1824 O

The hill appears to have been a habitation site, that of 'Tōk's farmstead', *v.* **tūn**. The ODan pers.n. *Tōk* (an original by-name 'fool') is deduced from p.ns. in Denmark, cf. DS **9** 40, **12** 22 and 125. Later, the area comprised one of the great fields of Easthorpe, hence: *the tawstinge hill feilde* 1625 *Terrier, Toston Hill Field* 1736 *ib, Tosternhill Field* 1772 *EnclA, v.* **hyll, feld**.

EASTHORPE COTTAGE. EASTHORPE LODGE. EASTHORPE MILL. MANOR HO., *Manor house* 1925 Kelly, *v.* **maner**. MILL POND. PENTNEY

COTTAGE, 1925 Kelly, *v.* **cotage**. RAMSLEY LODGE, 1925 Kelly, *v.* **loge**. TEMPERANCE HOTEL (lost), *Temperance Hotel* 1877 White; instituted by the later 19th cent. Temperance Movement which aimed to dissuade people from the consumption of alcohol. WASHDIKE BRIDGE, 1824 O; the site of a sheep-dip, *v.* **wash-dyke**.

FIELD-NAMES

Forms in (a) dated 1772 are *EnclA* and 1824 are O. Forms throughout dated 1236[1], 1236[2], 1531, 1544 and 1626 are *Rut*; 1427, 1567, 1625 and 1736 are *Terrier*; 1442 are *Comp*.

(a) Coneygree Cl, Coneygreen Leys (sic) 1772 (*Conynggre leys* 1567, *the Cunnygrey leis* 1625, *the Coneygree Lays*, ~ ~ *Leys* 1736, *v.* **coningre, leys**); Easthorpe Gorse 1824 (*v.* **gorst**); Far Pasture 1772 (cf. *the Far Field* 1736); Hall Cl 1772; Hungerhill Fd 1772 (*Hungerhil* 1236[1], 1236[2], *hungerhyll'* 1427 bis, *hungerhylle* 1427, *Hungirshill'* 1442, *hongerhyll* 1567, *Hungerhyl* 1625, *Hungar hill* 1626, *Hunger hill* 1736, *hongerhyll forlonge* 1567, *Hungar hill forlong* 1625 (*v.* **furlang**) (*v.* **hungor, hyll**); Middle Fd 1772 (*the middle feild* 1625, *the Midle Field* 1736, *v.* **middel, feld**; one of the great fields of the village); Sands Pasture 1772 (*the sandes* 1625, *the Sands* 1736, *v.* **sand**); Sheep Pasture 1772 (*the Pasture* 1736).

(b) *the Becke* 1625, *bekfurlong'* 1427, *the Beck furlonge* 1625 (*v.* **bekkr, furlang**; with reference to Winterbeck *supra*); *Blackmiles* 1736 (*v.* **blæc, mylde**); *Castell gate* 1625, *Castle Gate* 1736 (*v.* **castel(l), gata**; the road to Belvoir Castle); *Cawdewell sike*, ~ ~ *furlong* 1625 (*v.* **cald, wella, sík** and *Caldwell* in Bottesford f.ns. (b)); *James Drings Headland* 1736 (*v.* **hēafod-land**); *Esthorpfelde* 1567 (*v.* **feld**); *the Fold Bridge* 1736, *fold brigge buttes* 1625 (*v.* **butte**) (*v.* **fald, brycg**); *the footway to Redmile* 1736 (*v.* **fote-waye**; Redmile parish adjoins to the south-west); *the grene gate* 1625 (*v.* **grene**[1], **gata**); *the hamstell* 1625 (*v.* **hām-stall**); *the Highway* 1736 (the main road from Nottingham to Grantham); *Hunton' close* 1515, 1519 *Wyg*, 1672 Nichols (*v.* **clos(e)**; perh. with the surn. *Hunton*, although the early date may point rather to a lost farmstead, *v.* **tūn**; cf. *hunton busshe* 1579 in adjoining Barkestone f.ns. (b)); *Inmere furlonge* 1567 (*v.* **furlang**), (*the*) *Inmears* 1736 (*v.* **in, (ge)mǣre**; referring to land immediately within the parish/county boundary); *Long Croft* 1544 (*v.* **lang**[1], **croft**); *Muston gate* 1625 (*v.* **gata**; Muston adjoins to the south); *Muston Lane End* 1736 (*v.* **lane-ende**); (*the*) *pinder peece furlonge* 1625, *the Short, Long Pinder piece* 1736 (*v.* **pinder, pece**); *the Rye wong(e)* 1625, 1736 (*v.* **ryge, vangr**); *the Sike feilde* 1625 (*v.* **sík, feld**; one of the great fields of the village); *Tawsten hyll forlonge* 1567 (*v.* **furlang** and Toston Hill *supra*); *Town End close* 1544 (*v.* **tūn, ende, clos(e)**); *the warlott furlong* 1625 (*v.* **warlot**); *the west poole* 1625, *the West Pooles*, 1736 (*v.* **pōl**[1]); *Wigstons close* 1672 Nichols (belonging to Wigston's Hospital in Leicester).

3. MUSTON

> *Moston'* c.1130 LeicSurv, e.Hy 3, 1260, 1270 *Rut et passim* to 1343
> Cl, 1363 Ipm, *Mostona* e.13 *Rut* bis, *Mostone* 1271 *ib*, *Mostun'*
> 1260, Edw 1 *ib*, *Moseton'* Hy 3 *ib*, *Mosston'* 1325 *ib* bis
> *Mustun* Hy 1 (1333) Ch, Hy 2 (e.15) *BelCartB*, l.12 *Rut et passim* to
> Hy 3 (freq), Edw 1 *ib*, *Mustuna* Hy 1 (1333) Ch, Hy 2 (e.15), 12
> (e.15) *BelCartB et passim* to Edw 1 *BelCartA*, *Muston*(*'*) 1191,
> 1192 P *et passim* to e.Hy 3 *Rut* (freq) *et freq*, (~ *iuxta Belvere*
> 1302 Ass, ~ *iuxta Botel*(*s*)*ford* 1381, 1389 *Rut*, ~ *in the Vale of*
> *Beauer* 1449 *WoCart*), *Mustona* e.13, e.Hy 3 *Rut et passim* to
> Edw 1 *ib*, *Mustonia* Hy 3 *ib*, *Mustone* 1232 RHug, Hy 3 *Rut et*
> *passim* to 1306 *ib*, *Musthon'* 1313 *ib*
> *Mouston'* l.13, 1317 bis, 1343 *Rut*, *Mousston'* 1333, 1343 *ib*,
> *Moustoun* 1317 *ib*
> *Musson* 1604 SR, 1610 Speed, 1612 *Rut*, 1613, 1719 LML

'The farmstead, village infested with mice', *v.* **mūs**, **tūn**. The settlement lies in the Vale of Belvoir, hence ~ *in le Vale of Beauer* 1449, *v.* **val**. The 17th- and 18th-cent. forms show the period's characteristic Leics. loss of *t* in the group *-ston*, a feature still preserved in local pronunciation of the name.

DEBDALE FM, *Debdale* 1850 *TA*, *v.* **dēop**, **dalr**. DUKE'S FM. HOSPITAL FM, *the Hospital farm* 1729 Nichols. In 1612, the fifth Earl of Rutland endowed the Earl of Rutland's Hospital in Bottesford with land in Muston, *v.* **hospital**. LONGORE BRIDGE, 1824 O, *Long Gores* 1850 *TA*, *v.* **lang**[1], **gāra**. MANSEL BARN. METHODIST CHAPEL, 1850 *TA*. MUSSON GAP (local), *Muston Gap* 1777 Map, *v.* **gap**. MUSTON GORSE, 1795, 1806, 1815 Map, 1824 O, 1877 White, cf. *the Gorste cloasse* 1601 Terrier, *the gorse close* 1605 *ib*, *the gosse close* 1625 *ib*, *the Gorze close* 1629 (1712), 1709 *ib*, (*the*) *Goss close* c.1700, c.1705 *ib*, (*The*) *Gorse Close* 18, 1825 *ib*, 1850 *TA*, *v.* **gorst**, **clos**(e). MUSTON GORSE BRIDGE, 1824 O. MUSTON GORSE COVERT is *Gorse Covert* 1850 *TA*, *v.* **cover**(**t**). MUSTON GORSE FM. MUSTON GORSE WHARF is *Coal Wharf* 1824 O, *v.* **hwearf**; on the Nottingham and Grantham Canal. THE RECTORY, 1877 White, 1925 Kelly, *The Rectory House* 1850 *TA*; its predecessor is *the Parsonage* 1601, 1625, 1629 (1712) *Terrier*, *The Parsonage House* 1712 *ib*, *v.* **personage**. ST JOHN THE BAPTIST'S CHURCH, *Church (St John)* 1863, 1877 White, *Church (St John the Baptist)* 1925 Kelly; it is earlier recorded as *ecclesiam de Mustuna* a.1219 RHug, *ecclesie de Muston* 1220 ib, 1355, 1356 *Pat, ecc' de Muston'* Hy 3 *Stix*. Note also *the churchyeard* 1601 *Terrier, the Churchyard(e)* 1605, 1625 *ib, (the) Church Yard* 1712 *ib*, 1850 *TA, v.* **chirche-3eard**. VICTORIA COTTAGE, 1850 *TA, v.* **cotage**; no doubt named to honour the accession of Queen Victoria in 1837. WHEATSHEAF (P.H.), *Wheatsheaf* 1824 O, 1925 Kelly, *Wheat Sheaf* 1846, 1863, 1877 White, *"Wheat Sheaf" public house* 1850 *TA*.

FIELD-NAMES

Undated forms in (a) are 1850 *TA*; 18 and 1825 are *Terrier*. Forms throughout dated John, e.13, e.Hy 3, 1239, 1254, 1262, Hy 3, 13, Edw 1, 1316, 1317, 1318, 1321, 1325, 1330, 1332, 1333, 1336, 1338, 1344, 1352, 1360, 1366, 1380 and 1427 are *Rut*; those dated e.13 (e.15), m.13 (e.15), Hy 3 (e.15), l.13 (e.15), 13 (e.15) and e.14 (e.15) are *BelCartB*; e.14 are *BelCartA*: those dated 1601, 1605, 1625, 1629 (1712), c.1700, c.1705, 1709 and 1712 are *Terrier*.

(a) Aston Cl (with the surn. *Aston*); Barbers Cow Cl (with the surn. *Barber*); The Barrows (*berihc* Hy 3, *berou* 1321, *Berugh*(') 1332, *berwe* 1333, *Berw* 1366, *(on) barrow* 1605, *Barrowe* 1625, *the Barrow* 1709, *Berig furlong'* Hy 3, *barrowe furl'* 1601, *Barrowe furlonge* 1625, *barrow furlong* 1629 (1712) (*v.* **furlang**), *barrow(e) hedge* 1601, 1629 (1712) (*v.* **hecg**), *Barrow close* c.1700, c.1705, 1712, *v.* **berg**); Bonnycrofts (*v.* **croft**; if not a late form of *Brennycroft* in f.ns. (b), then with the surn. *Bonny/Bunny*, cf. Bunny's Spinney in Lt. Dalby); Bottom Cl (*v.* **bottom**); Brags Cl (with the surn. *Bragg*); Browns Cl (with the surn. *Brown*); Church Fd (*Chirchefeld, chyrchefeld'* 1352, *v.* **cirice, feld**; one of the great fields of the township); Clay pit; The Cliff (*Clif* Edw 1, *le Clyff'* 1352, *the hyghe cliffe* 1601, *the hyghe Clyffe* 1605, *highe Clife* 1625, *the Highcliff* 1629 (1712) (*v.* **hēah**[1]), *cliuishende* e.13, *Cliueshend'* 1352, *le Clifesend'* 1427 (*v.* **ende**), *v.* **clif**); Cottage Cl (*v.* **cotage**); Cow Cl; Over ~ ~, Craven Hills (*v.* **uferra**; prob. with the surn. *Craven*, cf. Craven Ho. in Bottesford); Dovecot Cl (*v.* **dove-cot**(e)); Epperstone Cl (with the surn. *Epperstone* of a family originating in the village of this name 12 miles to the north-west in Notts.); Fag Cl (cf. *Feggakyr* 1352 bis, *Feggeacre* 1427 in f.ns. (b) *infra*); First Wong (*v.* **vangr**); Flat Cl (referring to level ground, cf. *Flatdayle, infra*); Four Leys (*v.* **leys**; when compounded with a numeral, *leys* represents grassland units of tenure corresponding to *lands* similarly used of arable); Gate Furlong (*gatefurlong'* Hy 3, 1332 bis, 1336, *Gatfurlang'* e.14, 1333, *Gateforlong'* 1352, *v.* **gata, furlang**); Greater, Lesser Home Cl 18, 1825, Great ~ ~, Home Cl (*v.* **home**); High Fd; Hinks Furlong (*Heinc* e.Hy 3, *hengforlang* Hy 3 *Stix, hengesfurlong'* 1332, 1344, *hengefurlong'* 1332, *hingfurlong'* 1366, *yngesforlang'* e.14, *ingefurlong* 1333, *Inges* *furl'* 1601, 1605, *Inggs furlonge* 1625, *Ings furl'* 1629 (1712), *v.* **eng, furlang**); The Holme (*le Holmis* Edw 1, *le Holme* 1352, cf. *holmforlong'* e.Hy 3, Hy 3, 13 (e.15) (*v.* **furlang**), *v.* **holmr**); Honey Wells (cf. *Hunnuell fur'* 1605, *honnywell furlonge* 1625, *Hony Well furl'* 1629 (1712); prob. 'spring or stream where honey is found', *v.* **hunig, wella**, cf. Honeybourne, Gl 1 245, but the Scand pers.n. *Hunni* is formally poss. as the first el.); Hunt Cliff (*v.* **clif**); Island Platt (*v.* **plat**; in late f.ns., **island** is used of a close completely surrounded by others); Lane End Cl (*v.* **lane-ende**); Lines Cl (beside the lines of *Nottingham and Grantham Railway* c.1860 O, *Grantham and Nottingham Railway* 1877 White); Little Land Dyke (*Landyche, Landyk'* 1352, *landyke* 1601, *Landike* 1605, 1625, *Land Dyke* 1629 (1712), cf. *Landykhill'* 1352 (*v.* **hyll**), *v.* **land, dīc, dík**); Long Lands (*langlandes* 1352, *v.* **lang[1], land**); Lynn Cl (with the surn. *Lynn*, *v.* Reaney *s.n.*); The Marsh (*Mersch* 1332, *merches* 1333, *le Merches* 1352, *Mersh'* 1366, *v.* **mersc**, cf. *le maris* in f.ns. (b) *infra*); Middle Beck (*middelbekkes* e.14, 1366, *middelbekkis* 1333, *Middlebek* 1344, *middle beckes* 1601, *Middle Beeckes* 1605, *Midlebeck* 1625, *Midle Becks* 1629 (1712), *v.* **middel, bekkr**); Middlebeck's Cl 1863, 1877 White (*v.* the previous f.n.); Middle Fd; Monks Cl (with the surn. *Monk(s)*, *v.* Reaney *s.n.*); Montserrat (a close at the north-eastern boundary of the township; a name indicating remoteness, transferred from that of one of the Leeward Islands in the West Indies; discovered by Columbus, Montserrat was a British colony from the 17th cent.); Nedgates (*le netegates* 1332, *netgate* 1352 bis, *Neate gates* 1601, 1605, 1625, *Neatgates* 1629 (1712), *v.* **nēat**; the recurring pl. form suggests that rather than 'the cattle road' (with **gata**), this may be an early style of the later *cow-gate* 'an allotment of pasture for a single cow', *v.* Field 127); Old Clay Pits; Oxhead Cl (*v.* **oxa, hēafod**; poss. referring to an earlier 'ox headland' for which there is no other evidence (cf. *neateshead furlong* in Sproxton f.ns. (b)); otherwise perh. alluding to the shape of the close); Pear Tree Cl; The Pinfold (*v.* **pynd-fald**); Pingle (*v.* **pingel**); First, Second Pitts Cl, The First Pitts Cl 1825, Pitts Cl 1850 (*le Pyttes* 1352, *lez Pyttes* 1427, *the pittes cloasse* 1601, *the Pittes close* 1605, 1625, *the Pitts close* 1629 (1712), *the Pits close* c.1700, 1712, (*The*) *Pitts Close* c.1705, 1709), *v.* **pytt, clos(e)**); Rail Road 1824 O (a private railway running from *Coal Wharf* (*v.* Muston Gorse Wharf *supra*) on the Nottingham and Grantham Canal to Belvoir Castle; at this date, the wagons were no doubt horse-drawn); The Reads (*v.* **hrēod**); Roses Cl (with the surn. *Rose*, *v.* Reaney *s.n.*); Rough Cl (*v.* **rūh[1]**; alluding to the land surface); The Row (*le Wro* 1262 *Rut*, 1262 *Fine*, e.14, 1338, *le Vro* Hy 3, *Mustone Wro* e.14, cf. *Vrohil* Hy 3, *wrohill'* 1352 (*v.* **hyll**), *v.* **vrá**); Running Furrow (*le renand furo* 1254 (e.14), *le renand forgh'* 1352 ('the flowing drain', *v.* **furh**; with the pres.part. of OE (*ge*)*rinnan* 'to run, to flow', which is influenced here by Scand *renna* 'to make run', *v.* **rinnende, rennandi**; the feature appears to have been a major drainage ditch); Little ~ ~ ~, Rye Grass Cl (the fodder crop **rye-grass** (*Lolium perenne*) was popular with 17th- and 18th-cent. agricultural improvers); Saintfoin Cl (referring to the fodder crop **sainfoin** (*Onobrychis sativa*)); Sand Cl; Sand Dyke (*v.* **dík**); Scalding Furlong, Little Scauding Furlong (*Scaldinge forlange* 1601, ~ *furlang* 1625, *the Scalding furl'* 1629 (1712), *v.* **furlang**; earlier forms are needed; perh. 'a shallow depression', with Scandinavianized OE **sc(e)ald** plus **-ing[2]** may be thought of; but note *Scaldeford' furlong* and *skaldewelforlang'* in f.ns. (b), either of which *Scalding* may be a late garbled reflex); Shepherd Cl (either with **scēp-hirde** or with the surn. *Shepherd*); Straight Fold (*v.* **strǣt, fald**; presum. with reference to Sewstern Lane, a Roman road); The Syke (*le Sick* 1330, cf. *abouethesyk'* e.14 (*v.* **aboven**), *Sicfurland'* Edw 1, *Sigkefurlong'* 1317 (*v.* **furlang**), *le sikeshend'* 1332 (*v.* **ende**), *v.* **sík**); Taylor Cl (with the surn. *Taylor*); Three Leys (*v.* **leys**; when compounded with a numeral, *leys* represents grassland units of tenure corresponding to *lands* similarly used of arable units); Top Cl; Town End Cl (*v.* **tūn, ende**); Well Hill (*v.* **wella**); West Croft (*Westcrofd* e.13, *Westcroft* Hy 3, 1325, *West Croftes* Hy 3, *le Westecroft* 1317 bis, *Vest Croft* 1317, *v.* **west, vestr, croft**); West End (*v.* **ende**); White Leys (*v.* **hwīt, leys**; prob. here is ModEdial. *white* used of dry, open pasture); Whites Yard (*v.* **geard**; with the surn. *White*); Whiting Cl (with the surn. *Whiting, v.* Reaney *s.n.*); Willow Holt (*v.* **wilig, holt**).

(b) *Algersic* Edw 1 (*v.* **sík**; with either the ODan pers.n. *Alger* (ON *Álfgeirr*) or its ME surn. reflex *Alger, v.* Reaney *s.n.* Algar); *Alingtonecliff'* 1366 (*v.* **clif**), *Alingtonmere* 1344 (*v.* **(ge)mǣre**) (Allington lies to the north-east beyond the county boundary in Lincs.); *Alueredwrofurlong* Hy 3 (*v.* **vrá, furlang**; with the OE pers.n. *Ælfrǣd*, cf. *Alredwro* in Bottesford f.ns. (b)); *le Bakehous* 1344 (*v.* **bæc-hūs**); *barlandis* 1333, *Barland* 1352, *barlandes* 1366, *longebarlant* Edw 1, *longbarland'* e.14, 1332, *longbarlande* 1332, *langbarlandis* 1333, *longbarlandes* 1366 (*v.* **lang**[1]), *schortbarland'* e.14, 1332, 1333, *schortebarland* 1332, *chortbarland'* 1366 (*v.* **sc(e)ort**, 'selions where barley is grown', *v.* **barr, land**); *Bermeswell* 1262 Cur (poss. an original OE **Beorneswell* 'Beorn's spring or stream', *v.* **wella**); *Bertts* 1262 Fine (perh. a metathesized **breiðr**, hence 'the broads'); *Botilde toft* e.hy 3 ('Bothild's homestead', *v.* **toft**; the ODan pers.n. *Bothild* (ON *Bóthildr*) is fem.); *Botlisforthehole* 1333, *Botilsfordehole* 1352, *Botelisfordehole* 1366 ('the hollow towards Bottesford', *v.* **hol**[1]); *Brennycroft* 1316, *Brynycroft'* e.14 (*v.* **croft**; the first el. appears to be an adj. **brenni** formed from the ME verb *brennen* 'to burn', giving a sense such as '(cleared by) burning' (*v.* **-ig**[3]), although OE **bryne** or ON **bruni** with the same meaning are also poss., *v.* Bonnycrofts in f.ns. (a) *supra*); *bretlond* e.13 (e.15), Hy 3, e.14 (e.15), *Brathlond* Hy 3 (e.15), *bretland* m.13 (e.15), *Bretlond'* 1352, *longbretland* l.13 (e.15) (*v.* **lang**[1]) (*v.* **breiðr, land**; note Bretland, Ru 58 and 162, where the first el. is incorrectly assigned); *atte brigge* 1381 SR (p) (*v.* **brycg**); *le Brodsykmer'* 1352 (*v.* **brād, sík, (ge)mǣre**); *bucstornfurlong'* Edw 1 (*v.* **buc-þorn, furlang**; the earliest citation for *buckthorn* in OED is for 1578); *Burnelandez* 1427 (*v.* **land**; the first el. is prob. OE **bryne**/ON **bruni** '(a place cleared by) burning', with metathesis, cf. *byrnelandis* in Bottesford f.ns. (b)); *iuxta Crucem in villa* 1360 ('next to the cross in the village', with MLat *crux* (*crucem* acc.sg.) and MLat *villa* 'a township'; the base of a medieval cross survives); *Cukewoldheuedlond* Hy 3, *chukeuuoldheuidlond* e.13, *Cokewoldheuidlond* Edw 1 bis ('cuckolds' headland', *v.* **cukewald, hēafod-land**; evidently a well-known secluded and grassy spot for illicit sexual intercourse, which presum. a monk, when making an entry referring to it in the Large Cartulary of Belvoir Priory, preferred to call *synnefulheuedland* e.14, *v.* **infra**); *dicfurlang'* Hy 3, *Netherdicfurlong'* 1316, 1317 (*v.* **neoðera**), *vuerdikfurlang'* Hy 3, *ouirdicfurlongk* 1316, *Houirdikfurlong* Edw 1, *Huwirdikefurlong'* Edw 1 bis, *ouerdykforlong'* 1352 (*v.* **uferra**) (*v.* **dík, furlang**); *edisch* 1333 (*v.* **edisc**); *Enghirst* 1352 (*v.* **eng, hyrst**); *Engwong'* 1352 bis (*v.* **eng, vangr**); *Feggakyr* 1352 bis, *Feggeacre* 1427 ('Feggi's plot of land', *v.* **æcer, akr**; the pers.n. *Feggi* is Scand, *v.* SPNLY 81); *Finelwong'*

1338 (*v.* **fynel, vangr**); *Flatdayle* 1254 (*v.* **flatr, deill**); *Froskfourres* 1352 bis, *ouerfroskfourres* 1352 (*v.* **uferra**) ('the furrows where frogs abound', *v.* **frosc, froskr, furh**); *Gerstaldyche, Gerstaldyk'* 1352 (perh. 'the ditch at the place where good grass grows', *v.* **gærs, stall, dīc, dík**); *goswelleforlong* 1352 (*v.* **gōs, wella, furlang**); *the Grange* 1601, 1605, 1625, 1629 (1712) (*v.* **grange**; poss. originally an outlier of Belvoir Priory); *la grene* e.13, Hy 3, Hy 3 (e.15), Edw 1, *atte grene* 1381 (p) (*v.* **grēne², atte**; a medieval cross base survives on the western green (*v. iuxta Crucem in villa, supra*)); *grensti* Edw 1 (*v.* **stīg**; poss. with **grēne²** 'a village green' rather than with **grēne¹** 'green'; a footpath still runs from the western green to the church); *Hallehedlandis* 1344, *halleheuedland* 1352 (*v.* **hall, hēafod-land**); *Harstone* 1601, 1629 (1712), *Harston* 1605, 1625, ~ *close* 1698 *Deed* ('the (grey) boundary stone', *v.* **hār², stān**; with reference to the county boundary with Lincs., cf. Harston (Belvoir parish) which lies on the same boundary four miles to the south); *Hassoches* Hy 3, *Hassokes* Edw 1 (*v.* **hassuc**); *Hatchenesse* 1605, *Hatchines* 1625, *Hatchins furl'* 1629 (1712) (*v.* **furlang**) (the recurring *a* in this f.n. suggests that rather than these late spellings representing the common ME **heching** 'part of a field ploughed and sown during the year in which the rest of the field lies fallow', we have a similar formation with a base either OE **hæc(c)** 'a hatch, a gate' or OE **hæcce** 'a fence'; earlier forms are needed, but a sense 'a fenced-in area' appears to be present); *Heinhalfakirsichesende* Hy 3 (*v.* **half-aker, sīc, ende**; the first el. may refer this name to *Heinc* (*v.* Hinks Furlong *supra*), otherwise from OE **hēah¹** (**hēan** wk.obl.) 'high'); *Hellewong'* 1352 bis (*v.* **hjallr, vangr**); *Herdston* Edw I, *Herston'* 1316, 1352 bis, 1380, *underherstun* 1332 (*v.* **under**) (perh. 'Hert's farmstead', *v.* **tūn**; the pers.n. *Hert* represents either OE **Heort* or Scand *Hjǫrtr*, cf. Hardstoft, Db 269); *hesterne* e.14 bis, *hersternehul* e.14, *Hersternhill* 1332 (*v.* **hyll**) (if these forms do not belong with the preceding name, then perh. 'the thorn scrub', *v.* **hæs, þyrne**); *le heyeclif* e.14, *Hyeclyff* 1352 bis (*v.* **hēah¹, clif**); *Hingkesplotte* 1318 (*v.* **eng, plot** and cf. Hinks Furlong *supra*); *hirneclif* e.Hy 3, 13 (e.15) (*v.* **hyrne, clif**); *holforw* e.14 bis, 1333, 1366 (*v.* **hol², furh**); *holgate* e.14 (*v.* **hol², holr, gata**); *holmold* e.13 *Rut*, Hy 3 *Stix*, *holemold* Hy 3 bis (*v.* **hol², molde**; the precise meaning of the compound is uncertain, but presum. soil of particularly good quality is indicated); *hollewong'* 1352 (*v.* **hol², holr, vangr**); *the Homestall* 1605, *the homestead* 1709 (*v.* **hām-stall, hām-stede**; the home buildings of *the Parsonage, v.* The Rectory *supra*); *the homestal of Bartholomew Cubley* 1605 (*v.* **hām-stall**); *le houwe* 1333, *Howeford* 1601, 1629 (1712), *Howforde* 1605, *howford* 1625 (*v.* **ford**) (*v.* **haugr**); *hullesgate* l.13 (e.15) (*v.* **gata**; with either OE **hyll** 'a hill' or OE **hyles** 'holly'); *hundecliff'* 1332, 1366, *houndecliff'* 1333, *Huntclyff* 1352 bis (*v.* **clif**), *hundewelleforlang* e.14 (*v.* **wella, furlang**) (either with **hund** 'a hound' or with the OE pers.n. *Hund*); *Hyl* Hy 3 (*v.* **hyll**); *le kelnehous* 1352 (*v.* **kylne-hous**; this instance predates the earliest OED citation by 65 years); *the Kinges highe waie* 1605, ~ ~ ~ *way* 1625 (*v.* **hēah-weg**; the Nottingham to Grantham road, with reference to James I, *v. the queenes highe waye, infra*); *Kyrkestedplot'* 1352 (*v.* **plot**), *Kyrkestedwong'* 1352 (*v.* **vangr**) (*v.* **ciricestede** 'the site of a church', here with the replacement of OE *cirice* by the cognate ON **kirkja**); *lambekote* Edw 1, *lambecotehil'* Hy 3 bis, Edw 1, 1317, *lambecotehille, lambecotehylle* 1317, *lambecotehull'* 1360 (*v.* **hyll**), *Lambcotewong, lamcotwong* 1352 (*v.* **vangr**) (*v.* **lamb, cot**); *Langecroft* 1239, Hy 3 (*v.* **lang¹, croft**); *langedic* Hy

3, *langdick* 1316, *langdik'* 1332 bis, *langedyk* 1352 bis, *underlangdik'* 1332 (*v.* **under**), *langedicgate, langdicgate* Edw 1, *langdikgate* 1332, *langdykgate* 1352 (*v.* **gata**) (*v.* **lang**¹, **langr, dík**); *le lid* Hy 3, *þe lid* Edw 1, *Lith, Lyth* Edw 1, *lythewong* 1352 bis (*v.* **vangr**) ('the slope or hillside', *v.* **hlið**¹, **hlíð**²); *long dooles in Normanton medowes* 1605 (*v.* **lang**¹, **dāl** and *Normanton medowes, infra*); *longate* 1352 (*v.* **lang**¹, **langr, gata**); *lyttelmersh'* e.14, *littelmersch'* 1332 bis (*v.* **lȳtel, mersc**); *le maris* Hy 3, Edw 1, *le Mares* 1427 (*v.* **mareis**); *mennessefurlong'* 1333, 1366 (*v.* **(ge)mǣnnes, furlang**); *Middelforlong'* e.14, *middelfurlong'* 1332, 1333, 1344, 1366 (*v.* **middel, furlang**); *molendinis . . . de Mostona* e.13 (with MLat *molendinum* 'a mill'); *milnestymere, mylnstimere* 1352 (*v.* **myln, stīg, mere**¹); *neudik'* 1333, *neudyk'* 1366, *newe dykes* 1601, *New deykes* 1605, *Newdikes* 1625, *New Dykes* 1629 (1712) (*v.* **nīwe, dík**); *Normanton medowes* 1601, 1605, *Northmanton meadowes* 1625, *Normanton Meadow* 1709, *Normington Meadow* 1712 (meadowland north of the village towards Normanton); *Pesecroft'* Edw 1, 1318 (*v.* **pise, croft**); *Pollardwong'* 1352 bis (*v.* **vangr**; with the surn. *Pollard, v.* Reaney *s.n.*); *Potter pit* Hy 3 (*v.* **pottere, pytt**); *Prystcroft'* 1352 bis (*v.* **prēost, croft**); *the queenes highe waye* 1601, *the Queens Highway* 1712 (the Nottingham to Grantham road, *v. the Kinges highe waie, supra*; the first record refers to Elizabeth I, the second to Queen Anne); *Randolfland* 1427 (the Scand pers.n. *Rannulfr* was brought to England by the Normans as *Randulf*, in this f.n. used either as a pers.n. or as its ME surn. reflex, *v.* **land** and Reaney *s.n.* Randolph); *Redde heuitland* Hy 3 (*v.* **hēafod-land**; with either **rēad**, referring to the colour of the soil, or **hrēod**); *Redefordeland* Edw 1 (*v.* **hrēod, ford, land**); *Redemere* e.14 (*v.* **hrēod, mere**¹); *le Redewong'* e.14, *le Redwong'* 1352 bis (*v.* **rēad, vangr**); *Scaldeford' furlong* 1317 (*v.* **sc(e)ald, ford, furlang**; the first el. influenced by Scand *sk-*); *schortecroft'* e.14, *Schortcroft* 1316 (*v.* **sc(e)ort, croft**); *seghaker* Hy 3 (*v.* **secg**¹, **æcer**); *the shyre meere* 1605, *the shier meare* 1625, *the Shire meere* 1629 (1712) ('the county boundary', *v.* **scīr**¹, **(ge)mǣre**); *Sigkefurlong'* 1317, *Sicfurland* (sic) Edw 1 (*v.* **sík, furlang**); *Sidebroke feild* 1625 (*v.* **brōc, feld**; with **sīd** or **sīde**); *skaldewelforlang'* e.14 (*v.* **sc(e)ald, wella, furlang**; the first el. influenced by Scand *sk-*); *solledeyle* Edw 1 (*v.* **sol**¹, **deill**); *Steinwad* m.13 (e.15), *Stenwithe* 1601, *the Stennithe* 1629 (1712), *steynwathsyke* Edw 1, *Steynwathesyk'* 1352 (*v.* **sík**) (naming land on the boundary with Stenwith in Lincs., the neighbouring village to the south-east); *Stirkerthorn* Hy 3, *Stirgarthorn* Edw 1 bis (*v.* **þorn**; with the ODan pers.n. *Styrkar* (ON *Styrkárr*)); *stodfolde* Hy 3, *Netherstodfold'* 1352 (*v.* **neoðera**), *ouerstodfold'* 1352 (*v.* **uferra**) (*v.* **stōd-fald**); *Sueynnissike forlong'* Edw 1 (*v.* **sík, furlang**; with the ON pers.n. *Sveinn*); *Swinestyfurlong'* Hy 3, *le swynstyforlang'* e.14, *swynstifurlong'* 1332, 1344, 1380, *swynestifurlong'* 1332, 1366, *Suenistifurlong'* 1333 (*v.* **swīn, stig, furlang**); *synnefulheuedland* e.14 (literally 'the sinful headland', *v.* **synneful, hēafod-land**, being a monastic copyist's rendering of *Cukewoldheuedland, supra*); *Thacdeile* Hy 3 (*v.* **þak, deill**); *Thacholm* John (*v.* **þak, holmr**); *thirneber'* Hy 3, *Thirneberwe* Edw 1, *Threnberugh'* 1352 (*v.* **þyrne, þyrnir, berg**); *thirneclif* e.Hy 3, *thirneclife* Hy 3, *Turneclif* 13 (*v.* **þyrne, clif**); *thorn(e)forlong'* 1352 (*v.* **þorn, furlang**); *thorsepytwong'* 1352 ('the in-field containing the giant's pit', *v.* **þyrs, þurs, pytt, vangr**; it is poss. here that the name has been influenced by that of the Norse god *Þórr*); *tuotherne* l.13 (e.15) (*v.* **twēgen, tū, þyrne**); *wacelinesholm* Hy 3 (*v.* **holmr**; with the Norman-French pers.n.

Walchelin or its ME surn. reflex, *v.* Reaney *s.n.* Wakelin); *Walworthehow* e.14, *Waluordehowe* 1316, *Walwordhowe* 1352 (*v.* **haugr**; *Walworth* appears to be an earlier p.n., i.e. 'the enclosure, farmstead of the serfs or Britons', *v.* **walh, worð**, cf. Walworth, Sr 27); *watefordhill'* 1352 (*v.* **hyll**; perh. to be compared with Watford, Nth 75 and Hrt 103, both of which may be derived either from OE (**ge**)**wæd** 'a place for wading' or OE **wāð** 'hunting'; DEPN *s.n.* Watford (Nth) suggests the alternative possibility that the original name was ON **vað** 'a ford' (or OE (**ge**)**wæd** Scandinavianized) to which was added an explanatory **ford**); *waterfurris* Hy 3, *le Waterfourres* 1352 (perh. 'furrows where water tends to lie', *v.* **wæter, furh**; but *v.* Field 50 who argues that these were deeper furrows so ploughed in order to carry off surface water; it should be noted, however, that such furrows appear to be called alternatively *Wet furrowes* in Coston f.ns. (b) and *Watriforowis* in Eaton f.ns. (b)); *watirplace* 1380 (*v.* **place**; perh. with the surn. *Walter* (the reflex of the OGer pers.n. *Walter*), since *Water* was its normal medieval pronunciation (*v.* Reaney *s.n.*), but **wæter** cannot be discounted as the first el., cf. *Graueleyplace* in Belvoir f.ns. (b)); *Westgate* Edw 1 (*v.* **west, vestr, gata**); *le Westheynges* 1254, *le Westhingk* 1318, *le Westyng'* e.14, *le Westheng'* 1332 (*v.* **west, vestr, eng**); *le weynhous* 1352 ('the wagon-shed', *v.* **wayn-hous**; this instance predates the earliest OED citation by 217 years); *wheate under lease* 1601, *Wheateunderleyes* 1605, *Wheat & Lease* (sic) 1629 (1712) (of uncertain meaning; the 1712 copyist resorted to & to represent a problematical second el.; perh. 'the wet place beneath the pastures', *v.* **wēt, under, leys**); *Wheytcross* 1352 bis ('the white cross', *v.* **hwīt, cros**, presum. referring to limestone construction; the surviving medieval cross base in Muston is of limestone, cf. *white cross* in nearby Knipton f.ns. (b)); *Wintirbecfurlong* e.Hy 3, *Winterbecfurlong'* Hy 3, Hy 3 (e.15), *Winterbecfurlang'* Hy 3 (e.15) (*v.* **furlang** and Winterbeck *supra*); *le Wong* Hy 3 (*v.* **vangr**); *wrongelonds* Hy 3 (*v.* **wrang, vrangr, land**).

4. NORMANTON

Normanton(') c.1130 LeicSurv, e.13 *Rut*, e.13 *Wyg*, 1203, 1205 Cur, e.Hy 3 *Rut et freq*, (~ *in le Vale* 1338 Hosp, ~ *iuxta Bottellesforde* 1395 *Rut*, ~ *iuxta Bot(t)elesford'* 1398 *ib*, 1420 *Wyg*, 1449 *Rut*), *Normantona* 1209 × 19 RHug, *Normantone* 1253 *Rut* (p), *Normantun* Hy 3 *ib*

Normanneton' 1230 Cur bis

Northmanton 1624 *Terrier*

Norminton 1625 *Terrier*, *Normington* 1712 *ib*

'The farmstead, village of the Norwegians', *v.* **Norðman** (**Norð-manna** gen.pl.), **tūn**. The settlement lies in the Vale of Belvoir, hence ~ *in le Vale* 1338, *v.* **val**. The 1230 form preserves the original gen.pl. construction.

LITTLE COVERT FM, *Little Covert farm* 1925 Kelly, *v.* **cover(t)**.
NORMANTON HALL. NORMANTON LITTLE FOX COVERT is *Normanton Fox Cover* 1824 O, *v.* **cover(t)**. NORMANTON LODGE is *The Lodge* 1877 White, *v.* **loge**. NORMANTON THORNS, 1824 O, 1877 White, *Normanton Thornes* 1846, 1863 ib, *v.* **þorn**. PINFOLD *v.* **pynd-fald**. THREE SHIRE OAK (THREE SHIRE BUSH 2½") is *Shire Bush* 1777, 1815 Map, 1831 Curtis, *Three Shire Bush* 1824 O, 1846, 1863, 1877 White, *v.* **scīr**[1], **busc**; at the meeting point of Leics., Lincs. and Notts. WILLOW FM, *Willow farm* 1925 Kelly, *v.* **wilig**.

FIELD-NAMES

Forms in (a) dated 1771 are *Plan*, 1772 are *EnclA* and 1824 are O. Forms throughout dated 1200 × 50 (e.15), 1292 (e.15) and 1374 (e.15) are *BelCartB*; e.Hy 3, 1253, 1258, Hy 3, 1304, Edw 1, 1310, 1316, 1321, 1353, 1449 and 1626 are *Rut*; 1252 (e.14) and e.14 are *BelCartA*; 1625 and 1736 are *Terrier*.

(a) Calving Hills 1771, 1772 (*Cauill ~, Cavill hill* 1625, *Calving hill hedge* 1736 (*v.* **hecg**), 'the hill where calves are pastured', *v.* **calf** (**calfra** gen.pl.), **hyll**, cf. *Calverhillwong'* in Bottesford f.ns. (b)); Chippendale 1771, 1772, Chippingdale 1824 ('valley with a cow-shed', *v.* **scypen, dalr**); Dale Fd 1771, 1772 (*the Dale feilde* 1625, ~ ~ *Field* 1736, *v.* **dalr, feld**; one of the great fields of the township); Hill Fd 1771, 1772 (*The Hill feilde, the hillfeild* 1625, *the Hill Field* 1736, *v.* **hyll, feld**; one of the great fields); Holyleys Pasture 1771, 1772 (*Holly Leaze* 1626, *v.* **hol**[2], **læs**); Marr Pasture 1771, 1772 (cf. *Marwong'* 1252 (e.14), 1374 (e.15), *Marwonge* e.14, *the Marr furlong* 1736 *v.* **marr**[1], **vangr**); Mary's Bridge 1771, 1772 (it is poss. that tolls from this helped to maintain the fabric of St Mary's Church in Bottesford); Normanton Mill 1824 (a windmill); Syke Fd 1771 (*Sike feild* 1625, *Normanton Sike Field* 1736, *v.* **sík, feld**; one of the great fields of the village).

(b) *Acre* 1625 (*v.* **æcer**); *Beggar Bush Furlong* 1736 (*v.* **beggere, busc**; prob. denoting worthless land, cf. *Beggars Bush* in Harby f.ns. (b), *Beggar Busk*, L 5 34 and *v.* Field 108); *Beneland* Hy 3, *Northbenelandis* Edw 1 (*v.* **norð**), *le Suthbenelandis* Edw 1 (*v.* **sūð**) (*v.* **bēan, land**); *le Boles* 1310, ~ ~ *iuxta Coluildeyle* 1321 (*v.* **bole** and *Coleuyldeyle, infra*); *Braytheynghend'* 1449 (*v.* **ende**), *Breathing* 1625, 1736, *Long Breathing* 1625, *breathing furlong* 1625 (*v.* **breiðr, eng**); *the Bridge that goes to Staunton* 1736 (i.e. to Staunton in the Vale, beyond the county boundary in Notts); *Francis Brownes headland* 1625 (*v.* **hēafod-land**); *Bucklandes* 1625, *Bootlands* (sic) 1736 (*v.* **bōc-land**; rare in the Midlands); *the Bull hurst* 1736 ('the hillock or bank where the bull is pastured', *v.* **bula, hyrst**); *Byristede* e.Hy 3 ('(at) the site of the stronghold', *v.* **burh-stede** (**byrig-stede** dat.sg.), cf. *ouerberu* in Bottesford f.ns. (b)); *Cattewellegate* 1200 × 50 (e.15) ('the road to Cattewell (i.e. the

spring or stream frequented by wild-cats)', *v.* **cat(t)**, **wella**, **gata**); *Chees(e)wong*
1736 (*v.* **vangr**; prob. with the surn. *Cheese*, *v.* Reaney *s.n.*; OE **cis** 'gravel' is
formally poss. as the first el., but there are otherwise no examples of this el. in
Framland Hundred); *Clartes* 1736 (*v.* **clot(t)**; used of heavy ground); *Coleuyldeyle*
1310, *Coluildeyle* 1321 (*v.* **deill**; *Henricus de Colevile* is cited e.14 *BelCartA*, cf.
Coluilewonge in Bottesford f.ns. (b)); *Croftgate* 1258 (*v.* **croft**, **gata**); *thearles
h(e)adland* 1625 (*v.* **eorl**, **hēafod-land**; referring to the sixth Earl of Rutland, d.
1632); *Le gatefurlanc* Hy 3 (*v.* **gata**, **furlang**); *Gafelokessiche* 1200 × 50 (e.15),
Gafelocsik' Hy 3, *Gauelok' sike* 1321, *Gafelokesyk'* 1353 (*v.* **sīc**, **sík**), *Gauelokeswell*
1200 × 50 (e.15) (*v.* **wella**) (*v.* **gafeluc** 'a small fork', poss. used topographically of
a fork in a stream or of the meeting at an angle of selions in a great field); *the
headlays* 1736 (*v.* **headley** and *John Forrests headley* in Bottesford f.ns, (b)); *the
backside of the Hill* 1736 (*v.* **bak-side**), *the further Side of the Hill* 1736, *below the
Hill* 1736 (all furlong names); *Hingehille* Hy 3 (*v.* **henge**, **hyll**); *le Holewong* Edw
1 (*v.* **hol²**, **holr**, **vangr**); *Howong* Edw 1 (*v.* **vangr**; the first el. is prob. **haugr** rather
than **hōh**); *Hubarde ~*, *Hubards hill* 1625 (with the surn. *Hubbard*); *hyweie gate*
1625 (presum. 'the road to the highway', *v.* **hēah-weg**, **gata**); *Kirck* 1625 (*v.* **kirkja**,
here used of land near to, or belonging to a church; no church survives in Normanton,
but note *capella de Normantona* a.1219 RHug, *capellam de Normanton* 1220 MHW
(with MLat *capella* 'a chapel')); *Kirckridge* 1625 (*v.* **kirkja**, **hrycg**); *leuinggesti*
1200 × 50 (e.15) ('Lēofing's pen', *v.* **stig**; the pers.n. *Lēofing* is OE); *Longdeyles*
1310, *Longdeyle* 1316 (*v.* **lang¹**, **langr**, **deill**); *Longelandes* 1625, *Longlands* 1736
(*v.* **lang¹**, **land**); *Longstripes* 1736 (*v.* **strīp**); *le long terne* Edw 1 ('the long patch of
thorn-bushes', *v.* **lang¹**, **langr**, **þyrne**, **þyrnir**, cf. Normanton Thorns *supra*); *Lucy
gate* 1625 (*v.* **gata**; with the surn. *Lucy*, cf. *Lusiaker* in Bottesford f.ns. (b)));
Lynstygate 1449, *Lynstigatefurlong'* 1321, *lynsie gate furlong* 1625 (*v.* **furlang**)
(poss. is **sty-gate** (*v.* **stígr**, **gata**), a Danelaw equivalent of ME *sty-way* 'a narrow
road', with as first el. either OE **hlyn**, ON **hlynnr** 'a maple-tree' or OE, ON **lind** 'a
lime-tree'; OE **līn**, ON **lín** 'flax' in this compound seems unlikely, while Lindsey
appears to be discounted because of the *t* in early spellings and since highways north
in Leics. refer rather to Lincoln); *Middelfurlong* 1449, *the Midle furlong* 1736 (*v.*
middel, **furlang**; belonging to the great Syke Fd); *le midfurlong'* Hy 3 (*v.* **midd**,
furlang); *Mikilsig* Hy 3, *Mikelsyktong* 1310 (*v.* **tang**, **tangi**, *v.* **micel**, **mikill**, **sík**);
Muston Hill 1625, 1736 (a hill towards Muston *supra*); (*the) New Dike* 1736 (*v.* **dík**);
Nine Lays Hedge 1736 (*v.* **leys**, **hecg**; when compounded with a numeral, *leys*
represents grassland units of tenure corresponding to *lands* similarly used of arable);
Norminton greate medowe 1625, *the great Meadow* 1736, *Norminton little medowe*,
the little medowe 1625, *the Little Meadow* 1736; *Northlanges* 1449 (*v.* **norð**, **lang²**);
Pacewong 1253 (*v.* **vangr**; with the surn. *Pace* (*v.* Reaney *s.n.*), cf. *Joh' Pais* 1219
RFL); *the pathway to Staunton* 1736 (i.e., to Staunton in the Vale to the north-west
in Notts.); *Peasill greene* 1625, *Pessel green* 1736 (*v.* **pise**, **hyll**, **grēne²**); *the Poor
of Dorkins Land* 1736 (charitable land to aid the poor of Dorking in Surrey, cf. *Dr
Whites Charity Land*, *infra*); *le Reddelandes* 1258, *Redelandis* 1304, *le Redlandis*
Edw 1 (*v.* **rēad**, **land**; alluding to the colour of the soil); *the Sand pittes*, *~ ~ ~
furlong* 1625, *the Sand pit furlong* 1736 (*v.* **sand-pytt**); *Scales dicke* 1625, *~ Dike*
1736 (with either ON **skáli** (ME **scale**) or with the surn. therefrom, *v.* **dík** and Reaney

s.n. Scales); *Sheep crew furlong* 1736 (with ModEdial. **crew** 'a pen, a hut'); *short furrowes* 1625, *Short furrows* 1736 (*v.* **sc(e)ort, furh**); *the Short Stripes* 1736 (*v.* **strīp**); *the Sike* 1736, *Sike ~, Syke furlong* 1625 (*v.* **sík**); *Spirlinghalfacre* Hy 3, *Sperlinghaluakir* Edw 1 bis (*v.* **half-aker**; with either the OE pers.n. *Spyrling* or its ME surn. reflex *Sperling, v.* Reaney *s.n.* Sparling); *Stedfold, ~ Hill* 1736 (*v.* **stōdfald**); *Sty Lays* 1736 (*v.* **leys**; with **stīg** or **stig**); *Twodales* 1449, *two dales* 1736 (*v.* **twēgen, tū, deill**); *Watergongfurlong* 1449 (*v.* **wæter, gang, furlang**); *Westirfurlong'* Edw 1 ('the western furlong', *v.* **wester, furlang**); *Dr Whites Charity Land* 1736 (poss. to be identified with *the Poor of Dorkins Land, supra*); *Woodgate* 1625 (*v.* **wudu, gata**); *Wrongelandis* 1353 (*v.* **wrang, vrangr, land**).

Broughton and Old Dalby

1. NETHER BROUGHTON

Broctone 1086 DB, 1223 RHug, *Brocton'* 1202 FF, 1203 Fine, 1212
Fees *et freq* to 1268 Fine, Hy 3 *Crox* (freq) *et passim* to Edw 1
CroxR bis, 1316 Ch, (~ *iuxta Warkeneby* 1262 (Edw 1) *CroxR*),
Broctona John Dugd, *Broctun* 1236 Fees, 1236 Berkeley (p)
Brochton 1220 MHW, 1209 × 35 RHug, 1242 RGros, 1260 Cur,
Brohton 1242 RGros
Brouton 1290 Inqaqd, 1301 IpmR, *Broutton* 1296 Ipm, 1316 FA
Broghton 1258, 1259 Cur *et passim* to 1355, 1382 Pat, (~ *iuxta*
Claxton 1382 ib), *Nethyr Broghton* 1342 ib, *Netherbroghton'*
1499 *RTemple*
Brughton 1351 Pat, *Nethyrbrughton* 1387 Dugd
Broughton(') 1330 FA, 1364 Pat *et passim* to 1520 *Crox*, 1539 *Deed*
et freq, (~ *in Valle* 1416 Nichols, ~ *in-the-Vale* 1615, 1616 LML),
(~ *inferior* 1609 LeicW), (*Lesser* ~ 1693 LML), *Brougthon* 1502
MiscAccts, *Netherbroughton* 1332 HB, *Nethyrbroughton* 1387
Dugd, *Nether Broughton* 1473 *CCR*, 1539 *Deed*, 1541 MinAccts
et freq
Netherbrowghton 1539 MinAccts, *Neyther Browghton* 1566 LeicW

'The farmstead, village by the brook', *v.* **brōc, tūn**. The stream from
which the settlement took its name is Dalby Brook which forms the
county boundary here. Upper Broughton lies beyond the boundary in
Notts. Nether Broughton is at the edge of the Vale of Belvoir, hence ~
in Valle (*v.* **val**) and is adjacent to Wartnaby and Long Clawson. Its site
is some 100 ft lower than that of Upper Broughton, hence *Nethyr* ~ (*v.*
neoðera). Note also the suffixed MLat *inferior* 'lower'.

ANCHOR INN is *Anchor and Horse Shoe* 1846, 1863 White, *The Anchor*
1877 ib, 1925 Kelly. BLEAK HILLS, *blacke hills* 1625 *Terrier*, *Bleake*
Hills 1674 *ib*, *v.* **blæc** 'black, dark-coloured', alluding to the escarpment
of the Wolds, here dark with woodland cover, cf. Blackberry Hill in

Belvoir parish. BOTANY BAY, a common name signifying remoteness from a village, transferred from the early 19th-cent. penal colony in south-eastern Australia. This instance is located at the south-eastern extremity of the parish, a well-wooded area on the escarpment of the Wolds, *v.* Field 161–2. BROUGHTON GRANGE, *v.* **grange**. The building does not appear on the 1st edn of the O.S. map of 1836 and is now demolished. BROUGHTON HILL, 1836 O. BROUGHTON LODGES, 1836 O, *The Lodges* 1758 *Rental*, 1877 White, 1925 Kelly, *v.* **loge**. CHAPEL LANE, named from the Wesleyan Methodist Chapel. CLAWSON LANE leading to Long Clawson. DALBY LANE, leading to Old Dalby. GREENACRES. GREEN HILL, 1836 O, *Green Hills* 1758 *Rental*, *v.* **grēne**[1]. GREENHILL FM. HATTON LODGE, cf. *Wm. Hatton, farmer* 1863 White. HECADECK LANE, a lane adjacent to 'a water-channel with a floodgate or hatch', *v.* **hæc(c)**, **dík**, cf. Heckdyke, Nt 39. KING ST. LODGE FM. OLD GRANGE is *Broughton Grange* 1617 *Dun*, *The Grange* 1674 *Terrier*, 1863 White, *ye Mannor house & Grounds called ye Grange* c.1680 *Rental* (*v.* **maner**), *The Old Grange* 1877 White, *v.* **grange**. The early grange was originally an outlier of Croxton Abbey. It evidently was renamed Old Grange on the building of the fashionable Broughton Grange *supra*. THE PENN (local) is *Penclose* 1660 *Deed*, *the penn closse* 1675 *ib*, *the Penne closse* 1676 *ib*, *Penn Close* 1726 *ib*, 1762 *EnclA*, *the Pen Close* 1740, 1798 *HDW*, *v.* **penn**[2], **clos(e)**. THE RECTORY, 1925 Kelly, *v.* **rectory**. ST MARY'S CHURCH, *the Church of Broughton* 1617 *Dun*, *the Church* 1625 *Terrier*, *Church (St Mary)* 1846, 1863, 1877 White, 1925 Kelly; it is earlier recorded as *ecclesie de Brochton* 1220 MHW, *ecclesiam de Brocton* 1235 RGros, *~ de Brochton* 1242 ib, *ecclesie de Nethyr Broghton* 1342 *Pat*, *~ de Broghton* 1355 *ib*, *~ de Broghton iuxta Claxton* 1382 *ib*. Note also *the Church yard* 1625 *Terrier*. WESLEYAN METHODIST CHAPEL.

FIELD-NAMES

Forms in (a) dated 1758 are *Rental*; 1762 are *EnclA*; 1763, 1782[1], 1782[2], 1784, 1785, 1786, 1789[1], 1789[2], 1791, 1797, 1798, 1804, 1808, 1809, 1826, 1838 and 1853 are *HDW*; 1764 are Nichols. Forms throughout dated Hy 3 are *Crox*; c.1268 are Nichols; 1316 are Ch; 1547 × 58 are ECP; l.16, 1625 and 1674 are *Terrier*; 1617 are *Dun*; 1641 are Ipm; 1661, 1675[1], 1675[2], 1712 and 1736 are *Deed*; c.1680, 1685 and 1686 are *Rental*.

(a) Brickhill Cl 1797 (*bridg(e)hill* 1625, *Brighill* 1674, *v.* **brycg, bryggja**; beside *Clauson Bridge, infra*); Broadhill 1778, 1785 (*v.* **brād**); Brungate Leys 1808, Nether, Top Brungate Leys Cl 1809, 1826 (*v.* **gata, leys**; the first el. may be **brún**[2] 'the brow of a hill', since the land drops sharply to the north-west of the village); Cants Sand Cl 1762 (cf. *Wm. Cant* 1712 of Nether Broughton; a close with sandy soil); Church Cl 1762; Church Headland Furlong 1762 (*the Church hadland* 1674, *v.* **hēafod-land**); Commonham Lane 1762 (*v.* **commun, hamm**); Cow Close Nook 1762 (*Cowclose* 1674, *v.* **nōk**); Crook(e) Dyke Furlong 1762 (*v.* **krókr, dík**); Flash Fd 1762 (*the flashe* 1625, (*ye*) *Water Flash* c.1680, 1685, 1686, *the Flash Feild* 1674, *v.* **flask, flasshe**; one of the great fields of the village, earlier called *the easte feilde*, *v. infra*); Little Flash Furlong 1762 (*v.* the preceding f.n.); Flaxland Cl 1763, 1782[2], 1789[2] (*flaxlandes* 1625, *Flaxland furland* (sic) 1674 (*v.* **furlang**) (*v.* **flēax, land**); Flaxleys Cl 1785, 1838 (*the flax leyes* 1625, *Flaxlayes* 1674, *v.* **flēax, leys**; but note the observations on *Flaxwell* and *Short Flax Leyes* in Stonesby f.ns. (b)); Fuzlehole 1758 (*Fosill hole* c.1680, *v.* **fossile, hol**[1]; in early usage, *fossil* was used of any rock or mineral substance dug out of the earth, *v.* OED *s.v.* fossil B. 1); the Grange Cl 1763 (*the graunge close* 1625), Great Grange Cl 1762, 1764 (*the greate graunge close* 1625, *the Greate Grange Closse* 1661, 1675, cf. *the greate grange close hedge* 1625 (*v.* **hecg**), *v.* Old Grange *supra*); Hall Cls 1762 (*the Hawle Close* 1625, *the Hall Close* 1674, *v.* **hall**); Highway Cl 1758 (*ye highway Close* c.1680, *highway close* 1685, 1686); Home Cl 1804 (*the Home Closes* 1712, *v.* **home**); Hill Furlong 1762 (*the Hill* 1674); Jewel(l) Cl 1762 (prob. with the surn. *Jewell, v.* Reaney *s.n.*); Lammas Cl 1762 (*v.* **lammas**); Little Cl 1804; the Lodge Cls 1762 (*the Lodge Close* l.16, 1617, *v.* **loge**, cf. Broughton Lodges *supra*); the Mill 1758, 1762 (1625, 1685, 1686, *ye Wind Mill* c.1680; the windmill is shown on the 1st edn O.S. map of 1836 on the headland opposite Hecadeck Lane), Mill Fd 1762 (*the Millfeild* l.16, *Millne feild* 1617, *the Milne feilde* 1674, *Mill Feild* c.1680, *Milnfeild* 1685, 1686, *v.* **myln, feld**; one of the great fields of the village, also called *the weste feild, v. infra*, cf. *the Milne furland* (sic) 1674 (*v.* **furlang**)), Mill Hill 1762 (cf. *the mill hill hades* 1625 (*v.* **hēafod**), *Millhill Furlong* 1674), Mill Hill Cl 1797, Mill Pasture 1762; Mott Cl 1762 (*Mott* is apparently a surn. here; no moated site (ME *mote*) is evident in the area of the village, unless what appears to be an embanked reservoir at SK62 689241 is referred to; nor is there evidence for a moot-site (OE *mōte*)); Nether Fd 1762; Old Mill Furlong 1762 (perh. cf. *le milnedam* Hy 3, *Milldam* 1674, *v.* **myln, damme**; this appears to refer to a lost watermill, presum. on Dalby Brook); Overhills 1758 (*v.* **uferra**); Sheep Coat ~, Sheep Cote Cl 1762 (*the sheepecoate* 1625, *Sheepcoat close* 1674, *v.* **scēp-cot**); Smite Fd 1762 (*the Smite Feild* 1674; one of the great fields of the township and lying towards R. Smite; it was earlier called *The Northe Feilde, v. infra*); Turners Cl 1762 (with the surn. *Turner*); Town Street 1762 (*v.* **tūn**; the main street of the village); the First ~ ~ ~, Wash Dyke Cl 1853 (*v.* **wash-dyke**; the site of a sheep-dip); White Wong 1763, 1782[2], 1785, 1789[2], 1808, 1809 (c.1680, 1743, *the white wonge* 1625, *White Wonge* 1674, 1685, 1686), Old, New White Wong 1853, White Wong Cl 1762, 1782[1], 1784 *et passim* to 1838 (1748), White Wong Nook now Little White Wongs 1797 (*the white wonge nooke* 1625, *Whitewong nooke* 1674 (*v.* **nōk**)) (*v.* **hwīt, hvítr, vangr**; perh. with ModEdial. *white* 'infertile' in contrast to *black* 'fertile'); Willow Row 1808, ~ ~ Cl 1826 (*v.* **wilig, rǣw**).

(b) *Aboue ye Brooke* 1674 (*v.* **aboven**; a furlong in Flash Fd *supra*); *Aboue the Smite* 1674 (*v.* **aboven**; a furlong in Smite Fd *supra*); *Bacons Meade* c.1680 (*v.* **mǣd**; with the surn. *Bacon*); *Barnes East* ~, *Barnes West Close* 1685, 1686 (with the surn. *Barnes*); *bastard leyes* 1625 (*v.* **bastard, leys** and *the bastard lays* in Bottesford f.ns. (b)); *Mr Belleyes headland* 1625 (*v.* **hēafod-land**); *Blewhill* 1674, *blewe hill hades* 1625 (*v.* **hēafod**), *v.* **blēo, hyll**); *a Close late Blunkleys* (sic) c.1680, *Buncly's Closes* 1685, *Buncklys* 1686 (with the surn. *Bunkley*); *Bottlepits* 1674 (*v.* **pytt**; *bottle* may refer to shape, otherwise *v.* **botl**); *Bradshawes Close* c.1680, *Bradshaws* ~ 1685, 1686 (with the surn. *Bradshaw*); *Brakyn Close* l.16 (*v.* **brakni, clos(e)**); *the land of Mr Brookesby, the leyes of Mr Brookesbye* 1625 (*v.* **leys**) (the *Brooksby* family originated in the village of this name six miles to the south-west); *Broughton brooke* 1625, *Broughton Bridge* 1674, *Broughton ditch* 1674 (with reference to a boundary ditch), *Broughton Wood* 1547 × 58, 1617, c.1680 (*v.* **wudu**); *Brownes Close* c.1680, *Robt. Brown(e)s* ~ 1685, 1686; *Henry Brownes headland* 1625 (*v.* **hēafod-land**), *the land of Henry Browne* 1625, *the leyes of Henry Browne* 1625 (*v.* **leys**); *Bullivants close* 1685, *bulivants* ~ 1686 (with the surn. *Bullivant, v.* Reaney *s.n.*); *Cants Woldes* c.1680 (*v.* **wald**; cf. *Wm. Cant* 1712 of Nether Broughton); *Clauson Bridge* 1625, *Claxton Bridge* 1674 (crossing R. Smite on Clawson Lane), *Clauson brooke* 1625 (prob. another name for R. Smite); *Cold morning close* 1641 (poss. a close in a hollow or in the shadow of woodland, where frost lingered or mist remained; alternatively, a name implying 'cold comfort'); *the Common hades* 1674 (*v.* **commun, hēafod**); *the common hedge* 1625 (*v.* **commun, hecg**); *New Conygree* l.16, *the Newe Conigrave,* ~ ~ *Conygrave* 1617, *the old Connigree* l.16, *the old Conygrave* 1617, *Cuningry* 1635, *the cunerie* 1686, *Cunnary Closes* c.1680 (*v.* **coningre**); *Copthorne* 1674 (*v.* **copped, þorn**); *Coopers close* 1685, 1686 (with the surn. *Cooper*); *Crookesome* 1674 (prob. 'Krōk's water-meadow', *v.* **holmr**; the pers.n. is Scand (ODan *Krōk*, ON *Krókr*)); *Dexters Close* 1685, *Dexsters* ~ 1686 (with the surn. *Dexter*); *Dockey Wonge* 1625, *Dockewong* 1674 (*v.* **docce, -ig³, vangr**); *Drapers Close* c.1680 (with the surn. *Draper*); *the land of my Lord Duke of Buckingham* 1625; *the easte feilde* 1625 (*v.* **ēast, feld**; one of the great fields of the village, later called Flash Fd, *v. supra*); *east woulds* 1685, 1686 (*v.* **wald**); *Francks Close* 1685, 1686 (with the surn. *Frank(s), v.* Reaney *s.n.*); *the gossy Close* 1625, *the Gossye close* 1674 (*v.* **gorstig**); *gomfree home* (sic) 1625, *Godfrys holme* 1674 (*v.* **holmr**; from their contexts in consecutive glebe terriers, the forms appear to refer to the same feature, with the 1674 spelling presenting the first el. as the surn. *Godfrey*; whether it is the 1625 or the 1674 spelling which is garbled is uncertain, but cf. *Gounfreyholme* 1428 in Leicester (and *Thomas Gounfrey* 1342, 1369 and *Agnes Gounfrey* 1416, both of Leicester), *v.* Lei **1** 201)); *Grange land* 1685, *the graung land* 1686 (*v.* Old Grange *supra*); *Hicklinge brooke* 1625 (presum. another name for Dalby Brook; Hickling parish in Notts. adjoins to the north-west, the brook forming the county boundary here); *the Hill Close* 1617 (cf. Hill Furlong *supra*); *Holts Close* c.1680 (with the surn. *Holt*); *Horse Close* c.1680, 1685, 1686; *Hubbards Closs* 1685, ~ *close* 1686, *Wid' Hubbards close* 1685, 1686 (i.e. *Widow* ~ ~); *the inclosed groundes* 1625 (*v.* **grund**: an otherwise unrecorded early enclosure); *kirk(e)seck* 1625, *Kirkesick* 1674 (*v.* **kirkja, sík**); *the land meere* 1625, *Landmeere* 1674, *Landmere hedge* 1674 (*v.* **land-gemǣre**; a boundary eventually marked by a hedge);

listers close 1685 (*v. Nobles Close, infra*); *the little furlong* 1674 (in Mill Fd); *longe furlonge* 1625 (in Mill Fd); *the long Furland* (sic) 1674 (*v.* **furlang**; in Smite Fd); *the long hedge* 1674; *Lousie Bush* c.1680, *Lousibush* 1686, *the lowsy bushe close* 1625, *Lowsy bushe close hedge* 1625 (*v.* **lowsy, busc**; poss. describing a piece of scrub infested by insects (cf. **lūs-þorn**)); *le Lund* 1316, *Lowne Hill* c.1680 (*v.* **lundr**); *Thomas Mans Close* c.1680, *Mans close* 1685, 1686, *mans little close* 1685, *Wid' Mans Close* 1685 (i.e. *Widow ~ ~*), *Will. Mans close* 1686; *the meadowe Close* 1625; *Nath. Meadows ground* 1685, *~ Medows ~* 1686; *Melton Bridge* 1625, 1674 (on the road to Melton Mowbray to the south); *the Nether end of the Smite* 1674 (a furlong in Smite Fd *supra*); *Nobles Close* c.1680 (in the possession of *Christopher Noble* c.1680), *nobles and listers close* 1685, *nobles & Listers* 1686 (jointly in the possession of the *Noble* and *Lister* families); *The Northe Feilde* 1625 (*v.* **norð, feld**; one of the great fields of the village, later Smite Fd *supra*); *Old Pasture* c.1680, 1685, 1686; *Parris Close* c.1680 (with the surn. *Parris*); *the parsonage close* 1625, *the Parsonage gap* 1674 (*v.* **gap**), *the Parsonage yard* 1674 (*v.* **geard**); *the pasture* 1674; *Pin(c)ks close* 1685, 1686 (with the surn. *Pin(c)k, v.* Reaney *s.n.*); *Pooles tenement* c.1680, 1686, *pools ~* 1685 (*v.* **tenement**; with the surn. *Pool(e)*); *the Quobs* 1674 (*v.* **cwabba**); *the land of Samuell Raye* 1625; *redbancks* 1625, *Redbankes* 1674 (*v.* **banke**; with **hrēod** or **rēad**); *Redhill* l.16, *Redhill al's Reed(e)hill* 1617, *Reedhill* c.1680, 1685, 1686 (*v.* **hyll**; with **hrēod** or **rēad**); *Richisons Close* c.1680, *Richardsons ~* 1685, 1686 (with the surn. *Richardson*); *St Mary headland* 1625, *Saint Maryes Hadland* 1674 (*v.* **hēafod-land**; abutting the parish church of St Mary); *Sakertoft* c.1268 bis, *Sacirtoft* c.1268 (p), *Sakirtoft* c.1268 (p) bis (*v.* **toft**; with the ME occupational surn. *Saker* 'a maker of sacks or of sackcloth', a derivative of OE *sacc* or ON *sekkr* 'a sack', *v.* Reaney *s.n.* Sacker); *(in) Stedfold Dale* 1625 (*v.* **stōd-fald, dalr**); *Sheperdsons Close* 1617, *farr, hither Sheppardsons Close* c.1680 (with the surn. *Sheperdson/Sheppardson, v.* Reaney *s.n.* Shepherdson); *William Simpsons headland* 1625 (*v.* **hēafod-land**); *Smallys Close* c.1680, 1685, 1686 (with the surn. *Smalley*); *the Smithes shop* 1625 (*v.* **smið, sc(e)oppa**); *Christofer Smithes land* 1625; *Henry Smiths Close* 1674; *John Smiths Close* 1685, 1686; *Alice Stringers close* 1685, 1686, *Stringers tenement* 1686 (*v.* **tenement**; with the surn. *Stringer*); *Festus Taylers hedge* 1625 (*v.* **hecg**; a boundary hedge); *Taylors penn* 1674 (*v.* **penn²**); *Thornney close* 1674 (*v.* **þornig**); *the land of Thomas Trentum* 1625; *Walkers Close* c.1680 (with the surn. *Walker*); *Water furrowes* 1625, 1674 (*v.* **wæter, furh**; perh. 'furrows where water tends to lie', but *v. waterfurris* in Muston f.ns. (b)); *the Waterplott* c.1680, *water plott* 1685, 1686 ('the plot beside the water', *v.* **wæter, plot**); *the land of John Watkin* 1625, 1674, *the pasture close of John Watkin* 1625; *Welseck* 1625, *Welsick* 1674 (*v.* **wella, sík**); *the weste feild, the west feylde* 1625 ('the west field', *v.* **west, feld**; one of the great fields of the village, later Mill Fd *supra*); *Williamsons Closs* 1685, *~ close* 1686 (with the surn. *Williamson*); *the wood* l.16, *the Wood Close* l.16 (*v.* **clos(e)**) (*v.* **wudu**); *Wrights close* 1685, 1686, *Wrights Cottage* 1685, 1686 (*v.* **cotage**) (with the surn. *Wright*); *Edward Wrights layes* 1674 (*v.* **leys**); *the land of Thomas Wright senr.* 1625, *the leyes of Thomas Wright* 1625 (*v.* **leys**); *the land of Richard Wright* 1625.

2. OLD DALBY

The settlement is included in Goscote Wapentake in 1086 DB. It later became part of the East Goscote Hundred. Kelly 1925 places Old Dalby in Framland Hundred.

> *Dalbi* 1086 DB, Hy 2 Berkeley (p), 1208 Cur, *Dalbia* c.1130
> LeicSurv, *Dalby* 1156 (1318) Ch (p), 1209 × 35 RHug, 1235 Pat
> *et passim* to 1316 *RTemple* bis, 1325 *MiD et freq*, *Daleby* 1251,
> 1254 Fine, Edw 1 *CroxR*, 1314 *GarCart*, 1324 *RTemple*
> *Daubi* 1206, 1207 P, 1214 Cur, John Berkeley (p), *Dauby* 1208 Cur,
> 1209 Derby, 1214 Cur, 1209 × 35 RHug *et passim* to Edw 1
> *CroxR*, 1338 Hosp, 1340 Ch, *Dawby* 1543 ExchAO

'The farmstead, village in the valley', *v.* **dalr, bȳ**. Spellings with *u* for *l* are due to AN influence. Old Dalby lies in a small valley at the edge of the Wolds. The current affix *Old* ~ is a late form of *Wold* (*v. infra*). The manor was given by Robert Bossu, Earl of Leicester, to the Knights Hospitallers of St John of Jerusalem in the reign of Henry II (cf. *Magister Hospitalis Jerlm' de Daubi* 1206 P). They had a preceptory here.

Affixes are variously added as: ~ *de Wauz* 1209 Derby, ~ *super Wald*(*as*) c.1130 LeicSurv, 1316 *RTemple*, 1325 *MiD*, 1327 SR, ~ *super Woldas* Edw 2 *MiD*, ~ *super* (*le*) *Wold*(*e*) 1316 FA, 1408 Inqaqd *et passim* to 1499, 1529 *RTemple*, ~ *on le Walde* 1408 Pat, ~ *de le Woldys* 1505 *RTemple*, ~ *on the Wold* 1510 CoPleas, 1526, 1529 *RTemple*, ~ (*up*)*on the Would*(*s*) 1576 Saxton, 1641, 1715, 1719 LML, ~ *super le Wold*(*e*)*s* 1604 SR, 1709 LML, ~ *super le Oldes* 1555 Pat, ~ (*vp*)*on* (*the*) *Olds* 1610 Speed, 1688 LML, *Old* ~ 1718 ib *et freq* (*v.* **wald**), ~ *Hospital*(*i*) 1254 Val, 1314 *GarCart*, 1340, 1344 Nichols, ~ *Pital* 1253 ×58 RHug (*v.* **hospital**).

BACK LANE, *v.* **back**. BRIDGET'S COVERT, *v.* **cover(t)**. CHURCH LANE, *v.* St John the Baptist's Church, *infra*. COPELAND COTTAGES, *v.* **kaupaland**. CROMPTON'S PLANTATION. CROWN INN, *Crown* 1846, 1863 White, 1925 Kelly. DALBY BROOK, *the Brok* 1316 *RTemple*, *a ryndill called Dalbie broke* 1533 Thoresby (*v.* **rynel**), *The Dalby Brook* 1836 O, *v.* **brōc**. DALBY LODGES, 1836 O, *v.* **loge**. DALBY WOLDS, *Dalby Wold* 1325, 1326 Ipm, *Wold' de Dalby* Edw 2, *le Oldez* 1543 ExchAO, *the Woulds* 1758 *Rental*, *v.* **wald**. DEBDALE HILL, *Depedale* 1316

RTemple (p), *v.* **dēop, dalr**. DRYPOT LODGE. DURHAM OX (P.H.) (lost), *Durham Ox (Six Hills)* 1846 White; at Six Hills on Fosse Way. FAIRHAM BROOK, 1836 O; the upper reach of the stream which flows into R. Trent at Wilford, *v.* Nt 4. FISHPOND PLANTATION. GIBSON'S LANE. GRANGE COTTAGES, *v.* Old Dalby Grange *infra*. THE GREEN, *sur le grene* Hy 3 *Crox* (p), *super le Grene* 1327 SR (p), *v.* **grēne**². HALL PLANTATION, *v.* Old Dalby Hall *infra*. HILLCREST. HILL TOP FM. HOME FARM LODGE, *v.* **home**. HOME LODGE HOLLOW, *v.* **home, holh**. LAWN LANE, *the Launde* l.16 *Terrier*, 1617 *Dun*, *The Lawne* 1666 *Rental*, *the laund* 1686 *ib*, *Lawnes* 17 *ib*, *The Lawns* 1925 Kelly, *v.* **launde**. LAWNFIELD, *v.* Lawn Lane. LONGCLIFF HILL, *Long Cliffe* l.16 *Terrier*, 1617 *Dun*, 17 *Rental*, *Long Clyffe* 1617 *Dun*, *long cliff* 1685, 1686 *Rental*, *Long Clift* 1758 *ib*, *v.* **lang**¹, **clif**. LOWER GRANGE FM, *v.* Old Dalby Grange *infra*. MARRIOTT'S SPINNEY, cf. *Edward and Robert Marriott, farmers* 1846 White. NORTH LODGE. NOTTINGHAM LANE, leading to Nottingham via Fosse Way. OLD DALBY GRANGE is *The Grange* 1877 White, *v.* **grange**. OLD DALBY HALL, 1925 Kelly, *Hall* 1836 O, *Dalby Hall* 1846, 1863, 1877 White, *v.* **hall**; it is preceded by *the Manner house* 1685, 1686 *Rental*, *v.* **maner**. OLD DALBY LODGE. OLD DALBY WOOD, 18 Nichols, *Dawby wood* 1543 ExchAO, *Dalby Wood* 1576 Saxton, 1720 MagBrit, 1806 Map, *v.* **wudu**. PADDY'S LANE. PARADISE LANE (local), *Paradise* 1720 Nichols, *v.* **paradis**. PLOUGH (P.H.) (lost), *Plough* 1846, 1863 White, *Plough Inn* 1877 ib. ST JOHN THE BAPTIST'S CHURCH, *Church (St John)* 1846, 1863, 1877 White, *Church (St John the Baptist)* 1925 Kelly; the earlier church is recorded as *ecclesie de Dalby*, ~ *de Dauby* 1220 MHW. SIX HILLS LANE, leading to *Six Hills* 1846, 1863, 1877 White; at the parish boundary on Fosse Way. STATION RD. THORNEY HOLLOW, *v.* **þornig, holh**. TIP COTTAGES are located at the end of a railway siding, where tipped waste has accumulated. TUNNEL LODGE, built above a railway tunnel. UPPER GRANGE FM, *v.* Old Dalby Grange *supra*. THE VICARAGE, 1925 Kelly; it is *The Parsonage* 1877 White. WAVENDON GRANGE, *v.* **grange**. WOOD'S HILL, 1836 O, cf. *Henry Wood* 1666 SR of Old Dalby.

FIELD-NAMES

Undated forms in (a) are 1758 *Rental*; forms dated 1782 and 1784 are *HDW*. Forms throughout dated 1210 are Nichols; 1262 are Fine; 13, Edw 2 and 1325 are *MiD*; 1316 are *RTemple*; 1543 are ExchAO; l.16 are

Terrier; 1617 and 1666 are *Dun*; 1670 are *Lease*; 1685, 1686, 17[1] and 17[2] are *Rental*.

(a) Adcock's Plat (*v.* **plat**; with the surn. *Adcock*); Tho. Bishops House & Homestead (*v.* **hām-stede**); Brook Cl (*v.* Dalby Brook *supra*); Hemsly's Plat (*v.* **plat**; with the surn. *Hemsley*); Hopkin Cl (with the surn. *Hopkin*); Long Cl (1666, cf. *west long close* 1686, *east, west midle long close* 1685, 1686, 17[2], *Upper Long Close* 1685, 1686, 17[2], *east, west neather long close* 1685, ~ *Nether* ~ ~ 1686, *Ann Flowers Long Close* 17[2]); Nether Fd (*the Nether feild* 17[2], ~ ~ *Field* 1670); Pasture Plat (*v.* **plat**); Pirkin Arbour (*Perkin Arbor* 1685, *Perking* ~ 1686, *Perkins* ~ 17[2] (*v.* **erber**; with the surn. *Perkin*); the Platt 1782, Platt Cl 1784 (*v.* **plat**); Poor's Cl 1846, 1863, 1877 White (*v.* **pouer(e)**; rents from this provided assistance for the village poor, *v.* Field 192); Sand Plat 1784 (*Sand plott* 1685, ~ *plot* 1686, *v.* **sand**, **plot**, **plat**); Shoby Hills (*Sholby hill* 1685, 1686, *Shoby hill* 17[2]; the lost settlement of Shoby was in Grimston parish which adjoins to the south); Woulds Cl (1685, 1686, *v.* **wald**).

(b) *Alsops house* 17[2] (with the surn. *Alsop*); *Banland* 1316 (*v.* **bēan**, **land**); *Bells Close* 1685, 1686, *Bells Cottage* 17[2] (*v.* **cotage**) (with the surn. *Bell*); *Blakewelleclif* 1325 (*v.* **blæc**, **wella**, **clif**); *Boothes feild* 1617, *Booth Close* 1666, 17[1] (with the surn. *Booth*); *Brandriffs tenement* 1685, 1686 (*v.* **tenement**; with the surn. *Brandriff*); *le Breche* 1316 (*v.* **brēc**); *Bullam Close* 1617, *Bulholme* ~ 1685, 1686, 17[2] (*v.* **bula**, **holmr**); *Campions house* 17[2] (cf. *Thomas Campion* 17[2]); *Anthony Church his shop* 17[1] (*v.* **sc(e)oppa**), *Churches yard* 1685 (*v.* **geard**); *Coleseed plott* 1685, 1686, ~ *Plot* 17[2] (*v.* **plot**; **colseed** (*Brassica oleifera*) was cultivated for its seed, the source of 'rape' or 'sweet' oil); *Coopers Close* 1685, 1686 (with the surn. *Cooper*); *the Cow Pasture* 17[2]; *Coxe close* 1685, 1686 (with the surn. *Cox*); *Crofts closes* 17[2] (with the surn. *Croft*); *Dalewang* 1210 *bis* (*v.* **dalr**, **vangr**); *lez demesne lands* 1543 (*v.* **demeyn**, **land**); *Douesing* 13 ('Duve's meadow', *v.* **eng**; the pers.n. *Duve* is ODan (ON *Dúfa*), cf. Dowthorpe, YW 1 16 and Dowthorpe Hall, YE 47); *Emanuell hook(e)* 1685, 1686, *Emanuel Hooke* 17[2], *Manuell Hooke* 17[1], ~ ~ *Close* 1666 (*v.* **hōc**; with the surn. *Emanuel*); *fattbutts* 1685, *fatbuts* 1686, *Fat Butts* 17[2] (*v.* **fætt**, **butte**); *Ann Flowers close* 1685, 1686; *Flyntilandes* 1316 ('selions with flinty soil', *v.* **flinti**, **land**; the earliest citation in OED for *flinty* in this sense is for 1626); *Gills yard* 1685, 1686 (*v.* **geard**; with the surn. *Gill*); *Glappewellegrif* 1210 (originally prob. an OE *Glappanwella 'Glappa's spring', *v.* **wella**, cf. Glapwell, Db 258; to this was later added Scand **gryfja** 'a pit, a deep valley'); *the Gores* l.16, 1685, 1686, *the Goores*, *Gores Close* 17[2] (*v.* **gāra**); *Grimston(e) hill* 1685, 1686, *Grimson* ~ 17[2] (Grimston parish adjoins to the south); *sup' le Heth'* 1327 SR (p) (*v.* **hǣð**); Holmes Close 17[2] (with either the surn. *Holmes* or **holmr** 'a water-meadow'); *Holts Close* 17[2], *Holts hill close* 1685, 17[2], *Hoult* ~ ~ 1686 (with the surn. *Holt*); *House Close* 1685; *Keens Crofft* 1685, ~ *croft* 1686 (*v.* **croft**; with the surn. *Keen*); *Kenewelle schicke* (sic) 1262 (*v.* **wella**, **sīc**, **sík**; with the OE pers.n. *Cēna*); *Knotts Close* 1617, 1685, *Knot(t)s closes* 1686, 17[2] (with the surn. *Knott*); *Land Close* 1666, 17[1] (*v.* **land**; the close comprised the consolidation of an unspecified number of 'lands' or selions of an earlier great field); *Lane close* 1666, 1685, 1686, 17[2] (*v.* **lane**); *Lealands* 1685, *Lelands* 1686, *lealand close* 1685, *leland close* 1686, *Leylands Close* 17[2] (*v.* **lǣge**, **land**)); *the Little Close* 1617; *the Meadowe* l.16 (*v.* **mǣd** (**mǣdwe** obl.sg.));

Medilforlong 1316 (*v.* **middel, meðal, furlang**); *Miln plott* 1685, *the Milln plott* 1686, *Mill Plot* 17² (*v.* **myln, plot**); *New close* 1543, 1686, 17², *the Newe Close* l.16, *ye new close* 1685 (*v.* **nīwe, clos(e)**); *the old orchard* 1617; *Old thorne* l.16, 1617, 1685, 17², *Ould thorne* 1617, *oldthorn* 1686 (*v.* **þorn**; the first el. may be **wald** rather than **ald**); *the Parke and Padock* 1617 (*v.* **paddock**), *the Parke* 1666, 1685, 1686, 17², *Dalby Parke* 1666, 17¹, *the Park* 17¹ (*v.* **park**); *Parsons Close* 17¹ (*v.* **persone**); *Peselandesick* 1210 (*v.* **pise, land, sík**); *the first plott* 1686, *the Second plott* 1685, *2d plott* 1686, *3d and 4th plotts* 1685, *3rd and 4th plots* 1686, *5th and 6th plott* (sic) 1685, ~ ~ ~ *plots* 1686, (*the*) *7th plott* 1685, 1686 (*v.* **plot**); *Rougholes* 1685, *rough holes* 1686 (*v.* **rūh¹, hol¹**); *Sallowes* 1617, *East Sallowes* 17², ~ *Sallows* 1685, 1686, *South and West Sallowes* 17², *Great Sallows* 1685, 1686, *Sallowes Close* l.16, *Sallow Close* 1666, *Salufurlong* 13 (*v.* **furlang**) (*v.* **salh**); *Sandy Close* 1666, 17², *Sandy Close Meadow* 17¹, *Sandy plott* 1685, 1686, ~ *Plot* 17² (*v.* **plot**) (*v.* **sandig**); *Shepecotte close* 1543 (*v.* **scēp-cot, clos(e)**); *Sletyng* 1316 (*v.* **sléttr, eng**); *Smalthorndale* 1262 (*v.* **smæl, þorn**; with the final el. either **dalr** or **deill**); *Stondale* Edw 2 (*v.* **stān**; with the final el. either **dalr** or **deill**); *Strethelbut'* 1210 (*v.* **stræt, hyll, butte**; with reference to the Roman road Margary 58a across the Wolds); *Sudstubbinges* 1210 (*v.* **sūð, stubbing**)); *Wallescliffe* 1543 (perh. for **Waldescliffe* 'the steep slope of the Wolds', *v.* **wald, clif**; formally the OE pers.n. *Walh* or the ODan pers.n. *Val* (ON *Valr*) are poss. as the first el., but pers.ns. are rarely compounded with *clif*); *Willow poole plott* 1685, 1686, *Willow Pool Plot* 17² (*v.* **wilig, pōl¹, plot**); *Woodhowse* l.16, *Waddowes* 1617, *the Woodhouse* 17¹, *Wadhouse* 17², *East, West Wadhouse* 17², *Great Wadhouse* 1685, 1686, 17², *Lane Wadhouse* 1685, 1686 (*v.* **lane**), *Woodhouse Close* 1666 (*v.* **wudu, hūs**); *the Wood Nooke* l.16 (*v.* **wudu, nōk**); *Wooldales* l.16, 1617, *the Neather end* ~ ~, *the Upper End of Wooledales* 1617, *Netherwolddales* 17¹, *Over wooldales* 1666 (*v.* **uferra**), *east and west neather wooldales* 1685, ~ ~ ~ *nether* ~ 1686, *East and West Nether Wouldales* 17², *east* ~ ~, *west over wooldales* 1685, 1686, ~ ~ *Wouldales* 17² (*v.* **wald, deill**).

1. BUCKMINSTER

Bvcheminstre 1086 DB, *Bucheminestr'* c.1130 LeicSurv
Buccemenistre 1180 P, *Buckeminster* 1236 RGros, *Buckeministr'*
 1236 ib, *Buckemynstre* 1360 Brase
Bukeministr' 1195 P, 1212 Cur *et passim* to 1240 RGros,
 Bukemenistr' 1196 ChancR, 1198, 1199, 1200 P, *Bukemenestr(e)*
 1212 RBE (p), 1242 Fees, *Bukeministr(e)* 1237 RGros, 1242 Fees,
 Hy 3 *Crox, Bukemynstre* 1319, 1323 Pat *et passim* to 1399 AD,
 Bukeminster 1320 Abbr, *Bukemynster* 1328 Ass, 1369 Banco
Bokeminster 1261 Cur (p), 1284 Ass (p) *et passim* to 1327 SR (p),
 Bokeministre 1298 Ipm, 1298 Fine (p), *Bokemynstr(e)* c.1291
 Tax, 1313 Pat *et passim* to 1428 FA, *Bokemynstir* 1316 ib,
 Bokemynster 1360 LAS
Bokminstre 1298 Fine (p), 1305 FA (p), 1306 IpmR, 1339 Banco,
 Bokmynstre 1307 Fine (p), 1324 Pat (p), 1333 Banco, *Bokmynster*
 1308 ib
Bucminstr' 1254 Val, *Bucministr'* 1266, 1272 RGrav, *Bukmynstr(e)*
 1276 RH, 1279 RGrav *et passim* to 1362 Pat (p) *et freq* to 1444
 AD, 1451 Pat, *Bukmynster* 1318 Inqaqd, 1451 Pat *et passim* to
 1502 *MiscAccts*, 1520 *Rental et freq* to 1549 Fine
Buckmynster 1491 Banco, 1528 Visit *et passim* to 1571 LEpis, 1576
 Saxton, *Buckmenster* 1507 LWills, *Buckmynstre* 1542 *Rut*,
 Buckminster 1575 LEpis, 1576 LibCl, 1580 LEpis *et freq*
Bukmyster 1537 MinAccts, 1539 *Deed*, 1549 Pat, *Bukemyster* 1539
 MinAccts, *Buckmyster* 1546 Ass, 1549 Pat

'Bucca's minster', *v.* **mynster**. The pers.n. *Bucca* is OE. Bucca was
presumably the founder and patron of the Anglo-Saxon minster church
from which the village took its name. The earliest fabric identified in the
present church is of the second half of the 13th century.

BLUE BULL (P.H.) (lost), *Blue Bull* 1846, 1863, 1877 White. BLUE COW
(P.H.) (lost), *Blue Cow* 1846, 1863 White. BOTTOM PLANTATION, 1841
TA, *v.* **bottom**. BUCKMINSTER HALL, 1831 Curtis, 1846 White, *Hall*
1841 *TA*, *v.* **hall**; note also *the Hall orchyeard* 1700, 1703 *Terrier*, *v.*
orceard. BUCKMINSTER LODGE is *The Lodge* 1877 White, *v.* **loge**.
BUCKMINSTER PARK, 1806 Map, 1824 O, cf. *the Park wall* 1700, 1703,
1788 *Terrier* (*v.* **wall**), *v.* **park**. DURHAM OX (P.H.) (lost), *Durham Ox*
1846 White. DYSART ARMS HOTEL (lost), *Dysart Arms Hotel* 1925
Kelly; named from the Earls of Dysart, resident at Buckminster Park.
GORSE CLOSE PLANTATION, *Gorse Close* 1841 *TA*, *v.* **gorst**. GORSE
PLANTATION. GRANGE FM, *Grange farm* 1925 Kelly, cf. *the grange of
Bukmynster* 1537 MinAccts, *the Grange* 1700, 1708, 1724, 1745, 1788
Terrier, 1841 *TA*, 1846, 1877 White, *v.* **grange**. By at least 1846 ib, *The
Grange* was the name of a field on the south side of the village where
there were 'some traces of a religious house which belonged to Kirby
Bellars Priory'. JACKSON'S PLANTATION. METHODIST CHAPEL. THE
ROOKERY, *v.* **rookery**. ST JOHN THE BAPTIST'S CHURCH is *The Church*
1708, 1708 (18) *Terrier*, *Church (St John)* 1846, 1863 White, *Church
(St John the Baptist)* 1877 ib; it is earlier recorded as *ecclesie de
Bukeministr'* 1220 MHW, 1240 RGros, *ecclesiam de Buckministr'*, ~ *de
Buckeminister* 1236 ib, ~ *de Bukeminstr'* 1237 ib, *ecclesie de
Bokemynstre* 1346, 1363 *Pat*, *ecclesie parochialis de Bukmynster*, ~ *de
Bukmynstre* 1451 ib. Note also *the Church yeard* 1605, 1700, 1703
Terrier, *the Church Yard* 1612, 1708 ib et passim to 1788 ib, *Church
Yard* 1841 *TA*, *v.* **chirche-ȝeard**. THE VICARAGE, 1877 White, 1925
Kelly; it is *the Vicarage House* 1605, 1708, 1724, 1745, 1788 *Terrier*,
~ ~ *howse* 1612 ib. Note also *the Vicarage Garden* 1745, 1788 ib, *the
Vicarage Orchard* 1605, 1612 ib, *the Vicaridg orchyeard* 1700, 1703 ib,
v. **orceard**.

FIELD-NAMES

Undated forms in (a) are 1841 *TA*; forms dated 1788 are *Terrier* and
1802 are *Deed*. Forms throughout dated 1561 (1700) are *Rental*; 1605,
1612, 1700, 1703, 1708, 1708 (18), 1724 and 1745 are *Terrier*; 1607,
1634, 1635, 1636, 1637, 1639 and 1641 are Ipm; 1682, 1682 (1791),
1686 and 1744 are *Surv*.

(a) The Three Acre 1788 (1745), Four Acres, the Seven ~, The Eight ~, The Twelve Acres (*v.* **æcer**); Annis's Cl (with the surn. *Annis*) ; Backside Cl (*v.* **bakside**); Barn Cl; the Beacon Hill 1788 (1700, 1745, *Beacon Hill* 1703, 1708, 1708 (18), *v.* **(ge)bēacon**); Bellam Dike (*v.* **dík**; cf. *Balam Close* 1679 Nichols); Berridges Cl (with the surn. *Berridge*); Beversham's Cl 1788 (*Bevershams Close* 1724, 1745, cf. *Widow Beversham* 1700, *Dr Beuersham* 1703); Blocks Cl (with the surn. *Block*); First, Second Bottom Cl (*v.* **bottom**); Boyfields Cl (with the surn. *Boyfield*); Brick Yard Cl; Brindleys Cl (with the surn. *Brindley*); Buckminster Cl; Burtons Cl (with the surn. *Burton*); Cawthórnes Cl (with the surn. *Cawthorne*); Church Plantation; Coleman Hill 1788 (1700, 1703, 1708, 1708 (18), 1724, 1745, *Colemans* ~ 1708 bis, 1708 (18), *Coleman's* ~ 1708 (18); with the surn. *Coleman*); First, Second Common Hill (*v.* **commun**); Cover Cl (*v.* **cover(t)**); Coverleys Cl (with the surn. *Coverley*); Cow Cl; Cow Row Cl (*v.* **vrá**); Coys Cl (with the surn. *Coy*); Crashleys Cl (with the surn. *Crashley*); The Draycott (cf. *Dracord Close* 1682, *Drackerds* ~ 1682 (1791), 1686, *Draycoat* ~ 1744; 'the shed where drays are kept', *v.* **dræg, cot**); Easts Cl (with the surn. *East*); Elder Dale (*v.* **ellern**; with the second el. either **dalr** or **deill**); The Fatnings (*v.* **fattening**; good pasture used for fattening livestock, *v.* Field 110); Fox Crofts (*v.* **croft**; the first el. is prob. the surn. *Fox* rather than the name of the animal); First, Second Goodacres Cl (with the surn. *Goodacre*); Goodland Cl (prob. with the surn. *Goodland*, *v.* Reaney *s.n.*; otherwise *v.* **gōd**², **land**); Bottom, Middle, Great Grange (cf. *le Graunge close* 1634, *v.* Grange Fm *supra*); Great Cl; the Great Ground 1788 (1745, *v.* **grund**); Grice's Hill (cf. *Ann Grice*, resident in the village in 1841); Hall Garden, Hall Yard (*v.* Buckminster Hall *supra*); First, Middle, Far Hammer Hill (*v.* **hamor, hamarr**); The Haven (prob. a complimentary name for a place of shelter or security for animals; but *v.* Field 111 who notes that some such names may be forms of *Heaven* (which expresses approval) or may even be derived from OE **hæfen** 'a holding of land'); the Head Land 1788 (*the Headland* 1700, 1703, 1724, cf. *the Headland Lane* 1745, *v.* **hēafod-land**); Hewerdines Cl (with the surn. *Hewardine*); Hicklings Cl (with the surn. *Hickling* of a family which originated in the village of this name, nine miles to the north-west in Notts.); High Dike (*v.* **dík**); Hill Cl; Hoe Hill (*v.* **hōh**); Home Cl (*le Home close* 1635, *le two Home closes* 1639, *v.* **home**); House Cl; Hovell Cl (*v.* **hovel**); Hull Lane 1788 (1605, 1700, 1703, 1724, 1745, *Hullane* 1612, *v.* **hyll**); Land Cl (*le Land close* 1635, *v.* **land**; a close made up of an unspecified number of selions or 'lands' of one of the former great fields of the village); Lane Cl (cf. *Atte Lane* 1327 SR (p), *v.* **atte, lane**); Little Mdw; Lodge Cl (*v.* Buckminster Lodge *supra*); Long Cups, Bottom, Middle, Top Long Cups (*Longe Cop* 1607, *v.* **lang**¹, **copp**); Bottom, Top Long Dale (*Longdale* 1537 MinAccts, *Longdale close* 1637, *v.* **lang**¹ ; with a second el. either **dalr** or **deill**); Far, Great, North, West Long Hill; Mansfields Cl (with the surn. *Mansfield*); Marsh Cl (*March Close* 1682, 1686, 1744, *Marshs Close* (sic) 1682 (1791), *Middle marsh close* 1639, *the High or Middle marsh close* 1639, *v.* **mersc**); Bottom Marshalls Cl (with the surn. *Marshall*); Melton Lane 1788 (1700, 1703, 1708, 1708 (18), 1724, 1745; earlier *Melton high(e) way(e)* 1605, 1612, *v.* **hēah-weg**; the road to Melton Mowbray); Mere Gate Cl (*v.* **(ge)mǣre, gata**; with reference to The Drift/Sewstern Lane, the county boundary); Middle Cl; The Mill Fd 1788, Great, Little Mill Fd 1841, the Mill Field Cl 1802 (*the milne feild* 1605, 1612, *the Millfield* 1700, 1703, 1708, 1708 (18), 1724, *the Mill*

Field 1745, v. **myln, feld**; one of the great fields of the township); (the) Old Cl 1788, 1802, 1841 (*the Old close* 1700, 1703, 1708, 1708 (18), 1724, 1745); Over Cl (v. **uferra**); The Paddock (v. **paddock**); The Parks (v. Buckminster Park *supra*); Pingle (*the Pingle* 1641, v. **pingel**); Plantation Cl; Rectors Cl (v. **rectour**); The Red Earth 1788, 1841 (*the Redearth* 1700, 1703, 1708, 1724, 1745, *Redearth* 1700, *Red Earth* 1708, 1708 (18), cf. *Redearth close* 1607 *Reeve, ~ Closse* 1628 *ib, le Red earth close* 1637, v. **rēad, eorðe**); Great, Little Reeves Cl (with the surn. *Reeve*); Roberts Cl (with the surn. *Roberts*); Rouses Cl (with the surn. *Rouse*); Rowleys Cl (with the surn. *Rowley*); Sallow Cl (v. **salh**); Seed Cl (v. **sǣd**; in f.ns. usually referring to sown grass); the Seven Lands 1788, 1841, ~ ~ ~ Cl 1802 (*Seauen lands* 1703, *Seven ~* 1708, 1708 (18), 1724, 1745, v. **land**; an enclosure consolidating seven selions or 'lands' of one of the former great fields of the village); First, Second Short Cobs (these may belong with Long Cups *supra*; otherwise, v. **cobb(e)**); Great, Little Skill Hill (*Skilling hill* 1607, v. **skil, eng, hyll**; on the county boundary with Lincs.); the Sow Green 1788, Bottom, Top Sow Green, Great Sow Green 1841, the Sow Green Cl 1802 (*the Sowe greene* 1612, *the Sow Green* 1700, 1708, 1708 (18), 1724, 1745, *the Sowgreen close* 1700, 1703, v. **sūð, grēne**[2]); Sproxton Cl (Sproxton parish adjoins to the north-west); Sproxton Lane 1788 (1700, 1703, 1708, 1708 (18), 1724, 1745, *Sproxton waye* 1605, *Sproson ~* 1612 (v. **weg**); the road to Sproxton); Steanby Lane 1788 (1700, 1703, 1724, *Steansby Lane* 1708; the road to Stainby in Lincs. which adjoins to the east); Suttons Cl (with the surn. *Sutton*); Taylors Cl (with the surn. *Taylor*); Three Cornered Cl (v. **three-cornered**); Top Plantation (cf. Bottom Plantation *supra*); the Town Homestalls 1788 (1745, cf. *the home inclosures of the Town* 1700, 1708, 1708 (18), ~ ~ *closures ~ ~ ~* 1703, *the Inclosures of the Town* 1724, y. **hām-stall, tūn, inclosure**); the Vicarage Cow Pasture 1788 (*the Vicaridg Cowpasture* 1700, 1703, ~ *Vicarage ~* 1708, 1708 (18), 1745); Wash Dike Cl (v. **wash-dyke**; the site of a sheep-dip); Water Furrows 1788 (1700, 1708, 1708 (18), 1724, 1745, *Waterfurrows closes* 1607, *Waterfurrows leasewes* 1607 (v. **lǣs (lǣswe** dat.sg.)), v. **wæter, furh** and *waterfurris* in Muston f.ns. (b)); Weaver's Cl 1788, First, Second Weavers Cl (*Weavers Close* 1708, 1708 (18), 1724, *Weaver ~* 1745; with the surn. *Weaver*); Wench Leas (*Wensloes ground* 1700, *the ground called Wenslows* 1703, *Wenchlys ground* 1724, v. **grund**; with the surn. *Wensley*, cf. *Thomas Wensley* 1605 of Buckminster); Winter Hill 1788, Great, Little ~ ~ 1841, Winter hill Cl 1802 (*Winter Hill* 1745; perh. a reduced form of **Winterwell Hill, v.* the following f.n.); Winter Well 1788, 1841, the little Winter Well Cl 1802 (*Winterwell* 1605, 1745, *Winterwel* 1708, *Winterwells* 1700, 1703, 1708 (18), *the winter wells* 1724, *Wynterwellfeild* 1561 (1700), *Winterwell feild* 1605, 1612 (v. **feld**), v. **winter, wella**; a spring or stream that flowed only in the winter months (cf. Winterbeck in Bottesford), it gave its name to one of the great fields of the village); Far, First, Middle Wilderness (v. **wildernesse**).

(b) *Mr Ascoughs ground formerly Browns ground* 1703 (v. **grund**); *Tho. Clarkes farme* 1682, *Clarkes farm* 1682 (1791) (v. **ferme**); *Coston Leas* 1637 (v. **leys**; Coston lies immediately to the west); *Cowe pasture* 1635, *the Cowpasture* 1708, 1708 (18), 1724; *Croftlinggate* 1634 ('the road to the little croft', v. **croft, -ling, gata**); *Edgecourt alias Edgcroft* 1542 *Rut* (prob. with the surn. *Edge* (v. Reaney *s.n.*) rather than with **ecg**; **court** may have replaced **croft**); *le Est more* 1520 *Rental* (v. **ēast**,

mōr[1]); *Fulwell* 1634 (*v.* **fūl, wella**); *le Gautreyhill close* 1637 (*v.* **galg-trēow, hyll**); *super le Grene* 1327 SR (p) (*v.* **grēne**[2]); *le Hether close* 1637 (*v.* **hider**); *the High close* 1639; *the Homestall* 1708, 1708 (18) (*v.* **hām-stall**; belonging to the Vicarage *supra*); *Hornesfeild* 1641, *le Hornfeild close* 1637 (*v.* **horn, feld**; one of the great fields of the village); *le Little close* 1637, *The Little Close* 1682, 1682 (1791), 1686, 1744; *Littledale* 1634 (*v.* **lȳtel, lítill**; with either **dalr** or **deill**); *Long close* 1635, 1682, 1682 (1791), 1686, 1744; *Meadow Green* 1724 (*v.* **grēne**[2]); *Mill Hill* 1745; *Long more* 1634, *the More closes* 1607, *Morehill* 1634 (*v.* **mōr**[1]); *Odeney feild* 1561 (1700) (poss. based on an early OE p.n. **Od(d)anēg* 'Od(d)a's raised ground in marsh', *v.* **ēg, feld**); *the Old House* 1637; *the Ox close* 1700, 1703, 1708, 1708 (18) (*v.* **oxa**); *Nottingham Highway* 1612, *Notingham road* 1700, 1708, *Nottingham rode* 1703, ~ *road* 1708 (18), 1724, 1745 (*v.* **hēah-weg**; the principal road to Nottingham which lies to the north-west); *Poleclose* 1561 (1700) (*v.* **pōl**[1], **clos(e)**); *le Shortmarshes* 1639 (*v.* **sc(e)ort, mersc**); *le Square Close* 1639 (*v.* **squar(e)**; referring to shape); *le Twists gates close* 1637 (OED *s.v.* twist sb.[1], 1, defines a *twist* as 'the flat part of a hinge, fastened on a door or gate, and turning on a hook or pintle fixed in the post'); *le Two akers close* 1637 (*v.* **æcer**); *Twocrosseplace* 1607 (*v.* **twēgen, tū, cros, place**); *le Wheateley Bush close* 1635 (*v.* **busc** and cf. *Francis Wheately* 1636 of Buckminster).

2. SEWSTERN

> *Sewesten* 1086 DB, *Sewesterna* 1166 P (p), *Sewestern(e)* 1203 Cur (p), e.13 *BHosp* (p), 1214 Cur (p) *et passim* to 1547 Chap, 1549 Pat, *Sewistern'* 1370 *Wyg* (p), *Sewysterne* 1541 MinAccts
> *Seuesterne* 1185 Templar, 1208 ChancR, 1242 Fees, 1360 Brase, *Seuestorn'* 1205 P (p), 1206 ib (p), *Seuestorne* 1208 ib (p), *Sustron* 1556 Pat
> *Seustern(e)* c.1130 LeicSurv, 1195 P (p), 1196 ChancR (p), 1199 Fine *et freq* to 1399, 1424 AD *et passim* to 1539 *Rut*, *Sesterne* 1522 LEpis
> *Sewstern(e)* 1298 Ipm, 1303 Pat (p), 1356 Banco (p) *et passim* to 1539 *Deed*, 1549 Fine, 1576 Saxton *et freq*
> *Sheusterne* 1412 PRep, 1412 Pat, *Shewesterne* 1609 LML

Probably 'Sǣwīg's thorn', *v.* **þyrne**. Ekwall in DEPN suggests that the second element may be an unrecorded OE **sterne*, possibly a metathesized form of *(ge)strēon* 'property'. However, OE *þyrne* 'a thorn-bush, a thorn-patch' is likelier. In the East Midlands, the ME reflex of *þyrne* frequently appears as *terne*. Voiceless initial *th* was unknown to Norman scribes who replaced it by *t*. For example, in nearby Normanton, *le long terne* Edw 1 is typical and unambiguous and may well represent the modern Normanton Thorns, originally a major stretch of thorn scrubland. A parallel to Sewstern is Kelstern in Lincs. (*Kelesterne* 1185 Templar, *Keylsterne* 1210 (1252) Ch, *Kaillesterna* 1212 Fees, 'Cǣgel's thorn', with an OE pers.n. as the specific). The specific of Sewstern appears to be the gen. sg. of the OE pers.n. *Sǣwīg*. Spellings in *-torn(e)* may represent the variant OE **þorn** 'a thorn-tree, a thorn patch'.

ANGEL INN (lost), *the Angel Inn* 1795 Nichols. BLAISE'S INN (lost), *Blases Inne* 1634 Ipm; the home of the *Blaise* family, with late use of **inn** in its sense 'a dwelling', cf. *Blases Moore* 1652 in neighbouring Wymondham f.ns. (b) and *John Blees* and *Widow Blees* 1745, both also of Wymondham, *v.* Reaney *s.n.* Blaise. BLUE DOG (P.H.) (lost), *Blue Dog* 1846, 1863, 1877 White, 1925 Kelly. THE DRIFT, *v.* **drift**; here, an alternative name for the ancient (later Roman) trackway Sewstern Lane which forms the county boundary with Lincs. HOLY TRINITY CHURCH, by Anthony Salvin, was completed in 1842. Earlier recorded is a *capellam Seusterne* 1220 MHW (with MLat *capella* 'a chapel'). RED LION INN (lost), *Red Lion* 1846, 1863, 1877 White, 1925 Kelly. SEWSTERN GRANGE, 1863 White, *grangiam de Seusterne* 1323 *Pat*, *grang' de Seustern* 1331 (c.1430) *KB*; originally an outlier of Vaudey Abbey in Lincs., *v.* **grange**. WAGGON AND HORSES (P.H.) (lost), *Waggon and Horses* 1846, 1863, 1877 White.

FIELD-NAMES

Undated forms in (a) are 1841 *TA*; those dated 1821 are *Terrier*. Forms throughout dated 1331 (c.1430), 1348 (c.1430), 1349 (c.1430), 1358 (c.1430), Edw 3 (c.1430), 1399 (c.1430) and c.1430 are *KB*; 1520 are *Rental*, 1628 are *Reeve*, while 1634 and 1637 are Ipm.

(a) The Three Acres, The Four ~, The Five ~, The Six ~, The Eight ~, The Ten ~, The Twelve ~, The Thirteen ~, The Eighteen ~, The Nineteen Acres (*v.* **æcer**); Bakers Cl (with the surn. *Baker*); (The) Barn Cl; Barn Hill; Bottom, Top Bass Cl (with the surn. *Bass*); Bede House Cl (*v.* **bed-hūs**; presum. either income from this close helped to support almshouses or almshouses stood adjacent, but if so, these have not been identified); Body Makers Cl (ostensibly a disparaging name for a field hard to till, but a garbled 'bottom acres' is also poss.); Far ~ ~, Broken Dale (*Brocham Dale* 1628; perh. **brōc**, **hamm**, with **dalr** or **deill**); Cheesecake Cl (*v.* **cheesecake**; a triangular enclosure with a curving short end; named from the shape of an individual portion of the confection); Christians Cl (with the surn. *Christian*); Church Cl; Church Gate (*v.* **gata**); Church Land; First, Second, Third, Fourth Common Leys (*v.* **commun, leys**); First, Second Cow Cl (*the Cowe close* 1634), Meer Cow Cl (*v.* **(ge)mǣre**); Far, Near Cow Leys (*v.* **leys**); First, Second Dale, Great, Little Dale (*liteldale* 1331 (c.1430), *lituldale* 1348 (c.1430), 1349 (c.1430), Edw 3 (c.1430), *Westlituldale* 1331 (c.1430) bis (*v.* **west**), *Far little Dale* 1634, *lituldalegate* 1348 (c.1430) (*v.* **gata**), *v.* **lȳtel, lítill**; prob. with **dalr** rather than **deill**); Dovecote Cl (*v.* **dove-cot(e)**); Easts Cl (with the surn. *East*); The Fullwells, Great, Little, Middle Fullwells (cf. *Fulwellegate* 1348 (c.1430), *Fulwellgate* 1349 (c.1430) (*v.* **gata**), *Fulwell close* 1634, *Fulewell* ~ 1745 *Deed*, *v.* **fūl, wella** and note *Fulwell* in Buckminster f.ns. (b)); Nether, Upper Glovers Cl (with the surn. *Glover*); Goodland Cl (*v.* Buckminster f.ns. (a) *s.n.*); Gorse Covert (*v.* **gorst, cover(t)**); Grice's Cl, Grices Hill (with the surn. *Grice*, *v.* Grice's Hill in Buckminster f.ns. (a)); First, Second Grange (*v.* Sewstern Grange *supra*); Hammer Hill (*v.* Buckminster f.ns. (a) *s.n.*); Hill Cl; Hoe Hill (*v.* Buckminster f.ns. (a) *s.n.*); Home Cl (*the Home close* 1634, *v.* **home**); Hovel Cl (*v.* **hovel**); Little ~ ~, Land Cl (closes made up of unspecified numbers of selions or 'lands' of one of the former great fields of the village, *v.* **land**); Lane Cl (*v.* **lane**); Laxtons Cl (with the surn. *Laxton*); Little Long Hill (cf. *Longhill close* 1634); Long Cl; Liver Cl (*v.* **lēfer**); Lows Cl (with the surn. *Low*); Maddox Cl (with the surn. *Maddox*, *v.* Reaney *s.n.* Maddock); Margotts Cl (with the surn. *Margott*, *v.* Reaney *s.n.* Margetts); Marshalls Bottom, Marshalls Top Cl, Marshalls Plantation (with the surn. *Marshall*); Meer Cl (*v.* **(ge)mǣre**); Mill Fd; Mock Beggar (on the boundary with Wymondham in the extreme south-west of the parish; this example appears to be the name of a close rather than of a building, which is more usual; associated with hunger and neglect, *v.* Mockbeggar, Ru 157–8); The Moor, First, Second Moor, (The) Great, (The) Little Moor (Little Moor 1821), (The) Long Moor (Long Moor 1821), First, Second, Third Long Moor (cf. *Long Moor Closse* 1628, *v.* **clos(e)**), Locks Moor (either with **loc** or with the surn. *Lock*), Nether, Upper Millers Moor (with the surn. *Miller*) (*mora de Seusterne* 1348 (c.1430) (with MLat *mora* 'a moor'), *Seusterne more* 1358 (c.1430), *v.* **mōr**[1]); New Cl; Norths Cl, Norths Homestead (*v.* **hām-stede**) (with the surn. *North*); Old Matthews Cl (presum. with the surn. *Matthews* rather than referring to an old person called Matthew); Old Piece (*v.* **pece**); Pickleweed (unexplained; *pickleweed* is unrecorded in EDD and OED; *pickleplant* occurs in the north-west of England, used of the jointed glasswort (*v.* EDD *s.v.* pickle sb², 1), but this plant is generally associated with the littoral; in Nth, *pikle* is a dial. form of *pightle*, used of 'a small corner of a field' and 'a long narrow strip of ground' (*v.* EDD *s.v.* pightle) and may form part of *pickleweed*, a local name for a tare of some sort); Pipers Wong (*v.* **vangr**; prob. with the surn. *Piper*, but note also **pīpere**); Plaster Lees (*v.* **leys**; prob. with **pleg-stōw** 'a place where people gather for play', *v.* Field 242); Plough Dale (*v.* **plōg, deill**); (The) Red Earth, Doubledays Red Earth (with the surn. *Doubleday*) (cf. *the Red Earth close* 1634, *v.* **rēad, eorðe**); Sallow Tree Cl (*v.* **salh**); (The) Sewstern(e) Cl; Smiths Cl; Square Cl (*v.* **squar(e)**; with reference to shape); First, Second, Stone Gate (cf. *Stangatdik* 1331 (c.1430) (*v.* **dík**), *Stangate close* 1634, *v.* **stān, gata**); Three Cornered Cl (*v.* **three-cornered**); Timber Hill Gardens (*v.* **timber**); Top Cl; Barley Kitty's Urn (*v.* **bærlic**), Hobbs Urn, Kitty's Urn (*v.* **hyrne**; with the pers.n. *Kitty* (a pet form of Katharine) and the surn.

Hobb(s) (a pet form of Robert, rhymed on *Rob*)); Waterlane Gardens (*v.* **wæter, lane**); Well Cl (*v.* **wella**) ; The Welling (*v.* **wella, eng**); Wests Cl (with the surn.*West*); (the) Willow Holt 1821, 1841 (*v.* **wilig, holt**); Wollertons Cl (cf. *George Woollerton* (sic) 1841 of Sewstern); The Wong (*v.* **vangr**); Workhouse and Yard (*v.* **weorc-hūs**; here referring to a Poor Law institute).

(b) *Asketelthirn'* bis, *-thirne*, *Asketulthyrn* 1331 (c.1430) ('Ásketill's thorn-bush or thorn-patch', *v.* **þyrne, þyrnir**; the pers.n. *Ásketill* is Scand); *Beasons closes* 1634 (with the surn. *Beason*); *ad le Brigge* 1290 Misc (p) ('at the bridge', *v.* **brycg**); *Brodebalk* 1399 (c.1430) (*v.* **brād, balca**); *Bukmynstrecroft* 1331 (c.1430) (*v.* **croft** and Buckminster *supra*); *Bukthern* 1358 (c.1430) bis (*v.* **buc-þorn**); *diuisam de Wymundham* 1358 (c.1430) (with MLat *divisa* 'a boundary'; the parish boundary with Wymondham which adjoins to the south-east); *Elrendalforlang'* 1348 (c.1430) (*v.* **elren, furlang**; the second el. is either **dalr** or **deill**); *Flaxland'* 1331 (c.1430) (*v.* **fleax, land**); *Flemynghull* 1331 (c.1430) (*v.* **hyll**; the first el. is either AN **Fleming** 'a Fleming' or more likely its ME surn. reflex *Fleming*); *Galgtregate* Edw 3 (c.1430) ('the road which leads to the gallows-tree', *v.* **galg-trēow, galga-tré, gata** and *le Gautreyhill close* in Buckminster f.ns. (b) *supra*); *Gilberts close* 1634 (with the surn. *Gilbert*); *Haindale* 1331 (c.1430) (*v.* **hegn**; with **dalr** or **deill**); *Heuedland Achardi* 1331 (c.1430) (*v.* **hēafod-land**; with the AN pers.n. *Achard* (which is either from OFr *Achart* or *Aichart* or OGer *Aichard*)); *langfurlang* 1331 (c.1430) (*v.* **lang¹, furlang**); *le longedeyl* 1358 (c.1430) (*v.* **lang¹, langr, deill**); *Mersforlong'* Edw 3 (c.1430) (*v.* **mersc, furlang**); *More Hills* 1628 (*v.* The Moor *supra* and cf. *Morehill* in Buckminster f.ns. (b) *supra*); *North holme* 1520 (*v.* **norð, holmr**); *le Old close* 1637 (*v.* **ald**); *atte Persones* 1392 Pat (p) (*v.* **atte, persone**); *Peseland'* 1331 (c.1430), Edw 3 (c.1430) (*v.* **pise, land**); *Peysforlang'* 1348 (c.1430) (*v.* **pise, furlang**); *Radishes close* 1679 Nichols (with the surn. *Radish* (*v.* Reaney *s.n.* Reddish) rather than with the name of the plant); *Redehowe* 1331 (c.1430) (*v.* **rēad, haugr**, cf. Red Earth *supra*); *Scroutesdeil* Edw 3 (c.1430) ('Skrauti's portion of land', *v.* **deill**; the Scand pers.n. *Skrauti* has been accorded a ME *-es* gen.sg.); *Seustern grene* 1331 (c.1430) bis, *o grene* c.1430 (p) (*v.* **grēne²**); *Shortcop'* 1331 (c.1430) (*v.* **sc(e)ort, copp**); *Shortwellhull* 1331 (c.1430) (*v.* **sc(e)ort, wella, hyll**); *Skyllynghull'* 1331 (c.1430) (*v.* Skill Hill in Buckminster f.ns. (a)); *Sywalholm'* 1331 (c.1430) (*v.* **holmr**; the first el. is a pers.n., either OE *Sigeweald* or more likely Scand *Sigvaldr*); *Tofthill'* 1520 (*v.* **toft, hyll**); (*lez*) *Waterforowes* 1348 (c.1430) bis (perh. 'furrows where water tends to lie', *v.* **wæter, furh**; but *v. waterfurris* in Muston f.ns. (b)); *Westestrete* 1331 (c.1430) (*v.* **west, strǣt**; with reference to King Street Lane, a road which is presum. of Roman origin, running from Sewstern Lane north-west through Waltham on the Wolds); *le Westereines ende* c.1430 (*v.* **west, rein, ende**); *Willytrewelle furlang* 1331 (c.1430) (*v.* **wilig-trēow, wella, furlang**); *Wranglandes* 1331 (c.1430) (*v.* **wrang, vrangr, land**); *Wyltrehullforlang'*, *-furlang'* 1348 (c.1430) (*v.* **wilig-trēow, hyll, furlang**).

Burton and Dalby

1. BURTON LAZARS

Burtone 1086 DB, 1229, 1232 RHug, c.1250 (1404) *Laz, Burtona*
   1170 × 75 Dane, 1.12 (1404), 1216 (1404), 1235 (1404) *Laz et*
   passim to 1286 (1404) *ib*, 13 (1404) *ib* (freq), *Burton'* c.1130
   LeicSurv, 1150 × 59 TutP, 1190 P *et freq* to 1516 *Wyg*, 1517
   Deed, 1520 *Wyg, Burton* 1208 Fine, 1210, 1212 FF *et freq*,
   Burtun' 1209 P, *Burttun'* 1235 Cl, *Burthun(a)* e.13 (1404), m.13
   (1404) *Laz*
Burgtun' 1237 Cl
Borton 1229 Nichols, *Borton'* a.1250 (1404) *Laz*, m.13 (1404) *ib*
   (freq), *Bortona(m)* 1229 Nichols, m.13 (1404) *Laz*
Brottun' 1235 Cl, *Bruton* 1276 RH
Bwrton 1522 *MiD*

'Farmstead or village near a fortification' or 'farmstead with a
palisade', *v.* **burh-tūn** and *Barnewerc* in f.ns. (b) *infra*. Burton Lazars
stands on a hill-top at a suitable site for an early defensive work. A
Hospital of St Lazarus for lepers was founded here c.1138 by Roger de
Mowbray, of which extensive earthworks remain. Peter Burdet held one
carucate of land in Burton in 1242 Fees and part of the fee of Pantouf
was also here in 1242 ib. Land belonging to the Hospital was granted to
John Dudley, Viscount Lisley, in 1535.
   Affixes to Burton are variously added as:
   ~ *iuxta Melton'* 1216 (1404) *Laz*, 1236 Cl, ~ *iuxta Meltona'* 1235
      (1404) *Laz*
   ~ *de Sancto Lazaro* c.1225 AAS, 1200 × 40 Rental, ~ *Sancti Lazari*
      a.1250 (1404) *Laz*, 1254 Val, 1262 (1404), 1271 (1404) *Laz et*
      freq to 1520 *Wyg*, 1535 VE, ~ *Sancti Lazari iuxta Melton'* m.13
      (1404), p.1250 (1404) *Laz*
   ~ *Seint Lazer(e)* 1322 Pat, 1336 (1404) *Laz*, 1374 *Deed*, ~ *Seynt Lazar*
      1351 (1449) *WoCart*, 1371 LPeace, 1383 (1449), 1449 *WoCart*, ~
      Seynt Lazer 1372 Cl, ~ *Se(i)nt Lazar'* 1406 (1449), 1449 *WoCart*,

~ *Saynt Lazar(i)* 1449 *ib*, 1516, 1520 *Wyg*, 1540 Derby
~ *Lazarus* 1537 MinAccts, 1557 Cl, 1589 DKR, ~ *Lazerous(e)* 1687,
  1700 LML
~ *Lazar(e)* c.1545 Leland, 1551, 1552 Pat
~ *Laysarse* 1522 *MiD*, ~ *Lezars* 1576 Saxton, ~ *Lazers* 1610 Speed,
  ~ *Lazars* 1441 (1449) *WoCart*, 1610 LML *et freq*
~ *Burdet* 1242 Fees
~ *Pantouf* 1242 Fees
~ *Lisley* 1546 AAS 1549, 1553 Pat, 1589 DKR, ~ *Lysley* 1548
  CoPleas, ~ *Liesley* 1553 *BHosp*, 1557 Cl, ~ *Leysley* 1561 FF, ~
  Lysle 1561 (17) *Rental*

HOSPITAL OF ST LAZARUS (lost)
  hospitalis Sancti Lazari de Brottun' 1235 Cl, ~ *de Burton'* 1236,
    1237 RGros, 1271 *Pat*, *hospitalis de Burton Sancti Lazari* 1319,
    1364 *ib et passim* to 1461 *ib*, *hospitalis de Burton Sancti Lazari*
    de Ierusalem in Anglia 1461, 1464 *ib*, *Hospital de Burton Sancti*
    Lazari 1554 *Deed*
  Domus S. Lazari de Burton 1422 BM, *domus vel hospital de Burton*
    Sancti Lazari de Ierusalem in Anglia 1473, 1477 *Pat*

  v. **hospital**. Note also MLat *domus* 'a hospice, a hospital, a religious
house' and MLat *hospital* (*hospitalis* gen.sg.) 'a hospice, a hospital'.

ASH PLANTATION, *v.* **æsc**. BLOWPOOL SPINNEY, *blowepull'* 1300 (1449)
WoCart, *Bloopole* 1550 *Pochin*, *Blow(e)pole*, *Blowepoole*, *Blowepoule*
1561 (17) *Surv*, 'the cold, cheerless pool', *v.* **blár, pōl**[1]. BOTTOM PARK,
v. The Park *infra*. BURTON BRIDGE. BURTON BROOK, 1786 SNav; it is
le Brok 13 (1404) *Laz*, *þe broghk* 1300 (1449) *WoCart*, *le brok'* 1309
(1449) *ib*, *the Brooke* 1550 *Pochin*, 1561 (17) *Surv*, *Le Bro(o)ke* 1561
(17) *ib*, *v.* **brōc**. BURTON LAZARS HALL is *Burton hall* 1925 Kelly; built
in 1881. BURTON LODGE COTTAGE. BURTON LODGE FM. CHESTNUT FM.
CROSS LANE, prob. with **cross** rather than **cros**, cf. *thwertgate* 1309
(1449) *WoCart*, 'the road lying athwart', *v.* **þvert, gata**. DOG LANE, *v.*
dogge. THE DRIFT, *Le Dryfte apud Nether Syke Leyes* 1561 (17) *Surv*,
Le Dryfte apud South Medowe 1561 (17) *Rental*, *Driftway* 1681 (1791),
1682 (1791), 1786 *Surv*, *Drift*, ~ *Road* 1848 *TA*, 'the droveway', *v.* **drift**.
EAST FM. ELLABY'S SPINNEY, cf. *Fras. Ellaby* 1846 White, of Little
Dalby. FELSTEAD'S SPINNEY, cf. *Samuel Falstead, farmer* (sic) 1863
White. GARTREE STUD, *v.* **stōd** and Gartree Hill in Great Dalby. THE

GRANGE is *Burton Grange* 1412 *Pat*, 1537 *Cl*, *Burton Graunge* 1416,
1445 Nichols, 1545 *MinAccts*, *le Grange* 1552 *BHosp*, *le graunge* 1555
Pat, *the Grange* 1648 *Surv*, 1686 *Rental*, *v.* **grange**; an outlier of
Vaudey Abbey in Lincs. and a moated site of which considerable
earthworks remain south of the village. GRAVEL HOLE SPINNEY, *v.*
gravel, hol[1]. GREAT CLOSE PLANTATION, *Great Close* 1786 *Surv*. HALL
FM, *v.* Burton Lazars Hall *supra*. HIGHFIELD SPINNEY, *le Highfelde* 1555
Pat, *(le) Highfeild* 1561 (1700), 1593 (17) *Rental*, *High Field* 1609 (18)
Terrier, 1747 *Rental*, 1786 *Surv*, 1848 *TA*, *the High feilds* 1648 *Surv*,
l.17 *Terrier*, 17 *Surv*, *High feildes* 1682 *ib*, *the Hiey Fillds* 1686 *Rental*,
the two Highfields 1646 (1791), 1668 (1791), 1681 (1791) *Surv*, *the 2*
High-feilds 1668 *ib*, *Great*, *Little High feild* 1682 *ib*, 1708 *Rental*, 1708
Terrier, ~ *field* 1682 (1791), 1685 (1791) *Surv*, 1683 × 88 *Terrier*, 1747
Rental, *Little High Field* 1848 *TA*, *v.* **hēah**[1], **feld**; one of the great fields
of the village. HOLLOW LANE is *a little inclosed Lane called the*
Holloway 1792 *Rental*, *v.* **holh**, **weg**. THE KILN CLOSE, *close by the Kill*
1682 *Surv* (with dial. *kill* 'a kiln'), *Killn Close* 1686 *Rental*, *Kiln Close*
1786 *Surv*, 1848 *TA*, *The Great Killen Close* 1686 *Surv*, *Great Kiln(e)*
Close 1747, 1792 *Rental*, *(The) Little Kilne Close* 1686 *Surv*, 1683 × 88,
1708 *Terrier*, ~ ~ ~ *or Freemans Close by the Kiln* 1747 *Rental* (with
the surn. *Freeman*, cf. *Richard Freeman* 1747 *ib*), *Little Kiln Close* 1848
TA, *v.* **cyln**. LIME ST. LITTLE BURTON, 1925 Kelly. LONG SPINNEY.
LOWER HALL FM, cf. *Nether Hall* 1682 *Surv*, *the Nether house* 1683 ×
88 *Terrier*, *the Neither Howse* 1686 *Surv*, *v.* **neoðera**, **hall**. NEW RD.
OLD HALL FM is *Over howse Farm* 1648 *Surv*, *Overhouse farm* 1682
(1791) *ib*, 1685 (1791) *ib* (*v.* **uferra**, **hūs**); cf. *the hall*, *Burton hall* 1550
Pochin, *the Old Hall* 1708, 1708 (18) *Terrier*, *v.* **hall**; note also *(the)*
Hall Yard 1708 *ib*, 1747 *Rental*, 1786 *Surv*. THE PARK, *þe parke* 1300
(1449) *WoCart*, *Le Parke* 1561 (17) *Surv*, *the Parke* 1686 *Rental*, *Park*
1786 *Surv*, 1848 *TA*, *The Big Park* 1848 *ib*, *Near Park* 1848 *ib*, cf. *parke*
hynde 1300 (1449) *WoCart*, *Parke Ende* 1561 (17) *Surv* (*v.* **ende**), *v.*
park; originally the park of the Hospital of St Lazarus. PEPPER'S FM, cf.
Matthew Pepper 1846 White and *George Pepper* 1863 ib of Burton
Lazars. PLOUGH (P.H.) (lost), *Plough* 1846, 1863 White. RACECOURSE
FM, referring to the former racecourse here. ST JAMES'S CHURCH, *(The)*
Church 1848 *TA*, 1877 White, *Church (St James)* 1925 Kelly; it is
earlier recorded as *ecclesia de Burton Lisley* 1549 *Pat*. Also earlier
recorded is *capellas Birton (Keteleby et Friseby)* 1220 MHW (with
MLat *capella* 'a chapel'). Note *the Church-yard* 1708 *Terrier*, *Church*
Yard 1848 *TA*. SAPCOAT'S LODGE, SAPCOAT'S SPINNEY, cf. *Wm.*

Sapcoat, farmer 1846 White of Burton Lazars and *Richard Sapcote* 1475 Nichols of neighbouring Eye Kettleby; the *Sapcote* family originated in the village of Sapcote, 22 miles to the south-west in Sparkenhoe Hundred. SAWGATE RD is *Saltgate* m.13 (1404), 1288 (1404), c.1288 (1404), 13 (1404) *Laz*, 1550 *Pochin, Saltegate* 1300 (1449) *WoCart*, 1561 (17) *Surv*, *(Le) Salgate* 1561 (17) *ib* bis, *Sawgate Road* 1761 *EnclA*, cf. *saltgatte bryge* 1300 (1449) *WoCart*, *saltegatebrigge* 1309 (1449) *ib*, *Saltegate bridge*, ~ *brygge, Saltgate brygge, Salgate* ~ 1561 (17) *Surv* (*v.* **brycg**), 'the salt road', *v.* **salt**[1], **gata**; a salt-merchants' route. TOP PARK, *v.* The Park *supra*. WELL (2½"), a holy spring and well dedicated originally to St Anne, cf. *Ancell Crosse* 1550 *Pochin, Annwell Crosse, Anncell Cross(e), Annsell Crosse* 1561 (17) *Surv*, 'the cross at St Anne's Well', *v.* **wella**, **cros**. St Anne, a patroness of wells, was believed to intercede for the childless and thus the well may once have been a site of fertility rituals, *v.* Ru liii. The cross is probably *not* to be identified with *le Wite Cros* listed with f.ns. (b) *infra*. THE WHITE HO. WILD'S LODGE, cf. *John Wild* 1725 LML of neighbouring Melton Mowbray, *Joseph Wild and Thomas Wild, farmers* 1846 White of Little Dalby, *John Wild, grazier* 1925 Kelly of Burton Lazars, *v.* **loge**.

FIELD-NAMES

In (a), forms dated 1761 are *EnclA*, 1786 are *Surv*, 1792 are *Rental* and 1848 are *TA*. Forms throughout dated 1216 (1404), e.13 (1404), m.13 (1404), 1288 (1404), c.1288 (1404), 13 (1404) and 1404 are *Laz*; a.1280 (1449), l.13 (1449), 13 (1449), 1300 (1449), 1309 (1449), 1328 (1449), 1333 (1449) and 1449 are *WoCart*; 1381 are SR; 1394, 1554 and 1555 are *Pat*; 1453 are Banco; 1517 and 1657 are *Deed*; 1537 are Cl; 1535 × 46 are *MinAccts*; 1550 are *Pochin*; 1561 (17), 1634, 1646 (1791), 1648, 1668, 1668 (1791), 1681 (1791), 1682 (1791), 1685 (1791), 1686 and 17 are *Surv*; 1561 (17)[2], 1593 (17), 1686[2], 1708[3] and 1747 are *Rental*; 1585 are Fine; 1586 and 1624 are Ipm; 1589 are DKR; 1609 (18), 1683 × 88, l.17, 1708, 1708[2], 1708 (18) are *Terrier*; c.1683 are *Clay*.

(a) Ash Cl 1786, 1848 (prob. with reference to ash-trees rather than to soil-conditioning by ash, cf. Ash Plantation *supra*); Banks Peice 1786, Bank Piece 1848 (*v.* **banke, pece**); Barn Cl 1786, 1848 (1747); Baxters Plat 1792 (*v.* **plat**; cf. *Baxter Hedland* 1561 (17) (*v.* **hēafod-land**); *Thomas Baxster* is cited 1561 (17), *John Baxter his howse and homeyard* 1669 (*v.* **home-yard**), (*John*) *Baxters House and Homested*

1668 (1791), 1682 (1791) (*v.* **hām-stede**), *Baxters farm* 1681 (1791), *John Baxters farme* 1682, *Baxters farm late in the tenure of John Baxter* 1685 (1791), *Baxter's farm* 1708 (*v.* **ferme**), *John Baxters Close* 1683 × 88); the Capital Mansion House called Berkley's 1792 (*Pauntons or Barkleis* 1624; a messuage so called, with the family names *Paunton* and *Barkley*, cf. *Morris Barkley knight* 1550 and *the lord Barkley lord of Melton* 1550); Berry Gorse 1848 (*v.* **gorst**; in compound with *gorst*, it seems unlikely that the first el. is OE *berige* 'a berry'; poss. is the surn. *Berry* or even *byrig*, dat.sg. of *burh* 'a fortified site', *v.* *Barnewerc* in f.ns. (b)); Blacks Cl 1786, Blacks Mdw 1786, 1848 (*Blacks Meadowes* 1648, *the Blacks medow* 1686²; with the surn. *Black*); Brentingby Mdw 1786, 1848, Brentonby ~ 1792 (*brentnby medow* 1686², *Brentingby Meadow* 1686, 1708, *Brentonby Medow* 1683 × 88), Brentonby Long Mdw 1792, Brentingby ~ ~ 1848 (*Brentonby Meadow or the Long Meadow* 1747), Brentonby Nether Mdw 1792, Nether Brentingby Mdw 1848 (*Brentonby Meadow Platt or the Nether Meadow* 1747, *Brentingby Meadow Plott* 1682, *v.* **plat, plot**) (Brentingby adjoins to the north-east); Bridge Cl 1786, Brig or Bridge Cl 1792 (*Bridge Close* 1683 × 88, 1708, *v.* **brycg, bryggja**); Bridge Peice 1786, ~ Piece 1848 (*v.* **pece**); Briggs Cl 1786, 1848, Little ~ ~ 1848 (perh. with the surn. *Briggs*, but this could belong with Brig Cl *supra*); Brook Cl 1786, 1792, 1848, Brooks ~ 1848 (*Brooke Close* 1686, 1683 × 88, *Bruck* ~ 1686², *Brook* ~ 1708), Brook Mdw 1786, 1848 (*v.* Burton Brook *supra*); Bull Cl 1786, 1848 ((*the*) *Bull Close* 1648, 1686², *v.* **bula**); Bull Nook 1786, 1848 (*Bullocks Nook* 1646 (1791), 1708, 1708³, *Bullockes nook* 1682, *Bullicke nowke* 1686², *Bullocks Nooke* 1683 × 88, *Bullock Nook* 1747, *v.* **bulluc, nōk**; the earlier forms presum. belong here, with *bullock* later replaced by *bull*); Bullock Wong 1848 (*Bullok Wong* 13 (1404), *bolloke wong'* 1300 (1449), *Bullocks Wong* 1550, 1668 (1791), 1681 (1791), 1682, 1682 (1791), 1685 (1791), 1708, 1708³, *Bol(l)ocke Wonge* 1561 (17), *Bullocks Wonge* 1683 × 88, *Bullock Wong, ~ ~ Platt* 1747 (*v.* **plat**), *v.* **bulluc, vangr** and *Short Leyes* in f.ns. (b)); Burrows Cl 1786 (perh. with the surn. *Burrow(s)*, but **borow** 'an animal burrow' is poss.); Childs Arse 1786, 1848 (1646 (1791), 1682, 1685 (1791) *et passim* to 1708, 1747, *Childes Arce* 1686²; if not a fanciful name for a topographical feature reminiscent of a child's posterior, then perh. 'the rounded hill where the young folk gather', *v.* **cild, ears**, cf. *Catsars* in Ab Kettleby f.ns. (b)); Chisseldines Cl 1786 (with the surn. *Chisseldine*, common in neighbouring Rutland, *v.* Ru 437 and 449 *s.n.*); Church Croft 1786 (c.1683, 1686², *le Churchecrofte* 1555, *v.* **circe, croft**; presum. a croft beside the parish church); Cook Stall, ~ ~ Pasture 1848 (*kokisdale* m.13 (1404), *Cokesdale* 13 (1404) bis, 1453, *Cochesdale* 13 (1404), *Cokesdal(l)e, Cookesdale* 1550, (*Le*) *Coks Dale, Cocks Dale* 1561 (17), *3 Cooks dales* 1682 (1791), *the Cookesdale, Hither or Over Cooksdale* (*v.* **uferra**), *Middle, Nether or Farr Cookedale* 1747, *Cokesdale brooke* 1550 (*v.* **brōc**), *Coksdale End* 1561 (17) (*v.* **ende**), *Coks Dale Hede, ~ ~ Head, ~ ~ Heyde* 1561 (17) (*v.* **hēafod**)), Cookstall Hill 1786, Cooksdale Hill in 2 parts called 3 Cooks dales or Land Cl 1792 (*v.* **land**) (*Coks Dale Hill, ~ ~ Hyll, Cocksdale hill* 1561 (17), *Coucksdale hill* 1682) (as first el., either OE *cocc¹* 'a hillock' or OE *cocc²* 'a cook, a woodcock' or even the OE pers.n. *Cocc* is poss., with **dalr** or **deill**; the brook and adjacent hill perh. favour **dalr** as the second el.); Cowpasture 1786, Cow Pasture 1848 (*the Cow Pasture* 1648, 1668 *et passim* to 1685 (1791), 1708); Damends 1786, Great ~ ~, Daming Cl 1848 (*the*

Damings 1648, c.1683, *farder damins, the Hetther damins* 1686[2] (*v.* **farther, hider**); either 'the dam meadow', *v.* **damme, eng,** or simply 'the dam', *v.* **damming** and *new meadow, infra*); Draw Rail 1848 (naming pasture beside The Drift *supra*, hence '(land beside) the drove-road fence', *v.* **drāf, raile**); Dunmors Cl 1786, Dunmore ~ 1848 (with the surn. *Dunmore*); Durance Cl 1786, Durrance ~ 1848 (with the surn. *Durrand/ Durrance,* cf. *John Durrand* 1848 of Burton Lazars, *v.* Reaney *s.n.* Durrand); Eight Acres 1786, 1848, Brentonby 8 Acres 1792, the 8 Acre Plat 1792 (*v.* **plat**) (*8 Acres Close* 1682, *the 8 Ackrs Close* 1686[2], *Eight Acre* 1708, ~ ~ *Platt* 1747, *Dickens Eight Acre Platt or Brentonby Meadow* 1747 (with the surn. *Dickens*); Brentingby adjoins to the north-east, *v.* **æcer**); (The) Feeding Cl 1786, 1848, Big, Little, Middle Feeding Cl 1848, Feeding Close Mdw 1786 (*the Feedinge Close* 1648, *v.* **feeding;** an enclosure especially noted as superior grazing for cattle); Fenmans Cl 1786, 1848 (with the surn. *Fenman*); Fox Covert 1848 (*v.* **cover(t)**); Fox Dale Hill, Little Fox Dale 1848 (*Foxwell hill* 1550, *Foxsulhill, -hyll, Foxsullhyll, Foxulhyll* 1561 (17), *Foxdale Hill* 1682 (1791), 1683 × 88, 1708, 1708[3], 1747, *Foxdale hill Closes* 1682, *v.* **fox, wella, hyll**); Freemans House & Homestead 1792 (*Mr John Freemans House, Orchard and Homestead* 1683 × 88, *v.* **hām-stede**); Gardeners Cl 1786, 1848 (with the surn. *Gardener*); Gorse Cl 1786, Lower, Middle, Upper Gorse Cl 1848, Old Gorse Cl 1848 (*v.* **gorst**); Grange Cl 1786, 1848 (c.1683, *v.* The Grange *supra*); (the) Great Ground 1786, 1792, Great Ground or New Fd 1848 (*v.* **grund**); Harvies ~, Harveys Mdw 1848 (with the surn. *Harvey*); Hay Gripps 1848 (*Hey grippes* 1550, *Eygrippis* 1561 (17), *Highgripps* 1682 (1791), *High Gripps* 1683 × 88, 1708, *High Gripes* 1708, 1708[3], ~ *Grips* 1708, 1747), Haygrips Cl 1786 (*Egripe Close* 1682), Haygrips Mdw 1786 (*v.* (**ge)hæg, gryppe**); Home Cl 1848 (1682, *Further, Hither* ~ ~ 1682, *v.* **home**); Hopyard 1786, Hop Yard 1792 (*The Hopp Yard* 1682, 1683 × 88, *Hop Yard* 1708, *v.* **hop-yard** and Field 129); Horse Hook 1786, Horse Cl or Horse Hooks 1848 (*horsehoc* e.13 (1404), 13 (1404), *horsehoke, horsehooke* 1550, (*le*) *Horse Hoke, Horshoke, Le Horse hooke* 1561 (17), *Horsehooks* 1682 (1791), *Horse hookes* 1686, *Horse Hooks* 1683 × 88, 1708, 1747, *Horse Hooke* 1708[3], *horsehooke haides* 1550 (*v.* **hēafod**), *Horse hookes Close* 1682, 'the hook or angle of land where the horses are grazed', *v.* **hors, hōc**; also called (*The) Horse Close* 1682); The Island 1848 (*v.* **island;** a triangular close, with R. Eye to the north and streams on the other two sides); Keepers Ho. 1848 (a gamekeeper's abode); Lamp Mdw 1786 (1668 (1791), *Lampe meadow* 1624, *v.* **lampe;** rent from this endowed land maintained an altar lamp or other lamps in the village church); Land Cl 1786 (1708, 1708[3], *Land Close or the Cookesdale* 1747 (*v.* Cook Stall *supra*)), Land Cl or Fox Dale Hill 1848 (*Land Close or Foxdale Hill* 1747 (*v.* Fox Dale Hill *supra*)), Land Cl in Bullock Wong 1848 (*v.* Bullock Wong *supra*), Land Close Plat 1786 (*v.* **plat**) (*v.* **land**; all were enclosures which consolidated unspecified numbers of selions or 'lands' of the former great fields of the township); Lees Homestead 1786 (*v.* **hām-stede**; with the surn. *Lee*); Leicester Cl 1786, 1848 (1648, *Lester close* 1686[2]; it is uncertain whether *Leicester/Lester* is a surn. here (*v.* Reaney *s.n.*); otherwise perh. a close at that extremity of the early parish nearest to the county town, cf. Melton Cl *infra*); Little Feild 1786 (poss. *Little High Field, v.* Highfield Spinney *supra*); the Long Great Fd 1761; Long Mdw 1786, 1848 (*the Long Meadow* 1747); Man Mill Peice 1786, ~ ~ Piece 1848 (*v.* **pece**) (*mannemilne* e.13 (1404), m.13 (1404), 13 (1404) bis, 1309 (1449), *manmilne* e.13 (1404), *mannismulne* l.13 (1449), *Mannemilin'* 13 (1404), *the Man Milne* 1550, *Manmylne abut' super Le Eye* 1561 (17), 1561 (17)², *Man Milne* 1589, *Man Mill* 1648, (*molendinum de Man* 13 (1404), with ML at *molendinum* 'a mill'), *Manmylne Close* 1561 (17) (*v.* **clos(e)**), *the Man Mylne field* 1550, *Manmylnefeild(e)* 1561 (17) bis (*v.* **feld**; one of the great fields of the village); a water-mill on R. Eye, *v.* **myln**; because of the form *molendinum de Man* 13 (1404), the first el. of the English compound appears to be a pers.n., either *Man* which may be OE or Scand, or Scand *Manni, v.* SPNLY 194 and cf. *molendinum Harewyni* in Withcote f.ns. (b); but either (**ge**)**mǣne** 'communal' or (**ge**)**mǣnnes** 'community' would make more satisfying sense); Merrills Homestead 1792 (*v.* **hām-stede**; with the surn. *Merrill,* cf. *Widow Merils Cottage* 1747, *v.* **cotage**); Melton Cl 1786, 1848, Melton Close Mdw 1786, 1848 (*Melton Close* 1648, c.1683, 1686²; situated at the edge of the parish adjoining Melton Mowbray); Mill Peice 1786 (*v.* **pece**), Upper Mill Cl 1792 (cf. *Mylne Close* 1561 (17), *v.* **myln**, **clos(e)**; the identity of this mill is uncertain); Mole Cl 1786 (*v.* **molle**; evidently a particular habitat for moles); (The) Moor 1786, 1848 (cf. *littelmore* 13 (1404), *lytill more* 1300 (1449) bis, *le litelmor'* 1328 (1449), *the Litle More* 1550, *Lyt(t)ull ~, Little More* 1561 (17) (*v.* **lȳtel**), *middulmore* 1328 (1449) (*v.* **middel**) (*v.* **mōr**¹); Mutton Hill 1786, ~ ~ or High Fd 1848 (*Mutton Hill* 1747; to the east of Burton Lazars and thus presum. a whimsical name for a sheep pasture rather than a garbled form of Melton Hill, *v.* Highfields Spinney *supra*); Great ~, Nest 1786, (the) Great Ness 1792, 1848, Upper Ness 1848 (*le Nesse* 1288 (1404), 1309 (1449), *Nesse* l.13 (1449), *the Nesse* 1550, *Le Nesse abutt' versus Le Eye* 1561 (17), *middilnesse* l.13 (1449) (*v.* **middel**), *uper nes* 1686², *Nesheuedes* m.13 (1404), *Nesse heuedis* 13 (1404), *Nesse haydes* 1550, *Nesseheydes, Nesse Heydis,* ~ *Heads* 1561 (17) (*v.* **hēafod**)), Man Mill Nest 1786, Upper Ness Cl or Man Mill Ness & Upper Cl 1848 (*v.* Man Mill Peice *supra*) (*The Lower, The Upper Nesse Close* 1686, *Over, Neither Nest* 1708 (*v.* **uferra, neoðera**), *Lower or Nether Nest Close, Upper Nest Close* 1747), Nest Mdw 1786, Ness ~ 1792, 1848 (*The Nesse Meadow* 1686, *Nest Meadow* 1708, *nether nes meadow* 1686², *Lower Nest Meadow* 1747 (*v.* **næss, nes** 'a projecting piece of land formed in the bend of a river', in this case R. Eye); Nether Cl 1786, 1848; Nether Mdw 1786 (*the Nether Meadow* 1747); New Cl 1786, 1848, Great ~ ~ 1848 ((*the*) *New Close* 1561 (17), 1648, c.1683, 1686², *v.* **nīwe, clos(e)**); Newfeild 1786, Newfield or the Great Ground 1792 (*v.* the Great Ground *supra*), New Fd 1848 (*the New-feild* 1683 × 88, *new filld* 1686², *New Field* 1708, ~ *Feild* 1708³, *Newfield or Hubberts Close* 1747 (*v.* *Hubberts Close* in f.ns. (b) *infra*), Newfeild Mdw 1792, New Field Mdw 1848 (*New Field Meadow* 1708, ~ *Feild* ~ 1708³, *Newfield Meadow* 1747); New Mdw 1848 (*new meadow alias the Damings* c.1683, *v.* Damends *supra*); New Peice 1786, ~ Piece 1792, 1848 (*v.* **pece**); Old Ground 1786, 1848 (*v.* **ald, grund**); Old Lane 1848 (a pasture so called); Ox Pasture 1786, 1848 (*Le Oxe pasture* 1561 (17), 1561 (17)², *the* ~ ~ 1561 (17), *v.* **oxa, pasture**); The Old Yard 1848 (*v.* **geard**); The Pasture Spinney 1792; Peggs Mdw 1786, Pegs ~ 1786, 1848 (with the surn. *Pegg*); Pingle 1786, 1792, 1848 (1646 (1791), 1682 (1791), 1685 (1791), 1708, 1747, *the Pingle* 1682, *v.* **pingel**); Platts 1786, ~ in Bullock Wong 1848 (*v.* Bullock Wong *supra*), Great Platt 1786, 1848, ~ ~ in Sick Leys 1848 (*v.* Sick Leys *infra*), Little Platt 1786, Old Platts or Park 1848 (*v*. The Park *supra*), Platt Cl 1848 (*v*. **plat**); Prestons Pasture 1848 (with the surn. *Preston*); Ram Cl 1786, 1848 (*the Rame Close* 1648, 1686², *v*. **ramm**); Sand Lands 1786, Sandland Cl 1848 (*Sandlandes* m.13 (1404) bis, *Sandlondis* 13 (1404), *Sandlands* 1561 (17), *inferior Sandlandes* 13 (1404) (with MLat *inferior* 'lower'), *Nether Sand lands* 1550, *Neyther Sandlands* 1561 (17) (*v*. **neoðera**), *middylsandland'* 1300 (1449), *Midle Sand landes* 1550, *Middle ~*, *Middull ~*, *Myddull Sandlands* 1561 (17) (*v*. **middel**), *owersandland'* 1300 (1449), *Over Sand Lands* 1550, *Over Sandlands, Hupper ~* 1561 (17) (*v*. **uferra, upper**), *Sandland hades* 1550 (*v*. **hēafod**), 'selions with sandy soil', *v*. **sand, land**); Upper, Nether Sawgate, ~ Mdw 1786, Bottom, Top Great Sawgates 1848, Little ~, Home ~ (*v*. **home**), Calfs Sawgates (*v*. **calf**) 1848 (*Saltegatelonge* l.13 (1449) bis (*v*. **lang²**), *Brode Saltgate* 1550 (*v*. **brād**), *Longe Saltgate* 1550, *Long Saltegate* 1561 (17) (*v*. **lang¹**), *Saltgate feilde*, (*le*) *Salgate feild*(*e*) 1561 (17) (*v*. **feld**), *Salgate Close* 1648, 1668 (1791), *v*. Sawgate Rd *supra*); School Garden 1848; Shepherds Ho. 1848 (prob. 'the shepherd's house' rather than with the surn. *Shepherd*, *v*. **scēp-hirde** and cf. Shepherd Ho. in Freeby f.ns. (a)); Sick Leys 1848, Sick Mdw 1786, 1848, Big, Little, Middle Sick Mdw 1848, Dickins Nethersick 1792 (with the surn. *Dickins/Dickens*), Nethersick Little Plat, ~ Great Plat, ~ Long Plat 1792 (*v*. **plat**), Nether Sick Leyes 1786, ~ ~ Leys 1848, Nethersick Leys called the 8 Acre Plat 1792, Nether Sick Leys formerly Thomas Kelhams Plat 1792 (*v*. **leys**) (*The Seicks* 1686², *the Sicks* 1708³, *the Sick*, ~ *Syke* 1708, *Le Hither ~*, *Le Hyther Syke* 1561 (17) (*v*. **hider**), (*le*) *Ouersike* bis, *Houersike* 13 (1404), *houersyke* 1300 (1449), *the Over Syke* 1550, *le Oversicke* 1555, *Le Over Sike*, ~ ~ *Syke* 1561 (17), *Over Sicke* 1593 (17), *Oversick* 1609 (18), 1646 (1791) *et passim* to 1685 (1791), *Over Sike* 1668 (*v*. **uferra**), *Upper Sike* l.17, ~ *sicke* 17, *the nether syke* 1550, *Le Nether ~*, *Le Neyther Syke* 1561 (17), *Nether Sicke* 1593 (17), *Nethersick* 1609 (18), 1646 (1791) *et passim* to 1685 (1791), *Neither Sick* 1648, *Nether Sike* 1668, l.17, *Merells Nether Sikes* 1683 × 88 (with the surn. *Merrill*, *v*. Merrills Homestead *supra*) (*v*. **neoðera**), *Neyther Syke Leas*, ~ ~ *Leyes* 1561 (17), *Neather ~ ~*, *Nether Sike Leyes* 1682, *Nethersick Leys* 1682 (1791), 1747, *Nether Sike Leas* 1683 × 88, *Neither Sick Leyes* 1708³, *Waites Nether Sick Leyes* 1747 (cf. *John Waite* 1681 (1791); all with Scand **sík** in its later sense 'a piece of meadow along a stream'); Small Hill 1786, 1848 (1609 (18), 1708, 1708³, *Smalhilles* 13 (1404) bis, *smallhillys* 1300 (1449), *Small Hills* 1593 (17), 1648, 1668 *et passim* to l.17, *Small hills (since called Small hill Edge or Smallage)* 1646 (1791), *Small hill or Smallage* 1682 (1791), 1685 (1791), 1747, *Small ledge* 1686², *v*. **smæl, hyll, ecg**); Snows Cl 1761 (perh. with the surn. *Snow*, but *v*. Snow Cl in Brentingby f.ns. (a) and *Snow Close* in Wymondham f.ns. (b), both poss. with **snāw** 'snow')); South Mdw 1786, 1848 (*Le South Medow*(*e*), ~ ~ *Meddow*, ~ ~ *Meadow* 1561 (17), *South Medowe* 1561 (17), *v*. **sūð, mæd** (**mǣdwe** obl.sg.)); Spinney Piece 1848 (*v*. **spinney, pece**); Stamford Gate Leyes 1786 (1593 (17), 1648, 1668 *et passim* to 1747, *Staunfordgate leys* 1555, *Stamforth gate Leyes* 1561 (17), *Stamford Gate Leazes* 1609 (18), *Stanfordgate Leys* 1646 (1791), *Stamford Gate Leys* 1668 (1791), 1681 (1791) *et passim* to 1708, ~ ~ *leeys* 1686², ~ ~ *Leas* 1683 × 88, *v*. **lǣs** and *Stanfordegate* in f.ns. (b) *infra*); Far, Near, Little, Stapleford Leys 1848 (*v*. **leys**; Stapleford lies to the east); Steel Cl 1786, 1848 (*Steeles Close* 1648; with the surn. *Steel*, cf. *Randall Steel* 1683 *Surv* of Great Dalby); Stock Cl 1786, (the) Stock Mdw

1786, 1792, 1848, Stock Peice 1786, ~ Piece 1848, Great Stock Peice 1786, ~ ~ Piece 1848 (*v.* **pece**), the Stock Plat 1792 (*v.* **plat**) (*Stoke* m.13 (1404), l.13 (1449), 13 (1404), *le Stoc* 1288 (1404), c.1288 (1404), *Stocke* 13 (1449), *Stok'* 13 (1404) bis, 13 (1449), *le stokes, le stokkes* 1309 (1449), *the Stoke* 1550, *Le Stocke, Farther, Heyther Stocke, Hyther Sto(c)ke* 1561 (17) (*v.* **farther, hider**), *Middle ~, Myddull Stocke, Mydull Stoke* 1561 (17) (*v.* **middel**), *the Nether Stoke* 1550 (*v.* neoðra), *Over Stocke* 1561 (17), *Over Stock* 1708, 1708[3] (*v.* **uferra**), *Dalby Stoke* 1300 (1449), 1561 (17) bis, *Dalby Stoake, ~ Stocke* 1561 (17) (i.e. the *stoc* towards Little Dalby, prob. *Westoc*), *Westoc* m.13 (1404) (*v.* **west**), *the Stock Close* 1668, 1668 (1791), 1682 (1791), *Stocke Close* 1682, 1686[2], *Great Stock Close, Nether Stocks Close* 1682 (1791), *Stock Close* 1683 × 88, l.17, 1708, 1708[3], *Stock Close or Overstock* 1747, *the Stock Meadow* 1747, *v.* **stoc** 'an outlying farmstead, a dairy-farm'); Stonehill 1786, 1792, Great ~, Stonehill 1848, Stonehill Pingle or Stock Plat 1792 (*v.* **pingel** and the Stock Plat *supra*) (*Stonhil* m.13 (1404), l.13 (1449), *Stonhul, Stonhyl, Stonnyl* m.13 (1404), *Stonhill'* l.13 (1449) bis, 13 (1404), *Stonnehill, -hyll* 1561 (17), *Ston Hill* 1686[2], *Stone Hill* 1686, 1683 × 88, 1708, 1708[2], *middull' stonyll* 1300 (1449), *Midle Stone hill* 1550, *Mydull Stonehill, Myd(d)ull Stonnehyll, Myddull Stonne Hill* 1561 (17) (*v.* **middel**), *Far, Hither Stonehill* 1747, *Stonhilheuedes* m.13 (1404), 1328 (1449) bis, *Stonhulheudes* m.13 (1404) (*v.* **hēafod**), *the Stonehill Close* 1686, 'the hill with stony soil', *v.* **stān, hyll**); Tallys Cl 1786 (with the surn. *Tallis* or *Tally*); Three Corned Cl (sic) 1786, Three Cornerd Peice (sic) 1786 (*v.* **pece**) (*v.* **three-cornered**); Tollgate Ho. and Garden 1848 (*v.* **toll-gate**); Triangle 1786 (*v.* **triangle**; a three-cornered enclosure); Upper Cl 1792, Upper Mdw 1786 (poss. identical); Watsons Cl 1786, 1848, Watson's ~ 1792 (*Watsons Close* 1682, 1708, 1747; with the surn. *Watson*); Well Lane 1792, ~ ~ Cl 1848 ((*the*) *Well Lane* 1668, 1686, 1683 × 88, 1747, *Well Lane Close* 1682, 1708 (*v. Dickens Well Lane Close, infra*), *Welles* m.13 (1404), 13 (1404), *Westere Welles* 13 (1404) (*v.* **westerra**), cf. (*le*) *Welleheuedes* m.13 (1404), 13 (1404), *Welleheuedeshend'* 13 (1404) (*v.* **hēafod, ende**), *Wellehil* 13 (1404) (*v.* **hyll**), *Wellesike* 13 (1404) (*v.* **sík**) (all with OE **wella** 'a spring, a stream')); West Hill 1786, 1848 (*Westhill, -hyll* 1561 (17), *West Hills* 1686[2], *le Westhyll close* 1555, *West Hyll Closse* 1561 (17), *West Hill Close* 1648 (*v.* **clos(e)**), *v.* **west, hyll**); West Mdw 1786, 1848 (*Westmedwe* 13 (1404), *old meadow close alias west meadow* c.1683, *West Meadowes* 1648, *the little, the grat west medow* 1686[2] (*v.* **grēat**), *v.* **west, mǣd** (**mǣdwe** obl.sg.)); Wrights Cl 1786, 1848 (with the surn. *Wright*).

(b) *abbotte gate* 1300 (1449), *Abottgate* 1561 (17) (*v.* **abbat, gata**; with reference to the Abbot of Vaudey, The Grange *supra* being an outlier of Vaudey Abbey in Lincs.); *abbott tonge* 1300 (1449), *the Abbots tongue* 1550, *Abbottstonge* 1561 (17) (*v.* **abbat, tunge** and the preceding f.n.); *Achirdike* 1216 (1404), *Est akerdic* 13 (1404) (*v.* **ēast**) (*v.* **æcer-dīc, dík**); *Alnotescroft* 13 (1404) bis (*v.* **croft**; with the pers.n. *Alnoð* (spellings in *Alnot* in DB, *v.* Feilitzen 149) which could represent the earlier OE *Ælfnoð* or *Æðelnoð* or *Ealdnoð* or *Ealhnoð*); *alewinwong'* a.1280 (1449), *Alwinewong* 13 (1404), *alwynwong'* l.13 (1449), 13 (1449) (*v.* **vangr**; with the pers.n. *Alwine* which may represent the earlier OE *Ælfwine* or *Æðelwine* or *Ealdwine* or *Ealhwine*); *Alyn Balke End, Alyn Closse, Alyn Clossehynd, Alyn Closse Syde, Alyn yarde End, ~ yards ~* 1561 (17) (*v.* **balca, ende, clos(e), sīde, geard**; all with the surn. *Allin*, from the OFr pers.n. *Alain*, OBret *Alan*, v. Reaney *s.n.* Allain); *Ambrecrofte* 1561 (17) (*v.* **ampre, croft**); *Apeltre* m.13 (1404), *appiltr'* a.1280 (1449), *apiltre* l.13 (1449), *appiltre* 13 (1449) (*v.* **æppel-trēow**; *Ashby Hedland* 1561 (17) (*v.* **hēafod-land**; with the surn. *Ashby*); *aungerleyes* a.1280 (1449), 13 (1449), *aungerleyesheudes* bis, *aungerleyis heudis* l.13 (1449) (*v.* **hēafod**) (*v.* **lǣs**; with the AN pers.n. *Aunger*, from OFr *Angier* (OGer *Ansger*), v. Reaney *s.n.* Anger and cf. Angersleigh, So); *Back close* 1681 (1791) (*v.* **back**); *Barnard Pittes* 1300 (1449) (*v.* **pytt**; with the AN pers.n. *Bernard*; from OFr *Bernart* (OGer *Bernard*)); *Barnewerc* 13 (1404), *Barnewarke, Bernewarke* 1561 (17), *Barnewarke Holmes, ~ Holmys* 1561 (17) (*v.* **holmr**) (*v.* **beorn, (ge)weorc**; this appears to represent the site of an early fortification, perh. that from which Burton took its name; as a first el., both the OE pers.n. *Beorn(a)* and OE *bern* 'a barn' seem unlikely); *bekholmeheuedes* 1328 (1449) (*v.* **bekkr, holmr, hēafod**); *becmilne* m.13 (1404) bis (*v.* **bekkr, myln**); *Benelands* 1561 (17) (*v.* **bēan, land**); *Bitwenegates* m.13 (1404) ('(the furlong) between the roads', *v.* **betwēonan, gata**); *blacpole* 1309 (1449) (*v.* **blæc, pōl¹**); *blakeseke* 1300 (1449) bis, *le blakesik'* 1328 (1449), *Black Syke* 1550, *(Le) Blake Syke* 1561 (17) (*v.* **blæc, sík**); *Bounholme* m.13 (1404), l.13 (1449) bis (*v.* **baun, holmr**); *Bradegate* m.13 (1404), 1404 (*v.* **brād, gata**); *Bramelhoke, Bramell hoke, Bramell Howke* 1561 (17) (*v.* **brǣmel, hōc**); *Brentby(e) Croft(e)* 1561 (17) (*v.* **croft**), *Brentbye Stonys* 1561 (17) (*v.* **stān**; poss. referring to boundary markers) (Brentingby adjoins to the north-east); *Brethers Pytt* 1561 (17) (*v.* **brōðor, bróðir (brœðra** gen.pl.), **pytt**; poss. with reference to the religious brothers of the Hospital of St Lazarus or of The Grange *supra* (of Vaudey Abbey)); *briggeforth* 1309 (1449) (*v.* **brycg, ford**, prob. *Stapleford bridge forth*, *infra*; the compound *bridgeford* is usually taken to mean 'bridge at the ford', with the bridge seen as a later addition at the ford's river crossing (cf. East, West Bridgford, Nt 222, 231), but poss. in such cases is *brycg* in its early sense 'a causeway', hence 'ford with a made or reinforced bottom'); *Brokfurlong* 13 (1404) (*v.* **brōc, furlang**), *Broke Heydes* 1561 (17) (*v.* **hēafod**) (both f.ns. alluding to Burton Brook *supra*); *Broketes Yard, Brokets Yard End* 1550 (*v.* **geard, ende**; with the surn. *Brocket, v.* Reaney *s.n.*); *Burton Marlepyttes* 1394 (*v.* **marle, pytt**); *del Castel* 1381 (p), *othe castell* 1381 (p) (*v.* **castel(l)**; these were the names of a husbandman and of a ploughman respectively, which may suggest their association with The Grange *supra*, as there is reference to a tower at The Grange in 1189 (*v.* Dugd **5** 491), presum. a stone tower-house; but note *Castelgate* following); *Castelgate* 13 (1404) bis, 1328 (1449), 1561 (17), *Castell' gate* 1300 (1449) (*v.* **castel(l), gata**; the road was in the north of the parish and presum. led to the ford at Wyfordby where the earthworks of a fortified site survive beside the church (cf. *Castell Close* 1560 and *Castle hads* 1634 in Wyfordby and *castle hades* 1601 in adjoining Brentingby); *Chapell Yard* 1561 (17) (*v.* **chapel(e), geard**); *Chewegappe, Chew(e)gape* 1561 (17) (*v.* **gap**; with the surn. *Chew*, cf. *Gill gappe*, *infra*); *Chew(e)gate* 1561 (17) (*v.* **gata**; with the surn. *Chew*, cf. the preceding f.n.); *Christian's House & Homestead* 1708 (*v.* **hām-stede**; with the surn. *Christian*); *Mrs Claytons house and home close* 1682 (*v.* **home**, cf. *Peter Clayton* 1682); *Clerkeson Lane End* 1561 (17) (*v.* **lane-ende**; cf. *Ricardus Clerkeson* 1561 (17)); *Coke Banke* 1561 (17) (*v.* **banke**), *Coke head* 1561 (17) (*v.* **hēafod**) (cf. *Bartholomew Coke, ~ Cooke* 1561 (17)); *Coleshenge* 13 (1404) bis ('Kol's meadow', *v.* **eng**; the pers.n. *Kol* is ODan (ON *Kolr*)); *The Common Pasture* 1682 (*v.* **commun, pasture**); *John Cooks farme* 1682, *Cooks farm late in the tenure of John Cook* 1685 (1791), *Cooks farm(e)* 1708, 1708³ (*v.* **ferme**), *John Cookes plott* 1686 (*v.* **plot**); *Cottiers Close* 1682 (*v.* **cottere**); *the Cow Close, Cow Closse* 1682; *Cranewater, kranewater* 13 (1404), *Cranewatt'* 1300 (1449), *Cranwater* 1550, *Crane Water* 1561 (17), *Cranwater lese* 1550 (*v.* **læs**) (*v.* **cran, wæter**); *Crosse wonge* 1561 (17) (*v.* **cross, vangr**); *crumdale, crunbedale* l.13 (1449) (*v.* **crumb, deill**); *dailles closes* 1686² (*v.* **deill**); *Dalby bothum* 13 (1404) (*v.* **botm**), *Dalby gate* 1550, 1561 (17) (*v.* **gata**), *Dalby hedge* 1561 (17) (*v.* **hecg**; a boundary hedge), *Dalby Mere* 1561 (17) (*v.* **(ge)mære**) (*v.* Little Dalby *infra*); *Daleacre* 13 (1404) (*v.* **dalr, æcer**); *Damforlong, Damfurlong'* m.13 (1404) bis, 13 (1404) bis, *Damfurlong* 1328 (1449), *damefurlong'* 1309 (1449) (*v.* **damme, furlong**); *Deroldescroft* 13 (1404) (*v.* **croft**; with the OE pers.n. *Dēorwald*); *Dewicks Cottage* 1683 × 88 (*v.* **cotage**; cf. *Richard Deweick* 1682 and *Dewicks Vinehouse, infra*); *Richard Dickens farme* 1682, *Richard Dickins farem* (sic) 1686², *Widdow Dickens her Farm* 1683 × 88 (*v.* **ferme**), *Dickins House and Homested (in the tenure of the Widdow Dickins)* 1686, *Widdow Dickins house & homestead* 1683 × 88 (*v.* **hām-stede**), *Dickens Well Lane Close* 1747 (*v.* Well Lane *supra*); *Eagleswood* 1550 (either with the surn. *Eagle*, a nickname from the bird (ME **egle** from OFr *egle*), or with the bird itself; the habitat of the sea-eagle from the Anglo-Saxon period included inland woods (cf. Earnwood (Sa) and Arnold (Nt), both with OE *earn* 'eagle'), *v.* **wudu** and Reaney *s.n.* Eagle); *the Earles land, ~ ~ ~ called the hall land, the Earles land late Vaudy* 1550 (*v.* **eorl, hall, land**; with reference to the Earl of Warwick and Vaudey Abbey); *E(a)st Mary end* 1682 (*v.* **ende**; perh. with **myry** or **(ge)mære** since the church is dedicated to St James); *Edwards Vineyard* 1685 (1791) (*v.* **vinȝerd**; with the surn. *Edwards*); *the farre gate haides, Faregate hades* 1550, *Fargate Heyd(e)s, ~ Heydis, ~ He(a)ds* 1561 (17) (*v.* **feor, gata, hēafod**); *Fattland* 1682, *Great & litle fatland, great and little Fatlands* 1682 (*v.* **fætt, land**); *flaxlandis* l.13 (1449) bis, *Flaxlands* 1561 (17) (*v.* **fleax, land**); *Flegelonge, Fleggelonge* bis 1561 (17) (*v.* **flegge, lang²**); *Folker Dole* 1550 (*v.* **dāl**; with a pers.n., either ODan *Folkar* or AN *Folcard/Folcerd* (OGer *Fulcard*)); *for(e)hil* m.13 (1404), l.13 (1449), *forehill'* 1449, *Forhills* 1550, 1561 (17), *Forhillis, -hyllis* 1561 (17) (**fore, hyll**); *Freemans Orchard or the Old Hall Orchard* 1747 (cf. *Rich. Freeman* 1747 of Burton Lazars); *Fressingholme* 13 (1404) (*v.* **fyrsen, holmr**); *Furborough ~, Furborow Syke* 1550, *Fyrborow(e) Syke* 1561 (17) (*v.* **berg, sík**; the first el. is either *feor* 'far' or *fyrs* 'furze'); *Furnesty* 1561 (17) (*v.* **fearn**; with **stīg** or **stig**); *Le Further hedge* 1561 (17) (*v.* **furðra, hecg**); *Gildenehauedland, -heuedland* 13 (1404), *the gilden ~, gyldon headland* 1550, *Gyldyn Headlande, ~ Hedland* 1561 (17) ('the golden headland', *v.* **gylden, hēafod-land**; alluding presum. to yellow or golden flowers); *Gill gappe, Gyllegappe* bis 1561 (17) (*v.* **gap**; with the surn. *Gill*, cf. *Chewegappe, supra*); *Golding forthe* 1550, *~ forth* 1561 (17), *Goldynge forth* 1561 (17) (*v.* **eng, ford**; the first el. is either OE *gold* in its sense 'golden-hued' with reference to flowers, or OE **golde** 'a (marsh) marigold'); *Gorbrode* 1550, *Gorbrod* 1561 (17) (*v.* **gorebrode**); *Goseholme* m.13 (1404) bis, 1561 (17), *Gosholme* 1561 (17) (*v.* **gōs, holmr**); *grat filld* 1683³ (*v.* **grēat, feld**); *Gregorys House & homested* 1681 (1791), 1682 (1791), *~ ~ ~ ~* in the tenure of John Gregory 1682 (1791) (*v.* **hām-stede**); *Grene* 13 (1404) bis, *othe grene* 1381 (p) (*v.* **grēne²**); *Grenegate* 1216

(1404), m.13 (1404), *Greengate* 1561 (17), *grenegatesende* 13 (1404) (*v.* **ende**) (*v.* **grēne**[1], **gata**); *Grenehousike* m.13 (1404), 13 (1404) bis, *Grenehou Syke* 13 (1404) (*v.* **grēne**[1], **haugr, sík**); *Gudlokestoft* m.13 (1449), *Gudelokestoft* l.13 (1449) (*v.* **toft**), *Guddelokescroft* 1335 (1449) (*v.* **croft**) (both with the OE pers.n. *Gūðlāc; croft* may have replaced *toft*); *the hall land* 1550 (*v.* **land**) (*v. the Earles land, supra*), *the hall meadow* 1550 (*v.* **mǣd** (**mǣdwe** obl.sg.)), *Hall Orchard* 1708, *the Old Hall Orchard* 1747 (*v.* **hall** and Old Hall Fm *supra*); *Hancock land* 1550, *Hancocks Land* 1561 (17), 1609 (18), *Hancockes land alias Hancockes Thing* 1624 (*v.* **land, thing**), (*John*) *Hancocks Orchard* 1682 (1791), 1685 (1791), *Hancocks Platt* 1747 (*v.* **plat**); *Hardy Balke* 1561 (17) (*v.* **balca**; with the surn. *Hardy*); *Hartopps Hedlande* 1561 (17) (*v.* **hēafod-land**, cf. *Thomas Hartopp* 1561 (17) of Burton Lazars); *le Hegge juxta Over Syke* 1561 (17) (*v.* **hecg** and Sick Leys *supra*); *Hengendehil* 13 (1404), *hengandhull* 1309 (1449) ('the hill with a steep slope', *v.* **hangende, hengjandi, hyll**); *hill close* 1682[2]; *Le Hodde Willowe, Hodde Wyllow(e), Hod(e)wyllow* 1561 (17) (*v.* **odde, wilig**); *Hody Lane, ~ ~ End* 1561 (17) (*v.* **lane, lane-ende**; the first el. is obscure, poss. the surn. *Oddie/ Oddy, v.* Reaney *s.n.*); *Holefurwe* m.13 (1404), *holowforou* a.1280 (1449), *hollouforou* l.13 (1449), *holuforu* 13 (1449), *Hollow Furrow, Holowe furrowe* 1561 (17) (*v.* **hol**[2], **holh, furh**); *Le Holmes, ~ Holmys* 1561 (17) (*v.* **holmr**); *Hubbard's ~* 1708, *Hubberts House* 1708, 1708[3], *Hubberts Close* 1747 (*v.* New Fd *supra*) (with the surn. *Hubbert/Hubbard, v.* Reaney *s.n.* Hubert); *Iuett(e) Hedlands* 1561 (17) (*v.* **hēafod-land**; with the surn. *Ivett*, cf. *Peter Ivet* 1550 and *the land of the heires of Ivet* 1550 in neighbouring Melton Mowbray, *v.* Reaney *s.n.* Ivatt); *Jacobs Close* 1747 (with the surn. *Jacob(s), v. Sand Pit Close, infra*); *Tho. Jervis House* 1747, *Tho. Jervis his plott* 1682 (*v.* **plot**), *Wd' Jervas's plott* 1682 (i.e. Widow ~ ~, *v.* **plot**), *Jervis Platt* 1747 (*v.* **plat**); *John Kellam his howse & homeyard* 1668 (*v.* **home-yard**), *John Callams plott* 1682 (*v.* **plot**), *Tho. Kelhams Cottage* 1691 (1791), 1685 (1791) (*v.* **cotage**), *Tho. Kelhams House & homested* 1682 (1791) (*v.* **hām-stede**) (the *Kelham* family no doubt originated in the village of this name 24 miles to the north in Notts.); *the kings wonge late Lewis* 1550 (*v.* **king, vangr**; the king (Edward VI) also held land in neighbouring Melton Mowbray); *Kirkeby gate* 1561 (17) (*v.* **gata**; the road to Kirby Bellars, otherwise Sawgate Rd *supra*); *Kvynnyfurlong* m.13 (1404), *Wynni-, Wynnyfurlong* 13 (1404), *Whinnyfurlong* 1550, *Wynny(e)furlong(e)* 1561 (17) (*v.* **whinny, furlong**; the earliest citation for *whinny* in OED is for 1483); *langedike* 1216 (1404), *langedikes* 13 (1404) bis, *longedikes* l.13 (1449) (*v.* **lang**[1], **dík**); *Lauedylane* 1288 (1404), *lauedilane* c.1288 (1404) (*v.* **lavedi, lane**); *The Leys* 17, *Long(e) Leyes, Long Leys* 1561 (17) (*v.* **lang**[1]), *Short Leyes* 1593 (17), 1648, 1668, l.17, *Shortleazes* 1609 (18), *the Shorte Leyes* 1648, *Short leies* 17, *Shortleys since called Bullocks nook* 1646 (1791), *Short Leys once called Bullocks Wong* 1668 (1791), *~ ~ since called ~ ~*1685 (1791), *Shortleys or Bullocks Wong* 1681 (1791), 1682 (1791) (*v.* **sc(e)ort**, Bull Nook and Bullock Wong, both *supra*), *the Leyes Meadow* l.17 (*v.* **leys**); *litlihenge(s)* 13 (1404) (*v.* **lȳtel, lítill, eng**); *littlmedue* m.13 (1404) (*v.* **lȳtel, mǣd** (**mǣdwe** obl.sg.)); *the litle river* 1550 (*v.* **lȳtel, rivere**; referring to R. Eye); *Le Lyttyl Hendryth* 1561 (17) (*v.* **lȳtel, henn, rīð**, cf. Hendred, Brk 479); *Lytullhill* 1561 (17)[2] (*v.* **lȳtel, hyll**); *Longe Balke, Long Balk End* 1561 (17) (*v.* **lang**[1], **balca, ende**); *long dyke wong* 1550 (*v.* **lang**[1], **dík, vangr**); *Longefurlong* m.13 (1404), *longefurlange* 13 (1404), *long furlong* 1550, *Neytherlong(e)furlong(e)*,

Overlong(e)furlonge 1561 (17) (*v.* **neoðera, uferra**) (*v.* **lang**[1], **furlang**); *Lynes Yards End* 1561 (17) (*v.* **geard, ende**, cf. *Robertus Lyne* and *Willielmus Lyne* 1561 (17)); *Mabell Walls* 1550, *Mablay Wallis* 1561 (17) (*v.* **wall**; with the surn. *Mable/Mabley*; the ME pers.n. *Mabel* or *Mabley* was the popular form of *Amabel* (MLat *amabilis* 'lovable') which by dissimilation also gave the pers.n. *An(n)abel*); *Mare furlonge* 1550, *Mere Furlonge* 1561 (17) (*v.* **(ge)mære, furlang**); *Mare Pytt(e)*, ~ *Pytts* 1561 (17) (*v.* **(ge)mære, pytt**); *Mare Wong next the Stoke* 1550 (*v.* **(ge)mære, vangr** and Stock Cl *supra*); *Markytt Gate* 1561 (17) ('the road to the market', *v.* **market, gata**; i.e. the road to Melton Mowbray); *Marlewonge* 1561 (17) (*v.* **marle, vangr**); *Mekylgate* 1561 (17) (*v.* **micel, mikill, gata**); *Melton Mere* 1550, 1561 (17) (*v.* **(ge)mære**; the Melton Mowbray parish boundary to the north); *Midlefurlong* 1550, *Middull furlong, Myddull Furlonge* 1561 (17) (*v.* **middel, furlang**); *Middilgate* 13 (1404) (*v.* **middel, gata**); *Molote Welle* 13 (1404) (*v.* **wella**; with the ME pers.n. *Molot*, diminutive of *Moll* (Mary), *v.* Reaney *s.n.* Mollet); *le morfurlong'* m.13 (1404), *morefurlong'* 13 (1449), *More furlong(e)* 1561 (17) (*v.* **furlang**), *Moregate* 1561 (17) (*v.* **gata**) (*v.* The Moor *supra*); *Mussulhoke, Mussull Hoke* 1561 (17) ('the hook of land at Mouse Hill (i.e. the mouse-infested hill)', *v.* **mūs, hyll, hōc**); *the Mylne, behinde the Mylne* (*v.* **behindan**; i.e. the furlong behind the mill), *Mylne Balke* (*v.* **balca**), (*Le*) *Mylne Dame, Myldame* (*v.* **damme**) 1561 (17), *le milneheuedis* c.1288 (1404) (*v.* **hēafod**) (*v.* **myln**); *Nether furlong* 1550, *Neyther furlong(e)* 1561 (17) (*v.* **neoðera, furlang**); *Le Neyther Feild(e)* 1561 (17) (*v.* **neoðera, feld**); *northefylde* 1300 (1449), *the North fielde* 1550 (*v.* **norð, feld**; one of the early great fields of the village); *old meadow close alias west meadow* c.1683; *the Overfield* 1550, *Le Overfield(e) versus Melton* 1561 (17) (*v.* **uferra, feld**); *Over furlonge* 1561 (17) (*v.* **uferra, furlang**); *Parke Dyke* (*v.* **dík**), *Parke Furlonge* (*v.* **furlang**), *Parke Heads* (*v.* **hēafod**), *Parke Syke* (*v.* **sík**) 1561 (17) (*v.* The Park *supra*); *Pauntons or Barkleis* 1624 (a messuage so called, *v.* Berkley's *supra*); *the land sometyme called Peter Ivet* 1550 (*v.* **land**); *Philpots House & Homested* 1685 (1791) (*v.* **hām-stede** and cf. *Fra.ˢ Philpot* 1685 (1791) of Burton Lazars); *Pitt Close* 1682 (*v.* **pytt**); *pitgate* m.13 (1404), l.13 (1404), *putgate* m.13 (1404) bis, *Pitgatte* 13 (1404), *le pitgate* 1309 (1449), *Pit gate* 1550, *Pittgate, Pytgate, Pytt(e)gate* 1561 (17), *Pytgate Syde* 1561 (17) (*v.* **sīde**) (*v.* **pytt, gata**); *the Plash* 1550, *Le Plash, Le Plasshe* 1561 (17) (*v.* **plæsc**); *Porte Headlands* 1561 (17) (*v.* **hēafod-land**, cf. *Johannes Porte* 1561 (17) of Burton Lazars); *Pounde acre* 1561 (17) (*v.* **pund, æcer**); *the Pryors headland* 1550, *Prior He(a)dlands, Priors Headlands* 1561 (17) (*v.* **hēafod-land**), *Pryor leyes* 1550 (*v.* **leys**), *Prior Wonge* 1561 (17) (*v.* **vangr**) (*v.* **prior**; presum. referring to the Prior of Chacombe Priory, Nth (*v.* Great Dalby *infra*) or to that of nearby Kirby Bellars Priory, but the surn. *Prior* is poss., if less likely); *quakefen* 1309 (1449), 1561 (17), *quack fenn* 1550, *quakefenne* 1561 (17) (*v.* **quake, fenn**); *Rackett Mires* 1747 (*v.* **mýrr**; the first el. is poss. ME **ragged** 'ragged, shaggy, rough'); *Saint Margaryts Meadow abbutant super Le Eye, Saynt Margytts Meade, Saynte Margytts Meadow,* ~ ~ *Medowe* 1561 (17) (*v.* **mǣd** (**mǣdwe** obl.sg.)), *Saynt Margytts Wylleus* 1561 (17) (*v.* **wilig**) (this land with willow-trees bordering R. Eye was presum. associated with a local chapel dedicated to St Margaret; none of the surrounding churches bear such a dedication); *Sand Pit Close* 1708, 1708[3], *Sandpytt Close* 1708, *Sandpitt or Jacobs Close* 1747 (*v.* Jacobs Close, *supra*); *scalderdeyles* l.13 (1449) ('Skjaldari's portions of land', *v.* **deill**; the Scand pers.n. *Skjaldari* is an original by-name meaning 'shield-maker'); *Schepestigate* m.13 (1404) (ambiguous; either 'the sheep track', *v.* **scēp, sty-gate** (from **stīg, gata**, cf. ME *sty-way, v.* Ch 5 1 (ii) 358 *s.v.*) or 'the road to the sheep pen', *v.* **scēp, stig, gata**); *seuordebrigg'* 1309 (1449) (*v.* **brycg**; prob. with the OE pers.n. *Sigeweard*, but ON *Sigvarðr* (ODan *Sigwarth*) is also poss.); *Seuuldecrofte* 1216 (1404) (*v.* **croft**; with the first el. a pers.n., either OE *Sigeweald* or ON *Sigvaldr*); *Sewell Pole,* ~ *Poylle* 1561 (17) (*v.* **pōl**[1]; poss. with the same pers.n. as first el. as in the preceding f.n.); *Sheppards Lane* 1561 (17), *Sheppards yard end* 1561 (17) (*v.* **ende**) (*v.* **lane, geard**, cf. *Henricus Sheppard* 1561 (17)); *Siding Close* 1686[2] (*v.* **sīd, eng**); (*le*) *Slede,* (*le*) *Sleyde* 1561 (17) (*v.* **slæd**); *Sleythenges* m.13 (1404) (*v.* **slēttr, eng**); *Small leayes* 1683 × 88 (*v.* **smæl, leys**); *smethemedwe* a.1280 (1449), *smethemedue* l.13 (1404), *Smith meadowe* 1550, *Smeth Meadow,* ~ *Med(d)ow, Smythe Medowe* 1561 (17) (*v.* **smēðe**[1], **mæd (mædwe** obl.sg.)); *Snodon yarde* 1561 (17) (*v.* **geard**, cf. *Thomas Snodon* 1561 (17)); *le Sough Medowe apud Dalby gate* 1561 (17) (*v.* **sōg, mæd (mædwe** obl.sg.) and *Dalby gate, supra*); *Souheudes* l.13 (1449) (*v.* **sōg, hēafod**); *Soure* ~, *Sowre Dole* 1561 (17) (*v.* **sūr, dāl**); *Southwell* 1561 (17) (*v.* **sūð, wella**); *sowthefylde* 1300 (1449) (*v.* **sūð, feld**; one of the early great fields of the village); *spitelgate* 1309 (1449) (*v.* **spitel, gata**; the road to the Hospital of St Lazarus *supra*); (*the*) *Spring Close* 1682 (*v.* **spring**[1]); *Squires Plat* 1708 (*v.* **plat**; with the surn. *Squire(s)*); *Stanfordegate* 13 (1404), *Stamforth gate* 1561 (17), *Stamfordgate Pingle* 1682 (1791) (*v.* **pingel**), *Stamfordgate Sick* 1642 (1791), 1682 (1791), 1685 (1791), 1747, ~ *Sikes* 1682, *Stamford Gate Sike* 1683 × 88 (*v.* **sīk**) ('the road to Stamford', *v.* **gata**); *Stapleford bridge forth* 17 (*v.* *briggeforth, supra*), *Stapleford hedge* l.17 (*v.* **hecg**; a boundary hedge), *Stapulforth* ~, *Stabulforth Mere* 1561 (17) (*v.* **(ge)mære**) (Stapleford adjoins to the east); *stowhilles, stowehilles* 1328 (1449) (*v.* **stōw, hyll**); *the Street* l.17 (*v.* **strǣt**; prob. referring to the east to west salt-merchants' road, *v.* Sawgate Rd *supra*); *Sudinges iuxta divisam de Dalby* m.13 (1404) (with MLat *divisa* 'a boundary'), *suthenges* a.1280 (1449), *Sudenges* bis, *Suthhenges, Southehenges* 13 (1404), *Southenges* 13 (1449), *Sudengesgate, Suthengegate, Suthingate* 13 (1404) (*v.* **gata**) ('the south meadows', *v.* **sūð, eng**); *Suthere Peselandes* 13 (1404) (*v.* **sūðer, pise, land**); *ten knowles* 1550 (*v.* **tēn, cnoll**); *Thirne-, Thyrneclif* 13 (1404) (*v.* **þyrne, clif**); *Thistelholm* l.13 (1404) (*v.* **þistel, holmr**); *Thorneyard end* 1561 (17) (*v.* **geard, ende**; with the surn. *Thorn(e), v.* Reaney *s.n.*); *threhowis, threowis* l.13 (1449), *threws* 1300 (1449), *Throwis* 1561 (17), *Mid threwis* 1550 (*v.* **mid**), *Overthrewys* 1550, *Overthrowis* 1561 (17) (*v.* **uferra**), *Neytherthrowis* 1561 (17) (*v.* **neoðera**) (*v.* **þrēo, haugr**); *Thurstoneswong* m.13 (1404), *Thrustyn wonge Holmes* 1561 (17) (*v.* **holmr**) (*v.* **vangr**; with the OE pers.n. *Þurstān*, the anglicized version of ON *Þorsteinn* (ODan *Thorsten*)); *Tingle hill* 1682 (*v.* **pingel**); *Trowelle* 13 (1404), *Trowell Brygge, Trowelbrygge* 1561 (17) (*v.* **brycg**), *Trowell gate* 1561 (17) (*v.* **gata**) ('the tree stream', *v.* **trēow, wella**; perh. one with a bridge formed by a tree-trunk, cf. Trowell, Nt 153); *Tuffordegate* m.13 (1404), *tofordgate, toforthgate* l.13 (1404), *thofordgate* a.1280 (1449), *Tufforthe gate* 1550, *Tufforth gate, Tuffurthgate, Turfurthgate* 1561 (17) (*v.* **twēgen, tū, ford, gata**); *Tunforlong'* 1216 (1404), 13 (1404), *Tunfurlong(g)ate* 1288 (1404), c.1288 (1404) (*v.* **gata**) ('the furlong(s) beside the township', *v.* **tūn, furlang**); *Tynkerybbis* 1561 (17) (*v.* **rybb** 'a narrow strip of land' (OED *s.v.* rib sb.[1], 6a, with earliest citation 1670); the first el. is the ME occupational surn. *Tinker, v.* Reaney *s.n.*); *Vaudy land* 1535 × 46 *MinAccts*, 1550, *the land late Vaudy* 1550 (Vaudey Abbey in Lincs. held land in Burton Lazars, *v.* The Grange *supra*); *the Vinehowse* 1668, l.17, *the Vinehouse & homested* 1668 (1791) (*v.* **hām-stede**), *Dewicks Vinehouse* 1685 (1791) (cf. *Widow Dewick* 1685 (1791)), *the Vyne howse Farme* 1648, *the Vinehouse farm* 1682 (1791) (*v.* **ferme**), *the Vinehouse Land* 1668, 1668 (1791) (*v.* **vine, hūs**); *the Vineyard* 1747 (*v.* **vinʒerd**); *Waites farm late in the tenure of John Waite* 1681 (1791), *John Waytes farme* 1682, *Waites Farm* 1682 (1791) (*v.* **ferme**), *John Waites Plott* 1686 (*v.* **plot**); *Walke Mill, ~ ~ mead, the Walke Mill Meadow* 1681 (*v.* **walke-milne, mǣd** (**mǣdwe** obl.sg.)); *walsemoresedis, -edes, walsimoresedis* l.13 (1404), *Walchemoresedes* 13 (1404) (*v.* **mōr**[1], **edisc**; the first el. appears to be the adj. **wǣlisc** 'British' rather than **wales**, the gen.sg. of **walh** 'a Briton, a serf', although the latter would make more satisfying sense; *v.* also *Walsemorland* in Leesthorpe f.ns. (b)); *Walters Hempland* 1685 (1791) (*v.* **hempland**), *Walters londe* 1554 (*v.* **land**) (with the surn. *Walter(s)*); *John Waltons House & Vineyard* 1682 (1791) (*v.* **vinʒerd**), *Jo. Waltons House & Hempland* 1747 (*v.* **hempland**); *waterfurwes* m.13 (1404), *Water Furrows* 1561 (17), *Waterfurrow leyes* 1550, *Water Furrowe Leas* 1561 (17) (*v.* **leys**) (perh. 'furrows where water tends to lie', *v.* **wæter, furh** and *waterfurris* in Muston f.ns. (b)); *Le Water Meadow(e), ~ ~ Medow(e)* 1561 (17) (*v.* **wæter, mǣd** (**mǣdwe** obl.sg.); land with an artificial system of irrigation, *v.* Field 90–1); *le Wayte* 13 (1404) ('the fishing place', *v.* **veiðr**; presum. a spot beside R. Eye); *Welpiswong* 13 (1404) ('Hwelp's infield', *v.* **vangr**; the pers.n. *Hwelp* is ODan (ON *Hvelpr*)); *West Closes* 1683 × 88; *the West field* 1550, *Westfield close* c.1683 (*v.* **west, feld**); *Westings* 1550 (*v.* **west, vestr, eng**); *Where head* 1561 (17) (*v.* **wer, hēafod**); *The Widdow(e) Close* 1683 × 88, *The Widows plat* 1682 (1791), *The Widdows Platt* 1683 × 88 (*v.* **plat**), *The Widdows Plott* 1683 × 88 (*v.* **plot**) (*v.* **widuwe**); *Wilds farm in the tenure of Wm. Wild* 1685 (1791) (*v.* **ferme**); *le Wite Cros* m.13 (1404), *Wytecros* 13 (1404), *Whit' Crose* 1300 (1449), *Whyte Crosse* 1561 (17), *White Crosse* 1561 (17), 1593 (17), *Whitecross* 1609 (18), 1668 (1791), (*apud lapideam crucem* m.13 (1404), *ad Crucem* 13 (1404); with MLat *crux* (*crucem* acc.sg.) 'a cross' and MLat *lapidea* 'made of stone'), *Whytecroseleys* 1555, *White Crosse Leyes* 1648, l.17, 17, *Whitecross Leys* 1646 (1791), 1668 (1791), 1682 (1791), 1685 (1791) (*v.* **leys**) (*v.* **hwīt, cros**; this white cross, presum. made of limestone, is unlocated); *Wrangeland'* m.13 (1404), *Wrongelondis* 13 (1404) (*v.* **wrang, vrangr, land**); *Wrangesik'* 1216 (1404), *Wrongesike* 13 (1404), *Wrong(e) Sicke, ~ Syke, Wrongge Syke* 1561 (17), *Wrongesicheshend* 13 (1404) (*v.* **ende**) (*v.* **wrang, vrangr, sík, sīc**); *Wynmylne* 1561 (17), *The Windmill* 1668 (1791), 1682 (1791), *Winmylne feild, Le Wynmylne Feild, Wynmylne feilde* 1561 (17) (*v.* **feld**), *Wynmylne hedis, ~ Heyds* 1561 (17) (*v.* **hēafod**), *Wyndmyllne hyll, Wynmyl(l)ne hill(e)* 1561 (17), *Wynnemylhyll* 1561 (17)[2] (*v.* **hyll**), *the Windmill Leyes* 1648 (*v.* **leys**) (*v.* **wind-mylne**); *yngoldiscroft* l.13 (1449) (*v.* **croft**; the first el. is the Anglo-Scand pers.n. *Ingald/Ingold* (ON *Ingjaldr*)).

2. GREAT DALBY

DB includes Great Dalby in Goscote Wapentake. The township later became part of East Goscote Hundred.

> *Dalbi* 1086 DB bis, 1229 Nichols, m.13 (1404), p.1250 (1404) *Laz*,
> 1272 RGrav, *Dalbia* c.1130 LeicSurv bis, *Dalby* 1086 DB, Hy 2
> Dugd, 1212 Cur *et passim* to p.1250 (1404) *Laz*, 1284 Cl *et freq*
> *Daleby* c.1130 LeicSurv, a.1250 (1404) *Laz*, 1275 RH
> *Daubi* l.12 Dane, e.13 (1404) *Laz* (freq), e.13 Berkeley, a.1250
> (1404), m.13 (1404) *Laz*, *Dauby* e.13 (1404) *ib*, 1231 Berkeley,
> 1209 × 35 RHug *et passim* to 1273 Ipm, 1276 RH, *Daulby* n.d.
> (1449) *WoCart*

'The farmstead, village in the valley', *v.* **dalr, bȳ**. Spellings in *-au-* for ON *-al-* for both Great Dalby and Little Dalby *infra* are due to AN influence.

Although both Great Dalby and Little Dalby were in existence by the date of the Domesday Survey, Great Dalby had the higher valuation and was probably the settlement from which Little Dalby, although in a different wapentake, was an offshoot. It lies at the head of a wide valley running north towards R. Wreake. Little Dalby, two miles to the east, is also tucked into the head of a small valley which opens to the north, and its name, although probably transferred from that of Great Dalby, is appropriate to its location. Great Dalby was held by *Hugo de Chaucumbe* 12 Nichols, by *Robertus de Chaucumb* 1212 Cur, e.13, 1231 Berkeley and by the *prior et conventus de Chaucumb(e)* 1233, 1235 RHug, 1238 RGros, 1272 RGrav (*v.* Chalcombe, Nth 50).

Affixes for Great Dalby are variously:

> *Magna* ~ c.1130 LeicSurv, 12 Nichols *et passim* to 1535 MinAccts
> ~ *Magna* 1238 RGros, 1404 *Laz et passim* to 1609, 1678 LML
> *Majore* ~ c.1450 TutP, *Majori* ~ 1535 VE
> ~ *Chaucumb(e)* 1220 MHW, 1233 RHug *et passim* to 1315 Cl, 1327
> Banco, ~ *Cha(u)combe* 1316 FA, 1320 Cl *et passim* to 1615, 1630
> LML, ~ *Jacomb(e)* 1611 ib, 1720 MagBrit, ~ *Chalcomb(e)* 1613,
> 1675 LML
> *Cha(u)co(u)mbe* ~ 1272 RGrav, 1315 Cl, 1329 Ipm, *Chakun* ~ 1295
> ib, *Checom* ~ 1436 Pat, *Chacum* ~ 1535 VE

BURROUGH HILL COVERT, *v.* **cover(t)**; referring to Burrough Hill, the Iron Age hill-fort site in neighbouring Burrough on the Hill. CROWN HILL, *v.* Crown Dale in f.ns. (a) *infra.* FIRST HILL, 1842 *TA, The Big Hill or First Hill* 1968 *Surv*; either with **fyrs** 'furze' or with **fyrst** 'first, chief, principal', cf. The First Hill in Wymondham f.ns. (a). FREEHOLD HO., *The Freehold* 1877 White, *v.* **frehold**; describing the nature of the tenure of the land holder. GARTREE HILL is *Gallow Tree Hill* 1750 *Surv, Garrely Hill* (sic) 1824 O, *v.* **galg-trēow**; the name has been attracted to that of the county's Gartree Hundred which has a different etymology. The later form *Gallows Hill* 1842 *TA*, 1968 *Surv* retains the old signification. GARTREE HILL COVERT, *v.* **cover(t)**. GARTREE HILL LODGE. GREAT DALBY LODGE, (x2). GREAT DALBY STATION. THE GREEN, 1842 *TA*, 1846 White, 1968 *Surv, v.* **grēne**[2]. MALT SHOVEL (P.H.) (lost), *Malt Shovel* 1846, 1863 White. MANOR HO., cf. *Manor farm* 1925 Kelly, *v.* **maner**. MARCH HO., *Le Marshe* 1561 (1700) *Rental, the Marsh* 1683, 1750 *Surv, ye March* 1686 *ib, the March* 1968 *ib, v.* **mersc**. NAG'S HEAD (P.H.) (lost), *Nag's Head* 1846 White. NETHER END, *v.* **ende**. PRINCE OF WALES INN, *Prince of Wales* 1877 White, 1925 Kelly, 1968 *Surv*. ROYAL OAK (P.H.), *Royal Oak* 1846, 1863, 1877 White, 1925 Kelly. ST SWITHIN'S CHURCH, *the Church* 1708, 1708 (18) *Terrier, Church (St Swithin)* 1846, 1863, 1877 White. Note also *the Church Yard* 1601, 1708 (18), 1736 *Terrier*, 1750 *Surv, v.* **chirche-ӡeard**. SANDY LANE, *v.* **sandig**. SIR FRANCIS BURDETT'S COVERT, *v.* **cover(t)**; named after the Radical reformer Sir Francis Burdett (1770–1844) some time before 1843 when it is mentioned in C.J. Apperley, *Nimrod's Hunting Reminiscences*, 40. STATION COTTAGES, at Great Dalby Station. STOCK LEYS BARN, *Stock Leys Barn and Stackyard* 1968 *Surv* (*v.* **stak-ӡeard**), *Stock leyes* 1682 *ib, Stockleys* 1683 *ib, Stocklees, Stock Leys* 1750 *ib, v.* **stoc, leys**. THORPE END VILLA, 1877 White, *v.* **ende**; Thorpe End or Upper End is on the south-west side of the village towards Thorpe Satchville. UPPER END, *v.* **ende**. THE VICARAGE, 1877 White, 1925 Kelly, *The Vicarage House* 1708, 1708 (18) *Terrier*; it is *the mansion house* 1601 *ib, v.* **mansion-house**. Note also *the Homestall* 1708, 1708 (18) *ib* (*v.* **hām-stall**), part of the Vicarage buildings. WOODGATE HILL, *Woodgate* 1750 *Surv, Wood Gate* 1842 *TA, v.* **wudu, gata**. YEW TREE FM, *Yew Tree Farm* 1968 *Surv*.

FIELD-NAMES

Undated forms in (a) are 1968 *Surv*; forms dated 1842 are *TA*. Forms throughout dated c.1545 and 1535 × 46 are *MinAccts*, 1561 (1700) are *Rental*, 1601, 1612, 1708, 1708 (18) and 1736 are *Terrier*, while 1682, 1682 (1791), 1683, 1686, 1750 and 18 are *Surv*.

(a) The 2 Acre (x2) (Two Acres 1842), The 3 Acre, The 4 ~ (x2) (Four Acres 1842), The 5 ~ (x2), The Five ~ ((The) Five Acres 1842), The 6 Acre (x3), The 7 ~ (x3), The Seven ~, The 8 ~, The 9 ~ (x2), The 10 ~ (x2), The Ten ~, The 12 ~ (x2), The 16 Acre 1968, Eighteen Acres 1842, The 30 Acre (*v.* **æcer**); Adcock's Slatters (*v.* **slétta**; with the surn. *Adcock*); The Aeroplane Fd (named from an aeroplane which was forced to land in this field in the Second World War); The Alfords, Halfords or Alfords, Parson's Holford (*v.* **persone**) (*v.* **ford**); Alltoft 1842, 1968, ~ Mdw 1842, Alltofts 1842 (*Alltoft*, ~ *Close* 1750, *v.* **toft**; with the Scand pers.n. *Alli* or *Áli*); Angle Fd 1842 (*v.* **angle**); The First, The Second Ashes (*v.* **æsc**); Auntie Madge's Big Hill, Auntie Madge's four acre (*Madge* is a pet form of the pers.n. Margery); Barn Cl 1842 (x4), The Barn Cl 1968 (*Barn Close* 1750 (x2)), Barn Close Mdw 1842, Front o'the Barn; Basses Cl 1842, Bass's ~ 1968 (*Basses Close* 1750, cf. *John Basses Cottage* 1682, 1686, 18, ~ *Bass's* ~ 1682 (1791), *v.* **cotage**); Bendales 1842, 1968 (*Boon dale* 1686, *Bundle Fur'* 1686 (*v.* **furlang**), *Bundales Close* 1750, *v.* **bēan, baun, deill**); Better Land 1842, The Better Lands 1968 (*Better Lands* 1750, *v.* **butere, land**); Big Cl; Big Fd; The Big Mdw; Bottom Mdw (*v.* **bottom**); Break Miles 1842, The Brakemiles, Fisher's Brakemiles (with the surn. *Fisher*) (*Black Miles* 1682, *Blackmiles Fur'* 1686 (*v.* **furlang**), *Blackmoils* 1750, 'the black soil', *v.* **blæc, mylde**); Broad Brook 1842 (*Broadbeck Fur'* 1682, *Broadback* 1683, *Broad back Fur'* 1686, *Broad Buck* 1750, *v.* **brād, bekkr, furlang**); Brook Cl 1842, Brook Mdw 1842 (*v.* **brōc**); The Bulldozer (presum. a field containing a defunct machine); Burrow Hedge 1842 (1750, *v.* **hecg**; referring to the boundary hedge with Burrough on the Hill), Burrow Hill Wood 1842 (*Burrow Hill* 1750; the site of the Iron Age hill-fort of Burrough Hill in neighbouring Burrough on the Hill), The Burrough Mdw (adjacent to Burrough Hill); Great, Little Burton Hedge 1842, Burton Hedges 1968 (*Burton Hedge* 1750, *v.* **hecg**; referring to the boundary hedge of Burton Lazars); Bush Mdw (*v.* **busc**); Calf Cl 1842 (*v.* **calf**); Church Farm Paddock (*v.* **paddock**); The Church Fd; Coleing Cl 1842 (*Coling Close* 1750; poss. with the surn. *Coling, v.* Reaney *s.n.*); The Cottage Cl (*Cottage Close* 1750), Cottage Pasture 1842, 1968 (*v.* **cotage**); Crane Cl 1842 (either with the surn. *Crane* or with **cran** 'a crane, a heron', cf. Crown Dale *infra*); The Cricket Fd (referring to the game of cricket); Croft 1842 (*v.* **croft**); Crown Dale 1842 (1682, 1686, 1750, *Crownedale* 1686; poss. **cran, cron** 'a crane, a heron', with **dalr**, cf. Crown Hill *supra* and Crane Cl *supra*); The Dalby Fd 1842, Great Dalby Fd 1968; The Little Dalby Cl (towards neighbouring Little Dalby); Dalby Mill 1824 O (a windmill); Dale Paddock (*v.* **dalr, paddock**); Dead Wife 1842, 1968 (1750, *v.* **dēad**; on the township boundary and either the site of a discovered early female burial or that of a more recent death); Deep Dale 1842, 1968 (*Depdale* 1750, *v.* **dēop, dalr**); Dennis Cl 1842 (with the surn. *Dennis*); Ealing's (the surn. *Ealing* in the possessive case); Eating Cl 1842 (*v.* **eating**; referring to good pasture); The First Eddish (*v.* **edisc**); (The) Far Cl 1842; Fat-nick 1842 (f.ns. with *fat* indicate good quality in soil or herbage; this example may be a garbled **fattening**, referring to the fattening of livestock, cf. The Fatnings in Buckminster f.ns. (a)); Fenn Cl 1842, First Fen Mdw (both with **fenn**); (The) First Cl 1842; Len Fisher's First, Second Fd, Fisher's Garden, Fisher's Orchard; Flat Mdw (x2), The Flat Mdw (cf. *Flattlands* 1682, *v.* **flatr, land**); Little ~ ~, Foot Cl 1842, The Foot Cl (*v.* **fōt**; referring to a close at the foot of a hill); The Forcelands (*v.* **land**), Forsells 1842 (cf. *Forsells Sick* 1683 (*v.* **sík**)) (the three f.ns. may contain **fyrs** 'furze', the second with **hyll**); The Galls, Top Galls (*Galls Fur'* 1682, *Goales* ~ 1686, *v.* **galla, furlang**); Far Gorse 1842, Peers Gorse 1842 (with the surn. *Peers, v.* Reaney *s.n.* Pierce), Gorse Hill 1968, Far, Near, Little, Gorse Cl 1842 (*v.* **gorst**); Gravel Pit 1842 (*Gravell pitts* 1682, *Gravill* ~ 1686, *Gravell Pitt furlong* 1683), Gravel Pit Cl 1842 (*Gravel Pitt Close* 1750), (The) Gravel Hole 1968 (*v.* **gravel**); Gray's (the surn. *Gray* in the possessive case); Great Cl 1842, The Great Cl (x2); Green Lane; Green Leys 1842, 1968 (*v.* **leys**); Halfords (*v.* The Alfords *supra*); Far, Further, Near, Hall Yard 1842 (*Hall Yard* 1750), Hallyards (*The Hall Yards* 1736) (*v.* **hall, geard**); The Hills (1682), Hill Cl 1842, Hill Mdw 1842, 1968; Holland Dale 1842, Hollandale 1968 (*Hollondale* 1601, *Hollandale* 1612, *Holland dale* 1682, 1683, 1686, *v.* **hol²**, **land**; with **dalr** or **deill**); Home Cl 1842, 1968 (x2), Far ~ ~, First ~ ~ 1842, Second ~ ~ 1842, 1968, (The) Home Fd (x4) (*v.* **home**); The Horse Cl; House Croft 1842 (*v.* **croft**); The Hovel, Hovel Fd (*v.* **hovel**); Hubbuck Cl 1842, Hubbuck Mead 1842, Hubbock Mdw (*v.* **mæd**), Hubbock 1968, Hubbrick Hill 1842 (*Hobeck hill* 1682, *How Back hill* 1686, *Nether, Upper Hubbuck Hill* 1750, *Hobeck Fur'* 1682, *Hoe Beck Fur'* 1686 (*v.* **furlang**), *Hobeck Riggit* 1682, *How Back Rickett* 1686 (*v.* **riggett**), 'the stream beside the ridge', *v.* **hōh, bekkr**, the first el. has been influenced by **haugr** in two 1686 forms); Huts (*v.* **hut**; a field containing temporary shelters when the railway was being constructed; Big ~ ~, Top of ~ ~, Ingle Hill (*Ingle hill* 1683, *Ingley hill* 1750, *Ingle Ridgett* 1683 (*v.* **riggett**), *v.* **ingel**); Jackson's Orchard formerly Lowe's Orchard; Joel's Paddock (*v.* **paddock**; with the surn. *Joel*); Kiln Yard 1842, The Kill Yard 1968 (with ModEdial. *kill* 'a kiln'); First, Second Leys 1968, Long Leys 1842 (1750), Short Leys 1842 (*v.* **leys**); Little Cl 1842; Lower Little Dales, Upper Little Dale 1842, Second Littledales, Littledills or Upper and Lower Littledales 1968 (*Little Dale* 1682, 1686, *Lower, Upper Little Dale* 1750; with **dalr** or **deill**); Little Fd (x2); The Little Hill (cf. *Little hill wong* 1682, 1686, *v.* **vangr**); Little Mdw 1842; Long Furlong 1842, 1968 (1682, 1686, 1750, *Long Furlong Sike* 1683, ~ ~ *Sick* 1686, *v.* **sík**); Long Mdw 1842; Long Thong 1842 (1750, *Long thong furl'* 1683, *v.* **þwang, furlang**); Lord Cl 1842, Lord's 1968 (*Lords Close* 1750; with the surn. *Lord*); Lowe's Orchard (with the surn. *Lowe, v.* Jackson's Orchard *supra*); Meadow 1968, Meadow Gate 1842 (1682, 1683, 1686, 1750, *v.* **gata**); Middle, Nether, Upper Marsh 1842, The Middle, The Top March 1968, The Middle, The Top March Flat 1968 (*v.* **flat**), The March Hill 1968, Marsh Mdw 1842 (*March meadow* 1682, 1686) (all with **mersc**, *v.* March Ho. *supra*); Marshes Cl 1842 (prob. with the surn. *Marsh*, but **mersc** is poss.); Mee's or Measures's (both are surns. in the possessive case); Mill Cl 1842; Millfield (*Mylnefeild* 1561 (1700), *Mill feild* 1682 (1791), 1683, 1686, *v.* **myln, feld**; originally the name of one of the great fields of the township); Mill Yard 1842 (1750, *v.* **geard**); The Moor 1842, 1968, Moor Furlong 1842 (*More Furl'* 1682, 1683, *Moor Fur(long)* 1686, 1750, *v.* **mōr**[1]); Mother Acre 1842, 1968 (1750, *Mother Acres* 1682, ~ ~ *Fur'* 1686, *v.* **modor, æcer, furlang**); Mother Cl 1968 (*v.* the preceding f.n.); The Muckle Furlong (*Muckley Fur(long)* 1682, 1683, 1686, 1750, cf. *Muckley Wells* 1682, *Mucley* ~ 1686 (*v.* **wella**) (with Scandinavianized **mycel** 'big', despite the recurring spellings with final *y*, cf. the pairs *Ingle/Ingley, Beck/Bakey, Hullock/ Hullekey* in Gt. Dalby f.ns.); Needham, ~ Hill 1842 (*Needham Hill* 1750; prob. with the surn. *Needham*, although the common early p.n. *Needham* (with *nēd* 'need, poverty' and *hām*) may also be thought of; earlier forms are needed); Nether Yard 1842, ~ Yards 1968 (*v.* **neoðera, geard**); Neville's Top Fd, ~ Top Ploughed Fd 1968 (with the surn. *Neville*); New Cl 1842, 1968 (1750); New Mdw; Newton Leys 1842, 1968, Great ~ ~ 1842 (*Great, Little Newton Leys* 1750, *v.* **leys**; prob. with the surn. *Newton* rather than with an earlier p.n. *Newton*); Old Fowl Pen (an enclosure named from a construction within it); Orchard Platt 1842 (*v.* **plat**); The Paddock (*v.* **paddock**); The Parks (towards The Park in Burton Lazars); Parsons Cl 1842, The Parson's Cl 1968 (*Parsons Close* 1750, *v.* **persone**); Pere Croft 1842 (*v.* **pere, croft**); Pick's Cl (with the surn. *Pick*); First, Second Piece, Small Piece 1842 (*v.* **pece**); The Pig Paddock (*v.* **pigge, paddock**); The Pingle 1842, Pingle 1968 (*v.* **pingel**); Plough Cl 1968 (*v.* **plōg**); Plowed Cl 1842; Great, Little Ploughed Cl 1842; Corner Ploughed Fd (*v.* **corner**), Second Ploughed Fd, Williamson's Ploughed Fd; Ploughed Gorse (*v.* **gorst**); Prince Paddock (*v.* **paddock**; beside the Prince of Wales Inn); Back of Railway (*v.* **back of**); The Ranksborough (no earlier forms, but cf. Ranksborough Hill four miles to the east on the county boundary with Rutland, *v.* Ru 91); Red Grass 1842, 1968 (*Redgrasse meadow* 1683, *Redgrass* ~ 1750, *v.* **hrēod, græs**); Road Cl 1842, Road 1968; Rodwell (1682, *Rodwells* 1686, *Rodwell furlong* 1683, *Rodwell Spring* 1682, 1686, *v.* **hrēod, wella, spring**[1]); The First, The Second, The Third Roods 1968, Great, Little Long Roads 1842 (*Long Roods* 1750, *v.* **rōd**[3]); Rough Cl, The Rough Mdw (*v.* **rūh**[1]); Round Cl 1842 (*v.* **round**; referring to shape); The Sand Pit (cf. *Sand pitt ban(c)k* 1682, 1686 (*v.* **banke**), *Sandpitt Close* 1750, *Sand pitt Rig(g)itt* 1682, 1686 (*v.* **riggett**), *v.* **sand-pytt**); Sanham 1842, 1968, Neville's Sanham Fds (with the surn. *Neville*), Sanham Hill 1842 (1750), Sanham Mdw 1842 (1750), Sannon Mdw 1842, 1968 (the early forms *Senholme* m.13 (1404), p.1250 (1404) *Laz, Senneholm* p.1250 (1404) *ib* for Sanham Ho. beyond the parish boundary in Frisby (East Goscote Hundred) indicate 'the water-meadow subject to dispute', *v.* **sænna, senna, holmr**; the final el. was later replaced by OE **hamm** with the same meaning); The Second Cl 1842, 1968; Second Paddock (*v.* **paddock**); Seed Cl 1842, 1968 (*v.* **sǣd**; in f.ns., usually indicating an enclosure with sown grass); Sharpe's Orchard, Sharpe's Paddock (*v.* **paddock**) (with the surn. *Sharpe*); Shreddies (*v.* **scrēad**); The Bottom, The Top Sics (*v.* **sík**); Slip (*v.* **slipe**); Small Croft 1842 (*v.* **croft**); Small Patch 1842 (*v.* **patche**); Smeath 1842 (*Smeath Meadow* 1750, *v.* **smēðe**[1]); Smiths 1842 (the surn. *Smith* in the possessive case); The Spinney 1968, Spinney Mdw 1842, 1968 (*v.* **spinney**); Spittal Cl 1842 (*Spittle Close* 1750, *v.* **spitel**; referring to the Hospital of St Lazarus in Burton Lazars *supra*); Spot (*v.* **spotte**; the close so called in 1968 was very small); Stains 1842, Staines's 1968 (either ON **steinn** 'stone' referring to stony ground or the surn. *Staines* (a reflex of the ON pers.n. *Steinn*) in the possessive case);

Station Mdw (beside the railway station); Staytons Cl 1842, Staton's ~ 1968 (cf. *Statons Homestead* 1750, *v.* **hām-stede**; with the surn. *Staton*); The Strip (*v.* **strīp**); Swan Land 1842, Swanland Cl 1842 (*Swanland Close* 1750, *v.* **land**; the first el. could be either **swan**[1] 'a swan' or **swān**[2] 'a herdsman, a swineherd, a peasant', or a pers.n., either OE *Swān* or Scand *Sveinn*); Little ~, Swanton (poss. an early name; if so, then either 'the herdsman's or peasant's farmstead' (with **swān**[2]) or 'Swān's farmstead' (with the OE pers.n. *Swān*), *v.* **tūn**); Long Swells 1842, 1968 (*Long(e) Swall* 1682, 1686, *Long Swell* 1750), Short Swells (*v.* **(ge)swell**); The 3 Cornered Cl (*v.* **three-cornered**); Tomlin's Hill (with the surn. *Tomlin*); Top Cl; Top Lane; Townend or Cricket Fd 1968, Townend Cl 1842, 1968 (*Townes end* 1686, cf. *Townes end Fur'* 1682 (*v.* **furlang**), *Townesend leyes* 1682, 1683, *Towns end* ~1686 (*v.* **leys**), *v.* **tūn, ende**); Warner's Paddock (*v.* **paddock**; with the surn. *Warner*); Washdyke Cl (a close with a sheep-dip, *v.* **wash-dyke**); West Brook 1842, 1968 (*Westbeck*, ~ *Fur'* 1682, *Weast beck Fur'*, *West Back* ~ 1686, *v.* **west, bekkr, furlang**; with ON *bekkr* later replaced by *brook*); The Wet Fds (*v.* **wēt**); Dale Willows 1842, 1968 (1750, *Deal Willows* 1750, *v.* **deill**), North, South Willows (*v.* **wilig**); The Wood Cl; Year Cl 1842 (perh. indicating the limit of the period of tenure for the close (i.e for one year only), but **gear** 'a yair, a dam made in a stream for catching fish' is also formally poss.).

(b) *Ashby Feild* 1682, *As(s)hebeyfeild, Ayssheby feild* 1561 (1700), *Ashbey Feild* 1686 (*v.* **feld**; one of the great fields of the village, that towards Ashby Folville which adjoins to the south-west); *Ashby Gate Close* 1750 (*v.* **gata**; beside the road to Ashby Folville); *Beck Fur'* 1682, *Bakey Fur'* (sic) 1686 (*v.* **bekkr, furlang**); *Edward Blowers Homestead* 1750 (*v.* **hām-stede**); *Blowthorn* 1750 (*v.* **blár, þorn**); *Brimble Fur'* 1682, 1686, *Brimbley Fur'* 1682 (*v.* **furlang**), *Brimble Sike* 1683 (*v.* **sík**) (*v.* **brembel**); *Browns Homestead* 1750 (*v.* **hām-stede**); *Burton Gate Close* 1750 (*v.* **gata**; beside the road to Burton Lazars); *Great, Short Caldwell* 1682, ~ *Caudell* 1683, ~ *Cawdwell* 1686, *Caudle* ~, *Cawdle Field* 1683, *Caudle Sick*, ~ *Sike* 1683 (*v.* **sík**) (*v.* **cald, wella**); *Cockley Wong furlong* 1683 (*v.* **coccel, vangr** and note the comments on The Muckle Furlong in f.ns. (a) *supra*); *the Common Pasture* 1682, ~ ~ *Paster* 1686 (*v.* **commun, pasture**); *Cooke Wong* 1682, *Cook Wong Fur'* 1686 (*v.* **vangr, furlang**; prob. with the surn. *Cook(e)*); *Cosnet Close* 1750, *Cosnet(t) Gorse* 1750 (*v.* **gorst**), *Cosnett Hole* 1750 (*v.* **hōl**[1]) (*Cosnet(t)* appears to be a surn.; otherwise, unexplained); *Cottage Meadow* 1750 (*v.* **cotage**); *Cowdams* 1750 (*v.* **cū, damme**; originally an artificially created pond for watering cows, but *v.* Field 116 who observes that such ponds did not always serve cattle, as for example *Horse Cowdam*); *Crapton Dale* 1682, 1686, *Crapendale* 1683, *Crappendale, Crappingdale* 1750 (prob. belongs with *Grafton Dale, infra*); *Cunnery Gate* 1750, *Cunnery Hedge* 1750 (*v.* **coningre**); *Aboue the Dale* 1682 ('(the furlong) above the hollow', *v.* **aboven, dalr**); *Dent Leyes* 1683 (*v.* **leys**; with the surn. *Dent*); *Dickens's yards end* 1682, *Dickins yard end* 1686 (*v.* **geard, ende**; with the surn. *Dickens/Dickins*); *Dunghill Fur'* 1682, *Dungill* ~ 1686 (*v.* **dong-hyll, furlang**); *Elder Stub Fur'* 1686 (*v.* **ellern, stubb, furlang**); *Foxland* 1328 Dugd (*v.* **fox, land**); *Gore Fur'* 1682, *Gare* ~ 1686 (*v.* **gāra, furlang**); *Grafton Dale* 1682, 1686 (*v.* **deill**; with the surn. *Grafton*, from the common p.n. Grafton, *v.* DEPN *s.n.*, Reaney *s.n.* and *Crapton Dale, supra*); *Top othe Green, Under Green* 1750, *Undergreen furlong* 1683 (*v.* **grēne**[2]); *Greens*

Cottage 1750 (*v.* **cotage**), *Greenes Furlong* 1682 (with the surn. *Green*(*e*)); *the Hall homestall* 1708 (18) (*v.* **hall, hām-stall**); *Hodgkins Homestead* 1750 (*v.* **hām-stede**; with the surn. *Hodgkin*); *Holland Furlong Close* 1750 (*v.* Holland Dale *supra*); *Hullekey leyes* 1682, *Hullock Leyes* 1686 (*v.* **hylloc, leys**; the adj. *hillocky* is first recorded in 1727 in OED, but note the comments on The Muckle Furlong *supra*); *Hunstons Sike* 1683 (*v.* **sík**; with the surn. *Hunston*); *Hunts Dale* 1682, ~ ~ *sick* 1686 (*v.* **deill, sík**; with the surn. *Hunt*); *Kelhams Homestead* 1750 (*v.* **hām-stede**; with the surn. *Kelham*, cf. *Tho. Kelhams House & homested* in Burton Lazars f.ns. (b)); *Kettleby hedge* 1683 (*v.* **hecg**; the boundary hedge with Eye Kettleby which adjoins to the north-west); *Lane Close* 1750 (*v.* **lane**; *Frances Lomleys Farm*(*e*) 1682, 18, *Fra.*ˢ *Lumleys farm* 1682 (1791) (*v.* **ferme**); *Lower Meadow* 1750; *March Ford*(*e*) 1682, 1686 (*v.* **ford**), *March Fur'* 1682, 1686 (*v.* **furlang**), *Marsh Close* 1750 (*v.* March Ho. *supra*); *Wido Marshs cottage* 1682 (1791), *Widowe Marches Cottage* 1686, *Wid. March Cottage* 18, *Marches Homestead* 1750 (*v.* **cotage, hām-stede**; with the surn. *Marsh*); *Melton Feild* 1561 (1700), 1682, 1686 (*v.* **feld**; one of the great fields of the village, that towards Melton Mowbray to the north); *Melton Gate Close* 1750 (*v.* **gata**; beside the road to Melton Mowbray); *Melton Meare* 1682, ~ *Meer* 1686 (*v.* (**ge**)**mære**; the boundary with Melton Mowbray); *Millgate* 1682, 1683, *Milln gate* 1683 (*v.* **myln, gata**; the road to a windmill which was sited on rising ground south of the village); (*the*) *Oat Close* 1683, 1750 (*v.* **āte**); *Old*(*h*)*ams Homestead* 1750 (*v.* **hām-stede**; with the surn. *Oldham*); *Ounds Close* 1750 (perh. with a poor form of the surn. *Hound* in the possessive case; otherwise unexplained); *Parkers Homestead* 1750 (*v.* **hām-stede**; with the surn. *Parker*); *Parting Grasse Ba*(*u*)*lke* 1683 (*v.* **parting, græs**; poss. alluding to allocation by lot, *v.* Field 23); *Pinching Green* 1682, *Pinchin* ~ 1686 (*v.* **grēne**[2] ; either with the surn. *Pinchin*(*g*) (*v.* Reaney *s.n.* Pinchen) or with *pinching* in its sense 'narrow', *v.* OED *s.v.* pinching, ppl.a., 4); *Robinsons Homestead* 1750 (*v.* **hām-stede**; with the surn. *Robinson*); *Sanham Corner* 1750 (*v.* **corner** and Sanham in f.ns (a)); *Shan*(*c*)*k Fur'* 1682, 1686 (*v.* **scanca, furlang**); *Sissleborough* 1682, *Sissleborow*, ~ *furl'* 1683, *Sisleborow Fur'* 1686 (*v.* **furlang**), *Sissleborough Seike* 1682, *Siselborow Sick* 1686 (*v.* **sík**) (*v.* **berg**; the first el. is prob. **þistel**); *Stack Wong*(*e*) 1682, 1686 (*v.* **stakkr, vangr**); *Stack Yard* 1682, 1686 (*v.* **stak-ȝeard**); *Henry Steeles Seike* 1682, *Haristeel Sike* 1686 (*v.* **sík**); *Steeles Yard*(*s*) *end* 1682, 1686 (*v.* **geard, ende** and cf. *Henry Steel* 1682, *Randall Steel* 1683); *Stock leyes Fur'* 1686 (*v.* **furlang** and Stock Leys Barn *supra*); *Thorp Ford* 1682, 1686 (*v.* **ford**; prob. to be identified with *thorpforth* in Lt. Dalby f.ns. (b) *infra*), *Thorp Meer* 1683 (*v.* (**ge**)**mære**) (Thorpe Satchville adjoins to the south); *Thurn*(*e*) *Hill* 1682, 1683, *Thorne hill* 1683, *Thurnhill Fur'* 1686 (*v.* **furlang**), *Far, Near Thornhill* 1750 (*v.* **þyrne, þorn**); *Thurn Sick* 1683 (*v.* **þyrne, þyrnir, sík**); *Upper Close* 1682, 1686, 1750; *Valdye landes* c.1545, 1535 × 46 (*v.* **land**; formerly the property of Vaudey Abbey in Lincs.); *Wat Yard* 1750 (*v.* **geard**; with the surn. *Watt*); *the West feild* 1683; *Woodgate Fur'* 1682, 1686 (*v.* **furlang**), *Woodgate piece* 1750 (*v.* **pece**) (*v.* **wudu, gata**); (*The*) *Yards End*, ~ ~ *Close* 1750 (*v.* **geard, ende**).

3. LITTLE DALBY

Dalbi 1086 DB (x4), Hy 2 Dane, 1215 Cur, *Dalbia* c.1130 LeicSurv,
   Dalbya p.1250 (1404) *Laz*, *Dalby* 1212 RBE, 1216 (1404) *Laz*,
   1229 Pat, a.1250 (1404) *Laz*, c.1291 Tax *et freq*
Daleby 1150 × 59 TutP, 1243 Fees *et passim* to 1353 Ipm, *Dalleby*
   1163 TutP
Daubi 1212 Cur, e.13 (1404) *Laz*, *Dauby* 1209 × 19, 1224 RHug,
   1229 Pat *et freq* to 1276 RGrav, 1278 RH

'The farmstead, village in the valley', *v.* **dalr**, **bȳ**, cf. Great Dalby
supra from which the name was presumably transferred, but the name
of the 'lesser' village is entirely appropriate to its location. Little Dalby
was in part *de feodo Paynel* 1242 Fees. *Robertus Paynel* held this in
1335 Fine, 1367 Banco. Part was *de feodo Perer* 1242 Fees and part *de
feodo de Tatishale* 1242 ib. Distinguishing affixes are variously added
as:
   Parva ~ 1212 RBE, 1209 × 19, 1224 RHug *et passim* to 1492, 1494
      Wyg
   ~ *Parva* 1209 × 19 RHug, 1254 Val *et passim* to 1483, 1517 *Deed et
      freq* to 1678 LML
   Petit ~ 1266 Pat
   Litul ~ 1444 Nichols, *Litle* ~ 1535 VE, *Litylle* ~, *Lytyle* ~ 1552 AAS,
      Little ~ 1610 Speed *et freq*
   ~ *Paynel* 1242 Fees, 1335 Fine, 1367 Banco
   ~ *Perer* 1242 Fees bis
   ~ *Tateshale*, ~ *Tatissale* 1242 Fees

v. **petit**, **lȳtel** and note MLat *parva* 'little, small'.

THE BEECHES. BUNNY'S LODGE, BUNNY'S SPINNEY, cf. *Bonye* 1577 PR
(forename unrecorded), *George Bunney* died 1771 Nichols, *Sarah
Bunney* and *Wm. Bunney* 1846 White, farmers; the *Bunny* family prob.
originated in the village of Bunny, 15 miles to the north-west in Notts.
BUTTERMILK HILL SPINNEY, *buttermilk* being a complimentary epithet
for pasture giving fine milk in cattle. DEBDALE LODGE, DEBDALE
SPINNEY, *Depedale* m.13 (1404) *Laz* bis, l.13 (1449) *WoCart*, 13 (1404)
Laz, *Deep(e)dale* 1605, 1612 *Terrier*, *magna depedale* m.13 (1404) *Laz*,
Magna Dep(e)dale 1561 (17) *Surv* (with MLat *magna* 'large, great'),
Mydull Dep(e)dale 1561 (17) *ib* (*v.* **middel**), *Littull* ~, *Lyttull*

Dep(e)dale, Little Deepe Dale 1561 (17) *ib* (*v.* **lȳtel**), *Parva Depdale* 1561 (17) *ib* (with MLat *parva* 'little, small'), 'the deep hollow or valley', *v.* **dēop, dalr**. THE GRANGE, 1877 White, *v.* **grange**. GREEN SPINNEY. THE HALL, 1795 Nichols, 1846, 1877 White, *Little Dalby Hall* 1863 ib, *Dalby hall* 1925 Kelly, *v.* **hall**. HOME FM, *v.* **home**. LAKE SPINNEY. LANDFIELD SPINNEY, cf. *Great Land Field* 1968 *Surv*, *v.* **land**, referring to an enclosure consolidating an unspecified number of selions or 'lands' of one of the great fields of the village. LITTLE DALBY LAKES. LITTLE DALBY LODGE. LODGE SPINNEY. MILL HILL SPINNEY, *v.* Mill Hill in f.ns. (a) *infra*. PUNCH BOWL COVERT, *v.* **cover(t)**; a name reflecting the bowl-shaped valley in which the covert lies. RISE HILL SPINNEYS, *Daubiris* 1229 Pat, *v.* **hrīs**. ST JAMES'S CHURCH, *Church (St James)* 1846, 1863, 1877 White, *the Church* 1707, 1707 (18) *Terrier*; it is earlier recorded as *ecclesiam de parua Dauby* a.1219 RHug, ~ *de Dauby Parua* 1342 *Pat, ecclesiarum de Parva Dalbye et Somerby* 1549 *ib*. Note also *the Church-Yard* 1707 (18) *Terrier*. SLEDGE SPINNEY, perh. with **slæd** 'a valley', *v.* The Slade in f.ns. (a) *infra*. THE VICARAGE, 1877 White, 1925 Kelly, *The Vycaridge House* 1612 *Terrier, the Vicarage House* 1821 *ib*, *v.* **vikerage**. WEST LODGE, 1863, 1877 White, *v.* **loge**. WHEAT HILL SPINNEY, *Wheat Hill* 1849 *TA, v.* **hwǣte**. WHITE LODGE, 1863, 1877 White, *v.* **loge**.

FIELD-NAMES

Forms in (a) dated 1792 are *Rental*, 1795 are Nichols, 1821 are *Terrier*, 1849 are *TA* and 1968 are *Surv*. Forms throughout dated 1229 are Pat, m.13 (1404), 1271 (1404) and 13 (1404) are *Laz*, 1271 (1449), l.13 (1449), 1300 (1449) and 1333 (1449) are *WoCart*, 1517 are *Deed*, 1550 are *Pochin*, 1561 (17) and 1634 are *Surv*, 1585 are Fine, 1586 are Ipm, while 1605 and 1612 are *Terrier*.

(a) Four Acres 1968 (*v.* **æcer**); First, Second Apple tree Cl 1849 (*v.* **æppel-trēow**); Barrs Cl 1849 (with the surn. *Barr*); Bell Cl 1792 (prob. land endowed to provide a bell fund for the local church, especially for renewing bell-ropes, *v.* Field 200); Church Lees 1821, ~ Leys 1849 (*v.* **leys**); Great ~, Cunnery 1968 (*v.* **coningre**); Debdale Mdw 1849 (cf. *Depedalefurlong* 1333 (1449) (*v.* **furlang**), *depedaleheuedes* l.13 (1449) (*v.* **hēafod**), *Depedale feilde* 1605, *Deepedale* ~ 1612 (*v.* **feld**; one of the great fields of the township), *v.* Debdale Lodge, ~ Spinney *supra*); Fallow Lees 1849 (*Fallow(e) leaes*, 1605, 1612, *v.* **fealu, leys**); Hall Cl 1795 (*the Hall close* 1605, ~ ~ *Closse* 1612, *Hall Close furlonge* 1605, 1612, *v.* The Hall *supra*); Home Cl 1821,

1968 (v. **home**); Little Land Cl 1968 (v. **land** and Landfield Spinney *supra*); Long Cl 1849; Lukes Cl 1849 (with the surn. *Luke*, v. Reaney *s.n.*); Mickledine Cl 1849 (cf. *Mickldine leaes* 1605, *Myceldene Leaes* 1612, v. **leys**; prob. with a surn. *Mickledine*, but 'large valley' may also be thought of, v. **micel, denu**); Middle Cl 1849; Middle Fd 1849; Mill hill 1795 (v. *Mylne feilde, infra*); Nether Fd 1849; First, Second, Third Nether Pasture 1849 (*the neather pasture* 1612, v. **neoðera, pasture**); Nook Cl 1849 (v. **nōk**); Old Barn Cl 1968; Orton's Cl 1795 (with the surn. *Orton*; Nichols notes that a *Mrs Orton* c.1730 of Lt. Dalby was a pioneer in making Stilton Cheese); Parallogram Cl (sic) 1821 (v. **parallelogram**; a close of such a shape, cf. Triangular Cl *infra*); Parker's Cl 1968 (with the surn. *Parker*); Parting Piece 1849 (v. **parting, pece**; *parting* may allude to allocation by lot, v. Field 23); Pearce's Cl 1968 (with the surn. *Pearce*); Pick's Cl 1968 (with the surn. *Pick*); the Plashes 1849 (v. **plæsc**); Ploughed Piece 1849 (v. **pece**); Pond 1968 (an enclosure containing a pond); Poor Part 1968 (v. **pouer(e), part**; presum. originally endowed for the support of the village poor, v. Field 192); Far Rough Cl 1968 (v. **rūh**[1]; with reference to the ground surface); Round Acres 1968 (v. **round, æcer**; at this date, a triangular enclosure), Upper Round Acres 1968 (a rectangular close), Lower Round Cl 1968 (also rectangular); The Slade, ~ ~ Cl 1849 (cf. *Slade feilde* 1605, 1612, v. **slæd, feld**; one of the great fields of the village, cf. Sledge Spinney *supra* and *the furlong(e) between(e) slades* in f.ns. (b) *infra*); Smiths Cl 1849, Smith's Mdw 1968 (with the surn. *Smith*); Spinney Cl 1968; Spring Cl 1795, 1821, 1849 (v. **spring**[1]); Stacey's Cl 1968 (with the surn. *Stacey*); Three Corner Fd 1849, 3 Cornered Cl 1968 (v. **three-corner, three-cornered**); Triangular Cl 1821 (v. **triangular**; perh. to be identified with the preceding); Vicarage Hill 1821 (v. The Vicarage *supra*); Far ~ ~, First ~ ~, Wheat Hill 1849, Wheat Hill Cl 1849, Wheat Hill Mdw 1849 (v. Wheat Hill Spinney *supra*); Whiny dale 1849 (*Whynny dole* 1605, v. **whinny, dāl**).

(b) *Acredike furlonge* 1605, *acardycke* ~, *Acredicke* ~ 1612 (v. **æcer-dīc, dík**); *Barret hegge* 1517 (v. **hecg**; with the surn. *Barrat/Barrett*); *Broadgate* 1605, *brodgate* bis, *broodgate* 1612, *broadgate fur'* 1605, *Brodgate furlonge* 1612 (v. **brād, gata**); *the Brook(e)* 1605, 1612, *(the) Brooke furlong* 1605, 1612 (v. **brōc**); *Borohades, Browehades* 1550, *Borow Heydes* 1561 (17), *burrow(e) hades* 1605, 1612 (v. **burh, hēafod**; presum. with reference to adjacent Burrough Hill); *Burton hedge* 1605, 1612 (v. **hecg**; the boundary hedge of Burton Lazars to the north); *Calfes pasture furlonge* 1612 (v. **calf, pasture**); *Chapple Furl'* 1605, *Chapell furlonge* 1612 (v. **chapel(e)**); *Church h(e)adland* 1605, 1612, *Church headland furl'* 1605, *(the) Church hadland(e) furlonge* 1605, 1612 (v. **cirice, hēafod-land**); *the common*, ~ ~ *side* 1612 (v. **commun, sīde**); *Coram Furlonge* 1605, 1612 (with the surn. *Coram*); *Crosse Furlonge* 1605, 1612 (v. **cross**); *Cross(e)gate* 1605, 1612, *Chrosse gate* 1612 (v. **gata**; with either **cros** or **cross**); *Deepedale becke* 1605, *depedale* ~ 1612 (v. **bekkr** and Debdale Mdw *supra*); *Drift Furlonge* 1605, *Drifte hill furl'* 1605, *Drifte hill* 1612 (v. **drift**); *le est Broke* 1517 (v. **ēast, brōc**); *Furbushe Furlonge* 1605, 1612 (v. **feor, busc**); *Gallowe tree hyll feilde, Gallowtre hill feild* 1605, *Gallowtrye hyll Feilde* 1612 (one of the great fields of the village; towards Gartree Hill (*q.v.*) in neighbouring Gt. Dalby); *Graunge fur(longe)* 1605, 1612, *graunge leaes* 1605, 1612 (v. **grange, leys**; lying towards The Grange (*q.v.*) in neighbouring Burton Lazars); *Grymeswonge furl(onge)* 1605, 1612 (v. **vangr**; with the ODan pers.n. *Grīm* (ON

Grímr)); *hanging hill furl'* 1605, *hanginge hyll furlonge* 1612 (*v.* **hangende, hyll**); *Hardlandes furlonge* 1605, 1612, *hardland* 1612 (*v.* **heard, land**; alluding to soil difficult to till); *Hassocks close* 1634 (*v.* **hassuc**); *headland furlonge* 1605, 1612 (*v.* **hēafod-land**); *Underholes furlonge* 1605, *under ho(o)les* ~ 1612 (*v.* **under, hōl**[1]); *Hullocke hill Leaes* 1605, *Hullock hil Leas* 1612 (*v.* **hylloc, leys**); *Hungerhill* 1605, 1612 (*v.* **hungor**); (*the*) *kirkegate* 1605, 1612 (*v.* **kirkja, gata**); *Leicesthrop hedge furlonge* 1605, *Leesthorp* ~ 1612 (*v.* **hecg**; the furlong adjoining the boundary hedge of Leesthorpe which lies to the east); *the meadow(e)* 1605, 1612, *the medowe* 1612; *Melton gate Leaes* 1605, 1612, *Mellton* ~ ~ 1605 (*v.* **gata, leys**; referring to the road to Melton Mowbray to the north); *midle furlonge* 1605, 1612, *middell* ~ 1612 (*v.* **middel**; the middle furlong of Paddock Pool Fd); *Mylne feilde* 1605, 1612 (*v.* **feld**; one of the great fields of the village), *Milne Furlonge* 1605, *the mylne furlonge* 1612, *the Mylne hedge* 1605, *Milne hedge* 1612 (*v.* **hecg**) (all with reference to a windmill on Mill Hill, *v.* **myln**); *the neate(s) pasture* 1605, 1612 (*v.* **nēat, pasture**); *the neather pasture* 1612 (*v.* **neoðera**); *the nether furlonge* 1612 (i.e. the lower furlong of Paddock Pool Fd); *Netherthorp, Nethirthorp* bis 13 (1404), *Netherthorpe* 1585, 1586 ('the lower farmstead', *v.* **neoðera, þorp**); *the Nine landes* 1612 (*v.* **nigon, land**; a close made up of nine selions or 'lands' of one of the former great fields of the village); *Nooke meere furl(onge)* 1605, 1612 (*v.* **nōk**; the second el. is poss. **mere**[1] 'a pool' (cf. Little Dalby Lakes *supra*) rather than (**ge**)**mǣre** 'a boundary')); *Okeham waye* 1612 (*v.* **weg**; the road to Oakham in Rutland); *le ouerthorpe* 1517, *Overthorpe* 1585, 1586 ('the upper farmstead', *v.* **uferra, þorp**); *Padock poole* 1605, *Paddock poole broke* 1612 (*v.* **brōc**), *Paddock poole feild(e)* 1605, 1612 (*v.* **feld**; one of the great fields of the township), *Paddock(e) pole furlonge* 1605, *Padock poole* ~, *Paddocke pool* ~ 1612, *Paddock poole upper furlonge* 1612, *Paddock pole leaes* 1605, *Paddock poole short(e) Leaes* 1605, 1612 (*v.* **leys**) ('the frog-infested pool', *v.* **padduc, pōl**[1]); *the pasture* 1605, 1612 (*v.* **pasture**); *Rice pastures* 1612 (*v.* **hrīs**); *risburgsike* m.13 (1404) bis, *risebursike* l.13 (1449), 13 (1404), *risbursik'* l.13 (1449), *riseburuesike* 13 (1404), *risburseke* 1300 (1449) (*v.* **hrīs, burh, sík**; no doubt referring to Burrough Hill's Iron Age hill-fort); *Seaveacers* 1612, *Seveacres nether furl'* 1605, *Upper Seveacres furl'* 1605, *upper seavacres furlonge* 1612 (*v.* **sef, æcer, akr**); *Senholme lees* 1612, ~ *leaes furl'* 1605 (*v.* **leys, furlang**), *Senholme pyttes* 1605, ~ *pittes* 1612 (*v.* **pytt**), *senholmsike* 13 (1404) (*v.* **sík**) ('water-meadow subject to dispute', *v.* **sænna, senna, holmr**; cf. Sanham in Gt. Dalby f.ns. (a) and *Senholm*, Ru 37); *the Sidlinge* 1605 (*v.* **sīdling**); *the furlong(e) between(e) slades* 1605, 1612, *great slade furl(onge)* 1605, 1612, *the litle slade furlonge* 1605, *Lytell slade* ~ 1612 (*v.* **lȳtel**), *Midle Slade Furlonge* 1605, *Mydle* ~ ~ 1612 (*v.* **middel**), *Wollandes slade* 1612, ~ ~ *furl'* 1605, *Wolland Slade Furlonge* 1612 (*v.* *Wollandes furlonge, infra*), *Great Slade Leaes* 1605, 1612 (*v.* **leys**) (all with **slæd** 'a valley', *v.* The Slade *supra*); *Sowbrook(e)* 1605, 1612, *Sowbrooke Furlonge* 1612 (*v.* **sūð, brōc**); *Stanwell* 1612, ~ *Furl(onge)* 1605, 1612, *Stanwell Leaes* 1605 (*v.* **leys**), *Stanwell sycke* 1605, 1612 (*v.* **sík**) ('the stony-bottomed spring or stream', *v.* **stān, wella**); *le Thorpes* 1517 (referring to *Netherthorpe* and *Overthorpe, supra*), *Thorpe Balke* 1561 (17) (*v.* **balca**), *thorpforth* l.13 (1449) (*v.* **ford**), *Thorpmilnemeduwe* m.13 (1404), 13 (1404) bis, *Torpmilnemeduwe, -midowe* 1271 (1449) (*v.* **myln, mǣd** (**mǣdwe** obl.sg.)) (all with **þorp** 'an outlying farmstead'); *thurnborow brook(e)* 1605, 1612, *Thurnborow(e)*

Brooke feilde 1605, ~ ~ *fylde* 1612 (*v.* **feld**; one of the great fields of the village) ('the thorn hill brook', *v.* **þyrne, berg, brōc**); (*the*) *Towne furlonge* 1605, 1612 (*v.* **tūn**); *Turlington Furl(onge)* 1605, 1612, *Turrlington furl'* 1605 (with the surn. *Turlington*, an early form of the p.n. Tur Langton, a village 12 miles to the south in Gartree Hundred, whence the family originally came); *upper furl(onge)* 1605, 1612; *Welhyll* 1612, *Welhill arr' furl'* 1605, ~ *arable furlonge* 1612 (*v.* **arable**), *welhill leaes* 1605, *wellhyll leaes furlonge* 1612 (*v.* **leys**) ('the hill at the spring or stream', *v.* **wella, hyll**); *the Well' Syke* 1517 (*v.* **wella, sīk**); *White Earth arr(able) Furl(onge)* 1605, 1612 (*v.* **hwīt, eorðe, arable**); *Wm. Willsforth close* 1605, *Wylliam Wyllfordes Closse* 1612, *George Wyllford headley* 1612 (*v.* **headley**) (the family presum. originated in Wilford, 19 miles to the north-west in Notts.); *Wolland(es) Furlonge* 1605, *Wollande(s) furland* (sic) 1612 (*v.* **wōh, land**).

Clawson, Hose and Harby

1. LONG CLAWSON

Clachestone 1086 DB bis

Clacstune 1174 × 82 *Rut*, 1235 × 53 (e.15) *BelCartB, Clacstun'* 12
(e.15) *ib, Clacston'* 1174 × 82 *Rut*, e.13 (e.15), p.1250 (e.15)
BelCartB, Clacstona e.13 (e.15) *ib*

Claxstun 12 ISLR bis, *Claxstuna* 12 (e.15) *BelCartB, Claxston'* 1243
Fees, 1262 Fine *et passim* to 1396, 1411 *BelCartB, Claxstona* Hy
3 (e.15) *ib*

Claxtun' 1236 Fees, Hy 3 (e.15) *BelCartB, Claxtone* Hy 2 *Rut*, 12
ISLR, Hy 3 *Rut*, Hy 3 (e.15) *BelCartB* bis, *Claxtona* m.13 (e.15),
Hy 3 (e.15) *ib*, Hy 3 *Rut*, Edw 1 *CroxR, Claxton* c.1130 LeicSurv,
Hy 2 *Rut*, 1199 Fine *et passim* to 1209 × 35 RHug, 1240 (e.15)
BelCartB et freq to 1795, 1815 Map, (~ *in vall* 1332 SR, ~ *in
Valle* 1416 Nichols, ~ *in le Vale* 1445 ib), *Long Claxton* 1632,
1710 LML *et passim* to 1718 ib, *Claxton Longa* 1705 ib

Claston' a.1150 (e.15) *BelCartB, Clastone* 1209 × 35 RHug,
Clastona e.13 *Rut, Clastuna* Hy 2 (e.15) *BelCartB* bis, 1.12 (14)
BrCart

Clauxstun 1154 × 59 *Rut, Claucstuna* 12 (e.15) *BelCartB, Clauxton*
Hy 3 *Crox*, e.14 *BelCartA* bis, (~ *in the Vale* 1564 Fine)

Clauston 1505 Ipm, 1528 Wills *et passim* to 1576 Saxton, 1610
Speed, (~ *in le Vale* 1505 Ipm), *Long Clauston* 1725 LML,
Clawston 1580 LEpis, 1582 *Deed*

Clawson alias Clauston 1539 *Deed, Clawson alias Claxton* 1546
AAS, 1581 LEpis, *Claxton alias Clauston* 1609 Nichols, *Claxton
alias Clawson* 1624 Fine

Clauson c.1545 Leland, *Longe Clauson* 1549 Pat, *Clawson* 1548 Pat,
Long Clawson 1710 LML *et freq*

'Klak's farmstead, village', *v.* **tūn**. The ODan pers.n. *Klak* (ON
Klakkr), an original by-name probably meaning 'a lump, a clod' (*v.*
SPNLY 173), is frequently found in the Danelaw, cf. Claxton, YN 173

and Claxby, L 3 17. The village is variously described as ~ *in the Vale* (*v.* **val**), referring to the Vale of Belvoir, and since c.1550 as *Long* ~ (*v.* **lang**[1]). The township is of linear formation and stretches for approximately one mile. Loss of *t* from the group -*ston* is typical of Leics. p.ns. from the 16th cent. onwards.

BACK LANE, *v.* **back**. BRIDGE FM, beside a bridge over R. Smite. BROCK HILL, *the Brockhills* 1780 *EnclA, Brockhill* 1796 *ib, v.* **brōc**. CANAL LANE, leading to *Nottingham and Grantham Canal* 1877 White. CASTLE FD (local), *v.* **castel**(l); contains a curving ditch which appears to have been defensive. CLAWSON HALL, *The Hall* 1925 Kelly, *v.* **hall**. CLAWSON HILL. CLAWSON HILL FM. CLAWSON LODGE, 1836 O, cf. *Clawson Lodge Farm* 1846 White, *v.* **loge**. CLAWSON THORNS, 1806 Map, 1824, 1836 O, *Claxton Thorns* 1795, 1815 Map, *v.* **þorn**. CROWN AND PLOUGH (P.H.), *Crown and Plough* 1846, 1863, 1877 White, 1925 Kelly. DOVECOAT HO., *Dovecote House* 1863, 1877 White, 1925 Kelly, cf. *Dovecoat Lane* 1780 *EnclA, Dovecoat Close* 1780 *ib, v.* **dove-cote**. EAST END, 1824 O, *v.* **ende**. FEALER FM. GLEBE FM, *v.* **glebe**. HAZLETONGUE LODGE. HOLME FM, *v.* **holmr**. HOLWELL MOUTH COVERT, *v.* **cover(t)** and Holwell Mouth in Holwell, Ab Kettleby parish. HOSE VILLA, towards Hose which lies north-east of Long Clawson. THE LODGE. LONG CLAWSON AND HOSE STATION. LONG CLAWSON BRIDGE, *Clawson bridge* 1877 White; crosses the Nottingham and Grantham Canal. THE MANOR, 1925 Kelly, *v.* **maner**. NEWCOMBE'S PARLOUR, cf. *Fredk. P. Newcombe, landowner* and *Thomas Newcombe, farmer* 1846 White; with **parlur** in its later topographical sense 'a secluded piece of ground'. OLD MANOR HO., *Old Manor house* 1925 Kelly, *v.* **maner**. OLD MILL HO. THE PINGLE, *v.* **pingel**. PRIMITIVE METHODIST CHAPEL. ROUND COVERT, *v.* **round, cover(t)**; descriptive of shape. ROYAL OAK. (P.H.) (lost), *Royal Oak* 1846, 1863, 1877 White. ST REMIGIUS' CHURCH, *Church (St Remegius)* 1846, 1863, 1877 White, *Church (St Remigius)* 1925 Kelly; it is earlier recorded as *ecclesie de Claxton* 1220 MHW, *ecclesie Sancti Remigii Claxton* 1414 *Pat, the Church* 1707 *Terrier*. Note also *the Church Yarde* 1601 *ib, the Church yearde* 1605 *ib, the churchyarde* 1612 *ib, the Church Yard* 1707, 1707 (18), 1821 *ib, v.* **chirche-ȝeard**. SANDPIT FM., *v.* **sand-pytt**. SHERBROOK FOX COVERT, *v.* **cover(t)**; on R. Smite, a local name for which may have been *Sherbrook* 'the boundary stream' (*v.* **scīr**[1], **brōc**), since it forms the county boundary at the north-west of the parish, but there are no early forms extant. SLYBOROUGH HILL, *Slyborowe* 1601 *Terrier, Slideborow*

(*Hill*), *Slideborrow Hill* 1780 *EnclA*, *Slyborough Hill* 1836 O, 1846 1863, 1877 White, *v.* **berg**; earlier forms are needed to explain the first element. SMITH'S LODGE, cf. *Randolph and Thomas Smith, graziers* 1925 Kelly. SQUARE COVERT, *v.* **squar(e)**, **cover(t)**; descriptive of shape. STAR (P.H.) (lost), *Star* 1863 White, *Star Inn* 1877 ib. THE VICARAGE, 1707, 1707 (18) *Terrier*, 1877 White, *the Vicaridge* 1605 *Terrier*, *the Vicarage House* 1601, 1625, 1821 *ib*, *v.* **vikerage**. WATER LANE, 1780 *EnclA*, *v.* **wæter**; in part, running beside a stream. WEST END, *v.* **ende**. WESLEYAN METHODIST CHAPEL. THE WINDMILL.

FIELD-NAMES

Undated forms in (a) are 1780 *EnclA*, while those dated 1763 are *Reeve*, 1781 are *Deed* and 1821 are *Terrier*. Forms throughout dated 1.13 are *CRCart*; Edw 1 are *CroxR*; 1601, 1605, 1612, 1625, 1703, 1707 and 1707 (18) are *Terrier*; 1675 are *Deed*.

(a) (the) Acre Hill Fd 1780, 1781 (*Akarill feilde* 1601, *v.* **æcer**, **hyll**, **feld**; one of the great fields of the village); Beeson Cl (with the surn. *Beeson*, *v.* Reaney *s.n.* Beeston); Birtle Beck Drain (*v.* **drain**), Birtlebeck Ford (*v.* **bekkr**, **ford**; the first el. is poss. **bitel** or **bitela** 'a (water-) beetle', cf. *Bittlewell*, Ru 100 and Bisbrooke, Ru 238); Breech Cl 1763, Breaches ~ 1780 (*v.* **brēc**); Bridge Lane Cl; Broad Moor Heron Drain (*v.* **brād**, **mōr**[1], **drain**; with either **heyron** 'a heron' or **hyrne** 'an angle, a corner'); Caunts Lane (with the surn. *Caunt*, also found as *Cant* in Leics., cf. Cant's Thorns in Wartnaby); Cowl Cl, Cowl Close Drain (*v.* **drain**) (prob. with the surn. *Cowl/Cowell*); Cuckow Lodge Furlong (the furlong beside a lost Cuckoo Lodge, but it is uncertain whether this refers to a building or is a fanciful name for a haunt of the cuckoo); the Cross Dam, Cross Dam Drain (*v.* **cross**, **damme**, **drain**); Denby Cl (with the surn. *Denby*); (the) East Mill Fd (*the East Mill* 1707); East Rd; Flinty Gate (*v.* **flinti**, **gata**); Foster Hedge Furlong (*v.* **hecg**; with the surn. *Foster*); Fox Cl (with the surn. *Fox*); Gorse Fd, the Gorze Fd, Gorse Pasture, the Gorze Pasture 1780, the Gorse Pasture 1821, Gorze Leys Cl 1780 (*v.* **leys**) (*v.* **gorst**); Gough Cl (with the surn. *Gough*); the Gravel Pit, East, West Gravel Pit Drain (*v.* **drain**) (*v.* **gravel**, **pytt**); Hawleys Hickling Bridge Cl (referring to a bridge across R. Smite; Hickling in Notts. lies to the north-west), Hawley Styehedge ~, Hawleys Stye Hedge Cl (*v.* **stig**, **hecg**; cf. *George Hawley* 1780, landowner); Headache Furlong (a disparaging f.n. indicating problems with tillage or growth of crops); Heron Drain, Heron Furlong (*v.* Broad Moor Heron Drain *supra*); Hills Pasture, (the) East, West Hills Pasture; (the) Hooks Drain (*v.* **hōc**, **drain**); Hoping ~, (the) Hopping Fd, Long Hopping Furlong (*v.* **hopping**); Izle Beck (*v.* **bekkr**; the first el. is prob. **ōsle** 'an ouzle, a blackbird', cf. *Owsell welles* in Harston f.ns. (b)); Kirkby Cl (with the surn. *Kirkby*); Langar Hill Pasture 1780, 1821, Langer ~ ~ 1780 (a hill which looks toward Langar, five miles due north in Notts.); Lintop Drain (*v.* **drain**; in Long Clawson f.ns., *drain* is usually compounded with a topographical name, hence **lind** 'a lime-tree' or **līn** 'flax', with

topp 'the top of a hill' may feature here); Little Cl; Littledale drain (*v.* **drain**) (*Litledale* 1605, *Litle dales* 1612, 1625, *v.* **lȳtel, lítill** with **dalr** or **deill**); Long Sike, ~ Drain (*v.* **sík, drain**); Lousy Bush (for earlier forms and discussion, *v. Lousie Bush* in neighbouring Nether Broughton f.ns. (b)); (the) Mill Fd 1780 *EnclA*, 1846, 1877 White (*the Milne Feild* 1703, *v.* **myln**); (the) Moor Mdw (*v.* **mōr**[1]); New Cl; New Dikes Furlong (*v.* **dík**); Nine Acres Lane (*v.* **æcer**); Old House Homestead (*v.* **hām-stede**); Outhall Lane (a lane leading to 'the hall lying on the outskirts of the village', *v.* **ūt, hall**); Pakes Cl, Pakes Lane (with the surn. *Pake*, cf. *Pakecroft* Hy 3 (e.15) *BelCartB* (*v.* **croft**) and *Roger Pake* 1195 P, *v.* Reaney *s.n.* Pack); Pigeon Holes Furlong (perh. descriptive of land pock-marked by small excavations, cf. *dowve pytts* in Bottesford f.ns. (b) and Dove Holes, Db 64 and 399); Roe Cl (*v.* **vrá**); Saltwell Drain (*v.* **drain**), Saltwell Lane (*v.* **salt**[2], **wella**; a spring or stream with brackish water from salt domes in the Lower Lias formations which underlie the Wolds, cf. Saltbeck in Belvoir parish); Sands (*v.* **sand**); Shortcroft (*v.* **sc(e)ort, croft**); Skirting Holme Lane, Skirting Holme Mdw (*v.* **holmr; skirting** 'that which skirts or borders' is poss. here (citations from c.1735 in OED), but Skirting Holme may be a much altered and rationalized form of *Scethesholm* in f.ns. (b) *infra*); Slideborow Hill Cl, Slidebor(r)ow Hill Fd, Slideborow Sike, ~ Drain (*v.* **sík, drain**) (cf. *Slyborowe Feild* 1601, *v.* **feld** and Slyborough Hill *supra*); Far(r) ~ ~, Stoney Lands, Stoney Lands Cl (*v.* **stānig, land**); Style Cl (with **stigel** or **stīg**); the Swallows Cl, Swallows Drain (*v.* **swalg, drain**); Little Thirty Leys, Great, Little Thirty Leys Cl (*v.* **leys**; when compounded with a numeral, *leys* represents grassland units of tenure corresponding to *lands* similarly used of arable); the Westend Fd 1763 (*the Westend feild* 1675, *v.* West End *supra*); West Mill (*The West Mill* 1707), (the) West Mill Fd 1780, 1821; West Rd; Whittles Lane (with the surn. *Whittle*); the Wong (*v.* **vangr**).

(b) *Colstundale* l.13 (*v.* **dalr**; the valley towards Colston Bassett which lies to the north-west in Notts.); *the foreyarde* 1625 (*v.* **fore, geard**; i.e. that of *the Vicarage House, supra*); *othe grene* 1381 SR (p) (*v.* **grene**[2]); *the Homestall* 1707, 1707 (18) (*v.* **hām-stall**; i.e. that of The Vicarage); *Hundehou* l.13 (prob. 'the hill haunted by dogs', *v.* **hund** (**hunda** gen.pl.), **haugr**; but formally the Scand pers.n. *Hundi* is also poss. as the first el.); *the Kings heighe waye* 1605 (*v.* **hēah-weg**; at this date referring to James I); *the Lower feild(e)* 1605, 1625 (*v.* **feld**; one of the great fields of the village, also called the *Neither Feild(e)* 1601, 1612 (*v.* **neoðera**)); *the Orcharde* 1625 (belonging to *the Vicarage House*); *Pease Hill* 1605, 1625, *Peashill* 1612 (*v.* **pise**); *The Queens land* 1601 (*v.* **land**; at this date referring to Elizabeth I); *Scethesholm* (or *Stechesholm* or *Scechesholm*) l.13, Edw 1 (*v.* **holmr**; the correct reading of the f.n. form is made difficult because of the similar shapes of lower case *c* and *t* in early scripts and because both instances of the name appear in cartulary copies; if *Scethesholm* is correct, then **skeið** in its sense 'a boundary' is poss. (cf. ODan *skede* 'a boundary'), though the genitival construction would be unusual; if *Stechesholm*, the Scand pers.n. *Steik* in the possessive case may be thought of as first el., and if *Scechesholm*, the Scand pers.n. *Skegg* also in the possessive case may be present, *v.* Skirting Holme *supra*); *sloteridemere* Edw 1 (*v.* **slōhtre**; perh. with **rīð** and **mere**[1]); *Swinelandes* l.13, Edw 1 (*v.* **swīn, land**); *the Upper Feild(e)* 1601, 1605, 1612, 1625 (*v.* **feld**; one of the great fields of the village); *Westwudegate* l.13, Edw 1 (*v.* **west, wudu, gata**).

2. HARBY

Herdebi 1086 DB, 1166 LN, l.12 *Rut*, 1202 Fine *et passim* to 1268
  RGros (p), 1277 (e.15) *BelCartB*, *Herdebia* c.1130 LeicSurv,
  Herdebie Hy 1 (1333) Ch, *Herdebeie* 12 AD, *Herdeby* c.1130
  LeicSurv, 1166 RBE, l.12 *Rut et passim* to 1208 Fine, e.13 (e.14)
  BelCartA, Hy 3 *Crox* (freq) *et freq* to 1413, 1415 *Comp et passim*
  to 1446 Banco, 1472 *Wyg*, *Herddeby* 1294 *ib* (p)
Hertebi 1086 DB, *Herteby* 1277 (e.15) *BelCartB*, l.13 *Wyg* (p),
  Hertheby 1282 OSut (p)
Herdbi c.1130 LeicSurv, *Herdby* c.1130 ib, a.1250 (1449) *WoCart*
  (p) *et passim* to 1415 Fine, 1520 *Crox*
Herby 1518 Visit, 1521 LWills *et passim* to 1553 Pat, *Herbye* 1541
  MinAccts
Hardeby 1363 Ipm, 1395 Cl, 1413 *Comp et passim* to 1466 *Rut*,
  1475 *Wyg*, 1535, 1537 CoPleas, (~ *in le Vale* 1453 Fine)
Hardby 1413 *Comp*, 1431 Fine, 1463 *Wyg et passim* to 1490 Ipm,
  1535 CoPleas
Hareby 1510 *Rut*, *Harebia* 1578 LEpis, 1585 LibCl
Harby 1508 Banco, 1516 Fine, 1519 *Wyg et passim* to 1535 VE,
  1535 CoPleas *et freq*

There appear to be four instances of this name in the Midland
Danelaw. In addition to our Leics. example, there are also Harby (Nt
205), a lost *Herdebi* (Db 570) and a lost *Hertheby*, a recently recognized
late 13th cent. Notts. instance (related to Tithby) which is recorded in
the Thurgarton Cartulary. Lindkvist 10 suggests that the first el. of
Harby in Notts. may either be *hjǫrð* (*hjarðar* gen.sg.) 'a herd' or
alternatively the Scand pers.n. *Herrøðr*, while *Herrøðr* is preferred for
this instance by Ekwall DEPN and by Gover, Mawer and Stenton, the
editors of the Notts. survey of the EPNS. DEPN also prefers *Herrøðr* as
the first el. of Harby in Leics. Kenneth Cameron (Db 570) suggests that
the lost *Herdebi* contains rather OE *heord* 'a herd'. Gillian Fellows-
Jensen (SSNEM 52) prefers Scand *hjǫrð* for the Leics., Notts. and
Derbys. examples (the recently discovered *Hertheby* of the Thurgarton
Cartulary postdating her publication). Carole Hough (NQ, September
1995, 264–5) who first noted the cartulary example, points out that
because of it, four instances of apparently identical names would seem
to preclude a recurring pers.n. in compound with *bý*. She interprets all
of these names as being a compound appellative *hjarðar-bý(r)* 'herd

farm', a Scand representation of the common OE *heorde-wīc* 'herd farm', i.e. 'that part of a manor devoted to livestock as distinct from ... that part devoted to arable farming'. John Insley (SNPh 9–23) argues strongly that the compound is rather *heŏrdabȳ* of Anglo-Scand formation and meaning 'the village, settlement of the herdsmen'. He sees these names as representing low status settlements of groups of herdsmen attached to important desmesnes. He suggests that ninth cent. lengthening of short vowels and diphthongs before homorganic groups would have given *heŏrde* 'a herdsman, a shepherd', with later shortening to *herde*, that spellings with *t* show AN substitution of *t* for *d*, while forms with *th* may be the result of formal contamination by the Scand cognate *hirðir* 'a herdsman'.

Hence, Harby is probably 'the farmstead or village of the herdsmen', otherwise 'the herd farm', *v.* **heorde, hjǫrð** (**hjarðar** gen.sg.), **bȳ**. The form *Hardeby in Staverne* 1343 Cl may indicate that the settlement was absorbed into or later belonged to neighbouring Stathern. Harby lies in the Vale of Belvoir, thus *Hardeby in le Vale* 1453 Fine, *v.* **val**.

PIPER HOLE, *Pyperhoale* 1625 Terrier, *Pyper Hole* 1703 *ib*, *Piper Hole* 1708, 1708 (18) *ib*, 1793 EnclA, 1806 Map, *Pipers Hole* 1795 Nichols, cf. *Piperhole Mouth* 1703 Terrier (*v.* **mūða**), *Top of Piper Hole* 1708, 1708 (18) *ib* (*v.* **topp**), *Piper Hole Road* 1918 *ib*. A small stream rises at Piper Hole and in descending to the Vale of Belvoir has cut deeply into the escarpment of the Wolds. In discussing Peppering (Sx 167) and Peppering Eye (Sx 498), Ekwall PN-ing 38 compares these names with Pebringe which occurs twice in Denmark. This is taken to derive from ODan *pipr-* 'stream, water-course' or 'spring', an el. found in several Danish nature-names beginning with Peber-. The el. also occurs in Norwegian names. Ekwall postulates a cognate OE **pipere* 'spring, stream' as the base of Peppering and Peppering Eye. Such an el. would satisfactorily explain Piper Hole, even though no early spellings are recorded. However, the surn. *Piper* cannot be discounted if the name is a later formation (cf. Pipers Wong in Sewstern f.ns. (a)), nor can OE *pīpere* 'a piper' which may have been early extended to describe a bird (cf. *sandpiper*, whose initial citation in OED is for 1674), *v.* **pipere**, **hol**[1].

BARLOW'S LODGE, cf. *James Barlow, farmer* 1846 White. HARBY COLSTON BRIDGE, crossing *Grantham Canal* 1863 White towards Colston Bassett to the north-west in Notts. HARBY HALL, *v. the Hall*

Close and *the Hall Leys* in f.ns. (b). HARBY HILL, *Harbye Hill* 1625
Terrier; it is *the Hill* 1703, 1703 (18) *ib.* HARBY LODGE, 1925 Kelly, *v.*
loge. HOSE LODGE, (x2). LANGAR BRIDGE, crossing the Nottingham and
Grantham Canal towards Langar to the north-west in Notts. MARQUIS OF
GRANBY (P.H.) (lost), *Marquis of Granby* 1863 White, *v.* Lei **1** 132 *s.n.*
MEADOWS LANE. METHODIST CHAPEL. THE MILL, 1703, 1708, 1708
(18) *Terrier*, 1925 Kelly, *v.* **myln.** NAG'S HEAD (P.H.), *Nag's Head*
1846, 1877 White, 1925 Kelly. OLD MANOR HO., *Manor House* 1846
White, *v.* **maner.** THE POPLARS. THE RECTORY, 1877 White, 1925
Kelly, *The Rectory House* 1792, 1821 *Terrier*; it is *The Parsonage*
House 1708, 1708 (18) *ib.* ST MARY'S CHURCH, *The Church* 1708, 1708
(18) *Terrier*, *Church (St Mary)* 1846, 1863, 1877 White; it is earlier
recorded as *ecclesiam ~ ~*, *ecclesie de Herdeby* 1220 MHW, 1235, 1251
RGros, 1343, 1344 *Pat et passim* to 1376 *ib*, *ecclesie Sancte Marie*
Herdeby 1299 *ib*, *ecclesiarum de Hardeby et Redmyld* 1462, 1464 *ib*, ~
de Hardeby Wolsthorpe et Redmylde 1467, 1475 *ib.* WASH DYKE, a
sheep-dip, *v.* **wash-dyke.** WHITE HART (P.H.), *White Hart* 1846, 1863,
1877 White, 1925 Kelly.

FIELD-NAMES

In (a), forms dated 1792, 18, 1821 and 1918 are *Terrier*, 1793 are *EnclA*
and 1806 are Map. Forms throughout dated 1284, 1296, 1.13^1, 1.13^2,
1.13^3, 13^1, 13^2, 13^3, 1318, 1321, 1322, 1323 and 1328 are *Gret*; 13^4 are
AD; 1605, 1703, 1708 and 1708 (18) are *Terrier*; 1653 are *Conant*.

(a) Ash Cl 1793 (1703, 1708, *backside Ash Close* 1708 (18), *v.* **æsc, bak-side**);
(the) Beck Fd 1798, 18 (*the Beck feild* 1703, ~ ~ *Field* 1708, 1708 (18), *v.* **bekkr,**
feld; one of the three later great fields of the township); Besk Fd 1793, Roger Besk
Lane 1793 (with the surn. *Besk*); Bottom Pasture 1918; The Breaches 1793 (*Breeches*
1708 (18), *at the bottom of the briches* 1703, ~ ~ ~ *of Breeches* 1708, *v.* **brēc**); Broad
Lane, ~ ~ End 1793 (*v.* **lane-ende**); Canal Cl 1793 (beside the Nottingham and
Grantham Canal); Co(u)lston Bassett Rd 1793 (Colston Bassett lies to the north-west
in Notts.); Cranwell Court Covert 1824 O (*v.* **court, cover(t)**, cf. *Crankwell lane*
1703, *Crankwel-lane-End* 1708, *Crankwell Lane End* 1708 (18) (*v.* **lane-ende**),
'spring or stream frequented by cranes', *v.* **cranuc, wella**); Frick's Cl 1793 (with the
surn. *Frick*); Harby Covert 1806 (*v.* **cover(t)**); Harby Hills 1806 (*Harby hilles* 1605),
the Hills 1792, 1793, 18 (*le hillis* 1.13^2, *the Hills* 1703, 1708, 1708 (18), *v.* **hyll**);
Hose Rd 1793 (Hose lies to the south-west); Ironstone Sidings 1918 (railway tracks
belonging to Eastwell Ore Co.); Langar Rd 1793 (Langar lies to the north-west in
Notts.); (the) Long Fd 1793, 18 (*the long feild* 1703, ~ ~ *Field* 1708, 1708 (18), *v.*

lang[1], **feld**; one of the three later great fields of the village); Long Hedge, ~ ~ Cl 1793; Mill Cl 1918; Millgate 1793 (*the Mill gate* 1703, 1708, 1708 (18)), *v.* **myln, gata** and Old Mill Gate *infra*); North Well 1793 (*Norwell* 1703, 1708, 1708 (18), cf. *Norwell Dike* 1703, 1708, 1708 (18) (*v.* **dík**), *Norþewellehil* 1.13[2], *Northwellehil* 13[1], 13[2], *Northwellehille* 1322 (*v.* **hyll**), *v.* **norð, wella**); Old Mill Gate 1793 (*v.* Millgate *supra*); Old Pasture 1793 (*the Paster* 1703, *The Pasture* 1708, 1708 (18)); Plungar Rd 1792, 1793 (Plungar lies to the north-east); Red Lane 1793 (cf. *le Redehil* 13[4], *Redhill* 1703, 1708, 1708 (18), *v.* **hyll**; with either **hrēod** 'reed' or **rēad** 'red', referring to the colour of the soil); The Row 1793 (*the Roe* 1703, 1708, 1708 (18), *v.* **vrá**); Sike Fd 1793, Sick ~ 18 (*The Syke Feild* 1703, *The Sick Field* 1708, 1708 (18), ~ *Syke* ~ 1708 (18), *v.* **sík, feld**; one of the three later great fields of the village); Thorney Park 1792, 1821, Thorny ~ 18 (*Thorny Park* 1708, 1708 (18), *v.* **þornig, park**; the name of a close, *v.* Field 25–8); Top Piece 1918 (*v.* **top, pece**); Town Street 1793 (*v.* **tūn, strǣt**); Waltham Rd 1793 (Waltham on the Wolds lies to the south-west); Willow Cl 1793 (*v.* **wilig**); The Wong 1793, Wong Garden 1918, Wong Top 1918 (*v.* **topp**) (*v.* **vangr**).

(b) *Amy Wong* 1703, 1708, 1708 (18) (*v.* **vangr**; with the surn. *Amy*, *v.* Reaney *s.n.* Amey); *Long, Short Arborow* 1703, ~ *Arbrow* 1708, 1708 (18), *Long Arborow* 1708, *Arborow Hades* 1703, 1708, *Arbrow* ~ 1708 (18) (*v.* **hēafod**) (such forms are sometimes the modern reflexes of OE *eorð-burh* 'fortification built of earth', but no suitable site for such a fortress is apparent in Harby; perh. here a meaning 'hill where oats are grown' (*v.* **hæfera, hafri, berg**) is the case, but these late forms may rather belong with *Horreberue, infra*); *at the ashtree* 1703, *Ash-tree* 1708, 1708 (18) (*v.* **æsc**); (*in*) *campo australi* 1.13[1], 1.13[2], 1321 ('the south field' (with MLat *campus* 'a field' and MLat *australis* 'south, southern'); one of the two recorded early great fields of the village); *the Becks* 1703, 1708, 1708 (18), (*the*) *Beck Dike* 1703, 1708, 1708 (18) (*v.* **dík**), *becks hill* 1703, *Beck Hill* 1708, 1708 (18), *the beck sike* 1703 (*v.* **sík**) (*v.* **bekkr**); *Beggars Bush* 1703, 1708, 1708 (18), *Beggar's* ~ 1703, *Beggers* ~ 1708 (*v.* **beggere, busc**, *Beggar Bush Furlong* in Normanton f.ns. (b) and Field 108); *berilandis* 1.13[1], 1.13[3], *Berry Lands* 1708 (*v.* **berige, land**); *blackelandisti* 1.13[1], *blaclandsti* 1.13[3] (*v.* **blæc, land, stīg**); *Blacmild* 13[4] (*v.* **blæc, mylde**); *le bolys* 1.13[3] (*v.* **bole**); (*in*) *campo boriali* 1.13[1], 1.13[3], 1318, 1322, ~ *boreali* 1.13[2] ('the north field' (with MLat *campus* 'a field' and MLat *borialis* 'north, northern'); one of the two recorded early great fields of the township); *at the botham,* ~ ~ *bothom* 1705 (*v.* **botm**; a furlong so called); *brunis(s)wong* 1.13[1], 1.13[3], *Burns-wong* 1703, 1708 (*v.* **vangr**; the first el. is a pers.n., either OE *Brūn* or ODan *Brun* (ON *Brúnn*), or poss. a nickname from OFr *brun* 'brown', of hair or complexion, cf. Burns Wong in neighbouring Eastwell f.ns. (a) which may record the same feature); *Bunting Wong* 1703, 1708, 1708 (18) (*v.* **vangr**; prob. with the surn. *Bunting*, *v.* Reaney *s.n.*, although the bird-name **bountyng** is recorded from c.1300, *v.* OED *s.v.* bunting); *Burtofts* 1703, 1708, 1708 (18) (*v.* **búr**[2], **toft**); *Byard cloace* 1703, *Biard Close* 1708, 1708 (18) (*v.* **clos(e)**; with the surn. *Byard*); *the Church gate* 1703, 1708, 1708 (18) (*v.* **gata**); *Cloven Balk* 1703, 1708, ~ *Baulk* 1708 (18) (*v.* **clofen, balca**); *Cocks wong* 1703, *Cox Wong* 1708, 1708 (18), *Coxwong Hades* 1708, 1708 (18) (*v.* **hēafod**) (*v.* **vangr**; with the surn. *Cocks/Cox*); *Coleacker* 1703, *Cole Acre* 1708, 1708 (18), *Coleacker dich* 1703, *Cole Acre Dike* 1708, 1708 (18) (*v.* **dīc, dík**) (*v.* **æcer**; the first

el. could be either of the pers.ns. OE *Cola*, ON, ODan *Koli* or the surn. *Cole* or OE
cole 'a hollow'); *Crocland* 1.13¹, 1.13³, 13⁴ (*v.* **land**; the first el. is either **crocc** or
krókr); *Cross Furlong* 1703, 1708, 1708 (18) (*v.* **cross**; in Beck Fd); *Cross furlong*
1703 (*v.* **cross**; in Long Fd); *Crosthorn* 1703, *Cross Thorn* 1708, 1708 (18), *schort
crosþorn* 1.13² (*v.* **sc(e)ort**) (*v.* **cross, þorn**; the earliest citation in OED for *cross* in
this sense 'lying across, athwart' is for 1523); (*the*) *Dale Side* 1703, 1708, 1708 (18)
(*v.* **dalr, sīde**); *Darker Nook* 1703, 1708, 1708 (18) (*v.* **nōk**; with the local surn.
Darker); *le dede hevidland* 13² (*v.* **dēad, hēafod-land**; poss. a site where pre-
Christian burials were discovered); *Dedwong* 1322, *Dead Wong* 1703, 1708, 1708
(18) (*v.* **dēad, vangr**; as for the preceding f.n.); *le Deycfourlong* 1284, (*le*)
Dikefurlong 1318, 1323, *Dikfurlong* 1328, *Dike Furlong* 1703, 1708, 1708 (18) (*v.*
dík, furlang); *le Ferdgate* 13⁴ ('the military road', *v.* **ferd, gata**; the road south
across Brock Hill to ford R. Wreake at Melton Mowbray); *Flatwellis* 1296 (*v.* **flat,
wella**); *flitlandis* 1.13¹ (*v.* **(ge)flit, land**); *forlandis* 1.13¹, 1.13³, (*the*) *Forlands* 1703,
1708, 1708 (18) (*v.* **fore, land**); *Foxholes* 1703, 1708, 1708 (18) (*v.* **fox-hol**); *the
furlongs* 1703, (*the*) *Forlongs* 1708, 1708 (18) (*v.* **furlang**; in Beck Fd); *into the Gate*
1703 (*v.* **gata**); *le est gore* 1.13¹, *le hestgore* 13¹, *le westgore* 1.13¹, 1.13³ (*v.* **ēast, west,
gāra**); *le goytres(s) iuxta friscas* 1.13¹, 1.13³ (*v.* **goter**; with MLat *frisca* (*friscas*
acc.pl.) 'newly broken land'); *the Hall Close* 1653, *the Hall Leas* 1703, ~ ~ *Lays*
1708, ~ ~ *Leys* 1708 (18) (*v.* **hall, leys**); *le Hassokys* 13², *le assokis* 13¹, *Hassocks*
1703, 1708 (18), *Hassacks* 1708 (18) (*v.* **hassuc**); *haugrimhole* 1.13³ (*v.* **hol¹**; with the
Scand pers.n. *Hafgrímr, v.* SPNLY 122); *between the Headlands* 1703, *betwixt* ~ ~
1708, 1708 (18) (*v.* **hēafod-land**; a furlong so called); *the High gate* 1708, 1708 (18),
the hyegate 1703 (*v.* **hēah¹, gata**); *the Highway* 1708, 1708 (18) (*v.* **hēah-weg**); *at
the bottom of the Hill* 1708, 1708 (18), *under the Hill* 1708, 1708 (18) (furlongs so
called), *the Hill Close* 1653, *the Hill's end* 1703, (*the*) *Hills End* 1703, 1708, 1708
(18) (*v.* **ende**) (*v.* Harby Hill *supra*); *The Homestal(l)* 1708, 1708 (18) (*v.* **hām-stall**;
relating to *The Parsonage House*); *Long Horreberue* 13⁴, *schorthorberoue* 1284,
schorthoreberu 1322 (*v.* **lang¹, sc(e)ort, horu, berg** and *Arborow, supra*);
Horssepole 1321, *Horsepools* 1703, 1708, 1708 (18) (*v.* **hors, pōl¹**); *Horthorn Hill*
1703, *Horthon* ~ 1708 (*v.* **hagu-þorn**; prob. pronunciation spellings, but note
Harthorndale in Somerby f.ns. (b)); *Hosemeer* 1703, *Hose mear* 1708 (*v.* **(ge)mǣre**;
the boundary with Hose which lies to the south-east); *le hou* 1.13², *le Howe* 1322, *the
Hoff* 1703, *the Hof(f)e* 1708, 1708 (18) (*v.* **hōh, haugr**); *Housalls* 1703, *Housalds*
1708, 1708 (18) (perh. from **hūs** with **halh**, but earlier forms are needed); *Jony lane
end* 1703, 1708 (*v.* **lane-ende**; the first el. appears to be a surn., a derivative of John
such as *Jone, v.* Reaney *s.n.* John); *backside Tho. Kirk's* 1703, ~ *Thomas* ~ 1708 (*v.*
bak-side); *Lambert Hill* 1703, 1708, 1708 (18) (with the surn. *Lambert*);
landemerehil 1.13³, *-hyl* 1.13¹ (*v.* **hyll**), *landemeresike* 1.13 (*v.* **sík**) (*v.* **land-
(ge)mǣre**); *Litilheng* 13⁴, *lutelhenge* 1.13², *Littling* 1703, 1708 (18), *Littlein* 1708,
Littlin 1708, 1708 (18), *litlingbecke* 1.13¹, *lytlingbecke* 1.13³, *Litillengbeck* 13¹,
Litillingbec 13² (*v.* **bekkr**) ('the little meadow', *v.* **lȳtel, lítill, eng**); *longe presteholm*
1.13¹ (*v.* **lang¹, prēost, holmr**); *le maresty* 1.13¹, *Mare Steeth*, ~ *Steith* 1708, 1708
(18) (*v.* **stig**; perh. with **mare** rather than with **(ge)mǣre**; cf. *one piece of a Stigh att
Burns-wong* 1708, *v.* **brunis(s)wong**, *supra*); *Melton gate* 1703, 1708, 1708 (18) (*v.*
gata; the road to Melton Mowbray, earlier called *le Ferdgate*, *supra*); *Mickilldales*,

Michkill dales 1703, *Mickledales* 1708, 1708 (18) (*v.* **micel, mikill, deill**); *between the Mills* 1703, 1708, 1708 (18), *beyond the Mill* 1703 (furlongs so called); *the Moor(e)* 1703, 1708, 1708 (18), *le longemor* l.13¹, l.13³, *the Long Moor(e)* 1703, 1708, 1708 (18) (*v.* **lang**¹), *le schortmor* 1284, *le scort mor* l.13³, *le scormor* (sic) l.13¹, *Short Moor(e)* 1703, 1708, 1708 (18) (*v.* **sc(e)ort**), *Moor Leas* 1703, ~ *Lays* 1708, ~ *Leys* 1708 (18) (*v.* **leys**) (*v.* **mōr**¹); *Muck(e)wellegate* l.13², 13¹, 13² (*v.* **muk, wella, gata**); *Mudwells* 1703, 1708, 1708 (18), *above Mudwells* 1708 (a furlong so called) (*v.* **mudde, wella**; poss. a later name for *Muck(e)welle-*); *Neatwaters* 1703, 1708, 1708 (18), *neatwater* 1703 (*v.* **nēat, wæter**); *Notingham gate* 13¹, 13² (*v.* **gata**; the road to Nottingham which lies to the north-west); *Parnham Close* 1703, 1708, 1708 (18), *Parnham Sheep-house* 1708, 1708 (18) (*v.* **shepe-hous**) (cf. *Widow Parnham* 1703, 1708); *Parsonage Stack* 1703, 1708, 1708 (18) (*v.* **stakkr**; presum. a stack-yard); *(the) Parsonage Steith* 1703, ~ *Steeth* 1708, 1708 (18) (*v.* **stig**; a piece of enclosed grassland); *peseland'* l.13², *Peas(e) Lands* 1703, 1708, 1708 (18) (*v.* **pise, land**); *phistilberu* l.13¹, *Thistle-borrow Hill* 1708, *Thistle-Burrow hill* 1708 (18) (*v.* **þistel, berg**); *Pine syke* 1703, *(the) Pine Sike* 1708, 1708 (18) (*v.* **pine, sík**; evidently land very difficult to till); *the Sand Gate* 1703, 1708, 1708 (18) (*v.* **sand, sandr, gata**); *the Sands* 1703, 1708, 1708 (18), *the Long, (the) Short Sands* 1703, 1708, 1708 (18) (*v.* **sand**); *the Syke* 1703, *the Sike* 1708, 1708 (18), *the Sicke* 1708 (18), *the bottom of the Sike* 1708 (18) (a furlong so called), *Sikedeylwong* 13³ (*v.* **deill, vangr**), *(the) Syke Mouth* 1703, *Sick ~, Sike ~* 1708, 1708 (18) (*v.* **mūða**) (*v.* Sike Fd *supra*); *le sigate* l.13¹, l.13³, *Sygate* 1322 (*v.* **sík, gata**); *le smalesik* l.13¹, l.13³ (*v.* **smæl, sík**); *Snow Wong* 1703, 1708, 1708 (18) (*v.* **vangr**; either with the surn. *Snow* or describing an enclosure where snow lay long (*v.* **snāw**, cf. *Snow Cl* in Brentingby f.ns. (a) and *Snow Close* in Wymondham f.ns. (b)); *Standard* 13⁴, *Standartvang* 13⁴ (*v.* **standard, vangr**); *Stathurn Hedge* 1703, *Stathern(e) ~* 1708, 1708 (18) (the parish boundary hedge with Stathern which adjoins to the east); *Steephill* 1703, 1708, 1708 (18) (*v.* **stēap**); *(the) Stone Bridge* 1703, 1708, 1708 (18); *Stony Hill* 1703, 1708, 1708 (18) (*v.* **stānig**); *Stubthorn(e)* 1703, 1708, 1708 (18), *Stubsthorne* 1703 (*v.* **stubb, þorn**); *suenwongsike* l.13³, *sweynwongsike* l.13¹ (*v.* **vangr, sík**; with the ON pers.n. *Sveinn* (ODan *Sven*)); *the Swinherds peice* 1703, *the Swineheard Piece* 1708, ~ ~ *Peice* 1708 (18) (*v.* **swīn-hirde, pece**); *thickthorn(e)* 1703, 1708, *thicke-thorne* 1708 (18) (*v.* **þicce**², **þorn**); *thurniakyr* l.13¹, l.13³ (*v.* **þyrniht, æcer**); *(the) Tofts* 1703, 1708, 1708 (18), *Toft hurn* 1703, 1708, 1708 (18) (*v.* **hyrne**), *toftsti* l.13³ (*v.* **stīg**) (*v.* **toft**); *(at) the Town(s) end* 1703, 1708, 1708 (18), *(att) the Townside* 1703, 1708, 1708 (18) (*v.* **tūn, ende, sīde**; furlongs so called); *Long ~ ~, Water Furrows* 1703, 1708 (*v.* **wæter, furh**; poss. a place where water tended to lie, but *v.* *waterfurris* in Muston f.ns. (b)); *Westebecke* 1322, *Westbecks* 1703, *West Beck* 1708, 1708 (18) (*v.* **west, vestr, bekkr**); *Westhil* 1326 (*v.* **west, hyll**); *West Steeth* 1703, ~ *Steath, ~ Steith* 1708 (*v.* **stig**); *Whiny Leas* 1703, *Whinny Leys* 1708, 1708 (18) (*v.* **whinny, leys**); *Wrongland* 13⁴ (*v.* **wrang, vrangr, land**).

3. HOSE

Hoches 1086 DB
Howes 1086 DB, Hy 1 (1333) Ch, Hy 2 *Rut*, Hy 2 (e.15) *BelCartB*,
   1199 Fine *et passim* to 1261 RGrav, 1268 Cur, Hy 3 *Crox* (freq)
   et freq to 1473 *CCR*, 1493 *Rut et passim* to 1551 Fine, 1553 Pat,
   Houues Hy 1 (1333) Ch, Hy 2 (e.15) *BelCartB*, *Howys* 1247 Ass,
   1320 Banco *et passim* to 1420 Misc, 1539 *Deed*
Houwes c.1130 LeicSurv, 1236 Berkeley *et passim* to 1333 Ch, 1349
   Rut, *Houwis* 1328 (e.15) *BelCartB*, *Houwys* 1316 FA, 1326 Ipm
   et passim to 1439 Fine, *Houes* a.1150 (e.15), Hy 2 (e.15)
   BelCartB, l.12 *Rut*, 12 AD, 1236 Fees, *Houis* l.12 (p), Edw 1 *Rut*
   (p)
Hous 1174 × 82 *Rut*, 12 (e.15), 1235 × 53 (e.15), p.1250 (e.15)
   BelCartB
Houus 1209 × 35 RHug, *Hows* Hy 3 *Crox*, e.14 *BelCartA*, 1328
   (e.15) *BelCartB*
Hoys 1534 *Rut*, *Hoyes* 1580 LEpis
Hoose 1535 VE, 1552 AAS *et passim* to 1599 *Rut*, 1610 Speed,
   Hoose alias Howse 1544 Fine, *Howse* 1535 VE, *Howyes* 1539
   Deed, *Hooes al. Howes* 1558 × 79 ECP
Hosse 1541 MinAccts, 1553 Pat, 1564 Fine, *Hose* 1544 *Rut*, 1554
   AD *et passim* to 1590 SR, 1611 *Rut et freq*

'The hill-spurs', *v.* hōh (hō(h)as, hōs nom.pl.). Scand **haugr** 'a hill'
has influenced forms from DB onwards. Hose lies in the Vale of Belvoir,
below the Wolds which form a series of spurs to the south of the village.

BAPTIST CHAPEL. BLACK HORSE (P.H.), *Black Horse* 1846, 1863, 1877
White, 1925 Kelly. BOSTON LANE, presum. with the surn. *Boston*, cf.
Boston hoale in Knipton f.ns. (b). BROCKHILL HALL, 1877 White, *v.* **hall**
and Brock Hill in Long Clawson *supra*. CANAL LANE, leading to the
Nottingham and Grantham Canal. THE CEDARS. DAM DYKE, *v.* **damme**,
dík. THE GRANGE, 1863, 1877 White, 1925 Kelly, *Grange of Howes*
1539 MinAccts, *Hoose Grange* 1597 *Rut*, *Hose Grange* 1795 Nichols,
1824 O, *v.* **grange**; poss. in origin an outlier of Croxton Abbey. HOSE
BRIDGE, a canal bridge. HOSE GORSE, *v.* **gorst**. MARRIOTT'S BRIDGE, a
canal bridge, cf. *Wm. Marriott, landowner* 1846 White; earlier are
recorded in Hose *Richard Maryett* 1524 SR, *Laurence Marrytt* 1543 ib,
Jervice Marriott 1666 ib and *Richard Marriatt* 1710 *Terrier*, while in

neighbouring Long Clawson are *Thos. Marriott* 1628 LML, *John Marriott* 1705, 1716 ib and *Richard Marriott* 1718, 1725 ib. MOUNT PLEASANT, 1877 White, 1925 Kelly; it is *Hose Lodge* 1824 O, *v.* **loge**. PASTURE LANE. ROSE AND CROWN (P.H.), *Rose and Crown* 1846, 1863, 1877 White, 1925 Kelly. ST MICHAEL'S CHURCH, *the Parish Church* 1821 *Terrier, Church (St Michael)* 1846, 1863, 1877 White; it is earlier recorded as *ecclesie de Houus* 1220 MHW. Note also *The Churchyard* 1625 *Terrier*, *(The) Church Yard* 1710 *ib*, 1796 *EnclA*, *v.* **chirche-ȝeard**. THE SUNDAY SCHOOL. THE VICARAGE, 1925 Kelly; it is *the parsonage* 1605 *Terrier* (*v.* **personage**), *The Vickeradge House* 1703 *ib*, *The Vicarage House* 1710 *ib*.

FIELD-NAMES

Undated forms in (a) are 1796 *EnclA*, while those dated 1780 are also *EnclA*. Forms throughout dated Hy 3 are *Crox*; Edw 1 are *CroxR*; 1601, 1605, 1625, 1703, 1710 and m.18 are *Terrier*; 1627, 1631, 1649 and 1653 are *Rut*.

(a) Barn Cl; Beck Fd 1780, 1796 (*the Beck Feild* 1703, *v.* **bekkr**; one of the great fields of the township, earlier called *South feilde*); Boughtin Cl (poss. with the surn. *Boughton*); (the) Brigg Hill (*v.* **bryggja**); Brockhill, ~ Cl, the Brockhill Cls, (the) Brockhill Pasture, Brockhills Pasture (*v.* Brock Hill in Long Clawson *supra*); Bullys Dyke, ~ ~ Cls, Bullys Dike Cl (*v.* **dík**; with the surn. *Bully*); Butcher Lane (with the surn. *Butcher*); Clock Lane (cf. *Clock lane end* 1710, *v.* **lane-ende**; the nature of *clock* here is obscure); Cumber, ~ Cl (the surn. *Cumber*, *v.* Reaney *s.n.* Comber); Dale Cls (*v.* **dalr**); Cottage ~ ~, Darker Plat (*v.* **cotage, plat**; with the local surn. *Darker*); Dry Cl(s) (*v.* **drȳge**); Frontl(e)y Cl (presum. with the surn. *Frontley*); Gorsey Cl (*v.* **gorstig**); Hall Gate (*v.* **hall, gata**); Harby Meadow Plat (*v.* **plat**; Harby adjoins to the east); Haynes('s) Cl (with the surn. *Haynes*); Heyside Cl, (the) Hey Side Cls (*v.* **(ge)hæg, sīde**); Hill Cl, (the) Hill Cls; Hillocky Cl (*v.* **hylloc, -ig**[3]); Hose Hills 1806 Map; Kirks Cl (with the surn. *Kirk*); Land Cl (a close formed by the consolidation of an unspecified number of selions or 'lands' of one of the former great fields of the village, *v.* **land**); Cottage ~, Rough ~, Lee Wong (*v.* **cotage, rūh**[1], **vangr**; *Lee* is presum. a surn. here); Lound Cl (*v.* **lundr**); Lown ~, Lawn Cls (*v.* **launde**); Linlands Plat(t) (*v.* **līn, land, plat**); Long Cl(s); Magstone (a close so called; poss. with ModEdial. *mag* 'the mark to aim at in quoits, etc.' (*v.* EDD *s.v.* mag sb.[2]), hence named from a stone used as a mark of some kind (in a rural game?)); Meadow (*Hose Meadow* 1627), Meadow Cl(s); Mill Cl(s); Mud Pit Cl (*v.* **mudde, pytt**); the Nether Fd (*the nether feild* 1605, *Netherfeild* 1649, *the Neither Feild* 1703, *the Neather field* m.18, *v.* **neoðera, feld**; one of the great fields, formerly *the north feilde*); New Cl; New Dykes Furlong 1780 (*v.* **dík**); Ox Cl (*v.* **oxa**); The Park (*v.* Field

25–8); (the) Great, Little Pingle (*v.* **pingel**); Potter Wong (*v.* **vangr**; prob. with the surn. *Potter*); Ricks Cl (a close used as a rickyard may be thought of (*v.* **hrēac**); otherwise with the surn. *Rick(s)/Rix*); the Road Cl, Road Cls; Nether, Upper Roger Wong (*Roger Wong* 1613, *v.* **vangr**; with the surn. *Roger*, the reflex of the pers.n. OFr *Roger/Rogier*, OGer *Ro(d)ger*); Rowley (a close so called; the surn. *Rowley*); (the) Saltmoor Fd (*Saltmore feild* 1703, ~ *Field* 1710, m.18, 'moorland where brackish water lies', *v.* **salt²**, **mōr¹**, **feld** and Saltbeck in Belvoir parish; one of the great fields of the village, formerly *the East feilde*); Seed Cl (*v.* **sǣd** 'seed'; in f.ns., frequently used of areas of sown grass); Henry Stokes Cl (cf. *Henry Stokes* 1796 and *Henry Stoke's Land* in f.ns. (b)); Thorney Lane (*v.* **þornig**); Town Cl 1846, 1863 White (*v.* **tūn**); the Town Street (*the Towne Street* 1625, *v.* **tūn**, **strǣt**); Wadhill Nook (*v.* **wād**, **hyll**, **nōk**); the Waste (*v.* **waste**); Wetmo(o)re ~, Whetmoore Furlong 1780 (*v.* **wēt**, **mōr¹**); Wheel Cl (*v.* **hwēol**; such f.ns. sometimes indicate the presence of an ancient circular earthwork (*v.* Field 214) but evidence for such appears to be lacking here; poss. simply a circular enclosure); Woodgate Plat(t) (*v.* **wudu**, **gata**, **plat**).

(b) *Alfnadgraue* Hy 3, Edw I ('Ælfnōð's grove', *v.* **grāf**; the pers.n. *Ælfnōð* is OE); *the Beck* m.18 (*v.* **bekkr**; *the East feilde* 1601, *East feild* 1605 (*v.* **ēast**, **feld**; one of the great fields, *v.* Saltmoor Fd *supra*); *gaddesland* Edw 1 (*v.* **land**; with the Scand pers.n. *Gaddr*); *the gleabe land* 1607 LAS (*v.* **glebe**, **land**); *green leies* 1601, *Green-Lays* 1710, *Green Leas* m.18, *greene layes furlong* 1625 (*v.* **grēne¹**, **leys**); *the halfeacres* 1601, *halfeacre feild* 1605, *long Have-acres* 1710 (*v.* **half-aker**); *atte hall* 1381 SR (p) (*v.* **atte**, **hall**); *the Homestall* 1605 (*v.* **hām-stall**), *the Homestead* m.18 (*v.* **hām-stede**) (both relating to *the parsonage/The Vicarage House*); *Hutshoces* Edw 1 (*v.* **hōc**; the first el. appears to be a pers.n. in the possessive case, perh. **Hut*, a hypocoristic form of OE *Ūhtrǣd*); *Ingelemer* Hy 3 ('Ingeld's boundary', *v.* **(ge)mǣre**; the pers.n. is ODan *Ingeld* (ON *Ingjaldr*)); *the Kinges highe waie* 1605 (*v.* **hēah-weg**; referring to James I); *Longelands* 1631 (*v.* **lang¹**, **land**); *Longe Wonge* 1653 (*v.* **lang¹**, **vangr**); *Richard Marriats Head-land* 1710 (*v.* **hēafod-land**); *Meltongatefeild* 1649, *Melton Gate Field* 1710, m.18 (*v.* **gata**, **feld**; one of the great fields of the village, this on the road to Melton Mowbray; it is earlier called *South feilde*); *Melton gate furlong* 1625 (*v.* the preceding f.n.); *Millfeild* 1649, *le Milnegate* 1326 AD (*v.* **gata**, *miln(e)holm* Hy 3, Edw 1 (*v.* **holmr**) (*v.* **myln**); *Nevylles land* 1555 LAS (*v.* **land**; with the surn. *Neville*); *the north feilde* 1601 (*v.* **norð**, **feld**; one of the great fields, later called *the nether feild*); *le Redland* 1340 AD (*v.* **rēad**, **land**; alluding to the colour of the soil); *Sandpittes* Edw 1 (*v.* **sand-pytt**); *Scarddeslande* l.13 (*v.* **land**; the first el. is either the ODan pers.n. *Skarth* (cf. ON *Skarði*) or ON **skarð** 'a gap, a cleft' (poss. influencing an earlier OE **sceard** with the same meaning)); *le Shyremer* 1340 AD (*v.* **scīr¹**, **(ge)mǣre**; the county boundary with Notts.); *South feilde* 1601 (*v.* **sūð**, **feld**; one of the great fields, later called *Melton Gate Field*); *Henry Stoke's Land* 1710 (*v.* **land**; cf. Henry Stokes Cl *supra*); *Thyrnclif* n.d. Nichols (*v.* **þyrne**, **clif**); *top well gate* 1625 (*v.* **wella**, **gata**; with **top** or **topp**); *the Town Furland* (sic) m.18 (*v.* **tūn**, **furlang**); *atte Welle* 1358 Banco (p) (*v.* **atte**, **wella**); *wormeacer leies* 1601 (*v.* **æcer**, **leys**; the first el. could be the OE pers.n. *Wyrma*, but is likelier to be **wyrm** 'reptile, snake', perh. in some later sense such as 'an earthworm' or 'a tick' or 'a gadfly' or one of various other kinds of grub).

Croxton Kerrial

1. CROXTON KERRIAL

Crohtone 1086 DB, *Crocton'* 1199 P

Crochestona 1177 ChancR, *Crocheston'* 1195 P, 1196 ChancR, 1197
   P, *Crokeston'* 1169, 1177, 1185 P *et passim* to 1223 Cur, Edw 1
   (e.15) *BelCartB*, *Crokestone* 1202 Ass, *Crokestun'* Hy 3 *Rut*,
   Crokeston 1611 *ib*

Crocstona c.1130 LeicSurv, *Crocston'* 1223, 1225 Cur *et passim* to
   1236 Fees, *Crocstone* 1233 (e.14) *BelCartA*, *Crocstun* 1203 Fine,
   1203 FF

Croston' 1203 Ass, 1224 Cur, c.1270 (1449) *WoCart*, *Crostona* e.Hy
   3 *Rut*

Croxston e.13 Berkeley, 1221 Cur *et passim* to 1454, 1500 *Rut*,
   Croxstona Ric 1 (1227) Ch, *Croxstun'* 1223 ClR, Hy 3 Berkeley

Croxton(') 1198, 1199 Cur, 1200 P *et freq*, *Croxtona* 1189 (1290)
   Ch, e.13 *BHosp*, 1285 ChPr, *Croxtone* 1224, 1231 RHug *et
   passim* to c.1400 HP, 1442 Visit, *Croxtun'* 1205 ChancR, 1217
   ClR *et passim* to 1241 (e.14) *BelCartA*, 1252 Cl, *Croxtuna* 1209
   × 19 RHug, *Chroxton'* 13 *MiD*

Crouxton 1541 *Rut*

Crawston 1577 *Terrier*, *Crawson* 1577 *ib*

'Krōk's farmstead, village', *v.* **tūn**. The ODan pers.n. *Krōk* (ON
Krókr) is an original by-name meaning 'crooked-backed' or poss.
'crooked-dealer' (*v.* SPNLY 181). The p.n. is to be compared with South
Croxton (Lei), Croxton (L) and Croxton (St). For extended discussion
of this name, *v.* L **2** 99 and SSNEM 375. The spelling *Crawson* (1577)
shows typical Leics. 16th cent. and later loss of *t* in the group *-ston*.
   Distinguishing affixes are variously added as:
   ~ *Sar(r)acene* 1201 P, 1201 ChancR
   ~ *Kyriel* 1247 Fees, 1285 Nichols *et passim* to 1444 *Rut*, ~ *Kiriel(l)*
      1290, 1338 IpmR, ~ *Keryall* 1500 *Rut*, 1535 VE, ~ *Ker(r)iall*
      1535 *ib et passim* to 1629 LML, ~ *Kyryell* 1516 Wyg, ~ *Kyryall*

1499 Banco, 1539 *Deed et passim* to 1549 AAS
~ *Roos(e)* 1590, 1609 *Rut,* ~ *Rosse* 1611 *ib*
Oliverus Sarazin held land in neighbouring Warwickshire in 1252 Fees,
but there is no record, apart from the feudal affix to the p.n., of the
Sarazin family's holding land in Croxton. *Bertramus de Cryoll* was
granted the manor in 1239 *Rut* and it was held by his family as late as
Margeria de Crioll 1319 ELiW and *Nicholas de Criel* 1328 Banco. The
manor was in the possession of *Lord Roose* of Belvoir in 1590 *Rut* and
later.

CROXTON ABBEY (lost)
   Sancti Johannis de Valle de Croxton(a) 1189 (1290), 1227 Ch, ~ ~
      ~ ~ *de Croxstona* Ric 1 (1227) ib
   Abbatie de Croxton 1220 MHW, 1359, 1448 *Pat*
   Croxton' Abbey 1519 *Wyg, Croxton-Abbay* c.1545 Leland

   Founded in 1162 by William, Earl of Mortaigne, Parcarius de Linus
and Sir Andrew Lutterel originally as a priory of Premonstratensian
Canons, the abbey became the mother house of Blanchland, Cockersand
and Hornby in the North, *v.* **abbaye** and note MLat *abbatia* 'an abbey'.

BLACKWELL LODGE, 1863, 1877 White, 1925 Kelly (*v.* **loge**), *Blackwell*
1601, 1625, 1674, 1700, 1704, c.1708, 1708 (18) *Terrier, v.* **blæc, wella**.
BUTCHERS' ARMS (P.H.) (lost), *Butchers' Arms* 1846 White. CEDAR
HILL, 1806 Map, 1824 O, *v.* **ceder**. CHURCH FM, *Church farm* 1925
Kelly, *v.* St John the Baptist's Church *infra*. CONYGEAR WOOD, 1806
Map, *Coneygear Wood* 1824 O, *the Cunnygraye,* ~ *Cunygrey* 1601
Terrier, the Cunnygree 1625, 1704, c.1708, 1708 (18) *ib, the Cunny
greey* 1625 *ib, the Cunn(e)grey* 1674 *ib, the Connigree* 1700 *ib, v.*
coningre. COOPER'S PLANTATION. CROXTON BANKS, 1795 Nichols,
1824 O, *v.* **banke**. CROXTON LODGE, 1863 White, *v.* **loge**. CROXTON
PARK, 1610 *Rut,* 1767 *EnclA,* 1782 *Reeve,* 1846, 1863, 1877 White,
parco de Croxtona 1189 (1290) Ch (with MLat *parcus* 'a park'),
Croxton parke 1612 *Rut, the Park* 1700, 1704, c.1708, 1708 (18)
Terrier, cf. *the parke pale* 1625 *ib* (*v.* **pale**), *v.* **park**. The house called
Croxton Park was built by John, Duke of Rutland, c.1730. FISH PONDS
are the surviving stews of Croxton Abbey. FOX (P.H.) (lost), *Fox* 1863
White. HALLAM'S WOOD, 1824 O, cf. *William Hallam* 1642, 1666 SR.
HEATH FM (1" only), *the Heath* 1674, 1700, 1704, c.1708, 1708 (18)
Terrier, 1767 *EnclA, the First, the Second Heath* 1822 *Terrier, v.* **hǣð**.

HIGHFIELDS FM, *Highfield farm* 1925 Kelly. HILLSIDE FM, *Hill Side farm* 1925 Kelly. KENNEL PLANTATION, *v.* **kenel**. KING LUD'S ENTRENCHMENTS, *King Lud's Intrenchments* 1795 Nichols; an undated linear earthwork of rampart and ditch forming part of the parish boundary on Saltby Heath. Lud was a legendary king of Britain who appears in Geoffrey of Monmouth's *Historia Regum Britanniae* as the eldest brother of Cassivelaunus. He succeeded Heli, his father, as king of Britain, replanned and rebuilt its capital Trinovantum and renamed it Kaerlud, later Kaerlundein, eventually London. Supposedly, he was in time buried at a gateway of his capital, now remembered as Ludgate; but *v. Ludforth* in Branston f.ns. (b). LAWN HOLLOW PLANTATION, *v.* **launde, holh**. OLD HALL, 1925 Kelly, *the Hall* 1674 *Terrier, v.* **hall**. THE OLD WINDMILL. OLD WOOD. OSIER HOLT, *v.* **oyser, holt**. PARK HO., *v.* Croxton Park *supra*. PEACOCK (P.H.) (lost), *Peacock* 1863 White, 1925 Kelly, *Peacock Inn* 1877 White; the peacock is part of the coat of arms of the Manners family, the Dukes of Rutland, cf. The Peacock in Belvoir and Peacock Inn in Redmile. ST JOHN THE BAPTIST'S CHURCH, *the parish church dedicated to St John* 1822 *Terrier, Church (St John)* 1846 White, *Church (St John the Baptist)* 1877 ib, 1925 Kelly; it is earlier recorded as *ecclesie de Croxton* 1220 MHW, *ecclesie parochialis de Croxton* 1237, 1242 RGros, 1503 *Pat*. Note also *The Churchyard* 1700, 1704, c.1708, 1708 (18), 1822 *Terrier*. SWALLOW HOLE, 1806 Map, 1824 O, *le Suelu* 13 Nichols, *le swelu* Edw 1 *CroxR, v.* **swalg**. TEMPERANCE HO. (lost), *Temperance House* 1877 White; instituted by the later 19th cent. Temperance Movement which aimed to dissuade people from the consumption of alcohol. TIPPING'S GORSE is *Tipping's* 1806 Map, cf. *Richard Typpin* 1700 *Terrier, Wm. Tippin* 1732 LML, *Elizabeth and Walter Tipping* 1925 Kelly, *v.* **gorst**. THE VICARAGE, 1877 White, 1925 Kelly, *The Vicaridge house* 1601, 1700, 1704 *Terrier, the vickeridge* 1625 *ib, The Vicarage house* 1700, c.1708, 1708 (18) *ib, v.* **vikerage**. WINDMILL HILL.

FIELD-NAMES

In (a), forms dated 1767 are *EnclA*, 1822 are *Terrier*. Forms throughout dated Hy 2, 13 and 1330 are Nichols; e.13, 1270 and Hy 3^1 are Berkeley; Hy 3 are *Crox*; 1246 (Edw 1) and Edw 1 are *CroxR*; 1362, 1463, 1609 and 1611 are *Rut*; 1473 are *CCR*; 1601, 1625, 1674, 1700, 1704, c.1708 and 1708 (18) are *Terrier*.

(a) Bank Cl 1767 (*the banke* 1625, *v.* Croxton Banks *supra*); the Barn Cl 1822; the first, the second Branstone Cl 1822, the Branstone Lane 1822 (Branston adjoins to the west); Croxton Pasture, the Pasture 1767 (*the (Common) Cowpasture* 1700, 1704, c.1708, 1708 (18), *v.* **commun**); the Drift or Skillington Rd 1822 (cf. *the dryfte syde* 1601, *the Driftside* 1674, 1704, c.1708, 1708 (18), *v.* **drift, sīde**; Skillington lies beyond the county boundary to the south-east in Lincs.); the Fishpond Cl 1767 (*the fishe pond* 1625); Grantham Gate Fd 1767 (*Grantham gate Feilde* 1601, 1625, ~ ~ *feild* 1674, ~ ~ *Field* 1704, *Grantham field* 1700, 1708 (18), ~ *feild* c.1708, cf. *Grantham Gate* 1625, 1700, 1704, c.1708, 1708 (18), *v.* **gata, feld**; one of the great fields of the village, on the road to Grantham some six miles to the north-east in Lincs.); Horsepool Furlong 1767 (*horespoole* (sic) 1601, *Horsepool(e)* 1625, 1704, c.1708, 1708 (18), *hors poole* 1674, *Horspool* 1700, *Horsepooll* c.1708, *horsepoole meddow* 1625 (*v.* **mǣd** (**mǣdwe** obl.sg.)), *v.* **hors, pōl**[1]); Humberston's 1806 Map, Humberston's Gorse 1824 O (*v.* **gorst**; with the surn. *Humberston* of a family which prob. came from the village of Humberstone, some 20 miles to the south-west in East Goscote Hundred); the Knipton Rd 1822 (*Knipton gate* 1601, ~ *yeate* 1625, *v.* **gata**; Knipton lies to the north-west); the Meadow Cl 1822; the Moors 1767 (*haldemor'* Edw 1, *the Old Moore* 1601, 1625, *the Ould More* 1674, *the Old Moor Close* 1700, 1704, c.1708, 1708 (18) (*v.* **ald**), (*le*) *Neumor* 1270, Edw 1, *Hiderneumor* 13 (*v.* **nīwe, hider**), *the Grange moore* 1625, *the Grange Moor Close* 1700, 1704, c.1708, 1708 (18) (*v. the Grange* in f.ns. (b) *infra*), *Hoults Moore* 1609 (with the surn. *Hoult*), *the moore hedg* 1625, (*the*) *Moor hedge* 1700, 1704, c.1708, 1708 (18) (*v.* **hecg**), *the Moore tonge* 1601, 1625, *More tounge* 1674, (*the*) *Moor tongue* 1700, c.1708, 1708 (18), *Moor tong* 1704 (*v.* **tunge**), *v.* **mōr**[1]); the Nether Fd 1767 ((*The*) *Neather Feilde* 1601, 1625, (*The*) *Nether feild* 1674, 1704, c.1708, ~ *field* 1708 (18), *v.* **neoðera, feld**; one of the great fields of the township); Parson's Cl 1822 (*v.* **persone**); the Publick Horse Pond 1767; the Ridge Cl 1822 (*v.* **hrycg**); Saltby Gate Fd 1767 (*Saltbygate Feilde* 1601, *Saltby gate feild* 1625, 1674, *Saltgate feild* 1700, 1708 (18), ~ *field* 1704, c.1708, *v.* **gata, feld**; one of the great fields of the village, on the road to Saltby which adjoins to the south-east; the 18th cent. forms in *Saltgate* ~ prob. arose because of the course through the parish of the Roman road Margary 58a, once used as a salters' way ((*le*) *Saltegate* Hy 3, Edw 1, *Saltgate* 1601, 1625, 1674, 1700, 1704, c.1708, 1708 (18), *v.* **salt**[1], **gata**)); the Saltby Rd 1822 (*saltby gate* 1625, *v.* **gata**); Saltby Heath 1767 (*v.* **hǣð**); Saltcellar Lane 1767 (presum. a folk style for the Roman road Margary 58a noted above, hence 'salt-seller lane', the salters' way); Salter's Ford 1795 Nichols (*Salterford* Hy 2, 1330, *v.* **saltere, ford**); the Sand-pit Cl 1822 (*v.* **sand-pytt**); Swinedales Cl 1767 (*v. Swin(e)sdale* in Branston f.ns. (b)); Three Queen's Lane (sic) 1822 (leading to Three Queens in Wyville cum Hungerton parish beyond the county boundary in Lincs.); the Turnpike Rd 1822 (*v.* **turnepike**); the Upper Fd 1767; the West Fd 1822.

(b) *Abrahamwelle* Hy 3[1] (*v.* **wella**; with either the pers.n. or the surn. *Abraham*; Reaney *s.n.* notes that '*Abraham*, the name of a priest in DB (1086), was not confined to Jews'); *analandhil* Edw 1 (*v.* **andlanges, hyll**); *analangdale, andelongdale, andelogdale* Edw 1, *the Lynges or Anlandale* 1601 (*v.* **lyng**), *Anlamdale gutter* 1625 (*v.* **goter**) (*v.* **andlanges, dalr**); *Backthurns* 1700, 1704, c.1708, *Backthorns* 1708 (18) (perh. 'the thorn-trees on the ridge', *v.* **bæc, þyrne, þorn**; but a poss. alternative is reference to the buckthorn (*Rhamnus catharticus*), the berries of which were used for sap-green pigment and as a cathartic, *v.* **buc-þorn**); *the Becke* 1625 (*v.* **bekkr**); *biscopewelledale* Edw 1 (*v.* **wella, dalr**; the first el. is presum. the surn. *Bishop* rather than *biscop* 'a bishop', but if so, it would be a rather early instance, *v.* Reaney *s.n.*); *brakendale* Edw 1 (*v.* **dalr**), *bracken leayes* 1601, 1625, *Bra(c)king Leas* 1674, 1700, 1704, c.1708, 1708 (18) (*v.* **leys**), *Bracken Wonge* 1601, 1625 (*v.* **vangr**) (*v.* **brakni**); *Brand Wonge* 1625 (*v.* **vangr**; either with the surn. *Brand* or with **brand** 'a place cleared by burning, a place where burning has occurred'); *Bra(u)nston gate* 1601 (*v.* **gata**), *Branson hedg* 1674 (*v.* **hecg**; a boundary hedge, with the form *Branson* showing typical 17th cent. Leics. loss of *t* in the group *-ston*), *Branstone Nooke* 1625 (*v.* **nōk**), *Braunston shrubbes* 1601 (*v.* **scrubb**) (Branston adjoins to the west); *the Brooke* 1625; *the Bushes* 1625 (*v.* **busc**); *buttwong'* Edw 1 (*v.* **butt**[1], **vangr**); *the Castlegate* 1700, c.1708, 1708 (18) (*v.* **castel(l), gata**; the road to Belvoir Castle which lies to the north-west; *Farr Caudhill* 1601, ~ *Cawdhill* 1625 (*v.* **feor, cald**; ostensibly with **hyll** as the generic, but such late forms sometimes disguise an earlier **wella**); *Church hill* 1674; *Church leayes* 1601, (*the*) *Church Leas* 1700, 1704, c.1708, ~ *Leys* 1708 (18) (*v.* **leys**); *Church Way* 1700; *Cleay Hill* 1601, *Clayhill* 1625 (*v.* **clǣg**); *the Common peice* 1625 (*v.* **commun, pece**); *the comon waye* 1625 (*v.* **commun, weg**); *Aboue the Cunygrey* 1601, *Above the Cunnygree* c.1708, *Connigree side* 1700, *Cunnygree side* c.1708, 1708 (18) (*v.* **sīde**) (*v.* Conygear Wood *supra*); *Coweclose* 1473 (*v.* **cū, clos(e)**); *at the Crabtree* 1601, 1625 (*v.* **crabtre**; a furlong so called); *Crawell'* Hy 3, *crawelle* Edw 1, *Crowell* 1625, 1700, 1704, c.1708, 1708 (18), *estrecrowelle* Edw 1 (*v.* **ēasterra**), *westrecrowelle* Edw 1 (*v.* **westerra**) (*v.* **crāwe, wella**); *Crokeswinstey, Crooke Swinsty* 1674, *Crook Swinstead* 1700, 1704, c.1708, 1708 (18), *Crookswinestead* 1704, *Crook Swinested* c.1708, 1708 (18), *Crook Swinestead Lands* c.1708 (*v.* **land**) (*v.* **krókr, swīn, svín, stig**); *Croo Poole* 1601, *Crowpool(e)* 1700, 1704, c.1708, 1708 (18), *Cropoole gutter* 1625 (*v.* **goter**) (*v.* **crāwe, pōl**[1]); *crosled'* Edw 1 (*v.* **crāwe, slǣd**); *Croxton Abbay Water* c.1545 (*v.* **wæter** and Croxton Abbey *supra*); *Croxton' milne* 1246 Fine, 1246 (Edw 1) (*v.* **myln**); *Croystys* 1463 (*v.* **cross, stīg**); *Cublyes gate* 1601 (cf. *Henry Cubly* 1601; with either **gata** or **geat**); *the Dall* 1700, c.1708, *the Dale* 1704, 1708 (18), *Dall gutter* 1700, 1704, c.1708, *West Dall Gutter* 1708 (18) (*v.* **goter**), *doale hades* 1625, *Dall heads* 1700, 1704, c.1708, 1708 (18) (*v.* **hēafod**) (*v.* **deill**; the spelling *doale* poss. shows the influence of OE **dāl**); *Dawbalke* 1674, *Dowbalk* 1700, 1704, c.1708, *Dow-baulk* 1708 (18) (*v.* **balca**; prob. with a surn., either *Daw* or *Dow*, but **daw(e)** 'a jackdaw' is also poss.); *Denton Street* 1700, 1704, c.1708, 1708 (18) (*v.* **strǣt**; Denton adjoins to the north-east, beyond the county boundary in Lincs.); *the doucoate cloasse* 1601, *the dovecoate cloase* 1625, *the Dufcoat closse* 1674, (*the*) *Dove Coat Close* 1700, c.1708, ~ *Cote* ~ 1708 (18), *the Dove house close* 1704 (*v.* **dove-cot(e), clos(e), dove-house**); *douewell* 1601, *Dovewell* 1700, 1704, c.1708, 1708 (18) (*v.* **dufe, wella**); *durtypits* 1601, *dirty pittes* 1625, ~ *pits* 1700, ~ *pitts* 1704, c.1708, 1708 (18) (*v.* **dyrty, pytt**); *Eldrens* 1625 (*v.* **ellern**); *Endforde* 1601 (*v.* **ende, ford**); *Farhill* 1601, 1674, 1704, c.1708, 1708 (18), *farr hill* 1625 (*v.* **feor, hyll**); *the feild hedg* 1625 (*v.* **hecg**; referring to Nether Fd); *Foale Forth* 1601, 1625, *Foalefoorth* 1601 (*v.* **fola, ford**); *le Foredale* 13 (*v.* **fore, deill**); *the Freholde* 1601, *the Freehold*, ~ ~ *ground* 1625 (*v.* **grund**) (*v.* **frehold**); *fritenwong'* Edw 1 (*v.* **friðen**, vangr); *gallohill* 1601, *Gallow Hill* 1700, 1704, c.1708, 1708 (18), *Gally hill* 1674 (*v.* **galga** and *galowtres* in adjoining Knipton f.ns. (b)); *Francis Gollins Headland* 1704, c.1708, 1708 (18) (*v.* **hēafod-land**), *Fra. Gollin's Headlea* 1700, *Fran. Gollins Head Lea* 1704, c.1708 (*v.* **headley**), *Robert Gollins Meadow* 1704, c.1708, 1708 (18) (with the surn. *Gollin(s)*, *v.* Reaney *s.n.* Jolin); *the Grange* 1625, *Grange gate* 1700, 1704, c.1708, 1708 (18), *Grangate, Grange yate* 1708 (18) (*v.* **gata**), *the Grange ~, the Graung ground* 1625 (*v.* **grund**), *the Grange hedge* 1625 (*v.* **hecg**), *the Grange Waye* 1625 (*v.* **weg**, cf. *Grange gate*), *the Grange Yard* 1700, 1704, c.1708, 1708 (18) (*v.* **geard**) (*v.* **grange**; presum. originally an outlier of Croxton Abbey); *At the graue* 1601, 1625, *Grave* c.1708, 1708 (18) (a furlong so called, prob. with **grāf** 'a copse, a grove' rather than with **græf** 'a digging, a trench'); *Greenegate* 1601, 1625, *Green Gate* 1700, c.1708, 1708 (18), *green gates* 1704 (*v.* **grēne**[1], **gata**); *greyndele* Edw 1 (either OE **grendel** 'a gravelly place or stream' or more likely Scand **grein** with **deill**, meaning perh. 'a portion of land in a fork'); *the Gutter* 1601, 1625 (*v.* **goter**); *the hades* 1625 (*v.* **hēafod**); *haliwell* 1246 (Edw 1), Hy 3, Edw 1 (*v.* **hālig, wella**); *harborow pitt* 1625 (*v.* **berg, pytt**; the first el. is either **hæfera, hafri** or **hār**[2]); *hardescroft* Edw 1 (*v.* **croft**; with the surn. *Hard*, *v.* Reaney *s.n.*); *Harenebb* 1601, *Hareneb* 1601, 1625, 1700, 1704, c.1708, *Harneb* 1674, c.1708, 1708 (18) (*v.* *hareneb* in adjoining Knipton f.ns. (b)); *Harewell* 1708 (18) (prob. 'boundary stream', *v.* **hār**[2], **wella**, cf. *Harewellesike* in Bottesford f.ns. (b) and Hardwell Cl (*harewell*) in Holwell f.ns. (a)); *Haston feild side* 1704, *Harestone feild side* c.1708, ~ *Field* ~ 1708 (18) (*v.* **sīde**; Harston adjoins to the north); *le hay* Edw 1 (*v.* (ge)hæg); *Haysty* 13 (*v.* **(ge)hæg, stīg**); *Hea(y) Leayes* 1601, 1625, *the hay leas* 1700, 1704, c.1708, ~ ~ *leys* 1708 (18) (*v.* **leys**), *the hay leas gutter* 1700, ~ ~ ~ *guttur* 1704, c.1708, *the hayleys gutter* 1708 (18) (*v.* **goter**) (with either (ge)hæg or hēg); *heay syke* 1601, 1625 (*v.* **sīk**; with either (ge)hæg or hēg); *hertistoft* Hy 3 (*v.* **toft**; with the ME surn. *Hert* (from OE *heorot*, ME *hert* 'a hart'), *v.* Reaney *s.n.* Hart); *Hillgate* 1625, 1700, 1704, c.1708, 1708 (18) (*v.* **hyll, gata**); *hodelgate* 1625 ('the road to Howdale', *v.* **gata** and *howdale* in neighbouring Branston f.ns. (b)); *The Homestall*, c.1708, 1708 (18) (*v.* **hām-stall**; i.e. that of *the Vicarage house*); *the horsedames* 1625 (*v.* **hors, damme**; artificially created watering-place(s) for horses); *Ivybanck* 1625 (*v.* **īfig, banke**); *Kilmecroft* Edw 1 (if not a poor form of the following f.n., then *v.* **cyln, croft**); *Kilmundiscroft* Edw 1, *Kilmundiscroftdig* Hy 3 (*v.* **dīk**) ('Cynemund's enclosure', *v.* **croft**; the OE pers.n. *Cynemund* in both forms shows dissimilation of *n* to *l* by *m* in the following syllable); *the kings high streete* 1625, *the street* 1625, *the kings highway* 1625 (*v.* **stræt, hēah-weg**; with reference to James I or to Charles I who succeeded in March 1625, and to the Roman road Margary 58a); *atte Kirk* 1379 Ipm (p) (*v.* **atte**), *Kirkhill* 1625 (*v.* **kirkja** and St John the Baptist's Church *supra*); *Knipton hedg(e)* 1674, 1704, c.1708, 1708 (18), *Knypton hedge* 1700, *Knipton hedge nook* 1704 (*v.* **nōk**) (*v.* **hecg**; the boundary hedge of Knipton which adjoins to the north-west); *Lamcoates* 1601, 1625 (*v.* **lamb, cot**); *Larkmore* 1700, *Larkmoor* 1704, c.1708, 1708 (18) (*v. Larkesmore* in Branston f.ns. (b)); *Lincoln gate* 1601, 1625 (*v.* **gata**; the road to Lincoln in the north-east); *Lingdale* Edw 1, 1674, 1708 (18), *Lyngdale* 1700, 1704, c.1708 (*v.* **lyng, dalr** and Lings Hill *supra*); *littelcome* 1674, *littlecomb* 1700, 1704, c.1708, 1708 (18), *Littell Comb banke* 1601, *lyttle comb banke* 1625 (*v.* **banke**) ('the little valley', *v.* **lȳtel, cumb**); *lyttelbeckes*

1601, *Lyttlebeckes, little beckes* 1625 (*v.* **lȳtel, lítill, bekkr** and *Litle beckes* in Branston f.ns. (b)); (*the*) *Long Swathes* 1601, 1625, 1674, ~ *Swath* 1700, 1704, c.1708, ~ *Swarth* 1708 (18) (*v.* **swathe**); *lysbancke* 1601, *lychbancke* 1625 (*v.* **lisc, banke**); *Mary Leayse* 1611 (*v.* **leys**; perh. with either **myry** 'miry, muddy' or (**ge)mǣre** 'a boundary', since Mary Lane (*q.v.*) forms part of the parish boundary with Sproxton); *the Meers* 1700, 1704, c.1708, 1708 (18) (*v.* (**ge)mǣre**); *Middle Feild* 1704; *Midshill* 1601, 1700, 1704, c.1708, 1708 (18), *myds-hill* 1625 (*v.* **middes, hyll**); *mikkelberue* Edw 1, *Michelborough, Michelborrow* 1601, *Micleborow* 1625 (*v.* **micel, mikill, berg**); *le miln' close* 1473, *the milne cloase* 1625, *Mill Close* 1625, 1700, 1704, c.1708, 1708 (18) (*v.* **clos(e)**), *At the Milne Cloasse gate* 1601 (*v.* **geat**; a furlong so called), *the milne doare* 1601, *the mylne dore* 1625 (*v.* **duru**; a furlong so called), *le milneholm'* Hy 3 (*v.* **holmr**), *milnes lease syde* 1625 (*v.* **leys, sȳde**) (*v.* **myln**); *Middell hill* 1601, 1674, *myddle* ~ 1625, *Middle* ~ 1700, 1704, c.1708, 1708 (18) (*v.* **middel, hyll**); *netherstie* Edw 1 (*v.* **neoðera**; with **stīg** or **stig**); *the new close* c.1708, (*the*) *New Close hedge* 1700, 1704, 1708 (18) (*v.* **hecg**), *the new closse syde* 1601 (*v.* **sȳde**); *the nooke* 1625 (*v.* **nōk**); *North pen* 1700, 1704, c.1708, 1708 (18) (*v.* **penn²**); *At the Oake* 1601, *at the oake tree* 1625 (*v.* **āc**; a furlong so called); *At the Path* 1601, *at the padd* 1625 (*v.* **pæð, pad**; a furlong so called); *Tho. Porter's hedge* 1700, ~ *Porters* ~ c.1708, 1708 (18) (*v.* **hecg**), *Porters Townsend* 1601, 1708 (18), *Porters townes-ende* 1625, *Porter's Townsend* 1700, *Porter* ~ 1704, *Porters town's end* c.1708 (*v.* **tūn, ende**); *prudeng'* Edw 1 (*v.* **eng**), *prudewang', prudwang* Edw 1, *Prudwong* 13 (*v.* **vangr**) (both f.ns. with the ME surn. *Prude*, from late OE *prūd* 'proud, arrogant', *v.* Reaney *s.n.* Proud); *quenepittes* Edw 1 (prob. 'pits where quern-stones are obtained', *v.* **cweorn, pytt**; neither *cwene* 'a woman' nor the OE pers.n. *Cwēna* is convincing as first el., although formally the surviving ME spelling could suggest either of these); *radiebidale, rattebidale* Edw 1 ('the valley where Hraði's farmstead is situated', *v.* **bȳ, dalr**; the pers.n. is Scand *Hraði* (ODan *Rathi*), an original by-name meaning 'the swift one', cf. Raithby by Spilsby, L); *John Raven's headland* 1700, 1704, ~ *Ravens* ~ c.1708, 1708 (18) (*v.* **hēafod-land**); *redeng'* bis, (*le*) *redheng'* Edw 1 (*v.* **eng**; with either **hrēod** 'reed' or **rēad** 'red', referring to soil colour); *Remmington's Close* 1700 (in the possession of *George Remington* 1700), *George Rimmingtons Close* c.1708, ~ *Rimmingtons* ~ 1708 (18), *Edw. Remington's Headland* 1700, *Edward Rimmingtons* ~ 1704, c.1708, ~ *Rimmington's* ~ 1708 (18) (*v.* **hēafod-land**); *renhow* Edw 1 bis (*v.* **haugr**; poss. with **wrenna** 'a wren' as first el.); *Ristie* 13 (*v.* **hrīs, stīg**); *the Rundell* 1625 (*v.* **rynel**); *Rus(s)hall Leayes* 1601, 1625 (*v.* **risc, halh, leys**); *Ruttewell* e.13 (*v.* **wella**; prob. with the OE pers.n. *Ruta*, but OE **hrūt** 'dark-coloured' is poss.); *salteford* Edw 1, (*molendinum de*) *sauteford'* Edw 1 (with MLat *molendinum* 'a mill'), *saltefordil* Edw 1 (*v.* **hyll**) (these copied cartulary forms may represent Salter's Ford in f.ns. (a) *supra* (this with *saltere* 'a salt merchant'), otherwise simply 'salt ford, ford with brackish water', *v.* **salt², ford**); *scharphou nunc vocatur southmerwong, scharphow* Edw 1 (*v.* **scearp, haugr** and *southmerwong, infra*); *schiredun* 13 (*v.* **scīr¹, dūn**; a large hill on the county boundary); *schirestrete* Edw 1 (*v.* **scīr¹, strǣt**; the Roman road, otherwise Sewstern Lane, which forms the county boundary); *Schortforlonges* 1463 (*v.* **sc(e)ort, furlang**); *Sharpedale* 1674 (either with **scearp** or the surn. *Sharp(e)* and **dalr** or **deill**); *Shepard close* 1473 (*v.* **scēp-hirde, clos(e)**); *Shippdammes* 1601 (*v.* **scēp,**

damme; artificially created watering-place(s) for sheep); *Shittopp(es)* 1601, 1625, *Shittop(p)dale* 1601, 1625 (*v.* **deill**) (*v.* **scite, topp**); *Middle ~, Showton* 1601, *Farr Showton* 1625 (*v. Shouedon'* in Branston f.ns. (b)); *southmerwong* Edw 1 (*v.* **sūð**, (ge)**mære, vangr** and *scharphou, supra*); *Spinkwell* 1601, 1674, 1700, 1704, c.1708, 1708 (18), *Spinkwell forth* 1625 (*v.* **ford**), *Spinkwell Hedge* 1601, 1625 (*v.* **hecg**), *Spinckweldaylforlong'* 1362 (*v.* **deill, furlang**) ('spring or stream frequented by finches', *v.* **spink, wella**); *stannewong'* Edw 1 (*v.* **stān, vangr**); *the Steares, Stears* 1674 (*v.* **stæger**); *the steppinge stones* 1601, 1625 (*v.* **stepping-stone**); *Mr Stevens headland* c.1708, 1708 (18) (*v.* **hēafod-land**); *stoch* Edw 1, *Stocke* 1674, *Stock leayes* 1601, 1625, *~ Leas(e)* 1700, 1704, c.1708, *~ Leys* 1708 (18) (*v.* **leys**) ('the cattle farm, the dairy farm', *v.* **stoc**); *Stony brinkes* 1601 (*v.* **stānig, brink**); *John Streetons wong* 1700, 1704, 1708 (18) (*v.* **vangr**); *le suthdeil, suddeiles, southdeiles* Edw 1 (*v.* **sūð, deill**); *Thornewell* 1601, 1625, 1674, *Thornwell* 1704, c.1708, 1708 (18), *Thornewelbanck* 1601, 1625, *Thornwell Bank* 1700, 1704, c.1708, 1708 (18) (*v.* **banke**), *Thornewell gutter* 1625 (*v.* **goter**), *Thornwell hades* 1625 (*v.* **hēafod**), *Thornwell Leas* 1700, 1704, c.1708, *~ Leys* 1708 (18) (*v.* **leys**) ('spring or stream among the thorn-trees', *v.* **þorn, wella**); *thorp* Edw 1, *Shorte thorpes* 1601, 1625, *~ Tharps* 1674, *Short Tharps* 1700, 1704, c.1708, 1708 (18), *~ thorps* c.1708 (*v.* **þorp**); *Thorpdalebec* e.13 (*v.* **þorp, dalr, bekkr**); *Thredikes* Hy 3[1] (*v.* **þrēo, dík**); *East Thurnes* 1601, 1625, *East Thornes* 1674, *Long(e) Thurnes* 1601, 1625, *Long Thornes* 1674, *Long Thurns* 1704, c.1708, *~ Thorns* 1708 (18), *North Thurnes* 1601, *Under Thurnes or North Thurnes* 1625, *North Thornes* 1674, *West thorn* 1463 (*v.* **west**), *Thurneshill topp* 1625 (*v.* **topp**), *Thurnes syke* 1601, *Thornes Sike* 1674, *thurnsike* 1700, 1704, *Thurn Syke* c.1708, 1708 (18), *Thorn Syke* 1708 (18) (*v.* **sík**), *Thurnsyk gutter* 1625, *Thurn Sike guttur* 1700, *~ ~ gutter* 1704, *Thurnsyke Guttur* c.1708, *~ Gutter* 1708 (18) (*v.* **goter**) (the forms are principally with **þyrne** 'a thorn-bush, thorn-scrub', but there is occasional variation with **þorn** 'a thorn-tree, a hawthorn'); *Thurspitt leayes* 1601, *Thirspitt leayes* 1625, *Thrushpit lease* 1674, *Thurstpit leas* 1700, 1704, c.1708, *~ Leys* 1708 (18) (*v.* **þyrs, pytt, leys**); *toft(e)s* 1625, *Toftes fordoles* 1625 (*v.* **fore, dāl**), *Toft Close* 1700, 1704, c.1708, 1708 (18) (*v.* **toft**); *Richard Typpin's Meadow* 1700, *~ Tippins ~* 1704, *Richd. Typpins meadow* c.1708 (*v.* Tipping's Gorse *supra*); *the Vicarage house close and orchard* 1700, *~ Vicaridge ~ ~ ~ ~* 1704; *vickeres well* 1601 (*v.* **vikere, wella**); *Watclyffe* 1601, *Watclife* 1674, *Watcliff(e)* 1700, c.1708, 1708 (18) (*v.* (ge)**wæd, clif** and *wadecliue* in neighbouring Knipton f.ns. (b)); *atte Welle* 1332 SR (p) (*v.* **atte, wella**); *westfeld'* Edw 1 (*v.* **west, feld**; one of the early great fields of the village, not to be identified with the West Fd in f.ns. (a) *supra*); *westcombe* 1625, *wescumbe overende* 13 (*v.* **uferra, ende**) (*v.* **west, cumb**); *wildestedes, wilestedes* Edw 1 (*v.* **wilde, stede**); *the Willow head(e)* 1601, 1625 (*v.* **wilig, hēafod**); *Willowtree* 1674 (*v.* **wilig-trēow**); *wodegate* Edw l, *the Woodgate* 1625 (*v.* **gata**), *the wood hedge* 1625 (*v.* **hecg**), *the Wood Nooke* 1601 (*v.* **nōk**) (*v.* **wudu**); *Wormehill* 1601, 1625 (*v.* **hyll**; the first el. is **wyrm** 'a reptile', perh. in some later sense such as 'a tick' or 'a gadfly'); *yauley buttes* 1601, *yawley buttes* 1625 (*v.* **lēah, butte**; earlier forms are needed to ascertain the first el., but **gearwe** 'yarrow' is poss.); *yellowpit balke* 1674 (*v.* **geolu, pytt, balca**; prob. with reference to the colour of ironstone).

2. BRANSTON

Brantestone 1086 DB, 1227 RHug, *Branteston'* c.1130 LeicSurv,
  1190 P (p), 1.12 (e.14) *BelCartA et passim* to 1285 FA (p),
  Brantestona 1209 × 19 RHug, *Brantestun* 1283 Ipm, *Brantestuna*
  12 (e.15) *BelCartB, Brantiston'* 1209 × 35 RHug, 1246 Fine *et*
  passim to Hy 3 *Crox*, 1276 RGrav, 1.13 *CRCart*
Brandeston' 1184 (p), 1185 P (p) *et passim* to 1317 *Rut*, 1378 Cl,
  Brandestun' 1226 Cur, *Brandiston'* 1242 Fees
Braunteston' 1221 Fine, Hy 3 *Crox et passim* to 1298 Banco, c.1316
  (e.15) *BelCartB, Brauntestona* 1234 RegAnt
Braundeston' 1284 Ch, 1287 Ipm *et freq* to 1410, 1413 *Rut*, 1413,
  1425 *Comp, Braundiston'* 1321 *Rut*
Braunceton 1412, 1442 *Rut*, 1577 LEpis
Braunston' Hy 3 *Crox*, 1276 RH *et freq* to 1413 *Comp*, 1428 FA *et*
  passim to 1615, 1618 LML, *Brawnston* 1362, 1456, 1462 *Rut*
Branstun 1.12 *Rut, Branstuna* Hy 1 (1333) Ch, Hy 2 (e.15) *BelCartB*,
  Edw 1 *BelCartA, Branston(')* 1246 (Edw 1) *CroxR*, 1263 *Rut*, Hy
  3 *Crox* (freq) *et passim* to 1473 *CCR*, 1500 *Rut* (freq) *et freq*
Braundson 1599 *Rut, Braunson* 1604 SR, *Branson* 1611 *Rut*, 1612
  LeicW, 1674 *Terrier*

'Brant's farmstead, village', v. **tūn**. The OE pers.n. *Brant* is common
in East Midland p.ns., cf. Braunston, Ru 74 and Braunstone in the
Sparkenhoe Hundred of Leics. AN influence is responsible for *-aun-*
spellings for *-an-*. Typical in Leics. are those forms which show 16th
and 17th cent. loss of *t* in the group *-ston*.
    Distinguishing affixes are variously added as:
~ *Wandevill'* 1242 Fees (?rectius *Mandevill'*)
~ *iuxta Belver* 1315, 1318 Banco *et passim* to 1347 ib, ~ *iuxta*
  Beauver 1406 Pat
~ *iuxta Croxton* 1315, 1335 Banco *et passim* to 1387 Fine, 1406 Pat
~ *le Vale* 1529, 1552 AAS, ~ *iuxta le Vale* 1505 Pat, ~ *in Vale* 1612
  LeicW, ~ *in the Vale* 1615, 1618 LML, 1666 LeicW
The fee of *Wandeville* (?rectius *Mandeville*) held four carucates of land
in Branston in 1242 Fees. The affixes ~ *iuxta Belver* (i.e. Belvoir), ~
iuxta Croxton (i.e. Croxton Kerrial), ~ *le Vale*, ~ *in the Vale* (i.e. The
Vale of Belvoir, v. **val**) served as an aid to distinguish Branston from
Braunstone in Sparkenhoe Hundred whose etymological development
is parallel.

BRANSTON LODGE, *Braunston Lodge* 1863 White, *v.* **loge**. BUNKERS WOOD, on *Bunkers Hill* 1806 Map, 1824 O; named from the Battle of Bunker Hill (1775) in the American War of Independence when British victory failed to break the colonists' siege of Boston. HIGH LEYS FM, *the high(e) lees* 1577 *Terrier, v.* **hēah**[1], **leys**. LINGS COVERT, 1806 Map, *Lings Cover* 1824 O, *v.* **lyng**, **cover(t)**. LINGS FM, LINGS HILL, *le linges* 1323 *Rut, the Linges* 1577 *Terrier, the Lynges* 1601 *ib, The Lings* 1625 *ib*, 1767 *EnclA*, 1877 White, *Lings* 1846, 1863 ib, *Netherlings, Upper Lings* 1825 *Terrier, v.* **lyng**. NURSERY PLANTATION, *v.* **nursery**. THE RECTORY, 1877 White, 1925 Kelly, *The Rectory House* 1825 *Terrier,* cf. *rectorie de Braunston iuxta Beauver* 1406 *Pat* (with MLat *rectoria* 'a rectory, a rector's house'); it is *the Parsonage* 1577 *Terrier, the Parsonage house* 1708 (18) *ib, v.* **personage**. RESERVOIR COTTAGE, 1846, 1863, 1877 White *v.* **cotage** and Knipton Reservoir. ST GUTHLAC'S CHURCH, *the Church* 1708, 1708 (18) *Terrier, Church (St Cuthbert)* (sic) 1846, 1863, 1877 White; it is earlier recorded as *ecclesie de Brantestona* a.1219 RHug, ~ *de Brantiston* 1220 MHW, *ecclesiam de Branteston* 1241 RGros, *ecclesie de Braunston* 1350 *Pat*, ~ *de Braunston iuxta le Vale* 1505 *ib*. Note also *The Churchyard* 1708, 1825 *Terrier*. SQUARE AND COMPASS (P.H.) (lost), *Square and Compass* 1846, 1863 White. TERRACE HILL FM is *Drapers House* 1806 Map (with the surn. *Draper*), TERRACE HILLS, *v.* **terrace**. WHEEL INN, 1877 White, 1925 Kelly, *Wheel* 1846, 1863 White.

FIELD-NAMES

Forms in (a) dated 1767 are *EnclA* and 1825 are *Terrier*. Forms throughout dated 1.13 are Nichols; Edw 1, 1308, 1317, 1321, 1323, 1583 and 1627 are *Rut*; 1577, 1704, 1708, 1708 (18) and 1724 are *Terrier*.

(a) Burley Thorn Cl 1825 (*Burlythorn* 1704, 1724, *Burlethorn(e)* 1708, *v.* **þorn**; poss. with the common OE *burh-lēah* 'woodland (clearing) close to or belonging to a fortified site' or even with the surn. *Burley* which derives from it (in this case perh. of a family originating in Burley, 12 miles to the south-east in Rutland); but note *brennandthorn* 1321 in f.ns. (b) *infra* which may be a precursor of these late (if garbled) forms; Cow Pasture Leys 1825 (*v.* **leys**); Garlands 1825 (1704, 1708, 1708 (18), 1724, *v.* **gāra**, **land**); Home Cl 1825 (*v.* **home**); Life Fd 1767 (1704, 1724, *the Lithe, the Lythe* 1577, *Life* 1704, cf. *Longlife* 1708, 1708 (18), *Neather Life or Sidlands* 1704 (*v.* **neoðera** and *le sydlandis* in f.ns. (b) *infra*), *the Upper Life* 1704, *under Lythe hill* 1577, *under Life Hill* 1704, *under Lif(f)e* 1704, 1708, 1708 (18), *under Short life* 1704, *Witlife, Whiteliffe* 1708 (18), *White life* 1724 (with dial. *white* 'dry open pasture'), *life furlong* 1704, *life hades* 1704 (*v.* **hēafod**) (*v.* **hlið**[1], **hlíð**[2] 'a slope, a hillside'; one of the later great fields of the village); Longlands 1825 (*le Longland* 1.13, *longlands* 1704, 1724, *Longlandes furlonge* 1577 (*v.* **furlang**)), Longlands Fd 1767 (1704, 1724, *Longland feild* 1708, *Long Land Field* 1708 (18), *v.* **lang**[1], **land**, **feld**; eventually naming one of the later great fields of the village); Mill Fd 1767 (1708 (18), *the Mill fielde* 1577, *Mylnefeild* 1627, *Milne feild* 1708, *Miln Field* 1708 (18), *The Mill Field* 1704, 1724, *v.* **myln**, **feld**; one of the early great fields of the village); Pasture 1767 (*the pasture* 1704); Pibdale 1825 (*Pippedale* 1308, *Pibdale* 1577, *Pibdales* 1704, *Pibdale gutter* 1577 (*v.* **goter**), *Pibdale land endes* 1577 (*v.* **land**, **ende**), *Pibdale Lees* 1577 (*v.* **leys**), *v.* **pīpe, dalr**); Red Brinks 1825 (1704, 1708 (18), *le Rede Brinck'* 1323, *Red brinkes* 1577, *v.* **brink** either with **rēad** 'red', referring to soil colour, or with **hrēod** 'reed'); Sharrowdale 1825 (*Shredale* 1577, *Sherrowdale* 1704, *Sharadale* 1708, 1708 (18), *Sheraddale* 1724, *the farr side Sherrowdale* 1704, *Mires Sharadale* 1708 (18) (*v.* **mýrr**), *the neather end of Sherrowdale* 1704 (*v.* **neoðera**), *Over Sharadale* 1708, 1708 (18), *Over Sharaddale* 1724 (*v.* **uferra**), *Shredaleford* 1577, *Sherrowdale Ford* 1704 (*v.* **ford**), *Shredale gutter* 1577 (*v.* **goter**), *Shredale stones* 1577, *Sherrowdale Stones* 1704, *Sheraddale Stones* 1724 (*v.* **stān**; poss. boundary markers), *Sherrowdale Stone pitts* 1704 (*v.* **stān-pytt**), *v.* **scearu, dalr**; with *scearu* prob. in its sense 'boundary'; the valley lay on the road to Stathern and may have been that later flooded in part to form Knipton Reservoir); the Sheep Walks 1767 (*v.* **walk**); Southgate 1825 (*Sowgates* 1577, 1704, *Sougates* 1577, *Sougate* 1708, 1708 (18), *Sow gate Fur'* 1724 (*v.* **furlang**), 'the south road', *v.* **gata**); Stathern Gate Fd 1767 (1704, *Statorngate feild* 1708, *Stathorn Gate Field* 1724, *v.* **gata**; one of the later great fields of the village, this on the road to Stathern which lies to the north-west); Westings 1825 (1708 (18), *Westinges* 1577, *Westins* 1708, 1708 (18), *Westinges lees* 1577 (*v.* **leys**), *v.* **west, eng**).

(b) *The Ashes* 1577 (*v.* **æsc**); *Barston gate* 1577, *Barkston ~* 1704, 1724, *Backs(t)on ~* 1708 (18) (*v.* **gata**; the road to Barkestone which lies to the north-west); *Ra. Barns hedland* 1708 (*v.* **hēafod-land**), *Barns's headley* 1704 (*v.* **headley**) (both with the surn. *Barn(e)s*); *le Bellandes* 1317 (*v.* **land**; with **bēan** or **belle**, *v.* Bellands in Bottesford f.ns. (a)); *Bersicoudale* Edw 1, *Bersikoudale* 1308, *Parsie cowdale, Parsye Cowdale(s)* 1577, *Parsy Cowdales* 1704, 1724, *Parse Coudals* 1708, *~ Cowdales* 1708 (18), *Parcy Cowdales* 1724 (perh. 'hedged dell where cows are pastured', *v.* **berse, cū, dalr**; but the name has echoes of forms for Bescaby which lies some three miles to the south-east (as *Berscoudebi* Hy 3 *Rut, Berscoudeby* 1259 (Edw 1) *CroxR*), although the persistent vowel appearing between [s] and [k] in the Branston f.n. suggests that such echoes may not be related to etymology and that the Scand pers.n. *Berg-Skáld* does not feature here); *Blackhill* 1577, 1704, *Blackhillandes* 1577 (*v.* **land**) (*v.* **blæc, hyll**); *Bradgates, Brodgates* 1577 (*v.* **brād**; the generic may be **geat** 'a gap, an opening' rather than **gata** 'a road'); *breakbacke* 1577, *Breakback* 1704, *Bra(c)keback* 1708, 1708 (18), *the farther side breakback* 1724 (presum. a disparaging name for land hard to till); *brennandthorn* 1321 (literally 'burning thorn', *v.* **brennand, þorn**; *brennand* is from the Scand pres.part. of *brenna* 'to burn', hence poss. meaning here 'cleared by burning' or otherwise alluding to thorn-scrub used for kindling; *v.* Burley Thorn Cl *supra*); *the Brode Bolk* 1708, *the broad baulk* 1708 (18) (*v.* **brād, balca**); *Bucktree fur(long)* 1708, 1708

(18), 1724 (v. bōc, trēow); *the Calfe pasture* 1577, *Calfpaster furlong* 1708, *Calfpasture Furlong* 1708 (18), *Calf pasture leas fur'* 1724 (v. **leys**) (v. **calf, pasture**); *the Causway* 1704, *the Coase* 1708, 1708 (18), *the Cose* 1708 (18) (v. **caucie**); *Cawdaw hill* 1577, *Caddow Hill* 1704, *Cado hil(l)* 1708, 1708 (18), *Cadday hill* 1724 (v. **cad(d)aw, cad(d)ow**); *Caudwell* ~, *Cawdwell dale* 1577, ~ ~ *ende* 1577 (v. **ende**) (v. **cald, wella, dalr**); *Long Clees* 1577, *the Clays* 1708, 1708 (18), *i' th' Clay* 1724 (v. **clǣg**); *Cockinpit Furlong* 1708 (18) (v. **cocking** 'cock-fighting', **pytt**; a variation on *cockpit*); *the Common piece* 1704, ~ ~ *peice* 1708 (18), *the comon peec* 1708 (v. **commun, pece**); *Councell* ~, *Cownsell dale* 1577, *Council dale* 1704, *Counsel dale* 1708, 1724, *Councel-dale* 1708 (18) (v. **dalr**), *Cowncell dale gutter* 1577 (v. **goter**), *Cownsell gutter* 1577, *Council gutter* 1704 (v. **goter**; perh. an abbreviated form of the previous name), *Cowncell* ~, *Cownsell hill* 1577, *Counsel hill* 1708, 1724, *Councel-hill* 1708 (18) (presum. with ME **conseil** 'consultation, deliberation', indicating negotiation as to agricultural use); *Crabtree fur(long)* 1704, 1724 (v. **crabtre**); *Crawston dyke* 1577, *Croxton Dike* 1704 (v. **dík**), *Craws(t)on hedge* 1577 (v. **hecg**), *Crawston gate* 1577 (v. **gata**) (boundary markers of, and road to Croxton Kerrial which adjoins to the east); *Cringelles* 1577, *Cringle* 1704, 1724, *Kringle furlong* 1708, 1708 (18), *Cringell gutter* 1577, *Cringle* ~ 1704 (v. **goter**), *Cringell lees* 1577, *Cringle leys* 1704 (v. **leys**), *Cringle side* 1704 (v. **síde**) (v. **kringla**; used of anything of circular shape); *(the) Crooked fur(long)* 1577, 1704, 1724 (v. **croked, furlang**); *against the dike* 1724 (v. **dík**; a furlong so called in Mill Fd); *long(e) dooles, the short doles* 1577 (v. **dāl**); *Dunesby, Dunnesby* l.13 ('Dunn's farmstead', v. **bȳ**; the pers.n. *Dunn* is OE, cf. *Dunesho* in adjoining Harston f.ns. (b)); *the Earle of Ruttland hedley* 1577 (v. **eorl, headley**; with reference to the third Earl); *the East feild, the Est feilde*, ~ ~ *field* 1577 (v. **ēast, feld**; one of the early great fields of the township); *Elder tree bolk* 1708, ~ ~ *Baulk* 1708 (18) (v. **ellern, balca**); *Etonne dale* 1577, *Eaton Dale* 1704, 1708, 1708 (18) (v. **dalr**), *Etonne dale heade* 1577, *Eatondale head* 1704, 1708 (18), 1724, ~ *hed* 1708 (v. **hēafod**), *Eatone meare* 1577, *Eaton Mere* 1704, ~ *Meair* 1708, ~ *Meer* 1708 (18), 1724 (v. **(ge)mǣre**), *Eaton Mill* 1704, 1708 (18), *Eaton Mill Ashes* 1708 (18), *the Mill Ashes* 1577 (v. **myln, æsc**) (Eaton parish adjoins to the west); *Foxholes* 1704, 1708 (18), *Fox hols* 1708 (v. **fox-hol**); *over the Gate* 1708, ~ ~ *Gates* 1708 (18), 1724 (v. **gata**; a furlong so called); *Thomas Geales hedley* 1577 (v. **headley**), *Thomas Geales whole land* 1577 (v. **hāl, land**; poss. referring to a whole yardland rather than to a whole selion, cf. *Robt Steels halfland, infra*); *Edwd. Georges headland* 1704, *Edw. Gorgis hedland* 1708, *Edward George's headland* 1708 (18) (in Longlands Fd), *Ed. Georges Headland* 1704 (in Stathern Gate Fd), *Edward Georges Headland* 1704 (in Mill Fd) (v. **hēafod-land**), *Edw. Georges headley* 1704 (v. **headley**); *Robert George (his) hedland, Robert Georges hedland* 1577 (v. **hēafod-land**), *Robert George his hedley* 1577 (v. **headley**); *Godecnauebreche, Godknauebreche* 1323 (v. **brēc**; with the ME surn. *Godecnave*, v. Reaney s.n. Goodenough); *the goores, the Goares* 1577, *the Gores* 1704, 1708 (18), *the Goers* 1708, *Gores* 1724, *Gore bracking* 1577 (v. **brakni**, cf. *Bra(c)king Leas* in Croxton Kerrial f.ns. (b)), *(the) Gore furlong* 1704, 1708, 1708 (18), *le Gore hyl* 1321 (v. **hyll**) (v. **gāra**); *Gorin neb* 1708, *Goringneb* 1708 (18), *Goreing Neb* 1724 (v. **gāra, eng, nebb**); *the gorste* 1577, *the High Gorss* 1704, 1724, *the hy gors* 1708 (v. **gorst**); *John Gowrton(e)s hedland* 1577 (v. **hēafod-land**),

Gowrtones hedley 1577 (*v.* **headley**) (with the surn. *Gowerton*); *Granbe steeh,*
Granby stighe, ~ *stithe* 1577, ~ *stigh* 1704, ~ *Stee* 1724 (*v.* **stīg**; Granby lies to the
north-west in Notts.); *atte Graunge* 1332 SR (p) (*v.* **atte**), *the Gra(u)nge* 1577,
Braunston Grange 1583, *the Graunge hedland* 1577 (*v.* **hēafod-land**), *the Graunge*
hedley 1577 (*v.* **headley**), *the Grange leyes* 1577 (*v.* **leys**), *the grange land wonge,*
the Gra(u)nge wonge 1577 (*v.* **land, vangr**) (*v.* **grange**; presum. an outlier of
Croxton Abbey, cf. *the Monkes wonges, infra*); *Greengate* 1704, 1708, 1708 (18),
1724, *Grengate* 1708, *Greengate furlong* 1708 (18) (*v.* **grēne**[1], **gata**); *Grindhill* 1577,
Grinddille gate 1577 (*v.* **gata** and *greyndele* in Croxton Kerrial f.ns. (b) *supra*); *the*
gutter 1577, 1704 (*v.* **goter**); *the Hades* 1577 (in East Fd), *the Hades* 1704 (in Life
Fd) (*v.* **hēafod**); (*Thomas*) *Hains's Headland* 1704 (*v.* **hēafod-land**); *Harals* 1708,
1708 (18), *Harewell* 1724 (*v. Harewell* in Croxton Kerrial f.ns. (b)); *Hertisbrinc* Edw
1, *Hertesbrink'* 1308, *Har(t)springes* 1577, *Hart Springs* 1704, 1708 (18), *hard*
springs 1708, *Heart Springs* 1724 (*v.* **brink**; with the ME surn. *Hert*, cf. *hertistoft* in
Croxton Kerrial f.ns. (b)); *heycliffe* 1577, *Hay Cliff* 1704, *hea(i)klif, heklif* 1708,
hekelif 1708, 1708 (18), *Heakliffe* 1708 (18), *Hayclif* 1724, *under heycliffe* 1577, ~
heaiklif 1708, *under Meers Heacliffe* 1708 (18) (*v.* **under, (ge)mǣre**), *heaklif dich*
1708, *Heacliffe ditch* 1708 (18) (*v.* **dīc**), *Hay cliff leys* 1704, *heaiklif* ~, *he(a)klif lays*
1708, *Heacliffe* ~, *hekelif leys* 1708 (18) (*v.* **leys**) (*v.* **clif**; with either **hēg** 'hay' or
(ge)hæg 'an enclosure'); *Hicklings Head Ley,* ~ *headley* 1704 (*v.* **headley**), *Tho.*
Hiklins hedland 1708 (*v.* **hēafod-land**) (with the surn. *Hickling* of a family
originating in the village of this name seven miles to the west in Notts.); *the highe*
~, *the heighe field* 1577 (*v.* **hēah**[1], **feld**; one of the earlier great fields of the village);
the high street 1577 (*v.* **hēah**[1], **strǣt**); *Hollowel dale* 1704, *Holweldale* 1708, 1708
(18), 1724, *over Hollowel Dale* 1704, *over Holwel(l)dale* 1708, 1708 (18), 1724 (*v.*
ofer[3]) (*v.* **hol**[1], **holh, wella, dalr**; but these late forms may belong rather with
Holywell dale following); *Holywell* ~, *Hollywell dale* 1577 (*v.* **dalr** and *haliwelle* in
Croxton Kerrial f.ns. (b) *supra*); *holmesbrinck'* 1317 (*v.* **holmr, brink**); *Long* ~,
Homehill 1577 (presum. the first el. is **holmr** since the ModE adj. *home* 'near home'
is not recorded before 1662 (*v.* OED *s.v.* home, sb. 14b, adj. 2)); *Horscott Lees* 1577
(*v.* **hors, cot, leys**); *Howdale* 1577 bis (*v.* **haugr, deill**); *Inckerfielde* ~, *Ingerfielde*
dale 1577, *Ingerfielddale* 1724 (*v.* **dalr**), *ingerfeild gors* 1708, *Ingerfield Gorss* 1724
(*v.* **gorst**), *Inckerfielde well* 1577, *Ingerfield Well* 1724 (*v.* **wella**) (*v.* **feld**; with a
pers.n., either OE **Hynkere* (a nickname meaning 'the limper', cf. OE *hellehinca*
'hell-limper, devil', ON *hinka* 'to limp, to hobble') or ODan *Ingvar* (ON *Yngvarr*));
Ingersall Gorss 1704, *Ingersall Well* 1704 (forms which are presum. garbled versions
of *Ingerfield Gorss* and *Ingerfield Well*, but cf. Inkersall, Db 302); *the kiln bolk* 1708,
~ ~ *baulk* 1708 (18) (*v.* **cyln, balca**); *Knipton dike* 1577 (*v.* **dík**), *Knipton hedg(e)*
1577, 1704, 1708, 1708 (18), 1724 (*v.* **hecg**) (boundary ditch and hedge of Knipton
which adjoins to the north-east); *kyglesberou* 1317, *Kickles Barowe, kiklesbarowe*
1577, *Kicklesborow* 1704, *kikelsboro* 1708, *Kickels-Borow* 1708 (18), *Kickles*
Burrow 1724, *long Kickle Barowe,* ~ *Kicklesbarow, long Kickles Barowe* 1577,
Mickelkyglesberou 1317 (*v.* **micel, mikill**), *under kiklesbarowe* 1577, *under*
Kicklesborow 1704, *under kikelsboro* 1708, *under Kicklesburrow* 1708 (18) (*v.*
under), *kikelsboro furlong* 1708, *Kickles burrow Furlong* 1708 (18),
kyglesberouheude 1317 (*v.* **hēafod**), *kikelsboro nether furlong* 1708, *Kiklesborow*

nether furlong 1708 (18), *the over furlong on kikelsboro* 1708, ~ ~ ~ *on Kiklesborow* 1708 (18) (*v.* **uferra**), *Kickleburrow thorns* 1724 (*v.* **þorn**), *Kicklesbarow tounge* 1577, *Kicklesborow Tongue* 1704 (*v.* **tunge**) (*v.* **berg**; recurring medial *s* indicates a pers.n. in the possessive case as the specific, so presum. ON *kikall* 'winding' may be rejected; poss. is the late OE pers.n. *Gicel* as in Kickle's Fm (Bk 21) or the Scand pers.n. *Gikel* (from an unrecorded OScand *Guðkell*) as in Giggleswick, YW 6 144); *the lands* 1704 (*v.* **land**); *Larkesmore* 1577, *Larksmore* 1708, 1708 (18), *Lark(e)smoor* 1724 (*v.* **lāwerce, mōr**[1]); *the lees* 1577, *the lays* 1704, *the Long lays* 1708, ~ ~ *Leys* 1708 (18), *Long leas Furlong* 1724 (*v.* **leys**); *over Lincolne gate* 1577 (*v.* **ofer**[3], **gata**; a furlong above the road to Lincoln, the Roman road Margary 58a across the Wolds to Ermine Street); *Litle beckes*, ~ ~ *gutter* 1577 (*v.* **lȳtel, lítill, bekkr, goter** and *lyttelbeckes* in Croxton Kerrial f.ns. (b)); *the Lordes headlandes* 1577 (*v.* **hēafod-land**), *the Lordes wonge(s)* 1577 (*v.* **vangr**) (the lord being the third Earl of Rutland whose seat was Belvoir Castle); *long(e)*, *short Ludforth* 1577, ~ *Ludford* 1704, *long ludfoarth* 1704, *Ludfeild furlong* 1708, *Ludfield* ~ 1708 (18) (a ford across a branch of the upper reaches of R. Devon; either 'loud ford' (*v.* **hlūd, ford**), referring to the noisy flow of the water, or 'ford across the *Hlūde*, i.e. "the loud one"', a name for the stream here (*v.* **hlūde**); the 1708 and 1708 (18) forms are presum. corruptions of the earlier *Ludford* rather than representing a different name, i.e. 'field beside the *Hlūde*'; note King Lud's Entrenchments in neighbouring Croxton Kerrial, the source of which folklore name lies here); *George Matthews Headland* 1704, ~ *Mathis* ~ 1708 (18), *Gorg Mathes headland, Go. Mathisis hedland* 1724 (*v.* **hēafod-land**), *Matthews's head-ley* 1704 (*v.* **headley**); *Melton Highway* 1704 (*v.* **hēah-weg**; the road to Melton Mowbray which lies to the south-west); *Mickelholm'* 1317 (*v.* **micel, mikill, holmr**; *mido milne feild* 1708 (*v.* **mǣd (mǣdwe** obl.sg.), **myln**); *miery doles, mire dole* 1708 (*v.* **myry, mýrr, dāl**); *the midle furlonge* 1577 (in East Fd), *the Middle Furlong* 1708 (18) (in Mill Fd), *the Mid(d)le Furlong* 1704, 1708, 1708 (18) (in Stathern Gate Fd) (*v.* **middel, furlang**); *the Monkes wonges* 1577 (*v.* **munuc, vangr**; with reference to the monks of Croxton Abbey); *Willm Morris's Headland* 1704, *Will Morisis hedland* 1708 (in Longlands Fd), *William Morris('s) Headland* 1704, 1708 (18), *Will Morisis hedland* 1708 (in Mill Fd), *Morris's Headland* 1708 (18) (in Stathern Gate Fd) (*v.* **hēafod-land**), *Morris's headley* 1704 (*v.* **headley**); *the Myll* 1577, *the Miln* 1708, *the Mill* 1708 (18), *behind the Mill* 1704 (a furlong so called), *the Millbanke, the millne banke* 1577, *the Mill bank* 1704 (*v.* **banke**), *mill banke side* 1577 (*v.* **sīde**), *the mill dikes* 1577, *the great mill dike* 1577 (*v.* **grēat, dík**), *Milldore Lees* 1577 (*v.* **duru, leys**) (*v.* **myln** and Mill Fd *supra*); *Myre Field Gores* 1708 (18) (*v.* **mýrr, gāra**); *Rob(er)t Neals Headland* 1704, 1708 (18), *Ro. Neails hedland* 1708 (in Longlands Fd), *Neals headland* 1704, *Ro. Neails hedland* 1708 (in Mill Fd) (*v.* **hēafod-land**), *Neals headley* 1704 (*v.* **headley**); *Neatepoole, Neetpooles* 1577 (*v.* **nēat, pōl**[1]); *the Neete pasture* 1577 (*v.* **nēat, pasture**); *the Nether furlong* 1704; *North Beck* l.13 (*v.* **norð, bekkr**); *the oulde Milles* 1577, *(the) old mills* 1704, 1708 (18), 1724, *the ould mills* 1708 (*v.* **ald, myln**); *Willyam Palmeres hedland, Palmers hedland* 1577 (in High Fd), *Palmers hedland* 1577 (in Mill Fd) (*v.* **hēafod-land**), *Pallmeres hedlee, Palmers hedley* 1577 (*v.* **headley**) (with the surn. *Palmer*); *the parsonage greensward* 1704 (*v.* **greensward**); *broad pennies* 1577, *Long, Short Broad-penny* 1704, *Short Broad* *penney* 1724, *Stony Broad-penny* 1704, *long peny* 1708, ~ *penney* 1724, *short peny* 1708 (*v.* **peni**; used in f.ns. of 'something paying a penny rent'; but in the late Middle Ages *peni* was used of money in general, so that lands named thus were held against a cash payment rather than in return for manorial service, *v.* Field 193); *Plummers headland* 1704 (*v.* **hēafod-land**; with the surn. *Plummer*); *Ransyegate, Raunsiegate* 1577, *Ransy gate* 1704 (*v.* **gata**; earlier forms are required to explain the first el., but **hramse** 'wild garlic' is poss.); *Christopher Reades hedland, ~ Reads ~, ~ Reedes ~* 1577 (*v.* **hēafod-land**), *Christopher Reads headley* 1577 (*v.* **headley**), *Willyam Reads wonge* 1577 (*v.* **vangr**) (with the surn. *Read*); *the red bankes* 1577 (*v.* **banke**; with either **hrēod** 'a reed' or **rēad** 'red', referring to soil colour, cf. Red Brinks *supra*); *Robin Hood fur(long)* 1704, 1724 (presum. alluding to the folk hero rather than to a local resident; names with *Robin Hood* sometimes indicated the presence of archery butts, *v.* Field 244); *Bryan Robinson his hedland, (Bryan) Robinson hedland* 1577 (*v.* **hēafod-land**), *Bryan Robinsons hedley* 1577 (*v.* **headley**), *Bryan Robinsons whole land* 1577 (*v. Thomas Geales whole land, supra*); *Severall lees* 1577 (*v.* **severall, leys**); *Schouedon'* 1317, *Showden, ~ side* 1577 (*v.* **sīde**), *Schoudon' Stye* 13 (with **stīg** or **stig**) (*v.* **dūn**; the first el. is either **scōh** 'a shoe', indicating a shoe-shaped hill-mass or **scēo** 'a shelter'); *William Sharpes hedland* 1577 (in West Fd), *Willyam Sharpes hedland* 1577 (in High Fd), *Willyam Sharpes hedland* 1577 (in Mill Fld) (*v.* **hēafod-land**), *Willm Sharpes hedley* 1577 (*v.* **headley**); *the Sheeptrack* 1724 (*v.* **trak**); *Shortcuttes* 1577 (*v.* **sc(e)ort, cut**; poss. referring to land assigned by cut or lot, *v.* Ox 438 *s.v.* **cut** and Field 23; but cf. Ch **2** 70 *s.n.* Cutts Mdw where it is noted that 'cuts are short furrows in the corners of great fields'); *the Shorte furlonge* 1577 (in East Fd), *the Shorte furlonge* 1577 (in West Fd), *(the) Short furlong* 1577, 1704, 1708, 1708 (18), 1724 (in Mill Fld), *the Short Furlong* 1704 (in Stathern Gate Fd), *Short Furlong* 1724 (in Life Fd) (*v.* **sc(e)ort**); *Silles hedley* 1577 (*v.* **headley**; cf. *William Sills* 1708 (18) of Branston); *Sixteen lands* 1704 (*v.* **land**; an enclosure comprising sixteen selions or 'lands' of a former great field); *Spenywod, Spenye woode* 1577 (*v.* **spinney, wudu**, cf. Spinney Wood, Ess 525); *Starkesmore* 1577 (*v.* **mōr¹**; the first el. is poss. the surn. *Stark* (from OE *stearc* 'stern, strong') in the possessive case, or a shortened form of the ?Anglo-Scand pers.n. *Starkulf, v.* SPNLY 263); *Stathorne gate* 1577 (*Stathorne way* 1577, *v.* **weg**), *Stathern gate* 1704, *Statorn gate* 1708, 1708 (18), *Stathorn Gate* 1724, *above, under Stathern gate* 1704, ~ *Statorngate* 1708, 1708 (18), *Stathern gate furlong* 1704 (*v.* **gata**; the road to Stathern which lies to the north-west), *Statorn pad* 1708, 1708 (18) (*v.* **pad**); *the over steeh* 1708 (*v.* **uferra**; with **stīg** or **stig**); *Robt Steels halfland* 1704 (*v.* **land**; poss. a half yardland, cf. *Thomas Geales whole land, supra*; but *v.* Ch **5** (1.ii) 219 *s.v.* **h(e)alf-land**), *Robt Steels headley* 1704 (*v.* **headley**); *the Stoned Medowe* 1577 bis, *the red bankes stoned medowe* 1577 (*v. the red bankes, supra*), *the Lords stoned medowe* 1577 (with reference to the third Earl of Rutland of Belvoir Castle), *(the) Stone Medow* 1704, ~ *Meadow* 1708 (18) (*v.* **stoned, stān**; meadows cleared of surface stones, presum. to facilitate mowing); *the Ston(e)pit furlong* 1708, 1708 (18) (*v.* **stān-pytt**); *the street(e)* 1577, 1704, *above, under the street(e)* 1577, 1704, 1708, 1708 (18), 1724, *betwixt the Streets* 1708, 1708 (18), *between the Streets* 1724, *Street more* 1724 (*v.* **mōr¹**) (*v.* **strǣt**); *John Sumners Headland* 1704, ~ *Sumner's* ~ 1708 (18), *Jo. Sumners hedland* 1708 (*v.* **hēafod-land**), *John Sumners headley* 1704 (*v.*

headley); *Swin(e)sdale* 1704, 1708, 1708 (18), 1724 (*v.* **swīn, svín, dalr**); *le sydlandis* Edw 1, *le sideland'* 1308, *Sidlands* 1704, 1708, 1708 (18), 1724 (*v.* **sīd, land** and Life Fd *supra*); *high thorntree* 1724 (*v.* **thorne-tree**); *John Towers's headland* 1704, 1708 (18) (*v.* **hēafod-land**), *Towers hedley* 1577 (*v.* **headley**); *Thomas Veroes headley* 1704 (*v.* **headley**; with the surn. *Vero(e)*)); *the waren* 1577, *the Warren* 1577, 1704 (*v.* **wareine**); *the Waterlane End* 1704, 1708, 1708 (18), 1724 (*v.* **wæter, lane-ende**); *watersleades* 1577, *Water Slades* 1704, *Waterslads* 1708, 1708 (18) (*v.* **wæter, slæd**); *The West feilde* 1577, ~ ~ *field* 1577 (*v.* **west, feld**; one of the early great fields of the township); *Westerdick'* 1317 (*v.* **vestr, vestri, dík**); *wind-, wyndhilles* 1577, *Windhills* 1704, *under wyndhilles* 1577, ~ *Windals* 1708 (18), ~ *Windhils* 1724 (*v.* **under**) (*v.* **wind**[1], **hyll**; for earlier forms, *v. wyndhillis* in adjoining Eaton f.ns. (b)); *Wooden Bridge* 1724 (*v.* **wooden**); *Woodyrith* 1724 (*v.* **wodi, rīð**).

Eaton

1. EATON

Aitona c.1130 LeicSurv, *Haitona* Hy 2 *Rut*, *Ayton'* 1229 Cur (p)
Eitona 1181, Hy 2 *Rut*, *Eiton'* e.13 B*Hosp*, 13 *GarCart*, *Eitun'* Hy 2
    Rut, *Eytona* Hy 2 Dugd, 1.12 (1449) *WoCart*, 1228 *Rut*, 1258
    Nichols, 1261 (Edw 1) *CroxR*, *Eytone* 1212 Dugd, 1222 RHug
    (p), 1241 (e.14) *BelCartA*, *Eyton'* c.1207 (e.15) *BelCartB*, 1220
    Nichols, e.13 *Deed et passim* to 1228 (Edw 1) *CroxR*, Hy 3 *Crox*
    (freq) *et freq* to 1423, 1427 *Comp et passim* to 1576 LibCl, 1606
    Ipm, (~ *iuxta Estwell* 1455 ECP), *Eytun'* e.Hy 3 *Rut*, 1241 (e.14)
    BelCartA, 1241 (e.15) *BelCartB*, *Eytton* 1511 *Rut*
Ettona 1156 (1318) Ch, *Etona* Hy 2 *Rut*, *Etone* Hy 3 *ib*, *Eton* 1473
    CCR, 1519, 1520 *Wyg*, 1520 *Crox*, *Etton'* 1500, 1508, 1509 *Rut*,
    1535 VE
Eattone c.1170 CartAnt, *Eaton* 1576 Saxton, 1599 *Rut*, 1604 LeicW,
    1610 Speed *et freq*

'Farmstead, village on a hill-spur', *v.* $\bar{e}g$, $t\bar{u}n$. The common p.n. Eaton has two chief sources; either OE $\bar{e}a\text{-}t\bar{u}n$ 'farmstead or village beside a river' or OE $\bar{e}g\text{-}t\bar{u}n$ 'farmstead or village on an island or on a spur of land'. The Leics. Eaton stands on the eastern tip of an impressive promontory which lies between one of the headwaters of R. Devon and a much smaller stream which runs into it from the north-west. However, neither of the streams at this point is large enough to be described as an $\bar{e}a$ 'river' and this may be discounted as the first el. or specific here. Gelling (PNL 35) points out that 'sites of villages with $\bar{e}g$ names were often the likeliest places for colonists to choose, and it might be worth the archaeologist's while to look for continuity of settlement from pre-English times'. Although this observation no doubt refers principally to p.ns. with $\bar{e}g$ as their generic rather than specific, it is worthy of note that Roman burials have been discovered in Eaton some 700 yards north of the parish church.

    For an extended discussion of the various meanings of the el. $\bar{e}g$, *v.* PNL 34–40.

CASTLE INN, *Castle* 1925 Kelly. EATON GRANGE, 1925 Kelly, *Grangie* 1228 *Rut*, v. **grange**; perh. originally an outlier of neighbouring Croxton Abbey, but more likely a grange of Leicester Abbey since *LTD* and *Charyte* are the principal sources of medieval minor names for Eaton. EATON LODGE, 1806 Map, 1824 O, 1863 White, v. **loge**. GREEN LANE, v. **grēne**[1]. ST DENYS' CHURCH, *Church (St Denis)* 1846, 1863, 1877 White; it is earlier recorded as *ecclesia ~ ~*, *ecclesie de Eyton* 1220 MHW, 1235 RGros, 1253 × 58 RTAL, *the Church* c.1708 (18), 1771, 1781 *Terrier*. Note also *the Church Yarde* 1625 *ib*, *The Church Yard* 1704, c.1708 (18), 1821 *ib*, *Churchyard* 1771, 1781 *ib*. THE VICARAGE, 1877 White; it is *the vicaradge house* 1625 *Terrier*, *the Vicari(d)ge house* 1698, 1704 *ib*, *The Vicarage House* c.1708 (18), c.1750, 1781 *ib*. WINDMILL (P.H.) (lost), *Windmill* 1846, 1863 White, *Windmill Inn* 1877 ib.

FIELD-NAMES

Forms in (a) dated c.1750, 1771 and 1821 are *Terrier*; 1769 (18) are Nichols (ex *EnclA*). Undated forms in (b) are 14 (1467 × 84) *LTD*. Forms dated Hy 2 and 1228 are *Rut*, Hy 3 are *Crox*, Edw 1 are *CroxR*, 1477 (e.16) are *Charyte*, 1625, 1698 and c.1708 (18) are *Terrier*, 1650 are AAS.

(a) Brackendale Cls 1769 (18) (v. **brakni, dalr**); Church Cl 1769 (18) Nichols, 1846, 1863 White (allotted for church repairs at the Enclosure of 1769); the Clay Fd 1821; the Cliff 1770 *Deed* (*le Clif* 14 (1467 × 84) *LTD*, v. **clif**); the Common Pasture c.1750 (*communam pasture de Eitona* Hy 2, *the Comon Pasture* 1625, v. **commun, pasture**); The Homestall c.1750 (c. 1708 (18), v. **hām-stall**; belonging to *The Vicarage House*); Hop Yard 1824 O (v. **hop-yard**); the parsonage yard c.1750; the Plain c.1750, Plain Meer 1769 (18) (v. **(ge)mǣre**) (v. **plain**); Plat Meer 1769 (18) (v. **plat, (ge)mǣre**); the Stonepit Cls 1771 (v. **stān-pytt**).

(b) *Aldefeeldale* (v. **ald, feld, dalr**); *Alnothesgraue* 1477 (e.16) (the first el. is the common OE pers.n. *Alnōð*, which could represent an earlier *Ælfnōð* or *Æðelnōð* or *Ealdnōð* or *Ealnōð*, cf. *Alnotescroft* in Burton Lazars f.ns. (b) and *Alfnadgraue* in Hose f.ns. (b); with **grāf** 'a copse'); *Assebymilne* ('the mill at Ashby', v. **myln**; the lost settlement called *Asseby* (v. **æsc, bȳ**) is otherwise unrecorded, but cf. *Eaton Mill Ashes* in adjoining Branston f.ns. (b)); *Blescop* (v. **copp**; with either the Scand pers.n. *Blesi* or ON **blesi** 'a bare spot on a hillside', cf. *grangia de Blesewelle* (Goadby Grange)); *le Blyndwell* (v. **blind, wella**); *Borw* (either **borg**[1] 'a fortified hill' or **burh** 'a fortified site'); *Bowebriggegate* (v. **boga, brycg, gata** and Bow Bridge Cl in neighbouring Eastwell f.ns. (a)); *Brakenhou* bis, *Ouerbrakenhou* (v. **uferra**) (v. **brakni, haugr**); *the Bracken peece* 1698 (v. **brakni, pece**); *Bytwnethebekes* (v.

betwēonan, bekkr; a furlong so called); *Campus australis* ('the south field', one of the great fields of the township; with MLat *campus* 'a field' and MLat *australis* 'south, southern'), *Campus borialis* ('the north field', another of the great fields, with MLat *borialis* 'north, northern'); *Casil crofte* n.d. Nichols (*v.* caste(l), croft); *Castelsty* (*v.* castel(l); with stīg or stig); *Cleypit* (*v.* cley-pytt); *Clippesclif, Clippesclifbrig* (*v.* brycg, bryggja) (*v.* clif; the first el. is the ON pers.n. *Klyppr* in the possessive case); *Clippesdale* (with dalr or deill; presum. the same individual is recorded here as in the previous names); *le Cros* (*v.* cros); *Crosfurlong'* (*v.* cross, furlang); *Cros(s)gate* (*v.* gata; with cros or cross); *Depedalebrode* (*v.* dēop, dalr, brǣdu); *Dockedam* 14 (1467 × 84), *Docchedam* 1477 (e.16) (*v.* docce, damme); *Eaton Cowpastures* 1650; *Eaton Parke* 1650 (*v.* park); *Fifefurlong', Ouerfifurlong'* (*v.* uferra) (*v.* fīf, furlang); *Fordegate* 1228 (*v.* gata), *Forthehull* (*v.* hyll), *Atteforthe ende* (*v.* atte, ende; a furlong so called) (all with ford); *Longe ~, Schorte ~, Foxhou* (*v.* lang¹, sc(e)ort, fox, haugr); *Fulesdale* 1228, *Foulesdale* bis (*v.* deill; with either the OE pers.n. *Fugol* or Scand *Fugl* both original by-names meaning 'bird'); *Gosedale* (*v.* gōs; prob. with dalr rather than with deill); *Attegraungeyatte* (*v.* atte, grange, geat and Eaton Grange *supra*; a furlong so called); *Greneclif, Greneclifouerende* (*v.* uferra, ende) (*v.* grēne¹, clif); *Hareclif* (*v.* clif; with either har² or hara); *Hildindam* (*v.* damme; perh. with an OE pers.n. such as *Hilda* or *Hilding* or even with hilder 'an elder-tree' if the name was poorly copied); *Horsladedale* (*v.* slæd; with hors or horu and deill); *le Hows* 14 (1467 × 84), *Hows medo* 1477 (e.16) (*v.* mǣd (mǣdwe obl.sg.) (the simplex may be the plural of either Scand haugr or OE hōh, cf. Hose *supra*); *kyrsinges* (*v.* cærsing); *le Longeling'* (*v.* lang¹), *Schortling* (*v.* sc(e)ort), *Northling'* bis (*v.* norð) (all with lyng); *Lusternegate* 1228, Edw 1, *Lusterngate* Edw 1, *Lustringate* (*v.* lūs-þorn, gata); *le Milnegate, Milngate* (*v.* myln, gate), *molendinum de Eyton* 1477 (e.16) (with MLat *molendinum* 'a mill') (*v.* Watermilne, *infra*); *le Mor* (*v.* mōr¹); *New(e)brigge, Newbriggebec* (*v.* bekkr) (*v.* nīwe, brycg); *Noreweldale* (*v.* norð, wella; with dalr or deill); *Oselaker* (*v.* ōsle, æcer); *Oxgang Cottages* c.1708 (18) (*v.* ox-gang, cotage); *Peyselandes, Peyslond'* 14 (1467 × 84), *Peselandes* 1477 (e.16) (*v.* pise, land); *Podeaker* (*v.* pode, æcer); *le Presteswong'* (*v.* prēost, vangr); *Rieclef* 14 (1467 × 84), *Rieclif sik* 1477 (e.16) (*v.* sík) (*v.* ryge, clif); *le Rydyʒhede* 1477 (e.16) (*v.* hrēodig, hēafod); *le Saltestrete* bis, *le Strete* bis (*v.* salt¹, strǣt; the Roman road across the Wolds, Margary 58a, later used as a saltway); *Schirnclif, Longeschernclif* (*v.* lang¹) (*v.* scearn, clif); *Schortredelond* (*v.* sc(e)ort, land; prob. with rēad 'red', referring to the colour of the soil, but hrēod 'reed' is poss.); *Seggedam* 1290 Ch, *Segdam* n.d. Nichols (*v.* secg¹, damme); *Shepehousyate* (*v.* shepe-hous, geat); *le Sikes* (*v.* sík); *Smalewelle* 1228, Edw 1, *Abouethesmalewelle* (*v.* aboven), *Smalewelleholm* (*v.* holmr) ('the narrow stream', *v.* smæl, wella); *Stanlande* (*v.* stān, land); *Stathernegate* (*v.* gata; the road to Stathern which adjoins to the north-west); *le Swathes* (*v.* swathe); *Swynesdale* (*v.* swīn, svín, dalr); *Thornende* (*v.* þorn, ende); *Thornwelgate* (*v.* gata), *Thornwellethornes* (*v.* þorn) ('the spring or stream among the thorns', *v.* þorn, wella); *Thurston Werkhous* ('Thurstan's workshop', *v.* weorc-hūs; the pers.n. is ODan *Thursten* (ON *Þorsteinn*) anglicized as OE *Þurstān*); *Wandilberwdike* (*v.* dík; the first el. is the OE pers.n. *Wændel*, while the second el. appears ostensibly to be berg 'a hill'; however, as only a solitary form survives, one may be tempted to consider *Wandilberw* as another example of the name of the Iron Age hill fort Wandlebury (with **burh**), *v.* Ca 88 *s.n.* Vandlebury and note *Borw*, *supra*); *Watermilne* (*v.* **water-mylne** and *molendinum de Eyton, supra*); *Watriforowis* 14 (1467 × 84), *Watrifurwes* 1477 (e.16) ('furrows where water tends to lie', *v.* **wæterig, furh**; perh. a variant of the common Water Furrows); *Wermland'*, *Nether-*, *Ouerwurmland'* (*v.* **neoðera, uferra**) (*v.* **wyrm, land**); *Wetecroft* (*v.* **hwǣte, croft**); *Wranglond* (*v.* **wrang, vrangr, land**); *wyndehill'*, *wyndhillis* Hy 3 (*v.* **wind**[1], **hyll** and *windhilles* in adjacent Branston f.ns. (b)); *Wyterthe* (*v.* **hwīt, eorðe**).

2. EASTWELL

Estwelle 1086 DB, 1162 × 70 *Rut*, l.12 *GarCart et passim* to 1380, 1381 Cl, *Estwell'* c.1130 LeicSurv, 1166 P (p), 1180, 1181 *Rut et passim* to a.1211 *ib*, 1235 RGros *et freq* to 1610 Speed, (~ *Edenishouere* 1242 Fees), (~ *Arraby* 1242 ib), *Estwella* 1156 (1318) Ch, 1176 P (p), Hy 2 *Rut*, 1209 × 19 RHug, *Estuell'* 1154 × 77 *Rut*, *Estuelle* Edw 1 *CroxR*
Esteuuelle 1086 DB, *Estewelle* Hy 3 *Crox*, *Estewell'* 1294 *Wyg*, 1312 *Rut*, 1313 *Wyg et passim* to 1364 (1449) *WoCart*, 1535 VE, 1539 MinAccts
Yestwell 1528 LWills
Eastwell 1603, 1616 Fine *et freq*

'The east stream', *v.* **ēast, wella**. Eastwell is on a headwater of R. Devon which from here flows roughly eastwards before turning north-east. *Thomas de Hendesovere* held land in Eastwell in 1236 Fees. The fee of *Arraby* held three carucates here in 1242 ib. *Robertus de Arraby* still held this land l.13 Nichols.

THE BELT is *The Belt Plantation* 1848 *TA*, *v.* **belt**. EASTWELL LODGE, 1824 O, *v.* **loge**. THE HALL, 1877 White, *Eastwell Hall* 1846, 1863 ib, *v.* **hall**. HALL FM. PIPER HOLE FM, *v.* Piper Hole in adjoining Harby. THE RECTORY 1877 White, 1925 Kelly; it is *the Rectors house* 1703 *Terrier*, *the Parsonage House* 1601 ib, *v.* **rectour, personage**. ROMAN CATHOLIC CHAPEL, 1848 *TA*; built in 1798. ST MICHAEL'S CHURCH, *Church (St Michael)* 1846, 1863, 1877 White; it is earlier recorded as *ecclesiam de Estwella* a.1219 RHug, *ecclesiam ~ ~*, *ecclesie de Estwell* 1220 MHW, 1235 RGros, *the Church* c.1708 (18) *Terrier*, 1848 *TA*. Note also *The Church Yard* c.1708 (18) *Terrier*, *(the) Churchyard* 1724 ib, 1848 *TA*.

FIELD-NAMES

Undated forms in (a) are 1848 *TA*. Forms throughout dated 1601, 1605, 1611, 1625, 1694, 1697, 1703, c.1708 (18) and 1724 are *Terrier*; 1706 and 1708 are Nichols.

(a) Ash Tree Cl ((*the*) *Ash Close* 1694, 1724, ~ *Closes* 1703, 1708, c.1708 (18), *Ash Closeing* 1697 (*v.* **closing**), *v.* **æsc**); Badger Cl (either with **badger** the animal or with the surn. *Badger*, *v.* Reaney *s.n.*); Barn Cl; Beck Cl (*the Beck*(*s*) *Close* 1694, 1697, cf. *Eaton becke*(*s*) 1601, 1605, 1625, *v.* **bekkr**); Bow Bridge Cl (*v.* *Bowebriggegate* in Eaton f.ns. (b)); Branston Ground, ~ ~ Mdw (*v.* **grund**; Branston lies to the north-east); Breaches Cl (*v.* **brēc**); Broad Leys (*broade leas* 1601, *v.* **brād, leys**); Burns Wong (*Brouneswong*' 14 (1467 × 84) *LTD*, *the Burnwong's Close* 1694, ~ *Burnswongs* ~ 1697, (*the*) *Burnswong Close* 1703, 1708, *the Brunswong Close* c.1708 (18), *Burns Wong* 1724, *v.* **vangr**; the first el. is a pers.n., either OE *Brūn* or ON *Brúnn* (ODan *Brun*) or a nickname from OFr *brun* 'brown' of hair or complexion; cf. *bruniswong* in neighbouring Harby f.ns. (b) which may be a late 13th cent. recording of the same feature); (The) Clay Ground, ~ ~ Mdw (*v.* **grund**; cf. *the Clayfield* 1601, *v.* **clæg, feld**; one of the great fields of the village); Church Cl, Church Leys (*the Church Leas* 1601, ~ ~ *leyes* 1605, 1611, ~ ~ *leies* 1611, *the Church*(*e*) *Leas* 1625, *v.* **leys** and St Michael's Church *supra*); Clover Cl (*v.* **clāfre**; a fodder crop enclosure); Bottom ~ ~, Little ~ ~, Cold Hill, Cold Hill Cl (*v.* **cald**); Corner Cl, Corner Pingle (*v.* **corner, pingel**); The Croft (*v.* **croft**); Dove Cote Cl (*v.* **dove-cot**(**e**)); Eastwell Hills 1806 Map; Eastwell Pasture 1824 O, The Pasture, The Far Pasture (cf. *the Commone Pasture* 1605, ~ *Common* ~ 1694, 1697, 1703, c.1708 (18), 1724, *v.* **commun, pasture**); Bottom Fish Pond Piece (*v.* **pece**); Fox Hole Cl (*v.* **fox-hol**); Great, Nether, Upper Foxie Dale (*Foxidale* 1601, *Foxdale* 1601, 1625, *Foxedale* 1605, 1611, *Foxedalle* 1611, (*the furlonge*) *aboue Foxedal*(*l*)*e* 1605, 1611, *above Foxdale* 1625, *Long Foxdale* 1601, *Foxdale Bushe* 1625 (*v.* **busc**), 'valley frequented by foxes', *v.* **fox, dalr**; there is no record of the use of the adj. *foxy* in a non-pejorative sense except with reference to colour and *Foxidale/Foxie Dale* as a reduction of *Foxholedale seems unlikely); The Green Yard (*v.* **grēne**[2], **geard**; note *Grenam* a.1211 *Rut* (MLat *grena* 'a village green')); Hands Cl (with the surn. *Hand*(*s*)); Hill Cl; Home Cl (*v.* **home**); Low ~ ~, Top ~ ~, Land Fd (*v.* **land**; an enclosure comprising originally an unspecified number of selions or 'lands' of one of the earlier great fields of the village); Lane Cl (*v.* **lane**); Ling Dale, ~ ~ Nook (*v.* **nōk**) (*Lingdale* 1601, 1625, *lingedale* 1611, *Lingdale Close* 1706, *Stone Pen Lingdale* 1706 (*v.* **penn**[2]), *Ten Pool Lingdale* 1706 (*v.* **pol**[1]), *The Lingdale Close now divided into three closes, viz. The Stone pen Lingdale, The Ten pool Lingdale, The Nether Lingdale* c.1708 (18), *v.* **lyng, dalr**); Little Mdw; Lodge House Cl (*v.* Eastwell Lodge *supra*); Long Cl; Mill Fd (*the mill* 1601, cf. *the milne furlonge* 1611, *the Mill furlong* 1625, *v.* **myln**); Bottom, Top Nether Cl (*Nether Cloase* 1605, (*the*) *Neither Cloase* 1605, 1625, ~ *close* 1611, *v.* **neoðera, clos**(**e**)); Occupation Rd (a common name, often dating from the Enclosure and meaning 'a private road for the use of the occupiers of the land', *v.* OED *s.v.* occupation, 7; it signified a green lane through what was originally a great field); Old Orchard; Open Plantation (*v.* **open**; presum. unfenced); The Ozier Bed (*v.* **oyser, bedd**); Paddams (perh. 'toad pond', *v.* **padde, damme**, but earlier forms are needed); Parsons Cl (*v.* **persone**); Pasture Cl (*v.* Eastwell Pasture *supra*); The Pingle (*v.* **pingel**); Piper Hole Cl (*v.* Piper Hole in Harby); The Pound (*v.* **pund**); Round Hill Cl (*v.* **round**); Sand Pit Cl (cf. *Sandpit Leas* 1601, *Sandpitt leyes* 1605, ~ *leies* 1611, ~ *leas* 1625, *v.* **sand-pytt, leys**); Savages Cl (with the surn. *Savage*); Sixteen Acres (1706, c.1708 (18), *v.* **æcer**); Spring Head Washpond (*v.* **spring**[1], **hēafod, wæsce**; prob. a pond used for washing the wheels of carts); Stone Pen Cl (*v.* **stān, penn**[2]; perh. to be identified with *Stone Pen Lingdale, v.* Ling Dale *supra*); Stone-pit, ~ Cl (*the stonepittes* 1601, *v.* **stān-pytt**, cf. *Stannyngdelf* 1415 Banco (*v.* **stāning, (ge)delf, stān-(ge)delf**)); Tenement Barn (*v.* **tenement**); Tent Pool, ~ ~ Cl (sic) (*v.* Ten Pool Lingdale, *supra*); Thorney Cl, Thorney Furlong, ~ ~ Cl, Bottom Thorney Furlong (*Thorney furlong* 1601, *Thorny(e) furlong(e)* 1605, 1611, 1625, *v.* **þornig**); The Walk Plantation (*v.* **walk**); Far ~, Westinghams (*West Innoms* 1601, *West Inghams* 1706, *the West Inhams* c.1708 (18), *v.* **innām**); Dry Woulds (*v.* **drȳge**), Fallow Woulds (*v.* **falg**) (*the Oldes* 1605, 1625, *the Wouldes* 1605, *the ouldes* 1611, *The Woulds* 1706, c.1708 (18) (a close so called), *the Farr, the hither wowldes* 1601 (*v.* **feor, hider**), *Middle, (The) Upper Woulds* 1706, c.1708 (18), *the wowlde leas* 1601, *the Would lease* 1605, 1611, ~ ~ *leyes* 1605, ~ ~ *leays* 1611, *the Oldes Leas* 1625 (*v.* **leys**), *the wowlde medowe* 1601, *(The) Woulds Meadow* 1706, c.1708 (18), *v.* **wald**); Woulds Cl (cf. *Parson's Would Close* 1706, *The Parsons Woulds Close* c.1708 (18), *v.* **persone, wald**).

(b) *William Blythes Cloase* 1625 (*v.* **clos(e)**); *brad micle way, Broad Micleway* 1605, *Broad Michelway(e)* 1611, 1625 (*v.* **brād, micel, weg**); *Burneshome (Close)* 1601, 1611, *Burnshome* 1605 (*v.* **holmr** and Burns Wong *supra* which contains the same pers.n. as first el.); *the Churche headland* 1625 (*v.* **hēafod-land** and St Michael's Church *supra*); *the Cliffe* 1601, 1605, 1611, *the Clyffe* 1625, *the Cliffe fielde* 1601 (*v.* **feld**; one of the great fields of the village), *(the) Cliffe furlong(e)* 1601, 1605, 1611, 1625, *the Clyffe furlong* 1625 (*v.* **clif**); *the Common(e) Heades* 1605, 1625, *the Common Hades* 1611, 1625, ~ ~ *Heads* 1625 (*v.* **commun, hēafod**); *the common headland* 1625 (*v.* **commun, hēafod-land**); *the Commone peaces* 1605 (*v.* **commun, pece**); *the Lady Compton Cloase* 1625 (*v.* **clos(e)**); *the Conygree* 1601, *Conygraue* 1605, 1611, *the Connigrave* 1625 (*v.* **coningre**); *Robt. Draper(s) Headland* 1605 (*v.* **hēafod-land**), *drapers yard* 1605 (*v.* **geard**; belonging to *Robt. Draper* 1605); *dunsteades* 1605, 1611, 1625, *Dunstead furlong* 1601 (*v.* **tūn-stede**; prob. with reference to a deserted site); *the fallowes* 1611, *the Fallow feild* 1605, ~ ~ *field* 1625 (*v.* **falg**); *Farredoles* 1601 (*v.* **feor, dāl**); *Gawterley furlong* (sic) 1601, *Gautery Furlonge* 1605, 1611, *Gautry Furlong* 1625 (perh. a much altered 'gallows-tree furlong', *v.* **galg-trēow**, cf. *le Gautreyhill close* in Buckminster f.ns. (b)); *Goadby* ~, *Goatby Cloase* 1605, 1625, *Goadby(e) Close* 1611, 1625, *Goadbie* ~ 1611 (*v.* **clos(e)**), *Gawdeby hedge* 1601 (*v.* **hecg**; a boundary marker) (Goadby Marwood adjoins to the south); *Hardall sike* 1601 (*v.* **heard, deill, sīk**); *Harp(e) Wong* 1601, 1605, 1611, 1625 (*v.* **hearpe, vangr**; prob. with reference to the shape of the enclosure); *the Homestall* 1605, 1611, 1625, *the Homestead* 1694, 1697, 1724 (*v.* **hām-stall, hām-stede**; naming the home buildings of *the Parsonage House*); *the High(e)way* 1605, 1625, *the kinges high(e) way(e)* 1605, 1611, 1625 (*v.* **hēah-weg**;

with reference to James I and poss. to Charles I who succeeded in March 1625); *the High Street* 1605, *the highe streat* 1625 (*v.* **hēah**[1], **strǣt**); *Lawsemore* 1601, *Lausemoore* 1605, 1611, *Long Lausmore* 1625, *Laus(e)more sike* 1601, ~ *syke* 1611, ~ *Sicke* 1625 (*v.* **sík**) (*v.* **lūs, mōr**[1]); *Longdale* 1605 (*v.* **lang**[1] ; with **dalr** or **deill**); *Longfarme* 1601 (*v.* **lang**[1], **ferme**); *longe linge* 1605, 1611, *long ling furlong* 1601 (*v.* **lang**[1], **lyng**); *Melton Gate* 1601, 1605, 1611, 1625, *Melton way* 1605 (*v.* **gata, weg**; the road to Melton Mowbray which lies to the south); (*the*) *Middle Furlong(e)* 1601, 1605, 1611, 1625, (*the*) *Short Middle Furlong(e)* 1605, 1611, 1625 (*v.* **middel**); *the Mo(o)re* 1611, 1625 (*v.* **mōr**[1]); *the Neatheard(e)s headland* 1625 (*v.* **hēafod-land**), *the Neatheards yard* 1625 (*v.* **geard**) (*v.* **neetherd**); *the neather close* 1611 (*v.* **neoðera**); *Neather Hills* 1601 (*v.* **neoðera**); *Netherdale* 1340 Ch (*v.* **neoðera**; with **dalr** or **deill**); *The Open Close* c.1708 (18) (*v.* **open**; presum. an enclosure without permanent gates, cf. Open Cl, Ru 271); *Mr Portmans Cloase* 1605, 1625, *Mr Portman's Close* c.1708 (18); *Puncheholes* 1601, *Puncholes* 1611 (*v.* **punche, hol**[1]; perh. descriptive of a land surface resembling holes punched in leather, where a series of small pits had been dug for the removal of stone or other minerals); *the Seventeen Acre(s)* 1703, c.1708 (18) (*v.* **æcer**); *Short Segraves* 1601, ~ *Seagraues* 1605, 1611, ~ *Seagraves* 1625 (poss. the same name as the problematical Seagrave in East Goscote Hundred, whose first el. may be (**ge**)**set** 'a fold', with **grāf** 'a grove, a copse'; otherwise the surn. *Seagrave* in the possessive case of a family originating in this village, 12 miles to the south-west); *Short Thorne* 1605, 1611, 1625 (*v.* **þorn**); *the Sleightes* 1605, 1625, *the slightes* 1611, *the Sleights* 1706, c.1708 (18), *Eastwell Sleightes* 1605, 1625, *east well slightes* 1611, *the Long Slytes* 1601 (*v.* **slétta**); *the South feild* 1605, 1611, ~ ~ *fielde* 1625 (*v.* **sūð, feld**; one of the great fields of the township); *the Street* 1605, (*the furlonge*) *aboue the Street(e)* 1605, 1611, (*the furlong*) *above the Street(e)* 1611, 1625, *beneath the street* 1601, *under the Street(e)* 1605, 1611, 1625, *Street furlong* 1601 (*v.* **strǣt**; furlongs beside the Roman road across the Wolds, Margary 58a); *Long, Shorte Syppins* 1601, *Longe, Short(e) Shippens* 1605, 1611, *Long, Short Shippines* 1625 (*v.* **scypen**); *Talepoole leyes* 1605, ~ *leas* 1625, *Tailepoole leeies* 1611 (*v.* **taile, pōl**[1], **leys**); *Tankett Sike* 1605, ~ *syke* 1611, *Tanket sick* 1625 (*v.* **sík**; poss. with the surn. *Tankard* (cf. John *Tancart* 1202 Ass), *v.* Reaney *s.n.* or ModEdial **tankert** 'a vessel used for carrying water', perh. in some transferred sense, *v.* **tankard**); (*at*) *the Townes End(e)* 1605, 1611, 1625 (*v.* **ende**), *the Towne(s) feild* 1605, ~ ~ *field* 1625 (*v.* **feld**), *the Towne welles* 1605, 1611, *the Town Wells* 1625 (*v.* **wella**) (all with **tūn** 'village'); *Sir Gorge Villiers Cloase* 1605 (*v.* **clos(e)**); *Mr Waldromes cloase* 1605, *Waldrames close* 1611, *Waldromes* ~ 1625 (*v.* **clos(e)**; with the surn. *Waldron*, cf. *Waldrons ground* in Goadby Marwood f.ns, (b)); *the west feild* 1605, 1611, ~ ~ *field* 1625 (*v.* **west, feld**; one of the great fields of the village); *Westhengfurlanc* a.1211 *Rut* (*v.* **west, eng, furlang**); *White Grasse* 1601, 1605, 1611, 1625 (*v.* **hwīt, græs**; with *white* prob. in its ModEdial. use of 'dry, open pasture' and *grass* as 'a piece of grassland').

3. GOADBY MARWOOD

> *Goutebi* 1086 DB, c.1130 LeicSurv, 1154 × 77 *Rut* (p), l.12 (freq),
> e.13 *GarCart*, Edw 1 *Rut* (p), *Goutebia* c.1130 LeicSurv, *Gouteby*
> l.12 *Wyg*, l.12 *GarCart*, 1202 FF *et passim* to 1265 *BHosp*, Hy 3
> *Crox* (freq) *et freq* to 1361 (1449) *WoCart*, 1381 Cl *et passim* to
> 1421 Fine, 1428 FA, (~ *Quartremars* 1242 Fees), (~ *iuxta*
> *Waltham* 1308 Banco, 1346 Pat), (~ *Maureward* 1311, 1380
> Banco), *Gowtebi* 1251 RGros, *Gowteby* l.13 *Wyg*, *Gouthebi* l.12
> *GarCart*, *Goutheby* p.1274 *BHosp*
> *Goltebi* 1086 DB
> *Gawteby* 1428 *MiD*, *Gauteby* 1429 Fine
> *Goudeby* 1346 Ipm, 1381 SR *et passim* to 1460 Hastings, 1504
> Banco, *Gowedeby* 1414 Pat, 1484 Cl
> *Gaudeby* 1473 *CCR*, *Gaudebe* 1528 LWills, *Gawdeby* 1526, 1530
> AAS *et passim* to 1539 *Deed*, 1546 *Rut*, *Gaudby* 1520 *Crox*, 1535
> VE
> *Godeby(e)* 1462, 1464 Pat *et passim* to 1606 Ipm, 1610 Speed, (~
> *Morwode* 1576 Fine), *Godby* 1535 VE, 1537 MinAccts, *Godby*
> *alias dicta Gawdby* 1541 Nichols, *Goodby* 1576 LibCl
> *Goadbye Maureward* 1629 *Surv*, *Goadby Maurewood* 1725 LML

'Gauti's farmstead, village', *v.* **bȳ**, cf. Goadby in Gartree Hundred.
The ON pers.n. *Gauti* either represents short forms of names in *Gaut-* or
is an original by-name meaning 'a man from Gautland', *v.* SPNLY 98.
The DB form *Goltebi* is an AN inverted spelling. Ante-consonantal *l*
was frequently vocalized to *u*. The substitution of *th* for *t* in late 12th
and 13th cent. forms is the result of AN orthographical interchange
between the symbols *th* and *t* for etymological *t*.

Ada de Quartremars, the last of the Quartremars family, lords of the
manor of Goadby, married *Gaufridus Maureward* in the reign of Henry
III. The Maureward family is recorded as holding Goadby from
Galfridus ~, *Gaufridus Maureward* 1247 Ass to as late as *Thomas*
Maureward 1428 FA. The village lies some one and a half miles north-
west of Waltham on the Wolds, hence ~ *iuxta Waltham* 1308, 1346.

GOADBY GRANGE (lost)
> *Godby grange* 1537 MinAccts, *Godeby grange* 1606 Ipm
> *grangia de Blesewelle* 1265 *BHosp*, *grangie de Bleswelle* Hy 3 *Deed*
> *Blisewell grange* 1361 Nichols, *Blesswell Grange* 1461 ib, *Bleswell*
> *Graunge* 1551 Pat

The grange was named originally from a spring: (*ad fontem qui vocatur*) *Blesewelle* 1265, a.1277 *BHosp* (with MLat *fons* (*fontem* acc.sg.) 'a spring, a well'), *Bleswelle* Hy 3 *Deed, Blisewell* 1577 Nichols. *Blesewelle* compounds either the Scand pers.n. *Blesi* (an original by-name meaning 'white spot (on a horse's forehead), blaze') or ON **blesi** 'a bare spot on a hillside', with OE **wella** 'a spring, a stream'. 'The spring at the bare spot on the hillside' seems the likelier explanation of the name. There are two such springs near the village, each topographically suitable, both developing into minor streams which converge. There are traces of earthworks near the spring at SK 768268. The grange was an outlier of Garendon Abbey, *v.* **grange**.

BELLEMERE FM is *Bellemere Lodge* 1863, 1877 White, cf. *The Belle Mere, Belle-meer* 1795 Nichols, *v.* **loge**. Also appear to belong here *Ballymer Hill* 1601 *Terrier, Bullimare hill* 1612 *ib, Bullimore Hill* 1638 *ib, Ballymore* 1795 Nichols, *v.* **belle**; with (**ge**)**mǣre** or **mere**[1]. CRANYKE FM, *Cranyke farm* 1877 White, *Crane Sick* 1708 *Terrier, Lower ~ ~, Upper ~ ~, Cransyke field* 1839 *TA, v.* **cran, sík**. GLEBE FM *v.* **glebe**. GOADBY GORSE, cf. *Goss cover, ~ ~ close* 1839 *TA, v.* **gorst, cover(t)**. GOADBY HALL, ~ ~ FM, *Goadby Hall* 1831 Curtis, 1863, 1877 White, 1925 Kelly, *the Hall* 1863, 1877 White, *v.* **hall**. METHODIST CHAPEL. THE RECTORY, 1877 White, 1925 Kelly; it is *the parsonage howse* 1601 *Terrier, the parsonidge howse* 1612 *ib*, (*the*) *Parsonag(e) House* 1625, 1690, 1708, c.1710 *ib*, 1839 *TA, v.* **personage**. ST DENYS' CHURCH, *Church (St Denis)* 1846, 1863, 1877 White, *Church (St Denys)* 1925 Kelly; it is earlier recorded as *ecclesie de Gouteby* 1220 MHW, 1356 *Pat, ecclesiam de Gowtebi* 1251 RGros, *ecclesie de Goudeby* 1421 *Pat, ecclesiarum de Overton Quartermars Godeby et Cunston* 1464 *ib, The Church* 1708, c.1710 *Terrier*. Note also (*the*) *Church Yard* c.1700, 1701, 1708 *ib*, 1839 *TA*. WHITE LODGE, 1795 Nichols, 1824 O, 1846, 1863, 1877 White, *v.* **loge**.

FIELD-NAMES

Undated forms in (a) are 1839 *TA*. Forms throughout dated 1265 and a.1277 are *BHosp*; 1601, 1612, 1625, 1638, 1674, 1660 × 80, 1690, 1680 × 98, 1700, c.1700, 1701, 1708, c.1710 and c.1745 are *Terrier*; 1630 are Ipm.

(a) Ables Fd (with the surn. *Able/Abel*, from Hebrew *Abel* which was a common 13th cent. Christian name); Six ~, Nine ~, Eleven ~, Twelve Acres (*v.* **æcer**); East, West Amby Cl (cf. *the Ambey Bridge* 1638 and *v. Alby* in f.ns. (b) *infra*); Ballimoor Cl, Ballimoor Pond, Ballimoor Head Cl (*v.* **hēafod**), Ballimoor Tail Cl (*v.* **taile**) (all presum. relate to Bellemere (Fm) *supra*); The Banks (*v.* **banke**); Barn Cl; Barn Fd; Bottom Cl (*v.* **bottom**); Bullmoor Fd (presum. also belonging with Bellemere (Fm) *supra*); Bull Paddock (*v.* **bula, paddock**); Clay Fd (*the clay felde* 1601, *the Claye Feild* 1625, *Clay Feilde* 1638, (*the*) *Clay Field* 1674, 1660 × 80, 1690, 1701, 1708, c.1710, *v.* **clæg, feld**; one of the great fields of the village); Cottage Cl (*v.* **cotage**); Cottagers Pasture (*v.* **cotager**); Long ~ ~, Dale Cl, Dale Fd (*v.* **dalr**); Dog Kennel Plantation (*v.* **kenel**; with reference to kennels for hounds); Dove Hills (*v.* **dūfe**); Draycarts Mdw (if not with the surn. *Draycot(t)* in the possessive case, with a spelling attraction to *cart* since a *dray* was a low-sided waggon, then *v.* **dræg, cot**); Fold Yard (*v.* **fald, geard**); Fordlelion Cl (sic) (beside the Eastwell to Waltham road; unexplained, but cf. Lionville just within the parish boundary of Scalford, near Cranyke Fm *supra*); Gamble Fd ((*the*) *Gamble Feild* 1674, 1660 × 80, 1690, 1700, 1708; a late name for one of the great fields of the village, this appears to represent Amby *supra* with prosthetic *g*); Garth (*v.* **garðr**); Goadby Park 1806 Map, 1831 Curtis (*the Park* 1690, 1680 × 98, 1700, c.1710), Great, Little Park (*v.* **park**); Grange Fd (*v.* Goadby Grange *supra*); Great Cart Lane (*v.* **carte**); Great Cl (1630); Great Fd; Hall Gardens (*v.* Goadby Hall *supra*); High Fd (1630); Hill Cl; Home Cl (*v.* **home**); Homestead Cl (*v.* **hām-stede**); Bottom ~ ~, Horse Cl; Hovel Cl (*v.* **hovel**); Little Ings, ~ ~ Wood (*v.* **eng**); Ivy Cl (*v.* **īfig**); Kitching Cl (freq) (*v.* **kicchen**; these usually refer to kitchen gardens, but note *Daniel Kitchins Farm* 1660 × 80 *infra*); Far, Near Lamb Cotts (*Lambcotes* 14 (1467 × 84) *LTD*, *the lambecotes*, *Lambcotes* 1601, *Lamcotes* 1601, 1612, 1638, *Lamcoates* 1625, ~ *furlonge* 1638, *Lamcoates Feilde* 1625, 1638, *the Lamcotes Feild* 1700, *v.* **lamb, cot, feld**; one of the great fields of the village); Lane Cl (*v.* **lane**); Little Mdw; Long Cl; Long Mdw; Lower Cl; Middle Cl; Mill Fd; Mill Mdw; New Cl; New Mdw; Nooks Cl (*v.* **nōk**); Little ~ ~, Oaty Cl (*the oaty closes* 1700, *v.* **āte**); Old Mdw; Pane Cl (with the surn. *Pane, v.* Reaney *s.n.* Pain); Bottom, Top Pasture Piece (*v.* **pece**); Pingle Cl, Pingle Pool Cl (*v.* **pingel**); Pitt Fd, Pitt Field Pasture (*v.* **pytt**); Far, Near Pond Cl; Rimington Mdw (with the surn. *Rim(m)ington*, cf. *Edward Rimmington* 1700 of Croxton Kerrial); Sand Pit Cl (*v.* **sand-pytt**); Scroggs (*v.* **scrogge**); South Hill; Far, Near Stackyard Cl (*v.* **stak-ȝeard**); Stone Bridge Hole (*v.* **hol**[1]); Stone Pen Cl (*v.* **penn**[2]); Street Cl (x2) (*v.* **strǣt**; both closes were beside principal roads, but only one related to the Roman road Margary 58a); Three Cornered Cl (*v.* **three-cornered**); Far, Near Well Cl, Great Field Well Cl (*v.* **wella** and Great Fd *supra*); Wheat Cl; Wilkinson Cl (with the surn. *Wilkinson*).

(b) *Little Alby* 1612 (*v.* **bȳ**; recording a lost farmstead, perh. named from a Scand *Áli* or *Alli* and poss. an earlier form of Amby *supra*); *Beaumonts closes alias Would closes* 1630 (with the surn. *Beaumont, v. Would closes, infra*); *atte Brigg* 1381 SR (p) (*v.* **atte, brycg, bryggja**; perh. to be identified with Stone Bridge (Hole) *supra*); *whereon the Buttes stand* 1625 (*v.* **butt**[2]); *the Church Lays* 1690 (*v.* **leys** and St Denys' Church *supra*); *the Clay Furlonge* 1638 (in Clay Fd); (*the*) *Crabbe layes* 1601, 1625, *Crab leas* 1612, ~ *Leyes* 1638 (*v.* **crabbe, leys**); *atte Grange* 1381 SR (p) (*v.* **atte, grange** and Goadby Grange *supra*); *greene gate* 1625, *greane gate hedge*

1601, (the) Greenegate hedge 1612, 1638 (v. **hecg**) (v. **grēne**[1], **gata**); hall woodes 1612 (v. **wudu** and Goadby Hall supra); othe hay 1381 SR (p) (v. **(ge)hæg**); the high way 1601, 1638 (v. **hēah-weg**); Shorte Home 1601, longe, short houme 1612, Long, Short Home 1625, Longe, Shorte holme 1638 (v. **holmr**); the Homestal(l) 1625, 1708 (v. **hām-stall**; the home buildings of the Parsonage house); the New, the Old Inclosure c.1745 (v. **inclosure**); Daniel Kitchins Farm 1660 × 80 (v. **ferme**); Lamstons Close c.1700 (with the surn. Lamston, evidently a p.n. in origin such as Lambton (Du) and Lampton (Mx)); langfurlanges l.12 GarCart (v. **lang**[1], **furlang**); the Leas 1674, 1660 × 80, the leeses 1700, the Lees 1708, c.1710 (v. **leys**; a close so called); the Mare Close c.1745 (with **mare** or **(ge)mǣre**); Melton balke 1612 (v. **balca**; presum. with the surn. Melton of a family originating in Melton Mowbray, five miles to the south-west); the myddle furlonge 1601, the middle furlong 1612, 1625 (v. **middel**; a furlong in South ~, later Clay Fd); the old Mill 1680 × 98, the Mill banke 1625 (v. **banke**), the Nether, the Upper Mill Closse 1674, 1660 × 80, the Mill Closes 1690, 1680 × 98, the Milne gappe 1601, the Mill gap 1612 (v. **gap**), the Mill gate 1625, over the Milne gate 1601, over the Millgate 1612 (v. **ofer**[3]), the Milngate Furlonge 1638 (v. **gata**), (the) Milln home 1674, c.1710, the Mill-home 1660 × 80 (v. **holmr**) (v. **myln**); the north feilde 1612 (v. **norð**, **feld**; an earlier name for Lamcoates Feilde, one of the great fields of the township, v. Windmill field, infra); the old Lane 1690; the Parsonadge Furlonge 1638, the Parsonage layes 1625, Parsonadge Leyes 1638, the Parsons Lays 1680 × 98 (v. **leys**) (v. **personage**, **persone**); Pesehouwe 1265 (v. **pise**, **haugr**); Porters ground 1660 × 80 (v. **grund**; with the surn. Porter); the Red Earth furlonge 1638 (v. **rēad**, **eorðe**); the South feilde 1612 (v. **sūð**, **feld**; an alternative name for Clay Fd, one of the great fields of the village); the Swannes neast 1601, the Swans nest 1612 (v. **swan**[1], **nest**); Syr George his closes 1601 (belonging to Sir George Villiers, cf. Sir Gorge Villiers Cloase (1605) in Eastwell f.ns. (b)); the 2 & twenty Acres 1680 × 98, the two and twenty Acres 1700, Twenty two Acres Close 1701 (v. **æcer**); Waldrons ground 1660 × 80 (v. **grund**; with the surn. Waldron); Westby hades 1601, 1612, Westbye Heades 1638 (if not with the surn. Westby (v. Reaney s.n.), then recording a lost farmstead, v. **west**, **vestr**, **bȳ**, **hēafod**); Wheywelle 1265 ('whey spring or stream', v. **hwæg**, **wella**; the precise implication of the name is uncertain, but the colour or nature of the water seems to be described); Wykham dale 1601, Wickham Dale 1612, 1625, Wichamdale 1638 (v. **dalr**), Wykham hill 1601, Wickam ~ 1612, Wickham ~ 1625 (Wycomb adjoins to the south-west); Windmill field 1701, 1708 (one of the great fields, prob. a later name for Lamcoates Feilde, supra); Would closes 1630 (v. **wald** and Beaumonts closes, supra).

Freeby

1. FREEBY

Fredebi 1086 DB, *Fredebia* c.1130 LeicSurv, *Fredeby* 1276 RH,
1280 Cl
Fretheby 1227, 1229 Ch, 1230, 1233 Cl, Hy 3 *Crox* (freq) *et freq* to
1417, 1419 *Comp et passim* to 1560 *Rut*, 1605 Ipm, *Frethebye*
1599 Fine
Fritheby 1303 Pat, 1322 Cl, 1331 Fine *et passim* to 1359 Pat, 1370
Cl, *Frytheby* 1361 Ipm, 1363 Inqaqd (p) *et passim* to 1467 *Deed*,
1477 Pat, *Frythby* 1395 Hastings (p), 1467 *Deed*
Frethby 1406 (1449) *WoCart*, 1488 Ipm, 1525 *Comp*, 1634 Fine,
Frethbye 1599, 1604, 1607 ib
Freythby e.14 (1449) *WoCart*, *Freytheby* 1415 Ass, 1416 *Comp*,
Freithby 1473 *CCR*, 1496 Ipm, *Freathbie* 1634 Fine, *Freathby*
1657 *Deed*, 1658 Fine
Freyby 1473 *CCR*, 1526 AAS, *Freybie* 1632 Fine, *Frayby* 1525
AAS, 1539 *Deed*, *Fraybe* 1539 MinAccts, *Fraybey* 1581 LEpis,
Fraby 1576 Saxton, 1622 Burton
Freby 1518 Visit, 1535 VE, 1575 Ipm, 1666 SR, *Frebye* 1552 AAS,
Freebie 1604 SR, *Freaby* 1620 LML, *Freeby* 1607 Fine *et freq*

'Fræthi's farmstead, village', *v.* **bȳ**. The pers.n. *Fræthi* (*Frethi*) is
ODan.

COVERMILL HILL, *v.* **cover(t)**, **myln**. FREEBY FOX EARTH, *v.* **eorðe**.
FREEBY LODGE. FREEBY WOOD, 1806 Map, 1844 *TA*. THE GRANGE, *v.*
grange. HIGHFIELD HO. NEW PLANTATION. POOLE'S LODGE FM (WOOD
FM 2½"), with the surn. *Poole*. THE SCHOOL, cf. *Schoolhouse Close*
1844 *TA*. ST MARY'S CHURCH, *The Church* 1877 White, *Church (St
Mary)* 1925 Kelly; it is earlier recorded in the group *capellas Burton
Ketylby et Fretheby* 1220 MHW (with MLat *capella* 'a chapel').WEST
LODGE (GLEBE LODGE 2½"), *v.* **glebe**.

FIELD-NAMES

Undated forms in (a) are 1844 *TA*. Forms throughout dated 1550 are *Pochin* and e.17 are *Rental*.

(a) Four ~, Six Acres (*the Six Acres* e.17), Seven ~, Fourteen ~, Sixteen Acres (*v.* **æcer**); Beckham (*v.* **bekkr, hamm**); Bellowsick, ~ Hill (*Bal(l)o Syke* 1550, *v.* **sík** and *Belawe* in adjoining Saxby f.ns. (b)); Bridge Cl; Brigg Close Mdw (*v.* **bryggja**); Broad Mdw; Brownshill (with the surn. *Brown*); Chiseldines Mdw (with the surn. *Chiseldine*, common in neighbouring Rutland); Corn Part (*v.* **corn**[1], **part**); Cottage Cl (*v.* **cotage**); Cottagers Pasture (*v.* **cotager**); the Cover (*v.* **cover(t)**); Cow Cl; Draycott ('the shed where drays are kept', *v.* **dræg, cot**); Egril(s) (*Egorhill* 1550, *Eager hill Close* e.17, *Egyrill hades* 1550 (*v.* **hēafod**), *v.* **æcer, hyll**); Ewe Cl (*v.* **eowu**); Freeby Gorse 1795 Nichols (*v.* **gorst**); Freeby Pasture 1806 Map (cf. *The Cow Pasture* e.17, *v.* **pasture**); Grantham Gate (1550, *v.* **gata**; the road to Grantham which lies to the north-east in Lincs.); The Great Cl; Great Mdw; Ham (*v.* **hamm**, cf. Ham Bridge in Wyfordby); The Hill (*del Hull* 1327 SR (p), *v.* **hyll**); Home Cl (*v.* **home**); The Homes (*v.* **holmr**); Bottom ~ ~, Top ~ ~, Horse Cl (*Horse close* e.17, *v.* **hors**); Lawn Mdw (*v.* **launde**); Little Fd; Little Mdw; Long Cl; Long Mdw; Far ~, Near ~, Mickendales (*micull dale* 1550, *v.* **micel, mikill**; with **dalr** or **deill**); Middle Gates, Great Middle Gate, Middle Gate Cl (*midle gate* 1550, *v.* **middel, gata**); Upper ~ ~, Mill Fd (*The Milne feild and Meadow* e.17, *v.* **myln**); Moldewarp (an enclosure regularly blighted by molehills thrown up by the **moldewarp** or mole); The Nest, Nest Mdw (*v.* **næs, nes** 'piece of land round which a river flows to form a headland', in this case R. Eye; cf. Great Nest further downstream in Burton Lazars); New Cl; New Dale (*v.* **deill**); New Fd; Old Ground (*v.* **ald, grund**); Old Salls Cl (poss. with the surn. *Sall/Salles*, *v.* Reaney *s.n.*); Great, Little Over Mdw (*v.* **uferra**); Peaseland Mdw (*Paisland* 1550, *Peaseland Close* e.17, *v.* **pise, land**); Pingle (*v.* **pingel**); Road Cl; Rough Piece (*v.* **rūh**[1], **pece**); Seed Cl (*v.* **sǣd**; in f.ns., often used of areas of sown grass); Shepherds Ho. (*v.* **scēp-hirde**); The Stock, The Bottom, The Top Stock, Stock Mdw (*v.* **stoc**); Three cornered Mdw (*v.* **three-cornered**); Top Orchard; Top Plough Cl (*v.* **plōg**); Townend Cl (*v.* **tūn, ende**); Upper Fd (*The Uppe feild* (sic) e.17; with either **uppe** or **upper**); Wades Cl (with the surn. *Wade*); Wallo Cl (sic) (this may contain the sb. *wallow* 'a swine-wallow etc.' or may belong with Bellowsick *supra*, from earlier confusion of upper case *B* with *W* (cf. *Ballo* 1550); but note *Nethersole dyke* in f.ns. (b) *infra*); Wheat Cl; Wood Cl.

(b) *Acherne Wong* 1550 (*v.* **æcern, vangr**); *the beck*, ~ *beke* 1550 (*v.* **bekkr**); *Bingborow leyes* 1550 (*v.* **bingr, berg, lǣs**); *Blake moulde* 1550 (*v.* **blæc, molde**); *bondlands* 1550 (*v.* **bond, land**); *Brent Clyff* 1550 (*v.* **clif**; prob. with **brant** rather than with **brente**, cf. Brentingby *infra*); *Brode gate* 1550 (*v.* **brād, gata**); *bull pyts* 1550 (*v.* **bula, pytt**; presum. a venue for bull-baiting); *Bys(se) dyke*, ~ *ha(i)des* 1550 (*v.* **dík, hēafod**; the first el. may be (**ge)bysce** 'a copse of bushes'); *the Cockle Close* e.17 (*v.* **coccel**); *the common hades* 1550 (*v.* **commun, hēafod**); *the Cottyers Close* e.17 (*v.* **cottere**); *at the Crose* 1550 (*v.* **cros**; a furlong so called); *the crosse greene gate* 1550 (*v.* **cross, grēne**[1], **gata**); *Croxton furlong* 1550 (*v.* **furlang**; either with the surn. *Croxton* (based on Croxton Kerrial or South Croxton, both in Leics.) or referring to lands of Croxton Abbey if The Grange *supra* is of monastic origin); *Curce gate* (sic) 1550 (*v.* **gata**; presum. the first el. is **caucie** 'a causeway' rather than a poor spelling of 'church', cf. *kirk(e)gate* of the same date *infra*); *Derby Wong* 1540 *Ct* (*v.* **vangr**; with the surn. *Derby*); *the Doue Coate & orchard* e.17 (*v.* **dove-cot(e)**); *long dowe* 1550, *Dow but* 1550 (*v.* **butte**) (*v.* **dowe**; presum. applied to describe the doughy texture of the soil here, *v.* OED *s.v.* dough sb. 3); *Dowkey wong* 1550 (*v.* **docce, -ig**³, **vangr**); *Dry holme* 1550 (*v.* **holmr**); *the earles land* 1550 (*v.* **eorl, land**; with reference to the second Earl of Rutland whose Compotus Rolls in Belvoir Castle refer to holdings here); *East field* 1550 (*v.* **ēast, feld**; one of the great fields of the village); *Flatland* 1550 (*v.* **flatr, land**); *the Fulbeckes* 1550 (*v.* **fūl, bekkr**); *Gon Wong* 1550 (*v.* **vangr**; the first el. may be the Scand pers.n. *Gunni*, with *o* for *u* perh. due to AN spelling or to later *o* for *u* before *n* in order to avoid minim confusion); *greene grasse* 1550 (*v.* **grēne**², **græs**; presum. a plot next to the village green rather than indicating superior fertility, otherwise **grēne**¹); *atte Grene* 1332 SR (p) (*v.* **atte, grēne**²); *hartes well* 1550 (*v.* **wella**; with either OE **heorot** 'a hart' or the ME surn. *Hart* which derives from it); *the highway* (*going from Freby to Melton*) 1550 (*v.* **hēah-weg**); *hill furlong* 1550 (*v.* **furlang**), *hill haydes* 1550 (*v.* **hēafod**) (*v.* **hyll** and The Hill in f.ns. (a) *supra*); *hounghill* (sic) 1550 (poss. 'hill with poor soil', *v.* **hungor, hyll** and *Hungerhyl* in neighbouring Wyfordby f.ns. (b); but the form may belong with *hundhill* following); *hundhill*, ~ *more* 1550 (*v.* **hund, hyll, mōr**¹); *kirk(e)gate* 1550 (*v.* **kirkja, gata**); *the kirke wong* 1550 (*v.* **kirkja, vangr**); *long breches* 1550 (*v.* **lang**¹, **brēc**); *longlands* 1550 (*v.* **lang**¹, **land**); *Melton gate* 1550 (*v.* **gata**; the road to Melton Mowbray which lies to the west); *Est More* 1550 (*v.* **ēast**), *the greate More* 1550 (*v.* **grēat**), *litle, mickle, Mykill More* 1550 (*v.* **lȳtel, lítill, micel, mikill**), *Milne More* 1550 (*v.* **myln**), *More Furlong* 1550 (*v.* **furlang**), *More gate* 1550 (*v.* **gata**), *More hades* 1550 (*v.* **hēafod**) (all with **mōr**¹, **mór**); *the Neather feild* e.17 (*v.* **neoðera, feld**); *the New Inclosure* e.17 (*v.* **inclosure**); *North fielde* 1550 (*v.* **norð, feld**; one of the great fields of the village); *Saxbie hades* 1550 (*v.* **hēafod**), *Saxby Mere* 1550 (*v.* **(ge)mǣre**) (Saxby adjoins to the east); *Sewardes wong* 1550 (*v.* **vangr**; the first el. may be an early pers.n., either OE *Sǣweard* or OE *Sigeweard* or ODan *Sigwarth* (ON *Sigvarðr*), but more prob. the surn. *Seward*, a ME reflex of any of these pers.ns.); *Small haides* 1550 (*v.* **smæl, hēafod**); *Nethersole dyke, Oversole dyke* 1550 (**neoðera, uferra, sol**¹, **dík**; referring to a wallowing place for cattle, perh. cf. Wallo Cl *supra*); *South field* 1550 (*v.* **sūð, feld**; one of the great fields of the village); *a headland called Sprekley* 1550 (*v.* **hēafod-land**; belonging to *Thomas Sprekley* 1550); *Standing furlong* 1550 (*v.* **standing, furlang**); *Stondale, Stondall* 1550 (*v.* **stān**; with **dalr** or **deill**); *Stonpittes leyes* 1550 (*v.* **stān-pytt, leys**); *Stowe furlong* 1550 (*v.* **stōw, furlang**); *Strykiswell, nether Strykeswell* 1550 (*v.* **wella, neoðera**; the first el. is a pers.n., either ON *Stríkr* (a by-name, cf. Norw dial. *strik* 'a bag') or, less likely, OE *Stric* which Redin (24) explains as a strong variant of OE *Stric(c)a*, cf. Strixton, Nth 197, where *Stríc* is taken as an Anglo-Scand version of ON *Stríkr*); *Thorne headland* 1550 (*v.* **þorn, hēafod-land**); *the towne furlonge* 1550 (*v.* **tūn, furlang**); *the tythe wong* 1550 (*v.* **tēoða, vangr**); *Tythow* 1550 (*v.* **haugr**; the first el. may be the ME bird-name **tit/tyt**, surviving in *tomtit, titmouse* and *titling* (the hedge-sparrow)); *the West field* 1550 (*v.* **west, feld**; one of the great fields of the village); *Wiverby dale* 1550 (*v.* **dalr**; Wyfordby adjoins to the south-west); *Woldall hill* 1550 (*v.* **wald, hyll**; with the second el. prob. **deill**); *Woodgate* 1550 (*v.* **wudu, gata**); *Wygacer* 1550 (*v.* **æcer**; the first el. is either the OE pers.n. *Wi(c)ga* or OE **wigga** 'a beetle' (surviving in *earwig*)).

2. BRENTINGBY

> *Brantingbia* c.1130 LeicSurv, *Brantingby* Hy 2 Dugd, 1209 × 35 RHug, m.13 (1404), 13 (1404) *Laz*, 1262 FineR, 1314 Banco (p), 1322 Hastings (p), *Brantyngby* 1305 Banco (p), 1316 Ch, 1414 (1449) *WoCart et passim* to 1488 Ipm, 1535 VE, *Brantyngbye* 1539 *Deed*
>
> *Brantingebi* 1190 × 1204 France, 1212 P (p), *Brantingeby* 1156 (1318) Ch
>
> *Brentingbi* l.12 Dane (p), Hy 3 *Rut*, m.13 (1404) (p), 13 (1404) *Laz* (p) bis, *Brentingby* e.13 (1404) *ib*, e.Hy 3 *Rut* bis, m.13 (1404) *Laz*, 1261 Ass, Hy 3 *Crox* (freq) *et passim* to 1542 Fine, 1610 Speed *et freq*, *Brentyngby* m.13 (1449), l.13 (1449) *WoCart*, 1272 Cur *et passim* to 1307 (1449), 1309 (1449) *WoCart et freq* to 1449 *ib*, 1473 *CCR et passim* to 1549, 1557 Pat, (~ *iuxta Melton'* 1306 (1449) *WoCart*), (~ *iuxta Thorpe Ernald* 1338 Banco)
>
> *Brentingebi* 1170 P (p), e.13 (1404) (p), 13 (1404) *Laz*, *Brentengebi* 1171 P (p), *Brentingeby* 1214 Cur (p), 1276 RH, 13 (1404) *Laz* bis, *Brentyngeby* 1228 × 43 Blore (p), 1428 FA

A name which presents several problems. The late OE pers.ns. *Branting* and *Brenting* are both recorded independently. *Branting* is present in DB (*v.* Feilitzen 207) while *Brenting* appears as a surety in the *Medeshamstede* (Peterborough) charter BCS 1130 of c.980 (not included in *Anglo-Saxon Charters* by P.H. Sawyer). If the p.n. were simply a compound of one of these late OE pers.ns. with **bȳ** 'a farmstead, a village', it would be difficult to make a positive choice between them because of AN interchange of *a* and *e* (*v.* Feilitzen 44).

Ekwall DEPN *s.n.* Brentingby notes the recurring forms with -*inge*- spellings and suggests that possibly we have here 'the *bȳ* of Brant's people', the whole based on an early OE -*ingas* formation *Brantingas. The creation of a p.n. consisting of an English folk-name compounded with a Scand habitative generic would be unusual (but note Tealby, L **3** 131–36 and the possible example of Beckingthorpe in Bottesford *supra*). However, there is no reason to posit -*inga*- > -*inge*- here. The -*inge*- spellings could be the result of strong Scand influence on the genitival structure of either of the late OE pers.ns. *Branting/Brenting*. Such influence is a common feature of Lincs. p.ns. For example, Audleby (with *Aldwulf*), L 2 88 and Barnetby le Wold (perh. with *Beornnōð*), L 2 8 both show a consistent genitival *e* rather than the usual *es*. Autby (perh. with *Æðelwald*), L 4 167 has *es* in its DB form but subsequently has only *e*. Ekwall (*Selected Papers* 66) believes that spellings with medial *e* as in *Adulvebi* (Audleby) stem from an original Scand gen.sg. in *-ar-* > *-a-* and that such names were created by Scandinavians, even where an OE pers.n. occurs as first el.

Finally, there is the possibility that the first el. of Brentingby may be an early OE p.n. **Branting/*Brenting*, compounding *brant* 'steep' with the p.n.-forming suffix *-ing*, hence 'the steep place, the steep hill' (cf. *Brenting(e)* 960 BCS 1054 (S 683) in Hampshire). Brentingby stands on a steep slope above the flood-plain of R. Eye. Note the similar possibility of an early base for Beckingthorpe in Bottesford *supra*, while Wyfordby which adjoins Brentingby is certainly an earlier English topographical p.n. with *bȳ* suffixed, cf. Blackfordby in West Goscote Hundred.

In sum, Brentingby may be explained either as 'Branting's or Brenting's farmstead, village' or as 'the farmstead, village at **Branting* (i.e. 'the steep place')', *v.* **bȳ**, (**brant, -ing**^{2}).

BELL'S PLANTATION, cf. *Bells Close* 1850 *TA*; with the surn. *Bell*. *George Bell* 1846 White farmed from Freeby. BRENTINGBY LODGE FM. BRENTINGBY WOOD is *Brentingby Spinney* 1824 O, 1850 *TA*, *v.* **spinney**. COTTAGE FM. GLEBE LODGE, cf. *Glebe Close* 1850 *TA*, *v.* **glebe**. THE HALL, *atte Hall* 1381 SR (p), *Brentingby Hall* 1850 *TA*, *v.* **hall**, **atte**. HILLS BARN FM. OLD CANAL is *the Oakham Canal* 1821 *Terrier*, *the Old Melton and Oakham Canal* 1850 *TA*. PINFOLD LEES HILL, *Pinfold* 1850 *TA*, *Pinfold Leys*, ~ ~ *meadow* 1850 *ib*, *v.* **pynd-fald**, **leys**. ST MARY'S CHURCH, *Brentingby Church and Churchyard* 1850 *TA*; with fabric of the early 14th cent., it is recorded as *capellam de Brantingb'* 1220 MHW (with MLat *capella* 'a chapel'), *The Chapel* 1877 White. WEST END FM, *v.* **ende**.

FIELD-NAMES

Undated forms in (a) are 1850 *TA*; 1848 are *Plan*. Forms throughout dated 1601, c.1630 and 1700 are *Terrier*; 1718, 1719 and 1744 are *Reeve*.

(a) Two ~, Three ~, Eight ~, Ten Acres (*v.* **æcer**); Barn Cl (x 3); Big Cl, ~ ~ Mdw; Bottom Cl (*v.* **bottom**); Brook Cl (*v.* **brōc**); Broom Cl (*v.* **brōm**); Cock Cl (*v.* **cocc²**); The Conery (*v.* **coningre**); The Copy (*v.* **copis**; the spelling *copy* is due to the popular reconstruction of a 'singular' form); Cow Cl; Cumberland Cl, Cumberland Flatt (*v.* **flat**), Cumberland Mdw (*v.* Cumberland Spinney in adjoining Wyfordby); Far Cl; Five Acre Moor (cf. *the moores* 1601, c.1630, *Moore nooke* c.1630 (*v.* **nōk**), *v.* **mōr¹**); Great Cl or Cumberland Cl (*v.* Cumberland Cl *supra*); The Gorse Cl, Nether, Upper Gorse Cl (*the Upper Goss Close* 1744, cf. *the goss or neates pasture* 1601, *little gosse leayes* c.1630 (*v.* **leys**), *v.* **gorst** and The Pasture *infra*); Hicklings Big Cl, Hicklings Mdw (with the surn. *Hickling* of a family originating in the village of this name nine miles to the north-west in Notts.); Home Cl 1848, 1850 (*v.* **home**); House Cl (cf. *Manor House* 1863 White, *v.* **maner**; no doubt with reference to The Hall *supra*); Hovel Cl (*v.* **hovel**); Ladies Cl (*v.* **lavedi**; a preceding def.art. is deleted in the MS); Lock Cl (x2) (*v.* **lock**; containing canal locks of the old Melton and Oakham Canal); The Meadow; Middle Fd; Middle Ground (*v.* **grund**); Nether Fd; Old Cl (*The Old Close* 1700, *v.* **ald**); Paddock (*v.* **paddock**); The Pasture (cf. *neates pasture* 1601, *v.* **nēat, pasture**); Bottom, Middle, Top Plough Cl (*v.* **plōg**); Ploughed Cl; Pump Mdw (*v.* **pumpe**); Seed Cl (*v.* **sǣd**; in f.ns., used of areas of sown grass); Sills's Cl (with the surn. *Sills*); Snow Cl (either with the surn. *Snow* or indicating a close where snow lay long, *v.* **snāw**, cf. *Snow Wong* in Harby f.ns. (b)); Spinney Cl (*v.* **spinney**); Three corner'd Piece 1848 (*v.* **three-cornered, pece**); Top Cl; The Upper Cl 1795 *Reeve* (poss. to be identified with Top Cl *supra*); Wash Dyke (*v.* **wash-dyke**; a close containing a sheep-dip).

(b) *(the) Bases Close* 1718, 1719 (cf. *Will'm Basse* 1564 *Gret* and *Edward Basse* 1630 *ib* of neighbouring Stapleford); *Belland Sycke* 1601 (*v.* **sík**), *Bellonds* c.1630, *Bellams Close* 1700 (*v.* **land** and Bellands in Bottesford f.ns. (a)); *castle hades* 1601, *Castell hades* c.1630 (*v.* **castel(l), hēafod**; there appear to survive the earthworks of a stronghold beside the parish church at Wyfordby; note *Castelgate* in the north of Burton Lazars parish which adjoins to the south-west, which may be explained with reference to this site); *the east fyelde* 1601, *the Easte feilde* c.1630 (*v.* **ēast, feld**; one of the great fields of the village); *Ellondes* 1601 (*v.* **ēa, land**; beside R. Eye); *Floritoft* 1351 Nichols (*v.* **toft**; prob. either with the ME fem. pers.n. *Flori(a)* (from MLat *flos* 'a flower') or its surn. reflex *Flory*, *v.* Reaney *s.n.*); *Mr Jacombs land* 1700 (*v.* **land**); *lytledale* c.1630 (*v.* **lȳtel, lítill**; with **dalr** or **deill**); *mooregate* 1601 (*v.* **mōr¹**, **mór**, **gata**; the road continued in Wyfordby); *the Midle Close* 1700 (*v.* **middel**); *the Parsons Close* 1700 (*v.* **persone**); *a wonge called St Nicholas* c.1630 (*v.* **vangr**; *St Nicholas* may have been an earlier dedication of the now defunct parish church, but otherwise perh. land assigned to the upkeep of a chapel so called in the church); *Shedgate*, c.1630 (*v.* **(ge)scēad, gata**; also recorded in adjoining Wyfordby); *the Vicars wonge* 1601, *~ Vickers ~* c.1630 (*v.* **vikere, vangr**); *Waulthamheuydland* Hy 3 *Crox* (*v.* **hēafod-land**; Waltham on the Wolds adjoins to the north); *the weast fyelde* 1601, *the West feilde* c.1630 (*v.* **west, feld**; one of the great fields of the village); *Wiverby open common* 1700 (*v.* **open, commun**; Wyfordby adjoins to the east).

3. SAXBY

> *Saxebi* 1086 DB, 1176 P, 1198 Cur *et passim* to 13 (1449) *WoCart*
> (p), 1362 BPR, *Saxebia* 1175 P, *Saxeby* c.1141 Dugd, 1150 × 59,
> 1163 TutP, c.1200 (14) *BrCart et passim* to 1254 Val, 1257 *Rut*
> *et freq* to 1348, 1349 Pat *et passim* to 1376 Cl, 1380 GR, 1428 FA
> *Saxenebi* 1175 ChancR, 1198 Cur
> *Sessebia* c.1130 LeicSurv, *Sessebi* 1202 P, *Sauceby* 1199 ib
> *Sexeby* 1220 Cur, 1209 × 35 RHug *et passim* to 1245 × 64 (14)
> *BrCart*, 1338 Pat
> *Saxby* c.1200 (14), 1218 × 45 (14) *BrCart*, 1278 Coram *et passim* to
> a.1350 *BrCart*, 1359 Pat *et freq*, *Saxbye* 1575, 1576 LEpis, 1576
> LibCl, 1576 Saxton, *Saxbye alias Sawsby* 1577 LEpis
> *Sawsby* 1690 *Terrier*, *Sausby* 1674, 1679, 1697 *ib*

Either 'the farmstead, village of the Saxons' or 'Saxi's farmstead,
village', *v.* **bȳ**. The common ON, ODan pers.n. *Saxi/Saksi* may be the
first el. of the name of this settlement, cf. Saxby All Saints, L **2** 54.
However, in view of the two surviving early forms in *Saxenebi*, more
likely is the folk-name **S(e)axe** (**S(e)axna** gen.pl.), although by the date
of such a name's formation, the Danes were unlikely to have been able
to distinguish between Angles and Saxons. They no doubt used the two
folk-names synonymously. W. Levison, *England and the Continent in
the Eighth Century* (Oxford 1946), 92, observes that as early as the first
half of the 8th cent., there did not seem to be any distinction between the
use of the names in England. A continuing strong Anglo-Saxon presence
in this area would account for such a name as neighbouring Wyfordby
(*q.v.*). Nearby Brentingby may be of a similar construction to Wyfordby,
with an early English p.n. compounded with *bȳ*. Also indicative of
strong English presence here is the extensive late 6th cent. pagan Anglo-
Saxon cemetery found near the railway station in 1823.

THE ELMS. THE GRANGE, *v.* **grange**. MANOR HO., *Manor House* 1877
White, *v.* **maner**. PILE BRIDGE FM, *v.* **pīl**, cf. Pile Bridge, Ru 155. THE
RECTORY, 1877 White, 1925 Kelly, *Rectory House* 1821 *Terrier*; it is
the mansyon house 1625 *ib*, *v.* **mansion-house**. RICKETT'S SPINNEY,
Riggates 1625, 1674 *Terrier*, *Riggotts* 1679 *ib*, *Riggots* 1690, c.1695,
1.17 *ib*, *v.* **riggett, spinney**. ST PETER'S CHURCH, *Church (St Peter)*
1846, 1863, 1877 White; the early church is recorded as *ecclesie de
Sexeby* 1220 MHW, *ecclesiam Sancti Petri de Sexeb'* 1237 RGros,

ecclesiam ~ ~, *ecclesie de Saxeby* 1239, 1245 ib, 1297, 1345 *Pat*. Note also *the chapel yard* 1568 *Gret* (*v*. **chapel(e)**, **geard**), *the churchyard* 1625 *Terrier*, *the Church-Yard* 1821 *ib*. SAXBY STATION.

FIELD-NAMES

Forms in (a) dated 1762 and 1821 are *Terrier*. Forms throughout dated 1625, 1674, 1679, 1690, c.1695, 1697, 1.17 and 1763 are also *Terrier*.

(a) (the) Church Cl 1762, 1821 (*v*. St Peter's Church *supra*); Gallow Hill 1762, 1821 (1625, 1679, 1690, c.1695, 1697, 1.17, *Gallie Hill* 1674, *upper-Gallow-Hill* 1736, *Gallow Hill Feild* 1679, 1690, 1697, 1.17, ~ ~ *field* c.1695, *Galie Hill feild* 1674 (*v*. **feld**; one of the great fields of the village), 'the gallows hill', *v*. **galga**).

(b) *Allens hades* 1625 (*v*. **hēafod**), *Allens Hedlea* 1625 (*v*. **headley**) (with the surn. *Allen*); *Badmore* 1674, 1679, 1690, c.1695, 1697, 1.17, *Badmore Feild* 1674, 1679, 1690, 1697, 1.17, ~ *field* c.1695 (*v*. **feld**; one of the great fields of the township, formerly *the west feild, infra*), *Badmore middle furlong* 1674 (*v*. **mōr**[1]; prob. with **badde** 'worthless', although the OE pers.n. *Badda* cannot be discounted as first el., *v*. VEPN *s.v*. ***badde**); *Barrows banke* 1625 (*v*. **banke**), *Barrowes* ~, *Barrowghes hades* 1625 (*v*. **hēafod**), *Barrows hedlea* 1625 (*v*. **headley**), *Barrowes wonge* 1625 (*v*. **vangr**) (all with the surn. *Barrow*); *Bartley Leas* 1625 (*v*. **leys**; prob. with a surn. *Bartley*, but otherwise with a p.n. *Bartley* 'birch wood' (*v*. **berc**, **lēah**, cf. Bartley Regis (Ha) and Bartley Green (Wo 348)), though modern local flora would argue against the latter interpretation); *the beckes* 1625, *the Becks* 1674, 1679, 1690, 1697, 1.17 (*v*. **bekkr**); *Belawe* 1297 Ipm ('the bell-shaped hill or mound', *v*. **belle**, **hlāw**); *Bellands* 1625, 1674, *Bellams* 1679, 1690, c.1695, 1697, 1.17, *Bellandes close* 1625, *Bellems Close* 1720 *Gret* (*v*. Bellands in Bottesford f.ns. (a)); *betwixt the* (*two*) *closses* c.1695, 1697 (*v*. **clos(e)**; a furlong so called); *the Black(e) ground* 1674, 1679, 1690, c.1695, 1.17 (*v*. **blæc**, **grund**; either referring to the colour of the soil or to its fertility (or both), since eModE dial. *black* was used in the sense 'fertile' in contrast to *white* 'infertile'); *the bridge* 1625, (*the*) *Brigg* 1679, 1690, c.1695, 1.17, *Great Brigg* 1674, *the Brigg Close* 1679, 1690, c.1695, 1.17, *Brig furlonge* 1625, (*the*) *Brigg furlong* 1674, 1679, 1690, *Brigg furloung* c.1695, 1.17, *the brig furloung* 1697 (*v*. **furlang**) (*v*. **brycg**, **bryggja**); *Brokesby hades* 1625 (in *the Easte feilde, infra*), *Broxsbey hades* 1625 (in *the west feild, infra*) (*v*. **hēafod**; with the surn. *Brooksby* of a family originating in the Leics. village of this name nine miles to the south-west); *Bowlling leyes* 1674, *boudling leys* 1697, *Bowling green Leys* 1690, *boudling green leys* c.1695, 1.17 (*v*. **bowling**, **bowling-green**, **leys**); *Caudell-heads* 1679, *Cawdle heads* 1690, *Caudale hades* c.1695, *Caudle h(e)ads* 1697, 1.17 (*v*. **cald**, **wella**, **hēafod**); *the Church Leas* 1625, ~ ~ *leyes* 1674, ~ ~ *Leys* 1690, c.1695, 1697, 1.17, *Church-Leyes* 1679, *-Lees* 1736 (*v*. **leys** and St Peter's Church *supra*); *Clarkes hades* 1625 (*v*. **hēafod**), *Clarkes hedland* 1625 (*v*. **hēafod-land**; in both *the north feild* and *the west feild*), *Clarkes hedlea* 1625 (*v*. **headley**) (with the surn. *Clarke*); *the Colepytt way* 1625, *Coalepitt waye* 1674, *Cole cart way* 1690, *the coale cart way* c.1695 (*v*.

col-pytt; the forms presum. refer to the same track leading from a place where charcoal was made); *Cowdale* 1625 (ostensibly 'cow valley' (*v.* **cū, dalr**), but this form may belong with *Caudell, supra*); *the Cow Dames* 1674, *Cowdams* 1679, 1690, 1.17, *cow dam* c.1695, *the Cow Dame Leys* 1697 (*v.* **leys**) (*v.* **cū, damme** and the *neatdames, infra*; an artificially created pool for watering cattle, situated in *the north feild*); *the Cow pole* 1625 (*v.* **cū, pōl**¹; in *the west feild* and not to be identified with *Cowdam(s)*); *the Crose Leas* 1625 (*v.* **cross, leys**); *the daile* 1690, c.1695, *North Daile* c.1695 (*v.* **deill**); *the Dale* 1625, 1679, 1690, c.1695, 1697, 1.17 (*v.* **dalr**), (*the*) *North Dale* 1625, 1674, 1690, c.1695, 1.17 (may belong with *North Daile, supra*, otherwise *v.* **dalr**); *Duuecroft* 1245 × 64 (14) BrCart, *Dovecrofte* 1625 (*v.* **croft**; either with the OE fem. pers.n. *Dūfe* or its ON equivalent *Dúfa* or OE **dūfe** (ON **dúfa**) 'a dove, a pigeon'); *Doveings* 1674 bis, *Douins* 1679, c.1695, 1.17, *Douins in the Dale* 1697 (*v. the Dale, supra*), *Dovins* 1690, *Douins Furlo(u)ng* 1697, 1.17 (*v.* **dūfe, dúfa, eng**; but a pers.n. as first el. as in the previous f.n. is poss.); *the drifte* 1625, *the Drift* 1674, 1679, 1690, c.1695, 1697, 1.17, (*the*) *Drift next Quickset(s) leyes* c.1695, 1697 (*v. Quicksett Leyes, infra*), *the neatdrift(e)* 1625 (*v.* **nēat**) (*v.* **drift**); *the Easte feilde* 1625 (*v.* **ēast, feld**; one of the great fields of the village, later *Gallow Hill Feild, v.* Gallow Hill *supra*); *flaxlandes* 1625 (*v.* **fleax, land**); *the foard* 1679, 1690, c.1695, 1697, 1.17 (*v.* **ford**; the original **stapol-ford*, the ford across R. Eye where there is now a bridge next to Bedehouses in Stapleford Park, cf. *att Stableford* 1674 (a furlong so called in *Badmore Feild, supra*) and *v.* Stapleford *infra*); *the for(e)swaiths* c.1695, 1697 (*v.* **fore, swathe**); *Fraybey beckes* 1625 (*v.* **bekkr**), *Fraybey Meare* 1625 (*v.* **(ge)mǣre**) (Freeby adjoins to the west); *fulbeckes* 1625, *Ful(l)becks* 1674, 1679, 1690, c.1695, 1.17 (*v.* **fūl, bekkr**); *the Feild next Garthorp(e)* 1674, 1679, 1690, 1.17, *the Field next Garthrop* c.1695, 1697 (*v.* **feld**; one of the great fields of the village, earlier called *the north feild, infra*), *Garthorpe hedg* 1674 (*v.* **hecg**; the parish boundary hedge), *Garthorpe waye* 1625 (*v.* **weg**) (Garthorpe adjoins to the north-east); *the gated Banke* 1625 (*v.* **gated, banke**; the earliest citation for *gated* in OED is for c.1630); *the gated Lea* 1625 (*v.* **gated, ley** and the preceding name); *Gore Wong* 1679, 1690, ~ *woung* 1.17, *goare woung* c.1695 (*v.* **gāra, vangr**); *Grantham Hades*, ~ *haid(e)s* 1674, c.1695, 1.17, ~ *heads* 1679, 1690, 1697 (*v.* **hēafod**; with the surn. *Grantham* of a family originating in the town of this name, 11 miles to the north-east in Lincs.); *de la Grene* 1327 SR (p), *super Le Grene* 1327 ib (p), *on the grene* 1332 ib (p) (*v.* **grēne**²); *the gutter* 1625 (*v.* **goter**); *Hedding Leas* 1625 (*v.* **heading, leys** and OED *s.v.* heading, vbl.sb. 6, whose earliest citation is for 1676); *the highway* 1625, 1679, 1690, c.1695, 1697, 1.17 (*v.* **hēah-weg**); *the Hole* 1625 (*v.* **hol**¹); *Hollinges* 1625, *Holings, Holleinges* 1674, *Hollings* 1674, 1690, c.1695, 1697, 1.17, *Holleins* 1679, 1690, *Hollins* 1690 ('pasture in the hollow' *v.* **hol**¹, **eng**); *the Kinges hades* 1625, *Kings haids* 1674, ~ *heads* 1679, 1690, 1697, ~ *hades* c.1695, *the Kings hads* 1.17 (*v.* **hēafod**; the dates of these forms cover the reigns on monarchs from James I to William III); *the kinges he(a)dland* 1625 (*v.* **hēafod-land**), *the kinges headlea* 1625 (*v.* **headley**) (with reference to James I or Charles I, the latter ascending the throne in March 1625); *Longe litle more* 1625, *Long Little more* 1674, 1690, ~ ~ *Moor* 1679, *Loung Little more* c.1695, 1.17, *loung litlemore* 1697 (*v.* **lang**¹, **lȳtel, mōr**¹); *Lyns Banke* 1625 (*v.* **banke**; prob; with OE **hlyn** (ON **hlynnr**) 'a maple-tree', but the surn. *Lynn* cannot be discounted, *v.* Reaney *s.n.*); *Mansdales* 1625 (*v.* (**ge**)**mǣnnes, deill**); *March Leas* 1625, (*the*) *March Ley*(*e*)*s* 1679, c.1695, 1697, 1.17, *the Marsh Leys* 1690 (*v.* **mersc, leys**); *Maxeys hedland* 1625 (*v.* **hēafod-land**; with the surn. *Maxey* of a family which originated in Maxey, Nth); *the Meare* 1625 (*v.* (**ge**)**mǣre**; the boundary between Saxby and Freeby); *Melton gate* 1625 (*v.* **gata**; the road to Melton Mowbray); (*the*) *Mill* 1674, 1679, 1690, 1.17, *the Milne* 1674, *at* (*the*) *Mill* 1690, c.1695, 1697 (a furlong so called), *the Mill Furlong* 1.17 (identical with the preceding), *the Milne Home* 1568 Gret, 1674 (*v.* **holmr**) (*v.* **myln**); *the More* 1625, 1674, c.1695, 1.17, *the Moor* 1679, 1690, *More gate* 1625 (*v.* **gata**), *more sick* c.1695, 1697, (*the*) *Moor Sick* 1679, 1690 (*v.* **sík**) (*v.* **mōr¹, mór**); *the neatheardes balke* 1625 (*v.* **balca**), *the Neatheardes land* 1625 (*v.* **land**) (*v.* **neetherd**); *the neatdames* 1625 (*v.* **nēat, damme**; an earlier name for *the Cow Dames, supra*); *neather ends* c.1695 (*v.* **neoðera, ende**); *the new brigg* 1625 (*v.* **brycg, bryggja**); *the north feild* 1625 (*v.* **norð, feld**; one of the great fields of the village, later known as *the feild next Garthorpe*); *the Parsonage hades* 1625 (*v.* **hēafod**), *the Parsonage Leas* 1625 (*v.* **leys**), *the parsonage more meadow* 1625 (*v.* **mōr¹**) (*v.* **personage**); *the parson wyllowes* 1625, *Parson Willows* 1674, 1679, 1690, *Person* ~ c.1695, 1697, 1.17 (*v.* **persone, wilig**); *the pasture* 1625, *the paster* 1674 (*v.* **pasture**); *the qui*(*c*)*ksete* 1625, *quicksetts* 1674, *Quickset*(*t*)*s Dale* 1674, c.1695, (*upon*) *Quickset*(*t*) *Dale* 1679, 1690, 1697, 1.17, (*on*) *Quickset Dale furloung* 1697 (*v.* **furlang**; in *the west feild*), *at quicksete* 1625, *Quickset*(*t*) *Dale* 1679, c.1695, *Quicksett dail* bis, *Quicksett deil* 1690 (in *the north feild*) (*v.* **quykset, deill**); *Quickset*(*t*) *Leyes* 1679, 1697, ~ *Leys* 1690, 1.17 (*v.* **quykset, leys**); *Mr Richardsons hades* 1625 (*v.* **hēafod**); *Easte or Old Saxbey* 1625 (*v.* **ēast**), *Old Sausb*(*e*)*y* 1674, 1679, *Old Sawsby* 1690, *Ould Saxby* c.1695, *Ould Sausby* 1.17, ~ ~ *Furloung* 1697 (*v.* **ald**; a furlong in *the Easte feilde*, later *Gallow hill Feild*, presum. referring to an earlier site of the settlement); *tofte hole* 1625, *Taft hole* 1674, 1679, 1690, c.1695, 1697, 1.17 (*v.* **toft, hol¹**); *the townes hades* 1625 (*v.* **tūn, hēafod**); *Tythe Wong end* 1679, 1.17, (*the*) *tyth*(*e*) *woung end* c.1695, 1697 (*v.* **tēoða, vangr, ende**); *Waltham Meare* 1625 (*v.* (**ge**)**mǣre**; Waltham on the Wolds adjoins to the north-west); (*the*) *Warrens* 1674, 1679, 1690, 1697, 1.17, *Warrings* c.1695 (*v.* **wareine**); *the Water Milne* 1625 (*v.* **water-mylne**); *atte Welle* 1381 SR (p) (*v.* **atte, wella**); *Mr Westcotes hades* 1625 (*v.* **hēafod**); *Westerlong*(*s*) 1625, 1674, *Westerloung*(*s*) c.1695, 1.17, ~ *Furlong* 1697, *Westernlong*(*s*) 1679, 1690 (*v.* **wester, lang²**); *the west feild* 1625 (*v.* **west, feld**; one of the great fields of the village, later called *Badmore Feild, supra*); *Whithouse Leas* 1625, *Whitehouse Leyes* 1679, c.1695, ~ *Leys* 1690, 1697, 1.17 (*v.* **leys**; prob. with the surn. *Whitehouse*); *wormwels hades* 1625 (*v.* **wella, hēafod**; the first el. may be the OE pers.n. *Wyrm* or **wyrm** 'a reptile', perh. in some later sense such as 'a tick' or 'a gadfly'); *Wymondham hedges* 1625 (*v.* **hecg**; a furlong at a boundary hedge of Wymondham which adjoins to the south-east); *the wyndmyll* 1625 (*v.* **wind-mylne**).

4. STAPLEFORD

Stapeford 1086 DB bis, 1159 France
Stapelford' 1087 × 1100, 1094 × 1123 TutP, c.1130 LeicSurv *et freq*
  to 1381 Pat, 1392 TutP *et passim* to 1507 Banco, 1514 CoPleas,
  (~ *super Yreck'* c.1200 (14) *BrCart*), *Stapel(l)forde* 1158 × 66
  TutP, 1227 RHug, *Stapelfordia* e.13 (1404) *Laz*, *Stapelfort* m.13
  (1404) *ib*
Estapleford c.1200 France, *Estapelforde* 1223 RHug
Stapilford' c.1141 Dugd, 1209 × 35 RHug, 1242 Fees *et passim* to
  1375 *Peake*, 1404 *Laz et freq* to 1441 (1449), 1449 *WoCart et
  passim* to 1507 Pat, (~ *iuxta Brendebrocc'* Hy 3 *Crox*),
  Stapilforde 1327 SR (p), 1375 *Deed*, 1433 (1449) *WoCart*,
  Stapylford 1428 FA, 1498 Ipm, 1526 AAS
Stapulford' 1307 (1449), 1309 (1449), 1336 (1449) *WoCart et
  passim* to 1486 Pat, 1498 Banco
Stapleford 1159 France, 1132 × 66 (14) *BrCart*, 1284 Banco *et
  passim* to 1308 Ch, 1319 Inqaqd, 1518, 1528 Visit *et freq*, (~
  super Wrethec c.1200 (14) *BrCart*), *Stapleforda* c.1200 (14) *ib*,
  Staplefordie 1218 × 25 (14) *ib*, *Stapleforde* 1535 VE, 1539 *Deed*,
  1549, 1553 Pat
Stabul(l)forth 1473 *CCR*, 1564 *Terrier*, *Stapelforth* 1548 Fine,
  Stapylforth 1549 Pat, *Staplefo(u)rth* 1561 ib, 1592 *Rut*

'The ford marked by a post', *v.* **stapol**, **ford**. The ford was presumably sited where the bridge beside Bedehouses stands. The affixes ~ *super Yreck'*, ~ *super Wrethec* (both c.1200 (14)) indicate that in the 14th cent. and earlier, the settlement was considered to lie beside R. Wreake. Nowadays, this reach of R. Wreake to the east of Melton Mowbray is known as R. Eye and the Eye may have been the pre-Scandinavian name for the whole stream. The affix ~ *iuxta Brendebrocc'* t. Hy 3 probably preserves the early name of the brook which forms the county boundary between Stapleford and Whissendine in Rutland. It is 'the brook of burnt colour, the brownish stream', *v.* **brende**[2], **brōc**, with reference to its muddy waters. Those early forms for Stapleford with prosthetic *E-* are due to AFr influence.

BEDEHOUSES is *the Hospital* 1846 White; endowed for six poor men by the first Earl of Harborough and built 1732–3, *v.* **hospital**, **bed-hūs**. BERRY COVERT is *Fox Cover* 1824 O, *v.* **cover(t)**. BRICKYARD

PLANTATION. COTTAGE PLANTATION. CUCKOO HILL, *v.* **cuccu**. DECOY
COTTAGE (BRICKYARD COTTAGE 2½"), *v.* **decoy**. THE GRANGE, *v.*
grange. HOLLYGATE, 1824 O, *holegate* 1564 *Gret*, cf. *Hollygatfelde*
1561 (1700) *Rental*, *holygate feld* 1564 *Gret, Halligate feild* 1612
Terrier, Hollow(e)gate Field 1630, 1632 *Gret, Holligat(e)* ~ 1638, 1674
Terrier (*v.* **feld**; one of the great fields of the township, also called *South
field, v.* f.ns. (b) *infra*), *v.* **hol**[2], **gata**. HOSE HILL, *v.* **hōh** (**hōs** nom.pl.).
JERICHO LODGE, 1863, 1877 White, *Jericho* 1714 LML, 1795, 1815
Map, 1824 O, *Jerico* 1786 SNav. Jericho is a 'remoteness' name,
sometimes denoting land on which sick animals were isolated; the lodge
lies at the south-western extremity of the parish, *v.* **loge** and Stapleford
Lodge *infra*. LAXTON'S COVERT, cf. *Mr Laxton* 1666 SR, *v.* **cover(t)**.
PAGET'S SPINNEY, with the surn. *Paget*. ST MARY MAGDALENE'S
CHURCH, *Church (St Mary)* 1877 White, *Church (St Mary Magdalene)*
1925 Kelly; this estate church was built in 1783 for the fourth Earl of
Harborough, but the earlier village church is recorded as *ecclesie de
Stapilford* 1220 MHW, *ecclesiam* ~ ~, *ecclesie de Stapelford* 1249
RGros, 1325 *Pat*, *the Church* 1708 (18) *Terrier*. SAWGATE RD,
SAWGATE LODGE FM (SAWGATE ROAD FM 2½"), *saugatt* 1564 *Gret*, cf.
Sawe gate furlong 1630 *ib*, *Saltgate Hedge* 1708 *Terrier*, 1708, 1744
Rental, 1744 *Surv* (*v.* **hecg**); the salters' way which continued through
adjoining Burton Lazars (*q.v.* for additional forms), *v.* **salt**[1], **gata**.
STAPLEFORD BARN. STAPLEFORD HALL, 1846, 1863, 1877 White; it is
Stapleford House 1720 MagBrit and earlier recorded as *the halle* 1564
Gret, v. **hall**. Note also *Nether Hall, infra*. STAPLEFORD LODGE, 1863
White; it is *New Jericho* 1824 O, *v.* **loge** and Jericho Lodge *supra*.
STAPLEFORD LODGE (BURTON ROAD LODGE 2½"). STAPLEFORD
MANOR, cf. *Manor farm* 1925 Kelly, *v.* **maner**. STAPLEFORD PARK,
1786 SNav, 1824 O, *v.* **park**.

FIELD-NAMES

Forms dated 1561 (1700), 1708[3] and 1744[2] are *Rental*; 1564, 1609,
1630, 1632 and 1635 are *Gret*; e.17, 1612, 1625, 1638, 1674, 1703,
1708[1], 1708[2] and 1708 (18) are *Terrier*; 1668 (1791), 1682 (1791) and
1744[1] are *Surv*.

(a) Bulham 1824 O (*Bullholme* 1632, *v.* **bula, holmr**); *Jerico hill* 1786 SNav (*v.*
Jericho Lodge *supra*).

(b) *accare dyk* 1564, *acredickes furlong* 1630, *Acre Dike Field* 1708[1], 1708 (18)
(*v.* **æcer-dīc, dík**); *Baggotts Holme* 1635 (*v.* **holmr**; with the surn. *Baggot*); *Barker
Seicke* 1632 (*v.* **sík**; with the surn. *Barker*); *Basses Cottage* 1630 (*v.* **cotage**), *Edward
Basse his Tenement* 1630 (*v.* **tenement**), *basses hades* 1564, 1630 (*v.* **hēafod**; *Will'm
Basse* is cited 1564); *Beryl Close* 1632 (prob. an earlier 'barley hill, hill where barley
is grown', *v.* **bere, hyll**); *bosard home* 1564, *Bussard holme* 1630 (*v.* **holmr**; the first
el. is either ME **bosard/busard** 'a buzzard' or the surn. *Buzzard* derived from it, *v.*
Reaney *s.n.*); *brech* 1564 (*v.* **brēc**); *brenles* 1564, *Hinging Brentley* 1630, *Hanging
Brentleys furlong* 1708[2], 1708[3], ~ *Brentleas* ~ 1744[1], ~ *Brentley* ~ 1744[2] (the prefix
hangende 'hanging' was used of places on a steep slope or hill-side, which suggests
that the first el. could be **brant** 'steep' rather than **brende**[2] 'burnt, cleared by
burning'; and it is uncertain whether the generic was originally a plural **leys** in the
sense 'pastures' or a singular **lēah** 'clearing in woodland' (by burning?)); *bresshome
dalle* 1564 (*v.* **brēosa, holmr**; with **dalr** or **deill**); *burtune gatt* 1564, *Burtongate
Furlonge* e.17 (*v.* **gata**), *Burton S(e)icke* 1630, 1632 (*v.* **sík**) (Burton Lazars adjoins
to the west); *the Chequer* e.17, 1612, 1638, *the Chicquor* 1674 (*v.* **cheker**; a meadow
so called); *the common balke* 1625 (*v.* **commun, balca**); *cros hades* 1564 (*v.* **hēafod**;
with either **cross** or **cros**, since a medieval standing cross survives north-east of the
church); *Cubleys Cottage* 1668 (1791), 1682 (1791), 1708[3], 1744[1], 1744[2], *Cubleys
Cottage and homestead* 1708[2], *Cubleys Homeste(a)d* 1744[1], 1744[2] (*v.* **hām-stede**) (*v.*
cotage; with the surn. *Cubley*); *Dallewelle* 1199 Fine, 1199 FF ('Dalla's spring or
stream', *v.* **wella**; the pers.n. *D(e)alla* is OE); *ouer* ~ ~, *overe the dalle* 1564 (*v.* **ofer**[3],
dalr); *gal(l)es balk(e)* 1564 (*v.* **balca**; prob. with the surn. *Gale*, but **galla** 'a barren
or wet spot in a field' is also poss.); *the gatwell* 1564 (*v.* **wella**; with **gāt** or **gata**); *the
greenes* 1630, *Greens Furland* 1708[2], 1708[3], ~ *Foreland* 1744[1], 1744[2] (*v.* **grēne**[2];
prob. with **furlang**); *beyond the hale* 1564 (*v.* **halh**; a furlong so called); *Half-acre
Leys* 1674 (*v.* **half-aker, leys**); *Hugh Harris's House and Homestall* 1708[1], 1708 (18)
(*v.* **hām-stall**); *Richard Harris's Farm* 1708 (18) (*v.* **ferme**); *Sherard Harris's house*
1674; *Hentofte* 1564 (*v.* **toft**; poss. with the surn. *Henn*, *v.* Reaney *s.n.*, otherwise
with **henn**); *Highfelde* 1561 (1700), *the hye fylde* 1564, *the high feilde* e.17, (*the*)
High Field 1612, 1632, 1638, ~ *Hie* ~ 1630 (*v.* **hēah**[1], **feld**; one of the great fields of
the village); (*the*) *Hie Sicke* 1630 (*v.* **hēah**[1], **sík**); *the highway(e)* 1612, 1625, 1674
(*v.* **hēah-weg**); *Hobcroft* 1612, 1638 (*v.* **croft**; with the first el. either **hobb(e)**
'hummock' or the surn. *Hob(b)*, *v.* Reaney *s.n.*); *Thomas Houghtons Close* 1609;
Jeffrey house furlonge 1630 (*v.* **hūs**), *Jeffery's Leys* 1708 (18) (*v.* **leys**) (with the surn.
Jeffrey); *Kelhams Farm* 1668 (1791) (*v.* **ferme**), *Kellams House* 1708[2], 1708[3], ~ ~
and homestead 1708[2] (*v.* **hām-stede**) (with the surn. *Kelham* of a family originating
in the village of this name, 25 miles to the north in Notts.); *longe draughtes* 1630 (*v.*
drag, cf. *Draughton*, Nth 112 and *Draughton*, YW **6** 65); *the longe hadeland* 1630
(*v.* **hēafod-land**); *the Lords Nursery & Warren* 1744[2] (*v.* **nursery, wareine**; with
reference to the second Earl of Harborough); *Lounge hades* 1564 (*v.* **lang**[1], **hēafod**);
Lowfelde 1561 (1700) (*v.* **la(g)h, feld**; one of the great fields of the village); *the
Mares* 1564, 1612, 1630, 1638, 1674, 1708[1], 1708 (18), *the flat of the mares* 1564 (*v.*
flat), *the Mares Feilde* e.17, *the meres fielde* 1625, (*the*) *Mares Field* 1630, 1632,
1674, 1708[1], 1708 (18) (*v.* **feld**; one of the great fields of the village, prob. North Fd),
Mares furlong 1708[2], 1708[3], 1744[1], 1744[2], (*the*) *Mares Meadow(e)* 1630, 1632, 1744[1]

(prob. with **mareis** rather than **marr**[1], both meaning 'a marsh', cf. *le maris* Hy 3, *le Mares* 1427 in Muston f.ns. (b)); *the meadow* 1612; *the medelbryng'* 1564 (*v*. **meðal, brink**); *melton gat, meltune gatte* 1564 (*v*. **gata**; the road to Melton Mowbray which lies to the west); *Midle field* 1683 (1791), *Middle Feild* 1708[2], 1708[3], ~ *Field* 1744[1], 1744[2] (*v*. **middel, feld**; one of the great fields of the village); *the mill furlonge* 1630; *Nether Hall* 1575 Nichols, 1640 ib, 1658 Fine (*v*. **neoðera, hall**); *New Penn* 1632 (*v*. **penn**[2]); *North Field* 1682 (1791), 1744[1], 1744[2], ~ *Feild* 1708[2], 1708[3] (*v*. **norð, feld**; one of the great fields, prob. *the Mares Feilde, supra*); *Oatelands* 1632, 1674 (*v*. **āte, land**); *the Pasture* 1708[3], 1744[1], 1744[2]; *Pylhall* 1497 × 1524 Nichols (this may be an earlier name for *Nether Hall, supra*, but the generic is likelier to be **halh**; the first el. is either **píll** 'a willow' or **pyll** 'a pool in a river'); *red landes* 1564 (*v*. **rēad, land**); *Robert Robinsons Homestall* 1708[1], 1708 (18) (*v*. **hām-stall**); *the Sheepe Walke* 1632 (*v*. **walk**); *short forloung* 1564 (*v*. **sc(e)ort, furlang**); *Smale* ~ ~, *Small Gate Hades* 1630, 1632 (*v*. **smæl, gata, hēafod**); *South Field* 1682 (1791), 1744[1], 1744[2], ~ *Feild* 1708[2], 1708[3] (*v*. **sūð, feld**; one of the great fields of the village, earlier *Hollygatfelde*, *v*. Hollygate *supra*); *Spreckley's Farm* 1708 (18) (*v*. **ferme**, cf. *Thomas Sprekley* 1550 of neighbouring Freeby); *Stapelford brigge* 1492 Will (*v*. **brycg**; either at the site of the modern Ham Bridge or of that at Bedehouses *supra*); *suwe fourlong* 1564 (*v*. **sōg, furlang**); *the syekes* 1564 (*v*. **sík**); *Toftis* l.13 (1449) WoCart, *Tafts Close* 1632 (*v*. **toft**); *True gate* 1638 (*v*. **trog, gata**); *the Vicaridge House* 1703, 1708[1], ~ *Vicarage* ~ 1708 (18); *the Vicars Close* 17 (*v*. **vikere**); *water furres* 1630 (*v*. **wæter, furh**; poss. a place where water tended to lie in the furrows, but *v*. *waterfurris* in Muston f.ns. (b)); *betwyne the welles* 1564 (*v*. **betwēonan, wella**; a furlong so called); *long Wharles* 1564, *longe Wharl Clif* 1630 (*v*. **hwerfel, clif**); *Whetstone's house* 1708 (18) (with the surn. *Whetstone* of a family presum. in origin from Whetstone, 20 miles to the south-east in Guthlaxton Hundred); *long Whortlye* 1612, *long Whartlie* 1638, *Longe Whartley Furlonge* e.17 (*v*. **wyrt, lēah**); *Wrangling leas* 1630 (*v*. **leys**; if this f.n. does not belong with *wrong landes* following, then *v*. **wrangling**; if indeed of a different origin, it is uncertain whether these pastures were subject to dispute or whether they were the site of village sports, as *Wrustleling leyes* in Ab Kettleby f.ns. (b)); *wrong landes* 1564 (*v*. **wrang, vrangr, land**); *Wylletts* 1564 (*v*. **weg-(ge)lǣte**).

5. WYFORDBY

Wivordebie 1086 DB, *Wivordeby* 1241 Fine, 1242 Fees, 1244 RGros, 1258 Nichols, *Wiuordeby* m.13 (1404) *Laz*, 1259 (Edw 1) *CroxR et passim* to 1303 (1449) *WoCart*, *Wyvordebi* 1244 RGros, *Wyvordeby* 1242 Fees, 1248 RGros *et freq* to 1304 Pat, 1306 Ass *et passim* to 1392 Banco, 1415 Ass, *Wyuordeby* e.14 (1449), 1309 (1449), 1310 (1449) *WoCart et freq* to 1352 *LCDeeds*, 1354 (1449) *WoCart et passim* to 1433 (1449), 1449 *ib*, *Wyuordebia* 12 (1449) *ib*

Wyfordebia c.1130 LeicSurv, *Wyfordeby* 1220 MHW, 1209 × 35
    RHug *et passim* to 1335 (1449), 1380 (1449) *WoCart, Wifordeby*
    1236 Fees
Wivordesb' 1236 Fees
Wyuordby e.14 (1449), 1307 (1449) *WoCart et passim* to 1441
    (1449), 1449 *ib, Wyvordby* 1402 Pat, 1402 Inqaqd *et passim* to
    1428 FA, *Wivordby* 1445, 1447 Nichols
Wiwordeby 13 (1404) *Laz, Wywordeby* Hy 3 *Crox, Wywordby* Hy 3
    ib, Wiworthebi e.13 (1404) *Laz* (p)
Wyfordby 1279 RGrav, 1316 FA *et passim* to 1526 AAS, 1535 VE
    et freq, Wyforby 1433 *Pat, Wyforbie* 1576 LibCl
Wyuerdeby 1318 (1449), 1406 (1449), 1446 (1449) *WoCart,*
    Wyuerdby 1336 (1449), 1446 (1449), 1449 *ib*
Wyuerby 1361 (1449), 1449 *WoCart, Wyverby(e)* 1456 Nichols, 1535
    Ipm, 1535 VE, 1547 Fine, 1559 Pat, *Wiuerb(y)e* 1576 Saxton,
    1604 SR, *Wiverby* 1610 Speed, 1628 Fine *et passim* to 1710 LML
Wyfordby or Wyverby 1925 Kelly

'The farmstead, village at Wigford', *v.* **bȳ**. Wyfordby is a hybrid p.n.
with Scand **bȳ** 'farmstead, village' added to a pre-existing English
topographical name **Wīg-ford*. OE *wīg* (*wīh*) could signify either 'a
battle' or 'a military force, an army' or 'an idol, a holy place, a shrine'
(cf. OSax *wih*, ODan *wī* 'holy place, temple'). The ford over the narrow
R. Eye at Wyfordby may once have been a strategic one because of
surrounding marsh and thus a place near which a significant early battle
could have been fought. There are the earthworks of a rectangular
fortified site south-west of the church and only some two hundred yards
from the river. Onomastic evidence for a stronghold here to defend the
ford is the lost *Castelgate* 'the road to the castle' which ran somewhere
in the north of adjoining Burton Lazars and the f.ns. *Castell Close* in
Wyfordby and *castle hades* 'the headlands near the castle' in both
Wyfordby and adjacent Brentingby. The location of this fortification
near the ford is an indication of its once having been an important
crossing point, although there is no surviving evidence for a pre-
Conquest long-distance military route leading to it. Neither is there any
concrete evidence for a pagan Anglo-Saxon sanctuary at the ford. There
was possibly a St Anne's Well in Wyfordby, if the late form *Annie Well*
of c.1638 indicates a sacred spring (and if this is not the St Anne's Well
of Burton Lazars), and it has been argued that holy springs with this
name may predate the arrival of the Anglo-Saxons and relate to a Celtic

mother goddess such as Anu (*v*. J. Scherr, 'Names of springs and wells in Somerset', *Nomina* 10 (1986), 85–7). Continuity of such names through the early Anglo-Saxon period would suggest some continuity of pagan religious association. One must also take into account a significant pagan English population hereabouts, judging from the extensive late 6th cent. cemetery less than two miles away between Saxby and Stapleford. Even so, the exact interpretation of *wīg* in *Wīg-ford as either 'battle' or 'army' or 'holy place, shrine' must as yet remain unresolved, *v*. **wīg**[1], **wīg**[2], **ford**. For discussion of p.ns. recording pagan Anglo-Saxon religious sites, *v*. M. Gelling, 'Further thoughts on pagan place-names', *Otium et Negotium*, ed. F. Sandgren, Stockholm 1973, 109–28 (with particular notice of Wyfordby at 113–14 and 127).

CUMBERLAND SPINNEY, cf. *Cumberland ~*, *Cumberlands Close* 1850 *TA*; prob. with the surn. *Cumberland*, but 'ground encumbered with stocks or stones' (*v*. **cumber, land**) is poss., although if so, earlier forms might have been expected, cf. Cumberland Cl in adjoining Brentingby f.ns. (a) and Cumberland Lodge in Scalford. DOVECOT NOOK HILL, *Dovecote Nook* 1850 *TA*, *v*. **dove-cot(e)**, **nōk**. HAM BRIDGE, *Ham* 1477 (e.16) *Charyte, the hamme* 1612 *Terrier*, *v*. **hamm**. JASMINE FM. MILL HILL, 1850 *TA*, *the Milne hill* c.1638 *Terrier*, *the Mill Hill* 1692 × 1701, c.1701, 1708, 1708 (18) *ib*, *v*. **myln**; the site of *the Wind Mill* c.1638 *ib*. THE OLD RECTORY is *The Rectory* 1877 White (cf. *The Rectory garden* 1850 *TA*); it is *The Parsonage House* 1674, 1679, c.1701, 1708, 1708 (18) *Terrier*. RIPPON'S PLANTATION, cf. *Mrs Catherine Rippin, farmer* 1925 Kelly. ST MARY'S CHURCH, *the Church* 1708, 1708 (18) *Terrier*, *Church (St Mary)* 1846, 1863, 1877 White; it is earlier recorded as *ecclesie de Wyfordeby* 1220 MHW, *ecclesiam de Wyvordebi* 1244 RGros, *~ de Wyvordeby* 1248 ib, *ecclesie de Wyforby* 1433 *Pat*; note also *the Church Yard* 1708, 1708 (18) *Terrier*. WOODBINE FM. WYFORDBY GRANGE, *~ ~* COTTAGE, *Wyfordby grange* 1925 Kelly, *v*. **grange**.

FIELD-NAMES

Undated forms in (a) are 1850 *TA*. Forms throughout dated Edw 1 (1449), 1309 (1449), 1414 (1449) and 1449 are *WoCart*; 1477 (e.16) are *Charyte*; 1540 and 1557 are *Ct*; 1634 are *Reeve*; 1612, c.1638, 1674, 1679, 1692 × 1701, c.1701, 1703, 1708 and 1708 (18) are *Terrier*.

(a) Three Acres, the Eight Acres (v. **æcer**); Bottom Barn Cl (v. **bottom**); Cottage Ham (v. **hamm**), Cottage Pasture, Cottage Plat(t) (v. **plat**) (v. **cotage**); Farm Cl (*the Farm Close* 1708, 1708 (18), v. **ferme**); Little ~ ~, Gorse Cl (*the Goss Close* 1674, 1679, 1703, 1708 (18), *the Gossie Close* 1692 × 1701, c.1701, v. **gorst, gorstig**); The Ground, Great Ground, Home Ground (v. **home**), Middle Ground (*Over Ground* 1708, 1708 (18) (v. **uferra**), v. **grund**); Hicklings Cl, Hicklings Mdw (with the surn. *Hickling*, v. Hicklings Big Cl in Brentingby f.ns, (a)); The Holme (v. **holmr**); Home Cl (v. **home**); Intake (v. **inntak**); Jenkinsons Cl (with the surn. *Jenkinson*); The Lane (v. **lane**; a close so called); Little Cl; Little Fd; Little Hill; Little Side (v. **sīde**); Long Mdw; Middle Fd (*the middle filde, midle fild* 1612, *the midle feilde* 1634, *the Middle Feild* c.1638, v. **middel, feld**; one of the great fields of the village); Moor Cl (*the Moores* c.1638, *the Mores* 1674, 1679, *Wifordby Moor* 1700 Nichols, 1708, 1708 (18), v. **mōr**[1]); New Cl; New Mdw; New Piece (v. **pece**); Old Mdw; Old Yard (v. **geard**); Ozier Bed (v. **oyser, bedd**); Pease Cl (v. **pise**); Ploughed Piece (v. **pece**); Road Cl; Severance (an angle of Mill Hill cut off or severed by the line of the *Syston and Peterborough Railway* 1850); Little ~ ~, Top Fd; Top Mdw; Town End Cl (cf. *Wyfordbey Townes end* c.1638, v. **tūn, ende**); Tup Mdw (v. **tup**); Upper Fd; Wifords Cl (sic); Wyfordby Gorse (*the common gorste,* ~ ~ *gorse* 1612, *the Comon gosse, the Gosse* c.1638, *Wiverby Gosse* 1700 Nichols, *the Goss* 1708, 1708 (18), v. **gorst, commun**); Wyverby Wong 1821 *Terrier*, Wyfordby Wong 1850 (v. **vangr**).

(b) *abbot dole* 1612 (v. **dāl**; with either the surn. *Abbot* (cf. Abbott Lodge in adjoining Garthorpe parish) or **abbat**, referring to the Abbot of St Mary de Pratis, Leicester, since Charyte's Rental lists lands held by the abbey in Wyfordby); *Annie well* c.1638 (v. **wella**; a poss. example of a (St) Anne's Well and thus a sacred spring which may predate Christianity, v. the discussion of the township name *supra*); *bellandes* 1612, *Belland* 1612, c.1638, *bellande end'* Edw 1 (1449) (v. **ende**) (v. Bellands in Bottesford f.ns. (a)); *bigdickes* 1612, *Bigdykes* c.1638, *bigdick gorst* 1612 (v. **gorst**), *bigdick gutter* 1612 (v. **goter**), *bigdick slade* 1612 (v. **slæd**) (v. **big, dík**); *brode dale* 1612, *the broade Dale* c.1638 (v. **brād**; with either **dalr** or **deill**); *the bushe* 1612, *the Bush* c.1638 (v. **busc**); *Butterlandes* 1540 (v. **butere, land**); *Castell Close* 1560 Ct (v. **clos(e)**), *castle ha(a)des,* ~ *haedes* 1612, ~ *hads* 1634 (v. **hēafod**) (v. **castel(l)**; presum. with reference to the fortified site south-west of the church, the latter f.n. occurring also in adjacent Brentingby); *the Closse* c.1638 (v. **clos(e)**); *the common drifte* 1612, 1634 (v. **commun, drift**); *the Cowdames* 1612, c.1638 (v. **cū, damme**; artificially created watering-place(s) for cattle); *the Cow pasture* c.1638; *the Cowpen hill* c.1638 (v. **cū, penn**[2]); *(the) Cotyers Pasture* 1708, 1708 (18) (v. **cottere**); *Crosse gate furlonge* 1634 (prob. 'furlong lying athwart the road', v. **cross, gata**); *the cuningrye* 1612, *the coningrye closse* 1612 (v. **clos(e)**), *the Coneygrey end* c.1638 (v. **ende**), *Coniegraie furlong* 1634 (v. **coningre**); *Douecote Close* c.1638, *the douecote hedge* 1612 (v. **hecg**), *Douecote wonge* c.1638, *the douecote wonge head* 1612 (v. **vangr, hēafod**) (v. **dove-cot(e)**); *the east feild* 1634 (v. **ēast, feld**; one of the great fields of the village); *Engcroft, Hyngcroft* e.14 (1449), *Yngcroft* Edw 1 (1449), 1414 (1449), *Incroft* 1309 (1449), *Ingcroft* 1449, *Incrofte* 1558 Ct, *incraft closse* 1612 (v. **clos(e)**) (v. **eng, croft**); *the farthing balke* 1612 (v. **fēorðung, balca**); *Freby Close* 1708, 1708 (18), *Fraybie dale* 1612, *Frebey Dale* c.1638 (v. **dalr**), *fraybie* ~, *frayby hedg* 1612, *Frebey hedge* c.1638 (v. **hecg**; a boundary hedge), *fraybie gutter*

1612 (v. **goter**), *fraybie meare* 1612 (v. (**ge**)**mǣre**) (Freeby adjoins to the north-east); *the gorst under moregate* 1612 (v. **gorst** and *moor(e)gate, infra*); *the grasse head land* 1612 (v. **grǣs, hēafod-land**); *Grasse headley* c.1638 (v. **grǣs, headley**; presum. this feature is to be identified with *the grasse head land*); *hamme howkes* 1612 (v. **hōc** and Ham Bridge *supra*); *hammerwong* 1612, *Hamer Wong* c.1638 (v. **hamor, hamarr, vangr**); *heygate* 1612, *heagate* ~, *heygate gutter* 1612 (v. **goter**), *Haygatwong'* Edw 1 (1449) (v. **vangr**) (v. **hēg, gata**); *the high more* 1612 (v. **hēah**[1], **mōr**[1]); *the highway* c.1638 (v. **hēah-weg**); *the Home closes* 1703 (v. **home**); *homedale*, ~ *gutter* 1612 (v. **home, deill, goter**); *Hungerhyl* 1477 (e.16) (v. **hungor, hyll**); *Hungurfurlong* 1477 (e.16) (v. **hungor, furlang**); *the Husbandmens Field* 1679 (v. **husbandman**); *Ilueston* ~, *Ylueston Close* 1557 (v. **clos(e)**; with the surn. *Ilveston* of a family which originated in Illston on the Hill, 13 miles to the south-west in Gartree Hundred, such spellings for Illston being current from the early 12th to the 15th cent.); *the Kylne Close othewyse called the Woodyard* 1557 (v. **cyln, clos(e)** and *the Woodyard, infra*); *lambmase close* 1612 (v. **lammas**); *little dale* c.1638 (with **dalr** or **deill**); *little gosse leayes* c.1638 (v. **gorst, leys**); *the markit way* 1612, *the markett waie*, ~ ~ ~ *furlonge* 1634 (v. **market, weg**; the road to Melton Mowbray, otherwise *Melton gate, infra*); *Longe meates* 1612, *long metes* 1634, *longe Mates* c.1638 (v. **lang**[1], **mete**); *Melton gate* 1612 (v. **gata**; the road to Melton Mowbray which lies to the west); *the Middle Close* 1674, 1692 × 1701, c.1701, 1703; (*the*) *Midle hill* 1612, c.1638, *midle hill furlonge* 1634 (v. **middel**); *midull' holme* Edw 1 (1449) (v. **middel, holmr**); *milneholme* Edw 1 (1449), *the Mill-holme* 1692 × 1701 (v. **myln, holmr**); *Mooregate* 1612, c.1638, *moorgate, moregate* 1612 (v. **mōr**[1], **mór**, **gata**; the road continued in Brentingby); *the neates wateringes* 1612 (v. **nēat**, **wateryng**; poss. an alternative name for *the Cowdames, supra*); *the Orchard end* 1634 (v. **ende**); *the parsonage barn* 1612, *the Parsonage hade leay* c.1638 (v. **headley**), *the Parsonage hades* c.1638 (v. **hēafod**), *the Parsonage Homestead* 1692 × 1701 (v. **hām-stede**; later called *The Homestall* 1708, 1708 (18), v. **hām-stall**), *the parsonage stackplace* 1612, *the Parsons stacke stead* 1634, *the parsonage stack stead* c.1638 (v. **stakkr, place, stede**; also styled *the vicarag stackplace* 1612 (v. **vikerage**)), *the Parsonage yard* c.1638 (v. **personage**); *le pitplassh'* Edw 1 (1449) (v. **pytt, plæsc**); *the pitt* 1612 (v. **pytt**); *Randles well* 1612 (v. **wella**; with either the surn. *Randle(s)* or the ME pers.n. *Randel*, a diminutive of *Rand* (Randolph), from which it derived, v. Reaney *s.n.* Randall); *rivers side* 1612 (v. **rivere, sīde**); *Long Routes* 1612, *Routdale* 1612 (v. **deill**) (poss. early recordings of ModEdial. *root* (1846 OED) 'a grubbing-up, a rooting-out' from the vb. (*w*)*root* (OED) 'to root out, to grub up' (OE *wrōtan*, ON *róta*), with reference to ground cleared of roots, tree-stumps etc.); *the Rye Close* 1692 × 1701 (v. **ryge**); *the settes* 1612 (v. (**ge**)**set**); *sheddgate* 1612, *Shedgates* 1612, c.1638 (also recorded in adjoining Brentingby f.ns. (b) *q.v.*); *the Shortes* c.1638 (v. **sc(e)ort**); *Mr Smithes headland* 1612 (v. **hēafod-land**), *Mr Smith his Lees* 1612 (v. **leys**); *standardhill'* Edw 1 (1449) (v. **standard, hyll**); *the storth* 1612 (v. **storð**); *stump bushe* 1612 (v. **stump, busc**); *thirnewong'*, *le Thornwong'* Edw 1 (1449) (v. **þyrne, þyrnir, þorn, vangr**); *Thorpcliues* 1477 (e.16) (v. **clif**), *Thorp(e) hedg(e)* 1612, c.1638, 1674, *Thorpe Arnold hedge* 1708, 1708 (18) (v. **hecg**; here a boundary hedge) (Thorpe Arnold lands lie in part to the north-west); *the tith headland* 1612 (v. **tēoða, hēafod-land**); *aboue the towne* 1612 (*v.* **aboven**), *between the townes* 1612 (*v.* **tūn**; furlongs so called); *Waltham Moor* 1692 × 1701, c.1701, 1703, 1708, 1708 (18) (*v.* **mōr**[1]), *Waltham Sallows* 1692 × 1701 (*v.* **salh**) (Waltham on the Wolds adjoins to the north); *wardes headland* 1612 (*v.* **hēafod-land**; with the surn. *Ward*); *the west feild* 1634 (*v.* **west, feld**; one of the great fields of the village); *westmede* Edw 1 (1449), *west medow* 1612, *the West Meadowe* c.1638 (*v.* **west, mǣd** (**mǣdwe** obl.sg.)); *the Woodyard* 1557 (*v.* **wodyard** and *the Kylne Close, supra*); *wranglandes* 1612, ~ *gutter* 1612 (*v.* **goter**), *wrangland close* 1612 (*v.* **clos(e)**) (*v.* **wrang, vrangr, land**).

Garthorpe

1. GARTHORPE

Garthorp c.1130 LeicSurv, 1175 Nichols, 1199 FF, 1206 Ass *et passim* to Hy 3 *Crox* (freq) *et freq* to 1535 VE, 1550 Pat, (~ *iuxta Waltham* 1326 Banco, 1330 Ass), *Garthorp'* 1242, 1247 Fees, 1265 RGrav, Hy 3 *Crox et passim* to 1449 *WoCart*, 1535 VE, (~ *iuxta Waltham* 1325 (1449), 1353 (1449) *WoCart*), *Garthorpe* 1228 RHug, 1264 IpmR, 1275 Pat *et passim* to 1574, 1580 LEpis *et freq*

Gartorp' e.13 (1404) *Laz*, 1219 ClR, 1220 MHW *et passim* to 1290 Ch, 1.13 *CRCart* (p), *Gartorpa* 1220 × 35 RHug

Garetorp 1184, 1185 P

Geretorp 1180 P, *Gertorp* 1187, 1207, 1208, 1209 ib

Garsthorp 1274 Cl

Gardethorp 1416 Nichols

Garthropp 1530 LWills, 1537 MinAccts, *Garthrop* 1576 Saxton, 1582 LEpis, c.1695, 1697 *Terrier*, 1714 LML, *Gartherope* 1722 ib, *Gartrope* 1725 ib

This is a name whose first el. presents problems. Lindkvist (48, n.2) suggests that the specific is either ON *geiri* 'a triangular, wedge-shaped piece of ground' or the Scand pers.n. *Geiri* (*v.* SPNLY 98). Ekwall DEPN offers the OE pers.n. **Gāra* or ON *garðr* 'an enclosure'; while Fellows-Jensen (SSNEM 109) prefers OE *gāra* 'a triangular piece of land'.

Both of Lindkvist's suggestions may be safely dismissed. If the first el. were either a non-anglicized *Geiri* or *geiri*, some spellings in *Geir-/Geyr-* beside *Ger-* would be expected. Also, the known forms in *Ger(e)-* amount to five only, compared with the great preponderance in *Gar-*. The few spellings in *Ger(e)-* are also confined to a single source, the Pipe Rolls, and may be explained as due to AN influence, because of which *a* and *e* before *r* frequently interchanged (*v.* Feilitzen 44). Exchequer records would have been particularly prone to such influence.

Ekwall's suggestion of an OE pers.n. *Gāra* as the specific must also be questioned. The name is not recorded independently but may otherwise feature in Goring (Ox 51), Goring (Sx 168) and Garford (Brk 410). In each of these cases, however, OE *gāra* may be present rather than a pers.n., although the topography of the Oxfordshire site would seem to preclude it. In each of these instances, the pers.n. (if present) would appear to be of early type and use, since two of the p.ns. are of *-ingas* formation, signifying a folk-name, while a p.n. in *-ford* in Berkshire would happily belong to an early stratum of name creation (*v.* Brk 819–20). However, the continued use of an early OE pers.n. *Gāra* to be compounded with Scand *þorp* seems unlikely. Noticeable too is the marked lack of forms with a medial *e* surviving from an original (weak) gen.sg. of *Gāranþorp* 'Gāra's farmstead'. A greater number of forms with medial *e* would also have been expected with an anglicized form of the Scand pers.n. *Geiri*.

Ekwall's alternative suggestion of ON *garðr* is formally possible as the specific of the p.n. if the dissimilatory loss *garð-þorp* > *gar-þorp* has occurred. This would explain the preponderance of spellings in *Gar-* and lack of medial *e*. The form *Garsthorp* 1274 may show dissimilation of *ð* to *s*, while the late *Gardethorp* of 1416 may unusually preserve *ð* > *d*, but such isolated spellings must be viewed with suspicion. However, as a first el., *garðr* is rare, *v.* Elements *s.v.* (but cf. Guardhouse, Cu 252).

Finally, OE *gāra* would have been expected to provide more numerous spellings with medial *e*. Only three survive in the editor's collection of some 150 forms *ante* 1400. However, topographically *gāra* 'a triangular piece of land' would suit the site of the settlement nicely if one assumes it to have been applied to the v-shaped valley lying to the north of the present village, in the mouth of which it is sited. This *gāra* may be alluded to in *Goring Botham* 1690, *Goreing bottom* 1703 in the village's f.ns. (b) *infra*.

Hence, either 'the farmstead within an enclosure' (with **garðr**) or, perhaps more preferably, 'the farmstead in the triangle of land', *v.* **gāra**, **þorp**, cf. Garton, YE 58 and Garton on the Wolds, YE 96 which present similar problems to Garthorpe.

ABBOTT LODGE, with the surn. *Abbot(t)*. BLUE PIG (P.H.), *Blue Pig* 1877 White. GIPSY NOOK, *v.* **gipsy, nōk**. HONEY POT PLANTATION, a pejorative name alluding to poor, sticky soil. OLD CLOSE PLANTATION, *the Old Close* 1679, 1690 *Terrier*, *v.* **ald**. ST MARY'S CHURCH, *the*

Church 1708, 1709, 1745, 1821 *Terrier, Church (St Mary)* 1846, 1863, 1877 White; it is earlier recorded as *capella de Garthorp* 1184 CartAnt (with MLat *capella* 'a chapel'), *ecclesie de Gartorp* 1220 MHW, 1238 RGros, *ecclesiam ~ ~, ecclesie de Garthorp(e)* 1238 ib, 1342 (c.1430), 1354 (c.1430), 1355 (c.1430), 1368 (c.1430) *KB,* 1378 *Pat.* Note also *the Church Yard(e)* 1605, 1625 *Terrier et passim* to 1821 *ib,* 1840 *TA, v.* **chirche-ȝeard.** STRIFTS PLANTATION is *Strive Gorse* 1840 *TA, v.* **strive, strift, gorst**; on the northern boundary of the parish and referring to an area of land formerly subject to dispute. THE VICARAGE, 1877 White, 1925 Kelly; it is *the Vicarage House* 1612, 1679, 1708, 1709, 1745, 1821 *Terrier, the vicaridge house* 1625 *ib, v.* **vikerage.**

FIELD-NAMES

In (a), forms dated 1821 are *Terrier* and 1840 are *TA.* Forms throughout dated 1541, 1543, 1547, 1550, 1558, 1559 and 1560 are *Ct*; 1546 are AAS; 1605, 1612, 1625, 1652 (1674), 1679, 1690, 1697, c.1700, 1703, 1708, 1709, 1709 (18) and 1745 are *Terrier*; 1675 × 1708 are Nichols.

(a) Two ~, Five ~, Ten Acre 1840 (*v.* **æcer**); the Home Cl 1821 (1690, *homeclose* 1679, *v.* **home**); The Homestall or Homestead 1821 (1709, *The Homestall* 1605, 1708, *v.* **hām-stall, hām-stede**; i.e. of *the Vicarage House*); Mason's Fm 1821 (*Mr Masons Farm* 1709, 1709 (18), *v.* **ferme**); Moors 1840 (*v.* **mōr**[1]); the Parsonage Yard 1821 (1709, 1709 (18), *v.* **geard**); Plough Cl 1840 (*v.* **plōg**); Swathes 1840 (*the Swaths* 1679, 1703, 1708, 1745, *the Swathes* 1690, 1697, c.1700, 1709, *The Swarths* 1709 (18), *v.* **swathe**).

(b) Acre Brigge 1652 (1674), ~ Bridge 1675 × 1708 (*v.* **æcer, brycg**); the Beck 1558, c.1700, *the Beckes* 1543, *the Becks* 1652 (1674), *le bekkeheudes* 13 (1449) WoCart (*v.* **hēafod**) (*v.* **bekkr**); (*the*) Bellams 1652 (1674), 1675 × 1708 (*v.* Bellands in Bottesford f.ns. (a)); *brockyard* 1546 (*v.* **brōc, geard**); (*the*) Church Close 1708, 1709, 1745; *the Common pounde* 1558 (*v.* **commun, pund**); *Coston mere* 1703, ~ *Mear* 1708, 1709, 1709 (18), 1745 (*v.* (**ge**)**mǣre**; Coston adjoins to the north-east); *Father ~ (sic), Hither Cutt* 1675 × 1708 (*v.* **farther, cut**; poss. with reference to land assigned by cut or lot, *v.* Ox 438 *s.v.* **cut** and Field 23; but cf. Ch 2 70 *s.n.* Cutts Mdw, where it is noted that 'cuts are short furrows in the corners of fields'); *Davys Close* 1560 (*v.* **clos(e)**; with the surn. *Davy(s), v.* Reaney *s.n.*); *the East Enclosure* 1703, *the New ~* c.1700, *the Old ~* c.1700, 1703, *the Second Enclosure* c.1700, 1703 (*v.* **enclosure**); *the feild towards Saxby* 1652 (1674) (*v.* **feld**; one of the great fields of the village, in the south-west of the parish); *the Feild next Coston* 1652 (1674) (*v.* **feld**; another of the great fields, this in the north-east); *atte gate* 1332 SR (p) (*v.* **atte, gata**); *Goring Botham* 1690, *Goreing bottom* 1703 (*v.* **gāra, botm**; the second el. is either the OE noun suffix **-ing**[1] or the OE p.n.-forming suffix **-ing**[2] or ON **eng** 'meadow, pasture'); *Great Field* 1675 × 1708; *the Hall Close* c.1700, *Hallyard* 1546 (*v.* **hall, geard**); *Haynes Homeclose* 1709, *Haynes Homestall* 1709 (18) (*v.* **home, hām-stall**; with the surn. *Haynes*); *Hawthorn Slade* 1652 (1674), *Haythorn* ~ 1675 × 1708 (*v.* **hagu-þorn, slæd**); *Mr Hubbards Beck Close* c.1700 (*v.* **bekkr**); *de la Hyde* 1307 Fine (p) (*v.* **hīd**); *the King high waie* (sic) 1605 (*v.* **hēah-weg**; with reference to James I); *Litle Becke* 1558, *Little Beck Leas* 1709 (18) (*v.* **leys**) (*v.* **lȳtel, lítill, bekkr**); *Long, Short Leas* 1652 (1674), 1675 × 1708 (*v.* **leys**); *the Middle feild* 1652 (1674), ~ ~ *Field* 1675 × 1708 (*v.* **middel, feld**; one of the great fields of the village); *Moredale* 1541 (*v.* **mōr**[1], **mór**; with **dalr** or **deill**); *le Nether pasture* 1550, 1559, *le Ouerpasture* 1550 (*v.* **neoðera, uferra, pasture**), *le Neyttes pasture* 1550, *the Neytes* ~ 1558, 1559 (*v.* **nēat, pasture**); *Ad Pontem* 1327 SR (p) ('at the bridge', with MLat *pons* (*pontem* acc.sg.) 'a bridge'); *Saxby Mear* c.1700, 1708, 1709, 1745, *the Mear* 1652 (1674) (*v.* **(ge)mǣre**; Saxby adjoins to the south-west); *Stony lands* 1652 (1674), ~ ~ *meadow* 1675 × 1708 (*v.* **stānig, land**); *longe, short sykes* 1559 (*v.* **lang**[1], **sc(e)ort, sík**); *thirnegate* 13 (1449) WoCart (*v.* **þyrne, þyrnir, gata**); *Nether, the Upper Thurn Hill* 1652 (1674), *Thurn Hill* 1675 × 1708 (*v.* **þyrne**); *Turners Close* 1690, *Wm. Turners Cottage* 1708, 1709 (*v.* **cotage**); *the Upper Deals* 1652 (1674) (*v.* **deill**); *Westgate* 1547 (*v.* **west, gata**); *Westmoreende* 1541 (*v.* **west, mōr**[1], **ende**); *le Wheatefild* 1550 (*v.* **hwǣte, feld**); *Thom. Wilmots Homestal* 1709 (*v.* **hām-stall**); *Worrowe leyes* 1558 (*v.* **leys**; prob. to be identified with Worrel Leys in adjoining Coston f.ns. (a), *q.v.*).

2. COSTON

> *Castone* 1086 DB, *Castona* 1087 × 1100, 1163, Hy 3 TutP, *Caston'* 1094 × 1123 ib, c.1130 LeicSurv, 1150 × 59 TutP *et passim* to 1242, 1247 Fees *et freq* to 1290 Ch, 1294 *GarCart*, Edw 1 *CroxR et passim* to 1392 TutP, 1428 AAS, *Kaston* 1238, 1239 RGros
> *Causton'* 1219 ClR, *Caustton* 1311 Ch, *Kauston'* 1219 ClR
> *Coston(')* 1254 Val, 1261 TutP, Hy 3 *Crox*, Hy 3 *Rut et passim* to 1296 Ipm, 1302 (1449) *WoCart et freq, Kosthon'* 13 (1449) *ib*
> *Cooston'* 1396 *Rut*, 1445 Nichols, 1487 *Pat*, 1520 *Rental*
> *Cosun* 1507 *Pat, Coson* 1547 × 51 ECP, 1576 Saxton, 1607, 1630 LML, 1660 *Surv*
> *Coaston* 1630, 1631 LML, *Coasen* 1631 ib

Probably 'Kátr's farmstead, village', *v.* **tūn**. The pers.n. *Kátr* (*Káts* gen.sg.) is Scand, presumably an original by-name from the adj. *kátr* 'glad', *v.* SPNLY 163. Typical of Leics. p.ns. is loss of *t* in the group *-ston* in forms from the 16th cent. onwards.

COSTON COVERT, *v.* **cover(t)**. COSTON LODGE. COSTON LODGE EAST, ~ ~ WEST, cf. *Coston Lodges* 1824 O, *v.* **loge**. EAST PLANTATION. THE GRANGE, 1877 White, *atte Grange* 1381 SR (p) (*v.* **atte**), *grange of Coiston* 1539 MinAccts, *Grange House* 1845 *TA*, *v.* **grange**; in the possession of the family of *Roger de Bret* in 1303 Nichols, and there is no record of monastic ownership; but the grange was prob. once an outlier of Croxton Abbey. GRANGE LANE, 1601 *Terrier, the Grange Lane* 1612, 1690, 1697, 1703 *ib*, *v.* **lane**. HALL FM, cf. *Aboue the Halle* 1327 SR (p) (*v.* **aboven**), *atte halle* 1381 ib (p) (*v.* **atte**), *The Hall* 1660 *Surv*, 1846, 1863, 1877 White, *v.* **hall**. KING STREET LANE is *the high street* 1578 *Terrier*, *v.* hēah[1], strǣt; this was a minor Roman road. MANOR HO., *v.* **maner**. THE RECTORY, 1877 White, 1925 Kelly, *Rectory House* 1845 *TA*; it is *The Parsonage House* 1612 *Terrier*, 1660 *Surv*, 1697, 1708, 1708 (18) *Terrier*, *v.* **personage**. Note also *The Homestall* 1708, 1708 (18) *ib*, the outbuildings of *The Parsonage House*, *v.* **hām-stall**. ROYCE'S PLANTATION, cf. *Robert Rowse* 1578 *Terrier*, *William Rouse* 1666 SR, *Wm. Royce, farmer* 1863 White. ST ANDREW'S CHURCH, *The Church* 1708, 1708 (18) *Terrier*, *Church (St Andrew)* 1846, 1863, 1877 White; it is earlier recorded as *ecclesie de Caston* 1220 MHW, *ecclesiam ~ ~*, *ecclesie de Kaston* 1238 RGros, *ecclesie de Cooston* 1487 *Pat*, *ecclesie parochialis de Cosun* 1507 *ib*. WHITE SWAN (P.H.) (lost), *White Swan* 1863, 1877 White.

In 1660 *Surv*, the following houses with their associated appurtenances are listed: *Beltons house and yard*; *John Browns house and homested*; *Thomas Clements house*; *Francis Eatons house and home closse*; *Robert Flowers house and yard*; *Edward Jessons house*; *Thomas Jessons house and homested*; *Thomas Johnsons house and homested*; *Wid. Lees house and homested* (i.e. *Widow ~*); *Mr Michaells house and grange-yards* (*v.* The Grange *supra*); *William Palins house and home closs*; *John Rubbins house*; *Mary Rubbins house and homested*; *James Sharps house*; *William Sprecleys house*; *Adam Wands house and home closs*; *Alice Wands house*; *Wid. Wathrall her house and homested* (i.e. *Widow ~*); *Thomas Watkins house and home closse*; *Mr Wiglys house, v.* **geard**, **hām-stede, home, clos(e)**. Note that the surns. *Belton* and *Eaton* are prob. based on local p.ns. Eaton lies five miles to the north-west. There are three nearby villages called Belton: that in Lincs. is 12 miles to the north-east, that in Rutland is 13 miles to the south, while the Leics. instance lies 25 miles to the west.

FIELD-NAMES

Undated forms in (a) are 1845 *TA*, while those dated 1821 are *Terrier*.
Forms throughout dated 1578, 1601, 1612, 1674, 1690, 1697, 1700,
1703, 1708 and 1708 (18) are also *Terrier*; those dated 1660 are *Surv*.

(a) Ash Cl (*Ash-closs* 1660, *v.* **æsc, clos(e)**); Barn Cl; Bastard Yards (*v.* **geard**,
cf. *Bastard closse, Basterd closs* 1660 (*v.* **clos(e)**); either with **bastard** or with the
surn. *Bastard, v.* Reaney *s.n.*); Great ~, Beck, Tylers Beck (poss. to be identified with
Taylors Beck closs 1660, otherwise with the surn. *Tyler*), Becks, Beck Cl (*Beck-closs
alias Brook-close* 1660, *the great Beck-closs* 1660, *Thomas Jessons Beck closs* 1660,
Adam Wands ~ ~, Wid. Wands Beck closs(e) 1660 (i.e. *Widow ~*), *v.* **bekkr, clos(e)**);
Bedlam (*v.* **bedlem** and VEPN 70; in 1845, the pejorative name of a tiny close in
Coston); Bretland, Little ~, Great ~, Lees ~ (with the surn. *Lee*), Parkers ~ (with the
surn. *Parker*) (*Little, Great Bretlands* 1660, *Wid. Lees Bretlands* 1660 (i.e. *Widow
~*), *Robt. Rylys Bretlands* 1660, *v.* **breiðr, land**); Calf Cl (*John Browns calfe closse*
1660, *v.* **calf, clos(e)**); Cheesecake (*William Spreckleys Cheescake closs* 1660, *v.*
cheesecake, clos(e); in 1845, a wedge-shaped enclosure with one curving side;
named from an individual portion of such a confection); Copdale (1578, *Coppe dale*
1578, *Cop-dale* 1578, 1660, *v.* **copp, deill**); Coston Gorse 1806 Map (*v.* **gorst**);
Cottagers Cl (*Cottiers Closse* 1660, *Will. Beltons Cottiers Closs* 1660, *v.* **cotager,
cottere, clos(e)**); Great Cow Cl, Top Cow Cl; Crow Dale (*Crow-dale* 1660, *v.* **crāwe**;
with **dalr** or **deill**); Far, Hither Doddings (*Far, Heither Doddings* 1660 (*v.* **hider**),
Greenberies dodins 1578 (with the surn. *Greenberry, v.* Reaney *s.n.*), *Richard Love
his dodins, love his dodins, loves dodins* 1578; perh. 'pasture on the rounded hill', *v.*
dodde, eng, but *-ings* may rather represent the OE noun suffix **-ing**[1] or the OE p.n.-
forming suffix **-ing**[2]); The Doles (1660, *v.* **dāl**); East Cl; Far Pasture (1660, *v.*
pasture); Fox Cover (*v.* **fox, cover(t)**); Fowlers Cl (with the surn. *Fowler*); Geesons
Home Yard, Geeson's Yard, Next Geeson Yard (cf. *Wid. Geeson* 1660 (i.e. *Widow
~*), *v.* **home, geard**); Gothing Bottom (*Gothing-bottome* 1660, *v.* **botm**; this may be
Goring Botham of adjoining Garthorpe f.ns. (b), otherwise the name must remain
unexplained); Grange Dales (*greate grange dale* 1578, *grange dale* 1612, *v.* **great,
deill** and The Grange *supra*); Grange Yards (1660, *v.* **geard** and The Grange *supra*);
Lees ~ ~, Great Cl (*Wid. Lees great closs* 1660 (i.e. belonging to Widow Lee), *Easton
great close* 1578 (with the surn. *Ea(s)ton*, cf. *Francis Eaton* 1660), *Thomas Johnsons
great closse* 1660, *Mr Michaells great closs* 1660, *v.* **great, clos(e)**); Highgate, ~ Fd
(*Hey gate* 1578, *Hey-gate Feild* 1660, cf. *Hay gate bush* 1578 (*v.* **busc**), *v.* **hēg, gata,
feld**), Little ~ ~, High Leys (*olde Robert Rowse high leies* 1578, *High Leys, Little
high-leys* 1660, *v.* **hēah**[1], **leys**); Home Cl (*v.* **home**); Homestead 1821 (*homested*
1660, *v.* **hām-stede**; belonging to *The Parsonage House, q.v.*); Horse Leys (*Horse-
leys* 1660, *v.* **hors, leys**); House Cl; Jessons Mdw (cf. *Edward Jesson* and *Thomas
Jesson* 1660); Great, Little, Upper Lammas (*Great, Little, Upper Lammous* 1660, *v.*
lammas); Little Cl (*lyttle close* 1601, cf. *Thomas Clements ~ ~, Thomas Johnsons ~
~, Wid. Lees little closs* (i.e *Widow ~*) 1660, *v.* **lȳtel, clos(e)**); Little Croft (*v.* **croft**);
Little Dale (1578, 1660, *v.* **lȳtel, lítill**; with **dalr** or **deill**); Long Cl (*long-close* 1660,

cf. *Thomas Jessons ~ ~*, *Thomas Johnsons long clos(e)* 1660, *v.* **clos(e)**); *Melton Gate* (1660, *v.* **gata**; the road to Melton Mowbray); Mill Bank (*v.* **banke**), Mill Cl (*Mill closse alias Ortone closse* 1660, *v.* **clos(e)** and Ortons Cl *infra*), Mill Ham (*v.* **hamm**), Little ~ ~, Mill Fd (*Little ~ ~*, *Mill Feild* 1660, *v.* **feld**) (*The Mill and holme* 1660, *ye Mil-holme* 1660 (*v.* **holmr**), *Mill-peece* 1660 (*v.* **pece**), *Milne Place* c.1440 TutP (*v.* **place**), *v.* **myln**; note also Mill Stream 1845 (*v.* **myln-strēam** 'a mill-race') and *the Flood-gate* 1660 (*v.* **flod-gate**)); Moor (*the Moore* 1578, *The Moors* 1660, *Bryans Moore* 1660 (with the surn. *Bryan*)), Long Moor (*Longe Moore* 1660, *the Easter-most long Moore* 1660 (*v.* **eastermost**)), Nether Moor (*Wigleys neither Moores* 1660, *v.* **neoðera**; with the surn. *Wigley*), Slipe Moor (*Slight moore* 1578, *Slipe moore alias Sleep-moore* 1660; if these belong together, then **sléttr** 'smooth, level' is replaced by **slipe** 'a slip, a narrow strip of land'), Wigleys Moor (with the surn. *Wigley*), Moor Cl (*Wigleys Moore closs East*, ~ ~ ~ *West* 1660, *v.* **clos(e)**) (note also *the Lyttle Moore* 1601, *the little more close* 1612, *v.* **lȳtel**, **clos(e)**) (all with **mōr**[1]); Nether Fd (*Neither Feild* 1660, *v.* **neoðera**); New Cl (*New-closse* 1660, *v.* **clos(e)**); Nutshell Fd (no doubt a jocular allusion to the field's very small size, cf. Nursling (Ha) with forms as early as *Nhutscelle* c.800 Boniface, *æt Nutscillinge* 877 (12) BCS 544 (S 1277), with OE **hnutu-scell** 'a nutshell', also with reference to a tiny place); Far ~ ~, Near ~ ~, Open Pasture (cf. *(John) Browns Open Pasture* 1660, alluding to unfenced land, *v.* **open**, **pasture**); Ortons Cl (*Ortons closse* 1660; with the surn. *Orton*, *v.* **clos(e)** and Mill Cl *supra*); Parsons Cl (*the Parsons close* 1660, *v.* **persone**, **clos(e)**); Pinfold (*v.* **pynd-fald**); Poles (*v.* **pōl**[1]); Raggs Pasture (cf. *Thomas Raggs Pasture closs* 1660, *v.* **clos(e)**); Rileys Cl (*Robert Ryleys close* 1660, *v.* **clos(e)**); Roberts Fd (*Roberts Feild* 1660; with the surn. *Roberts*, *v.* *Adams Feild* in f.ns. (b)); Wid. Leys ~ ~, Middle ~ ~, Nether ~ ~, Upper ~ ~, Sorrel Dale (*Wid. Lees Sorrell-dale* 1660 (i.e. *Widow ~*), *Middle*, *Neither Sorrell-dale* 1660 (*v.* **neoðera**), *(the) Upper Sorrell dale* 1578, 1660, *v.* **sorell**; with **dalr** or **deill**); Little ~ ~, Stonebridge Cl (*Ston-Bridg closse* 1660, *v.* **stān**, **brycg**, **clos(e)**); Little ~, Thorney (*Little ~ ~*, *Thorny closs(e)* 1660, *v.* **þornig**, **clos(e)**)); Toft Dale, ~ ~ Mdw (*Toft-Dale* 1660, *v.* **toft**; with **dalr** or **deill**); Top Cl; Upper Fd (*Upper Feild* 1660); Upper Leys Cl (perh. to be identified with *Wid. Lees Upper closse* 1660, *v.* **clos(e)**, i.e. that belonging to Widow Lee, otherwise *v.* **leys**); Upper Pasture (*Browns upper Pasture* 1660; with the surn. *Brown*); Water Furrows 1821, 1845 (1690, *Water furrowes* 1578, 1601, 1612, prob. 'furrows where water tends to lie', *v.* **wæter**, **furh**; these are alternatively designated *Wet furrowes*, *v.* f.ns. (b) *infra*, but note Field 50 who treats Water Furrows as deeper furrows so ploughed to carry off surface water); Water Mdw (an irrigated meadow, *v.* **wæter** and Field 90); West Cl; Worrel Leys (*Worell-leys* 1660, *v.* **leys**; prob. to be identified with *Worrowe leyes* 1558 in adjoining Garthorpe f.ns. (b); the surn. *Worrell* seems unlikely in view of the date of the Garthorpe form, so perh. identical with Worrall, YW **1** 230 and Wirral, Ch **1** 7 ('nook of land where bog-myrtle abounds', *v.* **wīr**, **halh**)).

(b) *Adams Feild alias Roberts Feild* 1660 (with the surn. *Adams*, *v.* Roberts Fd *supra*); *Avington-closse* 1660 (*v.* **clos(e)**; with the surn. *Avington* of a family originally from Evington, 17 miles to the south-west in Gartree Hundred, which evidences p.n. forms in *Avin-* during the 12th cent., *v. Coson old-closs, infra*); *Bartle-Bridge* 1660 (presum. with the surn. *Bartle*, a diminutive of *Bart*, from *Bartelmew*

(Bartholomew), *v.* Reaney *s.n.* Bartlet); *William Beltons close* 1660 (*v.* **clos(e)** and *Beltons house and yard, supra*); *Black buttes* 1578 (*v.* **blæc, butte**; alluding to soil colour); *Brigge plotte* 1578 (*v.* **brycg, plot**); *John Browns neither-Pasture* 1660 (*v.* **neoðera**); *Buckmynster Meere* 1601, *Buckminster* ~ 1612 (*v.* **(ge)mǣre**; (land at) the parish boundary with Buckminster which adjoins to the east); *Tho. Clements closse* 1660 (*v.* **clos(e)**); *Coson old-close alias Avington-closse* 1660 (*v.* **ald, clos(e)** and *Avington-closse, supra*); *Cox Clos(s)e* 1578, 1674, 1690, 1697, 1700, 1703, 1708, *Cockes close* 1612 (*v.* **clos(e)**; with the surn. *Cox*); *crucem de Caston'* 13 TutP (an early standing cross; with MLat *crux* (*crucem* acc.sg.) 'a cross', *v. the Wooden Crosse, infra*); *The Deals closs* 1660 (*v.* **deill, clos(e)**); *(the) Far(r) close* 1690, 1697, 1700, 1703, 1708, 1708 (18) (*v.* **feor**); *(Robt.) Flowers closs* 1660 (*v.* **clos(e)**); *Fulbeckegate* 1578 (*v.* **fūl, bekkr, gata**); *Geesings-leys* 1660 (*v.* **leys**; with the surn. *Geeson*); *Wid. Geesons clos* 1660 (i.e. *Widow* ~ ~) (*v.* **clos(e)**); *the great dale* 1578 (*v.* **grēat**; with **dalr** or **deill**); *Gribbel dale* 1578 (*v.* **gribbele** (otherwise recorded from 1589 OED), **deill**); *High-Field* 1660 (*v.* **hēah**[1], **feld**); *holme yards* 1660 (*v.* **holmr, geard**); *Home yards* 1660 (this may belong with the previous f.n., otherwise *v.* **home**); *Edward Jessons closs* 1660 (*v.* **clos(e)**); *Kirke Hayd* 1578 (*v.* **kirkja, hēafod**); *Middle close* 1578, 1697, 1700, 1703, 1708, 1708 (18), *the Midle close* 1690, *the Parsons middle close* 1578 (*v.* **persone**); *Mr Mitchells greatest fielde* 1578 (*v.* **greatest**); *the Northfielde* 1578 (*v.* **norð, feld**; one of the great fields of the village); *Nyne acres* 1578 (*v.* **nigon, æcer**); *(the) Nyne lei(e)s* 1578, *the nine leas* 1612, *9 leaes* 1674, *Nine Lays* 1690, 1697, 1700, 1703, ~ *layes* 1708, ~ *Leys* 1708 (18), *the Nyne leies close* 1578, ~ ~ *leas* ~ 1601, *the Parsons Nyne leis close* 1578 (*v.* **persone**) (*v.* **nigon, leys, clos(e)**; an enclosure of nine former units of grassland); *Will. Palins clos* 1660 (*v.* **clos(e)**); *Parkers closse* 1660 (*v.* **clos(e)**; with the surn. *Parker*); *the Parsonage lane* 1660, 1697, 1708, 1708 (18), *the parsonage lane ende* 1578 (*v.* **lane-ende**) (*v.* **personage, lane**); *the Parsons lane* 1660 (*v.* **persone**; presum. to be identified with the previous lane); *the Parsons peece* 1578 (*v.* **persone, pece**); *John Rubbins closse* 1660 (*v.* **clos(e)**), *John Rubbins great doles,* ~ ~ *little doles* 1660 (*v.* **dāl**); *William Rubbins closse* 1660 (*v.* **clos(e)**); *James Sharps closs* 1660 (*v.* **clos(e)**); *the Sowthe fielde* 1578 (*v.* **sūð, feld**; one of the great fields of the village); *Spondale bush* 1578 (*v.* **spann**[1], **deill, busc**); *William Spreckleys closse* 1660 (*v.* **clos(e)**); *Sproxton Shrubs* 1578 (*v.* **scrubb**; Sproxton parish adjoins to the north); *Stone pittes* 1578, *Mr Mitchells ston-pittes* 1578, *Stone pitt hill* 1578 (*v.* **stān-pytt**); *the street furlong* 1578 (*v.* **furlang**), *the streete side* 1578 (*v.* **sīde**) (*v.* **strǣt**; with reference to King Street Lane *supra*, a Roman road); *le suaþes* Hy 3 Rut, *the Swathes* 1578, *The Swaths* 1660 (*v.* **swathe**); *Synnomes* 1578 ('water-meadow subject to dispute', *v.* **sænna, holmr**, cf. *Synnams* Ru 37, *Sanams* Ru 188 and Sanham Ho. in Kirby Bellars, East Goscote Hundred); *the Towne headge* 1578 (*v.* **tūn, hecg**); *Sir Charles Tuftons ground* 1690 (*v.* **grund**); *vestings* Hy 3 Rut (*v.* **vestr, eng**); *Wid. Wands close adjoyning to long-closs* 1660, *Wid. Wands middle-closs* 1660, *Wid. Wands upper close* 1660 (*v.* **clos(e)**; all belonging to Widow Wand); *Wedow Place* c.1440 TutP (*v.* **widuwe, place**); *the West fielde* 1578 (*v.* **west, feld**; one of the great fields of the township); *Westhorp* 1268 Ch, *Westorp* 1290 ib ('the west farmstead', *v.* **west, þorp**; lying between Coston and Garthorpe and not to be identified with the latter); *Wet furrowes* 1578, 1674, 1708, *Wetfurrows* 1697, 1700, 1703, 1708, 1708

(18), *the Parsons Wetfurrowes* 1578 (*v.* **persone**) ('furrows where water tends to lie',
v. **wēt, furh**; in this parish, an alternative name for Water Furrows *supra*); *Thomas
Wilsons closse* 1660 (*v.* **clos(e)**); *the Wooden Crosse* 1578 (*v.* **wooden, cros**; perh.
a later replacement for *crucem de Caston'*, *supra*; the stone crosses of the medieval
period in Framland Hundred appear to be usually of limestone); *Would(e) gate* 1578,
Woulde gate waye 1601, *Woul(d)gate lane* 1612 (*v.* **wald, gata, weg, lane**).

Ab Kettleby

1. AB KETTLEBY

Chetelbi 1086 DB, Hy 1, Hy 2 Dugd, *Chetelby* c.1130 LeicSurv,
   1166 RBE, *Chetlebi* 1166 LN, *Chetilbi* 12 (e.15) *BelCartB* (p)
Ketelbi l.12 Dane, 1199, 1200 Cur, *Ketelbia* c.1160 BM, *Ket(t)elby*
   c.1130 LeicSurv, 1209 × 19 RHug, 1242 RGros, 1243 Fees,
   a.1277 *BHosp* (p) *et freq* to 1535 VE *et passim* to 1610 Speed,
   Ketlebi l.12 *GarCart*, 1237 RGros, *Ketleby* c.1130 LeicSurv,
   1201 Cur *et passim* to 1449 *WoCart*, *Kettleby* 1576 Saxton, 1604
   LML *et freq*
Ket(t)ilby 1242 Fees, Hy 3 *Crox*, 1277 Banco *et passim* to c.1310
   (1449) *WoCart*, 1316 FA *et freq* to 1535 VE *et passim* to 1582
   Ipm
Katylby 1518 Visit, 1525, 1528 AAS, 1615 Ipm

The affix is usually added as:
Abbe- 1236, 1237, 1242 RGros *et passim* to 1433 Pat, 1615 Ipm,
   Abe- 1236 RGros, *Ab-* 1236 ib, 1274 Cl *et passim* to 1518 Visit
   et freq
Appe- 1327 SR, 1378 Banco, 1413 BM, *Ape-* 1351 Cl, 1392 ELiW,
   1449 *WoCart et passim* to 1610 Speed, *Ap-* 1358 *Rut*, 1397 Pat *et
   passim* to 1613 Fine
Abby- 1333 Inqaqd, 1556 Ipm, *Abbey* ~ 1524 SR, 1564 Nichols,
   Abbie ~ 1666 SR
~ *Abbatis* 1291 OSut
~ *on the hill* 1591 Nichols

'Ketil's farmstead, village', *v.* bȳ. The ODan pers.n. *Ketil* (ON *Ketill*)
is an original by-name (cf. OIcel *ketill* 'a cauldron, a cauldron-shaped
helmet') and was very common in England, *v.* SPNLY 166–70. Here, the
pers.n. is linked in stem-form to the generic, a structure which has many
certain parallels in the Danelaw.

The prefix Ab (ME *Abbe*) which distinguishes the village from Eye Kettleby some four miles to the south is the name of an early owner of the estate. Possible sources for *Abbe* are the OE pers.n. *Abba* or the Scand pers.ns. *Abbi* (ODan), *Abbe* (OSwed). *Abbe* appears as a by-name, as in *Gaufridus Abbe* 1199 Cur of Leics.; and in 1287, it is even found as a Notts. woman's forename in *Abbe ux' Henr' Lotefyn* (i.e. 'Abbe, wife of Henry Lotefyn'), in this case being a pet form of *Albrei* or *Aubrey* (Lat *Albreda*, OGer *Alberada*, OFr *Albree*, *Aubree*), *v.* P. McClure, 'The interpretation of hypocoristic forms of Middle English baptismal names', *Nomina* 21 (1998), at 115–6. From c.1220 to c.1433, the Prior and Convent of Launde Priory (later popularly called Launde Abbey) were patrons of the parish church. This gave rise through folk etymology to the affixed forms *Abbey* ~ (*v.* **abbaye**) and ~ *Abbatis* (MLat *abbas* (*abbatis* gen.sg.) 'an abbot').

HOME FM, *v.* **home**. LANDYKE LANE, *Landike Lane or Street Road* 1828 *Plan*, the Roman road Margary 58a across the Wolds, linking the Fosse Way and Ermine Street. It is *Lincoln(e) street* 1601, 1737 *Terrier*, *the street* 1601 *ib*, (*the*) *Street Road* 1764 *EnclA*, 1827 *Plan*, 1828 *Terrier*. The road led to Lincoln via Ermine Street, *v.* **strǣt, land, dík**. MAIN RD is *the towne streete* 1612 *Terrier*, *the Town Street* 1679, 1690 *ib et passim* to 1724 *ib*, *v.* **tūn, strǣt**. MANOR HO., *v.* **maner**. MILL LANE (lost), *Mill Lane* 1828 *Plan*. There are two mills recorded for the township. A windmill is shown on the higher ground to its north, west of the Nottingham road, in 1836 O. This was presumably the site of *the Milne* 1601, 1612 *Terrier*, *the Milln* c.1700, 1724 *ib*, *the Mill* 1674, 1690 *ib et passim* to 1709 *ib*. It lay in the East Redearth Fd. To its south-west was *the old(e) Milne* 1601, 1612 *ib et passim* to 1709 *ib*, *the old Milln* 1697, c.1700 *ib*, *the ould Milln* 1724 *ib*, *the old Mill* 1674, 1679, c.1700 *ib*, *the ould Mill* 1.17, 1724 *ib*, which was sited in the West Redearth Fd, *v.* **ald, myln**. NEW ROW COTTAGES. NOTTINGHAM RD, *Nottingham Road* 1828 *Plan*; it is *the Quenes hye waie* 1601 *Terrier*, *the kinges high waie* 1605 *ib*, *the kinges hie waye*, ~ ~ *hye waye* 1612 *ib*, *the kings hieway*, ~ ~ *hyghway*, ~ ~ *hyway* 1690 *ib*, (*the*) *Kings highway* 1674, 1690, 1697 *ib et passim* to 1724 *ib*, *v.* **hēah-weg**; referring to monarchs from Elizabeth I to George I. PINFOLD (lost), *Pinfold* 1828 *Plan*, *v.* **pynd-fald**. THE PREFABS, alluding to post-World War Two prefabricated dwellings. ST JAMES'S CHURCH, *Church (St James)* 1846, 1877 White; it is earlier recorded as *ecclesiam de Kethelby* a.1219 RHug, *ecclesie de Ketelby* 1220 MHW, *ecclesiam de Abketleby* 1236

RGros, *ecclesie de Abbekettleb'* 1236 ib, *ecclesiam de Abbeketlebi* 1237 ib, ~ *de Abbeketelby* 1242 ib, *ecclesie de Apketylby* 1397 *Rut*, ~ *de Abbeketelby* 1433 *Pat, ecclesie parochialis de Abketelby* 1476 *ib* and in the group *ecclesiarum de Bukmynster Disworth et Abkettylby* 1558 *ib*. SOUTH LODGE. SUGAR LOAF (P.H.), *Sugar Loaf* 1828 *Plan*, 1846, 1877 White, 1925 Kelly, *Sugar Loaf Inn* 1863 White. THE VICARAGE, 1877 White, *the vicaridge howse* 1601 *Terrier*, ~ ~ *hous* 1612 *ib*, ~ ~ *house* 1690, 1709 *ib*, *the Vicerage House* 1724 *ib*, *the Vicarage House* 1821 *ib*, *v*. **vikerage**. WELBY LANE, the road to Welby which lies to the south in neighbouring Asfordby parish. WELL LANE, cf. *well rundle* 1601 *Terrier, wel rundle* 1612 *ib, the Well Rundle* 1690, 1697 *ib et passim* to 1724 *ib*, 'the stream flowing from the spring', *v*. **wella, rynel**; the stream still flows from near the end of the lane. WHITE LODGE. WHITE LODGE FM is *The Lodge* 1828 *Plan, Ab Kettleby Lodge* 1836 O, *v*. **loge**.

FIELD-NAMES

Forms dated 1601, 1605, 1612, 1674, 1679, 1690, 1697, l.17, c.1700, 1709, 1724 and 1737 are *Terrier*.

(a) Church Lane 1828 *Plan* (*v*. St James's Church *supra*); Clerk's Cl 1846, 1863 White (Reaney *s.n*. Clark notes that the spelling *Clerk* is now rare in surns.); Hollow Street 1828 *Plan* (1674, 1679, 1690 *et passim* to 1724, *hollowe streete* 1601, 1612, *Hollowe Street* 1605, cf. *hollowe streete hades* 1612 (*v*. **hēafod**), 'the road running in a hollow, the sunken road', *v*. **holh, strǣt**; 1828 *Plan* shows this to be a field road, north-west of the village, and although termed *street*, unrelated to Margary 58a, the Roman road in the north of the parish); Holt 1830 Farnham (*v*. **holt**).

(b) *Bare Leys* 1737 (*v*. **bær**[1], **leys**; presum. referring to treeless pasture); *Baumborrowes* 1601, *Bawmborrowes* 1612, *Bamberis* l.17, *Bombros* 1690, 1697, *the top* ~, *Bomberarce* 1724, *Bambruss*, ~ *side* 1737 (*v*. **sīde**) (poss. 'hill where beans are grown' (*v*. **baun, berg**), but these late spellings parallel the later development of the p.n. Baumber (*Badeburg* 1086 DB) in Lincs., which may be an example of the series of hill-forts called Badbury 'Badda's fortress', perh. associated with an eponymous Anglo-Saxon warrior hero; the name *Baumborrowes* may have belonged to what was eventually called Arbour (*q.v.*), a poss. **eorð-burh** 'fortress with earthen ramparts' in adjacent Holwell; it should be noted, however, that later spellings for Baumber may have been influenced by Scand *baun* 'bean', *v*. **burh** and Barrie Cox, 'Baumber in Lindsey', JEPNS 30 (1997–8), 27–32); *Blankley headland* 1737 (*v*. **hēafod-land**; cf. *Robt. Blankley* 1690); *Bransick* 1601, 1612 *et passim* to 1709, *Brainsick* 1724, *Bran-sike* 1737 (*v*. **brant, sík**); *Broughton gate* 1601, 1605 *et passim* to 1724 (*v*. **gata**; the road to Nether Broughton which lies to the north-west); *at the Busk(e)* 1605, 1612 *et passim* to 1724 ('(the furlong) beside the bush or scrub', *v*. **buskr**);

Catsars 1601, *Catserce* 1.17, *Cats-arse* 1737, *Catsars hill* 1601, 1612, *Katsarse hill* 1674, *Catts arce hill* c.1700, *Catsarse hill* 1709, 1737, *Catsarce Hill* 1724 ('the rounded hill frequented by wild cats', *v.* **cat(t), ears**); *Chervins* 1690, *Keruins* 1697, 1724, *Kerbins* c.1700, *Kiruins* 1709, *Kervines* 1737 (*v.* **kervinge**); *the Church Hadland* 1601, 1612, 1674, 1697, ~ ~ *Headland* c.1700, 1709, 1724, 1737 (*v.* **hēafod-land**); *the Church Land end* 1690 (*v.* **land, ende**); *the Cley feilde* 1612, ~ ~ *feild* c.1700, *the Clay Feild* 1674, 1679 *et passim* to 1724, *the Clayfield* 1690, 1.17, *the East Cley* 1601, ~ ~ ~ *field* 1605, 1612, ~ ~ ~ *Feild* 1.17, 1709, 1724, *the East Clay Field* 1690, 1737, *the Middle Cley field* 1601, 1605, *the Midel clay feild* 1.17, *the Middle Clay field* 1690, ~ ~ ~ *feilde* 1709, *the Midle Clay Feild* 1724 (also called *the South Clay Field next Welby* 1737), *middlecley baulke* 1601 (*v.* **balca**), *the West Cley* 1601, ~ ~ ~ *fielde* 1612, (*the*) *West Clay feild* 1674, 1.17, 1700, 1709, 1724, ~ ~ *field* 1690 (also called *the Clay Field next Wartnaby* 1737) (*v.* **clǣg, feld**; one of the great fields of the village, later subdivided into three); *the Commond Baulk* 1.17 (*v.* **balca**), *the Common Ground* 1.17, 1697, c.1700, ~ *Commond* ~ 1724 (*v.* **grund**), *the Common Hades* 1612, 1690, 1697, c.1700, ~ ~ *hads* 1690, *the Commond Hades* 1.17, 1724 (*v.* **hēafod**), *the Common mere* 1601 (*v.* **(ge)mære**) (*v.* **commun**); *atte Croyz* 1308 Cl (p), *atte Cros* 1319 Inqaqd (p), 1327 SR (p), *atte Crosse* 1392 Pat (p) (*v.* **atte, cros**); *Crosse baulk* 1601, 1612, *the crosse baulke* 1605, *Cross Balk* 1690, 1697, 1709 (*v.* **cross, balca**); *Curstdole* 1601 (perh. 'the cursed portion of land', a pejorative name for poorly-yielding ground, or for land associated with misfortune of some kind, *v.* **cursed, dāl**); *the Dale* 1612, 1674 *et passim* to 1724, *top of* ~ ~, *the bottom of the Dale* 1737, *the dale syde* 1601, *the Dale Side* 1737 (*v.* **sīde**) (*v.* **dalr**); *the Dike* 1612, 1690 *et passim* to 1724, *the deke* 1697, *Dikes-End* 1737 (*v.* **ende**) (*v.* **dík**); *Estheng'* 1292 OSut (*v.* **ēast, eng**); *fitland(e) sick(e)* 1601, 1612, 1690, 1697 (*v.* **fit, land, sík**); *hanging baulk* 1737 (*v.* **hangende, balca**); *Heygate* 1601, 1612, 1674, 1690, *Heay gate* 1709, 1724, *Heigate Busk* 1737 (*v.* **buskr**) (*v.* **hēg, gata**); *Hesland* 1601, 1605, 1612 *et passim* to 1737, *Heasland* 1690, 1697, *hessland* 1724, *Heslands* 1.17, c.1700, 1709, 1737, *Heaslands* 1697, *hesslands* 1724, *hesland broade* 1612, *Hesland Broad* 1.17, *Heasland broad* 1690, 1697 (*v.* **brǣdu**), *Heslands side* 1737 (*v.* **sīde**) ('land growing with brushwood', *v.* **hǣs, land**); *High Gate* 1697, 1.17, *Highgate* c.1700 (*v.* **hēah**[1], **gata**); *Holwell meer(e)* 1601, 1605, 1612, c.1700, *Hollwell Meer(e)* 1690, 1697, 1.17 *et passim* to 1724, ~ *Mere* 1.17 (*v.* **(ge)mære** and Holwell *infra*); *the homestall* 1612, *the homestall or scite of the vicaridge* 1690, 1697, *the Homested or seat of the vicaridge* 1697 (*v.* **hām-stall, hām-stede** and The Vicarage *supra*); *Humberstone close hedge* 1737 (a boundary hedge; with the surn. *Humberstone* of a family originating in the village of this name, 12 miles to the south-west in East Goscote Hundred); *del Hull* 1308 Cl (p) (*v.* **hyll**); *Jennet Leys* 1737 (*v.* **leys**; most prob. with the surn. *Jennett* (*v.* Reaney *s.n.*) but note also the possibility of *jennet* 'a small Spanish horse', *v.* OED *s.v.* jennet[1]); *John pitts* (sic) 1697 (*v.* **pytt**; belonging to *John Spick* 1697); *Kettleby hedge* 1.17 (*v.* **hecg**; the parish boundary hedge), *Kettlebie meere* 1601, 1612, *Kettleby Meer(e)* 1690, 1697, 1709 (*v.* **(ge)mære**), *Ketylby woldes* 1403 Nichols, *Kettleby wouldes* 1601, *Kettlebie Woulds* 1674, 1697, 1709, 1737, *Kettleby Wolds* 1690, *Ab Kettleby Woulds* 1741 Nichols, *le Woldes* 1537 MinAccts, *the Woulds* 1.17, 1724, 1737 (*v.* **wald**); *the Lands Ends* 1.17 (*v.* **land, ende**); *Little-land-sike* 1737 (*v.* **land, sík**); (*the*) *Long hades* 1601, 1605,

1612 *et passim* to 1724, *the Longe hades* l.17 (*v.* **hēafod**); *long landes* 1601, 1612, *Longlands* 1612, 1674 *et passim* to 1724, *Langlands* 1690 bis, *longlandes furlong* 1601 (*v.* **lang**[1], **land**); *Marle pittes* 1601, 1.17, *Marlepitts* 1674, 1690, 1697, *Marlepits* 1612, c.1700, 1709, *the Marlepittes* 1679, *Marlpits* 1724, *Marl-pitts* 1737 (*v.* **marle-pytt**); *meere hill* 1601 (*v.* (**ge)mǣre**; at the boundary with Wartnaby to the west); *Melton gate* 1601, 1612 *et passim* to 1737, *Melton-Gate furlong* 1737 (*v.* **gata**; the road to Melton Mowbray and the adjoining furlong); *the Middle furlong* 1737; *the Mill-baulk* 1737 (*v.* **balca**), *the Mill-hole* 1737 (*v.* **hol**[1]) (*v.* Mill Lane *supra*); *mabbe wong* 1601, *Mab Wonge* 1612, 1690, 1697, 1709, *Mob Wong* l.17, c.1700, 1724, 1737 (*v.* **vangr**; with the surn. *Mabb*, originally a pet-name for Mabel, *v.* Reaney *s.n.* Mabb); *parchinshere leas* 1697, *parchinger leas* 1724, *Papenger Leys* 1737, *parchin leays* l.17, *Parchin leas* c.1700 (*v.* **leys**; the diverse forms indicate early misunderstanding; the first el. is perh. AFr **parcener** 'a joint tenant; one who shares' or a surn. derived from it, but earlier forms are needed; the l.17 and c.1700 spellings are the result of an initial miscopying followed by a repetition of the error in an ensuing glebe terrier); *Parrs Close* 1737, *Parrs Thorns* 1737 (*v.* **þorn**) (with the surn. *Parr*); *poors land* 1697, *the poors land* c.1700, 1709, 1724, *the poors ground* c.1700, *the poors land headland* 1690, *the poors headland* 1697, 1709, 1724 (*v.* **pouer(e)**, **land**, **grund**, **hēafod-land**; the income from the land was assigned to give assistance to the township's poor, *v.* Field 191–3); *Potter Close Leys* 1737 (*v.* **leys**), *potters dik(e)* 1601, *potter dik* 1612, *Potter dike* 1690, 1697 *et passim* to 1724, *the Potter dike* l.17 (*v.* **dík**) (towards Potter Hill on the boundary with Asfordby parish to the south-east; either with **pottere** 'a potter' or less likely with the surn. *Potter*); *the Redyearth* 1612, *the Redearth* 1612, 1674 *et passim* to 1724, *the East Redyearth* 1601, 1605, (*the*) *East Redearth* 1612, 1674 *et passim* to 1737, *the East Read Earth* l.17 (one of the great fields of the village), *the West Red Earth* 1601, *West Redyearth* 1605, (*the*) *West Redearth* 1612, 1674 *et passim* to 1737, *the West Read Earth* l.17 (one of the great fields) (*v.* **rēad, eorðe**); *the Redland End* l.17 (*v.* **rēad, land, ende**); *Red leare* 1612, *redlere* 1690, *Redlare* 1697, *Redlaire* 1709, 1724 (*v.* **rēad, leirr**); *Roadleays* l.17 (*v.* **leys**; pasture beside the Nottingham road); *Rush-land-Leys* 1737 (*v.* **leys**; this f.n. may belong with *Wrustleling leyes, infra*; but if not, *v.* **risc, land** and cf. Rush land dike in neighbouring Holwell f.ns. (a)); *Sheep-pen Croft nook* 1737 (*v.* **scēp, penn**[2], **croft, nōk**); *Showbredes* 1601, *Showbreds* 1612, l.17, 1724, *Shobrods* l.17, 1737, *Showbrends* 1690, *Shobreds* c.1700, 1724, *Showbread* c.1700, *Showbroads* 1709, *Shobreds furlonge* 1612, *the Showbread furlong* 1674, *Showbrends furlong* 1690, *Shobrods furlong* 1697, *showbred hades* 1601 (*v.* **hēafod**) (*v.* **scōh-brǣdu**); *Short-arm* 1737 (*v.* **arm**; referring to a short projection of land); *Short Cuttes* 1674, 1709, (*the*) *Short Cutts* 1690, 1697, l.17, c.1700, 1724 (*v.* **cut** and *Shortcuttes* in Branston f.ns. (b)); *Sidland sick* 1709, 1724 (*v.* **sīd, land, sík**); *sideholms* 1697, *the Side Holmes* 1724 (*v.* **sīd, holmr**); *Spick hadland* 1601 (*v.* **hēafod-land**; cf. *Wm. Spick* and *Richard Spicke* 1612); *Stacys Headland* 1737 (*v.* **hēafod-land**; with the surn. *Stacey*); *Roger Steele h(e)adland* 1601 (*v.* **hēafod-land**); *the Steeple end* 1737 (*v.* **ende**; it is uncertain whether **stēpel** here is in its early sense 'a steep place' or in its later sense 'a (church) tower'); *Robert Stokes hadland* 1601 (*v.* **hēafod-land**); *the stone pittes* 1601, 1679, *the stone pitts* 1612, 1674 *et passim* to l.17, 1709, *the stonepits* 1690 (*v.* **stān-pytt**); *by the streete* 1601 ('(the furlong) beside the Roman road', *v.* **stræt**); *Cross Town-end Leys* 1737 (*v.* **cross, tūn, ende, leys**); *atte Toneshevede* 1308 Cl (p) (*v.* **atte, tūn, hēafod**); *by the towne syde* 1601 ('(the furlong) beside the township', *v.* **tūn, sīde**); *the vicars headland* 1690, 1709, ~ ~ *hedland* 1724 (*v.* **hēafod-land**), *the vicars land* 1709, 1724 (*v.* **land**) (*v.* **vikere**); *wartnambie gate* 1601, *wartnabie gate* 1612, *Wartnaby Gate* 1674, 1679 *et passim* to 1737, *Wartnoby gate* 1709, *warpnabie gate furlonge* (sic) 1612, *Wartnobygate furlong* c.1700, *Wartnaby Gate Furlong* 1674, 1709, 1724, 1737 (*v.* **gata**; the road to neighbouring Wartnaby and the adjoining furlong), *wartnabie hedge* 1601, 1605, 1612, *warpnabie hedge* (sic) 1612, *Wartnaby hedge* 1690, 1697, l.17, 1737, *Wartnoby hedg* c.1700 (*v.* **hecg**; the boundary hedge with Wartnaby), *wartnambie* ~, *wartnamby meere* 1601, *Wartnabie meere* 1605, 1612, *Wartnaby Meer(e)* 1674, l.17, 1709, 1724, ~ *Mear* 1690, 1737, ~ *Mere* 1679, *Wartnoby Meer* c.1700 (*v.* **(ge)mǣre**; the boundary with Wartnaby); *weeteforrowes* 1612, *weetfurrows* 1690, 1697, 1709, *Wetfurrurs* l.17, *Weetfurows Furlong* 1724, *Wet furrow Ridge* 1737 (*v.* **hrycg**) ('wet furrows, furrows where water tends to lie', *v.* **wēt, furh**); *Whenham* 1737, *Whenham nook* 1737 (*v.* **nōk**) (poss. an early name in **hām** for an English estate preceding Kettleby, with OE **wenn** 'a wen, a tumour' used of a barrow or mound; this would be entirely in keeping with the distribution of p.ns. in *-hām* in relation to Roman roads in the East Midlands, *v.* JEPNS 5 (1972–3), 15–73); *Wrustleling leyes* 1601, *Rusling Leays* 1724 (*v.* **wrastling, leys** and Field 244; these meadows were the sites of wrestling matches, the spellings here from dial. *wrustle, russel* 'to wrestle'); *Yellow Leys* 1737 (*v.* **geolu, leys**; prob. indicating pasture where yellow flowers grew).

2. HOLWELL

> *Holewelle* 1086 DB, 1166 LN, 1242 Fees *et passim* to 1340 Ch, *Holewella* Hy 2 Dugd, *Holewell'* c.1130 LeicSurv, 1193 P (p), l.12 *GarCart et freq* to 1243 Fees, *Holewell* Hy 2 Dugd, 1199 Cur *et passim* to 1402 Banco, *Holewel* c.1130 LeicSurv
> *Hollewelle* 1166 RBE, 1285 Nichols, 1308 Ipm, 1312 Banco, *Hollewell* 1421 Fine, 1428 FA
> *Olewelle* 1265 Misc, *Olewell* 1326 Cl, 1326 Ipm
> *Holiwelle* 1324 Inqaqd, *Holywell* 1502 MiscAccts, 1523 LAS
> *Holwell'* 1331 (1449) WoCart, *Holwell* 1332 SR (p), 1345 Coram, 1368 Ipm *et passim* to 1411, 1412 Pat *et freq*

'The stream running in the deep hollow', *v.* **hol²**, **wella**.

ARBOUR (2½" only), sited near a spring in what is now a tree-filled dell at the top of Holwell Mouth *infra*. In 1795 Nichols, it is recorded that *there is a large and commodious harbour adjoining the spring with seats all around it and a stone table in the middle*. Ostensibly, then, the name represents ME **erber**. But it is possible that there are the ploughed-out remains of a prehistoric fortification on the headland forming the eastern side of Holwell Mouth. If this identification is correct, then perhaps Arbour really represents a forgotten adjacent **eorð-burh** 'fortification built of earth', *v. Baumborrowes* in Ab Kettleby f.ns. (b).

BEN'S COTTAGE. BROWN'S HILL, cf. *William Brown* c.1730 Nichols, patron of Ab Kettleby's parish church, and *John Cave Brown* 1756 ib, another patron; cf. also *Thom. Brown* and *Wm. Brown* 1846 White, both graziers of Holwell. CLAWSON LANE, 1828 *Plan*, the road to neighbouring Long Clawson to the north. FOX HOLES, *foxhooles* 1612 *Terrier*, *v.* **fox-hol**; for f.ns. arising, *v.* f.ns. (a) *infra*. HALL FM, cf. *The Hall Place* 1556 Ipm, *v.* **hall, place**. HOLWELL HUTS, *v.* **hut**. HOLWELL MOUTH, 1601, 1612, 1674 *Terrier et passim* to 1877 White, *Hollwel(l) Mouth* 1690, 1697 *Terrier et passim* to 1724 *ib*, *Holwel Mouth* 1737 *ib*; the head of a valley which rises into the escarpment of the Wolds from the Vale of Belvoir, *v.* **mūða**. IRONSTONE FM, named with reference to the ironstone that is quarried locally. IVY HOUSE FM. LANDYKE LANE FM, *v.* Landyke Lane in Ab Kettleby. MANOR FM, *v.* **maner**. METHODIST CHAPEL, 1849 *TA*. NURSERY LANE, *v.* **nursery**. OLD HILLS, 1806 Map, 1849 *TA*, *v.* **wald**. OLD HILLS WOOD. ST LEONARD'S CHURCH, cf. *Church & Churchyard* 1849 *TA* and note the earlier *capellam de Holewell* 1220 MHW (with MLat *capella* 'a chapel'). SCALFORD GORSE, *Scalford Gorse Plantation* 1849 *TA*; on the boundary with Scalford parish which adjoins to the east, *v.* **gorst**. WHITE HOUSE FM. WILLIAM IV (P.H.) (lost), *William IV* 1846, 1863, 1877 White, 1925 Kelly.THE WILLOWS, cf. *Willow Holt* 1849 *TA*, *v.* **wilig, holt**. YEW TREE FM is *Yewtree house* 1877 White.

FIELD-NAMES

Undated forms in (a) are 1849 *TA*. Forms throughout dated 1601, 1612, 1674, 1690, 1697, 1709, 1724 and 1737 are *Terrier*.

(a) The three ~, The four ~, The six ~, The seven ~, The eight ~, The Nine Acres, First, Second nine Acres (*nyne acre* 1601, *The Nyne Acre* 1612, *the Nine Acre* 1697, cf. *Nine Acre Lane* 1737, *v.* **nigon**), Fourteen Acres, Bottom,Top Sixteen Acres (*v.* **æcer**); Big ~ ~, Little ~ ~, Barn Cl; Barn Ground Cl (*Barn Ground* 1824 O, *v.*

grund); Big Cl; Middle Bottom Cl (*v.* **bottom**); Brimming Lees, ~ Leys (*v.* **leys**; the difficult *brimming* may refer to the breeding of pigs (*v.* OED *s.v.* brimming, vbl.sb.[1]) or allude to fertility of growth in a transferred sense of 'overflowing' (*v.* OED *s.v.* brimming vbl.sb.[2]); otherwise an earlier name based on **brimme** 'an edge, a border' may be thought of); Second ~ ~, Canks Cl (sic) (presum. with the local surn. *Cant*, cf. Cant's Thorns in neighbouring Wartnaby); Middle ~ ~ ~, Clawson Lane Cl (*v.* Clawson Lane *supra*); Clover Fd (*v.* **clāfre**); Crab tree Leys (*Crabtree Leys* 1745 *Reeve*, *v.* **crabtre**, **leys**); Croft hill East, ~ ~ North, ~ ~ West (cf. *Holewell Croft* 1271 *Fine*, *v.* **croft**); Crowtrees, ~ Spinney (*v.* **crāwe**, **trēow**); Dunkerk (in this instance, not a name signalling remoteness, since sited towards the village, but one presum. associated with misfortune or discomfort of some kind, *v.* Ch **4** 176 *s.n.* Dunkirk (Wood) and Field 153); Ewe Fd (cf. *Mr Welby's Ewe Grounds* 1727 *Reeve*, *v.* **eowu**, **grund**; the surn. *Welby* was that of a family originating in the settlement of this name three miles to the south-west in Asfordby parish); Far Gate Cl (*v.* **gata**); First Mdw; Flat Cl (*v.* **flatr**); Foot path Cl; Fox Covert or Old Hills (*v.* **covert** and Old Hills *supra*); Far ~ ~, First ~ ~, Foxes Cl (prob. with the surn. *Fox*); First, Second Fox Holes, Great, Little Fox Holes, Bridle road Fox Holes (*v.* **brigdels**), Tylers Fox Holes (with the surn. *Tyler*), the Fox Holes Mdw, the Fox Holes Redhill (*v.* Redhill *infra*) (*v.* Fox Holes *supra*); Middle ~ ~, Top ~ ~, Great Cl, First, Second Ploughed Great Cl; Hardwell Cl (*harewell* 1601, 1612; prob. 'boundary stream', *v.* **hār**[2], **wella**, cf. *Harewell* in Croxton Kerrial f.ns. (b) and *Harewellesike* in Bottesford f.ns. (b)); Hill Cl (x2), Hill Close Mdw; First, Second Holwell Cl; Far ~ ~, Middle ~ ~, Second ~ ~, Home Cl (*v.* **home**); Honey Pot (a name often given to sites with sticky soil, *v.* **hunig**); Hop Yard (used of a small field for growing hops, *v.* **hop-yard** and Field 129); Horse Cl; Intake (x3) (*v.* **inntak**); Far, Long, Great Land Dike, The Acre Land Dike (*v.* **æcer**), Hovel Land Dike (*v.* **hovel**), Red Land Dike (*v.* **rēad**), Rush Land Dike (*v.* **risc**), Great ~ ~ ~, Little ~ ~ ~, Land Dike Cl (*v.* **land**, **dík** and Landyke Lane in Ab Kettleby); Little Cl; Little Mdw; Big ~ ~, Long Cl (x2), Long Close Mdw; Lowning, The Lownings, Bottom, Middle, Top Lowning, Bottom, Middle Lowning adjoining Scalford Gorse, Top Lowning by Scalford Gorse, Bottom, Top Seven Acre Lowning, First, Second Eight Acre Lowning, The Fifty Strimes Lowning (*v.* **strime**) (*v.* **loning**); The Meadow; Mill Fd; New Fd; Bottom ~ ~, Top ~ ~, New Mdw; Old Dike (*v.* **dík**); First, Second Old Hill (*v.* Old Hills *supra*); Over Mdw (*v.* **uferra**); Pen Cl (*v.* **penn**[2]); Ploughed Cl; Ploughed Piece (*v.* **pece**); Pound (*v.* **pund**); The Poor's Cl 1846, 1863, 1877 White (*v.* **pouer(e)**; the income from the close provided funds to assist the village poor, *v.* Field 191–3); Red Hill (*v.* **rēad**; alluding to red soil); Far ~ ~, First ~ ~, Road Cl; Round Hill (*v.* **round**); Sand-pit Cl 1847, 1877 White; Far Seeds, Little Seeds (*v.* **sǣd**; in f.ns. often used of areas of sown grass); Nether, Over Shoot (*v.* **scēat**, **uferra**); Spring Cl (*v.* **spring**[2]; referring to a copse within the close); Stackyard Cl (*v.* **stak-ʒeard**); Stone Bridge Cl; Stone-pit, ~ Cl (x2) (*Stone pit close* 1691 Nichols, *v.* **stān-pytt**); Top Fifty Strimes (*v.* **strime**); Thirks Cl (prob. with the surn. *Thick(s)*, *v.* Reaney *s.n.*); Three Cornered Cl (*v.* **three-cornered**); Middle ~ ~, Top Cl; Top Mdw; Two Acre Cl; Undale (perh. 'Húni's portion of land', *v.* **deill**; the pers.n. *Húni* is Scand); Eight acre ~ ~, Ten acre Upper Mdw; Wand Cl (poss. with the surn. *Wand* rather than with **wand** 'a measure of land (a yardland or 30 acres)', cf. *Adam Wand* and *Alice Wand* 1660 *Surv* of Coston); Well Cl (cf. *le Well dole* 1403

Nichols, *v.* **wella**, **dāl**); Far, First Wold, First, Long Wolds, Leadbitters Wolds (with the surn. *Leadbitter, v.* Reaney *s.n.* Leadbeater), The Wolds Mdw (cf. *Holwell wold* 1403 Nichols, *Holwell Would* 1537 MinAccts, *Holwell wouldes* 1601, 1612, *Holwell Woulds* 1612, 1674, 1709, 1737, *Hollwell woulds* 1697, 1724, *v.* **wald**); Wool dale (*v.* **wald**, **deill**); Great, Little Whinhorne (*v.* **hvin**, **horn**); Big ~ ~, White Hill (*White Hill* 1601, 1612 *et passim* to 1737, *Whitehill* 1690, 1697; literally 'white hill', but here, as with dial. *white*, 'dry open pasture' may be indicated, *v.* **hwīt**).

(b) *the Acres* 1601, 1612 (*v.* **æcer**); *the East Hollwell Mouth* 1724 (*v.* Holwell Mouth *supra*); *the Gore* 1737 (*v.* **gāra**); *Holwell feilde* 1601, 1612, *Hollwell Feild* 1697, 1709, 1724 (*v.* **feld**); *Laund Dike* 1669 *Deed* (*v.* **dík**; poss. with **launde**, but may belong with Land Dike Cl *supra*); *Redding Lees* 1601 (*v.* **ryding**, **leys**); *Le Sikes*, ~ *Sykes* 1403 Nichols (*v.* **sík**); *atte Smythe* 1332 SR (p) (*v.* **atte**, **smiðde**).

3. WARTNABY

DB includes Wartnaby as a member of the manor of Rothley in Goscote Wapentake. The township later became part of East Goscote Hundred. White in 1846 notes that Wartnaby 'belongs to the Parish and Peculiar Jurisdiction of Rothley, though distant 12 miles from that village'.

Worcnodebie 1086 DB
Wargnodebi 1102 × 06 Reg, Hy 1 Nichols
Wartnadeby c.1130 LeicSurv, *Wartnathebi* 1273 RGrav (p), *Wartnothebi* 1227 GildR
Warcnatebi 1169 P, *Warcnathebi* 1207 ib, *Warknateby* 1271 *Wyg* (p), *Warknathby* 1276 RH
Warcnodbi c.1200 BM
Warknotheb' e.13 Berkeley (p), *Warknothebi* 1226 GildR
Warkeneteby 1209 × 35 RHug, 1278 RGrav, *Warkenetheby* 1285 Banco, *Warknetheby* 1294 Nichols, *Warkenetby* 1327 SR (p)
Warknedeb' 1253 × 58 RHug, *Warknedeby* 1315 ChancW, *Warkenedby* 1377 Pat
Warkeneby 1262 (Edw 1) CroxR, 1262 Ass, 1502 *MiscAccts*, 1523 LAS, *Warkenaby* 1355 GildR (p), 1381 Cl
Warnoteby 1328 *Pat*, 1338 Hosp, *Warnotby* 1382 *Pat*
Warkneby 1444, 1445 Nichols, 1523 LAS, *Warknaby* 1507 Ipm
Wartnamby 1472 Hastings, 1529 Fine, 1537 CoPleas, *Wartnambie* 1601 *Terrier*
Warkenamby 1504 Ipm
Werkeneby 1510 *Rental*, *Werkneby* 1523 LAS
Wartnaby 1507 Ipm, 1524 CoPleas *et passim* to 1601 LibCl, 1610 Speed *et freq*, *Wartnabye* 1570 Rental, 1576 Saxton

The village lies on high ground beside the Roman road Margary 58a across the Wolds. Its name is difficult. Ekwall in DEPN *s.n.* notes, 'The place is in a high situation. The first element may be a word meaning "watch hill" or the like, e.g. an OE *weard-cnotta* (cf. Knott End) or an OScand *varð-knǫttr* "hill with a cairn". But the first element is perhaps better explained as an OE personal name *Weorcnōþ, Worcnōþ* (cf. Workington) though the usual *a* in the first syllable offers difficulty.' Neither of the OE pers.ns. Ekwall suggests is recorded. The OE pers.n. *Weorc* is only found monothematically, never as the first theme of a dithematic name.

As the early forms with *d* and *th* indicate, the second element is probably OE *nōð* 'daring, boldness', a typical OE pers.n.-forming theme. Ekwall's *cnotta* or *knǫttr* are unlikely. In the case of *varð-knǫttr*, consistent early loss of *ð* would not be expected (cf. Warcop, We 2 82). The surviving forms seem more consistent with an unrecorded OE pers.n. **Wærcnōð*. Hence, 'Wærcnōð's farmstead, village', *v.* **bȳ** and SSNEM 76.

ASHLEIGH. BERLEA, ~ FM. CANT'S THORNS, 1828 *Terrier, Cants Thorns* 1806 Map, 1827 *Plan*. It is *Cants Cover* 1836 O, *v.* **þorn, cover(t)**. *William Cant* is resident in neighbouring Saxelby in 1706 LML, *Ann Cant* and *John Cant* in Wartnaby in 1764 *EnclA*. CHURCH FM, *v.* St Michael's Church *infra*. FISH POND, 1846, 1863 White. FISHPOND HO. FRIARS WELL, ~ ~ FM, cf. *Well Lane Close* 1828 *Terrier, v.* **wella**. LAMLEA. LITTLE BELVOIR, 1925 Kelly; it is *Wartnaby House* 1877 White. This lies on the edge of the Wolds escarpment and was renamed Little Belvoir in reflection of Belvoir Castle's similar position. ST MICHAEL'S CHURCH, *The Church* 1877 White; it is *the Chapel* 1764 *EnclA* and recorded earlier in the group *capellarum de Gaddesby . . . Warnoteby Caudwell et Wykeham* 1328 *Pat, capellarum de Gayddesby . . . Warnotby Caudewell et Wykam* 1382 *ib* (with MLat *capella* (*capellarum* gen.pl.) 'a chapel'). Note also *Chapelyard* 1764 *EnclA*. STONEPIT HOUSES. STONEPIT SPINNEY is *Stone Pit Covert* 1806 Map, *Stonepit Fox Covert* 1827 *Plan, Stonepit Covert* 1828 *Terrier,* ~ *Cover* 1836 O, *v.* **stān-pytt, cover(t)**. THE VICARAGE, 1925 Kelly. WARTNABY HALL, 1828 *Terrier*, 1846, 1863 White, 1925 Kelly, *The Hall* 1877 White, *v.* **hall**.

FIELD-NAMES

Undated forms are 1828 *Terrier*. Forms dated 1764 are *EnclA* and 1827 are *Plan*.

(a) Adam's homestead (*v.* **hām-stede**; with the surn. *Adam*); Asfordby Lane (Asfordby parish adjoins to the south); Far, Near Ash Holt (*v.* **æsc, holt**); Ash Spinney; Bottom Cl, ~ ~ Plantation, Bottom Mdw (*v.* **bottom**); Brewsters Lane 1764, Brewsters Lane Plantation (with the surn. *Brewster*); Broughton Road Cl (Nether Broughton lies to the north-west); Bull Cl (*v.* **bula**); Churchsick Fd 1764, the Church Sitch Fd (*v.* **sīk, sīc**; one of the great fields of the village); Far, Middle, Near Clay Cl (*v.* **clǣg**); Daft's Cl (with the surn. *Daft*); Far, Middle, Near Dale (*v.* **dalr**); Dickens Cl (with the surn. *Dickens*); Far, Near Double Pool Cl (*v.* **duble, pōl**[1]); Far Mdw; Far Pasture; Fasewell Fd 1764 (*v.* **fæs, wella**; one of the great fields of the village); Fishpond Cl (*Fishe poole close* 1605 *Conant, v.* **fisc, pōl**[1]), Fishpond Spinney; Frisby's Croft (*v.* **croft**; with the surn. *Frisby* of a family prob. originating in Frisby on the Wreake, some three miles to the south-west); Gorse Cl (*v.* **gorst**); Great Cl; Lower, Upper Hall Cl (*v.* Wartnaby Hall *supra*); Hay Cl (*v.* **hēg**); Hay Common 1764 (*v.* **hēg, commun**); Bottom, Top Hays, Little Hays, Middle Hays, Hays Plantation (prob. with **(ge)hæg**); Headland Cl (*v.* **hēafod-land**); Far, Near Hill Mdw, Hill Meadow Plantation; Lower ~ ~, Upper ~ ~, Home Cl (*v.* **home**); Great Homestead (*v.* **hām-stede**); the Horse Pasture 1764; House Cl, House Close Plantation; Hydes Orchard (with the surn. *Hyde*); Little Mdw (x2); Long Furlong 1764, 1828; Middle Fd 1764 (one of the great fields of the village); Near Pasture, Far ~ ~ ~, Near Pasture Cl; the Pinfold (*v.* **pynd-fald**); Pingle (x2) (*v.* **pingel**); Potatoe Pleck (*v.* **potato, plek**); the Red Earth Fd 1764 (*v.* **rēad**, one of the great fields), Far, Middle, Near Redearth, Great Redearth, ~ ~ Plantation; Round Plott 1764, Far, Near Round Plot, Great Round Plot (*v.* **round, plot**); Short Cut Hill, ~ ~ ~ Plantation (*v. Shortcuttes* in Branston f.ns. (b)); Short Furlong; Spilsbys Cl (with the surn. *Spilsby* of a family originating in the village of this name 50 miles to the north-east in Lincs.); Stonepit Cl (x2) 1828, Stone Pit Furlong 1764, Stonepit Mdw, ~ ~ Plantation 1828 (*v.* Stonepit Spinney *supra*); Top Cl; Top Mdw; Townend Cl (*v.* **tūn, ende**); Far, Near Vicars Cl, Vicars Mdw (*v.* **vikere**); Wartnaby Cl, ~ ~ Plantation; Wartnaby Gorse 1827, 1828 and 1834 O (*v.* **gorst**); Far, Near Wartnaby Hill Cl, Wartnaby Hill Plantation; Wartnaby Woulds 1764, 1828 (*v.* **wald**); Water Gall (*v.* **wæter, galla**); Far Woulds (*Farr Woulds* 1745 *Reeve, v.* **feor**), Bottom, Top Flewitts Woulds (with the rare surn. *Flewitt*, prob. the reflex of the OGer pers.n. *Hlodhard*, surviving in France as *Floutard*; note *Hubert flohardus* 1130 P of Leics., *v.* Reaney *s.n.*), Long Woulds (cf. *Woulds Close* 1686 *Deed*) (*v.* **wald**); the Wronglands (*v.* **wrang, vrangr, land**).

Melton Mowbray

1. MELTON MOWBRAY

Medeltone 1086 DB bis
Mealton' 1174, 1199 P *et passim* to 1214 ib, 1307 Cl
Meauton' 1198 Cur, 1202 FF, 1202 Ass *et passim* to 1256 RegAnt,
   1282 Cl
Miautune c.1200 AD, *Miauton'* 1202 Ass
Meltuna 1121 AC, *Meltune* e.Hy 2 BM, *Meltun'* Hy 2 Dane, e.13
   Dixie, m.13 (1404) *Laz, Meltone* l.12 *GarCart*, Hy 3 RBE *et*
   passim to 13 (1404) *Laz, Melton(')* c.1130 LeicSurv, 1198, 1200
   Cur *et passim* to 1222 AD, 1227 Ch *et freq*
Maltun 1155 × 66 BM, *Maltunam* 1166 Dane, *Malton'* l.12 *GarCart,*
   Mauton 1202 Ass (p), John Abbr
Meuton' l.12 *GarCart*, 1199 P, 1202 Ass *et passim* to 1276 RH, 1288
   Cl, *Meutun(e)* e.13 Berkeley, 1243 AD
Meelton' 1353 Cl, 1353 Ipm, 1411 PRep, 1425 Pat, *Meylton'* 1520
   Wyg
Milton 1410 Fine, 1415 Pat

'The middle farmstead, village', *v.* **meðal, tūn**. The Scand adj. *meðal*
'middle' may have replaced OE *middel*. Forms with *u* for *l* are due to
AN influence. The affix ~ *Mubray,* ~ *Moubray,* ~ *Mowbray* (with
various other spellings) is common from 1282 Cl. *Rogerius de Moubray*
held the manor c.1130 LeicSurv, *Robertus de Mulbrai* in l.12 *GarCart*
and *Willelmus de Mobray* in 1200 Cur.

STREETS, ROADS AND LANES

ASFORDBY RD, 1877 White, *Ashfordby gate* 1550 *Pochin, v.* **gata**;
the road to Asfordby which lies to the west.
   BECK MILL ST was *Bekmylnelane* 1477 (e.16) *Charyte, Beck Mill*
Lane 1842 TA, *v.* **lane** and Beck Mill *infra*.

BENTLEY ST, 1877 White; it is *Bentley Lane* 1761 *EnclA*, 1842 *TA*, 1846, 1863 White. *Bentley* presum. is a surn.

BROOK LANE, *v.* **brōc**; it gives access to R. Eye.

BURTON RD is *Burton Gate* 1550 *Pochin*, 1682, 1686 *Surv*, 1761 *EnclA*, *the kinges highe way called Burton* (sic) 1550 *Pochin*, *v.* **gata**, **hēah-weg**; the road to Burton Lazars which lies to the south-east. The 1550 record refers to Edward VI.

BURTON ST, 1877 White; it continues as Burton Rd *supra*.

CHAPEL ST, 1842 *TA*, 1846, 1877 White; named from the *Independent Chapel*, *infra*.

DALBY RD, 1682 *Surv*, 1761 *EnclA*, *Great Dalby road* 1877 White. It is *Dalbie ~*, *Dalby gate* 1550 *Pochin*, *v.* **gata**; the road to Great Dalby which lies to the south.

HIGH ST, 1842 *TA*, 1846, 1863 White, *the Hye Streete* 1607 *Reeve*, *the High Street* 1621, 1631 *ib*, *v.* **hēah**[1], **strǣt**; it is *The Town Street* 1707, 1708 (18) *Terrier*. Originally, the principal street of the township, leading into the Market Place.

KING ST, 1716 *Pochin*, 1846, 1863, 1877 White, *le kynges streate* 1540 *Ct*, *the King Street* 1782 *Fane*, 1795 *Reeve*, 1842 *TA*, *Kings ~*, *King's ~* 1842 *ib*. No doubt the monarch (in 1540 Henry VIII) held a deal of property here, *v.* **king**, **strǣt**.

LAG LANE, *v.* **lagge** (cf. So dial. *lag* 'a narrow marshy meadow by a stream'); this low-lying lane traverses R. Eye.

LEICESTER ST, 1846, 1863, 1877 White; the road to Leicester which lies to the south-west.

MARKET PLACE, 1842 *TA*, 1877 White, *le Merketsteade* 14 (1449) *WoCart*, *v.* **market**, **stede**. It is uncertain whether *the Beast Market* 1782 *Fane*, 1795 *Reeve* was located here, *v.* **beste**.

MILL ST is *Miln Lane* 1761 *EnclA*, *Mill lane* 1842 *TA*, 1862 White, *v.* **myln** and Eye Mills *infra*.

NOTTINGHAM RD, 1842 *TA*, 1863, 1877 White, *Not(t)ingham ~*, *Nottinghams Gate* 1550 *Pochin*, *v.* **gata**; the road to Nottingham which lies to the north-west.

NOTTINGHAM ST, 1842 *TA*, 1846, 1863, 1877 White; a continuation into the town centre of Nottingham Rd (via Park Rd).

PALL MALL, 1842 *TA*, 1863, 1877 White; a name transferred from the City of Westminster.

PARK RD is *Park Lane* 1863 White; beside Egerton Park *infra*.

REGENT ST, 1877 White; a common urban street-name honouring the Prince Regent, who became George IV in 1820. As late as c.1877, poss.

a transferred name from the City of Westminster, cf. Pall Mall *supra* and *Soho*, *infra*.

RUTLAND ST, 1842 *TA*, 1846, 1863, 1877 White; named in honour of the Duke of Rutland of Belvoir Castle, the county's senior peer of the realm.

SANDY LANE, *v.* **sandig**.

SCALFORD RD, 1846, 1863, 1877 White; it is *Skalford* ~, *Skalforth(e) gate* 1550 *Pochin*, *v.* **gata**; the road to Scalford which lies to the north.

SHERRARD ST, 1842 *TA*, 1846, 1877 White, *Sherard street* 1863 ib; with the surn. *Sherrard*.

SNOW HILL, 1877 White, 1925 Kelly. Since available forms are of late date, this may be a transferred name from the City of London. However, the road called Snow Hill curves gently and diagonally across a slight south-facing gradient which rises some 25 ft in 300 yards, so that the name may be an early survival, with OE *snōr* as first el., derived from a root meaning 'to twist', the road thus curving in order to negotiate the rise, *v.* **snōr** and M. Gelling, 'The hunting of the *snōr*', *Names, Places and People*, ed. A. R. Rumble and A. D. Mills, Stamford 1997, 93–5.

THORPE RD, 1846, 1877 White; it is *Thorpe gate* 1550 *Pochin*, *v.* **gata**; the road to Thorpe Arnold which lies to the north-east.

VICTORIA ST, cf. *Victoria place* 1863 White; named in honour of Queen Victoria.

WELBY LANE, cf. *Olebysti* 13 *Pochin*, *Oleby sty(e)* 1550 *ib*, *v.* **stīg**, **stígr** 'a narrow road'; Welby adjoins to the north-east.

WILTON RD, cf. *Wilton terrace* 1877 White, *v.* **terrace**; named from the Earl of Wilton who built Egerton Lodge as a hunting-lodge.

The following street-, road- and lane-names have not survived and have not been related with certainty to modern thoroughfares:

Ann street 1863, 1877 White.

Assebygate 13 *Pochin*, *v.* **gata**; the road to Ashby Folville, some six miles to the south-west.

the Back Street or Eye Gate 1782 *Fane*, *Back street* 1842 *TA*, 1863 White, *v.* **back** and *le Egate*, *infra*.

Bakhous lane 1335 Nichols, *v.* **bæc-hūs**, **lane**.

Baxterlane 1334 (1449), 1335 (1449), 1336 (1449), 1361 (1449) *WoCart*, *v.* **bæcestre**, **lane**.

Baytlane 1335 Nichols, *v.* **beit**, **lane**.

Birmingham road 1846 White.

Bradley's Row 1842 *TA*, *Bradley* ~ 1846 White, *v.* **rāw**; with the surn. *Bradley*.

Brentebigate, *Brentibigate* 1340 Nichols, *Brentingby Road* 1761 *EnclA*, *v.* **gata**; the road to Brentingby which lies to the east.

Caldwell Place 1842 *TA*, *v.* **place**.

Cappe Lane 1561 (17) *Rental*, *v.* **lane**; with the surn. *Capp*, cf. *Cap*(*e*) *place* in Domestic Buildings *infra*.

Cardigan terrace 1863, 1877 White, *v.* **terrace**; named in honour of James Brudenell, seventh Earl of Cardigan, who led the charge of the Light Brigade at Balaclava (1854) in the Crimean War.

Cheapside 1863, 1877 White; a transfer of the name of the City of London's Cheapside ('market side'), *v.* Lei **1** 27 *s.n.*

the Church lane 1550 *Pochin*, *Church lane* 1846 White, *v.* **lane** and St Mary's Church *infra*.

Coal Pitt Lane 1761 *EnclA*, *v.* **col-pytt**; presum. this refers to a place where charcoal was made rather than to an early mineral coal mine, even though nowadays coal is mined at Asfordby, some two miles west of Melton Mowbray.

Cornhill 1842 *TA*, 1846, 1863, 1877 White; prob. as for *Cheapside*, a transferred name from the City of London, indicating an area where corn was traded.

Dead ~, *Dede lane* 1550 *Pochin*, *v.* **dēad**, **lane**; perh. referring to the discovery of human bones at this location or to a lane with a dead-end, *v.* Dead Lane, Lei **1** 30-1 and Dean's St, Ru 104.

le Egate 1404 *Laz*, *v.* **gata**; a road leading to R. Eye (OE *ēa* 'a river, a stream'), *v. the Back Street*, *supra*.

Framland gate 1550 *Pochin*, *Framland way* 1669 *Reeve*, *Fram-land Lane* 1806 Map, *v.* **gata**, **weg**; the road due north from Melton Mowbray, leading to Great Framlands, the moot-site of the Framland Hundred (*q.v.*).

Goodrich street 1846, 1877 White, *Goodricke street* 1863 ib; with the surn. *Goodrich*, for which *Goodricke* is an alternative spelling, *v.* Reaney *s.n.*

Halford road 1877 White; with the surn. *Halford*.

Horngate 13 *Pochin*, *v.* **horn**, **gata**, cf. *Horn Lane* (Queen St) in Uppingham, Ru 212.

Ketleby ~, *Ketylby gate* 1550 *Pochin*, *v.* **gata**; the road to Eye Kettleby which lies to the south-west, rather than to Ab Kettleby to the north-west, since this road in 1550 was *Nottingham Gate* (*v.* Nottingham Rd).

Lambert Lane 1842 *TA*; with the surn. *Lambert*, cf. *Lamberts Meadow* 1744 *Rental*.

Little London 1842 *TA*, 1863 White; perh. used ironically of a square crowded with tenements.

Long gate 1550 *Pochin*, 1761 *EnclA*, *Longate* 1550 *Pochin*, 1761 *EnclA*, *Long Gate Road* 1761 *ib*, 1782 *Fane*, *Longate Road* 1842 *TA*, *v.* **lang**[1], **gata**.

Loundegat 1366 *Pochin*, *v.* **lundr**, **gata**, cf. *Lundewelle* and *Loundeinges* in f.ns. (b) *infra*.

Meer Lane 1761 *EnclA*, *v.* **(ge)mǣre**.

Melbourne street 1842 *TA*, 1863 White; named in honour of William Lamb, second Viscount Melbourne, who was Prime Minister in 1834 and 1835–41, a trusted adviser to the young Queen Victoria and whose wife, Lady Caroline Lamb, is chiefly remembered for her tempestuous love affair with Lord Byron.

Mill Lane Road 1842 *TA*, *v.* Mill St *supra*.

the Neate Drift 1664 *Reeve*, *the Drift* (*Way*) 1761 *EnclA*, *v.* **nēat**, **drift**.

New Street 1842 *TA*, 1846, 1863, 1877 White.

Norman street 1863, 1877 White; with the surn. *Norman*.

Northampton Gate 1550 *Pochin*, *v.* **gata**; the road to Northampton which lies to the south.

Nursery place 1863 White, *v.* **nursery**, **place**.

Park terrace 1863 White, *v.* **terrace** and Egerton Park *infra*.

Pigeon Row 1842 *TA*, 1863 White, *v.* **rāw**; whether with the surn. *Pigeon* or naming a location where pigeons congregated is uncertain.

Pinfold Lane 1761 *EnclA*, *v.* **pynd-fald** and Pinfold Cl in f.ns. (b) *infra*.

Play Close Lane 1842 *TA*, *v.* Play Close *infra*.

Queen Street 1842 *TA*, 1846, 1863 White, *Queen's ~* 1842 *TA*; honouring either the accession of Queen Victoria in 1837 or her marriage to Prince Albert of Saxe-Coburg-Gotha in 1840.

Ross Street 1842 *TA*, 1863 White; with the surn. *Ross*.

Rutland terrace 1863 White, *v.* **terrace**; named from the Duke of Rutland of Belvoir Castle, the county's senior peer.

(*the*) *Sage Crosse streete* 1631, 1634 *Conant*, *Sage Crose Streete* 1652 *ib*, *Sage Cross Street* 1842 *TA*, 1846, 1863, 1877 White, *v.* The Sage Cross *infra*.

Saltegate 13, 1334 *Pochin*, 1445, 1449 Cl, *Saltgate* 14 (1449) *WoCart*, 1550 *Pochin*, *Salgate* 1541, 1550 *ib*, *v.* **salt**[1], **gata**; the salt-merchants' road running from east to west across the parish south of the river, through Burton Lazars and Kirby Bellars. It is also recorded as *Saltergate* 1449 Cl, *v.* **saltere**.

Shamlys 1550 *Pochin*, *v.* **sceamol**; the butchers' shambles.

Soho 1842 *TA*, 1925 Kelly; opening from *Little London* and clearly a borrowing of the City of Westminster name.

Southern lane 1863, 1877 White.

South parade 1863, 1877 White, *v.* **parade**.

ye street called Spitle End 1708 *Terrier*, ~ ~ ~ *Spittle End* 1708 (18) *ib*, *Spittle End* 1733 LAS, 1761 *EnclA*, *v.* **spitel**, **ende** and *Hospitalis de Melton* in Charitable Institutions *infra*.

Spytelgate 1309 Cl, *le Spetylgate*, *le Spitelgate* 1404 *Laz*, *v.* **spitel**, **gata** and *Hospitalis de Melton* in Charitable Institutions *infra*.

Swyneslane 1293 (1449) *WoCart*, *le Swynlane* 1349 (1449), 1357 (1449), 1363 (1449) *ib*, *v.* **swīn**, **lane**.

Sydney street 1877 White.

Temperance terrace 1863 White, *v.* **terrace**; named from the 19th cent. Temperance Movement which aimed to persuade people against the consumption of alcohol.

Timber Hill 1733 LAS, 1842 *TA*, 1846, 1863, 1877 White, *v.* **timber**.

Union street 1863 White; perh. named in celebration of Pitt's Act of Union of 1801, uniting the parliaments of Britain and Ireland, cf. Union St (x2), Lei **1** 67; but note *Union House* in Civic Buildings *infra*.

Water lane 1550 *Pochin*, 1628 (1791), 1648, 1681 (1791), 1682, 1685 (1791), 1686 *Surv*, *v.* **wæter**, **lane**; leading to, or close by the river.

The Wharf 1863 White, *Canal Wharf* 1877 ib, *v.* **hwearf**; on the *Melton Mowbray and Leicester Navigation* 1846, 1863 White, a canalized portion of R. Eye.

No early forms have been found for the following Melton Mowbray street-names:

ABINGDON RD, ALBERT ST, ALGERNON RD, ALVASTON RD, ANKLE HILL RD (*v.* Ankle Hill), ARDEN DRIVE, BALDOCK'S LANE, BALMORAL RD, BARKER CRESC, BEACONSFIELD RD, BEECHWOOD AVE, BELVOIR ST, BLAKENEY CRESC, BOWLEY AVE, BRAMPTON RD, BRIGHTSIDE AVE, BROOK ST, CAMBRIDGE AVE, CHARNWOOD DRIVE, CLUMBER ST, COLLEGE AVE, COLLINGWOOD CRESC, CONISTON RD, CONWAY DRIVE, CRAVEN ST, THE CRESCENT, DOCTOR'S LANE, DOROTHY AVE, DULVERTON RD, EAST AVE, EASTFIELD AVE, EGERTON RD (*v.* Egerton

Lodge), ELMHURST AVE, ELMS RD, FERNIE AVE, FERNELEY CRESC, FIELD CL, FIRWOOD RD, GARDEN LANE, GARTREE DRIVE, GLOUCESTER AVE, GLOUCESTER CRESC, GLOUCESTER RD, GRANGE DRIVE, GRANTWOOD RD, GRANVILLE RD, GREAVES AVE, HADFIELD DRIVE, HAMILTON DRIVE, HARTLAND DRIVE, HARTOPP RD, HIGHFIELD AVE (*v.* Highfield Ho.), HILLSIDE AVE, HUNTERS RD, JARVIS DRIVE, KING'S RD, LAKE TERRACE, LAYCOCK AVE, LEICESTER RD, LIMES AVE, LUDLOW DRIVE, LYNTON RD, MAYFIELD ST, MEADOW WAY, MELBRAY DRIVE, MELTON SPINNEY RD (*v.* Melton Spinney), MORLEY ST, NEEDHAM CL, NEWBURY AVE, NEWPORT AVE (*v.* Newport Lodge), NORFOLK DRIVE, NORTH ST, OAK RD, OXFORD DRIVE, PADDOCK CL, PALMERSTON RD, PETERSFIELD RD, PRINCESS DRIVE, QUEENSWAY, QUORN AVE, RIVERSIDE RD, ROSEBERY AVE, RUDBECK AVE (*v.* Rudbeck Cl in f.ns. (a)), ST JOHN'S DRIVE, SALISBURY AVE, SAPCOTE DRIVE, SAXBY RD, SHERWOOD DRIVE, SPRINGFIELD, STANLEY ST, STAFFORD AVE, STAVELEY RD (*v.* Staveley Lodge), STIRLING RD, SUSSEX AVE, SYSONBY ST, TENNIS AVE, TENNYSON WAY, TUDOR HILL, VICTORIA ST, WARWICK RD, WELBY RD, WEST AVE, WICKLOW AVE (*v.* Wicklow Lodge), WOODLAND AVE, WYCLIFFE AVE (*v.* Wycliffe Ho.).

BRIDGES

BURTON END BRIDGE, *Burton Bridge* 1550 *Pochin*, 1761 *EnclA*, 1782 *Fane*, *v.* **brycg**; crossing R. Eye on the road to Burton Lazars which lies to the south-east.

LEICESTER BRIDGE, 1842 *TA*; carries Leicester Rd across R. Eye. Known locally as Lady Wilton's Bridge, *v.* Egerton Lodge *infra*.

THORPE BRIDGE, 1761 *EnclA*, *Thorp(p) Bridge* 1550 *Pochin*, *v.* **brycg**; on the road to Thorpe Arnold to the north-east. It is the site of *Ailmeresbrigge* 13 (1404) Laz, *v.* **brycg**; the first el. is ME *Ailmer/Ailmar*, from the OE pers.n. *Æðelmǣr*, *v.* Feilitzen 184–5.

The following bridges are either unlocated or unidentified:

Becebrigge m.13 (1449), 13 (1449) *WoCart*, *v.* **brycg**; since both forms are cartulary copies and thus may have been mistranscribed, the first el. could be either OE **bece**[1] 'a stream' or Scand **bekkr** with the same meaning. The bridge was situated between Melton Mowbray and Sysonby.

Foleville brigge 1340 Nichols, *v.* **brycg**; with the feudal surn. *Foleville,* cf. Ashby Folville which lies to the south-west in East Goscote Hundred. The bridge is unlocated.

Ketleby bridge 1550 *Pochin, Kettleby Bridge* 1761 *EnclA, v.* **brycg**; on the road to Eye Kettleby which lies to the south-west of Melton Mowbray.

Stone Bridge 1761 *EnclA.*

ECCLESIASTICAL BUILDINGS

St Mary's Church
  ecclesie de Meltuna 1121 AC, *ecclesiam de Melton'* 1200 Cur, *ecclesie de Meuton* 1220 MHW, ~ *de Melton'* 1310 *Pat, ecclesie paroch' de Melton Moubray* 1415 (c.1430) *KB, ecclesia de Melton Mowbray* 1563 *Pat*
  the Church 1550 *Pochin, the Parish Church of Melton* 1707 *Terrier St Mary's Church* 1842 *TA, Church (St Mary)* 1846, 1863, 1877 White
  the Church yard 1550 *Pochin,* 1707, c.1720 *Terrier, Churchyard* 1863, 1877 White

v. **cirice, chirche-ȝeard**.

St John The Baptist's Chapel (lost), *capelle Sancti Johannis Baptiste Melton Moubray* 1374 *Pat, capelle libere Sancti Johannis Baptiste Melton Moubray* 1400 *ib, capelle libere de Melton Moubray* 1405 *ib*; with MLat *capella libera* 'free or privileged chapel', presum. a royal foundation, cf. *the kynges land late Saynt Johannes* in f.ns. (b) *infra.*

Note also: *Independent Chapel* 1842 *TA; Methodist Chapel* 1842 *TA; Primitive Methodist Chapel* 1842 *TA; Roman Catholic Chapel* 1842 *TA.*

CROSSES

the Corn Cross 1733 LAS, 1795 Nichols, *v.* **corn**[1]; located at the west end of the town.

the Hye Crosse 1607 *Reeve, the High Cross(e)* 1621, 1631 *ib, the Market Cross* 1736 *Terrier, the Buttercross* 1795 Nichols (*v.* **butere**);

the principal market cross of the town, sited in the Market Place. This is referred to earlier in *atte Crosse* 1330 Pat (p), *atte Crose* 1335 (1449) *WoCart* (p), *atte Cros* 1348 Pat (p), 1369 ib (p), 1404 *Laz* (p), *del Cros* 1384 Pat (p), *v.* **hēah**[1], **cros, atte**.

the Sage Cross(e) 1660 *Reeve*, 1795 Nichols, *v.* **sauge, cros**; sited at the east end of the town. It is uncertain whether *ye Womans Market Cross* 1708 *Terrier*, *the Womens Market-Cross* 1708 (18) *ib* is to be identified with *the Sage Crosse*.

Shepe Cross 1577 AAS, *v.* **scēp, cros**; unlocated, but presum. at the site of the sheep market.

CHARITABLE INSTITUTIONS

HUDSON'S BEDE HOUSE (lost), *Hudsons Hospital* 1761 *EnclA*, *Hudson's Almshouse* 1846, 1863 White, *Hudson's Bede House* 1863, 1877 ib, *v.* **hospital, almes-hous, bed-hūs**; founded in 1671 by Robert Hudson.

MELTON HOSPITAL (lost), *Hospitalis de Melton'* 1254 Val; with MLat *hospital* 'a hospice, a hospital'. Note also *the Spittell Chapell* 1548 Pat, *Spyttell Chappell* 1548 AAS, *Spittall Chappell* 1577 ib, *the Chapel Howse alias the Spittell Chappell* 1548 Pat, *the Chappill house* 1549 AAS, *v.* **spitel, chapel(e), hūs**; the chapel of this early hospital.

STORER'S ALMSHOUSE (lost), *Storer's Alms Houses* 1842 *TA*, ~ *Almshouse* 1846, 1863, 1877 White, *v.* **almes-hous**; endowed in 1720 by Henry Storer.

CIVIC BUILDINGS

Burgate m.13 (1404) *Laz*, *v.* **burh-geat** 'a town gate'; perh. to be identified with *le yate howse* 1540 *Ct* (*v.* **gate-hous**) and *an ancient gateway called Leicester Gate* 1761 *EnclA*, located presum. towards Leicester Bridge. Town gateways imply a former defensive enceinte; note *the towne dyke* 1550 Pochin (*v.* **tūn, dík**) which appears to record a surrounding ditch.

County Bridewell 1842 *TA*, *v.* **bridewell** 'a place of forced labour for prisoners', cf. Bridewell, Lei **1** 109.

Union House 1824 O, *Union Workhouse* 1846, 1877 White; a Poor Law institute, it became St Mary's Hospital.

INNS AND TAVERNS

BELL AND SWAN (lost), *Bell and Swan* 1846, 1863, 1877 White. BELL HOTEL (lost), *Bell hotel* 1925 Kelly. BISHOP BLAZE (lost), *Old Bishop Blaize* 1846, 1863 White, *Bishop Blaze Inn, Bishop Blaise* 1877 ib, (*Old*) *Bishop Blaze* 1925 Kelly, v. Lei 1 122. BLACK HORSE (lost), *Black Horse* 1846, 1863, 1877 White, 1925 Kelly. BLACK MOOR'S HEAD (lost), *Black Moor's Head* 1846, 1863 White, *Black's Head* 1877 ib, 1925 Kelly. BLACK SWAN, 1846, 1863, 1877 White, 1925 Kelly. BLUE BELL (lost), *The Blue Bell* 1662 Nichols. BOAT INN, 1925 Kelly, *Boat* 1846, 1863 White; it is *Boatman Inn* 1877 ib. BRICKLAYERS' ARMS (lost), *Bricklayers' Arms* 1846, 1863, 1877 White, 1925 Kelly. CROWN (lost), *Crown* 1846, 1863 White, 1925 Kelly, *Crown Inn* 1877 White. EIGHT BELLS (lost), *Eight Bells* 1846, 1863 White, 1925 Kelly, *Eight Bells Inn* 1877 White. FOX AND HOUNDS (lost), *Fox and Hounds* 1846 White. FOX INN, 1877 White, *Fox* 1846, 1863 ib, 1925 Kelly. GENEROUS BRITON, 1846, 1877 White, 1925 Kelly, *Old Generous Briton* 1863 White. GEORGE AND DRAGON (lost), *George and Dragon* 1846, 1863 White. GEORGE HOTEL, 1863, 1877 White, 1925 Kelly, *George* 1846 White. GOLDEN FLEECE, 1846, 1863, 1877 White, 1925 Kelly. GRAPES, *The Grapes* 1925 Kelly. HALF MOON, 1846, 1863 White, *Half Moon Inn* 1877 ib. HARBOROUGH ARMS (lost), *Harborough Arms* 1846, 1863 White, *Harbro' Hotel* 1877 ib; named from the Earls of Harborough of Stapleford Hall. KING'S HEAD, 1846, 1863, 1877 White, *King's Head Hotel* 1925 Kelly. LORD NELSON (lost), *Lord Nelson* 1846, 1863 White. LORD WARDEN (lost), *Lord Warden* 1877 White; prob. a later name for the Lord Nelson, since both were in Leicester St. MALT SHOVEL (lost), *Malt Shovel* 1846, 1863, 1877 White. MARQUIS OF GRANBY (lost), *Marquis of Granby* 1846, 1863 White, 1925 Kelly, *Granby Inn* 1877 White; named from the title of the eldest son of the Duke of Rutland, v. Lei 1 132 *s.n.* NOEL ARMS, *Noel's Arms* 1846, 1863, 1877 White; named from the Noel family of Exton in Rutland, the Earls of Gainsborough. PEACOCK (lost), *Peacock* 1846, 1863, 1877 White; the peacock is part of the coat of arms of the Manners family, the Dukes of Rutland. RAILWAY (lost), *Railway* 1863 White, *Railway Inn* 1877 ib. RED LION (lost), *Red Lion* 1846, 1863, 1877 White, 1925 Kelly. ROUND TABLE (lost), *the Round Table* 1551 × 53 ECP, 1621 Reeve, *The Rownde Table* 1607 *ib*; presum. named with reference to the legend of King Arthur and the Knights of the Round Table, cf. *mess' voc' le Rounde Table* 1544 in Beausale, Wa 367.

RUTLAND ARMS, 1846, 1863, 1877 White, 1925 Kelly; named from the Dukes of Rutland of Belvoir Castle. STAR (lost), *Star* 1846, 1863 White. SWAN (lost), *le Swan* 1540 *Ct, the Swan* 1550 *Pochin.* SWAN AND SALMON (lost), *Swan and Salmon* 1846, 1863 White. THREE CROWNS (lost), *Three Crowns* 1863, 1877 White. THREE TUNS (lost), *Three Tuns* 1925 Kelly. WHEATSHEAF (lost), *Wheat Sheaf* 1846, 1863, 1877 White, *Wheatsheaf* 1925 Kelly. WHITE HART, 1925 Kelly. WHITE LION HOTEL, 1877 White, 1925 Kelly, *White Lion* 1846, 1863 White. WHITE SWAN (lost), *the White Swan Inn* 1705 *Reeve.* WOOLPACK (lost), *Woolpack* 1846 White.

DOMESTIC BUILDINGS

ANNE OF CLEVE'S HO. (local) is situated beside the parish church and was presum. the priest's house in origin. It is so named because the revenues of Lewes Priory, to which the living was appropriated, became the jointure of Henry VIII's queen. It is prob. to be identified with *the Churchehowse* 1554 Pat *infra.* THE BEECHES. CATHERINE DALLEY HO. CRAVEN LODGE 1873 *Sale, v.* **loge**. DORIAN LODGE. EGERTON LODGE, 1842 *TA*, 1846, 1863 White, *v.* **loge**; with Egerton Park, named from Francis Egerton, third Duke of Bridgewater (1736–1803), the British canal builder responsible for the Bridgewater Canal from Liverpool to Manchester. Egerton Park constitutes the island formed by R. Eye and the canal of the former Melton Mowbray and Leicester Navigation which cuts across the large sweep of the river south-west of Egerton Lodge. The house was the hunting-lodge of the Earl of Wilton. HIGHFIELD HO., cf. *Highfield* 1682, 1686 *Surv, v.* **hēah**[1], **feld**. HIGH VIEW. THE HOMESTEAD. THE MANOR HO., *The Manor House* 1842 *TA, v.* **maner**; built as a hunting-box for Lady Lawson. NEWPORT LODGE, 1863, 1877 White, *v.* **loge**. NORTHFIELD HO., *v. North field* in f.ns. (b) *infra*. PENARTH. SCALFORD ROAD LODGE. STAVELEY LODGE, with the surn. *Staveley.* The Staveley monument stands in the churchyard and was erected by this family of masons in 1747 to contain their burials dating from 1670 to 1747. THE VICARAGE, *(The) Vicarage House* 1625, 1707, 1707 (18), 1724 *Terrier*, 1842 *TA, the Vicaridge house* 1605 *Terrier, v.* **vikerage** and *the mansion howse of the Parsonage, infra.* WICKLOW LODGE. WYCLIFFE HO. is *Wycliffe Cottage* 1863 White, *Wycliffe House* 1877 ib; presum. named from John Wycliffe, the religious reformer, who made the first translation of the Bible and was

Rector of Lutterworth in the south of the county 1375–84. WYNDHAM
LODGE, 1873 *Sale*, v. **loge**.

The following domestic buildings are early and lost: *Bromwells place*
1550 *Pochin* (v. **place**; with the surn. *Bromwell*); *Cap(e) place* 1550
Pochin (v. **place**; with the surn. *Capp*, cf. *Cappe Lane, supra*); *the
Churchehowse* 1554 Pat, *le Churche House* 1558 ib (v. **cirice, hūs**); *atte
Hall* 1350 Nichols (p), *ad Aulam* 1327 SR (p) (with MLat *aula* 'a hall')
(v. **atte, hall**); *Mr Irelands House* 1716 *Pochin*; *Lamberts house* 1719
Nichols; *the mansion howse of the Parsonage* 1550 *Pochin, the
Parsonage House* 1669 *Reeve* (v. **mansion-house, personage** and The
Vicarage *supra*); *Monkes howse, Monkys howse* 1550 *Pochin* (v. **hūs**;
presum. with the surn. *Monk*, unless formerly the property of a religious
order); *Paccheplace* 1320 *Pochin, Pesshonplace* 1363 (1449) *WoCart*
(v. **place**; these messuage names appear to belong together since the ME
surn. *Pesshon/Pachon* is a diminutive of the ME surn. *Pacche* (a form
of *pasches* 'Easter'), the former giving the modern surn. *Patchin* and the
latter the surn. *Patch*; they poss. name a father and son or a grandfather
and grandson, v. Reaney *s.n.* Patch and Patchin); *(the) Parke House*
1616, 1718, 1719 *Reeve, the Park House* 1716, 1744 *ib* (v. **park**); *atte
Sale* 1330 Pat (p), 1345 ib (p), 1347 ib (p), 1348 *ib* (p) (v. **atte, salr**);
Storers House 1716 *Pochin* (cf. Henry Storer who endowed Storer's
Almshouse in 1720); *the Tythe howse* 1550 *Pochin* (v. **tēoða, hūs**; this
was perh. a house from which the parish priest received cash payments
as tithe, but otherwise his tithe barn, though less likely).

MILLS

BECK MILL (lost), *becmilne* m.13 (1404) *Laz, Beckemylne* 1561 (17)
Rental, Beck Milne 1648 *Surv, Beck Mill or the over Shott Milne* 1648
ib, the Water Milne called the Beck milne or the overshot Milne 17 *ib,*
(Two Milnes under one Roofe called) the Beck Milnes 1682, 1686 *ib,*
(the) Beck mill 1668 (1791), 1682 (1791), 17 *ib*, 1718 Nichols, 1744
Surv, 1761 *EnclA*, 1842 *TA*, 1877 White, *the Beck Mill with the dams*
1681 (1791) *Surv, a water Grist Mill called the Beck Mill* 1744 *ib*, 1744
Rental, v. **bekkr, myln, damme**; a corn water-mill with an overshot
wheel.
    EYE MILLS (lost), *(le) Emylyn* 1400 Ipm, *(the) Eye Mill* 1648, 1682
(1791), 17 *Surv, Eye Milne* 1682 *ib, Eye Milln* 1686 *ib, a Fulling Mill*

called Eye Mill 1744 *ib*, 1744 *Rental, Eymylnes* 1561 (17) *ib, The two Ey(e) mills* 1668 (1791), 1681 (1791), 1682 (1791), 1685 (1791) *Surv*, 1795 Nichols, *v.* **myln**; located on R. Eye.

THE MALT MILL (lost), *the mault milne* 1550 *Pochin, Maltemylne* 1561 (17) *Rental, v.* **malte-mylne**; the earliest citation for such a mill in OED is for 1607.

WARWELLMILL (lost), *Warwellemilne* 14 (1449) *WoCart, v.* **wer, wær, wella, myln**.

THE WINDMILL (lost), *the Windmill* 1681 (1791), 1682 (1791), 1685 (1791) *Surv, Wind Miln* 1686 *ib, Burton Windmill* 1744 *ib*, 1744 *Rental, v.* **wind-mylne**; located in Burton Fd on high ground to the south of the town towards Burton Lazars.

EARLY FARMS

Framlands farm 1877 White (*v.* Great Framlands); *Haynes farm(e)* 1674 *Reeve* (the property of *Lorance Haynes* 1674 *ib, v.* **ferme**); *Spring farm* 1877 White (cf. *wellesprynges* in f.ns. (b) *infra*); *Frances Walthoms Farm* 1682 *Surv, Francis Walthhoms Farm* 1682 (1791) *ib* (*v.* **ferme**; the surn. is *Waltham*, no doubt of a family originally from Waltham on the Wolds, five miles to the north-east of Melton Mowbray).

ANKLE HILL, 1925 Kelly, *Ankley ~, Anklie hill* 1550 *Pochin, Anchor hill* 1863 White, 'hill at the river bend', *v.* **angle, hyll**, cf. *Aungelwonge* in f.ns. (b) *infra*. BOUCH'S COVERT, *v.* **cover(t)**; with the surn. *Bouch, v.* Reaney *s.n.* BURBAGE'S COVERT (NEW COVERT 2½"), *v.* **cover(t)**; with the surn. *Burbage* of a family prob. originating in the village of this name, 25 miles to the south-west in Sparkenhoe Hundred. BURTON END, 1550 *Pochin*, 1705 *Reeve*, 1842 *TA*, 1846, 1863 White, *v.* **ende**; that end of the town towards Burton Lazars which adjoins to the south-east. BURTON HILL is rising ground south of the town on the road to Burton Lazars. EGERTON PARK (FRONT PARK 2½"), cf. *The Parks* 1842 *TA* (also with reference to New Park *infra*), *The Park* 1925 Kelly, *v.* **park** and Egerton Lodge *supra*. GRAMMAR SCHOOL FM (WYMONDHAM GRAMMAR SCHOOL FM 2½"), the former Wymondham Grammar School having been founded in 1637 by Sir John Sedley. GREAT FRAMLANDS, 1842 *TA, Framelande* 1400 Ipm, *Framland* 1550 *Pochin*, cf. *Little Framlands* 1842 *TA*. Great Framlands was the moot-site of the Framland Hundred (*q.v.*). Also recorded are *bosco de Framelund* 1276 RH (with

MLat *boscus* 'a wood', perh. the original *lundr* 'a small wood' of Framland), *Framland(e) hedge* 1550 *Pochin*, 1682, 1686 *Surv* (*v.* **hecg**; the boundary hedge of Framland), *Framland olde* 1541 *Ct* (*v.* **wald**; the high ground on which Framland is situated), *Framland Sike*, ~ *Syke* 1550 *Pochin* (*v.* **sík**). MELTON SPINNEY, 1806 Map; also may belong here *Lytle Spynney* 1539 Nichols, *Litle Spynes* 1550 *Pochin*, (*the*) *Farr Spinney(s)*, *the Farther* ~, *Further Spinneys* 1761 *EnclA*, *v.* **lȳtel**, **spinney** and The Spinney *infra*. MELTON SPINNEY FM. THE MOUNT, the earthworks of a motte and bailey castle. MOUNT PLEASANT (2½"), *Mount Pleasant* 1842 *TA*, 1846, 1863, 1877 White; a name for the locality of The Mount. NEW PARK, *v.* Egerton Park *supra*. PLAY CLOSE, (*the*) *Play Close* 1761 *EnclA*, 1842 *TA*; beside the parish church and thus a traditional popular location for games of various kinds, *v.* Field 243–4. SCALFORD BROOK, 1842 *TA*; it is *Scalford Dyke* 1831 Map, *v.* **dík**. This flows south from Scalford parish, which adjoins to the north, through Melton Mowbray into R. Eye. SHIPMAN'S BARN STUD, *v.* **stōd**; with the surn. *Shipman*. THE SPINNEY, *Speneye* 1272 Ch, *la Spyne* 1318 Pat, *Speney* 1445, 1449 Cl, *Spynee* 1535 Hastings, *Greate Spynney* 1539 Nichols, *the greate Spynys* 1550 *Pochin*, *Near Spinney* 1761 *EnclA*, cf. *the Lytil and Gret Spyney* 1501 AD, *the Spynis* 1550 *Pochin*, *v.* **grēat**, **lȳtel**, **spinney** and Melton Spinney *supra*. SPINNEY FM, SPINNEY FARM COTTAGE (SPINNEY FM 2½"), both near Melton Spinney *supra*. SWAN'S NEST, *le nesse* 1540 *Ct*, *Swanne Nesse*, *Swannesse*, *Swannys Nesse* 1561 (17) *Surv*, *v.* **swan**[1], **næss**, **nes**; in a major bend of R. Eye. THORPE END, 1842, 1845 *TA*, 1846, 1863, 1877 White, *v.* **ende**; that portion of the town towards Thorpe Arnold which lies to the north-east.

FIELD-NAMES

In (a), forms dated 1753 are *Pochin*; 1761 are *EnclA*; 1782 are *Fane*; 1786, 1795[1], 1796 and 1810 are *Reeve*; 1792 are *Rental*; 1795[2] are Nichols; 1806, 1824 and 1831 are Map; 1842 and 1845 are *TA*; 1873 are *Sale*. Forms throughout dated m.13 (1404), 13 (1404) and 1404 are *Laz*; m.13 (1449), 1293 (1449), l.13 (1449), 13 (1449), 1329 (1449), 1334 (1449), 1335 (1449), 1336 (1449), 1348 (1449), 1349 (1449), 1351 (1449), 1357 (1449), 1361 (1449), 1363 (1449) and 14 (1449) are *WoCart*; 1254 are Val; 1272 are Ch; 1276 are RH; 13, 1320, 1331, 1334, 1366, 1716[1] and 1717 are *Pochin*; 1309, 1310[1], 1341, 1359, 1392, 1445 and 1449 are Cl; 1310[2], 1374, 1400[2], 1405 and 1563 are *Pat*; 1318,

1330, 1345, 1347[1], 1348, 1369, 1384, 1548[1], 1549[1], 1554 and 1558 are
Pat; 1326 and 1400[1] are Ipm; 1335, 1340, 1350, 1363, 1539, 1718[1] and
1719[1] are Nichols; 1347[2] are Fine; 1351 are *Wyg*; 1441 are Banco; 1477
(e.16) are *Charyte*; 1501 are AD; 1535 are HMCVar; 1540 and 1541 are
Ct; 1548[2], 1549[2], 1567 and 1577 are AAS; 1550, 1605, 1625, 1707,
1707 (18), 1708, 1708 (18), c.1720, 1724 and 1736 are *Terrier*; 1551 ×
53 are ECP; 1561 (17) and 1744[1] are *Rental*; 1607, 1616, 1621, 1631[1],
1649, 1660, 1664, 1669, 1674, 1705, 1716[2], 1718[2], 1719[2], 1744[2] and
1750 are *Reeve*; 1631[2], 1634 and 1652 are *Conant*; 1648, 1668 (1791),
1681 (1791), 1682, 1682 (1791), 1685 (1791), 1686, 17 and 1744[3] are
Surv; 1733 are LAS.

(a) Almonds Piece 1782 (*v.* **pece**; with the surn. *Almond*); Ancle Hill Cls 1761,
Ankle Hill Cl 1782, Ancle Hill Furlong 1761 (*v.* Ankle Hill *supra*); Ashbys Cl 1761,
Ashbys Longate ~, Ashbys Long Gate Cl 1761 (*v. Long gate* in Streets, Roads and
Lanes), Ashbys Wong 1761 (*v.* **vangr**) (all with the surn. *Ashby*); Ballance Sick 1761
(1744[1], 1744[3], *Baland* ~, *Balond Syke* 1550, *Balon Sike,* ~ *Syke* 1550, *Ballande Sicke*
1669, *v.* **bēan**, **land**, **sík** and Bellands in Bottesford f.ns. (a)); (the) Beck Mill Cl
1761, 1842 (17, 1718[1], *Beckemylne Close* 1561 (17), *v.* **clos(e)** and Beck Mill *supra*);
Binghams Leys 1761 (*v.* **leys**; with the surn. *Bingham* of a family originally from
Bingham, 13 miles to the north in Notts.); The Black Dike 1842 (*v.* **blæc, dík**); The
Bridge Leys 1795[2] (*v.* **leys**); the Broadings, Broadings Mdw 1761 (*the brodenge,
Broding alias Crodyke, Broding(e)s, Broddings* 1550, *v.* **brād, eng** and *Crodyke* in
f.ns. (b)); Brockleburys Cl 1761 (with the surn. *Brocklebury*, poss. a late form of the
p.n. Brocklesby in Lincs., although no identical spellings are found in L 2 61–2 *s.n.*);
Burton Bridge Highway Cl, ~ ~ Nether Cl, ~ ~ Upper Cl 1782 (*v.* Burton Bridge
supra); Burton Fd 1761 (1540, 1682 (1791), 1718[1], 1744[1], 1744[3], *Burton Felde*
1549[1], ~ *Feild* 1681 (1791), 1682, 17, *in campo de Burton'* 1550 (with MLat *campus*
'a field'), *v.* **feld**; one of the great fields of the town, lying south-east towards Burton
Lazars); Burton Gate Sick 1761 (*Burton gate Seike* 1682, ~ ~ *Sike* 1686, *v.* **gata, sík**;
on the road to Burton Lazars); Burton Hedge Furlong 1761 (*Burton hedge* 1682,
1686, *v.* **hecg**; the parish boundary hedge with Burton Lazars), Burton Hedge
Gateway 1761 (a gate through the aforementioned boundary, poss. an early toll-gate);
Causeway Hill 1761, Causey-Hill Cl 1795[2] (cf. *le Causehyshend* 1340 Nichols, *v.*
caucie, ende); Chapel Cl 1753 (*v. the Spittell Chapell* in Charitable Institutions
supra); Crumpton's Cl 1782 (with the surn. *Crumpton/Crompton* of a family perh.
originating in Crompton (La), 13th cent. spellings of which show *Crumpton*); Dike
~, Dyke Mdw 1761 (*the dyke* 1550, cf. *le dicforlang* 13 (1449), *le dikforlong* 1310,
Dyke furlong(e) 1550, *v.* **dík, furlang**); the Drift Land 1761 (*v.* **land**), Drift Wongs
1761 (*v.* **vangr**) (*v. the Neate Drift* in Streets, Roads and Lanes *supra*); (the) Fish
Pond Cl 1761, 1782, 1795, 1796; Framlands Cls 1761 (*v.* Great Framlands); Gravel Pit(t)
Cl 1761, the Gravel Pit Wongs 1761 (*v.* **vangr**) (*v.* **gravel, pytt**); the Green 1782,
1795 (*v.* **grēne**[2]); Henshaws Cl 1782 (with the surn. *Henshaw*); High Leys, ~ ~ Cl
1761 (*High Leyes* 1682, 1744[1], 1744[3], *(the) High Leys* 1686, 1716[1], *High leyes Close*
1682, ~ *leys* ~ 1686, *v.* **hēah**[1], **leys**), High Leys Gateway 1761 (cf. Burton Hedge

Gateway *supra*); Hither Sick Furlong 1761 (1686, *Hither Seike* 1682, *Hithersike* 1718[1], *v.* **hider, sík**); (the) Hole Sick alias Long Gate Cl 1782, 1795[1], 1796, Hole Sike Cl 1796 (*holsyke* 1366, *holesyck* 1541, *Hole Syke* 1550, ~ *Seike* 1682, ~ *Sick* 1686, *v.* **hol**[2], **holr, sík** and *Long gate* in Streets, Roads and Lanes *supra*); Ivets Slip 1792 (*v.* **slipe**; cf. *the land of the heires of Ivet* 1550 and *Peter Ivet* 1550); Ladys ~, Lady's Mdw 1761 (*la Ladymede* 1441, *Our Ladyes medow* 1567, cf. *the towne land called Our ladies land* 1550, *v.* **lavedi, mǣd** (**mǣdwe** obl.sg.), **land**; land dedicated to the service of Our Lady, the Virgin Mary); Leicester Gate Furlong 1761 (presum. adjacent to *an ancient gateway called Leicester Gate*, *v.* **Burgate** in Civic Buildings *supra*); Levetts Cls 1782, 1795[1], Livetts Cls 1796, Levetts Wongs 1761 (*v.* **vangr**) (with the surn. *Levett*); Long Fd 1761 (1744[1], 1744[3]); Long Gate Cl 1782 (cf. *Long gate side* 1550, *v.* **sīde**, (the) Hole Sick *supra* and *Long gate* in Streets, Roads and Lanes *supra*); Long Mdw 1753; the Lords Hades 1761 (*v.* **hēafod**), Lords Mdw 1761 (1685 (1791), *the Lords Meadow(e)* 1648, 1669, 1681 (1791), 1744[1], 1744[3]; with reference to *the lord Barkley lord of Melton* 1550, *Morris Barkley knight* 1550); Lucy Cl 1761, Lucy alias Pinfold Cl 1782, 1795[1] (*v.* **pynd-fald**) (*lucy close* 1541, *v.* **clos(e)**; with the surn. *Lucy*); Matchetts Cl 1782 (with the surn. *Matchett*); Midsummer Piece 1761 (*v.* **pece**; poss. indicating seasonal use, *v.* Field 117–18, or else with the surn. *Midsummer*, *v.* Reaney *s.n.*); (the) Mill Brook 1761, 1842 (i.e. Scalford Brook), Mill Pond 1842 (i.e. of Beck Mill); Mill Cl 1761, 1842, Mill Close Homestead 1795[2] (*v.* **hām-stede**) (*Milne Close* 1550, *Mylne Close* 1561 (17), *Mill Close* 1744[1], 1744[3], *the Eye Milne Close* 1648, 1682, 1686, 17, *the Eye Mill Close* 1681 (1791), 1682 (1791), 1685 (1791), *v.* **myln, clos(e)**); Mill Holme 1753, the Mill Holme Cl 1761 (*the Mill holme*, (*the*) *Milne holme* 1550, *the Mill Holmes* 1648, 1681 (1791), *The Eye mill & Holmes* 1682 (1791), *Eye Milne homes* 1686, *Eye Mill Holmes* 1744[1], 1744[3], *v.* **myln, holmr**), Mill Leys 1761 (*v.* **leys**), Miln Lane Cl 1761 (*v.* Eye Mills *supra*); Nest Leys 1753 (*v.* **leys** and Swan's Nest *supra*); Norths Cl 1761 (with the surn. *North*); Olivers Cl 1782 (with the surn. *Oliver*); (the) Open Close alias Red Gate Mdw 1782, 1795[2] (*Open Close* 1716[1], 1717, *v.* **open**; originally an enclosure without a permanent gate, perh. closed off by hurdles as necessary; presum. Red Gate was a road-name (i.e. with **gata**), although there is no earlier evidence for such); Orgar Leys 1761, ~ Lays 1846 White (*Orgar Leyes* 1669, 1718[1], *v.* **leys**; with the surn. *Orgar*, cf. *John Orger* 1400[1]); Ormond's Piece 1795[2] (*v.* **pece**; with the surn. *Ormond*); Parke Cl 1753, Park ~ 1782 (*v.* **park**); Pinfold Cl 1782 (cf. *Pinfold leyes* 1682, ~ *leys* 1686, *v.* **pynd-fald, leys**, Lucy Cl *supra* and Pinfold Lane); the Pingle 1782 (1682, 1682 (1791), 1686, cf. *Rowses Pingle* 1744[1], 1744[3], *v.* **pingel**; with the surn. *Rowse/Rouse*); Plantation Cl 1782; Prior ~, Pryor Cl 1761, Priors Cl 1795[1], (The) Prior's Cl 1795[2], 1810 (*the Priors* ~, *Pryors Close* 1550, *Priors Close* 1716[1], cf. *Priourscroft* 1400[1] (*v.* **croft**), *v.* **prior, clos(e)**; either with reference to the Prior of Kirby Bellars Priory or to the Prior of Chacombe Priory, *v. the Pryors headland* in Gt. Dalby f.ns. (b)); Red Gate Mdw 1782 (*v.* Open Cl *supra*); Roes Cl 1761 (cf. *Francis Roe* 1761); Rudbeck Cl, Rudbeck Furlong 1761 (*Rudbeck(e)* 1541, 1550, *v.* **hrēod, bekkr**); Sand Pits 1782, Sand Pit Leys 1761, 1782 (*v.* **leys**) (cf. *Sandpitt Fur'* 1682, 1686, *Sandpit(t)* ~, *Sandpyt* ~, *Sond(e)pitt haydes, Sond pit hades* 1550, *v.* **sand-pytt, furlang, hēafod**); Joel Shuttlewoods piece 1761 (*v.* **pece**); Spinney Brook 1761 (*Speneybroke* 1445, 1449, *Spyny Broke* 1541, *Speny Brooke, the*

Spyne Broke, ~ ~ *Brooke* 1550, *v.* **brōc**), Spinney Hill 1761 (1682, *Spiney hill* 1686) (*v.* The Spinney *supra*); Spittle Leys 1761 (*v.* **leys**), Spittle (Town) Wong 1761 (*v.* **vangr**) (*v.* **spitel** and *Hospitalis de Melton* in Charitable Institutions *supra*); Stone Bridge furlong 1761 (*v. Stone Bridge* in Bridges *supra*); Thirty Leys 1761, 1782, 1795[1], 30 leys 1796 (*Thirty Leys* 1716[1], 1717, *v.* **leys**; an enclosure comprising thirty former grassland units of tenure); Thorney Cl 1753 (*v.* **þornig**); Thorpe Brook 1761 (flowing through Thorpe Arnold and beneath Thorpe Bridge into Melton Mowbray and R. Eye); Thurbans Cl 1761 (1716[1], cf. *Thurborns Fur'* 1682, *Thorborns* ~ 1686, *v.* **furlang**; with the surn. *Thurban*, the modern reflex of the ON pers.n. *Þorbjǫrn* (ODan *Thorbiorn*)); Traffic ~, Traffack Furlong 1761 (cf. *Straffick hades* 1682, 1686, *v.* **hēafod**; perh. with **trafficke** used in the sense 'exchange, bargaining' (*v.* OED *s.v.* traffic sb. 2), with the 17th cent. forms showing prosthetic *s*, cf. *Skawcy* in f.ns.(b)); Triggs Cl 1761, 1782, 1795[1], 1796 (with the surn. *Trigg*, a modern reflex of the Scand by-name *Tryggr* (ON *tryggr* 'true, faithful, trustworthy'), cf. *Trygebarne* in Knipton f.ns. (b)); Tythe Hookes 1753, (the) Tithe Hook 1795[1], 1796 (*the Tythe hoke* 1550, *pasture calle the Tith Hooks* 1669, *v.* **tēoða, hōc**); Wadd Cl 1753, Wadds ~ 1761 (either with the surn. *Wadds* (*v.* Reaney *s.n.*) or with **wād** 'woad'; woad was widely grown as a source of blue dye until the 19th cent., *v.* Field 102–3); West Mdw (*the West Medowe* 1541, (*the*) *West Meadow*(*e*) 1550, 1664, 1682, 1682 (1791), 1686, *v.* **west, mǣd (mǣdwe** obl.sg.)); Whaley Fd 1761 (*Warlou* m.13 (1449), *Warlow* 1400[1], *Wharlowe* 1541, *Wharloe, Wherloo* 1550, *Worley* 1561 (17), *Whalley field* 1718[1]), Whaley Furlong 1761 (1686, *Whalley* ~ 1682), Whaley Hades 1761 (*Wharloe hades, Wharlo ha*(*i*)*des*, ~ *haydes* 1550, *v.* **hēafod**) (*v.* **hlāw** 'a hill, a mound'; the first el. may be **waru** 'defence, guard' since the consistent absence of *d* tells against the more obvious **weard** 'watch').

(b) *Almescroft*(*e*) 1400[1], 1445, 1449 (*v.* **croft**; the first el. appears to be **ælmesse** 'alms, charity', and if so would signify an enclosure the rents from which were distributed to the poor; but with *croft*, a pers.n. in the possessive case would be more usual as the specific, here perh. the ME fem. pers.n. *Almus* as proposed for Great Alms Cliff, YW **5** 44; it is suggested that *Almus* is poss. of Scand origin, perh. based on an earlier fem. pers.n. *Álmveig*; a third alternative may be interpreted as 'the croft beside, or containing, the elm-tree(s)', *v.* **elm, almr (alms** gen.sg.), but both OE and ON words are otherwise almost always compounded with topographical terms); *Ancle Hill Close* 1733 (*v.* Ankle Hill *supra*); *Andrewscrofte* 1561 (17) (*v.* **croft**; at this date, prob. with the surn. *Andrew*(*s*) rather than with the pers.n. *Andrew*); *Ashby Crosse ha*(*y*)*des* 1550 (*v.* **cross, hēafod**), *Assheby plott* 1541 (*v.* **plot**) (with the surn. *Ashby*); *Mr Ashby's Garden* 1724; *Aungel*(*l*)*wong* 1445, 1449 (*v.* **angle, vangr** and Ankle Hill *supra*); *Balnesfyld* 1400[1] (*v.* **feld**; the first el. appears to be **balne** 'a bathing place', the earliest OED citation for which is dated 1471, *v.* Balne, YW **2** 14–15); *Barkeley hades* 1541, *Barkley haides*, ~ *haydes* 1550, *Barcle Had*(*e*)*s* 1682, 1686 (*v.* **hēafod**), *Barkeley syck* 1541, *Barkley Syke* 1550 (*v.* **sík**), *the land of the lord Barkley lord of Melton* 1550, cf. *the heires of Maurice* ~ ~, *Morris Barkley knight* 1550 (it is poss. that the f.ns. with **hēafod** and **sík** belong with *Berclyue, infra*, and have been attracted to the important surn. *Barkley*); *Barneyarde* 1541 (17) (*v.* **barne-yarde**); *Bates ground, Bates land, the lande of Bates* 1550 (*v.* **grund, land**, cf. *John Bate* 1550); *Becks* 1561 (17), *the Beck* 1682 (*v.* **bekkr**); *Berclyue* 1348 (1449),

Berclyff 1400[1], *long Barkliff, long(e) Barkl(e)y, Shorte Barcliff* 1550 (v. **lang**[1], **sc(e)ort**), *long Barcliffe haydes, Barkliffhades* 1550 (v. **hēafod**), *Barkliffe Syke, Barclifs Syke haydes* 1550 (v. **sík**), v. **bere, clif**; the 16th cent. forms have been attracted to the name of *the lord Barkley lord of Melton*, v. *Barkeley hades, supra*); *the blind(e) forth* 1550 (v. **blind, ford**); *brantclyf* 13 (1449) (v. **brant, clif**); *Brentingby Stones* 1540 (v. **stān**; Brentingby adjoins to the east and the stones were poss. boundary markers; but otherwise referring to stony ground); *Brigende* 1400[1] (v. **brycg, bryggja, ende**; with reference to Burton Bridge *supra*); *Netherbrynkes* 1400[1], *Neather, Over Brincks Wong* 1664, *Kettleby Crosse Wong or Over Brincks Wong* 1664 (v. **neoðera, uferra, brink, vangr** and *Kettleby Crosse Wong, infra*); *the brode, the Brode nye Dalby mere* 1550 (v. **nēah**), *the brode nye Saltgate* 1550 (v. **brǣdu**; referring to the same ground on the boundary ((ge)mǣre) with Gt. Dalby, presum. south of *Saltgate* (q.v. in Streets, Roads and Lanes *supra*)); *be esthalf the brok'* 1331 (v. **ēast, half** 'side', **brōc**); *Broke furlonge* 1550, *Brook(e) fur(long)* 1550, 1686, *Bruck Fur'* 1682 (v. **brōc, furlang**; with reference to Scalford Brook); *the land of Barthilmew Brokesbie, the meadowe of Bartilmew Brookesbie* 1550, *the land of William Brokesbie* 1550 (v. **land, mǣd** (**mǣdwe** obl.sg.); the *Brooksby* family came originally from the village of Brooksby, five miles to the south-west in East Goscote Hundred); *Brown(e)s meadow* 1682, 1686; *Burton Bridge Wong* 1716[1], 1717 (v. **vangr** and Burton Bridge s*upra*); *Burton hall land, the hall land of Burton called Orton land* 1550, *the hall land of Burton pertaining to the mault milne* 1550 (property of Burton Lazars Hall, v. **hall** and *the mault milne, supra*; with the surn. *Orton*); *Burton Me(a)re* 1550 (v. **(ge)mǣre**; the parish boundary with Burton Lazars); *Calfe(s) pasture* 1550 (v. **calf, pasture**); *Clot hades* 1550 (v. **clot(t), hēafod**); *Codland* 1550 (v. **land**; prob. with the surn. *Codd* (v. Reaney *s.n.*), but **codd** 'a hollow' is poss.); *the wong of John Coke* 1669 (v. **vangr**); *Croddins Garden* 1707, 1724, *Crodins ~* 1707 (18) (cf. *Ralph Crodwyn* 1605 of Melton Mowbray); *Crodyke* 1550 (v. **crāwe, dík**); *Custland* 1550 (v. **land**; with the surn. *Cust*); *Daymesonecroft* 13 (1449) (v. **damesene, croft**; the earliest citation for *damson* in OED is for 1398); *Dalby Mere* 1550 (v. **(ge)mǣre**; the parish boundary of Gt. Dalby to the south); *the land of the Earle of Warwick* 1550; *East Field* 1541 (v. **ēast, feld**; one of the great fields of the town); *the lande sometyme called John Edwardes* 1550; *Fenn Seike* 1682, *~ Sick* 1686, *Fensike* 1718[1] (v. **fenn, sík**); *Flaxland(s)* 1550 (v. **fleax, land**); *la Garthe* 1400[1] (v. **garðr**); *gor wong* 1550 (v. **gāra, vangr**); *the greate wong* 1669 (v. **vangr**); *Mr Gregorys Wong* 1744[2] (v. **vangr**); *Hardynghet* 1400[1] (v. **hetta**; perh. with the surn. *Harding*, the reflex of the OE pers.n. *Hearding*); *Harlonds, Arlond(es) Syke* 1550 (v. **sík**) (v. **hār**[2], **land**); *Hasle lands* 1550, *Shorte haselandes* 1541 (v. **sc(e)ort**) (v. **land**; either with **hæsel** or its derivative surn. *Hasel*, v. Reaney *s.n.* *Hazel*); *Hebbe lands* 1550 (v. **land**; with the ME surn. *Hebbe* (from *Hebb*, a short form of Herbert), v. Reaney *s.n.* Hebb); *(the) highfeild hedge* 1682, 1686 (v. **hēah**[1], **feld, hecg**); *ye High hades* 1541, *(the) high(e) hades, ~ haydes* 1550 (v. **hēah**[1], **hēafod**); *Hills land* 1550 (v. **land**; either with the surn. *Hill(s)* or **hyll**); *hither Wroo* 1550 (v. **hider, vrá**); *the Hoke* 1501, *the hock* 1550 (v. **hōc**); *lez Holmes* 1561 (17) (v. **holmr**); *Holwell ~, Howell hill* 1550 (v. **hol**[2], **wella, hyll**); *the Homestall* 1605 (v. **hām-stall**; belonging to *the Vicaridge house*); *the horse shoe* 1550 (the name of a meadow, perh. meaning 'the horse shelter', v. **hors, scēo**; *horseshoe*, i.e. the U-shaped plate of iron fitting the rim of the hoof, is recorded in OED from 1387, but it seems unlikely that the f.n. described a meadow with such a shape (*v.* **hors-sho**)); *atte Howe* 1330 (p) (*v.* **atte, haugr**); *the Lady Hudsons Garden* 1707, 1707 (18); *super le Hull* 1310[1] (p) (*v.* **hyll**); *hyder ~, hyther hades* 1550 (*v.* **hider, hēafod**); *Kettleby Crosse Wong or Over Brincks Wong* 1664 (*v.* **cross, vangr** and *Netherbrynkes, supra*), *Ketleby hedg(e)* 1541, 1550, *~ hege* 1550, *Ketylby hedg(e)*, *~ hegge* 1550 (*v.* **hecg**; the boundary hedge of Eye Kettleby), *Ketalbymere* 13 (*v.* **(ge)mǣre**; Eye Kettleby's original parish boundary); *the king(e)s land* 1550, *the kynges land late Saynt Johannes, ~ ~ ~ ~ Saynt Jones* 1541, *the kinges land St Johns* 1550, *the kings meadow St Johns* 1550 (the property of Henry VIII and his son Edward VI, previously assigned to finance St John the Baptist's Chapel, *q.v.*), *the kinges land Lewis* 1550, *the kings meadow Lewis* 1550 (the property of Edward VI out to farm by a man with the surn. *Lewis*) (*v.* **king, land, mǣd (mǣdwe** obl.sg.)); *Lamberts Meadow* 1744[1], 1744[3] (with the surn. *Lambert*); *in the lane* 1341 (p), 1359 (p), 1392 (p) (*v.* **lane**); *Levats pece* 1685 (1791) (*v.* **pece**), *Levitts yard land* 1716[1] (*v.* **yardland**) (with the surn. *Levett*, cf. *Levetts Cl supra*); *Loundeinges, Loundynges* 1400[1] (*v.* **lundr, eng**); *Loundewelle* 1293 (1449), *Lundewelle* 13 (*v.* **lundr, wella**); *Lowthes* 1550, *Under Lowthe* 1550, *Under Louth* 1682, 1686, *Lowth(e) ha(i)des, ~ haydes, Louth hades* 1550 (*v.* **hēafod**) (poss. an original stream-name *Hlūde* 'the loud one' from OE *hlūd* 'loud, noisy'; perh. the lost name of the major stream which flows through Thorpe Arnold from higher ground to the north-east or even the early name of Scalford Brook, *v.* **hlūde**, cf. *Ludforth* in Branston f.ns. (b) and Louth in Lincs.); *Lytlinges* 1550, *Littleing* 1682, *Littling* 1686, *Littlein(g) Fur'* 1682, 1686 (*v.* **furlang**), *littilhinghedes* 1.13 (1449), *Litling ~, Lytling hades* 1550 (*v.* **hēafod**) (*v.* **lȳtel, lītill, eng**); *Maltemylne close* 1561 (17) (*v.* **clos(e)** and *The Malt Mill supra*); *Manloves Land* 1750 (*v.* **land**; with the surn. *Manlove*); *Manndale Fur'* 1682, *Mondale ~* 1686 (*v.* **(ge)mǣne, deill, furlang**); *le Mar* 13, *le Mare, the Mare* 1561 (17), *Marefurlong(e)* 1541, 1550 (*v.* **furlang**), *Mare hades* 1550 (*v.* **hēafod**), *Mare Syke* 1550 (*v.* **sīk**) (*v.* **marr**[1]); *the Marsh(e)* 1541, 1550, *the Mershe* 1550 (*v.* **mersc**); *Meltonmedowe* 1400[1] (*v.* **mǣd (mǣdwe** obl.sg.)); *midlefurlong of the Stoke* 1550 (*v.* **middel, furlang** and *Stoc, infra*); *Middelhefdis* (14) (1449), *(the) Midle ha(y)des* 1550 (*v.* **middel, hēafod**); *a furlong called Monkys howse* 1550, *Monks house furlong* 1718[1], *Monkes howse ha(i)des, Monks howse hades, Monkyhowse haydes* 1550 (*v.* **hēafod**) (*v.* *Monkes howse* in Domestic Buildings *supra*); *Neþerdikes* 13 (1404) (*v.* **neoðera, dík**); *Nether Seike* 1682, *~ Sick* 1686, 1744[1], 1744[3], *Nethersike* 1718[1] (*v.* **sík**); *the new brooke* 1550 (*v.* **nīwe, brōc**); *(the) North field* 1541, 1550, 1632 (1791), *Northfelde* 1561 (17), *(the) North Feild* 1669, 1682, 1686 (*v.* **norð, feld**; one of the great fields of the town); *Old Broke, the old(e) brooke* 1550 (*v.* **ald, brōc**, cf. *the new brooke, supra*); *Orgar Close* 1718[1], *Orgerpark* 1400[1] (*v.* **park**) (cf. *Johannes Orger* 1400[1] of Melton Mowbray); *in Orto* 1351 (p) (with MLat (*h*)*ortus* 'a garden'); *Orton land* 1550 (*v.* **land**; with the surn. *Orton, v. Burton hall land, supra*); *Osborne land* 1561 (17) (*v.* **land**; with the surn. *Osborne*); *Overend Acres* 1550 (*v.* **uferra, ende, æcer**); *the Parke close* 1616, *Park Close* 1716[2], *(the) Park(e) Closes* 1718[2], 1719[2], 1744[2] (*v.* **park**); *the Park Wonge or the Scawcey Wong* 1664 (*v.* **park, vangr** and *Skawcy, infra*); *Pars(e)ley Syke, ~ ~ hades, Parsley Sike haydes, ~ Syke ~* 1550 (*v.* **hēafod**) (*v.* **persely, sík**); *the Parsonage Wonges* 1550 (*v.* **personage, vangr**);

peseclif 13 (*v.* **pise, clif**); *Pinquath* 1550, *Pinqueth hades* 1550 (*v.* **hēafod**), *the Pynkewathe meade* 1541 (*v.* **mǣd**) ('ford frequented by finches', *v.* **pinca, vað**; in R. Eye); *the plough land pasture* 1550 (*v.* **plōg, land, pasture**); *Plucked croft* (sic) 1550 (*v.* **croft**; presum. with the participial adj. *plucked,* alluding to the gathering of a fruit crop of some sort); *the Pooleyard* 1649 (*v.* **pōl**[1], **geard**); *Redbutt Fur'* 1682, *Rod-butt Fur'* 1686 (*v.* **hrēod, butte, furlang**); *St Johns Wonge, the towne wong of St Johns* 1550, *S. Johns Wonges* 1567 (*v.* **vangr, tūn** and St John the Baptist's Chapel *supra*); *Saltgate Syke* 1550 (*v.* **sík** and *Saltegate* in Streets, Roads and Lanes *supra*); *Sand* ~, *Sond haydes* 1550 (*v.* **sand, hēafod**); *Shamble hole* 1550 (*v.* **sceamol, hol**[1]; towards Sysonby); (*the*) *Short*(*e*) *hades* 1550 (*v.* **sc**(**e**)**ort, hēafod**); *Simson close* 1686, *Simsons* ~ 1744[1], 1744[2] (with the surn. *Simson*); *Sirholt* 14 (1449) bis, *Sherholde, Sherholds, Sheroldes* 1550, *Sherholdes mede* 1541, *the meadow called Sherolds* 1550 (*v.* **mǣd** (**mǣdwe** obl.sg.) (*v.* **scīr**[2], **holt**); *Sixtenebyheuedis* 1293 (1449) (*v.* **hēafod**), *Sixtenbywold* 1400[1] (*v.* **wald**) (Sysonby adjoins to the west and north-west); *Skawcy* 1550 bis, *the Scawcey Wonge* 1664 (*v.* **vangr**), *Scaucey meadow* 1718[1] (presum. **caucie** with a later prosthetic *s, v.* Causeway Hill *supra* and cf. Traffic Furlong in f.ns. (a)); *Skyrbeck* 1541 (*v.* **skírr, bekkr**); *the Sonde* 1550 (*v.* **sand**); (*the*) *South Field*(*e*) 1541, 1550, *the South Fielde against Burton* 1550, (*the*) *South Feild*(*e*) 1561 (17), 1669 (*v.* **sūð, feld**; one of the great fields of the town, also called Burton Fd); *Speny forthe* 1550 (*v.* **ford**), *Speny hedge* 1550 (*v.* **hecg**), *Spenyside* 1550 (*v.* **sīde**), *Spynnyhades* 1669 (*v.* **hēafod**), *Spinney close* 1718[1] (all named from The Spinney *supra*); *Spilemaneswang* m.13 (1404) (*v.* **vangr**; with a ME nickname *Spileman* from OE *spilemann* 'a jester, a juggler', which eventually gave the surn. *Spil*(*l*)*man, v.* Reaney *s.n.*); *Stake hades* 1550, 1718[1] (*v.* **hēafod**; perh. with **staca**, but the f.n. may belong with *Stoc, infra*); *Stanhills* 1550, *Stonehill Fur'* 1682, 1686 (*v.* **furlang**) (*v.* **stān, hyll**); *Staple land* 1550 (*v.* **land**; prob. with the surn. *Staple*, since **stapol** 'a post' would be unconvincing in this compound); *Stoc, Stocke* 13, *the Stoke* 1550, *Le Stocke* 1561 (17), *Stoke wong* 1550 (*v.* **vangr**) (*v.* **stoc**); *le Stonemeade* 1541 (*v.* **stān, stoned, mǣd** and *the stone middow* in Branston f.ns. (b)); *Sunne hades, Sonne ha*(*i*)*des* 1550, *Sun hades* 1718[1] (*v.* **sunne, hēafod**; alluding to ground which caught the best of the sunshine); *Lonkesuþingis* 13, *Long Sowthinges* 1541, 1550, *Long*(*e*) *Southings* 1550, 1682, 1686 (*v.* **lang**[1]), *Shorte Sowthynges* 1541 (*v.* **sc**(**e**)**ort**), *Southing lane* 1669 (*v.* **lane**) (*v.* **sūð, eng**); *Swaludale* 13, *Swallowdale, Swalow Dale* 1550, *hie Swalowdale* 1550 (*v.* **hēah**[1]) (*v.* **swalg**; with **dalr** or **deill**); *the Syke of Melton* 1550 (*v.* **sík**); *between the Sykes* 1550 (*v.* **betwēonan, sík**); *Sysonbe* ~, *Sysonby Mere* 1550 (*v.* (**ge**)**mǣre**; the boundary of Sysonby); *le Templegore* 1329 (1449), *Temple gore* 1550 (*v.* **temple, gāra**; sometime property of the Knights Templars); *Tenter Close* 1660 (*v.* **tentour**); *Ten Acres* 1718[1] (*v.* **æcer**); *Ten Acre Wong* 1669 (*v.* **æcer, vangr**; perh. to be identified with the previous field); *Thakholm* 1326 (*v.* **þak, holmr**); *Thorpe Crosse Wong* 1664 (*v.* **cross, vangr**), *Thorpe ditch* 1669 (*v.* **dīc**; a boundary marker), *the Meere of Thorpe Arnold* 1550 (*v.* (**ge**)**mǣre**) (Thorpe Arnold adjoins to the north-east); *Thurmans Close* 1744[1], 1744[3] (apparently with the surn. *Thurman*, a reflex of the ODan pers.n. *Þormund*; but the f.n. may belong rather with Thurbans Cl in f.ns. (a)); *the towne balke* 1550 (*v.* **balca**), *the towne dyke* 1550 (*v.* **dík**), *the towne headland* 1550 (*v.* **hēafod-land**), *the Wonge of the Townes* 1550 (*v.* **vangr**) (*v.* **tūn**); *Twenty Acres* 1718[1] (*v.* **æcer**); *the tythe* *meadowe* 1550 (*v.* **tēoða, mǣd** (**mǣdwe** obl.sg.)); *Upper Fur'* 1682, 1686 (*v.* **furlang**); *Vaud(e)y hill* 1682, 1686 (land belonging previously to Vaudey Abbey in Lincs., of which Burton Grange in neighbouring Burton Lazars was an outlier); *John Waltons Yard* 1707, 1707 (18) (*v.* **geard**); *Le Warren feild* 1561 (17) (*v.* **wareine, feld**; note the earlier *warennam apud Meuton* 1276 (with ML at *warenna* 'a warren')); *Warwellesik'*, *Warewelsik'* 14 (1449), *Warewell syck* 1541, *Warwell Syke* 1550 (*v.* **wer, wær, wella, sík** and Warwellmill in Mills *supra*); *Waterforous, Waterfurrowes* 1550 (*v.* **wæter, furh**; usually interpreted as 'furrows where water tends to lie', but *v. waterfurris* in Muston f.ns. (b)); (*the*) *Water Lane Close* 1648, 1681 (1791), 1682, 1682 (1791), 1686 (*v. Water Lane* in Streets, Roads and Lanes *supra*); *wellesprynges* 14 (1449), *Welspringes* 1541, *Welsprings, Well Springs* 1550 (*v.* **wella, spring¹**); *Westdale* 13 (1404), 1550, 1669, 1716¹, ~ *Furlonge* 1541 (*v.* **furlang**), *upon West dale against Framland* 1550 (*v.* Great Framlands), *Westdalehyl* 1320, *West dalle hill* 1550 (*v.* **hyll**), *Westdale Syke* 1550 (*v.* **sík**) (*v.* **west**; with **dalr** or **deill**); (*the*) *West field* 1550, 1669, 1682 (1791), 1718¹, ~ *Feild* 1669, 1682, 1686 (*v.* **west, feld**; one of the great fields of the town); *Wilby hedge* 1550 (*v.* **hecg**; the boundary hedge of Welby which adjoins to the north-west); *the Windmill Leys* 1681 (1791), *Wind Miln Leys* 1686, *the Windmill and Leys in Burton feild* 1682 (1791), *The Windmill & Leys* 1685 (1791) (*v.* **wind-mylne, leys**); *Woolings* 1716¹ (*v.* **wald, eng**); *Worteley ~, Wortley syck* 1541, *Wortley Sike, ~ Syke* 1550 (*v.* **wyrt, lēah, sík**).

2. EYE KETTLEBY

Chitebie 1086 DB

Chetelbia c.1130 LeicSurv

Ketelbi c.1130 LeicSurv, 1198 Cur *et passim* to 1215 ib, *Ketelby* 1199 Fine, 1200 FF, e.13 (1404) *Laz* (freq) *et passim* to 1312 *Rut*, 1334 AAS, *Kettelby* a.1250 (1404) *Laz*, 1290 GarCart *et passim* to 1327 SR

Ketelebi e.13 (1404), a.1250 (1404) *Laz*, *Ketellebi* 13 (1404) *ib*, *Keteleby* e.13 (1404) *ib*, 1220 MHW, 1209 × 35 RHug

Kedlesby 1236 Fees

Ketilby 1242, 1247 Fees *et passim* to 1548 Ipm, 1610 Fine, *Kettilby* m.13 (1404) *Laz*, 1303 Ipm, 1324 Hastings, *Ketylby* 1332 SR, 1421 Banco, 1428 FA *et passim* to 1521 Ipm, 1561 Pat, *Kettylbye* 1554 *Rut*, 1556 Fine, 1559 Pat, *Ketulby* l.13 (1449), 1309 (1449) WoCart

Ketlebi e.13 (1404), a.1250 (1404) *Laz*, *Ketleby* m.13 (1404), 13 (1404) *ib et passim* to 1315 *Rut*

Kettleby m.13 (1404), 1262 (1404), 1308 (1404) *Laz*, 1549 AAS, 1613 LML, 1622 Burton *et freq*

'Ketil's farmstead, village', *v.* **bȳ**. The ODan pers.n. *Ketil* (ON *Ketill*), common in England, is an original by-name, cf. Scand *ketill* 'a cauldron, a cauldron-shaped helmet'. It is noteworthy that, with the exception of only a single instance with the gen.sg. *-es*, the pers.n. is linked in stem-form to the generic.

Distinguishing affixes are variously added as:

Parua ~ m.13 (1404) *Laz* (i.e. MLat *parva* 'little, small')

~ *Beler* 1303 Ipm, 1324 Hastings, 1332 SR

E- 1345 Banco, 1420 ELiW *et freq* to 1554 *Rut*, 1556 Fine *et passim* to 1603 LeicW, 1613 LML, *Ey-* 1559, 1561 Pat, *Eie* ~ 1610 Speed, *Eye* ~ 1610, 1619 Fine, 1622 Burton *et freq*

Willielmus Beler held the manor a.1250 (1404) *Laz* and *Hamo Beler* m.13 (1404) *ib.* It remained in that family as late as *Johannes Beler* 1381 Banco. The present habitation site called Eye Kettleby stands on a tributary of R. Wreake/R. Eye, over one mile from its confluence with the main stream. It is uncertain at what point R. Wreake was thought to become R. Eye and it may be that Eye (OE *ēa* 'a stream') was the pre-Scandinavian name for the entire river as far as its junction with R. Soar. One presumes, therefore, that the affix *E-*, *Ey-*, *Eye* ~ referred originally to R. Eye rather than to the tributary (as *ēa*) on which modern Eye Kettleby stands. It is also possible that the early settlement was sited at Chapel Nook (*v.* White House Fm *infra*) beside the main stream where its chapel is recorded in 1220 and where the disused water-mill stands. The affix distinguishes the village from Ab Kettleby some four miles away to the north-west.

BROOKSIDE COTTAGE. EYE KETTLEBY HALL, ~ ~ ~ FM, *the Hall* 1925 Kelly, *v.* **hall**. EYE KETTLEBY HO., *Eye Kettleby house* 1925 Kelly. EYE KETTLEBY LODGE (lost), *Eye Kettleby Lodge* 1714 LeicW, 1824 O, *v.* **loge**. EYE KETTLEBY MILL, 1870 *Sale*. KIRBY LANE, leading to Kirby Bellars. NEW GUADALOUPE, 1824 O, 1846, 1863 White. OLD GUADALOUPE, 1863 White, *Guadalupe* 1795 Nichols, 1806, 1815 Map, *Guadaloupe* 1824 O. Guadaloupe is one of the Leeward Islands in the West Indies. The site of the farmstead is at the edge of the parish and thus this is a 'remoteness' name. RYDAL MANOR, *v.* **maner**. SUNNYSIDE FM. WHITE HOUSE FM (CHAPEL NOOK 2½"), *the Chapel Nook* 1874 AAS, *v.* **nōk**; note also *the Chappel(l)* 1707, c.1720 *Terrier* (and *the Chappel Yard* 1707 *ib*, *v.* **geard**), earliest recorded in the group *capellas Birton Keteleby et Friseby* 1220 MHW (with MLat *capella* 'a chapel'), *v.* **chapel(e)**. WOODLANDS.

FIELD-NAMES

Forms dated 1529 are LD; those dated 1548 and 1626 are Ipm.

(a) High Fd 1761 *EnclA* (*the highefeld, the highe felde, the high felde* 1529, *Highfields* 1626, *v.* **hēah**[1], **feld**; one of the great fields of the village); Mary Dykes Lower Mdw 1848 *TA* (*v.* **dík**; poss. with **myry** 'miry, muddy'); the Park 1874 AAS (*The Parke* 1541 MinAccts, *v.* **park**; a wood so called in 1541, but a meadow in 1874).

(b) *cranwell close* 1529, *Craunwell* ~ 1548 (*v.* **cran, wella, clos(e)**); *Est medow* 1548 (*v.* **ēast, mǣd** (**mǣdwe** obl.sg.)); *the fogge felde* 1529, *Foggefeld* 1626 (*v.* **fogge, feld**; one of the great fields of the village); *the hall close* 1529 (*v.* **hall, clos(e)**; with reference to an earlier hall than Eye Kettleby Hall *supra*); *Kettleby grounds* 1657 *Deed* (*v.* **grund**); *kirkeby bridge* 1529, *Kirby bridgge* 1548 (*v.* **brycg**; Kirby Bellars adjoins to the east, beyond the tributary of R. Wreake/R. Eye); *Melton lane* 1529, 1548 (*v.* **lane**; the road to Melton Mowbray); *the ueste leys* 1529, *Westleys* 1548 (*v.* **west, vestr, lǣs**).

3. SYSONBY

Sistenebi 1086 DB bis, p.1250 (1404) *Laz* (p)

Sixtenebi 1086 DB, c.1130 LeicSurv *et passim* to 1228 *Rut*, m.13 (1404), p.1250 (1404) *Laz*, *Sixtenebia* c.1130 LeicSurv, *Sixteneby* e.13 (1404) *Laz* (freq), 1212, 1214 Cur *et freq* to 1327, 1332 SR (p) *et passim* to 1362 (1449) *WoCart*, 1368 Cl, *Syxtenebi* l.12, e.13 *GarCart*, a.1211 *Rut*, *Syxteneby* c.1300 AD, *Sixstaneby* m.13 (1404) *Laz*, *Syxtaneby* p.1250 (1404) *ib*, *Sixtanaby* m.13 (1404) *ib*, *Sixtaneby* m.13 (1404) *ib*, *Sixtineby* 1327 SR (p), *Sixtuniby* 1325 (1449) *WoCart*

Sixtenesbi 1196 Cur (p), *Sixtenesby* 1236 Fees

Sextenebi l.12 *GarCart* (freq), 1200 P *et passim* to 1211 *ib*, 1212 Cur, *Sexteneby* 1201, 1206 Cur *et passim* to p.1250 (1404) *Laz*, 1257 Ch (p), *Sexstenebi* 1201 ChancR, *Sextanebi* 1206, 1207 Cur, *Sextaneby* 1207 *ib* (p), 1276 RH (p)

Sixtenby 1242, 1243 Fees *et freq* to 1428 FA, 1477 FF, (~ *Perer* 1242 Fees), *Syxtenby* e.13 *BHosp* (p), 1233 Fees *et passim* to 1473 Hastings, 1514 Fine, *Sixtinby* 1326 Ipm, 1336 (1449), 1349 (1449) *WoCart*, *Sixtonby* 1349 *LCDeeds* (p), *Sixstonby* 1535 VE

Sextenby 1298 Banco (p), 1435 Fine, *Sextonby* 1344 Cl (p)

Sistonby 1475 × 85 ECP, 1485 Fine, 1494 Will, 1496 Ipm, *Systonby* 1475 × 85 ECP, 1505 Ipm, *Systenbie* 1623 Fine

Sextenby alias Seyssenby 1541 Nichols
Sysonby 1529 LinDoc, 1535 VE, 1552 AAS, 1610 Speed *et freq,*
   Sysunbye 1556 Fine, *Sysonbie* 1604 SR, *Sisonbie* 1605 Ipm

'Sigsteinn's farmstead, village', *v.* bȳ. The pers.n. *Sigsteinn* is
Swedish and is recorded in a number of runic inscriptions, *v.* SPNLY
235. The 16th cent. loss of *t* in the group *-ston-* > *-son-* is typical in
Leics. p.ns., but is usually to be found when genitival *s* precedes the
generic *-ton* < *-tūn.*
Willielmus de Pereres held land in Sysonby in 1266 Cur.

ASFORDBY HILL, overlooking Asfordby which adjoins to the west. BUTT
CLOSE, cf. *(The) Butt Green* 17 *Terrier,* 1843 *TA, But Green* 1870 *Sale,*
Butt Meadow 1843 *TA, v.* **butt**², **grēne**². THE COTTAGE (SYSONBY
COTTAGE 2½"). THE GRANGE HO., *v.* Sysonby Grange *infra.* HALFWAY
COTTAGES, HALFWAY HO., presum. once halfway between Asfordby
and Melton Mowbray. PLYMOUTH LODGE, 1870 *Sale, v.* **loge**.
RIVERSIDE FM (2½"), at the location of SYSONBY (6"). SYSONBY
CHURCH is *The Chapel* 1795 Nichols, but with church plate of 1568, cf.
the Church headland in f.ns. (b) *infra.* SYSONBY FM. SYSONBY GRANGE
FM (SYSONBY GRANGE 2½"), *Sixtinby graunce* 1349 (1449) *WoCart,*
Sextonby Graunge 1561 *Pat, Sysonby grange* 1597 Ipm, *grangiam de*
Sextonby(e) 1537 MinAccts, 1559 *Pat* (with MLat *grangia* 'a grange'),
v. **grange**; an outlier of Garendon Abbey. SYSONBY GRANGE LANE.
SYSONBY HALL, 1843 *TA, The Hall* 17 *Terrier, v.* **hall**. SYSONBY
KNOLL, 1925 Kelly, *v.* **cnoll**. SYSONBY LODGE, 1925 Kelly; it is *Melton*
Lodge 1824 O, *v.* **loge**. SYSONBY LODGE FM is *Sysonby Lodge* 1824 O,
v. **loge**. SYSONBY UPPER LODGE (lost), *Sysonby Upr. Lodge* 1824 O, *v.*
loge.

FIELD-NAMES

Undated forms in (a) are 1843 *TA;* those dated 1870 are *Sale.* Forms
throughout dated 1550 are *Pochin* and 17 are *Terrier.*

(a) Six Acre Cl, Bottom, Top Six Acres, Eleven Acre (*v.* **æcer**); Asfordby Mdw,
Upper Asfordby Cl (Asfordby adjoins to the west); Ash Spinney (*v.* **æsc**); Barlows
Cl (with the surn. *Barlow*); Barn Ground (*v.* **grund**); Bass's Cl 1761 *EnclA,* 1870,
Basses ~ 1843 (with the surn. *Bass*); Bisnalls Cl (with the surn. *Bisnall*); Brestals Cl
(with the surn. *Brestal* (a poss. form of *Bristol*)); Brigg's or Captain's Cl 1870,

Briggs Little Cl (with the surn. *Brigg(s)*, *v.* Captain's Cl *infra*); Near, Further Brook Cl 1843, 1870 (*v.* **brōc**); Burnt Cl (poss. burnt over in preparation for tillage, *v.* Field 86–8); Captain's Cl 1870 (*v.* **capitain**; named from an owner with captain's rank, cf. Captains Cl in Burrough on the Hill f.ns. (a)); Carver Cl (with the surn. *Carver*); Coal pitt Lane Cl 1843, Coal-pit ~ ~ 1870 (*v.* **col-pytt** and *Coal Pitt Lane* in Melton Mowbray, Streets, Roads and Lanes); Cold Harbour Ground (literally 'cold shelter', *v.* **cald-herber**(3), **grund**; a name of reproach for an exposed place); Cooks Cl 1843, Cooke's ~ 1870 (*Cookes Close* 17; with the surn. *Cook(e)*); Coopers Cl (with the surn. *Cooper*); Corn Cl 1843, 1870 (*v.* **corn**[1]); Great, Little Cottage Pasture 1843, 1870 (*v.* **pasture** and The Cottage *supra*); Little Upper ~, Nether Dale (*v.* **deill**); First, Second Digbys Wong (*v.* **vangr**; with the surn. *Digby*); The Drift Way (*v.* **drift**); Fensick Cl (*Little* ~, *Fensick* 17, *v. Fenn Seike* in Melton Mowbray f.ns. (b)); Fox Covert (*v.* **cover(t)**); Goodmans Cl (with the surn. *Goodman*); Grange (*v.* Sysonby Grange *supra*); Hillockey Cl (*v.* **hylloc**, **-ig**[3]); Hinds Cl 1843, Hind's ~ 1870 (with the surn. *Hind(s)*); Holwells Cl (lying next to the boundary with Holwell which adjoins to the north); Home Cl, Home Mdw (*v.* **home**); Lodge Cl, Lodge Mdw (*v.* Sysonby Lodge *supra*); Marsons Cl (with the surn. *Marson*, perh. the result of typical Leics. treatment of the group *-ston* in *Marston*; the family may have originated in Potters Marston, some 20 miles to the south-west in Sparkenhoe Hundred, the p.n. showing forms in *Marson* from the early 17th cent.); Mere Cl (*Melton Mere* 1550, ~ *Meer* 17, *v.* **(ge)mære**; on the original boundary with Melton Mowbray); Upper ~ ~, Middle Fd 1843, 1870 (*midle field* 17); Milking Cl 1843, 1870 (*v.* **milking**; denoting a place where cows were milked or where milch-cows were specially pastured); Moundrell 1761 *EnclA*, Further Moundrell, ~ Maundrell 1843, ~ Maundrell's 1870, Middle Moundrell, ~ Maundrell 1843, ~ Maundrell's 1870, Nearer Moundrell, ~ Maundrell 1843, Moundrell ~, Maundrell Cl 1843, Maundrell's ~ 1870 (*Morwyndale* m.13 (1404) *Laz*, *morn dale* 17; the first el. is **morgen** 'morning', but its implication is unclear; it may represent **morgen-gifu** 'a morning gift', i.e. a piece of land or the like given by a man to his bride on the morning after their marriage; if so, then compounded with **deill** 'a portion of land', otherwise with **dalr** or **deill**); Noons Mdw (with the surn. *Noon*); Nuttalls Mdw (with the surn. *Nuttall*, poss. of a family originating in Nuthall in Notts., some 20 miles to the north-west); Pages Cl (with the surn. *Page*); Peaches Cl (with the surn. *Peach*); Peters Cl (with the surn. *Peters*); Pingle (*v.* **pingel**); The Poor Cl, Poor's Cl, Poor House and Garden (*v.* **pouer(e)**; land and accommodation for the support of the parish poor, *v.* Field 191); Bottom, Top, Nether Rowdike (*v.* **rūh**[1], **dík**); Rudbeck (*v.* Rudbeck Cl in Melton Mowbray f.ns. (a)); Shoulder of Mutton (a common f.n. describing shape); Bottom, Top Shrub Fd (*v.* **scrubb**); Smith's Cl (with the surn. *Smith*); Spells Cl 1843, 1870 (if not with the surn. *Spells* (*v.* Reaney *s.n.*), this may contain **spell** 'speech, discourse' and refer to a close neighbouring the moot-site of the Framland Hundred at Great Framlands (*q.v.*)); Stokes Little Cl, ~ Great Cl (either with the surn. *Stokes* or referring to *the Stoke* (**stoc**) in Melton Mowbray f.ns. (b)); Sysonby Nook 1870, ~ ~ Cl 1843 (*v.* **nōk**); Three Corner Cl 1870 (*v.* **three-corner**); Toons Homestead (*v.* **hām-stede**; with the surn. *Toon*); Turners Cl (with the surn. *Turner*); Twelve Pound Cl 1843, 1870 (referring to the cost of the close's rental); Wall's Cl (either with the surn. *Wall* or with **wall**); The Warren 1843, 1870 (*Conney Warren* 17, *v.* **coni**, **wareine**); Welby

Lane 1870 (Welby lies close by to the west); Whitsunday Pasture 1843, 1870, Whitsun ~ 1870 (earlier called *Whitsontide pasture* 17, *v.* **pasture**; the site of the village Whitsuntide festival which was marked by feasting, sports and merry-making); Far, Middle, Bottom Wortleys, First, Second, Third Wortleys (*v. Wortley Sike* in Melton Mowbray f.ns. (b)); Great, Little, Middle, Nether Woulds, First, Great Would Cl, Second Woulds Cl (*the Woulds* 17, *in valdis de sexteneby* c.1200 *Deed* (with MLat *walda* 'wold, woodland'), *v.* **wald**); Wood Cl (*v.* **wudu**).

(b) *Brokholetonge* 1336 (1449) *WoCart* (*v.* **brocc-hol, tunge**); *the Church headland* 1550 (*v.* **cirice, hēafod-land**); *Hacks Close* 17 (presum. with the surn. *Hack*, from the ON pers.n. *Haki*, an original by-name, cf. OSwed *haki* 'chin'; the *hack* or common saddle-horse is not recorded before the 18th cent. (*v.* OED *s.v.* hack, sb³, 1 b)); *Hall Close* 17 (*v.* Sysonby Hall *supra*); *Johnsons Closes* 17 (with the surn. *Johnson*); *Miltons Close* 17 (perh. a close adjoining the Melton Mowbray boundary rather than one with the surn. *Milton*); *le mirewell'* 1334 (1449) *WoCart* (*v.* **mýrr, wella**); *Oleby Mere* 1550 (*v.* **(ge)mǣre**; the boundary of neighbouring Welby); *Shamble hill* 1550, *Shamble hole* 17 (*v.* **sceamol, hyll** and *Shamble hole* in Melton Mowbray f.ns. (b), which refers to the same feature); *Stanages Close* 17 (presum. with the surn. *Stanage*, which occurs as a p.n., *v.* Db 93 and 157 *s.n.* and Stanedge, Db 369 (from *stān-ecg* 'stone edge'), but such a topographical feature may be discounted here); *Sysonbe brooke* 1550 (*v.* **brōc**); *Sysonbe feilde* 1550, *Sysonfelde* (sic) 1561 (17) *Rental, in campo de Sextenebi* 1.12 *GarCart* (with MLat *campus* 'a field'), *v.* **feld**).

Redmile

1. REDMILE

Redmelde 1086 DB, *Redmeld'* 1343 Cl, 1388 Pat *et passim* to 1400, 1413 *Rut et freq* to 1486, 1533 *ib*

Redmild' a.1166 (e.15) *BelCartB*, 1208 FF, e.13 (e.14) *BelCartA et passim* to 1236 *Rut*, 1242 Cl *et freq* to 1300, 1308, 1319 *Rut*, 1427 *Terrier, Redmilda* Stephen *Rut*, 1.12 (e.14) *BelCartA et passim* to 1222 (e.15) *BelCartB, Redmilde* 1230 RHug, 1240 *Rut et passim* to 1.13 (e.15) *BelCartB*, 1363 Ipm, *Redmyld'* 1285 ib, 1289 *Rut et passim* to 1404 *Wyg*, 1410 *Rut et freq* to 1525 *ib*, 1535 VE, 1544 *Rut*, (~ *in le Wall* 1519 *Wyg*), *Redmylde* 1397, 1421 Cl *et passim* to 1483 *Rut*, 1518 *Wyg*

Redemild' 1254 Val, 1292 *Rut et passim* to 1343 (e.15) *BelCartB*, 1363 Ipm, *Redemilde* 1233 (e.14) *BelCartA*, m.13 (e.15) *BelCartB et passim* to 1308, 1312 *Rut, Redemyld'* m.13 (e.15) *BelCartB*, 1274 Ass (p) *et passim* to 1370, 1411 *Rut, Redemylde* 1300 *ib*, 1321 (1449) *WoCart et passim* to 1428 FA, 1440 Cl, *Redemeild'* Edw 1 *Rut, Reddemild* 1300 IpmR, *Reddemyld'* e.14 *BelCartA, Reddymyld* 1427 *Terrier, Reddemeld* 1486 *Rut*

Redmelna Hy 1 (e.15) *BelCartB, Redmelina* c.1155 Dugd, *Redmelne* e.13 *Rut, Redmilne* Hy 2 *ib*, 1230 RHug, *Redmuln* c.1155 *Rut*

Redmilla Hy 1 (1333) Ch, Hy 2 (e.15), p.1250 (e.15) *BelCartB, Redmill* 1239 Cur, 1599 *Wyg, Redmyll* 1519 Fine, *Redemilla* Hy 1 (1333) Ch, Hy 2 (e.15), 12 (e.15) *BelCartB*, Edw 1 *BelCartA*

Radmilda Hy 2 (e.15) *BelCartB, Radmild'* m.13 *Wyg*, 1359 Pat, *Radmilde* 1288 Coram, *Radmyld'* 1371 *Rut*, 1482, 1489 *Wyg*, *Radmylde* 1409 PRep

Rademilde 1294 AD, 1343 Ipm, *Rademylde* c.1306 *Wyg*, 1343 Ipm, 1343 Fine, 1352 Ipm, *Rademeld(e)* 1350 Pat

Radmell 1524, 1525, 1531, 1532 *Wyg, Radmeyll* 1518, 1530, 1531 *ib*, (~ *in le Vale* 1530 *ib*), *Radmyle* 1502, 1521 *ib*

Redmella 1172 × 82 *Rut*, 12 (e.14) *BelCartA*, *Redmell'* 1448 *Rut*,
1516 *Wyg et passim* to 1582 LEpis, 1616 LML, *Redmeill* 1530
Wyg, *Redmyle* 1604 SR, 1610 Speed, 1613 LML, *Redmile* 1582
LEpis *et freq*

'(The place with) red earth', *v.* rēad, mylde, cf. Rodmell, Sx 325 and
note *Redlond* 1252 in f.ns. (b) and Red Furlong 1795 in f.ns. (a) *infra*.
Redmile lies in the Vale of Belvoir, hence ~ *in le Wall* 1519 *Wyg*, ~ *in
le Vale* 1530 *ib*, *v.* **val.** Some 12th and 13th cent. forms for the generic
have been attracted to *myln* 'a mill'.

ALLHALLOWS, 1697, 1724 *Terrier*, 1729 Nichols, 1824 O, 1846, 1863
White, *all hallowes* 1579 *Terrier*, *Alhallowes* 1579, 1601 *ib*, *Alhallows*
17 *ib*, *Allhalowes* 1700 *ib*, *holehalous* (sic) 1709 *ib*, *Hall Hallows*
c.1725 *ib*; this is a church dedication to All Saints (OE hālga 'a saint'),
cf. forms for All Saints, Lei **1** 82. The name is attached to a moated site,
half destroyed by a former railway line. White 1846 describes the
remains as 'the foundations of an ancient building supposed to have
been a religious house', while Nichols 1795 quotes from a note of 1725,
'In this parish was formerly a small house of nuns. The place where it
stood is yet called All-hallows, but there are no remains of the fabrick.'
No earlier references than the 1579 forms of the name have been found.
The site remains unexcavated.

CHURCH THORNS, *v.* þorn; perh. so called because at the edge of the
former *Churchfield*, but *v. Halythornfurlong* listed in adjoining
Barkestone f.ns. (b). DRIFT HILL, cf. *The Drift* 1729 Nichols, *v.* **drift**.
GLEBE FM is *Rectory F.* 1824 O, ~ *farm* 1877 White, cf. *the Gleabe
barne* 1625 *Terrier*, *v.* **glebe**. OLD HILL FM, *Old Hill farm* 1925 Kelly,
(the) Old Hill 1697, 1700, 1724, c.1725 *Terrier*, 1795 *EnclA*, *the houd
hill* 1709 *Terrier*; the first el. is poss. **hald²** 'sloping', since the rise of
the land is slight, but long and gradual, otherwise and more likely **wald**.
PEACOCK INN, 1877 White, *Peacock* 1846, 1863 *ib*, 1925 Kelly; the
peacock is part of the coat of arms of the Manners family, the Dukes of
Rutland, of neighbouring Belvoir Castle, cf. The Peacock in Belvoir
parish. PINFOLD, *the Pinfold* 1697, 1724, c.1725 *Terrier*, *the pinfould*
1700, 1709 *ib*, *v.* **pynd-fald**. THE RECTORY, 1824 O, 1877 White, 1925
Kelly; it is *the parsonage howse* 1601 *Terrier*, *v.* **personage, hūs**.
REDMILE AND BELVOIR STATION is *Redmile Station* 1854 O; now
demolished, but originally the Duke of Rutland's private station to serve

Belvoir Castle. REDMILE WINDMILL. ST PETER'S CHURCH, *The Church*
1877 White, *Church (St Peter)* 1925 Kelly; it is earlier recorded as
ecclesie de Reddemilde 1220 MHW, *~ de Rademelde* 1350 *Pat*, and with
that of Harby and Woolsthorpe in *ecclesiarum de Hardeby et Redmyld*
1462, 1464 *ib*, *~ de Hardeby Wolsthorpe et Redmylde* 1467, 1475 *ib*.
WINDMILL INN, 1877 White, *Wind Mill* 1846 ib, *Windmill* 1863 ib, *Old
Windmill* 1925 Kelly.

FIELD-NAMES

Undated forms in (a) are 1795 *EnclA*. Forms throughout dated 1252[1],
1289, 1305 and 1420 are *Rut*; 1252[2] are *Misc*; 1257, 1308 and 1729 are
Nichols; e.14 are *BelCartA*; 1424 and 1532 are *Wyg*; 1579, 1601, 1625,
1697, 1700, 1709, 1721, 1724 and c.1725 are *Terrier*.

(a) All Hallows Cl (*v.* Allhallows *supra*); Bridge Rd (cf. *Briggegate* 1257, *v.*
brycg, gata); The Drove (*v.* **drāf**; prob. a later alternative name for The Drift *supra*);
Grimmer Mdw (*v.* The Grimmer in adjoining Bottesford); Houghs Leys (*v.* **leys**; cf.
Henry Hough 1795 of Redmile); Little Fd ((*the*) *Little Field* 1601, 1724, c.1725, *the
Little feild(e)* 1625, 1700, *the litle field* 1697, *Littell feld* 1709, *v.* **lȳtel, feld**); Lords
Cls (*the Lords Close* 1697, 1700, 1724, *the Lord Close* 1700, *~ ~ closs* 1709, *the
Lordes clos* 1709, *the Lords Closes* c.1725, cf. *the Lordes Closse syde* 1601 (*v.* **sīde**);
with reference to the fifth Earl of Rutland (died 1612) and later to the Dukes of
Rutland of Belvoir Castle); The Meadows (1724, *the Medowes* 1625, 1700, *the
meddows* 1709); Mill Cl 1877 White; Mill Fd; Moor Leys (*long more leaes* 1601,
Long, Short More Leas 1700, *~ ~ Leas* 1697, 1724, *long more lease, short morles*
1709, *Long, Short Moor Leas* c.1725, *Morelease furlong* 1697, *~ forlong* 1700,
morles furlong 1709, *Moor-Leas furlong* 1724, *More lea furlong* c.1725 (*v.* **mōr[1]**,
leys); Nether Bullgates (a **bullgate** was an allotment of pasture for a single bull, cf.
cowgate, v. Field 116, 127); Nether Fd (1601, *the neather feilde* 1625, *~ ~ ~ feld* 1709,
the Nether Field 1697, 1724, *~ ~ feild* 1700, *Neather Field* c.1725, *v.* **neoðera, feld**;
one of the great fields of the township); Old Hill Leys (*v.* **leys** and Old Hill Fm
supra); Old Mill Fd (*the Mill feild* 1601, 1700, *the Milne feilde* 1625, *~ ~ ~ fild* 1709,
the Mill Field 1697, 1724, *Miln Field* c.1725, *v.* **myln, feld**; one of the great fields,
referring to a windmill); The Old Park, Old Park Wood (*v.* Old Park Wood in
adjoining Belvoir parish); Over Fd (*v.* **uferra**); The Pasture (*Redmell pasture* 1579,
Redmile Pasture Dike 1721 (*v.* **dík**)), Upper Pasture (*Redmile Upper Pasture* 1721)
(*v.* **pasture**); Red Furlong (*v.* **rēad**; referring to the colour of the soil); Open Roe
Wong (*v.* **open**), Roe Wong (*v.* **vangr**; with either **rūh[1]** 'rough' or **vrá** 'a nook, a
corner of land'; the 'open' wong was either unfenced or did not have permanent
gates, cf. *The Open Close* in Eastwell f.ns. (b) and Open Pasture in Coston f.ns. (a)).
Thorpe Fd (1724, c.1725, (*the*) *Thorpe field* 1601, 1697, *the tharp feild*, 1700, *tharp
fild* 1709, *v.* **feld**; one of the great fields of the village, named from *Redmylthorp*

1252¹, 1252², *Redmyldthorp* 1257, *v.* **þorp**); Town Cls, Town Street (*v.* **tūn, strǣt**); The Wong (*v.* **vangr**); Wood Fd (1724, c.1725, *the Wood feild* 1601, 1625, 1697, 1700, *wood feld* 1709, *v.* **wudu, feld**; one of the great fields of the village).

(b) *acherdich* e.14, *Akerdike* 1700, *acker dickes* 1709, *Acre-Dykes* 1724, *Acre Dikes* c.1725 (*v.* **æcer-dīc, dík**); *Allen well* 1697, *Alingwell* 1700, *Allonwell* 1724, *Allinwell* c.1725, *Allen well furlonge* 1601, *allinwell forlang* 1709 (*v.* **furlang**) (*v.* **wella**; either with the OFr pers.n. *Alain/Alein* (OBret *Alan*), or with its surn. reflex *Allen/Allin*); *Alwoldecroft* e.14 (*v.* **croft**; with an OE pers.n., either *Alwald* or *Ælfwald*, cf. *Alfwold* 1086 DB who held land in Somerby, Burrough on the Hill and Withcote TRE); *Barestones* 1420 (*v.* **bær¹, stān**); *barrowgate hurste* 1601 (*v.* **berg, gata, hyrst**); *the Beck* 1697, 1700, 1709, 1724, c.1725 (*v.* **bekkr**); *the Bell Headland* 1697, 1724, *the Bellhedlang* (sic) 1700 (*v.* **hēafod-land**), *the Bell Land* 1697, c.1725, *the belland* 1709 (*v.* **land**), *Bell Lea* 1697, *belle leay* 1709, *the Bell leay* 1700, ~ ~ *Ley* 1724 (*v.* **ley**) (all with **belle** 'a bell-shaped hill'); *John Bende his headland* 1601, *Bend head land* 1697 (the property of *William Bend* 1697), *Bends headland* 1700, *bend hedland* 1709 (belonging to *Thomas Bend* 1700, 1709), *Bends Head Land* c.1725 (that of *John Bend* c.1725) (*v.* **hēafod-land**), *Bend hedge* 1697, *Bends hedg* 1700, ~ *heg* 1709, ~ *Hedge* 1724, c.1725 (in 1724, bordering the property of *Thomas Bend* and c.1725, that of *William Bend*); *beneholm* e.14 (*v.* **bēan, holmr**); *Bergate* 1252 (*v.* **bere, gata**); *the Blacks* 1697, 1700, 1724, c.1725, *the blackes* 1709 (*v.* **blæc**; prob. referring to selions with very dark soil; in eModE, *black* also had the sense 'fertile' in contrast to *white* 'infertile', and black earth would no doubt have had a high organic content); *Brier Hill* 1697, 1724, c.1725, *Brear* ~ 1700, *Brare* ~ 1709 (*v.* **brēr**); *The Butt Close* 1729 (*v.* **butt²**); *in campo aquiloni* (sic) e.14 ('the north field'; with MLat *aquilonalis* 'northern' and *campus* 'a field'; one of the early great fields of the township); *in campo australi* e.14 ('the south field'; with MLat *australis* 'southern'; another of the early great fields); *castelgate* e.14 (*v.* **castel(l), gata**; the road to Belvoir Castle which lies to the south-east), *Castlegate Stones* 1601, 1697, 1724, c.1725, *Castilgate Stons* 1700, *castelgat stones* 1709 (*v.* **stān**; poss. boundary markers, but otherwise referring to stony ground; cf. *Brentingby Stones* in Melton Mowbray f.ns. (b)); *Catackeres* 1601, *Catakers* 1700, *catackers* 1709, *Katacres* 1724, *Catt Acres* c.1725, *Cat Acres furlong* 1697, *Catakers forlong* 1700, *catackers forlang* 1709, *Katacre furlong* 1724 (*v.* **æcer**; the first el. could either be **cat(t)** 'the (wild) cat' or the OE pers.n. *Catta*); *Chaldewellebech* e.14 (the final el. could be either OE **bece¹** (ME **beche**) or ON **bekkr**, both meaning 'a stream', since the e.14 cartulary often shows *ch* for *c/k*, cf. *acherdich supra*); *Caldewellesiche* 1257, *Kaldewellsike* 1252¹, *Kaldewellesyke* 1252² (*v.* **cald, wella, sīc, sík**); *the Churchfield viz. the field towardes Belvoyre* 1601, *the Church hill feilde* 1625 (*v.* **cirice, feld**; one of the later great fields, lying towards Belvoir Castle); *Cokhow(e)* 1424 (*v.* **haugr**; with either **cocc¹** or **cocc²**); *collpit forlang* 1709 (*v.* **furlang**), *the Cole pitt Waye, the Coalepitt Way* 1601 (*v.* **weg**) ('the pit where charcoal is made', *v.* **col-pytt**; the road continued in Barkestone, *v. the Colepytgate* in Barkestone f.ns. (b)); *the Cole Cart(e) Way* 1697, 1700, c.1725, *the Coal Cart Road* 1724 (no doubt later names for *the Cole pitt Waye*); *derholm* e.14, *Deerham close* 1697, *Dearham* ~ 1700, *dear holm* ~ 1724, *Derholm Close* c.1725, *dearam clos* 1709, *Dearham Field* 1697, 1724, *Dereholm Field* c.1725, (*the*) *dearam feild* 1700, ~ ~ *feld* 1709 (*v.* **feld**; one of the later great fields of the village), *dearhoulme furlonge* 1601, *deerham furlong* 1697, *dearam forlong* 1700, *~ forlang* 1709, *Dearham Furlong* 1724, *Derholm ~* c.1725 (*v.* **dēor, holmr**); *thearle of Rutland his great lande* 1601 (*v.* **eorl, land**; at this date, that of the fifth Earl); *enggate* e.14 (*v.* **eng, gata**); *fattebenelond'* e.14 (*v.* **fætt, bēan, land**); *flaxland'* e.14, *Flax Land* 1697, 1709, c.1725, *Flaxlands* 1700, 1724 (*v.* **fleax, land**); *Willm. Freckingham his headland* 1601 (*v.* **hēafod-land**), *Willm. Freckingham his wong* 1601 (*v.* **vangr**); *gildewong* e.14 (ostensibly 'in-field for which a payment is made', *v.* **gild, gildi, vangr**; but poss. is 'in-field with golden flowers' with a reduced **gylden**); *super le grene* 1289 (p), *de la Grene* 1308 (p) (*v.* **grēne**[2]); *grenemerebech* e.14 (the final el. of this f.n. could be either OE **bece**[1] or ON **bekkr**, both meaning 'a stream' (*v.* *Chaldewellebech, supra*); perh. 'the green, weed-covered pool' is referred to (with **grēne**[1], **mere**[1]), but the second el. could be (ge)**mǣre**, of a name alluding to a strip of grassland forming a boundary); *hallwonge* 1601, (*the*) *Hall Wong Clos(e)* 1697, 1700, 1709, 1724, c.1725 (*v.* **hall, vangr**); *Hawetorne mere* l.13 (e.15) *BelCartB, hawethornemere* e.14 (*v.* **hagu-þorn**, (ge)**mǣre**; bordering Barkestone for which the same name is recorded); *The hermitage field* 1601 (*v.* **ermitage**; perh. the site of Allhallows *supra*); *against the Hill* 1601, 1697, 1700, 1709, c.1725 (a furlong so called next to Mill Hill in Mill Fd); *hilleclaye* e.14 (*v.* **hyll, clǣg**); *the Holmes* 1700, *the Holms* 1724, c.1725 (*v.* **holmr**); *horshulles* e.14, *Shorthorsheales* 1700, *Short Hossils* 1724, *Short Horse Hills* c.1725, *horse hill leaes* 1601 (*v.* **leys**) (*v.* **hors, hyll**); *Horne Crosse leaes* 1601, *Hornkas leayes* (sic) 1700, *honcassles* 1709, *Honcass Leys* 1724, *Horn Castle Leas* c.1725 (*v.* **horn, cross, leys**); (*the*) *Kinwell feild* 1700, *~ field, Kinuell feld* 1709, *Kinwell forlang* 1700, *~ furlong* 1724, *Kinuell forlang* 1709 (*v.* **wella**; as first el. the OE pers.n. *Cynna* is poss., but cf. *Kilnewelle-* in Wycomb and Chadwell f.ns. (b)); *Kirk hill* 1729 (*v.* **kirkja**; cf. *the Church hill feilde, supra*); *Lincolne gate* 1601 (*v.* **gata**; the road to Lincoln); *littlebeck* 1601, *letelbeck, ~ forlang* 1709, *Little Beck forlong* 1700, *~ ~ furlong* 1724, c.1725 (*v.* **lȳtel, lítill, bekkr**); *longeboygate* e.14 (*v.* **lang**[1], **boia, gata** and *boigate* in Barkestone f.ns. (b) *infra*); *the longe furlonge* 1601, *the long forlang* 1700, 1709, *the Long furlong* 1724 (in *the Churchfield*, later *Kinwell feild*), *the longe furlonge* 1601, (*the*) *Long forlang* 1700, 1709, *the Long furlong* c.1725 (in Mill Fd), *the longe furlonge* 1601 (in Wood Fd) (*v.* **lang**[1], **furlang**); *Mannebrigg* 1252[1], 1252[2], *Manesbrigge* 1257, *mannesbrigge* e.14 (*v.* (ge)**mǣnnes, brycg**); *against the Mear(e)* 1700, 1709, c.1725, *~ ~ Meer* 1724 (*v.* (ge)**mǣre**; a furlong so called in Little Fd); *michelho* e.14, *miclehowsiche* e.14, *micklye syke* 1601 (*v.* **sīc, sík**) (*v.* **micel, hōh**); *middleacre ditch* 1601 (*v.* **middel, æcer, dīc**); *the Middle feilde* 1625; *the Midle of the feild* 1700, *the medel of the feld* 1709, *the Middle of the Field* 1724, c.1725 (a furlong so called in Nether Fd); *milne hyll, the mill hill* 1601, *mill hill steigh* 1601 (with or **stīg** or **stig**) (*v.* **myln, hyll**); *the Mill-Spring* 1724 (*v.* **spring**[1]); *Muston mere* 1601, *Musson meare* 1700, 1709, *~ Meer* 1724, *Muston Mear* c.1725 (*v.* (ge)**mǣre**; the boundary with Muston which adjoins to the north-east); *the newe field* 1601 (*v.* **nīwe**); *the Nine Rode* 1601 (*v.* **nigon, rōd**[3]); *normangate* e.14, *normangatehil* e.14, *Normangate hill* 1601 (*v.* **hyll**) (*v.* **gata**; prob. with **Norðman**, but **Norman** is also poss., cf. *Norman Bridge* in Knipton; the road continued through Bottesford as *Normangatt* 1427); *peseland'* e.14 (*v.* **pise, land**); *presthou* e.14 (*v.* **prēost, haugr**); *le Priouresgores, le Pryouresgores* 1424 (*v.* **prior, gāra**; presum. with reference to the Prior of Belvoir Priory); *the Quenes highway* 1601, *the highway* 1697, 1700 (*v.* hēah-weg; the earliest citation is with reference to Elizabeth I); *Redlande* 1252², *Redlond* 1252¹ (*v.* rēad, land; alluding to the colour of the soil); *Redmildeheng* 1305 (*v.* eng), *Redemyld' Saltbek* 1420, *Redmyld Saltbek'* 1424 (*v.* Saltbeck in Belvoir parish); *Hugh Restes headland* 1601 (*v.* hēafod-land); *the Rincks* 1697, 1709, *the Rinks* 1700, 1724, c.1725 (*v.* wrink; cf. *the wrinckes* in Stathern f.ns. (b)); *Sandes* e.14 (*v.* sand); *Sandpitt furlonge* 1601, *Sanpite forlong* 1700, *Sanpit(es) forlang* 1709, *Sand pit(t) furlong* 1724, c.1725 (*v.* sand-pytt); *seaven leaes* 1601, *Seuen leayes* 1700, *sefon les* 1709, *Seven Leys* 1724, ~ *Leas* c.1725 (*v.* seofon, leys; an enclosure comprising seven former grassland units of tenure); *Schepegate* 1424, *Shepegate* 1424, 1601, *Sheep Gates* 1697, 1700, 1724, c.1725, *ship gates* 1709 (*v.* scēp, gata and shepe-gate); *Shittlemyres* 1601, *Shitlemire forlong* 1697, 1700, *shittellmyers forlang* 1709, *Shuttlemire furlong* 1724, *Shittlemire* ~ c.1725 ('the unstable, shaky mire', *v.* scytel², mýrr); *sichewelle* e.14 (*v.* sīc, wella); *the Sike* 1697, 1700, 1724, c.1725, *the si(c)k* 1709 (*v.* sīk); *Slechtenge* 1252¹, 1252², *Slethenge* 1257 (*v.* sléttr, eng); *the Soke* 1724 (*v.* soc); *le Souchbek, le Soughbek* 1424 (*v.* sōg, bekkr); *the South forlong* 1700, ~ ~ *forlang* 1709, ~ ~ *Furlong* 1724, c.1725 (a furlong in Wood Fd); *Sowerbeck* 1601, *sowerbeck bush* 1601 (*v.* busc) (*v.* bekkr; this may belong with *le Soughbek* above, but if not, then either with sūr 'sour', referring to unpleasantly-tasting water (cf. Saltbeck in neighbouring Belvoir), or less likely with sūre 'sorrel, dock'); *stanes* e.14 (*v.* stān; perh. to be identified with *Castlegate Stones, supra*); *le stanwelle* e.14, *stanwellehille, stanwalhille* e.14 (*v.* hyll), *Stanwellewong'* e.14 (*v.* vangr) ('the stream with a stony bed', *v.* stān, wella); *stone bridge* 1601, *Stonebrigg Lane* 1729 (*v.* stān, brycg); *stonegate* 1601 (*v.* stān, gata); *stonhoupol* e.14 (*v.* stān, haugr, pōl¹); *suntland* e.14 bis (*v.* sunt, land); *Swarfurowes* 1601, *Suarforas* 1697, 1709, *Swarfuroes* 1700, *Swar furrows* 1724, c.1725 (*v.* swār, furh); *þistelwelle* e.14 (*v.* þistel, wella); *le Toftes* 1424, *Toftys* 1532, *toftes* 1601, 1700, *tofes* (sic) 1709, *the Tofts* c.1725, *South toftes* 1700, ~ *tofes* (sic) 1709, *Sow Tofts* 1724, *(the) South Tofts* c.1725 (*v.* toft); *the towne close* 1601, *the towne headland* 1601 (*v.* hēafod-land) (*v.* tūn); *the Tyth barne* 1625 (*v.* tēoða, bern); *longewatelond, scortewelond* (sic) e.14, *shorte wheatlandes* 1601 (*v.* lang¹, sc(e)ort, hwǣte, land); *witegresse* e.14 (*v.* hwīt, græs; 'white grass' here may indicate dry pasture); *withacre* e.14 (perh. 'white field', *v.* hwīt, æcer; the form parallels 13th cent. spellings for Whitacre, Wa 94); *woodgate* 1601 (*v.* wudu, gata); *wronglond'* e.14, *Wronglands* 1697, 1724, *Ronglands* 1700, 1709, c.1725 (*v.* wrang, vrangr, land).

2. BARKESTONE

Barchestone 1086 DB, Hy 1 Dugd, *Barchestona* 1116 RegAnt, 1174 × 82, l.12 *Rut*, *Barcheston'* 1116 RegAnt, c.1130 LeicSurv, l.12 (e.14) *BelCartA* (freq) *et passim* to John *Rut* (p), *Barchestun'* Hy 2 (e.15) *BelCartB*, *Barchestuna* Hy 2 (e.15) *ib*, l.12 *Rut*, l.12 (e.14) *BelCartA*, *Barchestune* Hy 1 (1333) Ch, Hy 2 (e.15), 1235 × 53 (e.15) *BelCartB*, *Barchiston'* Hy 3 *Rut* (p)

Barkestona Hy 2 (e.15) *BelCartB*, 1.12 *Rut* (p), 1.12 (e.14) *BelCartA et passim* to 1317, 1340 *Wyg, Barkestone* 1.12 *Rut*, 1209 × 19, 1225 RHug *et passim* to 1410 *Rut*, 1517, 1520 *Wyg et freq*, (~ *in le Wall'* 1517 *ib*), *Barkeston'* 1.12 (e.14), e.13 (e.14) *BelCartA* (freq) *et passim* to 1252, 1277 *Rut et freq* to 1477, 1486 *ib et passim* to 1546, 1556 *ib*, 1580 LEpis, (~ *in le Vale de Beluero* 1511 *Wyg*, ~ *in the Vale* 1556 *Rut*), *Barkestun'* e.13, c.1236 *ib et passim* to a.1290, 1293 *Wyg, Barkestuna* 12 (e.15) *BelCartB, Barkiston'* e.Hy 3 *Rut*, 1243 Fees *et passim* to 1307 *Rut*, 1320 (e.15) *BelCartB, Barkistona* 1347 *Wyg, Barkistone* Hy 3 *Rut, Barkistun'* 1299 *Wyg, Barkyston'* Hy 3, e.14 *Rut*, 1311, 1340, 1518 *Wyg*, 1518 *Rut, Barkystu'* 1294, 1.13 *Wyg*

Barkstone 1209 × 35 RHug, 1599 *Rut, Barcston'* Hy 3 *ib, Barkston'* 1306 Ass, 1344 Coram, 1381 SR *et passim* to 1411, 1413 *Rut et freq* to 1517 EpCB, 1534 *Rut et passim* to 1599 *ib*, 1605 LML, *Barxston* 1612 *Rut*

Bargston 1531 *Rut*

Barston' 1352 Ipm, 1364 *Wyg et passim* to 1425, 1427 *Rut et freq* to 1539 *Deed*, 1541 *Rut et passim* to 1579 LEpis, 1610 Speed, (~ *in le Vale* 1451, 1472, 1480, 1484 *Wyg*, ~ *in the Valle of Bever* 1516 *ib*, ~ *in le vale of Bever* 1520 *ib*, ~ *in the Wayll'* 1552 AAS)

Berkeston' 1408 Pat, 1420 *Rut, Berston* 1510, 1525 *Wyg*, 1549 *Pat*, 1550 *Rut*, (~ *in the Vayle* 1510 *Wyg*)

Backson 1708 *Terrier*

'Bark's farmstead, village', *v.* **tūn**. The Scand pers.n. *Barkr, Bǫrkr* is an original by-name, cf. *bǫrkr* (gen.sg. *barkar*) 'bark'. *Bark* occurs as a by-name in Sweden, while a settler in Iceland bore the name *Bǫrkr, v.* SPNLY 48. In this Leics. p.n., the OE gen.sg. *Barkes* has replaced the normal Scand gen.sg. *Barkar*. Note the typical Leics. loss of *t* from the group *-ston* in the early 18th cent. form *Backson*. For the 15th and 16th cent. affix ~ *in le Vale* (with various spellings), *v.* **val** and Redmile *supra*.

BARKESTONE BRIDGE, crossing the Nottingham and Grantham Canal. BARKESTONE WHARF, beside the canal, *v.* **hwearf**. BARKESTONE WOOD, 1796 *EnclA*, 1806 *Map, the woodd(e)* 1579 *Terrier, Barkestone Woods* 1824 O, *v.* **wudu**. CHEQUERS (P.H.), *Chequers* 1863, 1877 White, 1925 Kelly. JERICHO COVERT, *Jericho* 1824 O, *v.* **cover(t)**, JERICHO LODGE, 1925 Kelly; with the covert, situated on the parish boundary, Jericho thus being a 'remoteness' name, *v.* **loge**. THE LODGE. MANOR FM, cf. *Manor House* 1877 White, *v.* **maner**. ST PETER'S AND ST PAUL'S CHURCH, *Church (St Peter and St Paul)* 1846, 1863 White, 1925 Kelly; it is earlier recorded as *ecclesiam de Barkestona* a.1219 RHug, *ecclesie de Barkisston* 1220 MHW, ~ *de Barkeston* 1245 RGros, ~ *de Barkiston* 1264 *Pat*, *ecclesia parochiali de Berston* 1549 *ib.* Note also *The Churchyard* 1612 *Terrier*. SMITH'S FREE SCHOOL (lost), *Smith's Free School* 1846, 1863 White; founded by Daniel Smith in 1814, the building is now part of the Church of England Primary School. SUN (P.H.) (lost), *Sun* 1846, 1863 White, *Sun Inn* 1877 ib, *The Sun* 1925 Kelly. THE VICARAGE, 1877 White; it is *the vicarige house* 1625 *Terrier*, *the Vicaridge House* 1674, 1679, 1697 *ib*, *v.* **vikerage**. THE WINDMILL, *the wyndmyll*, *the wyndemyllys* 1579 *Terrier*, *v.* **wind-mylne**; evidently, more than one in 1579.

FIELD-NAMES

Undated forms in (a) are 1796 *EnclA*. Forms throughout dated 1154 × 59, 1.12, c.1250, Hy 3, Edw 1, e.14, 1480, 1532, 1611 and 1629 are *Rut*; a.1166 (e.15), 12 (e.15), Edw 1 (e.15) and 1358 (e.15) are *BelCartB*; 1.12 (e.14) and e.13 (e.14) are *BelCartA*; e.13, p.1273, a.1290, 1292, 1294, 1.13, 1299, 13, 1341, 1347 and 1364 are *Wyg*; 1421 are Cl; 1579, 1612, 1625, 1674, 1679, 1697 and 17 are *Terrier*.

(a) Dale Fd (*the Dale* 1579, *v.* **dalr**); Dam Fd (*v.* **damme**); Lincoln Gate Furlong (*Lyncolne gate* 1579, *v.* **gata**; the road to Lincoln); Lindsey Cl (cf. *Mr Linsey his land* 17, *v.* **land**); Meadow Wood (*the meadowe woodde* 1579, *the Meadow Wood* 17, *v.* **mǣd** (**mǣdwe** obl.sg.), **wudu**); Middle Fd ((*le*) *Myddle Fyelde*, *the Myddle Fyeld*, *Myddlefield* 1579, *the Midle Field* 17, *v.* **middel**, **feld**; one of the great fields of the township); Mill Fd (*the mylne* 1579, *the Mill* 17, *v.* **myln**); Mill Field Pasture; Moor Gate (*More* 1579, *v.* **mōr¹**, **mór**, **gata**); Nether Fd (*le Netherfeild* 1629, *the Neather feild* 1674, ~ *Neither* ~ 1679, *v.* **neoðera**, **feld**; one of the great fields, earlier called *South Felde*, *infra*); Ox Cl (*v.* **oxa**); The Pasture; Redlands Cls (*Redlands* 1611, *v.* **rēad**, **land**; with reference to the colour of the soil); Nether ~ ~, Roe Bushes, Roe Bush Cls (cf. *Rowbush field* 17, *v.* **vrá**, **busc**, **feld**; one of the great fields of the village, earlier called *the Northeast fyelde*, *infra*); Nether Row Bullgates (*v.* **vrá**, **bullgate**); Warren Cls (cf. *the Warren hill* 1579, *v.* **wareine**).

(b) *Acherdich* c.1250, (*le*) *akirdich* Edw 1, Edw 1 (e.15) (*v.* **æcer-dīc**); *de aula* e.14 (p), Edw 1 (e.15) (p) (with MLat *aula* 'a hall'); *le Bek* 1.13, *le Bekis* Edw 1, Edw 1 (e.15), *the Beck(e)* 1579, 17, *the Becknooke furlong* 17 (*v.* **nōk**), *the beckside* 1579 (*v.* **sīde**), *the becksyck* 1579, *Lower beckesyck furlonge* 1579 (*v.* **sík**, **furlang**) (*v.*

bekkr); *Belhous Place* 1421 (*v.* **bell-hūs, place**; this was the name of the manor house of Barkestone, so that it is worthy of note that for the Anglo-Saxons 'if a freeman had five hides, a church, a kitchen, a bell-house . . . he was worthy of thane-rights', *v. Ancient Laws and Institutes of England*, ed. B. Thorpe (London, 1840), 2 190); *long* ~, *bellandes* 1579, *Bellands*, ~ *furlong* 17 (*v.* **land** and Bellands in Bottesford f.ns. (a)); *le blakeland* e.13, *blacklandes* 1579, *Blacklands furlong* 17 (*v.* **blæc, land**; referring to the colour of the soil); *boigate* a.1166 (e.15), l.12, 12 (e.15), *boiegate* l.12 (e.14), e.13 (e.14), *boygate* 1579, *Boyegate furlong* 1579 (*v.* **boia, gata**; the road continued in Redmile, *v. longeboygate* in Redmile f.ns. (b)); *Branstongate* 17 (*v.* **gata**; the road to Branston which lies to the south-east); *le Bretland* Edw 1, Edw 1 (e.15) (*v.* **breiðr, land**); *brodegate* 1579, *Broadgate*, ~ *furlong(e)* 1579, 17 (*v.* **brād, gata, furlang**); *Henry Bugges Land* 17 (*v.* **land**); *Long, Ouer Bullgate, Bullgate furlong* 17 (*v.* **uferra, bullgate**); *le castelgate* p.1273, 13, *le Castilgate* l.13, *le Castelgat'* 1364, *Castell gate, the Castle gate* 1579, *Castlegate furlong* 1579 (*v.* **furlang**), *Castlegate hole* 17 (*v.* **hol¹**) (*v.* **castel(l), gata**; the road to Belvoir Castle); *Wm. Chesters land* 17 (*v.* **land**); *the Colepytgate* 1579 (*v.* **col-pytt, gata**; the road continued in Redmile, *v. the Cole pitt Waye* in Redmile f.ns. (b)); *the common streete* 1612, 1625 (*v.* **commun, strǣt**); *le Dritakir* l.13, *Dirte* ~, *Durt(e) Akers* 1579 (*v.* **drit, æcer**); *Rich' Dunmore his Land, Rich' Dunmores Land* 17 (*v.* **land**); *Andrew Dyxsons house* 1579; *Edlingstye* 1579 (*v.* **stig**; with the surn. *Edling*, the reflex of the ME fem. pers.n. *Edelina* (OGer *Adelina*), *v.* Reaney *s.n.* and Forssner 8); *Edmondstigh furlong* 17 (*v.* **stig**; with the surn. *Edmond*, the reflex of the OE pers.n. *Ēadmund*); *ye eight leys* 17 (*v.* **leys**; an enclosure made up of eight former grassland units of tenure); *therles Newe Close* 1579 (*v.* **eorl, nīwe, clos(e)**; with reference to the third Earl of Rutland who died in 1587), *the Erles Land* 17 (*v.* **land**); *Fishers Land* 17 (*v.* **land**; with the surn. *Fisher*); *le fyuefurlong* p.1273, *le Fifourlong* l.13, *le fiuefurlong* 13 (*v.* **fīf, furlang**); *Godiuhauedlond* 13 (*v.* **hēafod-land**; with the OE fem. pers.n. *Godgifu*); *Gorsye layes* 1579 (*v.* **gorstig, leys**); *Granby gate* 1629 (*v.* **gata**; the road to Granby, which lies to the north-west in Notts.); *Granthamgate* Edw 1 (*v.* **gata**; the road to Grantham which lies to the east in Lincs.); *a la Grene* Hy 3 (p) (*v.* **grēne²**); *Halythornfurlong* Hy 3, e.14, Edw 1 (e.15) (*v.* **hālig, þorn, furlang**; the location of the 'holy thorn' is unknown, as is the nature of its sanctity, but perh. the name relates in some sort to Church Thorns included with neighbouring Redmile minor names *supra*); *Harleston furlong* 1579, *Harlexton* ~ 17 (*v.* **furlang**; with the surn. *Harlexton* of a family originating in the village of Harlaxton which lies seven miles to the south-east in Lincs.); *Hawthornehill* 1579, ~ *Plaine* 17 (*v.* **plain** and *Playne, infra*), *Hawethornmere* Edw 1 (*v.* **(ge)mǣre**) (*v.* **hagu-þorn**); *Hawbysike Furlong* 17 (*v.* **sīk**; since Harby lies three miles to the south-west beyond Plungar, the *sīk* may once have been a small stream running between the townships, but the drainage pattern of the area is now much altered because of the construction of the Nottingham and Grantham Canal); *le Haygate* Hy 3, e.14, Edw 1 (e.15), *Heigate* e.13 (e.14), *le Heygate* Edw 1, Edw 1 (e.15), *Heygate* 1579, ~ *furlong* 17, *Heygate Shrubbs* 17 (*v.* **scrubb**) (*v.* **hēg, gata**); *le hengefurlong(e)* Edw 1, Edw 1 (e.15) (*v.* **henge, furlang**); *le holm* Edw 1, *the holmes* 1579, ~ ~ *furlong* 17, *the furlong Below the holmes* 17 (*v.* **holmr**); *the Homestead* 1674, 1679 (*v.* **hām-stede**; belonging to *the Vicaridge House, supra*); *le Houlholm* 1299 (*v.* **hulu, holmr**); *Hungerhil* p.1273,

Hungeril 1.13, *Hongerhil* 13, *Hungerhill* 1579, ~ *furlong* 17, *Hungerhilhefdis* 1299 (*v.* **hēafod**) (*v.* **hungor, hyll**); *hunton busshe* 1579, *Huntinbush furlong* 17, *Huntinbush Leys* 17 (*v.* **leys**) (*v.* **busc** and *Hunton' close* in neighbouring Easthorpe f.ns. (b)); *Hycksons hedley* 1579 (*v.* **headley**), *Hycksons house* 1579 (cf. *Willm. Hyckson* 1579); *Kaldewellefurlong'* 1.13 (*v.* **cald, wella, furlang**); *Langelayehil* Edw 1 (*v.* **lang**[1], **lēah, hyll**); *langwrth hill* 1579, *Langworth Hill* 17 (*v.* **lang**[1], **worð, hyll**, cf. *Stoneworth hill, infra*); *long layes* 1579, ~ *leays* 17 (*v.* **leys**); *the lytle beck* 1579 (*v.* **lȳtel, lítill, bekkr**); *Lyttle hill* 1579, *Litlehill* 17 (*v.* **lȳtel, hyll**); *Many Welles* 1579, *Maniwell furlong* 17, *Maniwellegate* 13 (*v.* **gata**) (*v.* **manig, wella**); *Rich. Marshall his Land* 17 (*v.* **land**); *the Meer* 17 (*v.* **(ge)mǣre**); *Mercie Close* 1674, 1679, *Marcie* ~ 1697 (with the surn. *Marcy, v.* Reaney *s.n.*; a poss. alternative *mercy*, perh. indicating the assignment of the close's rentals to assist the village poor, seems somewhat fanciful for this period); *Mikelhenge* Hy 3 (*v.* **micel, mikill, eng**); *Moreland(e)s* 1579, 17, *le morelandhende* Edw 1, Edw 1 (e.15) (*v.* **ende**) (*v.* **mōr**[1], **land**); *the furlong beneath the mylne* 1579 (*v.* **myln**); *le nedermylne* 1532 (*v.* **neoðera, myln**; a windmill); *Nomans furlong* 1579 (*v.* **nān-mann, furlang**; the nature of such a furlong is unclear); *the North Felde* 1579, ~ ~ *field* 17 (*v.* **norð, feld**; one of the great fields of the village); *the Northeast fyelde* 1579 (*v.* **norðēast, feld**; one of the great fields, later called *Rowbush field, v.* Roe Bushes *supra*); (*le*) *notebusk* 1.13, Edw 1, Edw 1 (e.15) (*v.* **hnutu, hnot, buskr**); *old parke nooke* 17 (*v.* **nōk** and Old Park Wood in Belvoir); *the ouerfurlong* 17 (of Middle Fd), *the ouerfurlong* 17 (of *Rowbush field*) (*v.* **uferra**); *the Overmylne* 1532 (*v.* **uferra, myln**; a windmill); *the Warren for deer called the Parke* 1579 (*v.* **wareine**), *the parke corner* 1579 (*v.* **corner**) (*v.* Old Park Wood in Belvoir); *Paticroft* 1358 (e.15) (*v.* **croft**; with the surn. *Patey* (a diminutive of *Pate* (Patrick)), *v.* Reaney *s.n.*); *Payncroft* 1480 (*v.* **croft**; with the surn. *Payn*, used in the 12th and 13th cents. as a Christian name, even though from OFr *Paien* (in turn from Lat *paganus* 'heathen'), *v.* Reaney *s.n.*); *Playne, the Towne playne* 1579 (*v.* **tūn**), *Walke playne* 1579 (*v.* **walk**) (*v.* **plain** and *Hawethornehill Plaine, supra*); *the Pyngle* 1579, *the Pingle furlong* 17 (*v.* **pingel**); *the quyckset hedge* 1579 (*v.* **quykset, hecg**); *Redemildgate* a.1290, 1347, *Redemeldgate* 1294, *Redmyldgate* 1364 (*v.* **gata**), *Redmell Close* 1579, *Redmile Close corner* 17 (*v.* **clos(e), corner**), *Redmell Layes* 1579 (*v.* **leys**), *Redmile Meer* 17 (*v.* **(ge)mǣre**) (Redmile adjoins to the north-east); *Edward Remingtons Land* 17 (*v.* **land**); *the Sandpytt furlonge* 1579, (*the*) *Sandpitt furlong* 17 (*v.* **sand-pytt, furlang**); *le Sandwong* Edw 1, *le sandewong* Edw 1 (e.15) (*v.* **sand, sandr, vangr**); *Sir Scroopes Land, Sir Scroop his Ground* 17 (*v.* **land, grund**; as early as 1413 Nichols, a *Roger le Scrop* held one carucate of land and a messuage in Barkestone but these f.ns. may refer rather to *Sir Skroop How* 1679 who held land in neighbouring Stathern); *Shortlands* 1629 (*v.* **sc(e)ort, land**); *the shrobbes* 1579 (*v.* **scrobb**); *Shrubbymeer furlong* 17 (*v.* **scrubb, -ig**[3], **(ge)mǣre**); *le Slade* 1341 (*v.* **slæd**); *Smythes pyngle* 1579 (*v.* **pingel**; with either the surn. *Smith* or *smið* 'a smith'); *Le South Fyeld*, (*the*) *South Felde* 1579, *the South Field or the field towards Plungar* 17 (*v.* **sūð, feld**; one of the great fields of the village); *Stacicroft* 1358 (e.15) (*v.* **croft**; with the surn. *Stac(e)y*); *Stanewoldehil* Edw 1, Edw 1 (e.15) (*v.* **stān, wald, hyll**); *le stangnum piscium* (sic) 1364 ('the fish pond', with MLat *stagnum* 'a pond' and MLat *piscis* (*piscium* gen.pl.) 'a fish'); *stochewille* 1154 × 59 ('stream with a footbridge consisting of a tree-trunk', *v.* **stocc, wella**); *the Stones* 1579, *the Midlestones* 17 (*v.* **middel**), *Neyther stones* 1579 (*v.* **neoðera**) (*v.* **stān**); *stone furlonge* 1579 (*v.* **stān, furlang**); *Stonewrth hill* 1579, *Long Stonworth hill* 17, *Broad Stonworth hill furlong* 17 (*v.* **stān, worð**); *Strawdales* 1579 (*v.* **strēaw, deill**; *straw* was used in later f.ns. as a term of contempt); *Tates house* 1579 (with the surn. *Tate*); *Thrawlhills* 17 (*v.* **þræll**); *Willm. Towers land* 17 (*v.* **land**); (*the*) *Trevers Gorse*(*s*), *the Trevayse Gorses* 1579, *Trevisgoss*, ~ *furlong* 17 (*v.* **travers, gorst**); *ye two Leys* 17 (*v.* **leys**; an enclosure consisting of two former grassland units of tenure); *the Vicaridge Yard* 1697 (*v.* **geard** and The Vicarage *supra*); *the Water stalles* 1579, *the Watterstalls* 17 (*v.* **wæter, stall**); *Watterbalke furlong* 17 (*v.* **wæter, balca**); *le Waylant* Edw 1 (e.15) (*v.* **weg, land**); *the west mere betwene Bareston & Plungar* 1579 (*v.* **(ge)mǣre**); *Wrongdeyl ende* 1364 (*v.* **wrang, vrangr, deill, ende**).

3. PLUNGAR

Plungar(*'*) c.1130 LeicSurv, 1225 RHug *et passim* to 1411 *BelCartB*, 1473 *CCR*, 1502 *MiscAccts et freq*, *Plungare* Hy 2 (e.15) *BelCartB*, l.12 *Rut*, 1209 × 35 RHug, 1529 *Rut*, *Pluncgar* 1220 MHW, 1209 × 35 RHug, *Plunger* Hy 3, e.14 *Rut et passim* to 1553 Pat, 1576 Saxton

Plumgar 1243 Fees, 1254 Val, 1525 *Wyg*, 1559 *Pat*

Ploungar l.13 *Rut*, *Plonger* 1480 *ib*, 1508 Ipm, *Plounger* 1541 *MinAccts*

Plumgath c.1130 LeicSurv, *Plumgarth* 1253 × 58 RHug, c.1291 Tax, e.14 *BelCartA et passim* to 1517 EpCB, 1518 *Rut*, *Plumgard* c.1130 LeicSurv, 1187 P (p) *et passim* to Hy 3 *Rut*, 1328 Banco

Plomgarth 1505, 1506, 1508 *Rut*

Plungard' 1155 × 68, 1174 × 82 *Rut*, 1186 P (p) *et passim* to 1253 FConc, 1260 Cur *et freq* to 1305, 1308 *Rut et passim* to 1328 (e.15) *BelCartB*, 1333 Ch, *Plungarde* 1302 *Rut*, *Plungarth'* Hy 3 *ib*, 1274 Ass, l.13 *Wyg et freq* to 1513, 1519 *ib et passim* to 1579 LEpis, 1604 SR, *Plungarthe* Hy 3 *Rut* bis, *Plungart'* 1312 *Wyg*, 1340 Ch (p), *Plungerthe* Edw 1 *Rut*

Plongarth' 1343 Cl, 1343 *Rut et passim* to 1502 *Wyg*, 1534 *Rut*, *Ploungart'* Edw 3 *ib*

The first el. of the name is OE **plūme** 'a plum-tree'. Spellings as late as the 17th cent. appear to show a continuing variation between OE **gāra** 'a gore, a triangular plot of ground' and Scand **garðr** 'an enclosure' as the generic. While the notion of an original OE compound **plūm-gāra* with the replacement of the OE generic by a Scand one is attractive, an original OE/Scand hybrid *plūm-garðr with later confusion of garðr and gāra cannot be discounted in this area, especially as the name may have been of relatively late creation. The concept of an enclosed plot planted with plum-trees makes reasonable sense, but it could be argued that a gore of ground growing with wild plum-trees may eventually have been enclosed, hence gāra was replaced by garðr to describe accurately this development in husbandry. That spellings in -gar may simply be the result of the reduction through loss of an original garðr seems unlikely. Hence, we have originally either 'the point of land growing with plum-trees' or 'the plum-tree enclosure'. The former may have given way to the latter, or else there was contemporary confusion between gāra and garðr, v. **plūme, gāra, garðr.**

ANCHOR INN (lost), *Anchor* 1846, 1863 White, *Anchor Inn* 1877 ib, 1925 Kelly. FAR BARN. GLEBE HO., v. **glebe.** MANOR HO., *Manor House* 1877 White, v. **maner.** NEWHOLME, v. **holmr.** PLUNGAR BRIDGE, crossing the Nottingham and Grantham Canal. PLUNGAR GRANGE, v. **grange.** PLUNGAR WOOD, 1824 O. THE POPLARS. RUNDLE BECK, *le bec* e.14 *Rut, le Bekke* 1410 *ib*, v. **rynel, bekkr.** ST HELEN'S CHURCH, *Church (St Helen, or Holy Cross)* 1846, 1863, 1877 White, *Church (St Helen)* 1925 Kelly; it is earlier recorded as *ecclesie de Pluncgar* 1220 MHW, ~ *de Plumgar* 1559 *Pat*. Note also the churchyard 1612 *Terrier*. VALE HO. THE VICARAGE, 1877 White, 1925 Kelly; it is *the Vicaridge house* 1679 *Terrier*.

FIELD-NAMES

The forms in (a) are 1796 *EnclA*. Forms throughout dated Hy 2 (e.15) are *BelCartB*; 1.12, Hy 3, e.14, 1343, 1410 and 1415 are *Rut*; 1311 are *Wyg*.

(a) Dale Fd (*le Dale* e.14, 1410, v. **dalr**; one of the great fields of the township); Mill Fd (one of the great fields); the Moor Gate (v. **mōr**[1], **mór, gata**); Nether Fd (one of the great fields); the Pasture; Wood Fd (another of the great fields).

(b) *Barkistonbec* e.14, *Barkistonbek'* 1343, *Barkeston' bek'* 1415 (v. **bekkr**), *Barkistonemere* Hy 3 (v. **(ge)mǣre**) (Barkestone adjoins to the north-east); *Bekkefurlong'* 1410 (v. **bekkr, furlang**); (*le*) *Beneland* e.14, 1415, *le Benelandis* 1343 (v. **bēan, land**); (*le*) *Blakeland* Hy 3, 1415 (v. **blǣc, land**; with reference to the colour of the soil); *Blakemoreacre* e.14, 1410 (v. **blǣc, mōr**[1], **æcer**); *Bretland'* e.14, 1410 (v. **breiðr, land**); *Atte Brigge* 1327 SR (p) (v. **atte, brycg**); *Catehil* e.14,

Catilhill' 1410 (*v.* **cat(t)el, hyll**); *le Cheldacre* 1415 (*v.* **celde, æcer**); *cortepit, choritepit* Hy 3 (*v.* **cort(e), pytt**); *Crossegate* 1410, *Crosse hill'* 1410 (*v.* **cros, gata, hyll**; the forms are adjacent in the text and evidently refer to the same unlocated wayside cross, since *cross* 'lying across, athwart' seems unlikely in this pairing); *Flaxland* e.14 (*v.* **fleax, land**); *Fulewellesike* e.14, *Fulwelsykehill'* 1343 (*v.* **hyll**) (*v.* **fūl, wella, sík**); *Gosecroft* e.14, 1311 (*v.* **gōs, croft**); *le groping'*, *le grouping* Hy 3, *le Groupingis* 1415 (*v.* **grōp, eng**); *Hauerhil* e.14 (*v.* **hæfera, hafri, hyll**); *Hengestland* 1410 (*v.* **land**; prob. with **hengest** 'a horse, a stallion, a gelding', but the OE pers.n. *Hengest* cannot be discounted); *le hepthorn* 1415 (*v.* **hēope, þorn**; the compound ***hēop-þorn** presum. refers to the dog-rose (OE *hēopa*)); *Herdebigate* 1311, 1410 (*v.* **gata**; the road to Harby which lies to the south-west); *le Heygate* e.14, 1343 (*v.* **hēg, gata**); *(le) Hillishende* e.14 (*v.* **hyll, ende**); *holdeb'akir* Hy 3, *holdberdacre* e.14, *Holdberdakir* 1415 (*v.* **æcer**; with the ME surn. *Holdebert*, which may derive from an unrecorded OE pers.n. *Holdbeorht, v.* Reaney *s.n.* Holbert); *le Holdehey* e.14 (*v.* **ald, (ge)hæg**); *le hundhakir* Hy 3, *Hundeacre* e.14 (*v.* **æcer**; the Fr def.art. *le* of the earlier form suggests that the first el. is **hund** 'a hound', but the generic **æcer** 'a plot of arable land' may argue rather for an OE or ON pers.n. *Hund, Hundi*, cf. Hounds Acre in Wymondham f.ns. (a)); *le kyrkefeld'* 1410 (*v.* **kirkja, feld**; one of the early great fields of the village, perh. to be identified with the later Dale Fd *supra*); *Lochiswellehil* Hy 3, *Lokkeswelhil* 1415 (*v.* **hyll**), *lokeswellegate* e.14, *Lokkeswelgate* 1415 (*v.* **gata**) (*v.* **wella**; the first el. is uncertain, perh. **loc** in its sense 'a fold', but the consistent genitival construction suggests rather a pers.n. such as the recorded OE *Loc*); *le Longehay* 1311 (*v.* **lang¹, (ge)hæg**); *Magothill'* 1415 (*v.* **hyll**; the first el. may be the ME surn. *Magot* which derives from the ME fem. pers.n. *Maggot*, a diminutive of *Magge*, a pet-form of Margaret; *Maggot* was also applied as a proper name to the magpie (cf. dial. *maggot-pie*) and it could have been the bird itself which was a frequenter of this hill, *v.* OED *s.v.* maggot² and Reaney *s.n.* Maggot); *le merefurlong'* e.14 (*v.* **(ge)mære, furlang**); *middelcroft* l.12, Hy 2 (e.15) (*v.* **middel, croft**); *super montem* Hy 3 (p) (with MLat *mons* (*montem* acc.sg.) 'a hill'); *Ogerstone* 1410 (the first el. is the OFr pers.n. *Ogier* (OGer *Odger*), cf. *Ogerus Brito* 1086 DB 'Oger the Breton' who held Kilby in Guthlaxton Hundred; with either **tūn** if a late farmstead or **stān** if a boundary marker); *le Oldemorlond* 1311 (*v.* **ald, mōr¹, land**); *Oxwelgate* 1410 (*v.* **oxa, wella, gata**); *Peseland* e.14, *le Peselandis* 1343 (*v.* **pise, land**); *Plungarbeck* Hy 3 (*v.* **bekkr**); *Plungar beastes pasture* 1579 *Terrier* (*v.* **beste, pasture** and the Pasture *supra*); *Radeland* e.14 (*v.* **rēad, land**; referring to the colour of the soil); *Rademoreacre* e.14 (*v.* **mōr¹, æcer**; with **hrēod** or **rēad**); *Sceldacre* e.14 (*v.* **sceld, æcer**; land with a shelter of some kind upon it); *le Schortehay* 1311 (*v.* **sc(e)ort, (ge)hæg**); *Shiremere* 1410, *le Shyremere* 1415 (*v.* **scīr¹, (ge)mære**; the county boundary with Notts.); *Smallewelgate* 1410, *Smalwelgate* 1415 (*v.* **smæl, wella, gata**); *Statherennegate* 1311 (*v.* **gata**), *Stathernemere* 1410 (*v.* **(ge)mære**) (Statherin adjoins to the south); *Stoueneshil* e.14, *Stoueneshyl* 1311, *Stouneshill'* 1410 (*v.* **hyll**; the first el. may be OE, ON **stofn** 'a tree-stump', but the consistent genitival forms point rather to a Scand pers.n. *Stofn* or *Stafn*, cf. Stonesby, six miles to the south-east and *v.* SPNLY 261 *s.n.* *Stafn* which cites *Stouenesbi* 12 (presum. identical with a.1158 Dane) for Stainsby in Lincs.); *Le Syke* 1343 (*v.* **sík**); *Thuerlondes* 1311 (*v.* **þverr, land**); *Tounefurlong'* 1410 (*v.* **tūn,** furlang); *Wadeland'* Hy 3 (v. **wād, land**); *le Waren* 1410 (v. **wareine**); *Warddeyle* 1410 (v. **deill**; with either the surn. *Ward* or Scand **varða** 'a heap of stones, a cairn'); *le Wellegate* Hy 3, e.14, *le Welgate* 1415 (v. **wella, gata**); *Westhillisende* Hy 3 (v. **west, hyll, ende**); *westwelle* Hy 2 (e.15) (v. **west, wella**); *le Wdegate* (sic) Hy 3 (v. **wudu, gata** and Plungar Wood *supra*).

Scalford

1. SCALFORD

Scaldeford' 1086 DB, 1107 Reg, c.1130 LeicSurv *et passim* to e.Hy
3 *Rut*, 1235 RGros *et freq* to 1405 Pat, 1416 Banco *et passim* to
1423 FA, 1430 *Deed, Scaldeforde* Wm 2 Dugd, 1122 Reg, 1219
RHug, *Scaldefort* 1147 BM, 1321 *Rut* (p), *Scaldeforth(e)* p.1250
Wyg, Edw 1 *Rut*
Scaudeford' Hy 2 *Rut*, 1200 OblR, e.13 *BHosp*, 1211 *Rut et freq* to
1270 RGrav, Hy 3 *Crox et passim* to 1340 Ch, 1351 BPR,
Scaudeforda c.1250 (1407) Gilb (p)
Schaldeford' 1201 P, m.13 (1404) *Laz et passim* to 1314 *GarCart*,
1317 *Rut, Schaldeforde* 1219 RHug, 1220 MHW, 1317 *Rut*,
Schalford 1440 *Wyg*, 1523 AAS
Skaldeford 1323 *Finch* (p), 1326 Ipm *et passim* to 1332 *Rut*
Scaldford' 1381, 1382 *RTemple*, 1420 (1449) *WoCart*
Scalford 1392 Fine, 1414 Pat *et passim* to 1440 *Wyg*, 1449 *WoCart*
et freq, Scalforth 1535 VE, 1541 MinAccts, 1552 AAS,
Schalfforthe 1527 LWills
Scawford 1574 Fine, *Scaulford* 1622 Burton, *Scofford* 1744 *Rental*

'The shallow ford', *v.* **sc(e)ald, ford**. Initial OE *sc* [ʃ] is replaced by
Scand *sk* [sk] in the first el., although the former sound seems to have
survived as late as the early 16th cent. Late 12th and 13th cent. forms
having *u* for *l* are due to AN influence.

RINGLETHORPE (later GOLDSMITH GRANGE)
Ricoltorp 1086 DB
Ringolfestorp c.1130 LeicSurv
Ringoldetorp l.12 *GarCart* bis, l.12 *BHosp*
Ringoltorp l.12, e.13 *GarCart, Ryngoltorp* 1204 *BHosp, Ringolthorp'*
1150 × 1200 *GarCh*, e.13 *Wyg*, a.1250 *BHosp, Ringolthorpe* 1340
Ch, *Ryngolthorp'* 13 *GarCart*, 1313 *Wyg*, 1340 Ch
Ringaltorp 1159 × 81 Nichols, l.12 *GarCart, Ringualtorp* l.12 *ib*

Ringeltorp 1.12 *GarCart* bis, Hy 3 *Rut, Ringelthorp'* e.13 *BHosp*,
1317 *Wyg*, 1467 × 84 *LTD, Ryngelthorp* 1315, 1343 Banco, 1374
AD, *Ryngelthorpe* 1551 Ipm
Ringilthorp p.1250 *Wyg*, l.13 *ib* bis, *Ringilthorpe* 1317 *ib*
Ringethorp Hy 3 *Rut*, 1276 RH, Edw 1 *CroxR, Ryngethorp* 1364 AD
Rynglethorp(p)e 1535 VE, 1537 MinAccts, *Rynglesthorpe* 1537
Dugd, *Ringlethorpe* 1558 × 79 ECP

Probably 'Hringwulf's outlying farmstead', *v.* þorp. Spellings from
c.1130 onwards point strongly to the OE pers.n. *Hringwulf* as the first
el. of the name. The isolated DB form with *Ricol-* may be due to scribal
error in the omission of *n* (with *c* representing the common AN
interchange of *k* and *g*) or else represents the OGer pers.n. *Ricolf* which
was replaced by *Hringwulf*. A possible alternative to OE *Hringwulf* as
first el. is the ODan/OSwed pers.n. *Ringulf*, but this is badly evidenced
in Scandinavia and it is worth noting that Feilitzen 293 takes the DB
instances of *Ringulf* to represent *Hringwulf*.

Ringlethorpe early became a grange of Garendon Abbey and is styled
as a grange from the 12th cent.: *grangia de Ringolthorp* 1150 × 1200
GarCh, Grang' de Ryngolthorp 13 *GarCart, grang' de Ringelthorp*
1467 × 84 *LTD, Ryngelthorpe Grange* 1551 Ipm, *Ringlethorp Grange*
1558 × 79 ECP.

From at least 1577, it is recorded as Goldsmith(s) Grange:
Goldsmiths graunge 1577 Ipm, ~ *Grange* 1609 LeicW, 1610 Speed,
1708 *Terrier, Gold(e)smithe graunge* 1601, 1605, 1612 *ib, Goldsmythe
graunge* 1605, 1612 *ib, (the) Goldsmith Grange* 1625 *ib*, 1657 *Deed*,
1674 *Terrier et freq* to 1730 *ib*, 1761 *EnclA et passim* to 1877 White,
Goldsmiths' ~ (sic) 1863 *ib*; it is *Scalford Grange* 1824 O. The grange
was renamed from *Joh' Goldsmith* 1463 Nichols who was a later owner,
v. **grange**.

BLACK HORSE (P.H.) (lost), *Black Horse* 1846, 1863, 1877 White.
BLACKSMITH'S SHOP (lost), *blacksmiths shop* 1848 *TA, v.* **blacksmith**,
sc(e)oppa. CHURCH FM, CHURCH ST, *v.* St Egelwin the Martyr's Church
infra. CLAYFIELD FM (x2), *the claye feilde* 1601, 1605, 1612 *Terrier*,
Clay Feilde 1625 *ib, the Clay feild* 1674, 1697, 1703 *ib, the Clay Field*
1704 *Reeve*, 1708, 1708 (18), 1730 *Terrier, v.* **clǣg, feld**; one of the
great fields of the township. THE COTTAGE, cf. *Cottage Gardens* 1969
Surv. CUMBERLAND LODGE, 1863, 1877 White, *v.* **loge**; it is
Cumberland Grange 1846 *ib, v.* **grange**; presum. with the surn.

Cumberland, cf. Cumberland Spinney in Wyfordby and Cumberland Cl in Brentingby f.ns. (a). DEBDALE FM (DEBDALE LODGE 2½"), *Debdale* 1824 O, *Debdale's Lodge* 1863 White, *Debdale* ~ 1877 ib, *v.* **dēop, dalr, loge**. THE ELMS. GATE LODGE, at the gateway to Scalford Hall. GLEBE FM, *Glebe farm* 1925 Kelly, *v.* **glebe**. THE GLOSSOMS, *Glossams* 1846 White. GOLDSMITH GRANGE, *v.* Ringlethorpe *supra*. GRANGE FM, *the Grange Farm* 1825 *Terrier*; in the north-west of the parish and unrelated to Goldsmith Grange, *v.* **grange**. KING ST. KING'S ARMS (P.H.), *King's Arms* 1846, 1863, 1877 White, 1925 Kelly, *King's Arms Inn* 1910 *Sale*. KING'S CLOSE, off King St. LIONVILLE, earlier the site of *The Lion Brick & Tile Co., Ltd.* 1925 Kelly. MANOR HO., *Manor House* 1846, 1863, 1877 White, 1925 Kelly, *v.* **maner**. MAWBROOK FM, *Moorebecke* 1601, 1605, 1612 *Terrier*, *Morebecke* 1625, 1674 *ib*, *Moorbeck* 1697, 1708, 1708 (18) *ib*, *Morebeck* 1704 *Reeve*, 1708, 1708 (18), 1730 *Terrier*, *the further side morebecke* 1625 *ib*, *the nearer side Moorbeck* 1708 *ib*, *moorebecke ditche* 1605 ib (*v.* **dīc**), *v.* **mōr**[1], **mór, bekkr**; *the Moorebecke feilde* 1601, 1605 *Terrier*, (*the*) *Morebeck(e) Feild(e)* 1612, 1625, 1674 *ib*, ~ *Field* 1704 *Reeve*, *the Moor Beck feild* 1697, 1703 *Terrier*, ~ ~ ~ *Field* 1708, 1708 (18), 1730 *ib*, *Mawbrook field* 1846, 1863 White, *v.* **feld**; one of the great fields of the village, with Scand *beck* late replaced by English *brook*. MAWBROOK LODGE, 1863, 1877 White, *v.* **loge**. MEADOWCROFT. MELTON RD is *Melton Gate* 1704 *Reeve* (*v.* **gata**); it is *the kinges hie way* 1605 *Terrier*, *the Kings highway* 1708, 1708 (18) *ib*, *v.* **hēah-weg**; the road to Melton Mowbray which lies to the south, with reference in 1605 to James I. Note that the reigning monarch in 1708 was Queen Anne. MILL HO., the site of *the windemille* 1612 *Terrier*, *the Wind Mill* 1704 *Reeve*, cf. (*the*) *Windmill Furlong*, 1697, 1708 (18), 1730 *Terrier*, *v.* **wind-mylne**. THE MISTE. NETHER HALL FM, *Nether Hall* 1863, 1877 White *v.* **hall**. NEW ST. OLDFIELDS LODGE, 1863, 1877 White (*v.* **loge**), *Olde feilde* 1601, 1605 *Terrier*, ~ *fyeld* 1612 *ib*, (*the furlong called*) *Old Feild* 1625, 1674, 1697 *ib*, ~ *Field* 1708, 1708 (18), 1730 *ib*, *v.* **ald, feld**; in the later *Breach Field*. PLOUGH INN, 1877 White, *Plough* 1863 ib, 1925 Kelly. PRIMITIVE METHODIST CHAPEL, 1848 *TA*. REDEARTH FM, *reedyearthe* 1601 *Terrier*, *the reede yearth, the read yearthe* 1605 *ib*, *the rede earthe, reede earthe* 1612 *ib*, *the redd earth, Readearth* 1625 *ib*, (*the*) *Red Earth* 1674, 1697, 1703, 1708, 1708 (18), 1730 *ib*, ~ ~ *Field* 1704 *Reeve*, 1846, 1863 White, *v.* **rēad, eorðe**; one of the great fields of the village. RED HOUSE FM is *Pitfield Lodge* 1824 O, the site of extensive ironstone quarrying, *v.* **pytt, loge**. ST EGELWIN THE MARTYR'S CHURCH, *Church (St Egelwin the Martyr)* 1846, 1863,

1877 White, 1925 Kelly; it is earlier recorded as *ecclesiam de Scaldeford(e)* 1219 RHug, 1235 RGros, *ecclesie de Schaldeforde* 1220 MHW, ~ *de Scaldeford* 1356, 1405 *Pat*, *The Church* 1708 (18) *Terrier*. Note also *the churcheyarde* 1605 *ib*, *the Church Yard(e)* 1625, 1674, 1697 *et passim* to 1708 (18) *ib*, *Church & churchyard* 1845 *TA*, *v.* **chirche-ʒeard**. SANDY LANE, *v.* **sandig**. SCALFORD BROOK, *the Brooke* 1601, 1605, 1612, 1625 *Terrier*, *the Brook* 1694 *ib*, 1704 *Reeve*, 1708, 1708 (18), 1730 *Terrier*, *v.* **brōc**. SCALFORD HALL, 1925 Kelly; an earlier hall is recorded in *othe Hall* 1306 Banco (p), 1344 ib (p), *v.* **hall**. SCALFORD HALL FARM COTTAGE. SCALFORD LODGE, 1846 White, *v.* **loge**. SCALFORD STATION, STATION COTTAGES, STATION HO., on the *Great Northern & London & North-Western Joint Railway* 1854 O, now dismantled. SCHOOL LANE, cf. *School house* 1848 *TA*. SOUTH ST. THORPE SIDE, *v.* **sīde**; referring to the lost Ringlethorpe *supra* (*v. Thorpe Gate* in f.ns. (b)). THE VICARAGE, 1877 White, 1925 Kelly; it is (*the*) *Vicarage House* 1708, 1708 (18) *Terrier*, 1848 *TA*. VICARAGE FM (2½"). WESLEYAN METHODIST CHAPEL, 1848 *TA*. WOLDS FM is *Wolds Lodge* 1863 White, *v.* **wald**, **loge**. YEW TREE HO.

FIELD-NAMES

In (a), undated forms are 1969 *Surv*; those dated 1825 are *Terrier*, while 1848 are *TA*. Throughout, forms dated 1.12 are *GarCart*; 1601, 1605, 1612, 1625, 1674, 1697, 1700, 1703, 1708, 1708 (18) and 1730 are *Terrier*; 1704 are *Reeve*.

(a) Four ~, 6 Acres, Middle 7 ~, Road 7 Acres, 8 ~, First 8, Second 8 Acres, 9 Acre, 10 ~, 11 Acres, 15 Acre (*v.* **æcer**); Barns Lane Paddock 1848 (*v.* **paddock**); Big Fd; the Black Sick, the South Black Sick (*v.* **blæc**, **sík**); Bottom Cl (*v.* **bottom**); Bridge Fd (*Bridge* 1704, cf. *Bridgehill* 1625, 1697, 1704, *the bridgehill forlonge* 1601, 1612, *bridghill furlonge* 1625, (*the*) *Bridgehill furlong* 1674, 1708, 1708 (18), *v.* **brycg**, **hyll**, **furlang**); Brook Fd (*v.* Scalford Brook *supra*); Bullimar (*v.* Bellemere Fm in adjoining Goadby Marwood); Calf Banks (*v.* **bank**), (the) Calf Cl 1848, 1969 (*v.* **calf**); Cat-tails (referring to Meadow Cat's tail Grass or Timothy Grass (*Pheleum pratense*), a native British grass introduced into cultivation in the North American colonies with great success by Timothy Hanson in 1720 and then developed by him in England); the Church Fd (*v.* St Egelwin the Martyr's Church *supra*); Chamberlains Cl 1848 (with the surn. *Chamberlain*); Copple Hill (*Copewell hill* 1601, 1612, *Coppill Hill* 1704, *Coppill Round Hill* 1704 (*v.* **round**), *Copphill furlong* 1674, (*the*) *Cop(p)ill hill furlong* 1697, 1708, 1708 (18), 1730, *Copehill tyngles* 1601, ~ *tingles* 1612, *cophill* ~, *coppill tingles* 1625, *Copphill tingles* 1674, *Copp(h)il Tingles* 1697,

Coppill Tingles 1708, 1708 (18), 1730 (*v.* **pingel**), *Copewell syke* 1605, *Coppill (Hill) Sick* 1704 (*v.* **sík**) (*v.* **copp, wella, hyll**); Cow Cl (*the kowe clos(s)e* 1601, 1605, 1612, *the Cow(e) Close* 1625, 1674, 1700, 1708 (18), *v.* **cū, clos(e)**); Cricket Fd (for the game of cricket); Croft (*v.* **croft**); Cross Hedge Cl (*v.* **cross**); Crosses or Football Fd (poss. with the surn. *Cross* in the possessive case, but note that *Stump Cross Furlong* survived until at least 1730, *v.* f.ns. (b) *s.n.*); Dutch Barn Seed Fd (*v.* **sǣd**; in f.ns., 'seed' was used of areas of sown grass); Duzzle (cf. *durdale forde* 1601, *dur(e)dalle foarde* 1601, 1605, *~ forde* 1612, *Durdall Forde* 1625, *Durdale fo(o)rd* 1674, 1697, 1708, 1708 (18), 1730, *~ Forde* 1704 (*v.* **ford**), *the nearer side durdalle foarde* 1601 (a furlong so called), *the farr ~ ~*, *Durdale Hill* 1704 (*v.* **feor**), *Durdale Round Hill* 1704 (*v.* **round**), *duredall(e) syke* 1605, *Durdall sike* 1612, 1625, *Durdale Sick(e)* 1697, 1708, 1708 (18), 1730, *the further side dur(e)dalle syke* 1601, 1605, *the further syde duredall sike* 1612, *further side Durdall Sike* 1625, (*the*) *further side Durdale Sick(e)* 1674, 1697, 1708, 1730 (*v.* **sík**; a furlong so called), *durdalle tingles* 1601, *duredall(e) tyngles* 1605, *Durdale tingles* 1674, 1708, 1708 (18), 1730, *Dur Dale Pingle, Durdale Tingle* 1704, *the hyther (side) duredalle tyngles* 1605, *the hether durdall tyngles* 1612, *~ ~ ~ tingles* 1625, *hither Durdale tingles* 1674, 1697, 1708 (18), 1730, *the heather Durdale Tingles* 1704 (*v.* **hider**), *the nearer durdalle tingles* 1601, *~ ~ Durdall tyngles* 1612, *~ ~ ~ tingles* 1625, (*the*) *nearer Durdale tingles* 1697, 1708, *Further Durdale tingles* 1697, (*the*) *further tyngles, ~ tingles* 1601, 1605, 1612 *et passim* to 1730, *middle Durdale tingles* 1708, *the middle tingles* 1601, *Middle Durdale Tingle Hill* 1704 (*v.* **pingel**); prob. 'the share of land in the gap in the hills', *v.* **duru, deill**; Scand *djúr* 'a beast' as the first el. would most likely have given ME and later spellings in *der-*); Far Mdw (cf. *the end Meadow* 1708 (18)); Football Fd (for the game of football); Germany (a humorous 'remoteness' name for a field towards the edge of the parish); Gorse Cl (m.18 *Plan*), Gorse pasture 1846, 1863 White (*v.* **pasture**) (*the Gorse* 1704, *v.* **gorst**); the Grange Cl 1825 (*v.* Goldsmith Grange *supra*); Gravel Pit; the High Leas (*the High Hall Leyes* 1704, *v.* **leys** and Scalford Hall *supra*); the Hollow (*v.* **holh**); Home Cl 1848, 1969, (the) Home Fd, Home Paddock (*v.* **paddock**) (*v.* **home**); the Hop yard 1848 (*v.* **hop-yard**); the Hornbuckle (*Horn Brockhill* 1704, *v.* **horn** and Brock Hill in Long Clawson); Horse Cl; Little House Cl; Hovel Cl (*v.* **hovel**); Lane Fd (*v.* **lane**); Leapers Cl 1848 (with the surn. *Leaper*); Middle Little Fds; Melton Hill (a hill towards, or with a view of Melton Mowbray, *v.* Wycomb and Chadwell f.ns. *s.n.*); Middle Cliff (*midleclife* 1601, 1605, *middleclife* 1612, 1625, (*the*) *Middle Cliff(e)* 1674, 1697, 1708, 1708 (18), 1730, cf. *Middle Cliffe Furlong* 1704, *Middle Cliff hedge* 1704 (*v.* **hecg**), *v.* **middel, clif**); Middle Cl; the Moors (*v.* **mōr**[1]); The Mowed Wong 1848 (*the molde wounge* 1601, 1612, *the mouldwonge* 1625, (*the*) *Mould Wong* 1697, 1708, 1708 (18), 1730, *ye Mouldong* (sic) 1674, 'the in-field infested with moles', *v.* **molle, mold, vangr**); Old Mills (*the Old Mill* 1704); Pettiphers Fd (with the surn. *Pettipher, v.* Reaney *s.n.*); the Pingle (cf. *The Pingle at the Yard End* 1704, *v.* **pingel**); Little Ploughed Fd; the Pound 1848 (*v.* **pund**); Bottom Redlands (*v.* **rēad, land**, cf. Redearth (Fm) *supra*); Road Cl; Round Hill(s) (*the Round Hill* 1704, *v.* **round**); Saker's Fd (with the surn. *Saker, v.* Reaney *s.n.*); Salter's Fd (*v.* **saltere**; the road forming the western boundary of the parish was a salters' way, climbing Brock Hill from the Vale of Belvoir and passing the hundred moot-site at Great Framlands on its way to the river crossing at Melton Mowbray); Sandpit Fd (*v.* **sand-pytt**); Seat, ~ Fd (earlier forms are needed, but the simplex suggests ME **sete** in the sense 'a lofty place'); First Seeds (*v.* **sǣd**; used of areas of sown grass); the Slang (*v.* **slang**); 1st, 2nd Slates, Middle, Top Slates (*the sleghtes* 1625, *the Sleights* 1674, 1697 *et passim* to 1730, *the longe sleghtes* 1601, 1605, *Longe slightes* 1612, *v.* **slétta**); Slip Fd (*v.* **slipe**); Smith's Fd (either with the surn. *Smith* or with **smið**); Spreckleys Cl 1848 (with the surn. *Spreckley*); Spring Cl 1848 (*v.* **spring**[1]); Stackyard Cl (*v.* **stak-ȝeard**); the Stendalls (*long(e), short(e) stendall(e)* 1601, 1605, 1612, 1625, *Long, Short Stendall* 1674, 1697, 1708 *et passim* to 1730, *Long Stendale*, ~ *Stendle* 1704, *Stendle Furlong* 1704, *stendall(e) syke* 1605 (*v.* **sík**) (*v.* **steinn, deill**); Stoney Fd (*v.* **stānig**); the Three-Cornered Fd (*v.* **three-cornered**); Top Cl; Tunnel Fd (in the extreme north-west of the parish where a railway line enters a tunnel in Brock Hill); the Turf (*v.* **turf**); the Far, the Middle, the Near Watchorn, Watchorns Fd (*v.* **wæcce, horn**; perh. cf. *Watch Bank* 1704 (*v.* **wæcce, banke**) and *Horn Brockhill s.n.* the Hornbuckle *supra*; poss. an early look-out place on a horn-shaped promontory of Brock Hill overlooking the Vale of Belvoir and the ancient trackway from the north later used as a salters' way, but Watchorns Fd *supra* and Watchorns in Wymondham f.ns. (a) suggest *Watchorn* as a surn. in the possessive case); Well Dale Spring 1795 Nichols (*v.* **spring**[1]) (*welldalle* 1601, 1605, 1612, *Weldale* 1697, *Welldale* 1708, 1708 (13), 1730, (*the) further side well dalles* 1601, ~ ~ *welldalle* 1605, 1612, ~ ~ *welldaile* 1625, ~ ~ *Weldal* 1697, ~ ~ *Welldale* 1674, 1708, 1708 (18), *the furlong called the further side weldale* 1730, *the nearer side welldalle* 1605, *the neerere side Well dalle* 1612, *the topp of welldall, toppe of welldaile* 1625, *Welldale Busk* 1704 (*v.* **buskr**), *welldaile furlonge* 1625, *welldalle gutter* 1605 (*v.* **goter**), *Welldale hole* 1704 (*v.* **hol**[1]), *welldalle tyngles* 1601, 1612, ~ *tingles* 1601, *welldaile* ~, *welldall tingles* 1625, *Welldale Tingle* 1704, ~ *tingles* 1674, 1697, 1704 *et passim* to 1730, *welldalle middle tyngles* 1605, *the nearer side weildaile tingles* 1625, ~ ~ ~ *Welldale tingles* 1674, *Welldale Tingle Hill* 1704 (*v.* **pingel**) (*v.* **wella**; prob. with **deill** rather than **dalr**, but note that all spellings with ~ *daile* are of 1625 only, cf. *Braunston dalle* in f.ns. (b)).

(b) *the ashe closse* 1605, 1612, ~ ~ *close* 1625, *the Ash Close* 1697, 1700, 1703, 1708 (18) (*v.* **æsc, clos(e)**); Bank Furlong 1704 (*v.* **banke**); *Bastard Leyes* 1704 (*v.* **bastard, leys** and *the bastard leys* in Bottesford f.ns. (b)); *beane furlonge* 1625, (*the) Bean Furlong* 1674, 1697, 1708, 1708 (18), 1730 (*v.* **bēan**); *Belwether Slade*, ~ ~ *Furlong* 1704 (*v.* **belleweder, slæd**; a bell-wether was the leading sheep of a flock upon whose neck a bell was hung); *Bernewanc, Bernewang* l.12 (*v.* **bern, vangr**); *Blackham* ~, *Blackholm Sick* 1704, *Far Blackham Sick Furlong* 1704 (*v.* **blæc, hamm, holmr, sík**); *blacke wong* 1601, *Blackewounge* 1605, 1612, *blakewong(e)* 1625, *blackewong* 1674, (*the) Black Wong* 1697, 1708, 1708 (18), 1730 (*v.* **blæc, vangr**; presum. referring to black, fertile soil); *Blewhils* 1601, *Blewe hils* 1612, *Blewhills* 1625, 1697, 1708, 1708 (18), 1730 (*v.* **blēo, hyll**); *Braunston dalle* 1601, 1605, ~ *dale* 1674, *Braunstone dalle* 1612, *Branston dalle, branstondaile* 1625, *Branston dale* 1697, 1708, 1708 (18), 1730, *braunstondale* 1697 (*v.* **deill**; Branston lies four miles north-east of Scalford, with other villages standing between, and thus *Bra(u)nston* here appears to represent the surn. of a family originating there or in Braunston, 18 miles to the south-west); (*the) Breache* 1605, 1612, 1697, (*the) Breach

1625, 1674, 1697, 1708, 1708 (18), 1730, *the neather end of the breache, the middle of the breache* 1601, *the lowere forlonge of the Breache* 1612, *the longe, the shorte breache* 1601, 1605, 1612, 1625, *(the) Long breach* 1674, 1697, 1704 *et passim* to 1730, *Long Breach Forlong* 1704 (v. **furlang**), *Short breach* 1708, 1708 (18), 1730, *the farr, the hither Breach Close* 1704, *the Breache feilde* 1601, 1605, 1612, 1625, *the Breach Feild* 1674, 1697, 1703, *(the) Breach Field* 1704, 1708, 1708 (18), 1730 (v. **feld**; one of the great fields of the village) (v. **brēc**); *the brooke forlong* 1601, 1612, ~ ~ *furlong(e)* 1605, 1625, 1674, *Brook Furlong* 1697, 1704 *et passim* to 1730 (v. **brōc** and Scalford Brook *supra*); *Bryare forlonge* 1601, 1612, *(the) Brier furlong(e)* 1625, 1674, *Bryer Furlong* 1697, 1708, *Briers* ~, *Bryers Furlong* 1704 (v. **brēr**); *the Land of Lady Castlehaven* 1704; *Clarkes well* 1601, 1605, 1612, 1625, *Clarkewell* 1674, 1704, *Clarks Well* 1697, 1708 (v. **wella**; with **clerc** or with the surn. *Clarke*); *the claye pasture* 1601, 1612, *the Clay Pasture* 1605, 1625, 1674 *et passim* to 1730 (v. **clǣg, pasture**); *the farre, the nearer closickes* 1601, *fare, nearer closykes* 1605, *the further, the neerere closikes* 1612, *farclosikes, the nearer closikes* 1625, *the further clossicks* 1674, *the farclose sicks, Near closicks* 1697, *the Far, the Nearer Close Sicks* 1708, 1708 (18), 1730 (v. **clos(e), sīk**); *the collpitt waie* 1605 (v. **col-pytt, weg**; with reference to a place where charcoal was made): *the Common Pasture* 1601, 1605, 1625 *et passim* to 1730 (v. **commun, pasture**); *the Common Street* 1625 (v. **commun, strǣt**); *the Constable Piece* 1704 (v. **conestable, pece**); *the Crayne Sick Gate* 1704 (v. **gata** and Cranyke Fm in neighbouring Goadby Marwood); *Cross Gate, ~ ~ Furlong* 1704 (v. **gata**; perh. with **cros** rather than **cross**, cf. *stumpcrosse, infra*; otherwise v. **cross**); *Driuers* ~, *Drivers Busk* 1704 (v. **buskr**; either with the surn. *Driver* or with **dryfer** 'one who drives a herd of cattle, a drover'); *the Dunmore piece* 1704 (v. **pece**; with the surn. *Dunmore*, cf. *Rich' Dunmore* 17 *Terrier* of Barkestone); *Eastely Sike* 1601, *eastelie* ~, *eastelye syke* 1605, *Eastly sike* 1625, ~ *Sick(e)* 1674, 1697, 1704, 1708, *Eastley sick* 1730 (v. **sīk**; poss. with the surn. *Eastley* (v. Reaney *s.n.*), otherwise v. **ēast, lēah**); *Farbuttes* 1306 Banco (v. **feor, butte**); *Farr Pingle* 1704 (v. **pingel**); *Mr Fishers Headland* 1704 (v. **hēafod-land**); *(the) flaxe pittes* 1601, 1605, 1612, *flax pittes* 1625, *Flaxpitts* 1674, *Flax Pits* 1697, 1708, 1730 (v. **fleax, pytt**; either pits containing water for retting flax or the gig-holes for drying the retted fibres); *ad Fontem* 1327 SR (p) (with MLat *fons* (*fontem* acc.sg.) 'a spring'); *Fould Sick, ~ ~ Furlong* 1704 (v. **fald, sīk**); *Frisby Pingle* 1704 (v. **pingel**; with the surn. *Frisby* of a family prob. originating in Frisby on the Wreake, six miles to the south-west); *Goadby Gate* 1625, 1674 *et passim* to 1730, *Goadby(e) upper(e) gate* 1601, 1612 (v. **gata**; two roads to Goadby Marwood which adjoins to the north-east); *Goldsmith grange closes* 1657 Deed, *the Graunge closse* 1605 (v. **clos(e)**), *the graunge forlonge* 1601, 1612, ~ ~ *furlonge* 1605, *Goldsmithe graunge hedge* 1601, 1605, 1612, *Goldsmith Grange hedge* 1625, 1674, 1708, 1708 (18), *the furlong called Lying upon the Goldsmith Grange Hedge* 1697, 1730, *the graunge hedge* 1605 (v. **hecg**; a boundary hedge) (v. Goldsmith Grange *supra*); *Hall Leyes* 1704 (v. **leys** and Scalford Hall *supra*); *Harrowe* 1601, 1605, 1612, *the furlonge called harro* 1625, *Harrow* 1674, *Harro* 1708, 1708 (18), 1730, *Long Harrow* 1704, *Harrowsyke* 1605, *Long ~ ~, Harrow Sick, ~ ~ Furlong* 1704 (v. **sīk**) (unlocated and earlier forms are needed, but formally *Harrow* could represent OE (Angl) **hærg** 'a heathen temple' (cf. Harrow on the Hill, Mx 51 and Peper Har(r)ow, Sr 207); however, 'the spur of land at the boundary', with hār[2] and hōh is also poss., or even **hara** 'a hare' as the first el.); *Haverwounge* 1601, 1612, *Haverwonge* 1625, *Haver Wong* 1697, 1708, 1708 (18), 1730 (*v.* **hafri, vangr**); *the High Way Balk* 1704 (*v.* **hēah-weg, balca**); *Hobstack(e) foard(e)* 1601, 1605, 1612, 1625, ~ *ford* 1674, 1697 *et passim* to 1730 (*v.* **staca, ford**; the first el. may be **hobb(e)** 'a hummock' which would suggest the site of a post signalling the ford; the ME pers.n. *Hobb* (a pet-form of Robert, rhymed on *Rob*) or its surn. reflex *Hobb(e)* seem less likely); *Holliwell gate* 1674 (*v.* **gata**; the road to Holwell which adjoins to the west); *the homestall* 1605, *the homesteade of the vicarige* 1612 (*v.* **hām-stall, hām-stede** and The Vicarage *supra*); *on the Hull* 1332 SR (p), *atte Hull* 1356 Pat (p), *atte Hill* 1343 Banco (p) (*v.* **hyll, atte**); *Knights Hedge* 1704 (with the surn. *Knight*; a boundary hedge); *longe ditche* 1601, 1605, ~ *dich(e)* 1612, 1625, *(the) Long Ditch* 1697, 1708, 1708 (18), 1730, *Longdike* 1674, 1704, *(the) shorter longe ditche* 1601, 1605, ~ ~ *diche* 1612, *shorte longe dich* 1625, *Short Long Ditch* 1697, 1708, 1708 (18), 1730, ~ ~ ~ *Furlong* 1704, *Shortlongdike* 1674, ~ *Furlong* 1704 (*v.* **dīc, dík**); *(the) longe forlonge* 1601, 1612, ~ *furlong* 1605, 1625, *(the) Long Furlong* 1674, 1697 *et passim* to 1730 (in *the Breache feilde*), *the longe forlonge* 1601, ~ ~ ~ *lyeing againste the towne* 1612 (*v.* **tūn**) (in *the Moorebeck feilde*); *(the) further loose* 1601, 1612, 1625, 1674, ~ *loosse* 1605, *Farther loose* 1697, 1708, 1708 (18), 1730, *the hither loose* 1601, *the hyther loosse* 1605, *(the) hether lo(o)se* 1612, 1625 *et passim* to 1730 (*v.* **hider**), *lo(o)sse heades* 1605 (*v.* **hēafod**) (*v.* **hlōse**); *Loughborow(e) gate* 1601, 1612, *Loughborrow Gate* 1674, 1697 *et passim* to 1730, ~ ~ *Furlong* 1704, *(the) upper side Loughborroe* ~, *Loughborowe gate* 1605, 1625, *Loughborowe gate heades* 1605 (*v.* **hēafod**) (*v.* **gata**; the road to Loughborough which lies 15 miles to the west); *Lown(e)s gate* 1605, 1625, 1674 *et passim* to 1730, *Lound(s)* ~, *Lounse Gate* 1704, *Lownesgatt* ~, *Lowenesgate forlonge* 1601, *Lownesgate furlonge* 1605, *Lownesgat(e) forlonge* 1612, *Lownse Gate furlong* 1697, *Lounds Gate* ~ 1704 (*v.* **lundr, gata**); *the Meadow* m.18 Plan, *meadow(e) foarde* 1601, 1605, 1612, *meadow forde* 1625, *Meddow foord* 1674, *Meadow ford* 1697, 1708, 1730, *the nearer side meadowe foarde* 1601 (a furlong so called) (*v.* **mǣd (mǣdwe** obl.sg.), **ford**); *meare furlonge* 1605 (*v.* **(ge)mǣre**); *the meare betwixt Goadbye and Scalford* 1601, *ye mear yt parts betwixt Scalford & Goadby* 1674, *the meare betwixt Hollwell and Scalforde* 1605 (*v.* **(ge)mǣre**; with reference to neighbouring Goadby Marwood and Holwell); *Medelholm* l.12, *Nordmedelhom* l.12 (*v.* **norð**) (*v.* **middel, meðal, holmr**); *the mill* 1601, *the milne* 1605, *the Water Mill* 1704 (*v.* **wæter-mylne**), *the Mill Bushes* 1704 (*v.* **busc**), *the mill dame* 1601, 1625, *the milne dame* 1605, 1612, *the Mill Damme* 1704, ~ ~ *dam* 1708, 1730 (*v.* **damme**), *the mill dame ende* 1601 (*v.* **ende**), *the Milne Hollow* 1708, *the Milln Hollow* 1730 (*v.* **holh**), *the Mill home* 1704 (*v.* **holmr**), *the milne hopeinges* 1601, 1605, 1612, ~ ~ *hopings* 1625 (*v.* **hopping**) (*v.* **myln**; all with reference to the water-mill); *the Milne Leyes* 1704 (*v.* **leys**), *the Mill Hill* 1704 (*v.* **myln**; both with reference to the windmill); *Morbell* 1396 Pat (*v.* **mōr**[1], **belle**); *nab hill* 1601 (*v.* **nabbi**); *the neather furlonge* 1605 (*v.* **neoðera, furlang**; i.e. of *the Breache feilde*); *Nearyearthe* 1601, *narearthe* 1612, *nar(e)yearth* 1625, *Naryearth* 1674, *Nary Earth* 1697, 1708, 1708 (18), 1730 (*v.* **nearu, eorðe**; with late metanalysis); *the New Close* 1704; *Nobles Nooke* 1704 (*v.* **nōk**; with the surn. *Noble*); *Nunriges* 1601, 1605, *Nunrigges* 1612, *nunridges* 1625, *(the) Nunriggs* 1674, 1697 *et passim* to 1730 (*v.* **hrycg, hryggr**;

presum. with **nunne** 'a nun' rather than with the surn. *Nunn* and referring to land belonging to the nunnery of Nuneaton which owned a grange in adjoining Waltham, *v.* Nun's Cl in Waltham on the Wolds f.ns. (a)); *old feilde layes* 1605 (*v.* **leys** and Oldfield Lodge *supra*); *the Oldes* 1601, 1605, 1612, 1625, (*one plott of ground called*) *the Olds* 1674, 1697, 1703 (*v.* **plot**), *the Woulds* 1704, *the Wolds* 1708, 1708 (18), 1730, *Scalford wouldes* 1601 (*v.* **wald**); *the Parkes* 1704, *the farr(e) parke* 1601, 1625, *fare parke* 1605, *the further parke* 1612, *the farr parks* 1674, *the Far Park* 1697, 1708, 1708 (18), 1730 (*v.* **feor**), *longe parke* 1601, 1605, 1612, 1625, *Long park(e)s* 1674, 1704, (*the*) *Long Park* 1697, 1708, 1708 (18), 1730 (*v.* **park**; poss. in its later sense 'an enclosed plot of ground, a paddock'); *Poplestoft* l.12 (*v.* **toft**; the first el. is ultimately from OE **popel** 'a pebble', but the -*es*- may represent a gen.sg. rather than a nom.pl. (we would expect **popel-toft* rather than **popelastoft*), in which case rather than describing a 'curtilage with pebbly soil', the name may be interpreted as 'Popel's curtilage', in which *popel* is used as a nickname, perh. for a bald-headed or squat, compact man; *Pople* survives as a surn.); *Preistdale* 1674, *Priest Dale* 1704, *prieste dalle forlonge* 1612, *preistdaile furlonge* 1625, *Preistdale furlong* 1697, 1708, *Priestdale* ~ 1708 (18), 1730, *prieste dalle hill* 1605, ~ ~ ~ *forlonge* 1601 (*v.* **furlang**) (*v.* **prēost**, **deill**); *Pryare clos(s)e* 1601, 1605, 1612, *Pryers close* 1625, *Prior* ~ 1674, *the Priors* ~ 1697, 1708, 1708 (18), *Priors Close Style* 1704 (poss. with **stīg** rather than **stigel**) (*v.* **clos(e)**; either with the surn. *Prior* or with **prior**, alluding to the Prior of Garendon Abbey which originally held the grange of Ringlethorpe); *reedehill* 1601, 1612, *Redhill* 1605, 1612, 1674 *et passim* to 1730 (*v.* **rēad**, **hyll** and cf. Redearth (Fm) *supra*); *reedyearth gate* 1605 (*v.* **gata** and Redearth (Fm) *supra*); *Rush Bush Furlong* 1704 (*v.* **risc**, **busc**); *Short Ditch Furlong* 1704 (*v.* **dīc**); *Spicers Bushes*, ~ ~ *Furlong* 1704 (*v.* **busc**; with the surn. *Spicer*); *Spong Bridge* 1704 (*v.* **spong**); *Stoke Barne and Yard* 1704 (*v.* **stoc**); *the Stone Pitt Close* 1704, *Stone Pitt Furlong* 1704 (*v.* **stan-pytt**); *the stonne medowe* 1605, *the Stone Meadow* 1704 (i.e. cleared of stones, *v.* **stān**, **stoned** and *the stone middow* in Knipton f.ns. (b)); *the streete forlonge* 1601, 1612, *street furlonge* 1625, *ye Strete furlong* 1674, (*the*) *Street* ~ 1697, 1708, 1730 (*v.* **strǣt**; with reference to the Roman road Margary 58a which runs through the north of the parish); *stumpcrosse* 1601, 1605, *Stump(e)cros* 1625, 1674, *Stump Cross* 1697, 1704 *et passim* to 1730, *stump(e)crosse forlonge* 1601, 1612, *Stumpecros furlonge* 1625, *Stumpcros furlong* 1674, (*the*) *Stump Cross Furlong* 1697, 1704 *et passim* to 1730, *stumpcrosse heades* 1605 (*v.* **hēafod**) (*v.* **stump**, **cros**; referring to a wayside cross, reduced to a stump of its shaft); *Swine Acres* 1704 (*v.* **swīn**[1], **æcer**); *the swineinge goares* 1601, 1612, *swineingoares, swineingors* 1625, *Swin(e)ing Goares* 1697, *Swinein gores* 1708, *Swine in Gores* (sic) 1708 (18), 1730, *the furlonge called the nether end of the swiningors* 1625, *the Furlong called the ne(a)ther end of Swine in gores* 1708, 1708 (18), 1730, *the Neither end of Swining Goares* 1697 (*v.* **neoðera**), *ye neither end, ye upper end of Swinegrass(e)* (sic) 1674, *the Topp of the Great Swinegores* 1704 (*v.* **swīn**, **svín**, **eng**, **gāra**); *Thorpe Bush Furlong* 1704 (*v.* **busc**; *Thorpe Gate* 1605, 1704, 1708, 1708 (18), *beneathe Thorpe gate* 1625, (*the furlonge called*) *the neather side Thorpe gate* 1601, 1605, ~ ~ ~ *the neether side* ~ ~ 1612, ~ *netherside* ~ ~ 1625, *ye neither side* ~ ~ 1674, 1697 (*v.* **neoðera**); *the upper side* (*of*) *Thorp(e) gate* 1601, 1605, 1612 *et passim* to 1730 (*v.* **gata**; all with reference to

Ringlethorpe); *Tingle Hill* 1704 (*v.* **pingel**); *Leys next the Town* 1708 (18) (*v.* **leys**), *the Towne Side* 1704 (*v.* **sīde**) (*v.* **tūn**); *Triggs headland* 1704 (*v.* **hēafod-land**; belonging to *Henry Trigg* 1704); *Mr Waldrones inclosure* 1601 (*v.* **inclosure**); *the Wall end* 1625, 1697, 1708 (18), 1730 (*v.* **wall, ende**); *weanegat(t)e syke* 1605 (*v.* **wægn, gata, sīk**); *Westbeck* 1697, 1708, 1730, *the further side westebecke* 1601, 1612, ~ ~ ~ *westbeck(e)* 1605, 1674, 1708, 1708 (18), *the Furlong called the further side of Westbeck* 1730, *the nearer side westebeck* 1601, 1605, 1625, ~ ~ ~ *of Westbecke* 1612, *the Neerer side (of) Westbeck* 1697, 1708, 1708 (18), *the Furlong called the nearer side of Westbeck* 1730, *ye hitherside Westbecke* 1674, *westebecke ditche* 1605 (*v.* **dīc**), *westebecke forlonge* 1601, 1605, 1612, *westbecke furlonge* 1625, *Westbeck Furlong* 1674, 1708, 1708 (18) (*v.* **west, bekkr** and the following f.ns.); *West brook(e)* 1704, *West Brook next the Forde* 1704, *Westbrook(e) Furlong* 1704, *Westbrooke Hill* 1704 (*v.* **west, brōc**; a restyled *Westbeck*, with English *brook* replacing Scand *beck*); *the West Piece* 1704 (*v.* **pece**); *the forlonge called Whettston(n)e* 1601, 1612, 1625, *the furlong called Whetstone* 1708, 1708 (18), 1730, *Whitstone* 1674, *Whetston* 1697 (*v.* **hwet-stān**; prob. referring to a place where rock suitable for whetstones was to be found); *White Wong* 1704 (*v.* **hwīt, hvítr, vangr**; denoting dry pasture); *winie meadowe* 1605 (*v.* **whinny**); *wollepittes* 1601, *woolle pites* 1612, *Wooll Pits* 1697, *Woolpit(t)s* 1708, 1708 (18), 1730 (*v.* **wulf-pytt**; alluding to the trapping of wolves which preyed on cattle and sheep in England as recently as the 17th cent.); *Wranglandes* 1601, 1612, 1625, *Wranglands* 1674, 1697 *et passim* to 1730, *Ranglands* 1704, *Rangland Furlong* 1704, *wranglande layes* 1605 (*v.* **leys**) (*v.* **wrang, vrangr, land**).

2. CHADWELL

DB includes Chadwell with Wycomb as a member of the king's manor of Rothley in Goscote Wapentake. Chadwell with Wycomb is said by White 1846 to form 'a chapelry and detached member of East Goscote Hundred, and the Parish and Peculiar Jurisdiction of Rothley'. Rothley lies in West Goscote Hundred.

> *Caldeuuelle* 1086 DB, *Caldewelle* 1184, 1195 P, 1220 MHW *et passim* to 1318, 1341 *Wyg, Caldewell'* c.1160 *Deed*, 1192, 1193 P *et freq* to 1313, 1317 *Wyg et passim* to 1353 *ib*, 1377 Pat, 1522 *RTemple*, (~ *iuxta Wicham* l.13 *Wyg*), *Caldewella* 1177, 1178 P *et passim* to 1192 ib, *Caldeuell'* 1284, l.13 *Wyg, Kaldewell'* e.13 *ib*
> *Chaldewell'* 1179, 1180 P *et passim* to 1200 Cur, 1210 Abbr, *Chaldewella* 1185, 1191 P
> *Caudewell'* 1201 Cur, e.13 *BHosp et passim* to 1505, 1519 *Wyg, Caudewelle* e.13 *BHosp, Kaudewell'* 1201 Cur, 1242 P (p)

Cawdewell 1502 MiscAccts, 1541 MinAccts, Kawdewell 1502
    MiscAccts
Caldwell 1317, 1351 Wyg et passim to 1831, 1836 Map, Calldwell
    1582 Terrier
Caudwell 1510 Rut, 1576 Saxton, 1710, 1716 Will, 1724 LML,
    Cawdwell 1440 Wyg, 1509 Deed, 1510 Rental et freq to 1604 SR,
    1610 Speed et passim to 1714, 1716 LML
Cauldwell 1778 EnclA
Chadwell 1721, 1727, 1731 Will et freq

'The cold spring', v. **cald, wella**. Early spellings (of Angl *cald*) with
Ch- for *C-* are due to AN orthography and do not represent a palatalized
ceald as in the WSax dialect of OE. Spellings with *u* for *l* are the result
of AN vocalization of pre-consonantal *l*, a pronunciation which survived
as late as the early 18th cent. Unusual is the 18th cent. appearance of
Chad- beside *Cald-* (the latter surviving until at least the middle of the
19th cent.). This emergence of the modern form *Chadwell* may be the
result of an 18th cent. antiquarian revival of AN forms and its continued
use based on spelling-pronunciation, with loss of *l* (*Chald-* > *Chad-*)
through dissimilation.

CLEMATIS COTTAGE. EASTWEST. MANOR FM, cf. *The Manor House*
1877 White, v. **maner**. ST MARY'S CHURCH, *Church (St Mary)* 1877
White, *The Chapel of St Mary* 1925 Kelly; it is earlier recorded in the
groups *capellis Cayham Grimston et Caldewelle* 1220 MHW,
*capellarum . . . de Gaddesby Kayham Grymeston Warnoteby Caudwell
et Wykeham* 1328 Pat, ~ ~ ~ ~ ~ ~ *Caudewell et Wykeham* 1382 ib (with
MLat *capella* 'a chapel'). Note also *the chapel yard of Cauldwell* 1778
EnclA. SPRINGFIELD FM, v. **spring**[1]; the only spring in the village which
is marked on the 2½" and 6" O.S. maps is adjacent to the farm and is
perh. the source of the township's name.

3. WYCOMB

With Chadwell *supra*, a detached member of East Goscote Hundred.

Wiche 1086 DB
Wicham l.12 Wyg, 1207 P, e.13 BHosp, 1282 Wyg (freq) et freq to
    1317 ib (freq), 1319 FA, 1341 Wyg, Wycham e.13 BHosp, 1284,

1296, l.13 *Wyg* (freq) *et passim* to 1351, 1353, 1519 *ib*, (~ *in Caudewell'* 1519 *ib*), Wichham 1282 × 91 *ib*

Wikham l.13, 1317 *Wyg et passim* to 1520, 1521 *ib*, *Wykham* 1278 RGrav, 1294 Nichols *et passim* to 1509 *Deed*, 1516 *Wyg et freq* to 1531 *ib et passim* to 1582 *Terrier*

Wicam p.1250, l.13 *Wyg*, *Wycam* p.1250, 1271, 1291, 1294 *ib*, 1510 *Rut*, *Wykam* l.13, 1310, 1317 *Wyg et passim* to 1382 Pat, 1505, 1519 *Wyg*, *Wicom* l.13 *ib*

Wikeham 1440 *Wyg*, 1610 Speed *et passim* to 1719 LML, *Wykeham* 1502 *MiscAccts*, 1510 *Rental et passim* to 1620, 1694 LML

Wyckham 1524, 1543 *Wyg*, 1558 Pat, 1567 CoPleas, *Wickham* 1543 *Wyg*, 1601 LibCl, 1604 SR

Wycomb(e) 1811 Nichols, 1846 White *et freq*

The place-name Wycomb represents the OE compound appellative **wīc-hām**, about 30 examples of which survive in place-names and field-names. Dr Margaret Gelling in two studies detailed below notes that three-quarters of known instances are situated directly on or not more than one mile from a major Roman road and that over half the examples are closely associated with Romano-British habitation sites, especially small towns. OE *wīc* in this compound appears to be very early and to have a close connection with Lat *vicus*, a term used by the Romans for the smallest unit of self-government in their provinces. Gelling observes that *wīc-hām* names tend to occur near RB sites in which later archaeological levels show no evidence of early Anglo-Saxon occupation and where sub-Roman survival seems particularly likely. Thus it is possible that *wīc-hām* was an OE term for a small RB town which survived without being swamped by Germanic settlers. Alternatively, it could have described an Anglo-Saxon settlement adjacent to a surviving RB *vicus* or even an early Anglo-Saxon estate comprising the *territorium* of a former RB *vicus* (cf. the later *biscop-hām* 'estate belonging to a bishop').

Wycomb fits the *wīc-hām* pattern in every respect. It lies roughly one mile south-east of the Roman road Margary 58a across the Wolds and one mile south of the important RB site at adjacent Goadby Marwood. Here, many RB burials have been discovered, as well as Roman buildings, wells, coins, brooches and other small finds, and also an area devoted to the smelting of ironstone, *v. Roman Small Towns in Eastern England and Beyond*, ed. A. E. Brown, Oxbow Monograph 52 (Oxford, 1995), 88.

It is worthy of note that Wycomb with Chadwell forms a land-unit in DB and retained its identity as a unit into the 19th century. Chadwell lies against the parish boundary and can never have been the principal township in the estate. Wycomb once lay at the centre of a compact land-unit until both townships were absorbed into Scalford parish.

Reference should be made to M. Gelling, 'English place-names derived from the compound *wīchām*', *Medieval Archaeology* XI (1967), 87–104; reprinted with addenda in *Place-Name Evidence for the Anglo-Saxon Invasion and Scandinavia Settlements: Eight Studies*, ed. K. Cameron (Nottingham, 1975), 8–26; also to M. Gelling, *Signposts to the Past*, 3rd edn (London, 1997), 67–74, which extends her earlier study of place-names in *wīc-hām*.

FIELD-NAMES OF WYCOMB AND CHADWELL

Wycomb and Chadwell appear to have shared their great fields, with Chadwell lying almost immediately on the boundary of the parish. No attempt here has been made to associate particular names with either of the townships, except where such association is recorded or obvious. Undated forms in (a) are 1812 *Plan*, while those dated 1778 are *EnclA*. Forms throughout dated e.13, 1271, 1282, 1282 × 91, 1291, 1293, 1294, 1296, l.13, 13, 1310, 1313, 1317, 1318, 1341, 1351 and 1353 are *Wyg*; 1561 (1700) and 1744 are *Rental*; 1582[1] and 1582[2] are *Terrier*; 1593 are *Nichols*; 1668 (1791), 1682, 1682 (1791) and 1686 are *Surv*.

(a) Great, Little Chadwell Hill; Church Cl (beside St Mary's Church at Chadwell); Cross Lands (1682, ~ ~ *Furlong* 1686, 1744, *v.* **cross, land**); The Dozzels (*v.* Duzzle in Scalford f.ns. (a)); High, Low, Middle Germany (a name signifying remoteness from the settlements, presum. lying at the edge of the parish, cf. Germany in Scalford f.ns. (a)); Goadby Cl (adjacent to Goadby Marwood to the north), Goadby Gate Fd 1778 (*Goadbygate Feild* 1682, *Goatbey* ~ 1686, *v.* **gata, feld**; one of the great fields of the townships, cf. *Goadbygate furlong* 1682, *Goatbey gate Fur'* 1686), Goadby Gorse (*v.* **gorst**); Headell Fd 1778 (*Heydale* e.13, *Head Dale* 1682, 1686, *haydallfeild, Hay(e) Dalle feild* 1582[1], 1582[2], *Headall Field formerly Grange Field* 1744, *v.* **hēg, deill, feld**; one of the great fields of the townships, cf. *Haydayll flatte* in f.ns. (b) *infra*); The Bottom, The Top Hill; The Long Hill 1812, Long Hill Fd 1778 (*Longe hill* 1582[1], 1582[2], 1686, ~ ~ *Fur'* 1686, *Longhill* 1682, ~ *Fur(long)* 1682, 1747); Far, Near Melton Hill (*Melton Hill* 1582[2], 1682, 1744, ~ ~ *Fur'* 1686, *v.* **furlang** and Melton Hill in Scalford f.ns. (a)); Middle Cl 1778; Old Yard (*v.* **geard**); the Pasture Cls 1778, Old, New Pasture 1812 (cf. *ye Beast pasture* 1682, ~ ~ *paster* 1686, *the Pasture Close* 1744, *the New Pasture* 1744, *v.* **best(e), pasture**); Pingle (cf. *Crosse pin(n)ggle* 1582[1], 1582[2], *v.* **cros, pingel** and *altam crucem, infra*); Stack Yard

(v. **stak-ȝeard**); Stone Pits, the Stone Pit Cl (cf. *Stonepitt Fur(long)* 1686, 1744, v. **stān-pytt**).

(b) *Acwellane* 1353 (v. **āc, wella, lane**); *le Balke* 1282, 1282 × 91, *le balcke* 1282 × 91 (v. **balca**); *Becks Fur'* 1682, 1686, *Beck Furlong* 1744 (v. **bekkr**); *Brakenousik(e)* 1282 × 91, 1318 (v. **brakni, haugr, sík**); *le Brock* 1317, *Bruck Fur'* 1682, 1686, *Brook Furlong* 1744 (v. **brōc**); *Caldewellebrok'* 1282 (v. **brōc**; the stream flowing beside Chadwell, which forms the parish boundary here); (*in*) *campo australi* e.13 ('the south field', with MLat *campus* 'a field' and MLat *australis* 'southern, south'; one of the early great fields of the townships), (*in*) *campo borialis* e.13 ('the north field', with MLat *borealis* 'northern'; another of the early great fields); *le Chart* 1294 (v. **cært, kartr**; the *Ch-* spelling is presum. due to AN orthography rather than representing a palatalized *ceart* as in the WSax dialect of OE, but if so, it is rather late, cf. the commentary on Chadwell *supra*; alternatively, it may represent the anglicizing of the Scand cognate *kartr*); *Church Fur'* 1682, 1686 (v. **furlang**; beside St Mary's Church at Chadwell); *the Churtch Layse* 1582², (*the*) *Churche Layse forlong(e)* 1582¹, 1582², *Church Ley(e)s Fur(long)* 1682, 1686, 1744 (v. **leys**; near St Mary's Church); *le Clif* e.13, 1282, 1282 × 91, 1.13, 1313, 1317, *le Clyf* 1282 × 91, *le clif apud Seuedale* 1282 × 91 (v. **clif** and *Seuedale, infra*); *Colepitte forthe* 1582¹ (v. **col-pytt, ford**); *Coles Cottage* 1744 (v. **cotage**; with the surn. *Cole(s)*); *Coppolle bushe* 1582², *Cophill Bush* 1682, *Copehill Bush*, ~ ~ *Fur'* 1686 (v. **furlang**) (v. **busc** and Copple Hill in Scalford f.ns. (a)); *Crathernesike* 1282 (v. **crāwe, þyrne, þyrnir, sík**); *the Crosse furlonge* 1582² (v. **cross**); *altam crucem, crucem de Wichham* 1282 × 91 ('the high cross' at Wycomb, with MLat *alta* 'high' and MLat *crux* (*crucem* acc.sg.) 'a cross'; this township shared the church at Chadwell, less than a half-mile away); *attedam* 1282 × 91 (v. **atte, damme**); *le dikesende* e.13 (v. **dík, ende**); *Doddisholm* 1318 bis, *Dodsdum Fur'* 1682, *Dodsdom*, ~ *Fur'* 1686 (v. **furlang**) (v. **holmr**; the first el. appears to be either the OE pers.n. *Dodd* or its ME surn. reflex *Dodd* (v. Reaney *s.n.*); also poss., but less likely in compound with *holmr*, is ME **dodde** 'the rounded summit of a hill'); *elyothou* 1282 × 91 (v. **haugr**; with the surn. *Eliot*, v. Reaney *s.n.*); *Emeloteslane* 1313 (v. **lane**; either with the ME fem. pers.n. *Emelot*, a double diminutive form of *Em* (i.e. *Em-el-ot*), a pet-form of Emma or Emeline, or with its ME surn. reflex *Emelote*, v. Forssner 88 and Reaney *s.n.* Emblott); *le foldecroft'* 1282 × 91 (v. **fald, croft**); *Folwelle* 1282, *Houerfolewellis* 1317 (v. **ofer³**) (v. **fūl, wella**); *le foredole* 1313 (v. **fore, dāl**); *le Fuleholm* e.13, *le Fouleholm* 1282 × 91, 1318 (v. **holmr**; the first el. may be either **fugol** or **fūl**; *Fullhill Fur'* 1682, 1686, *Fullhills Furlong* 1744 (this may be a late form of *Folwelle* above, otherwise v. **fūl, hyll**); *le gategreynis* e.13 (v. **gata, grein**); *Goadby Field formerly Hegham Field* 1744 (v. *Hyghham feild, infra*); *the gootter* 1582² (v. **goter**); *le Goris* 1313 (v. **gāra**); *Goutibimere* 1282 × 91, *Goutebymere* 1317 (v. **(ge)mǣre**; Goadby Marwood adjoins to the north); *Grange Feild* 1682, 1686, ~ *field* 1682 (1791), 1744 (v. **feld**; referring to Goldsmith Grange, v. Headell Fd in f.ns. (a)), *Grange Fur'* 1682 (v. **furlang**), *Grange ley(e)s* 1682, 1686, *Grange Leyes Furlong* 1744 (v. **leys**), *Grangemere* 1282 (v. **(ge)mǣre**; at this date, Ringlethorpe Grange); *Wid. Hanleys Farme* 1682 (v. **ferme**; belonging to Widow Hanley); *Hauereholm* 1282 × 91, 13, 1310, *haurholm* 1282 × 91, *Haveram Fur'* 1682, *Haverryne* ~ 1686 (v. **furlang**) (v. **hafri, holmr**); *Haydayll flatte* 1582², *Headall*

Flatt 1744 (v. **flat**), *haidall hedge* 1582² (v. **hecg**) (v. Headell Fd *supra*); *Heyning* 1282, *le Heininge* 1317, *ye hayninges, Hayninges feild* 1582² (v. **hegning, feld**; one of the later great fields of the townships; note also *Henings Furlong* 1682, 1686); *le Holm* 1282 × 91 (v. **holmr**); *le holucoumbe* 1289 × 91, *holecumbe* 1294 (v. **holh, cumb**); *le hopinc* e.13 (v. **hopping**); *horspolle hyll* 1582², *Horsepool(e) hill* 1682, 1686, *Horsepool(e) ley(e)s* 1682, 1686, *Horseball Leys Furlong* (sic) 1744 (v. **leys**) (v. **hors, pōl**¹); *Huncerhil'* e.13, *Hungerhil* 1282, 1282 × 91, 13, *Hung(g)erhill* 1582², 1682, *Hongerhill* 1582¹, 1686 (v. **hungor, hyll**); *Hundeholm* 1291 (v. **holmr**; prob. with **hund, hundr**, but the Scand pers.n. *Hundi* is formally poss.); *Huneisbalke* 1293 (v. **balca**; the use of the gen.sg. suggests that the first el. is the ME surn. *Hon(e)y*, which derives from OE *hunig* 'honey' used as a term of endearment, 'sweetheart, darling' (v. Reaney *s.n.* Honey), but OE **hunig** itself may be present (in f.ns. alluding to places where honey was to be found); note also the later garbled form *Honey Bud Furlong* 1744); *Hyghham,* ~ *feild* 1582², *Hyems Feild* 1682, *Hyams field* 1682 (1791), *Heyghems Feild* 1686, *Hegham Field* 1744 (v. **feld**; one of the great fields of the townships, v. Goadby Field, *supra*), *Hyems Fur'* 1681, *Heyghems* ~ 1682 (v. **furlang**), *higham gorse* 1582² (v. **gorst**) (earlier forms are needed, but this may well represent OE **hēah-hām*, recording a lost early Anglo-Saxon settlement on the Wolds adjacent to the Roman road Margary 58a and would be entirely in keeping with the locations of p.ns. in *-hām* in relation to such roads in the Midlands and in East Anglia, v. **hēah**¹, **hām** and Barrie Cox, 'The significance of English place-names in *hām* in the Midlands and East Anglia', JEPNS 5 (1972–3), 15–73, reprinted in *Place-Name Evidence for the Anglo-Saxon Invasion and Scandinavian Settlements: Eight Studies*, ed. K. Cameron (Nottingham, 1975), 55–98); *Kerisholm* 1271, 1317 (v. **holmr**; the first el. may be either the ME surn. *Ker* in the possessive case (from ON *kjarr* 'brushwood', ME *ker* 'a bog, a marsh, especially one overgrown with brushwood') or OE **cærse** 'cress, water-cress'); *Kilnewellehil* e.13 (v. **cyln, wella, hyll**); *le kirkeclyf* 1313 (v. **kirkja, clif**; referring to the church at Chadwell, since Wycomb only had a standing cross); *Lambecotes* e.13, 1282 × 91, 1294, 1318, 1341, *Lambcotis* 1282 × 91, *Lambecote'* 1318, *Lambecotehil* 1282 × 91 (v. **hyll**) (v. **lamb, cot**); *Langethorn* 1282 × 91, 1318, *Langetharn* 13, *langthorn* 1582¹, 1582², *Langton Fur(long)* 1682, 1686, 1744 ('the long patch of thorns', v. **lang**¹, **þorn**); *le lesegore* e.13 (v. **lǣs, gāra**); *The Little Close* 1744; *le Loetraues* e.13, *le Lowetraues* 1282 (v. **la(g)h, træf**, cf. *le Trauecroftes, infra*); *le longeholm* e.13, 13 (v. **lang**¹, **holmr**); *Low leyes furlong* 1682, *Law leys Fur'* 1686, *Law Leyes Furlong* 1744 (v. **la(g)h, leys**); *le Merefurlonges* 1317 (v. **(ge)mǣre, furlang**); *Middle Leyes* 1744 (v. **leys**); *Mill hades* 1682, ~ ~ *Fur'* 1686 (v. **hēafod, furlang**), *le Milnetonge* 1318 (v. **tunge**) (v. **myln**); *Mirewellesike* 1291 (v. **mýrr, wella, sík**); *le more* 1282, 1282 × 91, 1318, *the more* 1582², *ye More* 1682, ~ *Moor* 1686, *(ye) more hall close* 1582¹, 1582² (v. **hall**) (v. **mōr**¹); *Netherfold Croft* 1317 (v. **neoðera, fald, croft**); *Osindale* 1282, *Owsendale* 1682, *Ousindale Fur'* 1686, *Ousledown Furlong* (sic) 1744, *osindaleheuid* 1282 × 91 (v. **hēafod**), *Hosendalehil* 1282, *Hosindalehil* 1282 × 91 (v. **hyll**), *osendaleouerende* 1282 × 91 (v. **uferra, ende**) (v. **ōsle, dalr**; note the surviving AN interchange of *l* and *n*, and cf. the pair *Owsell welles* 1601 / *oowsin wells* 1605 in Harston f.ns. (b)); *Perkynyerd'* 1313 (v. **geard**; with either the ME pers.n. *Perkin* (from *Per* (*Peres*) with the diminutive *-kin*) or its surn. reflex *Perkin*); *Ponton ley(e)s*

1682, 1686 (v. **leys**; with the surn. *Ponton* of a family originating in the village of Ponton, ten miles to the north-east in Lincs.); *Prestisdale* 1313 (v. **prēost, deill**); (*le*) *redehou* e.13, 1282 × 91, *le redhou* 13 (v. **haugr**; prob. with **rēad** 'red', alluding to the colour of the soil, rather than with **hrēod** 'reed', cf. Redearth (Fm) in Scalford); *Ringiltorpmere*, *Ringilthorpemere* 1282 × 91, *Ryngolthorpmere* 1313, *Ringelthorpemere* 1317 (v. **(ge)mære**; the boundary with Ringlethorpe *supra*); *Roofclose Nook Furlong* 1744 (v. **nōk**; with the surn. *Roof*, a reflex of the ON pers.n. *Hrólfr* (ODan *Rolf*), v. Reaney *s.n.*); *le Sandpittes* 1313, *Sandpites* 1582[2] (v. **sandpytt**); *Scaldeford gate* 1294, *Scofford Gate* 1744 (v. **gata**), *Scaldefordmere* 1282, 1282 × 91, *Scaldeforthemere* 13 (v. **(ge)mære**), *Scofford Field Hill* 1744 (Scalford adjoins to the south-west); *Scharthforlong'* 1282 × 91, *le scarfurlong* 1294, *Scartheforlong'* 1313, *Scarthfurlong'* 1318 (v. **skarð, furlang**); *le Scortefurlonges* e.13, *Schortforlong'* 1282 × 91 (v. **sc(e)ort, furlang**); *le Scorteholm* e.13, *le Schortholm* 1282 × 91, 1318 (v. **sc(e)ort, holmr**); *Schouelebrod'* 1282 × 91, *Scouilbrode* 1313, *Schouelbrod'* 1317, *Schowelbrode* 1318, *Chouelbrode* 1282, *le Sowelebrodeheuedes* e.13 (v. **hēafod**) (v. **scofl-brædu**); *Seuedal(e)* 1282 × 91 (v. **sef**; with **dalr** or **deill**); *Shepherd boord Leyes* 1744 (v. **scēp-hirde, bord, leys** and *Shepperd board* in Somerby f.ns. (b)); *Shortham ley(e)s* 1682, 1686 (v. **leys**; poss. with **sc(e)ort, hamm**); *le Sike* 1282 × 91, *le Sikefurlong'* 1282 × 91 (v. **furlang**) (v. **sík**); *benethe Henry Simpsones gate* 1582[2] (v. **gēat**; a furlong so called); (*le*) *Slatelandes* e.13, 1282 × 91, 1582[2], *Slateland'* 1294, *Slatlands* 1682, *Slatelands* 1686, ~ *Furlong* 1744, *netherslatelandes* 1282 × 91 (v. **neoðera**) (v. **sléttr, land**); *slothornes* 1282 × 91, *Slouthorn* 1313 (v. **slōh, þorn**); *Spiceley Hill* 1593 (earlier forms are needed; perh. 'clearing where aromatic herbs grow', v. **spīce, lēah**); *le stonforde* e.13, *Stonforthe* 1282 × 91, *le stonforth* 1294, *le Stanforth* 1318 ('ford with a stony bottom', v. **stān, ford**); *Stikbrere, Stykebrere* 1282 × 91, *Styckbrayars* 1582[2], *Stickbriers Fur'* 1682, *Stickbryers* ~ 1686, *Stickbury Furlong* (sic) 1744, *Houirstikebrere* 1282 (v. **ofer**[3]) (v. **sticca, brēr**); *le swelupitte* 1282 × 91, *Swallowpitts* 1682, 1686, *Swallowpitt Furlong* 1744 (v. **swalg, pytt**); *toorpites* 1582[2], *Turfepitt Fur'* 1682, 1686 (v. **furlang**) (v. **turf-pytt**); *ye Towne* 1682, 1686 (v. **tūn**; a furlong so called in *Grange Feild*); *Townesend Fur'* 1682 (v. **tūn, ende, furlang**); *le Tounwelle* 1282, *le tunwelle de Wycham* 1282 × 91 (v. **tūn, wella**); *le Trauecroftes* e.13 (v. **træf, croft**, cf. *le Loetraues, supra*); *le Turues* l.13 (v. **turf**); *le Wadh* e.13, *le Wath* 1282 × 91 bis (v. **vað**; evidently replacing OE **(ge)wæd**); *Walke hill* 1582 , 1682, ~ ~ *Fur'* 1686, *Walkhill Furlong* 1744 (v. **walk**); *Waltham Dyke* 1582[2] (v. **dík**), *Waltham mere* 1313 (v. **(ge)mære**) (boundary markers of Waltham on the Wolds which adjoins to the east); *Warinhou* 1294, *Warinhoue* 1317 (v. **haugr**; perh. with the AFr pers.n. *Warin*, but an early instance of **wareine** 'a warren' (whose earliest citation in OED is for 1377) is poss.); *Watmore* 1294 (v. **vátr, mór**); *le Welle Croft* 1351 (v. **wella, croft**); *atte Wellehous* 1282 (p), *at the wellehus* 1282 × 91 (p), *al Wellehus* 1282 × 91 (p), *ad le Wellehus* l.13 (p), *a le Welhous* l.13 (p), *of Welhous* 1310 (p), *atte Wellehus* 1317 (p), *at le Welhous* 1318 (p) (v. **atte, welhous**; the earliest OED citation for *welhous* is dated 1355; the building was in Wycomb); *Whitestone Furlong* 1744 (appears to parallel *Whettstonne* (*Whitstone* 1674) in neighbouring Scalford f.ns. (b); v. *Wystonbrigge, infra*); *Wicham Sike* 1282 (v. **sík**); *Willowbed(s)* 1682, 1686 (v. **wilig, bedd**); *Windmill Hill Furlong* 1744; *Witewelle*

1282 × 91, (le) *Wytewell'* 1282 × 91, 1294, 1313, *Whitwell lay(e)s* 1582[1], 1582[2], *Whittle leyes* 1682, *Whittell* ~, *Whittill leys* 1686 (v. **leys**) (v. **hwīt, wella**); *Wystonbrigg(e)* 1282, 1282 × 91, *Wystonbrygge* 1282 × 91, *Wyston'brigge* l.13 (v. **brycg**; it is uncertain whether the bridge was one built of white stone (i.e. **hwīt, stān**) or built of a type of stone from which whetstones could be made (i.e. **hwēt-stān**) or alternatively was at a place where such whetstone materials could be found; cf. *Whitestone Furlong, supra* and *apud le Whiteston* in Burrough on the Hill f.ns. (b); the form *Wyston* appears frequently in early spellings for Whetstone (in Guthlaxton Hundred) which is derived from *hwēt-stān*).

Somerby

White 1846 notes that part of the parish of Somerby is in the Peculiar Jurisdiction of Rothley in West Goscote Hundred.

1. SOMERBY

Sumerlidebie 1086 DB

Summerdebie, Svmmerdebi, Svmerdeberie 1086 DB, *Sumerdebi* 1169
P, Hy 2 Dane, Hy 2 *Rut et passim* to 1268 RGrav, 1268 Abbr,
Sumerdebia 1177 P, *Sumerdeby* 1227 ClR, 1242 Fees *et passim*
to 1308 Ipm, 1323 Abbr, (~ *Tatisale* 1242 Fees), (~ *iuxta
Herdeburgh* 1301 Ass), *Sumardebi* Hy 2 Dane (p), *Sumardeby*
1203 Cur (p)

Sumeredebi 1193 × 1207 Dugd, *Sumeredeby* 1209 × 35 RHug, 1243
Fees, 1247 RGros, 1254 Val, *Sumeretebi* 1194, 1195, 1199, 1200
P, *Sumeretteby* 1266 RGrav

Sumeresdeby 1150 × 59 TutP, *Sumerisdeby* 1163 ib

Someredebia c.1130 LeicSurv, *Someredeby* c.1276 *LCDeeds*, 1292,
1295 Ipm

Somerdeby 1209 × 35 RHug, c.1250 RGros *et freq* to 1377, 1391 Pat
et passim to 1412 Cl, 1441 Banco

Sumerdby 1242 Fees, (~ *Quatremars* 1242 ib), (~ *Tateshal'* 1242 ib,
1247 Brase)

Somerdby m.13 (1404) *Laz*, 1323 Misc, 1381 Fine, 1382 Cl

Sumerby 1268 Cur, *Summirby* 1402 Brase

Somerby 1329, 1361 Ipm *et passim* to 1378, 1382 Cl *et freq*,
Somerbye 1535 VE, 1537 MinAccts *et passim* to 1576 Saxton,
Somerbie 1571, 1578 LEpis

Probably 'Sumarliði's farmstead, village', *v.* **bȳ**. The Scand pers.n.
Sumarliði is an original by-name meaning 'summer-traveller'. Fellows-
Jensen (SSNEM 70) suggests that instead of *sumarliði* being used as a
pers.n., it could rather be an appellative referring to one who pursued the
Viking way of life. She also notes a suggestion by Þorhallur

Vilmundarson that the first el. of Somerby could be a Scand compound appellative *sumar-hliðar* 'summer slopes', alluding to pastures originally used only in summer (cf. the Icelandic p.n. *Sumarliðabœr* which Vilmundarson considers to be a precise parallel to the East Midland p.ns. Somerby and Somersby). However, there is no reliable evidence for *sumar-hlið* as a p.n. element in England, although it may reasonably be argued that the fragmentation of the wapentake territories in the east of Leics. is the result of transhumance. There are five known instances of Somerby/Somersby, four of these in Lincs., while the pers.n. *Sumarliði* is recorded six times in Lindsey alone in DB.

Somerby became part of two distinct tenures. The fee of *Tateshall* contained three carucates less two bovates, while the fee of *Quatremars* comprised one carucate and six bovates in 1242 Fees.

GODTORP (lost), GILLETHORP' (lost)
>   *Godtorp* 1086 DB
>   *Gillethorp'* c.1130 LeicSurv

The lost *Godtorp* is cited in DB as being in the jurisdiction of Somerby and Pickwell. Slade (49–50) in his analysis of the LeicSurv assessment of *Gillethorp'* with Burrough on the Hill and the remaining vills of Cold Overton hundred as compared with their assessment in DB, shows that *Godtorp* and *Gillethorp'* are names for the same settlement. Slade (69, map) locates *Gillethorp'* between Somerby and Newbold.

The first el. of the DB name of the farmstead appears to be the adj. OE **gōd**[2], Scand **góðr** 'good', but this has been replaced c.1130 LeicSurv by the Scand pers.n, *Gilli*, a short form of Irish pers.ns. in *Gilli-* and found in Iceland at the time of its settlement. Fellows-Jensen notes that it is probable that the majority of the bearers of this pers.n. were of Celtic descent, *v.* **þorp** and SPNLY 100–1, cf. Gilroes, Lei **1** 221.

ALL SAINTS' CHURCH, *Church (All Saints)* 1846, 1863, 1877 White, 1925 Kelly; it is earlier recorded as *ecclesie de Somerdeby* 1220 MHW, *~ de Sumeredeb'* 1247 RGros, *ecclesia parochiali* 1549 *Rut*. Note also *The Church Yard* 1821 *Terrier*. THE GROVE, 1925 Kelly, *Somerby Grove* 1846, 1877 White, *le Grob* (sic) 1258 (1795) Nichols (rectius *le Grov*), *v.* **grāf**. THE HALL, 1846, 1863 White, 1925 Kelly, *Somerby Hall* 1877 White, cf. *atte Halle* 1358 Brase (p), *at Alle* 1358 ib (p), *v.* **atte**, **hall**. HAUGHLEY HO., *Haughley house* 1925 Kelly. ROSE AND CROWN (P.H.) (lost), *Rose and Crown* 1846, 1863, 1877 White, 1925 Kelly.

Somerby Grange, v. **grange**. Somerby Ho., *Somerby House* 1863
White. Southfields, 1925 Kelly. Three Crowns (P.H.) (lost), *Three
Crowns* 1846, 1863, 1877 White. The Vicarage, 1877 White, 1925
Kelly; it is *the Vicaridge howse* 1625 *Terrier, the Vicarage house* 1708,
1821 *ib.*

FIELD-NAMES

Undated forms in (a) are 1971 *Surv*; those dated 1761 are *EnclA*; 1780,
1781, 1795 and 1802 are Brase, while 1853 are *TA*. Forms throughout
dated 1247, c.1320, 1324, c.1330, a.1340, c.1340, 1358, 1374, c.1400,
1470, 1673 and 1732 are Brase; 1258 are Nichols; 1291 are Coram;
1524 are SR; 1549 are Pat; 1551 are Hastings; 1601, 1627, 1703, 1708,
1736 and m.18 are *Terrier*.

(a) the Five ~, 8 ~, the Twelve Acre (*v.* **æcer**); Adcocks Garden 1853 (in the
possession of *William Adcock* 1853); Andrews (the surn. *Andrew(s)* in the possessive
case); Anstey Bridge (*Hans(e)y-bridg* 1703, 1708, *Hannsy Bridge* m.18, cf. *Hansty
Hill* 1703, *Hansey* ~ 1708, *v.* **ānstīg**); Barn Cl, Barn Mdw; Barrel's Nook (*Barwell
Nook* 1761, *v.* **nōk**, cf. *Denny Barall* 1627; the surn. is a late form of *Barwell*, that
of a family originating in the village of Barwell, 23 miles to the south-west in
Sparkenhoe Hundred, *v.* Reaney *s.n.* Barrell); Bullocks Cl 1853 (the property of *John
Bullock* 1853); Burrow foot stile 1761 (with **stīg** 'a path' in origin rather than with
stigel 'a stile', to which it has been attracted), Burrow Hill Cl 1761 (*Burrough hills*
1703, 1708, *Burrow* ~ m.18), Burrow Hill Gate 1761 (*Erburgate, Erd(e)burghgate*
1291, *v.* **gata**) (Burrough on the Hill adjoins to the west); Cold Overton Gate 1761
(*v.* **gata**; Cold Overton adjoins to the east); Coles headland furlong 1761 (*v.* **hēafod-
land**; with the surn. *Cole(s)*); Cooke's ~, Cooks Lane 1761 (with the surn. *Cook(e)*);
the Coomes 1761 (*the Koomes* 1703, 1708, *ye Coomes* m.18, *v.* **cumb**); Cow Cl;
Cricket Fd (for the game of cricket); the Croft (*v.* **croft**); Cross Wong 1761, ~ Wrong
1781, 1802 (*v.* **cross, vangr**); Crow Castle 1802, 1971, ~ ~ Cl 1781 (*Crow Castle*
m.18, *v.* **crāwe, castel(l)**; a place frequented by crows, with 'castle' presum. used in
the sense 'a high safe place'); Crowding Leys Cl 1761 (*Croders Leas* 1703, 1708, *v.*
leys; with the surn. *Crowder, v.* Reaney *s.n.* Crowther); Double Dykes 1761 (*v.*
duble, dík); Thompson's ~ ~, Dry Hills (*v.* **drȳge**); Ewe Cl (*v.* **eowu**); Foresters Cl
1853 (with the surn. *Forester*); Goodfellow's Spring 1761 (*v.* **spring**[1]; either with the
surn. *Goodfellow* or named from *Robin Goodfellow*, the 'drudging goblin', who
threshes corn and does domestic chores while the farmer and his household are
asleep, and who also appears as *Robin-round-cap* or as *Robin-a-tiptoe* in the name
Robin-a-Tiptoe Hill in Tilton, four miles to the south-west, *v.* E. M. Wright, *Rustic
Speech and Folk-Lore*, Oxford 1913, 201); Greengate Cl 1781, 1802 (*Grenegate*
c.1330, 1470, *Green-gate* 1703, 1708, m.18, *v.* **grēne**[1], **gata**); the Haggs 1761 (*v.*
hǫgg); Hill Cl 1780; Hill Falls (cf. *hillfall hole* m.18, *v.* **hyll, (ge)fall, hol**[1]); the

Home Close of William Baxter 1761, Home Cl, Home Fd (*v.* **home**); Homestead 1802 (*v.* **hām-stede**); House Cl; Huttons Cl (with the surn. *Hutton*); Knossington Gate 1761 (*Knawston Yate* m.18, *Knawston way* m.18 (*v.* **weg**), *v.* **gata**; the road to Knossington which adjoins to the south-east); Leeks Cl, Leeks Mdw (with the surn. *Leek(s)*, *v.* Reaney *s.n.*); Little Dalby Bridle Gate 1761 (a bridle-way, *v.* **brigdels**, **gata**), Little Dalby foot stile called Rice Stile 1761 (*v.* **stīg**, Burrow foot stile *supra* and Rice Stile *infra*) (Little Dalby lies two miles to the north); Little Lane 1761; the Marr Fd 1761 (*the Marrfeilde* 1601, (*the*) *Mare field* 1703, 1708, m.18, *v.* **marr**[1], **feld**; one of the great fields of the village, earlier recorded as *campo australi* 1374 (with MLat *campus* 'a field' and MLat *australis* 'southern')); Meadows's Cl, Meadows's Garden 1853 (the property of *James Meadows* 1853); Melton Rd, the Melton Mowbray waggon road 1761 (*v.* **wægn**) (*Melton gate* 1601, *Melton Way* m.18, *v.* **gata**, **weg**; Melton Mowbray lies five miles to the north-west); Middle Fd; the Mill Gate 1761 (*v.* **gata**); Newbold foot stile 1761 (*v.* **stīg** and Burrow foot stile *supra*), Newbold Gate 1761 (*v.* **gata**), Newbold Hedge 1761 (*Newbald hedge* m.18; a boundary hedge) (Newbold adjoins to the south-west); Owston Gates (sic) 1761 (*Oston Yat* m.18, *v.* **gata**), Owston Stock Gate 1761 (*v.* **stock**, **gata**), Owston waggon road 1761 (*v.* **wægn**) (Owston adjoins to the south); Pickwell foot stile 1761 (*v.* **stīg** and Burrow foot stile *supra*), Pickwell Gate 1761 (*v.* **gata**) (Pickwell adjoins to the north-east); Pingle Cl 1780 (*v.* **pingel**); Ploughed Cl; the Pool 1802, Pool Cl 1795 (*v.* **pōl**[1]); Quakers Cl 1853 (the Quakers held land in Somerby according to m.18 *Terrier*); Ram Fd (*v.* **ramm**); Redland (*v.* **rēad**, **land**; alluding to the colour of the soil); the Rice Cl 1761, Rice Fd 1761 (*the Rice Feild* 1627, *Rice field* 1703, *Rise ~* 1708, m.18, *v.* **hrīs**, **feld**; one of the great fields of the township, earlier recorded as *campo boriali* 1374 (with MLat *campus* 'a field' and MLat *borealis* 'northern')), Rice Stile 1761 (*v.* **stīg** and Burrow foot stile *supra*); Little ~ ~, Round Hill (*v.* **round**, cf. *Attons Roundhill* m.18; with the surn. *Atton*, also found in Rutland, *v.* Ru 435); Sharpe's Cl 1761, Sharpes Cl or Home Spot 1853 (*v.* **home**, **spotte**; with the surn. *Sharpe*); Short Leys (m.18, *the Short Leas* 1703, 1708, *v.* **leys**); Shutoe Cl 1780 (*Sowter* 1627, *Souto* m.18; perh. 'the southern spur of land', *v.* **sūð**, **hōh**); Skerritts Home Spot 1853 (*v.* **home**, **spotte**; the property of *Robert Skerritt* 1853); Spring Cl (*v.* **spring**[1] and Goodfellow's Spring *supra*); Syke Cl (*v.* **sík**); Thompson's Seed (*v.* **sǣd**; in f.ns., used of areas of sown grass); Three Corner Fd (*v.* **three-corner**); Twival Dam 1761 (*Twivills* m.18, *Twivill Dambe* m.18, cf. *a Dame* 1524 (p), *v.* **damme**), Twival Fd 1761 (*the Twivell feilde* 1601, *Twiwell Feild* 1627, *Twivill Field* 1703, 1708, m. 18, *v.* **feld**; one of the great fields of Somerby, earlier recorded as *campo occidentali* 1374 (with MLat *campus* 'a field' and MLat *occidentalis* 'western')) (*v.* **twī-**, **wella**); Ward's Mdw (with the surn. *Ward*); Westcroft 1781, 1795, 1802 (1703, 1708, m.18, *Westcroftes* 1601, *the west crofts* 1703, *v.* **west**, **croft**); Withcot Rd 1761 (Withcote lies three miles to the south-east); Woodgate Meer 1761 (*v.* **wudu**, **gata**, **(ge)mǣre**).

(b) *Anclewarlot* c.1330 bis (*v.* **angle**, **warlot**); *Ancliff* m.18, *Ancliffe furlonge* 1627 (*v.* **ān**, **clif**); *Annuler Bank* (sic) m.18 (*v.* **banke**; perh. with *annular* 'forming a ring, ring-like', which would be in the style of some 'learned' 18th cent. f.ns., cf. Parallogram Cl (sic) and Triangular Cl in Little Dalby f.ns. (a)); *Ashby Leas* 1703, 1708 (*v.* **leys**; with the surn. *Ashby*); *Ashwels* m.18 (*v.* **æsc**, **wella**); *Asschemarebrock* a.1340, *Assemerebro(c)k* c.1340 (*v.* **æsc, (ge)mǣre, brōc**); *ye Bastards* m.18 (*v.* **bastard** and *the Bastardes* in Bottesford f.ns. (b)); *the beggars bushe* 1601, *Beggars Bush* 1703, 1708 (*v.* **beggere, busc**; a recurring name that may indicate poor, impoverished land); *Bellerys hedge* m.18 (a boundary hedge; with a surn., prob. a miswritten *Bellerby* in the possessive case, *v.* Reaney *s.n.*); *George Black's headland* 1708 (*v.* **hēafod-land**); *the black leas* 1601, *Black Leas* 1627, 1703, 1708 (*v.* **leys**; although *leys* is freq. preceded by a surn. in Framland Hundred f.ns., the use of the def.art. in the earliest form suggests that rather than the surn. *Black* (cf. the preceding f.n.), we have **blæc**, either in its sense 'dark-coloured' or in its later sense 'fertile'); *Brakenholm* c.1400 (*v.* **brakni, holmr**); *the Breche* 1374, *Breach leys* m.18 (*v.* **brēc, leys**); *Briggebec* 1258, *Brigbecke* 1601, *Brickback* 1703, *Brig-back* 1708 (*v.* **brycg, bryggja, bekkr**); *Brodmans ford* m.18 (*v.* **ford**; with the surn. *Bradman*); *Brogeland* c.1400 (*v.* **land**; the first el. is poss. **brōc**, but more forms are needed); *brokendikes* 1601 (*v.* **brakni, dík**); *the brook* 1703; *burdowe lees* 1601, *neather, (the) over Burdeleas* 1703, 1708 (*v.* **neoðera, uferra**), *Hither, Over, Short Burdyleys* m.18 (*v.* **byrde, haugr, leys**); *Burrough Mere* 1703, *~ Meer* 1708 (*v.* **(ge)mǣre**; the boundary with Burrough on the Hill which adjoins to the west); *Calde Wellys* c.1320 (*v.* **cald, wella**); *the Cheesecake piece* m.18 (*v.* **cheesecake, pece**; such closes were usually wedge-shaped and so named from an individual portion of the confection); *the Church headland* 1703, 1708, *Church hadland* m.18 (*v.* **hēafod-land**); *Church Middows* m.18 (*v.* **mǣd (mǣdwe** obl.sg.)); *the Clint(s)* 1703, 1708 (*v.* **klint**); *cole cart way* m.18 (a development of *col-pytt*, a place where charcoal was made, cf. *the Colepytt way* > *the coale cart way* in Saxby f.ns. (b)); *Cooks willow* 1708 (*v.* **wilig**; with the surn. *Cook*); *the dale* 1601, *between the dales* 1627, *Hither Dales* m.18, *the dale bauke* 1601 (*v.* **balca**) (*v.* **dalr**); *Neather, Over Danceing leys* m.18 (*v.* **neoðera, uferra, dauncing, leys**; the venue for local country dancing); *ye Dike* m.18 (*v.* **dík**); *Dinghill* m.18, *~ Feild* 1627, *dingil gate* 1247, *Dyngel ~, Dyngul Gate* 1374 (*v.* **gata**) ('the assembly hill', *v.* **þing, hyll**; a local moot-site); *le Estelane* 1358 (*v.* **ēast, lane**); *Fetherbeds* m.18 (*v.* **feather-bed**; used in f.ns. of spongy ground or soft, yielding areas of moorland peat-moss); *Flaxlands* m.18 (*v.* **fleax, land**); *Garbrod* 1374 (*v.* **gorebrode**); *the goare leyes* 1601, *Goar Leys* m.18 (*v.* **gāra, leys**); *Godson hey* 1374 (*v.* **(ge)hæg**; with the surn. *Godson, v.* Reaney *s.n.* for an extended discussion of various origins for the name); *greate sick* 1627, *(the) Great Seek* 1703, 1708, m.18 (*v.* **grēat, sík**); *Leonard Green's headland* 1708, *Leonard Greens headleas* 1703, *William Green's headland* 1703, *~ ~ headley* 1708 (*v.* **hēafod-land, headley**); *atte Grene* 1358 (p), *a grene* 1524 (p) (*v.* **atte, grēne**²); *Grimisholm* 1247 (*v.* **holmr**; with the Scand pers.n. *Grímr*, an original by-name that was often used of *Óðinn* in disguise, cf. OIcel *gríma* 'a mask'); *Gueyne Well* 1374 (*v.* **wella**; either with the pers.n. *Gawayn*, or by this date, poss. with its ME surn. reflex, cf. *Emma Gawayn* 1379 of Yorks., *v.* Reaney *s.n.* Gavin); *Halle Balke* 1708 (*v.* **hall, balca** and The Hall *supra*); *Harthorndale* c.1400 (*v.* **hār**², **þorn**, with **dalr** or **deill**; the tempting *hagu-þorn* 'hawthorn' appears to be discounted by the *r* in the first syllable; cf. the late *Horthorn Hill* in Harby f.ns. (b) which may parallel this construction); *the Harps* 1708 (*v.* **hearpe**); *herburo furlong* 1247 (*v.* **furlang**; adjacent to Burrough on the Hill); *Heyererforlange* (sic) 1374 (*v.* **herre, furlang**); *the hilles* 1601, *~ ~ side* 1703 (*v.* **hyll, sīde**); *hoke gate* 1247 (*v.* **hōc, gata**); *the holmes* 1703 (*v.* **holmr**); *the*

Homestall 1708 (*v.* **hām-stall**; i.e. that of The Vicarage *supra*); *Honny Acres* m.18 (*v.* **hunig, æcer**; poss. alluding to land where honey was found, or figuratively to 'sweet land', but alternatively *honey* could be used pejoratively of sticky soil, *v.* Field 42); *Keldervelde* 1374 (*v.* **kelda, feld**); *the Kilnes* 1703 (*v.* **cyln**); *Knossyngton mere* 1374 (*v.* **(ge)mǣre**; Knossington adjoins to the south-east); *Levielands* m.18 (*v.* **land**; with **levi** or **lēfer**); *Little hades* 1703 (*v.* **hēafod**); *(the) Little Seek* 1703, m.18, *Little sick* 1708 (*v.* **sīk**); *the long-dooles* 1708, *Long dols* m.18 (*v.* **dāl**); *the Long Leas* 1703, 1708 (*v.* **leys**); *Masons Yard* 1551 (*v.* **geard**; with the surn. *Mason*); *Maydenstede* 1549 (*v.* **mægden, stede**; poss. naming a place frequented by girls of the village, but could refer to a farm or building owned by a young unmarried woman); *the Meare* 1601 (*v.* **(ge)mǣre**; the boundary of Marr Fd *supra*); *the Medow* 1374 (*v.* **mǣd** (**mǣdwe** obl.sg.)); *Moore Huske* 1736 (*v.* **mōr¹, hyrst**); *More Bushes* m.18 (*v.* **mōr¹, busc**); *Mussike* 1258, 1601, *Mussyk* 1374, *Musseek* 1703, *Musses* 1708 (*v.* **mūs, mús, sīk** and *Mussicke* in Pickwell f.ns. (b)); *Mydelmor(e)* 1374 (*v.* **middel, mōr¹**); *Mylnesholme* 1374 (*v.* **myln, holmr**); *Newboll Meare* 1601, *Newbold Meere* 1703, *Neobald-meer* 1708 (*v.* **(ge)mǣre**; Newbold adjoins to the south-west); *neather-furlonge* 1708 (i.e. of Twival Fd *supra*), *the nether furlong* 1703, 1708 (i.e. of Marr Fd *supra*); *Nomonysland* c.1330 (*v.* **nān-mann, land**); *the old Mill furlonge* 1601; *Olmehou* c.1330 (*v.* **almr, haugr**); *Osolvistonesty* 1258 (*v.* **stīg**), *Ouston hedge* 1703, 1708, m.18 (*v.* **hecg**; a boundary hedge) (Owston adjoins to the south); *Palmers Bushes* m.18 (*v.* **busc**; with the surn. *Palmer*); *the Parsonage land* 1601 (*v.* **personage, land**); *Pease hill* m.18 (*v.* **pise**); *Peppy Leys* m.18 (*v.* **leys**; a surn. freq. precedes *leys* in f.ns. and here is prob. *Pepper*, common in Leics. and in neighbouring Rutland, *v.* Ru 456; ModEdial. *pepper* 'a peddler' is less likely); *peselandys* c.1330 (*v.* **pise, land**); *Pickwell hedge* 1601, 1703, 1708, m.18 (*v.* **hecg**; the boundary hedge of Pickwell which adjoins to the north-east), *Pickwell Mill Furlong* m.18 (beside a windmill towards Pickwell); *Pruste hyll* 1374 (*v.* **prēost, hyll**); *Red earth* 1703, 1708, m.18 (*v.* **rēad, eorðe**; referring to the colour of the soil); *Red Hill* 1703, 1708, m.18 (*v.* **rēad** and cf. the previous name); *Rushy Furrows* m.18 (*v.* **riscig, furh**); *Sir Rowland St John's balk* 1703 (*v.* **balca**); *Shepperd board* m.18 (*v.* **scēp-hirde, bord** in its sense 'a board, a table' and thus alluding to good grazing for sheep; cf. *Shepherd boord Leyes* (1744) in Wycomb and Chadwell f.ns. (b), *Shepheard Board* (1703) referring to leys in Kimcote, Guthlaxton Hundred and *Shepherds Tables* (1770), situated around Croft Hill in Croft, Sparkenhoe Hundred); *Smethe medue* 1247, *Smith Medow* 1703 (*v.* **smēðe¹, mǣd** (**mǣdwe** obl.sg.)); *Steyn* 1470 (*v.* **steinn**; alluding either to a specific stone or to stony ground); *Stobclif* 1374 (*v.* **stobb, clif**); *the Stone pits* 1703, 1708 (*v.* **stān-pytt**); *Stony Brink* m.18 (*v.* **stānig, brink**); *Sty(e) balk hole* 1703, 1708 (*v.* **stīg, balca, hol¹**); *Thyrneberowe* 1374 (*v.* **þyrne, þyrnir, berg**); *Towne forleng* 1374 (*v.* **furlang**), *the towne land* 1627 (*v.* **land**) (*v.* **tūn**); *the upper furlong* 1703, 1708 (in the Marr Fd *supra*); *Velsow* 1374 bis (*v.* **wella, sōg**); *atte Welle* 1324 (p) (*v.* **atte, wella**); *Westolmes* 1374 (*v.* **west, vestr, holmr**); *Whardloe* 1374, *Wharlow* m.18 (*v.* **weard, hlāw**); *Wood croft* 1732 (*v.* **wudu, croft**).

2. BURROUGH ON THE HILL

Bvrg 1086 DB, *Burg* 1213 Abbr, 1236 Fine *et passim* to 1303, 1308
  Ipm, *Burg'* c.1130 LeicSurv, 1184 Dane *et passim* to 1248 RGros,
  1254 Val, *Burgo* 1086 DB, 1184 Dane *et passim* to c.1291 Tax,
  1316 FA
Bvrc 1086 DB bis, *Burk* a.1250 (1404), m.13 (1404), Hy 3 (1404)
  . *Laz*, *Burk'* Hy 3 (1404) *ib*, *Burk(g)h* Hy 3 (1404) *ib*
Burgh 1193 × 1207 Dugd, 1242 Fees *et passim* to 1325 Inqaqd, 1330
  Cl *et freq* to 1388 Misc, 1398 Pat (p) *et passim* to 1522 Fine,
  1536 *Braye*, *Burgh alias Erdeborough* 1615 Ipm
Erdburg 1201 OblR, 1251 Fine, *Erdburgo* c.1290 Dugd, *Erdburgh*
  1288 Coram, 1321 Brase *et passim* to 1514 Ipm, 1518 CoPleas,
  Erdborow 1306 *Deed*, *Erdborou* 1306, 1361 *ib*, *Erdeburgh* 1245
  Fine, 1302 Cl (p) *et passim* to 1336 (c.1430) *KB*, 1346 *RTemple*
  et freq to 1398 Pat, 1398 Cl *et passim* to 1428 FA, 1431 *Braye*,
  Erdeburghe 1537 MinAccts, *Erdeborowght* 1572 LeicW,
  Erdeborowe 1604 SR
Erburg 1251 Cur, 1270 Fine, 1292 Ipm, *Erburgh* 1262 RGrav, 1288
  Ass, 1494 Pat, *Erborough* 1510 *Rental*
Erthburg c.1247, 1283, 1285 *RTemple*, 1327 SR, *Erthboru* 1281
  RTemple, *Erth(e)burgh* 1313 Banco, 1327 SR, 1330 Cl
Ardburght 1475 × 85 ECP, *Ardbrogh* 1480 Pap, *Ard(e)borough* 1510
  LP, 1626 Fine, *Ard(e)borowe* 1578, 1583 LEpis
Borow(e) 1323 Inqaqd, 1518 Visit, 1526 AAS *et passim* to 1574
  LEpis, (~ *alias Ard(e)borowe* 1578, 1583 ib), (~ *alias*
  Erdborough 1614 Ipm), *Boro* 1535 VE, *Borrow(e)* 1536 Dugd,
  1537 MinAccts, *Borough(e)* 1541 ib, 1614 Ipm, (~ *alias*
  Erdeboroughe 1588 Fine), *Borowgh* 1571 LeicW
Burow or Erdeborow 1537 MinAccts, *Burrow(e)* 1576 Saxton, 1576
  LibCl *et passim* to 1610 Speed, 1621 LML, *Burrough* 1612
  Nichols, (~ *alias Ardborough* 1626, 1627 Fine), *Burrough-on-*
  the-Hill 1641 LML

'The fortress', *v.* **burh**; and 'the fortress built of earth', *v.* **eorð-burh**.
There is a superb Iron Age hill-fort on Burrough Hill north of the
village, possibly the *caput* of the Corieltauvi, *v.* Lei **1** 3–4. The location
of the present settlement, with its 13th century church, lies on a hill
across a deep valley from the earthwork. There is no evidence that the
hill-fort itself was ever the site of an early Anglo-Saxon village.

However, traces of Romano-British occupation have been discovered there.

BURROUGH COURT, 1925 Kelly, *v.* **court**. BURROUGH HILL, 1846, 1863, 1877 White, *Barow ~, Borow Hilles* c.1545 Leland, *Burrough Hills* 1709 *Terrier, Burrow hill* 1720 MagBrit, 1824 O, 1846 *TA, v.* **burh, hyll**; the hill on which the Iron Age hill-fort stands. BURROUGH HILL HO. BURROUGH HILL LODGE is *Somerby Lodge* 1824 O, *v.* **loge**. FOX AND HOUNDS (P.H.) (lost), *Fox and Hounds* 1846 White. MANOR HO., *Manor House* 1863 White, *v.* **maner**. PEAKE'S COVERT, cf. *Thomas Peak, grazier* 1863 White, *Thomas Peak, farmer* 1877 ib, *v.* **cover(t)**. THE RECTORY, 1877 White, 1925 Kelly, *the Rectory House* 1846 *TA*; it is *the Parsonage House* 1709, 1742, 1821 *Terrier*. ST MARY'S CHURCH, *Church (St Mary)* 1846, 1863, 1877 White; it is earlier recorded as *ecclesiam ~ ~, ecclesie de Burgo* a.1219 RHug, 1220 MHW, *ecclesiam de Burg'* 1239, 1248 RGros, *ecclesie de Erdeburgh* 1336 (c.1430) *KB, Borrough Church* 1607 Brase, *ye Church of Burrough* 1697 *Terrier, ~ ~ ~ Burrow* 1699 *ib, Burrough Church* 1709 *ib*. Note also (*the*) *Churchyard* 1709, 1821 *ib*, 1846 *TA*. SALTER'S HILL, 1968 *Surv, Salters ~* 1846 *TA, v.* **saltere**, cf. *Salters Gate* in f.ns. (b) *infra*. STAG AND HOUNDS (P.H.) (lost), *Stag and Hounds* 1846, 1863, 1877 White, 1925 Kelly. TWYFORD RD is *Twyfordegate* Edw 3 (c.1430) *KB, Twiforde gate* 1607 *Brase, viam de Twyford* Edw 3 (c.1430) *KB* (with MLat *via* (*viam* acc.sg.) 'a road'), *v.* **gata**. Twyford adjoins to the south-west.

In 1709 *Terrier*, the following village dwellings are recorded: *Joseph Ashton House, Beanes ~, John Beeson ~, Mr Dilkes ~, James Frisby ~, Thomas Frisby ~, Mr Halford House, The Hall House* (*v.* **hall**), *Huttons ~, Richard Knapp ~, Mr Lane ~, Benjamin Palmer ~, Miss Pelcher ~, James Preston ~, Wido' Preston ~, Thomas Scarborrow ~, Mr Seaton ~, Frances Sharp ~, John Simson ~, Thomas Simson ~, Michell Stacey ~, Charles Tyre ~, Adam Walker ~, Mr Woolston House.*
   Note also in 1709 *Terrier: Allens Farme, Brigges Farme, Joseph Porter his farme* (*Porters Farme* 17 *Surv*), *v.* **ferme**.

FIELD-NAMES

Undated forms in (a) are 1968 *Surv*; those dated 1802 are *Map*, while 1846 are *TA*. Forms throughout dated Hy 3 (1404) are *Laz*; 1327 and 1381 are SR; 1336 (c.1430), 1338 (c.1430), 1340 (c.1430), 1343 (c.1430) and Edw 3 (c.1430) are *KB*; 1350 are Banco; c.1600, 1674, 1697, 1699, 1700, 1703, 1709 and 1742 are *Terrier*; 1607 are *Brase*; 17 are *Surv*; 1736 are *Deed*.

(a) Allens Cl 1846, Allen's ~ 1968 (*Allens close* 17, *Allens Clossinge* 1709, *v.* **closing**), Allens Mdw 1846, Allen's ~ 1968 (with the surn. *Allen*, cf. *Allens Farme* 1709 *supra*); Bottom, Top(p) At(t)cliff 1846, Bottom, Top Atcliffe 1968 (prob. with the surn. *Atcliff(e)*); otherwise *v.* **atte**, **clif**); Aveys Mdw 1846, Avey's ~ 1968, Aveys Wong 1846, Avey's ~ 1968 (*Aveyes wonge* 1607, *v.* **vangr**; with the surn. *Avey* (poss. from the OFr pers.n. *Avice*), *v.* Reaney *s.n.* Avis); Barn Cl 1846, 1968 (*The Barn Close* 1742); Bates Mdw 1846, 1968 (with the surn. *Bates*); Beans Cl 1846 (*Beanes Closse* 1709; with the surn. *Bean*, cf. *Beanes House* 1709 *supra*); the Breach 1846, 1968 (*Breache* 1607, *The Breaches* 1736, *v.* **brēc**); Broken Dikes 1846 (*Brakendikes* 1607, *Brokendikes* 17, *Brokindikes* 1709, *v.* **brakni**, **dík**); Brook Cl 1846 (*v.* **brōc**); Caesar's Camp 1831 Curtis (a fanciful name for the Iron Age hill-fort on Burrough Hill); Calf Cl 1846 (*v.* **calf**); Captains Cl 1846 (*the Captains close* 17, *v.* **capitain**); the Clinths 1846, 1968, Far Clinth 1846 (*the Clints* 1607, *(ye) Clint* 1674, 1709, *Faulkners Clint* 1708 (with the surn. *Faulkner*), *Little Clint* 17, cf. *the Clintil* 1709 (*v.* **hyll**), *v.* **klint**); Debdale, ~ Mdw 1846 (*Depedale* Edw 3 (c.1430), *Depdale* 1607, *Debdale* 17, 1709, *v.* **dēop**, **dalr**); Dove Hole Cl, Dove Hole Mdw 1846 (*Doue hole & meadow* 1709, *v.* **dūfe**, **hol**[1]; 'dove-holes' were presum. the effects of small excavations for minerals, reminiscent of the holes in a dove-cote, cf. Dove Holes, Db 64 and 399); Elder Holms 1846, 1968 (1709, *Elderholm* 1607, *v.* **ellern**, **holmr**); Elm Cl 1802 (*v.* **elm**); Elm Leys 1846, 1968 (*Elme leas* 1607, *v.* **elm**, **leys**); Far End Cl 1846, 1968; Far Mdw 1846; Featherbed Nook (*v.* **feather-bed**, **nōk** and *Fetherbeds* in Somerby f.ns. (b)); Fox Covert 1846 (*v.* **cover(t)**); Frisbys Cl 1846 (cf. *James Frisby House* and *Thomas Frisby House* 1709 *supra*; the *Frisby* family presum. originated in Frisby on the Wreake, six miles to the north-west, or in Frisby (by Galby), six miles to the south-west); Gees Lane 1846, Gee's Lane Cl 1846, 1968, Gees Lane Mdw 1846, Gee's ~ ~ 1968 (with the surn. *Gee*); Far ~ ~, Gorse Cl 1846, 1968 (*The Goss Close* 1742, *v.* **gorst**); Grandmothers Mdw 1846 (meadowland assigned for the benefit of a late owner's widow); The Gravel Hole 1968, Gravel Pit Cl 1846 (*v.* **gravel**, **pytt**); Great Cl 1846, 1968; Hall Cl 1839 VCHL, 1846, 1968 (*the Hall-Close* 1709, cf. *The Hall House* 1709 *supra*); Hassocky Cl 1846 (*v.* **hassuc**, **-ig**[2]); Highway Cl; Neather, Upper Hills (*the hilles, within ye hilles* 1607; furlongs so called); Holme Cl (*le holmes* Edw 3 (c.1430), *v.* **holmr**); Home Cl 1846, 1968 (*the Home Close* 1742, *v.* **home**); Honey Go Dale 1846, 1968 (*Honye acre dale* 1607, *Hunnicar Dale* 1674, *Honey Acre Dale* 1742, *v.* **hunig**, **æcer**, **dalr**; *honey* may describe 'sweet land', but alternatively may refer to sticky soil, arduous to till); The Hook 1846 (*the Hookes* 1709, *the Old Hook* 1709, *Gamble his Hooke* 1709 (with the surn. *Gamble*), *v.* **hōc**); Hookers Cl 1846 (17; poss. with the surn. *Hooker*, but note *Hookes Closse* 1709 which may belong with the previous f.n. or relate Hookers Cl to it); House Cl 1846; Husk leys 1846 (*v.* **hyrst**, **leys**); Huttons Cl 1846, Hutton's Cl or Featherbed Nook 1968 (cf. *Huttons House* 1709 *supra* and *v.* Featherbed Nook *supra*); Jacobs Cl 1846, Jacob's ~ 1968 (with the surn. *Jacob*); Kennys Cl 1846 (1709), Kennys Close Mdw 1846, Kennys Old Mdw 1846 (with the surn. *Kenny*);

Land Mdw 1846 (v. **land**; a meadow comprising an unspecified number of the selions of one of the former great fields of the township); Langerdale 1846, 1968 (17, *Langardale* 1607, v. **lang**[1], **gāra**; with either **dalr** or **deill**); Little Mdw 1846, 1968; Mar Hill 1846, 1968 (*Marehill* 1607, 1736), Marsick 1846, 1968 (*Mare Syke* 1607, v. **sík**) (v. **marr**[1]); Far, Near Mill Hill 1846, 1968 (*Millne Hill* 1607, *the Old Mill hill* 17, *the ould mill hill* 1709, v. **myln**; the site of a windmill); Lower, Upper Mill Fd 1846 (*Milne Fielde* 1607, *the Millfeild* 17, v. **myln**, **feld**; one of the great fields of the village); The Moors 1846, 1968, Ne(a)ther, Upper Moor 1846, 1968 (*the More* 1340 (c.1430), *le mor* Edw 3 (c.1430), *Moore aboue ye Close*, ~ *beneath ye Close* 1607, v. **mōr**[1]); Bottom, Top Moor Husk 1846, 1968 (*Morehurst* 17, *Moorehurst Close* 1607, *Moorehurste furl*. 1607 (v. **furlang**), *Moorehurst Syke* 1607 (v. **sík**), v. **mōr**[1], **hyrst**; note the late local dial. development of *hurst* > *husk* which explains the group of previously obscure Rutland names with *husk* listed in Ru 432, section T.; v. also Husk leys in f.ns. (a) *supra* and *Moore Huske* in Somerby f.ns. (b)); Narrow shred 1846 (v. **nearu**, **scread**); (the) New Mdw 1846, 1968; Nether Hill 1846; Occupation Rd 1846 (a common name, dating from the Enclosures and meaning 'a private road for the use of the occupiers of the land', v. OED *s.v.* occupation, 7; it signified a green lane, an access road through a former great field); Ogden, Ogdens Mdw 1846 (*Hogden* 1607, 17, 1709, *Hogden end* 17 (v. **ende**), *Hogden Syke* 1607 (v. **sík**), *Hogden hedge* 1607 (v. **hecg**; a boundary hedge); it is uncertain whether or not one is dealing with a surn. here (cf. *William Ogdin* 1612 RFL), otherwise v. **hogg**, **denu**, cf. *Norden* in f.ns. (b) *infra*); Old Pasture 1846 (*the Old Pasture* 17, 1709, v. **pasture**); Lower, Top Palm Hill 1802, 1846, 1968, Little Palm Hill 1846, 1968 (*Palme Hill* 1607, 1736, *Palm-Hill*, ~ *Close* 1709, v. **palme**; poss. referring to the goat-willow (*Salix caprea*), used for the true palm in northern countries in celebrations of Palm Sunday, v. OED *s.v.* palm sb.[1], 4); Peake's Flats (v. **flat**; with the surn. *Peak(e)*, cf. *Thomas Peak, grazier* 1863 White); Pinfold 1968, ~ Mdw 1846 (*Pinfolde* 1607, *Pinfould Close* 1709, v. **pynd-fald**); Pingle 1846 (v. **pingel**); Ploughed Cl 1846, 1968; Powers Great Cl, Powers Mdw 1846 (with the surn. *Power(s)*); Road Cl 1846; Sallow Bed 1846 (v. **salh**, **bedd**); Salters Hill Mdw 1846 (v. *Salter's Hill supra*); Sharpes Cl 1846, Sharp's ~ 1968 (with the surn. *Sharp*, cf. *Frances Sharp House* 1709 *supra*); The Slang (v. **slang**); Bottom, Middle, Top Slidings 1846 (*Sleything'* 1340 (c.1430), *Sleyting'*, *Sleytyng'* Edw 3 (c.1430), *Slidinges, the Slydinges* 1607, *Slyden* 17, *litulsleyttheynges* 1340 (c.1430) (v. **lȳtel**, **lítill**), v. **siéttr**, **eng**); Steprill 1846, 1968 (*Stirpirhull* 1343 (c.1430), *Steperhill* 1607, *Stepporhill* 1674, *Steeperhill* 1742, v. **stīpere**, **hyll**); Stonebridge Ford, ~ Cl 1846, 1968 (*Stanbrigge* Edw 3 (c.1430), *Stone bridg* 1607, *Stonebridg forde* 1607, v. **stān**, **brycg**, **ford**); Far, Near Thorpe Hill 1846, Thorpe Hill Mdw 1846 (*Thorpe hill* 1607; with reference to Thorpe Satchville which adjoins to the north-west); Townsend Ground 1846, 1968, Townsend Mdw 1846 (*the townesend ground* 17, *The Townsend Ground and Midow* 1709, v. **tūn**, **ende**, **grund**); The Triangle (v. **triangle**; a three-cornered close); Upper Hill 1846; Wheat Cl 1802, 1846, 1968 (v. **hwǣte**); Whetstones Cl, ~ Mdw 1846 (it is uncertain whether *Whetstone* is a surn. here (of a family originating in the village of Whetstone 15 miles to the south-west) or belongs with *apud le Whiteston* in f.ns. (b) *infra*); Willow Tree Cl 1846, 1968 (v. **wilig-trēow**).

(b) *Acres* 1607 (*v.* **æcer**); *Armdale* Edw 3 (c.1430), *Arndale* Edw 3 (c.1430) bis, *Arundell hole* 1607 (*v.* **hol**[1]) (*v.* **earm, deill**); *Bare Arse* 1607 (*v.* **bær**[1], **ears**; perh. alluding to barren soil, either lacking in vegetation, or causing its cultivator ultimate penury; otherwise a jocular name for a bare, rounded hill); *Mr Barfoots lease* 17 (*v.* **leys**); *Basterdes* 1607 (*v.* **bastard** and the *Bastardes* in Bottesford f.ns. (b)); *Beane hill* 1607 (*v.* **bēan**); *Belloes* 1607 (prob. the surn. *Bellow/Beloe* in the possessive case); *Blabies Close* 1607 (with the surn. *Blaby* of a family originally from the township of this name 14 miles to the south-west); *Brecklands* 1736 (*v.* **land**; if this f.n. is not a later form of the following f.n., with attraction to dial. *breck* 'uncultivated land', then its first el. is **bræc**[1] 'brushwood', cf. *Breclondes* in Thorpe Arnold f.ns. (b)); *Nether, Upper Bretlands* 1607 (*v.* **breiðr, land**); *Thomas Briges his close* c.1600; *Brigg-Close* 1709 (*v.* **brycg, bryggja**); *Brimbles* 1607 (*v.* **brembel**); *Betweene Brookes* 1607 (a furlong so called), *Brook tonges* 1607 (*v.* **tunge**) (*v.* **brōc**); *Bukkysthorn'* 1340 (c.1430), *Buckesthorne* 1607 (*v.* **buc-þorn**); *le Burnhassokis* 1340 (c.1430) (*v.* **bryne, hassuc**); *Burnforlong* Edw 3 (c.1430) (*v.* **bryne, furlang**); *Burrough Hill close* 17 (*v.* Burrough Hill *supra*); *Caddalehull* Edw 3 (c.1430) bis (*v.* **hyll**; formally, the first el. could derive from the OE pers.n. *Cada*, the Scand pers.n. *Kā* (an original by-name, cf. ON *ká* 'a jackdaw') or the OE sb. **cā** (ON **ká**) 'a jackdaw'), with either **dalr** or **deill**); *Chandlours Closse* 1709 (with the surn. *Chandler*); *Close Syke* 1607 (*v.* **clos(e), sík**); *the Colledge land* 1674, *Colidge Lease* 1709 (*v.* **leys**) (the property of *Brasen-nose College, Oxford* 1709, i.e. Brasenose College); *the Common pasture* 1607 (*v.* **commun, pasture**); *Cote lane* 1340 (c.1430) (*v.* **cot, lane**); *le Crosse in the More* 1340 (c.1430) (*v.* **mōr**[1]), *atte Cros* 1381 (p) (*v.* **atte**), *Crosse ford* 1607 (*v.* **ford**), *Crosse leaes* 1607 (*v.* **leys**) (*v.* **cros**; at least two standing crosses are indicated here); *Cumbe* 1340 (c.1430), *Coombes* 1607 (*v.* **cumb**); *Dale Mires* 1607 (*v.* **dalr, mýrr**); *Duckettes Close* 1607, *Ducket(t)s* ~ 17, 1709 (with the surn. *Duckett*); *Emneys Close* 1736 (with the surn. *Emney*); *Estdalsykouerende* Edw 3 (c.1430) (*v.* **ēast, dalr, sík, uferra, ende**); *Fallow holmes* 1607 (*v.* **falg, holmr**); *Falk(e)ners close* 17, 1709 (with the surn. *Falkener/Falkner/Faulkner*, cf. *Faulkners Clint* 1708 (*v.* **klint**)); *Flatte peece* 1607 (*v.* **flatr, pece**); *Nether, Ouer Flaxelandes* 1607 (*v.* **uferra**) (*v.* **fleax, land**); *Foxholys* 1340 (c.1430), *Foxholes* 1607 (*v.* **fox-hol**); *Galles, the Galls* 1607 (*v.* **galla**); *Garebred wong'* 1340 (c.1430) (*v.* **gorebrode, vangr**); *Gilhome Lane* 1709 (*v.* **holmr**; the first el. is poss. the Scand pers.n. *Gilli, v. Gillethorp'* and SPNLY 100); *Godwifisgore* Edw 3 (c.1430), *Goodwife Gore* 1607 (*v.* **gāra**; with the ME surn. *Godwyf* (from ME *good-wife* 'mistress of a house'), *v.* Reaney *s.n.* Goodiff); *Goose Syke* 1607 (*v.* **gōs, gás, sík**); *Grassie place, Grassye place furlonge* 1607 (*v.* **grassie, place**); *Grenedik* Edw 3 (c.1430), *Greene Diche* 1607, *Grenesdyk balke* 1350 (*v.* **balca**) (*v.* **grēne**[2], **dík, dīc**); *the Greenlands, Brecklands or Willows* 1736 (*v.* **grēne**[1], **land**; and *Brecklands* (*supra*) and *Willows* (*infra*)); *Grennewell* Edw 3 (c.1430), *Greene welles* 1607, *litulgrenwell* Edw 3 (c.1430) (*v.* **lȳtel**), *Grenewellehill* 1340 (c.1430), *Greenewell hill* 1607, *Greenewell leaes* 1607 (*v.* **leys**), *Greenewell wonge* 1607 (*v.* **vangr**) (*v.* **grēne**[1], **wella**); *le Greybrug'* 1340 (c.1430) (*v.* **græg**[1], **brycg**; referring to the colour of the stone of which the bridge was built); *Guylde holme leaes* 1607 (*v.* **holmr, leys**; with **gild, gildi** or **gylde**); *Haliwell broc* Edw 3 (c.1430) (*v.* **hālig, wella, brōc**); *Hall townes end* 1607 (*v.* **hall, tūn, ende** and *The Hall House*

1709 *supra*); *Hansaxbrigge* 1340 (c.1430) (*v.* **brycg**; the first el. is either **handseax** 'a dagger, a short sword' or **handaxe** 'a battle-axe' (if the cartulary copyist misread the fourth letter as *s* for *d*), but the implication of either in compound with 'bridge' is unclear); *under Harborow* 1607 (a furlong so called lying beneath Burrough Hill); *Hareclif* Edw 3 (c.1430) (*v.* **clif**; with **hār²** or **hara**); *Haselden Syke* 1607 (*v.* **sík**; if first el. is not the surn. *Hazelden*, then *v.* **hæsel, denu**); *Hastenglayes* 1335 (*v.* **læs**; either with the Norman pers.n. *Hastang/Hasten*(*c*) (from ON *Hásteinn*) or with its ME surn. reflex (cf. *Aitrop Hasteng* 1194 of Staffs), *v.* Reaney *s.n.* Hasting); *Hawthorn gate* 1607 (*v.* **hagu-þorn, gata**); *hennehou* Edw 3 (c.1430), *Henoe* 1607 (*v.* **henn, haugr**); *hennehul* Edw 3 (c.1430) (*v.* **henn, hyll**); *Hensoe bridg* 1607 (*v.* **brycg**; *Richard Henshoe* is cited 1607, but note *hennehou* above which may have given rise to the surn.); *herdale* Edw 3 (c. 1430) (*v.* **deill**; poss. with ME **herre** 'higher' (OE Angl **hēr(r)a**)); *High leaes* 1607 (*v.* **leys**); *le Hillimedue* 1343 (c.1430), *Hyllye meadowe* 1607 (*v.* **hyllig, mǣd** (**mǣdwe** obl.sg.)); *Hippelisdale, Hippelisdall'* 1340 (c.1430), *hiplisdale* Edw 3 (c. 1430), *Hibsdale* 1607 (*v.* **hyppels, dalr**); *Hissock hill* 1709 (*v.* **hassuc**); *Hodeclif* 1340 (c.1430), Edw 3 (c.1430), *Hotclyffe* 1607, *Hotcliffe end* 1607 (*v.* **ende**) (*v.* **hōd, clif**; poss. with reference to the Iron Age fortress on Burrough Hill); *the Homestalls of the town* 1709 (*v.* **hām-stall, tūn**); *Impewell*(*e*) Edw 3 (c.1430) (*v.* **impa, wella**); *Iohnsons yardes ende* 1607 (*v.* **geard, ende**; with the surn. *Johnson*); *Joice Lane Close* 1709 (with the surn. *Joice*); *atte Kirkestile* 1327 (p) (*v.* **atte, kirkja, stigel**); *Knapps Close* 1709 (the property of *Richard Knapp* 1709); *kyngeswellhull* Edw 3 (c.1430) (*v.* **wella, hyll**; by this date, the first el. is poss. the surn. *King* rather than the ME sb. **king** (cf. *Kingesbush* in neighbouring Pickwell f.ns. (b)), but note that *Herbert' ten' de rege IIII car' t'ræ in Bvrc* 1086 DB, i.e. Herbert was holding four carucates of land in Burrough directly from the king); *Lecester gate* 1607 (*v.* **gata**; the road to Leicester); *Leeste lane,* ~ ~ *end* 1607 (*v.* **lane-ende**), *Leeste well* 1607 (*v.* **wella**) (with the surn. *Leest, v.* Reaney *s.n.*); *litulgatte* Edw 3 (c.1430) (*v.* **lȳtel, lítill, gata**); *Long holmes* 1607 (*v.* **holmr**); *longelandhok'* 1340 (c.1430) (*v.* **lang¹, land, hōc**); *Longe tongues* 1607 (*v.* **tunge**); *Mardefeilde brok'* Edw 3 (c.1430), *Marefield Brook* 1709, *Marfeild Brooke close* 17 (*v.* **brōc**; the depopulated village of Old (or North) Marefield lay one mile to the south-west); *Michilstanbrigg'* Edw 3 (c.1430) (*v.* **mícel, stān, brycg**); *the Middle close* 17; *Mikelbereu* 1340 (c.1430), *Michilberu* Edw 3 (c.1430) bis, *Mikeleberwebroc* Hy 3 (1404), *Mikulberoubrok'* 1340 (c.1430) (*v.* **brōc**), *Miccilberuhill* c.1260 VCHL (*v.* **hyll**) (presum. 'the great hill' (*v.* **micel, mikell, berg**) rather than 'the great wood' (*v.* **bearu**), although DB does record in Burrough *Silua XIII quarentis longa et IIII lata*, that is 'woodland 13 furlongs long and 4 wide', of unusual extent in poorly wooded north-east Leics.); *Milnehooke,* ~ *leaes* 1607 (*v.* **myln, hōc, leys**); *le Milnesikenetherende* 1340 (c.1430) (*v.* **myln, sík, neoðera, ende**); *milnestonlane* Edw 3 (c.1430) (*v.* **milne-stone, lane**; a lane prob. paved with worn millstones, cf. Millstone Lane, Lei **1** 50); *Moore Close* 1607, *Moore Gates* 1607 (*v.* **gata**), *Morhougatte* 1340 (c.1430) (*v.* **haugr, gata**) (all with **mōr¹, mór**); *Mr Moulsoes close* 17, *Mr Moulsoes lease* 1607 (*v.* **leys**) (cf. *Richard Moulshoe* 1607); *Nether Close,* 1607; *Neubolde broke* 1343 (c.1430) (*v.* **brōc**; Newbold lies one mile to the south-east); *Newball Fielde* 1607 (*v.* **feld**; one of the great fields of the village, lying towards Newbold); *Newe Bridge, Newebrig* 1607, *Newbrig leaes* 1607 (*v.* **leys**) (*v.* **brycg, bryggja**); *the New milfeild* 17, *The New mill field* 1709 (*v.* **myln, feld** and Mill Fd *supra*); *Newells* 1607 (poss. the surn. *Newell* in the possessive case; otherwise *v.* **nīwe, wella**); *Nordalehull* Edw 3 (c.1430) (*v.* **norð, dalr, hyll**); *le Northcrouft* 1338 (c.1430), *North Croft* Edw 3 (c.1430), *Northcroftwong* 1350 (*v.* **vangr**) (*v.* **norð, croft**); *ye Nooke furlonge* 1607, *Nooke leaes* 1607 (*v.* **leys**) (*v.* **nōk**); *Norden* 1607 (*v.* **norð, denu**, cf. Ogden in f.ns. (a) *supra*); *the old mylne* Edw 3 (c.1430) (*v.* **ald, myln**); *Olde hill furlonge* 1607 (*v.* **wald**); *Olde Syke* 1607 (*v.* **sík**); *Ouer Close* 1607 (*v.* **uferra**); *Oyster leyes, ~ ~ furlonge* 1607 (*v.* **eowestre, leys**, cf. Oyster Bridge, Ess 506); *Parsonage wonge* 1607 (*v.* **personage, vangr**); *ye Parsons Close* 1674; *Parsons hill wonge* 1607 (*v.* **persone, vangr**); *Partingrasse* 1607 (*v.* **parting, græs**; presum. alluding to grassland of which portions were allocated by lot); *Pasture side furlonge* 1607 (*v.* **pasture, sīde**); *Pauntonwong* 1350 (*v.* **vangr**; with the surn. *Paunton*); *Pease holme* 1607 (*v.* **pise, holmr**); *le personyssyk'* 1340 (c.1430) (*v.* **persone, sík**); *Pinfolde leaes* 1607 (*v.* **pynd-fald, leys**); *Ploumanmedwe* 1340 (c.1430) (*v.* **plouman, mǣd** (**mǣdwe** obl.sg.); the meadow was that in which the ploughmen pastured their oxen for the night during seasonal ploughing); *Porters-Close* 1709 (with the surn. *Porter*); *le Portgatte* 1340 (c.1430) (*v.* **port**[2], **gata**; the road to the market town of Melton Mowbray which lies five miles to the north); *the Ram meadow* 17, *~ ~ Midow* 1709 (*v.* **ramm**); *Rangelandes* 1607 (*v.* **wrangr, vrangr, land**); *Rapthorne* 1607 (*v.* **þorn**; the name is prob. a late garbled form of the following f.n.); *Rattisthorn* Edw 3 (c.1430) (*v.* **þorn**; as the specific, an owner with the surn. *Rat(t)*, an original by-name from the rat, is poss., but so is **rǣt**); *Rigatehull* Edw 3 (c.1430) (*v.* **ryge, gata, hyll**); *Ringesdonland* 1336 (c.1430) (*v.* **land**), *Ryngedoncroftes* 1350 (*v.* **croft**) (cf. *Ric' de Ringisdon* Edw 3 (c.1430); it is uncertain whether *Ringesdon* is an early name for Burrough Hill, referring to the circle (OE *hring*) of the Iron Age ramparts of the hill-fort, but its first el. appears likelier to be the OE pers.n. *Hring* in the possessive case (with OE *dūn* 'a hill')); *Roule Toppes* 1607 (*v.* **topp**; the first word is poss. a reduced 'rough hill' (*v.* **rūh**[1], **hyll**)); *Roundaboute* 1607 (*v.* **roundabout**; a name given to circular features such as a group of trees surrounded by cleared land, or less frequently, to a small piece of land completely surrounded by trees); *under ~ ~, Salters Gate* 1607 (*v.* **saltere, gata**; a salters' way (earlier *le Ferdgate, v.* Harby f.ns. (b)) which skirted the Hundred moot-site at Great Framlands and ran south from the ford at Melton Mowbray across the ridge of Salter's Hill *supra*); *ye vii headelandes* 1607 (*v.* **hēafod-land**); *John Sharpes close* 17; *Shelbreds* 1607 (*v.* **scofl-brǣdu**); *Shittendale Syke* 1607 (*v.* **shitten, sík**; with **dalr** or **deill**); *Shorte meere* 1607 (*v.* **(ge)mǣre**); *Sideholm* Edw 3 (c.1430) (*v.* **sīd, holmr**); *Smaledalehull* Edw 3 (c.1430) (*v.* **hyll**), *Small dales* 1607 (*v.* **smæl, smal(r)**; with **dalr** or **deill**); *Richard Stacy close* 17; *stagnum molendini* Edw 3 (c.1430) ('the mill pool'; with MLat *stagnum* 'a pool' and MLat *molendinum* 'a mill'); *Stanbriggegate* 1340 (c.1430) (*v.* **gata**), *Stanbriggemore* 1340 (c.1430), *Stanbrigg'mor* Edw 3 (c.1430) (*v.* **mōr**[1]) (*v.* Stonebridge Ford *supra*); *atte Standeluis* 1340 (c.1430) (*v.* **atte, stān-(ge)delf**); *Standerd hooke* 1607 (*v.* **standard, hōc**); *Steeperhill Meadow* 1742 (*v.* Steprill *supra*); *Steynwordhoc* Edw 3 (c.1430) (*v.* **stān, steinn, worð, hōc**; an original OE *stān-worð* 'stone-built enclosure', with a Scandinavianized first el., cf. *Stonewrth Hill* in Barkestone f.ns. (b)); *Stockewell* 1607 ('stream with a footbridge consisting of a tree-trunk', *v.* **stocc, wella**); *Strewhull* Edw

3 (c.1430) (v. **strēaw, hyll**); *Litle Teale acres* 1607 (v. **æcer**; with the surn. *Teal(e)*); *Thorpe woldes* 1607 (v. **wald**; lying towards Thorpe Satchville which adjoins to the north-west); *le Thwerbrech* 1340 (c.1430) (v. **þverr, brēc**); *Toughs little Closes* 1709 (with the surn. *Tough*); *Tunforlong'* 1340 (c.1430), Edw 3 (c.1430), *le Tunforlongesende* 1340 (c.1430) (v. **ende**) (v. **tūn, furlang**); *Twyforde fielde* 1607, *Twyford feild* 1697, *Twiford field* 1699, 1700, 1703, 1709 (v. **feld**; one of the great fields of the village, lying towards Twyford which adjoins to the south-west); *the Vicar of Somerbyes close* c.1600; *the vicaridge close* 1709; *Wadhou, Wadhowe* Edw 3 (c.1430), *Waddow* 1607 (v. **wād, haugr**); *the washpit hooke* 17 (v. **wæsce, pytt, hōc**; either referring to a sheep-dip or to a place for washing the wheels of farm carts); *Wauefenhull* Edw 3 (c.1430), *Waferne hill* 1607, *Waferne Botome* 1607 (v. **botm**), *Wauefenetunge* Edw 3 (c.1430) (v. **tunge**) ('the quaking bog', v. **wæfre, fenn**); *Welbechull'* 1340 (c.1430), *Wellebekhull* 1343 (c.1430), *Wellebechull* Edw 3 (c.1430) (v. **wella, bekkr, hyll**; cf. Welbeck, Nt 103), *Beneathe ~ ~, welhowse leaes* 1607 (v. **welhous, leys**); *Wellelane* 1336 (c.1430) (v. **wella, lane**); *Weteland'* Edw 3 (c.1430) (v. **hwǣte, land**); *Whitlondis* 1340 (c.1430), *Whiteland* Edw 3 (c.1430) (v. **hwīt, land**; presum. alluding to the colour of the soil); *apud le Whiteston* 1340 (c.1430) (with MLat *apud* 'at, by'), *Whitston Leaes, White Stone ~* 1607, *Whitstons lease* 17, *Whitestone Leyes* 1709 (v. **leys**); ostensibly 'the white stone' (v. **hwīt, stān**) rather than 'whetstone' (v. **hwēt-stān**), but v. Whetstones Cl, ~ Mdw in f.ns. (a) *supra* and *Whitestone Furlong* in Wycomb and Chadwell f.ns. (b)); *Willows* 1736 (v. **wilig**); *Windmill* 1607 (v. **wind-mylne**); *Wodegate* Edw 3 (c.1430), *Woodgate* 1607 (v. **wudu, gata**).

3. LEESTHORPE

Leesthorpe (with Pickwell *infra*) is a detached part of Gartree Hundred.

Lvvestorp 1086 DB, *Luvestorp'* 1214 Cur, *Luuestorp'* 1258 Abbr (p)
Lucerthorp c.1130 LeicSurv, *Lichestorp* 1243 Fees
Leuestorp' e.13 (1404) *Laz*, *Levestorp'* 1276 RH, *Leuesthorp'* e.13, c.1240 Berkeley *et passim* to 1347 Cl, 1392 Pat, *Leuesthorpe* p.1250 (1404) *Laz*, 1321 (1449) *WoCart*, *Levesthorp(e)* 1294 Coram (p), 1361 Ipm *et passim* to 1428 FA, *Leuisthorp(e)* p.1250 (1404) *Laz*, c.1270 *RTemple* (p) *et passim* to 1337 Nichols, 1404 *Laz*
Livestorp' 1213 Abbr, 1214 Cur *et passim* to m.13 (1404) *Laz*, *Liuesthorp'* 1235 (1404), m.13 (1404) *ib*, *Livesthorp* 1240 Fine, 1295 OSut (p), *Lyvestorp* 1276 RH, *Lyvesthorp* 1273 Fine (p), 1279, 1304 Banco, *Lyuesthorp(e)* 1326 Cl, 1391 Pat, 1404 *Laz*, *Liuistorp* Hy 3 Crox, *Lyuisthorpe* 1326 Ipm, *Lyvysthorp* 1318 Inqaqd

Lifesthorp c.1235 (1404) *Laz*
Liuethorp c.1225 AAS, 1200 × 40 Rental, *Leuithorp* c.1275 *RTemple*
  (p), 1299 Ipm, *Levithorp* 1301 Cl
Lyestorp 1276 RH, *Lysthorpe* 1534 *RTemple*, 1537 Cl
Leisthorp(e) 1366 Banco, 1535 VE, 1555 Pat, 1557 Cl, *Leysthorp(e)*
  1498 Banco, 1499 Brase *et passim* to 1535 VE, 1557 Pat
Lesthorp(e) 1381 SR (p), 1415 Cl, 1535 VE, 1537 MinAccts,
  Lesethorpe 1492 Cl, 1606 *Terrier*, *Lesethorpp'* 1536 *Braye*
Leesthorp(e) 1422 Cl, 1506 Banco *et passim* to 1610 Speed *et freq*

'Lēof's outlying farmstead', *v*. **þorp**. According to Redin (14), there is no absolutely certain instance of the OE pers.n. *Lēof* on independent record. It does occur, however, in the p.n. Lewsey (*v*. BdHu 155) and is a strong variant of the recorded *Lēofa*. In this Leics. instance, it may have been used as a short form of OE *Lēofhēah*, as the spellings *Lucerthorp* and *Lichestorp'* suggest (cf. *Leofus* who is alternatively recorded with the dithematic pers.n. *Leofhēah*, *v*. Redin 15).

Pickwell and Leesthorpe are assessed together in DB and the two places are juxtaposed in this order in a range of medieval records. This indicates that originally Leesthorpe was an outlying dependent of Pickwell.

From the late 15th century, Leesthorpe is recorded only as pasture, following the depopulation of the township for sheep-farming: *pastura voc' Lesethorpe* 1492 Cl, ~ ~ *Lysthorpe* 1537 ib, ~ ~ *Leisthorpe* 1552 Pat, *Leisthorpe Pasture* 1557 Nichols, *v*. **pasture**.

ASH POLE SPINNEY, *v*. **æsc**, **pāl**, cf. Ash Pole Spinney in Cosby, Guthlaxton Hundred. BRICKFIELD FM (BRICKFIELD HO. 2½"). BROCKER HO., *Brochoh* c. 1235 (1404) *Laz*, *v*. **brōc**, **hōh**; the house is *Pickwell Lodge* 1824 O, *v*. **loge**. THE GRANGE, 1877 White, *Leesthorpe Grange* 1877 ib, *v*. **grange**. THE HALL is *Leesthorp(e) Hall* 1803 Nichols, 1846, 1863, 1877 White, 1925 Kelly, *v*. **hall**. LEESTHORPE HILL. LEESTHORPE HO. LEESTHORPE LODGE (lost), *Leesthorpe Lodge* 1616 *Terrier*, *v*. **loge**. LOWER LEESTHORPE.

FIELD-NAMES

Forms dated e.13 (1404), c.1235 (1404), m.13 (1404) and p.1250 (1404) are *Laz*; 1327 and 1337 are Nichols; 1334 are AD.

(b) *Benehill* e.13 (1404), m.13 (1404) (*v.* **bēan, hyll**); *Depedale* e.13 (1404), m.13 (1404) (*v.* **dēop, dalr**); *Erlesdole* 1327, 1334, 1337, *Erlisdole* 1337 (*v.* **eorl, dāl**); *foredoleford* e.13 (1404), m.13 (1404) (*v.* **fore, dāl, ford**); *la gyhereland* m.13 (1404) (*v.* **land**; poss. with **geiri**, but more forms are needed); *holewong* e.13 (1404), m.13 (1404) (*v.* **hol²**, **holr, vangr**); *litelho* e.13 (1404), m.13 (1404) (*v.* **lȳtel, hōh**); *longepoleslade* e.13 (1404), m.13 (1404) (*v.* **lang¹, pōl¹, slæd**); *Medlisdale* m.13 (1404) (*v.* **middes, middel, meðal, dalr**; cf. Middlesdale in Belvoir and *Middles dale* in Pickwell f.ns. (b)); *la mire* e.13 (1404), m.13 (1404) (*v.* **mȳrr**); *molendinum de Torp'* p.1250 (1404) (with MLat *molendinum* 'a mill'); *Northgore* e.13 (1404), m.13 (1404) (*v.* **norð, gāra**); *Opol* m.13 (1404) (*v.* **á, pōl¹**); *thothornes* e.13 (1404), m.13 (1404) (*v.* **twēgen, tū, þorn**; cf. *tuotherne in* Muston f.ns. (b)); *Walsemorland* e.13 (1404), m.13 (1404) (*v.* **wælisc, walh, mōr¹, land** and *walsemoresedis* in Burton Lazars f.ns. (b)); *le Wellehill'* m.13 (1404) (*v.* **wella, hyll**); *Weragland* m.13 (1404) (*v.* **land**; since this is prob. a cartulary miscopying, the first el. could represent either **wrang, vrangr** or the Scand pers.n. *Wraggi* (ODan *Wraghi*)); *Wihledale* c.1235 (1404) (*v.* **wilig, dalr**).

4. PICKWELL

Pickwell (with Leesthorpe *supra*) is a detached part of Gartree Hundred.

Picheuuelle, Pichewelle 1086 DB, *Pichewell'* e.13 (1404), c.1235 (1404), m.13 (1404) *Laz, Pichewella* e.13 (1404) *ib, Picheuell'* m.13 (1404) *ib*
Pychauilla c.1190 *MiD*
Picawella l.12 (1404) *Laz* bis
Picwell' c.1130 LeicSurv, 1214 Cur, 1220 *Hazlerigg et freq* to 1301 Ipm, 1316 FA *et passim* to 1373 Banco, 1404 *Laz, Picwelle* 1221 Fine, 1209 × 35 RHug *et passim* to 1328 Pat, 1334 AD, *Picuuella* e.13 (1404) *Laz* (p)
Pikewell' 1202 P, 1213 Abbr *et freq* to c.1260 Nichols, *Pikewella* e.13 (1404) *Laz*, 1214 Cur *et passim* to Hy 3 RBE, 1276 RH, *Pikewelle* 1209 × 35 RHug, m.13 (1404) *Laz, Pykewell'* 1257 *Rut*, 1257 Ch *et freq* to 1304 Banco, 1307 Abbr *et passim* to 1532 Fine, 1535 VE
Pickewell 1295 Cl, 1303 Ipm, 1535 VE, *Pyckewell* 1535 ib
Pikwell' 1248 RGros, 1259 Cl *et passim* to 1391 Pat, 1428 AAS, *Pykwell'* m.13 (1404) *Laz*, 1276 RH *et freq* to 1412 PRep, 1428 FA *et passim* to 1532 Ipm, 1536 *Braye*
Pickwell 1535 VE, 1575 LEpis *et freq*, (~ *Magna* 1585 LibCl)

'The spring or stream at the peak(s)', *v.* **pīc, wella**. The village lies at the head of a stream and beneath conical hills to the south and east. In relation to the unique form *Pickwell Magna* 1585, no Pickwell Parva is recorded.

ALL SAINTS' CHURCH, *Church (All Saints)* 1846, 1863, 1877 White; it is earlier recorded as *ecclesiam de Pikewella* a.1219 RHug, *ecclesie de Picwelle* 1220 MHW, 1328 *Pat*, *ecclesiam de Pikwell* 1248 RGros, *ecclesie de Pyckwell* 1559 *Pat*. Note also *the Churchyard* 1606, 1625, 1694 *Terrier, v.* **chirche-ȝeard**. KYTE HILL (local), *Kitehill* 1606 *Terrier*, 1616 *Plan*, 1625 *Terrier, v.* **cȳta**. MANOR HO., *Manor House* 1846, 1863, 1877 White, *The Manor* 1925 Kelly, cf. *Manor Farm* 1971 *Surv, v.* **maner**. OUNDLE HO., *Oundel house* 1925 Kelly, *Little ~*, *Oundle* 1971 *Surv*. PICKWELL GRANGE, *v.* **grange**. PICKWELL LODGE FM. THE RECTORY, 1925 Kelly; it is *the Parsonage House* 1606, 1625 *Terrier, the Parsonage* 1616 *Plan, v.* **personage**. Note also *the Parsonage Yard* 1674, 1679 *Terrier*. STONEFIELD HO. (local), *Stonefield house* 1925 Kelly. STONEPIT TERRACE, cf. *the Stonepitts* 1606 *Terrier*, *stone pits* 1625 *ib, v.* **stān-pytt, terrace**. WHITE HORSE (P.H.) (lost), *White Horse* 1846, 1863, 1877 White, 1925 Kelly.

FIELD-NAMES

Undated forms in (a) are 1765 *Surv*; those dated l.18 and 1822 are *Terrier*; 1971 are *Surv*. Forms throughout dated 1381 are SR; 1606, 1625, 1674, 1679 and 1694 are *Terrier*; 1615 and 1630 are Ipm; 1616 are *Plan*; 1726 are Nichols; 1744 are *Lease*.

(a) the Allotment 1971 (*v.* **allotment**); Barwells Cl (with the surn. *Barwell* of a family originating in the Leics. village of this name, 23 miles to the south-west); Baxters Cl (with the surn. *Baxter*); Brigg Leys l.18, Bridge Leys Cl 1822 (*bridgeleases* 1606, *Brigg lees* 1674, *~ leas* 1679, *~ ley(e)s* 1690, 1694, *Brigge Lees* 1726, *v.* **brycg, bryggja; leys**); Broad Mdw 1765, 1971; Browns Cl (with the surn. *Brown*); Bullock Yard (*v.* **bulluc, geard**); Bull Piece (*v.* **bula, pece**); Cold Overton Cl, Cold Overton Mdw 1971 (Cold Overton adjoins to the south-east); Farr Hill Cl, Far Hill Mdw 1765, Far Hill 1971; the Flat 1971 (*v.* **flat**); Garden Fd 1971; Great Ground Hill, Great Ground Mdw, Great Ground Seeds (*v.* **sǣd**; in f.ns., used of areas of sown grass) 1971 (*v.* **grēat, grund**); Hall Hill Cl (*v.* **hall**); Handen (*the Hounden* 1616, *v.* **hund, denu**); the Home Cl l.18, 1822 (1694, *v.* **home**); Ladys Mdw (*v.* **lavedi**; such names usually allude either to dedication to the Blessed Virgin or to a female proprietor or to a dowager or to the lady of the manor, *v.* 6 Acre Cl *infra*);

Lambing Mdw 1971 (*v.* **lambing**); Langhill Fd l.18 (*Langehylles* 1606, *Langhill* 1606, 1625, *~ feild(e)* 1606, 1615, 1616, 1625, 1630, *~ field* 1726, *v.* **lang**[1], **hyll, feld**; one of the great fields of the village); Little Brook Hill (*Brockhill* 1615, 1616, *v.* **brōc, hyll**); Great Langdale Ground (*v.* **grund**), Great Langdale Mdw (*v.* **lang**[1], **dalr**); Mill Dam Cl (*Milnedam* 1606, *Mildam* 1625, *v.* **myln, damme**); Mill Fd 1765 *Surv*, 1846, 1863, 1877 White, 1971, Mill Field Great Cl, Mill Field Mdw (*Mill Feild(e)* 1616, 1630); Mr Edward Muxloes Farm (*v.* **ferme**); New Cl (1694); the North Brook Fd (1744, *North brooke* 1606, *Northbrook feild* 1606, 1615, 1625, *v.* **norð, brōc, feld**; one of the great fields of the village); Pullens Little Pasture, Pullens Pasture Mdw (with the surn. *Pullen*); Great Red Earth (*v.* **rēad, eorðe**; alluding to the colour of the soil); Robin i'the Clay 1765, *~* in the Clay 1971 (*Robin in the Clay* 1606, 1625, *Robin yth Claye* 1616, *v.* **clǣg**), Little Robin Holme l.18 (*Robynholme* 1615, *Robin home or the parsons close* 1625, *Robbenholme* 1630, *Little Robin holme* 1616, *Little Robin home* 1625, *Little Robbinholme* 1630, *Little Robin Holm* 1726, cf. *Great Robin holme* 1616, *v.* **holmr**) (either with the pers.n. *Robin* (a diminutive of *Rob* (Robert)) or with its ME surn. reflex; however, more specifically, the reference may be to *Robin Goodfellow*, the drudging goblin, *v.* Goodfellow's Spring in neighbouring Somerby f.ns. (a) and cf. Robin-a-Tiptoe Hill in Tilton, East Goscote Hundred); the Ryce Fd l.18 (*the rise feild* 1606, 1625, *v.* **hrīs, feld**; one of the great fields of the village); Sandholms 1765, Bottom, Top Sandholmes 1971 (*Sandholmes* 1606, 1630, *Sands-holmes* 1616, *sandhomes* 1625, *v.* **sand, sandr, holmr**); 6 Acre Cl or Ladys Mdw (*v.* **æcer** and Ladys Mdw *supra*); Great Stain Hill (*Stenhill* 1630, *v.* **steinn** and *at the great stone*, *infra*); Stephenson's Mdws 1846, 1863, 1877 White; Great Styegate Cl 1765, Big, Little Stygot 1971 (*Stygate* 1679, 1690, *Great Stygate* 1694, *Styegate Feild(e)* 1616, 1630, *Stigate ground* 1674 (*v.* **grund**), *v.* **sty-gate** 'a narrow road' (*v.* **stīg, gata**), a Scandinavianized version of ME *sty-way*); the Wad Cl 1822 (*v.* **wād**).

(b) Ash Close 1616 (*v.* **æsc**); Ashwell sicke 1606, 1625 (*v.* **æsc, wella, sík**); Bartles Close 1616 (with the surn. *Bartle* (from *Bartelmew* (Bartholomew)); *the Brake* 1606 (*v.* **brǣc**[1]); *over Borrough way* 1606, *~ Burrough ~* 1625 (*v.* **ofer**[3]; a furlong above the road to Burrough on the Hill); *Breach Sike* 1616 (*v.* **brēc, sík**); Brewins Close 1616, 1630 (with the surn. *Brewin*); *Brickwoods Close* 1616, 1630 (the property of *Thomas Brickwood* 1616, 1625); *against the Bridge* 1606, 1625 (a furlong so called), *Brigg Close* 1616 (*v.* **brycg, bryggja**); *Broadacre* 1606, 1625 (*v.* **brād, æcer**); *Brockhill Sike* 1616 (*v.* **sík** and Little Brook Hill *supra*); *the Brooke* 1606, 1625 (*v.* **brōc**); *Broom(m)an Hill* 1616, 1630 (with the surn. *Brooman*, a reflex of the OE pers.n. *Brūnmann*); *George Brownes yard end* 1606, 1625 (*v.* **geard, ende**); *the Bull lee* 1625 (*v.* **bula, ley**); *Cants Close* 1616, 1630 (cf. *Robert Cante* 1616, *~ Kant* 1625 of Pickwell); *the Causey* 1606, *the Cawsey* 1625 (*v.* **caucie**); *Robert Clays homestead* 1674 (*v.* **hām-stede**); *Coldhill* 1606, 1625 (*v.* **cald, hyll**); *the Common Pasture* 1606, 1625 (*v.* **commun, pasture**); *Cottiers Close* 1616, *Cothers ~* 1630 (*v.* **cottere** and *Hoback(e)s*, *infra*); *Cowe Feilde* 1616, *Cow feild* 1630 (*v.* **cū, feld**); *Cros(s)es High meadow* 1616, 1630 (*v.* **hēah**[1] and cf. *Gabriel Crosse* 1625); *Dalby Bridge* 1606, 1625, *Dalby bridge leases* 1606, *Dalby leases* 1625 (*v.* **leys**) (Little Dalby adjoins to the north-west; but note also *James Dalby* 1606 of Pickwell, whose surn. may be compounded in the last f.n.); *Deadmans graue*

1616, *at the grave* 1606, 1625 (*v.* **dede-man, græf**; at the township's boundary and evidently the site of discovered early burials); *Deep(e)dale* 1606, 1625 (*v.* **dēop, dalr** and Debdale Spinney in Little Dalby which is named from the same valley); *Dinghill Close* 1630, *Steeles* ~ ~, *Dinghillwell Close* 1616, *Dingwel Close* 1674, 1679 (cf. *Stephen Steele* 1616, *George Steele* 1625) (*v.* **Dinghill** in Somerby f.ns. (b) for earlier forms; it is uncertain whether the **wella** 'stream' of some of the Pickwell forms refers to an actual watercourse or is simply a garbled *hill*); (*Mr*) *Dunmores Close* 1674; *Esses* 1606, 1625, *Drye Esse* 1616 (*v.* **drȳge**) (*v.* **æsc**; *Fetherbedes* 1606, 1625 (*v.* **feather-bed**, used in f.ns. of spongy ground or of soft, yielding areas of moorland peat-moss); *Frostlandes* 1606 (*v.* **forst, land**; presum. describing selions where frost remained long, but ON **froskr** 'a frog' may also be thought of as the first el.); *Fullilhill* 1606 (*v.* **fūl, wella, hyll**); *the Great close* 1674, 1679, *the Great close or Mill close* 1694; *at the great stone* 1606, 1625, *Great ston Close* 1616, *Great Stonneclose* 1630 (*v.* **stān**; it is uncertain whether these forms relate to Great Stain Hill *supra*); *Greavesfeild* 1615 (*v.* **feld**; poss. with the surn. *Greaves*, but more likely to belong with *Grives, infra*); *the greene swore* 1625 (*v.* **greensward**); (*on top of*) *Grives* 1606, 1625, *Grives banke* 1616 (*v.* **banke**), *Grives close* 1616, *Grivesford* 1606, *Grives foard* 1625 (*v.* **ford**), *Grives hole* 1616, 1630 (*v.* **hol**[1]), *Grives leases* 1606, ~ *leyes* 1616 (*v.* **leys**), *over Grives way* 1625 (*v.* **ofer**[3], **weg**; a furlong so called) (*v.* **gryfja** 'a pit, a hole'; presum. referring to small quarries for stone); *the Hades* 1606, 1625 (*v.* **hēafod**; in Langhill Fd); (*the*) *Hall close* 1616, 1630 (*v.* **hall**); *Highbrinke hole* 1606, 1625 (*v.* **hēah**[1], **brink, hol**[1]); *the High meddow* 1606, 1625, *High meadow Close* 1616, 1630, *High meadow gate* 1616 (*v.* **gata**) (*v.* **hēah**[1], **mǣd** (**mǣdwe** obl.sg.)); *the High street* 1625 (*v.* **hēah**[1], **strǣt**); *the Highway* 1625 (*v.* **hēah-weg**); *the other* ~, *Hoback(e)s* 1606, 1625, *Holbeck Close al's Cottiers Close* 1616, *Hobecks or Cothers close* 1630, *Holbeck Streame* 1616 (*v.* **strēam**) (*v.* **hol**[2], **holr, bekkr** and *Cottiers Close, supra*); *the Homestead* 1694 (*v.* **hām-stede**; prob. that of *the Parsonage House, v.* The Rectory *supra*); *Honyacres* 1606, 1625 (*v.* **hunig, æcer**; either referring to a place where honey was found or alluding to sticky soil or even to 'sweet land'); *Mrs Hudsons ground* 1674 (*v.* **grund**); *the Hull wonges* 1625 (*v.* **hyll, vangr**); *Keyes close* 1690 (with the surn. *Keyes*); *Kingesbush* 1606, *Kings bush* 1625 (*v.* **busc** prob. with the surn. *King*, but cf. *kyngeswellhull* in Burrough on the Hill f.ns. (b)); *on Kirkegate* 1606, 1625, *Beneath on Kirkegate* 1606 (*v.* **kirkja, gata**; furlongs so called); *Kirks Close* 1616 (in the possession of *Lawrence Kirke* 1616); *Langhillsicke* 1606, *Langhill Sike* 1616 (*v.* **sík** and Langhill Fd *supra*); *Lees close* 1606, 1625, *Leighs* ~ 1616, 1630 (in the possession of *George Leigh* and *Symon Leigh* 1616); *Leesthorpe gate* 1616 (*v.* **gata**), *Leesthorpe Groundes* 1616 (*v.* **grund**), *Leesthorpe hedge* 1606, 1625 (*v.* **hecg**; a boundary hedge) (Leesthorpe adjoins to the north); *Lincolne gate* 1606, 1616 (*v.* **gata**; the road to Lincoln), *Lincolne Hades* 1625 (*v.* **hēafod**; headlands abutting the road to Lincoln); *Little Dolby forde* 1616 (*v.* **ford**; Little Dalby adjoins to the north-west); *Longhoe* 1606, 1625 (*v.* **lang**[1], **hōh**); *Longlandes* 1606, 1625, *Longland leases* 1606, 1625, ~ *leys* 1615 (*v.* **leys**) (*v.* **lang**[1], **land**); *the Marre* 1606, 1625, *the Marr Close* 1616, *Marclose* 1630, (*the*) *Mar(r) Lane* 1674, 1679, 1694 (*v.* **marr**[1]); *Meddow gate* 1606, 1625 (*v.* **mǣd** (**mǣdwe** obl.sg.), **gata** and *High meadow gate, supra*); *Melton Way* 1606, 1625 (*v.* **weg**; the road to Melton Mowbray which lies to the north-west);

Middles dale 1606, *Middle* ~ 1625 (*v.* **middes, middel, dalr**; cf. Middlesdale in Belvoir and *Medlisdale* in Leesthorpe f.ns. (b)); *the Middle ford* 1606, *Middle foard* 1625 (*v.* **middel, ford**); *the Middle furlong* 1625 (i.e. of the Ryce Fd); *Mill Close* 1694, (*the*) *Milne Hill* 1606, 1625, *Mill-hill Close* 1616 (*v.* **myln**); *le Mores* 1615, *the Moores* 1616, 1630, *the Middle more* 1606 (*v.* **mōr**[1]); *Mussicke* 1606, 1625 (*v.* *Mussike* in Somerby f.ns. (b)); (*the*) *Nether ford* 1606, ~ *foard* 1625 (*v.* **ford**); *New Meadow* 1616, 1630; *Mr Nixes ground* 1694 (*v.* **grund**); *the North Close* 1690; *Opoole* 1606, *Opole* 1625 (*v.* *Opol* in Leesthorpe f.ns. (b)); *Orton meare* 1625 (*v.* **(ge)mǣre**; Cold Overton adjoins to the south-east); *the close of Faustin Paddy* 1606, *Paddies close* 1625 (*Faustin Paddy* is cited 1606, 1625); *the Parsonage great close* 1674; *the Parsons close* 1625 (*v.* **persone**); *Peaselands* 1606, 1625 (*v.* **pise, land**); *the pittes* 1606 (*v.* **pytt**); *Prestlandes* 1625 (*v.* **prēost, land**); *the Rise Close* 1616 (*v.* **hrīs**); *Risegores* 1606, *Rosegores* 1625 (*v.* **hrīs, gāra**); *Rosgalls* 1615 (this may belong with the preceding f.n., otherwise, *v.* **hross, galla**); *the Sandpittes* 1625 (*v.* **sand-pytt**); *le Save acres* 1615, *Nether, Upper Savacres* 1606, 1625 (*v.* **sef, æcer** and *Seaveacres* in Little Dalby f.ns. (b)); *Sharp(e)s Close* 1616, 1630 (the property of *Ruben Sharpe* 1625); *the Sicke* 1606 (*v.* **sīk**); *Sleight(e)s* 1606, 1625, *Sleight leases* 1606, 1625 (*v.* **leys**) (*v.* **slétta**); (*Richard*) *Smithes close* 1606, 1625, *Smiths* ~ 1625, 1726; *Somerby way* 1606, 1625 (*v.* **weg**; the road to adjoining Somerby); *Springwells* 1606, 1625, 1726, *Springwell Close* 1616, 1630 (*v.* **spring**[1], **wella**); *Stambardes* 1606, 1625 (*v.* **standard**); *Steele(s) close* 1616, 1630 (cf. *Stephen Steele* 1616, *George Steele* 1625), *the yard of George Steile* 1606 (*v.* **geard**); *Stenhill Close* 1616 (*v.* Great Stain Hill *supra*); *Stockins* 1616 (*v.* **stoccing**); *Stockhill* 1606, 1625 (*v.* **stocc, hyll**); *Stiletoppe* 1606, *Styletop* 1625 (*v.* **topp**; prob. with **stīg** rather than with **stigel** as the specific, otherwise with a reduced **stig, hyll**); (*the*) *Swans Nest* 1606, 1616, 1625 (*v.* **swan**[1], **nest**); *Swinedale* 1606, 1625 (*v.* **swīn, svín, dalr**); *Thonborrough* 1606, *Thornborowe* 1615, *Thunborrow* 1625 (*v.* **þorn, berg** and the earlier *Thyrneberow* in Somerby f.ns. (b)); *Thorny wong(e)* 1606, 1625 (*v.* **þornig, vangr**); *the mid tofthe* 1625 (*v.* **midd, toft**); *Townes end* 1625, *Town(e) end close* 1616, 1630 (*v.* **tūn, ende**); *the Towne streete* 1606 (*v.* **tūn, strǣt**); *twene dikes* 1625 (*v.* **betwēonan, dík**); *twene gates* 1625, *twenegate leases* 1606 (*v.* **leys**) (*v.* **betwēonan, gata**); *twene sickes* 1606, 1625 (*v.* **betwēonan, sīk**); *the Upper furlong* 1625 (i.e. of the Ryce Fd); (*Willm.*) *Walkers headland* 1606, 1625 (*v.* **hēafod-land**); (*the*) *neates watering* 1606, *Neates wattring* 1625 (*v.* **nēat**), *the neather wattring* 1625 (*v.* **neoðera**) (*v.* **wateryng**); *atte Welle* 1381 (p) (*v.* **atte, wella**); *Short(e)whytes* 1606, 1625, *Long* ~ 1625 (*v.* **hwīt**; poss. referring to the colour of the soil, but in eModE, *white* 'infertile' is used in contrast to *black* 'fertile'); *Willow Doles* 1616 (*v.* **wilig, dāl**); *Wronges* 1606, 1625 (*v.* **wrang, vrangr**); *Yates Close* 1616 (with the surn. *Yates*).

Sproxton

1. SPROXTON

Sprotone 1086 DB

Sproxcheston c. 1130 LeicSurv, *Sprokeston'* 1183 P (p), e.13 (1404)
   Laz (p), 1236 Fees (p), *Sprokestona* 1197 (e.14) RydCart (p),
   Sprokestun e.13(1404) *Laz* (p)

Sproxton(') 1166 P (p), 1190 ib (p), 1200 Cur (p) *et passim* to 1210
   FF, 1215 Cur *et freq*, (~ *Boby* 1242 Fees), (~ *Paynell* 1534 Fine,
   ~ *Painell* 1548 ib), *Sproxtona* 1147 BM, 1155 × 58 (1329) Ch (p),
   1.13 *CRCart* (p), *Sproxtone* 1209 × 19 RHug, 1221 Cur (p), 1232
   RHug, *Sproxtuna* 1209 × 19 ib, *Sproxtun'* 1226 Cur (p), 1236
   Fees

Sprochton' 1184 P (p), 1185 ib (p), *Sprocton* 1202 ChancR (p)

Sprostona c.1154 *Rut*, *Sprouston'* 1201 Cur (p), *Sprowston* 1523 Ipm

Sprauston 1549 *Pat*, *Sprawston* 1603 Fine

Sprawson 1539 *Rut*, *Sproson* 1612 *Terrier*

This p.n. also occurs in the North Riding of Yorkshire. Ekwall
(DEPN) interprets the first el. in both names as a Scand pers.n. *Sprok*
and notes that 'OSw *Sprok* seems to occur'. Smith (YN 70), following
Ekwall's suggestion, draws attention to *Sproxmire* (13th cent.) in
Crakehall (YN) and *Sproxstatha* (1376) recorded by Lundgren-Brate,
which also appear to contain the OSw pers.n. *Sprok* and associates the
pers.n. with OFris, LGerm *sprock* 'brittle'. However, Fellows-Jensen
(SSNEM 187) asserts that 'there is no evidence for the pers.n. *Sprok* in
Scandinavia' and suggests that it seems more satisfactory to take the first
el. of both p.ns. as an unrecorded ODan **sprogh* 'brushwood, twigs',
cognate with the independently unrecorded OE **spræg* which occurs in
several p.ns. in the south of England, especially in Devon and Wiltshire
(*v.* Elements *s.v.*). Formally, the Scand *Sprógr*, an original by-name (cf.
OIcel *spróga* 'to amble (of a horse)'), also deserves consideration as the
first el. of the p.ns. However, it only occurs as the name of a horse in
Sturlunga saga but is not recorded in Scandinavia as a pers.n. or as a by-
name (*v.* SPNLY 261).

245

Sproxton in Leics. occupies a favourable site on a south-west-facing hillside towards the head of a tributary valley of that of R. Eye. It was without doubt a major pre-Scandinavian English settlement with its own *tōt-hyll* 'look-out hill' and *stōw* 'place of assembly' (*v. Toote hill* and *the Stooe* in f.ns. (b) *infra*). In the churchyard of St Bartholomew's Church is a fine Anglo-Saxon standing cross, the only complete example in the county. A mile and a half to the south-west on R. Eye itself lies Coston, another former English settlement occupying a similar favourable site and restyled with the name of a Scandinavian overlord, probably *Kátr*. Both settlements, with surrounding villages with names in *bȳ* and *þorp*, appear to be of the Grimston-hybrid type, i.e. former Anglo-Saxon villages/estate centres appropriated by Scandinavians at the disbanding of the Great Army in 877 and renamed to particularize their new Scandinavian owners.

The preponderant spellings for Sproxton with genitival *s* point to a pers.n. in the possessive case as the first el. rather than to a substantive. It may also be argued that a Scandinavian word for 'brushwood, twigs' being used in renaming a major Anglo-Saxon settlement is scarcely conceivable. We may think, then, of Sproxton as probably 'Sprok's village, estate', *v. tūn*. 'Sprógr's village, estate' cannot be discounted, but is much less convincing. It is worth noting that the 16th and 17th cent. forms *Sprawson* and *Sproson* show typical Leics. loss of *t* from the group *-ston* in the 16th cent. and later.

Hugo de Boby a.1250 *CroxR* held the manor in the first half of the 13th cent., while *Thomas Paynell* held land in Sproxton in 1534 Fine.

CROWN (P.H.), *Crown* 1863 White, 1925 Kelly, *Crown Inn* 1877 White. THE DRIFT, *the Drift Road leading from Stamford to Newark upon Trent* 1772 *EnclA, v.* **drift**; otherwise known as Sewstern Lane. MANOR HO., *v.* **maner**. ST BARTHOLOMEW'S CHURCH, *Church (St Bartholomew)* 1846, 1863, 1877 White, 1925 Kelly; it is earlier recorded as *ecclesia de Sproxtuna* a.1219 RHug, *ecclesie de Sproxton* 1220 MHW, 1238, 1241, 1245 RGros, 1310 *Pat, ecclesia parochiali de Sprauston* 1549 *ib, the Church* 1708 (18) *Terrier*, 1772 *EnclA*. Note also *the Church(e) yeard* 1601, 1605, 1612 *Terrier, (the) Church Yard* 1703, 1708, 1708 (18) *ib*, 1772 *EnclA, v.* **chirche-ȝeard**. SPROXTON HEATH GORSE, 1806 Map, 1824 O, *the Heath* 1772 *EnclA, v.* **hǣð, gorst**. SPROXTON LODGE. SPROXTON THORNS, 1806 Map, 1824 O, *v.* **þorn**. THREE HORSESHOES (P.H.) (lost), *Three Horse Shoes* 1846, 1863, 1877 White, *Three Horseshoes* 1925 Kelly. THE VICARAGE, 1925 Kelly; it is *the Vicarage*

House 1605, 1612, 1625, 1708, 1708 (18), 1821 *Terrier*, *v.* **vikerage**.
Note also *the Vicarage Yard* 1708 (18) *ib* and *The Homestall* 1708, 1708
(18) *ib*, i.e. that of *the Vicarage House*, *v.* **hām-stall**.

FIELD-NAMES

Undated forms in (a) are 1772 *EnclA*. Forms throughout dated l.12 and
13 are Nichols; 1601, 1605, 1612, 1625, 1703, 1706, 1708, 1708 (18)
and 1712 are *Terrier*; 1602 and 1608 are *Rut*; 1664 and c.1665 are
Rental.

(a) the Church Fd (one of the great fields of the village, earlier the *Northe Feyld*
1601, *the North feild* 1602, 1605, 1612, ~ ~ *Field* 1703, 1706, 1708, 1708 (18), 1712,
v. **norð, feld**); the Fish Pool Cl (*Fishpoole* 1664, c.1665, 1708, *Fish pool* 1708 (18),
v. **fisc, pōl**[1]); Goldcroft (1664, 1708, 1708 (18), *Gould Croft* c.1665, *v.* **croft**; the first
el. could be the surn. *Gold* or *golde* 'a marigold' or **gold** 'golden-hued', presum. with
reference to the colour of flowers); the Kilne Cl (*v.* **cyln**); the Middle Fd (1703, 1706,
1708, 1708 (18), 1712, *the Middle feild* 1602, 1605, 1612, 1625, *v.* **middel, feld**; one
of the great fields of the village); a certain ancient Inclosure... called the Old Walls
(*the Ould Walls* 1602, *Ould Wales* 1664, c.1665, *the Old Walls* 1708, 1708 (18), *v.*
ald, wall); the Pasture (*the Common Pasture* 1708, 1708 (18), *v.* **commun, pasture**);
the Town Green (*the Green* 1708, 1708 (18), cf. *the Green close or Nether close*
1602, *v.* **tūn, grēne**[2]); Underhill Fd.

(b) *Joseph Ascouch his house & hom(e)steed(e)* 1664, c.1665 (*v.* **hām-stede**; the
form of the surn. is normally *Ascough*); *Ashe Close* 1608 (*v.* **æsc**); *Barrow Hill* 1712
(*v.* **berg**); *Batel Close forland* 1712 (*v.* **furlang**; with the surn. *Battel*, *v.* Reaney *s.n.*);
the Becke's Breach 1712 (*v.* **bekkr, brēc**); *Berrill Bridge* 1712 (the first word in
origin is prob. 'barley hill', *v.* **bere, hyll**); *Blackamiles* 1712 (*v.* **blæc, mylde**); *The
Breach* 1712 (*v.* **brēc**); *John Bullivant's Farm* 1712 (*v.* **ferme**); *Burntlands* 1712 (*v.*
brende[2], **brente, land**; poss. land cleared by burning in preparation for tillage);
Canter's Piece 1712 (*v.* **pece**; with the surn. *Canter*); *Church Lane End Wong* 1712
(*v.* **lane-ende, vangr**), *the Church pece* 1601, 1605, 1612, ~ ~ *peece* 1625, ~ ~ *piece*
1706 (*v.* **pece**) (with reference to St Bartholomew's Church *supra*); *Clarke Closse*
1664, ~ *close* c.1665 (with the surn. *Clarke*); *Clendalls* 1712 (*v.* **clǣne, deill**); *Coms
or Coms Wong* 1712 (*v.* **vangr**; either with the surn. *Combe(s)*/*Coom* (*v.* Reaney *s.n.*)
or **cumb** from which the surn. derives); (*the*) *Crabtre(e) pece* 1601, 1605, 1612,
Crabtree peece 1625 (*v.* **pece**), (*at*) *the Crabtree* 1703, 1706, 1708, 1708 (18) (*v.*
crabtre); *Croftesheag* 13 (*v.* **croft, hecg**); *Crosgates* 1712 (*v.* **cross, gata**);
Crosslayes 1712 (*v.* **cross, leys**); *the Cross Wongs* 1712 (*v.* **cross, vangr**); *the
Cuningrey(e)* 1601, 1612, *the Coningraye* 1605, *Conygreave* 1664, c.1665, *Connery*
1708, 1708 (18), *Cunery* 1712 (*v.* **coningre**); *Cutmon Leys* 1712 (*v.* **leys**; with the
surn. *Cotman*, *v.* Reaney *s.n.*); *Deadin* 1712 (prob. **dēad** with **eng**; usually in p.ns.,
'dead' is used in reference to a place of violent death or to the discovery of human
bones, cf. *Deadman leyes* in neighbouring Stonesby f.ns. (b)); *Doade Toft* l.12 (*v.*

toft; at this date, prob. with the OE pers.n. *Dodda* rather than with its ME surn. reflex *Dod(d)e* (*v*. Reaney *s.n.* Dod), but note the following local surn.); *Mr Dod's Wong* 1708 (*v*. **vangr**); *the East feld* 1601 (*v*. **ēast, feld**; one of the earlier great fields of the township); *the far wong* 1712 (*v*. **vangr**); *Fulin Hole* 1712 (*v*. **fulling, hol**[1]; cf. *Walke milne peece*, *infra*); *Garats* 1712 (the surn. *Garratt* in the possessive case); *grantham gate* 1601 (*v*. **gata**; the road to Grantham which lies seven miles to the north-east); *Greengaytes* 1712 (*v*. **grēne**[1], **gata**); *Hall Closes* 1664, c.1665, *the Hall Close* 1703, 1708, 1708 (18) (*v*. **hall**); *Hedge Croft* 1664, c.1665, 1708, 1708 (18) (*v*. **hecg, croft**); *the Hither Wong* 1712 (*v*. **vangr**); *Holmebeck* 1602 (*v*. **holmr, bekkr**); *Holwells* 1712 (poss. the surn. *Holwell* in the possessive case, otherwise *v*. **hol**[2], **wella**); *Howlayes* 1712 (the surn. *Howley* in the possessive case); *Rich. Ingleton his house & hom(e)steed(e)* 1664, c.1665 (*v*. **hām-stede**); *the kinges highe way* 1605 (*v*. **hēah-weg**; with reference to James I); *Lankolne Dale* 1703, *Lancoln(e)-Dale* 1708, 1708 (18), *Lanekindale* 1712, *Lankin dale furlong* 1625 (*v*. *Lankin dalle* in Saltby f.ns. (b)); *Long Ends* 1712 (*v*. **ende**); *Long Steanes* 1712 (*v*. **steinn**); *Lupton Shrubs* 1712 (*v*. **scrubb**; the first word is presum. a surn. taken from the name of the Westmorland village (*v*. Lupton, We **1** 46), otherwise the name of a lost farmstead, *v*. **tūn**); *the Marsh(e)* 1602, 1712, *the marshe feild* 1625 (*v*. **mersc, feld**; one of the earlier great fields of the village); *meadows leas* 1605 (*v*. **mǣd** (**mǣdwe** obl.sg.), **leys**); *the Mill* 1708, 1708 (18), 1712, *beyond the Mill* 1625, *behind the Mill* 1703, 1706 (furlong(s) so called), *the Milne Hoome* 1602 (*v*. **holmr**) (*v*. **myln**); *the more* 1601, *the Moore* 1602, 1625, *the Ne(a)ther Moor* 1703, 1706, 1708, 1708 (18) (*v*. **neoðera**), *the Moore Close* 1608, *Moregate* 1712 (*v*. **gata**) (*v*. **mōr**[1], **mór**); *Narrow eares* 1625, *~ ears* 1703, 1706, *Narears* 1708, 1708 (18) (*v*. **nearu, eare**); *Neatshead* 1703, 1706, 1708, 1708 (18), *neateshead furlong* 1625 (*v*. **nēat, hēafod**); *Nether close* 1602; *Nether End* 1712 (*v*. **ende**); *Nine Lands* 1712 (*v*. **land**; a close comprising nine selions of a former great field; but note that Sproxton's Enclosure Award is of 1772); *Ox Pasture* 1712 (*v*. **oxa**); *Potterhill* 1712 (*v*. **pottere** and Potterhill in Stonesby f.ns. (a); a Potter Hill is also present in Asfordby, East Goscote Hundred); *Pottwell Leas* 1608 (*v*. **potte, wella, leys**); *Rich. Ro(o)se his house & hom(e)steed(e)* 1664, c.1665 (*v*. **hām-stede**); *St Maries close* 1602 (*v*. **clos(e)**; it is unclear to what St Mary refers, since none of the surrounding churches are dedicated to her; a chapel in the local parish church may have been funded by proceeds from the rental of the close); *Saltby gate* 1601 (*v*. **gata**), *Saltbye meare* 1605, *Saltby meere* 1612 (*v*. **(ge)mǣre**), *Saltby Mear Wong* 1712 (*v*. **vangr**) (Saltby adjoins to the north); *Sheeprow* 1712 (*v*. **scēp, vrá**; the second el. may have the later dial. sense 'a shelter for animals'); *Sleets* 1712 (*v*. **slétta**); *the Southe Feyld* 1601, *the South feild* 1602, *~ ~ field* 1703, 1706, 1708, 1712 (*v*. **sūð, feld**; one of the great fields of the village); *Stone meadow* 1602 (presum. a meadow cleared of stones, *v*. **stān, stoned** and *the stone middow* in Knipton f.ns. (b)); *the Stooe* 1605, 1612, *the Stow* 1703, 1706, 1708, 1708 (18), 1712, *the Far Stow* 1703, 1706 (*v*. **stōw**); *the Street* 1625 (*v*. **strǣt**; referring to the Roman road King Street Lane (*q.v.*)); *Tafsike* 1712 (*v*. **toft, sík**); *Ten Acres* 1712 (*v*. **æcer**); *Thorndall* 1712 (*v*. **þorn**; with **dalr** or **deill**); *Toote hill* 1605, 1612, 1625, *Toot-hill* 1708, 1708 (18), *Twotill* 1712, *Toothill furlong* 1703, 1706 (*v*. **tōt-hyll**); *Vickerry Nook* 1712 (*v*. **nōk**; with the surn. *Vickery*, an adaptation of MLat *vicarius* 'vicar, sheriff', *v*. Reaney *s.n.*); *Walke milne peece* 1602 (*v*. **pece**), *Walke*

Mill Layes 1712 (*v.* **leys**) (*v.* **walke-milne** 'a fulling mill', cf. *Fulin Hole, supra*); *Water Furrows* 1712 (*v.* **wæter, furh**; usually interpreted as 'furrows where water tends to lie', but *v.* *waterfurris* in Muston f.ns. (b)); *the water milne* 1605, 1612 (*v.* **wæter-mylne**); *Waulk More* 1712 (*v.* **walk, mōr**[1]); *the West Feyld* 1601, ~ ~ *feild* 1612 (*v.* **west, feld**; one of the earlier great fields of the township); *the West Marshe* 1712 (*v.* **mersc**); *Willow beds* 1712 (*v.* **wilig, bedd**); *the Windye milne* 1605, *the wyndye milne platt* 1612 (*v.* **plat**), *Wind Mill Hill* 1712 (*v.* **wind-mylne**).

2. BESCABY

Berthaldebia (? rectius *Berchaldebia*) c.1130 LeicSurv
Berscaldeby c.1150 TutP, 1226 Fine, 1242 Fees *et passim* to 1.13 CRCart, *Berskaldeby* 1278 Cl
Berscaudebi 1195 P, Hy 3 *Rut*, *Berscaudeby* 1220 MHW, 1229 Cur, Hy 3 *Rut*, Hy 3 *Crox et passim* to 1.13 CRCart, Edw 1 *CroxR* (freq), *Berschaudeby* 1229 Cur, *Berscaudeby* Hy 3 *Crox*
Berscoldebi e.Hy 3 Berkeley (p), *Berscoldeby* Hy 3 *Crox* (freq), 1299 Banco *et passim* to 1356 (1449) *WoCart*, 1417 *Rut*
Berscoudebi Hy 3 *Rut*, *Berscoudeby* 1259 (Edw 1) *CroxR*
Bergaldebi 1196 ChancR, 1197 P
Bescaldebi 1195 P, *Bescaldeby* 1242 Fees, 1246 Fine *et passim* to 1290 Inqaqd (p), 1363 ib, *Bescaldby* 1285 Nichols (p)
Bescaudeby 1236 Fees, Hy 3 *Crox et passim* to p.1250 *Rut*, Edw 1 *CroxR* (freq), *Besckaudeby* m.13 (1404) *Laz*, *Bescaudby* 1559 *Rut*
Bescoldeby Hy 3, 1320 *Rut et passim* to 1367 Misc, 1416 Nichols
Bescoudeby 1257 (Edw 1), 1259 (Edw 1), Edw 1 *CroxR*
Bescoldby 1345 Ipm, 1356 (1449) *WoCart et passim* to 1365 (1449) *ib*, 1336 *Rut*
Bescolby 1445 Nichols, 1460 Pat
Bescoby 1539 *Rut*, 1539 *Deed*, 1539 MinAccts, 1609 *Rut et passim* to 1824 O, *Beskoby* 1540 *Rut*, *Bescobie* 1599 *ib*, *Bescaby* 1877 White *et freq*

'Berg-Skáld's farmstead, village', *v.* **bȳ**. The unrecorded Scand pers.n.*Berg-Skáld* is parallel in construction to the pers.ns. ON *Skóg-Ketill*, ON *Skóga-Skeggi* and Anglo-Scand *Skóga-Hreinn* (*v.* Feilitzen 417 *s.n.* *Wudu-Brūn*) in which a topographical term is prefixed to an independently recorded pers.n. In the case of *Berg-Skáld*, ON *berg* 'hill' is prefixed to *Skáld*, an original by-name (i.e. *skáld* 'poet'). For the prefix *Berg-*, *v.* NordKult VII 163, n. 278. Ekwall (DEPN) is clearly incorrect in basing his interpretation of the p.n. ('Hill Saltby') on the single erratic form *Bersaltebi* 1194 P, which may be simply explained as omitting *c* before *a* rather than referring to the lower-lying neighbouring Saltby. The form *Berthaldebia* c.1130 appears to show confusion with the ContGerm pers.n. *Berthold*, but is more likely to represent a misreading of *t* for *c*. Many spellings of the p.n. contain AN *u* for *l*.

BESCABY HO., *Bescaby House* 1877 White. BESCABY OAKS, 1877 White, *Bescoby Oaks* 1824 O, *v.* āc. HAMWELL SPRING is *Holwell Spring* 1795 Nichols, 1925 Kelly, *v.* **hol²**, **wella**, **spring¹**; the source of R. Eye. MARY LANE. Since the lane forms a short portion of the parish boundary, **(ge)mǣre** 'a boundary' is perh. the first el., but **myry** 'miry, muddy' may also be thought of.

FIELD-NAMES

Forms dated Hy 3 are *Crox*; those dated Edw 1 are *CroxR* and 1559 are *Rut*.

(a) Friars Walk 1846, 1863, 1877 White (*v.* **walk**; with the surn. *Friar*).

(b) *capellam de Berscaudeby* 1220 MHW (with MLat *capella* 'a chapel'; no chapel or church survives); *Drie Lees* 1559 (*v.* **drȳge**, **lǣs**); *Fogclose* 1559 (*v.* **fogge**, **clos(e)**); *grangia de Bescoby* 1539 MinAccts (with MLat *grangia* 'a grange'; this was presum. an outlier of Croxton Abbey and may be represented by the moated site immediately east of the present settlement); *Lytelmore* 1559 (*v.* **lȳtel**, **mōr¹**); *Sletheng'* Hy 3 (*v.* **sléttr**, **eng**); *ulueswong'*, *uluiswong'* Hy 3, *vlueswong'*, *Wluesuong'*, *Wlueswong'* Edw 1 (*v.* **vangr**; with the common Scand pers.n. *Ulfr*, an original by-name 'wolf', or a short form of compounds in *Ulf-*, *-ulfr*; the later forms may show anglicization to *Wulf*).

3. SALTBY

Saltebi 1086 DB, 1194 P *et passim* to m.13 (1404) *Laz,* 1301 Ipm, *Saltebia* c.1130 LeicSurv, *Salteby* c.1150 TutP (p), 1211 FF, 1222 RHug *et freq* to 1364 IpmR, 1367 Cl *et passim* to 1539 *Deed*, 1549 Pat, *Saltheby* Hy 3 *Crox*, 1311 Ch
Sautebi 1185 Templar, 12 Dugd, 1200 OblR, 1208 Cur, *Sauteby* 1220 MHW, 1228 *Rut*, 1228 RHug *et freq* to 1259 Cur, Hy 3 *Crox* (freq) *et passim* to Edw 1 *CroxR*, 1328 (e.15) *BelCartB* (p)

Saltby 1328 Banco, 1345 Cl *et passim* to 1535 VE, 1539 *Deed et freq*, *Saltbye* 1549 Pat, 1576 Saxton, 1611 *Rut*

Formally, this p.n. could derive from the ON pers.n. *Salt*, from the OE (Angl), ON sb. *salt* 'salt' or from an adj., OE (Angl) *salt*, ON *saltr* 'salty'. There are salt domes in the Lower Lias formations which underlie the Wolds and a stream-name such as Saltbeck (*q.v.*) in Belvoir parish some five miles to the north and the erstwhile spa there indicate iron salts and other mineral salts in solution draining from the high ground on which Saltby is situated into the Vale of Belvoir. Ironstone has been worked at Saltby for many years and there is a major chalybeate spring plus several other minor springs immediately south-west of the present village. It seems, therefore, less likely that the p.n. was formed from a Scand pers.n. *Salt*.

A possible interpretation of the name could be 'the farmstead at the salty spring', *v.* **salt**², **saltr**, **bȳ**. Whether, prior to the development of the countrywide salters' routes in the Middle Ages, salt could have been produced in any quantity at Saltby by the evaporation of brine from the mineral springs is uncertain; but if this were the case, then we would have rather 'the salt-making farmstead, village', *v.* **salt**¹, **bȳ** and note *Saltputes* in Wymondham f.ns (b).

Spellings of the p.n. with *u* for *l* are due to AN influence.

EGYPT PLANTATION runs along the north-eastern boundary of the parish and is thus poss. a fanciful name indicating remoteness from the township; but the name may allude to land on which gipsies habitually camped, *v.* Field 157. HERRING GORSE, 1806 Map, 1824 O, *v.* **gorst**; with the surn. *Herring*, cf. Herring's Lodge, two miles to the east in neighbouring Skillington, Lincs. NAG'S HEAD (P.H.) (lost), *Nag's Head* 1846, 1863, 1877 White, 1925 Kelly. ST PETER'S CHURCH, *Church (St Peter)* 1846, 1863, 1877 White, 1925 Kelly; it is earlier recorded as *ecclesie de Sauteby* 1220 MHW, *the Church* 1704, 1707 (18), 1788 *Terrier*. Note also *the Churchyard* 1704, 1707 (18) *ib*. SALTBY HEATH FM, *the He(a)th* 1605 *Terrier*, *Saltby Heath* e.18, 1795 Nichols, 1846, 1863, 1877 White, *v.* **hǣð**. SALTBY HEATH LODGE (lost), *Saltby Heath Lodge* 1824 O, *v.* **loge**. SALTBY LODGE, 1806 Map, 1846 White, *v.* **loge**. SALTBY PASTURE, *the Pasture* 1605, 1674, 1697, 1700, 1703, 1707 (18), 1788 *Terrier*, *the Pastor* 1704 *ib*, *v.* **pasture**. SWALLOWHOLE COVERT, *v.* **cover(t)** and Swallowhole in neighbouring Croxton Kerrial. THE TENT, 1795 Nichols, *King Lud's Tents* 1811 *ib*; fanciful names for tumuli at the eastern end of King Lud's Entrenchments (*q.v.*) in Croxton Kerrial parish. THE VICARAGE, 1605 *Terrier, the Vicaridge House* 1704, 1709 *ib*, ~ *Vicarage* ~ 1707 (18), 1788 *ib*, *v.* **vikerage**; note also *the Homestall* 1605, 1612, 1704, 1707 (18), 1709 *ib, the Vicaridge Homestall* 1697 *ib, v.* **hām-stall**.

FIELD-NAMES

Forms dated 1601, 1605, 1612, 1625, 1674, 1697, 1700, 1703, 1704, 1707 (18), 1709 and 1788 are *Terrier*.

(a) the Allottments 1788 (*v.* **allotment**); the Butts 1788 (cf. *shortbuts* 1601, 1605, 1612, 1674, *Short Butts* 1697, 1700, 1703, *v.* **sc(e)ort, butte**); the Folding Dykes 1811 Nichols (*v.* **falding, dík**); Lords Gorse 1806 Map (*v.* **gorst**; cf. *William Lord* 1605 of Saltby); the Mill Cl 1788; the Mill Fd 1788 (*the milne feilde* 1625, *ye Mill field* 1697, *v.* **myln, feld**; one of the great fields of the village, later called *the South field* and *the Croft field*); The Moor 1771 Nichols, 1788 (*the Moore* 1601, 1605, 1625, 1674, *the More* 1697, 1703, *the Moor* 1700, *v.* **mōr**[1]).

(b) *the aker furlong* 1601, ~ ~ *forlonge* 1605, 1612, *the acker furlonge* 1625, *Acar furlong* 1674, *the Acre furlong* 1697, 1700, 1707 (18), ~ ~ *furlung* 1704, 1709 (*v.* **æcer**); *atte Becke* 1327 SR (p), *atte Bek* 1328 Banco (p) (*v.* **atte**), *the beks* 1605, (*the*) *beck forlong* 1601, 1612, *the beck furlonge* 1625, *the Becke furlong* 1674, *the Beck Furlong* 1697, 1700, 1707 (18), ~ ~ *furland* 1703, ~ ~ *furlung* 1704, 1709 (*v.* **bekkr**); *Billinge wong* 1605, *byllinge* ~ 1612 (*v.* **vangr**; prob. with the surn. *Billing*, but *v.* Billinge Hill, Ch 1 138–9); *Blackwell* 1601, 1605, 1612, 1625, 1697, 1700, 1703, *blakwell* 1601, 1625, *blacwell* 1612, *blacke well* 1674, *blakwell leies* 1605, *Blackwell Leas* 1704 (*v.* **leys**), *Blackwell side* 1697, 1703 (*v.* **sīde**), *blackwell tythe* 1605 (*v.* **tēoða**) (*v.* **blæc, wella**); *atte Brigh* 1332 SR (p) (*v.* **atte, brycg**); *brod(e)by forde* 1601, 1612, *brodby forthe* 1601 (*v.* **ford**), *bro(o)dbye hill* 1601, *brodby hill* 1605, 1674, *brodeby* ~, *broodby hill* 1612, *Broadby Hill* 1700, 1703 (*v.* **brād, bȳ**; as first el. the Scand pers.n. *Broddi* in the possessive case would make happier sense than 'the broad, spacious farmstead', but the apparent continuing long vowel of the specific as well as lack of *dd* in any of the recorded forms argue against this; a lost early farmstead); *above the bush* 1612 (*v.* **busc**; a furlong so called); *castell gate* 1605 (*v.* **castel(l), gata**; the road via Croxton Kerrial to Belvoir Castle five miles to the north); *the tyth(e) called the chesecake*, ~ ~ ~ ~ *chisecake* 1605 (*v.* **tēoða, cheesecake**; such closes were originally wedge-shaped and thus named from a cut portion of the confection); *the church headland* 1605 (*v.* **hēafod-land** and St Peter's Church *supra*); *Clarkwell Side* 1674 (*v.* **wella, sīde**; either with the surn. *Clark* or with **clerc**); *Coggle Baulk* 1704, 1707 (18), 1709 (*v.* **balca**; the first el. may be a surn. *Coggle/Coghill*; otherwise, but less likely, an original topographical name, *v.* **cogg, hyll**); *the Common* 1605 (*v.* **commun**); *the Commond pasture* 1674 (*v.* **commun, pasture**); (*the*) *Cowdam hollow* 1674, 1697, 1700, 1703 (*v.* **cū, damme, holh**; the 'cow-dam' was an artificially created watering-place for cattle); (*at*) *the Crabtre*

1601, 1605, 1612, (*at the*) *Crabtree* 1704, 1707 (18), 1709 (*v.* **crabtre**; a furlong so called); *croft* 1601, (*the*) *Croftes* 1605, 1612, *Craftes* 1674, *the Croftfield* 1704, 1707 (18) (one of the great fields of the village, earlier *the milne feilde, infra*), *Croftes furlong* 1625, *ye Craft furlong* 1697, *Croft furlong* 1700, 1707 (18), *~ furlung* 1704, 1709, *Croft hedings* 1605 (*v.* **heading**; a recurring local alternative for *headland*) (*v.* **croft**); *Crosse furlong(e)* 1601, 1605, 1612, *the Crosforlongs* 1625, *Crose furlong* 1674, *Cross furlong* 1697, 1700, 1707 (18), *~ furland* 1703, *~ furlung* 1704, 1709 (*v.* **cross, furlang**); *Crowbush* 1704, 1707 (18), 1709 (*v.* **crāwe, busc**); *Croxton hedg* 1605 (*v.* **hecg**; the boundary hedge of Croxton Kerrial which adjoins to the north); *the dale* 1605 (*v.* **dalr**); *de la Dounhalle* 1292 Abbr (p) ('the lower hall', *v.* **dūne, hall**; the upper hall is unrecorded); *drake ashe* 1601, *~ eshe* 1612, *the drake eshe heding* 1605 (*v.* **heading**) (*v.* **æsc**; it seems unlikely that in compound with 'ash-tree', *drake* is OE *draca* 'a dragon', alluding to local folklore, or that it is ME *drake* 'the male duck'; poss. is the surn. *Drake*, with the tree as a boundary marker); *Drywell* 1700, 1703, *drywell head(e)* 1601, 1612, *driewellhed* 1605, *Driwell head* 1674 (*v.* **hēafod**) (*v.* **drȳge, wella**); *Dudg(e)well* 1625, 1674, 1697, *Dudgwell lease* 1601, *~ lees(e)* 1601, 1612, *~ Leas* 1700, 1704, *~ Leys* 1707 (18), *Dudgewell Leas* 1703 (*v.* **leys**) (*v.* **wella**; perh. with the surn. *Dudge/Dodge* (originally a pet-name for Roger, rhymed on *Rodge* and *Hodge*), cf. the pairs Dodgen/Dudgen and Dodgson/Dud(g)son; but note the OE pers.n. *Dodda* which may appear in *Doade Toft* in adjoining Sproxton and could feature here also in an earlier **Doddewell* > *Dudgewell*); *the east fielde* 1601 (*v.* **ēast, feld**; one of the great fields of the village, later *the middell field, infra*); (*at*) *the Eldar Stump* 1704, 1707 (18), 1709 (*v.* **ellern, stump**; a furlong so called); *the five roodes* 1601, 1605, 1612, *the fiue Roods* 1674, (*the*) *Five Roods* 1697, 1700, 1703, 1707 (18), *Five Rudes* 1709, *the fiue rood ends* 1674, *the Five Rood(s) ends* 1700, 1703 (*v.* **ende**) (*v.* **fīf, rōd**[3]); *Between the Gates* 1700, *Betwixt ~ ~* 1703 (*v.* **gata**; a furlong so called); *the goores* 1601, 1605, 1612, (*the*) *Gores* 1674, 1697, 1700, 1704, 1707 (18), 1709, *the Gores furland* 1703 (*v.* **furlang**) (*v.* **gāra**; *the gra(u)nge* 1601, 1605, 1612, 1625, *Saltby Graunge* 1610 Rut, *Saltbie Grange* 1611 ib, *grangiam de Saltby* 1410 PRep (with MLat *grangia* 'a grange'), *Grange balk* 1697, *~ baulk* 1704, 1707 (18), 1709 (*v.* **balca**), *the grange furlong* 1674, *the gra(u)nge gate* 1605, 1612 (*v.* **gata**), *graingegate furlonge* 1625, *the graunge gate syd* 1601 (*v.* **sīde**) (*v.* **grange**; prob. in origin an outlier of Croxton Abbey); *Grantham gate* 1605, 1697 (*v.* **gata**; the road to Grantham which lies seven miles to the north-east); *super Grenam* 1311 Ch (p) (with MLat *grena* 'a village green'); *gren(e)dikes* 1601, 1605, 1612, *greendikes* 1625, *the grenedike forlonge* 1601 (*v.* **furlang**) (*v.* **grēne**[1], **dīk**); *hawbrig(g)* 1601, 1605, *hawbriggs* 1612, *Hobrig(g)s* 1674, 1697, 1703, *Hoe Brigge* 1700 (*v.* **bryggja**; perh. with **haugr** rather than with **haga**[1], cf. *Herneshou* in Stonesby f.ns. (b) where *-hou* > *-haw* in the 17th cent.); *the Home Closes* 1674 (*v.* **home**); *Inge well* 1605 (*v.* **wella**; the first el. may be the Scand pers.n. *Ingi*, a short form of masc. names in *Ingi-*; the Scand pers.n. *Inga*, a short form of fem. names in *Ingi-* seems less likely, as does their ME surn. reflex *Ing(e)*, *v.* SPNLY 149 and Reaney *s.n.* Ing); *kenn(s) yate* 1605, 1612 (*v.* **geat**; with the surn. *Kenn*, *v.* Reaney *s.n.*); *Lankin dalle* 1605, *Lanckondale* 1709, *Lanckindale furlonge* 1625 (poss. 'the valley of the young lambs', *v.* **lambkin, dalr**; but note also the surn. *Lambkin* (cf. John *Lamkyn* 1379 of Colchester), a diminutive of *Lamb* (Lambert), *v.* Reaney *s.n.*; if with the surn., then *v.* **deill**; and *v.* *Lankolne Dale* in Sproxton f.ns. (b)); *Leake hedle* 1605 (*v.* **headley**; with the surn. *Leake*, *v.* Reaney *s.n.*); *Longlandes* 1601, 1605, 1612, *Longlands* 1674, 1697, 1700, 1703 (*v.* **lang**[1], **land**); *Lord his yard* 1605 (*v.* **geard**; the property of *William Lord* 1601, 1605), *Lordes yate* 1601, 1612 (*v.* **geat**; that of *Edward Lord* 1612); *the maner hedge* 1605 (*v.* **maner**, **hecg**); *(the) Meares* 1601, 1605, 1612, 1674, 1697, *(the) Meres* 1704, 1709, *the Meers* 1707 (18), *the Meares furlonge* 1625, *Meres Furlong* 1700 (*v.* (ge)**mǣre**; referring to the boundary with Croxton Kerrial); *middeldale, -dall* 1601, *middell dale* 1605, 1612, ~ *dall* 1605, *mideldale* 1612, *Middledale* 1674, 1697, 1700, 1703, 1704, 1707 (18), 1709, *Middle dale and west* 1674, *Middledale furlonge* 1625, *midel dale heding* 1605 (*v.* **heading**) (*v.* **middel**, **deill**); *the middell field* 1612, *(the) Middle Feild(e)* 1625, 1674, ~ *Field* 1697, 1700, 1704, 1707 (18), 1709 (*v.* **middel**, **feld**; one of the great fields of the township, earlier *the east fielde, supra*); *the Middle furlong(e)* 1625, 1674, 1697, 1700, 1707 (18), ~ ~ *furlung* 1704, 1709, *the Midle furland* 1703 (i.e. of *the middell field, supra*), *the Middle furlong* 1674, 1697, 1707 (18), ~ ~ *furlung* 1704, 1709 (i.e. of *north feeld, infra*, later *the Sevenrood field*) (*v.* **middel**, **furlang**); *the mill* 1601, 1612, *the mill water* 1605 (*v.* **wæter**) (*v.* **myln**); *the moore gate* 1605 (*v.* **gata**), *the greate more hedg* 1605 (*v.* **grēat**, **hecg**), *the More Meadow* 1704, 1707 (18) (*v.* The Moor *supra*); *the Morter pit(t)s* 1601, 1605, 1612, 1674, 1703, *the Mortar Pit(t)s* 1704, 1707 (18), 1709, *Morter pit furlong* 1700, *morter pit(s) heding(s)* 1605 (*v.* **heading**) (*v.* **morter**, **pytt**; the precise nature of these pits is uncertain, but poss. are (i) rounded pits having a resemblance to the shape of mortars, (ii) pits in rock used for the primitive grinding of ore etc. (cf. *mortar-hole*, *v.* OED *s.v.* mortar, sb.[1], 4b), (iii) pits from which sand or clay or limestone or other materials were extracted for agricultural use or for the manufacture of mortar for building purposes, *v.* Field 227); *neate heades* 1605, *the Neats head furlong* 1674, *Neathead Furlong* 1700 (*v.* **nēat**, **hēafod**); *Nicholsons Bush* 1704, 1707 (18), 1709 (*v.* **busc**; with the surn. *Nicholson*); *Norbeckes* 1674, *Northbecks gate* 1697, 1700, *norbecks yeat* 1703 (*v.* **gata**) (*v.* **norð**, **bekkr**); *north feelde* 1601, *the north fielde* 1612, ~ ~ *feild(e)* 1625, 1674, ~ ~ *Field* 1700, 1703 (*v.* **norð**, **feld**; one of the great fields of the village, later *the Sevenrood field, infra*); *the north ford* 1601 (*v.* **norð**, **ford**); *the orchard* 1674 (belonging to The Vicarage *supra*); *the Pole* 1704 (*v.* **pōl**[1]); *the seven(e) roodes* 1601, 1612, *the Seven Roods* 1605, 1697, 1703, *the Seuen Roodes* 1674, *the Seaven Roods* 1700, *Seven Rudes* 1704, 1709, *the Sevenrood Field* 1697, 1707 (18), *the Seven Rude* ~ 1704, 1709 (*v.* **feld**; one of the great fields of the village, earlier *north feelde, supra*), *sevenrood hedings* 1605 (*v.* **heading**), *Seaven Roode furlonge* 1625 (*v.* **seofon**, **rōd**[3]); *Shepherds Bush* 1704, 1709, *Shephards* ~ 1707 (18) (*v.* **busc**; either with the surn. *Shepherd* or with **scēp-hirde** and perh. to be compared with Shepherds Bush, Mx 109); *(the) South field* 1601, 1612, ~ *Feild* 1674 (*v.* **sūð**, **feld**; one of the great fields of the village, also called *the milne feilde* and later *the Croft field*); *spick close* 1605 (*v.* **clos(e)**), *spikes heading* 1605 (*v.* **heading**) (with the surn. *Spick*, cf. *John Spick*, *Wm. Spick* and *Richard Spicke* of Ab Kettleby, cited in 1612 *Terrier*); *Sproxton meare* 1601, 1605, 1612, ~ ~ *furlong(e)* 1625, 1674, *Sproxton Mere Furlong* 1700, *Sproxstonmear furlong* 1697 (*v.* (ge)**mǣre**), *Sproxton neathead* 1612 (*v.* **nēat**, **hēafod** and *neate heades, supra*) (Sproxton adjoins to the south-east); *stone brigg* 1601, 1605, ~ *bridge* 1612 (*v.* **stān**, **brycg**, **bryggja**); *stonay*

1601, 1605, 1612, *Stonye furlonge* 1625, *Far Stonie* 1674, ~ *Stonny* 1697, ~ *Stony* 1700, 1704, 1707 (18), 1709 (*v.* **stānig**); (*the*) *Stony dalle* 1601, 1605, *the stony dale* 1601, 1612, *Stonny dale* 1697, (*on*) *Stonydale* 1704, 1707 (18), 1709, *Further, Hither Stony Dale* 1700, *the Stoneydale furlonge* 1625, *Stoniedale forlong* 1674 (*v.* **stānig, deill**); *the stonepits* 1601, *the stonpittes* 1612, *stonpit gate* 1605 (*v.* **gata**), *stonpit hades* 1605 (*v.* **hēafod**), *the stonpit hedings, stonepit heading* 1605 (*v.* **heading**) (*v.* **stān-pytt**); *Stonsby hedg*(*e*) 1601, 1605, 1612, 1700 (*v.* **hecg**; a boundary hedge), *Stonsbye hedg furlong* 1674, *Stonsby hedge furland* 1703 (*v.* **furlang**), (*at*) *Stonsby mear* 1697 (*v.* (**ge**)**mǣre**) (Stonesby adjoins to the south-west); *the Stripes* 1704, 1707 (18), 1709 (*v.* **strīp**); *thefe pit* 1601, 1605, 1612, *Theife pitts* 1674, 1703, *Theef pitt*(*s*) 1697, 1700 (*v.* **þefa, pytt**); *the three roodes* 1601, *the thre roods* 1605, (*the*) *Three Roods* 1674, 1700, ~ *Rudes* 1704, 1709 (*v.* **þrēo, rōd**[3]); *thruspits* 1605 (*v.* **þyrs, pytt**); *the towne furlong*(*e*) 1625, 1674, *the Town Furlong* 1697, 1700, 1707 (18), ~ ~ *furlung* 1704, 1709, *the Towns End* 1704, 1707 (18), 1709 (*v.* **ende**) (*v.* **tūn**); (*the*) *vicar dale* 1601, 1605, 1612, 1674, 1700, ~ *dall* 1605, *Vicardale head* 1697 (*v.* **hēafod**) (*v.* **vikere, deill**); *the Walke* 1605 (*v.* **walk**); *Ward hedle* 1605 (*v.* **headley**; with the surn. *Ward*); (*above*) *the weanegates* 1601, 1605, 1612, *the wainegates* 1612, *the Wainegate furlonge* 1625, (*the*) *Waingate furlong* 1674, 1700, *the weangate furland* 1703 (*v.* **furlang**) (*v.* **wægn, gata**); *the West field*(*e*) 1601, 1612 (*v.* **west, feld**; one of the early great fields of the village); (*the*) *Whiny meare* 1601, 1612, *the whyny meare* 1601, (*the*) *wini*(*e*) *mear*(*e*) 1605, *winy meare* 1605, 1612, *Whinn*(*e*)*y Mere* 1700, 1704, 1707 (18), 1709, *Whinnie Meare* 1703, *whinnye meare forlonge* 1625, *the whinnimeare forlong* 1674, *Whinnymear furlong* 1697, *Whinnie Meare furland* 1703 (*v.* **furlang**) (*v.* **whinny, (ge)mǣre**); *woddend bridg* 1612 (*v.* **wudu, ende, brycg**); *Workman hedle* 1605 (*v.* **headley**), *Workman his ground* 1605 (*v.* **grund**), *Workmans land* 1605 (*v.* **land**) (the property of *William Workman* 1605); *William Wright headland* 1605 (*v.* **hēafod-land**); *wronglandes* 1601, 1605, 1612, *Wronglands* 1674, 1700, 1703, 1704, 1709, *ronglands* 1697, *Wranglands* 1707 (18), *Wronglandes furlonge* 1625 (*v.* **wrangr, vrangr, land**).

4. STONESBY

Stovenebi 1086 DB
Stouenesbia c.1130 LeicSurv, *Stouenesbi* Hy 3 *Rut* (p), e.13 (e.15) *BelCartB* (p), *Stouenesby* 1220 MHW, 1237 RGros, Hy 3 *Rut*, 1276 RH, *Stovenesbi* 1204 Cur, *Stovenesby* 1209 × 35 RHug
Stounesby 1245 FConc, 1248 Cl *et passim* to Hy 3 *Crox* (freq), 1275 Pat *et freq* to 1361 (1449) WoCart, 1366 *Rut et passim* to 1548 Fine, 1574 LEpis, *Stounesbi* 1272 RGrav (p), 1297 Coram (p), *Stounisby* Hy 3 *Crox*, Edw 1 *CroxR et passim* to 1317 *Wyg*, 1320 (1449) WoCart, *Stounysby* l.13 (1449), 1302 (1449) *ib*, 1317 *Wyg*, 1333 (1449) WoCart

Stownesby 1202 FF, c.1291 Tax, 1396 *Rut, Stownisby* p.1250 (1449) *WoCart*

Stounsby 1320 *Rut*, 1333 (1449),1336 (1449) *WoCart*

Stonesby 1317 *Wyg*, 1325, 1359 *Pat et passim* to 1502 *MiscAccts*, 1578 LEpis, 1610 Speed *et freq*, *Stonesbye* 1553 Pat, 1574 LEpis, 1576 Saxton, *Stonesbie* 1576 LibCl, 1578 LEpis, 1599 *Rut*, *Stonysby* 1502 *MiscAccts*, 1509 Fine *et passim* to 1535 VE, *Stonysbye* 1484 *Rut*

Ekwall (DEPN) suggests that the first el. of this p.n. may be OE (or ON) **stofn** 'the stump of a tree', poss. as an earlier OE p.n. *Stofn* (cf. Stoven in Suffolk, with forms *Stoune, Stouone* 1086 DB). He is followed in this interpretation by Fellows-Jensen (SSNEM 71). Insley (SNPh 70 (1998) at 19 n.) believes rather that 'as the first el. we must look to an elliptical OE locative p.n. in the dat.sg., i.e. **Stofne* '(settlement) at the tree-stump', to which Scand *bȳ* was added in a genitival formation subsequent to the Scandinavian settlement.

The ubiquitous forms with a genitival construction may indicate alternatively that the first el. is an unrecorded pers.n. *Stofn* (also proposed by DEPN), poss. a Scand by-name formation derived from the substantive, to be compared with the similar, but recorded, Scand pers.n. *Stúfr*, an original by-name from OIcel *stúfr* 'a stump' (*v.* SPNLY 267), *v.* **bȳ**.

THE DRIFT, 1744 *Rental*, *v.* **drift**; an alternative name for Sewstern Lane. FOX (P.H.) (lost), *Fox* 1846, 1863 White, *Fox Inn* 1877 ib. MANOR HO., *Manor house* 1877 White, *v.* **maner**. METHODIST CHAPEL. ST PETER'S CHURCH, *Church (St Peter)* 1846, 1863, 1877 White; it is earlier recorded as *ecclesie de Stouenesby* 1220 MHW, 1237 RGros, ~ *de Stounesby* 1340 *Pat*, ~ *de Stonesby* 1359 *ib*. Note also *the Churchyard* 1625, 1822 *Terrier*. STONESBY GORSE, 1806 Map, *v.* **gorst**. STONESBY LODGE, 1824 O, *v.* **loge**. STONESBY SPINNEY, 1806 Map, 1824 O, *v.* **spinney**. THE VICARAGE is *the Vicarage house* 1674, 1822 *Terrier*.

FIELD-NAMES

Undated forms in (a) are 1782 *Reeve*; those dated 1781 are *EnclA* and 1822 are *Terrier*. Forms throughout dated 1320 are *Rut*; 14 are *Gox*; 1561 (1700) and 1744 are *Rental*; 1625 are *Terrier*; 1682, 1682 (1791) and 1686 are *Surv*; 1738 are *Reeve*.

(a) Bamptons Cl (with the surn. *Bampton*); Near Beskaby 1782, Beskabby Bridle Road 1781 (*v.* **brigdels**), Beskabby Foot Road 1781 (*v.* **foot-road**), Beskabby Red Land (*v.* **rēad, land**) (Bescaby adjoins to the north); Bridgewell Leys (*v.* **leys**), Bridgewell Hill (*Bridgewell* is poss. a surn., otherwise *v.* **brycg, wella**); Long Butsall (*Longbutstall ~, Shortbutstall Furlong* 1744, *Shortbutts hill* 1682, *Short butsill* 1686, *v.* **butte, hyll**); Buttermilk Lane (*v.* **buttermilk**; a lane leading to good pasture, productive of rich milk, *v.* Field 110); Coston Foot Road 1781 (*v.* **foot-road**; Coston adjoins to the south-east); Garthorpe Gate Cl 1782 (*Garthorp(e) Gate* 1682, 1686, *v.* **gata**), Garthorpe Gate Fd 1781 (*v.* **feld**; one of the great fields of the township, earlier called *Nether Feild, infra*), Garthorpe Rd 1781, Garthorpe Foot Road 1781 (*v.* **foot-road**) (Garthorpe adjoins to the south); Far, Nether Ingleborough, Ingleborough Cl (*Nether, Upper Ingborough* 1682, *~ Ingborrow* 1686, *v.* **berg**; the first el. may be an early OE hill-name **ing** 'hill, peak', with the 1782 forms containing either the derivative variant **ingel** or representing **ing-hyll*; it is doubtful whether in 1782 the forms would have been influenced by the now well-known Ingleborough, YW 7 242); Nether, Upper Knowlands, Knowlands Cl (*Noelands Fur'* 1682, *Nolands Fur(long)* 1686, 1744, *v.* **land**; perh. with the ME pers.n. *Noe* (Hebrew *Noah* 'long-lived') or its surn. reflex, or with the ME pers.n. *Noel* (OFr *noël* 'Christmas', a name given to one born at that festival) or its surn. reflex, *v.* Reaney *s.n.* Noy and Noel; but earlier forms are needed); Richard Linneys Farm, James Loves Farm, George Mans Farm, Widow Masons Farm (*v.* **ferme**); Melton Rd 1781, Melton Foot Road 1781 (*v.* **foot-road**) (Melton Mowbray lies five miles to the south-west); Mill Fd 1781 (*Mill Feild* 1682, 1686, *Milfield* 1682 (1791), *v.* **myln, feld**; one of the great fields, later called *Saltbynook Field, infra*); The Moor (cf. *In the More, Through ye More* 1682, 1686, *v.* **mōr¹**; furlongs so called); New Home Cl (*v.* **home** and *the Home Close, infra*); New House Foot Road 1781 (*v.* **foot-road**); The Pasture 1781 (1744, *the beast pasture* 1682, *ye Beast paster* 1686, cf. *the Pasture side* 1744 (*v.* **sīde**), *v.* **beste, pasture**); Potter Hill alias Street Cl (*v.* **pottere**, Street Cl *infra* and *Potterhill* in Sproxton f.ns. (b)); Pyewhit Hill, Pye Wipe Hill (with eModE **pewit**, ModEdial. **pyewipe** 'the lapwing'); Ranglands (1682, 1686, 1744, *Wrangland'* 1320, *Wrancland'* 14, *v.* **wrang, vrangr, land**); Red Earth Cl (*v.* **eorðe**), Red Hill, Red Land, *~ ~* Cl (*v.* **rēad**; all referring to the colour of the soil); The Round Hill, Top of Round Hill (*v.* **round**); Saltby Rd 1781 (Saltby adjoins to the north-east); Sproxton Rd 1781 (Sproxton adjoins to the east); Stamford Rd 1781 (i.e. King Street Lane (*q.v.*), leading to Stamford, 17 miles to the south-east); the Stone-pit 1822, the Stonepit(t) Cl 1782, Stone-pit alias Red Land Cl 1782 (*Aboue the Stone pitts* 1682, 1686 (*v.* **aboven**; a furlong so called), *Stonepitt Fur'* 1682, 1686 (*v.* **furlang**), *the Stonepitts* 1744, *v.* **stān-pytt**); Stony Cross (*Stoney Cross* 1686, *Stonycross Furlong* 1744; it is uncertain whether this name represents a 'stony furlong lying athwart' (with **stānig, cross**) or more likely '(furlong at) the stone cross' (with **stān, cros** and an intrusive *y*, cf. *the Windye milne* 1605 in Sproxton f.ns. (b)); Stony Dale (*v.* **stānig**; prob. with **deill** rather than **dalr**); Spring Cl (*v.* **spring¹**); Street or Buttermilk Lane, Street Cl (*Street Fur'* 1682, 1686 (a furlong name in both *Mill Feild* and *Nether Feild, infra*), *Streetway, ~ Furl'* 1744 (*v.* **weg, furlang**), *v.* **strǣt**; with reference to the Roman road King Street Lane (*q.v.*) which runs immediately south-west of the village); the Vicar's Cl 1822; Wadland Hill (1682, *Waddland Hill* 1686, *Woodland*

Hill (sic) 1744, *v.* **wād, land**); Waltham Foot Road 1781 (*v.* **foot-road**), Waltham
Gate 1782 (*v.* **gata**), Waltham Gate Fd 1781 (*Waltham Gate Feild* 1682, 1686,
Walthamgate Field 1744, *v.* **feld**; one of the great fields of the village) (Waltham on
the Wolds adjoins to the west).

(b) *Ash Fur'* 1682, 1686 (*v.* **æsc, furlang**); *Aslakaker* 14 (*v.* **æcer, akr**; with the
ON pers.n. *Áslákr*); *Lez Balkes* 1561 (1700), *le Balke voc' the Grett Marke* 1561
(1700) (*v.* **balca, grēat, mearc**); *Blackborough* 1682, *Blackbor(r)ow* 1686, 1744 (*v.*
blæc, berg); *Black Mold* 1744 (*v.* **blæc, molde**); *Brenthill* 1744, *Under Brentill*
1682, 1686, *Brenthill baulke* 1682, *Brintill balke* 1686 (*v.* **balca**), *Brenthill Fur'*
1682, *Brentill* ~ 1686 (*v.* **furlang**) (*v.* **hyll**; prob. with **brant** rather than with
brente,); *Butcher Leyes* 1744 (*v.* **leys**; with the surn. *Butcher*); *Church Baulk* 1744
(*v.* **balca** and St Peter's Church *supra*); *Cookoe Hedge* 1744 (*v.* **hecg**; perh. with the
surn. *Cuckow* (*v.* Reaney *s.n.*) rather than with *cuccu* 'the cuckoo'); *othe dale* 1381
SR (p) (*v.* **dalr**); *Deadman ley(e)s* 1682, 1686, 1744 (*v.* **dede-man, leys**; evidently
alluding either to the discovery of a pagan burial ground or to a place where a corpse
was found, cf. Deadin in neighbouring Sproxton f.ns. (a)); *Dry(e)hill Fur'* 1682,
1686, *Dryall Furlong* 1744 (*v.* **drȳge, hyll**); *Eldern Stump* 1744 (*v.* **ellern, stump**);
Esshees Furlong 1744 (*v.* **æsc**); *Far(r) Close* 1682, 1686 (*v.* **feor**); *Flaxland* 14 (*v.*
fleax, land); *Flaxwell* 14 (*v.* **wella**; ostensibly, the first el. is **fleax** 'flax', but this
marches oddly with **wella** 'spring, stream', so that poss. is a metathesized ODan
flask 'swampy grassland, pool'); *Gartrope gate Furlong* 1744 (*v.* Garthorpe Gate Cl
supra); *Between the gates* 1682, 1686 (*v.* **gata**; furlongs so called in Mill Fd and
Waltham Gate Fd); *the glebe yard land* 1738 (*v.* **glebe, yardland**); *Goss Fur'* 1686
(*v.* **gorst, furlang**); *Granthamgate* 1744 (*v.* **gata**; the road to Grantham which lies
nine miles to the the north-east); *le Gren(e)* 1320, 14, *the towne comon greene* 1625
(*v.* **tūn, commun**) (*v.* **grēne**²); *Greengate* 1744, *Green gate Fur'* 1682, 1686 (*v.*
furlang) (*v.* **grēne**¹, **gata**); *Hall Nook(e)* 1682, 1686 (*v.* **hall, nōk**); *Herneshou* 14,
Longherne Shaw, Shortherne Shaw 1682, *Longehernshaw, Shorthernshaw* 1686,
long, short Herenshaw 1744 (the later forms here presum. belong with that of the
14th cent.; if so, the generic is **haugr**, the later forms showing attraction to *shaw* (OE
sceaga 'a small wood') through metanalysis or misdivision; the specific may be the
Scand pers.n. *Hjarni* with an anglicized gen.sg. inflexion, cf. *Scroutesdeil* in
Sewstern f.ns. (b)); *holdeland* 14 (*v.* **hald**², **land**); *the Home Close* 1738, ~ ~ ~
Pasture 1744 (*v.* **home** and New Home Cl *supra*); *Huuergate* 14 (*v.* **uferra, gata**; cf.
Upper gate, infra); *longat'* 14 (*v.* **lang**¹, **gata**); *Tho. Lodintons Farme* 1682 (*v.*
ferme; the surn. *Loddington* was that of a family which originated in the village of
this name 14 miles to the south in East Goscote Hundred); *longwongesend* 14 (*v.*
lang¹, **vangr, ende**); *More Beck* 1682, 1686, 1744 (*v.* **mōr**¹, **mór, bekkr**); *Upper* ~,
Neatgate 1682, 1686, *Hollow neatgates*, ~ *Furlong* 1744 (*v.* **holh**) (*v.* **nēat**; it is
uncertain whether this name means 'the cattle road' (with **gata**) or whether it is
another style of *cowgate* 'an allotment of pasture for a single beast', *v.* Field 127);
Nether Feild 1682, 1686, ~ *Field* 1682 (1791), 1744 (*v.* **neoðera, feld**; one of the
great fields of the township, later called Garthorpe Fd *supra*); *New Close* 1682, 1686;
Newhynger 1320, *Nethyrnewhynger* 1320 (*v.* **neoðera**) (*v.* **nīwe, hangra**); *Peasefelde*
1561 (1700) (*v.* **pise, feld**); *terram de Riges* 14 (prob. with the surn. *Ridge* (ME
Rigge) and MLat *terra* 'land'); *Saltbynook Field* 1744 (*v.* **nōk**; one of the great fields

of the village, lying towards Saltby and earlier called Mill Fd *supra*); *Setcop* 1320, 14 (*v.* **set-copp**); *Short Flax Leyes* 1744 (*v.* **leys**; poss. with **fleax**, but note the problem with *Flaxwell, supra*, which may pertain with *leys* and cf. also Flaxleys Cl in Nether Broughton f.ns. (a) which may relate to **flask**); *Smallongland* 1320 (*v.* **smæl, lang**[1]**, land**); *Smerberdal* 14 (*v.* **smeoru, smjǫr, berg, deill**, cf. Smarber, YN 272); *Spilmandail* 1320 (*v.* **deill**; with the ME surn. *Spilman* (from OE *spilemann* 'jester, juggler'), *v.* Reaney *s.n.*); *Sproxton baulke* 1682, ~ *Balke* 1686 (*v.* **balca**), *Sproxtonemere* 1320 (*v.* **(ge)mǣre**) (Sproxton adjoins to the east); *Stonland* 14, *netherstonland* 14 (*v.* **neoðera**), *Mid(d)le Stoneland* 1682, 1686, *Middlestone Lands* 1744 (*v.* **stān, land**); *Tenter ley(e)s* 1682, 1686 (*v.* **tentour, leys**); *Thack Dale* 1682, 1686 (*v.* **þæc, þak**; with **deill** or **dalr**); *Upper gate* 1682, 1686 (*v.* **gata**; cf. *Huuergate, supra*); *Viccar Bush* 1682, *Vicker* ~ 1686, 1744 (*v.* **busc**; either with **vikere** 'a vicar' or with the surn. *Vicar/Vicker* derived from it, *v.* Reaney *s.n.*); *Waltham Meare* 1682, *Waltom* ~ 1686 (*v.* **(ge)mǣre**; Waltham on the Wolds adjoins to the west); *Water Furrowes* 1682, *Waterfurrows* 1686, 1744, ~ *hedge furlong* 1744 (*v.* **hecg**) (*v.* **wæter, furh**; usually interpreted as 'furrows where water tends to lie', but *v. waterfurris* in Muston f.ns. (b)); *Wetfur'* 14, *Wheat Furrowes* 1682, ~ *forrows* 1686 (*v.* **wēt, furh**); *Wheatefeild* 1561 (1700) (*v.* **hwǣte, feld**).

Stachedirne 1086 DB, *Stachederna* Hy 1 (1333) Ch, Hy 2 (e.14)
  BelCartA et passim to 1.12 (e.15), 12 (e.15) *BelCartB*,
  Stachedern' a.1166 (e.15) *ib, Staccheturn* 1220 MHW
Stacthirn' c.1130 LeicSurv, *Stacthierne* 1209 P, *Stacthern(e)* 1226
  RHug, 1299 Ipm, 1301 Cl, *Stacthurna* 1236 Fees, *Stacthurne*
  1236 ib
Stacderne 1236 Fees, *Stakdern'* e.14 *BelCartA*, 1310 (e.15), 1328
  (e.15) *BelCartB*
Stakederna 12 (e.15) *BelCartB*, John *Rut, Stakedern'* e.13 (e.14)
  BelCartA, 1.13 *Wyg et freq* to 1337 *Rut*, 1346 (e.15) *BelCartB*,
  Stakederne Hy 3 *Rut*, 1276 RH *et passim* to 1302 (e.14)
  BelCartA, 1345 (e.15) *BelCartB*
Staketherna 1226 RHug, *Stakethern(e)* 1235 Cl, 1257 (e.15)
  BelCartB et freq to 1302 (e.14) *BelCartA*, 1325 (e.15) *BelCartB*
  et passim to 1333 Ch, 1472 *Wyg, Stakethirn(e)* 1242, 1243 Fees,
  1252 *Rut et passim* to Hy 3 *Crox*, 1292 OSut (freq), 1.13 *CRCart*,
  Stakethurn(e) John Berkeley, 1249 RGros, 1260 Cur, *Staketurn'*
  e.14 *Rut, Staketurna* 1316 Cl, *Stakethyrn(e)* 1243 Cl, 1316 FA
Stakethorn 1542 MinAccts, *Stackthorne* 1553 Pat, *Stathorne* 1535
  VE, 1592 *Rut et passim* to 1618 *ib*, 1630 LML
Stathern(e) 1325 (1449) *WoCart*, 1327 SR *et passim* to 1344 *Rut*,
  1352 Ipm *et freq*, (~ *in le Val(l)e* 1541 MinAccts, 1553 Pat)

The p.n. comprises two OE elements, **staca** and **þyrne**, literally 'the
stake-thorn'. It is uncertain what precisely the compound signified.
Perhaps one might think of a type of thorn with a well-defined stem,
useful in the construction of fencing; but if OE **stacaþyrne* were indeed
a compound describing a specific type of thorn, then its nature is lost.
OE **staca** was sometimes used in p.ns. with the meaning 'boundary
post', but it is unclear what boundary a **stacaþyrne* would have
indicated if this compound indeed meant 'boundary thorn', since the

present township lies on the lower slope of the escarpment of the Wolds at the edge of the Vale of Belvoir, hence ~ *in le Valle* 1541, *v.* **val**. Note that some 16th and 17th cent. spellings show attraction to *þorn* 'the hawthorn'.

THE BELT, *v.* **belt**. BLACKSMITH'S LANE, *v.* **blacksmith**. COMBS PLANTATION, occupying a valley in the escarpment of the Wolds, *v.* **cumb**. HARBY AND STATHERN STATION, on the former *London & North-Western Joint Railway* 1854 O, now disused. KING'S ARMS (P.H.) (lost), *King's Arms* 1846, 1863, 1877 White, 1925 Kelly. METHODIST CHAPEL. MILL HO. MOOR LANE is *the Moor Road* 1799 *EnclA*, *v.* The Moor in f.ns; (a) *infra*. NOTTINGHAM AND GRANTHAM CANAL, 1846, 1863, 1877 White, now disused. PASTURE LANE, cf. *Hills Pasture Road* 1799 *EnclA*, *the Pasture* 1674 *Terrier*, *the beast pasture* 1682 *ib*, ~ ~ *paster* 1686 *ib* (*v.* **beste**), *the Com(m)on Pasture* 1625, 1697, 1700, 1703, 1709 *ib* (*v.* **commun**), *Cowe paster* 1659 LAS (*v.* **cū**), *Hills Pasture* 1784 *Surv*, 1792 *Plan*, 1799 *EnclA*, *Nether Pasture* 1744 *Rental*, 1784 *Surv*, 1792 *Plan*, *Toftes pasture* 1709 *Terrier* (*v.* **toft**), *Wood Pasture* 1784 *Surv*, 1792 *Plan*, *the Pasture hedg(e)* 1674, 1679 *Terrier* (*v.* **hecg**), *v.* **pasture**. PLOUGH (P.H.) (lost), *Plough* 1846, 1863 White,1925 Kelly, *Plough Inn* 1877 White. THE RECTORY, 1877 White, 1925 Kelly; it is *the parsonaidge howse* 1605 *Terrier*, *(the) Parsonage house* 1625, 1709 *ib*, *v.* **personage**. RED LION (P.H) (lost), *Red Lion* 1846, 1863, 1877 White, 1925 Kelly. ST GUTHLAC'S CHURCH, *Church (St Guthlake)* 1846, 1863, 1877 White, *Church (St Guthlac)* 1925 Kelly; it is earlier recorded as *ecclesie de Staccheturn* 1220 MHW, *ecclesia(m) de Stakethurn'* 1249 RGros, *ecclesia de Staketherne* 1292 *Pat*, ~ *de Stathern(e)* 1340, 1380 *ib*. Note also *the Churchyard* 1709 *Terrier*. STATHERN BRIDGE, crossing the Nottingham and Grantham Canal. STATHERN JUNCTION, the meeting of *Great Northern Railway* 1854 O and *Great Northern & London & North-Western Joint Railway* 1854 ib; both disused. STATHERN LODGE, 1824 O, *v.* **loge**. STATHERN WOOD, 1795 Nichols, 1824 O, *the Wood* 1625 *Terrier*, 1744 *Rental*. TOFT'S HILL, TOFT'S LANE, *(the) Toftes* 1605, 1625 *Terrier*, 1634 LAS, *the toffts* 1674, 1679 *Terrier*, *the tofts* 1697, 1700, 1703, 1709 *ib*, 1784 *Surv*, *v.* **toft**. WHITE HO.

FIELD-NAMES

In (a), forms dated 1784 are *Surv*, 1791 are *FB*, 1792 are *Plan* and 1799 are *EnclA*. Forms throughout dated Hy 3 are *Crox*; 1284 (e.15) and 1302 (e.15) are *BelCartB*; 1285 (e.14) and 1302 (e.14) are *BelCartA*; 1292 are OSut; 1302 and 1346 are *Rut*; e.14 are *Gret*; 1337 are Ch; 1605, 1625, 1674, 1679, 1682, 1682 (1791), 1686, 1697, 1700, 1703 and 1709 are *Terrier*; 1630, 1631, 1633, 1634, 1641, 1643, 1644, 1646, 1649, 1650, 1653, 1658, 1659, 1660, 1667, c.1671 and 1680 are LAS; 1744 are *Rental*.

(a) Nether Ash 1784, 1791, 1792, Upper Ash 1791, 1792, Short Ash 1784 (*Short Eash* 1697, 1703) (*v.* **æsc**); Ashby Leys 1791 (1686, *Ashby Leyes* 1682, 1744, ~ *Leas* 1709, *Eashbee leyes* 1697, 1700, *Eashby leyes* 1700, ~ *Lees* 1703, *v.* **leys**; with the surn. *Ashby*); Barn Leys Furlong 1791, 1792 (*v.* **bern**, **leys**); Barnston Rd, Barnston Bridle Rd (*v.* **brigdels**), Barnstone Foot Road 1799 (*v.* **foot-road**) (the roads and path to Barnstone, four miles to the north-west in Notts.); Over Bastards 1784 (*v.* **uferra**), Upper Bastards 1791 (*v.* **bastard**); the Becks 1784 (1682, 1703, 1709, 1744, *ad le Becke* 1302 SR (p), *the Beckes* 1605, 1625, 1674, 1679, 1697, 1700, *In ye Becks* 1686, *v.* **bekkr**); Bells Leys 1791 (*v.* **leys**; either with the surn. *Bell* or referring to land whose rental was assigned to the maintenance of the bells of the parish church, *v.* Field 200–202); Belvoir Rd, Belvoir Foot Road 1799 (*v.* **foot-road**; Belvoir Castle lies some three miles to the north-east); Black Ground 1791, 1792 (*the Blacke ground* 1674, 1679, 1697, 1700, (*the*) *Black Ground* 1682, 1686, 1703, 1709, 1744), Black Ground Furlong 1791, 1792 (1744) (*v.* **blæc**, **grund**; poss. referring to the colour of the soil, but in eModE, *black* was also used of 'fertile' in contrast to *white* 'infertile'); Bleaklands 1784, 1791, ~ Furlong 1792 (*the blacke landes* 1625, *blackelands* 1700, *v.* **blæc**, **land**); Bottom Furlong 1791 (i.e of the West Fd); Bramble Cl 1846, 1863, 1877 White (*v.* **bræmbel**); the Nether furlong in the Breaches 1784, Nether Breach, Upper Breach Furlong 1791 (*the Breaches* 1605, 1625, 1682, *the Breeches* 1674, 1744, *the breches* 1679, *Middle Fur' in* ~ ~, *Upper Fur' in the breaches* 1682, *Midle Fur' in* ~ ~, *Upper Fur' in ye Breaches* 1686 (*v.* **furlang**), (*the*) *Breches Furlong* 1697, 1700, 1703, *v.* **brēc**); Broad Sike 1791, 1792 (1605, 1625, *Bradesike*, *Bradesyke* e.14, *Broade Sike* 1605, *Broad sicke* 1674, 1679, ~ *Seike* 1682, *Brod Sick* 1703, *Broad Syke* 1744, *Broad Sick Fur'* 1686 (*v.* **furlang**), *v.* **brād**, **sík**); Bull Sty 1784 (*the bull stie* 1653, 1709, *Bull stie(e)* 1697, 1700, 1709, *v.* **bula**, **stig**); Buskey Furlong 1791, Buskey Leys 1791 (*v.* **leys**) (*v.* **buski**); Butcher Leys 1791 (*bucher leyes* 1674, 1700, *Butcher leyes* 1679, 1682, 1697, 1744, ~ *leys* 1686, *Buchor Leys* 1703, *Butchor Leas* 1709, *v.* **leys**; with the surn. *Butcher*); Case Lane Cl 1846, 1863 White, Cake ~ ~ (sic) 1877 ib (presum. originally with the surn. *Case*, although *Cake* is also current as a surn., *v.* Reaney *s.n.*); Castle Wong Furlong 1791 (*Castle Wong* 1682, 1744, *Castlewonge Fur'* 1686, *v.* **vangr**, **furlang**; adjacent to Belvoir Castle); Clark Sty 1784 (*Clarke stie(e)* 1605, 1625, 1674, 1679, (*the*) *Clearkes stie* 1625, *the Clarkestie* 1679, *Clarkes Stye* 1744, *v.* **stig**; either with the surn. *Clarke* or with **clerc**); Coldhill 1784 (1605, 1674, 1679 *et passim* to 1744, *Cowdhill* 1625, (*on*) *Coldhill gauel* 1674, 1679 (with either **gafol**[1] or, more likely, **gafol**[2]) (*v.* **cald**, **hyll**); Coney Gray Hill 1791 (*the Coneygrie* 1625, *Coneygreue* 1709, *Coniger hill* 1605, *Conigree* ~, *Conigrey* ~ 1625, 1682, *Conninger* ~ 1649, *Cuneger* ~ 1674, *Con(e)gree* ~ 1686, 1744, *Cun(n)egar* ~ 1697, 1703, *Cunneger* ~ 1700, *Coney Greve Hill* 1709, *v.* **coningre** and *the Coniger cloose* in f.ns. (b) *infra*); Crabtree Furlong 1784, 1791 (1625, 1697, 1703, 1709, 1744, *Crabbtree furlonge* 1605, 1700, *Crabtre Fur'* 1686, *v.* **crabtre**; an instance present in each of the three great fields of the township); Cranor 1784, ~ Leys 1791 (*v.* **leys**) (*Crana* 1674, 1679, 1697, 1700, *Crane* 1679, *Cranoe* 1682, *Crano* 1686, 1744, *Crannor* 1703, 1709, *Crano(e) Fur'* 1682, 1686 (*v.* **furlang**), *Cranner Nest* 1703 (*v.* **næss, nes**), poss. 'headland where crows abound', *v.* **crāwe** (**crāwena** gen.pl.), **hōh**, cf. Cranoe in Gartree Hundred); Crokeleys 1784 (*Crokland'* 1292, *Crocklandes* 1605, 1625, *Crocklands* 1674, 1679, *Crockleayes* 1697, *Crockleyes* 1700, *Croakleys* 1703, *Croak leas* 1709, *v.* **krókr, land**; in the later forms, *lands* is replaced by **leys**, poss. because of the swarding over of arable); Cross Furlong 1791, 1792 (*the Cross(e) furlong* 1697, 1700, 1703, 1744, *v.* **cross**; an instance present in each of the great fields); The Cuts 1791 (*v.* **cut** and *Shortcuttes* in Branston f.ns. (b)); Deadhill Sike 1791 (*v.* **dēad, hyll, sík**; in p.ns. 'dead' usually refers to a place of violent death or to the discovery of human bones, and as this is a hill site, early burials are more likely); The Drabble 1784 (*the Drable* 1674, 1679, 1697, 1700, *The Drabbyell* 1680), Drabble Furlong 1791, Drabble Leys 1791 (*v.* **leys**) (perh. 'mire hill' or 'mire stream', *v.* **drabbe**, with **hyll** or **wella**; an eModE *drabbe* in the sense 'mire' is unrecorded, but cf. LGerm *drabbe* 'dirt, mire' and eModE *drabbe* 'a dirty woman, a slut'; the recurring def.art. in the early forms would seem to preclude the surn. *Drabble, v.* Reaney *s.n.*); Drift Ford 1784, 1791 (*the Dryft* 1605, *the Drift(e)* 1625, 1709, *v.* **drift, ford**); Dry Leys 1791 (*v.* **drȳge, leys**); Eastwell Rd 1799 (Eastwell lies one and a half miles to the south); Eaton Rd 1799 (Eaton lies two miles to the south-east); Edmanholes 1784, Long ~ ~, Short ~ ~, Edmund Knowles 1791 (*Edmund Knowle* 1605, (*on*) *Eadmond Knowell* 1674, *Edmon(d) Knowles* 1679, 1697, *Eadmonknowles* 1700, *Edmond knols* 1703, *Edmon nols* 1709, *v.* **cnoll**; either with the OE pers.n. *Ēadmund* or with its surn. reflex *Edmond/Edmund, v.* Reaney *s.n.*); Flaxhill 1784 (1605, 1630, 1674, 1679, 1697, 1700, 1703, 1709, 1744, *Flaxhul* 1292, *flaxen hill* 1625, *Flaxhilles* 1686, *Flaxe hill* 1700, cf. *Flaxhulgoris* 1292 (*v.* **gāra**), *v.* **fleax, hyll**); Fold furlong 1784, 1791 (*le Foldefurlong'* 1302, 1302 (e.15), *le foldforlong'* 1302 (e.14), *Fold(e) Fur'* 1682, 1686, *the Foald Furlong* 1744, *v.* **fald, furlang**); Foster Hill Furlong 1791 (with the surn. *Foster*); Fulleyhill 1784, Fulley Hill North ~, Fulley Hill South Furlong 1791 (*ful(l)well hill* 1605, 1625, *Folleehill* 1674, 1700, *Follow hill* 1679, *Fulloe hill* 1682, *Fullow hill* 1686, 1703, *Fullhill* 1709, *Fully Hill* 1744, *ful(l)well sike* 1605, 1625, *Folleehill Sicke* 1674, 1700, *Followhill sicke* 1679, 1697, *Fullowhill Sicke* 1703, *Fullhill sick* 1709 (*v.* **sík**), *Fulleehill yate* 1697 (*v.* **gata**) (*v.* **fūl, wella, hyll**); (Furlong) between the Gates 1784, 1791 (*Between(e) the gates* 1674, 1697, 1700, 1708, *betwixt the gates* 1679, *Between ye gates* 1682, *Between Gates* 1703, *v.* **gata**; a furlong in Long Fd *infra*); Golden Furlong 1791 (*v.* **gylden**; presum. complimentary in terms of productive land rather than descriptive of flowers or other vegetation); Grange Cl 1792 (*the Grange* 1625, *Granges Close* 1633), Grange Close Furlong 1784, 1791, 1792, Grange Wong 1791 (*the granges woong* 1625, *v.* **vangr**) (*v.* **grange**; prob. in origin an outlier of Belvoir Priory or Croxton Abbey); Grantham Bridle Rd 1799 (*v.* **brigdels**), Grantham Foot Road 1799 (*v.* **foot-road**) (Grantham lies nine miles to the north-east in Lincs.); Greensyke 1925 Kelly (*Greensyke* 1744, *Greene sike* 1605, *Green(e)sicke* 1625, 1697, 1700, 1703, *Green Sick* 1709, cf. *Greensick had* 1667 (*v.* **hēafod**)), Greensike

Slade 1784 (*v.* **slæd**) (*v.* **grēne**[1], **sík**); Harby Rd 1799, Harby Bridle Rd 1799 (*v.* **brigdels**), Harby Foot Road 1799 (*v.* **foot-road**), Harby Gate Furlong 1791, 1792 (*harbie gate* 1605, *Harby*(*e*) ~ 1625, 1630, *v.* **gata**), Harby Meer Furlong 1792 (*harbie meare* 1605, 1630, *Harby*(*e*) *Meare* 1625, 1674, *Harby mere* 1679, *Harbee Meer* 1744, *v.* **(ge)mǣre**; the former Harby parish boundary), Harby Moor Cl 1792, Harby Moor Furlong 1784, 1791 (*harbie moore* 1605, *Harby more* 1674, 1679, 1697, ~ *Moor*(*e*) 1700, 1703, 1709, *v.* **mōr**[1]), Near, Long, Short Harby Tofts 1784, 1791 (*harbie toftes* 1605, *Harby*(*e*)*toftes* 1625, 1679, *Harby Tofts* 1682, 1686, 1697, 1700, 1703, 1709, 1744, *v.* **toft**) (Harby adjoins to the west); Hellin Lands 1784, Helley Lands Furlong 1791 (*Hollylandes* 1605, 1625, *Healeylands* 1674, *Halleelands* 1679, *Helleelands* 1697, 1700, *Hollelands* 1703, *Hollilands* 1707, *Hellhilands* 1744, *Hely leyes* 1682, *Hely leys Fur'* 1686 (*v.* **furlang**), *v.* **land**; the first el. may be **hālig** 'holy, dedicated to sacred use' rather than **hol**[2] 'lying in a hollow', indicating land belonging to the Church, poss. originally to Belvoir Priory or to Croxton Abbey; in some later forms, *lands* is replaced by **leys**, cf. Crokeleys *supra*); Hookings 1784, 1791, ~ Furlong 1792 (*Hookins* 1674, 1697, *Hookings* 1679, 1703, 1709, *Hookeins* 1700, *v.* **hōc**; with either **-ing**[2] or **eng**); Hop Yard 1824 O (*v.* **hop-yard**); Hulcoat Sty Furlong 1784, 1791 (*Hul*(*l*)*coate stighe* 1605, 1625, *Hullcoate Stie*(*e*) 1605, 1674, 1697, *Hulcoat*(*e*) *stie*(*e*) 1630, 1679, 1700, 1703, 1709, *Hullcoate Sty* 1682, *Hulkcoate Stie* 1709, *Hulcoate Stee*, *Hulcourt Stye* 1744, *Hulcoatestie end* 1674 (*v.* **ende**), *v.* **hyll**, **cot**; prob. with **stīg** rather than with **stig**); Hurst Nook 1792, ~ ~ Leys 1791 (*v.* **leys**), Hurst Nook Rd 1799 (*v.* **hyrst**, **nōk**); Long, Short Kervings 1784, 1791 (*v.* **kervinge**); Hayes 1784 (*the haies, the hayes* 1605, *the heayes* 1674, 1679, *The Hays* 1744, *the middel*(*l*) *furlong in* ~, *the ouer furlong in* (*the*) *heayes* 1674, 1679 (*v.* **uferra**), *Middle Fur' in* ~ ~, *Upper Fur' in the Hayes* 1682, *Midle Fur' in* ~ ~, *Upper Fur' in ye Hays* 1686, *the Middel*(*l*) *furlong in* ~ ~, *the Nether furlong in the heayes* 1697, 1700, *afarside the heayes* 1697, *Farside heayes* 1700, *the Hea*(*y*)*s field* 1703, *the heyeslandes* 1625 (*v.* **land**), poss. **hǣse** 'land overgrown with brushwood' rather than the plural of **(ge)hæg** 'an enclosure, a fenced-in piece of ground'); Lammas Cl 1799 (*v.* **lammas**); Little Hill 1784 (1605, 1625, 1682, 1686, 1703, 1709, 1744, *littel*(*l*) *hill* 1674, 1679, 1697, 1700, *Little Hill Furlong* 1682, 1686, *little hill gutter* 1605 (*v.* **goter**), *v.* **lȳtel**, **hyll**); Littleing, ~ Furlong 1791 (*littling* 1605, 1625, *littel*(*l*)*in* 1679, 1697, 1700, *Littlein* 1703, *Little Inn* 1744), Little Inn Banks 1784 (*v.* **banke**), Little Inn Side 1784 (*v.* **sīde**) (*v.* **lȳtel**, **lítill**, **eng**); Long Fd 1791, 1792, 1799 ((*the*) *Long Feild* 1674, 1679, 1682, 1686, 1697, 1700, 1744, ~ *Field* 1703, 1709, *v.* **lang**[1], **feld**; one of the great fields of the village, also called Middle Fd *infra*); Long Hill 1784, 1791 (1744), Longhill Furlong 1791, 1792 (*Longhill Fur'* 1682, 1686) (*v.* **lang**[1], **hyll**); Long Lands 1791, 1792 ((*the*) *Longlands* 1682, 1744, cf. *Longlands Fur'* 1686 (*v.* **furlang**)), Long Lands Hades 1791 (*v.* **hēafod**) (*v.* **lang**[1], **land**); the Mare 1784 (1605, 1625, 1674, 1679, 1697, 1700, 1703, 1744, *the Mars* 1682, 1686, cf. *the Mare butts* 1744 (*v.* **butte**)), Mar Furlong 1791 (*Mars Fur'* 1686), Mar Leys 1791 (*v.* **leys**) (*v.* **marr**[1]); Melton Foot Road 1799 (*v.* **foot-road**; the path to Melton Mowbray which lies eight miles to the south); Mickleholms 1784 (*Mickle ho*(*l*)*mes* 1682, 1686, *nether, upper Mickleholmes* 1744, *v.* **micel**, **mikill**, **holmr**); (the) Middle Fd 1784 ((*the*) *Middle Feild*(*e*) 1605, 1625, *v.* **middel**, **feld**; one of the great fields of the township, also called Long Fd *supra*);

Middle Gate 1784 (*v.* **gata**); Mill Furlong 1791; the Moor 1784, 1791, 1792, Moores 1791 (*the Moore* 1605, 1674, 1700, 1703, 1709, *the Moare* 1625, *the More* 1674, 1679, 1682, 1684, 1686, 1709, *the Moor* 1686, 1744, *Bottom of the Moore* 1703, 1709, *the Farside the More* 1679, *the upper end of the moore* 1700 (furlongs so called), *the broadley in the moore* 1700 (*v.* **brād, ley**), *ye greatley in the more* 1697 (*v.* **grēat, ley**), *the hedley in the more* 1674, *ye headley in ye more* 1697 (*v.* **headley**), *the Throw(w)ley in the more* 1674, 1679, 1697, *the Throwe ley in the moore* 1700, *Thorow Ley* 1703 (*v.* **þurh, ley**), *the Moare end* 1625, *the Moore end* 1709, *Moor End* 1744 (*v.* **ende**), *(the) More hedge* 1674, 1686, 1697, *Moor(e) Hedge* 1700, 1703, 1744 (a boundary hedge), *Aboue More hedge* 1682 (*v.* **aboven**), *the Moor side* 1744 (*v.* **sīde**)), Middle Moore 1784 (*Middle More* 1682, *Midle Moor* 1686, *Middlemoor* 1744, cf. *midlemore stie* 1630 (*v.* **stīg**)), West Moore 1784 (1703, *West More* 1605, 1658, 1674, 1682, 1697, *Westmoare* 1625, *Westmoor* 1709, 1744), (the) Moor Piece 1784, 1791, Furlong above ~ ~, Furlong Bottom of Moor Piece 1791, Moor Piece Cl 1791 (*v.* **pece**) (*v.* **mōr¹** and Moor Lane *supra*); Long, Short Mosshill 1784, 1791, Long Mosshill Furlong 1792, Mosshill Lands 1784 (*v.* **land**) (*Mossill* e.14, *Moysshill* 1605, *Moshill* 1625, *Morsshill* 1700, *Mosshill* 1744, *Long Morsshill* 1674, 1679, 1697, ~ *Morsell* 1682, 1686, 1744, ~ *Mossell* 1703, ~ *Mossul* 1709, *Short Morsell* 1682, 1744, ~ *Morshill* 1686, *the Hither side Mossell* 1709 (furlongs so called), *Moysshill stighe* 1605, *Moshill stie* 1625, 1630 (*v.* **stīg**), *v.* **mos, hyll**); Nether Furlong 1784, 1791 (in West Fd); New Cl 1792; New Pit 1791, Newpit Wong 1784 (*v.* **pytt, vangr**); New Rd 1799; Nickman Acres 1791 (*Nick(e) my Naker* (sic) 1605, 1625, *Nickmenacar* 1674, *Nickmaynacar* 1679, *Nickmanacre* 1682, 1686, 1744, *Nickmanacar* 1697, *Nickmanaker* 1700, *-akers* 1709, *v.* **æcer**; with the surn. *Nickman, v.* Reaney *s.n.*); the Ninepenny Leys 1784 (*v.* **leys**; referring to a holding for which a ninepenny rent was once paid, *v.* Field 193–4); North Long 1784, 1791 (*Northlang* 1697, *Northlong* 1700, *Norlong* 1709), North Long Furlong 1791, North Long Wong 1784 (*v.* **vangr**) (*v.* **norð, lang²**); Occupation Rd 1799 (a common name, often dating from the Enclosures and meaning 'a private road for the use of the occupiers of the land', *v.* OED *s.v.* occupation, 7; it signified a green lane, an access road through what was originally a great field); the Over Furlong 1784 (1703, *the ouer furlong* 1674, 1679, 1697, 1700, 1703, *v.* **uferra**; in Wood Fd); the Over Gate 1784 (*v.* **uferra, gata**); Parsons Cl 1799 (*v.* **persone**); Long, Short Peaselands 1784, 1791, 1792 (1674, 1679, 1682, 1686, 1700, 1703, *pease landes* 1605, 1625, *Peas(e)lands* 1697, 1709, *v.* **pise, land**); Pen Lane Gate Rd 1799 (*pen(n) lane* 1605, 1625, *v.* **penn², lane**); Pigeon Hole Furlong 1791 (*Pigeon Hole* 1682, *Pigin hole* 1686, *Pigeon holes* 1744, *v.* **pigeon, hol¹**; it is uncertain whether this describes literally a hollow frequented by pigeons or names figuratively a small recess of some sort); Plungar Foot Road 1799 (*v.* **foot-road**), Plungar Tofts 1784, Long ~ ~, Short ~ ~ 1791 (*plungerthetoftes* 1284 (e.15), 1285 (e.14), *Plungardetoftes* 1302, 1302 (e.14), 1302 (e.15), *Plungar Toftes* 1605, *Plunger Toft(e)s* 1625, 1679, 1686, 1697, 1700, ~ *toffts* 1674, *Plungar Tofts* 1682, 1703, 1709, *Plonger* ~ 1744, *v.* **toft**; Plungar adjoins to the north); Redhill Furlong 1791 (*v.* **rēad, hyll**; alluding to the colour of the soil); Redlands 1784, 1791 (1625, 1674, 1679, 1682, 1686, 1697, 1700, 1703, 1709, 1744, *Redelant* e.14, *Readlandes* 1605, *High Red(d)land(e)s* 1605, 1625, 1697, 1700, 1709, *Lower, High Redlands* 1682, 1686, *Red(d)landes furl(onge)* 1605, 1625,

Redlandsik' 1292, *readlandes sike, Reddlandes syke* 1605, *Redland(es) sike* 1625, *Redland sick(e)* 1641, 1686, 1697, 1700, 1703, 1709, ~ *Seike* 1682, *Redlands sicke* 1700, *Red Land Syke* 1744, *Redland(s) sick(e) end* 1674, 1679, 1709 (*v.* **ende**), *v.* **rēad, land, sík**; with reference to the colour of the soil); Redmile Foot Road 1799 (*v.* **foot-road**; the path to Redmile which lies three miles to the north-east); Sand Holes 1791 (*v.* **sand-hol**); Sandpit hill 1784, 1791 ((*the*) *Sand pitts* 1674, 1679, *Sandpitt hill* 1605, 1625, 1674, 1679, 1682, 1686, 1697, 1700, 1703, 1709, 1744, cf. *Sandpitt hill gap* 1697, 1700 (*v.* **gap**), *Sandpitt hill gate* 1605 (*v.* **gata**), *Sand pitts hill landes* 1625 (*v.* **land**), *Sandpit hill moore* 1709 (*v.* **mōr**[1]), *Sandpitthill troffe* 1674 (*v.* **trog**), *v.* **sand-pytt, hyll**); the Sands 1784 (1744, *v.* **sand**); Short Leys 1791 (1686, *Short leyes Fur'* 1682 (*v.* **furlang**), *v.* **sc(e)ort, leys**); Silver Hill 1791 (*v.* **seolfor, silfr**; poss. an elliptical form of an older plant-name (cf. *silver-thistle*) or perh. a jocular reference to the richness of the ground or even an allusion to the rent paid for it; *Silver* also occurs as a surn., *v.* Reaney *s.n.*); Smithill 1784 (1697, *Smithhill* 1605, 1625, 1674, 1679, 1703, 1709, *Smiethhill* 1605, *Smithehill* 1700, *Smith(e)y hill* 1682, 1744, *Smythey* ~ 1686, cf. *Smithill hole* 1674, *Smith hill(e)* ~ 1679, 1700 (*v.* **hol**[1]), *Smiethhill Sieck, Smieth hill syeecke* 1605, *Smithhill sike* 1625, ~ *Sicke* 1697, 1703, 1709 (*v.* **sík**), *Smiethhill sike ditch* 1605 (*v.* **dīc**), *Smiethhill syke hole* 1625 (*v.* **hol**[1]), *v.* **hyll**; it is difficult to distinguish **smēðe**[1] 'smooth' from **smið** 'a smith' as the first el., but some later forms have been influenced by **smiððe** 'a smithy'; and note Blacksmith's Lane *supra*); Spring Furlong 1784, 1791, 1792, ~ *Lands* 1784 (*v.* **land**) (*v.* **spring**[1]); Stathern Point 1806 Map (*v.* **point**); Stockleys 1784 (*Stockeleyes* 1625), Stock Leys Furlong 1791 (*Stockleyes furlong* 1674, 1679) (*v.* **stoc, leys**); Stone Hill 1791, ~ ~ Furlong 1792 (*stonnie hill* 1605, *stonye* ~ 1625, *Stoney* ~ 1700, cf. *Stonehill stie, stonnehill stye* 1630, *Ston(e)yhill stiee* 1674, 1679 (*v.* **stīg**), *v.* **stānig, stān, hyll**); Stoney Beck Furlong 1791, 1792 (*Stonnie Beckes* 1605, *Stoney beck(e)* 1697, 1700, *Stony Beck* 1703, *aboue* ~ ~, *beneath Ston(e) beck* 1674, 1679 (*v.* **aboven**), cf. *stonnie beck(e) ditch* 1625 (*v.* **dīc**), *v.* **stānig, bekkr**); Street Bridge 1784, 1791, ~ ~ Furlong 1791 (*the street bridg* 1709, *the ouerside, the Nether Side* (*the*) *Street Bridge* 1703 (*v.* **uferra, sīde**)), the Street Rd 1799 (*the Street* 1605, 1625, *the streete* 1631, *ye street waye* 1697, *the street way* 1697, 1700, 1703, 1709, *aboue, beneath the streetway* 1674 (*v.* **aboven**), *the ouerside, the netherside the streetway* 1697 (*v.* **uferra, sīde**) (furlongs so called in *the Long feild, infra*), *v.* **stræt, weg**; an unlocated Roman road through the Vale of Belvoir, poss. a continuation via Waltham on the Wolds of King Street Lane (*q.v.*)); Long, Short Stripes 1791, 1792 (*v.* **strīp**); Swine Balk, ~ Baulk Furlong 1791 (*v.* **swīn**[1], **balca**); Taslands 1784, 1791, Tasland Furlong 1791 (*Tasslandes* 1605, 1625, *Tasslands* 1674, 1679, 1700, 1744, *Teayes lands* 1682, *Teaselands* 1686, *Taslands* 1697, 1703, 1709, *v.* **tǣsel, land**; teasel (*Dipsacus fullonum*) nowadays grows abundantly on the verges of the Roman road Sewstern Lane, five miles to the east; cf. *Tasleclif* in Kirby Bellars, East Goscote Hundred); Thorney Slade 1784 (1679, *Thirnie slade* 1605, 1625, *Thornslade* 1674, *Throney slade* (sic) 1697, *Thornney* ~ 1700, *v.* **slæd**; with the original first el. **þyrniht** later replaced by **þornig**); Thorn(e) Tree Furlong 1791, 1792, Thorn Tree Wong 1784 (*v.* **vangr**) (*v.* **thorne-tree**); Thrumpton Balk Furlong 1791, 1792 (*v.* **balca**; with the surn. *Thrumpton* of a family originally from the Notts. village of this name 16 miles to the west); the Tofts Cl 1784 (*the Toftes close* 1625), Tofts Furlong,

Tofts South Furlong 1791 (*Tofts Fur'* 1682, 1686, *v.* **toft** and Toft's Hill *supra*); the
Tongues 1784 (1682, 1703, 1709, 1744, *the toung(e)s* 1625, 1674, 1679, 1697, 1700,
The Tonges 1686, *v.* **tunge**); Top Furlong 1791 (that of West Fd *infra*); The Town
Street 1799 (*v.* **tūn, strǣt**); Long, Short Tumberhill 1784, 1791, ~ Tumbrell 1791,
~ Tumbrill 1792 (*Tumberhil'* 1284 (e.15), *Tumbyrhil* 1285 (e.14), 1302 (e.14),
Timberhul' 1292, *Timbirhil(l)* 1302, 1302 (e.15), *Tumbrill* 1605, 1625, 1703, 1744,
Tumberhill 1649, 1674, 1679, 1697, *Toumberhill* 1700, *Tumbrill Fur'* 1682, 1686 (*v.*
furlang), *Tumbrell gate* 1605, *Tumbrill* ~ 1605, 1625 (*v.* **gata**), *Timberhulslad'* 1292
(*v.* **slæd**), *v.* **timber, hyll**); Upper Furlong 1791 (1744, *the upor furlong* 1703, ~ *uper*
~ 1709; that of Wood Fd *infra*); Walker Leys 1791, 1792 (*walkar leys, walker lease*
1630, *v.* **leys**; prob. with the surn. *Walker*, but **walcere** is poss.); (the) West Fd 1784,
1791, 1792, 1799 (1682 (1791), 1703, 1744, (*the*) *West feild* 1605, 1625, 1674, 1679,
1682, 1686, 1697, 1700, *v.* **west, feld**; one of the great fields of the village); Whittle
Sty 1784, 1792, Whittle (or Wheathill) Sty 1784 (*Wethul'* 1292, *Wheat hill* 1625,
1674, 1700, 1703, *Wethilgate* 1292 (*v.* **gata**), *Wetenhulsty* 1292 (*v.* **hwǣten**), *Wheatle
stie* 1605, *Wheate hill stie, White hill stye* 1625, *Wheattill stie, Whittell* ~ 1630,
Wheathill sty(e) 1630, 1682, 1686, ~ *stie(e)* 1674, 1679, 1697, 1700, 1703, 1709,
Whittle(s) Stye 1744, *Whittel stie end* 1674 (*v.* **ende**)), Whittle Sty Furlong 1791,
1792 (*Wheatle stie furlonge* 1605, *White hill stie furlong* 1625) (*v.* **hwǣt, hyll, stīg**);
Wood Fd 1784, 1791, 1792, 1799 (*the Wodd feilde, Woodd feild* 1605, (*the*) *Wood
feild* 1625, 1674, 1679, 1682, 1686, 1700, *the wood feeld* 1633, *ye Wodfeild* 1697,
the Wood field 1703, 1709, 1744, *v.* **wudu, feld**; one of the great fields of the
township); Short Woodgate 1791 (*Woddgate, the Wodd gates* 1605, (*the*) *Woodgate*
1625, 1674, 1679, 1697, 1703, 1709, *the Woodyate* 1700, *v.* **wudu, gata**); Woodside
1784 (1682, 1686, 1744, (*att*) *the wood side* 1625, 1709, *v.* **wudu, sīde** and Stathern
Wood *supra*).

(b) *Barnes his Close* 1625, *Richd. Barnes Close* 1744 (seemingly a long-held
family property); *Bebing'* 1292 (the first el. appears to be the early OE pers.n. *Bebbe*,
which suggests that this f.n. may be the sole surviving evidence of a local folk-name
*Bebbingas 'the people of Bebbe', *v.* **-ingas**; otherwise *v.* **eng**); *Becke Closse* 1700,
Becks Close 1703, (*the*) *Beckes ditch* 1605, 1625, *the Becks Dike* 1659 (*v.* **dīc, dík**),
Beckes gate 1682, *Becks* ~ 1686, 1744 (*v.* **gata**) (*v.* **bekkr**); *Billinglye nooke* 1625 (*v.*
nōk; if not with the surn. of a family originating in Billingley (YW), then *v.* **billing,
lēah** and *Billinge wong* in Saltby f.ns. (b)); *the Bottoms* 1605, 1625 (*v.* **botm**); *the
bridge lane* 1625, *the Bridg lane end* 1605, *breglane end* 1630, *Briglane end* 1674,
1679, 1703, *Brigelane end* 1697, 1700 (*v.* **lane-ende**), *bridge lane gate* 1625 (*v.*
brycg, bryggja); *Bretland'* 1284 (e.15), 1285 (e.15), 1302, 1302 (e.14), 1302 (e.15)
(*v.* **breiðr, land**); *Tom Buggs Head Ley* 1744 (*v.* **headley**; with the surn. *Bugg* (ME
bugg(e) 'hobgoblin, scarecrow'), *v.* Reaney *s.n.*); (*in*) *campo boriali* e.14 ('the north
field', with MLat *campus* 'a field' and MLat *borialis* 'northern, north'; one of the
early great fields of the village); *Castelgate* 1292 (*v.* **castel(l), gata**; the road to
Belvoir Castle); *Caunt headland* 1697, 1700, *Caunts* ~ 1703 (*v.* **hēafod-land**; with
the surn. *Cant/Caunt*, cf. Cant's Thorns in Wartnaby); *Chantry land* 1700 (*v.*
chaunterie); *Cheescake* 1744 (*v.* **cheesecake** and *chesecake* in Saltby f.ns. (b));
Chitilishill e.14 (*v.* **hyll**; the first el. is the Anglo-Scand form *Cytel* of the Scand
pers.n. *Ketill* in the possessive case, *v.* Feilitzen 305, n.5); *the Church lane* 1605,

1625; *(the) Church headland* 1605, 1697, 1700, 1703, *~ Headlands* 1744 (*v.* **hēafod-land**) (*v.* St Guthlac's Church *supra*); *Cliffordlong'* 1292 bis (*v.* **clif, ford, lang**[2]); *Between the Closein* 1682, *~ ye Closin* 1686 (*v.* **closing**); *Cokkecroft* 1302, 1302 (e.15) (*v.* **croft**; with either **cocc**[1] or **cocc**[2]); *the Common gate* 1605 (*v.* **gata**), *the Com(m)on highe way, ~ ~ highwaie* 1625 (*v.* **hēah-weg**) (*v.* **commun**); *the Coniger cloose* 1605, *Cunnegar Closse* 1700, *Cony Groue Close* 1709, *Coneygrey ~, the Cunigree ditche* 1625 (*v.* **dīc**), *Coninger ~, Connegar Gate* 1605 (*v.* **gata**), *Coninger ~, Connegar hades, Conneger Hads* 1630 (*v.* **hēafod**), *Cuneger hedge* 1697, *Cunnegar he(d)ge* 1700, 1703 (a boundary hedge), *Cuneygree lane* 1625, *Coneygree side* 1625 (*v.* **sīde**), *Cony Groue Slade* 1709 (*v.* **slæd**) (*v.* Coney Gray Hill in f.ns. (a) *supra*); *the cougate* 1660 (this may be dial. **cowgate** 'an allotment of pasture for a single cow' (*v.* Field 127) but the def.art. suggests rather 'the cow road', *v.* **cū, gata**); *Crabb tree stigh* 1605, *Crabtree stigh* 1625, *~ stee* c.1671 (*v.* **crabtre**; with **stīg** or **stig**); *James Dixons Wong* 1744 (*v.* **vangr**; *littell Eash furlong* 1674, *Short eash* 1700 (*v.* **æsc**); *Eashbecks* 1700, *Ashbecks* 1709 (*v.* **æsc, bekkr**); *Eash sike, ~ syke* 1605, *Eashy sike* 1625, *Each sick(e)* 1674, 1679, 1697, 1700, 1703, *Ash Sicke* 1709, *~ Syke* 1744 (*v.* **æsc, sík**); *East(e) beckes* 1605, 1625, *the East beckes peece* 1625, *East Becks peice* 1703 (*v.* **pece**) (*v.* **ēast, bekkr**); *Eastwell leyes* 1625 (*v.* **leys**), *Eastwell meare* 1605, 1625, 1630, 1709, *~ meere* 1625 (*v.* **(ge)mǣre**; the parish boundary of Eastwell which adjoins to the south); *El(l)is leyes* 1674, 1679, 1697, *~ leayes* 1700, *Eles Leaes* 1680, *Ellis Leys* 1703 (*v.* **leys**), *Ellis Nook* 1709 (*v.* **nōk**) (with the surn. *Ellis*); *Engeheuedes* Hy 3 (*v.* **eng, hēafod**); *Farr hill* 1682 (*v.* **feor**); *Fencroftes* 1605, 1625, *Fencrafts* 1674, 1679, 1697, 1700, *Fencraft* 1703, 1709 (*v.* **fenn, croft**); *le flagforlong'* 1285 (e.14) (*v.* **flegge, flagge, furlang**); *James Gelstrupes hedge* 1605 (*v.* **hecg**; a boundary hedge); *Granbye furlong* 1625 (Granby in Notts. adjoins to the north-west); *graunt forlonge* 1605, *Grant furlong* 1697, 1700, 1703, 1709, *graunt woung* 1674, *grant wong* 1679 (*v.* **vangr**; with the surn. *Grant*); *Grantham gate* 1605, 1625 (*v.* **gata**; the road to Grantham which lies nine miles to the north-east in Lincs.); *Greenea* 1659, *Greena* 1674, 1679, *Greenea end* 1659 (*v.* **ende**) (*v.* **grēne**[1]; poss. with **hōh** but earlier forms are needed to identify the second el., cf. Cranor *supra*); *Between the hadlands* 1682, *Bettween ye hadlands* 1681 (*v.* **hēafod-land**); *(the) Hall Clos(s)e* 1697, 1700, 1703 (*v.* **hall**); *Harby hedge* 1674, 1679, *Harbee hedge end* 1744 (*v.* **ende**) (the parish boundary hedge of Harby which adjoins to the west); *Harrod hedg* 1709 (*v.* **hecg**; with the surn. *Harrod*); *Hauerholm* 1285 (e.14), 1302 (e.14) (*v.* **hafri, holmr**); *the Hills* 1679, 1744, *~ ~ feild* 1674; *Hiltons Wong* 1744 (*v.* **vangr**; with the surn. *Hilton*); *Hobbesyke* 1346 (*v.* **sík**; with either **hobb(e)** 'a hummock' or with the ME pers.n. *Hobb* (a pet form of Robert, rhymed on *Rob*); *Holewellecroft* 1284 (e.15), 1285 (e.14), 1302 (e.15) (*v.* **hol**[2], **wella, croft**); *(the) holland hurst* 1605, 1625, 1674, *holand hurst* 1679, *holland hurst furlonge* 1605 (*v.* **hol**[2], **land, hyrst**); *Holmes gate* 1605, 1625 (*v.* **holmr, gata**); *the holmestall* (sic) 1605, *the homestall* 1625, 1709 (*v.* **hām-stall**; belonging to the Parsonage house, *v.* The Rectory *supra*); *Hopbak furlong* 1709 (*v.* **hop**[1], **bæc**); *Hopsik'* 1292 (*v.* **hop**[1], **sík**); *Esquire Howe headland* 1674, *Sir Skroop How headland* 1679 (*v.* **hēafod-land**); *Husband leyes* 1605, 1674, 1679, 1682, 1744, *~ leas* 1625, 1697, 1703, 1709, *~ leys* 1686, *~ leayes* 1700, *Aboue Husband ley(e)s* 1682, 1686 (*v.* **aboven**) (*v.* **leys**; prob. with the surn. *Husband* rather than with ON *húsbóndi*, late

OE *husbonda* 'a farmer, a husbandman'); *Jarvis close* 1682, *Girvas* ~ 1686, *Gervas* ~ 1744 (with the surn. *Jarvis/Gervase/Gervis, v.* Reaney *s.n.* Jarvis); *Julyan Lane* 1605, *gillian lane* 1625 (*v.* **lane**; earlier with the surn. *Julian*, confused later with the surn. *Gillian.* Reaney *s.n.* Julian notes, 'In ME, *Julian* was both masculine and feminine . . . Lat *Julianus* . . . and *Juliana*, its feminine, were both names of saints and both names were popular, the latter particularly as *Gillian.*' And *s.n.* Gillian, he observes that its various modern styles result from 'colloquial pronunciations of *Julian* or, more commonly *Juliana*'.); *Kirkegate* 1337 (*v.* **kirkja, gata** and St Guthlac's Church *supra*); *the leyes* 1625, *the laies Bushe* 1605, *the layes bush* 1625 (*v.* **busc**) (*v.* **leys**); *Littelbeksik'* 1292 (*v.* **lȳtel, lítill, bekkr, sík**); *Longcroft* 1337 (*v.* **lang**[1], **croft**); *the long headland of thearle of Ruttlande* 1625, *the Long headland* 1674, 1679, 1709 (*v.* **hēafod-land, eorl**; with reference to the sixth Earl of Rutland, died 1632, whose grandiose tomb stands in Bottesford parish church); *the longe hedge* 1625; *the ground of Lowghborow Bridges* 1605, *Loughbrough bridges ground*, ~ ~ *land* 1625, *Lowbrowbrige* 1697, *lowbrow land* 1700, *lowbrow leys* 1700 (*v.* **leys**) (the income from rents from this land was assigned to the maintenance of the bridges over R. Soar at Cotes by Loughborough); *the Mere* 1625, *the meare* 1674, 1679, *Meares* 1703 (*v.* **(ge)mǣre**); *Melton gate* 1605 (*v.* **gata**; the road to Melton Mowbray which lies some eight miles to the south); *le Milnewong* 1284 (e.15), 1285 (e.14), 1302, 1302 (e.14), 1302 (e.15) (*v.* **myln, vangr**); *Moreaker Meare* 1644, *Moracker* ~ 1650 (*v.* **mōr**[1], **æcer, (ge)mǣre** and The Moor in f.ns. (a) *supra*); *the Nether furlong* 1679, 1703 (in Wood Fd); *Oliuercroft* 1284 (e.15), 1302, 1302 (e.15) (*v.* **croft**; either with the surn. *Oliver* or with its pers.n. antecedent which became common through the influence of the name of the peer of Charlemagne in the *Chanson de Roland*); *Richard Pachetes headland* 1625 (*v.* **hēafod-land**); *the parsonage headleye* 1625 (*v.* **headley**), *the Parsonaige Troughe* 1605, *the Parsonage troughe* 1625, *the Trough* 1605, *the trouf* 1674, *the truffe* 1679 (*v.* **trog**, here used of a hollow resembling a trough) (*v.* **personage**); *the parsons headland* 1625 (*v.* **hēafod-land**), *the Parson(s) Willowes* 1605, 1625 (*v.* **wilig**) (*v.* **persone**); *Peterhowse lande* 1605, *Peterhouse land* 1625 (*v.* **land**), *the headland of Peterhouse* 1625 (*v.* **hēafod-land**) (the property of the college called Peterhouse in Cambridge); *the pinder stie* 1660, *Pinder Sty(e)* 1682, 1686 (*v.* **pinder, stig**); (*on*) *Next Plunger* 1700, *Plungar field side* 1709 (both were names for the same furlong), *Plungar gate* 1605, 1625 (*v.* **gata**), *Plungar Meare* 1605, 1625, 1709, *Plunger meare* 1625, 1679, ~ *meere* 1625 (*v.* **(ge)mǣre**) (Plungar adjoins to the north); *the pouch* 1625, *the pouch peice* 1674, 1679, 1697, 1700 (*v.* **pece**), (*the*) *bawech headland* (sic) 1674, 1700, (*the*) *bauch* ~ 1679, 1697, *pauch* ~ 1703, *poach headland* 1709 (*v.* **hēafod-land**) (*v.* **pouche** 'a pouch', here used of a small, bag-shaped hollow); *Redmile Seike* 1682, ~ *Sick* 1686 (*v.* **sík**; Redmile lies three miles to the north-east and the stream running from that village still flows almost to the Stathern boundary, despite modern drainage); *The Round Hill* 1744 (*v.* **round**); *John Rowses close* 1625; *Richard Rowses headland* 1625 (*v.* **hēafod-land**); *the shier meare* 1625, 1653, ~ ~ *meere* 1625, (*the*) *Shire Mear(e)*1686, 1697, 1703, *Shire meer* 1709 (*v.* **scīr**[1], **(ge)mǣre**; the county boundary with Notts. forms the north-western boundary of the parish); *the Bottom(e) of the Sick(e)* 1697, 1700, 1703, *the Nether Sick* 1709 (*v.* **sík**); *Shornhill Slade* 1703 (*v.* **scoren**[2], **hyll, slæd**); *Stanewelsty* 1292 (*v.* **stān, wella, stig**);

Stanewoldehill e.14 (*v.* **stān, wald, hyll**); *between the sties* 1697 (*v.* **stīg**; a furlong so called); *little stye* 1625 (*v.* **stig**); *Stathorne hedge* 1605 (*v.* **hecg**; the parish boundary hedge); *Stokfurlong'* 1292, *Stockfurlong* 1605 (*v.* **stoc, furlang**; cf. Stockleys in f.ns. (a) *supra*); *swinerd stee* 1680 (*v.* **swīn-hirde, stig**); *Thornedeil* Hy 3 (*v.* **þorn, deill**); *Thornie close* 1625 (*v.* **þornig**); *Thirnie stie* 1605, *Thirnye ~* 1625, *Thrunie stie* (sic) 1646, *thorny stye* 1650 (*v.* **stīg**; with the original first el. **þyrniht** replaced by **þornig**, cf. Thorney Slade in f.ns. (a) *supra*); *the Towne headland* 1605, 1625 (*v.* **hēafod-land**), *the Towne(s) land* 1605, 1625 (*v.* **land**), *the Town side* 1744 (*v.* **sīde**) (*v.* **tūn**); *le Wedirlandsik'* 1292 (*v.* **weðer, land, sík**); *Wederhorn* 1337 (*v.* **weðer, horn**); *Frances Whitels Farme* 1682, *Fra. Whitwells farm* 1682 (1791) (*v.* **ferme**; the property of a family prob. originating in Whitwell, 15 miles to the southeast in Rutland); *Wind Mill seales* 1605, 1625, (*the*) *Wind(e)millne seales* 1674, 1700, (*att*) *the windmilne seales* 1679, *Windmilen seales* 1697, *Windmill seals* 1703 (*v.* **wind-mylne, segl**; a piece of grassland so called); *wodd leyes* 1605, *Wood leas* 1625, *Woodleyes* 1674, 1679, *Woodleayes* 1697, 1700, *the Wood Lays* 1703, (*the*) *nether woodleyes* 1625, 1674, 1679 (*v.* **wudu, leys** and Stathern Wood *supra*); *the wrinckes* 1605, (*the*) *Wrinkes* 1625 (*v.* **wrink** and cf. *the Rincks* in Redmile f.ns. (b)).

Waltham

1. WALTHAM ON THE WOLDS

Waltham 1086 DB, c.1130 LeicSurv, c.1150, a.1158 Dane *et passim*
to Hy 2 *Rut*, 1.12 *GarCart*, 1204 *BHosp et freq*, (~ *super le Wolde*
e.14 *BelCartA*, 1413 Inqaqd, 1539 *Deed*, ~ *on le Wolde* 1540
MinAccts, ~ *on the wowld* 1576 Saxton, ~ *on the would* 1610
Speed, ~ *on the Ould* 1613 Polyolbion, ~ *on the Wolds* 1441
ISLR, 1607 LML, ~ *on the Woldys* 1552 *Rut*, ~ *on the Olds* 1707
LML)
Waltam a.1158, c.1200, Hy 3 Dane, *Waltamia* c.1160 ib
Valthona 1163 CartAnt
Wautham 1201, 1246 (Edw 1) *CroxR*, 1271 Ipm, Hy 3 *Crox* (freq) *et*
passim to Edw 1 *CroxR*, c.1316 (e.15), 1328 (e.15) *BelCartB*

'The forest estate', *v.* **wald-hām**. Rhona Huggins in a detailed study
of all surviving examples of the name Waltham has demonstrated
convincingly that the appellative *wald-hām* represented a royal (hunting)
estate situated close to forest. That such names belong to the early
Anglo-Saxon period is suggested by their distribution which is closely
related to the Roman road system and is limited to those regions of the
country settled earliest by the English. Names in *wald-hām* are confined
to Kent, Sussex, Hants., Berks., Essex, Lincs. and Leics. That each
example of *wald-hām* was a royal estate is indicated by its being held by
the Church or by the king or by his deputy in the 11th cent., when each
was an important vill of from 30 to 50 ploughs and among the largest in
its county. Huggins also notes the close relationship between *wald-hām*
and extensive meadowland, which was of great importance to a
community dependent on oxen and horses. DB records 100 acres of
meadow at Waltham on the Wolds. This township lies just over one mile
from the major Roman road Margary 58a across the Wolds and is
precisely on the line of the lesser Roman road, now called King Street
Lane, which runs north-west from Roman Sewstern Lane, *v.* R. Huggins,
'The significance of the place-name *wealdhām*', *Medieval Archaeology*
19 (1975), 198–201.

OE (Angl) *wald* in early usage denoted 'woodland, high forest land'. With the clearing of forest tracts, some of which were on high ground, it came in ME to mean 'an elevated stretch of open country or moorland'. In the modern name Waltham on the Wolds, both usages are evident. OE (Angl) *wald* 'high forest land' is compounded in Waltham (with *wald* > *walt* before the *h* of the generic), while later ME *wold* 'elevated open country' is used in the suffix to describe the location of Waltham, i.e. ~ *on the Wolds*. Early spellings of Waltham with *u* for *l* are due to AN influence.

ANGEL (P.H.) (lost), *Angel* 1846, 1863 White. CRESSWELL SPRING FM, *v.* **spring**[1] and *Cresswell* in f.ns. (b). FISH POND, 1968 *Surv.* GEORGE AND DRAGON (P.H.) (lost), *George and Dragon* 1846, 1863, 1877 White, 1925 Kelly. GRANBY HOTEL (lost) is *Granby's Head* 1846, 1863 White, *Granby Inn* 1877 ib, *Granby Hotel* 1925 Kelly; originally with reference to John Manners, Marquis of Granby from 1721 to 1770, who became a popular hero as leader of the victorious cavalry at Warburg in 1760. He had many English hostelries named in his honour. The Marquis of Granby is the title of the heir of the county's senior peer, the Duke of Rutland, resident at Belvoir Castle. KING'S ARMS (P.H.) (lost), *Kings Arms Inn* 1823 *Deed.* MANOR FM, 1968 *Surv,* cf. *Manor house* 1877 White, *v.* **maner.** MOOR LEYS LANE, *More Leys* 1833 *Plan,* cf. *More Lays Close* 1833 ib, *v.* **leys** and Moor Cl in f.ns. (a) *infra.* THE RECTORY, 1877 White, 1925 Kelly, cf. *The Rectory House* 1821 *Terrier* and *Old Rectory* 1877 White, presum. to be identified with *the Parsonage howse* 1605 *Terrier,* ~ ~ *house* 1625, 1700, 1703 *ib, v.* **personage.** ROYAL HORSE SHOES (P.H.), *Royal Horse Shoes* 1846, 1863, 1877 White, 1925 Kelly. ST MARY MAGDALENE'S CHURCH, *Church (St Mary)* 1846, 1863 White, *Church (St Mary Magdalene)* 1877 ib, 1925 Kelly; it is earlier recorded as *ecclesiam de Valthona* 1163 CartAnt, *ecclesie de Waltham* 1220 MHW, 1344 (c.1430) *KB,* 1374 *Pat, ecclesiam de Wautham* 1239 RGros. Note also *the Churcheyeard* 1605, 1625 *Terrier, v.* **chirche-ȝeard.** SHEEPWASH, *sheepwasse* 1601 *Terrier, Top Sheepwash, Sheepwashes* 1968 *Surv, v.* **scēp-wæsce.** WALTHAM HO. WALTHAM LODGE. WALTHAM NEW COVERT, *Waltham New Co.* 1806 Map, *Waltham Cover* 1824 O, *v.* **cover(t).** WALTHAM PASTURE FM, *Waltham Pasture* 1806 Map, 1824 O, cf. *the Common Pasture* 1605, 1625 *Terrier, v.* **commun, pasture.** WALTHAM THORNS, cf. *East, North, South Thorns* 1833 *Plan, Thorns Field* 1968 *Surv, v.* **þorn.** WHEEL (P.H.) (lost), *The Wheel* 1846, 1863 White, *Wheel Inn* 1877 ib.

THE WINDMILL, *v. Windmill furlong* in f.ns. (b) *infra.*

FIELD-NAMES

Undated forms in (a) are 1968 *Surv*; those dated 1833 and 1862 are *Plan*, while 1851 are *Surv*. Forms throughout dated Hy 3, 1462, 1552 and 1606 are *Rut*; Edw 1 are *CroxR*; 1539 are MinAccts; 1601, 1605, 1625, 1700, 1703 and 1709 are *Terrier*.

(a) 4 Acres, 6 Acre, 8 Acre Cl (1862), 9 Acre, The 9 Acres, The 10 Acres (1862), 32 Acres (*v.* **æcer**); Abbey gate 1833 (*Abbie gate* 1625, *v.* **abbaye, gata**; the road to Croxton Abbey); Plough ~ (*v.* **plōg**), Annacre (*v.* **æcer**; with the OE pers.n. *Anna*, cf. *Onneacre* in Thorpe Arnold f.ns. (b)); Arch Cl (alluding to a railway arch); South ~ ~, Ashy Cl 1833 (*the Ash Closes* 1709, *v.* **æsc**); Barn Cl, Barn Fd; Bee Gate (*Bay Gate* 1709, *v.* **bēo, gata**; evidently a road where bees abounded); Bell Cl 1795 Nichols, 1833, Filling's Fd now called Bell Cl 1877 White (according to 1846 ib, 'originally the source of revenue to pay a clock winder and bell ringer' for the parish church); Bellands 1833, Bottom, Top Bellings (cf. *Shorte bellandes* 1601, *Short Bellans* 1605, *Bellans* 1709, *v.* Bellands in Bottesford f.ns. (a)); Benchy Cl 1833, Banshee ~ 1968 (*the Benchy Closes* 1709; poss. with **benc** 'a bank'); Big Fd; Freeman Bishop (the name of the close's owner or tenant); Blue Gate (poss. 'exposed, cold road', *v.* **blár, blo, gata**); Botterills Home Fd (*v.* **home**; with the surn. *Botterill*); Brackley Cl 1833 (*Bracklee* 1601), Brackley Furlong 1862 (1625, 1709, *Brackeley furlonge* 1605, *Brackly furlong* 1700, 1703) (*v.* **bracu, lēah**, cf. Brackley, Nth 49); Branston Road Cl 1833 (Branston adjoins to the north); Braythorne Cl 1833 (*Brathorn(e)* 1601, 1605, 1625, 1700, 1703, *Brathen* 1709, *v.* **breiðr, þorn**); Brickyard Cl; Bull Cl, Bull Mdw (*v.* **bula**); Middle, North, South Bunhills 1833, First, Second Bunnels (*Bunwelles* 1601, 1605, *Baunelles* 1625, *Short* ~, *bunnils* 1700, *long bunnals* 1703, *Bunnalds, Bunhils* 1709, *v.* **bune, wella**, cf. Bunwell, Nf); the Butts (either **butt²** 'an archery butt' or **butte** 'a short strip or ridge at right angles to other strips'); Carters Fd (with the surn. *Carter*); Cattle Arch (cf. Arch Cl *supra*); Coach Road Cl 1833 (prob. referring to the modern A607 road); Common Land Cl 1851 (*v.* **commun**); Cookes Fd (with the surn. *Cooke*); North Part, South Part Deepdale 1833 (*v.* **part**) (*dipdall(e)* 1601, *depdall, depedale* 1605, *depdale* 1605, 1625, cf. *Debdale field* 1700, 1703, 1709 (*v.* **feld**; one of the great fields of the village), *Debdale hill* 1709, *v.* **dēop, dalr**); Doubledays (the surn. *Doubleday* in the possessive case); Dovecote Fd (*v.* **dove-cote**); Drurys Far (*v.* **feor**), John Henry Drury (fields belonging to or tenanted by J. H. Drury); Bottom, Top Eaton Dale (*Eaton dall(e)* 1601, ~ *Dale* 1605, 1625, 1709, *v.* **dalr**), Eaton Lane Cl 1968, Eaton Road Cl 1851 (Eaton adjoins to the north-west); The Egypt (either a 'remoteness' name for a field far from the village or a name for land on which gipsies habitually camped, *v.* Field 157); Extons Cl 1862 (cf. *Thomas Exton Wong* 1709, *v.* **vangr**; the family *Exton* prob. originated in the village of this name eleven miles to the south-west in Rutland); Fair Fd (*uppon the Faire* 1703), Neat Fair 1833 (*Neat Fare* 1709, *v.* **nēat**) (*v.* **feire**; presum. the site of an annual fair and cattle market, *v.* Field 237); Filling's Fd 1846, 1863, 1877 White, The Fillings, Bottom ~, Fillings (*Fillinges* 1601, 1605, *Fillings* 1625, 1700, 1703, 1709; poss. OE **fille** 'thyme' (or some such plant), with the p.n.-forming suffix **-ing**[2] or **eng**; otherwise *v.* **filands**); Fox Cover Cl 1833 (*v.* **cover(t)**); Harry George 1968, Georges Cl 1833 (with the surn. *George* of a local family of long standing); Godbrows Cl 1833 (with a surn., perh. *Godber/Godbeher*, *v.* Reaney *s.n.* Godbear); Glenns Cl (with the surn. *Glenn*, poss. of a family originating in either Great Glen (Gartree Hundred) or Glen Parva (Guthlaxton Hundred), both some 20 miles to the south-west); Goodings (the surn. *Gooding* in the possessive case); Gore Lease (*gooreleesse* 1601, *gore leyes* 1605, 1625, 1700, *Gore Layes* 1709, *v.* **gāra, leys**); 1st, 2nd Gorse (*v.* **gorst**); Great Cl 1833 (*the Great Close* 1709); Guide Post Cl, Guide Post Fd (referring to a signpost); Haywoods Bottom Fd, ~ Top Fd, Haywoods Flats, ~ Bottom Flats (*v.* **flat**) (with the surn. *Haywood*); Hell Hole (a term of disparagement, poss. for a damp hollow, *v.* Field 40); Nether Long Hennings (*Long Hen(n)ings* 1700, 1703, 1709, *Long hening layes* 1700, 1703, *v.* **leys**), Burgins Hennings, Allen's Ennings (sic), Doubledays, Haywoods, Lord's Ennings (with the surns. *Burgin, Allen, Doubleday, Haywood, Lord*) (cf. (*the*) *west hen(n)inges* 1601, 1605, 1625, *the North Heninges* 1605, *Northhennings* 1625, *North Hen(n)ings* 1700, 1709, ~ *hennins* 1703, *henins field* 1703, *the Hennings field* 1709 (*v.* **feld**; one of the great fields of the township)) (*v.* **henn, eng**); Hill Side (*v.* **sīde**); Hoebecks (*Holebeck* Hy 3, *v.* **hol**[2], **holr, bekkr**); Home Cl 1862, 1968 (*v.* **home**); the House Fd, First House Fd; Horse Dam 1833 (*v.* **hors, damme**; an artificially created watering-place for horses); Hovel Fd (x2) (*v.* **hovel**); Kellams (cf. *Stephen Kelhams piece* 1709, *v.* **pece**; the family *Kelham* presum. originated in the village of this name 19 miles to the north in Notts.); Kirton Holm 1833 (*Kirton Holmes* 1462, *The Kirton Homes* 1709, *v.* **holmr**; perh. with the surn. *Kirton* of a family from the village of this name near the medieval port of Boston in Lincs., directly accessible to Waltham on the Wolds via the Roman road Margary 58a; but note *Kertonhill* (1467 × 84) in Thorpe Arnold f.ns. (b) which may suggest rather a lost farmstead called *Kirton* that once lay between the two townships of the modern parish (*v.* **tūn**), although hill-names are sometimes compounded with surns. in Framland Hundred); Lings Cl 1833, The Rough Lings (*v.* **rūh**[1]) (cf. *the Lynge furlong* 1601, *Linge furlonge* 1605, 1625, *Ling Furlong* 1703, 1709, *the Ling Field in Eaton Dale* 1703, 1709 (*v.* **feld**; one of the later great fields of the village), *v.* **lyng**); Little Mdw; Lock-Allens (with the surn. *Allen* in the possessive case; *lock* may refer to a fold (OE **loc**)); The Lussacks, Sharp's Lussacks (with the surn. *Sharp*) (*Lussacks* 1709; presum. a late form of *Hassock(e)s* 1601, 1605, 1625, 1700, 1703, *Hassacks* 1709, *v.* **hassuc**); Mares Cl (this may belong with The Morris *infra*; otherwise with the surn. *Mares* (in some instances from OFr *mareis* 'a marsh', *v.* Reaney *s.n.* Marris) or **mare** or **(ge)mǣre**)); 1st Tom Marriotts, Far Tom Marriott; Mathers Cl 1833 (with the surn. *Mather(s)*); Mausoleum Fd (*v.* **mausoleum**); Short Mere 1862 (*short(e) mare* 1601, 1605, *Longe mare* 1601, *long(e) meare* 1605, 1625, *Longmare* 1703, *Long Mere* 1709, *v.* **(ge)mǣre**)); Maryans (the surn. *Maryan* in the possessive case, *v.* Reaney *s.n.*); Nether Middle Fd 1833, Bottom, Top Middle Fd 1968; Upper Middle Cl 1833; Mill Fd, Behind Mill Cl, Mill Holmes (*v.* **holmr**); Mire Wells 1833 (*Myrewels* 1700, *Mirewel(l)s* 1703, 1709, *Weste Myerwelles* 1601, *West mirewell(e)s* 1605, 1625, *v.*

mýrr, **wella**); Allens Moors, Carters ~, Dolby ~, Haywoods ~, Lords ~, Wrights Moors 1968 (all with surns. in the possessive case, except for *Dolby*, a local form of the surn. *Dalby* of a family originating in nearby Old Dalby or Great, Little Dalby), Moor Cl 1833 (*the more* 1601, 1700, 1703, *the Moore* 1709), More Halls (*Morehale* 1539, *More Hall* 1552, *v.* **halh**) (*v.* **mōr**[1]); The Morris (*v.* **mareis** and Mares Cl *supra*); Upper ~ ~, Morrisons Cl 1833 (with the surn. *Morrison*); The Neck (*v.* **hnecca**; used topographically of 'a neck of land'); Nether Cl 1833; North Buck 1833, First Norbuck 1862, Far ~ 1968, Norbuck Cl 1833 (*betwixte Norbeckes* 1601, *betwixt bothe (the) Norbexe* 1605, *Norbe(c)ks* 1625, 1700, 1703, 1709, *v.* **norð, bekkr**); Nun's Cl 1795 Nichols, Nun's Lane 1795 ib (*the Nuns* 1709, *atte Nunnes* 1327 SR (p), *atte Nonnes* 1363 Inqaqd (p), *v.* **nunne, atte**; by 1709, *the Nuns* was the name of a farmstead, which earlier was a grange of the nunnery of Nuneaton); Osbourne Cl (with the surn. *Osbourne*); Lower ~, Ousledale 1833, Upper ~, Ouseldale, Ousledale (*the Ousledales* 1709, *v.* **ōsle**; with **dalr** or **deill**); Far, Near Oxburrow Cl 1833 (*Oxbarrowe* 1601, *Oxeborrowe* 1625, *Oxbourah* 1700, 1703, *Oxborough* 1709, *v.* **oxa, berg**); Pasture Cl (*v.* Waltham Pasture Fm *supra*); Pinfold Leys 1833 (*Pinfold* 1709, *v.* **pynd-fald, leys**); Plough Fd (*v.* **plōg**); Pond Cl; Pony Paddock (*v.* **pony, paddock**); Prestons (the surn. *Preston* in the possessive case); Queens Dales 1833, Queendale (poss. an early name dating from the period when Waltham was a royal vill (*v.* **cwēn**); otherwise with **cwene** and **dalr** or **deill**); Rectory Fd (*v.* The Rectory *supra*); Red Earth Cl 1862 (*v.* **rēad, eorðe**); Roses (cf. *W. E. Rose* 1968, owner or tenant); Rough Fd (*v.* **rūh**[1]); Round Table (1703, 1709, *the rounde table* 1625; describing a topographical or man-made circular feature and alluding to The Round Table of Arthurian legend); Sand Cliff Cl 1833 (*Sandcliff* 1709, *v.* **sand, clif**); Seed Cl (*v.* **sǣd**; in f.ns. used of areas of sown grass); Share Wells 1833 (*Sharwell(e)s* 1601, 1605, 1625, 1709, *Sharewels* 1700, *Sharrels* 1703; prob. 'boundary stream', *v.* **scearu, wella**); Bottom, Middle, Top Shaws (with the surn. *Shaw* in the possessive case); Shelton's (the surn. *Shelton* in the possessive case); Side Hill (poss. '(the field on) the side of the hill' (with **sīde**), otherwise *v.* **sīd**); Signal Box Fd (beside a now defunct railway line); 1st, 2nd Skibbecks, Nether Skibbeck 1968 (*Skibecke* 1601, *Middle Skibeck* 1606), Skibbecks Cl 1833 (*Skibeck close* 1606) ('boundary stream', *v.* **skil, bekkr**); First, Second Slatings (*Sleyting'* Hy 3, *Sletheng'*, *Sleytheng*, *Sleytyng* Edw 1, *Oversleightinges* 1601, 1605, 1625 (*v.* **uferra**), *Shorte sleightinges, Short slightinges* 1601, *Short Sleighting(e)s* 1605, 1625, *Sleighting Hook* 1709 (*v.* **hōc**), *Sleighting weare* 1601, *Sleightinge weere* 1605, *Sleightings were* 1625 (*v.* **wer**), *v.* **slēttr, eng**); The Slip (*v.* **slipe**); Sodgate One, ~ Two (*v.* **sodde, gata**); Southbecks (*v.* **sūð, bekkr**); Spring Cl, Spring Fd (*v.* **spring**[1]); Anthony Stennett (the name of the close's owner or tenant); Stone Pit Cl 1833, 1851 (*the Stonpites* 1601, *the Stonpittes* 1605, *att the Stone pittes* 1625 (a furlong so called), *Stonepits* 1700, 1703, 1709, *v.* **stān-pytt**); Bottom, Top Swallow (*Swallowe* 1601, 1605, 1625, *Swallow* 1700, 1703, 1709, *Shorte Swallowe* 1601, *v.* **swalg**); Talbotts, ~ Cl (with the surn. *Talbot* in the possessive case); Thirty Lands 1833 (*30 lands* 1709; a close comprising thirty selions of one of the former great fields); Bottom, Top Togar 1968, Togar Cl 1833 (*Toggwooe* 1601, *Toggoe* 1605, 1625, *Towgoe* 1700, *Toggow* 1703, *Tuggoe* 1709, *v.* **hōh**; with the OE pers.n. *Tocga*); (The) Top Fd; Toll Bar Cl 1862 (beside a toll-bar on a former turnpike road); Well Cl (*v.* **wella**); Middle ~, Wilfords (presum. with the surn. *Wilford* in the possessive case, poss. that of a family formerly from the village of Wilford, 16 miles to the north-west in Notts., otherwise *v.* **wilig, ford**); The Willows (*Willows* 1709), Far Willows, Willow Paddock (*v.* **paddock**) (cf. *the Willow(e) Close* 1605, 1625, 1703, *v.* **wilig**); Wool Breakers 1833, Grass ~ ~, Plough Wool Breakers 1968 (*v.* **græs, plōg**) (*Wolverakers* 1601, *woluueracres* 1605, *Wollveracre*s 1625, *Woolveracre*. 1700, 1703, *Wolveracres* 1709, *v.* **æcer**; with an OE pers.n., prob. *Wulfhere*); First, Second Wyndriggs 1833 (*v.* **hrycg, hryggr**; prob. with **wind**[1], **vindr**, used to denote a place in a windy position, cf. *Windisers* in Thorpe Arnold f.ns. (b)).

(b) *Mr George Alcockes Wong* 1709 (*v.* **vangr**); *John Baker his homestall* 1605 (*v.* **hām-stall**); *the Barsey Closes* 1709 (perh. with ME **berse** 'a hedge made with stakes', cf. Bearse Common, Gl 3 243; otherwise unexplained); *Bartin Hole* 1709 (*v.* **hol**[1]; prob. with the surn. *Barton*); *Brackinspole* 1601 (*v.* **brakni, pōl**[1]); *Brincthyrne* Hy 3, Edw 1 (*v.* **brink, þyrne, þyrnir**); *the Brooke* 1601, 1625 (*v.* **brōc**); *Buddle acre* 1625, *butlacre stile* 1703, *Bucklacre* ~ 1709 (*v.* **stīg, stig**) (*v.* **æcer**; either with the surn. *Buddle* (from OE *bydel* 'a beadle'), *v.* Reaney *s.n.* Beadel, or from **bydel** itself); *upon the butcher* 1703, *Butcher Lay* 1709 (*v.* **ley**) (with the surn. *Butcher*); *Caldwell* 1601, *Caudwell* 1709 (*v.* **cald, wella**); *Calvacre* n.d. Nichols (*v.* **calf** (**calfra** gen.pl.), **æcer**); *Caversicke* 1601, *Cawver sike* 1605, 1625, *Calversick* 1700, 1703, 1709 (*v.* **calf** (**calfra** gen.pl.), **sīk**); *Luke Coates his Headland* 1709 (*v.* **hēafod-land**), ~ ~ *his wong* 1709 (*v.* **vangr**); *Constables Hades* 1625, 1703, 1709 (*v.* **conestable, hēafod**); *Cresswell* 1709, *Creswell gatte* 1601, ~ *gate* 1605 (*v.* **gata**), *Creswell hille* 1601, ~ *hill* 1700, 1709, *Cresswell hill* 1605, 1625 (*v.* **cærse, wella**); *Cristen howse* 1539 (*v.* **hūs**; with the surn. *Christin, v.* Reaney *s.n.*); *the dalles* 1601 (*v.* **deill**); *deadmore* 1601 (*v.* **dēad, mōr**[1]; evidently moorland at the edge of the parish where early burials were discovered, but *v.* Dead Moor Leys in Wymondham f.ns (a)); *the edge of thurn hill* 1700, 1703, *upon the Edge* 1709 (*v.* **ecg**; a furlong so called, *v.* Thurn hill, *infra*); Flint 1601, 1700, 1703, 1709, *Flint hill* 1605, 1625 (*v.* **flint**); *Fullings* 1700, *Fullonpits* 1703, *Fulling Pits* 1709 (*v.* **fulling, pytt**); *Fulwell hill* 1601, *Fullewell* ~ 1605, 1625 (*v.* **fūl, wella**); *Jonathan Georges Balk* 1709 (*v.* **balca**); *Thomas Goodwins Wong* 1709 (*v.* **vangr**); *the grange wonge* 1601, *graunge wong* 1605 (*v.* **grange, vangr**; the grange was either an outlier of Croxton Abbey or that belonging to the nunnery of Nuneaton, *v.* Nun's Cl in f.ns. (a) *supra*); *Hanly's Close* 1709 (with the surn. *Hanley*); *the homestall* 1605 (*v.* **hām-stall**; i.e. that of *the Parsonage howse, v.* The Rectory *supra*); *hornwell crosse* 1601, *Harnoll Crosse* 1605, 1625, *Horne Cross* 1709, *Hornycross Close* 1700, 1709, *Harnycross* ~ 1703 (*v.* **horn, wella, cros**); *John Jeffryes Balk* 1709 (*v.* **balca**); *the kinges highe waye* 1605, *the kings highe waie* 1625 (*v.* **hēah-weg**; with reference to James I); *Melton gate* 1601 (*v.* **gata**; the road to Melton Mowbray which lies five miles to the south-west); *Mor(e)gates* 1601, 1605, 1625, 1703, *Moore gates* 1709 (*v.* **mōr**[1], **mór**, **gata** and Moor Cl *supra*); *Long Furlong* 1709; *the Northe feilde* 1605 (*v.* **norð, feld**; one of the great fields of the village); *Old Meadow* 1709 (*v.* **ald**); *Peaseland(s)* 1703, 1709, *Over Peasslandes* 1601, ~ *Peaseland(e)s* 1605, 1625 (*v.* **uferra**) (*v.* **pise, land**); *Saltgates* 1601, 1605, 1625, 1703, 1709 (*v.* **salt**[1], **gata**; referring to the Roman road called King Street Lane which was used in the medieval period as a salters' way); *Sawsdall* 1601, *Saucedall* 1605, *Saucedale* 1625, 1700, 1709, *Sasedale* 1703,

Sawce Dale 1709 (*v.* **deill**; the first el. appears to be a Scand pers.n., ON *Sǫlsi* (OSw *Salsi*), with AN *u* for *l*); *Shelbordes* 1601 (*v.* **scofl-brǣdu**); *Shortsmythe homes* 1601, *Short Smithey homes* 1605, ~ *Smithes holmes* 1625 (*v.* **sc(e)ort, smið, smiððe, holmr**); *Smithy pits* 1709 (*v.* **smiððe, pytt**); *the Sparrow lane* 1605, *the Sparrowe laine* 1625 (*v.* **spearwa**; with **lane** or **leyne**); *the Stonye wonge* 1601, *the Stoney wounge* 1605, *the Stone wonge* 1625 (*v.* **stānig, vangr, stān**); *the Street* 1601, 1709 (*v.* **strǣt**; the main street of the village); *Thorney Closses* 1703, *the Thorny Closes* 1709 (*v.* **þornig**); *Thurn(e)gate* 1601, 1605, 1625 (*v.* **þyrne, þyrnir, gata**); *(the) Thurn(e) hill* 1601, 1625, 1700, 1703, *Thorne Hill* 1709 (*v.* **þyrne, hyll**; the 1709 form has **þorn**); *the towne side* 1601 (*v.* **tūn, sīde**); *Waterfur(r)ows* 1703, 1709 (*v.* **wæter, furh** and *waterfurris* in Muston f.ns. (b)); *littell welbecke* 1601 (*v.* **lȳtel, lítill, wella, bekkr**); *Westfeld'* Hy 3, Edw 1 (*v.* **west, feld**; one of the early great fields of the township); *Windmill furlong* 1700, 1703, 1709 (*v.* **wind-mylne** and The Windmill *supra*); *the old windmilhill* 1601, *the olde mill hill* 1605, *Windmill hill* 1709 (*v.* **wind-mylne**; it is uncertain whether the sites of the windmills of 1601 and 1709 are identical); *the homestall of George Wollerton* 1625 (*v.* **hām-stall**; prob. of a family originating in Wollaton, 19 miles to the north-east in Notts., although Reaney *s.n.* prefers to refer the surn. to Wollerton in Shropshire); *Robert Wrights Balk* 1709 (*v.* **balca**).

2. THORPE ARNOLD

> *Torp* 1086 DB, Hy 2 Dugd, p.1150 *GarCh*, l.12 *GarCart*, c.1200
>   *Sloane et passim* to 1253 × 58 RHug, Hy 3 *Rut* (p)
> *Thorp(e)* c.1130 LeicSurv, 1208, 1219 Cur, 1238 RGros *et freq*
> *Arnoldestorp* 1214 P
> *Erlesthorp(e)* 1371 Cl, 1404 *Laz*, 1456 Nichols, 1547 Fine, (~ *al'*
>   *Thorparnold* 1535 VE), *Erllesthorp* 1420 Cl, *Harlesthorpe* 1537
>   Ipm, *Erlestroppe* 1603 Ipm, *Erlesthorpe* 1809 *EnclA*

'The outlying farmstead', *v.* **þorp**. Thorpe Arnold was a secondary settlement, presum. related in origin to Melton Mowbray rather than to Waltham on the Wolds, although by 1086 DB, Walter held Waltham and Thorpe together from Hugo de Grentemaisnil.

The principal affixes are added as follows:

> ~ *Ernaldi* Hy 2 Nichols, ~ *Ernald* 1238 RGros, 1261 RGrav *et freq*
>   to 1347 Cl, 1352 (1449) *WoCart et passim* to 1420 Inqaqd, 1449
>   *WoCart*, ~ *Ernaud* 1277 Ipm, 1296 Pat, ~ *Ernold'* c.1310 (1449),
>   1318 (1449) *WoCart et passim* to 1361 (1449) *ib*
> ~ *Arnald(e)* 1254 Val, c.1291 Tax *et passim* to 1445 Cl, 1449
>   *WoCart*, ~ *Arnold(e)* c.1291 Tax, 1309 (1449) *WoCart et passim*
>   to 1449 *ib*, 1453 Cl *et freq*
> ~ *iuxta Melton(a)* c.1200 *Sloane*, 1318 Pat *et passim* to 1445 Cl

Ernald de Bosco held the manor in 1156 Ch, followed by three successors of the same name until at least 1318 Pat. They were stewards of the Earls of Leicester, hence the alternative name *Erlesthorpe*, *v.* **eorl**.

ASHLEIGH. BROOMWOOD. CROSHER'S FM, with the surn. *Crosher*. HALL FM, *Hall farm* 1925 Kelly, cf. *Hall Close* 1849 *TA*, *v.* **hall**. HOME FM, *v.* **home**. LINACRE GRANGE, *v.* **grange**. LODGE FM (THORPE LODGE 2½"), *Thorpe Lodge* 1824 O, cf. *Lodge Close* 1849 *TA*, *v.* **loge**. ST MARY'S CHURCH, *Church (St Mary)* 1846, 1863, 1877 White, 1925 Kelly; it is earlier recorded as *ecclesie de Torp* 1220 MHW, ~ *de Thorp Ernald* 1238 RGros, *ecclesia de Torp Ernald* 1253 × 58 RTAL, *ecclesie de Thorpe iuxta Melton* 1318 *Pat*. Note also *(the) Churchyard* 1601, 1700, 1703 *Terrier*, 1849 *TA*, *v.* **chirche-ȝeard**. THORPE ASHES, *v.* **æsc**. THORPE HINDLES, HINDLE TOP FM, *Hindale*, *Hyndale* 1467 × 84 *LTD*; prob. 'the monks' valley', *v.* **hīwan (hī(g)na** gen.pl.), **dalr**, presum. a property originally of Leicester Abbey, the source of the 1467 × 84 spellings. THE VICARAGE, 1877 White, 1925 Kelly; it is *the Vicaredge howsse* 1601 *Terrier*, *the Vicaridge house* 1625, 1700 *ib*, *(the) Vicarage House* 1703 *ib*, 1849 *TA*, *v.* **vikerage**, **hūs**. WEST VIEW. WOLD HO., *v.* **wald**.

FIELD-NAMES

Undated forms in (a) are 1849 *TA*. Forms throughout dated 13, e.14 and 1309 are Nichols; 13 (1404) are *Laz*; 1309 (1449), 1321 (1449), 1324 (1449), 1325 (1449) and Edw 2 (1449) are *WoCart*; 1467 × 84 are *LTD*; 1477 (e.16) are *Charyte*; 1540 are *Ct*; 1583 and 1605 are Ipm; 1601, 1625, 1700 and 1703 are *Terrier*; 1628 (18), 1653 (18) and 1656 (18) are *Deed*; 1716 are *Pochin*.

(a) The Acres, Four Acres, Fifteen Acre Mdw (*v.* **æcer**); Adcocks Cl (with the surn. *Adcock*); (The) Barn Cl (x3); Booth Cl (presum. with the surn. *Booth*, although in 1849 *TA*, surns. are usually in the possessive case; otherwise *v.* **bothe** 'a temporary shelter' (dial. **booth** 'a cow-house')); Bull Pit Cl (*the Bullpit Close* 1700, 1703, *le Marche bullpitt* 1583 (*v.* **mersc**), *v.* **bula**, **pytt**; a venue for bull-baiting); Burton Road Bridge (on the road to Burton Lazars to the south); Corn Cl (*v.* **corn**[1]); The Cow Cl; Cow Dam Mdw (*v.* **damme**; an artificially created watering-place for cattle); Deadmans Grave (*v.* **dede-man**, **græf**; on the north boundary of the township and thus poss. the site of a pagan Anglo-Saxon cemetery); Dennis Yard (*v.* **geard**; with the surn. *Dennis*); Georges Ground, ~ ~ Mdw (*v.* **grund**; with the surn. *George*); Hackets Yard (*v.* **geard**; with the surn. *Hackett*); The Ham (*v.* **hamm**; beside R. Eye);

Middle ~ ~, Hanging Cl (v. **hangende**); Far, Lane, Little, Middle Hindall, Far Long,
Middle Long, Near Long Hindall (v. Thorpe Hindles *supra*); Holt Leys (v. **leys**; either
with the surn. *Holt* or with **holt**); Home Cl (v. **home**); Horse Cl, Horse Close Pingle
(v. **pingel**), Horse Holme (v. **holmr**) (v. **hors**); House Cl; Hubbards Pingle (cf. *the
pingle* 1625 v. **pingel**; with the surn. *Hubbard*); Jacksons Cl (with the surn. *Jackson*);
Ley Cl (1703, v. **ley**); Leys Cl (poss. with the surn. *Ley(s)*); Little Mdw; Long Cl (*the
Long Close* 1700, 1703); Mellams (*Medelholm, Nordmedelholm* 13 (v. **norð**),
Estirmelham 1467 × 84 (v. **ēasterra**), *Middelmelham* 1467 × 84 (v. **middel**), *mellome*
1601, v. **meðal, holmr**); Melton Wong (1716, *Meltonwong'* 1467 × 84, v. **vangr**; an
in-field towards Melton Mowbray); Hanging Moor (v. **hangende**), Hindall Moor (v.
Thorpe Hindles *supra*), Far, Middle, Near Moor Cl, Bottom, Top Great Moor Cl (v.
mōr¹); New Cl 1791 Nichols; New Mdw; New Piece (v. **pece**); The Nursery (*Nursery*
1700, v. **nursery**); Oat Cl (v. **āte**); Over Cl (v. **uferra**); Park Leys (*Parkleyes* 1601,
v. **park, leys**), Park Leys Pingle (v. **pingel**); Parsons Piece (v. **persone, pece**); The
Pasture (cf. *the neates pasture* 1601, v. **nēat, pasture**); Pool Banks (*the pool banks*
1700, *the Poole Bankes* 1703, v. **pōl**¹, **banke**); Red Mdw (*Redmedowe* 1583, *the Red
Meadow* 1700, 1703, v. **hrēod, mǣd** (**mǣdwe** obl.sg.)); Road Piece (v. **pece**); The
Row (*the wro* 1467 × 84, v. **vrá**); Shepherds Cl (either with the surn. *Shepherd* or,
more likely, with **scēp-hirde**); Shoemakers Cl (*the Shoemakers Close* 1700, 1703,
v. **shomakere**); Lower, Middle, Over (v. **uferra**), Southern Mdw; Little ~ ~, South
Fd, South Field Mdw (*the South fyelde* 1601, *the Southfield* 1700, 1703, v. **sūð, feld**;
one of the great fields of the township, earliest recorded as (*in*) *campo australis* 1467
× 84, with MLat *campus* 'a field' and MLat *australis* 'southern, south'); Southing
Lane 1761 *EnclA* (v. **sūð, eng**); Spa Cl (v. **spa**); Lower, Middle, Top Spinney Cl,
Great, Upper Spinney Fd, Upper Spinney Mdw (v. **spinney**; adjacent to Melton
Spinney); Stone Cl; Stone Mdw (v. **stān, stoned**; freq. such names refer to the
removal of stones, i.e. 'stoned', v. *the stone middow* in Knipton f.ns. (b))); Thistley
Cl, ~ Mdw (v. **thist(e)ly**); Three Corner Piece (v. **three-corner, pece**); Top Cl; Wash
Dyke Mdw (v. **wash-dyke**; the site of a sheep-dip); Whitings Mdw (with the surn.
Whiting); Woad Cl (v. **wād**; woad was widely grown in the 19th cent. as a source of
blue dye).

(b) *Apethirne* 1467 × 84 (v. **þyrne, þyrnir**, with the Scand pers.n. *Api*, an original
by-name meaning 'fool'); *Barlilandis* 1467 × 84 (v. **bærlic, land**); *Becfurlong'* 1467
× 84 (v. **bekkr, furlang**); *Belland* 1325 (1449) (v. Bellands in Bottesford f.ns. (a));
le Hiderbendolis 1467 × 84 (v. **hider**), *le Yendirsbeyndoles* 1467 × 84 (v. **yondir**) (v.
bēan, dāl); *Bernewang* 13 (v. **bern, vangr**); *Blackcroft* 1583 (v. **croft**; with the first
el. either the surn. *Black* or **blæc** 'black' referring to the colour of the soil or even to
fertility, since in eModE, *black* could have the sense 'fertile' in contrast to *white*
'infertile'); *Bradedik'* 1467 × 84 (v. **brād, dík**); *Breclondes* 1467 × 84, *Brecklandes*
1601, *Breckland rigget* 1601 (v. **riggett** 'a water channel, a surface drain', v. OED
s.v. **riggot**²) (v. **bræc**¹, **land**); *Brentingbye hedge* 1601 (v. **hecg**; a boundary hedge),
Brentingbie mores 1625 (v. **mōr**¹) (Brentingby adjoins to the south-east); *the brooke
fyeld(e)* 1601 (v. **brōc, feld**; one of the great fields of the village); *Bull close* 1583 (v.
bula, clos(e)); *le Cleyland'* 1467 × 84, *claylandes* 1601, *Nethercleylond'* 1467 × 84
(v. **neoðera**) (v. **clæg, land**); *Coningerend* 1467 × 84 (v. **coningre, ende**); *Cootys*
1477 (e.16) (v. **cot**); *Court Wong or Court Furlong* 1628 (18) (v. **court, vangr**);

Cringeldale 1467 × 84 (*v.* **kringla**; with **dalr** or **deill**); *the Croft* 1467 × 84 (*v.* **croft**); *Croklokhull* 1467 × 84 (*v.* **loc, loca, hyll**; the first el. is either **crocc** 'a crock, an earthenware pot', alluding either to a place where pots were made or to a place where pots and sherds were discovered, or **krókr** 'a nook, a secluded corner of land'); *Damesyngdale* 1540 (*v.* **damesene**; with **dalr** or **deill**); *Diuekir* 1467 × 84 (*v.* **dyfe, æcer**); *Dry Lane* 1628 (18) (*v.* **drȳge**); *Eforlong'* 1324 (1449), *le Efurlong'* 1467 × 84 (*v.* **ēa, furlang**); *Erlunstubbe* 1321 (1449), *Elronstobbe* 1325 (1449) (*v.* **ellern, stubb**); *le Estfurlong* 1324 (1449) (*v.* **ēast, furlang**); *Fattemold'*, *Faytemold'* 1309 (1449) (*v.* **fætt, molde**); *Fifteneleyes* 1467 × 84 (*v.* **fiftēne, leys**); *flynting meddowe* 1601 (*flynting* is prob. 'meadow with flints' (*v.* **flint, eng**) to which 'meadow' was later added); *gosse leyes* 1601 (*v.* **gorst, leys**); *the great ground* 1700, 1703 (*v.* **grēat, grund**); *le Halfackres, Halfakerres* 1467 × 84 (*v.* **half-aker**); *Hardhull* 1467 × 84 (*v.* **heard, hyll**); *Hassebriggates* 1467 × 84 (*v.* **æsc, brycg, bryggja, gata**); *Hauedlondes* 1477 (e.16) (*v.* **hēafod-land**); *heefeldlong'* 1324 (1449) (*v.* **hēah**[1], **feld, lang**[2]); *Herincroft'* 1467 × 84 (*v.* **croft**; with the surn. *Her(r)ing, v.* Reaney *s.n.*); *Heythirne* 1467 × 84 (*v.* **hæg-þyrne**); *Holecleues* 1467 × 84 (*v.* **hol**[1], **clif**); *Hook* 1583 (*v.* **hōc**); *the hoover furlong* 1601 (*v.* **uferra**); *Hungirhill* 1467 × 84 (*v.* **hungor, hyll**); *Kertonhill* 1467 × 84 (*v.* **hyll**; poss. with the surn. *Kirton*, but the name of a lost farmstead may be present, *v.* Kirton Holm in Waltham on the Wolds f.ns. (a)); *Knaphildale* 1467 × 84 (*v.* **cnæp, hyll**; with **dalr** or **deill**); *le kyrkwong* 1477 (e.16), *le Kirkwong'* 1467 × 84 (*v.* **kirkja, vangr**; with reference to St Mary's Church *supra*); *Langelandis* 1467 × 84 (*v.* **lang**[1], **land**); *langham rigget* 1601 (*v.* **lang**[1], **hamm, riggett** and *Breckland rigget, supra*); *Limpitt'* 1467 × 84 (*v.* **lyme-pytt**); *Litelbek'* 1467 × 84 (*v.* **lȳtel, lítill, bekkr**); *Litteldale(s)* 1467 × 84 (*v.* **lȳtel, lítill, deill**); *Lytilmore* e.14, *litilmore* Edw 2 (1449), *le Litelmor* 1467 × 84 (*v.* **lȳtel, lítill, mōr**[1], **mór**); *meddowonge leyes* 1601 (*v.* **mǣd** (**mǣdwe** obl.sg.), **vangr, leys**); *mellome rigget* 1601 (*v.* **riggett**, Mellams in f.ns. (a) *supra* and *Breckland rigget, supra*); *the middle fyeld* 1601 (*v.* **middel, feld**; one of the great fields of the village); *middle sicke* 1601 (*v.* **middel, sík**); *le Milnegate* 1467 × 84 (*v.* **gata**), *le Milnehull* 1467 × 84 (*v.* **hyll**) (*v.* **myln**); *Moredole* 1477 (e.16) (*v.* **dāl**), *le Morgate* 1467 × 84, *Moregate* 1540, *under* ~, *Mooregate* 1601 (*v.* **gata**) (*v.* **mōr**[1], **mór**); *Nedurholme* 1477 (e.16), *le Nether Holme* 1583, *the netherhome* 1601, *Nether holmes* 1605, *the netherhome lane* 1601 (*v.* **lane**) (*v.* **neoðera, holmr**); *Nordole* 13 (*v.* **norð, dāl**); *North head Land* 1628 (18) (*v.* **hēafod-land**); *Onneacre, Onneaker* 13 (*v.* **æcer**; with the OE pers.n. *Anna*; this may be the Annacre listed in Waltham on the Wolds f.ns. (a)); *the Parkes* 1628 (18), 1653 (18), 1656 (18), *Parkforlong'* 1325 (1449), *Parkfurlong'* 1467 × 84 (*v.* **furlang**) (*v.* **park**); *Penbutt'* 1467 × 84 (*v.* **penn**[2], **butte**); *Penidolis* 1467 × 84 (*v.* **peni, dāl**; referring to lands for which a penny rent was paid); *Peyslandis* 1467 × 84 (*v.* **pise, land**); *le Rede* 1467 × 84 ('the reed-bed', *v.* **hrēod**); *Redyngwald* 1318, *Redinwalde* e.14 (*v.* **wald**; the first el. is **hrēod** 'reed', with either **eng** 'a meadow' or the OE p.n.-forming suffix -**ing**[2], and if so meaning 'the reed place')); *Rigate* 1309, *Riggate* 1309 (1449) bis (*v.* **ryge, gata**); *le Sike* 1467 × 84 (*v.* **sík**); *Simpsons Meadow* 1716 (with the surn. *Simpson*); *Spinney Feild* 1628 (18) (*v.* **spinney**; adjacent to Melton Spinney); *the springe hedge* 1601 (*v.* **spring**[2], **hecg**); *Steynlandys* 1325 (1449), *Staynland'* 1449, *Steinlond(e)* 1467 × 84 (*v.* **steinn, land**); *the Street* 1700, 1703 (the main street of the township); *the Sty Yard* 1700, 1703 (*v.*

stig, geard); *le Thwertfurlong'* 1467 × 84 (*v.* **þvert, furlang**); *(le) Thirne* 1467 × 84
(*v.* **þyrne**); *Thorpmede* 13 (*v.* **mǣd**); *toadale rigget* 1601 (*v.* **riggett** and *Breckland
rigget, supra; toadale* may simply be a late form of *Todhow* following, but if not (and
more likely), *v.* **twēgen, tū, deill**); *Todhow* 1467 × 84 (*v.* **todd, haugr**); *the Tythe
yard* 1628 (18) (*v.* **tēoða, geard**); *Wilcokkes Wong', Wilkokkeswong'* 1309 (1449) (*v.*
vangr; with the surn. *Wilcock*); *Windisers, Windsers* 1467 × 84 (literally 'the wind's
arse', *v.* **wind**[1]**, ears**; perh. used of a conformation of hills resembling buttocks lying
in a windy, exposed situation and which funnelled the wind, cf. *Windesers* (1086 DB)
in Long Whatton, West Goscote Hundred); *le Winniwong'* 1467 × 84 (*v.* **whinny,
vangr**); *Wranglandes, Wranglonde* 1467 × 84 (*v.* **wrang, vrangr, land**).

Withcote

The parish is a small detached south-eastern member of Framland Hundred.

<small>WITHCOTE</small>

> *Wicoc* 1086 DB
>
> *Wythecok* 1229 Hastings, e.13 *Rut et freq* to 1420, 1479 FF, 1510 LP, *Wythecocke* 1552 AAS, 1561 CoPleas, *Withecok* 1263 RGrav, 1375 Ass, 1406 AD, 1406 Pat, *Wythycok* 1544 BodlCh
>
> *Withcoc* 1199 FF, 1205 P (p) *et passim* to 1226 ClR, 1236 Cl, *Withkoc* e.13 (1404) *Laz*, *Withcok* 1238 RGros, 1280 Fine *et passim* to 1610 Speed, 1622 Burton, *Withkoke* 1430 *MktHPR*, *Withco(c)ke* 1510 LP, 1518 Visit *et freq* to 1586 *Plan*, 1610 LibCl, *Withcock* 1606, 1608 LML *et freq* to 1713, 1717 ib, *Wythcok'* 1235 RGros, 1240 Cl *et freq* to 1395, 1396 Pat, 1529 AAS, 1544 BodlCh, *Wythcoc'* 1237, 1238 Cl
>
> *Witcoc* 1209 For (p), 1236 Cur, *Wytcoc* Hy 3 BM, *Wytcok* 1284 AAS
>
> *Wytecoc* 1220 MHW, *Wytecok* 1251 Cl, 1254 Val, 1267 Cur, 1268 Abbr
>
> *Wicote* 1086 DB
>
> *Wythecot(e)* 1236 Pat, Hy 3 Nichols, 1375 Ass, *Withecot* c.1260 Nichols, *Withekot(e)* 1241 BM, c.1260 Nichols
>
> *Witkot* Hy 2 Nichols, *Witcot* 1203 Ass, *Wytecot(e)* 1209 × 35 RHug, 1274 Ass, *Whytecot* 1258 Cl
>
> *Withcot'* 1235 RGros, *Wythcot'* 1236 Pat, 1414 PRep, *Withcott* 1661 AAS, 1715 LML, (~ *alias Withcocke* 1661 AAS), *Withcote* 1720 LML *et freq*

'The hillock growing with willows', *v.* **wīðig, cocc**[1]. Since at least 1086 DB, the generic has been confused with **cot** 'a cottage', but spellings with *cocc* greatly predominate. That the area was one where willows once grew in profusion is otherwise indicated by the name of Sauvey Castle *infra*.

SAUVEY CASTLE

Saluéé (sic) 1211, 1212 P, *Salvee* 1229 Cl, *Salveye* 1239 ib, *Salveie*
1247 Nichols, *castra sua de Rokingham et de Salveia* 1220 Pat,
Salveia(m) 1247, a.1250 Nichols, *Salveyam* a.1250 ib

castrum de Sauueie 1211 P, *castrum suum de Sauveye* 1230 Pat,
castro de Sauveye 1238 Cl, *Sauveye* 1235 Pat, 1244 Lib *et freq* to
1261 Pat, 1328 Fine, *Sauveie* 1237 Cl, *Sauvee* 1248 Pat, *Sauvey*
1246, 1254 ib *et passim* to 1267 Cur, *Sauweye* 1316 Fine

castri de Sawueye 1269 For, *Sawveye* Hy 3 Nichols

Sawaie 1401, 1407 Pat, *Sawaye* 1437 Fine, *Savaye* 1462 Pat, *Savey*
1566 AAS, *Sauey* 1586 *Plan*

Seway 1406 AD, *Seuay* 1406 ib, *Seway alias Sevay* 1483 Fine, ~
alias Seuay 1510 LP, *Seyvaye* 1561 AAS

Saywaie 1561 AAS, *Sayway* 1620 Ipm

Sauvoye 1347 Fine, *Savoye* 1566 AAS

Sauvey Castle 1846, 1863 White

castra nostra de Rokingeham et de Salvata 1218 Pat, *castrum*
nostrum de Salvata 1219, 1220 ib, *castro de Salvata* 1224 ib

Sabaud' 1255 Cl, 1275 Fine, 1276 Cl, *castrum de Sabaudie* 1290
Misc

Built by King John in 1211 principally for use as a hunting lodge,
Sauvey is the finest Norman motte and bailey castle in Leicestershire,
occupying a strong position, with ravines to the north and south
containing streams which meet at the east end of the site. The name
Sauvey appears to be OE in origin and probably means 'the road through
the willows', *v.* **salh, weg**. However, rather than the generic's being *weg*,
a final el. **ēg** 'land partly surrounded by water' to describe the castle's
exact site (hence 'willow island') would seem more appropriate to the
location, but in that case an intrusive *v* would be difficult to explain.

The range of the surviving forms shows strong AN influence. Thus
the vocalization of *l* to *u* (*Sal-* > *Sau-*) is due to AN modification, as is
the change of medial *w* to *v* (*-weg* > *-vey*), cf. Sanvey Gate, Lei **1** 61–2.
The form *Salvata* is the result of scribal false etymology, from MLat
salvata 'safe' (cf. MLat *salvatio* 'protection'), alluding to the strength
of the castle's position. A further medieval confusion was the
identification of the English name with Savoy in France. Hence the
Latin form for Savoy (i.e. *Sabaudia*) is also ascribed to the castle,
appearing as *Sabaud'* and *Sabaudie*.

Note the presence of ML at *castrum* 'a castle' with several 13th cent. forms.

ASH HILL PLANTATION, *Ash Hill* 1661 AAS, 1849 *TA*, 1853 *Deed*, v. æsc. AVENUE FM, v. **avenue**. CASTLE HILL, *Castell hill* 1620 Ipm, *Castle Hill* 1853 *Deed*, v. **castel(l)** and Sauvey Castle *supra*. THE CHAPEL is *The Church* 1877 White; this is a detached manor chapel of early Tudor date. The early church of Withcote is recorded as *ecclesia de Wytecoc* 1220 MHW, *ecclesiam de Withcot'* 1235 RGros, *ecclesie de Wythecot* 1236 *Pat*, ~ *de Witcok'* 1236 Cur, ~ *de Withkok* 1238 RGros, *ecclesiam de Withcok'* 1238 ib, *ecclesie de Wythecok(e)* 1376 *Pat*, 1560 *Pat*; note also *the Churchyarde* 1612 *Terrier*. COTTAGE FM, *The Cottage* 1877 White, v. **cotage**. DOWRY COTTAGE, cf. *Dowery Field* 1849 *TA*, *Dowry ~* 1853 *Deed*, *Dowry Field Meadow* 1849 *TA*, *Dowry Hill* 1853 *Deed*, ~ ~ *East* 1885 *ib*, *Dowery Hill Field* 1849 *TA*, v. **dowarie**; referring to land assigned to a woman on her marriage, v. Field 196. SAUVEY CASTLE FM, v. Sauvey Castle *supra*. SHEEPWASH, v. **scēp-wæsce**. WITHCOTE HALL, 1846, 1863, 1877 White, 1925 Kelly, *Hall* 1824 O, v. **hall**; it is *Withcock house* 1586 *Plan*, *the mansion house* 1625 *Terrier*, v. **mansion-house**. WITHCOTE LODGE, 1824 O, 1877 White, v. **loge**.

FIELD-NAMES

Forms in (a) dated 1849 are *TA*, while those dated 1853 and 1885 are *Deed*. Forms throughout dated 1558, 1561, 1566 and 1661 are AAS; 1560 are Pat; 1565 are DKR; 1586 are *Plan*; 1612 are *Terrier*; 1620 are Ipm; 1684 are Wright.

(a) Arable Field Rd 1885 (v. **arable**); Bottom Cl 1885 (v. **bottom**); Castle Hill Cl 1853 (v. Castle Hill *supra*); Chapel Cl 1885 (v. The Chapel *supra*); Great, Little Cockboro' Cl 1853 (v. **cocc**[2], **berg**); Nether, Upper Coppice 1885 (v. **copis**); Great Cl 1853, 1885; Far, Near Hall Mdw 1853 (v. Withcote Hall *supra*), Hall Mdw 1849, ~ ~ or Kemps 1885 (the surn. *Kemp* in the possessive case); Hill Mdw 1885; Home Cl or Pond Cl 1853 (v. **home, ponde**); House Cl 1849; Kings Cl (South, Middle and North) 1853 (with the surn. *King*); Land Cl 1849, 1853 (v. **land**; a close consolidating an unspecified number of 'lands' or selions of a former great field); The Large Pond 1853 (v. **ponde**); North Mdw 1853; The Paddock 1853 (v. **paddock**); Pool Cl 1853 (*the pooles* 1612, v. **pōl**[1]), Pool Close Orchard 1885 (cf. *the greate Orcharde* 1612, v. **orceard**); Rough Cl 1849, 1853 (*the great Rough closse* 1661, v. **rūh**[1]); Rushey Cl 1853, Rushey Mdw 1885 (v. **riscig**); Middle, Nether, Upper Sale 1849, 1885,

Middle, Nether, Upper Sale Cl 1853 (*Withcocke Sale* 1566, *Withcot sail* 1684, *v.* **sale** 'a division of a wood of which the underwood is cut down and sold', *v.* Nth 157 and EDD *s.v.*); Savis Cl 1853 (*Sauey close* 1586, *Sayway* ~ 1620, *v.* **clos(e)** and Sauvey Castle *supra*); Shoulder of Mutton 1885 (alluding to the shape of the close); South Hill 1853; Spinney Cl 1853 (*v.* **spinney**); Upper Cl 1885; West Fd 1853 (*Westfeild* 1620, *v.* **west, feld** and *Borowefilde, infra*); Wheat Cl 1853, 1885 (*v.* **hwǣte**); Wood Mdw 1849, 1853, 1885.

(b) *Borowefilde* 1558, *Burfytt alias Burfielde* 1586 (*v.* **burh, feld**; one of the great fields of the township, later West Fd *supra*; presum. this is a late use of *burh* applied to Sauvey Castle which was still in use in the early 14th cent.); *Brackley close* 1620 (*v.* **bracu, lēah**); *Haull Close* 1565 (*v.* **clos(e)** and Withcote Hall *supra*); (*le*) *Heigh meadow(e)* 1620 (*v.* **hēah**[1]); *Heighwood* 1620 (*v.* **hēah**[1], **wudu**); (*the*) *Laundetofte* 1560, 1561, *Laundetoft* 1620 (*v.* **toft**; formerly belonging to nearby Launde Priory in East Goscote Hundred); *othe lye* 1381 SR (p) (*v.* **lēah**); *molendinum Harewyni* 1269 For ('Herewine's mill'; with MLat *molendinum* 'a mill' and the OE pers.n. *Herewine*); *the Moore Close* 1586 (*v.* **mōr**[1], **clos(e)**); *the New Close* 1586 (*v.* **nīwe, clos(e)**); *Roppederne* 1227 ClR (*v.* **þyrne**; with the OE pers.n. *Hroppa/Roppa*); *Mr Smythes great garden* 1612; *Whirle Lake* 1586 (*v.* **hwerfel, hvirfill, lake**; an early name for the great pool south of Withcote Hall); *Wispyate* 1566 (*v.* **gata**; the road leading to The Wisp (OE *wisp* 'brushwood') beyond the county boundary in Rutland, *v.* Ru 74); *Withcocke feildes* 1566 (*v.* **feld**); *Withecocke wood, Withcocke woode* 1566 (*v.* **wudu**; it is earlier recorded as *boscum de Widkoc* 1227 ClR, with MLat *boscus* 'a wood').

Wymondham

1. WYMONDHAM

Wimvndesham 1086 DB, *Wymundesham* 1274 Abbr, *Wymondesham*
1330 FA, 1358 Pat

Wymundeham 1094 × 1123 TutP, c.1130 LeicSurv, 1159, 1163 TutP
et freq to 1296 Ipm, 1338 Pat *et passim* to 1409 PRep, 1450 TutP,
Wimundeham c.1141 Dugd, 1150 × 59 TutP, 1185 Templar *et
passim* to 1227 Fine, 1236 Fees, *Wimundaham* 1159 France,
Wymondeham 1262 Ass, 1318 Pap, 1374 Fine, *Wymoundeham*
1502 *MiscAccts*

Wymundham c.1130 LeicSurv, 1226 Fine *et passim* to 1259 (Edw 1)
CroxR, Hy 3 *Crox* (freq) *et freq* to 1409 Banco, 1415 *Rut et
passim* to 1510 LP, 1550 Ipm, *Wimundham* c.1160 Dane, 1180 P
et passim to Hy 3 *Crox*, 1290 Misc, *Wymondham* 1298 Ipm, 1304
Ch *et passim* to 1328 Banco, 1330 *Deed et freq*

Wymunham Hy 3 *Crox*, *Wymonham* 1296 Ipm, *Wimonham* 1652 *Gret*
Wymundam 1449 Pat, *Wymondam* 1473 *CCR*, 1530 AAS
Womandham 1470, 1487 AD, *Womondham* 1510 LP, 1609 LML,
1625 *Pochin*, 1626, 1627 LML, *Womanhame* 1608 *Rut*

'Wīgmund's village or estate', *v.* **hām**. The OE pers.n. *Wīgmund* also
appears in the p.n. Wymeswold, 15 miles to the west in East Goscote
Hundred.

BURROWCHURCH (lost)

Burchirche 13 TutP bis, *Borughkirk'* 1332 HB, 1332 *Pat*, *Burghkirke*
1332 Inqaqd, 1333 HB, *Borowkyrke* 1462 *Gret*, *Borokyrk* 1534
ib, *Burrowchurch* 1601 *Terrier*
capellam Sancti Petri Burghkirke 1332 *Pat*, *Burghkirke capella extra
Wymundeham* n.d. Nichols

A glebe terrier of 1612 locates the great field which took its name
from the lost *Burrowchurch* to the west of Wymondham (*v. Borokyrkfeld*

in f.ns. (b) *infra*), while the undated citation *Burghkirke capella* (with MLat *capella* 'a chapel') in Nichols places the chapel *extra* 'outside' the township. The *viam de Burchirche* 13 TutP (MLat *via* 'a road') led to the site which had its own fresh water supply, as indicated by *fontem de Burchirche* 13 TutP (MLat *fons* (*fontem* acc.sg.) 'a spring'). The chapel itself was dedicated to St Peter (*capellam Sancti Petri Burghkirke* 1332 *Pat*) and is not to be confused with the parish church of St Peter, Wymondham.

Burrowchurch is a compound of OE **burh** 'a fortified place', later 'a fortified house or manor' and OE **cirice** 'a church', the generic in the 14th, 15th and 16th centuries varying with or being replaced by ON **kirkja** 'a church'. No evidence of a major fortified site is obvious to the west of Wymondham. It may well be that the chapel was once the upstanding survivor of an early manor house. It is recorded as *the Chappell* 1601 *Terrier*. Note also the *Burrow Churche feilde* in Edmondthorpe f.ns. (b) *infra*.

ANGEL (P.H.) (lost), *Angel* 1846, 1863 White, 1925 Kelly, *Angel Inn* 1877 White, 1910 *Sale*. BLUE POINT, 1844 *TA*, 1863, 1877 White, 1968 *Surv*. Early maps indicate that it is *Crown Point* 1781 *Terrier*, 1795 Nichols, 1806 Map, 1815 Nichols, 1824 O, 1846 White, cf. *Crown Point Gap* 1801 Map (*v.* **gap**); but Blue Point coexisted with *Crown Point Close* 1844 *TA*, 1968 *Surv*, which suggests that Blue Point and Crown Point may have been adjacent features, with *Blue* representing ON **blár** (ME **blo**) in the latter's extended sense 'cold, exposed' and Crown as either from eModE **crowne** used of a rounded summit (*v.* OED *s.v.* crown IV 18; earliest citation in this sense 1583) or OE **cran, cron** 'a crane, a heron', since *Crown Point* is beside a stream which flows east into R. Witham, *v.* **point**. BUTT LANE, *v.* **butt**[2] and The Butt in Edmondthorpe f.ns. (a). CORD HILL is *Caldewald'*, *Caldewold'* 13 TutP and later *Cawde Hill* 1601 *Terrier*, *Caude hill* 1625 *ib*, *Caudhill* 1652 *Gret*, *Cauld Hill* 1968 *Surv*, *v.* **cald**, **wald**, **hyll**. CRIBB'S LODGE, 1968 *Surv*, *Lodge* 1824 O, *v.* **loge**; with the surn. *Cribb*, *v.* Reaney *s.n.* CROSSING COVERT is sited at a road-crossing of the former *Syston and Peterborough Branch Railway* 1850 O, *v.* **cover(t)**. DAY'S PLANTATION, *Days Plantation* 1968 *Surv*, cf. *Tho. Day* 1708 *Terrier*, *Mr Day* 1745 *ib*, *Wm. Day, farmer* 1846 White. DRIFT HILL, cf. *Womondham drift* 1625 *Pochin*, *The Drift* 1.18 *Plan*, (*The*) *Drifts* 1844 *TA*, *ye Drift Lane* 1679 *Terrier*, *v.* **drift**. GRANGE FM (local), *grangia apud Wymundeham* 13 TutP, cf. *Graung Bridge Close*, *Graunge Brigge Close* 1634 *Pochin*, *the*

Grange bridge close 1650 *ib*, *Grange Hill* 1652 *Gret*, 1844 *TA*, *v.*
grange; the grange was an outlier of Tutbury Priory. HORSE AND
GROOM (P.H.) (lost), *Horse and Groom* 1846 White. THE HUNTERS
ARMS (P.H.) is *Hunter's Inn* 1863, 1877 White. THE LODGE, *Lodge*
1824 O, *The Park Lodge* 1844 *TA*, *v.* **park**, **loge**. MANOR HO., *Manor*
house 1925 Kelly, *v.* **maner**; it is *Wymondham Hall* 1720 MagBrit, *v.*
hall. METHODIST CHAPEL, *The Methodist Chapel* 1844 *TA*. MOUNT
PLEASANT, 1846, 1863 White. THE POPLARS. THE RECTORY, 1877
White, 1925 Kelly, *Rectory House* 1844 *TA*; note earlier *the parsonage*
howse 1601 *Terrier*, *the Parsonage House* 1612, 1674, 1708, 1745 *ib*,
v. **personage**. ROOKERY HO., *Rookery House* 1846, 1863 White, *The*
Rookery 1925 Kelly, *v.* **rookery**. ST PETER'S CHURCH, *Church (St Peter)*
1846, 1863, 1877 White, 1925 Kelly; it is earlier recorded as *ecclesiam*
de Wymundeham 1235 RGros, *ecclesie de Wymundham* 1293 *Pat*, and
together with the church of Edmondthorpe as *ecclesiarum de*
Wymundeham et de Torp 1220 MHW, ~ *de Thorpe Edmer(e) et*
Wymond(es)ham 1355, 1358 *Pat*. Note also *The Churchyard* 1844 *TA*.
THREE HORSE SHOES (P.H.) (lost), *Three Horse Shoes* 1846, 1863, 1877
White, 1925 Kelly. WYMONDHAM BANKS, *The Banks* 1968 *Surv*, *v.*
banke. WYMONDHAM GRAMMAR SCHOOL, in the churchyard north of
the church and founded in 1673. Note Wymondham Grammar School
Farm in Melton Mowbray parish. WYMONDHAM HO., *Wymondham*
house 1877 White, 1925 Kelly. WYMONDHAM LODGE. WYMONDHAM
ROUGH, *Wymondham Roughs* 1968 *Surv*, *v.* **rūh**[2]. WYMONDHAM
WINDMILL, *Wimonham Windmill* 1652 *Gret*, cf. *Windmill (Granary) and*
Yard 1844 *TA*, *v.* **wind-mylne**.

HOUSES, OUTBUILDINGS, GARDENS AND ORCHARDS

The following are cited in 1745 *Terrier*: *Widow Andrews House*; *Mr*
Barlows House; *Peter Barnetts House and Home Stall* (*v.* **hām-stall**);
John Becks House and Garden; *Widow Becks House*; *John Blees House*;
Widow Blees House; *Mr Bullivants House and Orchard*; *William*
Burbages House; *James Bursnalls House and Home Stall*; *William*
Burtons House and Home Stall; *Edmund Burys House and Orchard*;
John Caunts House; *Henry Croslands House and Orchard*; *Robert*
Croslands House and Orchard; *Widow Croslands House*; *John Daines*
House and Home Stall; *Mr Days House and Garden*; *Mrs Days House*
and Garden; *Francis Derrys House and Home Stall*; *Samuel Dickmans*

House; *William Edgsons House* (*v. Jn." Edgson Toft* in Edmondthorpe f.ns. (b)); *Mr Extons House* (the *Exton* family no doubt originally came from the village of this name six miles to the south-east in Rutland); *John Fardells House*; *Mrs Gills House and Garden*; *John Graves Sen'. House and Home Stall*; *John Halls House and Home Stall*; *Robert Haucers House and Orchard*; *Widow Hollingworths House and Home Stall*; *John Horspools House and Home Stall*; *Christopher Huddlestones House and Orchard*; *Mr Hursts House*; *Anthony Leesons House and Home Stall*; *George Lords House*; *Mr Pawletts House*; *Widow Peers and Edward Stapleforths House* (sic); *Mr Rice Sen'. House and Garden*; *James Rippins House*; *Thomas Rippins House*; *Widow Rippins House and Home Stall*; *Widow Shaws House and Bowling Green* (*v.* **bowling-green**); *John Simpsons House*; *Joseph Sissons House and Home Stall*; *Widow Steels House and Home Stall*; *William Swansons House*; *Mr Taylors House*; *Joseph Thurlbys House*; *Widow Thurlbys House* (the surn. *Thurlby* was that of a family which originated in the village of this name 15 miles to the east in Lincs.); *Francis Tomlins House*; *Robert Tomlins House*; *John Toones House and Garden*; *Widow Turners House and Garden*; *Edward Wards House and Home Stall*; *Mr Wards House*; *William Wiles House*; *Hannah Wilfords House and Garden* (the surn. *Wilford* was presum. that of a family which originated in the village of this name 21 miles to the north-west in Notts.); *Thomas Williams House and Home Stall*; *Henry Williamsons House*; *Elizabeth Wormhill and Thomas Stapleforths House* (sic); *Robert Wormhills House and Home Stall*.

FIELD-NAMES

In (a), forms dated 1753 are *Pochin*; 1844 are *TA*; 1968 are *Surv*. Forms throughout dated 1221 are Fine; 1223 (l.13) are *Stix*; Hy 3 are *Crox*; 13 are TutP; Edw 3 (c.1430) are *KB*; 1462, 1534 and 1652 are *Gret*; 1601, 1612, 1674, 1679, 1690, 1697, c.1700, e.18, 1708 and 1745 are *Terrier*; 1611, 1625, 1634 and 1650 are *Pochin*; 1683 are *Wyg*; 1744 are *Rental*.

(a) Two ~, The Ten Acre 1968, Fifteen Acres 1844, The Fifteen ~, The Sixteen ~, Nineteen Acre 1968, Twenty Acres 1844, The Twenty Acre 1968 (*Twenty Acres* 1652), Forty Acres 1844 (*Fortye acres* 1611, *Fowerty Acres* 1652), Forty five Acres 1844, The Fifty Acre 1968 (*v.* **æcer**); Allotments 1968 (*v.* **allotment**); Far, Near Andrews 1968 (cf. *Widow Andrews* 1745); Baines Slip 1968 (*v.* **slipe**; with the surn. *Baine(s)*); Barlows Cl 1844, Barlows Middle, Barlows Far, Barlows First Platt 1844 (*v.* **plat**) (cf. *Mr Barlow* 1745); The Barn Fd 1968; Bassetts Plat 1844 (*v.* **plat**; with the surn. *Bassett*); Far, Near Bastards 1844, The Bastards 1968 (*v.* **bastard**); Far ~ ~, Little ~ ~, Middle ~ ~, South ~ ~, Beach Stones 1844 (*Heither* ~ (*v.* **hider**), *Beech Stone, Lower Beach Stone* 1652, *v.* **bece**[1], **stān**); Far, Near Beanlands 1844 (*Benelond'* 13, *Benlands* 1652, *v.* **bēan, land**); Far, Near Becks 1753, Bottom, Top Becks 1844, 1968, Gill's Becks 1968 (cf. *Robert Gill* 1745) (either with the surn. *Beck* in the possessive case, cf. *John Beck* and *Widow Beck* 1745, or with **bekkr**); The Bedlams 1968 (*v.* **bedlem**; a derogatory name for unproductive land, which only a madman would attempt to cultivate); Top ~ ~, Belchers Cl 1844, Top ~, Belchers 1968 (with the surn. *Belcher*); Beltside 1968 (*v.* **belt, sīde**); Berridges Cl 1844 (with the surn. *Berridge*); Berriffs Cl 1844 (with the surn. *Berriff*); Berrys Cl 1844, Berry Cl 1968 (cf. *Edward Berry* 1708 and prob. *Edmund Bury* and *Leonard Bury* 1745); (The) Big Fd 1968; Blaby Cl 1968 (with the surn. of a family originating in the village of this name, 22 miles to the south-west in Guthlaxton Hundred); Blacks Fd 1968 (with the surn. *Black*); East Blue Point 1968 (*v.* Blue Point *supra*); Bobs Cl 1844, Bob's ~ 1968 (either with the surn. *Bobb* (*v.* Reaney *s.n.*) or with the pet form *Bob* of the pers.n. Robert); Bodger's Cl 1844 (with the surn. *Bodger*); First, Second Botany Bay 1968 (used of land of poor quality or of remoteness from the township and named from the penal colony in south-eastern Australia to which British law-breakers were transported in the early 19th cent.); Bowrings Fd 1968 (with the surn. *Bow(e)ring*); High Brinks 1844 (*Great* ~, *Highbrink(e)* 1652, *Maxes high brinke* 1652 (with the surn. *Maxey* of a family originating in the village of this name, 18 miles to the south-east and formerly in Northants.), *v.* **hēah**[1], **brink**); Brockens Mdw 1844 (evidently with the surn. *Brocken*, rare in the Midlands; alternatively, the surn. *Bracken* may be thought of, *v.* Reaney *s.n.*); Bromleys Cl 1844 (with the surn. *Bromley*); Browns Cl, Browns Little Cl 1844 (with the surn. *Brown*); Bulls Cl 1844, 1968 (1652), Great, Little Bulls Walk 1844, 1968, Nether, Over Bulls Walk 1844, 1968 (*v.* **uferra**) (*Buls Walke* 1652, *v.* **walk**; with the surn. *Bull*); Burley Furze 1844 (*Purleyfurs, Great, Little Purley Furs* 1652, *v.* **fyrs**, cf. *William Purley* 1466 Nichols); Bushy Fds 1968 (*v.* **busshi**); Bursnell's 1844, ~ Paddock 1968 (*v.* **paddock**) (cf. *James Bursnall* 1745); The Canal 1968 (referring to the defunct *Oakham Canal* 1824 O); Upper Cliff(e) Bushes 1844 (*v.* **clif, busc**); Briggs ~ ~, Maxeys Cauld Hill 1844 (*Maxes Caudhill* 1652) (with the surns. *Briggs* and *Maxey*, *v.* Cord Hill *supra* and High Brinks *supra*); Cheese Cake Piece 1844, Cheesecake ~ 1968 (cf. *Cheesecake More* 1652 (*v.* **mōr**[1]), *v.* **cheesecake, pece**; in 1652 a triangular close, in 1844 rectangular and by 1968 square in shape); Christians Cl 1844, Christian's Leys 1844 (*v.* **leys**) (with the surn. *Christian*); Clarks Piece 1844 (*v.* **pece**; with the surn. *Clark*); Cocks Hill Cl 1844, North, South Cox's Hill 1968 (either with the surn. *Cocks/Cox* or with **cocc**[2]); Conery 1844, Big Coneygre 1968, Little Conery 1844, ~ Cunnery 1968 (*Andrews Cunnery* 1745 (cf. *Widow Andrews* 1745), *Little* ~ ~, *Connery Close* 1652, *Cunnery Close* 1708), Conery Hill 1844 (*Connery hill* 1652) (*v.* **coningre**); Little ~ ~, Cooks Cl, Cooks Little Cl 1844 (cf. *Beniamin Cooke* 1652); The Cottage Fd 1968 (*v.* **cotage**); Cowslip 1968 (poss. a f.n. styled from the plant-name *cowslip* (OE **cū-sloppe** (*Primula veris*)) referring to the dominant flower in the field; otherwise and more likely, *v.* **cū, slipe**); First ~, Crosslands, Crosslands Cl 1844 (cf. *Henry Crosland, Robert Crosland* and *Widow Crosland* 1745); Cross's

Barn 1968 (with the surn. *Cross*); Dead Moor Leys 1844 (*v.* d$\bar{e}$ad, m$\bar{o}$r[1], leys; evidently moorland at the edge of the parish where early burials were discovered, cf. *deadmore* in Waltham on the Wolds f.ns. (b); however, the compound 'dead moor' may rather indicate infertile wasteland); Dexters Cl 1844, 1968 (with the surn. *Dexter*); Dog Leg 1968 (descriptive of a close angled like a dog's hind leg, shaped as a dogleg); Doubledays Cl 1844 (with the surn. *Doubleday*, cf. *William Dubilday* 14 AD of Leics.); Doves Cl 1968 (with the surn. *Dove*); Dysarts 1968 (the property of the Earl of Dysart, resident at neighbouring Buckminster Park); Eddish Hill 1844 (*v.* edisc); Fardells Barn Cl 1844 (cf. *John Fardell* 1745); The Far Hill 1968; (The) First Hill 1844, 1968 (poss. with fyrs, cf. First Hill in Gt. Dalby, otherwise with fyrst 'first, chief, principal'); Flavills Platt 1844 (*v.* plat; with the surn. *Flavill*); The Footpath Fds 1968; Ford Cl 1968 (*v.* ford); Fowlers Cl 1844 (1745, *cf. Fowlers Pasture Close* 1652, cf. *Jack Fowler* 1652); Fox Cover 1844, Fox Cover Cl 1968 (*v.* cover(t)); Franers Cl 1844 (with a surn., prob. *Franey, v.* Reaney *s.n.*); Franks Cl 1968 (either with the surn. *Frank(s)* or with *Frank*, the pet form of the pers.n. Francis); Frisbys 1968 (the surn. *Frisby* in the possessive case, of a family originating in either Frisby on the Wreake or Frisby by Galby, both Leics.); Gambles Hill 1844 (with the surn. *Gamble*); Gann's Cl 1968 (with the surn. *Gann*); Gents, ~ Piece 1968 (*v.* pece; with the surn. *Gent*); Gauze Well 1844, Gorswell 1968 (*Goswell* 1652, *v.* prob. with g$\bar{o}$s rather than gorst); Gill's Paddock 1968 (*v.* paddock), Gill's Slip 1968 (*v.* slipe) (cf. *Robert Gill* 1745); Glebe 1844, East, West, Little Glebe 1844, Grass, Ploughed Glebe 1968, Glebe Cl 1844 (*The Gleabe, Gleabe Lands* 1652, *v.* glebe); The Gold Diggings 1968 (presum. a jocular name for a local mineral excavation); Gorse Cl 1968 (*v.* gorst); Gorsey ~, Garsey Cl 1844 (*v.* gorstig); Goslings 1844 (the surn. *Gosling* in the possessive case); Grave's Cl 1968, Graves Nether, Graves Upper Cl 1844 (with the surn. *Graves*); Far ~ ~, Grays Cl 1844, 1968 (cf. *Great, Little Grayes Close* 1652; with the surn. *Gray*); Great Cl 1968; Great Hill 1844, Bottom ~ ~ 1968; Great Mdw 1968; Great Walk 1844 (*Great Walke* 1652, *v.* walk); The Green 1844 (*v.* gr$\bar{e}$ne[2]); Grenfell's 1968 (the surn. *Grenfell* in the possessive case); Gretton's 1968 (the surn. *Gretton* in the possessive case); Grices Home Cl 1844 (*v.* home; with the surn. *Grice*); Gunthorpe Platt 1844 (*Guntraps Plott* 1652, *v.* plot, plat; with the surn. *Gunthorpe*, of a family prob. originating in the village of this name eight miles to the south in Rutland, although there is also a Gunthorpe 19 miles to the north-east in Notts.); Hacketts First, Hacketts Second Platt, First Hacketts Platt, Second ~ ~ 1844, Hacketts Hovel Platt 1844 (*v.* hovel) (*Hackets Further, Hackets heither Plott* (*v.* hider), *Hackets Middle Plott* 1652, *v.* plot, plat; with the surn. *Hackett*); Harleys Fds 1968 (with the surn. *Harley*); Hewitts Cl 1968, Middle Hewitts Platt 1844 (*v.* plat) (with the surn. *Hewitt*); Hickman's Slip 1968 (*v.* slipe; with the surn. *Hickman*); Far, Near Hill Cl 1753 (*Hill Closse* 1652, *v.* hyll, clos(e)); Hill Pit Leys 1844 (*Hellpitt leyes* 1634, *Helpit Layes* 1652, *Edward Berrys Helpit Leys* 1708, *Hellpitt Leys* 1745, *v.* leys and *Helpitt* in Edmondthorpe f.ns. (b)); Hills Far Cl 1844, Hills First Platt 1844 (*v.* plat) (with the surn. *Hill(s)*); Hollingworth's Cl 1844 (cf. *Widow Hollingworth* 1745); The Holme 1844, Holmes 1968 (*The Home* 1652, *v.* holmr); (The) Home Cl 1844, 1968, Great, Little Home Cl 1844 (*Home Close* 1652, *v.* home); Home Cl and Wong 1844 (*v.* home, vangr); The Home Fd 1968 (*v.* home); Hopkins Cl 1844, Hoppins ~ 1968 (*Hopkins Close* 1652; with the surn.

Hopkin(s)); Hornsbys 1968 (the surn. *Hornsby* in the possessive case); Hounds Acre 1844 (1652, *Great Howns Acre, Littlehounds Acre* 1652, *Maxes Houndsacre* 1652 (with the surn. *Maxey, v.* High Brinks *supra*)), Hounds Acre Garden 1844, 1968, Hounds Acre Pingle 1844 (*v.* **pingel**) (*v.* **æcer, akr**; the first el. is a pers.n., either OE *Hund* or Scand *Hundr*); Huntleys Cl 1844 (with the surn. *Huntley*); Hursts First, Hursts Second Platt 1844 (*v.* **plat**; cf. *Mr Hurst* 1745); Intake 1844 (*v.* **inntak**); Jacksons Platt 1968 (*v.* **plat**), Little Jacksons 1968 (with the surn. *Jackson*); Jarratts 1968 (the surn. *Jarratt* in the possessive case); Johnsons Piece 1968 (*v.* **pece**), Johnny Johnson's Fd 1968; Kirks Fd 1968 (with the surn. *Kirk*); Kitson's 1968 (the surn. *Kitson* in the possessive case); Leesons Pasture 1844 (cf. *Anthony Leeson* 1745); (The) Lineside 1968 (a field beside the former *Syston and Peterborough Branch Railway* 1850 O); Little Cl 1968; Littlers, ~ Fd 1968 (with the surn. *Littler* in the possessive case); Great, Little Lodge Cl 1844 (*v.* The Lodge *supra*); Lone Creek 1968 (*v.* **lone, crike**); Long Cl 1844, 1968, Browns ~ ~ 1844 (with the surn. *Brown*), Esther's ~ ~, Hesters ~ ~ 1844 (with the surn. *Hester*, confused with the fem. pers.n. *Esther*); The Long Fd 1968; The Long Slip 1968 (*v.* **slipe**); Loves Mdw 1844 (*Loues Meadow* 1652), Loves Platt 1844 (*Loues Plott* 1652, *v.* **plot, plat**) (with the surn. *Love*); Malt Office and Paddock 1844 (*v.* **paddock**) (cf. *The Malt Mill house* 1652, *v.* **malte-mylne**); Mans Bones 1844 (1652, 1708, 1745, *Mannes Bones* 13, *Manysbanes* 1462, *v.* **mann, bān**; situated due east of the village, half-way to the parish boundary, this is poss. the site of an early pagan Anglo-Saxon cemetery); Mantles Cl 1844 (with the surn. *Mantle*); Markham Platt 1844 (*Markhams Plott* 1652, *v.* **plot, plat**; in the possession of *Mathew Markham* 1652); North, South Maxeys Shrubs 1844, 1968, Maxeys Shrubbery 1844 (*Maxes Shroubes* 1652, *Max(i)es Shrubs* 1708, 1745, *v.* **scrubb**; with the surn. *Maxey, v.* High Brinks *supra*); Meer Cl 1844 (*The Meere* 1652, *ye Meer next to South Withum feild* 1679, *v.* **(ge)mǣre**; the boundary with South Witham (Lincs.) which adjoins to the east); Mill Cl 1844, Far ~ ~, Mill Fd 1968, Mill Hill 1844, Mills Platt 1844, Mill Platts 1968 (*v.* **plat**); The Minefield 1968 (so called because a German parachute mine exploded here 19 November 1940); Mitchells 1968 (the surn. *Mitchell* in the possessive case); First, Second Moor 1844 (*More* 1523 LAS, *Wymondam Moore* 1683, *in mora de Wymundham* Edw 3 (c.1430) (with MLat *mora* 'a moor')), Fine, Rough Moor 1844, 1968 (*v.* **fin, rūh**[1]), High Moor 1844, 1968 (*the high(e) more* 1601, 1612, cf. *High Moore Cliffe* 1652 (*v.* **clif**), *high moore gate* 1652 (*v.* **gata**), *ye High More Glebe close* 1679 (*v.* **glebe**), *ye high moor grounds* 1708, *High Moor Grounds* 1745 (*v.* **grund**), *the high or west more* 1612 (*v.* **hēah**[1]), *Westmor(e)* 1199 FF, 1200 Fine, 13 TutP, c.1350 Nichols, *Further ~ ~, Heither ~ ~* (*v.* **hider**), *West Moore* 1652 (*v.* **west**)), Harris Moor 1844, Harris's ~ 1968 (with the surn. *Harris*), Bottom ~ ~, Upper ~ ~, Pickards Moor 1844 (with the surn. *Pickard*), West Rudkins Moor 1844 (with the surn. *Rudkin*) (*v.* **mōr**[1]); Muse's Mdws 1968 (with the surn. *Muse*); Naylors Fds 1968 (with the surn. *Naylor*); Nearnought Cl 1844, Nearnought New Cl 1844 (a jocular name for a very small enclosure, i.e. 'nearly nothing'); Needhams 1968 (the surn. *Needham* in the possessive case); Nether Grounds 1844 (*v.* **grund**); Big ~ ~, Far ~ ~, New Cl 1844 (*New Close* 1652); New Hill 1844, 1968, ~ ~ or Pingle 1844 (*v.* **pingel**), New Hill Cl 1753; New Plantation 1968; New Seeds 1968 (*v.* **sǣd**; in f.ns. used of areas of sown grass); Nobles Cl 1844 (*Westons Nobles Close* 1745; earlier in the possession of a family called *Noble*, later acquired by the *Weston* family); Middle ~ ~, Nether ~ ~, Normans Hill 1844 (either with the surn. *Norman* or with **nān-mann** 'no man, nobody', often used of locations at boundaries); Old Cl 1844 (1652, *v.* **ald**); Oldhams 1968 (*Oadhams Close* 1652; (with) the surn. *Oldham* in the possessive case); Old Hill Cl 1753, Old Hill Steep Cl 1753 (*v.* **stēap**) (prob. with **wald** rather than **ald**, cf. Woulds *infra*); Old Lane, ~ ~ Garden 1844; Old Road and Waste 1844 (*v.* **waste**; described as arable in *TA*); Oldsworth Cl 1844, 1968, Oldsworths ~ 1844 (*Holdsworth Close* 1652; with the surn. *Holdsworth*, *v.* Reaney *s.n.*); East ~ ~, Great ~ ~, Middle ~ ~, West ~ ~, Open Ground 1844, 1968 (*the Open Grounds* 1745, *v.* **open, grund**); Palmers Cl, Palmers First, Palmers Second, Palmers Third Cl 1844 (with the surn. *Palmer*); The Park 1844, East, West Park 1844, The Parkes 1968 (*The Parke* 1652, *v.* **park**); Loves ~ ~, Love's Parting Cl 1844, Mans ~ ~, Man's Parting Cl 1844 (with the surns. *Love* and *Man*) (*a close commonly called Parting Close because divided betwixt ye Rector of Wymondham and Rector of Thorpe* 1690, (*ye*) *Parting Close* 1697, 1745, *Tho. Corners Parting Close* 1708, *v.* **parting**); Pasture Cl 1753, 1844 (1652, *Pasture Closse* 1652, *Neither Pasture Close* 1652 (*v.* **neoðera**), *Fowlers* ~ ~ 1652 (cf. *Jack Fowler* 1652), *the Parsonage* ~ ~ 1612 (*v.* **personage**), *v.* Wymondham Pasture *infra*); Pauletts Cl 1844 (cf. *Mr Pawlett* 1745); Paynes Cl 1844, 1968 (*Paines Close* 1652; with the surn. *Payne*); Pecks Fds 1968 (cf. *Pekesholm, Pekholm* Hy 3, *v.* **holmr**; with the ME surn. *Pecke* (ModE *Peck*)); Pedlars Cl 1844 (prob. with the surn. *Pedlar*; otherwise *v.* **pedlere**); Pegs Cl 1968 (with the surn. *Pegg(s)*); Peppercorn Cl 1844 (alluding to the liability for a peppercorn rent for the close, at a time when payment of some kind, however trivial, was necessary to validate the tenancy); (The) Pingle 1968 (*The Pingle* 1652, *v.* **pingel**); Pit Garden 1844 (*v.* **pytt**); Plantation Close Fds 1968; Platts 1968 (*v.* **plat**); The Poor Fd 1968 (*v.* **pouer(e)**; the rent from this field provided funds for assistance given to the village poor, *v.* Field 191–3); Porters Cl 1844 (with the surn. *Porter*); Priestmans (Far) Cl 1968 (with the surn. *Priestman*); Ram Cl 1844 (*the Ram Close* 1745, *v.* **ramm**); Red Earth 1844, The Reddiths 1968 (*v.* **rēad, eorðe**); Rickyard 1844 (*v.* **rick-yard**); The Ridgeway 1968 (*v.* **hrycg, weg**); Turners Roadside 1968 (a close beside a road; with the surn. *Turner*); North ~ ~ ~, Sand Pit Walk 1844, Nether, Upper Sandpit Walk 1844, 1968 (*Sandpitt Walke* 1652, *v.* **sand-pytt, walk**); St ~, Saint Ledger 1844 (*St Leagers* 1652; described as a close in 1652 and pasture in 1844; this is the surn. *St Leger* (earlier in the possessive case), cf. Colonel Barry St Leger who instituted the annual flat horse-race for three-year-old colts and fillies in 1776, held at Doncaster, now called The St Leger; and *v.* Reaney *s.n.* Salinger); Saunders Paddock 1968 (*v.* **paddock**; with the surn. *Saunders*); School Cl 1968 (cf. *Schoolhouse* 1844; referring to Wymondham Grammar School, north of the church, founded in 1637); The Seedfield 1968 (*v.* **sæd**; in f.ns., often used of areas of sown grass); Selbys Cl 1844, 1968, Selbys Fd 1968 (with the surn. *Selby*); First, Second Sewstern Rd 1968 (closes beside the road to Sewstern which lies three miles to the north-east); Upper ~, Shrovesdale, Upper Shroes Dale 1844 (*v.* **scrobb, dalr**; the first el. appears to be that in Shrewsbury and has a parallel development, with interchange of *b* and *v*, *v.* Sa **1** 267–71; Ekwall DEPN argues for an OE pers.n. *Scrobb* in Shrewsbury, rejected by Gelling); Siddans Fd 1968 (poss. with the surn. *Siddons*, but this f.n. may be a later garbled form of the following); Sissons Cl 1844 (cf. *Joseph*

Sissons 1745); Slades 1844 (*Estesled* 13 (*v.* ēast), *Westesled'* 13, *Westslaade* 1652 (*v.* **west**), *v.* **slæd**); Far, Near Smith's Cl 1968 (with the surn. *Smith*); Spreckleys Great Cl, ~ Little Cl 1844 (with the surn. *Spreckley*); Spring Cl 1968 (*v.* **spring**[1]; the field contains a fresh-water spring); The Stackyard 1968 (*v.* **stak-ȝeard** and Rickyard *supra*); Stanleys 1968 (the surn. *Stanley* in the possessive case); Stapleford Cl 1844 (Stapleford adjoins to the west); Steels Cl 1844 (cf. *Widow Steel* 1745); Steep Lane 1844 (*v.* **stēap**); Stokes's Fd 1968 (with the surn. *Stokes*); Great ~ ~ ~, Stone Pit Cl 1844, Stonepit Cl East, ~ ~ West 1968 (*le Stonepit'* 1462, *Stonpit Close, Stone Pitt Closse* 1652, *v.* **stān-pytt**); Stivesdale 1844, 1968, Styesdale 1844 (*Sthisdale, Stisdale* 13, *le Stisdale* 1462, *Crossers* ~ ~, *Styles Dale* 1652 (with the surn. *Croser*), *v.* **stig, dalr**); Sumptors Cl 1844 (with the surn. *Sumpter*); First ~ ~, Second ~ ~, Swills Platt 1844 (*v.* **plat**; the first el. may be OE *swille* 'a sloppy mess, a swilling', transferred topographically to boggy waterside land or to flat waterside land which is liable to flooding; however, as *plat* is invariably preceded by a surn. in Wymondham, indicating ownership or tenancy, the uncommon south-western surn. *Swill* (a variant of *Swell*?) must be preferred, although the 1881 census shows no families with the name resident in Leics.); Talton's Fd 1968 (with the surn. *Talton*); Tank Fd 1968 (referring to a water tank); Far, Near Thirty Stone Cl 1844, Thirty Stones 1844, 1968 (*Thirtie Stone* 1611, *Thirty Stone* 1652, 1745, *30 Ston* 1708; poss. a late garbled form of Thistleton (Ru) which has a common boundary with Wymondham parish; otherwise perh. referring to a boundary with 30 stones as markers); Thistle Fd 1968 (*v.* **þistel**); Thistly Cl 1844 (*v.* **thist(e)ly**); The Thorns 1968 (*v.* **þorn**); Three Cornered Cl 1844 (*v.* **three-cornered**); Todds Cl 1968 (with the surn. *Todd*); Lower ~ ~, Toft Dyke 1968 (*Toftes* 13, 1462, *v.* **toft, dík**); Tomlins Cl 1844 (cf. *Robert Tomlin* 1745); Pawletts ~ ~ (cf. *Mr Pawlett* 1745), Townsend Cl 1844 (*Heither* (*v.* **hider**), *Middle, Vpper Townes ende Closse* 1652, *v.* **tūn, ende**); Trainer's Cl 1968 (with the surn. *Trainer, v.* Reaney *s.n.*); Waddingtons 1968 (with the surn. *Waddington* in the possessive case of a family which prob. originated in the township of this name 30 miles to the north-east in Lincs.); Wards Cl 1844 (cf. *Edward Ward* 1745); Washdike ~, Wash Dyke Cl 1844 (*v.* **wash-dyke**; a close containing a sheep-dip); Watchorns 1968 (apparently the surn. *Watchorn* in the possessive case, but cf. Watchorn in Scalford f.ns. (a)); Water Cl 1844, 1968 (1652, *Watter Close* 1652, *v.* **wæter**; beside a stream and poss. alluding to an irrigation system, cf. *Water medow* in Edmondthorpe f.ns. (b) and *v.* Field 90–1); Big, Little Waterloo 1968 (on the parish boundary, but rather than being a 'remoteness' name, prob. commemorating Wellington's victory over Napoleon at Waterloo in 1815); Weston's Cl 1844, Bennet Westons, ~ ~ Land 1968 (with the surn. *Weston*); Nether, Upper Whitmores Platt 1844 (*v.* **plat**; with the surn. *Whitmore*); Williams Cl 1844 (cf. *Thomas Williams* 1745); Willow Holt 1844 (*v.* **wilig, holt**); Woodcock Island 1844 (*v.* **wudu-cocc, island**; prob. referring to a small piece of woodland surrounded by open country); Woodgate 1844 ((*le*) *Wodegate* Hy 3, 13, *le Wodgate* 1462, *v.* **wudu, gata**); Woulds 1844 (*v.* **wald**); Wrights Cl 1844 (with the surn. *Wright*); Wymondham Pasture 1806 Map, 1824 O (*the kowpasture* 1601, *Wymondham Cowpasture* 1612 (*v.* **cū**), *The Pastures* 1674, *Cooks Pasture, Edgsons* ~ (cf. *William Edgson* 1745 and *v. Jn.*[n] *Edgson Toft* in f.ns. (b) *infra*), *Fishers* ~ (cf. *Robert Fisher* 1612 of Edmondthorpe), *Fowlers* ~ (cf. *Jack Fowler* 1652), *Hopkins* ~, *Nobles* ~ (cf.

Henry Noble 1652), *Waits Pasture* 1652, *v.* **pasture**); Wyres Cl 1844 (with the surn. *Wyer(s)*, cf. *Wyers Towns End Close* in adjacent Whissendine (*v.* Ru 61, where a poss. derivation from *weyour* 'a pond' should be discounted)).

(b) *Alfricheston* 13 (*v.* **tūn**; with the OE pers.n. *Ælfrīc* (cf. *Alfriston*, Sx 415); a lost farmstead or settlement); *Baggot holme alias Boyholme* 1601 (*v.* **holmr**; with the surn. *Baggott, v. Boyholme, infra*); *Barkbyes* 1652 (the surn. *Barkby* in the possessive case of a family which originated in the township of this name 14 miles to the southwest in East Goscote Hundred); *Bells Close* 1652, (*Thomas*) *Days Bells Close* 1708, 1745 (prob. the rents from this close were originally assigned to the maintenance of the parish church bells or payments for their being rung; but the surn. *Bell* in the possessive case is also poss. as the earlier first el.); *Blackhill Bushes* 1652 (*v.* **blæc, hyll, busc**); *Blind Lane* 1652 (*v.* **blind**; used of a road closed at one end); *Boddy Close* 1652 (with the surn. *Boddy, v.* Reaney *s.n.*); *Bondebreches* 13 (*v.* **bond, brēc**); *Borokyrkfeld* 1534, *burowgh church feild* 1612 (*v.* **feld** and Burrowchurch *supra*; one of the great fields of the township); *Boyholme* 1601 (*v.* **holmr**; perh. a particular playing field for the village boys (*v.* **boia**), although the ODan pers.n. *Boie* cannot be discounted as the first el.); *Brethlondale* 13, *Northhalfbretlondale* 13 (*v.* **norð, half**), *v.* **breiðr, land, dalr**); (*The*) *Bridge Close* 1652, 1745, *Bridg* ~ 1708; *Lower Bromfielde, Vpper Brome Field* 1652, *Bromfield further, Bromfield great, Bromfield Heither Plott* 1652 (*v.* **hider, plot**) (*v.* **brōm, feld**); *Bulls Meadow* 1652, *Bulls Pingle* 1652 (*v.* **pingel**) (with the surn. *Bull*); *Leonard Burys Close* 1745; *Cattmoredale* 1611, *Catmoore dale* 1652 (*v.* **cat(t), mōr**[1]; with **dalr** or **deill**); *Caudhill gate* 1652 (*v.* **gata**), *Caudhill Lane* 1652 (*v.* Cord Hill *supra*); *Cleywong* 13 (*v.* **clæg, vangr**); *Clipsum Pitt* 1652 (*v.* **pytt**), *Clipsum Well* 1652 (*v.* **wella**) (with the surn. *Clipsham* of a family originating in Clipsham (Ru), eight miles to the east); *Connery Bridge* 1652 (*v.* Conery in f.ns. (a) *supra*); *Cookes great, Cookes heither Plott* (*v.* **hider**) 1652 (*v.* **plot** and cf. *Beniamin Cooke* 1652); *ye old Cottagers Close* 1679 (*v.* **cotager**), *ye Cotiers Close* c.1700, *the Cotier's-Close* e.18 (*v.* **cottere**); *Cow Close* 1652; *Cowpasture Close* 1612 (*v.* Wymondham Pasture *supra*); *Cowperdale* 1708, *Cauperdale* 1744 (*v.* **deill**; with the surn. *Cowper* (ME *couper* 'a maker or repairer of wooden casks and buckets'))); *Crabtree Holm(e)* 1611, 1745, ~ *home* 1652, *Mrs Days Crabtree Holm* 1708 (*v.* **crabtre, holmr**); *Dannycrosse* 1462 (*v.* **cros**; with the surn. *Danny* (OFr *daneis* 'Danish'), *v.* Reaney *s.n.*); *Dedborow Layes* 1652 (*v.* **dēad, berg, leys**; the hill was presum. either the place of a violent death or more likely a site where early burials had been discovered, cf. Dead Moor Leys in f.ns. (a) *supra*); *The Douehouse* 1652 (*v.* **dove-house**); *Drinchehull* 13 (*v.* **hyll**; the first el. is either ME **dreng** or the ON by-name *Drengr* (from *drengr* 'a warrior')); *the Eighteen Acres* 1745 (cf. *Eighteene Acre More* 1652 (*v.* **mōr**[1]), *18 Acre Pingle* 1652 (*v.* **pingel**), *v.* **æcer**); *Estmore* Hy 3, *Estmor(a)* l.13 (*v.* **ēast, mōr**[1]); *Est parkvall* 1462 (*v.* **ēast, park, wall**); *fifurlang* l.13, *Fyuefurlang'* Edw 3 (c.1430) (*v.* **fīf, furlang**); *Fordeyles* 13 (*v.* **fore, deill**); *Fordoles* 1221 (*v.* **fore, dāl**; this may represent the same feature as the preceding f.n., with **dāl** for **deill**); *Foster Close* 1652, *the homesteede of Randle Foster* 1634 (*v.* **hām-stede**); *Fyve leyes* 1611 (*v.* **fīf, leys**; when compounded with a numeral, *leys* represents grassland units of tenure corresponding to *lands* (i.e. selions or strips) similarly used of arable); *Gamballs hill* 1652 (cf. *Will'm Gamball* 1652); *Gillams Close* 1652 (cf. *Widdow Gillim* (sic) 1652); *Robert Gills Farm* 1745 (*v.* **ferme**); *Gooselees* 1652 (*v.* **gōs, leys**); *The Great Home* 1652 (*v.* **holmr**); *Green Close* 1745 (*v.* **grēne**²); *Gunby gate* 1652 (*v.* **gata**; the road to Gunby which lies four miles to the north-east in Lincs.); *Guneheng* l.13, Edw 3 (c.1430) (*v.* **eng**; with the Scand pers.n. *Gunni*, a short form of names in *Gunn-*, *v.* SPNLY 116); *Guntraps Meadow* 1652 (*v.* Gunthorpe Platt *supra*); *atte Hegge* 1327 SR (p) (*v.* **atte, hecg**); *de la Hegh* 1332 SR (p) (*v.* **(ge)hæg**); *Hendepit* 13 (*v.* **(ge)hende, pytt**); *Thomas Henslowes close* 1611; (*le*) *Holegate* Hy 3, 13 (*v.* **hol**², **gata**); *holemanhill* 1462 (*v.* **hyll**; with the surn. *Holman*); *le holking* 1462 (*v.* **holc, eng**); *Hunerfurlonge* (sic) 13 (prob. a scribal error for *Hungerfurlonge*, *v.* **hungor, furlang**); *Imery Close* 1652 (cf. *Thomas Imery* 1652); *Katerinedal* 1221 (*v.* **deill**; with the ME surn. *Caterin* (from OFr *Caterine*, a French form of Catherine, introduced into England in the 12th cent.), *v.* Reaney *s.n.* Catlin); *Lampery Home* 1652 (*v.* **holmr**; with the surn. *Lamprey*, *v.* Reaney *s.n.*); *Lampol* 13 (*v.* **lām, pōl**¹); *Further, Heither* (*v.* **hider**), *Lower Land Plott* 1652 (*v.* **land, plot**); *langhamgate ende* 1462 (*v.* **gata, ende**; Langham (Ru) lies five miles to the south); *Listern Bridge* 1652 (*v.* **lūs-þorn**; *þorn* > *tern* is a typical development in north Leics., cf. Sewstern); *Lit(t)elclif* 1221, 13 (*v.* **lȳtel, clif**); *Magdaunce hous* 1521 CoPleas (*v.* **hūs**; cf. *Henry Magdaunce* 1521 ib); *Maxes Close* 1652, *Maxes Home Close* 1652 (*v.* **home**), *Maxes Home Plott* 1652 (*v.* **plot**), *Maxes further, Maxes heither Plott* 1652 (*v.* **hider**) (with the surn. *Maxey*, for which *v.* High Brinks in f.ns. (a) *supra*); *The Meere Stone* 1652 (*v.* **(ge)mǣre, stān**; a parish boundary marker); *merfurlang* 1223 (l.13) (*v.* **(ge)mǣre, furlang**); *Mikildeyl* Hy 3, *Mikeldeyl* l.13, *Miclede(i)le* Edw 3 (c.1430) (*v.* **micel, mikill, deill**); *Adcocks Moore* 1745 (with the surn. *Adcock*), *Blases Moore* 1652 (with the surn. *Blaise*), *Wm. Dickmans Moor* 1708, *Samuel Dickmans Moor* 1745, *Fishers Moore* 1652 (cf. *Robert Fisher* 1612 of Edmondthorpe), *Heards Moore* 1652 (with the surn. *Heard*, *v.* Reaney *s.n.* Herd), *Ope Moore* (sic) 1652 (*v.* **ope**; a reduced form of *open* (cf. *bespoke*) and evidently referring here to unenclosed moorland; in the context of this group of names, a surn. might have been expected, but no such surn. is recorded and neither the approximate *Hope* nor *Opie* are surns. which relate to this county), *Palmer Moore* 1652 (cf. *Widd. Palmer* 1652 (i.e. *Widow* ~)), *Richardsons Moore* 1652 (with the surn. *Richardson*), *Whits Moore* 1652 (with the surn. *Whitt*) (*v.* First, Second Moor in f.ns. (a) *supra*), *Moore Close* 1652 (*v.* **mōr**¹); *le Moreherne* 1462 (*v.* **mōr**¹, **hyrne**); *Mucleberwe* 13, *Mucleberfurlong* 13 (*v.* **furlang**), *Mikelebersty* 13 (*v.* **stīg**), *Mykelbarowdale* 1462 (*v.* **dalr**), *Mekylbarowdale ende* 1462 (*v.* **ende**) (*v.* **micel, berg**); *Nixes Lower, Nixes Vpper Plott* 1652 (*v.* **plot**; with the surn. *Nix*); *Noble Cow Close* 1652, *Nobles First, Nobles Second Plott* 1652 (*v.* **plot**; cf. *Henry Noble* 1652); *Northgate* 13 (*v.* **norð, gata**); *Oadhams further, Oadhams heither* (*v.* **hider**), *Oadhams middle Plott* 1652 (*v.* **plot**; with the surn. *Oldham*, cf. *John Oldham* 1594 of North Luffenham (Ru), 11 miles to the south-east and Oldhams in f.ns. (a) *supra*); *The Oold Orchard* (sic) 1652 (*v.* **ald**); *Oxeclos(s)e* 1611 (*v.* **oxa, clos(e)**); *Pabelynglond* 1506 Banco (*v.* **land**; poss. added to an earlier p.n., an OE *Papoling 'place where pebbles abound', *v.* **papol, -ing**²); *Parke Lane* 1652, *The Parke Yard* 1652 (*v.* **geard**) (*v.* The Park in f.ns. (a) *supra*); *the Parsonage Glebe land platt* 1601 (*v.* **glebe, land, plat**), *the Parsonage ground* 1612 (*v.* **grund**) (*v.* **personage**); *Paynes Bridge* 1652 (with the surn. *Payne*, *v.* Paynes Cl in f.ns. (a) *supra*); *Peneyard* 1523 LAS (*v.* **geard**; the first el. is poss. an earlier spelling of the surn. *Payne*, otherwise

v. **penn**[2]; the holding is described as a toft); *Mrs Gills Persons Yard* 1745 (*v.*
persone, geard); *Peselonde* 13 (*v.* **pise, land**); *de ponte* l.13 (p) (with MLat *pons*
(*ponte* abl.sg.) 'a bridge'); *pratum Henrici Grim* l.13 (with MLat *pratum* 'a meadow,
meadowland'); *Prestheng', Pristheng* Edw 3 (c.1430) (*v.* **prēost, eng**); *Redehill'*
1462 (*v.* **hyll**; prob. with **rēad** 'red' (cf. Red Earth in f.ns. (a) *supra*), but **hrēod** 'a
reed, a reed-bed' is poss.); *Redeholle* 1462 (*v.* **hrēod, hol**[1]); *Redehou* 13 (*v.* **haugr**;
prob. with **rēad**, but **hrēod** is poss.); *Redfordes Pingle* 1634 (*v.* **pingel**; with the surn.
Redford); *Rigathe* 13 (*v.* **ryge, gata**); *Russells Close* 1745, *Russells Plott* 1652 (*v.*
plot) (with the surn. *Russell*); *Rygges* Edw 3 (c.1430) (*v.* **hrycg, hryggr**); *Saltputes*
1213 (*v.* **salt**[1], **salt**[2], **pytt**; it is uncertain whether the name refers to the production of
salt by evaporation or to brackish, salty water which accumulated in the pits, *v.*
Saltby); *terra Scatergod* l.13 (with MLat *terra* 'land', cf. *Willielmus Scatergod* l.13);
Segers way 1612 (*v.* **weg**; with the surn. *Seger*, *v.* Reaney *s.n.*); *Sheepwashe Close*
1652 (*v.* **scēp-wæsce**); *Smete* 13 (*v.* **smēðe**[1]); *Sir Roger Smith his lands* 1652, *Smiths
Goldsons hills* 1652 (with the surn. *Goldson*); *Snow Close* 1652 (either with the surn.
Snow or referring to a close where snow lay long, *v.* **snāw**, cf. Snow Cl in Brentingby
f.ns. (a) and *Snow Wong* in Harby f.ns. (b)); *Stapleford Bridge* 1652 (Stapleford
adjoins to the west; presum. a bridge across R. Eye); *Stonehull'* 13 (*v.* **stān, hyll**);
Taylors Plott 1652 (*v.* **plot**; cf. *Widdow Taylor* 1652); *terra Henrici de Thebeltoft*
l.13 (with MLat *terra* 'land'; *Henrici de Thebeltoft* is the *Henricus de Tybetoft* who
held land in neighbouring Edmondthorpe in 1242 Fees; *Thebeltoft* and *Tybetoft*
represent the same messuage, with the varying forms of the first el. being from the
OFr pers.n. *Theobald/Tibaut, v.* Reaney *s.n.* Theobald and Tibbet; *v.* **toft**); *Thirty
Acres* 1652 (*v.* **æcer**); *Thistleton more* Edw 3 (c.1430) (*v.* **mōr**[1]; Thistleton (Ru)
adjoins to the east); *Thorsedale* 1611 (*v.* **deill**; the first el. is either the Scand pers.n.
Þórir or the Anglo-Scand pers.n. *Þórr*); *Great Walke* 1652, *Neither Walke* 1652 (*v.*
neoðera) (*v.* **walk**); *Wallets* 1652 (cf. *Richard Wallet* 1652); *Weitte Caudhill* 1652
(*v.* Cord Hill *supra*), *Weate Lower, Weate Middle, Weate Vpper Plott* (*v.* **plot**) (with
the surn. *Wait*); *le Westbryge* 1462 (*v.* **west, brycg**); *Whitworths Plott* 1652 (*v.* **plot**;
with the surn. *Whitworth*); *WilleclifEdw* 3 (c.1430), *WesterewillecliftEdw* 3 (c.1430)
(*v.* **westerra**) (*v.* **wilig, clif**); *Nixes Guntree Wombe* 1652 (with the surn. *Nix* and a
debased form of the surn. *Gunthorpe, v.* Gunthorpe Platt in f.ns. (a) *supra*), *Stoney
Wombe* 1652 (*v.* **stānig**) (ostensibly with **wamb** 'a womb', used topographically in
the sense 'a hollow', but *wong* < **vangr** may be thought of); *Woodcat Close* 1652 (*v.*
Woodgate in f.ns. (a) *supra*); *Wrangeland'* 1462 (*v.* **wrang, vrangr, land**).

2. EDMONDTHORPE

Edmerestorp 1086 DB, 1165 P, *Eadmeristorp* 1223 (l.13) *Stix,*
   Edemeresthorpe 1380 Ipm
Edmeretorp 1183 P (p), *Edmer(e)thorp* 1344 Pap, 1345 Banco *et
   passim* to 1404 *Laz,* 1437 Banco
Thorp(e) Ed(e)mer(e) 1290 Inqaqd, 1291 TutP *et passim* to l.13
   (1404) *Laz et freq* to 1523 Ipm, 1526 AAS *et passim* to 1617 LML

Torp 1094 × 1123, 1150 × 59, 1159 TutP *et passim* to Hy 3 *Crox*,
1298 Ipm
Thorp(e) c.1130 LeicSurv, 1158 × 66 TutP *et passim* to 1323 Pat,
1326 Ipm, (~ *Chauers* 1242 Fees), (~ *Tybetoft* 1242 ib)
Torp Edmundi 1298 Ipm, *Thorp Edmund* 1298 Cl, 1358 Brase
Edmon(d)thorp(e) 1487 AD, 1490 Banco *et passim* to 1610 Speed,
1707 LML *et freq*, *Edmoundthorpe* 1502 *MiscAccts*,
Edmund(e)thorp(e) 1535 VE, 1550 Ipm *et passim* to 1619, 1702
LML
Thorpe Edmer alias Edmondthorp 1564 Fine, *Edmonthorpe alias
Thorp Edmer* 1604 ib

'Ēadmǣr's outlying farmstead', *v.* þorp. The pers.n. *Ēadmǣr* is OE.
Willelmus de Chawars and *Henricus de Tybetoft* held land in
Edmondthorpe in 1242 Fees. The manor was of the fee of *Edmund*, Earl
of Leicester and brother of Edward I, in 1298 Ipm.

BLACKSMITH'S SHOP (lost), *Blacksmiths Shop* 1844 *TA*, *v.* **blacksmith,
sc(e)oppa**. CORDHILL LANE, *v.* Cord Hill in Wymondham.
EDMONDTHORPE DRIFT, *Edmon(d)thorpe Drift* 1623, 1629, 1630
Pochin, Drift c.1740 *ib*, 1844 *TA*, *v.* **drift**. EDMONDTHORPE HALL, 1804
Nichols, 1925 Kelly, *The Hall* 1877 White, *v.* **hall**. EDMONDTHORPE
MERE, *v.* **(ge)mǣre**. HALL FM, *v.* *Edmondthorpe Hall*. MANOR HO.,
Manor House 1846, 1863 White, *v.* **maner**. OLD CANAL, the defunct
Oakham Canal 1824 O. PRINCE'S HOVEL, *v.* **hovel**; with the surn.
Prince. THE RECTORY, 1877 White, 1925 Kelly; earlier *the Parsonage
house* 1605, 1625, 1634, 1679, 1700 *Terrier*, *v.* **personage**. ST
MICHAEL'S CHURCH, *Church (St Michael)* 1846, 1863, 1877 White,
Church (St Michael and All Angels) 1925 Kelly; it is earlier recorded in
ecclesiarum de Wymundeham et de Torp 1220 MHW and as *ecclesie de
Thorpedmer* 1297 Pat, ~ *de Thorpe Edmer* 1340, 1402 *ib*, ~ *de
Edmerthorp* 1375 *ib*, ~ *de Thorpedmere* 1403, 1449 *ib*. Note also *the
Church yard* 1605, 1612, 1679 *Terrier, the Churchyeard* 1634, 1700 *ib*,
v. **chirche-ȝeard**. WOODWELL HEAD, 1629, 1767 *Pochin*, 1795, 1815
Map, 1824 O, *Woodwelhead* 1691 *Pochin*, cf. *Great, Little Woodwell
head* c.1740, 1753, 1768 *ib*, *Thick Woodwell head* c.1740, 1753 *ib* (*v.*
þicce[1]), *Thickett* ~ ~ 1768 *ib* (*v.* **þiccett**), *v.* **wudu, wella, hēafod**.

FIELD-NAMES

In (a), forms dated 1753, 1767, 1768 and 1775 are *Pochin*; 1769 are *Reeve*; 1844 are *TA*. Forms throughout dated 1550, 1620, 1623, 1625[1], 1629, 1630, 1631, 1634[1], 1650, 1691, 1731 and c.1740 are *Pochin*; 1601, 1605, 1612, 1625[2], 1634[2], 1679, 1700 and 1745 are *Terrier*; 1627 are ChPr; 1651 are Nichols; 1729 are *Map*.

(a) Half Acre 1753, 1769 (c.1740), ~ ~ Cl 1753, 1768, 1769 (c.1740), Two Acre(s) 1753, 1769 (c.1740), ~ ~ Cl 1753, 1769 (c.1740), Five Acre 1753, 1769 (c.1740, *5 acre* 1691, *Mr Garnons Five Acres* 1729 (cf. *Thomas Garnon* c.1740)), Seven Acres 1753, 1768, 1769 (*Seven Acre* c.1740), the Eight acre 1844, (the) Nine Acres 1753, 1768, 1769, 1844, Nine acres abutting on drift 1844 (*9 acre* 1691, *Wm. Andrews Nine Acres* 1729, *Nine Acre* c.1740, *v.* Edmondthorpe Drift *supra*), (the) Ten Acres 1753, 1844, ~ ~ Cl 1769 (*Ten acre* 1691, c.1740, *Ten Acres* 1729), (the) Eleven Acres 1753, 1768, 1769, 1844 (*11 acre* 1691, *Wm. Andrews Eleven Acres* 1729, *Eleven Acre* c.1740), (the) Thirteen Acres 1753, 1768, 1769 (*13 acre* 1691, *Wm. Andrews Thirteen Acres* 1729, *Thirteen Acre* c.1740), (the) Fourteen Acres 1769, 1844, Fourteen acres adjoining Nine acres 1844 (*14 acre* 1691, *Mr Garnons Fourteen Acres* 1729, *Fourteen Acre* c.1740), (the) Nineteen Acres 1753, 1768, 1769, 1844 (*19 acre* 1691, *Wm. Andrews Nineteen Acres* 1729, *Nineteen Acre* c.1740), Forty Acre(s) 1753, 1768, 1844 (c.1740, *40 Acres* 1691) (*v.* **æcer**); Asker hill 1767 (1691, *Askar hyll* 1550, *v.* **hyll**; the first el. is either the Scand pers.n. *Ásgeirr* or its surn. reflex *Asker*, found also in Lincs., Notts. and Norfolk); Austens Platts 1753, ~ Platt 1768 (*Austens ~, Austins Platt(s)* c.1740, *v.* **plat**; with the surn. *Austen*); Bakers Cl 1753, 1768 (c.1740; with the surn. *Baker*); Barn Cl 1844 (c.1740); Bean Lands Cl 1753, 1768 (c.1740), Bean Land Cl 1844 (*Banlandes al's Beanelandes* 1629, *Beane Lands* 1650, *Beanlands* 1691, 1729, c.1740, *little beanelands* 1625, *v.* **bēan, land**); Blaby Cl 1753, 1768, 1769, 1844 (c.1740; with the surn. *Blaby*, *v.* Blaby Cl in Wymondham f.ns. (a)); Ecobs Bottom Cl 1844 (with the surn. *Ecob*), Top Bottom Cl 1844, Top Long Bottom Cl 1844; Bottom hill 1844 (i.e. 'the close at the bottom of the hill'); Brick Yard, ~ ~ Cl 1844; Bridge Cl 1753, 1768, 1769 (c.1740, *ye bridge close* 1691); Broad Cl 1753, 1768, Long Broad ~ 1844 (*Broad Close* 1691, c.1740, *v.* **brād**); Bull Grass 1753, 1844, Bulls ~ 1767 (*Bullgrasse* 1601, *Bulgrass* 1691, *Bull Grass* c.1740, *v.* **bula, græs**); Butt Cl 1753, 1769, The Butt 1844 (*But close* 1691, *But(t) Close* c.1740, *v.* **butt**[2]); Caudhill 1753, 1769 (*Cawde Hill* 1601, *Caude hill* 1625[2]), Great Caudhill 1753, 1769 (1729, c.1740, *Grand Caudhill* c.1740, *v.* **grand**), Lower, Upper Caudhill 1753, 1768, 1769 (c.1740), West Caudhill 1753, 1768 (1691, 1729, c.1740), Simpson's Caudhill 1753, Simpsons ~ 1768 (*Sim(p)sons Caudhill* c.1740, cf. *John Simpson* 1745 of Wymondham), Snoden's Caudhill 1753, Snowdens ~ 1768 (*Snowdens ~, Snowdons Caudhill* c.1740; with the surn. *Snowden*, *v.* Reaney *s.n.*), Caudle Cl 1753 (c.1740), Caudhills Cl 1768, 1769, Cawdhill Cl 1844 (1634, *Caudhill Close* 1691, *Cawdhill little Close* 1629, *East, North, South, West Caudhill Close* 1691), Far Cawdhill Cl 1844, Caudhill Two Acres Cl 1768 (*v.* **æcer**) (*v.* Cord Hill in Wymondham); (the) Chees(e)cake Cl 1753, 1768, 1769, Cheesecake or Hunts

Cl 1844 (with the surn. *Hunt*) (*Chescake Close* 1691, c.1740, *v.* **cheesecake**; in 1844, the close was still wedge-shaped); Church Yard Cl 1753, 1768 (*the Church Yard Close* 1729, c.1740); Great Cloud hill 1844 (*v.* **clūd**); Cockpit Nook 1844 (*v.* **cockpit, nōk**); Great, Little Con(e)gree 1753, 1768, 1844, Great Coney Grey 1769, Great Coneygrees 1844 (*Great, Little Coneygree* c.1740, *the Great, the Little Cunigree* 1745, *little conygree* 1691), the Lodge Coneygree 1767 (*the Lodge Connygraye* 1650, *lodge connigree* 1691, *v.* **loge**), New Coneygree 1767 (*New connigree* 1691) (*v.* **coningre**); Conyers Cl 1753, 1769, 1844 (c.1740, *Conyer Close* 1729; with the surn. *Conyer*); Cottagers Pasture 1753, Cottage ~ 1844 (*the Cottiers pasture Close* 1629, *the Cottyers pasture* 1650, *Cottagers Pasture* c.1740, *v.* **cottere, cotager**); Cottagers Platt 1753, 1769 (1729, c.1740, *Cottiers plat* 1691, *Cottagers Plat* c.1740, *v.* **cottere, cotager, plat**); Cow Cl 1753, 1768 (1729, c.1740); Cow Common or Drift 1844 (*v.* **commun** and Edmondthorpe Drift *supra*); Crop of Leys (sic) 1753, Crop Leys 1768, Far, Near Cropper Leas 1844 (*v.* **leys**, the first el. may be **crop(p)** 'hump, hill', otherwise the surn. *Cropper*); Crossen's Cl 1753, Crosens ~ 1768, 1769 (*Crossens Close* c.1740), Crozens Pingle 1769 (*v.* **pingel**) (with the surn. *Crossen*); Dovecote 1844 (*v.* **dove-cot(e)**); Great Drift 1844, Drift Cl 1753, 1768, 1769 (*the Drift Close* 1629, *Drift close(s)* 1691, *Mr Rices Drift Close* 1729, *v.* Edmondthorpe Drift *supra*); Dry Cl 1753, 1844 (1691, c.1740, *Mr Rices Dry Close* 1729, *v.* **drȳge**); Bottom of Ecobs 1753, Bottom ~ ~, Ecobs Cl 1844 (*Ecobs* c.1740, cf. *Jn. Ecob* 1691 and *William Ecob* 1753); Edmondthorpe Pasture 1806 Map, 1824 O, The Pasture 1844 (*the pastures* 1601, *the ould cowpasture* 1612 (*v.* **ald**)), (the) Pasture Cl 1753, 1768, 1769, 1844 (1623, 1625, 1629, 1630, 1691, c.1740, *East, West pasture close* 1691) (*v.* **pasture**); Far Close near Melton hill 1844; Fardells Cl 1844 (cf. *John Fardell* 1745 of Wymondham); Fizgigs Cl 1753, Fisgigs 1769 (OED *s.v.* fizgig 2 and 3 offers disparate alternatives for interpreting this f.n.; a *fizgig* was (i) a kind of top with which boys played, a whirligig, and (ii) a kind of firework, a squib; in either case, village games or festivities are indicated; the enclosure was poss. the precursor of *the Play close, infra*); Flat Mdw 1844 (*v.* **flatr**); Flower's Cl 1753, Flower ~ 1844 (*Flowers close* 1691, c.1740; with the surn. *Flower*); Fox Covert 1844 (*v.* **cover(t)**); Gage's Cl 1753, Gages ~ 1768, 1769 (*Gages close* 1691, cf. *Clement Gage* 1630, *Christopher Gage* 1691); Gamble's Cls 1753, Gambles Cl 1844 (*Gambles Close* c.1740, cf. *John Gamble* 1631); Goatherd Cl 1844 (*v.* **gāthyrde**); Great Cl 1753, 1769, 1844 (c.1740); The Great Wood 1844; Green 1844 (*super la Grene* 1296 Ipm (p), *de la Grene* l.13 (1404) *Laz* (p), 1296 Ipm (p), 13 TutP (p), *atte Grene* 1375 GauntReg (p), 1381 SR (p) (*v.* **atte**), *the common greene* 1620 (*v.* **commun**), *v.* **grēne²**); Green Cl 1767, 1769, 1844 (1691, c.1740, *the greate Greene Close* 1623, 1629, 1630), Camm's Green Cl 1753, Camms ~ ~ 1768, 1769 (*Camms Green Close* c.1740, cf. *James Camm* 1768), Home Green Cl 1844 (*v.* **home**), Neither, Upper Green Cl 1753 (c.1740), Simpson's Green Cl 1753 (cf. *John Simpson* 1745 of Wymondham) (*v.* **grēne¹, grēne²**; it is uncertain whether these closes were butting on the village green or were swarded over); Holgate Leys 1767, Hollygate Leas 1844 (*Holgate* 1601, *Hollowgate waie* 1625 (*v.* **weg**), *Hollorgate* 1634², 1700, *Hollowgate* 1679, *Holy gatte & leas* 1691, *Holgate Lees* 1601, *Holygate leas* 1691), Drift Holygate Leys 1753 (c.1740), Drift Holgate Leys 1769, Drift Hollygate Leas 1844 (*holgate dryfte* 1601, *v.* Edmondthorpe Drift *supra*), Goss Holygate Leys (c.1740),

Gorse Hollygate 1844 (*v.* **gorst**), Great Holygate Leys 1753, 1768, Great Holgate Leys 1769, Great Hollygate Leas 1844 (*Great Holygate Ley* c.1740), Little Holygate Leys 1753, 1768 (*Little Holygate Ley* c.1740) (*v.* **hol²**, **holh**, **gata**, **leys**); Home Cl 1768, 1769, 1844, Bottom, Top Long Home Cl 1844 (*the home closes* 1650, *v.* **home**); Home Platts 1753, 1844, ~ Platt 1769 (*the home plotts* 1625, *Home plat* 1691, *Home Platt* c.1740, *v.* **home**, **plot**, **plat**); Hookers Cl 1769 (cf. *Robert Haucer* 1745 of Wymondham); Hopkins Cl 1753, 1768, 1769, 1844 (1729, c.1740; with the surn. *Hopkins*); Horse Park 1753, 1768 (*Horse Parke* c.1740, *v.* **hors**, **park**); Hunts Cl 1844 (with the surn. *Hunt*, *v.* the Cheesecake Cl *supra*); Land Cl 1753, 1769, 1844 (c.1740 *v.* **land**; a close comprising an unspecified number of 'lands' or selions of one of the former great fields of the village); The Lane Cl 1844; Lintills Mdw 1753, 1769, Lintalls ~ 1844 (*Lintells ~*, *Lintills Meadow* c.1740; with the surn. *Lintill*); Litlings 1753, Litlins 1769 (*lyttlynge* 1550, *Littellinges* 1601, *Littleinges* 1605, *Littlonds* (sic) 1612, (*the*) *Litlinges* 1623, 1625², 1630, 1634², (*the*) *Litlings* 1650, 1700, c.1740, *Littlins*, ~ *meadow* 1691), Litlings Cl 1844 (*Litleinges Close* c.1740) (*v.* **lȳtel**, **lítill**, **eng**); Little close abutting on Park 1844 (*v.* The Park *infra*); Little Fd 1768, 1769, Upper ~ ~ 1753, Upper Part of Little Fd 1768 (*The Litell felde* 1601, *the little ~*, *the lyttle or Common Feild* 1623, 1630, (*the*) *Little Feild(e)* 1625, 1629, 1631, 1650, 1691, *Upper Little Field* c.1740, *v.* **lȳtel**, **feld**); The Lock piece 1844 (*v.* **lock**, **pece**; beside the now defunct *Oakham Canal* 1824 O); Long Cl 1753, 1768, 1769 (1691, c.1740); Mans Cls 1768 (1691), Manns Cl 1769, Manns or Money Cl 1844 (cf. *George Mann* 1844 and *v.* Money Cl *infra*); Masons Cl 1844 (with the surn. *Mason*); Melton Cl 1769, Melton Hill 1753, 1768, 1844 (1691, 1729, c.1740, *Milton Hill* 1601, *Melton hils* 1691), Far, First, Top Melton Hill 1844 (cf. *Melton hill Close* 1623, 1629, 1630, *the Melton hill Closes* 1650), Fardell's Melton Hill 1753, Fardells ~ ~ 1844 (c.1740, cf. *James Fardell* 1753), Toon's Melton Hill, Toons ~ ~ 1768 (c.1740), Toons near Melton hill 1844 (cf. *John Toon* 1745 of Wymondham) (either with the surn. *Melton* or naming a hill with a distant view of Melton Mowbray, six miles to the west); Mill Cl 1753, 1768, 1769 (c.1740, *the Mill close* 1691); Millers Cls 1753 (c.1740), ~ Cl 1769, 1844 (with the surn. *Miller*); Money Cl 1844 (*Monyes close* 1691), Money close the less 1844 (with the surn. *Money*); New Cl 1753, 1768, 1844 (1691, c.1740); The Nook 1844 (*v.* **nōk**); North Side 1767, 1769, 1844 (1691, *v.* **norð**, **sīde**); Norwell's Cl 1753, Norwells ~ 1844 (*Norwells* 1691, *Norwells close* c.1740, cf. *Norwells furlonge* 1623, 1630; if not the surn. *Norwell*, then *v.* **norð**, **wella**); The Park 1844 (*v.* **park**); The Parting Cl 1844 (*v.* **parting**); Pennywell Cl 1753, Painywell ~ 1768 (*Pennywell Close* c.1740, *Pener wall* 1601, 1650, *Penner wall* 1605, *a furlonge called Pannar wall* 1612, *v.* **wall**; with the surn. *Penner*, *v.* Reaney *s.n.*; evidently the boundary wall of a property); the Pingle 1753 (*v.* **pingel**); the Platt Cls 1753 (*the Platt Close* c.1740), Bottom, Far, First, Middle, Top Plat(ts) 1844 (*v.* **plat**); Priestmans Cl 1844 (with the surn. *Priestman*); Ram Cl 1753, 1767, 1769, Rams ~ 1844 (*Ram Close* 1691, c.1740, *v.* **ramm**); Red Earth 1768 (*the red earthe* 1601, 1625², 1634², *the Red Earth* 1612, 1679, 1691, 1700), ~ ~ Fd 1753 (c.1740, cf. *the Reddearth Close* 1631) (*v.* **rēad**, **eorðe**); Robinsons Cl 1844 (with the surn. *Robinson*); Rough Mdw 1753, 1844 (1729, c.1740), Rough Piece 1844 (*v.* **pece**) (*v.* **rūh¹**); Schoolhouse 1844; Sheep Cl 1844; Sheep or Manns Cl 1844 (with the surn. *Mann*); Shelbread Cl 1753, Shelbriggs 1844 (*East*, *West sholbreds* 1691, *Shelbreds*

Close c.1740, *v.* **scofl-brǣdu**); Simpsons Home and Green Cl 1753, Simpsons Cl 1844 (cf. *Simsons Home & Great Close* c.1740, *v.* **home**, cf. *John Simpson* 1745 of Wymondham); Slipe Cl 1844 (*v.* **slipe**); the Smeeth 1769 (1623, 1630), Great, Little Smeeth 1753, 1768, 1769, the Great Smeathe 1844 (*Mr Garnons Great Smeeth*, ~ ~ *Little Smeeth* 1729, *Great, Little Smeath* c.1740), Smeeth Cl 1753 (c.1740), Great, Little Smeaths Cl 1844 (*v.* **smēðe**[1]); Snadons Cl 1844 (with the surn. *Snawdon*); Southside 1767, 1769 (1691, *v.* **sūð, sīde**); Spring piece 1844 (*the Spring* 1634[2], *v.* **spring**[1], **pece**); Steep Lane Cl 1753, 1769 (1729, c.1740, *v.* **stēap**); Stone Pit Cl 1753, 1768 (1650, 1691, *Stonepitt Close* c.1740, *v.* **stān-pytt**); The Far Lock Spinney 1844 (*v.* **lock**; beside the former *Oakham Canal* 1824 O), Little Spinney 1844, The Little Long Spinney 1844, The Long Spinney 1844 (*v.* **spinney**); Teigh Mill Cl 1753, Teigh Mill Platts 1768, 1769, Far, First Teigh Mill Platt 1844 (*teigh plat* 1691, *Hither Teigh Mill Platt* 1729, *v.* **plat**; Teigh in Rutland adjoins to the south-east); Thistleton Gap Cl 1844 (*v.* **gap**; Thistleton in Rutland adjoins to the east); Thornhill Cl 1753, 1769, 1844 (c.1740, cf. *Thornhill Bottom* c.1740 (*v.* **botm**), *v.* **þorn, hyll**); Thorpe Brook 1795 Nichols; Great, Little Tofts 1753, 1768, 1844 (1691, c.1740), Watkin's Tofts 1753, Watkins ~ 1768, 1769 (*Stephen Watkins Toft* 1729, *Watkins Tofts* c.1740), Tofts Cl 1753, 1769 (c.1740), Lower ~ ~, Upper ~ ~, Tofts Sink 1753, 1768, 1769 (*Tofts Sink* 1691, 1729, *Lower, Upper Toft Sinks* c.1740, *v.* **sinke**), Lower ~ ~, Toft Sykes 1844 (poss. an altered form of the previous f.n., otherwise *v.* **sík**) (*v.* **toft**; Toon's House 1753, Toon's Mdw 1753, 1844, Toons ~ 1768 (*Toones Meadow* c.1740, cf. *John Toone* 1745); Great, Little Top of Hill 1753, 1768 (c.1740), Great, Little Top Hill 1844; The Vineyard 1753, 1769, Vine yard 1844 (*The Vineyard* c.1740, *v.* **vinȝerd**); Wadlands Platt 1753, 1769 (*Wadland plat* 1691, *Wadlands, ~ Platts* c.1740, *v.* **wād, land, plat**); Water Cl 1844 (*v.* **wæter**; beside the former *Oakham Canal*, but *v.* Water Cl in Wymondham f.ns. (a)); Westland hill 1844 (if not with the surn. *Westland*, then *v.* **west, land**); White Earth 1775, 1844 (*v.* **hwīt, eorðe**); Wood Cl 1844; Woodville Hill Cl 1844, Peat ~ ~ ~ (*v.* **pete**), Woodville Mead 1844 (*v.* **mæd**) (*v.* Woodwell Head *supra*; this 1844 spelling of Woodwell may have been influenced by the official change of the name Wooden Box on the Leics. border to Woodville (now in Derbys.) at almost exactly this date, *v.* Db 670); Wragdale Cl 1844, ~ ~ next Drift 1844 (*v.* Edmondthorpe Drift *supra*) (if Wragdale is an early name, then prob. 'Wraggi's portion of land', *v.* **deill**; the pers.n. *Wraggi* is ON (ODan *Wraghi*), cf. perh. *Weragland* in Leesthorpe f.ns. (b)); Wymondham Platt 1753, 1769, ~ Plot 1844 (*Wimond' plat* 1691, *Wymundham Platts* c.1740, *v.* **plat, plot**; Wymondham adjoins to the north-west).

(b) *Barbers Close* 1729 (with the surn. *Barber*); *Barkin platte alias Lane platt* 1627 (*v.* **plat**; *Barkin* is presum. a surn.); *barpit hades* 1601 (*v.* **pytt, hēafod**; a greater range of forms is needed to identify the first el. which could be either **bær**[1] 'bare, without vegetation' or **bār** 'a boar' referring to a place where wild boar were trapped (*v.* Field 75 *s.n.* Boarpits) or even **bera** 'a bear', alluding to the sport of bear-baiting); *James Bells house* 1691; *Berrys close* 1691 (in the ownership of *Wm. Berry* 1691); *Bilberry Lane* 1731 (a location for the **bilberry** (*Vaccinium Myrtillus*) which grows on stony moors and heaths); *brend lees* 1601 (*v.* **brende**[2], **leys**); *Little Bretstone* 1691 (*v.* **breiðr, stān**); *brodpenne* 1601 (*v.* **brād, penn**[2]); *Bullane ende* 1601 (*v.* **lane-ende**; either with the surn. *Bull* or with **bula** 'a bull'); (*Willm.*)

Burnbies hadland 1623, 1630 (*v.* **hēafod-land**), *Burnbyes hedge* 1601 (*v.* **hecg**; a boundary hedge), *Wid. Burnbys house* 1691 (i.e. *Widow* ~ ~), *Burnbyes little Close* 1650; *Burrow Churche feilde, Borrow Church feild* 1601 (*v.* **feld**; one of the great fields of the village, adjacent to the lost Burrowchurch *supra*); *the clay furlonge* 1601 (*v.* **clæg**); *Claie Wonge* 1623, *Clay* ~ 1630 (*v.* **clæg, vangr**); *Coles close* 1691 (with the surn. *Cole(s)*); *the common* 1612 (*v.* **commun**); *the nether Conigree* 1629, *the Conigre Hill* 1605, *the cuningray side* 1612, *the Cuningrye side* 1625 (*v.* **sīde**) (*v.* Great, Little Con(e)gree *supra*); *Conys close & medow* 1691 (either with **coni** 'a rabbit' or with the surn. *Cony* (*v.* Reaney *s.n.*) or belonging with Conyers Cl *supra*); *Tho. Cooks Hither Plat* 1691 (*v.* **hider, plat**), *Tho. Cooks Pingle* 1691 (*v.* **pingel**); *Jn. Collingtons caudhil* 1691, *Lambs* ~, *Ormes* ~, *Willowes Caudhill* 1691 (with the surns. *Lamb* and *Orme*; and cf. *John Willowes* 1679 and *Wm. Willows* 1691), *East Caudhill* 1691 (*v.* Cord Hill in Wymondham); *Deas vineyard* 1691 (poss. to be identified with The Vineyard in f.ns. (a); cf. *Mr Day* 1745 of Wymondham); *Dennycross close* 1691 (this relates to *Dannycrosse* listed in Wymondham f.ns. (b)); *the dike* 1625[1], *the dike side* 1601 (*v.* **sīde**) (*v.* **dík**); *East medow* 1691; *East plot* 1691 (*v.* **plot**); *Jn.*[n] *Edgson Toft* 1729 (*v.* **toft**; *Edgson* is a later local form of Egleton (*v.* Ru 84), six miles to the south, whence the family originally came); *Edward Wonge* 1623, 1630 (*v.* **vangr**; with the surn. *Edward*); *Figgins Close* c.1740 (with the surn. *Figgins, v.* Reaney *s.n.*); *Fishers close* 1605, 1634[2], 1691, 1700, *Fishars* ~ 1612 (*v.* **clos(e)**), *Fishers farme* 1650 (*v.* **ferme**), (*Robert*) *Fishers hedge* 1601, 1605, 1625, 1634[2], 1700 (*v.* **hecg**; a boundary hedge) (cf. *Robert Fisher* 1612, 1625[2], *Eliz. Fisher widow* 1634[2], *Widow Fisher* 1650, *Christopher Fisher* 1691); *Formans Close* 1623, 1629, 1630, 1691, *Formans headland* 1601 (*v.* **hēafod-land**), *East, West Forman plat* 1691 (*v.* **plat**) (cf. *Fra(u)ncis Forman* 1625, 1630); *Fosewell Syke* 1601, *Foswell sike* 1625[2], *Fossellsike* 1631, *Foswell sick* 1634 , 1679, 1700 (*v.* **foss**[1], **wella, sík**); *Mr Garnons Long Close* 1729 (cf. *Thomas Garnon* c.1740); *between gates* 1601, 1623, 1630, *betwixt* (*the*) *gates* 1612, 1625[2], 1634[2], 1679, 1700 (presum. to be identified with the furlong called *betwix the high wayes* 1605, *v.* **hēah-weg**), *under gates* 1623, 1630 (*v.* **gata**); *atte Goters* 1296 Ipm (p) (*v.* **atte, goter**); *Neither Green Platt* c.1740 (*v.* **neoðera, grēne**[1], **plat**); *greenplek hades* 1601 (*v.* **grēne**[1], **plek, hēafod**); *Helpitt* 1627 (*v.* **hell, pytt** and Hill Pit Leys in Wymondham f.ns. (a)); *the High Street(e)* 1605, 1625[2], 1634[2], 1679, 1700, ~ ~ *strete* 1612 (*v.* **hēah**[1], **stræt**; the main street of the village, also called *the Towne streete* 1625[2] (*v.* **tūn**)); *the high way(e)* 1605, 1612, 1625[2], 1634[2], 1700 (*v.* **hēah-weg**); *the Homestall* 1605, 1625[2], 1634[2], 1700 (i.e. of *the Parsonage house, v.* The Rectory *supra*), *the Homestall of Henry Hough* 1679, *the Homestall of John Pickwell* 1634[2] (his family no doubt originated in Pickwell, six miles to the south-west) (*v.* **hām-stall**); *Horse Close* 1650 (*v.* **hors**); *Jenkinsons close* 1691 (with the surn. *Jenkinson*); *Kerchein Leys* 1627 (*v.* **leys**; with the surn. *Kirchen*); *Kings close* 1691 (with the surn. *King*); *Lample penne* 1601 (*v.* **penn**[2] and Lampol in Wymondham f.ns. (b)); *Lane platt* 1627 (*v.* **lane, plat**); *Latimers close* 1691 (with the surn. *Latimer, v.* Reaney *s.n.*); *Linnyes close* 1691 (cf. *Wid. Linny* 1691, i.e. *Widow* ~); *Litell tofte* 1601 (*v.* **lȳtel, lítill, toft**); *Lysters farme* 1691 (*v.* **ferme**; with the surn. *Lister/Lyster, v.* Reaney *s.n.* who identifies it as 'an Anglian surname'); *the Mere* 1623, 1630, (*the*) *Mere close* 1691 (*v.* **(ge)mǣre**); *michelbor(r)ow dale* 1601 (*v.* **micel, mikill, berg**; with **dalr** or **deill**); *the middell* *feild* 1601 (*v.* **middel, feld**; one of the great fields of the township); *middell hill* 1601 (*v.* **middel, hyll**); *Milne leyes* 1623, 1630 (*v.* **leys**), *Milpole* 1601 (*v.* **pōl**¹) (*v.* **myln**); *Tho*(*mas*) *Moores hadland* 1623, 1630 (*v.* **hēafod-land**), *Moors farme* 1691 (*v.* **ferme**); *the High Mo*(*o*)*re* 1601, 1605, 1612, 1625², 1634², 1679, 1700 (*v.* **hēah**¹), *the West Mo*(*o*)*re* 1605, 1679, *Cardigans* ~ ~, *Moor Close* 1691 (with the surn. *Cardigan*), *morgate hades* 1601 (*v.* **gata, hēafod**) (*v.* **mōr**¹, **mór**); *napporons dale* 1601 bis (*v.* **napperone**; with **dalr** or **deill**; the first el. is an early form of *apron*, before metanalysis or misdivision moved the initial *n* to become part of the indefinite article *an* < *a* (*a napron* > *an apron*, cf. *a naranja* > *an orange*); it is perh. used here of a platform placed at the bottom of a sluice to intercept the fall of water and prevent the washing away of the bottom (*v.* OED *s.v.* apron 4a; earliest citation is for 1721) and may relate to the irrigation system represented by *Water medow* below and *Water Cl* in Wymondham f.ns. (a); otherwise it may allude to the perceived shape of a portion of land); *the nether furlonge* 1601 (i.e. of *the middell feild*); (*the*) *New Hall* 1650, 1651 (built c.1620 and now represented by the ruins of Edmondthorpe Hall *supra*; cf. *the old hall*, *infra*); *Tho. Nobles close* 1691; *the north*(*e*) *feild*(*e*) 1601 (*v.* **norð, feld**; one of the great fields of the village); *the oate plott* 1650 (*v.* **āte, plot**); *Okeham waie* 1625 (*v.* **weg**; the road to Oakham in Rutland, five miles to the south); *the old hall* 1650 (*v.* (*the*) *New Hall*, *supra*); *the ould way* 1601 (*v.* **weg**; with **ald** or **wald**); *the parke wall* 1601 (*v.* **park, wall**); *the parsonage close* 1631 (*v.* **personage**); *Peppers close* 1691 (with the surn. *Pepper*); *Petts Close* 1729 (with the surn. *Pett*(*s*)); *Pickwells close* 1691, *Pickwells house & homested* 1691 (*v.* **hām-stede** and *the Homestall of John Pickwell*, *supra*); *pinder hades* 1601 (*v.* **hēafod**; either with the surn. *Pinder* or with **pinder** 'an officer of a manor who impounded stray beasts' upon which the surn. is based); *the Pingle* c.1740 (*v.* **pingel**); *the Play Close* 1729 (used for village games, *v.* **plega**, Fizgigs Cl *supra* and Field 243–4); *Purlefurres close* 1627 (*v.* Burley Furze in Wymondham f.ns. (a)); *Thomas Ravens Homestead and Yard* 1729 (*v.* **hām-stede**); *Rigate ford*(*e*) 1601 (*v.* **ford**), *Rigate furlonge* 1601 (*v.* **ryge, gata**); *Russells close* 1691 (with the surn. *Russell*); *Ryse headland* 1601 (*v.* **hrīs, hēafod-land**); *Seneschalls close* 1691 (presum. with the surn. *Seneschall* rather than with **seneschal** 'a steward, a major-domo' which gave rise to the surn., *v.* Reaney *s.n.*); *Shorn Hill Close* 1729 (*v.* **scoren**²); (*a messuage howse called*) *Smith*(*e*)*s Farme* 1620, 1623, 1629, 1630 (*v.* **ferme**), *Mr Smithes Close* 1623 (cf. *Edward Smith* and *Roger Smith* 1630), (*Wid.*) *Smiths cottage* 1691 (i.e. *Widow* ~ ~, *v.* **cotage**); *Stamford Waie* 1623, 1630 (*v.* **weg**; the road to Stamford which lies 12 miles to the south-east in Lincs.); *Stiles close* 1691 (prob. with the surn. *Stile*(*s*); otherwise *v.* **stigel**); *Stonborow hades* 1601 (*v.* **stān, berg, hēafod**); *Stonehill* 1623, 1630 (*v.* **stān, hyll**); *the two streete waies* 1623, 1630 (*v.* **street-waie**); *Stubb furlonge* 1623, 1630, 1631 (*v.* **stubb**); *Taylors close* 1691, *Wm. Taylors house* 1691; *Teigh Close* c.1740 (Teigh in Rutland adjoins to the south-east); *Thirty Stone* 1601, *Thirtyston* 1612, 1634², *Thirtie Stone* 1700 (*v.* Thirty Stones in Wymondham f.ns. (a)); *Thorney Close or Formans Close* 1623, 1630, *thornie closes* 1630, *Thorny* ~ 1691 (*v.* **þornig** and *Formans Close*, *supra*); *the Townes end* 1625² (*v.* **tūn, ende**); *the upper furlonge* 1601 (i.e. of *the middell feild*); *Betwixt* ~, *Wadlands* 1601, *Longe Wadlandes* 1601 (*v.* **wād, land**; woad was widely grown until the 19th cent. as a source of blue dye); *Waterfurrowes* 1623, 1630 (*v.* **wæter, furh** and *waterfurris* in

Muston f.ns. (b)); *Water medow* 1691 (*v.* **wæter**; prob. a meadow through which channels controlled by sluices were constructed for irrigation, *v. napporone dale, supra*, Water Cl in Wymondham f.ns. (a) and Field 90–1); *Richard Wats close* 1691; *atte well* 1381 SR (p) (*v.* **atte, wella**); *West medow* 1691; *West plot* 1691 (*v.* **plot**); *the Willow Close* 1625 (*v.* **wilig**); *John Willowes close* 1679, *John Willowes hedge* 1679, *Willowes Tofte* 1691 (*v.* **toft**); *Windmill* 1650, *Edmondthorpe Windmill* 1652 (*v.* **wind-mylne**); *Woodgate* 1601, ~ *close* 1627, *Woodgate hill* 1601 (*v.* **wudu, gata**); *Austyn Woodkeeps hadland* 1623, 1630 (*v.* **hēafod-land**); *Worths close* 1691 (with the surn. *Worth*).

THE ELEMENTS, OTHER THAN PERSONAL NAMES, IN THE FRAMLAND HUNDRED'S PLACE-NAMES, FIELD-NAMES AND STREAM-NAMES

This list includes the elements in uncompounded and compounded place-names, field-names and stream-names. The names quoted in each entry are arranged in alphabetical order, with no distinction between uncompounded and compounded names. Names which survive on modern maps and also lost major names are listed first, followed by a summary of the use of the elements in field-names and stream-names. Although a concise translation of each element is provided, for a fuller discussion of its significance and use, reference should be made to *English Place-Name Elements* (EPNS, vols. 25 and 26, amended in JEPNS 1), *The Vocabulary of English Place-Names* (CENS, in progress), M. Gelling, *Place-Names in the Landscape*, 1984 and M. Gelling and A. Cole, *The Landscape of Place-Names*, 2000.

The elements are often given in an OE, ON or OFr form, but it should be remembered that many of these elements continued as common nouns in the English language and that many of the names in Leicestershire's Framland Hundred are of more recent origin than the periods represented by the lexical head-forms used. Many terms are included which are not listed in the above mentioned volumes, but it has not been felt necessary to distinguish these. Those elements marked * are not independently recorded in the head-forms cited or are hypothetical reconstructions from the place-name evidence.

á ON, 'a river, a stream'. *Opol* (f.n. Leesthorpe).

abbat OFr, ME, 'an abbot'. *?abbot dole* (f.n. Wyfordby), *abbotte gate* (Burton Lazars), *abbott tonge* (f.n. Burton Lazars).

abbaye ME, (OFr *abbaie*), 'an abbey'. *Abbey Ketylby* (Ab Kettleby), *Croxton Abbey*. *Abbey gate* (Waltham on the Wolds).

aboven ME, **above** eModE, prep., 'above, over'. Freq. in f.ns., e.g. *Aboue the Dale* (Gt. Dalby), *Abouethesmalewelle* (Eaton), *abouethesyk'* (Muston), *aboue the towne* (Wyfordby).

āc OE, 'an oak-tree'. Bescaby Oaks. *Acwellane* (f.n. Wycomb/Chadwell), *At the Oake* (f.n. Croxton Kerrial).

æcer OE, 'a plot of cultivated land'; also 'an acre, a specific measure of ploughland', originally the unit which a yoke of oxen could plough in a day. The OE el. is generally indistinguishable from ON **akr** 'a plot of arable land'. The general sense 'arable land' is found in the compound *acre-land*. Very freq. in f.ns.: as a simplex, e.g. *Acre* (Normanton), *(the) Acres* (Burrough on the Hill, Holwell); with a numeral indicating size, e.g. *le Two akers close* (Buckminster), The Four Acre (Harston), Eight Acres (Burton Lazars), *nyne acre* (Holwell); with an early pers.n. or its ME surn. reflex, e.g. Annacre (Waltham on the Wolds), *Aslakaker* (Stonesby), *Feggakyr* (Muston), *holdberdacre* (Plungar), *Lusiaker* (Bottesford); with reference to crops, e.g. *Barliakir* (Bottesford) or to natural vegetation, e.g. *Seaveacres* (Lt. Dalby), *Seghaker* (Muston), *thurniakyr* (Harby); to the nature or condition of the soil, e.g. *le Dritakir* (Barkestone), Mother Acre (Gt. Dalby), *withacre* (Redmile); to fauna, wild or domestic, e.g. *Catackeres* (Redmile), *le hundhakir* (Plungar), *Oselaker*, *Podeaker* (Eaton), *Swine Acres* (Scalford); to shape, e.g. Round Acres (Lt. Dalby), *swerdeacre* (Bottesford). Acrelands Lane (Bottesford) and The Acre Land Dike (f.n. Holwell) contain the compound *acre-land*.

æcer-dīc OE, perh. 'the ditch surrounding an arable plot' or 'the ditch marking the limit of ploughland'. Spellings with final *k* are due to Scandinavian influence. *accare dyk* (f.n. Stapleford), *Acherdich* (f.n. Barkestone, Redmile), *Achirdike* (f.n. Burton Lazars), *akerdick'* (f.n. Bottesford), *Acredike furlonge* (f.n. Lt. Dalby).

æcern OE, 'an acorn', perh. also 'a beech-nut, a chestnut'. *Acherne Wong* (f.n. Freeby).

ælmesse OE, 'alms, charity'. *?Almescrofte* (f.n. Melton Mowbray).

æppel-trēow OE, 'an apple-tree'. *Apeltre* (f.n. Burton Lazars), Apple tree Cl (f.n. Lt. Dalby).

æsc OE, 'an ash-tree'. Ash Plantation, Ash Pole Spinney, *Assebymilne* (Eaton). Freq. in f.ns.: signifying small stands of ash-trees, e.g. *The Ashes* (Branston), Ash Holt (Wartnaby), Ash Spinney (Sysonby); boundary marks and perh. boundary streams, e.g. *Ashwell sicke* (Pickwell), *Ashwels*, *Asschemarebrock* (Somerby), *drake ashe* (Saltby); identifying individual closes, e.g. *Ash(e) Close* (Pickwell, Sproxton), *the ashe closse* (Scalford), Ash tree Cl (Eastwell). Spellings in *e-* may indicate either the raising of *æ* to *e* before the palatal consonant in ME dialects from Norfolk to Northumberland or be owing to the influence of ON **eski** 'an ash-tree'; an OE collective **esce* 'a group of ash-trees' may also have existed: e.g. *Eashbecks*, *Eash sike* (f.ns. Stathern), *Esses* (f.n. Pickwell), *Esshees Furlong* (f.n. Stonesby).

akr ON, 'a plot of arable land', v. **æcer.**

ald OE (Angl), adj., 'old'. Common in indicating former or long use, as: Old Close Plantation, Oldfields Lodge, Old Park Wood. In f.ns., e.g. *Aldefeeldale* (Eaton), *Aldemulne* (Knipton), *le Holdehey* (Plungar), *le Old Close* (Sewstern), Old Ground (Burton Lazars, Freeby), *The Oold Orchard* (Wymondham). Referring to a former course of a stream: *Old Broke* (f.n. Melton Mowbray). As an affix to distinguish an original from a newer settlement: *Old Saxbey* (f.n. Saxby).

allotment ModE, 'a portion of land assigned to a particular individual', especially in names recording the redistribution of land at Enclosure, as in the Allotment (f.n. Pickwell), the Allottments (f.n. Saltby); and later 'a small portion of land let out to an individual (e.g. by a town council) for cultivation', as in the Allotments (f.n. Wymondham).

almes-hous ME, 'an almshouse, a house founded by a private charity for the reception and support of the aged poor'. Earl of Rutland's Hospital. *Hudson's Almshouse, Storer's Alms Houses* (Melton Mowbray).

almr ON, 'an elm-tree'. ?*Almescroft(e)* (f.n. Melton Mowbray), *Olmehou* (f.n. Somerby).

ampre OE, 'dock, sorrel'. *Ambrecrofte* (f.n. Burton Lazars).

ān OE, num., adj., 'one, single'; in p.ns., presum. used sometimes with the sense 'alone, isolated'. *Ancliff* (f.n. Somerby).

andlanges OE, prep., 'along'. *analandhil, analangdale* (f.ns. Croxton Kerrial).

angle ME, 'an angle, a corner, a point of land'. Ankle Hill. *Anclewarlot* (f.n. Somerby), Angle Fd (f.n. Gt. Dalby), *Aungellwonge* (f.n. Melton Mowbray).

ānstīg OE, 'a narrow (ascending) pathway'. Anstey Bridge (f.n. Somerby).

arable ModE, adj., 'being, or capable of being ploughed; fit for tillage'. Arable Field Rd (Withcote), *Welhill arable furlonge, White Earth arrable Furlonge* (f.ns. Lt. Dalby).

arm OE, **arme** ME, 'an arm'; topographically 'a projecting piece of land'. *Short-arm* (f.n. Ab Kettleby).

āte OE, 'oats'. *the Oat Close* (f.n. Gt. Dalby), Oat Cl (f.n. Thorpe Arnold), *Oatelands* (f.n. Stapleford), *the oate plott* (f.n. Edmondthorpe), Oaty Cl (f.n. Goadby Marwood).

atte ME, prep. with masc. or neut. def.art., 'at the'. Common in f.ns. and often used for ME toponymic surnames. Examples in f.ns. are *attedam* (Wycomb/Chadwell), *atte Smythe* (Holwell), *atte Toneshevede* (Ab Kettleby); while toponymic surnames include *atte grene* (Muston), *atte hall, atte Welle* (Hose), *atte Kirk* (Croxton Kerrial).

austr ON, adj., '(to the) east'. *osbutterlands* (f.n. Bottesford).

avenue ModE, 'a tree-lined approach'. The Avenue, Avenue Fm.

back ModE, adj., 'hindmost, lying behind'. Back Lane (Long Clawson, Old Dalby), Back St (Bottesford), *the Back Street* (Melton Mowbray). *Back close* (f.n. Burton Lazars).

back of ModE, prep., 'behind'; elliptically 'that which lies at the back of, or behind, something'. Back of Railway (f.n. Gt. Dalby).

*****badde** ME, adj., 'bad, worthless' ?*Badmore* (f.n. Saxby).

badger ModE, 'a badger'. ?Badger Cl (f.n. Eastwell).

bæc OE, **bakke** ME, 'a back; a ridge'. ?*Backthurns* (f.n. Croxton Kerrial), *Hopbak furlong* (f.n. Stathern).

bæcestre OE, **bakester, baxter** ME, 'a baker'. *Baxterlane* (Melton Mowbray).

bæc-hūs OE, 'a bake-house, a bakery'. *le Bakehous* (Muston), *Bakhous lane* (Melton Mowbray).

bær[1] OE, adj., 'bare, without vegetation'. *Bare Arse* (f.n. Burrough on the Hill), *Bare Leys* (f.n. Ab Kettleby), *Barestones* (f.n. Redmile), ?*barpit hades* (f.n. Edmondthorpe).

bærlic OE, **barli** ME, 'barley'. Barley Kitty's Urn (f.n. Sewstern), *Barlilandis* (f.n. Thorpe Arnold), *Barlyakir* (f.n. Bottesford).

bak-side ME, 'property behind a dwelling; the back, the rear'. *backside Ash Close* (f.n. Harby), Backside Cl (f.n. Buckminster), *the backside of the Hill* (f.n. Normanton), *backside Tho. Kirk's* (f.n. Harby).

balca OE, 'a ridge, a bank; a ridge of unploughed land that marked the boundary between adjacent strips of the common field'. Freq. in f.ns.: often compounded with a surn., e.g. *Alyn Balke End* (Burton Lazars), *Annisbalkes* (Knipton), *Jonathan Georges Balk* (Waltham on the Wolds). Reference may be made to structures, e.g. *Church Baulk* (Stonesby), *the Kiln bolk* (Branston), *the Mill-baulk* (Ab Kettleby); to flora, e.g. *Elder tree bolk* (Branston); to topographical features, e.g. *Brenthill baulke* (Stonesby), *galles balke* (Stapleford), *yellowpit balke* (Croxton Kerrial). Freq. also are compounds describing the nature of the balk, e.g. *Brodebalk* (Sewstern), *Cloven Balk* (Harby), *Crosse baulke, hanging baulk* (Ab Kettleby). The names of larger habitation sites may also be compounded, e.g. *Grange balk* (Scalford), *Halle Balke* (Somerby), *Thorpe Balke* (Lt. Dalby).

balne OFr, ME, poss. 'a bathing place in a river'. *Balnesfyld* (f.n. Melton Mowbray).

bān OE, 'a bone'. Mans Bones (f.n. Wymondham).

banke ODan, ME, 'a bank, the slope of a hill or ridge'. Croxton Banks, Wymondham Banks. Common in f.ns.: with fauna or flora, e.g. Caddow Bank (Bottesford), Calf Banks (Scalford), *Ivybanck, lysbancke* (Croxton Kerrial); with locational features, e.g. *Grives banke* (Pickwell), Pool Banks (Thorpe Arnold), *Sand pitt banck* (Gt. Dalby); with a surn., e.g. *Coke Banke* (Burton Lazars), *Barrows banke* (Saxby). Note also the recurring Mill Bank (Coston), *the Mill banke* (Goadby Marwood).

barne-yarde eModE, 'a barn-yard'. *Barneyarde* (f.n. Melton Mowbray).

bār OE, 'a (wild) boar'. ?*barpit hades* (f.n. Edmondthorpe).

barr ON, 'barley'. *barlandis* (f.n. Muston).

bastard OFr, ME, 'a bastard'; toponymically, used of fields of abnormal shape or poor yield and occasionally of selions of former great fields not completely swarded over. *the Bastardes* (f.n. Bottesford), *ye Bastards* (f.n. Somerby), Bastards (f.n. Stathern, Wymondham), *Basterdes* (f.n. Burrough on the Hill), *Bastard Leyes* (f.n. Nether Broughton, Scalford), *the bastard leys* (f.n. Bottesford), ?Bastard Yards (f.n. Coston).

baun ON, 'bean'. ?*Baumborrowes* (f.n. Ab Kettleby), Bendales (f.n. Gt. Dalby), *Bounholme* (f.n. Burton Lazars).

(ge)bēacon OE, 'a beacon'. Beacon Hill. *the Beacon Hill* (f.n. Buckminster).

bēan OE, 'bean'. Freq. in f.ns.: in the compound *bean-lands* (with various spellings in Bottesford, Burrough on the Hill, Burton Lazars, Old Dalby, Edmondthorpe, Normanton, Plungar, Wymondham, cf. *fattebenelond'* in Redmile) and note the prob. reduction of this compound to *bellands* (with various spellings in Barkestone, Bottesford, Branston, Brentingby, Garthorpe, Saxby, Thorpe Arnold, Waltham on the Wolds, Wyfordby, cf. Ballance Sick in Melton Mowbray). Recurring is *bean-hill* (with various spellings in Bottesford, Burrough on the Hill, Leesthorpe). Note also *beane furlonge* (Scalford), ?*Beaneleas* (Knipton), *beneholm* (Redmile), *le Hiderbendolis* (Thorpe Arnold).

bearu (bearwe dat.sg.) OE, 'a wood'. ?*Mikelbereu* (f.n. Burrough on the Hill).

beau OFr, adj., 'beautiful', *v.* **bel**[2].

bece[1] OE, **beche** ME, 'a stream, a stream-valley'. Beach Stones (f.n. Wymondham), ?*Becebrigge* (Melton Mowbray), ?*grenemerebech*, ?*Chaldewellebech* (f.ns. Redmile).

bedd OE, 'a bed, a plot where plants grow or are grown'. (The) Ozier Bed (f.ns Eastwell, Wyfordby), Sallow Bed (f.n. Burrough on the Hill), *Willowbeds* (f.n. Sproxton, Wycomb/Chadwell).

bed-hūs OE, 'a prayer-house, a chapel'; in ME, sometimes 'an almshouse'. Bedehouses. Bede House Cl (f.n. Sewstern), *Hudson's Bede House* (Melton Mowbray).

bedlem ME, 'a mental hospital; a lunatic asylum, a madhouse', derived from ME *Bedlem* 'Bethlehem', a word used in the medieval period as a proper name for the Hospital of St Mary of Bethlehem, London, which became a mental institution sometime before 1402. In f.ns., used as a derogatory name for unproductive land which only a madman would attempt to cultivate. Bedlam (f.n. Coston), The Bedlams (f.n. Wymondham).

beggere ME, 'a beggar'; the recurring f.n. *Beggar's Bush* appears to denote poor or unproductive land (cf. EDD *beggar* 'to impoverish land, to exhaust soil of nutrients'). *Beggar Bush Furlong* (f.n. Normanton), *Beggars Bush* (f.n. Harby), *the beggars bushe* (f.n. Somerby).

behindan OE, prep., 'behind, at the back of'. *behinde the Mylne* (f.n. Burton Lazars).

beit ON, 'pasture'. *Baytlane* (Melton Mowbray).

bekkr ON, 'a stream, a beck'. Rundle Beck, Saltbeck, Winterbeck. Very freq. in f.ns.: commonly as a simplex, e.g. *the Beck(e)* (Easthorpe, Freeby, Hose), (the) Beck Fd (Harby, Harston); prefixed by an el. indicating location, e.g. *Hobackes* (Pickwell), Middle Beck (Muston), *Westebecke* (Harby); or by a settlement name, e.g. *Barkistonbec* (Plungar), *Eaton becke* (Eastwell), *Mustonbek* (Bottesford). Recurring is compounding with OE *fūl* 'foul, dirty, filthy', e.g. *Fulbeckegate* (Coston), *Fulbeckes* (Freeby, Saxby) and with OE *lȳtel*, ON *lítill* 'little, small' (with various spellings in Barkestone, Branston, Croxton Kerrial, Garthorpe, Redmile, Stathern). In Framland Hundred, stream-names with ON *bekkr* outnumber those with OE *brōc* 'a brook, a stream' at a ratio of 2:1 and in names recorded only before 1600, at a ratio of 3:1. No doubt in the medieval period, *bekkr* often replaced *brōc* in already existing compounds, but the reverse process can be seen post-1600, e.g. *Broadbeck* > Broad Brook, *Westbeck* > West Brook (Gt. Dalby), *Moorebecke* > Mawbrook (Wyfordby).

bel[2], **beau** OFr, adj., 'fair, beautiful'. Belvoir.

belle OE, 'a bell'; topographically 'a bell-shaped hill, a knoll'. Bellemere Fm. *Belawe* (f.n. Saxby), *the Bell Headland, the Bell Land, Bell Lea* (f.ns. Redmile), *Morbell* (f.n. Scalford). Note that f.ns. in *bellands* (with various spellings in Barkestone, Bottesford, Branston, Brentingby, Garthorpe, Saxby, Thorpe Arnold, Waltham on the Wolds, Wyfordby) may belong here, *v*. Bellands in Bottesford f.ns. (a) and **bēan** *supra*.

bell-hūs OE, 'a bell-house, a belfry'. Belhouse Place (Barkestone).

belleweder ME, 'the leading sheep of a flock, on whose neck a bell is hung'. *Belwether Slade* (f.n. Scalford).

belt ModE, 'a belt (of woodland), a screen of trees, a plantation'. The Belt (Eastwell, Stathern). *Beltside* (f.n. Wymondham).

benc OE, 'a bench'; topographically 'a ledge, a terrace, a bank'. ?Benchy Cl (f.n. Waltham on the Wolds).

bēo OE, 'a bee'. Bee Gate (Waltham on the Wolds).

beorn OE, 'a warrior'. ?*Barnewerc* (f.n. Burton Lazars).

bera OE, 'a bear'. ?*barpit hades* (f.n. Edmondthorpe).

berc OE (Angl), 'a birch-tree'. ?*Bartley Leas* (f.n. Saxby).

bere OE, 'barley'. *Berclyff* (f.n. Melton Mowbray), *Bergate* (Redmile), Berrill Bridge (Sproxton), *Beryl Close* (f.n. Stapleford).

berg OE, 'a rounded hill, a mound, a burial mound', **berg** ON, 'a hill'. Blackberry Hill, Slyborough Hill. Freq. in f.ns.: as a simplex and referring either to a hill or burial mounds upon a hill, e.g. Barrow Hill (Sproxton), The Barrows (Muston); compounded with an el. signifying flora or fauna, e.g. *phistilberu* (Harby), ?*Sissleborough* (Gt. Dalby), *thirneber'* (Muston), *thurnborowe brooke* (Lt. Dalby), *Thyrneberwe* (Somerby), Cockboro' Cl (Withcote), Oxburrow Cl (Waltham on the Wolds); occasionally with a pers.n., e.g. *kyglesberu* (Branston), ?*Wandilberwdike* (Eaton); with an el. signifying the physical aspect of the hill, e.g. *Bingborow leyes* (Freeby), *Blackborough* (Stonesby), *Stonborow hades* (Edmondthorpe); commonly compounded with OE *micel, mycel* or ON *mikill* 'big, great', e.g. *michelborrow dale* (Edmondthorpe), ?*Mikelbereu* (Burrough on the Hill), *mikkelberue* (Croxton Kerrial), *Mucleberwe* (Wymondham). Note the interesting *Baumborrowes* (Ab Kettleby).

berige OE, 'a berry'. *berilands* (f.n. Harby).

bern OE, 'a barn'. Barn Leys Furlong (f.n. Stathern), *Bernewanc* (f.n. Scalford), *Bernewang* (f.n. Thorpe Arnold), *Gudwynbarns* (f.n. Bottesford), *the Parsonage Barne, Trygebarne* (Knipton), *the Tyth barne* (Redmile).

*berse ME, 'a hedge made with stakes'. ?*the Barsey Closes* (f.n. Waltham on the Wolds), ?*Bersicoudale* (f.n. Branston).

beste OFr, ME, 'a beast'; by the 16th cent., generally restricted to livestock. *the Beast Market* (Market Place, Melton Mowbray), *the beast pasture* (Pasture Lane, Stathern; The Pasture, f.n. Stonesby), *ye Beast pasture* (the Pasture Cls, f.n. Wycomb/Chadwell), *Plungar beastes pasture* (f.n. Plungar).

betwēonan OE, prep., 'between, amongst'; usually occurring in compound p.ns. with the elliptical sense 'the place between'. *between the Sykes* (f.n. Melton Mowbray), *betwyne the welles* (f.n. Stapleford), *betwynne ye myllnes* (f.n. Bottesford), *Bitwenegates* (f.n. Burton Lazars), *Bytwnethebekes* (f.n. Eaton), *twene dikes, twene gates, twene sickes* (f.ns. Pickwell).

big ME, adj., 'big'. *bigdickes* (f.n. Wyfordby).

bilberry ModE, 'a bilberry (-bush)'. *Bilberry Lane* (Edmondthorpe).

***billing** OE, 'a hill, a prominence, a promontory, a ridge'. ?*Billinge wong* (f.n. Saltby), ?*Billinglye nooke* (f.n. Stathern).

bingr ON, 'a heap'. *Bingborow leyes* (f.n. Freeby).

bitel, bitela OE, 'a (water-) beetle'. Birtle Beck Drain (f.n. Long Clawson).

blacksmith ModE, 'a blacksmith'. Blacksmith's Lane, Blacksmith's Shop (Edmondthorpe, Scalford).

blæc OE, **blak(e)** ME, **black** ModE, adj., 'black, dark-coloured, dark'; in eModE also 'fertile' as against *white* 'infertile'. Blackberry Hill, Black Holt, Blackwell Lodge, Bleak Hills. Freq. in f.ns.: principally combined with an el. signifying soil, e.g. *the Blacke grounde* (Saxby), *le Blakeland* (Barkestone, Plungar), *Black(a)miles* (Easthorpe, Sproxton), *Blacmild* (Harby), *Blake moulde* (Freeby); also with an el. signifying water, e.g. *Blackwell* (Saltby), *blacpole* (Burton Lazars); or with an el. meaning a hill, e.g. *Blackborough* (Stonesby), *Blackhill* (Branston, Wymondham); note also *Black buttes* (Coston), ?*Blackcroft* (Thorpe Arnold), The Black Dike (Melton Mowbray), *blakeseke* (Burton Lazars). In *the Blacks* (f.n. Redmile), the substantive use of the adj. is evidenced.

blár ON, adj., 'dark, lead-coloured'; by extension as ME **blo**, 'cheerless, cold, exposed'. Blowpool Spinney, Blue Point. *Blowthorn* (f.n. Gt. Dalby), ?Blue Gate (Waltham on the Wolds).

blēo OE, adj., 'coloured, variegated'. *Blewhill* (f.n. Nether Broughton), *Blewhils* (f.n. Scalford).

blesi ON, 'a bare spot on a hillside'. *grangia de Blesewelle* (Goadby Grange, Goadby Marwood). *Blescop* (f.n. Eaton).

blind OE, **blindr** ON, adj., 'blind'; topographically, 'concealed, overgrown'; 'closed at one end'. *le blinde forthe* (f.n. Melton Mowbray), *le Blyndwell* (f.n. Eaton), *Blind Lane* (Wymondham).

bōc OE, 'a beech-tree'. *Bucktree furlong* (f.n. Branston).

bōc-land OE, 'land held by royal charter'. *Bucklandes* (f.n. Normanton).

boga OE, **bogi** ON, 'a bow, an arch; an arched bridge'; topographically 'a curving hillside or headland'. *Bowebriggegate* (Eaton), ?*Filbowe well* (f.n. Knipton).

boia OE, 'a boy; a servant'. *boigate* (Barkestone), *longeboygate* (f.n. Redmile), ?*Boyholme* (f.n. Wymondham).

bole ME, 'a tree-trunk, a stump'. *le Boles* (f.n. Normanton), *le bolys* (f.n. Harby).

bond ME, adj., 'held by tenure of bond service'. *bondlands* (f.n. Freeby), *Bondebreches* (f.n. Wymondham).

bondeman ME, 'a husbandman, an unfree villager, a serf'. *bondemanisbrode* (f.n. Bottesford).

***bor**[1] OE, a hill, an eminence'. ?*borland forlonge* (f.n. Bottesford).

bord OE, 'a board, a table'. *Shepherd boord Leyes* (f.n. Wycomb/Chadwell), *Shepperd board* (f.n. Somerby).

bord-land ME, 'demesne land, land which supplied food for the lord's table'. *Bordland'* (f.n. Bottesford).

borg[1] ON, 'a fortified place'. ?*Borw* (f.n. Eaton).

borow ME, 'a burrow'. ?Burrows Cl (f.n. Burton Lazars).

*bōs (*bōsum dat.pl.) OE, 'a cow-stall'. *boosam wonge* (f.n. Bottesford).

bosard ME, 'a buzzard'. *?bosard home* (f.n. Stapleford).

bothe ME, 'a temporary shelter', **booth** ModEdial., 'a cow-house'. Booth Cl (f.n. Thorpe Arnold).

boðl, botl OE, 'a house, a dwelling'. Bottesford. *?Bottlepits* (f.n. Nether Broughton).

botm OE, 'the bottom'; topographically, also 'a flat alluvial area forming the floor of a valley'. *at the botham* (f.n. Harby), *the Bottoms* (f.n. Stathern), *Dalby bothum* (f.n. Burton Lazars), *Goring Botham* (f.n. Garthorpe), *Gothing Bottom* (f.n. Coston), *Thornhill Bottom* (f.n. Edmondthorpe), *Waferne Botome* (f.n. Burrough on the Hill).

bottom ModE, adj., 'bottom, lowermost'. Bottom Plantation. Freq. in f.ns.: esp. compounded with ME *clos(e)* 'a close, an enclosure', e.g. (The) Bottom Cl (Brentingby, Goadby Marwood, Harston, Muston, Scalford, Wartnaby, Withcote), Middle Bottom Cl (Holwell), Bottom Close Plantation (Wartnaby); note also Bottom Mdw (Gt. Dalby, Wartnaby), Bottom Bass Cl (Sewstern), Bottom Pasture (Harby).

bountyng OE, 'a bunting (the seed-eating bird)'. *?Bunting Wong* (f.n. Harby).

bowling eModE, vbl.sb., 'playing at bowls, the action of rolling a bowl'. *Bowlling leyes* (f.n. Saxby).

bowling-green ModE, 'a smooth, level piece of grass upon which to play bowls'. *Bowling green Leys* (f.n. Saxby), *Widow Shaws House and Bowling Green* (Wymondham).

bracu OE, **brake** ME, 'bracken, fern'. Brackley Cl (f.n. Waltham on the Wolds), *Brakley close* (f.n. Withcote).

brād OE, adj., 'broad, spacious'. Common in f.ns.: with an el. typifying a unit of land, e.g. *bradeland* (Knipton), the Broadings (Melton Mowbray), *Brodebalk* (Sewstern); in the names of watercourses, e.g. *bradebeck'* (Bottesford), Broad Brook (Gt. Dalby), *Brodesyke* (Knipton); esp. compounded with *gata* 'a road', e.g. *Bradgates* (Branston), *Broadgate* (Lt. Dalby), *Brodegate* (Barkestone, Bottesford, Freeby). Note also *brodeby forde* (Saltby).

bræc¹ OE, 'a brake, a thicket, brushwood'. *the Brake* (f.n. Pickwell), *?Brecklands* (f.n. Burrough on the Hill), *Breclondes* (f.n. Thorpe Arnold).

brǣdu OE (Angl), 'breadth', **brode** ME, 'a broad stretch of land, a broad strip of land, a broad cultivated strip of a great field'. *bondemanisbrode* (f.n. Bottesford), *the brode* (f.n. Melton Mowbray), *Depedalebrode* (f.n. Eaton), *hesland broade* (f.n. Ab Kettleby).

bræmbel, brǣmel OE, 'a bramble', v. **brembel** *infra*.

brakni ON, **braken** ME, 'bracken, fern'. Brackendale Cls, *the Bracken peece* (f.ns. Eaton), *bracken leayes*, *brakendale* (f.ns. Croxton Kerrial), *Brackinspole* (f.n. Waltham on the Wolds), *brakendole* (f.n. Knipton), *Brakenholm* (f.n. Somerby), *Brakenhou* (f.n. Eaton), *Brakenousike* (f.n. Wycomb/Chadwell), *Brakyn Close* (f.n. Nether Broughton), *?Brockens Mdw* (f.n. Wymondham), Broken Dikes (f.n. Burrough on the Hill), *brokendikes* (f.n. Somerby), *?Gore bracking* (f.n. Branston).

brand OE, 'fire, flame, a brand'; also 'a place cleared by burning, a place where burning has occurred'. *?Brand Wonge* (f.n. Croxton Kerrial).

brant OE, *brant ON, adj., 'steep, steep-sided'. ?Brentingby. *Bransick* (f.n. Ab Kettleby), *le brantpyttys* (f.n. Knipton), ?*brenles* (f.n. Stapleford), ?*Brent Clyff* (f.n. Freeby), ?*Brenthill* (f.n. Stonesby).

brēc OE (Angl), **breche** ME, 'a breaking, a breach, land broken up for cultivation, newly broken-in ploughland'. Common in f.ns. as a simplex, e.g. the Breach (Sproxton), the Breaches (Harby, Stathern), *brech* (Stapleford), *le Breche* (Old Dalby, Knipton, Somerby), *le Breches* (Bottesford); occasionally with a qualifier, e.g. *long breches* (Freeby), *le Thwerbrech* (Burrough on the Hill); or with an indication of location, e.g. the Becke's Breach (Sproxton), *Wheathill breache* (Knipton); or of tenure or ownership, e.g. *Bondebreches* (Wymondham), *Godecnauebreche* (Branston).

breiðr ON, 'broad, spacious'. *Braytheynghend'* (f.n. Normanton), Braythorne Cl (f.n. Waltham on the Wolds), *Brethlondale* (f.n. Wymondham), Bretland (f.n. Coston), *(le) Bretland'* (f.ns. Barkestone, Plungar, Stathern), *Bretlands* (f.n. Burrough on the Hill), *bretlond* (f.n. Muston), Little Bretstone (f.n. Edmondthorpe).

brembel, bræmbel, brǣmel OE, 'a bramble, a blackberry bush'. Bramble Cl (f.n. Stathern), *Bramelhoke* (f.n. Burton Lazars), Brimbles (f.n. Burrough on the Hill), *Brimble Fur'*, *Brimble Sike* (f.ns. Gt. Dalby).

brende², **brente** ME, pa.part., adj., 'burnt', used often in the sense 'cleared by burning'. In a stream name, it prob. signifies 'of a burnt colour, brownish'. *Stapilford' iuxta Brendebrocc* (Stapleford). *Brendelandes* (f.n. Bottesford), *brend lees* (f.n. Edmondthorpe), ?*brenles* (f.n. Stapleford), ?*Brent Clyff* (f.n. Freeby), ?*Brenthill* (f.n. Stonesby), *Burntlands* (f.n. Sproxton).

brennand ME, pres.part., 'burning'; prob. in p.ns. 'cleared by burning'. *brennandthorn* (f.n. Branston).

brenni ME, adj., poss. 'cleared by burning'. ?*Brennycroft* (f.n. Muston).

brēosa OE, 'a gadfly'. *breeshome dalle* (f.n. Stapleford).

brēr OE (Angl), 'briars'. *Brier Hill* (f.n. Redmile), *Bryare forlong* (f.n. Scalford), *Stikbrere* (f.n. Wycomb/Chadwell).

***brērig** OE (Angl), adj., 'growing with or overgrown with briars'. Briery Wood.

bridewell eModE, 'a house of correction'. *County Bridewell* (Melton Mowbray).

brigdels OE, 'a bridle' (used in the sense 'fit for a horse to pass', as in *bridle-path*). Barnston Bridle Rd, Grantham Bridle Rd, Harby Bridle Rd (Stathern), Beskabby Bridle Rd (Stonesby), Bridle road Fox Holes (f.n. Holwell), Croxton Bridle Rd, Woolsthorpe Bridle Rd (Harston), Little Dalby Bridle Gate (Somerby).

brimme ME, 'an edge, a border'. ?*Brimming Leys* (f.n. Holwell).

brink ODan, ME, 'a brink, the edge of a bank'. *Brincthyrne* (f.n. Waltham on the Wolds), *the brinke* (f.n. Knipton), *Hertisbrinc, holmesbrinck'*, Red Brinks (f.ns. Branston), *Highbrinke hole* (f.n. Pickwell), High Brinks (f.n. Wymondham), *the medelbryng'* (f.n. Stapleford), *Netherbrynkes* (f.n. Melton Mowbray), *Stony brinkes* (f.n. Croxton Kerrial), *Stony Brink* (f.n. Somerby).

brōc OE, 'a brook, a stream'. Nether Broughton, Brocker Ho., Brock Hill, Burton Brook, Mawbrooke Fm, Scalford Brook, Sherbrook Fox Covert. Freq. in f.ns.: esp. compounded with a settlement name and thus prob. identifying a more major watercourse, e.g. *Bottesforde browke* (Bottesford), Burton Brook (Burton Lazars), Dalby Brook (Old Dalby), *Newbolde broke* (Burrough on the Hill), *Sysonbe brooke* (Sysonby); common as a simplex, e.g. *the Brook(e)* (Croxton Kerrial, Lt.

Dalby, Pickwell, Somerby, Waltham on the Wolds); occasionally with a directional adj., e.g. *le est Broke* (Lt. Dalby), *North brooke* (Pickwell), *West Brook* (Gt. Dalby); or compounded with a minor name, e.g. *Asschemarebrock* (Somerby), *Caldewellebrok'* (Wycomb/Chadwell), *Haliwell broc* (Burrough on the Hill), *thurnborow brooke* (Lt. Dalby). In names recorded only before 1600, stream-names with *brōc* are outnumbered by those with Scand *bekkr* 'a stream' at a ratio of 1:3. In the medieval period, presum. *bekkr* replaced *brōc* in many instances in already existing compounds; but stream-names recorded post-1600 show a marked increase in the use of *brook*, a process which appears to have been in progress from the earlier 16th cent., as the example *the new brooke* (Melton Mowbray) of 1550 suggests, *v.* **bekkr**.

brocc-hol OE, 'a badger hole, a sett'. *Brokholetonge* (f.n. Sysonby).

brōm OE, 'broom'. *Bromfielde* (f.n. Wymondham), Broom Cl (f.n. Brentingby).

brōðor OE, **broðir** (**brœðra** gen.sg.) ON, 'a brother'; in later p.ns., also 'a religious brother, a monk'. *Brethers Pytt* (f.n. Burton Lazars).

brún[2] ON, 'the edge, the brow of a hill'. ?Brungate Leys (f.n. Nether Broughton).

bruni ON, 'burning; a place cleared by burning'. ?*Brennycroft* (f.n. Muston).

brycg OE, 'a bridge; a causeway'; in the Danelaw, the spellings of p.ns. with *brycg* are often influenced by ON **bryggja** 'a jetty, a quay'. Winterbeck Bridge. Sometimes prefixed by a settlement name, e.g. *Harston brigge* (Knipton), *Ketleby bridge* (Melton Mowbray), *kirkeby bridge* (Eye Kettleby), *Stapelford brigge* (Stapleford). Commonly compounded with *stān* 'stone', as *Stone Bridge* (Melton Mowbray), *stone brigg* (Saltby), *Michilstanbrigg'* (Burrough on the Hill); or with a directional adj., e.g. *northebrige* (Knipton), *Sowthbrygge* (Belvoir), *westbryg* (Bottesford); occasionally with a pers.n or surn., e.g. *Ailmeresbrigge* (Thorpe Bridge, Melton Mowbray), *Foleville brigge* (Melton Mowbray), *seuordebrigg'* (Burton Lazars); or shape may be indicated, e.g. *Bowebriggegate* (Eaton), *Hansaxbrigge* (Burrough on the Hill). Common in f.ns., e.g. *Brigg Close* (Burrough on the Hill, Pickwell), Brigg Leys (Pickwell), *Brigge plotte* (Coston), *bryggefurlonge* (Knipton). Note *briggeforth* (Burton Lazars), an example of the common *bridge-ford*, perh. indicating a ford with a made-up causeway or else a ford replaced by a bridge at the stream's crossing-place, cf. Stonebridge Ford (Burrough on the Hill).

bryne OE, 'burning'; prob. in p.ns. 'a place cleared by burning'. ?*Brennycroft*, *Burnelandez* (f.ns. Muston), *Burnforlong, le Burnhassokis* (f.ns. Burrough on the Hill), *byrnelandys* (f.n. Bottesford).

buc-þorn ME, 'the buckthorn', the shrub *Rhamnus catharticus*, the berries of which yielded sap-green and other pigments, and were formerly used as a cathartic. *bucstornfurlong'* (f.n. Muston), *Bukkysthorn'* (f.n. Burrough on the Hill), *Bukthern* (f.n. Sewstern).

bula OE, 'a bull'. Common in f.ns.: Bulham (Stapleford), *Bulholme Close* (Old Dalby), Bull Cl (Burton Lazars, Waltham on the Wolds, Wartnaby), *Bull close* (Thorpe Arnold), Bull Grass (Edmondthorpe), *the Bull hurst* (Normanton), *the Bull lee* (Pickwell), Bull Paddock (Goadby Marwood), *the bull swayth* (Knipton), Bull Sty (Stathern). Bull-baiting is evidenced in Bull Pit Cl (Thorpe Arnold), *bull pyts* (Freeby).

bullgate ModEdial., 'pasturage for a single bull'. *Bullgate*, Nether Row Bullgates (f.ns. Barkestone), Bullgates (f.n. Redmile).

bulluc OE, 'a male calf, a bullock'. *Bullocks Nook* (Bull Nook, f.n. Burton Lazars), Bullock Wong (f.n. Burton Lazars), Bullock Yard (f.n. Pickwell).

bune OE, 'a reed'. Bunhills (f.n. Waltham on the Wolds).

búr² ON, 'a store-house'. *Burtofts* (f.n. Harby).

burh OE, 'a fortified place; a pre-English earthwork; a Roman station; an Anglo-Saxon fortification; a fortified house or manor; a manor'. Burrough on the Hill, Burrough Hill, *Burrowchurch.* ?*Baumborrowes* (f.n. Ab Kettleby), *Borohades* (f.n. Lt. Dalby), *Borowefilde* (f.n. Withcote), ?*Borw* (f.n. Eaton), ?Burley Thorn Cl (f.n. Branston), ?*ouerberu* (f.n. Bottesford), *risburgsike* (f.n. Lt. Dalby), ?*Wandilberwdike* (f.n. Eaton).

burh-geat OE, 'a town gate'. *Burgate* (Melton Mowbray).

burh-stede (**byrig-stede** dat.sg.) OE, 'the site of a fortification'. *Byristede* (f.n. Normanton).

burh-tūn OE, 'a fort enclosure; a farmstead with a palisade'. Burton Lazars.

*****busc** OE, **bush** ME, 'a bush, a shrub', also 'ground covered with bush'. Three Shire Bush. Freq. in f.ns.: as a simplex, e.g. *the bushe* (Wyfordby), *above the bush* (Saltby), *the bushes* (Croxton Kerrial), Bush Mdw (Gt. Dalby); with a surn. indicating ownership, e.g. *John Calcroftes Bushes* (Bottesford), *Nicholsons Bush* (Saltby), *Palmers Bushes* (Somerby); prefixed by a p.n. indicating location, e.g. *Blackhill Bushes* (Wymondham), *Coppolle bushe* (Wycomb/Chadwell), *Hay gate bush* (Coston), *sowerbeck bush* (Redmile). Note also *Beggar Bush Furlong* (Normanton), *Beggars Bush* (Harby), *the beggars bushe* (Somerby), *v.* **beggere**.

buski ME, 'growing with bushes'. Buskey Furlong (f.n. Stathern).

buskr ON, 'a bush, a shrub'. *at the Buske*, *Heigate Busk* (f.ns. Ab Kettleby), *Drivers Busk* (f.n. Scalford), *le notebusk* (f.n. Barkestone), *Welldale Busk* (Well Dale Spring, f.n. Scalford), *Withinbusc* (f.n. Bottesford).

busshi ME, 'growing with bushes'. Bushy Fds (f.n. Wymondham).

butere OE, 'butter'; in f.ns., referring to rich pasture. *the Buttercross* (Melton Mowbray). the Better Lands (f.n. Gt. Dalby), *Butterlandes* (f.n. Wyfordby), *osbutterlands* (f.n. Bottesford).

*****butt¹** OE, 'a tree-stump, a log'. *buttwong'* (f.n. Croxton Kerrial).

butt² OFr, ME, 'an archery butt'. Butt Close, Butt Lane. Butt Cl (f.n. Edmondthorpe), *The Butt Close* (f.n. Redmile), ?the Butts (f.n. Waltham on the Wolds), *whereon the Buttes stand* (f.n. Goadby Marwood).

butte ME, 'a strip of land abutting on a boundary'; also 'a short strip or ridge at right angles to other ridges, a short strip of ploughed land in the angle where two furlongs meet'. *Black buttes* (f.n. Coston), the Butts (f.n. Saltby, ?Waltham on the Wolds), *Coldellebuts*, *withins buttes* (f.ns. Bottesford), *Dow but* (f.n. Freeby), *Farbuttes* (f.n. Scalford), *fattbutts*, *Strethelbut'* (f.ns. Old Dalby), *fold brigge buttes* (f.n. Easthorpe), Long Butsall (f.n. Stonesby), *the Mare butts* (the Mare, f.n. Stathern), *Penbutt'* (f.n. Thorpe Arnold), *Redbutt Fur'* (f.n. Melton Mowbray), *yauley buttes* (f.n. Croxton Kerrial).

buttermilk ModE, 'buttermilk; whey; milk from which the butter has been churned out'; in f.ns., applied to land with rich pasturage. Buttermilk Hill Spinney. Buttermilk Lane (Stonesby).

bȳ ON, 'a farmstead, a village'. Bescaby, Brentingby, Great Dalby, Little Dalby, Old Dalby, Freeby, Goadby Marwood, Harby, Ab Kettleby, Eye Kettleby, Saltby, Saxby, Somerby, Stonesby, Sysonby, Wartnaby, Wyfordby. Occasionally recording sites of lost farmsteads: *Little Alby*, ?*Westby hades* (f.ns. Goadby Marwood), *Assebymilne* (f.n. Eaton), *brodeby forde* (f.n. Saltby), *Dunesby* (f.n. Branston), *radiebidale* (f.n. Croxton Kerrial).

bydel OE, 'a beadle'. *Bidilhawedland* (f.n. Bottesford), ?*Buddle acre* (f.n. Waltham on the Wolds).

****byrde** OE, 'a border, an edge, a bank'. *burdowe leyes* (f.n. Somerby).

(ge)bysce OE (Angl), 'a copse of bushes'. ?*Bysse dyke* (f.n. Freeby).

****cā** OE, ****ká** ON, **cā** ME, 'a jackdaw'. ?*Caddalehull* (f.n. Burrough on the Hill).

cad(d)aw, cad(d)owe ME, 'a jackdaw'. Caddow Bank (f.n. Bottesford), *Cawdaw hill* (f.n. Branston).

cærse, cresse OE, 'cress, water-cress'. *Cresswell* (f.n. Waltham on the Wolds), ?*Kerisholm* (f.n. Wycomb/Chadwell).

****cærsing** OE, 'a place where cress grows, a cress bed'. *kyrsinges* (f.n. Eaton).

cært OE, 'rough ground, stony ground', **kartr** ON, 'rough, rocky, sterile ground'. *le Chart* (f.n. Wycomb/Chadwell).

cald OE (Angl), **kaldr** ON, **cald, cold** ME, adj., 'cold'. Chadwell, Cord Hill. In f.ns., freq. compounded with *wella* or *hyll*: *Calde Wellys* (Somerby), *Caldwell* (Bottesford, Waltham on the Wolds), Short Caldwell (Gt. Dalby), *Caudell-heads* (Saxby), *Caudwell dale* (Branston), *Cawdewell sike* (Easthorpe), *Chaldewellebech* (Redmile), *Kaldewellefurlong'* (Barkestone), Cold Hill (Eastwell, Stathern), *Coldhill* (Pickwell), *le Coldhyl* (Knipton), Far Caudhill (Croxton Kerrial).

****cald-herber(3)** ME, 'a cold shelter'. Cold Harbour Ground (f.n. Sysonby).

calf (calfra gen.pl.) OE, 'a calf'. Calf Banks (f.n. Scalford), Calf Cl (f.n. Burrough on the Hill, Coston, Gt. Dalby, Scalford), *the Calfe pasture* (f.n. Branston), *Calfes pasture* (f.n. Lt. Dalby, Melton Mowbray), Calfs Sawgates (f.n. Burton Lazars), *Calvacre, Caversicke* (f.ns. Waltham on the Wolds), *Calverhillwong'* (f.n. Bottesford), Calving Hills (f.n. Normanton).

capitain OFr, ME, 'a military leader, a commander of a body of troops, or of a fortress'; later, the military rank between major and lieutenant. Captains Cl (f.n. Burrough on the Hill), Captain's Cl (f.n. Sysonby).

carte ME, 'a cart'. Great Cart Lane (Goadby Marwood).

castel(l) ME, 'a castle, a stronghold'. Belvoir Castle, Sauvey Castle. *Casil crofte, Castelsty* (f.ns. Eaton), *(le) Castelgate* (Bottesford, Burton Lazars, Redmile, Stathern), *Castell gate* (Easthorpe, Saltby), *the Castlegate* (Croxton Kerrial), Castle Fd (f.n. Long Clawson), *castle hades* (f.n. Brentingby, Wyfordby), Crow Castle (f.n. Somerby).

cat(t) OE, 'a cat', **catte** OE, 'a she-cat'. ?*Catackers* (f.n. Redmile), *Catewade* (f.n. Bottesford), *Catsars* (f.n. Ab Kettleby), *Cattewellegate* (Normanton), ?*le cattisterne* (f.n. Knipton), *Cattmoredale* (f.n. Wymondham), The Cutwells (f.n. Harston).

cat(t)el ME, 'cattle, livestock'. *Catelhil* (f.n. Plungar).

caucie ONFr, **cauce**, **cause** ME, 'an embankment or dam, a raised way across marshy ground or along a dyke; a (raised) paved way'. *the Causey* (f.n. Pickwell), Causeway Hill, ?*Skawcy* (f.ns. Melton Mowbray), *the Causway* (f.n. Branston), *Curce gate* (Freeby).

ceder OE, **cedre** ME, 'the cedar-tree'; the evergreen conifer *Cedrus Libani*. Cedar Hill.

celde OE (Angl), 'a spring'. *Cheldacre* (f.n. Plungar).

chapel(e) OFr, ME, 'a chapel'. Baptist Chapel, The Chapel, Chapel Lane, Chapel Nook, Methodist Chapel (Buckminster, Goadby Marwood, Holwell, Hose, Ab Kettleby, Muston, Stathern, Stonesby, Wymeswold), Primitive Methodist Chapel (Long Clawson, Scalford), Roman Catholic Chapel, Wesleyan Methodist Chapel (Nether Broughton, Long Clawson, Scalford); *the Chapel* (Brentingby, Sysonby), *the Chapel of St Mary* (St Mary's Church, Chadwell), *the Chappel Howse alias the Spittell Chapell*, *Independent Chapel*, *Methodist Chapel*, *Primitive Methodist Chapel*, *Roman Catholic Chapel* (Melton Mowbray). *the chapel yard* (St Peter's Church, Saxby), *Chappell Yard* (f.n. Burton Lazars), *the Chappel Yard* (Chapel Nook, Eye Kettleby), *chapill pitts* (f.n. Knipton), *Chapple Furl'* (f.n. Lt. Dalby).

chaunterie ME, 'a chantry'. *Chantry land* (f.n. Stathern).

cheesecake ModE, 'a tart usually made with eggs and cheese'; applied to a wedge-shaped field in humorous reference to a portion of such a confection. *Cheescake* (f.n. Stathern), Cheesecake (f.n. Coston), *the tythe called the chesecake* (f.n. Saltby), (the) Cheesecake Cl (f.ns. Edmondthorpe, Sewstern), *the Cheesecake piece* (f.n. Somerby), Cheese Cake Piece (f.n. Wymondham).

cheker ME, 'a chequer', (OFr *escheker* 'a chequer, a chess-board, the Exchequer'); in later f.ns., used to denote ground of chequered appearance. *þe checer* (Bottesford), *the Chequer* (f.n. Stapleford).

cheri(e) ME, 'a cherry-tree'. the Cherry Yard (f.n. Knipton).

chirche-ȝeard ME, 'a church-yard'. Freq., earlier instances being *the Church yard(e)* (belonging to the parish churches of Melton Mowbray (1550), Long Clawson, Gt. Dalby, Knipton (1601), Garthorpe, Harston, Scalford (1605)), *the Churchyeard* (Muston (1601), Buckminster (1605)).

cirice OE, 'a church'. Parish churches with their various dedications are not listed. *Burrowchurch*, Church Fm (Bottesford, Croxton Kerrial), Church St, Church Thorns. Common in f.ns., e.g. Church Croft (Burton Lazars), Church Fd (Muston), *the Churchfield* (Redmile), *Church headland* (Lt. Dalby, Sysonby), Church Hill (Harston). Note also *le Churche House* (Melton Mowbray).

cirice-stede OE, 'the site of a church'. *Kyrkestedplot'*, *Kyrkestedwong'* (f.ns. Muston).

*cis OE, 'gravel'. ?*Cheesewong* (f.n. Normanton).

clæg OE, 'clay, clayey soil'. Clayfield Fm. Common in f.ns.: e.g. Clay Fd (Goadby Marwood), *Claie Wonge*, *the clay furlonge* (Edmondthorpe), *clayfurlonge* (Knipton), The Clay Ground (Eastwell), *Clayholm* (Bottesford), *the clay pasture* (Scalford), Cleay Hill (Croxton Kerrial), *the Clefeld, Cleforlonge* (Bottesford), *the Cleyes* (Harston), *the Cley feilde* (Ab Kettleby), *le Cleyland'* (Thorpe Arnold), *Cleywong* (Wymondham), *hilleclaye* (Redmile), *Long Clees* (Branston), *le Witeclais* (Bottesford). Note the intriguing Robin i'the Clay (Pickwell).

clæne OE, adj., 'clean, clear of weeds'. *Clendalls* (f.n. Sproxton).

clāfre OE, 'clover'. Clover Cl (f.n. Eastwell), Clover Fd (f.n. Holwell).

clerc OE, OFr, 'an ecclesiastic, a cleric'; also in ME, 'a scholar, a secretary'. ?Clark Sty (f.n. Stathern), ?*Clarkewell* (f.n. Scalford), ?*Clarkwell Side* (f.n. Saltby).

cley-pytt ME, 'a clay-pit'. *Cleypit* (f.n. Eaton).

clif OE, 'a cliff, a bank, a steep hillside'. Longcliff Hill. Freq. in f.ns.: often as a simplex, e.g. *le Clif(f)* (Bottesford, Wycomb/Chadwell), the Cliff (Eaton, Muston), *the Clyffe* (Harston); or with an el. identifying a crop, e.g. *Berclyue* (Melton Mowbray), *Rieclef* (Eaton), or natural flora, e.g. *Thirneclif* (Burton Lazars, Muston), *Thyrnclif* (Hose), *Willeclif* (Wymondham); or with an el. indicating shape, e.g. *brantclyf* (Melton Mowbray), *le heyeclif* (Muston), *le Longclif* (Bottesford); or with a pre-existing p.n., e.g. *Alingtonecliff'* (Muston), *Blakewelleclif* (Old Dalby); or with a simple locational identifier, e.g. *le kirkeclyf* (Wycomb/Chadwell), *wadecliue*, *Westcliffe* (Knipton), *Watclyffe* (Croxton Kerrial). *Clippesclif* (Eaton) is the only sure instance in Framland Hundred with a compounded pers.n.

clofen OE, pa.part., 'cloven, split'. *Cloven Balk* (f.n. Harby).

clos ME, adj., 'close, narrow'. *closickes* (f.n. Scalford).

clos(e) ME, 'a close, an enclosure'. Very freq. in f.ns.: early examples are *le Croft Close* (1253, Bottesford), *Coweclose, Shepard close* (1473, Croxton Kerrial), *Hunton' close* (1515, Easthorpe), *Blakke Borowe close* (1525, Knipton), *cranwell close, the hall close* (1529, Eye Kettleby).

closing eModE, 'an enclosure'. *Allens Clossinge* (Allens Cl, f.n. Burrough on the Hill), *Ash Closeing* (Ash Tree Cl, f.n. Eastwell), *Between the Closein* (f.n. Stathern).

clot(t) OE, 'a mass, a lump, a clod; a hill'. *Clartes* (f.n. Normanton), *Clot hades* (f.n. Melton Mowbray).

clūd OE, 'a rock, a mass of rock, a (rocky) hill'. Great Cloud hill (f.n. Edmondthorpe).

cnæpp OE (Angl), 'a hill-top; a short, sharp ascent'. *Knaphildale* (f.n. Thorpe Arnold).

cnoll OE, 'the summit of a hill'; later 'a knoll, a hillock'. Sysonby Knoll. Edmanholes (f.n. Stathern), *the Round Knowl* (f.n. Harston), *ten knowles* (f.n. Burton Lazars).

***cobb(e)** OE, 'a round lump, a cob', **cob** ModEdial., 'a mound, hillock, tumulus'. ?*Cobbecroftes* (f.n. Belvoir), ?*Short Cobs* (f.n. Buckminster).

cocc[1] OE, 'a heap, a hillock'. As a first el., difficult to distinguish from **cocc[2]** *infra*. Withcote. ?*Cokhowe* (f.n. Redmile), ?*Cokkecroft* (f.n. Stathern), ?Cook Stall (f.n. Burton Lazars).

cocc[2] OE, 'a cock, a woodcock'; difficult to distinguish from **cocc[1]** *supra*. Cockboro' Cl (f.n. Withcote), Cock Cl (f.n. Brentingby), ?Cocks Hill Cl (f.n. Wymondham), ?*Cokhowe* (f.n. Redmile), *Cokeswrogate* (Bottesford), ?*Cokkecroft* (f.n. Stathern), ?*coksty* (f.n. Bottesford), ?Cook Stall (f.n. Burton Lazars).

coccel OE, 'tares'. *the Cockle Close* (f.n. Freeby), *Cockley Wong furlong* (f.n. Gt. Dalby).

cocking eModE, 'cock-fighting'. *Cockinpit Furlong* (f.n. Branston).

cockpit ModE, 'a pit for cock-fighting'. Cockpit Nook (f.n. Edmondthorpe).

codd OE, 'a bag, a sack', used topographically as 'a hollow' in later f.ns. ?*Codland* (f.n. Melton Mowbray).

*cogg OE, **cogge** ME, 'a cog-wheel, a mill; a protuberance or projection; a hill', *v.* Löfvenberg 43. ?*Coggle Baulk* (f.n. Saltby).

cole OE, 'a hollow'. ?*Coleacker* (f.n. Harby).

coleseed ModE, 'coleseed, oilseed rape', the plant *Brassica oleifera* cultivated for its seed which produces 'rape' or 'sweet' oil. *Coleseed plot* (f.n. Old Dalby).

col-pytt OE, 'a coalpit', i.e. a place where charcoal is made. *Coal Pitt Lane* (Melton Mowbray), Coal pitt Lane Cl (f.n. Sysonby), *Colepitte forthe* (f.n. Wycomb/Chadwell), *the Cole pit gate* (Bottesford), *the Colepytgate* (Barkestone), *the Colepytt way* (Saxby), *collpit forlang* (f.n. Redmile), *the collpitt waie* (Scalford).

commun ME, used both as a sb. as 'common land' and as an adj. as 'shared by all, of a non-private nature'. Freq. in f.ns.: *the Common* (Lt. Dalby, Edmondthorpe, Saltby), *the Common at the Mill* (Knipton), Common Hill (Buckminster), Hay Common (Wartnaby), *Wiverby open common* (Brentingby); the adj. is perh. to be assumed in such instances as *the common drifte*, *the common gorste* (Wyfordby), *the Common gate* (Bottesford), Commonham Lane (Nether Broughton), *the Common Me(e)re* (Harston, Ab Kettleby), the Common Pasture (Gt. Dalby, Eaton), *the Common peice*, *the comon waye* (Croxton Kerrial), but there is often ambiguity when the el. is used as a qualifier.

conestable OFr, ME, 'a constable'. *the Constable Piece* (f.n. Scalford), *Constables Hades* (f.n. Waltham on the Wolds).

coni ME, 'a rabbit'. *Conney Warren* (The Warren, f.n. Sysonby), ?*Conys close* (f.n. Edmondthorpe).

coningre, coninger ME, 'a rabbit warren'. Conygear Wood. (The) Conery (f.ns. Brentingby, Wymondham), Coney Gray Hill (f.n. Stathern), Coneygree (Cl) (f.ns. Easthorpe, Edmondthorpe), *Coningerend* (f.n. Thorpe Arnold), *Conygree* (f.n. Eastwell), *the Cuningr(e)ye* (f.n. Sproxton, Wyfordby), Cunnery (f.n. Lt. Dalby), *Cunnery Gate* (Gt. Dalby), *the old Connigree* (f.n. Nether Broughton).

conseil OFr, ME, 'consultation, deliberation'. *Cownsell dale* (f.n. Branston).

copis ME, (OFr *copeiz*), 'a coppice'. The Copy (f.n. Brentingby), Upper Coppice (f.n. Withcote).

copp, cop OE, 'a summit, a hill or ridge which has a narrow, crest-like top'. *Blescop* (f.n. Eaton), Copdale (f.n. Coston), Copple Hill (f.n. Scalford), Long Cups (f.n. Buckminster), *Shortcop'* (f.n. Sewstern).

copped ME, pa.part., adj., 'having had the head removed, pollarded', (OE *coppian 'to pollard'). *Copthorne* (f.n. Nether Broughton), Copton Fd (f.n. Knipton).

corn[1] OE, 'corn, grain'. *the Corn Cross* (Melton Mowbray), Corn Cl (f.n. Sysonby, Thorpe Arnold), Corn Part (f.n. Freeby).

corner ME, 'a corner, a nook'. Corner Cl, Corner Pingle (f.ns. Eastwell), Corner Ploughed Fd (f.n. Gt. Dalby), *the parke corner*, *Redmile Close corner* (f.ns. Barkestone), *Sanham Corner* (f.n. Gt. Dalby).

cort(e) OE, poss. 'a short plot of ground, a piece of land cut off'. *cortepit* (f.n. Plungar).

cot OE, 'a cottage, a hut, a shelter'. Withcote. *Cootys* (f.n. Thorpe Arnold), *Cote lane* (Burrough on the Hill), ?Draycarts Mdw (f.n. Goadby Marwood), (The) Draycott (f.ns. Buckminster, Freeby), *Horscott Lees* (f.n. Branston), Hulcoat Sty Furlong (f.n. Stathern), *Lamcoates* (f.n. Croxton Kerrial), *Lambcotewong* (f.n. Muston), Lamb Cotts (f.n. Goadby Marwood), *Lambecotes* (f.n. Wycomb/Chadwell), *ouercotestys* (f.n. Bottesford).

cotage ME, 'a cottage, a hut, a shelter'. Ben's Cottage, Brookside ~, Burton Lodge ~, Clematis Cottage, The Cottage, Cottage Fm, Dowry Cottage, Easthorpe Cottage, Grange Cottages, Halfway Cottage, Knipton Cottage, New Row Cottages, Providence Cottage, Pultney ~, Reservoir ~, Spinney Farm ~, Sysonby Cottage, Tip Cottages, Victoria ~, Vine Cottage. Commonly prefixed by a surn., e.g. *Basses Cottage*, *Cubleys Cottage* (Stapleford), *Bells Cottage* (Old Dalby), *Dewicks Cottage* (Burton Lazars); note also *Oxgang Cottages* (Eaton). Freq. in f.ns.: e.g. (The) Cottage Cl (Gt. Dalby, Freeby, Goadby Marwood, Muston), Cottage Ham, Cottage Pasture, Cottage Platt (Wyfordby), Cottage Lee Wong (Hose), *Cottage Meadow* (Gt. Dalby).

cotager eModE, 'one who lives in a cottage', used especially of the labouring population in rural districts. Cottagers Cl (f.n. Coston), Cottagers Pasture (f.n. Edmondthorpe, Freeby, Goadby Marwood), Cottagers Platt (f.n. Edmondthorpe), *ye old Cottagers Close* (f.n. Wymondham).

cottere OE, 'a cottar, a cottager'. *ye Cotiers Close* (f.n. Wymondham), *Cottiers Close* (f.n. Burton Lazars), *Cottiers Closse* (Cottagers Cl, f.n. Coston), *the Cottiers pasture Close* (Cottagers Pasture, f.n. Edmondthorpe), *the Cottyers Close* (f.n. Freeby), *the Cotyers Pasture* (f.n. Wyfordby).

court OFr, ME, 'a large house, a manor house'. Burrough Court. *Edgecourt* (Buckminster), *Court Wong* (f.n. Thorpe Arnold), Cranwell Court Covert (f.n. Harby).

court-hous ME, 'a house where manorial courts were held'. *le Courtehous Yerde* (Belvoir Castle).

cover(t) ME, 'a covert, a shelter for game'. Bridget's Covert, Sir Francis Burdett's ~, Burrough Hill Covert, Covermill Hill, Crossing Covert, Holwell Mouth ~, Jericho ~, Laxton's Covert, Little Covert Fm, Muston Gorse Covert, Peake's ~, Punch Bowl ~, Round ~, Sherbrook Fox ~, Square ~, Swallowhole Covert. *Cants Cover* (Cant's Thorns, Wartnaby), Cover Cl (f.n. Buckminster), Cranwell Court Covert, Harby Covert (Harby), Fox Covert (Burrough on the Hill, Burton Lazars, Edmondthorpe, Holwell), Gorse Covert (Sewstern), *Stone Pit Covert* (Stonepit Spinney, Wartnaby).

cowgate ModEdial., 'pasturage for a single cow'. ?*the cougate* (f.n. Stathern).

crabbe ME, 'a crab-apple-tree', cf. **crabtre**. *the Crabbe layes* (f.n. Goadby Marwood), ?*Crabbesforowes* (f.n. Bottesford).

crabtre ME, 'a crab-apple-tree'. *Crabb tree stigh*, Crabtree Furlong (f.ns. Stathern), *at the Crabtre(e)* (f.n. Croxton Kerrial, Saltby), *Crabtree furlong* (f.n. Branston), *Crabtree Holme* (f.n. Wymondham), Crab tree Leys (f.n. Holwell), *the Crabtree pece* (f.n. Sproxton).

cran, cron OE, 'a crane, a heron'. Cranyke Fm, ?*Crown Point* (Blue Point, Wymondham). Crane Cl, Crown Dale (f.ns. Gt. Dalby), *Cranewater* (f.n. Burton Lazars), *cranwell close* (f.n. Eye Kettleby).

cranuc OE, 'a crane'. *Crankwell lane* (Cranwell Court Covert, Harby).
crāwe (crawena gen.pl.) OE, 'a crow'. ?*Cranor* (f.n. Stathern), *Crathernesike* (f.n. Wycomb/Chadwell), *Crawell'*, *Croo Poole*, *crosled'* (f.ns. Croxton Kerrial), *Crodyke* (f.n. Melton Mowbray), *crouthorn* (f.n. Bottesford), *Crowbush* (f.n. Saltby), Crow Castle (f.n. Somerby), Crow Dale (f.n. Coston), Crowtrees (f.n. Holwell).
crew ModEdial., 'a pen, a hut, a shed'. *Sheep crew furlong* (f.n. Normanton).
crike ME, **creek** ModE, 'a nook, a corner, a secluded recess'. Lone Creek (f.n. Wymondham).
crocc OE, 'a crock, an earthenware pot', prob. alluding to places where pots and sherds were discovered or where pots were made. ?*Crocland* (f.n. Harby), ?*Croklokhull* (f.n. Thorpe Arnold).
croft OE, 'a small enclosed field, a small enclosure near a house'. Very freq. in f.ns.: especially with pers.ns. and surns., e.g. *Alnotescroft, Deroldescroft, yngoldiscroft* (Burton Lazars), *Alwoldecroft* (Redmile), *Andrewscrofte* (Melton Mowbray), *wlruncroft* (Knipton); with crops or flora, e.g. *Ambrecrofte* (Burton Lazars), *Daymesonecroft* (Melton Mowbray), Pere Croft (Gt. Dalby), *Pesecroft'* (Muston); with structures indicating location, e.g. Church Croft (Burton Lazars), *le foldecroft'* (Wycomb/Chadwell), *milnecroft* (Bottesford); with an ecclesiastical specific, e.g. *Priourscroft* (Melton Mowbray), *Prystcroft'* (Muston); with an adj. of size or shape, e.g. *Long(e)croft* (Belvoir, Easthorpe, Stathern), *schortecroft'* (Muston), Little Croft (Coston), Small Croft (Gt. Dalby); with an indicator of direction, e.g. *le Northcrouft* (Burrough on the Hill), *Southcroftes* (Belvoir), West Croft (Muston, Somerby). Occasionally as a simplex, e.g. (The) Croft (Gt. Dalby, Eastwell, Scalford), *croft* (Saltby).
croked ME, adj., 'crooked, twisted'. *the Crooked furlong* (f.n. Branston).
crop(p) OE, 'the sprout or top of a plant, a bunch of blooms, a cluster of berries'; also 'a swelling, a mound, a hill'. ?Crop of Leys (f.n. Edmondthorpe).
cros late OE, ME, 'a cross'; difficult to distinguish from **cross** *infra* when acting as a qualifier. *Ancell Crosse* (Well, Burton Lazars), *the Corn Cross, the Hye Crosse, the Sage Crosse, Shepe Cross* (Melton Mowbray), *le Cros* (Eaton), *at the Crose* (f.n. Eaton), *le Crosse in the More* (Burrough on the Hill), *Crosse ford* (f.n. Burrough on the Hill), *Crosse hill'* (f.n. Plungar), *Crosse pinnggle* (Pingle, f.n. Wycomb/Chadwell), *Dannycrosse* (Wymondham), *hornwell crosse* (Waltham on the Wolds), *stumpcrosse* (Scalford), *Twocrosseplace* (Buckminster), *Wheytcross* (Muston), *white cross* (Knipton), *le Wite Cros* (Burton Lazars), *the Wooden Crosse* (Coston). The common *Cross(e)gate* (as in Lt. Dalby, Eaton, Plungar, Scalford) may contain **cros** or **cross**.
cross ME, adj., 'athwart, lying across, crosswise'. Freq. in f.ns., e.g. *Crosfurlong'* (Bottesford, Eaton), *(the) Cross(e) furlong(e)* (Lt. Dalby, Harby, Saltby, Wycomb/Chadwell); *Crosse gate furlonge* (Wyfordby), *the crosse greene gate* (Freeby); *the Crose Leas* (Saxby), *Crosslayes* (Sproxton); *Crosthorn* (Harby); Cross Wong (Somerby), *Crosse wonge* (Burton Lazars), *the Cross Wongs* (Sproxton), *Kettleby Crosse Wong, Thorpe Crosse Wong* (Melton Mowbray), *v.* **cros**.
crowne eModE, 'a rounded summit'. ?*Crown Point* (Blue Point, Wymondham).
crumb OE, adj., 'crooked, twisted'. *crunbedale* (f.n. Burton Lazars).

*crymel OE, 'a small piece of land'. *Crunbull'* (f.n. Bottesford).

cū OE, 'a cow'. Common in f.ns.: *Cooslades* (Bottesford), *the cougate* (Stathern), Cow Cl (Scalford), *Coweclose* (Croxton Kerrial), *Cowdale* (Saxby), *(the) Cow Dam(e)s* (Gt. Dalby, Saxby, Wyfordby), *the Cowdam hollow* (Saltby), *Cowedoles* (Bottesford), *Cowe Feilde* (Pickwell), *Cowe paster* (Pasture Lane, Stathern), *the Cowpen hill* (Wyfordby), *the Cow pole* (Saxby).

cuccu ME, 'the cuckoo'. Cuckoo Hill.

cukewald ME, 'a cuckold'. *Cukewoldheuedland* (f.n. Muston).

cumb OE, 'a valley, a short, broad valley with three steeply rising sides'. Combs Plantation. ?*Coms or Coms Wong* (f.n. Sproxton), *the Coomes* (f.n. Somerby), *the Cowmes* (f.n. Knipton), *Cumbe* (f.n. Burrough on the Hill), *le holucoumbe* (f.n. Wycomb/Chadwell), *littelcome, westcombe* (f.ns. Croxton Kerrial).

cumber ME, 'an encumbrance'; prob. used of ground encumbered with rocks, stumps etc. ?Cumberland Spinney.

cursed ME, 'accursed, execrable'. *Curstdole* (f.n. Ab Kettleby).

cū-sloppe OE, 'the cowslip', the wild flower *Primula veris*. ?Cowslip (f.n. Wymondham), *Cowslophyll'* (f.n. Bottesford).

cut ME, 'a lot'; in f.ns., poss. used of common land, the shares in which were assigned by lot. The Cuts (f.n. Stathern), *Father ~* (sic), *Hither Cutt* (f.ns. Garthorpe), *Shortcuttes* (f.n. Branston, Ab Kettleby).

*cwabba OE, 'a marsh, a bog'. *the Quobs* (f.n. Nether Broughton).

cwēn OE, 'a queen'. ?Queens Dales (f.n. Waltham on the Wolds).

cwene OE, 'a woman'. ?Queens Dales (f.n. Waltham on the Wolds), ?*quenepittes* (f.n. Croxton Kerrial).

cweorn OE, 'a quern, a hand-mill'. ?*quenepittes* (f.n. Croxton Kerrial).

cyln OE (Angl), 'a kiln, a furnace for baking or burning'. The Kiln Close. ?*Kilmecroft* (f.n. Croxton Kerrial), *the kiln bolk* (f.n. Branston), the Kilne Cl (f.n. Sproxton), *the Kilnes* (f.n. Somerby), *Kilnewellehil* (f.n. Wycomb/Chadwell), ?*Kinwell feild* (f.n. Redmile), *the Kylne Close* (f.n. Wyfordby).

cȳta OE (Angl), 'a kite'. Kyte Hill.

dāl OE, **dole** ME, 'a share, a portion; a share in the common field'. Freq. in f.ns.: prefixed by a pers.n., surn. or el. indicating rank/occupation, e.g. *Folker Dole* (Burton Lazars), *Typold doles* (Bottesford); *abbot dole* (Wyfordby), *Erlesdole* (Leesthorpe), *Smyth doles* (Bottesford); by an el. indicating the nature of possession, e.g. *the Parteable dole* (Knipton), *Penidolis* (Thorpe Arnold); by an el. identifying natural or cultivated flora, e.g. *brakendole, whinydole* (Knipton), *Willow Doles* (Pickwell), *le Hider bendolis* (Thorpe Arnold); by an el. describing the nature of the soil, e.g. *miery doles* (Branston), *Soure Dole* (Burton Lazars). Recurring are instances of *Longdole(s)* (Bottesford, Knipton), *long(e) dooles* (Branston, Muston, Somerby) and *(le) foredole* (Leesthorpe, Wycomb/Chadwell), *Fordoles* (Wymondham), *Toftes fordoles* (Croxton Kerrial).

dalr ON, 'a valley'; in later spellings, very difficult to distinguish from **deill**, 'a share, a portion of land'. Great Dalby, Little Dalby, Old Dalby, Debdale Fm, Debdale Hill, Debdale Lodge, Debdale Spinney, Middlesdale. Very freq. in f.ns., of which some of the principal types are: prefixed by a major p.n., e.g. *Colstundale* (Long Clawson), *Mustundale* (Bottesford), *Wiverby dale* (Freeby),

Wykeham dale (Goadby Marwood), or by a minor p.n., e.g. *biscopewelledale*, *radiebidale* (Croxton Kerrial), *Thorpdale* (Knipton); compounded with an el. indicating wild flora, e.g. *brakendale, Lingdale* (Croxton Kerrial), Ling Dale (Eastwell); or wild fauna, e.g. Crown Dale (Gt. Dalby), Foxie Dale (Eastwell); or agricultural buildings, e.g. Chippendale (Normanton), *Stedfold Dale* (Nether Broughton). The el. often appears as a simplex, e.g. *the Dale* (Ab Kettleby), *Aboue the Dale* (Gt. Dalby), or with a suffixed el. describing a land unit, e.g. Dale Cl (Bottesford), Dale Fd (Barkestone, Goadby Marwood, Normanton, Plungar), Dale Paddock (Gt. Dalby) and earlier *Daleacre* (Burton Lazars), *Dalewang* (Old Dalby). Debdale/Deepdale, with various spellings, occurs in f.ns. in Bottesford, Burrough on the Hill, Gt. Dalby, Eaton, Knipton and Waltham on the Wolds, as well as in the minor names listed above.

damesene ME, 'the damson-tree'. *Damesyngdale* (f.n. Thorpe Arnold), *Daymesonecroft* (f.n. Melton Mowbray).

damme ME, 'a dam', usually created either for use at mills or for the watering of farm livestock. *attedam* (f.n. Wycomb/Chadwell), *the Cowdames* (f.n. Saxby, Wyfordby), *the Cowdam hollow* (f.n. Saltby), Cow Dam Mdw (f.n. Thorpe Arnold), *Cowdams* (f.n. Gt. Dalby), the Cross Dam (f.n. Long Clawson), Dam Dyke (f.n. Hose), ?Damends (f.n. Burton Lazars), Dam Fd (f.n. Barkestone), *Damforlong, Mylne Dame* (f.ns. Burton Lazars), *Dockedam, Hildindam, Seggedam* (f.ns. Eaton), Horse Dam (f.n. Waltham on the Wolds), *the horsedames, Shippdammes* (f.ns. Croxton Kerrial), Mill Dam Cl (f.n. Pickwell), *the mill dame* (f.n. Scalford), *le milnedam* (f.n. Nether Broughton), *the neatdames* (f.n. Saxby), *Neate dammes* (f.n. Knipton), ?*Paddams* (f.n. Eastwell), Twival Dam (f.n. Somerby).

*damming ME, 'a dam'. ?Damends (f.n. Burton Lazars).

dauncing ME, vbl.sb., 'dancing'. *Danceing Leys* (f.n. Somerby).

daw(e) ME, 'a jackdaw'. ?*Dawbalke* (f.n. Croxton Kerrial).

dēad OE, adj., 'dead'; usually in p.ns. in reference to a site of violent death or to the discovery of human bones. Deadhill Sike (f.n. Stathern), *Deadin* (f.n. Sproxton), Dead Moor Leys (f.n. Wymondham), *deadmore* (f.n. Waltham on the Wolds), Dead Wife (f.n. Gt. Dalby), *Dedborow Layes* (f.n. Wymondham), *le dede hevidland* (f.n. Harby), *Dede lane* (Melton Mowbray), *Dedwong* (f.n. Bottesford, Harby).

decoy ModE, 'a decoy, a pond into which wild fowl are lured for capture'. Decoy Cottage.

dede-man ME, 'a dead man, a corpse'. *Deadman leyes* (f.n. Stonesby), *Deadmans graue* (f.n. Pickwell), Deadmans Grave (f.n. Thorpe Arnold).

deill ON, 'a share, a portion of land'; in later spellings, difficult to distinguish from **dalr** 'a valley', but pl. forms with *-dales* are sometimes indicators of *deill*. Very freq. in f.ns.: compounded with a pers.n., e.g. *Sawsdall* (Waltham on the Wolds), *scalderdeyles* (Burton Lazars), *Scroutesdeil* (Sewstern); or with a surn., e.g. *Coleuyldeyle* (Normanton), *Katerinedal* (Wymondham), *Spilmandail* (Stonesby); or with an el. indicating a crop, e.g. *Bendales* (Gt. Dalby), *Peesdal* (Knipton) or wild flora, e.g. *Thacdeil* (Muston), *Thornedeil* (Stathern); or with an el. specifying the nature of the land, e.g. *Clendalls* (Sproxton), *Flatdayle, solledeyle* (Muston), *harddeyles* (Bottesford); or shape or size, e.g. *crunbedale* (Burton

Lazars), *Wrongdeyl* (Barkestone), *longedeyl(e)* (Bottesford, Sewstern), *Mickilldales* (Harby), *scamdeyll* (Bottesford); or direction, e.g. *North Daile* (Saxby), *le suthdeil* (Croxton Kerrial); or location particularized by an earlier p.n., e.g. *Horsladedale* (Eaton), *Shittopdale, Spinckweldayl* (Croxton Kerrial). The nature of tenancy is sometimes suggested, e.g. *Mansdales* (Saxby), *le Smithiedeil* (Bottesford).

(ge)delf OE, 'a digging, a pit, a quarry', v. **stān-(ge)delf**. *Stannyngdelf* (f.n. Eastwell).

demeyn OFr, ME, 'demesne'. *lez demesne lands* (f.n. Old Dalby).

denu OE, 'a valley'. Handen (f.n. Pickwell), ?*Haselden Syke, Norden*, ?Ogden (f.ns. Burrough on the Hill), ?Mickledine Cl (f.n. Lt. Dalby).

dēop OE, **djúpr** ON, adj., 'deep'. Debdale Fm, Debdale Hill, Debdale Lodge (Lt. Dalby, Scalford), Debdale Spinney, Debdales. Debdale (Fd) (f.ns. Burrough on the Hill, Knipton), Debdales (f.n. Bottesford), Deepdale (f.n. Gt. Dalby, Waltham on the Wolds), *De(e)pedale* (f.n. Leesthorpe, Pickwell), *Depedalebrode* (f.n. Eaton), *Depslade* (f.n. Harston).

dēor OE, 'an animal, a beast', **der** ME, 'an animal'. *derholm* (f.n. Redmile).

dīc OE, 'a ditch'. *the Beckes ditch, stonnie becke ditch* (f.ns. Stathern), *Branston Dyche, long dytche* (f.ns. Knipton), *Gerstaldyche, Landyche* (f.ns. Muston), *longe ditche, Short Ditch Furlong* (f.n. Scalford), *the medow dyche* (The Meadows, f.n. Bottesford), *thirndich* (the Thurn, f.n. Harston), *Thorpe ditch* (f.n. Melton Mowbray).

dík ON, 'a ditch'; the el. varies with OE **dīc** in some f.ns. Dam Dyke, Heckadeck Lane, Landyke Lane. The Black Dike (f.n. Melton Mowbray), Bullys Dyke (f.n. Hose), *Croxtondikes, longedyke* (f.ns. Knipton), *the Dike* (f.n. Harston, Ab Kettleby), *Gerstaldyk'*, Little Land Dyke, *neudik'* (f.ns. Muston), *the great mill dike* (f.n. Branston), *hallewongedyke, medowdyke* (f.ns. Bottesford), Land dike Cl, *Laund Dike, Old dike* (f.ns. Holwell), *potters dike* (f.n. Ab Kettleby), *Scales dicke* (f.n. Normanton), *Thredikes* (f.n. Croxton Kerrial). Note also *the towne dyke*, presum. the defensive ditch of Melton Mowbray.

docce OE, 'a dock' (the plant); poss. also 'a water-lily' when combined with an el. denoting water. *Dockedam* (f.n. Eaton), *the dockes* (f.n. Bottesford), *Dockey Wonge* (f.n. Nether Broughton), *Dowkey wong* (f.n. Freeby).

dodde ME, 'the rounded summit of a hill'. Doddings (f.n. Coston), ?*Doddisholm* (f.n. Wycomb/Chadwell).

dogge ME, 'a dog'. Dog Lane.

dong-hyll ME, 'a heap of dung or refuse'. *Dunghill Fur'* (f.n. Gt. Dalby).

dove-cot(e) ME, 'a dove-cote'. Dovecoat Ho., Dovecot Nook Hill. *the doucoate cloasse* (f.n. Croxton Kerrial), *the Doue Coate & orchard* (f.n. Freeby), *Douecote Close, Douecote wonge* (f.ns. Wyfordby), Dovecot Cl (f.n. Muston), *Dovecote* (f.n. Edmondthorpe), Dovecote Cl (f.n. Eastwell, Sewstern), Dovecote Fd (f.n. Waltham on the Wolds).

dove-house eModE, 'a dove-cote'. *the Douehouse* (f.n. Wymondham), *the Dove-house close* (f.n. Croxton Kerrial).

dowarie ME, 'a dowry'. Dowry Cottage.

dowe ME, 'a soft, pasty mess'. *Dow but, long dowe* (f.ns. Freeby).

drabbe eModE, '?mire'. The Drabble (f.n. Stathern).

dræg OE (Angl), 'a drag; a dray'. ?*Draycarts* Mdw (f.n. Goadby Marwood), (The) Draycott (f.ns. Buckminster, Freeby).

drāf OE, 'a herd, a drove; a road on which cattle are driven'. Draw Rail (f.n. Burton Lazars), The Drove (f.n. Redmile).

drag ON, 'a gentle slope; a portage'. *longe draughtes* (f.n. Stapleford).

drain eModE, 'a channel for carrying off water'. Birtle Beck Drain, Cowl Close ~, Cross Dam ~, Gravel Pit ~, Heron ~, the Hooks ~ Lintop ~, Littledale ~, Long Sike ~, Saltwell ~, Slideborough Sike ~, Swallows Drain (f.ns. Long Clawson), Cadowbanks drain, *Winterbeck drain* (f.ns. Bottesford).

dreng ME, 'a man holding land by a particular form of free tenure combining service, money payments and military duty' (*v.* OED *s.v.*). ?*Drinchehull* (f.n. Wymondham).

drift ModE, 'a track along which cattle are driven'. The Drift (Burton Lazars, Sewstern, Sproxton, Stonesby), Drift Hill (Redmile, Wymondham), Edmondthorpe Drift. *the common drifte* (Wyfordby), the Drift (Croxton Kerrial), *the drifte* (Saxby), Drift Ford (f.n. Stathern), *Drifte hill* (f.n. Lt. Dalby), The Drift Way (Sysonby), Far, Middle Drift (f.ns. Harston), *the neatdrifte* (Saxby), *the Neate Drift* (Melton Mowbray).

drit OE, 'dirt'. *le Dritakir* (f.n. Barkestone).

dropi ON, 'a drop, a drip, that which drips'. Dropwell Hill (f.n. Harston).

dryfer ME, 'one who drives a herd of cattle'. ?*Drivers Busk* (f.n. Scalford).

drȳge OE, adj., 'dry, dried up; well-drained'. *Drie Lees* (f.n. Bescaby), Dry Cl (f.n. Edmondthorpe), *Dry Esse* (f.n. Pickwell), *Dryehill Fur'* (f.n. Stonesby), Dry Hills (f.n. Somerby), *Dry holme* (f.n. Freeby), *Dry Lane* (Thorpe Arnold), *Dry Leys* (f.n. Stathern), *Drywell* (f.n. Saltby), Dry Woulds (f.n. Eastwell).

duble ME, adj., 'double'. Double Dykes (f.n. Somerby), Far, Near Double Pool Cl (f.ns. Wartnaby).

dūce OE, 'a duck'. *the Ducks Nest* (f.n. Bottesford).

dūfe OE, **dúfa** ON, 'a dove'; prob. also 'a pigeon'. *douewell* (f.n. Croxton Kerrial), Dove Hills (f.n. Goadby Marwood), Dove Hole Cl (f.n. Burrough on the Hill), ?*Dovins*, ?*Duuecroft* (f.ns. Saxby), *Duuepittis* (f.n. Bottesford).

dūn OE, 'a tract of hill-country, an upland expanse; upland pasture'. *schiredun* (f.n. Croxton Kerrial), *Schouedon'* (f.n. Branston).

dūne OE, adv., 'down'; used elliptically of 'a place below, a place lower down (at a lower level) than another'. *la Dounhalle* (Saltby).

duru OE, 'a door, a gate, a gap'. The Dozzels (f.n. Wycomb/Chadwell), Duzzle (f.n. Scalford), *Milldore Lees* (f.n. Branston), *the milne doare* (f.n. Croxton Kerrial).

***dyfe** OE, prob. 'a hollow'. *Diuekir* (f.n. Thorpe Arnold).

dyrty eModE, adj., 'dirty'. *durtypits* (f.n. Croxton Kerrial).

ēa OE, 'a river, a stream'. *Eforlong'* (f.n. Thorpe Arnold), *Ellondes* (f.n. Brentingby).

eare eModE, 'a piece of arable tilth'. *Narrow eares* (f.n. Sproxton).

earm OE, adj., 'wretched, poor'. *Armdale* (f.n. Burrough on the Hill).

ears OE, 'a buttock; a rounded hill'. *Bare Arse* (f.n. Burrough on the Hill), *Catsars* (f.n. Ab Kettleby), *Childs Arse* (f.n. Burton Lazars), *Windisers* (f.n. Thorpe Arnold).

ēast OE, adj., 'east, eastern'. Easthorpe, Eastwell. *the Easte Feilde* (f.n. Nether Broughton, Harston), *le est Broke* (Lt. Dalby), *le Estelane* (Somerby), *(le)*

Estfurlong(e) (f.ns. Knipton, Thorpe Arnold), *Estheng'* (f.n. Ab Kettleby), *estsandes* (Sands Pasture, f.n. Bottesford), *þe est syd etty* (Eady Fm, Bottesford).

eastermost eModE, adj., 'most easterly, situated farthest to the east'. *the Easter-most long Moore* (f.n. Coston).

ēasterra OE, comp.adj., 'more eastern'. *Estirmelham* (Mellams, f.n. Thorpe Arnold), *estrecrowelle* (f.n. Croxton Kerrial).

eating ModE, vbl.sb., 'the action of taking food'; in f.ns., presum. referring to grass available only for grazing and not for a hay crop. *Eating Cl* (f.n. Gt. Dalby).

ecg OE, 'an edge; the edge of a hill, an escarpment'. *upon the Edge* (f.n. Waltham on the Wolds), ?*Edgecourt alias Edgcroft* (f.n. Buckminster), *Small hill Edge or Smallage* (f.n. Burton Lazars).

edisc OE, 'an enclosure, an enclosed park', **eddish** ModEdial., 'aftermath, stubble'. *Eddish Hill* (f.n. Wymondham), *edisch* (f.n. Muston), *The First Eddish* (f.n. Gt. Dalby), *walsemoresedis* (f.n. Burton Lazars).

ēg OE (Angl), 'an island, a piece of raised ground in wet country, land partly surrounded by water'. *Eaton*, ?*Sauvey Castle*. ?*Odeney feild* (f.n. Buckminster).

egle OFr, ME, 'an eagle'. ?*Eagleswood* (Burton Lazars).

ellern OE, 'an elder-tree'. *at the Eldar Stump* (f.n. Saltby), *Elder Dale* (f.n. Buckminster), *Elder Holme* (f.n. Burrough on the Hill), *Eldern Stump* (f.n. Stonesby), *Elder tree bolk* (f.n. Branston), *Elder Stub Fur'* (f.n. Gt. Dalby), *Eldrens* (f.n. Croxton Kerrial), *Erlunstubbe* (f.n. Thorpe Arnold).

elm OE, 'an elm-tree'. ?*Almescroft(e)* (f.n. Melton Mowbray), Elm Cl, Elm Leys (f.ns. Burrough on the Hill).

elren OE, adj., 'overgrown with or near to alder-trees'. *Elrendalforlang'* (f.n. Sewstern).

enclosure ModE, 'land surrounded by a fence or marked off by a boundary', with particular reference to the enclosing of common land following an Enclosure Act. *the East Enclosure, the New Enclosure, the Old Enclosure, the Second Enclosure* (f.ns. Garthorpe).

ende OE, **endi** ON, 'the end of something', 'the end of an estate, a district or quarter of a village or town', *v.* **lane-ende**. Burton End, East End, Nether End, Thorpe End, Upper End, West End. Freq. in f.ns., e.g. *Braytheynghend'* (Normanton), *the Church Land end, Dikes-End, the Redland End, the Steeple end* (Ab Kettleby), *Thornende* (Eaton); recurring in the compound *town(s)end* (with various spellings in Burrough on the Hill, Gt. Dalby, Easthorpe, Eastwell, Edmondthorpe, Freeby, Harby, Harston, Ab Kettleby, Pickwell, Saltby, Wartnaby, Wycomb/Chadwell, Wyfordby, Wymondham).

eng ON, 'a meadow, a pasture'. Freq. in f.ns.: with a pers.n., e.g. *Coleshenge* (Burton Lazars), *Douesing* (Old Dalby), *Guneheng* (Wymondham); with an el. indicating shape or size, e.g. *Braytheynghend'* (Normanton), The Broadings, *Lytlinges* (Melton Mowbray), *Mikelhenge* (Barkestone), *Smaleeng* (Bottesford); with a directional adj., e.g. *Estheng'* (Ab Kettleby), *Southynges* (Belvoir), *le Westheynges* (Muston). Recurring is prefixed *sléttr* 'level' as in Slatings (Waltham on the Wolds), *Sletheng* (Bescaby), *Sletyng* (Old Dalby), *Sleythenges* (Burton Lazars), Slidings (Burrough on the Hill). As a first el., e.g. *Engcroft* (Wyfordby), *Enggate* (Redmile), *Enghirst, Engwong'* (Muston).

eorl OE, 'a nobleman', late OE, 'a high-ranking officer of state'; ME, 'a count, an earl'. *Erlesthorpe* (an alternative style for Thorpe Arnold). *the Earles land* (f.n. Burton Lazars, Freeby), *Erlesdole* (f.n. Leesthorpe), *herle acres* (f.n. Bottesford), *the land of the Earle of Warwick* (f.n. Melton Mowbray), *the long headland of thearle of Ruttlande* (f.n. Stathern), *thearle of Rutland his great lande* (f.n. Redmile), *thearles headland* (f.n. Normanton), *therles Newe Close* (f.n. Barkestone).

eorð-burh OE, 'an earthwork; a fortification built of earth'. Burrough on the Hill, ?Arbour.

eorðe OE, 'earth, soil, ground, a plot of ground'; later also 'an animal lair in the earth'. Freeby Fox Earth, Redearth Fm. *Nearyearthe* (f.n. Scalford), White Earth (f.n. Edmondthorpe), *White Earth arrable Furlonge* (f.n. Lt. Dalby), *Wyterthe* (f.n. Eaton). In Framland Hundred, commonly prefixed by OE *rēad* 'red' (f.n. with various spellings in Bottesford, Buckminster, Edmondthorpe, Goadby Marwood, Ab Kettleby, Pickwell, Sewstern, Somerby, Stonesby, Waltham on the Wolds, Wartnaby, Wymondham).

eowestre OE, 'a sheep-fold'. *Oyster leyes* (f.n. Burrough on the Hill).

eowu OE, 'a ewe'. Ewe Cl (f.n. Freeby, Somerby), *Mr Welby's Ewe Grounds* (Ewe Fd, f.n. Holwell).

erber OFr, ME, 'a grass-covered piece of ground, a garden, an orchard'. ?Arbour. Pirkin Arbor (f.n. Old Dalby).

ermitage OFr, ME, **hermitage** ME, 'a hermitage'. *The hermitage field* (f.n. Redmile).

ete OE, 'grazing, pasture'. Eady Fm.

fæs OE, 'the fringe of a garment'; poss. used topographically of 'the border or edge of something'. Fasewell Fd (f.n. Wartnaby).

fætt OE, adj., 'fat, rich'. *fattbutts* (f.n. Old Dalby), *fattebenelond'* (f.n. Redmile), *Fattemold'* (f.n. Thorpe Arnold), *Fattland* (f.n. Burton Lazars).

fald OE, 'a fold, a small enclosure for animals'. *the Fold Bridge* (Easthorpe), *le foldecroft*, *Netherfold Croft* (f.ns. Wycomb/Chadwell), Fold furlong (f.n. Stathern), Fold Yard (f.n. Goadby Marwood), *Fould Sick* (f.n. Scalford), Straight Fold (f.n. Muston).

*falding OE, 'the action of folding animals'. the Folding Dykes (f.n. Saltby).

falg, falh OE (Angl), 'land broken up for cultivation, ploughed land'; later 'ploughed land left uncultivated for a year, fallow land'. *the fallowes*, Fallow Woulds (f.ns. Eastwell), *Fallow holmes* (f.n. Burrough on the Hill).

*(ge)fall OE (Angl), 'a falling, a place where something falls', whence 'a felling of trees, a clearing'. Hill Falls (f.n. Somerby).

farther ModE, adj., 'farther off'. *farder damins* (f.n. Burton Lazars).

fattening ModE, vbl.sb., 'the process of making fat'. ?Fat-nick (f.n. Gt. Dalby), The Fatnings (f.n. Buckminster).

fealu OE, adj., 'fallow, pale-brown or reddish yellow'. Fallow Lees (f.n. Lt. Dalby).

fearn OE, 'a fern; ferns; a ferny place'. *Furnesty* (f.n. Burton Lazars).

feather-bed ModE, sb., adj., 'a feather-bed; something soft and yielding; a peat-bog or spongy ground'. Featherbed Nook (f.n. Burrough on the Hill), *Fetherbed(e)s* (f.n. Pickwell, Somerby).

feeding ModEdial., vbl.sb., 'grazing ground, pasturage'. Feeding Cl (f.n. Burton Lazars).

feire OFr, ME, 'a fair; a gathering of merchants'. Fair Fd, Neat Fair (f.ns. Waltham on the Wolds).

feld OE, 'open country', **feld(e)** ME, 'land for pasture or cultivation; a common or great field of a township', **field** ModE, 'an enclosed or fenced-in plot of land'. Clayfield Fm, Highfields Spinney, Landfield Spinney, Oldfields Lodge, Springfield Fm. Of the Framland Hundred's 53 townships, 27 have their great fields designated by combinations of the simple directional adjectives *north*, *south*, *east*, *west*, and of these Eaton, Harby, Redmile, Somerby, Stathern, Thorpe Arnold and Wycomb/Chadwell have the medieval Latin spellings recorded. Otherwise, the great fields were named from topographical features, e.g. *Akarill feilde*, *Slyborowe Feild* (Long Clawson), *Coppethorne Feilde*, *Wheathill Feilde* (Knipton), *Hornesfeild*, *Wynterwelle feild* (Buckminster); in this category, watercourses are prominent, e.g. *the Beck feild* (Harby), *Moorebecke feilde* (Scalford), *Sidebroke feild* (Muston), as are marshlands, e.g. *the Mares Feilde* (Stapleford), the Marr Fd (Somerby), *(the) Marshe Feild(e)* (Knipton, Sproxton). Soil type may be indicated, e.g. *the Clay feilde* (with various spellings in Bottesford, Eastwell, Goadby Marwood, Ab Kettleby, Scalford), the Red Earth Fd (Ab Kettleby, Wartnaby); or flora, e.g. *the fogge felde* (Eye Kettleby), *the Heays field* (Stathern), *the Ling Field* (Waltham on the Wolds), Rice ~, Ryce Fd (Somerby, Pickwell). Major buildings are often specified, e.g. *Borokyrkfeld* (Wymondham), *Chirchefeld* (Muston), *le kyrkefeld* (Plungar), *the milne feild* (with various spellings in Branston, Buckminster, Burrough on the Hill, Gt. Dalby, Lt. Dalby, Redmile, Saltby, Stonesby), *Winmylne feild* (Burton Lazars), as are roads to neighbouring townships, e.g. *Goadby Gate Feild* (Wycomb/ Chadwell), *Grantham gate Feilde*, *Saltbygate Feilde* (Croxton Kerrial), Waltham Gate Fd (Stonesby). Three great fields were the norm for each township in the medieval period, hence the common *middle* field recorded in Barkestone, Easthorpe, Edmondthorpe, Garthorpe, Saltby, Sproxton and Wyfordby. Changes in the names of a township's great fields may or may not indicate the reorganization of the township's arable, but such changes of names or alternative names are evidenced in Barkestone, Harby, Hose, Plungar, Redmile, Somerby, Stathern, Thorpe Arnold and Wycomb/Chadwell.

fenn OE, 'a fen, a marsh, marshland; mud, mire'. *Fencroftes* (f.n. Stathern), Fenn Cl (f.n. Gt. Dalby), *Fenn Seike* (f.n. Melton Mowbray), *quakefen* (f.n. Burton Lazars), *Wauefenetunge*, *Wauefenhull* (f.ns. Burrough on the Hill).

feor OE, **fur(re)** ME, **fur** ModEdial., **far** ModE, adj., 'far, distant'. *Farbuttes*, *Farr Pingle* (f.ns. Scalford), *Farhill*, Farr Caudhill (f.ns. Croxton Kerrial), *Farr Close* (f.n. Stonesby), *the farr Durdale Hill* (Duzzle, f.n. Scalford), *Farredoles* (f.n. Eastwell), *the farre gate haides* (f.n. Burton Lazars), *Farr hill* (f.n. Stathern), Far Woulds (f.n. Wartnaby), *Furborough Syke* (f.n. Burton Lazars), *Furbushe Furlonge* (f.n. Lt. Dalby).

feorðung, feorðing OE, 'a fourth part, a quarter'; in later f.ns. it may denote either a measure of land or a rental of a farthing. *the farthing balke* (f.n. Wyfordby).

ferd OE (Angl), 'an army'. *le Ferdgate* (Harby).

ferme OFr, ME, 'rent', eModE, 'land held on lease, a farm, an agricultural tenement'. Common in modern minor p.ns. In earlier instances, usually prefixed by a surn., e.g. *Allens Farme, Brigges Farme* (Burrough on the Hill), *Kelhams Farm, Spreckley's Farm* (Stapleford); or with pers.n. plus surn., e.g. *Frances Lomleys Farme* (Gt. Dalby), *John Waytes farme* (Burton Lazars). Farm Cl (f.n. Wyfordby), *Longfarme* (f.n. Eastwell).

fīf OE, num., 'five'. *Fifefurlong'* (f.n. Eaton), *fifurlang, Fyve leyes* (f.ns. Wymondham), *the five roodes* (f.n. Saltby), *le fyuefurlong* (f.n. Barkestone).

fiftēne OE, num., 'fifteen'. *Fifteneleyes* (f.n. Thorpe Arnold).

filands ModEdial., 'tracts of unenclosed arable, open selions'; prob. from OE (ge)*filde* 'a plain' or OE *feld* 'open country' and *land*, cf. ModE *field-land* (OED) 'level, unenclosed land'. ?Filling's Fd (f.n. Waltham on the Wolds).

fille OE, 'thyme' or some such plant, (*v.* OED *s.v.* fill). ?Filling's Fd (f.n. Waltham on the Wolds).

fin ME, adj., 'fine'. Fine Moor (f.n. Wymondham).

firr ME, 'a fir-tree'. Fir Holt (f.n. Belvoir).

fisc OE, 'a fish'. Fishpond Cl (f.n. Wartnaby), the Fish Pool Cl (f.n. Sproxton).

fit ON, 'grassland on the banks of a stream'. *fitlande sicke* (f.n. Ab Kettleby).

fjǫl ON, 'a board, a plank'. *felbrygreins* (f.n. Bottesford).

flask ODan, 'a swamp, swampy grassland', **flasshe** ME, 'a swamp'. Flash Fd, ?Flaxleys Cl (f.ns. Nether Broughton), ?*Flaxwell*, ?*Short Flax Leyes* (f.ns. Stonesby).

flat ON, 'a piece of flat, level ground'. Cumberland Flatt (f.n. Brentingby), the Flat (f.n. Pickwell), *Flatwellis* (f.n. Harby), *Haydayll flatte* (f.n. Wycomb/Chadwell), Peake's Flats (f.n. Burrough on the Hill), The Top March Flat (f.n. Gt. Dalby).

flatr ON, adj., 'flat, level'. Flat Cl (f.ns. Holwell, Muston), *Flatdayle* (f.n. Muston), *Flatland* (f.n. Freeby), (The) Flat Mdw (f.ns. Gt. Dalby, Edmondthorpe), ?Flatten Cl (f.n. Harston), *Flatte peece* (f.n. Burrough on the Hill).

fleax OE, **flax** ME, 'flax'. Fairly freq. in f.ns.: *the flaxe pittes* (Scalford), Flaxhill (Stathern), *Flaxlandes* (with various spellings in Burrough on the Hill, Burton Lazars, Melton Mowbray, Plungar, Redmile, Saxby, Sewstern, Somerby, Stonesby), Flaxland Cl, ?Flaxleys Cl (Nether Broughton), ?*Flaxwell*, ?*Short Flax Leyes* (Stonesby).

flegge, flagge ME, 'the flag-iris; a reed or rush; a place where reeds grow'. *le flagforlong'* (f.n. Stathern), *Fleggelonge* (f.n. Burton Lazars).

Fleming AN, 'a Fleming, a native of Flanders'. ?*Flemynghull* (f.n. Sewstern).

flint OE, 'flint'. Flint, Flint hill (f.ns. Waltham on the Wolds), *flynting meddowe* (f.n. Thorpe Arnold).

flinti ME, adj., 'flinty, full of flint stones'. Flinty Gate (Long Clawson), *Flyntilandes* (f.n. Old Dalby).

(**ge**)**flit** OE, 'strife, dispute', used in p.ns. of land in dispute. *flitlandis* (f.n. Harby).

flod-gate ME, 'a flood-gate, a sluice'. *the Flood-gate* (Mill Bank, f.n. Coston).

fogge ME, 'aftermath, the long grass left standing during the winter'. *Fogclose* (f.n. Bescaby), *the fogge felde* (f.n. Eye Kettleby).

fola OE, **foli** ON, 'a foal'. *Foale Forth* (f.n. Croxton Kerrial).

foot-road ModE, 'a footpath'. Barnston Foot Rd, Belvoir ~ ~, Grantham ~ ~, Harby ~ ~, Melton ~ ~, Plungar ~ ~, Redmile Foot Rd (Stathern), Beskabby Foot Rd, Coston ~ ~, Garthorpe ~ ~, Melton ~ ~, New House ~ ~, Waltham Foot Rd (Stonesby), cf. **fote-gate** and **fote-waye** *infra*.

ford OE, 'a ford'. Bottesford, Scalford, Stapleford, Wyfordby. Freq. in f.ns. combined with the name of the stream forded, e.g. Birtlebeck Ford (Long Clawson), *Spinkwell forth* (Croxton Kerrial); with locational prefix, e.g. *Colepitte forthe* (Wycomb/Chadwell), *Marche Forde* (Gt. Dalby), *Speny forthe* (Melton Mowbray), and in this category are those examples combined with a minor agricultural habitation site, e.g. *brodeby forde* (Saltby), *Thorpe Ford* (Gt. Dalby), *thorpforth* (Lt. Dalby); with an el. describing the physical nature of the ford, e.g. *the blinde forth* (Melton Mowbray), *Scaldeford'* (Muston), *le stonforde* (Wycomb/Chadwell). Note *briggeforth* (Burton Lazars) and Stonebridge Ford (Burrough on the Hill) which perh. indicate a ford later replaced by a bridge. Note also the local example of the common Salters Ford (Croxton Kerrial). Spellings in *-forth(e)*, arising from late ME *-rd* > *-rth* in unstressed syllables, which occur only in the Danelaw, may well be due to Scand influence.

fore OE, prep., 'in front of, before'; elliptically '(land, place, thing) in front of, or standing or lying before something'. *le Foredale, Toftes fordoles* (f.ns. Croxton Kerrial), *Fordeyles, Fordoles* (f.ns. Wymondham), *le foredoles* (f.n. Wycomb/Chadwell), *foredoleford* (f.n. Leesthorpe), *forehil* (f.n. Burton Lazars), *forlandis* (f.n. Harby), *the foremedowes* (f.n. Bottesford), *the foreswaiths* (f.n. Saxby), *Forewonge* (f.n. Belvoir), *the foreyarde* (f.n. Long Clawson).

forst OE, 'frost'. ?*Frostlandes* (f.n. Pickwell).

***foss**[1] OE, **fosse** ME, 'a ditch, an artificially-made water-channel'. *Fosewell Syke* (f.n. Edmondthorpe).

fossile eModE, 'a fossil'; in early use, 'any rock, mineral or mineral substance dug out of the earth'. Fuzlehole (f.n. Nether Broughton).

fōt OE, **fótr** ON, 'a foot; the foot of something; the bottom of a hill'. The Foot Cl (f.n. Gt. Dalby).

fote-gate ModEdial., 'a footpath'. *Orston foote gate* (Bottesford), *v.* **foot-road** *supra*.

fote-waye ModE, 'a footpath'. *Orson foot way*, *Redmile Footway* (Bottesford), *v.* **foot-road** *supra*.

fox OE, 'a fox'. Fox Cover (f.n. Coston), Fox Covert (f.n. Holwell), *Foxhou* (f.n. Eaton), Foxie Dale (f.n. Eastwell), *Foxland* (f.n. Gt. Dalby).

fox-hol OE, 'a fox-hole, a fox's earth'. Fox Hole Cl (f.n. Eastwell), Fox Holes (f.n. Holwell), *Foxholes* (f.n. Branston, Harby), *Foxholys* (f.n. Burrough on the Hill).

frehold ME, 'a tenure in absolute possession'; adjectivally, 'held by freehold'. Freehold Ho. *the Freholde* (f.n. Croxton Kerrial).

***friðen** OE, adj., 'protected; fenced in'. *fritenwong'* (f.n. Croxton Kerrial).

frogga OE, 'a frog'. Frog Hall Hollow (f.n. Knipton).

froskr ON, 'a frog'. *Froskfourres* (f.n. Muston), ?*Frostlandes* (f.n. Pickwell).

fugol OE, 'a bird'. ?*le Fuleholm* (f.n. Wycomb/Chadwell).

fūl OE, adj., 'foul, filthy, dirty'. *Folwelle*, ?*le Fuleholm* (f.ns. Wycomb/Chadwell), *Fulbeckgate* (Coston), *(the) Fulbeckes* (f.ns. Freeby, Saxby), *Fulewellesike* (f.n. Plungar), Fulleyhill (f.n. Stathern), *Fullilhill* (f.n. Pickwell), *Fulwell hill* (f.n.

Waltham on the Wolds), The Fullwells (f.n. Sproxton), Fulwell (f.n. Buckminster), *Fulwellehill'* (f.n. Knipton).

fulling ModE, vbl.sb., 'the process of cleansing and thickening cloth by washing and beating'. *Fulin Hole* (f.n. Sproxton), *Fulling Pits*, *Fullings* (f.ns. Waltham on the Wolds).

furh OE, 'a furrow, a trench'; in ME also used of 'a piece of arable land'. *Cooke furrowes*, *Crabbesforowes* (f.ns. Bottesford), *Froskfourres*, *holforw*, Running Furrow (f.ns. Muston), *holowforou* (f.n. Burton Lazars), Rushy Furrows (f.n. Somerby), *short furrowes* (f.n. Normanton), *Swarfurowes* (f.n. Redmile), Water Furrows (f.n. Buckminster, Coston), *Waterfurrowes* (f.n. with various spellings in Nether Broughton, Burton Lazars, Edmondthorpe, Harby, Melton Mowbray, Muston, Sewstern, Sproxton, Stapleford, Stonesby, Waltham on the Wolds), *Watriforowis* (f.n. Eaton), *weeteforrowes* (f.n. Ab Kettleby), *Wetfur'* (f.n. Stonesby), *Wet furrowes* (f.n. Coston).

furlang OE, 'the length of a furrow, a furlong, a piece of land the length of a furrow (esp. in the great field)'; in ME 'a division of the great field cultivated as a unit'. Very freq. in f.ns., e.g. *Benhillforlang'*, *borland forlonge*, *Bradebekeforlong*, *Cleforlonge* (Bottesford), *bryggefurlonge*, *gorefurlonge*, *longefurlonge*, *stonfurlonge* (Knipton). Many of the 'field-names' in ME sources are furlong-names.

furðra OE, adj., 'more distant'. *Le Further hedge* (Burton Lazars).

fynel ME, 'fennel'. *Finelwong'* (f.n. Muston).

fyrs OE, 'furze'. ?First Hill. Burley Furze, ?The First Hill (f.ns. Wymondham), The Forcelands (f.n. Gt. Dalby), ?*Fyrborowe Syke* (f.n. Burton Lazars).

*fyrsen OE, adj., 'growing with furze'. *Fressingholme* (f.n. Burton Lazars).

fyrst OE, adj., 'first, chief, principal'. ?First Hill. ?The First Hill (f.n. Wymondham).

gærs OE, 'grass', v. **græs** infra.

gafeluc ME, 'a fork'. *Gafelokessiche* (f.n. Normanton), *Geueloks* (f.n. Bottesford).

gafol¹, **gafel** OE, 'a fork', used topographically of 'a fork in a stream'. ?*on Coldhill gauel* (Coldhill, f.n. Stathern).

gafol² OE, 'rent', later perh. 'rented land'; difficult to distinguish from **gafol¹**. ?*on Coldhill gauel* (Coldhill, f.n. Stathern).

galga OE, **galgi** ON, 'a gallows'. Gallow Hill (f.n. Saxby), *Gally hill* (f.n. Croxton Kerrial).

galg-trēow OE, **gálga-tré** ON, 'a gallows-tree, a gallows'. Gartree Hill. *Galgtregate* (Sewstern), *galowtres* (f.n. Knipton), *le Gautreyhill close* (f.n. Buckminster), ?*Gautry Furlong* (f.n. Eastwell).

galla OE, 'a sore; a wet or barren place in a field'. *Galles* (f.n. Burrough on the Hill), *galles balke* (f.n. Stapleford), The Galls (f.n. Gt. Dalby), ?*Rosgalls* (f.n. Pickwell), Water Gall (f.n. Wartnaby).

gang OE, **gangr** ON, 'a passage, a way, a path, a track'. *Watergongfurlong* (f.n. Normanton).

gap ON, 'a gap, an opening', **gappe** ME, 'an opening in a wall, fence or hillside'. Crown Point Gap (Blue Point), Musson Gap. *Chewegappe*, *Gill gappe* (f.ns. Burton Lazars), *the Milne gappe* (f.n. Goadby Marwood), *the Parsonage gap* (f.n. Nether Broughton), *Sandpitt hill gap* (Sandpit hill, f.n. Stathern), Thistleton Gap Cl (f.n. Edmondthorpe).

gāra OE, 'a gore, a triangular plot of ground, a point of land'. ?Garthorpe, Plungar, Longore Bridge. Freq. in f.ns.: with a directional adj., e.g. *le est gore* (Harby), *Northgore* (Leesthorpe); with an el. or surn. specifying ownership, e.g. *le Priouresgores* (Redmile), *le Templegore* (Melton Mowbray), *Godwifisgores* (Burrough on the Hill); preceded by an earlier minor name indicating location, e.g. *Flaxhulgoris, Myre Field Gores* (Branston), *the swineinge goares* (Scalford); often as a simplex, e.g. *the Gore* (Holwell), *the goores* (with various spellings in Branston, Old Dalby, Saltby, Wycomb/Chadwell); as the specific in a compound, e.g. *Garlands, le Gore hyl* (Branston), *gorefurlonge* (Knipton), *the goare leyes* (Somerby), *gor(e) wong* (Melton Mowbray, Saxby).

garðr ON, 'an enclosure'; later 'a courtyard'. Plungar. Garth (f.n. Goadby Marwood), *la Garthe* (f.n. Melton Mowbray), *Hallegarth'* (Belvoir Castle).

gás ON, 'a goose', *v.* **gōs**.

gāt OE, 'a goat'. ?*the gatwell* (f.n. Stapleford).

gata ON, 'a way, a road, a street'. From its later use in the sense 'a right of way for leading cattle to pasture, a right of access to pasture-land', the el. came to mean 'right of pasturage' and 'an allotment of pasture' as in **bullgate** and **cowgate** (*q.v.*). Hollygate, Sawgate Rd, Woodgate Hill. In road-names, the dominant el.: it may be prefixed by a settlement name (as destination), e.g. *Barstongate, Belvor gate* (Knipton), *Bingham gate* (Bottesford), or compounded with an el. indicating topography, e.g. *Horngate* (Melton Mowbray), *Moregate* (Burton Lazars), *Woodgate* (Gt. Dalby, Hose); or with a minor name defining a more precise location, e.g. *benehilgate, brodebeke gatt* (Bottesford), *Cattewellegate* (Normanton). The local flora may be specified, e.g. *Hawthorn gate* (Burrough on the Hill), *Lusternegate* (Eaton), *Thurnegate* (Waltham on the Wolds). Grassy tracks are freq. recorded, e.g. *Grenegate* (with various spellings in Croxton Kerrial, Easthorpe, Knipton, Somerby); or the size of the track, e.g. *le Brodegate* (with various spellings in Bottesford, Lt. Dalby, Freeby), *Long gate* (Melton Mowbray). Man-made structures are often represented, e.g. *castelgate* (with various spellings in Barkestone, Bottesford, Burton Lazars, Croxton Kerrial, Redmile, Saltby), *the Church gate* (Harby), *Galtregate* (Sewstern), *the kirkegate* (Lt. Dalby), *le Milnegate* (Eaton, Harston, Hose), *Spytelgate* (Melton Mowbray); and human occupations or identities are sometimes recorded, e.g. *abbotte gate* (Burton Lazars), *Prestegate* (Bottesford), *Salters Gate* (Burrough on the Hill), *normangate* (Redmile). The road surface may be described, e.g. Flinty Gate (Long Clawson), *the Sand Gate* (Harby), Sodgate (Waltham on the Wolds). Compounding with a directional adj. is sometimes found, e.g. Southgate (Branston), *Westgate* (Belvoir, Muston). Note the important *le Ferdgate* (Harby). Many of these road-names have survived as furlong-names, even when not specifically designated as such; but sometimes a furlong-name is clearly indicated, as e.g. *Brode Saltgate, Long Saltgate* (Burton Lazars), *under Salters Gate* (Burrough on the Hill), *over the Gate* (Branston).

gated ModE, ppl.adj., 'furnished with gates'. *the gated Banke, the gated Lea* (f.ns. Saxby).

gate-hous ME, 'a gate-house'. *le Gatehouse* (Belvoir Castle), *the gate howsse* (Bottesford), *le yate howse* (Melton Mowbray).

gāthyrde OE, 'a goatherd'. Goatherd Cl (f.n. Edmondthorpe).

*__gear__ OE, 'a yair, a fish-weir'. ?Year Cl (f.n. Gt. Dalby).

__geard__ OE, 'an enclosure; a yard; a courtyard'. Freq. in f.ns.: with a surn. indicating ownership or tenancy, e.g. *Broketes Yard* (Burton Lazars), *Gills Yard* (Old Dalby), *Perkynyerd'* (Wycomb/Chadwell); with reference to principal buildings, e.g. *Chapell Yard* (with various spellings in Burton Lazars, Eye Kettleby, Saxby), *le Courthous Yerde* (Belvoir Castle), *Le Hallȝerd* (with various spellings at Belvoir Castle, Gt. Dalby, Garthorpe), *the Parsonage Yard* (Nether Broughton, Pickwell); with reference to agricultural activities, e.g. *Fold Yard* (Goadby Marwood), *the Grange Yard* (Croxton Kerrial), *the Neatheards yard* (Eastwell), *the Sty Yard* (Thorpe Arnold); with an el. indicating a small orchard, e.g. *the Cherry Yard*, *the Nut Yard* (Knipton).

__gearwe__ OE, 'yarrow'. ?*Yauley buttes* (f.n. Croxton Kerrial).

__geat__ OE, 'an opening, a gap, a passage; a gate'. *At the Milne Cloasse gate* (f.n. Croxton Kerrial), *Attegraungeyatt* (f.n. Eaton), *benethe Henry Simpsones gate* (f.n. Wycomb/Chadwell), *Kenns yate*, *Lordes yate* (Saltby), *Shepehousyate* (Eaton).

__geiri__ ON, 'a triangular plot of ground'. ?*le gyhereland* (f.n. Leesthorpe).

__geldyng__ ME, 'a castrated horse'. *Geldyngcroft* (f.n. Belvoir).

__geolu__ OE, adj., 'yellow'. Yellow Leys (f.n. Ab Kettleby), *yellowpit balke* (f.n. Croxton Kerrial).

__gild__ OE, __gildi__ ON, 'payment'. ?*gildewong* (f.n. Redmile), ?*Guylde holme leaes* (f.n. Burrough on the Hill).

__gipsy__ ModE, 'a Romany'; a member of a wandering people coming originally from India to Europe in the early 16th cent. and believed at that time to have come from Egypt. Gipsy Nook.

__glebe__ ME, 'glebe', i.e. land belonging to an ecclesiastical benefice. Glebe Fm (Long Clawson, Goadby Marwood, Redmile), Glebe Ho., Glebe Lodge. *the Gleabe barne* (Redmile), *the gleabe land* (f.n. Hose), Glebe, *ye High More Glebe close*, *the Parsonage Glebe land platt* (f.ns. Wymondham), *Glebe Close* (f.n. Brentingby), Glebe Wongs (f.n. Bottesford), *the glebe yard land* (f.n. Stonesby).

__gnípa__ ON, 'a steep rock or peak'. Knipton.

__gōd__² OE, __goðr__ ON, adj., 'good'. *Godtorp. godegate* (Bottesford), ?Goodland Cl (f.n. Buckminster).

__gold__ OE, 'gold'; poss. used also in the sense 'gold-hued'. ?Goldcroft (f.n. Sproxton), ?*Golding forthe* (f.n. Burton Lazars); but difficult to separate from __golde__ *infra*.

__golde__ OE, 'a marigold, a marsh-marigold'. ?Goldcroft (f.n. Sproxton), ?*Golding forthe* (f.n. Burton Lazars).

__gorebrode__ ME, 'a broad strip in a gore of a great field'. *Garbrod* (f.n. Somerby), *Garebred wong'* (f.n. Burrough on the Hill), *Gorebrode* (f.n. Bottesford, Burton Lazars).

__gorst__ OE, 'gorse, furze'; freq. in modern minor names and f.ns. in the sense 'a piece of ground covered with gorse, a fox-covert of gorse bushes'. Goadby Gorse, Gorse Close Plantation, Gorse Plantation, Herring Gorse, Hose ~, Muston ~, Scalford ~, Sproxton Heath ~, Stonesby ~, Tipping's Gorse. Freq. in f.ns.: with settlement names, e.g. Coston Gorse, Easthorpe Gorse, Freeby Gorse, Goadby Gorse (cf. the minor names *supra*); common in Gorse Cl (Brentingby, Burrough on the Hill, Burton Lazars, Harston, Scalford, Wartnaby, Wyfordby, Wymond-ham). Note the dial. form *goss(e)*, e.g. *Goss Fur'* (Stonesby), *gosse leyes* (Thorpe Arnold).

*gorstig OE, adj., 'overgrown with gorse'. Gorsey Cl (f.n. Hose, Wymondham), Gorsey Close Wood (f.n. Knipton), *Gorsye layes* (f.n. Barkestone). The spellings in *the Gossie Close* (f.n. Wyfordby), *the Gossye close* (f.n. Nether Broughton) record dial. *gossy* (cf. *goss(e)* in **gorst** *supra*).

gōs OE, **gás** ON, 'a goose'. ?*Gasgell medow* (f.n. Bottesford), ?Gauze Well, *Gooselees* (f.ns. Wymondham), *Goose Syke* (f.n. Burrough on the Hill), *Gosecroft* (f.n. Plungar), *Gosedale* (f.n. Eaton), *Goseholme* (f.n. Burton Lazars), *goswelleforlong'* (f.n. Muston).

goter ME, 'a gutter'. Fairly freq. in f.ns.: as a simplex, e.g. *the gootter* (with various spellings in Croxton Kerrial, Harby, Knipton, Saxby, Wycomb/Chadwell); but more usually with a locational minor name, e.g. *Cropoole gutter, Thornewell gutter, Thurnsyk gutter* (Croxton Kerrial), *little hill gutter* (Stathern), *Pibdale gutter, Shredale gutter* (Branston).

græf OE, 'a digging, a grave, a trench'. ?*At the graue* (f.n. Croxton Kerrial), *at the grave, Deadmans graue* (f.ns. Pickwell), Deadmans Grave (f.n. Thorpe Arnold).

grǣg¹ OE, adj., 'grey'. *le Greybrug'* (Burrough on the Hill).

græs, gærs OE, 'grass'. Bull Grass (f.n. Edmondthorpe), *Gerstaldyche* (f.n. Muston), *the grasse headland, Grasse headley* (f.ns. Wyfordby), *greene grasse* (f.n. Freeby), *Partingrasse* (f.n. Burrough on the Hill), *Parting Grasse Baulke*, Red Grass (f.ns. Gt. Dalby), *White Grasse* (f.n. Eastwell), *witegresse* (f.n. Redmile).

grāf OE, 'a grove, a copse, a coppiced wood'. The Grove. *Alfnadgraue* (f.n. Hose), *arkelgraue* (f.n. Bottesford), *Arnothesgraue* (f.n. Eaton), ?*At the graue* (f.n. Croxton Kerrial), ?*Short Segraves* (f.n. Eastwell).

granary ModE, 'a storehouse for grain'. *the Granary Close* (f.n. Bottesford).

grand OFr, adj., 'great, big'. *Grand Caudhill* (f.n. Edmondthorpe).

grange, graunge OFr, ME, 'a grange, an outlying farm belonging to a religious house or a feudal lord, where crops were stored'; often used in modern minor names, usually with an older p.n. prefixed, to convey a pretence of antiquity. Broughton Grange, Eaton ~, Old Dalby ~, Goadby ~, Goldsmith Grange, The Grange (Burton Lazars, Coston, Lt. Dalby, Freeby, Hose, Leesthorpe, Saxby, Stapleford), Grange Fm (Buckminster, Scalford, Wymondham), Old Grange, Pickwell ~, Plungar ~, Sewstern ~, Somerby ~, Sysonby ~, Wavendon ~, Wyfordby Grange; *Braunston Grange* (Branston), *Cumberland Grange* (Cumberland Lodge, Scalford), *the Grange* (Croxton Kerrial, Muston), *Saltby Graunge* (Saltby). *Grange Feild* (f.n. Wycomb/Chadwell), Grange Wong (f.n. Stathern), *the grange wonge* (f.n. Waltham on the Wolds), *graunge leaes* (f.n. Lt. Dalby).

grassie ModE, adj., 'covered by grass, abounding in grass'. *Grassye place furlonge* (f.n. Burrough on the Hill).

gravel ME, 'gravel'. The Gravel Hole (f.n. Burrough on the Hill), Gravel Hole Spinney (f.n. Burton Lazars), (the) Gravel Pit (f.ns. Long Clawson, Gt. Dalby, Scalford), Gravel Pitt Cl (f.n. Melton Mowbray), *Gravill furlong, Gravill pittes* (f.ns. Harston).

graveli ME, adj., 'abounding in gravel'. ?*Graueleyplace* (Belvoir).

grēat OE, adj., 'massive, bulky', ME, 'big in size'. *grat filld, the grat west medow* (f.ns. Burton Lazars), *the great dale, greate grange dale* (f.ns. Coston), *the greate More* (f.n. Freeby), *Greate Spynney* (The Spinney, Melton Mowbray), *the greate wong* (f.n. Melton Mowbray), Great Ground Hill (f.n. Pickwell), *the great mill dike* (f.n. Branston), *Grete Close* (f.n. Belvoir), *le Balke voc' the Grett Marke* (f.n. Stonesby), *Thomas Johnsons great closse* (f.n. Coston).

greatest ModE, adj., sup., 'largest, greatest'. *Mr Mitchells greatest fielde* (f.n. Coston).

greensward ModE, 'turf on which grass is growing'. *the greene swore* (f.n. Pickwell), *the parsonage greensward* (f.n. Branston).

grein ON, 'a fork (of a stream)'. *?felbrygreins* (f.n. Bottesford), *le gategreynis* (Wycomb/Chadwell), *?greyndele* (f.n. Croxton Kerrial).

grendel OE, 'a gravelly place or stream'. *?greyndele* (f.n. Croxton Kerrial).

grēne[1] OE, adj., 'green, grass-grown'. Green Hill, Green Lane. *Greenegate* (with various spellings in Croxton Kerrial, Easthorpe, Knipton, Sproxton, Stonesby), Greengate Cl (f.n. Somerby), Green Hills (f.n. Harston), *le Grenecrofte* (f.n. Knipton), *grenedikes* (f.n. Saltby), *grene layes* (f.n. Bottesford), *grenemerebech* (f.n. Redmile), *le Grenlane* (Bottesford).

grēne[2] OE, 'a grassy spot; a village green'. The Green (Bottesford, Gt. Dalby, Old Dalby). Fairly freq. as a simplex, e.g. (the) Green (Edmondthorpe, Melton Mowbray, Wymondham), *the greenes* (Stapleford), *(la ~)*, *(le ~) Grene* (Bottesford, Burton Lazars, Knipton, Stonesby) and *atte Grene* (recorded in various styles for Barkestone, Buckminster, Long Clawson, Freeby, Muston, Somerby). Note also *The Butt Green* (Sysonby), *Peasill greene* (Normanton), *Pinching Green* (Gt. Dalby), *Seustern grene* (Sewstern), the Sow Green (Buckminster), *Stowegren* (Bottesford), the Town Green (Sproxton), *Under Green* (f.n. Gt. Dalby).

gribbele ME, 'a crab-apple-tree'. *Gribbell dale* (f.n. Coston).

*grím̄a[1] ON, 'a mark or blaze on a tree to denote a boundary'. The Grimmer.

grōp OE, 'a ditch, a drain'. *le groping'* (f.n. Plungar).

grund OE, 'ground; a stretch of land', **grund** ON, 'earth, a plain'; later also 'an outlying farm, outlying fields' and 'a piece of land enclosed for agricultural purposes'. Freq. in f.ns., esp. indicating ownership/tenancy, e.g. *Bates ground* (Melton Mowbray), *Porters ground, Waldrons ground* (Goadby Marwood), *Sir Scroop his ground* (Barkestone); or soil type, e.g. *the Blacke ground* (Saxby), The Clay Ground (Eastwell); or location, e.g. Cold Harbour Ground (Sysonby), *High Moor Grounds* (Wymeswold), *Stigate ground* (Pickwell); or indicating the nature of ownership, e.g. *the Common Ground, the poors ground* (Ab Kettleby), *the Freehold ground* (Croxton Kerrial); or enclosure or otherwise, e.g. *the inclosed grounds* (Nether Broughton), Open Ground (Wymondham). Association with buildings may be specified, e.g. Barn Ground Cl (Holwell), *the Grange ground* (Croxton Kerrial), *the haull grounde* (Knipton); or settlements, e.g. Branston Ground (Eastwell), *Kettlelby grounds* (Eye Kettleby), *Leesthorpe Grounds* (Pickwell). Recurring compounds are: (the) Great Ground (Buckminster, Burton Lazars, Pickwell), Middle Ground (Brentingby, Wyfordby). Note *Mr Welby's Ewe Grounds* (Holwell).

gryfja ON, 'a hole, a pit'. *Glappewellegrif* (f.n. Old Dalby), *Grives* (f.n. Pickwell).

gryppe ME, 'a ditch, a drain'. *the grippes* (f.n. Bottesford), Hay Gripps (f.n. Burton Lazars).

*gylde OE, 'a golden flower'. ?*gildewong* (f.n. Redmile), ?*Guylde holme leaes* (f.n. Burrough on the Hill).

gylden OE, 'golden'; literally as to material or colour, figuratively as to richness or fertility. *Gildenehauedland* (f.n. Burton Lazars), Golden Furlong (f.n. Stathern).

hæc(c) OE (Angl), 'a hatch, a grating, a half-gate'; also 'a sluice-gate'. Hecadeck Lane. ?*Hatchenesse* (f.n. Muston).

hecce OE, 'a fence'. ?*Hatchenesse* (f.n. Muston).

*hæfera OE, **hafri** ON, 'oats'. ?*Arborow* (f.n. Harby), ?*harborow pitt* (f.n. Croxton Kerrial), *Hauerhill* (f.n. Plungar), *Hauereholm* (f.n. Wycomb/Chadwell), *Hauerholm* (f.n. Stathern), *Haverwounge* (f.n. Scalford).

(ge)hæg OE, **hay** ME, 'a fence, an enclosure'. *Bottesford heye* (f.n. Bottesford), *Godson hey* (f.n. Somerby), *le hay, Haysty,* ?*Heay Leayes,* ?*heay sike* (f.ns. Croxton Kerrial), *the hay* (Goadby Marwood), ?Hayes (f.n. Stathern), Hay Gripps (f.n. Burton Lazars), ?Bottom, Top Hays (f.ns. Wartnaby), *la Hegh* (Wymondham), Heyside Cl (f.n. Hose), *le Holdehey, le Longehay, le Schortehay* (f.ns. Plungar).

hæg-þyrne OE, 'the hawthorn, the whitethorn'. *Heythirne* (f.n. Thorpe Arnold).

hænep OE, ***hemp** ON, **hemp** ME, 'hemp'. *the hemp landes* (f.n. Bottesford).

hærg OE (Angl), 'a heathen temple'. ?*Harrowe* (f.n. Scalford).

*hæs OE (Angl), 'brushwood'. *Hesland* (f.n. Ab Kettleby), ?*hesterne* (f.n. Muston).

*hæse OE (Angl), 'land overgrown with brushwood'. ?*Hayes* (f.n. Stathern).

hæsel OE (Angl), **hesli** ON, 'a hazel'. ?*Haselden Syke* (f.n. Burrough on the Hill), *Hasle lands* (f.n. Melton Mowbray).

hǣð OE (Angl), 'a heath, a tract of uncultivated land'. Heath Fm, Saltby Heath (Croxton Kerrial, Saltby), Sproxton Heath Gorse. *super le Heth'* (p) (Old Dalby).

hafri ON, 'oats', *v.* ***hæfera**.

haga¹ OE, 'an enclosure', **hagi** ON, 'a grazing enclosure, a pasture'. ?*hawbrigg* (f.n. Saltby).

hagu-þorn OE, **hag-þorn** ON, 'the hawthorn, the whitethorn'. *Hawethornmere, Hawthornehill* (f.ns. Barkestone), *Hawetorne mere* (f.n. Redmile), *Hawthorn gate* (Burrough on the Hill), *Hawthornstye* (f.n. Knipton), *Hawthorn Slade* (f.n. Garthorpe), ?*Horthorn Hill* (f.n. Harby).

hāl OE, **hole** ME, **whole** ModE, adj., 'entire, undivided'. *Thomas Geales whole land, Bryan Robinsons whole land* (f.ns. Branston), *v.* **half-land**.

hald² OE (Angl), adj., 'sloping'. ?Old Hill Fm.

half OE (Angl), sb., 'side, part'. *be esthalf the brok'* (f.n. Melton Mowbray), *Northhalfbretlondale* (f.n. Wymondham).

half-aker ME, 'a half-acre'; in early f.ns., poss. 'a measure of land which a yoke of oxen could plough in half a day'. *le Halfackres* (f.n. Thorpe Arnold), *the halfeacres* (f.n. Hose), *Half-acre Leys* (f.n. Stapleford), *Heinhalfakirsichesende* (f.n. Muston), *Lusihalfaker* (f.n. Bottesford), *Spirlinghalfacre* (f.n. Normanton).

half-land ME, 'a half-size selion, half a selion'. *Robt Steels halfland* (f.n. Branston).

hālga OE, 'a saint'. Allhallows.

halh (**hale** dat.sg.) OE (Angl), 'a nook, a corner of land; a water-meadow; a tongue of land between two streams; a hollow, a secluded valley' etc. As a final el., it usually appears as ME -*hale* (from the dat.sg.), later -*hall*, -*all* (when it is confused with **hall**). *beyond the hale*, *Pylhall* (f.ns. Stapleford), ?Frog Hall Hollow (f.n. Knipton), ?*Housalls* (f.n. Harby), More Halls (f.n. Waltham on the Wolds), *Northalls* (f.n. Harston), *Russhall Leayes* (f.n. Croxton Kerrial), ?Worrel Leys (f.n. Coston), *Wylnehall* (f.n. Bottesford).

hālig OE, adj., 'holy, sacred, dedicated', *haliwell* (Croxton Kerrial), *Haliwell broc* (Burrough on the Hill), *Halythornfurlong* (f.n. Barkestone), ?Hellin Lands (f.n. Stathern).

hall OE (Angl), 'a hall, a manor house'. Brockhill Hall, Buckminster ~, Burton Lazars ~, Clawson ~, Old Dalby ~, Edmondthorpe Hall, Goadby Hall Fm, The Hall (Brentingby, Lt. Dalby, Eastwell, Goadby Marwood, Leesthorpe, Somerby), Hall Fm (Coston, Holwell), Harby Hall, Normanton ~, Old Hall, Old Hall Fm, Scalford Hall, Stapleford ~, Sysonby ~, Wartnaby ~, Withcote Hall. Note also *la Dounhalle* (p) (Saltby), *atte Hall*(e) (p) (Bottesford, Hose), *Knypton Hall*, *le Stonhalle* (Knipton), *Nether Hall* (Stapleford). Occasionally in f.ns., e.g. *Halle Balke* (Somerby), *the hall close* (Eye Kettleby), *the hall land* (Burton Lazars), *the haull grounde*, *the haull peece* (Knipton), *Outhall Lane* (Long Clawson). With *hall* as part of a castle: *Hallegarth'*, *le Hallȝerd* (Belvoir Castle).

hām OE, 'a village, an estate, a homestead', cf. **wald-hām**, **wīc-hām**. Wymondham, ?*Hygham* (Wycomb/Chadwell), ?*Whenham* (Ab Kettleby).

hamm OE, 'a water-meadow, land hemmed in by water or marsh, wet land hemmed in by higher ground'. Beckham (f.n. Freeby), *Blackham Sick* (f.n. Scalford), Broken Dale (f.n. Sewstern), Commonham Lane (Nether Broughton), (The) Ham (f.ns. Freeby, Thorpe Arnold), Ham Bridge, Cottage Ham, *hamme howkes* (f.ns Wyfordby), *langham rigget* (f.n. Thorpe Arnold), Mill Ham (f.n. Coston), Sanham (f.n. Gt. Dalby), ?*Shortham leyes* (f.n. Wycomb/Chadwell), ?*Thornham hadland* (f.n. Bottesford).

hamor OE, **hamarr** ON, 'a hammer'; in p.ns., also 'a place with a forge or smithy'; and from Scand usage, 'a steep rock, a cliff, a hammer-shaped crag'. Hammer Hill (f.n. Buckminster), *hammerwong* (f.n. Wyfordby).

hām-stall OE (Angl), 'a homestead, home buildings; the enclosure of a homestead'; surviving as ModEdial. **home-stall** 'a farm-yard'. A common compound el., e.g. *the Hall homestall* (Gt. Dalby), *the hamstell* (Easthorpe), *the Homestall* (with reference to the vicarage or rectory buildings of Buckminster, Harston, Ab Kettleby, Knipton, Muston), *Haynes Homestall*, *Thom. Wilmots Homestal* (Garthorpe), *Hugh Harris's House and Homestall*, *Robert Robinsons Homestall* (Stapleford), the Town Homestalls (Buckminster). Note the 16 instances dated 1745 listed in the Wymondham section 'Houses, Outbuildings, Gardens and Orchards'.

hām-stede OE, 'a homestead, the site of a dwelling', **homestead** ModE, 'home buildings'. Adam's homestead (Wartnaby), *John Baxters House and Homested*, Merrills Homestead (Burton Lazars), Tho. Bishops House & Homestead (Old Dalby), Browns ~, Hodgkins ~, Kelhams Homestead, *Statons Homestead* (Gt. Dalby), *Robert Clays homestead* (Pickwell), *Cubleys Cottage and homestead*, *Kellams House and homestead* (Stapleford), *the Homestead* (Eastwell, Harston,

Hose, Muston; with reference to dependent buildings and offices of the vicarage or rectory), *the homesteade of the vicarige* (Scalford), *the Homested or seat of the vicaridge* (Ab Kettleby), *Rich. Ingleton his house & homesteede* (Sproxton), Norths Homestead (Sewstern), Old House Homestead (Long Clawson). Occasionally in f.ns., e.g. Great Homestead (Wartnaby), Homestead Cl (Goadby Marwood), Homested (Coston). Note the 6 instances dated 1660 of such dependent building complexes listed in Coston.

*hamstra OE, 'a corn-weevil'. *?hamstryll* (f.n. Bottesford).

handaxe ME, 'a battle-axe; an axe to be wielded by one hand'. *?Hansaxbrigge* (Burrough on the Hill).

handseax OE, 'a dagger'. *?Hansaxbrigge* (Burrough on the Hill).

hangende OE, **hengjandi** ON, pres.part., 'hanging', used of places on a steep slope or hillside. *hanging baulk* (f.n. Ab Kettleby), Hanging Cl, Hanging Moor (f.ns. Thorpe Arnold), *hanging hill furl'* (f.n. Lt. Dalby), *Hengendehil* (f.n. Burton Lazars), *Hinging Brentley* (f.n. Stapleford).

hangra OE, 'a wood on a (steep) hillside'. *Newhynger* (f.n. Stonesby).

hār² OE, adj., 'hoar, grey', esp. 'grey through being overgrown with lichen'; prob. came to mean 'boundary' because of its freq. use with features forming boundary marks or lying on boundaries. Difficult to distinguish from **hara**. Harston. *?harborow pitt* (f.n. Croxton Kerrial), *?Hareclif* (f.n. Burrough on the Hill, Eaton), *harelonds*, *Harewellesike*, *?Harewong'* (f.ns. Bottesford), *?harenab* (f.n. Knipton), *Harewell* (f.n. Croxton Kerrial, Holwell), *Harlond(e)s* (f.n. Belvoir, Melton Mowbray), *?Harrowe* (f.n. Scalford), *Harstone* (f.n. Muston), *Harthorndale* (f.n. Somerby).

hara OE, 'a hare'; difficult to distinguish from **hār²**. *?Hareclif* (f.n. Burrough on the Hill, Eaton), *?Harewong'* (f.n. Bottesford), *?Harrowe* (f.n. Scalford).

hassuc OE, 'a clump of coarse grass'. *le Burnhassokis*, Hassocky Cl, *Hissock hill* (f.ns. Burrough on the Hill), *Hassoches* (f.n. Muston), *Hassocks close* (f.n. Lt. Dalby), *Hassockes* (The Lussacks, f.n. Waltham on the Wolds), *hassokes* (f.n. Bottesford), *le Hassockys* (f.n. Harby).

haugr ON, 'a hill, a hill-top; a burial-mound'; sometimes difficult to distinguish from OE *hō(e)*, dat.sg. of **hōh**. *Brakenhou*, *Foxhou* (f.ns. Eaton), *Brakenousike*, *elyothou*, *le redhou*, *Warinhou* (f.ns. Wycomb/Chadwell), *Cokhowe*, *presthou*, *stonhoupol* (f.ns. Redmile), *hennehou* (f.n. Burrough on the Hill), *Herneshou* (f.n. Stonesby), *le houwe*, *Howeford*, *Walworthehow* (f.ns. Muston), *Howdale* (f.n. Branston), *atte Howe* (p) (Melton Mowbray), *Hundehou* (f.n. Long Clawson), *Olmehou* (f.n. Somerby), *Pesehouwe* (f.n. Goadby Marwood), *Pesowe* (f.n. Knipton), *Redehowe* (f.n. Sewstern), *scharphou* (f.n. Croxton Kerrial), *threhowis* (f.n Burton Lazars), *Todhow* (f.n. Thorpe Arnold), *Tythow* (f.n. Freeby), *Wadhowe* (f.n. Burrough on the Hill).

heading ModE, vbl.sb., 'the highest part, that which is at the top; a headland'. *Crofte hedings*, *the drake eshe heding*, *midel dale heding*, *morter pit hedings*, *sevenrood hedings*, *spikes heading*, *the stonpit hedings* (f.ns. Saltby), *hedding Leas* (f.n. Saxby).

headley ModEdial., perh. 'a swarded-over headland; an end unit of grassland'. Earliest forms in Framland Hundred are from 1577, cf. *Ric. Niccolles leyehadland*, *a ley hadland* (1606, Kimcote, Guthlaxton Hundred). Freq. in f.ns.:

usually with a surn. to specify ownership, tenancy, e.g. *Allens ~, Barrows ~,*
Clarkes hedlea (Saxby), *Leonard Greens headleas* (Somerby), *Robert George his*
hedley, Thomas Geales hedley, Gowertones hedley (Branston), *John Forrests*
headley (Bottesford), *George Wyllford headley* (Lt. Dalby); occasionally with
title of rank, e.g. *the Earle of Ruttland hedley* (Branston), *the Kinges headlea*
(Saxby). Note *Grasse headley* (c.1638, Wyfordby).

hēafod OE, 'a head; the (top) end of something, a headland, unploughed land at the
end of the arable where the plough turns', cf. **hēafod-land**. Freq. in f.ns., e.g.
blewehill hades (Nether Broughton), *Borohades* (Lt. Dalby), *Whyttmoore heades*
(Harston), *Mannisheuid* (Bottesford), *atte Toneshevede* (Ab Kettleby). Note also
the Common(e) H(e)ades (Eastwell, Ab Kettleby, Sproxton), *neate heades*
(Saltby), *neateshead furlong* (Sproxton), *the Spring heade in Powell* (Knipton),
Where head (Burton Lazars).

hēafod-land OE, 'a strip of land at the head of a furlong, left for turning the plough'.
Freq. in f.ns.: usually with an early pers.n. or later surn. prefixed, e.g.
Godiuhauedlond (Barkestone), *Godwynhedland* (Bottesford), *Baxter Hedland,*
Iuette Hedlands (Burton Lazars), *Frances Brownes headland* (Normanton),
James Drings Headland (Easthorpe); or with an el. indicating occupation, e.g.
Bidilhawedland, ye person hedlande (Bottesford), *the Neatheardes headland*
(Eastwell), *the vicars headland* (Ab Kettleby). The parish church may be
specified, e.g. *the Church Hadland* (Ab Kettleby), *Church headland furl'* (Lt.
Dalby), *St Mary headland* (Bottesford); or human behavioural associations
indicated, e.g. *Cukewoldheuedlond, synnefulheuedland* (Muston), *le dede*
hevidland (Harby); or an el. descriptive of flora may be prefixed, e.g.
Gildenehauedland (Burton Lazars), *Redde heuitland* (Muston); or shape, e.g. *the*
long h(e)adland (Bottesford, Harston); or occasionally a locational minor name,
e.g. *the poors land headland* (Ab Kettleby), *Sandhilhedland* (Bottesford).

hēah[1] (**hēan** wk.obl.) OE, **hēh** (Angl), **high** ModE, adj., 'high, tall, important; lying
high up, standing in a high place'. Highfields Spinney, The High Leys. Fairly
freq. in f.ns., e.g. *Highfelde* (Stapleford), High Gate (Ab Kettleby), *the Highe*
Thorne (Knipton). Note also *heynehowys* (Knipton), *the high street* (King Street
Lane, Coston), *the Hye Crosse* (Melton Mowbray).

hēah-weg OE, 'a highway, a main road'. *the Highway(e)* (Easthorpe, Goadby
Marwood, Knipton), *hyweie gate* (Normanton), *the Kinges highe waie* (with
various spellings in Bottesford, Long Clawson, Ab Kettleby, Melton Mowbray,
Muston), *Nottingham Highway* (Buckminster), *the queenes highe waye* (Muston),
the Quenes hye waie (Ab Kettleby).

heard OE, adj., 'hard; hard to till; cheerless'. *Hardall sike* (f.n. Eastwell),
harddeyles, Hardhilles (f.ns. Bottesford), *Hardhull* (f.n. Thorpe Arnold),
hardland (f.n. Lt. Dalby).

hearpe OE, 'a harp'; topographically, used of something resembling a harp in shape.
Harpe Wonge (f.n. Eastwell), *the Harps* (f.n. Somerby).

hechinge ME, 'part of a field ploughed and sown during the year in which the rest
of the field lies fallow'. *?Hatchenesse* (f.n. Muston).

hecg OE, 'a hedge'. Freq. used with reference to the boundary hedges of adjoining
townships, e.g. *Branston hedge, Croxton hedge* (Knipton), *Burton hedge* (Lt.
Dalby), *Garthorpe hedg* (Saxby), *Kettleby hedge* (Gt. Dalby). Topographical

features may be prefixed, e.g. *the moore hedg* (The Moors, f.n. Croxton Kerrial), *Calving hill hedge* (Calving Hills, f.n. Normanton), *Hogden hedge* (Ogden, f.n. Burrough on the Hill), *Speny hedge* (Melton Mowbray). A surn. may be prefixed indicating private property, e.g. *Barret hegge* (Lt. Dalby), *Foster Hedge Furlong* (f.n. Long Clawson); or a larger habitative feature, e.g. *Goldsmith graunge hedge* (Scalford), *the Grange hedge* (Croxton Kerrial), *the maner hedge* (Saltby). Note the early *Croftesheag* (13, Sproxton) and *under þe hege* (1427, f.n. Bottesford).

hēg OE, 'hay, mowing grass'. Hay Cl, Hay Common (f.ns. Wartnaby), *le Haygate* (Barkestone), Headall Fd (f.n. Wycomb/Chadwell), *?Heay Leayes, ?heay syke* (f.ns. Croxton Kerrial), *(le) Heygate* (Ab Kettleby, Plungar, Wyfordby), Highgate (Coston).

*hegn ON, 'an enclosure'. *Haindale* (f.n. Sewstern).

hegning ON, 'enclosed land'. *Heyning* (f.n. Wycomb/Chadwell).

hell OE, 'hell'. *Helpitt* (f.n. Edmondthorpe).

hempland eModE, 'land appropriated to the growth of hemp'; later 'a piece of land held by a small tenant, irrespective of the produce of the soil'. *the hemp landes* (f.n. Bottesford), *Walters Hempland, Jo. Waltons House & Hempland* (f.ns. Burton Lazars).

(ge)hende OE, adj., 'near at hand'. *Hendepit* (f.n. Wymondham).

*henge OE, adj., 'something hanging; steep'. *le hengefurlonge* (f.n. Barkestone), *Hingehille* (f.n. Normanton).

hengest OE, 'a horse, a stallion'. *?Hengestland* (f.n. Plungar).

henn OE, 'a hen (esp, of wild birds); a water hen' etc. *Le Lyttyl Hendryth* (f.n. Burton Lazars), *hennehou, hennehul* (f.ns. Burrough on the Hill), Hennings (f.n. Waltham on the Wolds), *?Hentoft* (f.n. Stapleford).

hēope OE, 'the fruit of the wild rose, a hip', **hēopa** OE, 'the dog rose, a bramble'. *le hepthorn* (f.n. Plungar).

heorde OE, 'a herdsman'. ?Harby.

heorde-wīc OE, 'a herd farm'. *Hardwick.*

heorot OE, 'a hart, a stag'. *?hartes well* (f.n. Freeby).

herre ME, **her** eModE, adj., comp. of **hēah**[1], 'higher'. *?herdale* (f.n. Burrough on the Hill), *Heyererforlange* (f.n. Somerby).

hetta ON, 'a hood', **hǫttr** ON, 'a hat'; used of a hill thought to resemble a hat. *Hardynghet* (f.n. Melton Mowbray).

heyron ME, 'a heron'. ?(Broad Moor) Heron Drain, ?Heron Furlong (f.ns. Long Clawson).

hīd OE, 'a hide of land; an amount of land for the support of one free family and its dependents'. *la Hyde* (p) (Garthorpe).

hider OE, adv., 'on this side'. *le Hether close* (f.n. Buckminster), *the Hetther damins, Heyther Stocke* (f.ns. Burton Lazars), *Hiderbendolis* (f.n. Thorpe Arnold), *Hiderneumor* (The Moors, f.n. Croxton Kerrial), *Hither Cutt* (f.n. Garthorpe), Hither Sick Furlong (f.n. Melton Mowbray).

hilder ME, 'an elder-tree'. *?Hildindam* (f.n. Eaton).

hīwan (hī(g)na gen.pl.) OE (Angl), 'a household; a religious community (of monks or nuns)'. Thorpe Hindles.

hjallr ON, 'a hut, a shed'. *Hellewong* (f.n. Muston).

hjǫrð (hjarðar gen.sg.) ON, 'a herd, a flock'. ?Harby.

hlāw OE, 'a burial-mound, a hill'. *Belawe* (f.n. Saxby), *lauutona* (f.n. Bottesford), Whaley Fd (f.n. Melton Mowbray), *Whardloe* (f.n. Somerby).

hlið¹ OE, **hlíð²** ON, 'a slope, a concave hillside'. *le lid* (f.n. Muston), Life Fd (f.n. Branston).

hlōse OE, 'a pigsty'. *loosse heades* (f.n. Scalford).

hlūd OE, adj., 'loud', **hlūde** OE, sb., 'the loud one'. *Lowthes* (f.n. Melton Mowbray), *Ludforth* (f.n. Branston).

hlyn OE, **hlynnr** ON, 'a maple-tree'. *Lyns Banke* (f.n. Saxby), *Lynstygate* (Normanton).

hnecca OE, 'a neck'; used topographically of 'a neck of land'. The Neck (f.n. Waltham on the Wolds).

hnutu OE, **hnot** ON, 'a nut; a nut-bearing tree'. *le notebusk* (f.n. Barkestone), the Nut Yard (f.n. Knipton).

hnutu-scell OE, 'a nutshell'. Nutshell Fd (f.n. Coston).

***hobb(e)** OE, 'a tussock, a hummock'. ?*Hobbesyke* (f.n. Stathern), ?*Hobcroft* (f.n. Stapleford), ?*Hobstacke foarde* (f.n. Scalford).

hōc OE, 'a hook, an angle, a projecting piece of ground'; cf. the later *hook-land* 'land ploughed and sown every year'. *Bramelhoke*, Horse Hook, *Mussulhoke* (f.ns. Burton Lazars), *Emanuell hooke* (f.n. Old Dalby), *hamme howkes* (f.n. Wyfordby), *the Hoke*, Tythe Hookes (f.ns. Melton Mowbray), *hoke gate* (Somerby), The Hook, *longelandhok'*, *Standerd hooke*, *Steynwordhoc*, *the washpit hooke* (f.ns. Burrough on the Hill), *Hook* (f.n. Thorpe Arnold), Hookings (f.n. Stathern), the Hooks Drain (f.n. Long Clawson), *Hutshoces* (f.n. Hose), *Milne hookes* (f.n. Harston), *Sleighting Hook* (Slatings, f.n. Waltham on the Wolds).

***hōd** OE, 'a shelter; a fortification'. *Hodeclif* (f.n. Burrough on the Hill).

hogg OE, 'a hog'. ?Ogden (f.n. Burrough on the Hill).

hǫgg ON, ' a felling of trees, a part of a wood marked off for cutting'. the Haggs (f.n. Somerby).

hōh (hōas, hōs nom.pl.) OE, 'a heel; a hill-spur'; in the Danelaw, difficult to distinguish from **haugr**. Hose, Brocker Ho., Hose Hill. Shutoe Cl (f.n. Somerby), ?Cranor (f.n. Stathern), *Dunesho* (f.n. Harston), ?*Harrowe* (f.n. Scalford), Hoe Hill (f.n. Buckminster), *Hoo* (p) (Bottesford), ?Hough Hedge, ?*Walkerhou* (f.ns. Bottesford), ?*Howong* (f.n. Normanton), ?*le Hows* (f.n. Eaton), Hubbuck Cl (f.n. Gt. Dalby), *litelho* (f.n. Leesthorpe), *Longhoe* (f.n. Pickwell), *michelho* (f.n. Redmile), Togar (f.n. Waltham on the Wolds).

hol¹ OE, **hol** ON, 'a hole, a hollow'. Piper Hole. Freq. in f.ns.: esp. prefixed by a locational name, e.g. *Castlegate hole* (Barkestone), *Highbrinke hole* (Pickwell), Stone Bridge Hole (Goadby Marwood); by a surn. or pers.n., e.g *Bartin Hole* (Waltham on the Wolds), *Bostone hoale*, *herring hole* (Knipton), *haugrimhole* (Harby); by an el. indicating industrial use, e.g. *Fulin Hole* (Sproxton), Fuzlehole (Nether Broughton), *Grives hole* (Pickwell). Note also the whimsical associations of Dove Hole Cl (Burrough on the Hill), Pigeon Hole Furlong (Stathern), *Puncheholes* (Eastwell), *v.* **holh**.

hol² OE, **holr** ON, adj., 'lying in a hollow, deep, running in a deep hollow'; esp. in stream-names and road-names, also 'sunken'. Holwell, Hollygate. Freq. in stream-names, e.g. *Hobackes* (Pickwell), *Howbecks* (Waltham on the Wolds), *Holwell* (with various spellings and compounding in Bescaby, Melton Mowbray, Sproxton, Stathern); and in road-names, e.g. *holgate* (with various spellings in Edmondthorpe, Muston, Wymondham); in f.ns., recurring in *holewong* (with various spellings in Bottesford, Leesthorpe, Muston, Normanton), Holland Dale (Gt. Dalby), *the holland hurst* (Stathern). Note also *holforw*, *holmold* (f.ns. Muston).

holc OE, 'a cavity, a hollow'. *le holking* (f.n. Wymondham).

holh OE, 'a hole, a hollow'. Hollow Lane, Home Lodge Hollow, Lawn Hollow Plantation, Thorney Hollow. Fairly common in f.ns., e.g. *the Cowdam hollow* (Saltby), Frog Hall Hollow (Knipton), The Hollow (Harston, Scalford), *the Milne Hollow* (Scalford), *holoforou* (Burton Lazars), *le holucoumbe* (Wycomb/Chadwell). Note also *Hollow neatgates* (Stonesby), Hollow Street (Ab Kettleby).

holmr ON, 'a small island, an inland promontory, a piece of drier ground amid marshes; a water-meadow'. Holme Fm. Very freq. in f.ns.: as a simplex, e.g. *le holm(e)* (Barkestone, Knipton, Muston, Wycomb/Chadwell, Wyfordby), the Holmes (Burton Lazars, Freeby, Redmile); with a prefixed pers.n., e.g. *Crookesome* (Nether Broughton), *Grimisholm* (Somerby), *Sywalholm'* (Sewstern), or surn., e.g. *Baggot holme* (Wymondham), *Bassett home* (Harston), *Paskedenholm* (Bottesford). Soil type may be specified, e.g. *Clayholm* (Bottesford), *Dry holme* (Freeby), Sandholms (Pickwell); or crops, e.g. *beneholm* (Redmile), *Bounholme* (Burton Lazars), *Pease holme* (Burrough on the Hill); or wild flora, e.g. *Brakenholm* (Somerby), Elder Holme (Burrough on the Hill), *Thakholm* (with various spellings in Bottesford, Melton Mowbray, Muston), *Thistelholm* (Burton Lazars); or (agricultural) buildings, e.g. *Barnewarke Holmes* (Burton Lazars), *le Houlholm* (f.n. Barkestone), *milneholme* (with various spellings in Croxton Kerrial, Hose, Knipton, Somerby, Wyfordby); or livestock, e.g. Bulham (Stapleford), *Bulholme Close* (Old Dalby), *derholm* (Redmile), *Goseholme* (Burton Lazars). Directional indicators also appear, e.g. *North holme* (Sewstern), *sowthholme* (Bottesford), *Westolmes* (Somerby).

holt OE, ON, 'a small wood, a single-species wood'. Black Holt, Fir Holt, Osier Holt. Ash Holt (f.n. Wartnaby), Holt (f.n. Ab Kettleby), ?Holt Leys (f.n. Thorpe Arnold), *the neither holte* (f.n. Bottesford), Priory Holt Wood (f.n. Belvoir), *Sirholt* (f.n. Melton Mowbray), Willow Holt (f.n. Harston, Holwell, Muston, Sewstern, Wymondham).

home ModE, adj., 'near home'. Home Fm (Lt. Dalby, Ab Kettleby), Home Lodge Hollow. Common in f.ns., e.g. Home Cl (Nether Broughton, Buckminster, Coston, Goadby Marwood, Harston, Holwell, Sewstern, Wartnaby, Wyfordby), The Home Fd (Gt. Dalby). Note also *homedale*, Home Ground (Wyfordby).

home-yard ModE, 'a yard attached to a dwelling'. *John Baxter his howse and homeyard*, *John Kellam his howse & homeyard* (Burton Lazars).

hop¹ OE, 'a small hemmed-in valley, esp. one opening into or overhanging the main one; a recess in a hill; a remote enclosed place; a plot of enclosed land, esp. in marsh or wasteland'. *Hopbak furlong*, *Hopsik'* (f.ns. Stathern).

*hopping OE, 'a hop-garden'. *le hopinc* (f.n. Wycomb/Chadwell), Hoping Fd (f.n. Long Clawson), *the milne hopeings* (f.n. Scalford).

hop-yard ModE, 'a hop-yard, a hop-garden, an enclosure where hops are grown'. Hop Yard. (the) Hop Yard (f.ns. Burton Lazars, Eaton, Scalford, Stathern).

horn OE, ON, *horna OE, 'a horn, a projection; a projecting feature or piece of land'. the Hornbuckle, ?Watchorn (f.ns. Scalford), *Hornecrofte close* (f.n. Belvoir), *Horne Crosse leaes* (f.n. Redmile), *Hornesfeild, le Hornfeild close* (f.ns. Buckminster), *Horngate* (Melton Mowbray), *hornwell crosse* (Waltham on the Wolds), Huntershorn (f.n. Bottesford), *Wederhorn* (f.n. Stathern), Whinhorne (f.n. Holwell).

hors OE, 'a horse'. *Horscott Lees* (f.n. Branston), *Horse Close*, Horse Park (f.ns. Edmondthorpe), Horse Cl (f.n. Freeby, Thorpe Arnold), Horse Dam (f.n. Waltham on the Wolds), *the horsedames* (f.n. Croxton Kerrial), Horse Holme, Horse Pingle (f.ns. Thorpe Arnold), Horse Hook (f.n. Burton Lazars), Horse Leys (f.n. Coston), *Horsepooles* (in various spellings and compounds in Croxton Kerrial, Harby, Harston, Knipton, Wycomb/Chadwell), *the horse shoe* (f.n. Melton Mowbray), *horshulles* (f.n. Redmile), ?*Horsladedale* (f.n. Eaton).

hors-sho ME, 'a horseshoe'. ?*the horse shoe* (f.n. Melton Mowbray).

horu OE, 'filth, dirt'. ?*Horsladedale* (f.n. Eaton), *Long Horreberue* (f.n. Harby).

hospital ME, 'a hospital, a hospice'. *Dalby Hospital* (Old Dalby). Earl of Rutland's Hospital, Fleming's Almshouses, Hospital Fm, *Hospital of St Lazarus* (Burton Lazars), *the Hospital* (Bedehouses, Stapleford), *Hudson's Hospital* (Melton Mowbray).

hovel eModE, 'a hovel, a shed; a frame or stand on which a stack of corn was built'. Hacketts Hovel Platt (f.n. Wymondham), Hovel Cl (f.n. Brentingby, Buckminster, Goadby Marwood, Scalford, Sewstern), Hovel Fd (f.n. Gt. Dalby, Waltham on the Wolds), Hovel land dike (f.n. Holwell), Prince's Hovel (f.n. Edmondthorpe).

hramse OE, 'wild garlic'. ?*Ransyegate* (Branston).

hrēac OE, 'a rick'. ?Ricks Cl (f.n. Hose).

hrēod OE, 'a reed, a rush; a reed-bed'; sometimes difficult to distinguish from **rēad** 'red'. ?*Rademoreacre* (f.n. Plungar), The Reads, ?*Redde heuitland, Redefordeland, Redemere* (f.ns. Muston), ?*redbancks*, ?*Redhill al's Reedhill* (f.ns. Nether Broughton), *Redbutt Fur'*, Rudbeck Cl (f.ns. Melton Mowbray), *le Rede*, Red Mdw, *Redyngwald* (f.ns. Thorpe Arnold), ?*Redehill'*, *Redeholle* (f.ns. Wymondham), Red Grass, Rodwell (f.ns. Gt. Dalby).

hrēodig OE, adj., 'growing with reeds'. *le Rydyʒhede* (f.n. Eaton).

hrīs OE, hrís ON, 'shrubs, brushwood'. Rise Hill Spinneys. the Rice Cl (f.n. Somerby), *Rice pastures* (f.n. Lt. Dalby), *the Rise Close, Risegores*, the Ryce Fd (f.ns. Pickwell), *Ristie* (f.n. Croxton Kerrial), *Ryse headland* (f.n. Edmondthorpe).

hross ON, 'a horse'. ?*Rosgalls* (f.n. Pickwell).

hrūt OE, adj., perh. 'dark-coloured'. ?*Ruttewell* (f.n. Croxton Kerrial).

hrycg OE, hryggr ON, 'a ridge'. *Kirckridge* (f.n. Normanton), *Nunriges* (f.n. Scalford), the Ridge Cl (f.n. Croxton Kerrial), The Ridgeway, *Rygges* (f.ns Wymondham), *Wet furrow Ridge* (f.n. Ab Kettleby), *Wyndriggs* (f.n. Waltham on the Wolds).

hulu OE, 'a shed, a hovel'. *le Houlholm* (f.n. Barkestone).

hund (hunda gen.pl.) OE, **hundr** ON, 'a hound', used often of places haunted by dogs. Difficult to distinguish from the OE pers.n. *Hund* or the ON pers.n. *Hundi*. Handen (f.n. Pickwell), ?Hounds Acre (f.n. Wymondham), ?*hundecliff*, ?*hundewelleforlang* (f.ns. Muston), ?*Hundeholm* (f.n. Wycomb/Chadwell), *Hundehou* (f.n. Long Clawson), ?*le hundhakir* (f.n. Plungar), *hundhill* (f.n. Freeby).

hundred OE, 'an administrative division of a county, prob. consisting originally of 100 hides', *v.* **hīd**. Framland Hundred.

hungor OE, 'hunger, famine', usually an allusion in f.ns. to 'barren ground'. *Huncerhil'* (f.n. Wycomb/Chadwell), *Hunerfurlonge* (f.n. Wymondham), *Hungerhil(l)* (f.n. Barkestone, Lt. Dalby), Hungerhill Fd (f.n. Easthorpe), *Hungerhyl, Hungurfurlong* (f.ns. Wyfordby), *Hungirhill* (f.n. Thorpe Arnold).

hunig OE, 'honey'; in p.ns. usually alluding to places where honey was found or produced, or perh. to 'sweet land'; but sometimes used of sites with sticky soil. Honey Go Dale (f.n. Burrough on the Hill), Honey Pot (f.n. Holwell), Honey Wells (f.n. Muston), *Honny Acres* (f.n. Somerby), *Honyacres* (f.n. Pickwell), ?*Huneisbalke* (f.n. Wycomb/Chadwell).

*****huntere** OE, 'a hunter'. Huntershorn (f.n. Bottesford).

hūs OE, **hús** ON, 'a house'; usually 'a dwelling house', but sometimes used of a building for special purposes; **house** ModE, 'a residence, a mansion, a manor-house', *v.* **maner, mansion-house**. Acacia Ho., Bescaby ~, Brocker ~, Burrough Hill ~, Catherine Dalley ~, Craven ~, Dovecoat ~, Fishpond ~, Freehold ~, Glebe ~, The Grange ~, Halfway ~, Haughley ~, Highfield ~, Knipton ~, Mill ~ (Scalford, Stathern), Old Mill ~, Park Ho., Red House Fm, Somerby Ho., Stonefield ~, Storers ~, Temperance ~, Waltham ~, (The) White Ho. (Burton Lazars, Stathern), White House Fm (Holwell, Melton Mowbray), Wold Ho., Wycliffe ~, Wymondham Ho. Early examples may be prefixed by a surn. indicating the residing family and/or ownership, e.g. *Cristen howse* (Waltham on the Wolds), *Magdaunce hous* (Wymondham), *Tates house* (Barkestone); or by an el. indicating ecclesiastical use, e.g. *the Chapell Howse alias Spittell Chapell*, *le Churche House* (Melton Mowbray), *le kirkehous* (Bottesford), *the Parsonage House* (with various spellings in Bottesford, Branston, Burrough on the Hill and 10 other townships), *the Rectory House* (in Holwell, Knipton, Muston and 4 other townships), *the Vicarage House* (with various spellings in Barkestone, Buckminster, Long Clawson and 14 other townships). Note the range of examples of dwellings in Coston (1660), in Burrough on the Hill (1709) and in Wymondham (1745). Note also *the Tythe howse, Union House* (Melton Mowbray), *Woodhowse* (Old Dalby) and the unusual *husemilne* (Bottesford).

husbandman ModE, 'a tenant farmer, a smallholder'. *the Husbandmens Field* (f.n. Wyfordby).

hut eModE, 'a hut, a shed'. Holwell Huts. Huts (f.n. Gt. Dalby).

*****hvin** ON, **whin** ME, 'whin, gorse'. Whinhorne (f.n. Holwell).

hwǣg OE, 'whey'. *Wheywelle* (f.n. Goadby Marwood).

hwǣte OE (Angl), 'wheat'. Wheat Hill Spinney. *longewatelond* (f.n. Redmile), *Wetecroft* (f.n. Eaton), *Weteland'* (f.n. Burrough on the Hill), Wheat Cl (f.n. Burrough on the Hill, Withcote), *Wheatefeild* (f.n. Stonesby), *le Wheatefild* (f.n.

Garthorpe), Wheat Hill Fd (f.n. Knipton), Whittle Sty (f.n. Stathern).

hwǣten OE, adj., 'growing with wheat'. *Wetenhulsty* (Whittle Sty, f.n. Stathern).

hwearf OE, 'a wharf'. Barkestone Wharf, Bottesford Wharf, Muston Gorse Wharf. *The Wharf* (Melton Mowbray).

hwēol OE, a wheel', whence 'something circular'. Wheel Cl (f.n. Hose).

hwerfel OE (Angl), **hvirfill** ON, 'a circle; something circular'. *long Wharles* (f.n. Stapleford), *Whirle Lake* (Withcote).

hwēt-stān OE, 'a whetstone'; alluding either to a particular rock or stone, or to a place where such stone was to be got. *the forlonge called Whettstonne* (f.n. Scalford), *?Wystonbrigge* (Wycomb/Chadwell).

hwīt OE, adj., 'white'; in eModE, *white* 'infertile' is contrasted with *black* 'fertile'. *Shortewhytes* (f.n. Pickwell), *le Wite Cros* (with various spellings in Burton Lazars, Knipton, Muston), *White Earth* (f.n. with various spellings in Lt. Dalby, Eaton, Edmondthorpe), *White Grasse* (f.n. Eastwell), White hill (f.n. Holwell), *Whiteland*, *le Whiteston* (f.ns. Burrough on the Hill), White Leys (f.n. Muston), White Wong (f.n. Nether Broughton, Scalford), *Whyttmoore heades* (f.n. Harston), *le Witeclais* (f.n. Bottesford), *witegresse*, *withacre* (f.ns. Redmile), *Witewelle* (f.n. Wycomb/Chadwell), *?Wystonbrigge* (Wycomb/Chadwell).

*hyles OE, 'holly'. *?hullesgate* (Muston).

hyll OE, 'a hill'. Ankle Hill, Ash Hill Plantation, Beacon Hill, Brock ~, Broughton ~, Brown's ~, Burrough ~, Burton Hill, Buttermilk Hill Spinney, Castle Hill, Cedar ~, Clawson ~, Cord ~, Covermill ~, Crown ~, Debdale ~, Drift ~, First ~, Gartree ~, Green ~, Harby Hill, Hillcrest, Hill Fm, Hill Top Fm, Hose Hill, Kyte ~, Leesthorpe ~, Lings ~, Mill Hill, Mill Hill Spinney, Old Hill Fm, Old Hills, Salter's Hill, Slyborough ~, Snow Hill, Terrace Hills, Toft's Hill, Toston Hill, Wheat Hill Spinney, Windmill Hill, Windsor ~, Woodgate ~, Wood's Hill. Very freq. in f.ns.: soil type may feature, e.g. *Clayhill* (Croxton Kerrial), *Flintehil* (Waltham on the Wolds), Stonehill (with various spellings in Burton Lazars, Edmondthorpe, Melton Mowbray, Pickwell, Stathern, Wymeswold); or size, shape, aspect, e.g. *Lyttle hill* (Barkestone, Stathern), Small hill (Burton Lazars), Longhill (Buckminster, Stathern, Wycomb/Chadwell), Round Hill (Eastwell, Holwell, Scalford), *Blewhill(s)* (Nether Broughton, Scalford), *Hengendehil'* (Burton Lazars), *Hingehill* (Normanton). Crops may feature, e.g. *Beane hill* (with various spellings in Bottesford, Burrough on the Hill, Leesthorpe), *Peashill* (Long Clawson, Normanton), Wheat Hill (Lt. Dalby, Knipton, Stathern); or wild flora, e.g. *Cowslophyll'*, *Hawthornehill* (Bottesford), Forsells (Gt. Dalby), *Thurn Hill* (Garthorpe, Waltham on the Wolds); or animal husbandry, e.g. *Catelhil* (Plungar), *the Cowpen hill* (Wyfordby), *Lambecotehil*, *Walke hill* (Wycomb/Chadwell). Wild birds may be specified, e.g. *Cawdaw hill* (Branston), *laferikhilles* (Bottesford), Pyewhit Hill (Stonesby). Religious edifices may be indicated, e.g. *Church hill* (Redmile), *Crosse hill'* (Plungar), Kirk Hill (Harston); or lay structures, e.g. Beacon Hill (Bottesford, Buckminster), Gallow Hill (Croxton Kerrial, Saxby), *le Gautreyhill* (Buckminster), Mill Hill (with various spellings in Nether Broughton, Buckminster, Burrough on the Hill, Lt. Dalby, Redmile, Scalford), Windmill Hill (with various spellings in Burton Lazars, Sproxton, Waltham on the Wolds, Wycomb/Chadwell). Settlement names are compounded, e.g. Chadwell Hill (Wycomb/Chadwell), *Grimston hill*, Shoby Hills

(Old Dalby), *Muston Hill* (Normanton); or minor names, e.g. *Fulwellehill'* (Knipton), *Normangate hill* (Redmile), *Stocbechil* (Bottesford). Surnames may feature, e.g. Brownshill (Freeby), Grices Hill (Buckminster), *Hubards hill* (Normanton); or pers.ns., e.g. Asker hill (Edmondthorpe), *Chitilishill* (Stathern). Note the recurring West Hill (Burton Lazars, Long Clawson, Hose, Plungar) and the important *Dinghill* (Somerby).

hyllig OE, adj., 'hilly'. *le Hillimedue* (f.n. Burrough on the Hill).

***hylloc** OE, **hillok, hullok** ME, 'a hillock'. Hillock(e)y Cl (f.n. Hose, Sysonby), *Hullocke hill Leaes* (f.n. Lt. Dalby), *Hullock Leyes* (f.n. Gt. Dalby).

***hyppels** OE, 'stepping stones'. *Hippelisdale* (f.n. Burrough on the Hill).

hyrne OE (Angl), 'an angle, a corner; a recess in a hill or in the hills, a corner in a valley, a spit of land in a river-bend'. ?Heron Drain, ?Heron Furlong (f.ns. Long Clawson), *hirneclif* (f.n. Muston), Kitty's Urn (f.n. Sewstern), *le Moreherne* (f.n. Wymondham), *Toft hurn* (f.n. Harby).

hyrst OE (Angl), 'a hillock; a wooded hill'. *barrowgate hurste* (f.n. Redmile), *the Bull hurst* (f.n. Normanton), *Enghirst* (f.n. Muston), *the holland hurst, Hurst Nook* (f.ns. Stathern), Husk leys, Bottom, Top Moor Husk (f.ns. Burrough on the Hill), *the Mill hurst* (f.n. Knipton), *Moore Huske* (f.n. Somerby).

īfig OE, 'ivy'. *Ivybanck* (f.n. Croxton Kerrial), Ivy Cl (f.n. Goadby Marwood).

-ig³ OE, suffix, mostly adj., **-ig, -i(e), -y(e)** ME, **-y** ModE, adj. suffix. *Brennycroft* (f.n. Muston), *Dockey Wonge* (f.n. Nether Broughton), *Dowkey Wong* (f.n. Freeby), Hassocky Cl (f.n. Burrough on the Hill), Hillock(e)y Cl (f.n. Hose, Sysonby).

impa, impe OE, 'a young shoot, a sapling'. *Impewelle* (f.n. Burrough on the Hill).

in OE, prep., 'in', sometimes with adj. force 'inner'. *Inmere furlonge* (f.n. Easthorpe).

inclosure eModE, 'an inclosing, an enclosure'; a variant form of **enclosure**, being the statutory form of reference to the inclosing of waste lands, commons etc. *the home inclosures of the Town* (Buckminster), the New Inclosure (f.n. Freeby, Goadby Marwood), *Mr Waldrones inclosure* (f.n. Scalford).

***ing** OE, 'a hill, a peak'. ?Ingleborough (f.n. Stonesby).

-ing¹ OE, noun suffix. ?Doddings (f.n. Coston), ?*Goring Botham* (f.n. Garthorpe).

-ing², -ling OE, toponymic suffix (adaptation of locative function of **-ing¹**). ?Beckingthorpe, ?Brentingby. ?Doddings (f.n. Coston), ?Filling's Fd (f.n Waltham on the Wolds), ?*Goring Botham* (f.n. Garthorpe), ?Hookings (f.n. Stathern), *Pabelynglond* (f.n. Wymondham), ?*Redyngwald* (f.n. Thorpe Arnold), ?Scalding Furlong (f.n. Muston).

-ingas OE, 'the people of ~, the people called after ~'; the patronymic function of **-ing¹**, used for forming folk-names. ?Beckingthorpe. ?*Bebing'* (f.n. Stathern).

***ingel** OE, 'a hill, a peak'. ?Ingleborough (f.n. Stonesby), Ingle Hill (f.n. Gt. Dalby).

inn OE, 'a dwelling, a lodging'. *Blaise's Inn*.

***innām** OE, **innám** ON, 'a piece of land taken in or enclosed'. Westinghams (f.n. Eastwell).

inntak ON, 'a piece of land taken in or enclosed', **intake** ModEdial., 'a piece of land enclosed from moor or waste'. Intake (f.n. Holwell, Wyfordby, Wymondham).

íri ON, 'an Irishman', prob. also used of Norsemen who had lived in Ireland. ?*the Iredale Furlong* (f.n. Harston).

island eModE, 'a piece of land completely surrounded by water, a piece of elevated land surrounded by marsh'; also 'a piece of woodland surrounded by open country'. The Island (f.n. Burton Lazars), Island Platt (f.n. Muston), Woodcock Island (f.n. Wymondham).

kaupa-land ON, 'purchased land'. Copeland Cottages. *Coupeland* (f.n. Bottesford).

kelda ON, 'a spring'. *Keldervelde* (f.n. Somerby).

kenel ME, 'a kennel'; sometimes relating to kennels in which hunting dogs were kept. Kennel Plantation, Kennels Wood. Dog Kennel Plantation (f.n. Goadby Marwood).

kervinge ME, 'a cutting, a carving out'. *Chervins* (f.n. Ab Kettleby), Kervings (f.n. Stathern).

kicchen ME, 'a kitchen'. *the Kechen close* (Belvoir Castle), Kitching Cl (f.n. Goadby Marwood).

king ME, 'a king'. King St. *the kinges land* (*Lewis*) (f.ns. Melton Mowbray), *the kings wonge* (f.n. Burton Lazars),*?kyngeswellhull* (f.n. Burrough on the Hill).

kirkja ON, 'a church'. *Kirck, Kirckridge* (f.ns. Normanton), *le kirkeclyf* (f.n. Wycomb/Chadwell), *kirkegate* (Lt. Dalby, Freeby, Pickwell, Stathern), *Kirke Hayd* (f.n. Coston), *le kirkehous* (Bottesford), *Kirkestile* (p) (Burrough on the Hill), *the kirkewong* (f.n. Freeby), Kirk Hill (f.n. Croxton Kerrial, Harston, Redmile), *le kyrkefeld'* (f.n. Plungar), *Kyrkestedplot'*, *Kyrkestedwong'* (f.ns. Muston), *le kyrkwong* (f.n. Thorpe Arnold).

klint ODan, 'a rocky cliff', used of 'a steep bank overlooking a river' and in ModEdial. **clint** of 'a hard rock projecting on the side of a hill'. the Clinths (f.n. Burrough on the Hill), *the Clints* (f.n. Somerby).

kollr ON, 'a hill, a top, a summit'. ?*colle lease* (f.n. Knipton).

kringla ON, 'a circle', used of 'the circular sweep of a river, a round hill, anything circular in shape'. *Cringelles* (f.n. Branston), *Cringledale* (f.n. Thorpe Arnold).

krókr ON, 'a crook, a bend; land in the bend of a river; a nook, a secluded corner'. ?*Crocland* (f.n. Harby), Crokeleys (f.n. Stathern), *Crokeswinstey* (f.n. Croxton Kerrial), ?*Croklokhull* (f.n. Thorpe Arnold), Crooke Dyke Furlong (f.n. Nether Broughton).

kylne-hous ME, 'a kiln; a building containing a kiln'. *le kelnehous* (Muston).

la OFr, fem.def.art., 'the'.

***læge** OE, adj., 'fallow, unploughed, lying untilled'. *Lealands* (f.n. Old Dalby).

læs (**læswe** gen.sg., dat.sg.) OE, 'pasture, meadowland'; extremely difficult to distinguish from the plural of **lēah** (**lēh** (**læs** nom.pl.) (Angl)) to which some of the following may rather belong, *v.* **leys**. *aungerleyes, Cranwater lese, Staunfordgate leys* (f.ns. Burton Lazars), *Bingborow leyes* (f.n. Freeby), *Chaveneis leasis* (f.n. Belvoir), *Drie Lees* (f.n. Bescaby), *grene lays, Hardwick Leys, Weyleys* (f.ns. Bottesford), *Hastenglayes* (f.n. Burrough on the Hill), Holyleys Pasture (f.n. Normanton), *le lesegore* (f.n. Wycomb/Chadwell), *the ueste leys* (f.n. Eye Kettleby), *Waterfurrows leasewes* (Water Furrows, f.n. Buckminster).

***lagge** OE, prob. 'a marsh' or the like. Lag Lane.

la(g)h ME, **low** ModE, adj., 'low, low-lying'. *le Loetraues, Low leyes furlong* (f.ns. Wycomb/Chadwell), *Lowfelde* (f.n. Stapleford).

laie ME, 'a pool'. *Leicroft* (f.n. Belvoir).

lake ME, 'a lake'. *Whirle Lake* (Withcote).

lām OE, 'clay, loam'. *Lampol* (f.n. Wymondham), *Lample penne* (f.n. Edmondthorpe).

lamb OE, 'a lamb'. *Lambcotewong* (f.n. Muston), Lamb Cotts (f.n. Goadby Marwood), *Lambecotes* (f.n. Wycomb/Chadwell), *Lamcoates* (f.n. Croxton Kerrial).

lambing eModE, vbl.sb., 'the parturition or yeaning of lambs'. Lambing Mdw (f.n. Pickwell).

lambkin ModE, 'a recently born lamb'. ?*Lankin dalle* (f.n. Saltby).

lammas eModE, 'Loaf Mass'; the 1st of August, in the early English Church observed as a harvest festival at which loaves of bread made from the first ripe corn were consecrated. In f.ns., referring to land which was under cultivation until harvest and reverted to common pasture from Lammas-tide until the following Spring. *lambmase close* (f.n. Wyfordby), Lammas Cl (f.n. Bottesford, Nether Broughton, Stathern), Upper Lammas (f.n. Coston).

lampe ME, 'a lamp'; in f.ns. referring to land endowed for the maintenance of an altar lamp in the parish church. Lamp Mdw (f.n. Burton Lazars).

land, lond OE, **land** ON, 'land', either in the general sense 'ground, part of the earth's surface' or 'an estate or small tract of land' or 'a strip of arable in a common field'. Acrelands Lane, Landfield Spinney, Landyke Lane, Woodlands. Very freq. in f.ns. The colour of the soil may be specified, e.g. *blackeland* (with various spellings in Barkestone, Harby, Plungar, Stonesby), *le Redlandes* (with various spellings in Holwell, Ab Kettleby, Normanton, Somerby, Stathern, Stonesby), *White land* (Burrough on the Hill), or its fertility may be indicated, e.g. *Butterlandes* (with various spellings in Bottesford, Gt. Dalby, Wyfordby), *Fattland*, Sand Lands (Burton Lazars), *Stanlande* (Eaton); or crops may be specified, e.g. *Barlilandis* (Thorpe Arnold), *Benlandes* (with various spellings in Bottesford, Burton Lazars, Edmondthorpe, Melton Mowbray, Normanton; and note *Bellands*, prob. an assimilated form of *Benlandes* in Barkestone, Bottesford, Branston, Brentingby, Garthorpe, Saxby, Thorpe Arnold, Waltham on the Wolds, Wyfordby), *flaxlandes* (with various spellings in Nether Broughton, Burton Lazars, Melton Mowbray and 5 additional townships), *peselandes* (with various spellings in Eaton, Freeby, Harby and 4 additional townships). Shape or extent is freq. indicated, e.g. *bretland* (with various spellings in Barkestone, Burrough on the Hill, Coston and 5 additional townships), *longlandes* (with various spellings in Branston, Burrough on the Hill, Knipton and 7 additional townships), *wranglandes* (with various spellings in Bottesford, Burton Lazars, Eaton and 12 additional townships). Wild flora may be indicated, e.g. *Hesland* (Ab Kettleby), Rush land dike (Holwell), *Taslands* (Stathern); or location, e.g. Crook Swinstead Lands (Croxton Kerrial), *Pibdale land* (Branston), *Redefordeland* (Muston); or ownership by larger institutions, e.g. *Grange land* (Nether Broughton), *the hall land* (Burton Lazars, Melton Mowbray), *Loughborough bridges land*, *Peterhowse land* (Stathern). Types of tenure may be specified, e.g. *bondlands* (Freeby), *lez demesne lands* (Old Dalby), *(the) Gleabe Land(s)* (Hose, Wymondham). Ownership may be specified by a pers.n. or a surn., e.g. *gaddesland* (Hose), *Custland* (Melton Mowbray), *Emmeslande*, *Hamsterley land*, *Lucaslande*

(Bottesford), *Nevylles land* (Hose), or by an el. signifying aristocracy, e.g. *the Earles land* (Burton Lazars), *the kinges land* (Melton Mowbray). In later f.ns., units made up of specified numbers of selions of former great fields appear, e.g. *the Seven Lands* (Buckminster), *(the) Nine Land(e)s* (Lt. Dalby, Sproxton), *sixteen lands* (Branston). Common is the close formed from unspecified numbers of selions of former great fields, e.g. Land Cl (Burton Lazars, Lt. Dalby, Old Dalby, Hose, Sewstern), Land Mdw (Burrough on the Hill).

land-gemǣre OE, 'a boundary'. *landemerehil* (f.n. Harby), *the land meere* (f.n. Nether Broughton).

lane OE, 'a lane, a narrow road'. Acrelands Lane, Back Lane (Long Clawson, Old Dalby), Barkestone Lane, Blacksmith's ~, Boston ~, Brook ~, Butt ~, Canal Lane (Long Clawson, Hose), Chapel Lane, Church ~, Clawson Lane (Nether Broughton, Holwell), Cordhill Lane, Dalby ~, Devon ~, Gibson's ~, Grange ~, Green ~, King Street ~, Kirby ~, Lag ~, Landyke ~, Lawn ~, Mary ~, Meadows ~, Mill Lane (Bottesford, Ab Kettleby), Moor Lane, Moor Leys ~, Nook ~, Nottingham ~, Paddy's ~, Paradise ~, Pasture Lane (Hose, Stathern), Sandy Lane (Melton Mowbray, Scalford), Six Hills Lane, Sysonby Grange ~, Toft's ~, Water ~, Welby Lane (Ab Kettleby, Melton Mowbray), Well Lane; and in lost street~names in Melton Mowbray (*q.v.*). Freq. in f.ns., e.g. with a hill- or stream-name, e.g. *Blackborow lane* (Knipton), *Acwellane* (Wycomb/Chadwell), *Crankwell lane* (Harby); with a directional adj., e.g. *le Estelane* (Somerby), *le West lane* (Belvoir); with the name of an adjacent township, e.g. Asfordby Lane (Wartnaby), the Branstone Lane (Croxton Kerrial), Melton Lane (Buckminster, Eye Kettleby); with a pers.n. or a surn., e.g. Roger Besk Lane (Harby), *Emeloteslane* (Wycomb/Chadwell), *Leeste lane* (Burrough on the Hill), *Phaskeden lane* (Bottesford); in a compound relating to the medieval salt trade, e.g. Saltcellar Lane (Croxton Kerrial), *Salt'lane* (Harston); with an el. describing a physical feature of the lane, e.g. *Blind Lane* (Wymondham), *milnestonlane* (Burrough on the Hill), *le Peterstone Lane* (Belvoir); with an el. relating to the Church, e.g. *Church lane* (Sproxton, Stathern), *the Parsonage lane* (Coston). Note also the simplex The Lane (Wyfordby), Lane Cl (Buckminster, Gt. Dalby, Old Dalby, Eastwell, Goadby Marwood, Sewstern).

lane-ende ME, 'a lane-end; (land at) the end of the lane' (*v.* Löfvenberg 117 and Ch **5** (l.ii), 262–3). *the Bridg lane end* (f.n. Stathern), Broad Lane End (f.n. Harby), *Bullane ende* (f.n. Edmondthorpe), *Church Lane End Wong* (f.n. Sproxton), *Clerkson Lane End, Hody Lane End* (f.ns. Burton Lazars), *Clock lane end* (f.n. Hose), *Crankwell Lane End, Jony lane end* (f.ns. Harby), Lane End Cl (f.n. Muston), *Leeste lane end* (f.n. Burrough on the Hill), *Muston Lane End* (f.n. Bottesford), *the parsonage lane ende* (f.n. Coston), *the Water-lane End* (f.n. Branston).

lang[1] OE, adj., **langr** ON, adj., 'long'. Long Clawson. Freq. in f.ns. with a range of units of agricultural land, e.g. *langelond* (Knipton), *long landes* (Ab Kettleby), *langewong', Longeclose, Longecroft'* (Belvoir), *longedeyle, Long doles* (Bottesford), *longefurlonge* (Harston, Knipton), *the Long Headland* (Harston). Note also the el. in compound with topographical features, e.g. *Langmore* (Belvoir), *le Longclif* (Bottesford), *long dytche* (Knipton).

lang² ME, 'a long strip of land'. *Cliffordlong'*, North Long (f.ns. Stathern), *Fleggelonge* (f.n. Burton Lazars), *heefeldlong'* (f.n. Thorpe Arnold), *Northlanges* (f.n. Normanton), *Westerlong* (f.n. Saxby).

launde OFr, ME, 'an open space in woodland, woodland pasture'. Lawn Hollow Plantation, Lawn Lane. *le laund* (f.n. Belvoir), ?*Laund Dike* (f.n. Holwell), Lawn Cls (f.n. Hose), Lawn Mdw (f.n. Freeby).

lavedi, ladi ME, 'a lady; Our Lady, the Virgin Mary'; often alluding to a female proprietor or a dowager or the lady of a manor. Ladies Cl (f.n. Brentingby), Ladys Mdw (f.n. Melton Mowbray, Pickwell), *Lauedilane* (Burton Lazars).

lāwerce, lāferce OE, 'a lark'. *laferikhilles* (f.n. Bottesford), Larkcliff Fd (f.n. Knipton), *Larkesmore* (f.n. Branston).

le OFr, masc.def.art., 'the'.

lēah OE, **lǣh (lǣs** nom.pl.) (Angl), 'woodland, a woodland glade, a clearing in a wood'; later 'pasture, meadow', *v.* **leys.** ?*Bartley Leas* (f.n. Saxby), ?*Billinglye nooke* (f.n. Stathern), Brackley Cl (f.n. Waltham on the Wolds), *Brackley close* (f.n. Withcote), ?*Eastely Sike* (f.n. Scalford), *Langelayehil* (f.n. Barkestone), *longe Whortlye* (f.n. Stapleford), *Spiceley Hill* (f.n. Wycomb/Chadwell), *Worteley syck* (f.n. Melton Mowbray), *yauley buttes* (f.n. Croxton Kerrial).

lēfer OE, 'a rush, a reed, a yellow iris, levers'. ?*Levielands* (f.n. Somerby), Liver Cl (f.n. Sewstern).

leirr ON, 'mud, clay', **leira** ON, 'a clayey place'. *Red leare* (f.n. Ab Kettleby).

levi ME, adj., 'leafy, abounding in foliage'. ?*Levielands* (f.n. Somerby).

ley ModE, 'a meadow, a pasture', *v.* **leys.** *the broadley* ~, *ye greatley* ~, *the headley* ~, *the Throwley in the more* (f.ns. Stathern), *the Bull lee* (f.n. Pickwell), *Butcher Lay* (f.n. Waltham on the Wolds), *the gated Lea* (f.n. Saxby), Ley Cl (f.n. Thorpe Arnold).

leyne, lain ME, 'a tract of arable land'. ?*the Sparrowe laine* (f.n. Waltham on the Wolds).

leys ModE, 'meadows, pastures; grassed-over selions of a common field (lying fallow)'. F.ns. with *leys* (spellings also in *layes, lays, leaes, leas, lease, leayes, leayse, leaze, leazes, lees, leies, leyes, leyis*) may have developed variously from the pl. of **lēah** (**lǣh** (**lǣs** nom.pl.) (Angl)) in its later sense 'pasture, meadow' and from **lǣs** 'pasture, meadowland' and it is very difficult to assign with confidence an individual name to either source, except where forms with *leasow* (from **lǣswe,** gen.sg. of the latter) survive. Professor K. Cameron argues that most later f.ns. with *leys* (*ley* sg.) are prob. from **lēah,** *v.* L 2 66 *s.n.* Carr Leys Wood. However, the modern sg. form *ley* (with spellings too in *lay, lea, lee*) may also be the result of the reduction of *leys* (from **lǣs** 'pasture, meadowland') as a perceived plural. Very freq. in f.ns., esp. with a locational prefix, e.g. *Sandpit Leas* (Eastwell), *Sheepcoate Lease* (Knipton), Spittle Leys (Melton Mowbray), *the Windmill Leyes* (Burton Lazars); or with a surn., e.g. *Dent Leyes* (Gt. Dalby), *Jeffrey's Leys* (Stapleford), Orgar Leys (Melton Mowbray), *Edward Wrights layes* (Nether Broughton). An indication of country games may occur, e.g. *Plaster Lees* (Sewstern), *Wrustleling leyes* (Ab Kettleby); or the quality or nature of the grassland, e.g. *Bare Leys,* Yellow Leys (Ab Kettleby), *Bastard ley(e)s* (Bottesford, Nether Broughton), White Leys (Muston); or local wild flora, e.g.

Crab tree Leys (Holwell), *Gorsye layes* (Barkestone). Cf. also *Deadman leyes*, *Tenter leyes* (Stonesby). When compounded with a numeral, *leys* represents grassland units of tenure corresponding to *lands* (i.e. selions or strips) similarly used of arable: e.g. *ye two Leyes* (Barkestone), *the Seven Lease* (Knipton), Thirty Leys (Melton Mowbray), *the Eighty-Three Leys* (Bottesford).

lez OFr, pl.def.art., 'the'. Infrequent in f.ns.: *Lez Balkes* (Stonesby), *lez demesne lands* (Old Dalby), *Lez Holmes* (Melton Mowbray), *lez meres* (Knipton), *lez Waterforowes* (Sewstern).

līn OE, **lín** ON, 'flax'. *linecroft* (f.n. Bottesford), Linlands Platt (f.n. Hose), ?Lintop Drain (f.n. Long Clawson).

lind OE, ON, 'a lime-tree'. ?Lintop Drain (f.n. Long Clawson), ?*Lynstygate* (Normanton).

-ling OE, diminutive suffix. Croftlinggate (Buckminster).

*lisc OE, 'reeds, reedy marsh'. *lysbancke* (f.n. Croxton Kerrial).

loc OE, 'a lock, a fold', **loca** OE, 'an enclosure'. *Croklokhull* (f.n. Thorpe Arnold), ?*Lochiswellehil* (f.n. Plungar), ?Lock-Allens (f.n. Waltham on the Wolds), ?Locks Moor (f.n. Sewstern).

lock ModE, 'an enclosed section of a canal which has gates at each end and in which water can be raised or lowered to move boats from one level to another'. Lock Cl (f.n. Brentingby), The Lock piece, The Far Lock Spinney (f.ns. Edmondthorpe).

loge OFr, **log(g)e** ME, 'a hut, a small house', later 'a house in a forest for temporary use (a forester's house or a hunting-lodge), a house at the entrance to a park'; freq. in modern house-names as a pretentious term for a country villa, often prefixed by an older p.n., by analogy with the names of genuine hunting-lodges, forest-houses or manorial estate-houses. Abbott Lodge, Barlow's ~, Blackwell Lodge, Brentingby Lodge Fm, Braunston Lodge, Broughton Lodges, Buckminster Lodge, Bunny's ~, Burrough Hill Lodge, Burton Lodge Fm, Clawson Lodge, Coston Lodge East, West, Craven Lodge, Cribb's ~, Croxton ~, Cumberland ~, Old Dalby ~, Debdale ~, Dorian ~, Drypot ~, Easthorpe ~, Eastwell ~, Eaton ~, Egerton ~, Gartree Hill ~, Glebe Lodge (Brentingby, Freeby), Harby Lodge, Hatton ~, Hazletongue ~, Home Farm Lodge, Home Lodge Hollow, Hose Lodge (x2, Harby), Jericho Lodge, Eye Kettleby ~, Knipton ~, Leesthorpe Lodge, The Lodge (Barkestone, Bottesford), Mawbrooke Lodge, Newport ~, Normanton ~, North ~, Oldfields Lodge, Pickwell Lodge Fm, Plymouth Lodge, Poole's Lodge Fm, Ramsley Lodge, Saltby ~, Saltby Heath Lodge, Sawgate Lodge Fm, Scalford Lodge, Smith's ~, South ~, Sproxton ~, Stapleford ~ (x2), Stathern ~, Staveley ~, Stonesby Lodge, Sysonby Lodge Fm, Sysonby Upper Lodge, Thorpe ~, Tunnel ~, Waltham West ~, White Lodge (Lt. Dalby, Goadby Marwood, Ab Kettleby), Wicklow Lodge, Wild's ~, Withcote ~, Wymondham Lodge; *Bellemere Lodge* (Bellemere Fm, Goadby Marwood), *Hose Lodge* (Mount Pleasant, Hose), *Pickwell Lodge* (Brocker Ho., Leesthorpe), *Pitfield Lodge* (Red House Fm, Scalford), *Wolds Lodge* (Scalford). the Lodge Cls (f.n. Nether Broughton), *Lodge Close* (f.n. Thorpe Arnold).

lone ModE, 'standing apart, isolated'. Lone Creek (f.n. Wymondham).

loning, laning ME, 'a lane'. Lowning (f.n. Holwell).

lowsy ME, adj., 'lousy; infested with lice or insects'. *Lousie Bush* (f.n. Nether Broughton), Lousy Bush (f.n. Long Clawson), cf. **lūs-þorn**.

lundr ON, 'a small wood, a grove'. Framland. Lound Cl (f.n. Hose), *Loundegat* (Melton Mowbray), *Loundeinges*, *Loundewelle* (f.ns. Melton Mowbray), *Lownes gate* (Scalford), *le Lund* (f.n. Nether Broughton).

lūs OE, **lús** ON, 'a louse'; in p.ns., poss. used to describe something small and insignificant. *Lawsemore* (f.n. Eastwell).

*lūs-þorn OE, 'a spindle-tree'. *Listern Bridge* (Wymondham), *Lusternegate* (Eaton), cf. **lowsy**.

lyme-pytt ME, 'a lime-pit'. *Limpitt'* (f.n. Thorpe Arnold).

lyng ON, 'ling, heather'. Lings Covert, Lings Fm, Lings Hill. Ling Dale (f.n. Eastwell), *Lingdale*, *the Lynges* (f.ns. Croxton Kerrial), Lings Cl (f.n. Waltham on the Wolds), *le Longeling'*, *Northling*, *Schortling'* (f.ns. Eaton), *longe linge* (f.n. Eastwell).

lȳtel, lītel OE, adj., **lítill** ON, adj., 'little, small'. Little Dalby. Freq. in f.ns., e.g. Little Dale (Sewstern), *littlemedue* (Burton Lazars), *Lyttledale*, *lyttle wonge* (Knipton), *lyttylgorebrod'* (Bottesford).

mǣd (mǣdwe obl.sg.) OE, **mēd** OE (Angl), 'a meadow'. Examples of f.ns. from the nom.sg. are few: *Bacons Meade* (Nether Broughton), Hubbuck Mead (Gt. Dalby), *la Ladymede*, *the Pynkewathe meade*, *Sherholdes mede* (Melton Mowbray), *Saynt Margytts Meade*, *Walke Mill mead* (Burton Lazars), *westmede* (Wyfordby). Freq. in f.ns. as *meadow* from the oblique case: with a locational indicator e.g. *benilmedow* (Bottesford), *Neathouse meadow* (Belvoir), *Thorpmilnemedue* (Lt. Dalby); or with a directional indicator, e.g. South Mdw, West Mdw, Brentingby Mdw (Burton Lazars), *Normanton medowes* (Muston). Size may be described, e.g. Great Mdw (Wymondham), Little Mdw (Eastwell), Long Mdw (Burton Lazars, Melton Mowbray, Wyfordby); or aspect, e.g. *the Hillimedue* (Burrough on the Hill), Rough Mdw (Edmondthorpe), *Smethe medue* (with various spellings in Burton Lazars, Gt. Dalby, Somerby), *winie meadowe* (Scalford). Agricultural usage may be indicated, e.g. *Ploumanmedwe*, *the Ram meadow* (Burrough on the Hill), Tup Mdw (Wyfordby), *the Stoned Medowe* (with various spellings in Branston, Knipton, Scalford, Sproxton, Thorpe Arnold), *Water medow* (Coston, Edmondthorpe). Ownership may be indicated, e.g. *the Kings meadow* (Melton Mowbray), Loves Mdw (Wymondham), Nuttalls Mdw (Sysonby). Common as a simplex, e.g. *the meadowe* (with various spellings in Lt. Dalby, Old Dalby, Holwell etc.).

mægden OE, 'a maiden, a young unmarried woman'; in p.ns., usually in allusion to places owned by them, or to places which they habitually frequented. *Maydengate* (Knipton), *Maydenstede* (Somerby).

(ge)mǣne OE, adj., 'common'; in p.ns. denoting property or land held communally. ?Man Mill Peice (f.n. Burton Lazars), *Manndale Fur'* (f.n. Melton Mowbray).

(ge)mǣnnes OE, 'a community'; in p.ns., used of 'common land, a common holding' ?Man Mill Peice (f.n. Burton Lazars), *mannesbrigg* (Redmile), *?Mannisheuid* (f.n. Bottesford), *Mansdales* (f.n. Saxby), *mennessefurlong'* (f.n. Muston).

(ge)mǣre OE, 'a boundary, a border; a strip of land forming a boundary'. Fairly freq. in f.ns.: most often with the name of an adjoining township, e.g. *Croxton Meere* (Harston), *Holwell meere* (Ab Kettleby), *Hosemeer* (Harby); with reference to the county boundary, e.g. *the shyre meere* (with various spellings in Harston, Hose,

Muston, Plungar); with a pers.n., poss. indicating a balk of ploughland, e.g. *hingoldysmer'*, *Jonismere* (Bottesford), *Ingelemere* (Hose); with wild flora, e.g. *Hawethornmere* (Barkestone, Redmile), Thorney Mere (Harston), *the Whiny meare* (Saltby). When found as a simplex pl. (e.g. *le meeres* (with various spellings in Croxton Kerrial, Knipton, Saltby)), the reference is presum. to land on a boundary. Note *The Meere Stone* (Wymondham); township boundaries were often marked by major stones in the 17th and 18th centuries.

malte-mylne ME, 'a mill for grinding or crushing malt'. The Malt Mill. *The Malt Mill house* (Malt Office, Wymondham).

maner ME, 'a manor (house), a mansion'. The Manor, Manor Fm (Barkestone, Chadwell, Waltham on the Wolds), Manor Ho. (Brentingby, Burrough on the Hill, Gt. Dalby, Easthorpe, Ab Kettleby, Melton Mowbray, Pickwell, Plungar, Saxby, Scalford, Sproxton, Stonesby, Wymondham), Old Manor Ho. (Long Clawson, Harby), Rydal Manor, Stapleford Manor. *the Manner house* (Old Dalby Hall), *the maner hedge* (f.n. Saltby).

manig OE, adj., 'many'. *Many Welles* (f.n. Barkestone).

mann OE, 'a man', cf. **dede-man, nān-mann**. ?*Mannisheuid* (f.n. Bottesford), Mans Bones (f.n. Wymondham).

mansion-house eModE, 'the house of a lord of the manor; an official residence, esp. that belonging to the benefice of an ecclesiastic'. *the mansion hous* (The Vicarage, Gt. Dalby; Withcote Hall), *the mansion howse of the Parsonage* (Melton Mowbray), *the mansyon house* (The Rectory, Saxby).

mare ME, 'a mare'. ?*the Mare Close* (f.n. Goadby Marwood), ?Mares Cl (f.n. Waltham on the Wolds), ?*le maresty* (f.n. Harby).

mareis OFr, ME, 'a marsh'. ?*the Mares* (f.n. Stapleford), *le maris* (f.n. Muston), The Morris (f.n. Waltham on the Wolds).

market ME, 'a market, a market-place'. Market Place. *the markit way* (Wyfordby), *Markytt Gate* (Burton Lazars).

marle-pytt ME, 'a marl-pit'. *Burton Marlepyttes* (f.n. Burton Lazars), *Marle pittes* (f.n. Ab Kettleby).

marr[1] ON, 'a fen, a marsh'. *le Mar* (f.n. Melton Mowbray), the Mare (f.n. Stathern), ?*the Mares* (f.n. Stapleford), *the Marre* (f.n. Pickwell), the Marr Fd (f.n. Somerby), Mar Hill, Marsick (f.ns. Burrough on the Hill), Marr Pasture (f.n. Normanton).

mausoleum ModE, 'a stately tomb'. The Mausoleum. Mausoleum Fd (f.n. Waltham on the Wolds).

mearc OE, 'a boundary; a boundary-mark'. *le Balke voc' the Grett Marke* (f.n. Stonesby).

mere[1] OE, 'a pool, a lake', also 'wetland'; difficult to distinguish from **(ge)mǣre**. ?Bellemere Fm. ?*grenemerebech* (f.n. Redmile), *milnestymere*, *Redemere* (f.ns. Muston), ?*Nooke meere furlonge* (f.n. Lt. Dalby), ?*sloteridemere* (f.n. Long Clawson).

mersc OE, 'watery land, a marsh'. March Ho. *lyttelmersh'*, The Marsh (f.ns. Muston), *le Marche bullpitt* (Bull Pit Cl, f.n. Thorpe Arnold), March Fd (f.n. Knipton), *March Leas* (f.n. Saxby), Marsh Cl, *le Shortmarshes* (f.ns. Buckminster), *the Marshe* (f.n. Melton Mowbray, Sproxton), The Top March (f.n. Gt. Dalby), *the West Marshe* (f.n. Sproxton).

mete OFr, ME, 'a boundary; a boundary-mark'. *Longe meates* (f.n. Wyfordby).

meðal ON, adv., 'among, between'; in p.ns. with adj. function 'middle', influencing or replacing **middel** in the Danelaw. Melton Mowbray. *the medelbryng'* (f.n. Stapleford), *Medelholm* (f.n. Scalford), *Medilewhytcleys* (f.n. Bottesford), *Medilforlong* (f.n. Old Dalby), *Medlisdale* (f.n. Leesthorpe), Mellams (f.n. Thorpe Arnold).

micel, mycel OE, adj., **mikill** ON, adj., 'big, great'; the OE el. is much influenced by the ON el. in the Danelaw, and difficult to distinguish. Freq. in f.ns., e.g. *Coleuillemiclewong, mickelmerehil, mikelgorebrod', myclemore dole, mykulplott* (f.ns. Bottesford), *michelho* (f.n. Redmile), *Mikilsig* (f.n. Normanton), *mikkelberue* (f.n. Croxton Kerrial), *myculclyf* (f.n. Knipton).

midd OE, adj., 'middle'. *(le) midfurlong'* (f.ns. Bottesford, Normanton), *the mid tofthe* (f.n. Pickwell).

middel OE, adj., 'middle'. Middlesdale, Middlestile Bridge. Freq. in f.ns., e.g. Middle Beck (Muston), Middle Cl (Buckminster), Middle Fd (Bottesford), *middelfurlong'* (with various spellings in Bottesford, Lt. Dalby, Harston, Knipton etc.).

middes ME, 'the middle of something'. Middlesdale. *Medlisdale* (f.n. Leesthorpe), *Middles dale* (f.n. Pickwell), Midshill (f.n. Croxton Kerrial).

milking eModE, vbl.sb., 'the drawing of milk from the udders of cows and other animals'. Milking Cl (f.n. Sysonby).

milne-stone ME, 'a millstone'. *milnestonlane* (Burrough on the Hill).

***modor** OE, 'mud, bog'. Mother Acre, Mother Cl (f.ns. Gt. Dalby).

molde OE, 'earth, soil'. *Black Mold* (f.n. Stonesby), *Blake moulde* (f.n. Freeby), *Fattemold'* (f.n. Thorpe Arnold), *holmold* (f.n. Muston).

moldewarp ME, 'the mole', literally 'earth-thrower'. Moldewarp (f.n. Freeby).

molle ME, **mold** eModE, 'the mole'. Mole Cl (f.n. Burton Lazars), the Mowed Wong (f.n. Scalford).

mōr¹ OE, **mór** ON, 'a moor; marshland, barren wasteland, barren upland'. Freq. in f.ns.: prefixed by the name of a township, e.g. *Easthorpmore* (Belvoir), *Wifordby Moor* (Wyfordby), *Wymondam Moore* (Wymondham); or by the surn. of an owner of a stretch of moorland, e.g. *Adcocks Moore, Richardsons Moore* (Wymondham), *Hoults Moore* (Croxton Kerrial), Wigleys Moor (Coston); or with an adj. indicating direction from a township, e.g. *(le) Est More* (Buckminster, Freeby), West Moore (Stathern), *Westmore* (Wymondham). Shape or size are often indicated, e.g. *le longemor* (with various spellings in Belvoir, Coston, Harby, Harston), *le schortmor* (Harby), *Short Moores* (Harston), *Cheesecake More* (Wymondham), *the greate More, Mykill More* (Freeby), *littelmore* (Burton Lazars); or the nature of the land, e.g. Saltmoor, Wetmoore (Hose), *Watmore* (Wycomb/Chadwell), *Whyttmore* (Knipton), Fine Moor, Rough Moor (Wymondham). Freq. as a simplex, e.g. *le more* (with various spellings in Burton Lazars, Coston, Gt. Dalby, Eastwell etc.), *the Moores* (Croxton Kerrial, Wyfordby). Note the interesting *deadmore* (Waltham on the Wolds, Wymondham) and *Walchemoresedes* (Burton Lazars). *Mooregate* (with **gata**) with various spellings occurs in 8 townships.

morgen OE, 'the morning'. Moundrell (f.n. Sysonby).

morgen-gifu OE, 'the principal gift by a husband to his wife in the morning after the wedding'. ?Moundrell (f.n. Sysonby).

morter ME, 'a mortar, a vessel having a cup-shaped cavity, used for grinding'; 'mortar, a mixture of cement, lime etc. with sand and water, that hardens and is used to join bricks and stones in building'. *the Morter pitts* (f.n. Saltby).

mos OE, **mosi** ON, 'moss, lichen'; also 'a bog, a swamp, a moss'. Mosshill (f.n. Stathern).

mote OFr, 'an embankment', **mote** ME, 'a moat, a protective ditch'. *le Mote* (Belvoir Castle).

mudde ME, 'mud'. Mud Pit Cl (f.n. Hose), *Mudwells* (f.n. Harby).

muk ME, 'dung, muck, dirt'. *Muckewellegate* (Harby).

munuc OE, **monke** ME, 'a monk'. *the Monkes wonges* (f.n. Branston).

mūs OE, **músi** ON, 'a mouse'. Muston. *Mussike* (f.n. Somerby), *Mussulhoke* (f.n. Burton Lazars).

mūða OE, 'a mouth'; in early p.ns., transferred as 'the mouth of a river', later 'a valley mouth' etc. Holwell Mouth. *Piperhole Mouth* (Piper Hole), *the Syke Mouth* (f.n. Harby).

***mylde** OE (Angl), 'soil, earth'. Redmile. *Blackamiles* (f.n. Sproxton), *Blackmiles* (f.n. Easthorpe), *Blacmild* (f.n. Harby), Break Miles (f.n. Gt. Dalby).

myln, mylen OE, 'a mill', cf. **water-mylne, wind-mylne**. Covermill Hill, Easthorpe Mill, Eye Kettleby Mill, The Mill, Mill Hill, Mill Hill Spinney, Mill Ho. (Scalford, Stathern), Mill Lane, Mill Pond, Old Mill Ho. Mills specified only in MSS sources are: *Aldemulne* (Knipton), *Assebymilne* (Eaton), *Beck Mill, Eye Mills, Warwellmill* (Melton Mowbray), Bottesford Mill, *husmilne* (Bottesford), *Croxton' milne* (Croxton Kerrial), Dalby Mill (Gt. Dalby), *the East Mill*, West Mill (Long Clawson), Knipton Mill (Knipton), *mannemilne* (Burton Lazars), *mido milne* (Branston), *the milne* (with various spellings in Barkestone, Branston, Nether Broughton, Coston, Eastwell, Ab Kettleby, Saltby, Saxby, Scalford, Sproxton), *le nedermylne, the Overmyln* (Barkestone), Normanton Mill (Normanton), *the olde Milne* (with various spellings in Burrough on the Hill, Goadby Marwood, Ab Kettleby, Redmile, Waltham on the Wolds); cf. *molendinum de Eyton* (Eaton), *molendinum Harwyni* (Withcote), *molendinis de Mostona* (Muston), *molendinum de Torp* (Leesthorpe). Very freq. in f.ns., usually as the first el.: most common are Mill Cl (with various spellings in Burton Lazars, Croxton Kerrial, Gt. Dalby and 8 other townships), Mill Fd (with various spellings in Barkestone, Branston, Buckminster and 16 other townships), Mill Hill (with various spellings in Nether Broughton, Lt. Dalby, Knipton and 6 other townships), Mill Holme (with various spellings in Coston, Goadby Marwood, Hose and 8 other townships). Water-mills are signalled by *le milnedam* (Nether Broughton, Pickwell, Scalford), *Milpole* (Edmondthorpe), Mill Pond (Burrough on the Hill, Melton Mowbray), *the mill water* (Saltby). The road-name *Mill gate* occurs in Gt. Dalby, Eaton, Goadby Marwood, Harby, Harston, Hose, Somerby and Thorpe Arnold.

myln-strēam OE, 'a mill-stream'. *Mill Stream* (Mill Bank, f.n. Coston).

mynster OE, 'the church of a monastery or religious body, a church served by secular clergy'. Buckminster.

mýrr ON, 'a mire, a bog, swampy ground'. *la mire* (f.n. Leesthorpe), *Dale Mires* (f.n. Burrough on the Hill), *mire dole, Mires Sharadale, Myre Field Gores* (f.ns. Branston), *le mirewell'* (f.n. Sysonby), *Mirewellesike* (f.n. Wycomb/Chadwell), Mire Wells (f.n. Waltham on the Wolds), *Rackett Mires* (f.n. Burton Lazars), *Shittlemyres* (f.n. Redmile).

myry ME, adj., 'miry, muddy'. ?Mary Lane. ?*East Mary end* (f.n. Burton Lazars), ?Mary Dykes Lower Mdw (f.n. Eye Kettleby), ?*Mary Leayse* (f.n. Croxton Kerrial), *miery doles* (f.n. Branston).

nabbi, nabbr ON, 'a projecting peak, a knoll, a hill'. *harenab* (f.n. Knipton), *nab hill* (f.n. Scalford).

næss OE (Angl), **nes** ON, 'a projecting piece of land (especially jutting into water or marsh)'. Swan's Nest. *Cranner Nest* (Cranor, f.n. Stathern), Great Ness (f.n. Burton Lazars), The Nest, Nest Mdw (f.ns. Freeby).

nān-mann OE, 'no man, nobody'. *Nomans furlong* (f.n. Barkestone), *Nomonysland* (f.n. Somerby), ?*Norman Bridge* (Knipton), ?Normans Hill (f.n. Wymondham).

napperone ME, 'an apron'; later, used amongst other things of 'a sluice-apron'. *napporons dale* (f.n. Edmondthorpe).

nēah OE, **nigh** eModE, adj., 'near, nigh'. *the Brode nye Dalby mere, the brode nye Saltgate* (f.ns. Melton Mowbray).

nearu OE, adj., 'narrow'. *Narrow eares* (f.n. Saltby), Narrow shred (f.n. Burrough on the Hill), *Nearyearthe* (f.n. Scalford).

nēat OE, 'cattle'. *the neatdames, the neatdrifte* (f.ns. Saxby), *Neate dammes, Neat Sike* (f.ns. Knipton), *the Neate Drifte* (f.n. Melton Mowbray), *neate heades, Sproxton neathead* (f.ns. Saltby), *Neatepoole* (f.n. Branston), *neateshead furlong* (f.n. Sproxton), *the neates pasture* (f.n. with various spellings in Bottesford, Branston, Brentingby, Lt. Dalby, Garthorpe, Thorpe Arnold), *the neates watering(es)* (f.ns. Pickwell, Wyfordby), Neat Fair (f.n. Waltham on the Wolds), *Neatwaters* (f.n. Harby), Nedgates (f.n. Muston).

nebb OE, 'a beak'; used topographically of 'a projecting peak', cf. **nabbi**. *Gorin neb* (f.n. Branston), *hareneb* (f.n. Knipton).

neetherd ME, 'a cowherd'. *the neatheardes balke, the Neatheardes land* (f.ns. Saxby), *the Neatheardes headland, the Neatheards yard* (f.ns. Eastwell).

neethowse ME, 'a cattle shed'. *Neathouse meadow* (f.n. Belvoir).

neoðera OE, adj., 'lower'. Nether Broughton. Fairly freq. in f.ns., e.g. *nedergorbrod, nedergreneleys, neder smyth deyls, the neither holte, le Nethermiddilforlong* (Bottesford), *le nedermylne, Neyther stones* (Barkestone), *Nether Hall* (Stapleford), *Netherthorp* (Lt. Dalby).

nest OE, 'a nest'. *the Ducks Nest* (f.n. Bottesford), *the Swannes neast* (f.n. Goadby Marwood), the Swans Nest (f.n. Pickwell).

nigon OE, num., 'nine'. *the Nine landes* (f.n. Lt. Dalby), *the Nine Rode* (f.n. Redmile), *Nyne acre(s)* (f.ns. Coston, Holwell), *the Nyne leies* (f.n. Coston).

nīðing OE, **níðingr** ON, 'a wretch, a villain, a coward; a mean or miserly person, a niggard; one who gives food grudgingly'; used adjectively, perh. 'sparing, niggardly'. the Nithingworth (f.n. Knipton).

nīwe OE, adj., 'new'. Fairly freq. in f.ns. and used of plots of land newly acquired, newly cultivated and, chiefly, newly reclaimed from the waste, e.g. *New close*

(Old Dalby), *therles Newe Close* (Barkestone), *the newe field* (Redmile), *le Neumor* (The Moors, Croxton Kerrial), *Newhynger* (Stonesby). Note also *Newebrigge* (Eaton), *Nuegate* (Harston), *Neuweye*, *New Parke* (Belvoir) etc.

nōk ME, 'a nook; a nook of land, a triangular plot of ground'. Chapel Nook, Dovecot Nook Hill, Nook Lane, The Nook. Freq. in f.ns.: with a sum. specifying ownership, e.g. Barrel's Nook (Somerby), Ellis Nook (Stathern), *Nobles Nooke* (Scalford); with the name of an adjacent township, e.g. *Branstone Nooke* (Croxton Kerrial), *Saltbynook* (Stonesby), Sysonby Nook (Sysonby); prefixed by an el. specifying a structure, e.g. the Church Nook (Knipton), Cockpit Nook (Edmondthorpe), *Hall Nooke* (Stonesby); or by a local minor name, e.g. Ling Dale Nook (Eastwell), *old park nooke* (Barkestone), Wadhill Nook (Hose); or prefixed by a minor topographical feature, e.g. Featherbed Nook (Burrough on the Hill), Hurst Nook (Stathern), *the Wood Nooke* (Old Dalby). Reference to farm animals sometimes occurs, e.g. Bull Nook (Burton Lazars), Cow Close Nook (Nether Broughton), *Sheep-pen Croft nook* (Ab Kettleby).

Norman ME, 'a Norman of Normandy'. *?Norman Bridge* (Knipton), *?normangate* (Redmile), *?Normangatt* (Bottesford).

norð OE, ON, adj., adv., 'northern, north'. Freq. in f.ns., e.g. Nordale Cl, *Northalls, The North Feild* (Harston), *Nordmedelhom* (Scalford), *northbellands, northbrendeland'* (Bottesford), *northebrige* (Knipton), *Northwel'* (Belvoir).

norðēast OE, adj., adv., 'northeastern, northeast'. *the Northeast fyelde* (f.n. Barkestone).

Norðman late OE, 'a Norwegian'. Normanton. *?Norman Bridge* (Knipton), *?normangate* (Redmile), *?Normangatt* (Bottesford).

nunne OE, 'a nun'. *Nunriges* (f.n. Scalford), Nun's Cl (f.n. Waltham on the Wolds).

nursery eModE, 'a piece of ground in which young plants or trees are reared until fit for transplantation; a nursery garden'. Bottesford Nursery, Nursery Lane, Nursery Plantation. *the Lords Nursery* (f.n. Stapleford), The Nursery (f.n. Thorpe Arnold), *Nursery place* (Melton Mowbray).

odde ME, adj., 'odd, the odd one (of three etc.)'. *Le Hodde Willowe* (f.n. Burton Lazars).

ofer[3] OE, prep., 'over, above, across'; difficult to distinguish from **uferra**. *Houerfolewellis* (f.n. Wycomb/Chadwell), *houerpols*, *?ouerberu, ouercotestys* (f.ns. Bottesford), *ouer the dalle* (f.n. Stapleford), *over Borrough way, over Grives way* (f.ns. Pickwell), *over the Milne gate* (f.n. Goadby Marwood).

ope ME, adj., adv., 'open, unenclosed'. *Ope Moore* (f.n. Wymondham).

open OE, adj., 'open, unenclosed'. the Open Cl (f.n. Melton Mowbray), *The Open Close* (f.n. Eastwell), Open Ground (f.n. Wymondham), Open Pasture (f.n. Coston), Open Plantation (f.n. Eastwell), Open Roe Wong (f.n. Redmile), *Wiverby open common* (f.n. Brentingby).

ōra[1] OE, 'a ridge with a rounded shoulder at one or both ends'. *?Windsor Hill.

orceard, ort-geard OE 'a garden'; later in OE, 'an orchard'. *the Hall orchyard, the Vicaridg orchyeard* (f.ns. Buckminster), *le horcharde wong, the Parsonage Orchyarde* (f.ns. Knipton), Pool Close Orchard (f.n. Withcote).

ōsle OE, 'an ouzle, a blackbird'. Izle Beck (f.n. Long Clawson), *Oselaker* (f.n Eaton), *Osindale* (f.n. Wycomb/Chadwell), *Ousledale* (f.n. Waltham on the Wolds), *Owsell welles* (f.n. Harston).

oxa OE, 'an ox'. Ox Cl (f.n. Hose), *the Ox close* (f.n. Buckminster), *Oxeclosse* (f.n. Wymondham), Oxburrow Cl (f.n. Waltham on the Wolds), Oxhead Cl (f.n. Muston), Ox Pasture (f.n. Burton Lazars), *Ox Pasture* (f.n. Sproxton), *Oxwelgate* (Plungar).

ox-gang OE, 'a measure of land of 10 to 30 acres; an eighth of a plough-land'. *Oxgang Cottages* (Eaton).

oyser ME, 'osier, willow'. Osier Holt. (The) Ozier Bed (f.ns. Eastwell, Wyfordby).

pad ModEdial., 'a path', *v.* **pæð**.

***padde** OE, **padda** ON, 'a toad'. ?Paddams (f.n. Eastwell).

paddock eModE, 'a small field or enclosure; a plot of pasture land usually adjoining a house or stable'. Barns Lane Paddock, Home Paddock (f.ns. Scalford), Bull Paddock (f.n. Goadby Marwood), Bursnell's Paddock, Gill's Paddock (f.ns. Wymondham), Church Farm Paddock, Dale Paddock, Joel's Paddock, The Pig Paddock, Prince Paddock, Second Paddock, Sharpe's Paddock, Warner's Paddock (f.ns. Gt. Dalby), (the) Paddock (f.ns. Belvoir, Brentingby, Buckminster, Gt. Dalby, Thorpe Arnold), *Padock* (f.n. Old Dalby), Pony Paddock, Willow Paddock (f.ns. Waltham on the Wolds).

***padduc** OE, **paddok** ME, 'a frog'. *Padock poole* (f.n. Lt. Dalby).

pæð OE, **pad** ModEdial., 'a path'. *at the padd*, *At the Path* (f.ns. Croxton Kerrial), *Statorn pad* (f.n. Branston).

pāl OE, 'a stake, a pole'. Ash Pole Spinney.

pale ME, 'a fence, a park-pale'. *the parke pale* (Croxton Park, Croxton Kerrial).

palme ME, 'a palm-tree'; in northern countries, the goat-willow was used in celebrations of Palm Sunday as a substitute for the true palm. Palm Hill (f.n. Burrough on the Hill).

***papol** OE, 'a pebble'. *Pabelynglond* (f.n. Wymondham).

parade ModE, 'a public square or promenade'. *South parade* (Melton Mowbray).

paradis ME, 'a garden, an enclosed pleasure ground'. Paradise Lane (Old Dalby).

parallelogram ModE, 'a quadrilateral with opposite sides parallel and equal'. Parallogram Cl (f.n. Lt. Dalby).

park OFr, ME, 'an enclosed tract of land for beasts of the chase'; later also 'an enclosed plot of ground, a field'. Croxton Park, Egerton Park, New Park, Old Park Wood, Stapleford Park, The Park. *Dalby Parke* (f.n. Old Dalby), *Eaton Parke* (f.n. Eaton), Goadby Park (f.n. Goadby Marwood), Horse Park, The Park (f.ns. Edmondthorpe), *New Parke* (f.n. Belvoir), *Orgerpark, the Park Wonge* (f.ns. Melton Mowbray), The Park (f.n. Eye Kettleby, Wymondham), *the Parkes* (f.n. Scalford, Thorpe Arnold), (the) Park Leys (f.ns. Knipton, Thorpe Arnold), Thorney Park (f.n. Harby). Note *Est parkvall* (Wymondham).

parlur ME, 'a parlour, a private room'; in later f.ns. 'a secluded piece of ground'. Newcombe's Parlour.

part ME, 'a part, a portion'. Corn Part (f.n. Freeby), North, South Part Deepdale (f.ns. Waltham on the Wolds), Poor Part (f.n. Lt. Dalby).

partable OFr, ME, adj., 'capable of being divided'. *the Parteable dole* (f.n. Knipton).

parting ModE, ppl.adj., in f.ns. prob. meaning 'that which may be divided or shared'. Love's Parting Cl, Man's Parting Cl (f.ns. Wymondham), The Parting

Cl (f.n. Edmondthorpe), *Partingrasse* (f.n. Burrough on the Hill), *Parting Grasse Baulke* (f.n. Gt. Dalby), Parting Piece (f.n. Lt. Dalby).

pasture OFr, ME, 'a pasture, a piece of pasture-land'. Knipton Pasture, Pasture Lane (Hose, Stathern), Saltby Pasture, Waltham Pasture Fm. Common in f.ns.: esp. with reference to cattle, e.g. *the Calfe pasture* (Branston), *Calfes pasture furlonge* (Lt. Dalby), *the neates pasture* (with various spellings in Bottesford, Branston, Lt. Dalby, Garthorpe), *Ox Pasture* (Burton Lazars, Sproxton), *Plungar beastes pasture* (Plungar); specifying a township, e.g. Freeby Pasture (Freeby), *Leisthorpe Pasture* (Leesthorpe), *Redmell pasture* (Redmile). Note also Old Pasture (Burrough on the Hill), *the plough land pasture* (Melton Mowbray), Whitsunday Pasture (Sysonby).

patche eModE, 'a small piece of ground'. Small Patch (f.n. Gt. Dalby).

pece OFr, ME, 'a piece; a piece or plot of land'. Freq. in f.ns.: with a surn. indicating ownership, e.g. *Canter's Piece* (Sproxton), Clarks Piece (Wymondham), *Levats pece*, Joel Shuttlewoods piece (Melton Mowbray); with the title of a township official, e.g. *the Constables Piece* (Scalford), *pinder peece* (Easthorpe); with common structures, e.g. *the Church pece* (Sproxton), *the hall peece* (Knipton), Man Mill Piece (Burton Lazars); with reference to shape or surface characteristics, e.g. *the Cheesecake piece* (Somerby), Three Corner('d) Piece (Brentingby, Thorpe Arnold), *Flatte peece* (Burrough on the Hill), Rough Piece (Freeby); with wild flora, e.g. *the Bracken peece* (Eaton), *the Crabtree pece* (Sproxton). Note also the recurring *the Common peice* (Branston, Croxton Kerrial, Eastwell), Ploughed Piece (Lt. Dalby, Holwell, Wyfordby).

pecok ME, 'a peacock'. ?*Pecok croft* (f.n. Belvoir).

pedlere ME, 'a pedlar'. ?Pedlars Cl (f.n. Wymondham).

peni ME, 'a penny; a penny rent'. *broad pennies* (f.n. Branston), *Penidolis* (f.n. Thorpe Arnold).

penn[2] OE, 'a small enclosure, a fold'. The Penn. *brodpenne, Lample penne* (f.ns. Edmondthorpe), *the Cowpen hill* (f.n. Wyfordby), *New Penn* (f.n. Stapleford), *North pen* (f.n. Croxton Kerrial), *Penbutt'* (f.n. Thorpe Arnold), Pen Cl (f.n. Holwell), ?*Peneyard* (f.n. Wymondham), Pen Lane Gate (Stathern), *Sheep-pen Croft nook* (f.n. Ab Kettleby), Stone Pen Cl (f.n. Eastwell, Goadby Marwood), *Stone Pen Lingdale* (f.n. Eastwell), *Taylors penn* (f.n. Nether Broughton).

pere OE, 'a pear, the fruit of the pear-tree'. Pere Croft (f.n. Gt. Dalby).

persely ME, 'parsley'. *Parsley Syke* (f.n. Melton Mowbray).

personage ME, 'a parsonage'. *the Parsonage* (Bottesford, Branston, Hose, Muston), *the parsonage howse* (with various spellings in Eastwell, Goadby Marwood, Harston, Knipton, Pickwell, Stathern). In f.ns.: *the Parsonage Balke, ~ ~ Barne, ~ ~ Cloase, ~ ~ meddow, ~ ~ Orchyarde, ~ ~ Pingle* (Knipton), *the Parsonadge Furlonge* (Goadby Marwood), *the Parsonage ground* (Harston), *the Parsonage hades, ~ ~ Leas, ~ ~ more medow* (Saxby), *the Parsonage land* (Somerby), *the parsonage stackplace* (Wyfordby), *Parsonage wonge* (Burrough on the Hill), *the Parsonage Wonges* (Melton Mowbray).

persone OFr, ME, 'a parson, a beneficed cleric'. *Mrs Gills Persons Yard* (f.n. Wymondham), *the Parsons Balke* (f.n. Knipton), Parsons Cl (f.n. Coston, Croxton Kerrial, Gt. Dalby, Eastwell, Stathern), *(the) Parsons Close* (f.ns. Brentingby, Old Dalby, Pickwell), Parson's Holford (f.n. Gt. Dalby), *the Parsons*

Lays (f.n. Goadby Marwood), *the Parsons middle close, the Parsons Nyne leis close, the Parsons peece* (f.ns. Coston), Parsons Piece (f.n. Thorpe Arnold), *The Parsons Woulds Close* (f.n. Eastwell), *the parson wyllowes* (f.n. Saxby), *ye person hedlande* (f.n. Bottesford), *le personyssyk'* (f.n. Burrough on the Hill), *atte Persones* (p) (Sewstern).

pete ME, 'peat'. Peat Woodville Hill Cl (f.n. Edmondthorpe).

peterstone eModE, 'a fossil encrinite'. *Le Peterstone Lane* (Belvoir).

petit OFr, 'little'. *Petit Dauby* (Little Dalby).

pewit eModE, 'a lapwing'. Pyewhit Hill (f.n. Stonesby).

pīc OE, 'a point; a pointed hill'. Pickwell.

pigeon ME, 'a pigeon'. Pigeon Hole Furlong (f.n. Stathern).

pigge ME, 'a young pig'. The Pig Paddock (f.n. Gt. Dalby).

pīl OE, 'a pile, a shaft'. Pile Bridge Fm.

píll ON, 'a willow'. ?*Pylhall* (f.n. Stapleford).

*pinca OE, 'a finch, a chaffinch'. *Pinquath* (f.n. Melton Mowbray).

pinder ME, 'a pinder, an officer of a manor who impounded stray beasts'. ?*pinder hades* (f.n. Edmondthorpe), *pinder peece furlonge* (f.n. Easthorpe), *the pinder stie* (f.n. Stathern).

pine ME, 'labour, toil, exertion, effort'. *Pine syke* (f.n. Harby).

pingel ME, 'a small plot of ground'. Fairly freq. in f.ns.: as a simplex, (The) Pingle (Buckminster, Burton Lazars, Long Clawson, Gt. Dalby, Eastwell, Freeby, Muston, Wartnaby), *the Pyngle* (Barkestone), *le Pyngull* (Bottesford); with a locational prefix, e.g. *Copehill tyngle* (Scalford), Hounds Acre Pingle (Wymondham), *Stamfordgate Pingle* (Burton Lazars); with a surn. indicating ownership, e.g. Crozens Pingle (Edmondthorpe), Hubbards Pingle (Thorpe Arnold), *Redfordes Pingle* (Wymondham). Note the local dial. form in *durdalle tingles, welldalle tyngles* (Scalford), *Tingle Hill* (Burton Lazars, Scalford).

pīpe OE, 'a pipe, a conduit'. Pibdale (f.n. Branston).

*pipere OE, 'a spring, a stream'. ?*Piper Hole*.

pīpere OE, 'a piper'; perh. extended to describe a bird, cf. *sandpiper*. ?*Piper Hole*. ?*Pipers Wong* (f.n. Sewstern).

pise OE, 'pease'. Freq. in f.ns.: esp. in the compound *Peaselands* (with various spellings in Burton Lazars, Old Dalby, Eaton, Freeby, Harby, Pickwell, Plungar, Redmile, Sewstern, Somerby, Stathern, Thorpe Arnold, Waltham on the Wolds, Wymondham). Note also *Peesdal* (Knipton), *peseclif* (Melton Mowbray), *Pesecroft'* (Muston), *Peasefelde* (Stonesby), *Peysforlang'* (Stathern), *Pease Hill* (Long Clawson), *Peasill greene* (Normanton), *Pease holme* (Burrough on the Hill), *Pesehouwe* (Goadby Marwood), *Pesowe* (Knipton).

place OFr, **place, plas** ME, 'an area surrounded by buildings'; later 'a plot of ground, a residence'. *Belhous Place* (Barkestone), *Bromwells place, Caldwell Place, Cape place, Nursery place, Paccheplace* (Melton Mowbray), *Grassye place furlonge* (f.n. Burrough on the Hill), *Graueleyplace, prattesplace* (Belvoir), *The Hall Place* (Hall Fm, Holwell), *Hamsterley place* (Bottesford), *Milne Place* (Mill Bank, f.n. Coston), *the parsonage stackplace* (f.n. Wyfordby), *Twocrosseplace* (Buckminster), *watirplace* (Muston), *Wedow Place* (Coston).

*plæsc OE, 'a pool', **plash** ModEdial., 'a marshy pool'. *le pitplassh'* (f.n. Wyfordby), *Le Plash* (f.n. Burton Lazars), the Plashes (f.n. Lt. Dalby).

plain OFr, ME, 'a great open tract'; also 'a piece of flat meadowland'. *Hawthornehill Plaine, Playne, the Towne playne, Walke playne* (f.ns. Barkestone), the Plain, Plain Meer (f.ns. Eaton).

plat ME, 'a plot, a small piece of ground'; varies with **plot**. Fairly freq. in f.ns.: very often with a surn. indicating ownership, e.g. Adcock's Plat (Old Dalby), Austens Platts (Edmondthorpe), Bassetts Platt, Flavills Platt (Wymondham); as a simplex, e.g. the Platt (Old Dalby), Platts (Burton Lazars, Wymondham); sometimes locational, e.g. *Brentonby Meadow Platt* (Burton Lazars), Cottage Platt (Wyfordby), Island Platt (Muston), Orchard Platt (Gt. Dalby), *the wyndye milne platt* (f.n. Sproxton).

plega OE, **plaga** OE (Angl), 'play, sport'; in p.ns. 'a place for games'. *the Play Close* (f.n. Edmondthorpe).

pleg-stōw OE, 'a sport-place, a place where people gathered together to play'. ?Plaster Lees (f.n. Sewstern).

plek ME, 'a small plot of ground'. *greenpleke hades* (f.n. Edmondthorpe), Potatoe Pleck (f.n. Wartnaby).

plōg OE, **plógr** ON, 'a plough'. Plough Cl (f.n. Brentingby, Gt. Dalby, Freeby, Garthorpe), Plough Annacre, Plough Fd (f.ns. Waltham on the Wolds), Plough Dale (f.n. Sewstern), *the plough land pasture* (f.n. Melton Mowbray).

plot late OE, ME, 'a small piece of ground'; varies with **plat**. Fairly freq. in f.ns.: with a surn. indicating ownership, e.g. *Assheby plott* (Melton Mowbray), *John Cookes plott* (Burton Lazars), *Loues Plott* (Wymondham); with a locational prefix, e.g. *Brigge plotte* (Coston), *Kyrkestedplot'* (Muston), *Miln plott, Willow poole plott* (Old Dalby); with an indication of size or shape, e.g. *mykulplott* (Bottesford), Round Plot (Wartnaby), or soil type, e.g. *Sand plott, Sandy plott* (Old Dalby), or crop, e.g. *Coleseed plott* (Old Dalby). Unlike **plat**, the el. does not occur as a. simplex.

plouman ME, 'a ploughman'. *Ploumanmedwe* (f.n. Burrough on the Hill).

plūme OE, 'a plum, a plum-tree'. Plungar.

pohha OE, 'a pouch, a bag'. ?*Powell* (f.n. Knipton).

pode ME, 'a toad'. *Podeaker* (f.n. Eaton).

point eModE, 'a promontory, a pointed headland'. Blue Point. Stathern Point (f.n. Stathern).

pōl[1] OE, 'a pool'. Freq. in f.ns.: esp. with farm animals, e.g. *the Cow pole* (Saxby), *Horssepol* (with various spellings in Croxton Kerrial, Harston, Knipton), *Neatepoole* (Branston); with fish or amphibians, e.g. *Fishe poole close* (Sproxton, Wartnaby), *Padock poole* (Lt. Dalby); with wild flora, e.g. *Brackinspole* (Waltham on the Wolds), *Willow poole plott* (Old Dalby); with an el. signifying location, e.g. *houerpole, the west poole* (Bottesford), *Talepoole leyes* (Eastwell); as a simplex, e.g. *the Pole* (Saltby), Poles (Coston, Somerby), Pole Cl (Buckminster, Withcote).

ponde ME, 'a pond, an artificial or natural pool'. The Large Pond, Pond Cl (f.ns. Withcote), *Westminster pondes* (Westminster, Belvoir).

pony ModE, 'a horse of any small breed'. Pony Paddock (f.n. Waltham on the Wolds).

***popel** OE, 'a pebble. ?*Poplestoft* (f.n. Scalford).

port^2 OE, 'a market-town, a market'. *le Portgatte* (Burrough on the Hill).

potato ModE, 'a potato'. *Potatoe Pleck* (f.n. Wartnaby).

potte ME, 'a deep hole, a pit, a deep hole in a river-bed'. *Pottwell Leas* (f.n. Sproxton).

***pottere** OE, 'a pot-maker'. *Potterhill* (f.n. Sproxton, Stonesby), *Potter pit* (f.n. Muston), *?potters dike* (f.n. Ab Kettleby).

pouche ME, 'a bag, a receptacle of small or moderate size'; used topographically of a small hollow or bag-like feature . *the pouch* (f.n. Stathern).

pouer(e) ME, adj., 'poor'; in modern f.ns. 'poor' for 'the poor' refers to land dedicated to poor-law relief or charity. (The) Poor('s) Cl (f.ns. Old Dalby, Holwell, Sysonby), The Poor Fd (f.n. Wymondham), Poor Part (f.n. Lt. Dalby), *poors land, the poors headland* (f.ns. Ab Kettleby).

prēost OE, 'a priest'. *Preistdale* (f.n. Scalford), *Prestegate, the prestes hadland, þe prest welows* (f.ns. Bottesford), *longe presteholm* (f.n. Harby), *le Presteswong'* (f.n. Eaton), *Prestheng'* (f.n. Wymondham), *presthou* (f.n. Redmile), *Prestisdale* (f.n. Wycomb/Chadwell), *Prestlandes* (f.n. Pickwell), *Pruste hyll* (f.n. Somerby), *Prystcroft'* (f.n. Muston).

prior OFr, late OE, ME, 'a prior of a religious house'. Prior Cl, *Priourscroft* (f.ns. Melton Mowbray), *le Priouresgores* (f.n. Redmile), ?*Pryare closse* (f.n. Scalford), *the Pryors headland* (f.n. Burton Lazars).

pumpe ME, 'a pump'. Pump Mdw (f.n. Brentingby).

punche ME, 'a tool for making holes in anything'. *Puncheholes* (f.n. Eastwell).

***pund** OE, **pund** ME, 'a pound, an enclosure into which stray cattle were put'. *the Common pounde* (f.n. Garthorpe), The Pound (f.n. Eastwell, Holwell, Scalford), *Pounde acre* (f.n. Burton Lazars).

pyewipe ModEdial., 'a lapwing'. Pye Wipe Hill (f.n. Stonesby).

pyll OE, 'a pool in a river, a small stream'. ?*Pylhall* (f.n. Stapleford).

***pynd-fald** OE, 'a pinfold'. Pinfold Lees Hill. (the) Pinfold (f.ns. Burrough on the Hill, Coston, Ab Kettleby, Muston, Normanton, Redmile, Wartnaby), *Pinfold Lane* (Bottesford, Melton Mowbray), *Pinfolde leaes* (f.n. Burrough on the Hill, Waltham on the Wolds).

pytt OE, 'a pit, a natural hollow, an excavated hole' etc., (cf. **cley-pytt, cockpit, col-pytt, marle-pytt, sand-pytt, stān-pytt, wulf-pytt**). Freq. in f.ns.: with an indication of ownership, e.g. *Barnard Pittes, Brethers Pytt* (Burton Lazars), *John pitts* (Ab Kettleby), or of location, e.g. *chapill pitts* (Knipton), *Clipsum Pitt* (Wymondham), *Wolstropp pittes* (Harston); with an el. signifying shape, e.g. *le brantepyttys* (Knipton), *Duuepittis* (Bottesford), *le swelupitte* (Wycomb/ Chadwell), or colour/condition, e.g. *blacpyt forlonge* (Bottesford), *yellowpit balke, durtypits* (Croxton Kerrial), Mud Pit Cl (Hose). Industrial use may be specified, e.g. *the flaxe pittes* (Scalford), Fulling Pits (Waltham on the Wolds), *Potter pit* (Muston); or mineral extraction, e.g. *Gravill pittes* (Harston), ?*quenepittes* (Croxton Kerrial), *Saltputes* (Wymondham); or village entertainment, e.g. Bull Pit Cl (Thorpe Arnold), *bull pyts* (Freeby), *Cockinpit*

Furlong (Branston). Superstitions concerning the supernatural are evidenced, e.g. *Helpitt* (Edmondthorpe), *Thurspitt* (with various spellings in Bottesford, Croxton Kerrial, Knipton, Muston, Saltby).

quake ME, 'a stretch of quake-ooze'. *quakefen* (f.n. Burton Lazars).

quykset eModE, 'a quickset hedge'. *the quicksete, Quicksetts Dale, Quicksett Leyes* (f.ns. Saxby), *the quyckset hedge* (Barkestone).

ræt OE, 'a rat'. ?*Rattisthorn* (f.n. Burrough on the Hill).

ræw OE, 'a row, a row of trees'. Willow Row (f.n. Nether Broughton).

ragged ME, adj., 'ragged, shaggy, rough'. ?*Rackett Mires* (f.n. Burton Lazars).

raile, reille OFr, ME, 'a bar of wood', later 'a fence, a railing'. Draw Rail (f.n. Burton Lazars).

ramm OE, 'a ram'. Ram Cl (f.n. Burton Lazars, Edmondthorpe, Wymondham), Ram Fd (f.n. Somerby), *the Ram meadow* (f.n. Burrough on the Hill).

rāw OE, 'a row, a range of buildings, a street lined with houses'. *Bradley's Row, Pigeon Row* (Melton Mowbray).

rēad OE, adj., 'red'; sometimes difficult to distinguish from **hrēod** in f.ns. Redmile, Redearth Fm. Freq. in f.ns., where it denotes the colour of soil, e.g. (The) Red Earth (with various spellings in Bottesford, Buckminster, Edmondthorpe and 9 other townships), Redhill (with various spellings in Holwell, Scalford, Somerby, Stathern, Stonesby, ?Wymondham), *Redehou* (Wycomb/Chadwell, ?Wymondham), *Redehowe* (Sewstern), Redlands (with various spellings in Barkestone, Belvoir, Holwell and 10 other townships), *Red leare* (Ab Kettleby), *le Redewong'* (Muston), *Redwong* (Bottesford).

rectory ModE, 'the residence appertaining to a rector'. The Old Rectory, The Rectory (Branston, Nether Broughton, Burrough on the Hill, Coston, Eastwell, Edmondthorpe, Goadby Marwood, Harby, Harston, Knipton, Muston, Pickwell, Redmile, Saxby, Stathern, Waltham on the Wolds, Wymondham), Rectory Covert, Rectory Fm.

rectour ME, 'a parson or incumbent of a parish whose tithes are not impropriate'. Rectors Cl (f.n. Buckminster), *the Rectors house* (The Rectory, Eastwell).

rein ON, 'a boundary strip'. ?*felbrygreins* (f.n. Bottesford), *le Westereines ende* (f.n. Sewstern).

rick-yard ModE, 'an enclosure containing ricks, a stackyard'. Rickyard (f.n. Wymondham).

riggett eModE, 'a furrow, a channel', ModEdial., 'a water-channel, a surface-drain'. Rickett's Spinney. *Breckland rigget, langham ~, mellome ~, toadale rigget* (f.ns. Thorpe Arnold), *Hobeck Riggit, Ingle Ridgett, Sand pitt Riggitt* (f.ns. Gt. Dalby).

rinnende OE, **rennandi** ON, pres.part., adj., 'running, flowing'. Running Furrow (f.n. Muston).

risc OE, 'a rush'. *heltun ruschus* (f.n. Bottesford), *Rush Bush Furlong* (f.n. Scalford), ?Rush land dike (f.n. Holwell), *Rush-land-Leys* (f.n. Ab Kettleby), *Russhall Leayes* (f.n. Croxton Kerrial).

*riscig OE, **rushy** ModE, adj., 'rushy, growing with rushes'. Rushey Cl (f.n. Withcote), *Rushy Furrows* (f.n. Somerby).

rīð OE, 'a small stream'. *Le Lyttyl Hendryth* (f.n. Burton Lazars), ?*sloteridemere* (f.n. Long Clawson), *Woodyrith* (f.n. Branston).

rivere ME, 'a river'. *the litle river* (f.n. Burton Lazars), *rivers side* (f.n. Wyfordby).

rōd[3] OE, 'a rood of land'. The First Roods (f.n. Gt. Dalby), *the five roodes, the sevene roodes, the three roodes* (f.ns. Saltby), *the Nine Rode* (f.n. Redmile).

rookery ModE, 'a colony of rooks'. The Rookery, Rookery Ho.

round OFr, ME, adj., 'round'; in modern f.ns. sometimes describing fields not necessarily circular, but equilateral rather than oblong or irregular polygons. Round Covert. *Copill Round Hill, Durdale Round Hill* (f.ns. Scalford), Round Acres (f.n. Lt. Dalby), Round Cl (f.n. Gt. Dalby), (The) Round Hill (f.ns. Eastwell, Holwell, Scalford, Somerby, Stathern, Stonesby), *the Round Knowl* (f.n. Harston), Round Plott (f.n. Wartnaby).

roundabout eModE, 'a circle, a circular object'. *Roundaboute* (f.n. Burrough on the Hill).

rūh[1] OE, adj., 'rough'. Common in f.ns., e.g. (Far) Rough Cl (Lt. Dalby, Muston, Withcote), Rough Fd (Waltham on the Wolds), (The) Rough Mdw (Gt. Dalby, Edmondthorpe), Rough Piece (Edmondthorpe, Freeby), Rowdike (Sysonby).

rūh[2] OE, 'a rough place' (a sb. use of **rūh**[1] , *v.* Löfvenberg 169), 'a piece of rough ground, ground left wild'. Wymondham Rough. *the Rofe* (f.n. Harston).

rybb eModE, 'a narrow strip of land'. *Tynkerybbis* (f.n. Burton Lazars).

***ryding** OE, 'a clearing'. *Redding Lees* (f.n. Holwell).

rye-grass ModEdial., 'rye-grass' (*Lolium perenne*). Rye Grass Cl (f.n. Muston).

ryge OE, 'rye'. *Rieclef* (f.n. Eaton), *Rigate* (Thorpe Arnold), *Rigathe* (Wymondham), *Rigate forde* (f.n. Edmondthorpe), *Rigatehull* (f.n. Burrough on the Hill), *the Rye Close* (f.n. Wyfordby), *the Rye wonge* (f.n. Easthorpe).

rynel OE, **rundle** ModEdial., 'a runnel, a small stream'. Rundle Beck. *the Rundell* (f.n. Croxton Kerrial), Rundle (f.n. Bottesford), *the Rundle* (f.n. Knipton), *well rundle* (Well Lane, Ab Kettleby).

sadol OE, 'a saddle'; topographically 'a saddle-shaped dip in hills'. ?*Sadelbridges* (f.n. Knipton).

sǣd OE, 'seed; sowing'; in modern f.ns. often used of areas of sown grass. Seed Cl (f.n. Brentingby, Buckminster, Gt. Dalby, Freeby, Hose, Waltham on the Wolds), The Seedfield (f.n. Wymondham), Dutch Barn Seed Fd (f.n. Scalford), Far Seeds (f.n. Holwell), First Seeds (f.n. Scalford), Great Ground Seeds (f.n. Pickwell), New Seeds (f.n. Wymondham), Thompson's Seed (f.n. Somerby).

sænna ODan, **senna** ON, 'a dispute, a quarrel'. Sanham (f.n. Gt. Dalby), *Senholme lees* (f.n. Lt. Dalby), *Synnomes* (f.n. Coston).

sainfoin ModE, 'the fodder plant sainfoin' (*Onobrychis sativa*) and occasionally 'lucern' (*Medicago sativa*). Saintfoin Cl (f.n. Muston).

sale eModE, 'a division or "quarter" of a wood, of which the underwood is cut down and sold' (*v.* Nth 157 and EDD *s.v.*). Upper Sale (f.n. Withcote).

salh, salig OE, 'a willow, a sallow'. Sauvey Castle. *le Salowe* (f.n. Knipton), *Sallowes* (f.n. Old Dalby), Sallow Bed (f.n. Burrough on the Hill), Sallow Cl (f.n. Buckminster), Sallow Tree Cl (f.n. Sewstern), *Salufurlong* (f.n. Old Dalby), *Waltham Sallows* (f.n. Wyfordby).

salr ON, 'a hall'. *atte Sale* (p) (Melton Mowbray).

salt[1] OE (Angl), ON, 'salt', poss. also 'a brine-pit, a salt-pan'. ?Saltby, Sawgate Rd (Burton Lazars, Stapleford). (*le*) *Saltegate* (Croxton Kerrial, Melton Mowbray),

Saltgates (f.n. Waltham on the Wolds), *le Saltestrete* (Eaton), ?*Saltputes* (f.n. Wymondham).

salt[2] OE (Angl), **saltr** ON, adj., 'salty, brackish'. ?Saltby, Saltbeck. the Saltmoor Fd (f.n. Hose), ?*Saltputes* (f.n. Wymondham), Saltwell Drain (f.n. Long Clawson).

saltere OE (Angl), 'a salt-merchant'. Salter's Hill. Salter's Fd (f.n. Scalford), Salter's Ford (f.n. Croxton Kerrial), *Saltergate* (Melton Mowbray), *Salters Gate* (Burrough on the Hill), *Salt'lane* (Harston).

sand OE, **sandr** ON, 'sand, sandy soil'. Common in f.ns., e.g. (the) Sands (Long Clawson, Harby, Stathern), (*le*) *Sandes* (Bottesford, Easthorpe, Redmile), *the Sonde* (Melton Mowbray), Sand Cliff Cl (Waltham on the Wolds), *the Sand Gate* (Harby), *Sand haydes* (Melton Mowbray), *Sandhill'* (Bottesford), Sandholms (Pickwell), Sand Lands (Burton Lazars), (*le*) *Sandwong(e)* (Barkestone, Bottesford).

***sand-hol** OE, **sand-hole** ME, ModE, 'a sand-pit'. Sand Holes (f.n. Stathern).

sandig OE, adj., 'sandy'. Sandy Lane (Gt. Dalby, Melton Mowbray, Scalford). *Sandy Close, Sandy Meadow, Sandy plott* (f.ns. Old Dalby).

sand-pytt OE, 'a sand-pit', cf. **sand-hol**. Sandpit Fm. The Sand Pit (f.n. Gt. Dalby), *the Sondpytt* (f.n. Knipton), Sand Pits (f.n. Melton Mowbray), (*the*) *Sandpittes* (f.ns. Bottesford, Hose, Normanton, Pickwell, Wycomb/Chadwell), (the) Sand Pit Cl (f.ns. Croxton Kerrial, Eastwell, Goadby Marwood), Sandpit Fd (f.n. Scalford), Sandpit Hill (f.n. Stathern), *Sandpitt furlonge* (f.n. Redmile), *the Sandpytt furlonge* (f.n. Barkestone), Sand Pit Walk (f.n. Wymondham).

sauge OFr, ME, 'sage' (*Salvia officinalis*). *the Sage Crosse* (Melton Mowbray).

scanca OE, 'a shank, a leg'; figuratively of long, narrow, bent selions in a great field. *Shanck Fur'* (f.n. Gt. Dalby).

(ge)scēad OE, 'a boundary'. *Shed(d)gate* (Brentingby, Wyfordby).

***sc(e)ald** OE, adj., 'shallow'. Scalford. *Scaldeford' furlong, skaldewelforlang'*, ?Scalding Furlong (f.ns. Muston).

sceamol, scamol OE, 'a bench, a (market) stall', ME, 'a stall for the sale of meat'. *Shamble hill* (f.n. Sysonby), *Shamble hole* (f.n. Melton Mowbray), *Shamlys* (Melton Mowbray).

sceard, scard OE, 'a cleft, a gap'. ?*Scarddeslande* (f.n. Hose).

scearn, scarn OE, 'dung, muck'. *Schirnclif* (f.n. Eaton).

scearp, scarp OE, adj., 'sharp, pointed', perh. also 'steep'. *scharphou*, ?*Sharpedale* (f.ns. Croxton Kerrial).

scearu, scaru OE, 'a share, a share of land; a boundary'. Share Wells (f.n. Waltham on the Wolds), Sharrowdale (f.n. Branston).

scēat, scēata OE, **shot(e)** ME, 'a corner of land, an angle, a projecting piece of land'. Over Shoot (f.n. Holwell).

sceld OE, 'a shield, a protection', whence 'a shelter'. *Sceldacre* (f.n. Plungar).

***scēo** OE, 'a shelter'. ?*the horse shoe* (f.n. Melton Mowbray), ?*Schouedon'* (f.n. Branston).

sc(e)oppa OE, 'a shop, a booth, a shed'. Blacksmith's Shop (Edmondthorpe, Scalford). *Anthony Church his shop* (Old Dalby), *the Smithes shop* (Nether Broughton).

sc(e)ort OE, adj., 'short'. Freq. in f.ns., e.g. *schortecroft'* (Muston), *schort grenelays, schortharelondeys, Schortwronglandes, shortclyf* (Bottesford), *le Scortefurlonges, le Scorteholm* (Wycomb/Chadwell) etc.

scēp OE (Angl), 'sheep'. *Schepegate* (Redmile), *Schepestigate* (Burton Lazars), *Sheep-pen Croft Nook* (f.n. Ab Kettleby), *Sheeprow* (f.n. Sproxton), *Shepe Cross* (Melton Mowbray), *Shippdammes* (f.n. Croxton Kerrial).

scēp-cot OE (Angl), 'a shelter for sheep'. Sheep Coat Cl (f.n. Nether Broughton), *Sheepcoate Lease* (f.n. Knipton), *Shepecotte close* (f.n. Old Dalby).

scēp-hirde OE (Angl), 'a shepherd'. *Scheperd well* (f.n. Bottesford), *Shepard close* (f.n. Croxton Kerrial), ?Shepherd Cl (f.n. Muston), ?Shepherds Cl (f.n. Thorpe Arnold), *Shepherd boord Leyes* (f.n. Wycomb/Chadwell), *Shepperd board* (f.n. Somerby), ?*Shepherds Bush* (f.n. Saltby), Shepherds Ho. (Burton Lazars, Freeby).

scēp-wæsce OE (Angl), 'a place for dipping sheep, a sheep-wash'. Sheepwash (Waltham on the Wolds, Withcote). *Sheepwashe Close* (f.n. Wymondham).

***schadel** ME, 'a parting of the ways; a cross-way'. ?*Sadelbridges* (f.n. Knipton).

scīr[1] OE, 'a shire, an administrative district'. Sherbrook Fox Covert, Three Shire Oak. *schiredun* (f.n. Croxton Kerrial), *schirestrete* (Croxton Kerrial), *Schyremere* (f.n. with various spellings in Harston, Hose, Muston, Plungar, Stathern).

scīr[2] OE, adj., 'bright'. *Sirholt* (f.n. Melton Mowbray).

scite OE, 'shit, dung'. *Shittoppes* (f.n. Croxton Kerrial).

***scofl-brǣdu** OE, 'a shovel's breadth', i.e. a narrow strip of land, cf. **scōh-brǣdu**. *Schouelebrod'* (f.n. Wycomb/Chadwell), *Shelbordes* (f.n. Waltham on the Wolds), Shelbread Cl (f.n. Edmondthorpe), *Shelbreds* (f.n. Burrough on the Hill).

scōh OE, 'a shoe'. ?*Schouedon'* (f.n. Branston).

***scōh-brǣdu** OE, 'a shoe's breadth', i.e. a very narrow strip of land, cf. **scofl-brǣdu**. *Showbredes* (f.n. Ab Kettleby).

scoren[2] OE, pa.part., 'cut, shorn', hence 'sharply cut off, precipitous, abrupt'. *Shorn Hill Close* (f.n. Edmondthorpe), *Shornhill Slade* (f.n. Stathern).

scrēad OE, 'a shred, a scrap', **shredd** ME, 'a shred, a strip', used figuratively of a small patch of land. Narrow shred (f.n. Burrough on the Hill), Shreddies (f.n. Gt. Dalby).

***scrobb** OE, 'scrubland, brushwood'. *Edlin his shrobbes* (f.n. Knipton), *the shrobbes* (f.n. Barkestone), ?*Shrovesdale* (f.n. Wymondham).

scrogge ME, 'a bush, brushwood'. Scroggs (f.n. Goadby Marwood).

***scrubb** OE, 'a shrub, brushwood, a place overgrown with brushwood'. *Braunston shrubbes* (f.n. Croxton Kerrial), Maxeys Shrubs (f.n. Wymondham), *Heygate Shrubbs* (f.n. Barkestone), Lupton Shrubs (f.n. Sproxton), Shrub Fd (f.n. Sysonby), *Sproxton Shrubs* (f.n. Coston).

***scrubbig** OE, adj., 'covered with brushwood'. *Shrubbymeer furlong* (f.n. Barkestone).

scypen, scipen OE, 'a cow-shed, a shippon'. Chippendale (f.n. Normanton), *Shippens* (f.n. Eastwell).

***scytel[2]** OE, adj., 'unstable', *Shittlemyres* (f.n. Redmile).

S(e)axe (S(e)axna gen.pl.) OE, 'the Saxons'. ?Saxby.

secg[1] OE, 'sedge, a reed, a rush'. *Seggedam* (f.n. Eaton), *seghaker* (f.n. Muston).

sef ON, **seave** ModEdial., 'sedge, a rush'. *le Save acres* (f.n. Pickwell), *Seaveacers* (f.n. Lt. Dalby), *Seuedale* (f.n. Wycomb/Chadwell).

segl OE, 'a sail'. *Wind Mill seales* (f.n. Stathern).

seneschal OFr, 'a steward, a major-domo, a chief administrator'. ?*Seneschalls close* (f.n. Edmondthorpe).

seofon OE, num., 'seven'. *seaven leaes* (f.n. Redmile), *the Seven Lease* (f.n. Knipton), *the sevene roodes* (f.n. Saltby).

seolfor OE, **silfr** ON, 'silver'. Silver Hill (f.n. Stathern).

(ge)set OE, 'a dwelling, a camp, a place for animals, a stable, a fold'. ?*sedygatt* (Bottesford), ?*Short Segraves* (f.n. Eastwell).

*****set-copp** OE, 'a hill with a fold', poss. also 'a seat-shaped hill', i.e. a flat-topped hill. *Setcop* (f.n. Stonesby), *Setcopp'* (f.n. Bottesford).

sete ME, 'a lofty place'. ?Seat (f.n. Scalford).

severall eModE, 'privately owned', referring to land in individual ownership as opposed to common land. *Severall lees* (f.n. Branston).

shepe-gate ME, 'pasturage for sheep' (*v.* Sheep Gates, L **2** 244). ?*Shepegate* (f.n. Redmile).

shepe-hous ME, 'a shelter for sheep'. *Parnham Sheep-house* (f.n. Harby), *Shepehousyate* (Eaton).

shitten ME, ppl.adj., 'defiled, foul, covered with excrement'. *Shittendale Syke* (f.n. Burrough on the Hill).

shomakere ME, 'a maker of shoes'. Shoemakers Cl (f.n. Thorpe Arnold).

sīc OE, 'a small stream', **siche** ME, 'a piece of meadow along a stream'; cf. **sík**, with which it sometimes varies. *Caldewellesiche, miclehowsiche, sichewelle* (f.ns. Redmile), the Church Sitch Fd (f.n. Wartnaby), *Gafelokessiche* (f.n. Normanton), *Heinhalfakirsichesende* (f.n. Muston), *Wrongesicheshend* (f.n. Burton Lazars).

sīd OE, adj., 'large, spacious, extensive, long'. ?*Sidebroke feild* (f.n. Muston), ?Side Hill (f.n. Waltham on the Wolds), *Sideholm* (f.n. Burrough on the Hill), *sidholms*, *Sidland sick* (f.ns. Ab Kettleby), *le sydlandis* (f.n. Branston).

sīde OE, 'a side; the long side of a hill, a hill-side; the land alongside a stream, village, wood, etc.'. *Alyn Closse Syde* (f.n. Burton Lazars), *Bambruss side, the dale syde, Heslands side, by the towne syde* (f.ns. Ab Kettleby), *the beckside* (f.n. Barkestone), *the common side* (f.n. Lt. Dalby), Drift Hill Side, Top Hill Side (f.ns. Harston), *the dryfte syde* (f.n. Croxton Kerrial), *þe est syd etty, þe west syde etty, the far medowe syde, the Meadow Side, prest gatt syde* (f.ns. Bottesford), Heyside Cl (f.n. Hose), Little Side, *rivers side* (f.ns. Wyfordby), *Long gate side* (f.n. Melton Mowbray), ?*Sidebroke feild* (f.n. Muston), ?Side Hill (f.n. Waltham on the Wolds), Southside (f.n. Edmondthorpe), *the streete side* (f.n. Coston), Thorpe Side (f.n. Scalford).

*****sīdling** OE, ME, 'a strip of land lying alongside a stream or some other piece of land'. *the Sidlings* (f.n. Lt. Dalby).

sík ON, 'a ditch', in the Danelaw often influencing or replacing **sīc**. Cranyke Fm. Freq. in f.ns.: principally with minor p.ns., e.g. *Lausemore sike* (Eastwell), *risburgsike* (Lt. Dalby), *sweynwongsike* (Harby), and with names for, or associated with, watercourses, e.g. *the becksyck* (Barkestone), *Caldewellesic*, *Harewellesike* (Bottesford), *the Well' Syke* (Lt. Dalby), *Gafelocsik'* (Normanton), *steynwathsyke* (Muston); with pers.ns. indicating ownership, e.g. *Algersic*, *Sueynnisike forlong'* (Muston), *Henry Steeles Seike* (Gt. Dalby); with an el. specifying wild flora, e.g. *Brimble Sike, Thurn Sick* (Gt. Dalby); or size, e.g. *Brodesyke, Long sike* (Knipton), *le smalesik* (Harby). Occurs also as a simplex, e.g. *Le Sikes* (Holwell), *The Syke* (Muston), *the Sike feilde* (Easthorpe).

sinke ME, 'a sink, a cesspool, a bog, a sump'. Tofts Sink (f.n. Edmondthorpe).

skáli ON, **scale** ME, 'a hut, a shed'. ?*Gasgell medow* (f.n. Bottesford), ?*Scales dicke* (f.n. Normanton).

skarð ON, 'an opening, an open place on the edge of something, a gap'. *Scharthforlong'* (f.n. Wycomb/Chadwell), ?*Scarddeslande* (f.n. Hose).

skeið ON, 'a track, a race-course'. ?*Scethesholm* (f.n. Long Clawson).

skil ON, 'a boundary'. Skibbecks (f.n. Waltham on the Wolds), Skill Hill (f.n. Buckminster).

skírr ON, adj., 'clear, bright, pure'. *Skyrbeck* (f.n. Melton Mowbray).

skirting ModE, ppl.adj., 'that skirts, that borders'. ?Skirting Holme Lane (Long Clawson).

slæd OE (Angl), 'a valley'. ?Sledge Spinney. *Belwether Slade* (f.n. Scalford), *bigdick slade* (f.n. Wyfordby), *Cony Groue Slade*, Greensike Slade, *Shornhill Slade*, Thorney Slade, *Timberhulslad'* (f.ns. Stathern), *Cooslades* (f.n. Bottesford), *crosled'* (f.n. Croxton Kerrial), *Depslade* (f.n. Harston), *Horsladedale* (f.n. Eaton), *longepoleslade* (f.n. Leesthorpe), *le Slade* (f.n. Barkestone), The Slade, *Wollandes slade* (f.ns. Lt. Dalby), Slades (f.n. Wymondham), *le Sleyde* (f.n. Burton Lazars), *watersleades* (f.n. Branston).

slang ModEdial., 'a long, narrow (sometimes sinuous) piece of land; a roadside verge; the ground beside a (winding) stream'. The Slang (f.n. Burrough on the Hill, Scalford).

slétta ON, 'a smooth, level field'. Adcock's Slatters (f.n. Gt. Dalby), Slates (f.n. Scalford), Sleets (f.n. Sproxton), *Sleightes* (f.n. Eastwell, Pickwell).

sléttr ON, adj., 'smooth, level'. *le Slatelandes* (f.n. Wycomb/Chadwell), Slatings (f.n. Waltham on the Wolds), *Slechtenge* (f.n. Redmile), *Sletheng'* (f.n. Bescaby), *Sleythenges* (f.n. Burton Lazars), *Sletyng* (f.n. Old Dalby), Slidings (f.n. Burrough on the Hill), *Slight moore* (f.n. Coston).

slipe, slippe ME, 'a slip, a narrow strip of land'. Baines Slip, ?Cowslip, Gills Slip, Hickman's Slip, The Long Slip (f.ns. Wymondham), Ivets Slip (f.n. Melton Mowbray), (The) Slip (f.ns. Gt. Dalby, Waltham on the Wolds), Slip Fd (f.n. Scalford), Slipe Cl (f.n. Edmondthorpe), Slipe Moor (f.n. Coston).

slōh OE, 'a slough, a mire, a muddy place'. *slothornes* (f.n. Wycomb/Chadwell).

*slōhtre OE, 'a slough, a mire, a muddy place'. *sloteridemere* (f.n. Long Clawson).

smæl OE, adj., 'narrow, thin', **smal(r)** ON, adj., 'small'. *Smaledalehull* (f.n. Burrough on the Hill), *smaleeng, smal furlong'* (f.ns. Bottesford), *Smalewelle* (f.n. Eaton), *Smallewelgate* (Plungar), *Small Gate Hades* (f.n. Stapleford), *Small haides* (f.n. Freeby), Small Hill, *Small leayes* (f.ns. Burton Lazars), *Smallongland* (f.n. Stonesby), *Smalthorndale* (f.n. Old Dalby).

smeoru OE, 'fat, grease, lard', **smjǫr** ON, 'grease, butter'; in f.ns. alluding to rich pasturage, productive of milk, butter, etc. *Smerberdal* (f.n. Stonesby).

smēðe[1] ON, adj., 'smooth'; also used as a sb. 'smooth ground'. Smeath (f.n. Gt. Dalby), the Smeeth (f.n. Edmondthorpe), *Smete* (f.n. Wymondham), *Smeth* *meadowe* (f.n. Burton Lazars), *Smethe medue* (f.n. Somerby), ?Smithill (f.n. Stathern).

smið OE, **smiðr** ON, 'a smith, a worker in metal'. *the Smithes shop* (Nether Broughton), ?Smithill (f.n. Stathern), *le Smithisdeil* (f.n. Bottesford), ?Smith's Fd (f.n. Scalford), ?*Smythes pyngle* (f.n. Barkestone).

smiððe ON, 'a smithy, a metal worker's shop'. *Shortsmythe homes, Smithy pits* (f.ns. Waltham on the Wolds), *Smithey hill* (f.n. Stathern), *atte Smythe* (p) (Holwell).

snāw OE, 'snow'. ?Snow Cl (f.n. Brentingby), ?Snows Cl (f.n. Burton Lazars), ?*Snow Close* (f.n. Wymondham), ?*Snow Wong* (f.n. Harby).

*snōr OE, 'something twisted; a road which deviates from a direct line in order to negotiate a slight hill'. ?Snow Hill.

soc OE, 'sucking', later 'the drainage of a dunghill, a drain, a soak-away, a sock pit'. *the Soke* (f.n. Redmile), *þe Soke, sukewonge* (f.ns. Bottesford).

sodde ME, 'sod, turf'. Sodgate (Waltham on the Wolds).

*sōg, *sōh OE, **sogh** ME, 'a bog, a swamp', **sough** ModEdial., 'a bog, a marsh; a drain'. *le Soughbek* (f.n. Redmile), *le Sough Medowe, Souhendes* (f.ns. Burton Lazars), *suwe fourlong* (f.n. Stapleford), *Velsow* (f.n. Somerby).

sol¹ OE, 'mud, a slough, a wallowing-place for animals', whence 'a dirty pond'. *Nethersole dyke, Oversole dyke* (f.ns. Freeby), *solledeyle* (f.n. Muston).

sorell ME, 'sorrel, dock'. Common sorrel (*Rumex acetosa*) is used for culinary purposes. Sorrell Dale (f.n. Coston).

spa emodE, 'a spa, a mineral medicinal spring'. *Belvoir Spa* (Belvoir), Spa Cl (f.n. Thorpe Arnold).

spann¹ OE, 'a hand's breadth, a span'; used in f.ns. prob. to denote something narrow, such as 'a strip of land'. *Spondale bush* (f.n. Coston).

spearwa OE, 'a sparrow'. *the Sparrow lane* (f.n. Waltham on the Wolds).

spell OE, 'speech, discourse'; used in p.ns. esp. of places where speeches were made in assemblies and freq. denotes a hundred moot-site or other meeting place. ?Spells Cl (f.n. Sysonby).

spīce OE, 'an aromatic herb'. ?*Spiceley Hill* (f.n. Wycomb/Chadwell).

spink ME, 'a finch'. *spincwelle* (f.n. Knipton), *Spinkwell* (f.n. Croxton Kerrial).

spinney ME, 'a copse, a small plantation, a spinney'. Ash Pole Spinney, Blowpool ~, Bunny's ~, Buttermilk Hill ~, Cumberland ~, Debdale ~, Ellaby's ~, Green ~, Highfields ~, Lake ~, Landfield ~, Long ~, Marriott's ~, Melton ~, Mill Hill ~, Paget's ~, Rickett's Spinney, Rise Hill Spinneys, Sapcoat's Spinney, Sledge ~, The Spinney, Stonesby ~, Stonepit ~, Wheat Hill Spinney. Note also Ash Spinney (Sysonby), *Brentingby Spinney* (Brentingby Wood), The Far Lock Spinney, Little ~, The Little Long ~, The Long Spinney (Edmondthorpe), *Spenywod* (Branston). Infrequent in f.ns.: Spinney Cl (Brentingby, Thorpe Arnold, Withcote), Spinney Fd (Thorpe Arnold), Spinney Mdw (Gt. Dalby, Thorpe Arnold).

spitel ME, 'a hospital, a religious house'. *spitelgate* (Burton Lazars), Spittal Cl (f.n. Gt. Dalby), *the Spittell Chapell, Spittle End, Spytelgate* (Melton Mowbray), Spittle Leys, Spittle Town Wong, Spittle Wong (f.ns. Melton Mowbray).

spitel-hous ME, 'the hospital of a religious house'. *Spittelhousclose* (f.n. Belvoir).

spong ModEdial., 'a long, narrow strip of land'. *Spong Bridge* (f.n. Scalford).

spotte ME, 'a small plot of ground'. Home Spot, Skerritts Home Spot (f.ns. Somerby), Spot (f.n. Gt. Dalby).

spring[1] OE, 'a spring, a well, the source of a stream'. Cresswell Spring Fm, Hamwell Spring, Springfield Fm. Goodfellow's Spring (f.n. Somerby), *the Mill-Spring* (f.n. Redmile), *Rodwell Spring* (f.n. Gt. Dalby), (the) Spring Cl (f.ns. Burton Lazars, Lt. Dalby, Scalford, Somerby, Stonesby, Waltham on the Wolds, Wymondham), Spring Furlong (f.n. Stathern), *the Springe heade in Powell* (f.n. Knipton), Spring Head Washpond (f.n. Eastwell), Spring Piece (f.n. Edmondthorpe), *Springwells* (f.n. Pickwell), Well Dale Spring (f.n. Scalford), *wellesprynges* (f.n. Melton Mowbray).

spring[2] ME, 'a young plantation, a copse'. Spring Cl (f.n. Holwell), *the springe hedge* (Thorpe Arnold).

squar(e) ME, adj., 'square'. Square Covert. *le Square Close* (f.n. Buckminster), Square Cl (f.n. Sewstern).

staca OE, 'a stake, a post'. Stathern. *Hobstacke foarde* (f.n. Scalford), ?*Stake hades* (f.n. Melton Mowbray).

stæger OE, 'a stair, a steep ascent'. *the Steares* (f.n. Croxton Kerrial).

***stak-ȝeard** ME, **stack-yard** ModE, 'a stack-yard, an enclosure for ricks'. (The) Stack Yard (f.ns. Wycomb/Chadwell, Wymondham), Stackyard Cl (f.n. Goadby Marwood, Holwell, Scalford), *Stack Yard, Stock Leys Barn and Stackyard* (f.ns. Gt. Dalby).

stakkr ON, 'a stack, a rick'. *Parsonage Stack* (f.n. Harby), *the parsonage stackplace, the parsonage stack stead, the Parsons stacke stead* (f.ns. Wyfordby), *Stack Wonge* (f.n. Gt. Dalby).

stall OE (Angl), 'a place', esp. 'a standing-place, a stall for cattle', 'a site (of a building or other object or feature)', 'a place for catching fish, a fishing pool' (*v.* Sandred 37–41). *Gerstaldyche* (f.n. Muston), *the Water stalles* (f.n. Barkestone), *waterstals* (f.n. Bottesford).

stān OE, 'a stone, stone, rock'; when used as a first el., often has the adj. function 'stony', esp. in names of roads, streams, fords, plots of ground; or may refer to something stone-built. Harston. Very freq. in f.ns.: referring to standing stones, boundary stones etc., e.g. *at the great stone* (Pickwell), *apud le Whiteston* (Burrough on the Hill), *Brentingby Stones* (Melton Mowbray), *Castlegate Stones* (Redmile), *Harstone* (Muston); to stone structures, e.g. *Stonebridge* (Burrough on the Hill, Coston, Redmile), *le Stonhalle* (Knipton), *Stonewrth hill* (Barkestone); to springs or streams, e.g. *(le) stanwell(e)* (Lt. Dalby, Redmile); to fords, e.g. *le stonforde* (Wycomb/Chadwell); to roads, e.g. Stone Gate (Sewstern), *Stongate* (Bottesford); to stony ground, e.g. *stannewong'* (Croxton Kerrial), *ston(e)furlonge* (Barkestone, Knipton), Stone Mdw (with various spellings in Branston, Knipton, Scalford, Sproxton, Thorpe Arnold) and *le Stonemeade* (Melton Mowbray), *v.* **stoned**.

standard ME, 'the standing stump of a tree'. *Stambardes* (f.n. Pickwell), *Standard, Standartvang* (f.ns. Harby), *standardhill'* (f.n. Wyfordby), *Standerd hooks* (f.n. Burrough on the Hill).

standing ME, 'a standing place, a place in which cattle and horses may stand under shelter'. *Standing furlong* (f.n. Freeby).

stān-(ge)delf OE, 'a stone-quarry'. *atte Standeluis* (f.n. Burrough on the Hill), *?Stannyngdelf* (f.n. Eastwell).

stānig OE, adj., 'stony, rocky, made of stone'. *stonay* (f.n. Saltby), Stoney Beck Furlong, *stonnie hill* (f.ns. Stathern), Stoney Fd (f.n. Scalford), Stoney Lands (f.n. Long Clawson), *Stoney Wombe* (f.n. Wymondham), *the Stoney wounge* (f.n. Waltham on the Wolds), *Stony Brink* (f.n. Somerby), *Stony brinkes* (f.n. Croxton Kerrial), ?Stony Cross, Stony Dale (f.ns. Stonesby), *Stony Hill* (f.n. Harby), *Stony lands* (f.n. Garthorpe).

*stāning OE, 'a stony place'. ?*Stannyngdelf* (f.n. Eastwell).

*stān-pytt OE, ***stan(e)pytt** ME, **stone-pit** ModE, 'a stone-pit, a quarry'. Stonepit Spinney, Stonepit Terrace. *Sherrowdale Stone pitts* (Sharrowdale, f.n. Branston), (the) Stone Pitt (f.ns. with various spellings in Eastwell, Harston, Holwell, Knipton, Stonesby), *(the) Stone pittes* (f.ns. with various spellings in Coston, Ab Kettleby, Saltby, Somerby, Wycomb/Chadwell), (the) Stonepit Cl (f.ns. Eaton, Scalford, Waltham on the Wolds, Wymondham), *Stonepitfurlong* (f.n. Branston), *Stonpittes leyes* (f.n. Freeby).

stapol OE, 'a pillar, a post'. Stapleford.

stēap OE, adj., 'steep'. Old Hill Steep Cl, Steep Lane (f.ns. Wymondham), *Steephill* (f.n. Harby).

stede OE, 'a place, a site, a locality'. *Kyrkestedplot'* (f.n. Muston), *Maydenstede* (f.n. Somerby), *le Merketsteade* (Market Place, Melton Mowbray), *the parsonage stack stead, the Parsons stacke stead* (f.ns. Wyfordby), *Stedfordsty* (f.n. Knipton), *wildestedes* (f.n. Croxton Kerrial).

steinn ON, 'stone, rock'; used adj. as 'stony'. Great Stain Hill (f.n. Pickwell), *Long Steanes* (f.n. Sproxton), Stains (f.n. Gt. Dalby), *Staynewong'* (f.n. Belvoir), *stenwytt' well* (f.n. Bottesford), the Stendalls (f.n. Scalford), *Steyn* (f.n. Somerby), *Steynlandys* (f.n. Thorpe Arnold), *Steynwordhoc* (f.n. Burrough on the Hill).

stēpel OE (Angl), 'a steep place', 'a steeple, a tower'. *the Steeple end* (f.n. Ab Kettleby).

stepping-stone ModE, 'a stone for stepping on, a stone placed in the bed of a stream or on muddy or swampy ground to facilitate crossing on foot'; usually pl., referring to a row or line of such stones. *the steppinge stones* (Croxton Kerrial).

sticca OE, 'a stick, a twig'. *Stikbrere* (f.n. Wycomb/Chadwell).

stīg OE, **stígr** ON, 'a path, a narrow road, an upland path' (*v.* **sty-gate**); almost impossible to distinguish formally from **stig** 'a sty, a pen', and as in some cases the el. develops late as *stile*, it thus may be confused also with names formed with **stigel**. In f.ns., the el. is best recognized when combined with names of townships, e.g. *Granbe steeh* (Branston), *Burrow foot stile, Little Dalby foot stile, Osolvistonesty* (Somerby), *Olebysti* (Melton Mowbray); or perh. where there are indications of flora associated with the paths, e.g. ?*Furnesty* (Burton Lazars), *Hawthornstye* (Knipton), *Thirnie stie* (Stathern). Names such as *Castelsty* (Eaton), *Croystys* (Croxton Kerrial), *grenesti* (Muston), *in tyll' Sty* (Bottesford) may also reasonably be assigned to the el., but a range of names in the text attributed to **stīg, stígr** may belong with **stig**.

stig OE, 'a sty, a pen'; also 'a hall, a dwelling'. Almost impossible to distinguish formally from **stīg, stígr**. Such f.ns. as the following may reasonably be attributed to this el.: Bull Sty, Clark Sty, *little stye, the pinder stie, swinerd stee* (Stathern), *Crokeswinstey* (Croxton Kerrial), *Edlingstye, Edmondstigh furlong* (Barkestone), Hawleys Stye Hedge Cl (Long Clawson), *le maresty, the Parsonage Steith, West Steeth* (Harby), *ouercotestys* (Bottesford), *the Stigh* (Knipton), Styesdale (Wymondham), *the Sty Yard* (Thorpe Arnold), *Swinestyfurlong'* (Muston).

stigel OE, 'a stile'. *atte Kirkestile* (p) (Burrough on the Hill), ?*Priors Close Style* (f.n. Scalford), ?Style Cl (f.n. Long Clawson).

stīpere OE, 'a post'. Steprill (f.n. Burrough on the Hill).

*****stobb** OE, 'a tree-stump'. *Stobclif* (f.n. Somerby).

stoc OE, 'a religious place; a place where cattle stood for milking in outlying pastures; a cattle farm; a dairy farm, esp. an outlying one; a secondary settlement'. *Stoc* (f.n. Melton Mowbray), *stoch* (f.n. Croxton Kerrial), The Stock (f.n. Freeby), Stock Cl (f.n. Burton Lazars), Stock Leys Barn (f.n. Gt. Dalby), *Stokfurlong', Stockleys* (f.ns. Stathern), *Stoke Barne and Yard* (f.n. Scalford).

stocc OE, **stokkr** ON, 'a tree-trunk, a stump, a log, a stock'. *Stocbechil, Stochil* (f.ns. Bottesford), *stochewille* (f.n. Barkestone), *Stockewell* (f.n. Burrough on the Hill), *Stockhill* (f.n. Pickwell), *stokbrig* (f.n. Knipton).

*****stoccing** OE, **stocking** ME, 'a piece of ground cleared of stumps'. *Stockins* (f.n. Pickwell).

stock ModE, 'livestock'. Owston Stock Gate (Somerby).

stōd OE, 'a stud, a herd of horses'. Gartree Stud, Shipman's Barn Stud. *Stodgate* (Bottesford).

stōd-fald OE, 'a stud-fold, a horse-enclosure'. *Stedfold* (f.n. Normanton), *Stedfold Dale* (f.n. Nether Broughton), *stodfolde* (f.n. Muston).

stofn OE, ON, 'a tree-stump'. ?Stonesby. ?*Stoueneshil* (f.n. Plungar).

stoned ModE, ppl.adj., 'stoned, cleared of stones'. *the Lords stoned medowe, the red bankes stoned medowe, the Stoned Medowe* (f.ns. Branston). Note *the stonne medowe* (f.n. with various spellings in Branston, Knipton, Scalford, Sproxton, Thorpe Arnold) and *le Stonemeade* (Melton Mowbray) in which *stone* may have the same force as *stoned*, v. *the stone middow* in Knipton f.ns. (b).

storð ON, 'a young wood, a plantation, land growing with brushwood'. *the storth* (f.n. Wyfordby).

stōw OE, 'a place, a place of assembly, a holy place'. *the Stooe* (f.n. Sproxton), *Stowe furlong* (f.n. Freeby), *Stowegate, Stowegren* (f.ns. Bottesford), *stowhilles* (f.n. Burton Lazars).

strǣt OE, **strēt** (Angl), 'a Roman road, a paved road, an urban road, a street'. High St, King Street Lane. *Denton Street, the kings high streete, schirestrete* (Croxton Kerrial), *the High Street* (Coston, Eastwell, Pickwell), Hollow Street, *Lincolne street* (Ab Kettleby), *le Saltestrete, le Strete* (Eaton), Straight Fold (f.n. Muston), *the Street(e)* (Branston, Burton Lazars, Croxton Kerrial, Eastwell, Harston, Ab Kettleby, Sproxton, Stathern), Street Bridge (Stathern), Street Cl (f.n. Goadby Marwood, Stonesby), *the streete furlong* (f.n. Coston, Scalford), *the streete side* (f.n. Coston), *Strethelbut'* (f.n. Old Dalby), *the Town(e) Street(e)* (Harby, Harston, Hose, Ab Kettleby, Pickwell, Stathern), *Weste strete* (Sewstern).

strēam OE, 'a stream'. *Holbeck Streame* (f.n. Pickwell).

strēaw OE, 'straw'. *Strawdales* (f.n. Barkestone), *Strewhull'* (f.n. Burrough on the Hill).

street-waie eModE, 'a paved road or highway'. *the two streete waies* (Edmondthorpe).

strift eModE, 'contention, strife'. Strifts Plantation.

strime ModEdial., 'a stride, a pace'. The fifty strimes Lowning, Top fifty strimes (f.ns. Holwell).

*****strīp** OE, 'a narrow tract of land'. *Longstripes, the Short Stripes* (f.ns. Normanton), The Strip (f.n. Gt. Dalby), Stripes (f.n. Stathern), *the Stripes* (f.n. Saltby).

strive, strif ME, 'strife, contention, dispute'. *Strive Gorse* (Strifts Plantation).

stubb OE, 'a stub, a tree-stump'. *Elder Stub Fur'* (f.n. Gt. Dalby), *Erlunstubbe* (f.n. Thorpe Arnold), *Stubb furlonge* (f.n. Edmondthorpe), *Stubthorne* (f.n. Harby).

*****stubbing** OE, 'a place where trees have been stubbed, a clearing'. *Sudstubbinges* (f.n. Old Dalby).

*****stump** OE, 'a tree-stump'. *at the Eldar Stump* (f.n. Saltby), *Eldern Stump* (f.n Stonesby), *stump bushe* (f.n. Wyfordby), *stumpcrosse* (f.n. Scalford).

*****sty-gate** ME, 'a pathway, a narrow road, a footpath' (*v.* **stīg, stígr, gata**). Great Styegate Cl (f.n. Pickwell), *Lynstygate* (f.n. Normanton), ?*Schepestigate* (f.n. Burton Lazars).

*****stynt** OE, 'stint, limit'. *the stint furlong* (f.n. Bottesford).

sunne OE, 'sun', alluding in f.ns. to ground which catches the best of the sun. *Sunne hades* (f.n. Melton Mowbray).

*****sunt** OE, 'a marsh, a swamp, boggy ground'. *suntland* (f.n. Redmile).

sūr OE, 'sour', 'damp, coarse' (of land). *Soure Dole* (f.n. Burton Lazars), ?*Sowerbeck* (f.n. Redmile).

sūre OE, 'sorrell'. ?*Sowerbeck* (f.n. Redmile).

sūð OE, adj., adv., 'south, southern'. Freq. in f.ns., e.g. *Southcroftes, southynges, Sowthell'* (Belvoir), *the Sowthe fielde* (Coston), *sowthholme* (Bottesford), *Sudstubbinges* (Old Dalby), *le Suthbenelandis* (Normanton) etc.

sūðer OE, **suðr** ON, adj., 'south, southern', *Suthere Peselandes* (f.n. Burton Lazars).

sviða ON, 'burning', used topographically as 'cleared by burning'. *swithmors* (f.n. Bottesford).

*****swalg** OE (Angl), 'a pit, a pool'. Swallow Hole. Swallow (f.n. Waltham on the Wolds), the Swallows Cl (f.n. Long Clawson), *Swaludale* (f.n. Melton Mowbray), *le swelupitte* (f.n. Wycomb/Chadwell).

swan[1] OE, 'a swan'. ?Swan Land (f.n. Gt. Dalby), *the Swannes neast* (f.n. Goadby Marwood), Swan's Nest (f.n. Melton Mowbray), *the Swans Nest* (f.n. Pickwell).

swān[2] OE, 'a herdsman, a swineherd, a peasant'. ?Swan Land, ?Swanton (f.ns. Gt. Dalby).

swār OE, adj., 'heavy'. *Swarfurowes* (f.n. Redmile).

swathe ME, 'a strip of grassland'. *the bull swayth, Long Swaythes* (f.ns. Knipton), *the foreswaiths* (f.n. Saxby), *the Long Swathes* (f.n. Croxton Kerrial), *le suaþes* (f.n. Coston), Swathes (f.n. Garthorpe), *le Swathes* (f.n. Eaton).

sweeting eModE, 'a sweet-apple tree'. *the Sweeting tree* (f.n. Knipton).

(ge)swell OE, 'a swelling'; topographically 'a rising piece of ground, a hill'. Long Swells (f.n. Gt. Dalby).

sweord OE, 'a sword'; poss. topographically 'a narrow strip of land of the shape of a sword, a headland'. ?*swerdeacre* (f.n. Bottesford).

swille OE, 'a sloppy mess, a liquid mess; a swilling'. ?Swills Platt (f.n. Wymondham).

swīn OE, **svín** ON, 'a swine, a pig'. *Crokeswinstey* (f.n. Croxton Kerrial), *Swine Acres, the swineinge goares* (f.ns. Scalford), Swine Balk (f.n. Stathern), *Swinedale* (f.n. Pickwell), *Swinelandes* (f.n. Long Clawson), *Swinesdale* (f.n. Branston), *Swinestyfurlong'* (f.n. Muston), *swynemore forlonge* (f.n. Bottesford), *Swynesdale* (f.n. Eaton), *Swyneslane* (Melton Mowbray)

swīn-hirde late OE, 'a swine-herd'. *swinerd stee* (f.n. Stathern), *the Swinherd peice* (f.n. Harby).

synneful OE, adj., 'wicked, corrupt, characterized by sin'. *synnefulheuedland* (f.n. Muston).

tǣsel OE, 'a teasel'. Taslands (f.n. Stathern).

taile ME, 'a tail'; topographically 'a tail of land; the bottom end of a pool or stream'. Ballimoor Tail Cl (f.n. Goadby Marwood), *Talepoole leyes* (f.n. Eastwell).

tang, ***tong** OE, **tangi** ON, 'a spit of land'. *etytong'* (Eady Fm), *Mikelsyktong* (f.n. Normanton), *þe stytong'* (f.n. Bottesford), *Wulverstang* (f.n. Knipton).

tankard ME, **tankert** ModEdial., 'a wooden tub, esp. used for carrying water, a drinking vessel'. ?*Tankett Sike* (f.n. Eastwell).

temple ME, 'a temple', in p.ns. usually in allusion to properties of the Knights Templars. *le Templegore* (f.n. Melton Mowbray), *Templewong'* (f.n. Bottesford).

tēn OE, num., 'ten'. *ten knowles* (f.n. Burton Lazars).

tenement ME, 'a tenement, a dwelling'; also in ModE 'a land-holding'. *Edward Basse his Tenement* (f.n. Stapleford), *Brandriffs tenement* (f.n. Old Dalby), *Pooles tenement, Stringers tenement* (f.ns. Nether Broughton), Tenement Barn (f.n. Eastwell).

tentour ME, 'a tenter, a frame for tenting cloth'. Tenter Cl (f.n. Bottesford, Knipton), *Tenter Close* (f.n. Melton Mowbray), *Tenter leyes* (f.n. Stonesby).

tēoða OE, 'a tithe, a tenth'. *blackwell tythe, the tythe called the chesecake* (f.ns. Saltby), *the tith headland* (f.n. Wyfordby), *the Tyth barne* (Redmile), Tythe Hookes, *the tythe meadowe* (f.ns. Melton Mowbray), *the Tythe howse* (Melton Mowbray), *the tythe wong* (f.n. Freeby), *Tythe Wong end* (f.n. Saxby), *the Tythe yard* (f.n. Thorpe Acre).

terrace ModE, 'a raised level place for walking; a horizontal shelf on the side of a hill; a row of houses on a level above the general surface, a row of houses of uniform style'. Stonepit Terrace, Terrace Hills. *Cardigan terrace, Park ~, Rutland ~, Temperance ~, Wilton terrace* (Melton Mowbray).

þæc OE, **þak** ON, 'thatching material', used in p.ns. of places where thatching materials were got. *Thacdeile, Thacholm* (f.ns. Muston), *Thack Dale* (f.n. Stonesby), *Thakholm* (f.n. Bottesford, Melton Mowbray), Thatch Mdw (f.n. Bottesford).

þak ON, 'thatch, material for thatching', *v.* **þæc**.

þe ME, def.art., 'the'.

*****þefa** OE, 'brushwood, bramble'. *thefe pit* (f.n. Saltby).

þicce[1] OE, 'a thicket, dense undergrowth'. *Thick Woodwell head* (Woodwell Head).

þicce[2] OE, adj., 'thick, dense'. *thickthorne* (f.n. Harby).

þiccett OE, 'a thicket, dense bushes or undergrowth'. *Thickett Woodwell head* (Woodwell Head).

þing OE, ON, 'an assembly, a council, a meeting'. *Dinghill* (f.n. Somerby).
thing ME, 'possession, property'. *blakethyng, harwythyng* (f.ns. Knipton), *Hancockes land alias Hancockes Thing* (f.n. Burton Lazars), *Tawstonthinge* (f.n. Belvoir).
þistel OE, 'a thistle'. *phistilberu* (f.n. Harby), ?*Sissleborough* (f.n. Gt. Dalby), *Thistelholm* (f.n. Burton Lazars), *þistelwelle* (f.n. Redmile), Thistle Fd (f.n. Wymondham).
thist(e)ly ME, adj., 'thistly'. Thistl(e)y Cl (f.n. Thorpe Arnold, Wymondham).
þorn OE, 'a thorn, a thorntree'; collectively, 'a stand or thicket or a wood of thorntrees'. Cant's Thorns, Church Thorns, Clawson Thorns, Sproxton Thorns, Waltham Thorns. Freq. in f.ns.: with an el. indicating the shape/size of the thorn-patch, e.g. *Langethorn* (Wycomb/Chadwell), *Short Thorne* (Eastwell); or the particular characteristic of the thorns, e.g. *Copthorne* (Nether Broughton), *le hepthern* (Plungar), *stubthorne, thickthorn* (Harby); or location, e.g. *Kickleburrow thorns* (Branston), *Thornwellethornes* (Eaton), *þe waren thorns* (Bottesford); with a pers.n. or surn. indicating ownership, e.g. *Stirkerthorn* (Muston), Parrs Thorns (Ab Kettleby), ?*Rattisthorn* (Burrough on the Hill). As a specific, the el. appears with a range of words specifying land units, e.g. *Thornedeil* (Stathern), *thorneforlong'* (Muston), *Thorne headland* (Freeby), *le Thornwong'* (Wyfordby). Note the unusual *Halythornfurlong* (Barkestone).
thorne-tree ME, 'a tree bearing thorns, a hawthorn-tree'. *high thorntree* (f.n. Branston), Thorn Tree Furlong, Thorn Tree Wong (f.ns. Stathern).
þornig OE, adj., 'thorny, growing with thorns'. Thorney Cl (f.n. with various spellings in Nether Broughton, Coston, Eastwell, Melton Mowbray, Stathern, Waltham on the Wolds), Thorney Hollow (f.n. Old Dalby), Thorney Lane (Hose), Thorney Mere (f.n. Harston), Thorney Park (f.n. Harby), Thorney Slade (f.n. Stathern), *Thorny wonge* (f.n. Pickwell).
þorp OEScand, ON, 'a secondary settlement, a dependent outlying farmstead or hamlet'. Beckingthorpe, Easthorpe, Edmondthorpe, *Erlesthorpe* (Thorpe Arnold), Garthorpe, *Gillethorp'*, *Godtorp*, Leesthorpe, *Ringlethorpe*, Thorpe Arnold, Westthorpe. *Netherthorp, le ouerthorpe, thorpforth* (f.ns. Lt. Dalby), *Redmylthorp* (f.n. Redmile), *thorp* (f.n. Croxton Kerrial), *Thorpdale, Thorpes* (f.ns. Knipton), *Westhorp* (f.n. Coston).
þrǽll ON, **þrǽl** late OE, 'a thrall, a serf, a villein, a bondman'. *Thrawlhills* (f.n. Barkestone).
three-corner ModE, adj., 'having three corners, triangular'. Three Corner Cl (f.n. Sysonby), Three Corner Fd (f.n. Lt. Dalby, Somerby), Three Corner Piece (f.n. Thorpe Arnold).
three-cornered ModE, adj., 'having three corners, triangular'. Three Cornered Cl (f.n. Buckminster, Burton Lazars, Gt. Dalby, Lt. Dalby, Goadby Marwood, Holwell, Sewstern, Wymondham), the Three-Cornered Fd (f.n. Scalford), Three cornered Mdw (f.n. Freeby), *Three corner'd Piece* (f.n. Brentingby).
þrēo neut., fem., **þrī** masc., OE, num., 'three'. *Thredikes* (f.n. Croxton Kerrial), *the three roodes* (f.n. Saltby), *threhowis* (f.n. Burton Lazars), *Threthorndale* (f.n. Knipton).
þurh OE, adv., prep., 'through'. *the Throwley in the more* (f.n. Stathern).
þurs ON, 'a giant', v. **þyrs**.

þverr (þvert neut.) ON, adj., 'athwart, lying across'. *Thuerlondes* (f.n. Plungar), *le Thwerbrech* (f.n. Burrough on the Hill), *le Thwertfurlong'* (f.n. Thorpe Arnold), *thwertgate* (Cross Lane, Burton Lazars).

þwang OE, 'a thong'; topographically 'a narrow strip of land'. Long Thong (f.n. Gt. Dalby).

þyrne OE, **þyrnir** ON, 'a thorn-bush'. Sewstern, Stathern. Fairly freq. in f.ns.: with a pers.n. indicating ownership, e.g. *Apethirne* (Thorpe Arnold), *Asketelthirn'* (Stathern), *Roppederne* (Waltham on the Wolds); esp. with an el. specifying a hill or hillside, e.g. *Thirneclif* (Burton Lazars, Muston), *Thurn(e) Hill* (Gt. Dalby, Garthorpe, Waltham on the Wolds), *thurnborow* (with various spellings in Lt. Dalby, Muston, Somerby); with fauna, e.g. *le cattisterne* (Knipton), *Crathernesike* (Wycomb/Chadwell); in road-names, e.g. *thirnegate* (Garthorpe), *Thurnegate* (Waltham on the Wolds). Note the ME reflex of OE **þyrne** which occurs in the Framland Hundred, as in *hesterne* (Muston), *le long terne* (Normanton) and in *le cattisterne* and Sewstern *supra*.

þyrniht OE, adj., 'growing with thorns'. *Thirnie slade* (Thorney Slade, f.n. Stathern), *Thirnie stie* (f.n. Stathern), *thurniakyr* (f.n. Harby), *Thurnye Meere* (Thorney Mere, f.n. Harston).

þyrnir ON, 'a thorn-bush', *v.* **þyrne**.

þyrs OE, **þurs** ON, 'a demon, a giant'. *thirspittes* (f.n. Knipton), *thorsepytwong'* (f.n. Muston), *thruspits* (f.n. Saltby), *Thurspitt leayes* (f.n. Croxton Kerrial), *Tyrspitwong'* (f.n. Bottesford).

timber OE, 'timber, trees'. *Timber Hill* (Melton Mowbray), Timber Hill Gardens (f.n. Sewstern), Tumberhill (f.n. Stathern).

tit, tyt ME, 'a tit, a small bird'. ?*Tythow* (f.n. Freeby).

*todd OE, 'a fox'. *Todhow* (f.n. Thorpe Arnold).

toft ODan, **topt** ON, **toft** late OE, 'a building site, a curtilage, a messuage'. Toft's Hill, Toft's Lane. Fairly freq. in f.ns.: esp. with a pers.n., e.g. *Basiltoftes* (Bottesford), *Botilde toft* (Muston), *Gudlokes toft* (Burton Lazars), *Thebeltoft* (Wymondham); or with a locational prefix, e.g. Harby Tofts, Plungar Tofts (Stathern), *the mid tofthe* (Pickwell). As a simplex (only in the pl.), (*le*) *Toftes* (with various spellings) occurs in Bottesford, Croxton Kerrial, Edmondthorpe, Harby, Harston, Redmile and Stapleford. Occurs occasionally as a specific, e.g. Toft Dale (Coston), Toft Dyke (Wymondham), *tofte hole* (Saxby), *Toft hurn*, *toftsti* (Harby).

toll-gate ModE, 'a gate across a road at which toll was payable, a turnpike-gate'. Tollgate Ho. and Garden (Burton Lazars).

top ModE, adj., 'topmost, upper, uppermost'. Top Piece (f.n. Harby), ?*top well gate* (Hose).

topp OE, 'top, the top of a bank or hill'. *the hill toppe* (f.n. Knipton), ?Lintop Drain (f.n. Long Clawson), *Roule Toppes* (f.n. Burrough on the Hill), *Shittoppes*, *Thurneshill topp* (f.ns. Croxton Kerrial), *Stiletoppe* (f.n. Pickwell), ?*top well gate* (Hose), *Wong Top* (f.n. Harby).

*tōt-hyll OE, 'a look-out hill'. *Toote hill* (f.n. Sproxton).

træf OE, 'a dwelling, a building'. *le Loetraues*, *le Trauecroftes* (f.ns. Wycomb/Chadwell).

trafficke eModE, 'bargaining, exchange'. ?Traffic Furlong (f.n. Melton Mowbray).

trak ME, 'a path, a way beaten by the feet of animals, a rough unmade road'. *the Sheeptrack* (Branston).

travers OFr, ME, adj., 'lying across, extending across, transverse'. *the Trevers Gorse* (f.n. Barkestone).

trēow, trēo OE, 'a tree'. *Bucktree furlong* (f.n. Branston), Crowtrees (f.n. Holwell), *Trowelle* (f.n. Burton Lazars), *Willytrewelle furlang, Wyltrehullforlang'* (f.ns. Sewstern).

triangle OFr, ME, 'a figure having three angles and three sides; something having the form of a triangle'. (The) Triangle (f.ns. Burrough on the Hill, Burton Lazars).

triangular eModE, adj., 'having the form of a triangle, three-cornered, three-sided, contained by three sides and angles'. Triangular Cl (f.n. Lt. Dalby).

trog OE, 'a valley, a trough, a long narrow vessel (for watering or feeding animals)'. *the Parsonage Troughe, Sandpitthill troffe* (f.ns. Stathern), *True gate* (Stapleford).

tūn OE, 'an enclosure, a farmstead, a village, an estate'. Barkestone, Branston, Nether Broughton, Long Clawson, Coston, Croxton Kerrial, Eaton, Knipton, Melton Mowbray, Muston, Sproxton, Toston; *Alfricheston* (Wymondham), *Herdston* (Muston), ?*Hunton* (Easthorpe), *lauutona* (Bottesford), ?*Ogerstone* (Plungar), Swanton (Gt. Dalby). Common in later f.ns. denoting land adjacent to a township, e.g. Townend Cl (Gt. Dalby, Freeby, Harston, Muston, Wartnaby), *the Towne furlonge* (with various spellings in Burton Lazars, Lt. Dalby, Freeby, Harston, Hose, Plungar, Somerby). Recurring is *the Towne Streete* (with various spellings in Nether Broughton, Harby, Harston, Hose, Ab Kettleby, Redmile, Stathern). Note also *the Towne welles* (Eastwell), *the tunwelle de Wycham* (Wycomb/Chadwell).

tunge OE, 'a tongue; a tongue of land'. *abbott tonge* (f.n. Burton Lazars), *Brokholetonge* (f.n. Sysonby), *Brook tonges, Longe tongues, Wauefenetunge* (f.ns. Burrough on the Hill), *Kicklesbarew tounge* (f.n. Branston), *le Milnetonge* (f.n. Wycomb/Chadwell), *the Moore tonge* (The Moors, Croxton Kerrial), the Tongues (f.n. Stathern).

tūn-stede OE, 'a farmstead'; later, poss. 'a deserted site'. *dunsteades* (f.n. Eastwell).

tup ME, 'a ram, a tup'. Tup Mdw (f.n. Wyfordby).

turf OE, 'turf', turf ModEdial., 'peat'. the Turf (f.n. Scalford), *le Turues* (f.n. Wycomb/Chadwell).

***turf-pytt** ME, 'a pit from which peat is dug'. *toorpites* (f.n. Wycomb/Chadwell).

turnepike ME, 'a turnpike, a revolving frame or pole bearing spikes and serving as a barrier', **turnpike** ModE, 'a road on which a toll is payable and along which movement is controlled by barriers'. the Turnpike Rd (Croxton Kerrial).

turnyard ModE, 'a yard containing a rotary apparatus such as a horse-mill'. *Thomas Worsdale his turneyarde* (Knipton).

twēgen (tū neut.) OE, **twey** ME, **two** ModE, num., 'two'. *thothornes* (f.n. Leesthorpe), ?*toadale* (f.n. Thorpe Arnold), *Tuffordegate* (Burton Lazars), *tuotherne* (f.n. Muston), *Twocrosseplace* (Buckminster), *Twodales* (f.n. Normanton).

twelf OE, num., 'twelve'. Twelve Acre Cl (f.n. Bottesford).

twī- OE, prefix, 'double, two'. Twival Fd (f.n. Somerby).

uferra OE, adj., comp., 'higher, upper'; difficult to distinguish from **ofer**[3] 'over, above'. Freq. in f.ns., e.g. Over Cl (Buckminster), Over Fd (Redmile), Over Ground (Wyfordby), Over Mdw (Freeby, Holwell), *the Overmylne* (Barkstone), Over Shoot (Holwell), *the over steeh* (Branston), *Over Stock* (Burton Lazars), *le ouerthorpe* (Lt. Dalby).

under OE, adv., prep., 'under, beneath, below'. *underherstun, underlangdik'* (f.ns. Muston), *Underholes furlonge* (f.n. Lt. Dalby), *under heycliffe, under kiklesbarowe, under wyndhilles* (f.ns. Branston), *under þe hege* (f.n. Bottesford).

untyll ME, prep., 'as far as, reaching to, up to'. *in tyll'* Sty (f.n. Bottesford).

uppe ME, adv., prep., 'up, higher up, the higher one'. ?Upper Fd (f.n. Freeby).

upper ME, adj., 'higher'. ?Upper Fd (f.n. Freeby).

ūt, ūte OE, **út, úti** ON, adv., 'outside, on the outskirts'; elliptically 'a place lying on the outskirts'; as adj., 'outer, more distant'. Outhall Lane (Long Clawson).

val OFr, **vale** ME, 'a vale, a wide valley'. Vale of Belvoir. Also as an affix in forms for Barkestone, Bottesford, Branston, Nether Broughton, Long Clawson, Harby, Muston, Normanton, Redmile, Stathern.

vangr ON, 'an in-field'. West Wong. Very freq. in f.ns.: with a pers.n., e.g. *alewinwong'*, *Thurstoneswong* (Burton Lazars), *Frethegestwong'* (Harston), *Swartketilwong'* (Bottesford); with a surn., e.g. Ashbys Wong, Levetts Wongs (Melton Mowbray), *Derby Wong* (Freeby), *Pauntonwong* (Burrough on the Hill); with an el. indicating ecclesiastical ownership, e.g. *the Monkes wonges* (Branston), *le Presteswong'* (Eaton), *Templewong'* (Bottesford), *the Vicars wonge* (Brentingby). Major township buildings may appear, e.g. *hallewonge* (Redmile), *the kirke wong* (Freeby), Spittle Wong (Melton Mowbray); or agricultural edifices, e.g. *Bernewang* (Scalford, Thorpe Arnold), *boosam wonge* (Bottesford), *Hellewong'* (Muston). Crops may be specified, e.g. *Finel wong'* (Muston), *Haverwounge* (Scalford), *the Rye wonge* (Easthorpe); or wild flora, e.g. *Bracken Wonge* (Croxton Kerrial), *Dockey Wonge* (Nether Broughton), *thirnewong'* (Wyfordby). Soil or fertility may be indicated, e.g. *(le) sandewong(e)* (Barkestone, Bottesford), *Staynewong'* (Belvoir), *blacke wong* (Scalford), White Wong (Nether Broughton); or size/shape, e.g. *Coleuillemiclewong* (Bottesford), *lyttle wonge* (Knipton), *langewong'* (Belvoir). Locational names are esp. common, e.g. *Burton Bridge wong*, Drift Wongs (Melton Mowbray), *Calverhillwong'*, *Diuenewong'*, *Herdwykwonge* (Bottesford), *Lambcotewong'* (Muston), *Saltbeckwong* (Belvoir). Note *Dedwong* (Bottesford, Harby) which may allude to the discovery of early burials.

vápnatak ON, **wæpengetæc** late OE, **wapentac** ME, 'a wapentake, a sub-division of a county', corresponding to OE **hundred**. Framland Wapentake.

varða, varði ON, 'a cairn, a heap of stones'. ?*Warddeyle* (f.n. Plungar).

vað ON, 'a ford'. *Pinquath* (f.n. Melton Mowbray), *stenwytt well'* (f.n. Bottesford), ?*watefordhill* (f.n. Muston), *le Wath* (f.n. Wycomb/Chadwell).

vatr ON, adj., 'wet'. Watmore (f.n. Wycomb/Chadwell).

vedeir OFr, 'a view'. Belvoir.

veiði ON, 'a place for hunting or fishing'. *le Wayte* (f.n. Burton Lazars).

vengi ON, 'a field'. *le Wenge, Wyngfurlong'* (f.ns. Bottesford).

vestr ON, adj., 'west', **vestri** ON, comp., 'more westerly'. *le ueste leys* (f.n. Melton Mowbray), *vestings* (f.n. Coston), *Westerdick'* (f.n. Branston).

vikerage ME, 'a vicarage'. The Vicarage (Barkestone, Buckminster, Long Clawson, Stonesby, Thorpe Arnold, Wartnaby).

vikere ME, 'a vicar'. *the Vicars Close* (f.n. Stapleford), *the vicar dale* (f.n. Saltby), *the vicars headland, the vicars land* (f.ns. Ab Kettleby), Vicars Mdw (f.n. Wartnaby), *the Vicars wonge* (f.n. Brentingby), ?*Viccar Bush* (f.n Stonesby), *vickeres well* (f.n. Croxton Kerrial).

vine OFr, ME, 'a vine'. *the Vinehowse* (Burton Lazars).

vinery ModE, 'a glass-house or hot-house constructed for the cultivation of the grape-vine'. Bottesford Vineries.

vinȝerd ME, 'a vineyard'. *Edwards Vineyard, the Vineyard* (f.ns. Burton Lazars), The Vineyard (f.n. Edmondthorpe), *John Waltons House & Vineyard* (Burton Lazars).

vrá ON, **wro** ME, 'a nook, a corner of land', **wro** ModEdial., 'a secluded spot; a cattle shelter'. *Alredwro, Cokeswrogate, þe wroo* (f.ns. Bottesford), *Alueredwrofurlong, wrohill'* (f.ns. Muston), *Castell Row* (f.n. Belvoir), Cow Row Cl (f.n. Buckminster), *hither Wroo* (f.n. Melton Mowbray), Roe Bushes (f.n. Barkestone), Roe Cl (f.n. Long Clawson), The Row (f.n. Harby, Muston, Thorpe Arnold), *Sheeprow* (f.n. Sproxton), *Wrogate, the Wrooes* (f.ns. Harston).

wād OE, 'woad'. the Wad Cl (f.n. Pickwell), ?*Wadd Cl* (f.n. Melton Mowbray), *Wadeland'* (f.n. Plungar), Wadhill Nook (f.n. Hose), *Wadhou* (f.n. Burrough on the Hill), Wadland Hill (f.n. Stonesby), *Wadlands*, Wadlands Platt (f.ns. Edmondthorpe), Woad Cl (f.n. Thorpe Arnold).

wæcce OE, **watch** ModE, 'a watch, a look-out'. *Watch Bank*, ?Watchorn (f.ns. Scalford), ?Watchorns (f.n. Wymondham).

(ge)wæd OE, 'a ford'. *Catewade* (f.n. Bottesford), *Wade, wadecliue,* ?*waudyng* (f.ns. Knipton), ?*le Wadh* (f.n. Wycomb/Chadwell), *Watclyffe* (f.n. Croxton Kerrial), ?*watefordhill'* (f.n. Muston).

wæfre OE, adj., 'unstable, shaking'; also used of 'swampy ground' and 'brushwood'(v. DEPN *s.n.* Waverley, Sr). *Wauefenhull, Waferne Botome, Wauefenetunge* (f.ns. Burrough on the Hill).

wægn, wægen, wǣn OE, **wag(g)on** ModE, 'a wagon, a cart'. *the Melton Mowbray waggon road, Owston waggon road* (Somerby), *above the weanegates* (f.n. Saltby), *weanegatte syke* (f.n. Scalford).

wælisc OE (Angl), adj., 'British (not Anglo-Saxon); unfree, servile'. ?*walsemoresedis* (f.n. Burton Lazars), ?*Walsemorland* (f.n. Leesthorpe).

wæsce OE, 'a place for washing'. Spring Head Washpond (f.n. Eastwell), *the washpit hooke* (f.n. Burrough on the Hill).

wæter OE, 'water; an expanse of water, a lake or pool, a stream or river' or, as first el., 'near to a stream or pool; wet, watery'. Water Lane (Branston, Long Clawson, Melton Mowbray, Sewstern). Fairly freq. in f.ns., e.g. *Cranewater* (Burton Lazars), *Croxton Abbay Water* (Croxton Kerrial), *the mill water* (Saltby), *neatwater* (Harby); Water Cl (Edmondthorpe, Wymondham), Water Mdw (Burton Lazars, Coston, Edmondthorpe). Common is *Waterfurrowes* (with various spellings in Nether Broughton, Buckminster, Burton Lazars plus 10 other townships). Note also Water Gall (Wartnaby), *Watergongfurlong* (Normanton), *the Waterplott* (Nether Broughton), *watersleades* (Branston), *(the) Waterstal(le)s* (Barkestone, Bottesford).

wæterig OE, adj., 'watery'. *Watriforowis* (f.n. Eaton).

walcere OE, **walkere** ME, 'a cloth-dresser, a fuller'. *Walkerhou* (f.n. Bottesford), ?Walker Leys (f.n. Stathern).

wald OE (Angl), 'woodland, a large tract of woodland, high forest-land', **wald, wold** ME, 'an elevated stretch of open country or moorland'. Old Dalby, Waltham on the Wolds; Dalby Wolds, ?Old Hill Fm, Old Hills, Wolds Fm. Freq. in f.ns.: with a township name, e.g. *Ketylby woldes* (Ab Kettleby), *Sixtenby wold* (Melton Mowbray), Wartnaby Woulds (Wartnaby); with an el. indicating the nature of the upland, e.g. *Caldewald'* (Wymondham), Dry Woulds (Eastwell), *Redyngwald* (Thorpe Arnold), *Stanewoldehil(l)* (Barkestone, Stathern); as a simplex, e.g. *the Oldes* (Scalford), Woulds (Sysonby, Wymondham), Woulds Cl (Old Dalby, Eastwell), *Would closes* (Goadby Marwood). Recurring is *Wooldale(s)* (Old Dalby, Holwell), *Woldall* (Freeby).

wald-hām OE (Angl), 'a forest estate'. Waltham on the Wolds.

walh (wales gen.sg.) OE (Angl), 'a Briton, a serf'. *?walsemoresedis* (f.n. (Burton Lazars), *?Walsemorland* (f.n. Leesthorpe), *Walworthehow* (f.n. Muston).

walk ModE, 'a walking-place; a range of pasture'. Bulls Walk, Great Walk, *Neither Walke*, Sand Pit Walk (f.ns. Wymondham), Friars Walk (f.n. Bescaby), *the Sheepe Walke* (f.n. Stapleford), *the Walke* (f.n. Saltby), *Walke hill* (f.n. Wycomb/ Chadwell), *Walke playne* (f.n. Barkestone), The Walk Plantation (f.n. Eastwell), *Waulk More* (f.n. Sproxton).

walke-milne ME, 'a walk-mill, a fulling mill'. *Walke Mill* (Burton Lazars), *Walke milne peece* (f.n. Sproxton).

wall OE (Angl), 'a wall'. *Est parkvall* (f.n. Wymondham), *Mabell Walls* (f.n. Burton Lazars), the Old Walls (f.n. Sproxton), *the Park(e) wall* (f.n. Buckminster, Edmondthorpe), Pennywell Cl (f.n. Edmondthorpe), *the Wall end* (f.n. Scalford), *the Warrande walle* (f.n. Knipton).

wallow ModE, 'a mud-hole or dust-hole where animals wallow'. ?Wallo Cl (f.n. Freeby).

wamb, womb OE, 'a womb, a belly', used topographically as 'a hollow'. ?*Nixes Guntree Wombe*, ?*Stoney Wombe* (f.ns. Wymondham).

wand eModE, 'a measure of land (a yardland or 30 acres)'. ?Wand Cl (f.n. Holwell).

warde ME, 'a castle ward, the circuit of a castle wall'. *le Castleward* (Belvoir Castle).

wareine ME, 'a game preserve, a piece of ground for the breeding of rabbits, a warren'. *the Lords Nursery & Warren* (f.n. Stapleford), *le Warenne* (f.n. with various spellings in Belvoir, Branston, Plungar, Saxby, Sysonby), *þe waren thorns* (f.n. Bottesford), ?*Warinhou* (f.n. Wycomb/Chadwell), *the Warrande walle* (f.n. Knipton), *the Warren for deer called the Parke*, Warren Cls (f.ns. Barkestone), *Le Warren feild* (f.n. Melton Mowbray).

warlot ME, 'a piece of land assessed to a specifically defined payment of geld' (*v.* L 2 67–8). *Anclewarlot* (f.n. Somerby), *the warlott furlong* (f.n. Easthorpe).

waru OE, 'a shelter, defence, guard'. ?Whaley Fd (f.n. Melton Mowbray).

wash-dyke ModEdial., 'a sheep-dip'. Wash Dyke. Washdike Bridge (f.n. Easthorpe), Wash Dike Cl (f.n. Buckminster, Wymondham), Wash Dyke (f.n. Brentingby), Wash Dyke Cl (f.n. Nether Broughton, Gt. Dalby), Wash Dyke Mdw (f.n. Thorpe Arnold).

waste ME, 'waste land'. Old Road and Waste (Wymondham), the Waste (f.n. Hose).

water-mylne ME, 'a water-mill'. the Watermill (Knipton, Scalford), *(the) Watermilne* (Eaton, Saxby, Sproxton), *Water Mill* (Mill Lane, Bottesford).

wateryng eModE, 'a place where cattle are taken to drink'. *the neather wattring, the neates watering(es)* (f.ns. Pickwell, Wyfordby).

wāð OE, 'the chase, hunting'. ?*watefordhill'* (f.n. Muston).

wayn-hous ME, 'a wagon shed, a cart shed'. *le weynhous* (Muston).

weard OE, 'watch, protection'. ?*Warlow* (Whaley Fd, f.n. Melton Mowbray), *Whardloe* (f.n. Somerby).

weg OE, 'a way, a road'. ?Sauvey Castle. Fairly freq. in f.ns., esp. with the name of a township, e.g. *Melton way* (Eastwell), *Okeham waye* (Lt. Dalby), *orson way* (Bottesford), *Sproxton waye* (Buckminster), *Stathorne way* (Branston). Cf. *broadsike waye* (Knipton), *the Cole pitt Waye* (Redmile), *the markit way* (Wyfordby). Occasionally occurs as first el., e.g. *le Waylant* (f.n. Barkestone), *Weyleys, weywyllis* (f.ns. Bottesford).

weg-(ge)lǣte OE, 'a junction of roads'. *Wylletts* (f.n. Stapleford).

welhous ME, 'a small building enclosing a well and its apparatus'. *welhowse leaes* (f.n. Burrough on the Hill), *atte Wellehous* (p) (Wycomb/Chadwell).

wella, well(e) OE (Angl), 'a well, a spring, a stream'. Chadwell, Eastwell, Holwell, Pickwell; Blackwell Lodge, Friars Well, Hamwell Spring, Well, Well Lane, Woodwell Head. Very freq. in f.ns.: with a pers.n. or surn., e.g. *hybaldwell'* (Knipton), *Ogberdeswell'* (Belvoir), *Strykiswell* (Freeby), *Abrahamwelle* (Croxton Kerrial), *Allen well* (Redmile), *Gueyne well* (Somerby); with a locational name, e.g. *Blakeborou wellis, Maydengatewelle* (Knipton), Denton Wells (Harston). Wild flora may be indicated, e.g. *Ashwels* (Somerby), *Thornewell* (Croxton Kerrial), *Willytrewelle* (Sewstern); or fauna, e.g. *Cattewellegate* (Normanton), *The Cutwells* (Harston), esp. birds, e.g. *Crawell'* (Croxton Kerrial), *Owsell welles* (Harston), *spincwelle* (Croxton Kerrial, Knipton). The nature of the spring/stream may be specified, e.g. *Caldwell* (with various spellings in Barkestone, Bottesford, Gt. Dalby, Easthorpe, Redmile, Saxby, Somerby), *Fulwell* (with various spellings in Buckminster, Knipton, Pickwell, Plungar, Sewstern, Stathern, Wycomb/Chadwell), *Muckewellegate, Mudwells* (Harby), Saltwell Drain (Long Clawson); or its function, e.g. *Harewell* (Bottesford, Croxton Kerrial, Holwell), Fasewell Fd (Wartnaby), *haliwell* (Burrough on the Hill, Croxton Kerrial). Direction from a township may be indicated, e.g. *Northwel'* (Belvoir, Harby), *Sowthell'* (Belvoir), *Westere Welles* (Burton Lazars). Note the important *Annwell* (Well, Burton Lazars) and *Annie well* (Wyfordby) which may have been pre-English sacred springs.

wenn OE, 'a wen, a tumour', perh. used topographically of a barrow or mound which might be thought to resemble such an excrescence. ?*Whenham* (f.n. Ab Kettleby).

(ge)weorc OE, 'a work, a building structure', esp. in p.ns. 'a fortification'. *Barnewerc* (f.n. Burton Lazars).

weorc-hūs OE, 'a workshop', **workhouse** ModE, 'a workhouse, a place of public employment for the poor'. *Thurston Werkhous* (Eaton), Workhouse and Yard (Sewstern).

wer, wær OE, 'a weir, a river-dam, a fishing enclosure in a river'. *Sleighting weare* (Slatings, f.n. Waltham on the Wolds), *Warwellmill, Warwellesik'* (Melton Mowbray), *Where head* (f.n. Burton Lazars).

west OE, **vestr** ON, adj., 'western, west'. *Westthorpe*, West Wong. Common in f.ns., e.g. *Westcliffe, the Weste Feilde* (Knipton), *Westgate* (Belvoir, Muston), *le Westheynges* (Muston), *Westhil* (Harby) etc.

*****wester** OE, **wester** ModEdial., adj., 'west, western'. *Westerlongs* (f.n. Saxby), *Westirfurlong'* (f.n. Normanton).

westerra OE, comp.adj., 'more westerly'. *Westerewilleclif* (f.n. Wymondham), *westrecrowelle* (f.n. Croxton Kerrial), *Westere Welles* (f.n. Burton Lazars).

wēt OE, adj., 'wet'. *weeteforrowes* (f.n. Ab Kettleby), *Wetfur'* (f.n. Stonesby), *Wet furrowes* (f.n. Coston), Wetmoore Furlong (f.n. Hose), The Wet Fds (f.n. Gt. Dalby).

weðer OE, 'a castrated ram, a wether'. *Wederhorn, le Wedirlandsik'* (f.ns. Stathern).

whinny ME, adj., 'growing with whins or gorse-bushes'. *kvynnyfurlong* (f.n. Burton Lazars), *Whiny dale* (f.n. Lt. Dalby), *Whinydole* (f.n. Knipton), *Whiny Leas* (f.n. Harby), *the Whiny meare* (f.n. Saltby), *winie meadowe* (f.n. Scalford), *le Winniwong'* (f.n. Thorpe Arnold).

wīc-hām OE, 'an Anglo-Saxon settlement adjacent to a surviving Romano-British small town; an early Anglo-Saxon estate comprising the territory of a former Romano-British small town'. Wycomb.

widuwe OE, 'a widow'. *Wedow Place* (Coston), *The Widdowe Close* (f.n. Burton Lazars).

wīg[1] OE, 'a battle; a military force, an army'. ?Wyfordby.

wīg[2] OE, 'an idol; a holy place'. ?Wyfordby.

wigga OE, 'a beetle'. ?*Wygacer* (f.n. Freeby).

wilde OE, adj., 'uncultivated or desolate'. *wildestedes* (f.n. Croxton Kerrial).

wildernesse ME, 'a wilderness, a wild place'; in modern minor names, perh. a designed wild area in a constructed landscape or park. Wilderness (f.n. Buckminster).

*****wilig** OE (Angl), 'a willow'. Willow Fm, The Willows. Fairly common in f.ns.: as a simplex, e.g. *Willows* (Burrough on the Hill, Waltham on the Wolds); with a prefixed surn. or ecclesiastical style indicating ownership, e.g. *colleuelwylows* (Bottesford), *Cooks willow* (Somerby), *the Parsons Willowes* (Saxby, Stathern), *þe prest welows* (Bottesford); with a generic specifying type of willow clump, e.g. *Willowbed* (Sproxton, Wycomb/Chadwell), Willow Holt (Harston, Holwell, Muston, Sewstern, Wymondham), Willow Row (Nether Broughton). Occasionally with an el. specifying farming units, e.g. Dale Willows (Gt. Dalby), *Willow Doles* (Pickwell) or topographical feature, e.g. *Willeclif* (Wymondham), *the Willow heade* (Croxton Kerrial), *Willow poole plott* (Old Dalby).

*****wiligen** OE, adj., 'growing with willows'. *Wylnehall* (f.n. Bottesford).

*****wilig-trēow** OE, 'a willow-tree'. *Willowtree* (f.n. Croxton Kerrial), Willow Tree Cl (f.n. Burrough on the Hill), *Willytrewelle furlong, Wyltrehullforlang'* (f.ns. Sewstern).

wind[1] OE, **vindr** ON, 'wind', used in p.ns. to denote places with windy, exposed situations. *Windisers* (f.n. Thorpe Arnold), *wyndhill'* (f.n. Eaton), *wyndhilles* (f.n. Branston), Wyndriggs (f.n. Waltham on the Wolds).

wind-mylne ME, 'a windmill'. The Old Windmill, Redmile Windmill, Scrimshaw's Windmill, The Windmill (Barkestone, Melton Mowbray), Wymondham Windmill. *Edmondthorpe Windmill* (Edmondthorpe), *the windemille* (with various spellings in Burrough on the Hill, Burton Lazars, Saxby, Scalford, Sproxton), *Windmill furlong, Windmill hill, the old windmilhill* (f.ns. Waltham on the Wolds), *the Windmill Leys* (f.n. Melton Mowbray), *Wind Mill seales* (f.n. Stathern).

winter OE, **vinter** OEScand, 'winter'; in. p.ns., referring to streams that ran or to places that were used in winter. Winterbeck. Winter Hill, Winter Well (f.ns. Buckminster).

wīr, wȳr OE, 'myrtle, bog-myrtle'. ?Worrel Leys (f.n. Coston).

wīðig OE, 'a withy, a willow'. Withcote.

*wīðign OE, 'a willow, a willow copse'. *Withinbusc, Withins* (f.ns. Bottesford).

wodi ME, adj., 'wooded, overgrown with wood, having a growth of trees or shrubs'. *Woodyrith* (f.n. Branston).

wodyard ME, 'an enclosure in which wood is chopped, sawn or stored'. *the Woodyard* (f.n. Wyfordby).

wōh OE, adj., 'crooked, twisted'. *Wollandes Furlonge* (f.n. Lt. Dalby).

wooden eModE, adj., 'made of wood'. *Wooden Bridge* (Branston), *the Wooden Cross* (Coston).

worð OE, 'an enclosure, a farmstead', *langwrth hill, Stonewrth hill* (f.ns. Barkestone), *the Nithingworth* (f.n. Knipton), *Steynwordhoc* (f.n. Burrough on the Hill), *Walworthehow* (f.n. Muston).

*wræs(t)el OE, 'something twisted'. *Nethurresduldal'* (f.n. Knipton).

wrang OE, **vrangr** ON, adj., 'crooked or twisted in shape'. In f.ns., almost invariably compounded with **land**, as *Ranglandes, Wranglandes, Wronglandes* (with various spellings in Bottesford, Burrough on the Hill, Burton Lazars and 14 other townships), *Wronges* (f.n. Pickwell), *Wrongdeyle ende* (f.n. Barkestone).

wrangling ModE, ppl.adj., 'marked by disputation'. ?*Wrangling leas* (f.n. Stapleford).

wrastling ME, vbl.sb., 'wrestling, the sport of grappling and throwing'. *Wrustleling leas* (f.n. Ab Kettleby).

wrenna OE, 'a wren'. ?*renhow* (f.n. Croxton Kerrial).

wrink ME, 'a sharp twist or turn'; in f.ns., prob. referring to sharply twisting selions (cf. **wrang** *supra* and ME *wrinkel* 'a wrinkle, a twisting, a winding'). *the Rincks* (f.n. Redmile), *the wrinckes* (f.n. Stathern).

wudu OE, 'a wood, a grove, a tract of woodland'; also 'wood, timber' sometimes when **wudu** is the first el. with words for buildings and other structures. Barkestone Wood, Brentingby ~, Briery ~, Bunkers ~, Conygear ~, Freeby ~, Granby ~, Hallam's ~, Harston ~, Kennels ~, King's ~, Old ~, Old Dalby ~, Old Hills ~, Old Park ~, Plungar ~, Reservoir ~, Sir John's ~, Stathern Wood; Woodgate Hill, Woodlands, Woodwell Head. *Broughton Wood* (Nether Broughton), *Eagleswood* (Burton Lazars), *Heighwood, Withecocke wood*

(Withcote), Meadow Wood (Barkestone). *Woodgate* is common (with various spellings in Burrough on the Hill, Croxton Kerrial, Gt. Dalby, Edmondthorpe, Normanton, Plungar, Redmile, Stathern, Wymondham), *Westwudegate* (Long Clawson). Occasionally in f.ns., e.g. *wodd leyes*, *att the wood side* (Stathern), the Wood Cl (Nether Broughton, Gt. Dalby, Sysonby), Wood Fd (Plungar, Redmile), Wood Mdw (Withcote). Note also *Wood croft* (Somerby), *the Wood Nooke* (Croxton Kerrial) and *Woodhowse* (Old Dalby).

wudu-cocc OE, **wodecok** ME, 'a woodcock'. Woodcock Island (f.n. Wymondham).

wulf-pytt OE, 'a wolf-pit, a wolf-trap'. *wollepittes* (f.n. Scalford).

wyrm, wurm OE, 'a reptile, a snake; a dragon; an insect', **worm** ME, 'an earthworm'. *Wermland'* (f.n. Eaton), *wormeacer leies* (f.n. Hose), *Wormehill* (f.n. Croxton Kerrial), ?*wormwels* (f.n. Saxby).

wyrt OE, 'a plant, a vegetable'. *longe Whortlye* (f.n. Stapleford), ?*Worteley syck* (f.n. Melton Mowbray).

yardland eModE., 'a square measure of about 30 acres of land'. *the glebe yard land* (f.n. Stonesby), *Levitts yard land* (f.n. Melton Mowbray).

yonder ME, adv., adj., 'over there, away there'. *le Yendirbeyndoles* (f.n. Thorpe Arnold).

INDEX OF THE PLACE-NAMES
OF FRAMLAND HUNDRED

This index includes all the major names and minor names in the Introduction and in the main body of the work but not in the section The Elements in the Framland Hundred's Place-Names. Field-names are not indexed. The names of the townships are printed in capitals. Lost names are printed in italic.